So Many Fish,
So Little Time

So Many Fish,

1001 of the World's Greatest

Backcountry Honeyholes, Trout Rivers,

Blue Ribbon Waters, Bass Lakes,

and Saltwater Hot Spots

So Little Time

Mark D. Williams

Collins
An Imprint of HarperCollinsPublishers

HarperCollins books may be purchased for educational, business, or sales promo-
tional use. For information, please write: Special Markets Department, HarperCollins
Publishers, 10 East 53rd Street, New York, NY 10022.

FIRST EDITION

Designed by Cassandra J. Pappas

Library of Congress Cataloging-in-Publication Data

Williams, Mark D., 1960–
    So many fish, so little time : 1001 of the world's greatest backcountry honeyholes,
    trout rivers, blue ribbon waters, bass lakes, and saltwater hot spots /
    Mark D. Williams. — 1st ed.
    p. cm.
    ISBN: 978-0-06-088239-6
    ISBN-10: 0-06-088239-5
    1. Fishing—Guidebooks. I. Title.

SH412.W55 2007
799.—dc22   2006051796

07   08   09   10   11   NMSG/RRD   10 9 8 7 6 5 4 3 2

I am blessed with amazing women in my life from my grandmothers (Mamaw and Granny Williams) to my beautiful daughter Sarah (who is closer and closer to college graduation) to all my lovely aunts and nieces. I have two women who especially made this book possible.

To my mother, Gwen, who, despite all my years of not listening to her, continued to imbue my life with salts of wisdom and gifts of unconditional love. She always said "you can." You're an amazing woman.

To my wife, Amy, who worked doubly hard as my researcher, photographer, and pre-editor, not to mention putting up with all the baggage that comes with the MDW package. You're my angel.

Contents

Introduction   xv

UNITED STATES OF AMERICA

Northeast   3

Connecticut   3
Farmington River   5
Housatonic River   5

Maine   8
Kennebec River   8
Rapid River   9
Sebago Lake   9
West Branch of the
    Penobscot River   10

Massachusetts   11
Boston   12
Cape Cod, Cape Cod Bay,
    Nantucket Sound,
    Nantucket Island   13
Deerfield River   14

Martha's Vineyard   15
Quabbin Reservoir   17
Westfield River   17

New Hampshire   18
Androscoggin River   18
Connecticut River, New
    Hampshire, and Vermont   19
Lake Winnipesaukee   20

New York   21
West Branch, Ausable
    River   22
Beaverkill River   23
Black Lake   25
Cayuga Lake   26
Delaware River   27
New York City   29
Montauk Point   32
Lower Niagara River   32
Salmon River   33
Willowemoc River   34

Pennsylvania   35
   Letort Spring Run   36
   Pennsylvania Trout Streams   37
   Philadelphia   38
   Pittsburgh   40
   Raystown Lake   41
   Susquehanna River   41
   Youghiogheny River   43

Rhode Island   44
   Wood River   44
   Newport   45

Vermont   45
   Batten Kill River   48
   Lake Champlain   49
   White River   51
   Winooski River   52

Southeast   54

Alabama   54
   Birmingham   56
   Lake Dannelly/Millers Ferry   56
   Lake Eufaula   57
   Lake Guntersville   58
   Pickwick Lake   59
   Smith Lake   60
   Tallapoosa River   60
   Wheeler Lake   61

Florida   62
   Bienville Plantation Lakes   63
   Charlotte Harbor and Boca Grande
      Pass   64
   Destin Village   65
   Everglades   66
   Homosassa River   67
   Florida Keys   68
   Jacksonville   69

Lake Tarpon   71
Lake Okeechobee   71
Miami   72
Orange Lake and
   Crooked Lake   73
Orlando   74
Pine Island Coast   76
Rodman Reservoir   76

Georgia   77
   North Georgia Trout Waters   79
   Atlanta   80
   St. Simons Island   87
   Lake Seminole   89
   Paradise Public Fishing
      Area   90
   Savannah   90
   Soque River   91

Kentucky   93
   Barren River Lake   94
   Cave Run Lake   95
   Cedar Creek Lake   95
   Cumberland River   97
   Dale Hollow Lake   97
   Kentucky Lake and
      Barkley Lake   98

Louisiana   99
   Calcasieu Lake   100
   Chandeleur Islands   101
   Venice   101
   New Orleans   102

Maryland   103
   Big Gunpowder Falls   104
   North Branch of the
      Potomac River   105
   Baltimore   106
   Savage River   107

Contents

Mississippi   108
    Lake Tom Bailey   108
    Biloxi and Gulfport   109

North Carolina   110
    Chattooga River   112
    Charlotte   113
    Davidson River   113
    Fontana Lake   114
    French Broad River   115
    Great Smoky Mountains
        National Park   116
    Nantahala River   120
    Watauga River   122
    Outer Banks   122
    South Toe River   124

South Carolina   124
    Lake Murray   124
    Santee Cooper   125

Tennessee   126
    Clinch River   127
    Duck River   128
    Hiwassee River   129
    Holston River, South Fork   130
    Nashville   130
    Nolichucky River   131
    Reelfoot Lake   131
    Tellico River   132

Virginia   137
    James River   140
    Mossy Creek   141
    Rappahannock River   142
    Richmond   143
    Shenandoah National Park   144
    Whitetop Laurel Creek   145

Washington, DC   146

West Virginia   148
    West Virginia Top Fishing
        Hot Spots   148
    New River   151

Midwest   152

Arkansas   152
    Buffalo River   154
    Crooked Creek   156
    Dry Run Creek   156
    Greers Ferry Lake   157
    Little Red River   158
    Norfork River   160
    Ouachita Lake   161
    Spring River   162
    White Oak Lakes   163
    White River   164

Illinois   167
    Chicago   167
    Rend Lake   168

Kansas   169
    Kansas City   169

Michigan   170
    Au Sable River   173
    Boardman River   174
    Fox River and the Upper
        Peninsula   175
    Detroit   176
    Grand River   180
    Manistee River   181
    Muskegon River   183
    Pere Marquette River   184
    Rifle River   186
    Saginaw Bay   186

Minnesota   187
   Boundary Waters Canoe
      Area   187
   Driftless Area   189
   Lake of the Woods   195
   Lake Vermilion   196
   Minneapolis-St. Paul   197
   Red Lake   198

Missouri   198
   Lake of the Ozarks   200
   North Fork of the White
      River   201
   Top Waters of Missouri:
      St. Louis to Branson   202
   Truman Reservoir   209

Nebraska   209
   Lake McConaughy Reservoir   209
   Merritt Reservoir   210

North Dakota   211
   Devil's Lake   211
   Missouri River   211

Ohio   212
   Lake Erie   212

Oklahoma   214
   Lake Eufaula   216
   Mountain Fork River   217

South Dakota   219
   Black Hills   219
   Lake Oahe   224
   Lake Sharpe   224

Wisconsin   225
   Milwaukee   226
   Bois Brule River   227

Namekagon River   228
St. Croix River   228

Southwest   230

Colorado   230
   Animas River   236
   Arkansas River   238
   Blue River   239
   Cochetopa Creek and Cebolla
      Creek   242
   Colorado River   245
   Conejos River   246
   Delaney Butte Lakes   248
   Denver   249
   Dolores River   250
   Durango Area   251
   East Fork of the San Juan River,
      Colorado   258
   Frying Pan River   259
   Gunnison River/Black
      Canyon   261
   Horsetooth Reservoir   266
   Rio Grande   266
   Roaring Fork   268
   Rocky Mountain National
      Park   270
   San Luis Lake   273
   South Platte River   273
   Taylor River   275
   Trappers Lake   276
   Twin Lakes   277
   Vallecito Reservoir   278

New Mexico   279
   Albuquerque   282
   Rio Chama   282
   Cimarron River   284
   Jemez Area   287

Contents

Red River   296
Rio Costilla   297
Rio Grande   300
San Juan River   302

Texas   306
   Lake Alan Henry   309
   Alligator Gar   311
   Lake Athens   312
   Austin   313
   Brazos River   314
   Choke Canyon Reservoir   315
   Dallas   317
   Devils River   318
   Falcon Lake   320
   Fayette County Lake   321
   Lake Fork   322
   Gibbons Creek Reservoir   323
   Hill Country   324
   Lake Meredith   330
   Houston   331
   Noodling in the South   333
   Richland-Chambers Reservoir   336
   Sabine Lake   336
   Sam Rayburn Reservoir   338
   Squaw Creek Reservoir   339
   Texas Coast   339
   Lake Texoma   342
   Toledo Bend Reservoir   344
   White Bass   345

West   347

Arizona   347
   The Lakes and Rivers of the White
     Mountains   348
   Roosevelt Lake   365
   Lees Ferry, Colorado   366

Phoenix   367
Oak Creek   368

California   370
   Barrett Lake   372
   Lake Berryessa   373
   California Delta   374
   Lake Casitas   375
   Castaic Lake   376
   Clear Lake   377
   Crowley Lake   378
   Lake Davis   379
   Diamond Valley Lake   380
   Dixon Lake   381
   Fall River   382
   Hot Creek   383
   Kings River   384
   Los Angeles   386
   Mammoth Lakes   387
   McCloud River   387
   Milton Reservoir   389
   Lake Nacimiento   390
   Owens River   391
   Oakland and San
     Francisco (Bay Area)   392
   Sacramento River   395
   Middle Fork San Joaquin
     River   397
   San Diego   398
   Shasta Lake   400
   Trinity Lake   401
   Truckee River   401
   Whiskeytown Reservoir   403
   Yosemite National Park   403

Nevada   405
   Crittenden Reservoir   406
   East Walker River   407
   Lake Mead   408

Contents

Lake Mohave   409
Pyramid Lake   410
Las Vegas   411
Ruby Lake   412
Wild Horse Reservoir   413

Utah   417
Flaming Gorge Reservoir   419
Green River   421
Upper Green River   424
Lake Powell   424
Strawberry Reservoir   426
Salt Lake City   427
Underrated in Utah   428

Yellowstone National Park   437
Hebgen Lake   459

Northwest   465

Idaho   465
Big Wood River   467
Brownlee Reservoir   468
Henry's Fork of the Snake
    River   469
Henry's Lake   472
Kelly Creek   473
Lochsa River   475
Middle Fork, Salmon River   476
Salmon River   479
Selway River   480
Silver Creek   481
St. Joe River   484
Teton River   485

Montana   490
Beaverhead River   494
Big Hole River   496
Bighorn River   497
Bitterroot River   500
Blackfeet Reservation Lakes   502

Blackfoot River   504
Clark Fork River   505
Flathead River   507
Fort Peck Reservoir   507
Jefferson River   508
Kootenai River   509
Other Montana Waters
    to Try   512
Rock Creek   514
Smith River   515
Sun River   516
Montana Spring Creeks   518

Oregon   522
Deschutes River   522
Grande Ronde River   525
High Desert Lakes   526
Crane Prairie Reservoir   526
John Day River   531
McKenzie River   532
Metolius River   533
Rogue River   534
Umpqua River   535
Wenaha River   537
Williamson River   538

Washington   539
Columbia River   539
Cowlitz River   540
Olympic Peninsula   541
Rocky Ford Creek   543
Seattle   544
Sprague Lake   545
Yakima River   545

Wyoming   547
Beartooth Plateau   549
Encampment River   550
North Platte River   551
South Fork Snake River

and the Jackson
Hole Area   553

Alaska   558

Hawaii   568

CANADA

Alberta   578
Bow River Drainage   578
Crowsnest River   581
Royal Canadian Pacific Fishing
Excursion   583
Oldman River   585
Castle River   585
North Raven River   585
Red Deer   586
Ram River   586

British Columbia   588
Dean River   588
Elk River   589
Iskut Chain Lakes   590
Prince Rupert   591
Queen Charlotte Islands   593
Skeena River System   593
Vancouver Island   596

Manitoba   599
Nueltin Lake   599
Silsby Lake   600

New Brunswick   601
Miramichi River   601

Newfoundland and
Labrador   602

Northwest Territories   606
Great Bear Lake   606
Tree River   608

Kasba Lake   609
Mosquito and Dubawnt
Lakes   609
Coppermine River   609
Great Slave Lake   609

Ontario   610
Lake Scugog   610

Quebec   611
Gaspé Peninsula   611
Gouin Reservoir   614

Saskatchewan   615
Lake Athabasca   615
Milton Lake   616
Selwyn Lake   617
Wollaston Lake   618

MEXICO
Baja California   625
Bass Lakes of Mexico   627
Cabo San Lucas   635
Cozumel   636
Puerto Vallarta   639
Yucatán Peninsula   641

CARIBBEAN

Bahamas   649

Bermuda   656

Cayman Islands   656

Dry Tortugas   657

Puerto Rico   659

Turks and Caicos   663

British Virgin Islands   664

Contents

CENTRAL AMERICA

Belize   671

Costa Rica   675

Guatemala   677

Honduras   681

Nicaragua   685

Panama   686

SOUTH AMERICA

Argentina   693

Brazil   700

Chile   703

Suriname   705

Venezuela   708

EUROPE

Andorra   713

Austria   716

Corsica   719

Croatia   725

England   727

France   729

Hungary   737

Iceland   738

Ireland   740

Lapland (Finland, Sweden)   745

Norway   748

Portugal and the Azores and
    Madeira Islands   751

Slovenia   754

Spain   757

ASIA

Hong Kong   773

India   775

Japan   780

Mongolia   782

Russia   784

South Korea   789

Sri Lanka   790

Thailand   791

AFRICA

Bom Bom Island   797

Egypt   798

Ethiopia   800

Gabon   803

Guinea-Bisseau   804

Kenya   806

Seychelles   807

SOUTH PACIFIC

Australia   817

Bikini Atoll   819

Christmas Island   822

Fiji   824

Midway Island   827

New Zealand   828

Papua New Guinea   833

Tahiti, French Polynesia   835

Tasmania   836

Acknowledgments   841

Credits   **845**

Contents

Introduction

Square the girth then multiply times the length and divide by 800. That should give you an amazingly close estimate of the weight of a fish without having a scale to measure.

ANONYMOUS

There is no monopoly on courage. It is the quality of courage found in fish that leads men to fish for them. And it is something of the same quality in man himself that keeps him wading bravely through swift waters even when the hour is late and shadows are closing in around him.

STEVE RAYMOND (1973)

You'll hear some anglers say they spend thousands of dollars on fishing each year in pursuit of fish for the "sport" of it. You'll hear fly fishers talk about how it's not about catching fish, it's all about the art of the sport.

Anglers fish for so many reasons—to fish with family; to fish with buddies; to fish alone; to catch big fish; to catch a lot of fish; to catch a rare species of fish; to catch several species of fish; to catch a fish on a new lure, a specific type of lure, a fly you tied yourself; to try a new strategy, a new technique.

Sometimes, anglers fish for something as simple as wanting to try out a new rod, to feel the lapping waves against the boat, to say they fished in Bolivia or Nevada because no one ever thinks about fishing in Bolivia or Nevada. Sometimes, anglers fish to enjoy the solitary, intimate pleasures of a creek; sometimes to mindlessly bounce a nymph along the river bottom; sometimes to dap and dance a Royal Wulff on the slick surface of an alpine lake. We all fish for many reasons.

I fish all over the world and meet a lot of anglers. I hear bass fishermen talk as much

about hardware and lake structure as they do the rush of fighting their big-lipped prey. I talk to those who go after exotic fish, those who fish in exotic places for any fish, those who hunt trophy fish, those who fish as an excuse to hang out by the water. Some folks fish only once or twice a year, to catch the white perch run or the crappie nesting or the salmonfly hatch or to be on a pond with their grandkids.

Most every angler dreams of fishing for wild cutts in the cold mountain streams of Yellowstone National Park. Every angler wishes to tighten the line on a monster 1,000-pound shark at the end of their bowed rod. Who wouldn't want to fish the best angling hot spots of the entire world? Land a leaping peacock bass from the Negro River of the Amazon? Fly fish for behemoth 100-pound taimen in the muddy cold waters of Mongolia? Tangle with voracious 150-pound tarpon off the coast of Florida? Or tackle trout in as diverse locations as Spain or Tasmania?

Time is but the stream I go a-fishing in. I drink at it; but while I drink, I see the sandy bottom and detect how shallow it is. Its thin current slides away, but eternity remains. I would drink deeper, fish in the sky, where the bottom is pebbly with stars.   HENRY DAVID THOREAU (1854)

Like every other angler I've ever fished beside or talked to over a beer, I dream about where to go fishing. The common act of planning? Fishing guidebooks all over the desk or floor. Yellow legal pad. Maps wrinkled and unfolded like multicolored carpet spread on the floor. You know the drill. Is this the year I fish Alaska? New Zealand? Belize? Montana?

I've fished in every state of the union, fished in countries all over the world for all kinds of species, and fished for all those reasons I previously mentioned. No fishing trip is ever like any other, even to the exact same fishing hole. From day to day, the fishing experience changes.

Fishing one spring creek in Pennsylvania is totally different from fishing a spring creek in Montana or in New Zealand or in the Driftless. Fishing an alpine creek in the Sierra Nevada is unlike (but no better or worse than) fishing a high country stream in the Appalachians. Just different. It's as useless as comparing the quality of the drinking experiences of a Beaujolais to a Burgundy, comparing the colors red to maroon, green to khaki, Chevys to Fords, or Ed Wood to Francis Ford Coppola. There exists merit and taste and idiosyncratic elements to each of these. I like hamburgers and I like steak. And so it is with anglers.

No fish ever gave the alarm in a burning building by barking or played with a ball of yarn on the hearth. The most you can say for the fish is that he has a certain icy composure and austere dignity.

S. J. PERELMAN (1958)

Clearly, comparing Athens Lake in Texas to Owen River in New Zealand is not apples to apples. Owen River trout live in infinitely more beautiful surroundings. When I put this book together, I had to figure out which fisheries I was going to include. A river or lake that's in close proximity to your house has a lot of value—you can get there more frequently, and that combined with good (not great fishing) can make a river/lake/inshore/offshore spot a superb fishing experience. I decided to include a good number of places to fish that were simply good because of where they lay.

Sometimes it's not about the size of fish, it's the numbers. Sometimes it's that the trout are wild. Sometimes it's a chance to catch a record. Sometimes it's because to a grandparent, this is a good family spot to take the grandchildren. Sometimes it's that underfished lake only you and a few friends know about, so you fish in solitude, beauty. Sometimes a river or lake has seen better days but it's a classic—like driving a '65 Mustang, it's worth it just to revisit the memories, the history.

There is value in a body of water that offers you multiple species in one day or on one trip. The scenery of a place to fish can be almost as important as what you're fishing for. Ditto the uniqueness of fishery or fish, or maybe the rarity of that species, or the extreme aspects, or the remoteness. I included Europe and a few other spots more for the atmosphere and culture than the fishing. Atlantic salmon fishing for sport has declined worldwide the last decade but the act of catching an Atlantic salmon was always difficult even in the heyday and takes place in such pretty places, I had to include some of the classic spots. So apples to apples? Nope. The San Juan has more fish and bigger fish than the small remote brook trout stream Lime Creek an hour to its north but both are valid, interesting, superb fishing experiences, just different.

Let's say you're on a business trip and you have some down time. Maybe you're visiting your Uncle Tom in Chicago and you are tired of his corny jokes and cramped 1950s house. Maybe you want an adjunct to a city vacation but you don't want to see another Off-Broadway play or visit a nondescript mall and you're all touristed out with historical monuments. Time to fish. I included some of the best fishing cities in America.

There were another 1,001 fisheries I just couldn't include. I wanted some balance to the book, as many geographic locales as possible, as many species, but with an eye on not overlooking the obvious, either. I love making lists, however at times crossing off rivers and lakes and bays I love for the sake of balance or numbers was frustrating. Still, putting this together was a blast. I picked the brains of my friends for their ideas, places they loved that I might have missed. No one person can fish all the thousand and one best places in the world but I've done my dead level best to knock off most everything on the list. That's why I talked to so many guides, outfitters, fly shops, tackle stores, captains, booking agents, clubs, and, of course, more friends.

Now, I hate it that some will be mad because I left this stream or that bay or this lake off the list. I hate it that some will be mad because I included their favorite place, their undiscovered or underfished fishin' hole. That's one of the dilemmas of the outdoors writing biz. And if you're wondering—yeah, I did leave out a couple of my favorite fishing holes around my cabin in Durango because I need a place to get away sometime. Hopefully, I didn't too greatly emphasize one of your spots.

I take no responsibility if one of the fisheries listed ends up suffering from degradation, pollution, safety issues, hurricanes, terrorism, civil war, regular war between two belligerents, disease, or political problems. This stuff happens but you can't always see it coming. There were numerous places I did leave out for all of these reasons but over time, some of them will be more available because of counteractions to all of these reasons.

■   ■   ■

I wrote *So Many Fish, So Little Time* with the idea that it wouldn't just be a planning book, but a book that inspires daydreams. Dreams. I was determined to write a book of fishing dreams. A book of dreams, a wish list of all the best places in the world to

fish. This is a sit-on-the-pot kind of book, the type of book that sometimes inspires you to get off your duff and make plans, the type of book that is fun to pick up, knowing full well you can't afford to visit New Zealand until little Bobby finishes college in ten years, but you still read it and wish.

Can you think of a better fishing wish list than this?

Dreamfishing. I'm always searching for dream places. Hell, I'm always searching for something.

I have been searching for the perfect fishing hat for twenty years, maybe longer. My closet is a graveyard of hats and caps I have disowned. I have tried the run-of-the-mill cap you buy off the rack. Some of these have logos that endorse soft drinks, sporting goods stores, fly fishing companies, rivers and lakes and fly shops, sports

teams. They all failed to become the perfect fishing hat. Some of the hats in my closet are straw hats. Some are torn and tattered, beaten by wind and heavy friends sitting on them before looking. Some are new and in the box, gifts from well-meaning friends who just don't understand what the perfect fishing hat means. I have some of those army-type floppy hats that you snap up on the side and they're okay at times but I look like a Rat Patrol wannabe or an Australian tour guide so they don't work either.

I have owned two perfect fishing hats but they both disappeared. Terry Moore and a couple of his buddies made the first one disappear, a ten-year-old cap that at one time was khaki and had a black logo with a stitching of some kind of colorful trout. After a decade, the cap was a nondescript color, kind of a gray, kind of a dirty blond, ragged, torn on the brim, sweat-stains ringing the cap and best of all, the cap fit to my head perfectly. I didn't get headaches or indentations or even hat-hair and it never blew off in the wind. It matched all my other dingy, ragged, worn clothes I love so much.

I sat in the duck blind on Lake Greenbelt waiting in the early morning cold with three guys I had never hunted with before. They had their own little hunting club, had hunted for years together. Terry Moore, my outdoor writer friend, my buddy who seemed so caring at times, took off my cap and flung it out as far as it would go. The three of them unloaded their shotguns and in a flash, the only thing left of the cap was a jagged piece of fabric two inches by two inches.

"Welcome to the club, Mark," Terry laughed.

He killed my perfect fishing cap.

So here I am, years later, minding my own business, fishing and catching a brown trout every so often, when a gust of wind picks my newest perfect fishing cap off my head and deposits it in the river behind us. A beautiful faded red worn torn ragged jobber that fit me so I didn't even know it was on my head.

We couldn't back up in time to retrieve it. The river took the cap's life, a cap I had worked so hard to turn into the perfect fishing hat. All those fishing trips in the cap, wasted, sunken at the bottom of the Clark Fork River. Look for my cap, guys.

■　■　■

There are many times when I fish with someone who is a much better caster than I am. They don't have tailing loops and they can place a size-20 Adams in a floating hula-hoop ring from 100 yards away. Two-handed spey casters who can cast from New Brunswick to Newfoundland. Double-haulers who obviously have PhDs in physics. On a bass lake, I always end up fishing with those guys and gals who can flip a lure underneath a boat dock back-handed while standing on their head or can cast from here to there across the river and hit a smallmouth in the head. I'm pretty lucky not to hook one of my big ears. But on a creek like Whitetop Laurel, I can hold my own.

My casting weaknesses are ideal on small intimate creeks where the casts are not long nor are they Krieger-perfect. My casts come from all angles. I make crooked casts that fly under the limb right in front of me but curve to miss the overhanging rhododendron and then land this side of the tangle of roots more like a putt-putt shot than a Masters approach at Amen Corner. I bow-and-arrow some casts on creeks like Whitetop Laurel and Robin Hood in Appalachia. You have to avoid a full cast or you catch the canopy of trees above you. If you can present your fly without hanging it up and do so in a two-to-one ratio, you will catch a lot of trout on streams like these. Turn your weakness into a strength.

Let those fancy-pants casters come and cast with me in a small, bunched-up stream. They may be able to hit a quarter with a size-22 RS2 emerger at a hundred yards but I bet they don't know how to do an *up-and-over-through-the-third-branch-tumble-down-boulder-splash-pile* cast.

United States
of America

Northeast

CONNECTICUT

I don't have a Connecticut patch. The trailer-park side of my family comes out in me more times than I want and one way it manifests is that I iron and sew patches on my ratty old fishing vest.

My late father-in-law Fred gave me my fishing vest as a Christmas present the year he died. My vest is no longer khaki; more a drab gray. Every pocket is frayed. The Velcro on the pockets rarely works anymore. Last count, the vest had five holes of significance. Leftover crumbs sit, powdery, in every pocket, vestiges of orange peanut butter–cheese crackers or what I usually call lunch on the stream. Second nature after all these years, I know where everything is on the vest: my extra Chapstick, ibuprofen, sinus pills, several safety pins, thread and needle (I pretend I might have

to one day sew up a wound which, if I or a fishing buddy ever did need that kind of medical attention, I do not think I would be able to do, at least not sober), toilet paper, wet wipes, five fly boxes, leaders, tippet, tiny shreds of my wife Amy's pantyhose I used to attach to flies as shucks, beef jerky wrappers, Xink, floatant, nippers, forceps, receipts from the road trip in '92 to the Driftless, splitshot, foam indicators, leaves and dried flowers I collect to give to Amy to show I am thinking about her but forget to give her, and an extra pair of clip-on polarized sunglasses. And most important, on this multipocketed fishing ragtag vest, for reasons beyond my control, all the patches.

From Idaho to New York, Cozumel to France, the patches are attached in various stages to my vest, on the shoulders, the

Connecticut R.   Androscoggin R.

Lake Champlain   Rapid R.   MAINE   ★ W Branch Penobscot

★ Winooski R.   Kennebec R.

★ White R.

Black L. ★   W Branch ★   Sebago L.

ADIRONDACKS   Ausable R.   VERMONT

LAKE ONTARIO   ★ Salmon R.   ★ Lake George   NEW HAMPSHIRE   ★ Lake Winnipesaukee

Niagara R.   ★ Cayuga L.   ★ Batten Kill   Boston ★   Quabbin Reservoir

★ NEW YORK   Deerfield R. ★   MASSACHUSETTS   Cape Cod

★ Westfield R. ★

CATSKILLS   Willowemoc ★ Beaver Kill   ★ Housatonic R.   R.I.

★ Slate Run   ★ Delaware R.   CONNECTICUT   ★ Newport   ★ Martha's Vineyard

★ Cedar Run   ★ Fishing Creek   Montauk Point

★ Spruce Ck.   ★ New York City

★ Penns Ck.   ★ Big Fishing Creek

★ Raystown L.   Philadelphia ★   NORTHEAST

★ Pittsburgh   ★ Letort   ★ NEW JERSEY

PENNSYLVANIA   ★

Youghiogheny R.   Susquehanna R.

pockets, under the armholes. Some have completely torn off but their die stained the vest after being dunked or rained upon and you can easily tell that a Bow River patch used to cling there. Some are curled up and threaten to fall off at any moment. Others are sewn in addition to being ironed on but they know that on this threadbare vest they could be expelled soon.

I don't have a Connecticut patch. I went all the way for a Northeast angling sojourn and had a blast that spring but I never got on the Farmington for the deluge, three days of heavy rain, and not the kind in which you can fish. If I don't fish it, I don't get a patch.

My patching habit is kinda reminiscent of those slow recreational vehicles you see on the road, the RVs you are behind on this single-lane road, the ones from the 1960s, beaten and worn, with a thousand colorful decals and stickers on the back so you can see all the neat places they have visited in their rust-bucket. You know sure as shootin' that the largest two stickers plastered on the RV will be from Yellowstone National Park and Good Sam's RV Club. KOAs are big players on these moving murals, too.

Maybe I am into this patch thing for the goal-oriented spirit, to satiate my list-making tendencies. Whatever it is, I have to guard my vest at home because Amy has threatened to throw it away. "It looks like rats have gotten ahold of it," she complains. Maybe they have, I don't know. But even so, it's a perfectly good vest. I'll get a Connecticut patch one day. I just hope the vest makes it long enough to iron or sew it on.

Farmington River

- **Location:** North central Connecticut
- **What You Fish For:** Brown and rainbow trout
- **Highlights and Notables:** The holdover trout reach trophy size

Farmington is one of the finest brown trout rivers in the East. The river is not an angler's homerun rising-up-the-charts bestseller but a solid novel that will keep selling a goodly number of copies each year.

Located in north central Connecticut, this medium- to large-sized river is one of the more picturesque, what with the clear river passing under covered bridges, past green forests and through rolling hills out in the peaceful countryside and all. Despite two dams, the Farmington doesn't suffer from major water fluctuations. Accessibility on the Farmington is a positive since the river has roads following it and intersecting it.

Two Trout Management Areas (TMAs) on the river were meant to create trophy trout and it appears they are doing their job. The upper reaches of the Farmington provide a wilderness setting that belies its proximity to the cities. Most don't believe that a river this close to major populated areas can be a fishery of quality trout fishing. They're sadly mistaken. The Farmington gets cold water releases from dams that keep the river fishable even through the hot days in summer.

With the cold water, the prolific insect hatches, plenty of holding water (pockets, pools, riffles), and the river management, it's no wonder the Farmington provides a healthy population of brown, rainbow, and brook trout. The holdover browns and rainbows reach 16 to 20 inches and they are able to hide out well—18-inch trout on the Farmington are reported daily, it seems.

The West Branch out of Hogback is one of the top streams in the East. The river's two branches meet in New Hartford and the Farmington fishes well to Lower Collinsville Dam. Farmington enjoys solid mayfly and caddis hatches.

CONTACTS
Classic and Custom Fly Shop,
    New Hartford,
    www.classicandcustomflyshop.com
UpCountry Sportfishing, New Hartford,
    www.farmingtonriver.com
Quiet Sports, Collinsville, 860-693-2214

Housatonic River

- **Location:** Western half of Connecticut, north to south
- **What You Fish For:** Brown and rainbow trout, smallmouth bass
- **Highlights and Notables:** Some of the most prolific hatches in the East. Big river with plenty of access and challenging fishing

For several of my friends, the Housatonic is their favorite river in the East. The Housatonic is a real joy to fish, miles and miles virtually unfished. The river is photogenic with its covered bridges, green riverside forests, and big boulders tossed out in the river with no rhyme or reason. Thick green tops of trees and green small trees form a 3-D multitextured wall of all the shades of green on a color wheel. This tailwater runs north to south in the western half of Connecticut and this river's beauty is accented by shady banks and boulders as big as my Uncle Bob.

Locals and regulars call this intricate, challenging trout stream the Housey. The Housey has good insect life, caddis and mayflies, and plenty of fat, brightly-colored

brown trout ready to refuse the angler's imitation of these caddis and mayflies.

The river is mineral rich, high in alkaline, made so from the filtering and additive effect of the regional limestone. The calcium and other parts of the witches' brew make the plants grow, that make for more and diverse insects and for a healthier trout population.

With all its famous pools—Split Rock Pool, Corner Pool, upper Elm Pool, Doctors Pool, Two Car Pool, Carse Pool, Sand Pool, Meat Pool, and Grave Pool—you can be assured the Housey has passed muster with the knowledgeable anglers of the East. If it's one thing eastern anglers know, is how to canonize a fishery and how to identify hatches. The hatches: Eastern fly fishers love to talk hatches. Set their sundials by them. Green drake mayfly. Hendrickson. Light Cahill. Slate Drake. Bluewinged Olive. Baetis. Caddis. Pale Afternoon Dun. The Housey is lousy with insects. The hatches are prolific and intimidating and a thing of wonder. I tricked the fish one time by *not* matching the hatch (because they were refusing my every offering) and caught two fat 13-inch browns on a Royal Trude, an ugly downwing western attractor that should never work on this or any other eastern river. Word spread underwater and after those two trout, the others laid off. Smart fish. Tie your flies, load your box—hatchmatchingheaven.

The Housey offers so much of a good thing, you understand why so many experienced fisherfolks find it hypnotizing: nice current, deep pools, riffles, wide flats, variety, cute scenic historic towns, Americana, holdover browns and rainbows that grow surprisingly large, up to 16 or so inches, and in parts, the river seems almost western.

Like most eastern rivers, the Housatonic heats up during the summer but the feeder stream mouths are regulated safe havens for summer-stressed trout. I haven't fished the Housey enough to be an expert but when I have been on the river, I was not crazy about the numbers of other anglers who crowded small sections with all that other water to cover. Or paddlers. That's the nature of eastern streams so close to metro areas, I know.

The regulations are catch and release in the best parts of the river, in the Trout Management Areas (no closed season in TMAs with a small exception). You can also float the Housey on a raft or other type of pontoon and reach water not many others do. There is so much water in so much unexplored area that much of the Housey doesn't get pressure. Hint: Don't forget about smallmouth bass population. Nice diversion.

The Housatonic offers so many different kinds of water. Great access. Lots of fish, browns and rainbows of all sizes. Various sections tumble over cascading waterfalls and others run slow and deep. The fish inhabiting these runs, riffles, and pools are educated, wary of leaders and big flies. The Housey is close to metro areas (Boston, New York, etc.) so you can steal away for a day of angling, a day of refuge. So can others, so be prepared.

CONTACTS

Housatonic Meadows Fly Shop, Cornwall
    Bridge, www.flyfishct.com
Housatonic River Outfitters, Cornwall
    Bridge, www.dryflies.com

Great site for Connecticut guides and fly shops: negetaway.com/connecticut/pr/ctflyfishing.html

I cut my right hand open on the West Branch, scrambling down to where a chute poured through two big rocks and formed the perfect plunge pool. The cut was in between where my two middle fingers (keep it clean, guys) met my palm. I washed the blood out in the river and no matter how I tried to hold the rod, it stung like the dickens. So I cast left-handed. Not that I am preternaturally ambidextrous. I am not. Not that I am an amazingly coordinated fellow who can pick up something at the drop of a fishing cap. I am not. It's because I hadn't yet bastardized my casting with that hand and once I tried it a couple of times, I found I was much more fundamental, tighter, more controlled, and yet weirdly fluid. I can toss a ball right-handed and I look like I know what I'm doing. Left-handed, it's a girly throw. But if you have never seen me cast, I could fool you with my left hand.

Kennebec River

- **Location:** Middle of Maine
- **What You Fish For:** Landlocked salmon, rainbow and brown and brook trout, smallmouth and shad, striper, too
- **Highlights and Notables:** The Kennebec is back from years of misuse.

Some say this river is being underfished, ignored perhaps because of notoriety from pollution two decades ago. She's clean and has been for a good while. A major dam removal has brought a saltwater tidal change to the river as well, and that bodes well for shad and striper.

The Kennebec, which drains Moosehead Lake, is a storied river but its reputation took a dive and hasn't recovered yet. Still a good trout stream, the river is fishing better than it has in quite a while.

Below Shawmut Dam is the water favored by many, but the river is rewarding throughout. Wyman Dam to Gadabout Gaddis Airport is another sweet stretch. The river is a series of tailwaters which keep the Kennebec's fish populations steady—landlocked salmon, smallmouth bass, brook, brown, and rainbow trout. Some browns, not many but some, grow to bragging size.

The Kennebec has the usual excellent eastern hatches and early in the season, dry fly action is good on Hendrickson and BWO patterns. Give it a go, cold water or warm or salt. Get in there before the crowds figure out the Kennebec is good again.

CONTACTS
Kennebec River Outfitters, Madison, www.kennebecriveroutfitters.com
Flyfishing Only Fly Shop, Fairfield, www.maineflyfishing.com
Mountain Valley Flies, Solon, www.mtnvalleyflies.com
Fly Anglers Guide Service, Clinton, www.flyanglersguide.com
Gateway Recreation and Lodging, Bingham, www.gateway-rec.com

Kingfisher River Guides, Kingfield,
www.kingfisherriverguides.com
Maine Wilderness Tours, Belgrade,
www.mainewildernesstours.com

Rapid River

- **Location:** Western Maine
- **What You Fish For:** Brook trout
- **Highlights and Notables:** These squaretails rival in size those found in Labrador.

The average-size brook trout in Rapid River is, now hold onto—or on second thought have a seat—an amazing, mind-boggling, unbelievable 3.5 to 4 pounds. Average size. In America, not Canada. Brookies.

The Rapid River is short but obviously one of the best trout-growing rivers in the world. Less than four miles long, the Rapid is one of those special fisheries. Enhanced by the helpful catch and release–only and fly fishing–only restrictions, the Rapid and its riffles and pocket water and wide glides produce brook trout almost the equal of Labrador. And not all Rapid's brook trout look the same—it's as much fun to see the different markings and color combinations as it is to hold a 5-pound brookie in your hands.

Below Richardson Lake, the Rapid River is rapid, mean, hurtful, and hurrying to escape downstream. The pocketwater is productive but you'd better be careful wading or you'll take a drink of cold natural water. Some of the best water is at the Pond when the river is sort of flat all the way across, flat like plaster on a wall with little divots here and there, with some flat water sitting on top of other flat water like ledge on ledge.

Even though the water doesn't immediately look inviting with its tumbling whitewater, there are the big brookies and also salmon and (unfortunately) smallmouth bass in its riffles and pools. Getting to the river and to some of the better pools involves some doing, both by boat (lasts forever) and hiking (you up for an hour's hike?), but the trek is worth it. Four-pound brook trout, wild as the hair in my ears, and that's the average size. What are you sitting here reading for? Book a plane trip already.

CONTACTS
Rapid River Flyfishing,
Andover, 207-650-3890,
www.flyfishingfantasy.com
Rob's Fly Shop, North Jay,
www.robs-fly-shop.com

Sebago Lake

- **Location:** Southern Maine
- **What You Fish For:** Togue, brown trout, landlocked salmon, smallmouth bass, brook trout, crappie, perch
- **Highlights and Notables:** Variety of fish, great location, super scenery

The large, clear waters of Sebago Lake are the central focus of the southern region of Maine, providing fishing for large togue (the regional sobriquet for lake trout), brown and brook trout, and landlocked salmon. The surrounding terrain around Sebago Lake is some of the prettiest in the state even though commercial interests like camps, motels, and hotels ring the lake.

Sebago is the second largest Maine lake and ever so deep, 315 feet at its deepest. Landlocked salmon used to be the big ticket item at Sebago and to catch a 15-pound landlocked did not rise above exceptional. Nowadays, a 3-pound landlock is a nice fish. Two other fish have supplanted the landlocked Sebago salmon, the *Salmo salar Sebago*: smallmouth bass and lake trout, known in these parts as togue.

Smallies run about 2 to 5 pounds, which is nothing to sneeze at, and Sebago is lousy with them. The lake has a lesser population of largemouth bass, too. Sebago is becoming better and better known for being a lake trout lake (say that three times fast) and while the size of the lakers won't challenge any records, you can expect to catch numerous 4- to 8-pound macks and possibly some in the double digits. Anglers also catch black crappie and white perch (which with lake trout is an ice fishing target in the winter). Sebago is probably the best ice fishing lake in the state.

Sebago is close to so much. Up the coast is Portland, Maine's largest city, and it works well as a base to reach many of the area's trout waters. Be sure to visit the L.L. Bean store in Freeport. Sebago is an ideal family lake, beautiful, with easy access, camping, and nearby lodging, and is not far from places tourists love, like Kennebunkport and Kittery, the southern gateway to Maine.

CONTACTS
L.L. Bean, Freeport, www.llbean.com
Sebago Lakes Region Chamber of
    Commerce, 207-892-8265, www
    .windhamchamber.sebagolake.org
Maine Department of Inland Fisheries and
    Wildlife in Gray, 207-657-2345

West Branch of the Penobscot River

- **Location:** Central Maine
- **What You Fish For:** Brook trout, landlocked salmon
- **Highlights and Notables:** Classic Maine scenery, big squaretails

West Branch is a large river with way-too-easy road access. The Golden Road follows the river forever and I love it when I want to move from here to there but hate it when I find some other angler is using the same road I am to fish my holes. But the wooded West Branch is worth it, the way the river slams down into rocks, plows through gorges, bubbles and drops, foams and plunges and energizes into long ferocious rapids. All this chop-water holds stream-bred brook and below Rip Dam, stream-bred landlocked salmon.

The scenic stretch of the West Branch from the famous tailrace below Ripogenus Dam to Nesowadnehunk is better known for its nationally-respected landlocked salmon fishing, but hiding around the boulders away from the strong Penobscot current are some wary trophy brook trout of 2 to 4 pounds. The 2- to 5-pound salmon in the West Branch are storied for their fighting power. They pack a mean punch, so quick and powerful that it reminds me of hunting quail or pheasant. You know that initial burst when the bird fans out and scares the crap out of you with its fury? That's what a West Branch salmon does to you, in a manner of speaking. Many anglers consider this to be the best river for landlocked salmon in the United States. And the Rip Gorge ranks up there with any in the East for scenery and drama, ideal for the adventurous fishing floater (hire a guide, don't be stupid).

The East Branch is typical Maine scenery: stunning mountain views, thick pine forests, clear-flowing waters. Brook trout grow big here, too, but the majority of squaretails will be under 14 inches. Since much of the East Branch is made up of deeper, faster water (as is the lower West Branch), traveling its course by canoe should include caution and experience. Both branches are heavily fished at times but canoeing and rafting can get anglers to relatively secluded parts of each.

CONTACTS
Maine Guide Fly Shop and Guide Service, Greenville, www.maineguideflyshop.com
Two Rivers Canoe and Tackle, Medway, www.tworiverscanoe.com
Mountain View Drifter Lodge and Outfitters, Millinocket, www.mountainviewdrifter.com
Penobscot Guide Service, 229 Center Street, Brewer, 207-989-8806
Penobscot River Company, 261 Stillwater Avenue, Old Town, www.PenobscotRiverCo.com
Fish Stalker Guide Service, Brewer, www.maineflyfish.com/fish_stalker/fish_stalker.htm

MASSACHUSETTS

I love this thing I do. I teach, I have summers off, I travel and write. I get to go to places like Cape Cod and I fish for migratory northerly stripers that pass through these waters, big stripers that eat everything that won't eat them, from squid to menhaden and probably little children.

I love this thing, this bodacious place, this awesome sport of fishing. Cape Cod has it all. Summer chic, cool breezes, fly shops

City Fishing

BOSTON
Boston Harbor

My cousin Jay went to Harvard (after making his undergraduate mistake by attending and graduating University of Texas). Because Jay went to Harvard, we got to go to Boston a couple of times more than we would have. I've been now to Beantown four times and I can't wait to go back again (although next time I will be fishing) because the town is alive, has an energy unlike few other American cities. The history, the people, the attitude. When I was in Boston previously, fishing Boston Harbor was not even a thought, it was so polluted. It's been cleaned up and it cleaned up well.

Boston Harbor has become a prime fishing destination, not just one of those places you fish because you're looking for fishing while staying over in this or that city. North and South Shore have great runs throughout the year of striper and bluefish (and at times, hickory shad). Of course, South Shore is close enough to Cape Cod and Martha's Vine-

yard (separate entries in the book), and the quality of fishing isn't all that different. Most of the stripers are schoolie size but you can still get into some monsters (15, 20 pounds, or bigger) at times. And the action on the surface can be thrilling on poppers and topwater lures and flies.

The North Shore has a variety of terrain and all kinds of water for stripers and bluefish. Much of South Shore is private but you can still find plenty of access through beaches like Plymouth and Duxbury (and many others). Would you believe that you can fish and catch nice fish near State Street or near the TD Banknorth Garden downtown (where the Celtics run up and down the floor). You can fish the shallows around any of the harbor's thirty-plus islands. The key is to find the fish, fish the season, and cover a lot of water. The stripers move into the warmer shallows come April, replaced by blues come July, then come the stripers again in fall. The Neponset River is a popular estuary/marshland fishery for Boston anglers.

and guides and talk of fishing, delectable food, bluefish, bonito, false albacore, giant bluefin tuna, celebrities, history, and souvenir t-shirts. What more could you want?

You can get a lot of the same ambience and seaworthiness and quality angling at

Martha's Vineyard. Amy and I did a lot less fishing and a lot more touristing than I wanted on one trip to Martha's Vineyard. I was there for inshore fishing. Now I am aware that I am lucky that I have Amy. It's not likely any other beautiful woman would be interested in me or put up with me or fish with me or indulge me. My friends tell me this all the time. I know, I know.

So there we were, holding hands and shopping and eating at cute restaurants and buying trinkets, walking beaches barefoot and climbing dunes and jealously eyeballing the colorful rows of beach houses, while out in the salt there were migrating stripers tearing up herring and squid. I took pics of the rocky coastline, the farmers' market, summer tourists with red cheeks and white tennis shoes. I like history and beauty and nature as well as the next person but I also like catching striped bass better than most.

I caught a few stripers in the 10-pound range but the weather turned foul and my mood turned foul and at the end of the day, I had Amy and we had Martha's Vineyard and I know, I know, I'm a lucky guy.

Caught off the surf, this striper put up a fight

Cape Cod, Cape Cod Bay, Nantucket Sound, Nantucket Island

- **Location:** Far eastern Massachusetts
- **What You Fish For:** You name it. Stripers are the big sport but you also fish for albacore, bonito, bluefish, and tuna.
- **Highlights and Notables:** Bodacious scenery, flats fishing, the atmosphere that only Cape Cod owns, trophy stripers

Roll up your sleeves and get to work. There's fish to be caught. I have a word

for Cape Cod and its islands and bays: *Bodacious.*

Thirty-pounders, no big deal. Forty-pounders, nice catch. Fifty-pounders, not quite a lifetime fish but let's get a photo or two. Sixty to seventy pounders, you know, we might need to weigh that sucker.

Giant bluefin tuna. Recently, they're back in good form, 7- to 10-foot long, the likes of which haven't been seen since the 1970s. While not the same or as many or as big, they're here. They school and you can see them and it's magnificent.

Get to know the northern end of Monomoy Island that lies in northeast Nantucket Sound, the western side of this Monomoy Island. Flats fishing. You read it right. Flats fishing for stripers, if you want to call them flats. I guess they are, three feet or less, pretty much clear with green and amber then darker to blue, sandy bottom and in these flats, you fish for 10- to 20-pound stripers but 30-plus pounders have been taken on these flats. A 20-pound striper in the flats is kinda like tying a tow-strap onto a trailer hitch of a souped-up, speeding pickup truck and trying to Rollerblade behind it.

You catch such a variety of species, you never know what you're going to catch, and you can get into fish so many seasons. Striper and bluefish are heaven May through July but tougher in August and September, so you fish for bonito and false albacore instead.

You could stay in Nantucket, a rich man's retreat replete with celebrities and surfcast. Nantucket is a one- to two-hour ferry ride from Cape Cod.

Cape Cod is simply one of the best places in the world to fish. Known for its shallow waters, you sight-cast a lot. You watch feeding diving birds for clues. You catch as many fish in the evening, at dusk, at night as you do in the clear of day.

Besides striper and bluefish and albacore and bonito and bluefin tuna, if you wanted to go offshore, you could also fish for yellowfin tuna and white marlin (at times depending on currents) and blue marlin, bigeye tuna, albacore tuna, wahoo, and mako sharks. You can fish brackish barrier ponds and clear bass ponds, estuaries, tidal creeks, jetties, rips, rock piles, sandy bottoms, islands, rocky beaches and sandy beaches, and river outlets. Access is easy and everywhere.

CONTACTS

Cape Cod National Seashore Park
    Headquarters, 508-349-3785
Cape Cod National Seashore,
    508-487-2100
Fishing the Cape, www.fishingthecape.com
Randy Jones, www.yankeeangler.com
Jeff Walther, 508-240-6602
Bob Luce, 508-432-4025
Nantucket On The Fly, www
    .nantucketonthefly.com

Deerfield River

- **Location:** Northwestern Massachusetts
- **What You Fish For:** brown and rainbow trout
- **Highlights and Notables:** Trophy-sized trout in a year-round tailwater

It's always nice to find a quality river in these parts whose name I can easily spell. The Deerfield River in northwestern Massachusetts is the top trout fishery in the state, heavily stocked, but holding browns and rainbows of note. In this year-round growing environment, the trout get bigger, some to 24, 25, 26 inches.

The river is year-round because the numerous power-generating dams are bottom-release, but fishing in cold winters means fishing to lazy trout. The water releases are up and down on the Deerfield and you have to take them into play, working hard and fishing hiding places when the water is up; when the water goes back down, the fish prowl and you should, too. When the water begins rising, you don't have long to make decisions to swim or get to high ground. Pay attention.

Pools and runs and riffles with some pocket water make up the configurations of the Deerfield. Good hatches, nice long clear pools, pretty water, catch and release, artificials only in places, some big water in parts—it's a nice experience located less than a three-hour drive from Boston. The Deerfield is a tributary of the Connecticut River and the best section of the Deerfield is below Fife Brook Dam, where legendary places along this catch-and-release area have names like Fisherman's Pool, the Swimming Hole, Lookout Run, Yankee Flats, and King's Rapids. As the names imply, there is a variety of trout water.

The catch-and-release areas can hold choosy, big rainbows and browns best caught with mayfly and caddis imitations. Favorite dry flies include Blue Quill, Elk Hair Caddis, Adams, Light Cahill, Blue Winged Olive, and wet flies work well, too. The river supports lots of insects, which sometimes makes fish finicky and fishing frustrating. Under normal conditions, anglers can wade most of the river, but it can be tricky. Chest waders and felt soles are recommended.

CONTACTS

Dave's Pioneer Sporting Center,
    Northampton, 413-584-9944
Walt Geryk, fly fishing guide, Hatfield,
    413-247-3380

Martha's Vineyard

- **Location:** Island southeast of Massachusetts
- **What You Fish For:** Stripers, bluefish, and much more
- **Highlights and Notables:** Rocky coast, New England atmosphere

Known for its unique New England summery beachy monied feel, Martha's Vineyard is an excellent fishery for striped bass in May and June as well as bonito, false albacore, and especially bluefish. Anglers can begin fishing South Shore for bluefish and striped bass as early as April and still take them into November. The 100-square-mile area is a blend of six towns, each with its own flair and atmosphere, beaches, and nature preserves. "Charming" is the best word to use to describe it.

More than 120 miles of rocky shoreline means that stripers are at home. When the birds circle and the squid and baitfish furiously leap to avoid being eaten, you can rest assured that a cast into the maelstrom will draw a striper strike. Most fish from boats, some from choice beaches, searching for the 10- to 20-pounders early in the season, the 30-pounders and up, later.

Come September and through October, Martha's Vineyard Striped Bass and Bluefish Derby takes over. All sorts of divisions shoot for prizes and honor, going after all species of fish.

One of the top guides of fly fishing is

the Vineyard's own Capt. Jeff Sayre, and this is what he tells me: May and June are great months to catch your first bluefish or striped bass on the fly!! By mid-May large bluefish move in, many of which can be sight-cast to in shallow water, and bass fill the rips around the island. The cinder worm hatch of May also provides an exciting opportunity to catch stripers. Cast to stripers as they blast squid all around the boat.

CONTACTS

Capt. W. Brice Contessa, Contessa Flyfishing, www.contessaflyfishing.com
Capt. Jeff Sayre, Fly Fishing the Vineyard, www.flyfishingthevineyard.com
Capt. Jamie Boyle, 508-922-1749

Capt. Tom Rapone, 508-922-1754
Cooper Gilkes, 508-627-3909
Ken and Lori VanDerlaske, 508-696-7551

For more guides and outfitters, try this Web site: www.mvgazette.com/directory/browse/bait_and_tackle/170.html

Ware and Quaboag Rivers
You've never heard of these outstanding trout waters, admit it. Stocked browns and rainbows in easy-access rivers not all that far from major urban settings.

Quabbin Reservoir

- **Location:** Central Massachusetts
- **What You Fish For:** Seventeen species and the top game include small-mouth and largemouth bass and white perch
- **Highlights and Notables:** Wilderness setting, diversity of fish

Old Reliable. You can go to Quabbin and know that, depending on the time of year, *something's* biting. In the spring, the land-locked salmon and lake trout are tearing up forage fish and all you have to do is unlock their locations. Come summer, the smallmouth and largemouth fishing heats up.

Quabbin Reservoir is a meandering, spread-out fertile fishery, a wilderness-type lake that's not quite in the middle of no-where. Most fishermen will be jigging or trolling for white perch and at Quabbin, they're fighting fools, resisting the boat be-cause they know they taste so good and are headed for the frying pan. The lake holds so many game fish, some seventeen total, that it's hard not to find fish to catch (and they include rainbow trout, pickerel, yellow perch, panfish, etc.). Quabbin Reservoir is over eighteen miles long, dotted with numerous islands and undeveloped shoreline.

CONTACTS
Quabbin Visitor's Center, 485 Ware Road, Belchertown, 01007, 413-323-7221

Westfield River

- **Location:** Western Massachusetts
- **What You Fish For:** Brown, rainbow, and brook trout
- **Highlights and Notables:** Out-of-the way small stream fishing

Out in western Massachusetts flows a three-headed creature, each of the head(waters) small and attractive, distant. At Huntington, the three become one, a fertile moving beast.

The Westfield River is formed by three branches (East, West, Middle), each which is fairly remote, small, scenic, not heavily fished. East Branch is the biggest of the three, referred to as the Westfield even though it's the East Branch, very fishable, with an artificials and catch-and-release section at Chesterfield Gorge all the way for eight miles to Knightville Reservoir.

In some areas, the road sucks and that means fewer anglers to park, hop out, and fish in the beautiful mountain scenery for brooks, browns, and rainbows. Most fish reach an average size but you'll get surprised every now and again by a 15-inch trout or bigger. The Gorge may be the most famous stretch but the better stretches are those where the trees shade big pools, where the river curls up behind rocks, swirls into eddies, stops and forms holding pockets. The West Branch is small but not tiny, and if you have different casts in your bag of tricks and you like to explore small streams, don't pass this up.

CONTACTS

Walt Geryk, Northeast Fly Fishing Guide
Service, 413-247-5579

BG Sporting, Westfield, 413-568-7569
Marla Blair's Fly Fishing Guide Service,
Ludlow, www.marlablair.com

NEW HAMPSHIRE

I had to finally get to the Androscoggin River in summer, in the heat, with Umbagog Lake shallow and hot and the water it releases as the Androscoggin was hotter than I wanted or the trout wanted.

The river is bigger than I expected. Wider. There's some heavy water in the Androscoggin. I saw many who kayaked and canoed and were not fishing. Some people, sheesk. I did see the most beautiful vehicle in the history of the world in one of the small towns, a Toyota Land Cruiser from the old days all tatted out, buffed up, racks and grills, army fatigue green, mean and stoked and ready to fish.

So you fish from a boss Toyota Land Cruiser, if you're lucky enough, for landlocked salmon—of which there are plenty, but they're on the Mickey Rooney side.

Androscoggin River

- **Location:** Northern New Hampshire
- **What You Fish For:** Landlocked salmon, brook and brown trout
- **Highlights and Notables:** Juicy floatable stream in the mountains

The river is a bit of everything a trout stream should be: long flats and glides and deep pools. Rapids that turn into riffles. Pocket water, juts and points and banks. You can wade it. You can float it. You should float it and get out and wade it.

This is one pretty clear river. The road runs along the west side but the eastern side is roadless. That means if you can float, you can cover water that gets fished less. I didn't see any prolonged hatches—some gray mayflies, some blonde caddis, and I missed the Alderfly hatch (really the zebra caddis), so it was prospecting time.

You're not gonna catch the big fish on the Androscoggin. It's not a big fish river. You fish for landlocked salmon. You catch lots of brook trout (mine weren't that colorful) and brown trout, some of size but not bragging size. Make sure you get a friend who is a good paddler and won't tip over the boat and everything in it, because there are some Class 2 and 3 rapids along the way. But who am I kidding—when I waded, I got to slippin' and slidin' and got in too deep and took a dunking.

While I enjoyed floating the river and catching a few landlocks, a lot of brookies, and a couple of browns, I enjoyed the feeder streams, Mollidgewock Brook and Clear Stream and Bog Brook, in a different way, too. Beautiful streams loaded with nice brookies. I found weighted streamers worked well, saw that spinning lures and big, bushy dry flies thrown around cover will produce strikes from the lurking browns. The Androscoggin has a lot of river to offer, and for its quality has little fishing pressure. Other streams in the area are small but are loaded with brook trout.

CONTACTS

North Country Angler, North Conway,
    www.northcountryangler.com
Ducret Sporting Goods, Colebrook,
    www.allroutes.to/ducrets
L.L. Cote, Errol, 603-482-7777
Ray Cotnoir, guide, 603-466-5179
Ken Hastings, guide, 603-922-3800
New Hampshire Fish and Game
    Department, Concord, www.wildlife
    .state.nh.us
Northern White Mountain
    Chamber of Commerce, www
    .northernwhitemountains.com

Connecticut River, New Hampshire and Vermont

- **Location:** Northern New Hampshire, northeastern Vermont
- **What You Fish For:** Landlocked salmon, brook trout especially in the upper reaches, brown and rainbow trout in the lower sections
- **Highlights and Notables:** Variety of water type, variety of fishing experience, near-wilderness feel

The Connecticut is one of the real finds of the Northeast. The river is no secret but it somehow has managed to remain rustic feeling, more wild than most top-notch eastern rivers. The Upper Connecticut River is a complex of water bodies, not a river in the sense you might think. The "river" flows from lake to lake—four lakes ingeniously named First, Second, Third, Fourth Connecticut Lakes—as well as Lake Francis.

In the upper reaches, the Connecticut is a wilderness stream, or pretty close to one anyway. You see the lodges and campgrounds and other vestiges of human intrusion, but the river is small and fairly wild and the trout are small. After the river picks up Perry Stream (fishable in its own right), the Connecticut leaves boyhood and becomes a man. I don't know if this says anything about me, but I still like fishing the smaller water between First and Second (bushwhack time) and between Second and Third Lakes. The woods are thick with fir and conifer, the solitude pleasing

(I like to fish alone sometimes), the stream small, the boulders big, the coolness of the air refreshing and the brook trout are meaty little kaleidoscopes, and the intimate pleasure of it all is like back-to-back Fridays. Some days, I don't want to think about hatches or technique or strategy—I just want to catch a bunch of little fish in pretty surroundings.

Somewhere when the water gets bigger, you can catch landlocked salmon, or so I am told. Perhaps it's the tailwater below First Lake which is the best overall water on the Connecticut to me. Especially where Perry comes in.

Below Murphy Dam at Lake Francis, the Connecticut River emerges wider and deeper, and from here downstream, there are many big browns and rainbows. Muddler Minnows and sculpin imitations get big results. As you move downriver, wading is more precarious, cleats and wading sticks often being used by experienced fishermen. The river is slower and meanders past picturesque dairy farms. It stays cold and fertile, resulting in heavy insect life. At Lyman Falls, the river has special regulations; the fish reach nice sizes in that stretch.

The Upper Connecticut has good fishing from ice-out all the way into autumn. Spin fishermen cover the water with spinners and spoons, and fly fishermen match the hatch and swing wets and streamers into likely looking pools and runs. All along its coldwater course, access is ridiculously easy.

Mayfly hatches include the big Hexagenia, the small Blue-Wing Olives, tricos, green drakes, Hendricksons and pale evening duns. The river also has bountiful hatches of caddis, stonefly, midges, and terrestrials. To top it off, many stretches of this river do not receive much angling pressure even on summer weekends and holidays. The river does have problems with low water flows in the mid to late summer. Anglers from New Hampshire and Vermont have reciprocal license privileges to fish the river, but New Hampshire regulations take precedence because they technically own the Connecticut River.

The lakes themselves are worthy diversions: lightly-fished blue dots in northern New Hampshire, holding stocked brook, rainbow and lake trout.

CONTACTS
Lyme Angler, Hanover, 603-643-1263
North Country Angler, North Conway,
   www.northcountryangler.com

Lake Winnipesaukee

- **Location:** East central New Hampshire
- **What You Fish For:** Landlocked salmon, largemouth and smallmouth salmon, rainbow trout, and more
- **Highlights and Notables:** Huge lake with big fish and awesome mountain scenery; great family getaway

Ask someone who fishes Lake Winnipesaukee why they fish the big lake and your answers will vary from angler to angler. Landlocked salmon as long as Elle McPherson, one of them will respond. Lake trout as heavy as Jack Palance in the

1950s, says another. Rainbow trout as big as lake trout. Largemouth bass and smallmouth bass by the dozens. Say what?

The lake with the crazy name. Lake Winnipesaukee. Why should anyone go to this lake? Easy: 44,500 acres with 374 islands; 26 miles long with 185 miles of shoreline. One hundred feet deep at its deepest, and more structure than a Hollywood actress including humps, points, and dropoffs (see? structure like an actress). Tree-lined shores, low-slung green mountains, the White Mountains.

Yep. The lake was so busy being one of the top salmon and laker lakes in the Northeast, the cold deep-water rocky bottom fostered healthy populations of black bass, where bronzebacks grow up to five pounds.

With so many quaint New England villages and their inclusive shopping, restaurants, and historical sites, with so much lodging on the lake, so many ramps and amenities and resorts, Lake Winnipesaukee is one of the top family fishing vacations in the country.

CONTACTS
NH Fish and Game Department, Concord,
    www.wildlife.state.nh.us
Ames Farm Inn, Gilford,
    www.amesfarminn.com
Silver Sands Motel & Marina, Gilford,
    www.silversands.com

This Web site lists all the numerous guides, lodges, tackle shops serving the lake: www.winnipesaukee.com/links/ Fishing.

NEW YORK

I cannot believe the hatches on the West Branch of the Ausable River. I got so caught up in deciphering the hatches throughout the day, my first day on the water, that I didn't much care if I caught trout or not. You ever do that? On one June day, I saw multiple mayfly hatches of all kinds of the eastern variety, two different caddis hatches, and a stonefly hatch.

Amy and I surf fished at Montauk watching clouds gray-silver, slate-blue, pregnant with water, portentous, bulked up, filling the horizon, cold and windy, moving our way.

What does Cheryl David see in Larry David anyway? He's mean-spirited, not all that handsome, anything can come out of his mouth. Montauk's weather can be mean-spirited (don't turn your back on this sea). Montauk's scenery doesn't compare to the Bahamas, the Teton, New Zealand. But you can catch just about anything out of these rough blue waters.

Surf fishing always reminds me of when Dad would wake me at four o'clock in the morning and we'd pick up Marshall Turner, Dad's best friend, and we'd drive to the Freeport Jetties or we'd surf fish near Port Aransas and the weather was always windy and cold and wet and the surf and salt burned my cheeks. But Dad and Mr. Turner waded out to their hips in that cold crashing water, slinging their shrimp on big curved pointy hooks as far out as they could and their smiles, their silly smiles. They loved the blurriness of it all.

We fished in the surf, the rocky beach behind us, the cold waves beating, beating against our waders, the birds diving, the high steep shoreline a barrier behind us but the wind in front of us, and nothing was stopping its merciless pounding. "Fishing is good when the weather is not" the bearded old man at the tackle shop told me, and the rain began, the waves became whitecaps, the air became colder and my rod bent violently, a salty beast at the other end.

I fished the Salmon River only one time and thought I did pretty good. I spilled my morning coffee in the rental car, got caught on the river in a freezing rain before I could take off my vest and take out my rainjacket, I slipped and fell and soaked my shirtsleeve, smoked two cigars during the wet cold day, and ate a Slim Jim and drank a juice box for lunch. I enjoyed the experience completely even though I didn't catch a single steelhead. But since most anglers don't, I felt like I fit right in.

My buddy Jorgen, who lives in upstate New York, has caught several browns of real size in the Willowemoc, but he has asked me not to write about this. I will say this, the bigger browns I have caught in the deeper pools of the Willowemoc have been the color of Aladdin's lamp. As for

Jorgen's big browns he catches there, well, I can't really say anything about something he doesn't want me to write about, can I?

West Branch Ausable River

- **Location:** Adirondacks in northeastern New York
- **What You Fish For:** Rainbow and brown trout
- **Highlights and Notables:** A classic trout stream

Legendary trout streams, you think of West Branch Ausable.

Though the quality of this freestone stream does not compare with days gone by, it is still one of our better fisheries. This beautiful stream is only a five-hour drive from New York City, so it endures heavy angling pressure. Because much of the river is public, access is good, but mostly by way of old logging roads and well-worn trails. Unfortunately, more and more of the West Branch is being posted.

The West Branch is known for its productive pocket water, but the river has long stretches of flat water and numerous deep pools. Brook trout inhabit the headwaters of the West Branch, rainbow and brown trout swim around the boulder-strewn lower section. The river relies on stocked trout to meet fishers' needs, but the river has a good population of wild trout. In fact, the West Branch could be a much better fishery if it were managed as a wild trout fishery. Unlike in the so-called good old days, the average trout caught in the West Branch does not measure 18 inches or weigh 2 pounds. Trout grow fast in these waters, and holdover trout grow to nice fighting sizes, up to 3 pounds or so. The average size fish runs 12 to 15 inches. Biggest I've caught is about 15 inches.

The best fishing begins below Highway 86 and is good all the way to the river's entrance into Lake Champlain. The river fishes best in spring and fall since the summers lower the water level and stress the fish. Anglers will need to wear felt-soled waders because the West Branch is rocky. Walking the stream bottom is like walking across a bed of greased bowling balls. The Ausable Wulff, a local creation, is the perfect fly to imitate the hatches, and meet the needs of the fast, foamy water. The pools require smaller, more exacting flies. Spinner falls in the late evening cause hundreds of dimples on the stillwater of these pools.

The river has the usual dependable eastern hatches of mayfly and caddis as well as an important hatch of stonefly. Fishers should fish the large black stonefly nymphs year-round, bumping the big fly off the bottom of the stream. Terrestrial patterns are important for fly fishers, too, especially ant patterns.

The small but charming town of Wilmington serves the needs of fishermen, has done so for years. Lake Placid also has adequate lodging and other services.

The sister river to the West Branch, the East Branch of the Ausable is a wide, shallow trout fishery but not nearly as productive. The East Branch is primarily a put-and-take river relying almost exclusively on heavy stocking. The main stem of the Ausable is thought to be troutless but it holds some decent populations. The river used to be tainted by sewage and pollution, but these unfortunate river additives have ceased. Atlantic salmon inhabit the river as they move in and out of Lake Champlain.

CONTACTS
Jones Outfitters, Lake Placid, www .jonesoutfitters.com
Ausable River Fly Shop Wilmington, www.ausableriversportshop.com
Tightlines Fly Fishing, Pine Brook, www.tightlinesflyfishing.com

Beaverkill River

- **Location:** In the Catskills, southeastern New York
- **What You Fish For:** You're fishing for the browns but you can also catch rainbow and brook trout.
- **Highlights and Notables:** One of the most legendary streams in America

To say the Beaverkill River is fabled is like calling the Great Wall of China long. There is no American river as storied, as much a part of fly fishing lore as this Catskill stream. The famous anglers fished and tied flies and wrote about this river, the famous pools like Hendrickson and Junction and Cairns and Acid Factory and Cemetery Pools. And after all, you couldn't have Roscoe as Trout Town USA if it wasn't really Trout Town USA, could you?

When you walk through the little town, fiddle in the fly boxes, see the sign, wade the river, you're hit by the force of history. So much of the sport so many of us love began here.

In the Catskill Mountains, in southern New York, the Beaverkill River flows toward East Fork Delaware, gentle, complex, familiar. There's an elegance about the intricate smooth-flowing surface, the river's relationship to the insects, the diversity the river displays.

Big long wide pools. Fuzzy riffles. Rocks and pockets.

Much of the upper Beaverkill is private, but below Livingston Manor down to Roscoe and for most of the river downstream, public water rules. In the heat of summer, the lower Beaverkill's trout have trouble with the warmer water. The trout fishing in Beaverkill has held up well considering that so many come from northeastern urban areas to visit the leg-

Adirondack Park
Lightly populated, but tourists certainly know about the huge wilderness area—they visit by the millions every year. The state park itself is 5.7 million acres, larger than any national park in the nation. Northern New York has lots of water, lots of big water, like the Hudson River, Lake Champlain, and Lake George. The scenery of the north country is grand, punctuated by the beauty of island-dotted lakes and the magnificent forested peaks.

endary waters. Some stretches, like the No-Kill section, offer superb angling. You can fish year-round and do well. You can do your best to match hatches and get skunked or you can get lucky and have a glorious day. To hold the heft of a brown trout caught from a Beaverkill pool, after you have identified the hatch, the stage of the hatch, made a great cast, kept the fly from dragging, set the hook, and brought this baby to hand, well, that's the cat's pajamas.

CONTACTS
Al's Wild Trout Ltd., Downsville,
   607-363-7135
Beaver Kill Angler, Roscoe,
   www.beaverkillangler.com
Catskill Flies Inc., Roscoe,
   www.catskillflies.com

Jorgen with a solid trout. Notice that while at first glance the river seems featureless, if you look below, you see an underworld of holding places.

Ultimate Fly Fishing Store, Hancock,
   607-637-4296
Wild Rainbow Outfitters, Starlight, PA,
   www.westbranchangler.com/
   WildRainbowLodge.html

Black Lake

- **Location:** Upstate New York, northern end, just this side of the Canadian border
- **What You Fish For:** Largemouth and smallmouth bass
- **Highlights and Notables:** Underrated, loaded with great habitat

Despite all the glitzy honors the lake receives (best bass lake in New York, that kind of thing), not many outside New York or neighboring villages just over the border have even heard of the lake. Boy-howdy, the islands on this lake!

Black Lake is shallow and warm, oxygenated and fertile, so scenic with the islands and forests and bays that it makes you wonder how this place hasn't blown up and become famous. The largest of the Indian River lakes, Black Lake fills 11,000 acres, is twenty miles long and has over sixty miles of shoreline. Black Lake has deep water, shallow water; flats and points; gravel bars and weed beds. In short, a little bit of every kind of habitat which works well for all the fish the lake holds.

Bass are Black Lake's calling card. The average bucketmouth is 2 pounds, the average smallmouth goes about a pound.

Catskill Park

This area of the Empire State is as storied as any other trout fishing region in the United States, and rightfully so. The Catskills have produced innovative angling techniques, classic fly patterns, and a host of famous and influential fly fishermen. The names of the rivers that flow through the Catskills are so intertwined with fly fishing literature and folklore, their reputations are often intimidating to the first-timer: the Beaver Kill, the Neversink, the Willowemoc, the Delaware, the Schoharie, the Esopus. Few places in the world have a set of trout fisheries this good, this fabled. The waters of the Catskills generally flow a little less turbulently than those of the Adirondacks, but the landscape through which they flow is no less majestic or impressive.

No trophies for either here but the largemouths do reach 4 to 7 pounds.

If you fish for crappie, you'll catch lots of them. If you are a northern pike, you will, too. Year-round fishing for pike up to 15 pounds. Bullhead catfish, a few walleye here and there, and mighty fine fishing for panfish. Ice fishing is popular on Black Lake. The lake is located in upstate New York, approximately two hours north of Syracuse.

CONTACTS
Black Lake Chamber of Commerce,
   Hammond, www.blacklake.org
Indian Head Point, Hammond,
   www.fishingresort.com

The eleven Finger Lakes from east to west: *Otisco Lake, Skaneateles Lake, Owasco Lake, Cayuga Lake, Seneca Lake, Keuka Lake, Canandaigua Lake, Honeoye Lake, Canadice Lake, Hemlock Lake, Conesus Lake,* and sometimes *Oneida Lake* (the thumb). Seneca Lake and Skaneateles Lake have the best fishing.

Cayuga Lake

- **Location:** Central New York
- **What You Fish For:** Brown trout, land-locked Atlantic salmon, lake trout, rainbow trout, and largemouth bass
- **Highlights and Notables:** One of the Finger Lakes, you're talking long and blue and steep and beautiful with a variety of game fish

Like eleven blue eels wriggling north across land to reach the sanctuary waters of Lake Ontario, the Finger Lakes spread out in central New York in their north-south narrowness, deep and glacial. The longest of the Finger Lakes, the one I like the best for fishing is Cayuga Lake, a steeply-shored across-the-board good fishery near the college-town of Ithaca (where Kurt Vonnegut attended Cornell).

Cayuga is long and slender, an ideal representation of a Finger Lake, up to 435 feet deep. That's deep. The lake is beautiful, typical of Finger Lakes, lined with trees and houses, cobalt-colored water.

The lake holds brown trout, landlocked Atlantic salmon, lake trout, rainbow trout, and largemouth bass, and all of them are worthy of any angler. Atlantic salmon average 2 to 5 pounds with the occasional bigger one. Brown trout are healthy, good size, deep fat bellies but don't expect to catch an 18-pounder like happened in 1997. Rainbow trout have been landed up to 9 pounds but are mostly of the 12- to 15-inch variety. Lake trout, with a 17.5 pound record, are taken deep but no world records here. Pike and perch, pickerel and bluegill and many more species also reside here and they all are worthy targets. Cayuga Lake has good fishing for everything.

Lake George

Lake George (28,000 acres) is one of the more scenic lakes in North America, despite the fact that it has become a major resort area. This storied lake is a 32-mile-long narrow lake, flanked by the Green Mountains to the east and the Adirondacks to the west. Like so

many northern New York lakes, Lake George has numerous islands sitting atop its aqua-blue, deep water, 365 islands by some counts. The lake is known better for its bass fishing, but anglers will also find lake trout and salmon.

Delaware River

- **Location:** Southeastern New York
- **What You Fish For:** Rainbow, brown, and brook trout where the water is cold enough and shad below
- **Highlights and Notables:** The hatches, man, the hatches and, oh yeah, the shad man, the shad, and don't forget about the underrated smallmouth angling in the lower stretches

This southeastern New York river holds rainbow, brown, and brook trout and you can fish them year-round. I have caught mostly browns and a handful of brookies. I find that I get lots of looks and rises but more snubs and refusals than most rivers.

The Delaware River and its upper two branches, the East and West, have been up and down over the years. They are in an up stage nowadays, constituting what might be the finest trout fishery in the East. Big-D holds wild rainbow and brown trout, known for their size and hard-fighting ability. Because the Delaware is a tailwater fishery, it receives summer water releases. The river stays downright cold despite the heat of summer, making it one of the few East Coast trout fisheries to remain productive throughout the length of summer. The Upper Delaware includes the two branches and it is the combined seventy-seven miles of fishable trout water where most anglers concentrate. The West Branch below Cannonsville Dam is the most noted and popular fly fishing water.

Even though the river has big fish, and lots of fish in the 15-inch range, and even though the river is within a couple of hours drive of most of the metropolitan areas, the Delaware is surprisingly underfished. Maybe the river has become too associated with the tremendous shad fishing. After leaving the Cannonsville Reservoir, the river forms the border between New York and Pennsylvania. The river is navigable and a good way to cover it is in a canoe.

On the Delaware River below the confluence of the East and West Branches, the river grows big, and pools are as long and wide as the eye can see. The Upper Branches are typically about thirty feet wide and are usually wade-fished, but they can be float-fished as well. The river is best broken down into two parts: the fifteen or sixteen miles above its junction with the Beaverkill and the river below it. The river has aforementioned abundant hatches, but these are smart fish and often require flies with less hackle and low profile. It could take an angler years to fully understand the different characteristics of the Upper Delaware.

The West Branch is often slow-moving and intimate before gaining speed and size, and the East Branch quickly realizes a big-water personality as it rushes to meet the main stem. The West Branch is generally the better midsummer water, while the East Branch fishes better early and late season. The main stem is just plain big water, and the fish you catch in this part will make you wonder why you only put seventy-five yards of backing on your reel. Hancock, where the East and West branches meet, offers you the nearest services.

If you hunt smallmouth bass, don't overlook the warm water Delaware in Pennsylvania. The Delaware Water Gap near Milford is unexpectedly scenic and natural given the river's closeness to so many urban centers. The lower Delaware stretches offer plenty of park and wade access but the most efficient method to fish is by floating the river, getting out every now and again and wading, floating again. This is much bigger water than the trout reaches above.

CONTACTS
Blaine Mengel, The Backwoods Angler,
    www.backwoodsangler.com
Brian Shumaker, Susquehanna River
    Guides, www.susqriverguides.com

City Fishing

NEW YORK CITY

New York is many things but one thing it is decidedly not, is a fishing destination. That said, did you know you can string up your rod and fish in any of the five boroughs and catch fish? Did you know that you can fish the surf in and around New York City? Striped bass are one of your spring quarries, followed in the summer by weakfish and bluefish, later false albacore and bonito. Anglers can fish from piers, in the surf, in flats, and from jetties in places around NYC including Queens (Little Neck Bay, the Lighthouse), Staten Island, the Bronx (Orchard Beach), Jamaica Bay, Brooklyn (Coney Island). Sheepshead Bay with its slips and piers has been a fishing favorite for the last century. That's the short list. You'll be amazed how many charters work the harbor and area waters.

Did you know that you can also drop a line in the Hudson and East Rivers in a variety of places too numerous to mention but including Battery Park City (Wagner Park), the Lighthouse, Gracie Mansion, and Long Island City.

So you can fish the salt in NYC. Crazy, I know.

Well, in that case, are there any lakes I can fish?

Yessiree Bob. You bet your sweet bippy. Here's a wild one: you can fish in Manhattan and it is perfectly legal and entirely plausible. Maybe not entirely sane but being different is a badge worn proudly in Gotham City. When it is warm and sticky in Central Park, the anglers come out and play: 59th Street Pond; Harlem Meer at East 110th; Boathouse Lake on West 72nd. You'll see rod-wielders fishing with everything from bamboo fly rods to cane poles. *Whatcha fishin' for?* Anything that bites. And that includes bass and bluegills mostly but you'll also find at the end of your line golden shiner, carp and chain pickerel. Catch-and-release fishing only (as if you'd want to eat something that came out of these lakes, right?). Manhattan's not the only borough where you can cast out a popper and catch a bass or bluegill. Some of the "standout" waters include Staten Island (Clove Lake, Wolf's Pond), Brooklyn (Prospect Park, where the bass are plentiful and thick, I am told), the Bronx (Crotona Lake), and Queens (Willow and Oakland Lakes; Oakland has a downlow rep for large cats and carp).

Gateway National Recreation Area: 26,000 acres of fishing pleasure right where New Yorkers live and breathe. From northern New Jersey into three boroughs, this is nature-lite at its best. Cast from jetties or work the flats. Brooklyn's Floyd Bennett Field and its marshy saltwater are ideal for flyfishermen. Crazy anglers catch blues, stripers, false albacore in the heavy cold wind of the Coney Island waters and watch the rollercoasters go up and down and all around.

Daytrippers, listen up. Long Island Sound is the prize fishing hole in the New York City area. Although shore access is limited, the west side urbanized, this body of water is productive most of the year for migratory, seasonal fish, real fighting fish like stripers (not the big ones like off Montauk or Cape Cod or Martha's Vineyard, but up to 30 inches long), bonito, false albacore, and bluefish (a real scrappy high-charged prey). You can fish in just about any kind of craft if the weather is good, targeting sheltered bays, flats, islands, and where rivers spill into the Sound. The western half is more developed but calmer; the eastern side has clearer water and is less developed but edgier and subject to windy conditions. In addition to the aforementioned species, you can also catch Spanish mackerel, weakfish, and hickory shad. And if that's not all, you can fish Long Island for trout on the Connetquot or Nissequogue Rivers.

Two Other Area Waters

Pepacton Reservoir
A 6,400-acre impoundment on the East Branch Delaware River, part of the water system of NYC. One hundred miles away from NYC. A 22-pound brown caught 1994. Strict regs. Rowboats only. Browns are big and a 5- to 6-pounder is not unusual.

Croton Waters
Twenty-five miles north of Manhattan (take the train). Connected lakes and rivers of the Croton River watershed. Putnam and Westchester counties. Largemouth and smallmouth bass in lakes. East Branch Croton River is a well-respected trout river. Need a permit from Environmental Conservation fisheries office.

CONTACTS
Capt. Ken Courtlangus, 516-932-0685
Capt. Dick Dennis, Backcast Charters, 732-929-0967
Capt. Tony DiLernia, 212-529-6910
Capt. Paul Eidman, 732-922-4077
Capt. Hobitzel, Outback Charters, 732-780-8624
Capt. Scott Holder, Dragonfly Charters, 516-840-6522
Capt. Barry Kanavy, 516-785-7171
Capt. John "Spot" Killen, Briny Fly Charters, 631-728-BASS (2277)
Capt. Ken Kuhner, 631-673-8937
Capt. Joe Mattioli, On The Bite Charters, 718-967-9095
Capt. Brendan McCarthy, 212-727-3166
Capt. John McMurray, One More Cast Charters, 718-791-2094

Glen Mikkleson's Atlantic Flies,
    631-878-0883
Capt. Bob Robl, Fly-A-Salt Charters,
    631-243-4282
Capt. Joseph Shastay, Jr., 201-451-1988
Shore Catch Guide Service,
    732-528-1861
Edwin Valentin, c/o The Urban Angler,
    212-979-7600 (knows Central Park
    well)
www.pflga.org is a great source for fly
    and tackle stores in the area

FLY SHOPS AND TACKLE STORES

Orvis, 522 Fifth Avenue (Corner of
    44th Street and Fifth Avenue),
    New York, NY 10017, 212-827-0698
Capitol Fishing Tackle, 218 West
    23rd Street, New York, NY 10011,
    212-929-6123
Paragon Sports, 867 Broadway, New
    York, NY 10003, 212-255-8036
Urban Angler, 206 Fifth Avenue
    (between 25th and 26th streets),
    3rd Floor, New York, NY 10010,
    212-979-7600

YOUR LOCAL GOVERNMENT
FISHING CONTACTS

New York State Department of Envi-
    ronmental Conservation, Region 2
    New York City (licenses, regs, and
    permits) 718-482-4922
www.dec.state.ny.us/website/reg1/
    nycfish.pdf (Comprehensive guide to
    using mass transit to freshwater fish

throughout the five boroughs of New
    York City)
New York City Department
    of Environmental Protection,
    www.ci.nyc.ny.us/html/dep/home.html
    or www.nyc.gov/html/dep/html/
    ruleregs/wsrecreation.html (You have
    to have a public access permit to fish
    the reservoirs in the Big Apple; here
    is a downloadable application and
    general information.)
New York State Department of Health,
    800-458-1158 ex. 27815
Battery Park City Parks Conservancy,
    212-267-9700, info@BPCParks.org
Dana Discovery Center, Harlem Meer,
    110th Street and Fifth Avenue,
    New York, NY, 212-860-1370
Gantry Plaza State Park, 48th Avenue
    and East River, Long Island City,
    718-786-6385
Gateway National Recreation Area,
    718-318-4300
Hudson River Park, Pier 40 at West
    Houston Street, New York, NY
    10014, 917-661-8740 www
    .hudsonriverpark.org, info@hrpt
    .state.ny.us
New York City Parks and Recreation
    Department, 800-201-PARK,
    www.nyc.gov/html/dpr/
The Waterfront Museum and Showboat
    Barge, 1290 Conover Street at Pier
    44, Brooklyn, NY 11231, 718-624-
    4719

Montauk Point

- **Location:** Easternmost point of Long Island
- **What You Fish For:** You name it, from shark to tuna, striper to albacore and everything in between
- **Highlights and Notables:** Surf fishing, hunting big stripers and tuna and other fish that challenge existing records, proximity to major urban areas

You can catch anything at Montauk. Bluefin tuna. Striped bass. Blue shark, brown shark, hammerhead, and mako, sometimes great white, tiger. Yellowfin tuna. Albacore, marlin, swordfish, dolphin, bonito, and on and on. Large fish, watery creatures that could eat you.

At Montauk, the easternmost point of Long Island, anglers have their best fishing opportunities on the entire seaboard for shark. A 1,080 pound mako off Montauk in 1979. A white shark in 1989 that weighed 3,427 pounds, more than the combined offensive lines of the Giants and the Jets. That kind of stuff makes you think when you are waist-deep in the angry ocean.

Large fish. Bluefin tuna of 500 pounds caught with scary regularity in the canyon grounds. Yellowfin tuna brought to the boat in the 50-plus pound class and up to 100 pounds. Blue marlin over 1,000 pounds. The big stripers come in spring and 40-pounders are common. Bluefish are a real player from May through November. Variety is the key at Montauk but quality variety. Reasons? The various migrating game

fish southern routes run right by Montauk, the tip of Long Island, and these fish find tons of bait to keep them there. Several water systems meet here, currents and streams. Montauk is one of the best fishing holes in the world.

CONTACTS
Capt. Peter Chan, Mostly Montauk,
   www.mostlymontauk.com
Capt. Frank Crescitelli and Capt. Dino
   Torino, Fin Chaser Charters,
   www.finchaser.com

For a list of other outfitters, guides, and shops visit this Web site:
www.onmontauk.com/fishing.html

Lower Niagara River

- **Location:** Western New York, north of Buffalo
- **What You Fish For:** Anything and everything
- **Highlights and Notables:** One of the best rivers for steelhead and smallmouth in America. The variety of big fish is amazing for such a short piece of water.

Is it really possible that the lower Niagara River is the best ten miles of any river in the world for multispecies trophy angling?

It is only ten miles long. Leaves Lake Erie, flows to Lake Ontario. Up to a dozen species you can catch, each possibly a trophy. You see some stalwart optimists fishing from the bank but the only way to fish

fifty fish a day, no problem. Four pounds on average for a smallie. That's huge. A great westerly wind and low barometric pressure is a good combo for you to have a field day.

The steelheading is a top-flight, too, with a healthy fishery—easy to catch and lots of them, not highly technical. From early to mid-October to April, you can find big steelhead. Catch Chinook salmon in spring. Most fish with salmon egg clusters/skein (eggs with membrane) or Glo-Bugs. There is also a lake trout run in May.

CONTACTS
Capt. Frank Campbell, Niagara Region
    Charter Service, www.niagaracharter.com
Bill Hilts, Jr., www.outdoorsniagara.com/
    bill_hilts_outdoors_weekly

this fast, deep, big water is by boat. Deep forbidding gorge. Treacherous river. Be prepared. Easy access from Toronto.

Smallmouth to 7 and 8 pounds. Brown trout as big as 30 pounds large. Ten-pound walleye, pike over 20 pounds and equally amazing and humongous steelhead, lake trout, muskie, sheepshead, and more. All on the same trip. Sometimes in bone-chilling weather.

You can fish this puppy all year long even when the Niagara Falls stretch freezes over. You use soft sensitive rods and invisible line. The smallmouth are so big and fat, they look like largemouth at first glance. Part of this is from the introduced gobi, a slow-moving, non-native fat baitfish—the smallmouth and walleye love them. If things are hot, you can catch twenty-five to

Salmon River

- **Location:** North central New York, east of Lake Ontario
- **What You Fish For:** Steelhead
- **Highlights and Notables:** One of the best winter steelhead fisheries in the East

While the steelheading has been up and down in recent years, the Salmon River is still a great winter fishery for steelies as well as a scenic and iconic river for the sport. You can fish the Black Hole or the Schoolhouse Pool or the private Douglaston Run stretch in Pulaski. The Salmon River has instituted rules and regulations and limits to help return the river to its former self (including a section of fly fishing

only). We're still talking several thousand fish caught each year, you can still catch whoppers up to 15 and even 20 pounds so it's one of the Northeast's finest steelhead rivers. You'll have to put in your time on the river, fifteen to twenty hours to catch one steelhead but that's part of the sacrificial fun of it. Best time to hit the Salmon is November and December.

CONTACTS

Oswego County tourism office,
    315-349-8322

Randy Jones, www.yankeeangler.com

Willowemoc River

- **Location:** Catskills, southeastern New York
- **What You Fish For:** Brown trout (as well as rainbow and brook)
- **Highlights and Notables:** One of the best trout streams in the Northeast

The upper Willowemoc is one of my favorite places to be in the East. I let the other Orvis-clad anglers squeeze into the crowded rivers of the Beamoc (the Beaver Kill and Willowemoc) while I play with wild brookies in the clear-yellow, often-shaded pocket waters of the upper river. The forests are so dark in places, you lose all color and the small river is a smooth copper sheen broken only by scattered gray rocks. A real test for my casting tricks and stealth. I often tie on a wet fly and that's about all I go with on the Willowemoc.

But to the part of the river *everybody* loves to fish, or talk about fishing. The Junction Pool where the Willowemoc River enters the Beaverkill, right? The Willowemoc has more public water than its sister river, the Beaverkill, but like sissy, the hatches dictate your success (or failure). The Willowemoc has the same pool-riffle-pool configuration, smaller overall.

Here we have the perfect eastern-city-getaway trout trip. Stay in a quiet Catskills motel with your fishing buddy, or in a romantic bed-and-breakfast with your significant other (but don't get the two options confused), visit any of a handful of fly shops in Roscoe or Livingston Manor or Decker-town, then get down to the business, the art, the science of insects. Figure out the hatch and you're almost there. Then you have to work to get in position, cast without getting lost in the thick streamside trees and vegetation, and see if those mayflies are Blue Quill or Hendrickson or March Brown or light Hendrickson, or hope and pray that maybe it's time for the grannoms to come out.

I suggest May or early June for the best angling memory. The river from Junction Pool down is usually referred to as the Big Beaverkill. Unlike the lower Beaverkill, come summer heat, the Willow is still cool and fishable.

The Beaverkill and Willowemoc Rivers are open year-round to fishermen. I also suggest getting upstream, hiking up some feeder creeks. Nearby streams worth visiting when the fishing is off or the fishermen are stacking up include the Little Beaverkill, Bush Kill, Trout Brook, Basher Kill Marsh, Fir Brook (a true Catskills test of your pocket water stealth against the wild browns), Catskill Creek, Callicoon Creek,

Mongaup Creek (high-mountain creek—not river—with easy road access for wild brookies).

PENNSYLVANIA

Letort Spring Run. It's like working on your stroke on the putting greens with professional golfers before the Masters and having one of them challenge you to a putt-around for a cool thousand. It's like the first time you ever played an action video game, on an X-Box or Playstation let's say, and you're playing your normal fifteen-year-old boy, which is akin to a gaming genius if he's like the fifteen-year-olds I know; you're facing a boy who knows what the buttons on the controller actually control and where the imbedded potions and weapons are hidden and how to sequence the buttons to maximize firepower and how to spin, drop, and roll so your character disappears.

Fishing this classic limestone stream is considered a rite of passage, perhaps because rites of passage by their very nature are meant to teach you a lesson, didactically important because to become a man, you must fail before you succeed. On Letort, you have a better chance at failure than success.

My Pennsylvania friends at Texas A&M always referred to their home state as P-A. Mike and Vinnie and Charlie, all with the hard-to-say and impossible-to-spell names that bespoke their Eastern European heritage. P-A boys partied hard, I'll say that much for them. One Halloween, we four got all dolled up in slips and combat boots, ·lit up cigars and walked proudly into the Texas A&M Library to find Amy (then my girlfriend). It's a wonder that girl married me.

Fishing Pennsylvania is a tough fun proposition. The streams have been fished and the trout are smart. So it ain't easy. Like when Tim Bollier and I would play one-on-one for hours in the driveway of his parents' Mineral Wells home (where I smoked my first cigar, a Swisher Sweet, and tried my first taste of liquor, something awfully sweet) and we'd just about always split the games. Letort. Raystown. Spruce Creek. Sometimes you get the bear, sometimes the bear gets you. Raystown is one of my favorite lakes in the Limestone State and it is brawlingly unabashedly P-A. Just like Mike and Charlie and Vinnie.

Letort Spring Run

- **Location:** South central Pennsylvania
- **What You Fish For:** Brown trout
- **Highlights and Notables:** Challenging chalkstream, one of the best spring creeks in the world

The combination of intricacies and unknowns on Letort Spring Run in south central Pennsylvania is overwhelming. Chalkstream. Spring creek. If those two delineations aren't enough to run you off to your favorite easy-to-fish freestone, then you are one of those spring-creek masochists. Welcome.

Letort Spring Run is one of the most famous rivers in America, having been the proving grounds for trout behavior by such noted fly fishermen and authors as Charlie Fox and Vince Marinaro. There are less than five miles of fishable stream, and the fertile stream is small, choked with watercress and other thick vegetation, the surface like polished marble.

Beginning anglers need not apply, because the Letort not only requires long, invisible leaders, tiny flies, and perfect casts to finicky fish finning in tricky currents, but it also is best fished with subsurface patterns. When I say long invisible leaders, I mean twelve-foot or longer, 7X or even 8X. Problem is, that if you were to raise a brown from his or her lair, that fish would snap off your fly with a small shake of the head. If you don't use long invisible leaders, you may not be able to entice them to even take a look at your offering.

Some Letort vets like to use shorter, heavier leaders and try to drop in streamers, get the brown trout's aggressive nature working for them. These vets know that they must stay far enough back from river's edge that the trout can't feel the footfall or see a shadow or any movement. If you put down a fish, you might as well smoke a pack of cigarettes before they'll show again.

The Letort holds wild browns, some of which weigh up to 5 pounds, feed on the abundant shrimp, scuds, and cress bugs moving about in the weedbeds. The trout get spooked easily so getting wet flies and nymphs to them without scaring them or lining them isn't easy. That's the reason the Letort is such a testing ground. About the only kind of dry fly fishing which can be done on the stream is with terrestrials like beetle, cricket, and ant patterns. The Letort is tucked away behind commercial development in Carlisle and has much more angling pressure now than then.

The Letort isn't the big-time trout fishery it once was due to many factors. The creek doesn't hold as many trout either. But because of the difficulties and complexities the angler confronts to catch any size brown trout—and some are still sizeable—this is the Rite of Passage East.

Pennsylvania Trout Streams

Little Juniata

This river will surprise you in many ways. For starters, big browns live here (although you'll have to match hatches and play the game just right to coax them to your fly). If you catch a brown trout 18 or 19 or 20 inches long, it won't be a big surprise. Re-

ally, you are going to be shocked at how big some of the browns are, and not the long skinny browns either. Fat and round and beautiful, like antique brass–colored Botticellis. For another, the Little Juniata isn't all that little. There are numerous limestone springs feeding the Little Juniata along its fifteen miles of good fishing water.

The river has recovered and with new vigilance and new regulations is back to becoming one of the finer trout streams in the state. The water once ran dark and smelly because of pollution. There are now wild brown trout swimming in these chalky limestone currents, swimming along with thousands of hatchery fish stocked by the state.

Route 453 runs alongside the river providing the angler with good access. Wading can be an adventure on this stream, like many Pennsylvania streams, for the underwater boulders are covered with slickness that will affect even felt-soled, cautious wading fishermen sooner or later.

Yellow Breeches Creek

Large trout in south central Pennsylvania. Yellow Breeches is part freestone, part limestone, all fun when it comes to catching the stocked and wild trout holding in the chalky water. You'll want to end up fishing the Boiling Springs–Allenberry Resort water.

You won't be fishing alone. Somehow, even though you see other anglers on the water, you don't feel as crowded as you do at some other streams, probably because this Yellow Breeches is larger than your average bear, forty feet wide in spots. Allenberry Resort is comfortable and the folks

City Fishing

PHILADELPHIA
Schuylkill River

You might be surprised (I was) to discover that Philly has one of the better urban fishing settings in the country. The Schuylkill River runs right through the city. In the upper reaches out of the city and on to Fairmount Dam flows a flirty scenic freestone stream that used to characterize the river for so many years. Anglers fish for smallmouth bass in scenic environs.

Below the nineteenth century dam, at the Fairmount Water Works, in full view of the Philadelphia skyline, the river is more moody, brawny, reliant on tides, estuarine and year-round. It's not unusual to see the base of the dam crowded with folks on shore casting for largemouth and smallmouth bass. Depending on the tide, the more determined fisherman can duel with everything from white perch to catfish to American shad to striper to sunfish and even the occasional brown trout.

The Schuylkill is so accessible it's amazing—the Loop runs along both sides of the river, a sort of walking-biking-jogging trail/path.

---

there know trout so this stretch becomes a touchstone, a place of trout renewal. Besides, it's an accessible and do-able getaway from urban centers, including during winter.

The river has great early season hatches, like caddis, Slate Drake, and Sulphur hatches. Fishing the river when no hatch is in progress can be challenging, but terrestrial, streamer, and midge patterns work on fished-over trout.

Penns Creek

This may be the most scenic river in Pennsylvania, with over fifty miles of good trout fishing water. Penns Creek is the longest limestone stream in the state, one of the widest, and is underrated compared to other limestone fisheries. The river can be difficult to fish because of its size, but Penns Creek has excellent hatches and is chock-full of wild and stocked trout to eat the abundant food. Some stretches hold trout where almost every trout you spot—and you can spot them easily—is 13 to 22 inches long. I've been with folks who caught trout much much bigger than that. I missed one that must have been 25 inches or longer.

These trout are finicky because they have so many choices; they can feed on Green Drake, Yellow Drake, Blue Quill, or Tricos. Penns Creek runs through the Bald Eagle State Forest, which has lots of hiking trails and puts the angler in the midst of beautiful stands of timber and hemlock. And if you hook up, the trout run for cover and bust you off.

The Green Drake hatch in late May is famous, and to fish the hatch means fishing shoulder to shoulder with other anglers. There are few trophy trout caught in Penns Creek, but plump 12-inchers and the occasional large brown make the stream blue-ribbon quality. Don't be surprised if you have days where you can't figure out the hatch and you come away with only wet waders.

Slate Run

Wild and rugged, scenic and green, Slate Run, for as well known and visited as it is, still gets my vote as my favorite Keystone State stream. Wherever you are on Slate, you are not where you easily scramble out. Wherever you are on the Slate, you feel you're in wild country, the slopes of the mountains right down upon you. Wherever you are on Slate, with its piles of flat rocks, ledges, green clear water, overhanging brush, dense stands of trees, big shaded emerald pools, pockets and riffles and runs, wild trout, lushness and fertility all around, you are glad you are there.

Seven miles of the north-central creek are catch-and-release, fly fishing–only. The hatches are typically eastern, good hatches of mayflies, caddisflies, and stoneflies.

Cedar Run

Neighbor to Slate Run, Cedar Run also offers prime fishing hidden in the folds of timbered mountains. Cedar Run flows crystal-clear, tumbling, stair-stepping over rocks into deep blue-green pools. Mossy rockfaces stand like primeval forest creatures.

Like Slate, this intimate river is pro-tected by special regulations. Almost all of Cedar Run's seven miles of remote water is under trophy-trout regulations and limited to artificial lures and flies. The pools hold some big trout, and average trout run 10 to 12 inches.

Falling Spring Branch

Wild trout stream that was banged around by civilization pretty good over the years. Falling Spring doesn't fall, it glides.

At one time, Falling Spring was one of the finest rainbow trout streams in the eastern United States, but heavy sedimentation and creeping civilization curtailed the continued success of the beautiful, small, gentle-flowing, limestone stream, known for its Trico and Sulphur hatches.

The stream was recovered and now has regained some of the hatches which fed its strong, colorful rainbow trout. There aren't many miles of fishable stream, but this short stretch requires a delicate touch, matching the hatch, and drag-free floats. Wading is easy on the narrow stream. The biggest I have caught since the meadow stretches are back in the game is a 12-inch rainbow but with snow on the ground, pretty as you please.

Fishing Creek

Pennsylvania has more Fishing Creeks than Pennsylvania has Rolling Rock bottles of beer. Five streams are ingeniously named Fishing Creek. Go figure.

One of the two best Fishing Creeks is Fishing Creek, the Fishing Creek located near the town of Lamar. The stream has the usual spectacular Pennsylvania mayfly hatches and annually produces some of bigger trout caught in the state. This Fishing Creek is a limestone stream even though it looks and acts like a freestone with its runs, pools, and riffles, and undercut banks and big boulders. Fall is a beautiful time to be on Fishing Creek, the Fishing Creek near Lamar, angling for wild and stocked brown, brook and rainbow trout in the trophy-trout designated section of the river. Sections of Fishing Creek are closed to angling on Sundays. I don't know why.

Big Fishing Creek

As if Pennsylvanians didn't make it difficult enough with all the Fishing Creeks, they have a Big Fishing Creek and a Little Fishing Creek. This Fishing Creek is in Columbia County. This Fishing Creek, excuse me, this Big Fishing Creek is a wadeable, cold freestone stream with nearly thirty miles of quality angling for stocked brown, rainbow, and brook trout, with many of the holdover trout reaching good size. The stream record is a 28-inch, 8-pound monster by none other than noted fly fishing writer/photographer Cathy Beck.

Access is good for most of the river with roads paralleling its course. Fishing Creek is a classic freestone stream, albeit colder than most eastern freestone streams. The pool/riffle/pool configurations make for ex-

City Fishing

PITTSBURGH
Ohio, Allegheny, Monongahela Rivers

Three Rivers. That's why they name everything in the city that way. The Ohio, Allegheny, and Monongahela Rivers. Surprisingly, you get outstanding catch rates for bass on these rivers and at times your catch seems small, but the average largemouth runs about 3 or 4 pounds. The smallies are small, with a whopper running 3 pounds.

Over 150 river miles to fish. Not too shabby. Even the Cheat River, which feeds the Mon (as the locals call it), has acquired a rep for largemouth bass. Sauger on the Mon are always good, and now they're showing up in the other two rivers, too. The Yough is nearby (see page 43). And if you haven't visited Pittsburgh or you did so thirty years ago, go back. It's cleaned up its act, the people are unique and as with Pittsburgh you can't help but love them.

Area waters worth dropping a hook for trout and bass include: Keystone Lake, Kooser Lake, Laurel Hill Lake, Linn Run, Laurel Ridge, McConnells Mill, Lake Arthur, Raccoon Lake, Raccoon Creek, Duke Lake, Yellow Creek Lake. And if you want quality trout fishing in rivers, less than three hours away are Little Juniata and Spruce Creek (see Pennsylvania Trout Streams entry.)

cellent fly fishing opportunities, especially when the varied insect hatches are ongoing. The lowest stretch holds some skittish, lurking huge brown trout.

Spring Creek

Fisherman's Paradise is paradise. Fish this lionized catch-and-release stretch from Bald Eagle Creek to Fisherman's Paradise for wild trout and wild crowds of anglers, too. An especially good choice in winter. Fish this just because of all the history, where catch-and-release, fly fishing–only and no-wading mentality all began, where legends like Joe Humphreys and Charlie Meck earned their chops.

Other Pennsylvania Trout Streams Worth Investigating
> Lehigh River
> Lackawanna River
> Quittapahilla Creek
> Kettle Creek
> Fishing Creek
> Spruce Creek
> Elk Creek
> Big Spring Creek

Raystown Lake

- **Location:** South central Pennsylvania
- **What You Fish For:** Smallmouth and stripers grow big but don't overlook the brown trout, lake trout, muskies, walleye, and largemouth bass.
- **Highlights and Notables:** Always a surprise at the end of your line

Raystown Lake winds through south central P-A, sinuously twisting for thirty-plus miles with the Appalachian Mountains descending right to water's edge. One hundred ten miles of steep deep shoreline. Not all that much lakeside development but the lake is heavily fished and with good reason. Pennsylvania's largest inland lake is an ideal challenge for the angler—she holds plenty of sporting fish, from smallies that run 3 to 6 pounds and stripers as big as 20 to 35 pounds (a 50-pounder was caught a few years back) and brown trout and lakers and muskies and walleyes (maybe the best fishery of the lot here) and largemouth; they're all healthy and deep in the lake, lots of trophies in fact, but they aren't easily caught or landed.

CONTACTS
Trophy Guide Service, www.trophyguide.com

Susquehanna River

- **Location:** Southern and south central Pennsylvania and a bit of Maryland
- **What You Fish For:** Smallmouth bass
- **Highlights and Notables:** One of the premier smallmouth bass rivers in America, this pretty stream is more about numbers than size.

The Susquehanna River has become an American fishing icon. After the river cleaned up its act (or others cleaned up the river's act) the smallmouth fishery took off and it has become one of the top bronze-back rivers in the country.

The Algonquian Indians called this river *Susquehanna* and the name means "muddy stream." It's not. It's green and clear.

The Susquehanna's reputation as a quality smallie stream is not based on trophy-sized fish but on the fantastic numbers of solid fish. Not many 5 to 6 pounders are caught. Big means 15, 16, 17 inches here. Each day is a heyday, full of bent rods and 14-inch emerald-sided slabs of fury, either diving or jumping.

Between the scenery (everything is so green, all shades of green in the early summer), diversity of habitat, diversity of light where you have some areas entirely in shade and others wide open bright, the length of the river, the opportunity to access, and the proximity to urban centers, the Susque-hanna is an amazing fishery. Hard to believe the river stays so clean, produces so many fish.

The Susquehanna is shallow, green, and clear with a bumpy rocky bottom. In places, the ledges and ridges are so perfect, they look man-made. I wet-waded but saw others in waders, many more in boats of all kinds. I like to be on the move and I waded miles and miles, looking for ideal lies. The dry fly action was good—they sipped more than slashed—but the locals say that the white fly hatch in late summer is the end-all. The river has profound food sources—insect life is rich with so much sun reaching the bottom of this shallow river; the bugs include mayfly, caddis, hell-grammite, damselfly, terrestrials and then you also have forage like crayfish, juvenile bass, dace, shiners, shad, etc.

When you consider the two forks, West and North, plus the main stem of the river, it all adds up to hundreds of miles of fishable river. Sunbury to Middletown is the most popular spot. You won't lack for places to eat or lodge. You won't necessarily need a guide but I can see where a boating trip would give you a great ride and super scenery, and cover a lot more water. Besides, these locals take their fishing seriously and have invented all kinds of flies and techniques for their little baby.

CONTACTS
Clouser's Fly Shop, 717-944-6541
Mike O'Brien, 717-322-8965
Dave Shindler, Jst Fishin' Guide Service,
   www.JSTFISHIN.com
Brian Shumaker, Susquehanna River
   Guides, www.susqriverguides.com

Youghiogheny River

- **Location:** Southwestern Pennsylvania, northwestern Maryland, northeastern West Virginia
- **What You Fish For:** Brown trout mostly but don't underestimate the rainbow trout
- **Highlights and Notables:** Trophy trout fishery with rough wild scenic water

The Casselman flows into one of the better tailwater fisheries in the East, the Youghiogheny River, also one of the most popular recreation rivers in the East. The "Yough,"

as it is known affectionately by canoeists, rafters, and anglers alike, is a powerful river. The river is more famous for its impressive whitewater than its holdover brown and rainbow trout, more famous for its polluted waters of two decades ago than its big fish. These trout are stocked by the state, adult trout in the first mile below the dam at Confluence, hundreds of thousands of fingerlings throughout the other twenty-six productive trout fishing miles to the dam at South Connellsville.

The Yough can be crowded with rafters and canoeists, but for miles and miles of it, anglers will see no other (or maybe few other) anglers. Because the river can only be accessed in parts by hiking, by biking on a nice bicycle trail, or by floating, fishermen often feel isolated, away from it all. There are only two villages on this twenty-seven-mile stretch of trout water, Confluence and Ohiopyle.

The river has all kinds of water character along this course, and provides good fishing for some pretty big holdover trout for fly fishermen, spin fishermen, and bait casters. If the water were more fertile, you'd see even better fishing. As it is, the hold-overs reach impressive sizes. The hatches are predominantly caddis hatches; the mayfly hatches are sporadic, even sparse. The river has lots of other trout food, including crayfish and minnows.

The river runs cool throughout the year, and it's a good idea to bring your Neoprene waders to the tailwater. The Yough is one of the few rivers in the state that remain fishable in July and August, and in fact, these are perhaps the best times to fish it. The currents can be deceptively strong, and footing tricky, so wear felt soles, use a wading staff, and stay respectful of the strength of the river. The last few years, anglers are seeing more and more 20-inch browns and rainbows.

RHODE ISLAND

Wood River

- **Location:** Western Rhode Island
- **What You Fish For:** Brown, brook, and rainbow trout
- **Highlights and Notables:** Proximity to urban areas, solid hatches, novelty of cute stream in Rhode Island

Rhode Island? Trout? I know, I had the same incredulity at one time.

On the west side of Rhode Island, kinda out in the country, away from the cities and shore crowds, flow eighteen miles of pretty trout water, freestone with little dams like stepping stones. If a river could be called "cute" then this one would be. The Wood River has delectable hatches, caddis and mayfly especially the Hex and the Hendrickson, which make the banks thick with them and those with rods.

Brown, rainbow, and brook trout rise to

carefully selected dry flies in the summer heat. Take a lazy canoe trip to cast your line or wade (wet wade) and cool off. The river has excellent access, and while not an eastern river of the quality of Farmington or West Branch Ausable, the Wood is surprisingly rich and rewarding made more so because it's so accessible, so close to urban east, and combined with the insect hatches, especially the Hex, the Wood makes the cut. The Fall River, a tributary to the Wood, is worth an afternoon of your time.

CONTACTS

Quaker Lane Bait and Tackle, North
   Kingstown, www.quakerlanetackle.com
Blackstone Fly Company, Johnston,
   www.blackstoneflies.com

City Fishing

NEWPORT

Listen to the jazz festival or cruise around on your yacht then go out and catch big stripers. The ideal habitat for striped bass, the waters around Newport have rocky islands, bony rock ledges, swift tide rips. You can fish casting from the surf or comfortably from a boat. Good starting points are Ocean Drive and Brenton Reef or Snug Harbor and south to Block Island. Hire a charter and you can fish close for tuna, black-fish, and billfish or go way offshore and pick up something bigger.

Inshore fishing includes fluke (summer and winter), flounder, porgie, sea bass, bluefish, scup, Spanish mackerel, striped bass (also called Striper), rockfish, tautog (also called blackfish), chubfish, weakfish (also called gray trout), summer trout, and sandbar shark. Offshore fishing includes blue marlin, white marlin, swordfish, yellowfin tuna, bluefin tuna, little tunny, bonito, and blue shark.

VERMONT

I think we must have time to waste despite the fact I hate to waste it. I see folks of all types wasting time in long lines at the cinema. You can't go into Starbucks without seeing young and old alike cradled in comfy chairs, sipping caffeine, talking about noth-ing or surfing the web. Ratings show that nations watch endless hours of soap operas and telenovelas and reality television. I think I hate to waste time but there I am giving up hours of my life to fantasy football, the E Channel and *Maxim*. We waste time.

So what made this guy who was driving the silver Beemer behind me in *Manchester* of all places get up on my ass, honk, gyrate his hands and head at me, and then speed around me shaking his fist? Gone, in a flash. Where in the world did this guy have to get in such a hurry? I bet he was late for *The Young and the Restless.*

I always go to the Orvis store. As much as I poke fun at the neophytes who spend hundreds or thousands of dollars to suit up, I understand their fervor. Over the years, I've spent enough money with Orvis that I feel I could be nicknamed "Perk" and have it stand up in court. At least I don't look like I just walked out of the catalog because I mix and match brands and I wear out my stuff in a year or two.

I always go to the Arlington section because I like bouncy water, rocky bottoms.

If you like sandy, silty bottom, fish above the Arlington section of water. I fish the banks, I fish in lowlight, early and late. I don't wear a watch. I don't care what time it is. When my stomach tells me, I eat lunch. When it's dark, I eat dinner and go back to the motel.

I watched one kid wade to his waist (not waste) and with amazingly accurate casts, enticed a brown to sip his fly (I couldn't tell what it was but it was small) and lifted quickly, confidently and before long, he had a brown trout in his net with a tail hanging over it. I hadn't caught a trout in hours. I was pretty sure the trout were sipping spinners but I couldn't see to take off my fly and tie on another, too dark at that point, and should have bought that really cool tiny flashlight that clips to the brim of your cap that I had seen in the Orvis store earlier in the day but I didn't buy it because I needed to hurry and get out on the river.

I started to ask what he saw that I didn't, the old "What are you using?" question, but he was just a kid and I had been fishing forever, the sky was pewter and I was tired and that just wasn't going to happen. I could see the trout dimpling but I didn't see any hatch and I guess the kid could. The kid caught two more heavy trout before it got too dark to fish and he walked out and walked down the road to his grammar school or job at the ice cream store while I slipped off my waders and wondered what the hell I was doing when I was sixteen.

Now if Silver Beemer Guy was rushing to the Battenkill to get on the river before the spinner fall was over, I understand fully. Can't afford to waste perfectly good time on the river, you know?

My wife Amy hates that commercial (the one I like), the one advertising a candy bar, the one where the guy drops off his date and she brushes him off and shuts the door on him, so he goes to his car, sees the Snickers bar in the glove box, opens it and a beautiful tiny woman pops out of the wrapper and asks "why so blue, panda bear?" and he replies sadly, "Whatev—" and she whispers to him "You're a buffet of manliness." He smiles and takes a big honkin' bite out of the Snickers/babe, and all is right with the world. Love it.

Lake Champlain is a buffet of manliness, a smorgasbord of tasty lake delights. All is right with the world. Amy dislikes the commercial and said it demeans women, diminishes them to sweets all wrapped up, opened just to make men feel better. I kinda

like the idea that you could get chocolate, caramel, and a hottie all in one package to pick you up when you're feeling blue.

Batten Kill River

- **Location:** Eastern New York, western Vermont
- **What You Fish For:** brown trout with brook and rainbow trout
- **Highlights and Notables:** Beautiful classic freestone trout stream

The Batten Kill won't waste your time. The Batten Kill is timeless.

From the headwaters in Vermont, twenty-five miles to the New York border and another twenty-four miles to the Hudson River in New York. Southwestern Vermont, eastern New York. Spring-fed limestone. Not very big as great trout streams go. Brook trout in the upper reaches, and brown trout throughout the course of the river. Timeless.

I had a fall day, where yellow and orange leaves were in the black-surfaced water, when I tricoed those trout into an autumn frenzy. You're not supposed to catch that many trout on the Batten Kill, wild browns don't fall this easily. Hadn't had a day like it again.

Think drag-free float. Think precise presentation. Think stealth. You often need to have the skills of the legendary names who made the Batten Kill famous, names like Jordan, Wulff, Schwiebert. The tricos obviously need long, light leaders, say 7X, and small flies, say #24. These are tough fish to catch, wary of anglers, conscious of insect hatch stages.

The Batten Kill is an extremely clear river, but does not run fast due to its slow gradient. It has plenty of pools to fish, and they are connected by shallow runs, flats, mild riffles, a few rapids, and bends in the river. The river has a low temperature most of the time, and it owes a lot to the heavy canopy of willows and alder. The banks are conveniently littered with rocks, shrubs, fallen limbs, overhanging bushes, and so on, making for good brown trout cover.

There are quite a few access points for the forty-nine miles of fabled river, many pull-outs along the roads that run beside the river, as well as both marked and unmarked trails leading to various pools. Private land is usually marked, in fact usually marked well, but most landowners are willing to grant permission to access the river if you are polite and not dripping water all over the front porch.

This river hasn't been put on the timeline of fly fishing just because it is another pretty river. It earned its way there by pro-viding consistent wild trout fishing, dependable hatches, and smart fish. These trout are often finicky to the point of absurdity, turning down a #20 Blue Winged Olive for a #22 instead, for turning away from a well-placed, match-the-hatch dry fly because of a 6X tippet instead of a 7X. The Batten Kill is one of those small, intimate blue-ribbon trout fisheries familiar enough where you can feel like it is your home river, yet mysterious enough that you never feel like you fully know it. There aren't many wild brown trout fisheries left in the East, and few can match the angling experience and challenge of the Batten Kill. At times, like more and more rivers everywhere, the stream gets crowded, and overall, the special regs areas get fished a lot more than some other more remote, unregulated areas. The river fights to maintain its pristine

The trees close in on this stretch of the Batten Kill.

water, fending off waste, creeping population, and overuse, but the conservation groups protecting the river are strong and determined. The river seems to have backbone and resiliency, and continues to hold on. A great midweek option.

CONTACTS

Orvis Company, Manchester, 802-362-3622
   and for more general info www.orvis.com
The Brookside Angler, Manchester Center,
   802-362-3538
American Museum of Fly Fishing,
   Manchester, 802-362-3300

Lake Champlain

- **Location:** Northwestern Vermont, northeastern New York
- **What You Fish For:** Everything
- **Highlights and Notables:** Unparalleled big lake beauty, trophy fish of all kinds

Survey time. What doesn't Lake Champlain have?

Local water monster? Check. Champ the sea-serpent is Loch Ness American-style but still a Plesiosaurus-like creature. Besides this friendly serpent, you see vestiges of fables and legends all around; Sleepy Hollow lives.

A great lake? Sometimes called the sixth Great Lake, Champlain has 271,000 surface acres, some 440 square miles, 120 miles long. That's great. One of the largest freshwater lakes on the continent. It's just so big, it's hard to fathom.

Does this buffet include lots of cute little villages replete with cozy bed and breakfasts and diners and cafés and quaint shopping? One can find these historic towns all around the lake, Vermont, New York, and Canada.

Can you catch many different kinds of fish, say as many as a dozen species? One, lake trout; two, landlocked salmon; three, brown trout; four, steelhead trout; five, largemouth bass; six, smallmouth bass; seven, pike; eight, walleye; nine, pickerel; ten, yellow perch; eleven, white perch; twelve, crappie; thirteen, bluegill; fourteen, channel catfish; fifteen, rock bass; sixteen, whitefish—I can keep counting, if you'd like; seventeen, smelt; eighteen, bowfin; nineteen, carp; twenty, gar; and the list continues.

Nice list but are these diverse species in healthy catchable populations and do they offer up quality in size for each, too? Yep and yep. Champlain produces pike, lake trout, largemouth and smallmouth bass, landlocked salmon, walleye populations that equal any in the Northeast, in both numbers and size. Quantity and quality. In fact, the quality of the largemouth bass fishery surprised many in the late 1990s after a successful professional fishing tournament held on the lake. The lake record for landlocked salmon is almost 13 pounds, for smallmouth bass, 6.8 pounds. The average size of a largemouth runs 2 to 3 pounds; for a bronzeback, 1 to 4 pounds.

Does this lake offer a variety of habitat? Holy cow, the lake is so many things, it's difficult to describe. The South Lake acts like a river, weedy and woody. Broad Lake is deep and wide, deep and wide, Broad

Lake is deep and wide. Mallets Bay ranges from shallow to deep. Inland Sea has bays and islands. Missiquoi Bay is shallow and rich. The waters change colors, green to dark green to inky blue. Like five different lakes, this Lake Champlain.

Is this buffet attractive, appealing? People seem to think so. They scuba dive in the clear waters tending to the bottom where they visit nineteenth century sunken ships, boat the blue waters in all kinds of craft from dingys to canoes to kayaks to sailboats. Steep bluffs with trees growing right out of the rock stand over the lake tall; the sunsets and sunrises are some of the most beautiful anywhere as the lake and the mountains move from the sharp greens and whites and blues into monochrome, but the nexus before, a pastel of soft reds and pinks and yellows and golds, that is the treat. And wildlife like turkey and deer and falcons are common sights.

On Champlain, with the expanse of blue water and the layers of gray-green mountains all around, it's easy to you lose your bearings and it's windy and it's so blue and all the shore looks the same. The wind kicks up and the lake is ocean-like and you are lost. Dangerous for most smaller boats so if it's windy, stay in coves and bays and rivers.

Besides the history and the beauty and the vastness and the quality of the fishery and the lake monster, you never know what's at the end of your line. Lake Champlain is everything that's neat and good about New England.

CONTACTS
Bronzeback Guide Service, 802-868-4459
Champ Charters, 802-899-3104
SureStrike Charters, 802-878-5074
Capt. Joe Greco, Justy-Joe Sport Fishing
    Charters, www.newyorkfishing.com

Contact for more fishing guides:
Burlington Chamber of Commerce, 802-
863-3489

White River

- **Location:** Central Vermont
- **What You Fish For:** Brook, rainbow and brown trout
- **Highlights and Notables:** So much water, so much scenery, easy to wade, big browns waiting to avoid your fly

If you can live with wild trout smaller than those you'd catch in freestone streams in

Wyoming and Montana, then there is nothing keeping you from drawing up a plan to fish the White River in Vermont because, except for the smaller versions of trout, the scenery and experience are equally as spectacular, rewarding.

There's this one snakey meadow part of the White, a shallow riffley gravelly section, that has braids, and it flows straight for fifty yards, turns right for seventy-five, back to the left for another seventy-five, and then curves back right again and it does this for a mile. I fish the banks and the riffles, of course, but I am biding my time until I fish the bend pools. If I can get the brown trout to jump on the beadhead as it passes over the drop edge, and I can get his head up quickly, I can get two fish out of the bend pool, maybe even three, up against where the river has undercut the banks. Sometimes, the browns are big enough to make me smile.

In the main stem, the road right there in sight, there is this one spot of plunging water, not quite pools, too big to be riffles, and I can cast into the foam over and over until I hook a colorful 13-inch rainbow, without fail. And the plungey-priffle right next to it, too. Same thing.

There's this section of the White where there are boulders the size and color of a DeLorean, streamside rocks as big as seals. I can dap a dry fly in the pocket water and around boulders, trying both not to fall and to also be stealthy, and I can catch trout as I move up the noisy river.

If you want to fish the one river in Vermont that best offers a diversity of water types, then the White River should be the one. There are five branches in the upper reaches of the White, and in them anglers can fish for wild brook, rainbow, and brown trout. The main stem runs for fifty-seven miles, dam free, until it empties into the Connecticut River. The White is known for its trophy browns, but the quality of the water is so good, so clear, you sometimes forget that the reason you're not catching many fish is because the trout can see you.

This is a wadeable river, where fishermen can work long, slow glides or fast whitewater or deep pools, where most of the big fish are caught. Because of the clarity of the water, White River trout can be spooky. Access is good from the state roads that generally follow the river's path. If nothing else, and there is so much more, the White is the perfect wading river.

CONTACTS

White River Guide Service, www
.whiteriverguide.com
Sportsman's Resort, www
.sportsmans-resort.com
Rainbow Drive Resort, www
.rainbowdriveresort.com
Cane Island Lodge and Fly Shop,
www.caneislandflyshop.com
Blue Ribbon Flies, www.mtnhome.net/brf/
For more guide and lodging info, visit
www.whiteriver.net

Winooski River

- **Location:** North central Vermont
- **What You Fish For:** Brown and rainbow trout, landlocked salmon
- **Highlights and Notables:** In the middle of trout fisherman's heaven with nearby Little, Mad, and Dog Rivers

I was on one of those fishing trips where you're supposed to be doing something else (visiting Burlington friends who don't fish), which I guess technically isn't a fishing trip but I've got to tell you, all trips are fishing trips to me, and I was trying to get in some fishing without making a big deal about it. The Winooski was becoming an impediment to my fishing. Reading the regs made me woozy. You can't fish here until this date, you can't access the river here, the regs start at this bridge (which bridge *is* this?) and ends at that one (I'm confused). I wasn't in time for salmon but I didn't even know Winooski held salmon, the river runs freestone and beautiful but there are so many dams and so on. I had driven upstream to just get in an hour or two fishing for wild brook trout but couldn't really figure out where to put in, what was public and private, probably more my fault than anything else, trying to drink my morning coffee and eat a pastry while driving.

I don't know if I ever figured things out but I was fishing, legal or not. Two other guys were fishing within eyesight, a good two hundred yards away and they were go-ing to jail with me if I was doing wrong. The river was clear and cool, not cold, and I wet waded. Greenery everywhere I looked, trees, bushes, grass, river rocks with slippery vegetation. I saw what looked like golden stoneflies fluttering, dapping the water then splatting in a splashdown to only drift and struggle a few feet or yards before gulp, gone.

I tied on a western fly, no way this will work, a size 14 yellow stimulator and caught twelve trout in two hours, about half and half browns and rainbows. The longest was probably about 15 inches. All were deeper, more colorful than I expected.

I had to keep sneaking out during my week-long visit. I hit the Winooski one more time, dropped in on Winooski feeder streams, the Little, the Mad, the Dog. A lot of the water on these three is posted but that that isn't, fishes well and is a worthy distraction.

I had fun fishing the Winooski (I keep thinking how it sounds like an offensive lineman from Penn State and in fact, it might have been) and made plans to return some time without telling my nonfishing Burlington friends. I'd fish for a couple of days on the Winooski, making sure to hit the Little, Mad, and Dog Rivers while I'm at it.

The Winooski River in north central Vermont is known for its spring-run rainbow action. Fall fishing for brown trout in the shallows and tributaries can be exciting on the Winooski as well. Many anglers float parts of the river in canoes, allowing them to get to tough lies. There are boul-

Many Vermont lakes freeze over for much of the winter allowing for plenty of opportunities to try out ice fishing.

ders, logs, and overhanging brush in many places; slow, deep runs and pools in the wider parts, and fast riffles in the narrows in others. The Winooski has lots of challenging water for the spin and fly fishermen alike. The river stays fishable through the summer, its cool waters satiated by confluences with willing streams.

CONTACTS
The Fly Shop, Stowe, www.flyrodshop.com
The Classic Outfitters, South Burlington, 800-353-3963
Pleasant Valley Flyfishing Guides, Jefferson-ville, www.pleasantvalleyflyfishing.com
Catamount Fishing Adventures, Stowe, www.catamountfishing.com

Southeast

ALABAMA

I'm from the South (we still count Texas as a southern state) and my heroes were often Southerners, people like Luis Rubin, Shelby Foote, Bill Dance, C. Vann Woodward, Flannery O'Connor.

It's funny when I fish in the South. I'm always finding characters. Doppelgangers.

The Harp Brothers. Hazel Motes. I've twice found Joy-Hulga except neither one of the big mean girls had a wooden leg. Joe Christmas. Flem Snopes. Binx Bolling. Ruby Turpin. The Misfit. Ignatius J. Reilly.

I know many of these characters I find are sometimes ugly, unlikeable characters but I find grace and redemption in all of them, real and imagined. They've been punished. They are also complex. Interesting. Real.

And on this trip, I found a character.

So check this out. Sunday afternoon and I need some lunch. I fished all morning instead of going to church and it's on my mind because at this country store are folks all dressed up who just came from church. There's this older lady and she's wearing white cotton gloves and a hat and a navy blue dress just like the grandmother in Flannery O'Connor's "A Good Man is Hard to Find." And she's getting on to the two kids who are likely her grandkids. These kids are running all over the store and I decide to sit back and wait because they keep getting in my way.

She grabs the boy's hand, he's maybe five or six, because he was digging around in the beef jerky bin and she says ear-

SOUTH/SOUTHEAST

nestly, disturbingly, as he let go a couple of pieces of jerky, "Get your hands out of there, young man. You don't know who all's hands been in there!" Now if that's not a tormented woman in need of redemption, I don't who is. I halfway expected to discover from Red Sammy as he hands me a plate of barbecue that this family was on a trip to find a secret panel in an old house in Georgia. Or Alabama.

Smith Lake was a struggle to include in the book because when I fished it a number of years ago, I guess the lake was on the wane with its spotted bass and not yet a clear trophy striper lake. Enough friends have con-

vinced me of its worthiness that here Smith Lake sits, right in the middle of this book. I do remember getting one of the best breakfasts I've ever eaten at a local café.

I broke a flyrod on the Tallapoosa, right near the rod butt. The story would be better if I claimed the rod snapped while fighting a huge bass, but the spotted bass was little. The log the fish dived under that subsequently snagged my fly was the culprit. Okay, I was the culprit because I pulled hard when I should have just cut the line and gone horizontal and snapped the fly off but noooooo, I had to think I could salvage the fly, heck, I thought I was clever enough to think I could yank the spotted bass clean out from under the logjam. Snap.

You know the old joke where the patient moves his arm in a circular motion and tells the doctor "It hurts when I do that," and the doctor says "Well, don't do that." Lake Guntersville, one of the top bass lakes in the nation (now that the vegetation is back), is a lot like the patient who moves his hurt arm—if you don't do what you're supposed to do, it's gonna hurt. If you do what you're supposed to do, when you're supposed to, then it won't hurt.

Lake Dannelly/Millers Ferry

- **Location:** Southwestern Alabama
- **What You Fish For:** Blue and channel catfish (and flatheads)
- **Highlights and Notables:** One of the better catfishing spots in the South

Lake Dannelly (aka Millers Ferry Reservoir) in southwestern Alabama is one of the best catfishing spots in the South. The best catfishing is actually in the tailrace below Millers Ferry Dam where blue and channel cats grow to perfect eating size (the average catch is 2 pounds) and you can just catch a lot of them. Blue cats are more common and run from 1 to 12 pounds with some 15- to 20-pounders. Flatheads to 75 pounds are also caught in the tailwater.

Thirty miles south of Selma, Lake Dannelly is chock-full of crappie and largemouth bass, worth a visit for them alone. The crappie average about a pound each (again, perfect eating size) and the bass run 2 to 4 pounds. The stripers (up to 20 pounds) and hybrid striped bass are an underrated fishery.

Lake Dannelly has good access and several launch ramps. The lake measures in at 17,200 surface acres and is situated on the

---

City Fishing

BIRMINGHAM

Lakes Guntersville, Wheeler, Wilson, Smith, Coosa River

Birmingham has cleaned its act up the last two decades and if you haven't been there, it's a pretty neat city set in beautiful scenery. If you like bass fishing, especially spotted bass, you won't find a better home base. The area lakes have two species, the northern spotted and the Alabama spotted bass.

Don't overlook the angling for smallmouth and largemouth bass just because the spotted bass is a local fave. Check out Guntersville, Smith, and Wheeler Lakes entries elsewhere in the book for more specific information. The Coosa River is wild and scenic, good for a great boat ride and a day of bass fishing. No less than ten quality waters lie within an hour or two drive from Birmingham including Lake Jordan, Weiss Lake, and Logan Martin Lake.

Alabama River between Jones Bluff Dam and Claiborne Lake, so with the Alabama River feeding it, the lake is rich and fertile. Between the great catfishing in the tailrace and the choice of four species in the lake, this is a hot spot few others outside southwest Alabama know about. Dannelly can be reached from Selma from Highway 41 to the southeast, Highway 5 to the northwest and Highway 28 to the southwest.

Lake Eufaula

- **Location:** Southeastern Alabama, southwestern Georgia
- **What You Fish For:** Largemouth bass, spotted bass
- **Highlights and Notables:** Legendary bass lake still kickin' it

Growing up, I knew Lake Eufaula was a big-name lake. I remember seeing Jimmy Houston and Bill Dance lip sowbellies and smile big for the cameras. I'd see photos of tourney winners holding up an unbelievable stringer of bass. Back then, Eufaula was the premier bass fishing destination in the nation. As with all great bass lakes, things that go up must come down.

With 45,000 acres straddling the border of Alabama and Georgia, Lake Eufaula is on the Chattahoochee River. Eufaula (more accurately named Walter F. George Reservoir but come on, Eufaula just rolls off the tongue better) is a structure lake and these features are what keep the largemouth bountiful and big. Flats, humps, channels, dropoffs, ledges.

Still, the biologists and fisheries managers know that with the increase of the spotted bass population and the great numbers of largemouth, and the possibility of overcrowding, they need to tinker with limits and harvesting and return the biomass to proper levels. On a spring or summer morning, you can still catch upwards of twenty-five bass, spotted and largemouth, a big one weighing about 3 or 4 pounds; you can still catch lots of crappie on Eufaula, especially the way I grew up doing it: night fishing for these fat crappie off docks under lights with minnows.

Lake Eufaula has a lot going for it. History and tradition. Structure. Spotted bass. And especially nostalgia and the promise of good things to come.

CONTACTS

Sam Williams, Hawk's Fishing Guide Service, www.fishingworld.com/iGuide/AL/Eufaula/HawksFishingGuide

Billy Darby, Billy Darby's Fishing Guide Service, www.dixiebass.com/billydarby

Tracy Beall, 334-687-2245 or 334-703-2570

Lake Eufaula Guide Service, 334-687-9595

Eufaula Guide Service, www.eufaulaguideservices.com

Doug Haynie, eufaulaguideserv@mindspring.com

Reed Montgomery, 205-787-5133, www.fishingalabama.com

Jackie Thompson, 334-686-9595

Sam Williams, Hawk's Guide Service, www.hawksfishingguideservice.com

Fishing license information may be found at: www.outdooralabama.com/fishing/freshwater/license

Lake Guntersville

- **Location:** Northeastern Alabama
- **What You Fish For:** Largemouth bass
- **Highlights and Notables:** The bass are back and mean and big.

Lake Guntersville (69,000 acres) is the largest lake in Alabama, an impoundment of the Tennessee River in northeast Alabama. A tournament favorite for years because of the abundant numbers of hefty largemouth bass. They'd catch them in the shallows in winter (where they really shouldn't be) and under or around the vegetation (especially hydrilla and milfoil) in the spring and summer (and then the vegetation died off). Alabamans like fishing for their bream, and Guntersville has colorful fat redear sunfish, and longear sunfish and bluegill. I know many fish for sauger and crappie and catfish, too. But Guntersville is about the bass and with little vegetation, the bass population was threatened.

The lake is reborn. The weeds are back. So are the 2- to 6-pound bass. And the occasional 7- to 10-pound bucketmouths. Probably holds more 5-pound bass than any other lake not in Texas, Florida, California, or Mexico. But catching them ain't easy. We have here a shallow large lake with plenty of hiding places. You really need to hire a guide but you probably won't. The lake sees more than its fair share of eager-beaver area anglers, tournaments, and hard-core sowbelly-chasers so these bass are wary and lure educated. These bass will turn off with weather changes, too. So you have a lot working against you. And when you locate the largemouth bass, when you hook one, they're going to take you into the submerged wood and rock and pop you off.

Challenging. Like I said, hire a guide.

CONTACTS

Guide Troy Jens, www.anglingalabama.com/seasonal.htmwww.anglingalabama.com

Chris McCollum, 256-974-6325

Barry Wilson, 256-678-2390

Tee Kitchens, www.alabamaoutdoors.net/tee.html

Capt. Chris Jackson,
www.finsngrinsfishing.com
Doug Campbell, Waterfront Tackle, 256-582-6060
C & B North Alabama Guide Service, www .angelfire.com/al2/fishingguideservice

Pickwick Lake

- **Location:** Northwestern Alabama and parts of Tennessee and Mississippi
- **What You Fish For:** Smallmouth bass, largemouth bass
- **Highlights and Notables:** Arguably the best smallmouth lake in the nation

I'm not sure smallmouth fishing in America has ever been in such good shape. From Lake Erie to Wilson Lake, Table Rock Lake to Devils River, Dale Hollow Lake to the Susquehanna River, Columbia River to Lake Champlain, brown bass fishing is superb in both quantity and quality. In every region of the nation, anglers have several options to choose from in order to catch thirty to fifty or have a legitimate shot at a 7- to 9-pounder or just have a grand time catching 1- to 3-pound bronzebacks. Some lucky fisherfolks have caught 10-pound smallmouth here. And Pickwick Lake in northwestern Alabama symbolizes all that is right with smallmouth fishing today.

Pickwick Lake is one of the top smallmouth lakes in the country. The water is warm, the growing season is long, and the lake has ideal habitat and food sources.

This impoundment of the Tennessee River is almost entirely located in Alabama. This place makes the difficult act of catching a 5-pound smallie seem easy. There's just a lot of 4- to 6-pounders. And for the trophy brown bass hunter? You have a legitimate shot at a 7-pounder. The lake has several line class IGFA records. You have a legit opportunity at reeling in a world record.

You'll know you're in the South when you're at Pickwick, if not from the drawl then at least from the comfort food and obsession with fishing and, of course, the characters. Another giveaway is that quite a few anglers on Pickwick use live bait. Shad. Works well if you like that sort of thing. For smallies, work the stump flats and the grassbeds; the rocky dropoffs and the channels; the creeks and the bluffs. Pickwick smallmouth bass are strong, bull-necked fish that put up a fight.

Pickwick is fifty miles long and 47,500 acres at full pool and also has respectable fishing for largemouth especially since all the other anglers are focused on catching a world record smallmouth. Nearly 500 miles of shoreline ring this impoundment of the Tennessee River. The lake also holds hybrid striper bass, walleye, sauger, spotted bass, white bass, yellow bass, crappie, and catfish. While at Pickwick, you may want to try the tailraces of Joe Wheeler and Wilson Dam.

CONTACTS
Roger Stegall, www.fishpickwick.com

For more information on the lake and other guides, www.pickwickoutdoors.com

Smith Lake

- **Location:** Northern Alabama
- **What You Fish For:** Striped bass, spotted bass, largemouth bass
- **Highlights and Notables:** One of the up-and-coming striper lakes in the country

Stripers are all the rage at this clear, deep impoundment of the Warrior River, a lake once known for producing record spotted bass including a spotted bass that weighed in at a whopping 8 pounds, 15 ounces. Today, the slow-growing spotted bass are typically much smaller and stripers have taken over as the prevalent target of anglers.

Twenty thousand acres in the hilly country of Alabama (some call the northern part of Alabama "mountainous" but come on, guys, let's keep this real), Smith Lake fills up its volume in deep river arms and sloping banks. That deep water works wonders for stripers, giving them a cool place to escape the Alabama summer heat. Depths to 200 feet and cool, clear water qualify as ideal striper habitat, I believe. (Clear deep water in Alabama? I know, by state law all fisheries in 'Bama are supposed to be mud-colored but this one got grandfathered in.)

The lake record stands at 46 pounds but many local regulars know there are stripers in Smith that bust the 50-pound mark. You can hunt for lunkers or in April, May, and June, catch 20-pounders on topwater lures. Anglers catch lots of 8- to 12-pounders and have a legit chance at a 30-pound striped bass.

The spotted bass fishery is still good (not great) and a 6-pound spotted bass is a large one. Largemouth bass are another option in Smith Lake. Both types of bass hold deep. My friends tell me all this and I believe them. Hope you do too. I've seen their photos but you know how computer programs can alter images nowadays.

CONTACTS
Alabama Department of Conservation, 334-242-3465
Speegle's Marina, 256-739-0364
Duncan Bridge Marina, 205-387-1208
Bruce Holcombe, www.alabamaoutdoors.net/smithlake.html
Reeds Guide Service, 205-787-5133
Dale Welch, www.alabamastriperfishing.com
Bill Vines, 205-647-7683
Patrick Crocker, 205-631-0026
John Eisenbarth, Riverside Fly Shop, www.1flyfish.com

Tallapoosa River

- **Location:** West of Atlanta about an hour
- **What You Fish For:** Spotted bass, red-eye bass, largemouth bass, striper
- **Highlights and Notables:** An easy drive from Atlanta, a diverse fishery, an ideal southern stream

Tallapoosa is a fine river for bass fishers cleverer than me. Spotted bass are the predominant bass, plentiful, easy to catch, pretty to hold. Redeye bass, a southern specialty, are located in upstream Tallapoosa where the waters are cool and clear, largemouth down low where the water is warmer, tintier.

I didn't catch any stripers but tried to because some 'Bama friends said they have. You can also catch rock bass, bluegill, and catfish. The Tallapoosa is a rocky, woody river that has both fast and slow waters and lies about fifty miles west of Atlanta, offering a variety of southern bass fishing hospitality.

Wheeler Lake

- **Location:** North central Alabama
- **What You Fish For:** Smallmouth, largemouth, white bass, catfish, sunfish, crappie, sauger
- **Highlights and Notables:** Scenic lake with an amazing variety of game fish

This is one of the entries that may not be readily agreed upon. Every angler goes through well-known stages where they want to catch all the fish, catch the biggest fish, catch the toughest fish, and so on. Wheeler Lake is not likely to produce the most or the largest or the toughest sporting game fish. But Wheeler Lake is a scenic lake, a surprising pleasure with excellent fishing for both smallmouth and largemouth bass, and in fact did have the world record for the biggest blue catfish

(1995), a titan that tipped the scales at 111 pounds. Wheeler Lake is pretty and has lots of interesting habitat and it's not well known. Wheeler is a find. You will enjoy your visit on many levels. That's good enough for me.

Wheeler Lake is an impoundment in north central Alabama, the second largest lake in the state, a big sucker that's seventy-five miles long, covers 67,000 surface acres, and provides over 1,000 miles of shoreline. Wheeler Lake sits in forested rolling hills, has beautiful bluffs, a variety of bass structure. The hills are mountains but more hills than mountains, the tail end of the Appalachians. I found it a few years ago, not that fishermen from the region didn't already know about it of course, but I was out for smallmouth on the Tennessee River, had some disappointing fishing, and ended up fishing Wheeler. I stayed an extra two days longer than I had planned.

The bass at Wheeler have a healthy shad population to chase after. They can swim in or around dropoffs, old river shoals, rocks, points, steep banks, flats, creek channels, stumps, grass, brushpiles, coves, and boat docks. That's a lot of hiding places.

Largemouth bass aren't of trophy size but 3- to 5-pounders are not uncommon. The bronzeback fishing is spectacular when you can find them, but their population isn't huge. The angling for bluegill, redear sunfish, and longear sunfish is top-notch. The lake also enjoys a healthy crop of crappie. Sauger, stripers, hybrid, and white bass run upstream as well.

FLORIDA

I read a lot. I always have two to three books I am working on. Some books, I give my full attention, like Eco's *Baudolino* or *The Time Traveler's Wife* by Niffenegger. And I reread many books, looking for what I missed the first time, looking for layers, for context, but often, I reread because it's familiar territory of places I like to visit. *World War II* by John Keegan. Must've read it ten times. I get something new out of it each go-round. *A Confederacy of Dunces, Hotel New Hampshire, Sex, Death, and Fly-fishing, Catch-22, The Collector, The Magus, Jude the Obscure, Slaughterhouse-Five, The Snows of Kilimanjaro, Foucault's Pendulum, Wise Blood, Lord of the Rings, Rainbow's Gravity, Finnegan's Wake, Red and the Black, The River Why,* and more. I tried and failed to finish *The Poisonwood Bible, The Corrections.* I didn't get *Baudolino* as much as I wanted to. I didn't get *The Crimson Petal and the White.* I intend to try them again down the line, see if I understand them better. Now my fishing buddy Jorgen Wouters has me hooked on the Patrick O'Brian novels.

I like to fish places I've fished before and yet I travel the world looking for new haunts. I do read new books, of course, and try to make them mine, make them familiar so I can revisit them.

The Everglades will at once seem familiar and foreign and will definitely haunt you. You'll want to revisit these waters over and over and you'll find new layers each time. Sure, like Shrek and the onion but hopefully a little more meaningful than that. The Keys are like that too. So many books, so many hidden layers.

I came to saltwater fishing late in life. Or later in life. I'm just forty-six so I'd hate to think anything is late in my life. I did surf fish off the Texas and Puerto Rican coasts when I was growing up but I always chose mountains over beaches when I got serious about the sport.

The Keys were instrumental in changing that view.

The Florida Keys are special and I wish I could have been there decades ago when they were still wild and woolly and undiscovered. You just can't believe all the water and islands and the sunsets. You just can't believe the profundity of the fishery. You just can't believe that this is America. You just can't believe how frustrating it was casting in the wind to a school of bonefish you know will scatter if you don't lead them just right. *Dem bones, dem bones, gonna walk around.*

I was once a kicker, a goat-roper, a cowboy. We had a farm where we raised about thirty or forty head of cattle so it was a definite hobby (and losing proposition). During my teen years, I showed steers, did Chapter Conducting in FFA, built barbed wire fences and barns, cut calves, branded cattle. So I always had boots. And big buckles. And hats, a summer and a winter.

I was not a very good cowboy but a cowboy I was.

It is expensive to outfit a cowpoke and was in the 1970s, too. A good kicker needs several pairs of boots: an everyday pair to wear to school (Justin, $150), a dress pair (my lizards, $250), and an exotic pair just for the hell of it (my sharkskins, $400). Dad wore all the cowboy gear, too, and dressing like you meant business wasn't unusual in Mineral Wells or Odessa or Longview. But how to outfit two cowboys in one family without breaking the bank?

Post, Texas.

This tiny Texas town used to have—and I say used to because I haven't been there in twenty years and I couldn't find out anything on the Internet that made me certain it's the same place—used to have a western store that encompassed two city blocks. You'd go in and it was like an Old West diorama: all around you, western wear. The place was so big, so inventoried, one huge room the size of a barn held only winter hats. One huge room just belts and buckles. Another room held only Wrangler jeans (no cowboy in his right mind wore Lees or Levis back then). This Post, Texas western wear store had the cheapest prices this side of Taiwan. And this store went on for two city blocks. I mention all this because of the angling options on the Pine Coast of Florida. It's so overwhelming, so diverse, it's like shopping in Post, Texas. You won't know where to start first. And it never seems to end.

Bienville Plantation Lakes

- **Location:** Northern Florida
- **What You Fish For:** Largemouth bass
- **Highlights and Notables:** A place to spoil you, lap of luxury, sportsman's dream, gourmet meals, luxury lodging, and trophy bass

Sometimes, camping just won't cut it. The moldy smell of the tent, the ticks and mosquitos, the smoke that gets in your clothes and hair, eating your own cooking, doing your business outside. Or fishing all night from the boat, with the beer and Vienna sausage gone and you're down to crackers and warm bottled water, your hands smell like fish and you smell like sweat or worse—sometimes you just want to be pampered. I've got just the place.

Bienville Plantation is a northern Florida resort of 14,000 acres of sportsman's paradise located a little over an hour's drive west from Jacksonville. The resort has over 4,000 acres of prime bass fishing, hawg heaven in lakes that are former phosphate pits, fertile as your Aunt Myrtle, rotated to keep things fresh, all catch-and-release. Catching twenty to fifty bass in a day is nothing and guides are disappointed if your average bass on the day's take isn't 4 to 6 pounds. It usually is. Not only that, but a 10- to 15-pound bass is a do-able deed. Crappie and bluegill are as fat as some small bass I've caught before.

Catering to corporate retreats and individuals who like solitude and the finer things in life, Bienville Plantation offers first-class lodging and gourmet meals. The resort is also well known for duck and quail hunting, deer hunting, even boar and alligator hunts. Bienville Plantation's luxury and bass fishing doesn't come cheaply but you kinda figured that out already I bet, but it's competitively priced with other luxury sports resorts. If you've the money and the time, they have the southern hospitality and the big bass.

CONTACTS

Bienville Plantation, White Springs, www .bienville.com

Charlotte Harbor and Boca Grande Pass

- **Location:** Southwest Florida
- **What You Fish For:** Tarpon
- **Highlights and Notables:** One of the top tarpon spots in the world

Catching a tarpon is like taking a hammer to the face, it's that shocking and powerful. Not as painful. Say you hook into a 6-footer. Your teeth are jarred, your brain scrambled, and as the silver leaps into the air over and over, your arms are tired and shaking. Charlotte Harbor calls itself 'the Tarpon Capital of the World' and with good reason.

At Charlotte Harbor, on the southwest side of Florida, anglers have a saltwater smorgasbord. This area where the Peace

Amelia Island Plantation, Florida
King mackerel are good eating, Southern-style. Relaxed atmosphere, scenic Amelia Island is one of the best places to catch king macks. Catch 'em and eat 'em.

River and Myakka River form the Peace River Basin and empty into the Gulf of Mexico at Boca Grande is one of the best shallow water angling experiences in America. Charlotte Harbor looks a lot like the Texas coast, only pretty.

Three-quarters of a million acres of estuary. Shorelines that are a tangle of mangroves. Backbays and rivermouths and hidden backwaters and channels. Clear shallow flats that spread out for eons and more nearshore and offshore species than you can fish for in a week if you just chose one type a day. Tarpon on Monday, redfish on Tuesday, snook on Wednesday, seatrout on Thursday, flounder on Friday, pompano on Saturday, amberjack on Sunday. I ran out of days—I still have grouper, tuna, snapper, kingfish, cobia, king mackerel (they'll take more line than you've got), tripletail (watch where you hold them, they'll slice you clean open), permit, barracuda, sheepshead, and many more fish you can fish for in and around Charlotte Harbor. The shallow water is incredibly rich with crustaceans and forage.

For shallow water species, you sight fish most of the time. You can wade much of the time but for the best way to get around, to get onto snook and into redfish, you'll do best in a flats boat or other shallow-draft boat. Fly fishers do well on these waters, too. Catching a powerful snook (you have no idea how powerful until you catch one of these fish shot from bazookas) and having him take you into the mangroves is a frustrating and jaw-dropping experience.

Because of the favorable food source (especially Pass crabs) and all the fish that feed on that food source, the silver kings make their way through Boca Grande Pass each summer by the thousands. This pass really gets packed as the tarpon move in to feed on crabs and finfish. They move in with numbers as big as rock concerts or bigger and the angling is sometimes combat fishing because 100-pounders are in the mix. These tarpon are sometimes so thick you could James Bond across their backs (surely you remember *Live and Let Die* where Roger Moore escapes by running across the backs of the crocs). They hold a huge tournament each year, the *World's Richest Tarpon Tournament* where the winners share a purse of $100,000.

CONTACTS
Boca Grande Outfitters, www
.bocagrandeoutfitters.com
Fishing Unlimited Outfitters and Fly Shop,
Boca Grande, www.4tarpon.com
Capt. James Wisner, www.tarponwiz.com
Capt. Ian Devlin, www.saltwaterflies
.com/devlin
Capt. Steve Futch, www.catchtheking.com

Destin Village

- **Location:** Southern coast of the panhandle, northwestern Florida
- **What You Fish For:** Speckled trout, redfish, grouper, snapper, amberjack, cobia
- **Highlights and Notables:** Underrated family fishing home base for inshore and offshore angling

I used to hear about Destin back in the 1980s as one of those unknown family getaways where things were comfortable and inexpensive and you got value for your money in the fishing and scenery. They'd tell me about Destin in guarded tones, unsure if I was worthy of the annual journey, if I might tell too many others about it.

The white beaches are of the fine sand

Grouper

variety, the people of the village of the still sweet, how-can-I-help-you variety. Amberjack, grouper, and snapper are abundant and of the man-that's-a-big-fish variety. There's a spring migration of giant cobia (an underrated sportfish) that you'll need a ten or eleven-weight rod to fight. Out in Choccolocco Bay, you fish for redfish and speckled trout on the hard flats and clear water and if you don't hook up with ten or fifteen of either or both during the day, you're doing something wrong. I checked it out and found it didn't live up to their hype so I wouldn't go visit if I were you. Really.

CONTACTS
Destin Florida Chamber of Commerce, 850-837-6241, www.destinchamber .com
Capt. Kelly Windes, Sunrise Charters, www.destin-charter-fishing.com/html/ important_info.htm

Everglades

- **Location:** Southern Florida
- **What You Fish For:** Snook, redfish, and tarpon are the targets but you can catch more species than Carter's has liver pills.
- **Highlights and Notables:** One of the world's natural wonders

One million acres of the country's largest wetland system. That's a number that is just too large to fathom and when you are in the thick of it, you can't even fathom how many more little coves like this there must be in one million acres of wetland. When you're in the Everglades, there is no other place on earth. This is it because you can't imagine that the grasses and canals and stained-water ever end.

The Everglades are one of the more special places on earth. You can imagine that with all this acreage, and with all the labyrinths you've seen in photos, the fishing pressure is almost nil, relative to its size. And the Everglades that cover much of the tip of southern Florida is not someplace you just hop in the boat and go fish, either—access is limited. Unless you know the Everglades, I wouldn't think of exploring the backwaters. You could get lost and not found forever. Go with a guide the first time and get a feel for this dwarfing marsh. If you do decide to follow some of those do-it-yourself articles, take the Wilderness Waterway, 100 miles of what's called a route, a water-highway that meanders through the backwaters of the Everglades. Daytripper do-it-yourselfing is fine. The longer backwoods trip is dicey without knowledgeable support.

You primarily fish for snook, reds, and tarpon in the Everglades but you also catch bass and bream, among other species (permit, sea trout, Jack crevalle, Spanish mackerel, black drum, ladyfish, grouper). This is the largest subtropical wilderness in America, one of the most beautiful and exotic and mysterious and sexy spots in the world. So many fish. So much wildlife. So precariously balanced. One-point-three million acres of mostly shallow water and low mangrove islands. The diversity of quarries is reason alone to enter the Everglades. And then, there's the alligator factor in the same way there's the grizzly factor in Yellowstone. The alligators won't get you unless you do something stupid. Now, the mosquitos? Well, that's a different story.

Typically, the snook run about 5 to 10 pounds but at times, you'll find a 20-pounder. The reds aren't big, just 2 to 6 pounds. The tarpon aren't world-breakers but 50 to 80 pounds is a lot of tarpon in these shallow waters. The deeper, the better.

Canoeing or kayaking, the two best ways to see the Everglades, to fish the Everglades. Wading is tough because the water is off-color and the bottom muddy, and the thought of sharks and alligators is enough to keep me in the boat. Fishing becomes secondary on this journey because it's all so overwhelming. You can camp at one of two campgrounds, Flamingo and Long Pine Key. Reservations and a per-night fee are required from December through May (800-365-CAMP). With a park permit, you can camp on your own. You'll sleep on a chickee, a platform that sits above water, a place to call home in this watery mosaic. The chickees have roofs and you can cook on them with a grill.

CONTACTS

Everglades National Park, Park Headquarters, 305-242-7700, www.nps.gov/ever
Flamingo Lodge (the only motel in the park), www.flamingolodge.com
Rick Murphy, 305-242-0099
Capt. Al Keller, Everglades Angler, Flamingo, www.evergladesangler.com
Jim Dupree, 352-371-6153
Adam Redford, www.captadamredford.com/charters

Homosassa River

- **Location:** West coast of central Florida
- **What You Fish For:** Tarpon, sharks, black bass, snook, and more
- **Highlights and Notables:** The Homosassa is a tarpon treat, a silver torpedo haven.

You ever get that weird feeling where your stomach knots up and you lose your breath? It happens when you look in the rearview mirror and you see that the big SUV hasn't seen that you've stopped and it's obvious they are going to smash into the rear of your car. Real pucker power. And then slam bang! All hell breaks loose.

It's not really a line you see, more a few dark silhouettes at first and then you see them, like those paintings at the mall where you have to concentrate and focus on one point and then the whole picture shows up—you can't believe your eyes.

That's tarpon fishing.

If the fishing for the giant tarpon that come up this clear spring-fed river each spring were more consistent from year to year, this amazing fishery would rank with any tarpon fishery in the world. This beautiful crystal-clear river spills out into lovely flats and while you can catch many other species in the river and the flats (like sharks, black bass, snook, jack, crevalle) and the surrounding waters, it's really all about the giant tarpon for destination anglers. Most locals fish the healthy fishery of both spotted sea trout and redfish. Homosassa is located on the west coast of Florida, about seventy miles north of Tampa.

The river and flats have numerous class tarpon records and five world-record tarpon have been caught. This is not Boca Grande for numbers (or tarpon or boats) but the fish, when in the river, are larger. The bay is saltwater fed by brackish and freshwater creeks. The mangrove labyrinth of Chassahowitzka National Wildlife Refuge is another prime fishing hotspot.

If you do decide to make a run at the giant tarpon run, plan on the first week of May, cross your fingers, pray, hope, wish, and hire a guide. If the fishing is on that particular year, you have a legit shot at a world record tarpon, a 200-pounder. Bring your heavy gear, eighty-pound shock tippets and a good attitude.

CONTACTS

Capt. Mike Locklear,
   www.homosassafishing.com
Earl Waters, 352-563-5001
Tommy Locke, 941-766-9070
Dan Malzone, 813-831-4052
Tommy Mohler, 727-527-3551

Steve Kilpatrick, 352-493-2279
Nature Coast Fly Shop, 352-795-3156
Citrus County Tourist Development
   Council, www.VisitCitrus.com

Florida Keys

- **Location:** Off the southern tip of Florida
- **What You Fish For:** Tarpon, bonefish, snook, and more
- **Highlights and Notables:** A true top-ten angling experience. Not many places in the world offer this much diversity and quality for shallow-water fishing.

The flats. Florida Bay. Mangroves. Islands. Beaches. Channels and reefs. The Florida Keys are the posterchild for the saltwater fishing jones. Thatch roof bars where we anglers clink beer mugs and toast and brag about the big one we caught or that got away.

First, you have to think bonefish. The Keys grow bonefish to be large and especially spooky. The Florida Keys is still one of the top handful of bonefish locales in the world.

Second, think tarpon.

Third, everything else: redfish, snook, permit, barracuda, sharks, wahoo, marlin, dolphin, tuna, and a lot more. Offshore provides angling for king mackerel, cobia, jacks. The underrated quarry are permit and redfish and snook.

The Florida Keys begin with Key Largo and reach south 123 miles to Key West.

The Keys are three-part harmony—Upper, Middle, and Lower. Upper is Key Largo, Lower is Key West. You hear the locals talk about ocean side and you'll soon figure out that means the southeastern side. By default, the bay side must be the opposite side, the side facing Florida Bay, right? Keys are islands, thirty-some odd keys. Bridges are everywhere: forty-seven of them along Highway 1 to Key West.

Fishing guides grow on palm trees in the Keys. They are legion. You need them like you need sunblock and cold beer. You won't catch much of anything until you figure out the ins and outs of the Keys. I can't imagine doing-it-yourself the first time out in the Keys.

The fishing is good year-round. The weather is good year-round. Islamorda is a hub for anglers, plenty of shops and guides. Motels and resorts and the like are hit and miss, sometimes overpriced, quality uneven.

City Fishing

JACKSONVILLE
St. Johns River, Trout River, Indian River, Charlotte Harbor

The city of Jacksonville still has some of that old-time southern charm, and as one of America's oldest cities, the combination of history and flavor make for an ideal home base from which to fish. You're not far from many of the same bass haunts that Orlando anglers are close to— Stick Marsh one of the top ones. A saltwater option close to Jax is Homosassa with its tarpon and cobia and sea trout. Charlotte Harbor and Indian River are two other top local choices (all three have entries in this book). Gator trout, they call them, speckled trout. It's gator everything in Jacksonville so you kinda get numb to it after a while. It's a sea trout.

The Johns River is the same St. Johns as the river in Orlando, but this is the lower version, the redfish version. The lower St. Johns has a healthy population of resident redfish; we're not talking trophies but they run 2 to 5 pounds (with 6 and up being large for these waters) and they are fishable year-round. You can also fish the Intracoastal Waterway for reds. What makes both St. Johns and the Intracoastal so much fun is that since the water is shallow, you can sight fish. Little Talbot Island is a popular place to drop a line. By the way, you can still catch bass in St. Johns toward Green Cove Springs and Black Creek.

Sisters Creek, Browns Creek, and other backwaters and coves and creeks and cuts and channels and waterways— they're everywhere in and around Jacksonville—are some of the prime gator-trout fishing spots.

Keys bones are spooky world-record bones that require long, accurate presentations. Ten- to 14-pound bonefish, some of the largest in the world. Only the lucky or the great catch bonefish this gigantic.

At other bonefish hotspots where you have big bones, you can still put newbies on smaller bonefish, on schools, and they can eventually catch a few. In the Keys, the schools are few and far between and you're usually casting to singles and doubles and these silvery ghosts are tough to spot, difficult to entice. Beginners need not apply. The casts need to be longer and more accurate than in other bonefish locales.

Here's a surprise for you: The flats of the Florida Keys are not always wadeable. Sure, you'll find some hard flats, but most are mucky and you'll sink to your knees or even your waist. So you're fishing from a boat, the bonefish are impossible to spot, nearly impossible to catch—you've got to hire a guide. They spot 'em, they move the boat into position, they know where the bones hang out (grass flats, baby), they advise you (a nice way to put it) where to cast, what you did wrong, how to do it better. They help you catch bonefish. Biscayne Bay, Marathon, and Key West are solid bonefish producers but Islamorda is the bonefish mecca.

You can catch snook and redfish in Florida Bay, in grass flats, shallow reefs, mangroves, channels, even in the wide open unprotected water. Redfishing is easy. Spot the tails. Pin the tail on the donkey.

I haven't fished for dolphin in the upper Keys yet but I hear it's fruitful and fun.

The permit fishery is underrated be-cause they are in numbers six months of the year and these flatsiders grow big here, but if you are masochistic and don't like catching fish, the Keys permit may just be for you. The Lower Keys hold the best numbers.

The tarpon fishing in the Keys is both good and dicey. Good because tarpon are there in numbers and in size (up to 170 pounds, the average about 80 pounds), but dicey because they're difficult to locate, more difficult to catch, crazy to land. Fun part? Many times you can get by with a floating line on your flyrod, the tarpon are so shallow. Bring an intermediate sinking line for those other times. Ten- to 12-weight rods recommended. Most bonefish in the Florida Keys have seen a fly more than once and will ignore Gotchas, Bonefish Charlies, and many other flies that work well on the flats at other bonefish destinations.

The best times to find great numbers of migrating tarpon is March through July, but you can find tarpon to break your heart all year long. A common practice in the Keys is to fish for tarpon at night, when they feed. Novel idea. Now bow to the king.

CONTACTS

Key West Chamber of Commerce, Old Mallory Square, Key West, 800-527-8539

Chambers of Commerce: Key Largo, 800-822-1088; Islamorada, 800-322-5397; Marathon, 800-262-7284; and the Lower Keys, 800-872-3722

Key West Visitor's Bureau, 800-FLA-KEYS

Two Web sites that have numerous listings for guides and outfitters include www.charternet.com/fishers/florida-keys.html *and* www.worldwidefishing.com/florida/fly.htm

Lake Tarpon

- **Location:** Ten miles west of Tampa, west coast of central Florida
- **What You Fish For:** Largemouth bass
- **Highlights and Notables:** Lots and lots of 5-pound bass

This bass lake has a misleading name. With all the businesses and traffic and houses, the quality of this fishery is also misleading. Lake Tarpon is one of Florida's best largemouth bass lakes, plenty of 3- to 6-pound buckets in here, in the Canal, near the islands and humps.

CONTACTS

Florida Fish and Wildlife Conservation Commission, South Region, 813-648-3203

Lake Okeechobee

- **Location:** Southern Florida near Orlando
- **What You Fish For:** Largemouth bass
- **Highlights and Notables:** The Big O is one of the best bass lakes in the country. Think lunkers and great numbers of big bass.

Can a place be sexy? This lake is sexy. No other bass lake in America looks fishy-er. Okeechobee is humongous, weedy, reedy, shallow, warm, inviting. This lake near Orlando is a heavy cover lake with so much vegetation, it looks like a vegan salad spilled in a bowl of water. Pencilgrass, lily pad weedbeds, cattails, sawgrass, eelgrass—green plants of all kinds rise up from the shallows, wickedly unique, like mats of prehistoric plants scattered all around the shore. Seven hundred square miles of ideal bass habitat.

You will catch fish.

You will catch bass.

You will catch bass that bend your rod.

You will catch bass that weigh 1 to 4 pounds and at Okeechobee, 20- to 50-fish days are not the dreams of Disney World. Reality. Three- to 7-pound largemouths are common. If you work it hard, move around, kinda know what you're doing, you'll hook up with numerous bass in the 7- to 10-pound range. Ten-pound largemouth bass and bigger? Oh yeah. Okeechobee is a

City Fishing

MIAMI
Biscayne Bay

Miami has it all, not just for fishing but for anything else you might want. Nightlife, great food, beautiful people, cool architecture, beaches, and more. The centerpiece for fishing is Biscayne Bay, where the city of Miami is right in front of you (or behind you, depending which way you are facing). The bay is easy to access (through Homestead Bayfront Park or Crandon Park), full of fish, and fruitful all year long.

In Biscayne Bay, anglers can fish for shark. Lemon shark. Up to 200 pounds large. Tarpon, bonefish, sea trout and permit and pompano. For pompano, use a lead-headed jig on the bottom and catch those pompano on the bottom all day long (looks like a permit but it's not). You'd pay a lot for a pompano in a Miami restaurant, an expensive dinner and extremely delicious. Flats flat flats flats. Channels for drifting. Lots of good sight fishing in the shallows. This habitat is mostly in the South Bay but don't discount the less famous, more urbanized North Bay with its grass beds and docks (and some flats). In North Bay, sea trout are abundant and on the small side. In South Bay, the bonefish are plentiful but smallish. Near mangrove trees and islands, sandy bottoms and that means fish.

In Miami, you can fish from lighted piers and docks, hoping to catch croaker, snapper, mackerel. Offshore in the Atlantic is a short boat ride for sailfish, swordfish, kingfish, mahi-mahi, etc. The Miami Canal Airport Lakes System (like Blue Lagoon and Lake Mahar) hold all kinds of fish including—get this—peacock bass. Check out the 836 shoreline if you get the chance. From Miami, you have close access to the Everglades, Key West, Okeechobee, and many other options.

trophy bass lake so you better be ready every time you cast (lake record is 14 pounds). Plain and simple, Lake Okeechobee is one of the best bass fishing lakes in the country.

Orlando, Florida. This is your greatest excuse ever to take the family on one of your fishing trips and they won't even care if you go fishing. And it won't be like you're fishing just to fish. Disney World, MGM Studios, Universal Studios, the Orlando Magic, sunshine, and so much more. The lake and area offers something for everyone. If you want to teach the kids to fish and have a reasonable chance of catching bass and crappie, this is your top choice. My first trip to the Big O was when I was fifteen and Dad dropped me off with a guide while he and the family went to Disney World all day long. I caught a 5-pound largemouth that at the time, looked belly-fat like a world record bass. I caught lots more in the 2–3 pound range and thought I must be the greatest angler in the world. That's how Okeechobee makes you feel.

Summer is the ideal time to fish the Big O. The bass fishing at Lake Okeechobee overshadows the crappie fishing and it shouldn't. The lake is chock-full of paper-mouths.

The Big O's deepest water is only about twelve feet, with the majority of the lake in the five to seven-foot range. You can imagine how scintillating the topwater fishing must be. It's 760,000 acres when full; the lake hit drought conditions a few years back but has recovered, and the fishing is awesome. Lake Okeechobee is the largest inland freshwater lake in America. This is real southern bass fishing, so good that more than twenty guides serve the lake.

Ninety miles northwest of Miami at the southern tip of the state, next to the Everglades, complete with alligators and snakes, Lake Okeechobee has something for everyone. Clewiston is the homebase for many and you have all kinds of lodging to choose from including legendary angler Roland Martin's marina and resort.

CONTACTS
Florida Game and Fresh Water Fish Commission, Tallahassee, 904-488-4676
Roland Martin, www.rolandmartinmarina .com
Florida Division of Tourism (for accommodations), Tallahassee, 904-488-9804

To find a guide or outfitter, this Web site is a good resource www.1fghp.com/okeechobee.html

CONTACTS
Capt. Ken Collette, 954-463-0512
Capt. Andy Thompson, 305-246-4669
Capt. Harry's Fishing Supply, www.captharry .com
Biscayne Bay Fly Shop,
    www.biscaynebayflyshop.com

Orange Lake and Crooked Lake

- **Location:** Northeastern Florida
- **What You Fish For:** Bass and crappie
- **Highlights and Notables:** Sister lakes with attitude

Scylla and Charybdis. A rose by any other name is still a rose. The River Styx.

Choosing between these two connected lakes is like being between a rock and a hard place. There's one reference down. Two to go.

Crooked Lake is the newest name for Lake Caloosa, aka Lochloosa Lake. Ah, the rose reference.

Orange Lake is fed by the River Styx. Hey, I couldn't make this stuff up.

These sister lakes, Orange (12,500 acres) and Crooked (5,700 acres) are a pair of hot-fishin' honeys located in northeastern Florida, with Orange best known for its

City Fishing

ORLANDO
St. Johns River, Kissimmee Chain of Lakes, Disney World

Within the city limits of Orlando there are more than 100 lakes. The world-famous Kissimmee Chain of Lakes (Toho, Toho, Toho) is but a short drive away. Stick Marsh/Farm 13, one of the hottest bass fisheries no one but hard-core bass anglers know about is only an hour away. Lots of water. Big bass. Easy to get to, year-round angling. A mix of big-name lakes and well managed municipal waters. Apopka, Clermont Chain, Harris Chain, East and West Tohopekaliga, Blue Cypress Lake, and numerous small in-town lakes like Turkey Lake, Baldwin, the Butler Chain and Lake Underhill, so many, you can have one all to yourself (almost).

There are so many bass lakes, phosphate pits (a Florida thing), ponds, and other bodies of fresh water of all sizes and shapes that hold 5- to 10-pound largemouth it would take a book to cover them all. I haven't found a city this big with this many quality fishing opportunities so close, period. And you have quality salt water fishing too. This city may be the best city to live in or visit for fishing in the nation.

Citizens and tourists have St. John's River too, one of the better bass rivers in the country, right out your back yard (and it flows south to north). This three-hundred mile long tortuous river produces high numbers of quality bass and bass of high quality in its labyrinth of sloughs and canals. St. John's even has populations of striper and shad. The most difficult aspect is deciphering access points, so it's a good idea to check with tackle shops to see where to set up shop.

Stick Marsh/Farm 13. Doesn't sound like much, does it? It is. Stick Marsh/Farm 13 is 6,000 surface acres of mean, nasty bass-water. The impoundment produces smashing numbers of double-digit catches of mean, nasty bass. A catch-and-release lake and it's not unusual to talk to anglers who catch fifteen to thirty bass in a day at this lake near Fellsmere (an hour from Orlando) and so many 7- to 12-pounders it's crazy, mean, and nasty.

And then there's Disney World. Don't laugh, don't skim over this. Disney World is for real. Don't plan a fishing trip to the land of Mickey Mouse, rather fish there, in Bay Lake, on your off day, while the kids are standing in line for Magic Mountain or the spinning teacups or that boat ride where you go past big fiberglass elephants and they spray you with water. You'll be out on the lake with a guide (if you want one) catching largemouth bass 1 to 5 pounds and bigger. Five- to 8-pound bucketmouths are common and the lake record is something in the neighborhood of 14 pounds.

Thing is, the guided trips are usually just for two hours but that's all the fishing you need anyway. Go back to the air conditioned hotel room and take a well deserved nap. If you want to book a Walt Disney World guided fishing trip, call their Recreation and Reservations Line. Call 407-WDW-PLAY.

The Kissimmee chain of lakes make up the headwaters for the Everglades. There are numerous lakes to choose from, but the best lakes are not in the Alligator chain but the lower chain—all good, all a bit different but similar, if that makes any sense. Tohopekaliga (aka Toho), Cypress, Hatchineha, Jackson, Marian, and of course Kissimmee. Kissimmee is also known for shellcracker angling.

Lake Toho (Tohopekaliga) is a personal fave—it flies under the national radar but is one of the more consistent big bass producers anywhere. The lake record hawg is 17 pounds large. What's fun is the average size bass that comes in around 4 or 5 pounds of fury.

CONTACTS
AJ's Freelancer, www.orlandobass.com
For a comprehensive list of guides, visit www.1fghp.com/florida/fltoho.html

numerous crappie and Crooked a quiet big bass producer.

Both lakes have water levels that have returned to normal after being down for a few years. Both have wide aquatic vegetation, especially lily pads that hide fish, especially crappie. Orange is not thought of as a lake with large largemouth but in the winter months, 10-pound bass are not rare. Crooked Lake's prize bass weighed in at almost 16 pounds. Seven- to 8-pound bass are frequently caught. Little Crooked Lake is the favored happy hunting grounds for hawg hunters, not bad for a lake that not all that long ago was thought to have crossed the River Styx. The locals know Crooked Lake is worthy but are glad the word's not out yet about its hefty bass. Ooops.

CONTACTS
South Shore Fish Camp, 352-595-4241
McIntosh Fish Camp, 352-591-1302
Gainsville Chamber of Commerce,
   904-372-4305

Pine Island Coast

- **Location:** Southwestern coast of Florida, just west of Fort Myers
- **What You Fish For:** Snook, tarpon, speckled trout and redfish
- **Highlights and Notables:** Undiscovered cool beach town with productive inshore and offshore angling

Pine Island Coast for anglers. Every kind of saltwater fish you ever wanted to catch and set in an easygoing, inexpensive environment. No big tourism here, few crowds, just an unassuming artist community, a throwback, in western Florida off the coast from Fort Myers. Snook, tarpon, speckled trout, tripletail, redfish, grouper, snapper, Spanish mackerel, and cobia swim in these waters, not as pretty as the Keys but much more scenic that you'd think. If you like light-tackle action or fly fishing in shallow water, the Pine Island Coast (Pine Island, Cayo Costa, Captiva, Pine Island Sound, various and sundry islands) is your place. This could be your Margaritaville before it becomes famous, no traffic lights, easygoing atmosphere, authors and musicians, unspoiled land and water, and few tourists.

There's no way to fish this water on your own the first few times. Navigation in this salt wilderness labyrinth is futile unless you know the nooks and crannies. Hire a guide. They'll take you to the island points and mangroves for snook; sneak up on tailing redfish; put you on tarpon in shallow water, sometimes grass flats (yeah, grass flats!), even sightcast to the schools of tarpon hanging out just off the beaches. Daisy chain. Rolling. Setting the hook like you mean it. Jumping and running. Fifty- to 140-pound silver streaks. Rattled nerves.

Rodman Reservoir

- **Location:** Northeast Florida
- **What You Fish For:** Largemouth bass
- **Highlights and Notables:** Don't bury this legendary bass lake just yet—there's still life in her.

Americans are the world's most fickle fans. They love the underdog but wear Yankees caps and Bulls jerseys, #23 of course. Rodman Reservoir, a 9,500-acre reservoir on the Ocklawaha River in northeast Florida, is consistently one of Florida's top largemouth producers. The lake is known for big bass and the water cabbage the big bass hide under. But so many whispers suggest that, oh my, Rodman isn't the last it was twenty years ago. Shhh.

Lake record for largemouth? A 17.27 pounder. Pretty decent, huh? And Rodman, aka Lake Oklawaha, has black bass of similar sizes caught in recent years, too. The lake just seems loaded with 8- to 10-pounders, which is why Rodman acquired such a reputation as a trophy bass destination the last two decades.

So we look to those critics who don't think Rodman is as good as it used to be. The quality and quantity are higher than most lakes in all of America. Rodman is certainly one of the best winter largemouth hotspots in the South. And in bad weather, the lake still fishes well. The lake has an amazing array of bass living quarters ranging from water channels, stump fields, mats of floating hyacinth, standing timber, river channels, hydrilla, and other vegetation. Plenty of shallow spawning flats for the black bass. The lake also holds bream, speckled perch, catfish, and many other species (and alligators, too, if you like that sort of moving predatory scenery).

Electroshocking shows the lake is healthy, that the bass population is in its upward cycle. Every few years, Rodman goes through drawdown and as a result, some of the choking vegetation dies off and the fishing becomes phenomenal again.

The biggest problem Rodman faces is an ongoing battle with those who want to return this lake to its natural state. Once part of a proposed but abandoned barge canal system, Rodman remains in jeopardy more from this threat than from any whispers from the peanut crowd.

To get to Rodman from Jacksonville, head south on US 17 to 19 West, then travel on 310 west to 315 west. You have about seventy-five miles to reach Rodman from Jacksonville.

CONTACTS
The Tackle Box, 352-372-1791 or 904-328-9311

GEORGIA

So I was talking to my fishing buddy Richie Santiago who fishes Dukes (and Smith and Noontootla and all the northern Georgia creeks) on a regular basis about what he thinks of Dukes Creek. I know I loved the stream and did pretty well but I missed more fish than I should have. Richie doesn't miss many. He's one of those young trout fishing bums who's read all the books, learned all he could and then gone out and put hours and hours into refining it. What are your secrets? Richie tells me "I've found that both big and tiny flies work the best at Dukes Creek. I usually go with something big and ugly up top followed by some tiny off the back." *Perfect. Dropper rigs are great prospecting tools.*

"For large flies," Richie continues, "I've had a lot of luck with zonkers and herl-less nymphs and for small flies you can't go wrong with a pheasant tail #20, various soft hackles usually #18 and up, a good crawdad pattern also works great up there. But if it rained heavy the day before then no one should leave the house without a pink San Juan worm." *Never would have thought of it. A pink San Juan worm on a southeastern stream.*

"I've found that walking while fishing super slow will produce more fish at Dukes Creek. Most of the time I'll leave the creek with a sore shoulder from high sticking all day but that and a good drag free drift are two of the best techniques for fishing Dukes.

Surprisingly typical fish for north Georgia

As far as what size tippet . . . if it's a clear day and the sun is shining then you better tie on something thin but if it is stained or if it's raining then you can get away with something thicker like 4X and sometimes 3X." *And there I was using 6X and 7X and wondering why I kept losing big trout.*

"It always surprises me to see so many huge fish in that small stream!" *Me, too.*

Amy and I had done the Atlanta thing. The quaint northern Georgia bed and breakfast thing. It was weird trying to find any of these northern Georgia streams because of the listing by county and by wildlife management area or wilderness management area and the forest service roads weren't always well marked and it was spring but late spring so it was hot and I was hungry and she didn't really want to fish. I was bitchy, she was bitchy.

We were walking the banks of the Conasauga, stopping and me casting, an Adams I think, not really caring if we caught anything. And then I caught something. A wild rainbow. Sitting right by the undercut bank. Tore the Adams up. Thirteen inches and fat as my thigh. Two more as we walked along. One rainbow, one brown. Twelve and fourteen. Beautifully colored. Now Amy wants to fish and it's a lot cooler since the clouds moved over and the scenery is beautiful and we aren't feuding and all is right with the world.

Amy caught six (including a nice 10-inch fat brook trout) in a 100-yard stretch (but should have caught twice that many) before she got tired of fishing (catching) and relinquished the rod. Me and the Conasauga got busy. Great afternoon. Better evening. Making up is always fun.

And Amy and I moved out of the agitated phase and into the "we're catching fish" phase and after we left the river, we ate at a diner and moved into the "we're so much in love" phase, which is our favorite phase of all. A beautiful wife who fishes and forgives me. Tell me I'm not one lucky guy.

For a change of pace, try the Georgia coast, a surprisingly fertile, scenic place to hunt big fish. David McDonald is a special projects carpenter on the Little St. Simons Island on the coast, pretty darned convenient for a guy who is eaten up with fishing fever. McDonald typically catches redfish and flounder and black drum. "We get great speckled trout in the winter months," McDonald confided. "There's never a shortage of things to catch in the abundant creeks and ponds on the island."

One fine July day (every day is fine on Little St. Simons), fishing for mullet, McDonald spotted two large tarpon in the creek, a little less than a mile from the ocean. He cast in their direction, his rod tip moved and a 100-pound tarpon "rocketed out of the water and shot toward the ocean." If you've never caught a tarpon in a river, it's similar to wrestling a greased hog in a half-filled bathtub.

"I was running along the bank of the creek, through the spartina, trying to set the drag and keep the huge fish from spooling out. About 200 yards from the ocean, the fish stopped and I was able to tighten the line," McDonald explained. "That was the first half-hour."

Then the tarpon turned and shot back upriver.

McDonald spent the next half-hour chasing his quarry along the bank when the fish stopped for another rest. A friend, Joe Taylor, took the rod while McDonald took a drink and caught his breath. By the time they hauled in the tarpon, took photos, and released it, nearly two hours had elapsed.

"We know of no one else who has ever done this on Little St. Simons Island. The line should have broken, but it didn't," McDonald confesses. "It was a great catch."

You want to know how comfortable (southern comfortable) you're gonna be at the Lodge? Check out a typical dinner: Artichoke Hearts & Calamata Olive Salad Dressed with Herb Vinaigrette & Feta Cheese, Pecan-Crusted Pork Loin with Port Wine & Pear Sauce, Fresh Sauteed Vegetable Medley, Southern Sweet Potato Souffle, Fresh Baked Whole-Wheat Rolls, Sweet Potato Gratin. Sweet southern cookin'.

North Georgia Trout Waters

- **Location:** Northern Georgia, mountains
- **What You Fish For:** Trout
- **Highlights and Notables:** Some of the best trout fishing in the South, a variety of creeks and streams, surprising sizes in these relatively small rivers

Chain pickerel can be caught in the backs of oxbow lakes and shallow areas with vegetation.

City Fishing

ATLANTA
Lake Sidney Lanier, Chattahoochee River, Soque River

Don't go to Atlanta just for the Chattahoochee. While it's very good, it's not that good. Go to A-Town for your business conference, to visit Aunt Marge, or to shop and while you're there, take a day and visit the Hooch or the hundreds of Georgian streams for trout and bass. Of these hundreds of rivers and creeks in Georgia that hold bass and trout, few are more than an hour or two drive from Atlanta.

Let's start with the Chattahoochee River, the new signature landmark for outdoors-minded tourists who find themselves in Atlanta. The Hooch runs right through ATL like it means business. Tailwater. Artificial. There shouldn't be good trout fishing this close to Atlanta, right? If you've been there in the summer, you know that Beelzebub rents a downtown condo in July and August, it's so hot. The Chattahoochee has its charms even as a put-and-take fishery. The mornings are fog and smoke, hardwood trees threaten to fall off the bluffs, the hardwood stands stand sentinel on rolling hills, the rhododendron and mountain laurel steal your breathing air, shoals expose to give you dry sanctuary.

Not much reproduction in the Hooch—most all of your catches are by virtue of stocking—brown, brook, and rainbow. The brown trout may or may not be reproducing but it's doubtful they're doing so in any meaningful way. The holdover browns grow to bragging size but they are far and few between. The record is an 18-pound brownie but that's an aberration if there ever was one. You'll hear about this old boy or that one catching an 8-pound brown but their scale must be broken. The rainbows are catchable size and that's about the best you can say. Bass converge around inlets and in oxygenated water.

In the upper Hooch, you fish midges all winter. Delayed harvest on the lower Hooch does create some nice fishing and fish that have had all summer to grow (usually November into March). Easy to wade, easy to float (belly boat), nothing fancy to figure out to fish, the Chattahoochee is a nice diversion for an afternoon, even a day.

Atlanta has several man-made lakes within an hour drive like Lake Lanier and Alltoona Reservoir. Lake Lanier (40,000 acres) is an older lake but good for largemouth and spotted bass. The Chattahoochee National Forest is north of the city and there you find more than two thousand miles of mountainous trout streams.

I can promise you that no other major city in the country has so many private and public waters that hold such large trout, trophy trout—pellet-fed trout to be sure—but trout so unbelievably large, they ought to be in the North Platte or the Bighorn but no, they live in small shallow mountain waters a couple of hours drive from Hotlanta, Georgia. Private trout waters worth looking into include the Soque River (see separate entry) and Frog Hollow on the Chestatee, Cannon Falls Lodge, and I know local fly shops have some other very exclusive, private, special trout streams and lakes, too.

Unicoi has access to plenty of private water that holds browns that will just blow you away with how large they are. The Nacoochee Bend of the Chattahoochee near Helen is one such spot, a slow-moving 1.5-mile section where the forest comes right up on the river and big pools hold big browns. The Frog Hollow of the Chestatee is quicker and enjoys long runs, pocket water, and big clear pools. Rainbows and browns in the mid-20-inch range, few rods on the water each week. Lots of 5-pound trout. Cannon Falls Lodge on the upper Chestatee doesn't hold the trout-hawgs of some of the other Georgia streams but is among the more beautiful with its 100-foot waterfall (and several other waterfalls) and wild, rugged surroundings and you can still catch numerous 12- to 18-inch brook trout and some big ol' 'bows.

CONTACTS

Fish Hawk tackle shop, Atlanta, 404-237-3473

Unicoi Outfitters, 706-878-3083, www .unicoioutfitters.com

Cannon Falls Lodge, 706-348-7919, www.cannonfallslodge.com

Toccoa River

Toccoa River above Blue Ridge Lake has marginal trout fishing on its public stretches. Most of the good fishing on the Toccoa is private. What is open is big water for Georgia, in some places 100 feet wide. The river is stocked with all three species but does have a population of wild brown and rainbow trout as well as smallmouth bass.

The Toccoa River tailrace below Lake Blue Ridge in northwest Georgia is a wide river, punctuated by long, deep pools, shoals, riffles, and rapidly changing water levels. The Toccoa is a high quality trout stream, less fished than its twin tailwater, the Chattahoochee. The Toccoa holds rainbows, browns, and brookies and is open all year long.

Float fishing is the best way to cover this deep, fertile river since access for the walking and wading angler is limited. Locals say that the river fishes best when the water levels are falling, as is the case with most tailwater trout fisheries. The trout here sometimes reach 17, 18, 19, even 20 inches but you have to work to find them. Most run about 9 to 13 inches and if you are a halfway decent angler, you can catch quite a few in a day. What's cool is that you can fish this tailwater successfully with dry flies. This is so because unlike the mountain streams that don't have great hatches, the Toccoa has plenty, especially mayflies.

CONTACTS
Mike Darnell, Morganton,
    www.troutshack.com/home.htm
Reel Angling Adventures, Suches,
    bborgwat@reelanglingadventures.com

Jacks Creek

Jacks River flows in northwest Georgia through primitive wilderness, with two of the best trout streams in the state, the Jacks and Conasauga Rivers. The Cohutta Wildlife Management Area is the largest in the state, and it is easily the most inaccessible. The streams flow through mixed hardwood forests and thickets of laurel and rhododendron. There are few roads, so the Cohutta is a backpacker's paradise. In fact, most of the people you'll run into in this wilderness will be hikers and backpackers.

Jacks River is a large wild trout stream for these parts. Like the Conasauga, Jacks is in rugged country with high quality fishing in its fifteen miles of valley stretches and miles and miles of trails all along the river including numerous stream crossings. The great amount of access/mileage combined with healthy populations of cautious wild rainbows and browns is why Jacks

is in the book, is an ideal fishing destination for loners and remote location lovers. The Cohutta WMA can be accessed from State Highway 52 east of Chatsworth, State Highway 5 and off US 411 onto several forest service roads. Access is not easy and the only access by road is at its junction with the Conasauga on FS 16 or in the headwaters off FS 64 on either the West or South forks.

Waters Creek

Isolated. Remote. In the middle of nowhere. Waters Creek is a freak of a stream. A small mountain stream five to ten feet wide, but it's a trophy trout fishery. Like Dukes, the trout get fat on supplemental food (pellets) but these fish are wild.

The unusual special regulations of Waters Creek regularly produce trout as long as 24 inches. Several state records have come out of this small stream, including the record brook trout, 5 pounds, 10 ounces. Many browns and rainbows from 8 to 12 pounds have been caught over the twenty years these regulations have been in place. Anglers must use artificial single-barbless lures or flies no bigger than size 6 in the nearly three miles of excellent trout habitat (but hatches are sporadic, uneven).

Open March to end of October, 6:30AM to 6:30PM each day. Fishermen must check in their fishing license to enter the area, and they are required to have a Georgia fishing license, a WMA stamp, and a trout stamp. Check your regulations for all the special restrictions that keep this place special. Waters Creek can be accessed from US 19 & 29 in the Chestatee WMA.

Dicks Creek

Waters Creek flows into Dicks Creek and some of the big Waters Creek trout make the trip downstream into the notable, crowded, high-use Chestatee WMA stream. Dicks Creek is heavily stocked and sees lots of bank fishermen on weekends and holidays. Even with all the pressure, anglers catch big trout every season, some over 20 inches. The swimmers and tubers will force anglers to alter casts on the medium-sized river, so the best fishing is early and late on Dicks Creek.

The upper section is typical overgrown Georgia mountain stream but as the stream moves down, things open up. If you want to get into wild trout or big trout, get away from the easy access points. Access is from US 19 to Waters Creek Road. Boggs Creek and Blood Mountain Creek are two other fishable streams in the Chestatee WMA, both of which hold wild trout hard to get to because of the streamside growth.

Dukes Creek

If I listed the good things and bad things about Dukes, I could list 100 things and have only one negative. For some anglers, this 1 percent will outweigh the 99 percent. I'll start with the 99 percent: Brown and rainbow trout that in the Smithgall Woods section average—and I have only anecdotal and personal evidence here, no state figures—about 15 or 16 inches or big-

ger. Probably bigger but I want to err on the side of caution. You catch an occasional brook trout and they are usually nice-sized. Not many brookies in this creek because with all the stocked rainbows and browns; the brook trout have been crowded out or eaten.

Brown and rainbows that are nearly wild, stocked as fingerlings in the Smithgall Woods, wild trout above it.

Brown and rainbow trout that grow to at least 28 inches long. The frequency of trout caught that are 17 to 24 inches long rivals the Green, the San Juan, the Big Hole, the Big Horn, the North Platte, and even Soque Creek.

All the fish are solid, fat, heavy, hefty, chunky, thick. Year-round fishing. Even in the snow. Dukes Creek, with its upper reaches overgrown with rhododendron, laurel, hemlock, pine, old-growth hardwoods, its clean clear water bouncing down the upper river's steep gradient, diving off in a 100-foot tall waterfall, cascading over rocks, crashing into pools, before settling down a bit, pool-riffle and then finally squeezing through a gorge. The small river is as pretty as any stream in Georgia.

Great management of the resource. Dukes Creek can only be fished with artificial lures and flies, barbless hooks only. Catch-and-release only for the creek and its tributaries. The creek is also limited to a little more than a dozen anglers at any one time and you must have reservations to even get on the water. Dukes Creek is probably the finest public trophy trout destination in the Southeast.

Ten or more miles of Dukes Creek and tributaries that run through the Smithgall Woods–Dukes Creek Conservation Area.

Now for the one negative element and you can judge for yourself if it turns you off or not: The reason why the trout are so drippingly fat is that they are supplementally fed pellets. This doesn't make them easy to catch because you have to present the right fly in the right way, but this fact does sometimes dampen the spirits of purists.

You know, when you get in the river and you sightcast to a 4-pound rainbow whose dorsal fin is sticking out the water, you tend to forget all that kind of negativity. Helen is the nearest real town but you can also stay in the Lodge at Smithgall Woods, a fancy-schmancy resort with lodgepole pine house, bungalows, and cottages all fixed up elegantly and such (www.smithgallwoods .com).

If you get the chance, fish the upper reaches above Smithgall Woods. The upper is beautiful and not as fished and wild and green and smells like a southern forest ought to smell and the waterfall is worth the hike.

If the pellets bother you enough not to try this trophy trout creek, that's fine with me. I understand fully. I have trouble with it every time I land one of those 20-inch Dukes Creek monsters.

Park Hours
7AM to 6PM. Trout fishing on Wednesday, Saturday, and Sunday only (daily for lodge guests). Reservations required.

All visitors must register at the Visitor Center. Dukes Creek and its tributaries within the Dukes Creek Conservation Area are open to fishing year-round by reservation only. For reservations, call 706-878-3087.

Noontootla Creek

Noontootla Creek holds wild rainbows and browns in a southern Appalachian setting with all the requisite heavy foliage and difficult casting and clear tumbling water. Set almost entirely in the Blue Ridge Wildlife Management Area, Noontootla does not receive the fishing pressure its fishery and scenery would normally demand. You can't camp, you must use artificials only, and there are other special regs including a limit on keeping fish that basically makes the stream a catch-and-release stream. Despite excellent access, these restrictions keep the crowds away.

Wading can be tricky in the rougher parts of this beautiful, productive, and underfished stream. Rock Creek is a high-use stream, full of plenty of rainbow and brown trout. The creek has some deep pools worth fishing where catchable-sized trout hang susceptible to corn or worms. Campgrounds and campsites dot the river's banks. Rock Creek Lake impounds the creek in its middle portion, and also gets planted hatchery trout.

CONTACTS

Fish Hawk, Atlanta, 404-237-3473
Unicoi Outfitters, 706-878-3083, www
.unicoioutfitters.com

Conasauga River

- **Location:** In the roadless Cohutta Wilderness Area
- **What You Fish For:** Rainbow and brown trout
- **Highlights and Notables:** Rugged scenery and excellent dry fly fishing for wild trout

Boy, what an underrated river. You hear more about Jacks Creek or Dicks Creek but to me, this one is better than both. Jacks may have bigger fish (it may not, too) and Dicks great water but the Conasauga has similar fish and beautiful water and a lot fewer anglers. The Conasauga is a pretty big trout stream by Appalachian standards. This is clean cold water full of wild trout, browns and rainbows. Fifteen miles of it.

And the wild trout get to some big sizes by Appalachian standards. You won't often have a legit shot at a 20-incher. A 16-inch trout shouldn't surprise you. If you fish long enough, put enough nice casts out there, you'll catch enough 12-inch trout to tell your buddies that your arm is tired.

What keeps this a great river is that it's not easy to get to parts of the Conasauga. This land is rugged and wild. I know, I know, you don't associate wilderness with Georgia. The Peach State? Well, that goes to show how much you know and why I'm telling you about this gem.

The Conasauga lies within the 34,000-acre Cohutta Wilderness Area, a roadless tract (the largest of its kind in the eastern United States) and if you travel here, you'll walk this high country (in places, you can ride a horse). It gets confusing because the Conasauga and the Cohutta Wilderness Area are part of the larger Cohutta Wilderness Management Area, one the WMAs in northern Georgia and ultimately, it's part of the Chattahoochee National Forest which is owned by the U.S. Forest Service. Told ya.

You won't see many other anglers on the Conasauga. You will see some strong hikers and backpackers but they generally take their strong legs on past you. Ridiculous access in places on steep mountains makes this a destination you really have to want to reach. Over a decade ago, *Trout* magazine named the Conasauga one of the top 100 trout streams in America. There hasn't been a true run on the river because you better be a strong hiker to fish here.

And you better be a pretty decent fly fisher. Spincasters won't fare as well because the water is as clear as club soda. To catch the 9- to 14-inch stream-bred trout, you're going to have to sneak around, stalk, sight cast, use light long tippet, hide behind the big boulders, be stealthy, and generally go commando.

You're going to get "I-need-to-pee" excited when you come up to a big pool of clear water and see half dozen to a dozen good-sized fish holding. Drag-free drifts. The browns are your best chance at a lunker and a 3- to 5-pounder wouldn't surprise any locals. It's in the South. It's primitive. It holds wild fish of size (and beauty). And it isn't all that far from Atlanta.

St. Simons Island

- **Location:** One of the barrier islands (the Golden Isles) off the Georgia coast
- **What You Fish For:** Tarpon, speckled trout, and redfish are the three top game fish but you can also catch drum, mackerel, flounder, croaker, yellowtail, and many others.
- **Highlights and Notables:** Stunning scenery, surprisingly great fishing for tarpon and reds, great getaway for you and your significant other

Sometimes, you need to show your wife how much you love her. Sometimes you have to get some brownie points. Sometimes work is too stressful and you have discretionary income and you need to get away from it all. Voilà! St. Simons Georgia.

This barrier island, part of the Golden Isles along the Georgia coast, just off from Brunswick, has been many things over the years ranging from a military outpost to cotton plantation to playground for the rich and famous. Think *Southern Living*, antebellum mansions, Spanish moss, cool breezes in summer and warmth in summer. The island is still many things today, too. An offshore refuge for golfers, beach-loungers, beachcombers, bicyclists, hikers, lighthouse-admirers, sunbathers, birdwatchers, shell-collectors, shoppers, tennis players, and anyone who likes the unhurried semitropical lifestyle. St. Simons is also a great base from which to fish for the numerous species available in the Golden Isles.

What species might you enjoy in those breaks from the pampered life? Red drum, black drum, Spanish mackerel, flounder, croaker, spot, yellowtail—but none of those will float your boat. How about tarpon? Speckled trout? Redfish? Tripletail? Shark, kingfish, barracuda? Now we're talking. The sleeper game fish in these Georgian waters is tarpon, some up to 200 pounds. Imagine driving six hours from Atlanta, enjoying a stroll on the beach, a southern-style dinner, drinks, the rhythmic murmur of the sea and waking up to a day where you catch three or four or five tarpon ranging from 70 to 150 pounds.

At times, the fishing around the nine barrier islands can be tough, other times, easy; either way, enhanced by the ambience and activities. The Golden Isle region holds fish in its inshore waters, surf, estuaries, bays, tidal creeks, and not far offshore, you can tangle for bigger, meaner fish and you can find some kind of game fish to angle for all year round. Both fly fishers and conventional anglers can ply their trade. If you go to St. Simons, and you should, get in touch with Larry Kennedy of St. Simons Outfitters on Frederica Road. Kennedy's one of those salty dogs who grew up on local waters and knows them like the back of his hand.

tarpon

St. Simon is the largest of the nine barrier islands but one is privately-owned, secluded and ideal for resort lovers, accessible only by boat: Little St. Simons.

Stay at the Lodge on Little St. Simons Island. Seven miles of unspoiled beaches. Limit of thirty visitors per day. All kinds of activities with an emphasis for naturalists. Romantic. Unless you're from Georgia, you probably haven't heard of it but the luxurious lodge has won numerous awards including *Condé Nast Traveller* 2000 Readers' Choice Award for "Best

Small Hotel, North America." Not too shabby.

Besides making Little St. Simons Island a home base for fishing the public waters, you can also find fish moving in Sancho Panza Creek, and Bass Creek on the island, especially redfish in season. Mosquito Creek runs east to west across Little Simons Island.

Like I say, at Little St. Simons Island, the fishing is fine and the digs are even better.

Captain Larry Kennedy III recommends

that you bring the ever-popular Clouser minnow in chartreuse/white, orange/red, orange/white, pink/white, white/white, and gray/white. Flies that emulate local white shrimp or bay minnows, anchovies, or glass minnows, and any other good small bait fish imitation may work.

CONTACTS

St. Simon Outfitters, St. Simons Island, www.tbssouth.com

The Lodge on Little St. Simons Island, Little St. Simons Island, Lodge@LittleStSimonsIsland.com

Simons Bait & Tackle Shop, www.coastalgeorgia.com

Coastal Island Charter Fishing, 888-288-5030

St. Simons Island, www.gacoast.com/navigator/ssi.html

Capt. Mark Noble Charter Fishing, St. Simons Island, 912-634-1219

Lake Seminole

- **Location:** Southwestern Georgia (shares parts with Alabama and Florida, too)
- **What You Fish For:** Largemouth bass
- **Highlights and Notables:** Real southern bass lake complete with hawgs and gators

On the southwestern tip of Georgia sits a lake that seems more at home in Florida than the Peach State. Alligators, lily pads, stumps, grass beds, and huge bass. Lake Seminole shares part of its water with Florida and Alabama but its national reputation as one of the top largemouth bass lakes in the country is all its own.

Year-round fishing in a semitropical setting for big bass. Aquatic vegetation like few other lakes in the nation. Three rivers form this lake, Flint (the famous one that produces so many big bass), Chattahoochee, and Spring Creek. The lake is shallow, fertile, and has about as much structure and cover as can be packed into a lake. The topwater action can be out of this world at times.

Seminole has plenty of bass tournaments, lots of boats and bassing bubbas on the lake so you need to share the 37,000 acres with others. Water clarity varies from clear to muddy. Stripers to 40 pounds and hybrid bass with average size of about 3 pounds are the other two main attractions.

CONTACTS

Wingate's Lunker Lodge, 229-246-0658

Paradise Public Fishing Area

- **Location:** Southwestern Georgia
- **What You Fish For:** An alphabet soup of game fish ranging from bass to perch
- **Highlights and Notables:** More than 70 ponds, super place to take a beginner, your family, or to get out for a pleasant day of angling and hiking and picnicking

One of the oddest fishing complexes in North America. In the rolling hills of southwest Georgia is a collection of some seventy-odd ponds and lakes that hold everything from panfish to bass, catfish to god-knows-what, totaling 550 acres. This system was built sixty years ago by an enterprising businessman and was for years a pay-to-fish collection of fishing paradise. The state took over twenty years ago, renovated the lakes and ponds, and stocked them with a variety of fish.

I can't imagine any better setup to teach your kids or an angling newbie how to fish. With so many bodies of water, you can pretty much find your own little lake and be assured that someone is going to catch something. I heard recently that the big bass program is going great guns and that in some of the ponds/lakes, several largemouths have been caught in the 8- to 10-pound range, even one that weighed over 11 pounds. Most of the lakes are ideal for bank fishing and a few are good for boating. The lakes are surrounded by easy-on-the-eye landscapes of open fields, forested hills, and lots of wildlife, especially birds. Trails interconnect many of the lakes. The Paradise Public Fishing Area is located eight miles east of Tifton on the Brookfield-Nashville Road, off US 82 near Brookfield. You can't miss the signs on the highway.

CONTACTS
Georgia Department of Natural Resources, Wildlife Resources Division, 912-533-4792

Savannah

- **Location:** Eastern Georgia on I-95
- **What You Fish For:** Redfish and speckled trout
- **Highlights and Notables:** One of the nation's most unique cities, coastal and southern influences, eye-popping architecture, and tummy-pleasing cuisine

Not only do you have the creepy cemeteries, the plantation-style homes, the huge trees, the odd recollections of Savannah characters and events in *Midnight in the Garden of Good and Evil*—not to mention my wife Amy's favorite television cook, Paula Deen—you also have outstanding angling in flats, around islands, and in channels for redfish, speckled trout, flounder, jack crevalle, tarpon, black-tip, and spinner sharks. Tybee Island ought to be your starting point and there are quite a number of outfitters there who can put you on great fish. If you've never been to Savannah and seen its beauty, eaten its creative and great food, especially its comfort food, you need to use a fishing trip as an excuse.

CONTACTS
Bass Pro Shops, 14045 Abercorn Street, Savannah, 31419, 912-961-4200, www.basspro.com/servlet/catalog .CFPage?appID=94&storeID=29
Miss Judy Charters, Savannah, 912-897-4921
Coastal River Charters, www.coastalrivercharters.com

Soque River

- **Location:** 90 miles northeast of Georgia, near Batesville and Helen
- **What You Fish For:** Rainbow and brown trout
- **Highlights and Notables:** The fattest, longest trout east of the Rockies

You say it "So-Kwee." I haven't seen many streams like this. At first, you think it's brochure hype, all this talk about catching 20- to 30-inch trout *regularly*. Twelve- to 20-pound trout, *no big deal*. The average size trout is close to *25 inches!* Not their exact words but you get the point. Easy to doubt, right? Three species of trout—brook, brown, and rainbow—and when you see the photos on their Web site, in the articles, of all the happy anglers holding not just big trout but behemoth near record–setting size trout, you just have to wonder where the hype ends and the truth begins.

It's the truth.

The Soque River is not wide nor is it deep. The river is beautiful and small, old-growth hemlock, rhododendron, trees that lay down across the river without touching the green water, dark forests— and they all conspire to form an intimate, unique angling experience. There's the inevitable question of authenticity here: instream-rehab, aeration dams, pools that have been hand-crafted, cutting back the river banks, add-in structure, feeding trout from time to time, and other land and water management practices. Catch-and-release only, single-hook arti-

ficial flies only (barbless, of course), and they're serious about protecting their fish, discouraging landing nets because—get this—most nets aren't designed to handle trout 12 pounds and over. They even ask you not to wade too much through the pools so as not to disturb the fishing for those who come after you.

If the water is low, the lodges avoid anglers putting undue stress on the trout since Georgia heat suffocates. The lodges also have limitations on the number of anglers per day and they rest the river, too, only putting anglers on their stretches three to four days a week. Anglers can use no fly rods lighter than six-weight rod because lighter rods would make the fight last too long and stress the trout.

Here's some more unbelievable information, bordering on lore: These are stream-bred trout. This best-kept-secret in America lies only 1.5 to two hours north of Atlanta.

Over the last few years, I had heard about it, this Soque, but it felt kind of like

an urban legend, this small stream with gargantuan trout, sort of dreamy fantasy like the fabled kingdom of Presbyter John.

It's okay. They made something special out of something mediocre. Before the rehab and the management, this was just a pretty little mountain stream. Check out this little bit of eye-opening data: Surveys indicate that certain stretches of the Soque have one of the highest number of catchable trout per mile in the nation, over 6,500 with an average size of 20 inches and an amazing 8.5 pounds.

I am still in awe. Soque is like New Zealand rivers in some ways, where there aren't as many but all are big, except Soque has lots of trout. Maybe more like Dry Run Creek in Arkansas, but no kids and the fish are bigger. Perhaps like the Bighorn or Big Hole and this is the Little Hole, the Littlehorn. Kinda like the Ridgway tailrace a few years ago, the Uncompahgre River two- to three-mile rehabbed stretch where the locals called it Jurassic Park for all the big dinosaurs they caught. It's really like no other trout fishery I've ever seen.

It's not a one-time deal either. There are just too many excellent anglers I've spoken to who caught several 5- to 12-pounders, 26-plus inches, and the smallest would be 17 to 19 inches—some very reliable people tell me they had a day where they caught twenty to forty fish. The trout, being natives, are more colorful than you would believe regarding trophy trout. They are not slow tolerant beasts like other artificial fisheries produce. They use the leverage of the small stream to jump, pull, dive, and create havoc.

The Soque River is spring-fed, limestone enriched, nutrient-rich but stained, and under its canopy of trees and streamside brush moves through bursts of rapids, fair-to-middling size pools, wide glides, chunky runs, and pillowy-slow water. The river has incredible insect hatches but that's expected in the South. Beginners will have a tough time without a guide and I wouldn't even think of doing that to them. Besides matching the hatch, the need for good casts and better presentations, the backcasts and bank-brush will eat up their flies.

Three "lodges" service their own private water on the Soque: Brigadoon Lodge, Blackhawk Lodge, Riverside Lodge. The two nicer ones are the first two but you're on the river not for the Montana lodge experience; you're there to catch more of the biggest trout than you ever have in your life. You have to see it to believe it.

Lodging

There's no reason not to enjoy your stay, right? Brigadoon Lodge has quite the reputation for making anglers feel right at home. Brigadoon is situated along its own private stretch of the Soque. You can stay at the main lodge or in one of two riverfront cabins, Oman and Cragganmore. You know that when your cabins have names like these, they are not your rustic western cabins (and they are not). Aristocratic is too stuffy a word for this place. Maybe southern sophistication.

Lodging at Brigadoon means Persian throw rugs and antiques and baby grand pianos and fly fishing décor and even a

Great Room. These folks do know how to manage a river and fishery as their stretch is flat-dab loaded with trophy trout.

CONTACTS

Brigadoon Lodge, Clarksville, www .brigadoonlodge.com

Blackhawk Flyfishing, Clarkesville, www .blackhawkflyfishing.com

Fish Hawk Fly Shop, Atlanta, www .fishhawk.com

Riverside Trophy Trout, Clarksville, 706-947-3364

River Through Atlanta, Roswell, www .riverthroughatlanta.com

Unicoi Outfitters, Helen, www.unicoioutfitters.com

KENTUCKY

I'm not a scientist nor do I play one on TV. I'm not even very good at science even though I find myself reading more and more books about science. *A Short History of Nearly Everything* by Bill Bryson. *Zero: The Biography of a Dangerous Idea* by Charles Seife. And one thing I have read the last decade, picked back up on what I read and forgot in college, something I read somewhere but now don't remember where, was about Schrodinger's Cat.

Ever heard of Schrodinger's Cat?

What we have with Schrodinger's Cat is a theoretical experiment. No animals are really harmed in this experiment because it is theoretical. You take a cat. Put him in a box. You can't see inside this box. The cat is in one compartment separate from this theoretical contraption. This contraption has two parts: a poison gas and a gizmo that has a radioactive nucleus. There is a 50 percent chance that the nucleus will decay in one hour and if it does that, the poison will be released and kill the cat. All theoretical mind you. Quantum mechanics horseplay.

So some of the famous scientists believe that because we, the observers, cannot see the cat, we cannot know if it is dead or alive. So they say the cat is both dead and alive. Only when we look inside the box and see the result—that the cat has died from the decaying nucleus causing the poison canister to release or the cat is alive because the nucleus did not live up to its 50 percent suggestion of decaying—only then can we know the result. Dead or alive. One or the other.

Fishing is like the cat. When we get to the lake or the river, we know that we could catch a lot of fish or not catch a lot of fish. And only when the day is done and we open the box do we know the status of the cat (or catfish). If we never look at the cat, if we never fish the lake or the river, then we have only possibilities, probabilities.

"I bet we would have caught a lot of fish in that lake" or "50-50 we'd have gotten skunked." So with the dead cat in mind, you come to Dale Hollow Lake. Big fish, the top smallmouth bass lake in the world. World records swim in these waters.

Is there a 15-pounder lurking in Dale Hollow waiting for you to catch it? Go ahead. Look in the box.

(Note: If you are a scientist who is an expert in quantum mechanics and I have not explained this theory to your liking, sorry. I'm doing the best I can. Skip the intro and then go fishing at Dale Hollow Lake.)

Potential is a funny thing. What you think something is versus what you think it will become. I think Barren River Lake is going to become a real gem, a top fishing lake. Maybe I'm right, maybe I'm wrong. You never know about these things until after you're right or wrong.

I attended my twenty-year high school reunion seven years ago. Bald and fat, both the guys and gals. Some of the cheerleaders looked more like the offensive linemen they used to cheer for. One beautiful, slender female was getting all the whispery talk but no one was going up to her to talk to her because no one remembered her. I did. I took her out three times but moved on because, vainly, I wanted to date someone more popular. This girl lived in a trailer, was an excellent student, wasn't in any crowd, much less the popular clique (but never seemed to care), and here she was at age thirty-eight looking like twenty-eight, all grown up, ugly duckling into swan, as much

dignity and comfort in her skin as when she was sixteen and told me when I dropped her off for the last time, "You haven't chosen to kiss me good night on any date so far. I think I get the picture." I missed out. I should have kissed her good night.

She became something special. Like Barren River Lake.

Barren River Lake

- **Location:** South central Kentucky
- **What You Fish For:** Hybrid striped bass, catfish, largemouth and small-mouth bass
- **Highlights and Notables:** Fish this gem while it's still becoming a great lake.

Barren Lake is on the list more for what I think it is becoming than for what it is.

What it is: the best hybrid striper bass fishery in the Commonwealth, probably the South. Hybrid bass are a cross between white bass and stripers, strong as bulls, mean as snakes. When hybrids hit shad close to the top, whoa, Nelly. A white bass on steroids. Also popular with Barren anglers: flathead catfish.

What it is becoming: This 10,000-acre lake (that backs up the Barren River) is hardly barren, and is, in fact, one of the more fertile lakes in the South. Besides the hybrids that weigh in excess of 10 pounds, some to 15 and up, the south central Kentucky lake is blessed with tremendous forage, a variety of cover and structure, a variety of lake habitat and features, rich nutrients from rich soil. Add all this up, toss in small-mouth and largemouth bass, and you have the makings of two fisheries that may one day rank with any in the South. (The Coen brothers should make a film here, a *film noir*, this time with a bass fisherman who isn't really there and the fish he catches illusory.)

Anglers already catch largemouth bass that regularly weigh 4 to 5 pounds. The smallmouth are growing in numbers (but are still a fishery in infancy) and are surprisingly fat, some 1 to 4 pounds. Throw in the beautiful scenery and this place is a real winner, lots of potential.

CONTACTS

Kentucky Department of Fish and Wildlife Resources, Southwestern District, 270-746-7127

Jeff Miller, F2K Guide Services, Louisville, 502-494-6706

Cave Run Lake

- **Location:** Eastern Kentucky
- **What You Fish For:** Muskie
- **Highlights and Notables:** Muskie hunters take notice: 44-pounders swim these waters.

Two reasons to enjoy Cave Run Lake. One, this 8,270-acre lake is scenic, set in the Daniel Boone National Forest. Two, if you fish for muskie, this is one of the best muskie lakes in the country.

The current record for muskie is a 44.75-pound giant. There have been other freshwater sharks over 40 pounds. Cave Run Lake has waterwolves in spades, big ones, lots of them over 30 inches long. The lake is known, for good reason, as the Muskie Capital of the South.

Several aspects of the lake make it ideal for the long predators. Cave Run Lake has acres and acres of flooded timber both in thirty feet of water and in shallow water. The lake has lots of arms and bays. The lake has lots of vegetation, including the rapid-growing pesky Eurasian milfoil. Muskies love to hide in and around and under weed cover, in shallow bays and around timber.

Sixty miles to the east of Lexington, an impoundment of the Licking River, Cave Run Lake is a thriving recreational outdoorsy community. Motels, cabins, lodges, campgrounds, marinas, bait and tackle, everything you want or need. There are hiking trails, rock climbing, and lots of other great things for the happy active family.

CONTACTS

Kentucky Department of Natural Resources, 606-784-6872

U.S. Army Corps of Engineers, 606-783-7001 or 606-784-9709

Cedar Creek Lake

- **Location:** East central Kentucky near Stanford and Crab Orchard
- **What You Fish For:** Largemouth bass
- **Highlights and Notables:** A lake drawn up, created, and regulated with the intent to produce a fertile bass lake, and this lake's best days are still to come.

A designer lake. The Kentucky Department of Fish and Wildlife Resources went and created us a designer trophy bass lake. They shut down the water supply, put on their bass-design thinking caps, drew up blueprints, and gave the bucketmouth brigade a trophy bass fishery to be proud of, one that should last for years to come.

Cedar Creek Lake is a relatively new 784-acre impoundment located in the Commonwealth. What did the powers-that-be do to ensure that bass would grow quickly and stay big?

Minimum size limit of 20 inches. No houseboats, jetboats, jetskis, or personal watercraft. No waterskiing. The state stocked the dry lake with more cover than a White House leak and artificially enhanced more structure than Orange County housewives. Rockpiles. Downed timber. Standing timber. Brushpiles. Road-beds, old. Ponds, submerged. Stumps, existing, untouched.

Boating lanes cut for easier navigation. Underwater hump. Underwater reef. Three hundred-foot neutral zone around the lake so that bank fishing doesn't suffer because of private property access or other obstacles. Structure in place close to shoreline. Overall, cover and structure in place strategically, not just willy-nilly like most state-owned operations. Three boat ramps. Marina coming.

I spoke to guide Jim Miller about Cedar Creek Lake and how it's coming along. Miller said "Last fall, biologists thought some anglers would start finding a few bass at the 20-inch mark, and for sure, there will be fish in the lake above 20 inches in 2006. Reports are that fish 12 to 17 inches are very plentiful already, and that come this spring, more fishermen are going to come home very happy campers with tales of boating some exceptional largemouths on this budding big-bass lake."

Miller calls Cedar Creek "an exceptional body of water." And why not? This 800-acre lake has to have some of the best largemouth fishing in the Southeast for quality and quantity of fish and it's still a baby.

"There are numerous fish in the 15- to 19-inch or 3- to 4-pound range. These fish are aggressive and just downright mean," Miller confides. "I have chased largemouth bass all my life and have yet to find any that pull as hard as these fish do for their size. I don't know if it is due to the fact that the lake is new and the fish are not used to being caught or what. We are starting to see more fish in the trophy range this spring." You always love to hear that, right?

Miller finishes by saying "The really cool aspect of this lake is that it offers every type of structure and cover known to man and bass. Grass—you got it, laydowns—plenty, standing timber—abundant, riprap banks—yes sir, road beds—absolutely. Not to mention humps, ditches, creek channels, point, flats, stake beds, etc. . . . ."

Time will tell how good Cedar Creek Lake will be but early reports are mouth-watering. Cedar Creek Lake is located in Lincoln County, between Stanford and Crab Orchard.

CONTACTS
Jeff Miller, F2K Guide Services, Louisville, 502-494-6706

Cumberland River

- **Location:** Southern Kentucky
- **What You Fish For:** Brown and rainbow trout
- **Highlights and Notables:** This trout-y tailwater is on the verge of becoming one of the best trout streams in the country.

If we're not careful, ten years from now we're going to be talking about the Cumberland in the same breath with the greatest of southern tailwaters, the Little Red and the White and the Hiwassee Rivers. The Cumberland is already in league with Clinch, Watauga, South Holston, and Norfork.

Not many anglers around the world know just how good this place is, Kentucky's Cumberland tailwater. The state record brown used to be 18 pounds but a landed 21-pounder busted that record to pieces. There are bigger browns than that in these wide waters.

Fourteen pounds, 6 ounces. State record rainbow trout caught in the Cumberland. Not too shabby, eh? Over 100,000 trout are stocked per year here, and the fertile waters combined with ideal habitat and great forage make this *the* tailwater to watch.

Over fifty miles of quality trout fishing is offered up by the cool tailrace below Wolf Creek Dam. In one section of river, surveys indicate that over 10 percent of all trout caught measure out at 20 inches or longer. And the Cumberland is only getting better. Downstream of Burkesville, the brown trout are huge and the fishing pressure light.

CONTACTS
Gerald McDaniel, 502-473-0080 or 502-895-3182

Dale Hollow Lake

- **Location:** Southern Kentucky and northern Tennessee
- **What You Fish For:** Smallmouth bass
- **Highlights and Notables:** Dale Hollow is arguably the best smallmouth lake in the world.

Dale Hollow Lake is the self-proclaimed *Smallmouth Capital of the World*. And with good reason. Dale Hollow has enough laurels to make that claim stick. The lake holds the world-record smallmouth bass, a tiny little brown bass weighing in at 11 pounds, 15 ounces. Catching 3- to 5-pound bronzebacks is ridiculously common and a 7-pounder only gets a smile.

This highland reservoir in northern Tennessee (but with a tad in southern Kentucky) is picturesque, a bountiful 28,000 acres with a long growing season like Pickwick, both in the southern-most range for smallmouth. The copper predators feed on threadfin and gizzard shad and alewives. The prey up top, the anglers have as many smallmouth catching theories and strategies and lures and techniques and tactics than you can shake a stick at, and if you don't have a strategy, if you just fish willy-nilly, you won't catch fish.

Dale Hollow's water is very clean and very clear and very deep. The fish can see you and you can see them. Will you have a fifty-fish day? Or a fishless day? Catch a mythical 10-pound smallie? Until you either catch a big bass or until the day ends with no fish, you really don't know, do you?

This sixty-one-mile-long lake is full of smallmouth, largemouth, and spotted bass as well as muskie, stripers, walleye, crappie, bluegill, and a few other game fish. I hear the muskie fishing is tremendously underrated.

How to catch Dale Hollow's smallmouth? You hear so much and the guides and locals preach with such conviction that you believe each theory when you hear it. An array of methods. Do this. Do that. Kentucky waters are no good in winter because the big boys move south. That's not true, we that fish the Kentucky side catch plenty of big boys in winter. Fish the Wolf River arm, no wait, fish Ilwill Creek. Dude, hit the Tennessee waters and fish Pulsey Creek, Sulphur Creek, Hendricks Creek. Suspend the XYZ-Lure and retrieve it slowly. Let the ABC-buzzbait drop to the bottom and let it rest. No, find a deep point and blah blah blah. Use this color, use that one.

And then all the advice changes with each season when the smallies start moving around the lake. Dale Hollow Lake has excellent, world-class angling for smallmouth all year long, great in winter, great in spring, great in summer, great in fall. There are so many variables based on structure and season that you really ought to hire a guide for a day to figure out this lake and the smallmouth. And that's half the fun of this lake.

The funny thing is, the various tactics are solid, and they work if you stay consistent within each strategy. Because of the size of the brown bass, the quantity and the challenge involved, the great care given the lake by regulators and anglers, Dale Hollow Lake probably *is* the best smallmouth bass fishery in the United States. (I'd say in the world but ah, there's Canada, you see.)

CONTACTS
Kentucky Department of Fish and Wildlife Resources, 800-858-1549
US Army Corps of Engineers, 931-243-3408
Robert Reagan, guide, 931-864-3699

Kentucky Lake and Barkley Lake

- **Location:** Western Kentucky
- **What You Fish For:** Smallmouth and largemouth bass
- **Highlights and Notables:** Double your pleasure with two top bass lakes

Recovering from drought in the 1980s and grasskill in the late 1990s, the water levels are better and the vegetation is back and growing and so are the bass populations. These twin lakes are connected by a canal and together provide nearly 218,000 acres of prime fishing grounds for smallmouth bass and to a lesser degree, largemouth and crappie.

Kentucky Lake has had the reputation for years as one of the top smallmouth lakes in the country. Rightfully so. Brown bass were plentiful and sizeable. Barkley Lake for years has had the reputation as a producer for both largemouth and crappie. Both had down cycles and now are in up cycles. Fish on.

Kentucky Lake impounds the Tennessee River for nearly 200 miles, resulting in a massive lake, a border lake between Kentucky and Tennessee, with 2,400 shoreline miles, 160,000 acres. Lake Barkley backs up the Cumberland River forming a 134-mile-long lake (another border lake of course) with 1,000 miles of shoreline. With the canal connecting the two huge lakes, together they form one of the top freshwater fishing complexes in the country. If they're not biting on Kentucky, then maybe Barkley—and then there's always the canal.

Barkley is usually off-color, Kentucky Lake clear. Barkley is shallower, heats up more quickly. Barkley is twenty years younger than Kentucky Lake and still has more cover. Kentucky Lake is deeper, plenty of rock and pea gravel, while Barkley has shallow flats, is narrower. Kentucky Lake has the healthier smallmouth population but Barkley is catching up. Smallmouths in the 5- to 7-pound range hold in Kentucky Lake's clear water. Barkley, with its swift currents that make it seem more riverine than lake, is still an excellent limit lake for largemouths.

CONTACTS
Kentucky Lake Online, www.kentuckylake
    .com
Capt. Weber,
    www.captainkirksguideservice.com.
Jeff Miller, F2K Guide Services, Louisville,
    502-494-6706

LOUISIANA

Casting to speckled trout in Calcasieu Lake is almost a rite of passage for Louisianans and for Baja Louisianans (also known as East Texans). I graduated from deep East Texas, from Longview High School, so I understand this weird attraction to all things Cajun. Home cooking in Longview was much more Cajun than Texan or Southern. Mr. Barnette's fish frys were golden things of spicy beauty but always included crawfish and shrimp. Lance Barnette and I and a few of the boys fished Lake Cherokee and a pond here and there (some of them where the owner knew, some of them the owner might not have known) and we used to sneak over the border and run down south a bit to Lake Charles to drink under age and to fish Lake Calcasieu. Being Cajun or even pretending to be Cajun is as much a state of mind as it is where you are at the time. Honestly, we never did much good on Calcasieu. We'd catch trout but the other anglers were catching them up 8 and 9 pounds. I'm positive we saw some that pushed the state record of 12 pounds and some-odd ounces. I know some of the boys in Tyler and in the East Texas Fly fishers have been fly fishing at Calcasieu for years now and do well there.

Calcasieu Lake

- **Location:** Southwest Louisiana on the coast
- **What You Fish For:** Redfish and speckled trout
- **Highlights and Notables:** Amazingly fertile estuary lake loaded with redfish

This estuary is just south of Lake Charles and is known for its large specks. Calcasieu is featureless, pretty only in the way it produces large speckled trout and redfish. Little development. The fishermen generally outnumber the residents who live around the lake. A few coves, some back lakes all grassy and shallow, and some hard shallow flats provide choices if you get tired of fishing the main body that stretches twelve miles long by nine miles wide and averages about six feet in depth. I hear

some bored anglers move into the Calcasieu Ship Channel. Why, I don't know. There's enough fish here for everyone, for all these Texans. What we have here is just a big ol' lake on flat land, made fertile by the swampy fecundity of marshes, the rich mucky stuff of B-movies.

You don't wade on Lake Calcasieu. You fish from boats for trout weighing in the double digits. You watch for tails of feeding reds or specks, you move around, fish the jetties, look for the commotion under diving gulls. Your average speck runs about 3 to 6 pounds but don't be surprised by an 8- or 9-pound trout or even if you break the state record with a trout over 12 pounds. You fish topwater lures and flies whenever you can, because you can. You sleep in a motel near Lake Charles, eat good Cajun food at a local eatery, and you go back home and get out the calendar and figure out when you can go back to Lake Charles and you just go on and on.

CONTACTS
Capt. Mark Huse, Hackberry Charter Service, www.hackberrycharters.com
Capt. Allen Singletary, Reel Men's Sports, 337-497-1029
Big Lake Guide Service, www .biglakeguideservice.com
Calcasieu Charter Service, www .calcasieucharters.com
Louisiana Department of Wildlife and Fisheries, 504-765-2800

For lodging information www .visitlakecharles.org

Chandeleur Islands

- **Location:** East of New Orleans
- **What You Fish For:** Redfish, speckled trout, jacks, and more
- **Highlights and Notables:** The islands were annihilated by Hurricane Katrina but the fishing is still some of the best in the Gulf.

You don't always see clear water in the Gulf of Mexico, especially water that's clear *and* blue-green.

Then came Hurricane Katrina in 2005 that destroyed so much of the islands. After the shock, the concern came the inevitable—how's the fishing?

Early reports are amazing. The fishing is better than ever. Reds tailing in less than a foot of water. The reefs got hit hard but the fish still hang around what's left. Trout, sharks, jacks and Spanish mackerel frequent the waters in as big of numbers as ever. Topwater fishing for specks is still super. The devastation of the islands is still hard to fathom, to process, to wrap your brain around.

CONTACTS
Southern Sports Fishing, Biloxi, MS, 866-763-7335
Southern Belle Fishing Tours, Gulfport, MS, 228-897-1317
Due South Fishing Charter, Biloxi, MS, 228-872-8422
Joka's Wild, Biloxi, MS, 228-769-5000

Venice

- **Location:** Southeastern-most Louisiana
- **What You Fish For:** Redfish, speckled trout and more
- **Highlights and Notables:** You don't visit Venice for the scenery. You go for the gold, a bounty of angling treasure.

Venice, Louisiana, is not your pretty postcard paradise. This coastal town is the southernmost point in Louisiana, the Gateway to the Gulf, an eyesore to be fair what with unsightly oil refineries, gas flares and fishing boats and the dirtiness of it all. Noisy and smelly Venice was hit hard by Hurricane Katrina, the fishery left in doubt as to how and if it would recover, the community ravaged by wind and water.

Hurricane Katrina damaged just about everything in and around Venice including marinas, boats, psyches, and everything else. Rebuilding is in full motion and a lot has been done for the most part. Early reports are that the fishing is back in this estuary and maybe better than before.

This is where the Mississippi spills

Grand Isle
A barrier island two hours south of New Orleans, this is one of the top Cajun sites for tarpon fishing. Used to harbor pirates, now harbors specks, reds, flounder, and of course, the Silver Kings.

its guts. All that the mighty river collects spreads out here at the delta, effluence and silt, canals and ponds, bayous and broken marshes and all. The fertility of the region is mind-boggling, so rich in bounty with its fecund marshes and deep bays. What can you catch? Any fish you can think of: striped and largemouth bass, catfish, crappie, flounder, cobia, king and Spanish mackerel, yellowfin and blackfin tuna, dolphin, wahoo, marlin, shark, and the big three, tarpon, redfish, and speckled trout.

The tarpon fishery should interest the angler the most even though at times, it's hit or miss. Tarpon 100 to 175 pounds own these waters at times but finding the

City Fishing

NEW ORLEANS
Myrtle Grove, Lake Ponchartrain

New Orleans must-dos: Beignets and chicory coffee at Café de Monde. Hurricanes at Pat O'Brien's. Bananas Foster at Brennan's. Oysters Rockefeller at Antoine's. Fish Myrtle Grove.

First time I went there I was eighteen, on a business trip working for my Uncle Stan and I promptly fell under the Big Easy's spell. I was supposed to be coordinating a dinner for clients and I got carried away trying local mixtures and all of a sudden, Uncle Stan and the entourage show up and well, lucky for me we were family. Second time, I was working on a graduate paper about John Kennedy Toole's *A Confederacy of Dunces*. Go Ignatius Reilly! Go Mardi Gras! (I guess I should be writing this entry on a Big Chief tablet if I stayed true to the book.)

Your first instinct should be to wonder what damage Hurricane Katrina did to any fishery in its path, including Myrtle Grove, twenty-five miles south of the city of jazz. Early reports are encouraging. The fishing has been hot and heavy in this labyrinth of marshes and canals on the periphery of the city. What you can catch at Myrtle Grove is as mixed as Louisiana gumbo. Largemouth bass and sizeable redfish are the two staples of this marshy area.

Lake Pontchartrain is a local hotspot for spotted seatrout, trophy sized. Trout 10 to 12 pounds have been caught in this big shallow lake and you can fish for trout and reds wintering in the lake. The north side of the lake is excellent for wade fishing for jacks and bull sharks with its hard flats. Other area fisheries include Biloxi Marsh, Lake Borgne, City Park, and Bayou Segnette. If you fish in the summer, consider yourself a masochist because few places on earth are as hot as this Mardi Gras town.

CONTACTS
Uptown Angler, New Orleans, 504-529-3597, www.uptownangler.com

schools as long as a Cajun party is not always easy what with the way the Mississippi muddies the water from time to time. When you do find them, belt in, harness up and hold on because a 200-pound silver king is a possibility.

The other consistently great fishing is for reds and specks. Silt is a problem so find clarity if you want sea trout and redfish. (Clear water I mean; finding clarity is more a life pursuit.) Spinnerbaits are the lures of choice for the specks and anything tipped with shrimp seems to work for reds. The specks are sizeable with a fair number in the 6- to 8-pound range, a good chance at breaking 10 pounds.

Some like to fish the "lumps" when the water is low or the Mississippi has mud-died the waters. The Midnight Lump is supposed to be a big-time feeding trough for humongous yellowfin tuna, a submerged salt dome. The guides say that if you hit the lumps right, these underwater holding areas between shallow and deep, you can really stick it to big specks. Take I-23 south out of New Orleans and stop before you hit the ocean.

CONTACTS

Venice Marina, www.venicemarina.com (I don't know if they've finished rebuilding just yet but I heard they were working on it and they know more about this area than anybody.)

Nicotri, guide, 504-453-7136

Cypress Cove Marina, 888-534-8777

MARYLAND

I love Baltimore. The city is so cool. I am your typical tourist, enjoying the seaport side of things, the Chesapeake Bay thing, eating crabcakes, chicken boxes and drinking cold beer, trying to capture some of the flavor of this historic city. And the city looks so different than two decades ago when I first visited—so much renovation, for better or worse.

Courtesy note: So I'm on the Savage River and I'm getting ready to fish this one deep green run, under the dogwood, in the shade. I'm tying on a fourteen-inch bead-head below my Patriot (thanks, Mr. Meck) and I'm anticipating several strikes and maybe a couple of wild fish to hand.

Two guys come out of nowhere, all of a sudden, loud, maybe in their early twenties. They never acknowledge me, just fish right through my run, knocking over rocks, putting down all the trout and keep on shuffling their big feet and talking and taunting each other. Guys, if someone has a spot on a river this size, just go around and bump upstream several pools to give breathing room to you both. (By the way, I sat on a rock and waited out the pool and caught two fish, two brookies, both about 10 inches long and quiet as mice.)

Big Gunpowder Falls

- **Location:** Northeastern Maryland
- **What You Fish For:** Wild brown trout
- **Highlights and Notables:** Quality trout river thirty minutes away from Baltimore

Big Gunpowder Falls River is a trout stream thirty-five minutes north from downtown Baltimore (but much closer from the suburbs), right off Highway 83. Big Gunpowder Falls River is a viable real-life trout fishery. Big Gunpowder Falls River is both enchanting and infuriating. Big Gunpowder Falls River is one of the top wild trout streams in the East and what's amazing is that it's this close to civilization.

The river below the dam doesn't seem much like a tailwater since it's rather wild, flowing through a canyon with boulders the size of Boog Powell. There are runs as long as Lenny Moore's scrambling eighty-yard touchdowns. Riffles as numerous as Cal Ripken's games-played streak. Okay, enough Baltimore sports-figure references.

Pools so big that even some of the old Bullets could hit it with a jumper. (Sorry, I couldn't resist.) You notice, while you wait for another canoe to pass, just how pretty this river is, just how green everything is around you and above you.

The trout above and below the dam are all stream-bred fish and not as big as they used to be. The fishing is fun and challenging on the year-round tailwater because the trout are angler-weary and environment-wary. A foot-long fish is a nice prize. Heck, just catching a brace of wild trout is a nice day's angling sometimes on this tantalizing river. Being so close to metro areas means you'll never be on the water alone. Then again, because the trout are wary and selective, fewer folks are on the water than would be if the fishing were easy. Free advice: when the hatches are off or they're not taking your offerings, look for big water and work it with a streamer or something big and subsurface. The seventeen miles from Pretty Boy Dam to Falls Road to York to Bluemont Road are the most popular of the fifty-plus miles of the river.

Big Gunpowder Falls River has commendable hatches, the usual array that an eastern stream enjoys. Hit a hatch correctly and you can tie into browns and maybe some rainbows. Spinfishermen find the river to be hit or miss, but they do have success in the pools and runs. This is a beautiful, fertile river rich with insect hatches, thick with streamside vegetation, full of stream-bred brown, brook trout, and rainbow trout holding in the pocket water, riffles, and runs, behind logjams, in the swirling eddies and in the medium-deep, olive green pools.

CONTACTS

Maryland Department of Natural Resources, Fisheries Service, Annapolis, 410-260-8281

Tochterman's, Baltimore, 888-327-7744

Hudson Trail Outfitters, Towson, 410-583-0494

Great Feathers, Sparks, 410-472-6799

Backwater Angler, Monkton, 410-329-6821

Fisherman's Edge, Catonsville, 410-719-7999

Gunpowder Bed and Breakfast, Monkton, 410-557-7594

Trout and About, Arlington, VA, 703-536-7494

Tollgate Tackle, Bel Air, 410-836-9262

On the Fly, Monkton, 410-329-6821

Wolf's, Ellicott City, 800-378-1152

Wolf's, Baltimore, 410-377-6759

North Branch of the Potomac River

- **Location:** Western Maryland
- **What You Fish For:** Four species of trout: brown, rainbow, and some cutthroat and brook trout
- **Highlights and Notables:** Beautiful, consistent, diverse trout fishery

Hard to believe, sometimes, that this wild a river flows in the Northeast (I call it the Northeast but I grew up thinking of Maryland as a southern state). All these trees. Thick green forests and all this beautiful green clear water. The river itself is notable in that it forms the border between Maryland and West Virginia.

The North Branch used to be great, then was decimated by acid rain from coal mining and various industrial pollution as well as siltation. The river was dammed by Jennings Randolph Lake and like the tainted Uncompahgre River in southern Colorado when Ridgway Reservoir was built, the North Branch became a tailwater and the lake-as-filter effectively screened out the acidity and silt and the river began to return to normalcy. The fishing gets better year after year.

Rainbows and browns are the main quarry but (and this is a cool "but") you can also catch cutthroat and brook trout. I don't know of another river this far east where you can catch cutts. Because North Branch is a tailwater, the cold waters are one of the few eastern streams good all year long, especially in summer. Plenty of access but much of it can only be reached by walking or biking. Adequate hatches but sparse compared to other area rivers. Azaleas, rhododendron, laurel. Fish bigger than you expect. Around the rocks in the stream, you can always find a trout or two.

You can wade (slippery, strong, deep) but the only way to consistently fish North Branch is by floating it. It's not so crazy you can't float it yourself (and many do, in all sorts of floatable craft including pontoons) but above the lake and when there are low flows below, wading is the only method to get around. The river has catch-and-release sections, no-kill sections (but only at certain times of the year), artificials-only, delayed harvest and a slurry of regs and rules. Check up on them before you fish. You can fish above the lake and sometimes not see another angler, but the big-trout water is below the lake. I think you're going to be surprised by how well the North Branch and its trout are doing in recovery.

City Fishing

BALTIMORE
Big Gunpowder Falls River, Chesapeake Bay

You can imagine that with nearly six million folks in the Baltimore metro area, the fishing hotspots nearby would be crowded. Yes and no. Big Gunpowder Falls River is minutes away and while you rarely fish by yourself, the tailwater is not as crowded as you think when you think about a crowded river, say, like Bennett Springs on opening day. (See Big Gunpowder Falls entry for more.) Pretty Boy Reservoir and Loch Raven Reservoir have decent-to-good bass fishing. The Potomac, Susquehanna, and Savage Rivers are an easy drive from Baltimore and somehow they survive the onslaught. Baltimore has so many piscatorial options within two hour's drive, the pressure is steady but dispersed.

One of the best and most interesting is Chesapeake Bay, which fronts over 200 miles of Baltimore County. Most know Chesapeake Bay for its extraordinary striped bass fishery, and with good reason. In spring, the stripers move *en masse* into the flats (and so do fishermen). Catches of 12 to 25 pounds are the norm, 30- and 40-pound stripers not unusual, fifty to one hundred fish in a day a loud but provable boast. Also in the spring, tidal black bass get active and jump on your hook.

Bluefish, channel catfish, largemouth and smallmouth bass, walleye, weakfish (gray trout), croakers, white perch, sea trout are a few of the other game fish in the Bay. Janes Island State Park is a popular access to the bay. Chesapeake Bay is tough to access in many places because of privately-owned waterfront but if you want on the Bay, you can find a way. The Bay is huge, the largest estuary in America and drains an unbelievable number of rivers.

CONTACTS
Janes Island State Park, 26280 Alfred Lawson Drive, Crisfield, MD, 21817, 410-968-1565
Fish Hawk Guide Service, 410-557-8801, fishhwk@aol.com
Capt. Norm Bartlett, 410-679-8790
Maryland Department of Natural Resources, 580 Taylor Avenue, Tawes State Office Building, Annapolis, MD 21401, 1-877-620-8DNR, customerservice@dnr.state.md.us

Savage River

- **Location:** Western Maryland
- **What You Fish For:** Brown, rainbow, and brook trout
- **Highlights and Notables:** Feisty wild fish in a wild racy river

This sassy, scenic river courses through old-growth forests in western Maryland, raging in places, whispering in others, a tale of two rivers. From the headwaters downstream to above the dam, the Savage is a bouncy eastern freestone stream. Below the dam, it's a solid tailwater with deep pools, foamy pocket water, and swift channels. The Savage is an ideal choice when other eastern waters are getting low and warm in the summer wilt. And you gotta love the name.

The Savage River is unusual for a tailwater in that it is on the small side and holds a great population of wild brook trout, wild and colorful and plump. Typical tailwaters don't have big solid boulders like linebackers shrugging off watery blockers, heavy water pooling up around these big rocks, pushing and shoving downstream like two kids fighting. Aptly named, this Savage River, one of the underrated and top trout fisheries in the East. My call and I'll stand behind it—the river is dense with catchable trout, denser than most people know.

Wild brown and brook trout (and rainbows, too, but to a lesser degree) are what you'll find at the end of your hook. The brook trout are nice-sized, bigger than you tend to catch in the East. Ten- to 12-inch brookies are common. Browns are the predominant catch. They aren't monsters (though there are some nice-sized fish) but anecdotally, the catches seem to be getting bigger the last few years. The browns are deep chestnut with golden bellies and brown and red spots while the brook trout are beautiful with scintillating swatches of greens and oranges and reds. Wild trout are just better, aren't they?

Fishermen will find that the river has excellent hatches of caddis, mayfly, and stonefly in its pools, pocket water, and riffles. The Savage is not wide, not slow in very many places but instead rocky and choppy and quick and bouncy and exciting. You have lots of rocks in lower stretches to cast around. There is good access to the six miles of tailwater below the Savage River Reservoir, and the three miles above it.

They'll tell you nymphing is the best method to catch trout on the Savage. Dries don't seem to do as well (they say) but I've had good luck when the Sulphurs, Cahills, drakes, and quills come out to play. Still, nymphing will catch you bigger trout and dries typically catch the smaller trout. Shortlining nymphs through the pocket water or squeezing a dry-dropper rig through the quick pockets are two ways to draw lots of strikes.

If you wade, prepare to dance. Felt-soled waders are good but cleats are better. You'll be doing the twist and the limbo as you try to negotiate the algae-slick rock bottom. Some carry a wading stick but for me that would just be one more thing to hold onto as I tried to right myself after falling face-first.

When low, you still find deep-enough

pools, pocket water, and undercut banks. I like to find the deeper runs and work them—the trout tend to stack up in those runs.

Savage River is not as crowded as many eastern streams and with the trout density and pocket water/pool configuration, you can fish a short stretch for a long time and not feel like you've properly covered it. From Savage Road, anglers have great access to this clean, cold river, six miles of tailwater below the Savage River Reservoir, and the three miles above it. Middle Fork, a super tributary with lots of small- to medium-sized trout, can be accessed from below or go to upper stretches via a hike-in (close to an hour).

Let's review: freestone and tailwater fishery loaded with lovely wild brown and brook trout, some of size, relatively uncrowded, with excellent access, diverse hatches, and did I mention that it flows through wooded and flowered hillsides and even a canyon? What's holding you back? Why are you bothering with other more difficult, less fruitful, less beautiful places? Get off your duff and go fish this spirited stream.

CONTACTS
William Bowen, 703-535-5992
Trout & About, 703-536-0017
Jay Sheppard, 301-725-5559
Whitetail Guide Service, 717-328-9400

MISSISSIPPI

Lake Tom Bailey

- **Location:** East central Mississippi, close to Meridian
- **What You Fish For:** Catfish
- **Highlights and Notables:** Plentiful and huge catfish

I first caught catfish the old-fashioned way, the southern way—I strung a trotline and baited it with goldfish. Papaw always stood over my shoulder, me at eight years old, watching as I struggled to catch the goldfish from the minnow bucket, fumbled trying to hook the goldfish with the big hooks

and then paddled in the small boat across the cove to drop the rock with the end of the line. I knew when I lifted the trotline and felt the wiggle, the weight, that we'd be eating good that night although I was more a flour fan than cornmeal, our family preference for frying catfish.

Catfish. The only reason Tom Bailey is on the list. Located in east central Mississippi, this 234-acre lake is on the small side but makes up for it with big channel catfish. While the lake has produced both a 48-pound and a 51-pound channel cat—both state records at the time—the lake also holds an amazing number of perfect eating-size catfish, those 2- to 6-pound ones.

City Fishing

BILOXI AND GULFPORT

- **Location:** Southern Mississippi
- **What You Fish For:** You name it; if it swims in saltwater, you can catch it here.
- **Highlights and Notables:** One major benefit for anglers has been that you can fish in the day, gamble at the casinos at night.

Hurricane Katrina. The infrastructure will recover long after the fishery for this area took a brutal hit from the powerful hurricane. The fishing is good to great, so say the guides in these early aftermath days.

Offshore, inshore, your options from Biloxi to Gulfport are limitless.

Inshore: Redfish, speckled trout, flounder, permit, yellow tail, black drum, red drum, snapper, snook, bluefish, striped bass, amberjack, and so many more.

Offshore: Blue marlin, white marlin, wahoo, dolphin, sailfish, cobia, king mackerel, grouper, greater amberjack, skipjack tuna, albacore, bluefin tuna, shark (yes, shark).

Need I write more? Okay, how about fishing around barrier islands (Chandeleur, Cat, Horn, Ship Islands), productive if ugly oil rigs, flats, strapping-in deep-sea fishing, stalking the numerous bays and backbays, light-tackle fishing in the surf. There are some other Gulf Coast communities where the diversity for inshore and offshore fishing is as good or even better—not many—but the coolest aspect of fishing from Biloxi-Gulfport, up until the hurricane, was the fun of gambling at Treasure Bay Casino one minute and casting off the bow another minute. Or fishing for reds in Biloxi Back Bay. Or fishing over an oyster reef or sunning on the white sand beaches or eating fresh seafood at a beachfront café. You could roll the dice some more, have a cold beverage, and then hit the Isle of Capri, win some more money, and hop on a charter boat to catch a sailfish or catch cobia at the oil rigs or fish some stumps or grassbeds or even enjoy a couple of hours casting to trout from a pier. Biloxi-Gulfport has it all, had it all, and it will again.

CONTACTS

Ocean Springs Marine Mart, 228-875-0072

The Bait Shop, 228-452-6592

Biloxi Harbor Bait & Fuel Dock, 228-863-1653

David's Fishing Camp, 228-392-1304

Brady's Bait House, 228-864-5338

Lil' Joe's Cedar Lake Fishing Camp, 228-392-0852

NORTH CAROLINA

Things I think of when I think of North Carolina: Luis Rubin; minor league baseball; the Triangle; accents; barbecue; salted ham; the curative heat; that Scottish-style restaurant near Linville where the cute waitress sloshed coffee as she handed it to me and she just about cried but I ate the best roast beef sandwich ever and I have no idea why it was so darned good; Michael Jordan; Coach K; waterfalls; the proverbial mist that covers the ridges in the mornings; insufferable humidity; how cool it was to find so much that was Scottish and so much that was Cherokee since that combination is my heritage.

You won't find a better state in America to visit and to fish. From the mountain trout streams to the rugged smallmouth rivers to the lowland shad rivers to surf fishing to the piers and inlets and sounds and islands, North Carolina is one of the finest fishing destinations in the world. (No, I am not forgetting the largemouth bass, a favorite in the state.) The people are friendly and cultured, down-to-earth sportsmen.

I've had the good fortune to spend a fair amount of time over many years in North Carolina. The state is a land of contrasts and surprises. Just when you're getting used to how modern the state is, how urban and educated, you run into a scene from 1873 rural America or some place as wild as any in the Rocky Mountain West. The gorge on the Nantahala River is one of those places.

When I think of the Chattooga River, I have this marquee in mind, *The Chattooga and the Trout*. Like two characters in a movie. I'm the third character. I have caught a lot of trout over the years but the encounter with this one trout sticks out in my mind. I'll tell you about the trout working backwards.

I held the brown in two hands, one wouldn't do. He went 21, 22 inches easily. Could've gone an inch more, I didn't measure, didn't want to. Probably pushed 4.5 to 5 pounds. He didn't wriggle or fight at this point, either tired or content to have lost this time, knowing I was about to release him back to his watery haunt. If I killed him, he was warrior enough to know he would die with dignity, a noble beast. I release all trout and I'm betting he knew this. Maybe it's corny or maudlin or hyperbolic, this idea of battle, but if you have ever fished in wilderness, where your moves are edgy and aware, primal, instinctive, and then you are the predator in these wilds, then you know exactly what I mean. That's the Chattooga. This brown looked me in the eye as if he had a soul and it scared the hell out of me. I looked around to see if anyone was looking.

It was as if he accepted the Muddler Minnow to finish the game we had started two hours before. From the left bank, I tied on a Muddler Minnow, the light dimming as the heavy woods blocked the sun even though it was only about four or five in the afternoon. He, on the right bank, holding in a tail of a bile green–colored chute-pool, feeding, mouth white. His spots were as dark as charcoal briquets. I estimated 24 inches but they always look bigger in the water or when they get away.

I cast up and across, more in the middle and let it swing in front of him, arcing, and he followed it then stopped right behind it, so I let it drop, picked it up again and he hit it, I could see the take and he dove, the rod bent, and he stayed on the bottom for a bit, I don't know how long, the rod was bent so far, a four-weight, that I actually worried the butt might break (I knew it wouldn't but I still thought it).

Thirty minutes earlier, this brown trout broke me off for the second time. A sowbug that always did well in Arkansas streams. Pocket water around a rock the size of a sumo wrestler took me under the boulder and the tippet broke. I kept thinking that someone was following me, stalking me somewhere out on the trail or in the thick dark woods. I knew nobody was there but I still thought it.

I hadn't caught but one other fish all day, a 10-inch rainbow, stocker and I was surprised he had made it to this stretch. I had spooked a couple of browns under a foot long and hadn't seen much. So I was determined with this fish.

A while before that, the titan had been finning in shallow riffle water, darting every so often to the deeper seam, then returning to the shoal. I had to go carefully back downstream and cross, not an easy or safe crossing, walk back up to get the right angle to present. Dry-dropper, #16 Royal Wulff with a beadhead below. Took the dry

hard and I never had a chance, never expected him to slash at the dry, no hatches anywhere for an hour. It was over before it happened. The Chattooga will do that to you. Spook you.

There is a lot of whitewater and mysterious, deep pools on the Chattooga and of course, lots of wild brown trout, some fairly large. There is also something out there, something primitive and penetrating and unseen and I can't explain it and I know it doesn't exist but that doesn't keep me from thinking it.

So I'm talking to Reese Stecher, owner and guide for Beach Bum Fishing, one of the hardcore-type Outer Banks guides who believes in putting anglers on fish rather than taking them for a boat ride and Reese starts in on this one special client he guided for years on these waters. I don't fall prey easily or often to personal interest stories but this one choked me up a bit. Here's what he told me:

Frank Rogers, an Outer Banks fishing legend passed away on 10/28/04. Frank was known to the small boat captains here on the beach as The All-Star. At 70 years old Frank was still a die-hard fisherman. You could not get The All-Star to cancel a trip regardless of how bad the weather was. He would fish under any conditions. He was the saltiest man that ever stepped foot on my boat. Frank was diagnosed with and had defeated Leukemia dating back to 1989. You would have never known that he had it. Frank treated cancer like he did bad weather. He didn't let it phase him. Frank died of a heart attack, not cancer.

Chad Lilly, one of Frank's many fishing partners, put it best when he said that Frank beat cancer with a baseball bat. I had the pleasure of fishing with Frank most recently during a September southwest gale. Perfect Frank weather. As always, Frank was just happy being on the water. As usual he caught fish. One could only hope to live half the life that Frank did. R.I.P. Frank Rogers.

So sayeth Reese Stecher. A testament to the man, a testament to the Outer Banks.

Chattooga River

- **Location:** Far western North Carolina (and borders up with South Carolina and Georgia)
- **What You Fish For:** Brown trout
- **Highlights and Notables:** One of the wildest rivers in the South, a super brown trout stream

The Chattooga is likely the wildest quality-fishable stream in Appalachia. While a few parts of the Wild and Scenic River are developed, most of it remains wild. Anglers might recognize something about the Chattooga River when they fish in its fast-moving trout waters. It was the setting for the movie *Deliverance* and its beauty and wildness is still evident. Dodge the numerous canoeists, and the primitive Chattooga River will give up rainbows, brooks, and browns. Access is easy to a few parts of the river but other sections are only accessible to backpackers or canoeists. The Chattooga is one of the most remote rivers in the eastern United States and provides the opportunity to land some big browns.

The upper section down to Burrells Ford is the prime water. Below that, the predominant catch is rainbow and that stretch is popular with anglers. Additionally, the water widens and downstream becomes the stuff of dreams for crazy whitewater paddlers. Chattooga begins in North Carolina, picks up streams and steam, then reaches Georgia and South Carolina where it forms their border. It sounds like I am minimizing this fourteen miles of water and I shouldn't because it's easy-access, big enough to handle pressure, and the holdover rainbows are colorful and fat and fun to catch. Don't think that just because you hike into the wilder parts of the Chattooga that you're going to catch a lot of big brown trout. You might, but you might only catch a handful of 10-inch browns or even nothing at all.

The East Fork of the Chattooga and Whetstone Creek are feeder streams to the Chattooga, and both make for interesting fishing destinations. The Walhalla Fish Hatchery is located on the East Fork in South Carolina. East Fork is a solid brown trout fishery that receives fairly heavy fishing pressure. The river is fishable year-round. There is plenty of access to the East Fork throughout its run.

West Fork of the Chattooga River is a large stream, a tributary to the productive Chattooga River, full of wild rainbows and browns, some which reach pretty fair size. It is a Wild and Scenic River. All fishing is catch-and-release with single-hook artificial lures only on delayed-harvest waters through May 15.

Davidson River

- **Location:** Western North Carolina
- **What You Fish For:** Rainbow, brown, and brook trout
- **Highlights and Notables:** Challenging complicated trout river with as much beauty as any southern stream

The Davidson River in western North Carolina's Blue Ridge Mountains has a national reputation as a blue ribbon trout fishery because of beautiful scenery and wild trout, but it's a great place to get fairly skunked, too. The trout are everywhere and chunky and smart. You'll see them and they'll see you and never the twain shall meet. This is not a stream for sissies or beginners.

The Davidson River is easy to find and access (too easy) and is visited by lots of anglers. Too close to cities, too well known now, roads that follow the river and provide too much access, veterans say the Davidson doesn't stack up to the good old days. Old-timers always say that, I know, but in this case, they're probably right. The Davidson is still a heavyweight for eastern streams and so challenging that this difficulty in hooking up with cautious big browns makes the Davidson an ideal stream for experienced longrodders. I think folks underestimate the chubby brook trout you can catch in places—a 13-inch brook trout is a thing of beauty.

I mean c'mon, you've got year-round fishing in a scenic mountain stream loaded with wild brown and rainbow and brook trout (supplemented by stocked browns) and these are some of the prettiest, healthiest, most colorful trout you'll ever see. The river stays shady and cool even in the heat of the North Carolina summers thanks to a canopy of rhododendron and mountain laurel, hardwood, and evergreen forests.

Characterized by deep pools, choppy riffles, and back eddies. Davidson fishes more like a spring creek so get in that frame of mind and you'll have a fighting chance. So here's the checklist: Long thin leaders. Match the hatch. Stalk. Perfect presentation.

There is no stocking from its headwaters thirteen miles down to Avery Creek. This section is tight on regulations: catch-and-release only, artificials only, single barbless hook only. Further downstream, the river is heavily stocked.

I'm a big fan of Avery Creek and Looking Glass Creek, two feeder creeks to the Davidson. The Looking Glass Pool is legendary and picturesque with the water dropping down, down, down into a massive green-clear pool. Photographer's wet dream. All I've ever caught on Looking Glass Creek and its tumbling pocket waters are wild rainbows that are carbon-copies, 11 inches long. Nothing wrong with that, right? (I think I might have caught a brown or two, too, but the rainbows stand out.)

I've been surprised by the nice-sized wild browns I've caught in Avery Creek. They must move up from the main river. Brilliantly colored and the best thing is, I wasn't fighting for my own water with other anglers.

Fontana Lake

- **Location:** Far western North Carolina, Great Smoky Mountains National Park
- **What You Fish For:** Smallmouth bass, rainbow trout, and many other odd species including walleye
- **Highlights and Notables:** Dramatically beautiful home base

I'm going to recommend Fontana Lake not based on the fishing, which is good but not great, but on its location. Treat this 11,000-acre highland lake in the middle of the Smoky Mountains in western North Carolina as an ideal outdoor vacation home base. You and your family can fish the lake, boat the lake, ski the lake. And from the lake, you can sightsee, hike, visit a national park, and enjoy just about any other outdoor endeavor you can imagine.

This is one of the most visually appealing lakes I have ever fished. The dam alone is impressive at some 480 feet, the tallest dam east of the Rockies.

Fontana is a clear, cool lake on the Little Tennessee River and is not especially fertile and doesn't support typical southern game fish. That's not a bad thing either. Fontana has big rocks, steep rocky shorelines, rocky dropoff points, pea gravel, cool water all year long, perfect for smallmouth. In Fontana Lake, smallmouth average 11 to 15 inches but have been caught up to 7 pounds.

This is stunning scenery, mountainous and forested. Development around the lake is limited and Fontana is jammed in between the Great Smoky Mountains

With almost half the Great Smoky Mountains National Park within the borders of Swain County, there are plenty of mountains, wildflowers, trees, and animals to enjoy. Half of Fontana Lake, shown here, is also in Swain County.

National Park and the Nantahala National Forest. Fontana also has rainbow trout, which is good, and also walleye, white bass, muskie, bream and lesser catfish, brown trout and crappie. Some big muskies and walleye have been caught in Fontana.

Busy. Fontana Lake is a busy lake. There are few boat ramps and lots of boaters, everything from jetskis to pontoon boats to house boats to ski boats. Still, the lake is large enough that you don't feel all that crowded. Fontana has many tributaries to explore, lots of deep water, twenty-nine miles long with 240 miles of shoreline. Mid-April into July are the best months to fish here. Warning: the shore drops off in a hurry, not to like ten feet but more like fifty to 100 feet. If you don't camp here or near here, Bryson City is a cool town to make your home base.

CONTACTS

Fontana Village Resort, Fontana Dam,
 704-498-2211
Smoky Mountain Fly Fishing, Cherokee,
 828-497-1555

French Broad River

- **Location:** Northwestern North Carolina
- **What You Fish For:** Smallmouth bass are your main prey.
- **Highlights and Notables:** If you like bronzeback river fishing, you won't find many better than this.

Unremarkable trout stream in its upper reaches, a nationally-prominent smallmouth stream for forty miles of its lowest reaches. Anglers enjoy year-round fishing on the lower French Broad, a large and deep river where thick slabbed smallmouth explode to take topwater lures and flies. These bronzebacks are some of the most wriggly, wiggly, powerful smallies in the country, short, stout, and strong like Basque men.

The smallmouth of French Broad River is best fished by boat (boats of all sorts) but bank fishing is pretty darned good in most places, too. The French Broad smallmouth water begins a bit above Brevard, moves through Asheville and on into Tennessee. Access points, raft and canoe launches, both free and fee, are easy to come by. The river also holds catfish, longnose gar, musky, sauger, and numerous sunfish, but you go to fish the French Broad River for its amazing smallmouth fishery.

Great Smoky Mountains National Park

- **Location:** Western North Carolina, eastern Tennessee
- **What You Fish For:** Wild trout
- **Highlights and Notables:** One of America's treasures, wild and forested with myriad cold clear mountain streams chock-full of trout

You catch so many trout, you never feel rushed, you can sit and take it all in, you remember to breathe. Your closest home bases, if you don't camp, are Bryson City, North Carolina and Gatlinburg, Tennessee. It's just hard to explain how much electricity is generated when a wild trout wriggles in your hand, the colors blurring like a Technicolor movie.

The thrill of catching native trout in a mountain setting with gurgling streams.

The thrill of floating a dry fly, a high-riding Royal Wulff and seeing the blur.

Great Smoky National Park is not just for fly fishers, although its streams are tailor-made for it—ultralight spin gear with light little lures are super, too. Some streams are still closed by the way.

The Great Smoky Mountains National Park is one of the most visited of our national parks. The park has over 500,000 acres that straddle the border between North Carolina and Tennessee. Most of the over 300 streams in the park require a trek to reach, and many of these are lightly fished. The small, swift streams hold wild brook, rainbow, and brown trout, most of them less than a foot long, but in some of the lower, wider, slower reaches of some of these waters, trout grow fairly big, some to 20 inches. In the Great Smoky Mountains National Park, no trout are stocked and only artificial flies and lures are allowed. Rainbow trout are now the predominate coldwater fish in the park's rivers and lakes, with brown trout still expanding their territory.

Because insect populations are not abundant in the park, these trout are not picky. Toss something in and they'll bite it. Still, the fish live in mighty clear water in streams no wider than a salmon fly rod, so they spook easily. A cautious approach is best. Dapping with attractor flies is a good way to enjoy angling on such productive streams.

The Great Smoky Mountains National Park gets heavy usage, including recreational use, but most of it is from campers, backpackers and hikers enjoying the Appalachian Trail. All these park visitors and so few anglers. Camping in the backcountry is free, but to ease overuse on the pristine wilderness, a permit is required to camp away from the crowds. Most of the streams in the park are located in the unspoiled backcountry, some several hours away by hiking. Many of the creeks and rivers in the eastern part of the park are shared by Tennessee and North Carolina.

Throughout the park, only single-hook artificial lures may be used or possessed, and a limit of five trout and minimum size of 7 inches apply. Except in eight designated open brook trout streams (four in each state), all brook trout must be released immediately.

Abrams Creek

One of the Smokies streams that has been written about in glorious terms, Abrams Creek deserves its accolades. Hazel and Abrams Creek are the two poster children of the park. Rainbow trout are the main trout of Abrams although anglers catch browns below the Cades Cove (only rainbows above), a few more browns below the Falls. Most are 6 to 10 inches but occasionally a large pool or deep run or plunge pool will deliver one much bigger. Go in at the Abrams Falls Trailhead and avoid the lower end flotsam and jetsam. Bring felt-soles because Abrams is as slippery as the Roaring Fork in Colorado. If you fish the Horseshoe, it's a full-day affair so be prepared. The water between the Cove and the Falls is the most productive (higher pH, so they say) because of the plethora of insects.

Hazel Creek

The most famous stream of the park. Hazel Creek is an overnighter since by the time you cross Fontana Lake and then hike in, you've used up the better part of the day. That is unless you want to hike in from Clingmans Dome, a long, tiring hike into the really small parts of this stream.

Located in the southeastern section of the park, Hazel Creek is the perfect backcountry overnight fishing trip of the East/Southeast. With isolation, the de facto Smoky Mountain beauty, the variety of water type and large rainbows and browns (brookies in the headwaters), it's a must-fish.

Take the shuttle, hike the trail. Easy enough. It's hard to pass up the Horseshoe, Sugar Fork Creek, Bone Valley Creek (don't pass this up), Walker Creek. You want to fish upstream and keep moving up to see what great pool or bend or plunge pool awaits you but at some point, you've got to settle down and get to the business at hand.

Little River (Little, Middle Prong, West Prong)

Three, three, three mints in one. The Little River, the Middle Prong Little River, and West Prong Little River. Great Smoky Mountain National Park.

Small waters each. Small stream enthusiasts' dream streams.

For the most part, the fish you catch will be on the small to middle size, 6 to 10 inches, wild trout, for the most part, rainbows. The water is skinny, the streams rocky and narrow, typically covered in a canopy where little light breaks through. Like halos on the water, the Little River sometimes lets anglers see the light with catches of large rainbows and browns, up to five pounds.

The Little River system is wonderful, so many pluses. Access by road along the river in the park. The streams have enough deep pools and pocket water that both fly rodders and spinfishermen can enjoy the wilderness, tree-lined and rocky. The Middle Prong is only slightly smaller than the main stem and the fish close in size and allotment. I mention West Prong because if you hike far enough upstream, well, you'll see about it for your own self if you do it. You might not ever leave.

Deep Creek

Famous for its brown trout fishing, Deep Creek is one of the larger streams in Great Smoky Mountains National Park. How large? You will see kids by the dozens tubing down the rough water.

You have trail access along the river so you can cast dries in the pools and pocket water. Expect to catch some nice browns—I've been surprised by some 15-inch browns holding in runs. Indian Creek feeds Deep Creek and it's full of catchable wild rainbows.

Raven Fork

At one time, Raven Fork owned state records for brook and brown trout (North Carolina) and being one of the largest streams in the park, big fish do reside here. Wild brook and rainbow trout. Three-mile hike up Hyatt Ridge to get into the Raven Fork is steep and tough (both ways) so this barrier keeps out all but the determined angler/mountain climber types.

Bunches Creek

Bunches feeds Raven Fork. Decent-sized stream with healthy population of brook trout, and with its slower sections, ought to hold some brook trout over 8 inches, big for the park. No trails reach the creek so you have to fish upstream and hike back downstream.

Cataloochee Creek

More wide open than most other Smokies' streams, Cataloochee flows through the eastern part of the park, a good-sized river. Because it's shallow and wide and fairly large, Cataloochee is ideal for fly fishing. Don't be surprised if you don't pick up a rainbow or brown that snaps your line or comes to hand in the mid-teens. This end of the park is less fished and Cataloochee is remote so you might be thinking this is a good place to hike to and catch larger trout than is normal for the park, and you'd be a very smart person.

Indian Camp Creek

Rugged wild stream off-the-beaten path, betwixt Gatlinburg and Cosby. This is a hiking stream, so load up the fanny pack and get to walking.

Fish Camp Prong

Camp time. Once one of the top brook trout streams in the park because of the occasional big squaretail, Fish Camp (part of the Little River system) will still hold some nice ones because it's just not close to anything. You'll walk upwards of six to seven miles from your starting point to get to the good fishing so you can deduce that you won't have much company. This is too long, IMO, for a day hike so hike in, catch your share of brookies and rainbows, enjoy the isolation, and make camp.

Cosby Creek

A few too many folks on the creek for my taste and a bit too close to stereotypical Cosby (Uncle Jed and Granny would feel right at home in Cosby), the creek is popular because you won't go home skunked. You will catch brook and rainbow trout in typical mountain surroundings.

Ramsey Prong

I've read where some don't think the fishing above the cascades is not all that good. Excellent, my plan is working.

Take the Ramsey Prong Cascades Trail and fish all the way up *but don't fish above the cascades, got it?*

Middle Prong of the Little Pigeon River

The Little River, not to be confused with the Little Pigeon River, flows through the park, and along with its main feeder stream, Middle Prong Little River (Ramsey Cascades Trail), offers trout anglers a chance to catch large rainbows (for the park), the occasional brown, and lots of brookies. Both rivers have some deep pools holding both small wild rainbow trout and some lunker trout. Anglers will often share the rivers with tubers, swimmers, and other fishermen. The Middle Prong is a favorite because it has more open room to cast, and fish hang out all around the big boulders strewn about the river.

Walker Camp Prong / West Prong of the Little Pigeon River

This may be the best all-around stream in the park. Big rocks and fast water mean great pocket water. Pocket water means fun fun fun with dry flies. West Prong is one of eight streams in the park where you can again fish for brook trout.

The creek is chock-full of rainbows and brookies. Plunge pools might hold three or four fish in them if you play it right. In some stretches, you'll catch almost exclusively rainbows, beautifully colored. The deep green pools are playgrounds for feeding trout and it's rare you come up to one of these emerald jewels and not see several fish on the surface or darting around.

Accessibility is great because Highway 441 runs right alongside it more or less, but the creek is always within easy walking distance. If you stay in Gatlinburg, you will see the West Prong of the Little Pigeon River because it runs right through town after it exits the park.

Porters Creek

Small wild rainbow trout, pocket water and drop pools, light fishing pressure, a fine trail and scenic wildflowers. Need I say more?

Noland Creek

Noland doesn't hold trophy trout nor does it have brookies, but the medium-sized creek is productive above the popular lower section. Browns and rainbows in the pockets and pools are chunky and the scenery is pretty darned good and the valley is serene. The biggest brown I've caught in the park was from Noland, a 16-inch beauty on a Patriot dancing through some choppy water.

Forney Creek

Here is a must-do stream in the park. No auto access. You reach Forney by boat (across Fontana Lake, upstream, north side), horseback, or hiking (from Bryson City area). While remote, it does see traffic but it's the adventure, the scenery that makes it worthwhile. Still, many creeks in the park get more pressure (Hazel Creek, for instance) and the fishing is just as good or better and I think the fish are a tad longer. The water is clear green and fishy-looking and between downed trees and big rocks and short pools, you will have a ball fishing here.

Big Creek

Big Creek is a rocky, cascading, mossy, typically beautiful Smoky Mountain trout stream highlighted by black, deep pools, white pocket water, and impressive ruggedness. The fishing is less than stellar, since the creek isn't particularly fertile and the road access is a little too good, but the scenery more than compensates.

CONTACTS
Little River Outfitters, Townsend, TN, 865-448-9459
Smoky Mountain Fly Fishing, Bryson City, 828-488-7665
Great Smoky Mountains National Park, 865-436-1200

List of NC guides: www.ncguide.com/outdoors/fishing.htm

Nantahala River

- **Location:** Western North Carolina, not far from Great Smoky Mountains National Park
- **What You Fish For:** Brown and rainbow trout
- **Highlights and Notables:** The gorge makes it all worthwhile for this trophy trout river.

The state's big-fish trout stream is the Nantahala River, a well known tailwater fishery in the far western part of the state, a river which has on occasion produced trophy trout from its big waters. The river flows slowly past thick bankside vegetation in its upper section where it holds mostly small rainbows, flows into Nantahala Lake, then is diverted by pipeline to a downstream powerhouse where the river is unleashed and where the flows can alternate between moderate levels and powerful, put-in-the-kayak levels. Even when water is being pumped in, anglers can still fish the river and do well. Trout aren't scared of the canoes, anyway—they hold near the shore, in the pools, eddies at the big rocks, and channels.

When you hear guide Mac Brown talk about his waters, he's as passionate as a preacher at a southern revival. The natives called the Nantahala the river of the noonday sun. The canyon walls rise up sheer, to the sky. When the shadows hit, the browns lose some of their wariness. Night fishing is allowed on this river to help stay away from the daytime canoeists and kayakers and rafters, which get thick at times.

The middle section gets little flow, and is reliant on rainfall and feeder streams. This section is heavily stocked and provides pretty good fishing of the put-and-take variety. There is a delayed-harvest section on the lower middle section, and at times, dry fly fishing can be exciting for rainbows, brooks, and browns, with some of the rainbows reaching 16 to 20 inches. Below the powerhouse, wild and stocked rainbow and brown trout grow to braggin' sizes in the fertile waters. Most are rainbows but the big-uns are the browns.

The Nantahala River has excellent hatches of mayfly and caddis, especially on the lower section, often requiring match-the-hatch precision. The lower section has lots of productive water to test, over eight miles flowing through the rugged gorge. Anglers have success fishing the pocket water, back eddies, and side channels.

With lots of pullouts and access points—US 19-74 runs right beside the tailwater—access is as good as it gets. Both fishing pressure and hatches get hot and heavy in summer. Fly fishermen do well but so do spinfishermen who employ rapalas, rooster tails, jigs, and mepps. The river is many things, and for anglers looking for blue ribbon trout water, a river with character where one can hook three species of trout, possibly a trophy trout, then this is the place.

CONTACTS

Mac Brown, McLeod's Highland Flyfishing, Bryson City, 704-488-8975

Hunter Banks Fly Shop, Asheville, www.hunterbanks.com/watauga.html

High Country Angler, Inc., Charlotte, 704-641-6815

North Carolina Wildlife Resources Commission, 919-733-7291

Pisgah and Nantahala National Forests, 828-257-4200

List of NC guides: www.ncguide.com/outdoors/fishing.htm

Watauga River

- **Location:** Western North Carolina, close to Asheville
- **What You Fish For:** Rainbow and brown trout
- **Highlights and Notables:** Tailwater river that is becoming one of the most productive southern streams for large trout

This ain't no small stream. The Watauga is a twenty-two-mile-long Tennessee tailwater with long deep pools and long deep trout. They catch some real whoppers out of the flat, wide, and relatively featureless stretches stocked with browns and rainbows, but it's the browns that grab your attention.

What also ought to grab your attention is that in 2000, a chemical spill occurred in the lower Watauga and killed all the fish. For all intents and purposes, the river was dead. The Watauga is back and getting better every year. Cycles.

If the Watauga is high, you float. If the Watauga is low, you wade. Trees sidle right up to the water and if you're wading they won't bother you. The unremarkable surface (but pretty scenery) gives few clues about where to cast so you've got to fall back on the magazine advice to use the old break-it-down-into-smaller-sections saw or "fish the edges" saw. Watauga does have the deep pools that go into chutes and runs and then back to riffles but there are these wide nothingness sections, too. In the summer, the trout will often hold in the shady pools. Your catch will mostly be stockier rainbows but the growth rate is good and they're bigger than your average planted rainbow. Reports indicate the browns are reproducing in the river. I've seen so many photos the last few years of anglers holding browns 5 to 10 pounds, real titans.

Fish Watauga in conjunction with nearby South Holston River. The Watauga holds up to 5,000 fish per square mile and when the fish are on, twenty-five to fifty fish days are possible. One reason is the delayed harvest program (where anglers can only catch-and-release fish) that takes place March to June, and October through November. The Watauga River is located just an hour north of Asheville, NC. I can't wait to go back. This river could be getting lots of headlines this next decade.

CONTACTS
Hunter Banks Fly Shop, Asheville,
  www.hunterbanks.com/watauga.html

Outer Banks

- **Location:** The waters off the eastern coast of North Carolina
- **What You Fish For:** Too many species to list but tops include false albacore, bluefish, and cobia
- **Highlights and Notables:** Inshore and offshore fishing rank with any American location

The North Carolina coast offers amazing angling opportunities with backdrop scenery that rivals more famous Massachusetts, with its white beaches and lighthouses.

The coast holds so many fabled and popular and worthy destinations—Hatteras, Lookout, Fear, the Point, Ocracoke Island. The best of the best of coastal North Carolina is what is known as the Outer Banks.

The Outer Banks is now synonymous with several seasons, several fish. The false albacore in the fall; bluefish in the fall; striped bass (rockfish) in the winter. All year long, fish move through these intricate waters, the watery playground for dead ships, ghostly captains, sunken treasures. A commonality to angling in the Outer Banks, in North Carolina waters, is fishing to wrecked ships, usually marked by yellow buoys. These wrecks are ideal hiding places for migrating fish, structure deluxe.

Bluefin tuna and marlin are the deep-water treasures found by seagoing anglers (arrgh) nowadays. Yellowfin tuna in November and December provide exciting action and great grilling treats (the Point is a famous hotspot for the yellowfin) and they run about 20 to 40 pounds. Bluefin tuna now show up around Cape Lookout in addition to the Outer Banks and anglers troll for the beefy fish.

Don't miss the Atlantic bonitos that belie their 4-pound average size by fighting like soccer hooligans once hooked. Bluefish are sometimes thought of as a trash fish but they run about 10 to 12 pounds and put up a good enough struggle. Spanish mackerel will surprise you with their aerial acrobatics as they chase baitfish. The striped bass (rockfish) winter along the Outer Banks in voluminous schools, bigger than city blocks. They also swim close to shore, then up the Roanoake River. Fifty or more in a day is not at all unusual.

Albacore, cobia, bull dolphin, and red drum are four more sporting fish that round out the year in the waters off the coast. Albies on light tackle is silly, outrageous fishing, like riding a charging tiger. They rival bonefish for the explosive fury and long athletic powerful runs. The cobia find their way to the Outer Banks and Hatteras in May, naïve fish, hard-fighters when hooked.

Spin casting, bait casting, and fly fishing are viable options for all the Carolina gamefish. Word is—and I need to try this—that tarpon are found in Pamlico Sound in late summer.

CONTACTS
Reese Stecher, Beach Bum Fishing, www .beachbumfishing.com

These Web sites both provide great contact information for bait shops, tackle stores and fishing guides: www.outerbanksfishing.com *and* www.outerbanks.nc.us/tgod/fishing/obfish.htm

South Toe River

- **Location:** Western North Carolina near Burnsville
- **What You Fish For:** Brown, rainbow, and brook trout
- **Highlights and Notables:** A perfect southern middle-sized trout stream

The South Toe River is durable and made by nature for fly fishers. An exemplary medium-sized mountain stream. With its cascading water that drops into pools, then rushes over and around rocks of all shapes and sizes, the pureness of the cold water, you can't help but love it. South Toe holds mostly wild rainbows and browns (brookies in some spots), but the more popular points get some stocked trout.

Mt. Mitchell is the highest peak east of the Rocky Mountains, some 6,680 feet high and the majestic mountain sits high above the river. Avoid the lower river where you find mostly planted trout and too many other anglers. Fish the middle section to try for one of the big trout (artificial flies only, single hook, year-round) then keep hiking into the upper reaches, watching for black bear and fish the feeder creeks (Upper, Lower, Rock Creeks). Go to South Toe for the middle to the upper, camp out or stay in a cabin on the lower river, take a buddy, catch lots of wild trout on dry flies, enjoy the beautiful scenery.

CONTACTS
Appalachian Ranger District, Burnsville, 828-682-6146

SOUTH CAROLINA

Lake Murray

- **Location:** Central South Carolina, just west of Columbia
- **What You Fish For:** Largemouth and striped bass
- **Highlights and Notables:** Big lake, big bass

For a good time, call BR-549-MURRAY. The lake was drawn down in 2003. *Yippee!* The lake was refilled in 2006. *Hooray!*

You know the drill, y'all—you get low water from drought or drawdown and then you fill 'er up. This means nutrients are released, means new submerged shoreline vegetation and brush and those two things mean better and bigger numbers of fish.

Located in central South Carolina, the big lake of nearly 50,000 acres is notorious for largemouth bass, large and angry, bounties of meanness. This Saluda River impoundment has plenty of docks and piers, houses and cabins, islands, 500-plus miles of shoreline, ideal cover for bass and bream and crappie.

But that kind of cover is not for stripers, and that particular lean, mean fighting machine is what is starting to draw anglers to Murray. Murray has become a striper mecca, with shad and blueback herring providing ideal forage for these roaming predators. The water is deep and clear and cool, ideal for striped bass that can reach sizes of 15 to 30 pounds in Murray. They do the usual striper things, early and late they menace shad in the shallows; when it gets hotter, they go offshore and deeper, finding the points and humps. Speaking of humps, I hear that the best baits to catch Loch Murray's resident serpent monster, Messie, are poodles and Chihuahuas. Good luck hunting.

For more information about the lake and guides and stores: www .lakemurraycountry.com

Santee Cooper

- **Location:** Southern South Carolina, southeast of Columbia
- **What You Fish For:** Catfish, crappie
- **Highlights and Notables:** Choices of lakes, choices of fish

Two lakes and a canal. Sounds like a new sitcom on the Outdoor Channel. Playing the lead parts are Lakes Marion and Moultrie and a seven-mile long diversion canal. The writers have segmented the shows into different months: come March and April, they'll show crappie and bream in their spawning beds. Another spring episode has the big stripers whizzing through the diversion canal chasing baitfish in a frenzy of laughter and hijinx complete with diving seagulls (no report if there will be appearances by Gertrude and Heathcliff but there is a rumor that Jonathan Livingston has signed on for one season). By midsummer, largemouth bass are auditioned in the flooded timber and swampy water (the cypress tree props look mighty real). By late summer and through the fall, the real stars of the situation-comedy will make their first appearance: the hilarious behemoth catfish (blue and channel) wearing Ernie Kovacs glue-on moustaches, some weighing in the 70- to 80-pound range (and some having appeared in various London acting companies so I expect some dramatic performances).

Set in scenic eastern South Carolina between Columbia and Charleston, the cast will include raucous scenes in the number of marinas on this complex of three waters that impound both the Santee and Cooper Rivers. Early reports suggest *Two Lakes and a Canal* will be a major hit, destined to be a classic. TV critic Gene Shalit raved about the realistic makeup used for the big cats that easily run about 10 to 20 pounds. I think we all better check this one out. Two thumbs up.

CONTACTS
Harry's Fish Camp, 843-351-4561
Santee-Cooper Country, www
.santeecoopercountry.org

For good information:
southcarolinalakes.net/santee3

TENNESSEE

I first fished the Clinch when I was stupid and young and invincible and didn't believe that the water releases from this dam would rise quickly enough that I couldn't get off the skinny water and the shoal before it got deep. I was wrong. I swam (excitedly, nervously, scared to death) to shore from the shoal and vowed never to be that stupid again. It'd sound like whining except that it was a valuable lesson for fishing in southern tailwaters and I did later catch a 6-pound rainbow, so who's complaining?

The biggest trout I've caught east of the White River, I caught in this year-round southeastern Tennessee tailwater. The Hiwassee doesn't always fish like a tailwater and in fact, may be the best dry fly fishing big river in the South (yeah, yeah, the South Fork of the Holston is a front-runner too, I know).

I caught this big rainbow on the back end of a month-long summer journey to walk Civil War battlefields in the South and East and meet relatives of mine on my mother's family who mostly lived in Tennessee. Gettysburg, Chancellorsville, Chattanooga, Shiloh. McCallums and Hubbells and Spanns. Rainbows and browns. The big bow went somewhere close to seven or seven and a half pounds.

I almost didn't stop to fish the Hiwassee on that trip. This was the third time I'd done the Civil War battlefield tour and like always, I tried to do too many places on one trip. I brought too many books and maps and it was a pain to haul them around. It's hot and humid in the East and South in the early summer and between the heat, and hooking up with friends, and walking the battlefields, and a bout of diarrhea that occurred after some Virginia ham at a lonely diner, and meeting my kinfolk, it wore me out. So I thought about not even fishing on my way back to Texas.

I'm glad I did.

When the fog comes off the Hiwassee like steam rising from the hot coffee you hold in your hands, and the green valley opens up before you and stands green and tall over the river, and the water is clear and cold and a big trout rises in the eddy behind a huge boulder and sips and porpoises back into the water, there's not much better. Try it and see if you don't agree. You can bypass the battlefields and my relatives if you want.

We all have in our mind our favorite celebrities based on looks. A vain and empty pursuit to be sure, but it is what it is. Doc's list includes more blondes than are on my list. He's got Kim Basinger and Pam Anderson and Jessica Simpson on his list. I think they are beautiful women and I'd be tongue-tied if I ever met any of them, but they're not on my list. Blondes typically aren't my thing. I can't explain it. It's not by design. I don't like Brussels sprouts or apricots or calamari or Thousand Island dressing or Roquefort cheese but none of these dislikes is on purpose. In case you're wondering, my list does include Rachel Ward, Bridgette Moynihan, Keira Knightley, Angie Harmon, Paz Vega, and Monica Belluci. I've obviously got too much time on my hands.

I didn't fall in love with the South Fork Holston.

I caught my share of 12- to 15-inch rainbows and one that went 17 inches or so. I caught a brown that was heavy but lost him against some rocks. The morning mist was beautiful and green. And I caught most of my trout on dry flies. So the lowland South Fork did its best to impress me.

It's all good and I can see that but the river didn't grab me, didn't affect me like I had hoped. Heck, I don't know, the South Fork is on someone else's list, not mine. That's all I'm saying. Well, it *is* on my list but only because so many tell me it should be.

Clinch River

- **Location:** Eastern Tennessee
- **What You Fish For:** Brown and rainbow trout
- **Highlights and Notables:** Trophy trout tailwater

The Clinch River below Norris Dam in eastern Tennessee is one big river. Dramatic. The Smoky Mountains at their finest.

Combine the woodsy, mountainous scenery, potential to catch a real whopper, and the likelihood that if you're worth your salt

you can catch upwards of forty or fifty fish on a full day's float, and you have the makings of a real trout destination. The Clinch is a bouillabaisse of trout food, rich in midges and scuds and the southern tailwater specialty, the sowbug. Fish grow quickly and 15 to 16 inches doesn't get any notice round these parts. Spincasters and baitfishermen can have a field day on the Clinch, too.

The Clinch is one hundred yards wide. Fishable all year long. Only twenty miles from Knoxville. Real deep. Real clear. Real slow.

The browns are the drawing card here. Some estimate brown trout that swim in the fourteen miles of trout-water to run over 30 pounds. Five- to 12-pound browns, while not the norm, are not at all unusual. Rainbows are typically smaller but do get up to 8 to 10 pounds. To be fair, most of the trout you're gonna catch, those forty to fifty I mentioned, will be stocked rainbow trout in the 10- to 13-inch range. You catch the large ones, those double-digit boys in the higher-water stages and when hatches are on. River record is also the state record: a 28-pound, 12-ounce brown in 1988.

The flows are gonna drive you crazy. It's tough to figure them out. Spring is typically a solid bet. The flows are more consistent, energy demands are less and not as much water is being released. Additionally, the Sulphur hatch takes place in April and May and if you fly fish, you'll want to taste this sweet treat of a hatch.

The river is an easy float but hire a guide the first go round. You'll see locals in john-boats and canoes but unless you are experienced, learn the river the old-fashioned way. The river moves slowly and you can cover a lot of water in eight hours. Don't be fooled into wading unless there's zero generation. When you do wade, look for shoals that are great trout hangouts. There is good access all along the tailwater's course including several trails. Be really careful when you see the water rise, okay?

Releases: To obtain information on water releases at Norris Dam, call the TVA's recorded message at 1-800-238-2264 or 865-632-2264. Touch-Tone phone is required for this service. The code for the Chia River system is 1. The code for Norris Dam is 17.

CONTACTS

The Creel, Knoxville, www.creelflyfishing .com

Duck River

- **Location:** Central Tennessee
- **What You Fish For:** Smallmouth bass
- **Highlights and Notables:** Laid-back scenic river with bluffs and lots of bronzebacks

At times, with the limestone bluffs overlooking the lazy green river, you'd swear you were on an Arkansas river. What we have with the Duck River is one excellent fishing experience where you enjoy the laid-back float and beautiful scenery as much as you enjoy catching smallmouth bass and eating-size channel catfish galore.

Duck River bends and turns, moving slowly west from Normandy Reservoir to the Tennessee River, over 150 miles of fishable water. You can catch twenty-five smallies in a day without too much exertion. The river is blanketed on either side by thick forests, overhanging trees and vegetation and pastoral farmland throughout its course through middle Tennessee. Yellow bass are one of your other quarries during this long, lazy, meandering, scenic float.

Hiwassee River

- **Location:** Southeastern Tennessee
- **What You Fish For:** Rainbow, brown, and brook trout
- **Highlights and Notables:** Humongous trout and plenty of them. One of the top twenty trout streams in the country.

Check the Hiwassee out. It's the premier southern river after the White. The river flows past green forested hills (brilliant colors of hardwood in the fall) and redbuds, dogwood and mountain laurel and azaleas. The river is close driving distance to Knoxville, Atlanta, and Chattanooga, but it flows through some of the more rugged land, forested and mountainous, in the Southeast. That said, the angler has plenty of access from the road and trails and put-ins along its flow.

The Hiwassee ranks with any stream in the East and with most in the West. The fishery is superb, loaded with healthy energetic trout, rainbow and brown (with a few brookies), some of which grow to prodigious sizes. You have a fighting chance of hooking up with a 20-inch rainbow and if you bring one to bear, you'll see the typical big Hiwassee rainbow trout—small head, broad shoulders, shaped like a football, thick as a smoked turkey. Brown trout are secondary in the scheme of things here but do get big as well. If you land a 5-pound trout, no one on the river will take a second look. If the Hiwassee has a drawback, purists might note, the river relies on heavy stocking to maintain this great fishery.

Rocks in places, wide glides, wide riffles,

nice easy flow. Easy to float—Mackenzie and canoes. Come summer, you'll have to cast between the canoes and rafts and tubes. When it's low, easy to wade. Like a totally different river.

You're going to think this when you first see it: "The Hiwassee is so big, so wide, I don't know where in the world to begin." Agreed. It's big and wide but you just have to find edges, seams, and attack them. Depending on the flow, says one generator, wading is a great way to manage these edges, find the fish. Two generators or more running and you better be in a boat because wading is difficult to impossible. And if you wade, you're going to think "damn, this is cold, much colder than I thought." Agreed. I sometimes wear a lightweight polar fleece even in the summer just to keep the chills off when I wade.

CONTACTS

Adams Fly Tackle, Reliance, 615-338-2162

Outdoor Guides Services, Inc., Kingston, GA, 404-386-0413

Hiwassee Outfitters, Reliance, 800-338-8133

Holston River, South Fork

- **Location:** Northeastern Tennessee
- **What You Fish For:** Rainbow and brown trout
- **Highlights and Notables:** One of the South's top tailwater trout rivers

The river favors other southern tailwaters. The water is not very diverse, not enough riffles or pockets or variance in water type,

---

City Fishing

NASHVILLE
Dale Hollow Lake, Percy Priest Reservoir, Barkley Lake, Kentucky Lake

Dale Hollow Lake is the centerpiece fishery for Tennessee and Nashville folks know it well (see entry for Dale Hollow in Kentucky). But the good fishing doesn't begin and end with Dale Hollow, no matter whether it's the top smallmouth fishery in the world or not (it is).

Percy Priest Lake, Kentucky Lake and Barkley Lake are just three of the quality fishing options if you're passing through the home of country-western music.

Percy Priest Lake is close so you need to consider it first. Located on the eastern edge of Nashville, this is a fine smallmouth fishery in its own right. Not far out west sit Barkley and Kentucky Lakes (see entry for both). They provide some of the best fishing in the South for three species: largemouth and smallmouth bass and crappie.

the river not winding enough, the fluctuations of water level too much up and down, but you can sure see the potential. You can see fish feeding in the long pools, the named pools.

The northeastern Tennessee tailwater is undoubtedly one of the top southern trout rivers producing rainbows that average about 13 inches and many close to 20 inches; and browns that grow to southern tailwater braggin' size due to the fertile waters and incredible insect hatches, the other aquatic food like scuds.

Big heavy rainbows and browns, the aeration weir to oxygenate the water, the insect hatches that rank with any in the South, the bucolic farming landscape, the anecdotes of fifty-fish days, of 10-pound trout, the shoals and big wide pools, the clearness, the sometimes-shallow nature, the eminently floatable wide water.

Nolichucky River

- **Location:** Northeastern Tennessee
- **What You Fish For:** Smallmouth bass
- **Highlights and Notables:** Remote floatable river with a chance at many smallies in a day

Born from mountain streams in northeastern Tennessee and western North Carolina, the Nolichucky River flows strong and long, through a spectacular gorge, plunging and cascading, and the powerful river provides one of the top overnight float trip adventures in the South. The Nolichucky

River is a strong contender to become one of the top smallmouth fisheries in the country. Already, given the pure numbers of smallies you can catch on the Nolichucky, the river is superb.

You probably are not aware that if you floated the Nolichucky, you'd catch twenty or thirty bronzebacks and you'd catch a few that weighed 3 or 4 pounds. You would do all this in splendid isolation, with soaring cliffs and big green pools.

The Nolichucky River also holds largemouth bass, crappie, bluegill, redeye, and catfish, but you need to forget all that and catch the smallies. The consistency along your float and the fury of these copper beasts is something to behold. Underrated aspects of this fishery are the rainbow trout holding in the faster currents, and the bass in the backwaters, the stillwaters, and sometimes right next to the rainbow trout. Fish to the banks, float and marvel, dangle your toes in the water but watch for muskie. They catch them over 20 pounds in the Nolichucky and your toes look like bait.

Reelfoot Lake

- **Location:** Northwestern Tennessee right up against the borders with Kentucky and Missouri
- **What You Fish For:** Crappie, bluegill, largemouth bass
- **Highlights and Notables:** Shallow lake with lots of structure, stupendous crappie fishing

This 15,000-acre woodsy lake located in the most extreme northwest corner of Tennessee is not all that well known outside of the state. But it should be.

Reelfoot is the largest natural lake in Tennessee, a series of hollowed out basins, created by earthquakes 200 years ago. A shallow lake with fertile mucky bottom, stumps and vegetation and cypress trees, Reelfoot has an amazing natural habitat and forage. She also has an amazing legend about how it came to be created—briefly, it involves a Chickasaw Indian chief who had a clubfoot, aka reelfoot, and who was denied the woman of his dreams because of his affliction. So he stole her and the gods shook the earth to punish him and thus the lake was created, burying the chief and his stolen bride and his people. The earthquakes were a part of the New Madrid earthquakes of 1811–1812. Things are still shaking at Reelfoot Lake today.

Twelve miles long but narrow, not big by southern standards, Reelfoot is only twenty feet deep at its deepest. Canals and ditches connect four main bodies of water. Underwater stumps dot the lake bottom like so many monolithic statues. The big tease that draws anglers here is the incredible crappie fishing. Second draw is the bountiful panfishing. I know, it doesn't sound all that fun to travel to northwest Tennessee just to go fishing for bluegill but two things to consider: 1) Reelfoot's bluegills are numerous, feisty, colorful, and great eating; 2) the bluegill population is so good that you can find them served up as vittles in local restaurants by the friendly population. Now that's a southern treat not to

miss. Besides, this scenery of cypress trees solitary and in clutches watch over the lake like ghostly sentinels.

Third on the list of things to do at Reelfoot is to target a fish that ought to be number one on your notepad: angling for largemouth bass. Years ago, one lucky angler caught a 14-pound black bass and the density surveys tell us that the lake is loaded with largemouth. The shallow water, natural hiding places everywhere including lily pads, food sources, year-round growing season—come on, you can see how good this place is, just don't go make a big deal to all your friends about a silly little ol' crappie factory.

Tellico River

- **Location:** Southeastern Tennessee, southwestern North Carolina, near Great Smoky Mountains National Park
- **What You Fish For:** Rainbow and brown trout
- **Highlights and Notables:** Excellent access on this shadowy, diverse, scenic, fun trout river

Eastern Tennessee has some of the best mountain fishing in the eastern United States, the majority of which lie in the Cherokee National Forest (600,000 acres) and Great Smoky Mountains National Park (500,000 acres). Most of these coldwater streams are subject to special regulations, especially those within the Cherokee Wildlife Management Area in the forest.

The Cherokee National Forest is a skinny stretch of rugged mountainous land in the Unaka and Great Smoky mountain ranges, characterized by colorful, dense hardwood forests spiced with thick undergrowth of rhododendrons, rich meadows, and remote wilderness trout streams reachable only by hiking.

When you enter one of the tunnels, those river sections where the Tellico River and its muted green water swirls and pushes through and past and over big gray rocks, rocks with green and rust and orange-colored lichen, where the trees sit on the bank with their limbs drooping over pools and backeddies, where treetops and rogue limbs shoot high into the sky and across the river forming a shadowy hidden fishery, well, when you enter one of these tunnels, you get goosebumps. You know you can fish a tunnel for hours, finding hiding trout in every place that can hold trout.

When you exit one of the tunnels is a shallow flat with a riffle here and a riffle there, with the water too shallow to hold fish, too clear to catch them if it did, the Tellico spread out like taking a deep breath, you see where the now crystal-clear water narrows again and where the two downed trees are and you see fish finning and you get goosebumps. You know you can work this stretch for hours and catch trout.

When you see the random shocks of boulders, the minipools formed by the ring of rocks, the pockets of popping white foam, the dark green pools and the brown bottom in the shallows, the trees leaning forward to watch you cast, the rainbows with more red in their coloration, the browns with more color than browns usually have, the overwhelming options of where to cast your fly to taunt you, well, this is the Tellico and you'll never want to leave.

The Tellico River in North Carolina and Tennessee is one of the best trout streams in the Southeast that few outside of the Southeast know about. Whether you are fishing for wild trout in tributaries like Bald or North Rivers or are casting to holdover browns in Tennessee or angling in the dead of winter wearing but a lightweight sweater, this is the Tellico. The hatches? Nothing to speak of, let's say light, unpredictable.

The river is talked about in three sections: the upper section is the origination of the Tellico, where the brook trout hold; the middle section is where the Bald and North come in, my favorite section; the lower is where you run into Grandpa Jones and his can o' corn, mostly put-and-take but with some wild trout and if you get away from the crowds, some good fishing.

CONTACTS
Green Cove Motel and Trailer Camp, 423-253-2069
Hiwassee Angler in Benton, 423-338-6263
Little River Outfitters in Townsend, 423-448-9459

Lake Calderwood
One of a necklace of impoundments of the Little Tennessee River. Unusually good for trout fishing with its clear water. Narrow, steep, full of plump rainbow trout.

Tennessee Fishing Records

The following list is according to Tennessee Wildlife Resources Agency as of January 26, 2005.

Species	Size	Location	Angler	Date
Bass (black)				
Coosa	1 lb. 14.5 ozs.	Parksville Lake	Harry E. Parker	Aug. 18, 1991
Smallmouth*	11 lbs. 5 ozs.	Dale Hollow Reservoir	D. L. Hayes	July 9, 1955
Largemouth	14 lbs. 8 ozs.	Sugar Creek	Louge Barnett	Oct. 17, 1954
Spotted	5 lbs. 8 ozs.	Center Hill Lake	Gary Martin	Feb. 4, 1989
Bass (true)				
Striper (Rockfish)	63 lbs. 12 ozs.	Bull Run Steam Plant	William L. Marsh, Jr.	Feb. 7, 1998
White	5 lbs. 10 ozs.	Mississippi River	Bill Nelson	Sept. 29, 2003
Cherokee (Hybrid)	23 lbs. 3 ozs.	Stones River	Ray Pelfrey	Apr. 17, 1998
Yellow	2 lbs. 9 ozs.	Duck River (near Waverly)	John T. Chappell	Feb. 27, 1998
Buffalo				
Bigmouth	52 lbs. 7ozs.	Percy Priest Reservoir	Greg Megibben	Apr. 28, 2001
Smallmouth	62 lbs. 7 ozs.	Percy Priest Reservoir	Jerry W. Young	Mar. 9, 1986
Black	55 lbs. 8 ozs.	Cherokee Reservoir	Ed H. McLain	May 3, 1984
Catfish				
Channel	41 lbs.	Fall Creek Falls Lake	Clint Walters, Jr.	July 30, 1982
Flathead	85 lbs. 15 ozs.	Hiwassee River	Larry Kaylor	July 25, 1993
Blue	112 lbs.	Lock C, Cumberland River	Robert E. Lewis	June 7, 1998
Brown Bullhead	2 lbs. 14 ozs.	Chickamauga Reservoir	John Thomas Hammond	June 5, 1980

Species	Size	Location	Angler	Date
Black Bullhead	3 lbs. 5.5 ozs.	Embertons Pond (Cannon County)	Hunter Chance Gaither	Feb. 20, 1997
Yellow Bullhead	4 lbs. 8 ozs.	Chickamauga Reservoir	Jessie R. Johnson	Apr. 21, 1979

Crappie

Species	Size	Location	Angler	Date
Black	4 lbs. 4 ozs.	Brown's Creek Lake	Clyde Freeman	Mar. 23, 1985
White	5 lbs. 1 oz.	Garner Brown's Pond	Clyde Freeman	Apr. 20, 1968

Gar

Species	Size	Location	Angler	Date
Longnose	38 lbs. 3 ozs.	Barkley Reservoir	Matthew A. Norton	Apr. 19, 2002
Shortnose	16 lbs. 6 ozs.	Kentucky Reservoir	Kay Lynn Butterfield	June 15, 2001
Spotted	4 lbs. .5 ozs.	Cross Creeks	Victor Robinson	June 27, 1999

Perch

Species	Size	Location	Angler	Date
Yellow	1 lb. 15 ozs.	Hiwassee River	Jerry Wills	Dec. 6, 1992
Yellow	1 lb. 15 ozs.	Melton Hill	David C. Lyons	Aug. 25, 1996
Sauger	7 lbs. 6 ozs.	Pickwick Tailwaters	Rayford D. Voss	Feb. 19, 1973
Saugeye	10 lbs. 12 ozs.	Melton Hill	Chris Vittetoe	July 18, 1998
Walleye*	25 lbs.	Old Hickory Reservoir	Mabery Harper	Aug. 3, 1960

Pike

Species	Size	Location	Angler	Date
Northern	24 lbs. 7.5 ozs.	South Holston	Frank Childers	Mar. 28, 1995
Muskellunge	42 lbs. 8 ozs.	Norris Reservoir	Kyle F. Edwards	Apr. 27, 1983
Chain Pickerel	7 lbs. 7 ozs.	Kentucky Lake	Burke Williams	Feb. 2, 1991

Sunfish

Species	Size	Location	Angler	Date
Bluegill	3 lbs.	Farm Pond	Brad Pendergrass	Dec. 19, 1987
Bluegill	3 lbs.	Fall Creek Falls Lake	Thelma Grissom	June 27, 1977
Pumpkinseed	5 ozs.	Dogwood Lake	Lynn Middleton	June 14, 1998

Species	Size	Location	Angler	Date
Green	1 lb. 4 ozs.	North Cross Creek	Dwight M. Lehman	June 8, 1991
Longear	12.75 ozs.	Pond, Overton County	Kay Fosberg	May 15, 1985
Redbreast	1 lb. 5 ozs.	Holston River	R. W. Gillespie	June 22, 1974
Redear	3 lbs. 5.5 ozs.	Private Pond	Annelise S. Houston	Sept. 1, 1979
Rock Bass	2 lbs. 8 ozs.	Stones River	Bill Sanford	1958
Warmouth	1 lb. 12 ozs.	Nolichucky River	Frank E. Garrett	May 26, 1984
Round Flier	8 ozs.	Kentucky Reservoir	Craig Ellis	June 8, 2001
Orange Spotted	5 ozs.	Nolichucky River	Donald Daryl Fox	May 30, 1982

Trout

Species	Size	Location	Angler	Date
Brook	3 lbs. 14 ozs.	Hiwassee River	Jerry Wills	Aug. 15, 1973
Brown	28 lbs. 12 ozs.	Clinch River	Greg Ensor	Aug. 30, 1988
Cutthroat	6 ozs.	Obey River, Below Dale Hollow Dam	Philip Neyman	June 1, 1969
Rainbow	16 lbs. .15 ozs.	Ft. Patrick Henry Reservoir	Ronnie Roaland	Sept. 6, 2002
Ohrid	14 lbs. .5 ozs.	Watauga Reservoir	Richard Lynn Carter	Mar. 28, 1986
Lake	20 lbs. .79 ozs.	Watauga Reservoir	Eddie Southerland	Apr. 2, 1994

Other

Species	Size	Location	Angler	Date
Golden Shiner	15 ozs.	Chickamauga Reservoir	Dave Littlejohn	Mar. 26, 1999
Slipjack Herring*	4 lbs.	Watts Bar Reservoir	Chris Vittetoe	Feb. 28, 2004
Common Carp	42 lbs. 8 ozs.	Boone Reservoir	Al Moore	Aug. 12, 1956
Bighead Carp*	73 lbs.	Reelfoot Lake	Michael C. Hicks	May 7, 2003
Israeli Carp	53 lbs.	Marrowbone Lake	John R. Pepper, Jr.	May 21, 1997

Species	Size	Location	Angler	Date
Drum	54 lbs. 8 ozs.	Nick-a-Jack Reservoir	Benny Hull	Apr. 20, 1972
Paddlefish	75 lbs.	Center Hill Reservoir	Shane S. Henery	Apr. 28, 1984
Bowfin	15 lbs. 7 ozs.	Reelfoot Lake	Charles Aaron	June 22, 1983
Redhorse	11 lbs. .01 oz.	Duck River	Cliff Crowell	Apr. 6, 1993
Golden Redhorse	2 lbs. 9 ozs.	Elk River	K. Daniel Boone	Oct. 10, 1998
Stoneroller	9.76 ozs.	Hiwassee River	Roy S. King	May 1, 1983
Goldeye	14 ozs.	Cumberland River	Harold A. Sanders	Apr. 17, 1993
Mooneye	1lb. 4 ozs.	Hiwassee River	Steve D. Moss	May 5, 2005
Northern Carpsucker	1 lb. 9 ozs.	Pickwick Tailwater	Jim Youmans	Feb. 28, 1980
White Amur	70 lbs.	Guntersville Reservoir (Nickajack tailwater)	Chad A. Killian	June 4, 2005

*Represents a World Record.

VIRGINIA

I used to love arguing when I was a kid. I have always loved making lists. I'm a list-maker. I still make lists but I don't argue much anymore. I explore. I debate. I analyze. Okay, sometimes I still argue but at least I try to have facts and logic nowadays.

You can't argue with these two points about Old Dominion: Virginia is for lovers. And Virginia is the best state in the union for smallmouth rivers. Quality. Scenery. No fewer than five rivers could make the claim for best smallmouth river in the state: James, Rappahannock, Shenandoah, New, Roanoke. Virginia is for anglers.

All my fly fishing friends have a problem with my fly box organization. Mac says it looks like a duck, an elk, and a calf stepped on a landmine inside of my fly box. They don't get how I can stick an Elk Hair Caddis into my beadhead nymph fly box, much

less how I didn't take the time to hook it in line with all the Prince Nymphs. I sometimes find a size-6 Stimulator in my San Juan box where no other fly is larger than size 20. Bothers the crap out of my fishing buds. "Willy-nilly," Kenny says. "Chaos," hollers KC-Masterpiece. Doc doesn't say much of anything, choosing instead to roll his eyes and harrumph derisively.

I say to my friends, "Gestalt."

They just don't understand the holistic method to my madness. Not everything is rigid, digital, numeric. I don't like lines and rows, I don't like matched things. I like wrinkled shirts and worn-out shoes and old holey jeans or khakis. I like spontaneity.

Mossy Creek destroys any sense of spontaneity. You better prepare to the nth degree like all my friends, lining up all the size 18 Tricos in rows in the fly box, putting the tippet spool back in the lower right pocket where it belongs, sharpening the hooks. You don't have time on the Mossy to dilly-dally or willy-nilly. Kaos kills. Myopia murders. Before the knee injury (ACL, MCL, meniscus, patella tendon, blown out baby), I could have jumped this brook in a single bound. Or close anyway.

I have this friend who doesn't want to be named because he sucked so badly at this fishery. So I won't name him. One day Doc and I were fishing on the Cimarroncita, a spring-creek–like stretch of the Cimarron River in New Mexico and we started talking about Mossy Creek, in that same way Atlantic salmon fishers talk about how many days they fished without landing a thing.

"I didn't even get a hit the first day," this unnamed friend bragged to me.

"I remember the day on the Rio San Antonio when you didn't catch a thing either," I countered.

"The currents go in a million different directions and I got moss on my fly almost every cast," the unknown angler complained while stripping in a 10-inch brown trout.

"We all said that there wasn't a fish in the San Antone and you left that next day and then Kenny and me each caught browns 'til our arms fell off," I chuckled.

"Mossy's like that. One day I'd swear that there wasn't a trout in the stream. But the next day . . . well . . ." He played a bigger brown, rod bent like an old man.

The next day does sometimes happen on Mossy Creek. It'll inevitably be the day after you got skunked, learned some lessons, ate crow, bowed your head.

"You know you can't wade, right?" The unnamed angler who I was fishing with on Cimarroncita was showing off again, wanting me to feel sorry for his lousy fishing day on Mossy. Shared misery.

"How did you locate your flies, you unnamed fisherman?" I had him and I knew it.

"What do you mean, how did I locate my flies?"

"You have your pretty little boxes, your flies all in a row."

He got it and nodded. Gestalt. Chaos. Sometimes order does not triumph. You can fail on Mossy Creek with a messy fly box just as easily as you can with a tidy fly box. Mossy Creek is mysterious moving in low light, a river no longer clear but shimmering mercury.

I first read about the Rappahannock in my books about the Civil War. The river took on legendary historic stature in my eleven-year-old mind. I imagined that since the river was a defensive line for each army in the War Between the States, that it was wide and deep, Mississippi-like in breadth and strength. So you can imagine when I first saw it, as an eighteen-year-old visiting Civil War landmarks, I was awestruck at the legacy of the river but somewhat bumfuzzled at how this sometimes shallow river was a major barrier between armies.

We all grow up sooner or later. The things we loved so much in childhood somehow fade from our lives as we graduate into real life, get married, have kids. Remember the pleasure of naptime in kindergarten? Remember sharing secrets with your best friend?

Well, most of us have rediscovered the sweet slumber of a nap but now instead of the cot, we fall asleep in the recliner. And what about best friends? We've still got 'em. It's just that now we just call them fishing buddies.

If you've got a fishing buddy, then you know what I mean. The fishing buddy is the guy who shares his sandwich (you forgot yours), tells you what they're biting on (fishing buddies aren't selfish), and doesn't complain (much) about horseflies, mosquitos, and fishing from dusk to dawn.

I have several friends I call fishing buddies but the one who has been to the most rivers and lakes with me, the one who's saved my butt more times than I can count is my brother-in-law, Kenny Medling, who has a head as big as a bison and a brain the size of a brook trout. We know certain things about each other, know what to expect from the other after traveling thousands of miles across the country. We know that one of us has surely tied up some extra size 22 Blue Winged Olive patterns; that we will eat Mexican food at some dive at least once on the trip; and that if one of us falls face-down in the river, no photos, never happened.

I do this thing that really bothers Kenny. He hates this and I don't understand why since he swears he's not superstitious. I will predict how many fish I'm going to catch on the river we're fixing to fish. I might throw him a curve and predict I'll catch the largest fish on the trip or—and he hates this worse of all—I might predict he's going to get skunked.

Kenny didn't go with me to fish the Susquehanna but before I left for my weeks-long fishing trip, I let him know I was gonna tear up the smallies on the famous Virginia river. He started to caution me, realized his error, and shook his head with a knowing smile, hoping I'd have to eat crow. Now that's a true fishing buddy.

I saw smallmouth all over the river but to catch them required hitting their hiding places, edges, fuzzy spots, seams, foamy water, near islands, in the braids, in cover and structure. They want to feel hidden because in places on the river, it's wide and wide-open.

When I go back with Kenny, we'll hire a guide so he can actually catch some fish. Heh heh heh.

James River

- **Location:** Flows across central Virginia and through Richmond on its way to the sea
- **What You Fish For:** Smallmouth and largemouth bass
- **Highlights and Notables:** Long productive bass river, two hundred miles of fertile habitat, one of the best smallmouth rivers in the country

The James River. Fishing and history all in the same pools.

In the evening, the river is dark and mysterious. She is not quiet, lapping and noisily sucking in the night air, flowing through Richmond and moving eastward, draining much of southern Virginia on its course to Chesapeake Bay. Colonial independence and Civil War, two pretty important histories that still run through the James River. Antebellum plantation homes overlooking the banks. The historic village of Jamestown. Top that.

Few rivers in America fish as well as the James for both smallmouth and largemouth bass. The James has incredible structure, cover of all kinds and variety of water. The James River is shallow, great for fly fishing, fishable year-round. Access is more limited than the other four top-notch

Virginia smallmouth rivers but you can find several ramps from which to launch canoes and rafts.

Two hundred miles of smallmouth water chock-full of diverse habitat ranging from old creek channels to downed trees, pier pilings to gravel pits long abandoned. The deep pools can hold an amazing amount of fat, healthy smallies and all will be holding closer to the top than you think. The bigger bronzebacks are tougher to find, hiding smartly under cover.

Below Richmond, the James changes and becomes a different river, a tidal river, much better for catfish (many over 35 pounds), crappie, perch, carp, and recently reintroduced populations of stripers. Put the James on your list.

CONTACTS

Tracy Asbury, Outdoor Adventures, www
   .wvoutdooradventures.com

A good source to locate guides:
www.1fghp.com/va

Mossy Creek

- **Location:** Western Virginia
- **What You Fish For:** Brown and some rainbow trout
- **Highlights and Notables:** You won't find many streams in America that will test your skills and patience more than this spring creek.

Mossy Creek is one of the finest, one of the most famous, one of the most challenging trout streams in America. All this fuss for three miles of a mossy, slow-moving, limestone narrow meandering *Schadenfreude.*

Odds are, you won't do well here. I don't care if you're one helluva fly fisher. Trouble awaits you. Silver Creek East. The Mossy flows near both the Washington National Forest and the Shenandoah National Park. Fishermen will not miss the similarities to central Pennsylvania or Wisconsin or even some English streams, where gentle-flowing flat water moves slowly past grassy pastureland. Not that many years ago, Mossy Creek was a muddy little creek degraded by cattle, pesticides, and other problems, a creek with little or no trout fishing value. One of the more visible trout stream restoration projects, cooperation between landowners, Virginia Game and Inland Fisheries and area trout lovers created (re-created) this green frustrating paradise of a stream.

It's not enough to have a challenging trout stream, even if it's a spring creek. You better have some braggin' size trout to watch refuse your flies. Mossy Creek has just that, wily colorful heavy-bodied browns, some over the magical 20-inch mark, a few up to 5 or 6 pounds. Rainbows and brook trout fill out the fare and they're rarely big enough to raise an eyebrow.

The fish are invisible, the vegetation thick, and the shoreline has tall grasses, jumpy brush that eat your offerings. Casting is nigh on impossible but if you do land a fly where you want, the multiple currents cause drag, keep the trout down. The trout might be under the cutbanks or they might be camouflaged against or under wavy vegetation.

There are almost no trees, just some big bushy things that might one day be trees. You're tired of fishing delicately as if with a scalpel instead of wielding your rod like a sword. So try it. Reach in the big fly box and tie on a streamer and run it past the undercut bank and see what happens. Anglers are restricted to fly fishing tackle and single-hook, artificial lures only. From Harrisonburg, travel south on I-81, then take Route 257 to Bridgewater. Take a left on Route 42, then west on Route 747. Written permission slips are available from the Virginia Department of Game and Inland Fisheries. Send a request, along with a self-addressed, stamped envelope to Fisheries Division, P. O. Box 996, Verona, VA 24482.

CONTACTS
Blue Ridge Angler, 540-574-FISH
Bob Cramer (Orvis-endorsed guide), 540-867-9310

Murray's Fly Shop, 540-984-4212
Mossy Creek Fly Shop, 800-646-2168
Virginia Commission of Game and Inland Fisheries, Richmond, 804-367-1000

Rappahannock River

- **Location:** Northern Virginia
- **What You Fish For:** Hickory shad and smallmouth bass
- **Highlights and Notables:** Historic, productive river close to several major cities, one of the top places anywhere to catch hickory shad on light tackle

The Rappahannock River is a beautiful river, wooded on both sides, running past old growth forests, the clear, clean blue water, gentle to plunging rapids, boulders and dancing riffles, pools and eddies and deep runs, all subject to the whims of the tides. The time to be on the Rapp is in the morning, a fuzzy blue tissue mist rising from the water. The time to be on the Rapp is in the spring, when the hickory shad run, when fishing to these throngs of silver bullets is a rite of passage for anglers in the East. Cool thing is that it's easy to get to from Washington, DC, Baltimore, and Richmond.

Hickory shad. *Alosa mediocris.* The hickory jack. Easy to dismiss. After all, they're just shad, not even the famous American shad of the Delaware or Susquehanna. Ah, but there's the rub about this herring—they are fighters, mercury balls of fury. Silver-colored with green around the head, gray-green on the back, they look like giant minnows. They strike with a force greater than a fish that size should be able to strike, greater than you believe a fish you didn't used to think of as a sporting fish could strike, and they jump as high as trout (they shouldn't jump should they?).

Make the historic town of Fredericksburg your home base. Fredericksburg has become a commuter home for Washington, DC, and it's grown a lot in the last twenty years. The town that has history from colonial to Revolutionary to Civil War times has many good restaurants, lodging that runs the gamut and includes historic inns and bed and breakfasts, historic places everywhere you turn and *way* too many antique stores.

The Rappahannock is wadeable for most of the Piedmont stretch but you'll see some in canoes and kayaks. Since the removal of the Embry Dam, the smallmouth fishing has returned to good form; still, the brown bass fishing doesn't hold up to nearby smallmouth rivers. You come here in the spring for the shad. Starting in March, the spawn, not the one by Todd McFarlane, but where the shad stack up by the hundreds of thousands, peaks in April and continues through May. You want the tide to be moving, you want cloudy conditions or you want morning and you want fish to the middle and to the deeper runs. Anglers go at the pods of shad with both conventional and fly fishing gear.

CONTACTS
Mike Theis, American Fly, 540-439-8281
Jeff Willow, Blue Ridge Kayak Fishing, 410-635-3957
Castaway Company, Culpepper, www.thecastawaycompany.com
Gander Mountain, Fredericksburg, www.gandermountain.com
Ken's Tackle Shop, Fredericksburg, 540-898-1011
Rappahannock Angler, Fredericksburg, www.playva.com

City Fishing

RICHMOND
James River

Richmond is one of the prettier cities of the country. If you can get past the beauty of the homes, the greenness of the surroundings, the growth of the city, then you can get to the James River, the centerpiece fishery of the area (see entry). Additionally, Richmond has several urban lakes that are a cut above the norm for cities—Bryan Park, Byrd Park, Dorey Park Lake. And in James Park, you have amazing in-town river fishing in a beautiful park.

CONTACTS
Richmond Dept. of Parks, Richmond, 804-646-5733
Virginia Beach Parks and Recreation, Virginia Beach, 757-563-1100
Virginia Department of Game and Inland Fisheries, Fredericksburg, 540-899-4169

Shenandoah National Park

- **Location:** Western Virginia
- **What You Fish For:** Trout
- **Highlights and Notables:** Even though the park sees millions of visitors annually, anglers can easily find solitude, a stream to call their own, choosing from the dozens of rivers. Great for dry fly fishing.

This is the forest primeval. The
  murmuring pines and the hemlocks,
Bearded with moss, and in garments
  green, indistinct in the twilight . . .
                            Evangeline,
  HENRY WADSWORTH LONGFELLOW

The typical Shenandoah brook trout isn't much bigger than a Twinkie. Many of the streams are no wider than your fly rod, no deeper than two fingers of tequila. The rhododendron, laurel, and hemlock form a frenzy of tentacles and sinewy arms and cascading green leaves and latticework of colorful flowers all around your tiny stream. Fishing this tangled tunnel is next to impossible. Roll casting is about the only way to present a fly to these tiny trout. To even reach this diminutive brook, you probably have to hike a few miles up and down trails. So this begs the question: Why in the world would you want to fish Shenandoah National Park?

Despite these difficulties, Shenandoah National Park is a must for anglers fishing Virginia's trout streams. Even though the park reportedly has the most traffic of any national park (some ten to twelve million visitors annually), solitary fishing is easy enough with a hike of a mile or two (well, sometimes considerably farther), and a topographic map is needed to reach many of the streams. The park sees lots of campers and hikers, but there are dozens of freestone streams to choose from to seek refuge from the visitors.

All streams in the Shenandoah National Park require anglers to use single-hook artificial lures and flies. Spincasters have success using small spinners, but the majority of fishermen are fly fishers. Flies should be bouncy and visible to both the angler and the small native brook trout found in every stream. The streams rush down steep gradients, rarely slowing down long enough for the small trout to become picky about the next meal. Spring is the best time to be on a SNP stream because the fish are active and the streams are full of water.

By summertime, the streams are desperately low and clear, the trout desperately scared and wary. The fall is the most intense time to be in the park what with the noisiness of the surrounding colors and impending winter and gorge-feeding by the spawning brook trout, but the water is even lower and clearer and you better be able to cast and present in order to catch these sparkling gems.

Go to Shenandoah National Park not for the fishing but to catch the native brook trout in their enclosed primitive environs. These wild trout are explosions of color, a Manet blown to pieces. Go to Shenandoah National Park to teach someone to fish because in the spring, the trout are easy enough that by day's end, the newbie will have caught enough trout to be hooked. Go to Shenandoah National Park to be away from it all, somewhere on a clear gurgling stream going through the motions of fishing, thinking about things. You can go for the hiking, the exercise, the communing with nature thing. Just go.

Some of the top streams to visit include:

North Fork Moorman's ▪ Rapidan River ▪ Rose River ▪ Hawksbill Creek ▪ Staunton River ▪ One Mile Run ▪ Jeremys Run ▪ Madison Run ▪ Robinson River ▪ Conway River ▪ North Fork Thornton ▪ East Branch Naked Creek ▪ Big Run ▪ Hughes River ▪ Piney River ▪ Ivy Creek ▪ Hogcamp Branch ▪ Hannah Run ▪ Paine Run ▪ Meadow Run

The Rapidan River is possibly the best of the park's waters and certainly one of its most scenic. It's an easy hike to the upper Rapidan, and the lower section can be reached by automobile. Special regulations apply to this boulder-strewn stream, but out of the park, there are no restrictions. The Rapidan does see its fair share of mayfly hatches in the spring, but terrestrials work on the pocket water and pools most of the season, especially in late summer. Meadow Run is a pleasant little stream worth hiking the three miles necessary to reach its wild brook trout population. Most all of the streams in Shenandoah National Park hold native populations of brook trout and a few hold wild brown trout.

Whitetop Laurel Creek

- **Location:** Southwestern Virginia
- **What You Fish For:** Brown and rainbow trout
- **Highlights and Notables:** Intimate wild trout stream

Whitetop Laurel Creek is one of the best examples of an Appalachian mountain stream, and it is tucked away remotely in the Thomas Jefferson National Forest. The trout are wild and chunky, colorful and feisty. These wild trout range in size from fit-in-the-palm-of-your-hand to better-hold-it-with-two-hands (6 to 14 inches) with some in the 16- to 20-inch range. I'm always surprised at the heft of the trout I catch here in just inches of water. But Whitetop Laurel isn't small by Appalachian standards; it's one of the bigger ones but by western standards, still on the small side.

This productive stream is fishable all season long, and holds primarily wild trout, rainbows mostly, with some nice, hard-

City Fishing

WASHINGTON, DC
Shenandoah, Potomac, Susquehanna, Rappahannock, upper James River

You'd be surprised just how many good fishing waters are within a two-hour drive from America's capital. Your first choice is the Potomac River, a unique fishery that runs right through town, 358 miles long of which 108 are tidal water, freshwater and tidal waters. Washington, DC is near the fall line of fresh/salt. The Potomac River is now one of the top ten or twenty smallmouth bass rivers in the nation. The bronzebacks thrive in the upper, fresher water, largemouth in the saltier, brackish lower water. Come on now, doesn't fishing with any of our national monuments in the background sound sort of fun?

Because it's only about an hour's drive from the suburbs of Washington, DC, the Shenandoah is Virginia's most popular smallmouth river. It's actually three rivers: the North Fork, the South Fork, and after they join near Front Royal, the main stem. The North Fork is about a third as large as the South Fork. It's a fertile river with abundant aquatic life. Access is limited on the North Fork, which makes it uncrowded.

The Susquehanna is still one of the best smallmouth fisheries in the East especially in the upper reaches. Upper Chesapeake Bay also has excellent bass fishing. Both are short drives away from DC. The Rappahannock is another of the region's top rivers. Head out north, west, or south and you'll run into a trout stream or a smallmouth bass river or a solid lake like Prettyboy or Liberty Reservoir in no time.

CONTACTS
Shenandoah Streamers,
    www.shenandoahstreamers.com
Murray's Fly Shop,
    www.murraysflyshop.com
Page Valley Flyfishing,
    www.pagevalleyflyfishing.com
Shenandoah River Outfitters, www
    .shenandoahriver.com

to-catch browns hiding around the rocks and deep in its pools. Whitetop Laurel is a mountainous freestone stream, running quick down its steep grade. The river has good access but to reach much of the river requires a decent bit of walking. Anglers will find pool after pool and riffle after riffle, connected in places with chutes and glides.

This freestone, tumbling creek has great trout fishing for predominantly rainbow, but also brown and brook trout all year long. The stream is blessed with deep pools, cascading waterfalls and pleasant riffles. It is easy to wade, with plenty of bankside trails that follow the stream. Every new stretch I come to is my new favorite stretch. I especially love the wide flats that move over a million multicolored rocks, where you can discern three trout holding, feeding. Man, that's a rush for a small-stream wild-trout enthusiast.

In between pools, among the rocks littering the river, the riffles and chutes churn white, hiding 10- to 12-inch wild trout. With all the rocks, drop pools, and small targets, short tight casts are required. If it rains, the river easily goes spate and may not clear till the next day.

Whitetop enjoys healthy, if sporadic, mayfly hatches with the Green Drake and Sulfur Dun hatches in early spring being especially notable. If you can match the hatch during the hatches, you can expe-rience a dry-fly braggin' rights day. But in most of the pools and riffles, barring a major hatch, anglers need only present drag-free artificials like a Royal Wulff or an Adams.

Whitetop Laurel has an artificials-only section (three and a half miles) and another special regulations section, so be sure to check regulations before fishing. Even though the road follows much of the river from Damascus to Konnarock, you never even hear the trucks and cars when you're on the river.

Much of the upper river is in virtual wilderness, reachable only by hiking. The Virginia Creeper Trail over a mountain and into Taylor's Valley is a good hike/backpacking trip for wild trout fishing. This upper section of Whitetop Laurel (also known as Little Whitetop Laurel) has plenty of pools, tight cover, and lots of smaller wild trout. From Roanoke, travel west on I-81, south on VA 91 into Damascus. Travel east on US 58.

CONTACTS
Thomas Jefferson National Forest, Roanoke, 703-982-6270
Virginia Creeper Flyshop, Abingdon, 540-628-3826
Virginia Commission of Game and Inland Fisheries, Richmond, 804-367-1000
Virginia Division of Tourism, Richmond, 804-786-4484

West Virginia Top Fishing Hot Spots

Seneca Creek

As remote and pristine as Seneca Creek is, it ought to be a western backcountry stream. This is a hiking, backpacking, camping experience, a wilderness trip. Seneca holds wild trout and is one of the top wild trout streams east of the Mississippi.

The lower end of Seneca, burdened with development, doesn't give you hope for a wild trout stream, but as you hike upstream, you won't be disappointed. You won't likely see any other anglers and if you do, you have many more miles of water to find and call your own. Camp near the stream, eat in the outdoors, fish from dawn to dusk.

Seneca Creek is rich. I've fished there before and did not move more than two

hundred yards all morning, rare for me because I like to hike. Then again, I've hiked for hours, never seeing anyone save a deer, dapping in the quick pools or dropping a dry-dropper through likely pocket water and moving, moving upstream. I've caught brook trout too big to expect to live in this small stream, over a foot long. The rainbows are brightly colored but rarely of any size. The brook trout are the typical most-beautiful-trout-in-the-world-Appalachian-variety of trout. And the falls are spectacular.

I also slipped and banged my knee hard into a rock the size of a record player and bruised it so much, I stayed in one two-hundred-yard stretch most of the morning and caught around fifteen or so wild trout. That's one rich stream.

Cheat River

In east central West Virginia, the Cheat River is a trout fishery virtually unknown outside of the state. What a stream. Wider than some WVA rivers, the Cheat and its Forks provide popular easy-access, put-and-take waters and dozens of miles of remote hike-in water. Formed by the wedding of Shaver's Fork and Dry Fork, the Cheat is big enough to entice whitewater paddlers.

Shaver's Fork is probably the most popular stretch of the Cheat, some twenty-five miles worth, some stretches heavily fished but still productive; the other reaches are off the beaten path, great destinations for day-hiking anglers. The catch-and-release section, some five miles of gloriously blessed water, has amazing hatches.

The Glady Fork of Dry Fork is a popular fly fishing stream, as is the Dry Fork. Laurel Fork, Black Fork, Gandy Creek, and the Blackwater River are regularly stocked and offer alternative fishing in both fastwater and their slower runs and pools. If the main stem is crowded move up the feeder creeks. Most of the streams are no wider than fifty feet, and most have overhanging vegetation keeping the water cool and providing trout hiding places. Spruce Knob Lake is a twenty-three-acre lake that offers year-round fishing for stocked trout, some that are big enough to make the angler next to you come over and ask what you're using (rainbow, golden, brook, brown trout).

South Branch of the Potomac River

The thick forests push the South Branch right on through, squeezing the green waters. Everything about it is green. The main river has trout (average quality but you can catch some whoppers, especially browns) and smallmouth (good to great), largemouth (middling), catfish and carp (excellent). Canoe this river and you'll catch a *lot* of fish. Pretty enough, the river is even prettier in the canyon and where the rock cliffs tower over the green river.

North Branch of the Potomac

For the most part, I haven't run into too many West Virginians who were disrespectful. Most are friendly enough and give directions and make small talk at the diner but I have picked up on a subtle undercurrent of a club mentality, it's ours and

Confluence of Shenadoah and Potomac

you're not in our club. This veiled protectionism isn't enough to keep me away; just an interesting aside.

The North Branch is the de facto border between West Virginia and Maryland. You won't see many more likely-looking trout waters east of the Mississippi. Boulders of all sizes. Clear cold water. Riffles that go on forever. Lazy pools against rock cliffs. Slippery rocks. As a tailwater, North Branch provides year-round quality fishing that seems to only be getting better each year. Another interesting draw to the North Branch: you can catch four species of trout, rainbow and brown and brook and cutthroat.

Elk River

In central West Virginia, there runs a stream that collectively is called Elk River but the river has many forks and many names for these forks even when the fork has joined the main. Whatever. The Elk River is a *tight* stream. *Tight*, as the kids today say when they like something a lot.

A spring-fed limestone stream, the Elk is one of my favorite streams in the East. There are sections where the clear water is about a foot deep and flat, like a shallow glide but bigger, wider than a glide, taking up the entire river for a hundred years, and then the solid foot-high slow water hits a natural weir of rocks and bunches up, not quite riffles, more chunky pocket water, then it spills into fifteen tiny plunge pools. You can pick a trout out of each little pool, move up and catch several in the bunchy pockets, and then work the glide for an hour, at times sightcasting to rising trout, browns and brooks and rainbows, wild and feisty, the brooks native, the rainbows stocked, the browns home-grown from fingerlings. The trout are plump (what my Mamaw called fat kids) but not large, except for the rare one living in one of the deep dark pools on the Elk. Other streams in the Elk River system worth fishing include Laurel Fork, Holly River, and the tailwaters below Sutton Lake.

Cranberry River

Once a great trout stream, the Cranberry has recovered enough to take its place among other eastern back country trout streams again. The deep frothy pools, the isolation and wildness, the amber clear water, the forty-plus miles (including forks) of primitive setting.

The Cranberry nearly died but has recovered from the acid rain problem that laid the trout population almost barren. Some of this back country is as wild as you can find east of the Mississippi except for all the hikers and bikers and recreationalists.

Sixteen miles with no vehicle access. The browns and rainbows are typical catches, 7 to 13 inches, the brookies a little less. The Cranberry is neither big nor small, the insect hatches good not great, the gradient neither fast nor slow, fishable year-round. In the upper reaches, the rhododendron and laurel make for tunnel fishing in the gray light that peeks through. Get your roll casts ready.

On your hike upstream, you'll see others camping, some in tents, others in shelters. The forest is dense, the spruce trees lightly scenting the air, the creek gurgling. A fine day for a hike and some fishing.

Williams River

Great name for a river. Sister river to the Cranberry, a little bigger, not so much year-round, easier to access, more reliant on stocking, mostly rainbows, some browns, hatchery size except for holdovers. The Middle Fork is the wildest branch, surrounded by forest, not close to roads like the main stem. In parts, the Middle Fork jumps and dances over rocks, pools up into big basins; other times it slides gently over smooth chunks of rock.

New River

- **Location:** Flows through West Virginia, Virginia, and North Carolina
- **What You Fish For:** Smallmouth bass
- **Highlights and Notables:** Largely unknown, this smokin' hot river is one of the top smallmouth streams anywhere, a real trophy bass treat.

Before you step into the boat to float the New River, prepare yourself. This is no ordinary smallmouth river. New River ranks with the other Virginia smallmouth bass rivers, with John Day, with Devils River.

The Three H's of my New River visit:

Hook in my hand (thank goodness I was barbless)

Hot, smokin' hot (I wished for a breeze but none came)

Headshakin' brown bass (angry bronzebacks)

I didn't catch many under 2 pounds and many went at least 4 pounds and all were difficult to catch, harder to land. They were fat, blown up like balloons, at the least measured a foot-and-a-half long. The scenery on the world's second oldest river is stupendous, wide and deep, exhilarating with its rugged rock faces, heavily wooded mountains, fantastic habitat like ledges and pools, deep runs (oh, these are sweet looking), pockets, drop pools, and riffles.

Catamarans and rafts work especially well on the New.

Only one other river on the continent flows northerly, the Shenandoah. The New River above Claytor Lake is considered the upper river; below it, naturally, the lower river. They'll tell you the lower has bigger smallies but it seemed pretty even to me. Lower is lovelier. In summer, the recreational boaters come out in droves but they don't seem to bother the fishing especially since the smallies fish best early and late. The New has other state records, a walleye at 15 pounds and a muskie at 45 pounds. Whatever. Fish for these angry fat smallmouths.

The Virginia state record bronze weighed over 8 pounds and came out of the New River. At this one ledge drop pocket water pool configuration, there lay one bigger, big enough that he wasn't scared of me, the raft or anything else. He was bigger than any 8 pounds. He ignored every offering even when I bumped him with a marabou muddler. He gave me one of those go-to-hell looks and slowly swam away. I'm telling you straight up, prepare yourself for the New.

Midwest

ARKANSAS

One of my favorite things to do is to take kids fishing. It's a tradition on both sides of my family. Let's go fishing with Uncle Mark. Dry Run Creek is the most special place I've ever seen to take children fishing.

I have this one nephew, Bryan. He belongs to Dave and Debbie. Dave's my wife's big brother and a frequent fishing buddy. Bryan is a unique kid. Smart as a whip but ornery as a ferret in a burlap sack. When he was four, he got the beginning fly fishing lesson we give all the kids: short fly rod with a worm tied onto short tippet fishing Soldier Creek, a step-across stream in southern Colorado loaded with tiny brook trout. Dave told Bryan to stay out of the water, walk along the bank and dap the worm in the river. Bryan waited until his father turned his head and jumped in the stream. That's Bryan.

Let's pick up nine years later. It's time to teach him to wade (carefully) and fish upstream (he's a decent fly fisher at this point). I give him and his cousin Chase the lesson and arm them with danger warnings and avuncular threats. *Do not, under any circumstances, get close to any water that goes over your knees. And Bryan, be careful with your new Sage rod and reel that cost your father so much moolah.*

This stream we're fixing to fish is small to medium but it has some deep pools and lots of fallen timber and beaver ponds. A fifty-two-year-old man had drowned a couple of weeks before on a similarly-sized

stream on the other side of the pass when he got caught up under a huge brush pile. This stream had plenty of those.

My plan was to keep the boys close but with enough room so I could watch both of them while also letting them get the sense they were fishing on their own. Chase caught a nice one and I was taking his picture when Chase went quiet and cocked his ear. Softly, we hear "Help, help."

I ran around a stand of alders and across the stream, at the absolute widest, deepest part of the entire stream, I saw the tip of a rod and a little white hand holding it up. Bryan's head slipped out of the water to call for help again and as he did, I threw the camera down (hey, it's a thousand-dollar camera and the boy still was able to lift out of the water), dived into the cold pool and grabbed hold of Bryan's shoulder. He was caught on a debris pile and couldn't shake loose. He was taking in a lot of water. His big eyes, his thrashing, his unflinching grip on the new Sage rod and reel—priceless. I should say priceless because we retrieved the cold, shaking, lucky young man. He told us, between deep breaths, that he slipped crossing the pool ("I know, I know") and got caught up in the current. He's been a careful wader ever since. Dry Run Creek is for kids, and you don't even have to be a careful wader.

There's something about comfortable things. I have these shoes I like to wear. Amy hates them. They are old slippers, moccasin-style suede-outs that slide on and off easily. They're not pretty. In fact, they're as beat up as the holy jeans (she'd say holey) I try to wear all the time. Sometimes, familiarity/comfort/safety is as important to an experience as is newness/discovery/excitement. There's something comfortable about fishing in Arkansas. It's an easy state to get around in and the rivers aren't menacingly powerful.

(I've got on my raggedy moccasins right now as I'm typing, by the way.)

I'm a skeptic. I am particularly a skeptic about brash claims. This detergent works better than this one. Rub this paste on your scalp and it grows hair in days (my mother actually bought me some of this and no, I did not try it). We had this guy at college who talked all the time about how he could have walked on to the team, NCAA Division One. I was skeptical the first time I fished Ouachita.

You may have had a different version of the same guy at your high school or college, bragging about invisible, unproveable exploits. My version was built like an extra from *Revenge of the Nerds III.* Skinny legs, floppy socks, chestless, large nose, peach fuzz on his face. I challenged him to a little game of one-on-one, me being a halfway decent hoopster—I was quick (then), could dribble and play defense (Lance says I fouled more than Chris Dudley but if you don't know who Chris Dudley was, you obviously never watched the "greatest" free throw shooter of all time).

Nerd kicked my ass. He dribbled between his legs and around mine. He pulled up and hit jump shots from anywhere in the half-court. He hit runners and banked fallaways. His hands were quick as flitting hummingbirds. He hadn't told me he could play defense and he blocked several of my shots. Guy had serious game. The floppy socks should have given it away—Nerd was Pete Maravich reincarnate.

Nerd lived up to the hype.

Regarding braggarts and look-at-me types, I like to call B.S. and most of the time I'm right. Every blue moon, you run into someone who can talk the talk and walk the walk. Lake Ouachita holds its own, exceeds it even. Ouachita is floppy socks and all.

Buffalo River

- **Location:** Northwestern Arkansas
- **What You Fish For:** Smallmouth bass
- **Highlights and Notables:** One of the favorite canoe trips in America because of the combination of beautiful mountain scenery and hot smallmouth fishing

I don't think there is a prettier river to float and fish east of the Rockies. The Buffalo National River has choppy, fast, clear oxygenated water, gravel bottom, and all kinds of rocks strewn about like a giant's marbles. This makes ideal habitat for smallmouth bass. The Buffalo's cool, clean waters also provide good living for channel catfish, green and longear sunfish, largemouth, and

spotted bass (as well as Ozark bass, rock bass, suckers, and gar, just in case you're wondering). It's weird how clear this water is when you look at it one way but how it turns so milky green when you look at it another way.

The smallmouth are in all the right places and there are great numbers of them but they don't grow as big as those in Crooked Creek. Buffalo will entice you with its natural beauty, its limestone bluffs that reach into the blue sky, its green looming mountains and dramatic canyons. Long gravel bars with gray-brown driftwood gnarled into anthropomorphic creatures sitting like sentinels. Elephant Head Bluff, Grayface Bluff. Aesthetics. One hundred fifty miles of a national treasure. No dams, no obstructions for any of its 132 miles of

national river designation. Float past caves. No development. You'll catch twenty smallies a day. Isn't that enough for you?

The Buffalo River is one of two Arkansas rivers designated an Ozark Zone Blue Ribbon Smallmouth Stream. Located in the northwest corner of the state, this designated National River is one of the wildest rivers not in the West, one of the most remote rivers in the South. The daily limit on smallmouth bass is two and each must be at least 14 inches long to creel. If you go, don't even think of not floating this gem.

CONTACTS
Terry Cook, Harrison Convention
    and Visitors Bureau, www
    .HarrisonArkansas.org

Crooked Creek

- **Location:** North central Arkansas
- **What You Fish For:** Smallmouth bass
- **Highlights and Notables:** A top bronzeback river

The reason they call it Crooked Creek is legit. This creek has more twists and turns than *Desperate Housewives*. Crooked Creek moves through north central Arkansas under a canopy of hardwood trees, past rolling hills, under rugged bluffs, through fertile pastures, and flows right through populated areas until it empties into the White River.

Let's be honest. Crooked Creek is not as good as it once was, back when it was mentioned as one of the top five smallmouth rivers in the country. Count on your hand and you can find things gone wrong: commercial interests that degrade the quality of the fishery, angling pressure increasing, recreational usage increasing, and creeping population. That leaves one finger up. That finger still has fast rocky riffles and runs and chutes that dump into deep pools that hold big, fat bronzebacks. That finger means you can see an amazing assortment of wildlife at any point along the cool spring-fed river, from kingfishers and osprey to beaver and deer.

Your finger points to smallmouth bass from a tree-lined river, bass that average 1 to 2 pounds, fat on crayfish and hellgrammites. Not as common as the old days, you can still catch obese brown bass from 2 to 5 pounds with the occasional 6-pound

smallie. Crooked Creek still holds lots of fish per mile, has a great catch rate per hour, and the fish population is strong and healthy.

Crooked Creek also holds other species including channel catfish and several varieties of sunfish. The clear creek is one of Arkansas's two Ozark Blue Ribbon Smallmouth Streams (the other is the Buffalo River). With its multitude of ideal smallmouth habitat and its long growing season and its abundance of forage food all combined with its incredible scenery, Crooked Creek is still one of the top river destinations in the country.

CONTACTS
Duane Hada, www.duanehada.com/
Crooked Creek Canoe Service, 870-449-6203
Dillard's Ozark Outfitters, www.dillards-outfitters.com
Roundhouse Shoals Fishing Services, www.roundhouseshoals.com

Dry Run Creek

- **Location:** North central Arkansas
- **What You Fish For:** Enormous trout
- **Highlights and Notables:** A unique fishery, a stream with huge trout, plenty of them and only kids under 16 can fish it

Kids. If you have children who fish and have a desire to catch a trophy-sized trout, there is probably no better place in the entire world than Dry Run Creek. If you want

a safe place where you can take your Bryan fishing, this is the place.

After thirty years of closure, Dry Run Creek was opened again in 1988 and the river was made into a catch-and-release, single-hook, artificial-lure stream ONLY FOR KIDS UNDER 16. That makes it unique, and the amazingly large trout make it special.

This rocky short stretch of only one half mile flows into the North Fork River. The Norfork National Trout Hatchery is adjacent to the river. The river is fertile with lots of trout holding places and when you add trout and lots of them, add the regulations, add in the Ozark beauty, you have the making of a high-quality fishery worth a trip with the kids. Browns and rainbows are the predominant catch but the river also holds brook and cutthroat trout. You hear of kids all the time getting a Grand Slam.

You won't believe how many large trout are in this short section. I mean really really big trout. Kids will hardly catch any under 15 inches and they stand a better than good chance at a titanic trout. With only a modicum of skill, young anglers will catch a lot of trout. I'm telling you, this place is just loaded with trout, 10-pound trout will be feeding just feet from your waders. Electroshocking surveys show that this short stream holds unbelievable totals of fish per mile, from 8,000 to 11,000 fish per mile *and up*. In a creek no more than twenty feet wide.

Don't fish yourself. You can teach, model, but the child needs to be there and you don't need to overdo it. It's tempting, but don't. Dry Run Creek is for those 16 years of age and younger and for those whose mobility is impaired. Several wheelchair ramps are in place and everything is user-friendly at this unusual stream.

To reach Dry Run Creek, take Arkansas Highway 5 to Salesville (Baxter County), then follow Arkansas Highway 177 almost two miles east out of Salesville toward Norfork Dam. The hatchery parking lot is on the north side of the road.

Greers Ferry Lake

- **Location:** North central Arkansas
- **What You Fish For:** Hybrid striped bass, walleyes
- **Highlights and Notables:** Touted as the best lake in the country for hybrid stripers, the walleye fishing is as good as it gets in the South

Greers Ferry is a comfortable place. The lake fits just right. Even though the walleye fishery is legendary, setting records, tributaries giving up 20-pound walleyes, even though Greers Ferry is probably still the top lake in America for hybrid striped bass, even though anglers have found out that the smallmouth population is loaded with chunky brown bass, even though Greers Ferry may wear the crown as best hybrid lake in the nation—there is something laid back and easy-going about this impoundment of the Little Red River.

Forty thousand acres of crappie, bream, largemouth and white bass, rainbow and brown trout, and catfish to go with the hybrids, walleyes, and smallies. Some say that Greers Ferry and its clear waters have the top crappie fishery anywhere. With 300 miles of shoreline drama, Greers Ferry ranks with most any lake for scenery with its bluffs and woods. The people of Heber Springs, Greers Ferry, and the other surrounding villages are connective tissue to the lake and its tailrace, the Little Red, proverbial hearts of gold, sweet sincere folks.

Seems like Greers Ferry fishes well all year long. When the creeks are full of moving walleye, big ones, ones that could be the next world record (25 pounds, baby), there's a palpable tension on the lake. Hooking into an 8-pound hybrid is akin to trying to land two 10-pound brown trout on the same rod. When one species is dropping in catch rates, another is on the rise. Greers Ferry is awfully comfortable year-round and if you fish it, you're not gonna want to leave.

CONTACTS

Greers Ferry Lake, Heber Springs, 501-362-9067, www.swl.usace.army.mil/parks/greersferry

Ozark Angler, Heber Springs, 501-362-3597

Charley's Bait and Sports, Heber Springs, 501-362-5413

Little Red Fly Shop, Heber Springs, 501-887-9988

Little Red River

- **Location:** North central Arkansas
- **What You Fish For:** Brown and rainbow trout and some cutthroats
- **Highlights and Notables:** Despite the fact the world-record brown trout was caught here, many anglers wrongfully overlook this fertile fishery in favor of the White River.

Tom Hawthorne guides on the Little Red. Tom owns The Ozark Angler Fly Shop. Tom is tall. He used to enjoy cigars and single-malt Scotch and could talk about any subject, especially the river he loves so much.

I haven't seen Tom in a few years so I don't know if he still partakes of cigars or Scotch, but I'll bet he's still espousing ways to make this great tailwater even better because as good as it is, Tom and others know it could even be better.

The White River isn't the only fishery capable of coughing up huge trout. A decade ago, the Little Red River relinquished a 40-pound, 4-ounce brown trout to a spin fisherman, setting a new world record.

For years this was one of the best-kept trout fishing secrets in the South. No longer. The Little Red, which flows from Greers Ferry Dam near Heber Springs, offers thirty miles of trout water from the dam. Anglers can fish for big rainbows pushing 15 pounds, and colorful browns of titanic proportions. The big brown trout is the golden calf of the Little Red, creating hordes of swarming pagans searching for another shining idol. They are Don Quixote. The smart ones, the Sancho Panzas, they know better. They know you go out, you catch a lot of 2- to 6-pound trout and you go home and smile about what a great day you just had and know that tomorrow, without fanfare, without posturing, without fighting windmills, you just might catch the big one. Just don't make it the end-all because the Little Red has far too much to offer.

There are all kinds of holding water along the Little Red, and the best way to try them all is to float this clear, blue-ribbon fishery from a boat, usually a johnboat—a long, narrow, shallow fiberglass or aluminum boat, the traditional craft on these waters.

Hatchery cutthroat were introduced in the early 1990s, and preliminary results show that these planted trout are thriving. Brook trout are now part of the regular catch, too. The river has islands, swift shoals, and big boulders, making for a variety of trout habitats. For your first time, I strongly recommend hiring a guide to learn the river and techniques.

Fish above the moss beds, under overhanging limbs, by submerged timber, to drop-offs, to the banks, to logjams, and to the heads and tails of pools, in deep slack water, off of shoals. The Little Red is crazy-in-love with holding water.

You'll probably hear that the Little Red has little or no dry-fly fishing, but don't believe it. Caddis flies hatch most of the warm months, stones come off in spring, and attractor patterns seem to work most of the summer.

The Little Red does have big brown trout 20 pounds and up. Maybe the river holds another world record. But look past that and enjoy the Ozark scenery, the twenty to forty trout you're going to catch that day and the character of a special fishery. Maybe you'll land a trophy and maybe not. Just fish, baby.

To reach the river, take US 67 North toward Memphis. Stay on US 67 to Heber Springs turnoff near Cabot. Travel north on Highway 5 heading north for nearly forty miles until you curve right on Highway 16/25 and cruise right into Heber Springs.

CONTACTS
Ozark Angler, Heber Springs, 501-362-3597
Charley's Bait and Sports, Heber Springs, 501-362-5413
Little Red Fly Shop, Heber Springs, 501-887-9988
Red River Trout Dock, Heber Springs, 501-362-2197

Duane Hada, Fort Smith, 501-452-3559

Lindsey's Rainbow Resort, Heber Springs, 501-362-3139

Lobo Landing, Heber Springs, 501-362-5802

Norfork River

- **Location:** North central Arkansas, feeds the White River
- **What You Fish For:** Rainbow, brook, and brown trout
- **Highlights and Notables:** Not many rivers have as many catchable trout nor offer a chance at a trophy trout.

There's no way you're going to plan a trip to the Norfork River without also fishing the White River. Not gonna happen. But if you make the trip all the way to the White River and don't take time to fish the Norfork, well pardner, you've missed out in a big way. The North Fork River (usually called the Norfork River) below Norfork Dam once held the world's brown trout record of nearly 39 pounds. In 1988, a pair of 38-pound browns were caught. Them's big fish, boys and girls. This is one of the world's top locations to have a chance to catch a world-record trout.

The Norfork is a nutrient-rich tailwater, ideal for wade-fishing and stalking trout. A bit less than five miles long, the Norfork is amazingly rich with rainbow trout to 15 pounds and brown trout on par with the giants in the White River. In many ways, I like the Norfork River better than the White River. More intimate (when the water is low or lower). Easier to work just one concentrated area. Consistent. More pocket water. Easier to wade (except when during big generation). The dam area is fun to work when it's not too crowded.

The trout are everywhere. Norfork has to have one of the highest densities of trout per mile in nation. I've had them feeding on creepy crawlies stuck to my neoprene waders before. The river is a curious mix of anglers: spinfishermen abound in Arkansas, so they're there in camouflage caps, contrasted by those longrodders in thousands of dollars of waders and boots and vests and polarized glasses.

The fishing is so darned consistent and consistent for trout that are stout (stout trout, heh heh) and run on average about 12 to 16 inches. Like the White River, rainbows are what you'll be catching most of the time but you can also tie into some big browns as well as stocked brook and cutthroat trout. The brook trout are some of the bigger average-sized brook trout in the South, running about 11 to 15 inches long.

In summer when the water gets warmer, the Norfork is a haven for trout that run up from the increasingly hotter waters of the White River. Like the White River, the Norfork has riverside resorts along its course that provide lodging, boat rentals, guides, and meals.

The riffles and pools (some really big pools) combined with the various trout havens like ledges, cracks, shoals and drop-offs create a fly fisher's dream. Emergers, nymphs, wets, and streamers are consistent producers, but the North Fork has some good dry-fly action. Midge fishing is good year-round. Spincasters find that everything from small jigs to largemouth bass stickbaits can be productive, but I see the most success with Rooster Tails and smallish spinners and slabs.

This short, fertile river is best fished from a drift boat when the water is up, best wade-fished when the generators aren't running and the water is low and clear. Usually Norfork Dam only runs two generators, but even with just those two, when the siren sounds, get to high ground; this is a narrow river and the water rises quickly, more quickly than you think. Have an escape route already planned out.

For recorded information about power generation at Norfork and Bulls Shoals dams, call 870-431-5311.

CONTACTS

Lindsey's Rainbow Resort, Heber Springs, 501-362-3139

McClellan Trout Dock, Norfork, 501-499-5589

Norfork Trout Dock, Norfork, 501-499-5500

John B. Gulley II, Norfork, 501-499-7517

Ouachita Lake

- **Location:** West central Arkansas, close to Hot Springs
- **What You Fish For:** Striped bass as well as smallmouth and largemouth bass
- **Highlights and Notables:** Beauty and the bass

Lake Ouachita bills itself as the "Striper Capital of the World." Not just of Arkansas or the South, but the best place on earth to catch striper.

This impoundment of the Ouachita River, this clear lake with the big boast, Arkansas's largest lake. You pronounce this funny-looking lake name "Wash-it-taw" although if you want to be local, you have to turn it into a four-syllable word instead of three. Forty thousand acres big, 970 shore-miles, clear and clean water, surrounded by the wilderness of the Ouachita National Forest. Largely undeveloped shoreline. Forty miles long and green, so green and pristine and woodsy and undeveloped that you'd swear you're on some big wilderness Oregon lake. The Ouachita Mountains are not as consistently pretty or dramatic as the Ozarks, but here, on this scenic lake, they're equal in drama.

Lake Ouachita, plain and simple, is one of the most beautiful lakes on the planet. Photos don't do the colors justice. The water looks blue in pictures but up close and personal, the water is so clear, it's as if it's not there (like when Nerd would pull a crossover dribble on me). The greens of the forest run the gamut from kelly green to tissue-paper green, emerald to jade.

Start with the striper fishery. Come February and on through May, the shad start moving and so do the stripers. Stocked, they don't reproduce here. If you striper fish, you know how they follow the shad, then chase them to the top, disorienting them and then in a frenzy of carnage and splashing water and athleticism and terror (on the part of the shad, that is), the stripers close in on the kill.

This was my first experience on Ouachita in the 1980s, winter fishing. We threw top-water lures, mostly pencil-poppers, and we grew weary of so many 10-pound stripers and our arms tired so we quit, went back to the shore, sat under a tree, and drank beer. We watched the fleeing shad tear up the water in a chaotic zig-zag pattern no more than twenty feet in front of us in a shallow lagoon as the sun went down.

Stripers average about 8 to 12 pounds on Ouachita but you shouldn't have any problem landing one or two in the 15- to 25-pound range. Thirty-pound striped bass are not rare. Forty-pound stripers are not common nor are they uncommon, a few this size caught each year. Largest I've caught went about 20 pounds, topwater, scared me half to death because the big fish hit the lure right at the boat when I was lifting up to cast.

Here's a surprise: Lake Ouachita's small-mouth fishery is getting good enough to rival that of its striper population. Makes perfect sense. Deep clear water, rocks, clean and cool.

Largemouth bass. The numbers are good per day but surprisingly, the size of each is better than most other Arkansas lakes. Lance caught an 8-pound bass that we spotted cruising back and forth under a grassbed near the banks. He sightcast to it and we watched through the invisible water as the big mouth opened and flash bang, the biggest 8-pound bass we'd ever seen. The crappie in Ouachita are as big as pork roasts, the catfish could eat little kids, and the walleye, well, they're walleye.

On Lake Ouachita waters sit 100 unin-habited islands. When you read 100 unin-habited islands, it's just a number but until you've boated Ouachita, you can't quite imagine what 100 islands looks like. What else to catch? No need to, not with the big three so good, but indulge you—bream and catfish, crappie and walleye (and rainbow trout in the spillway). The lake never seems all that busy but reports have it getting as many as five million visitors annually. Some of those comes from Hot Springs, a pretty tourist town with racing and hot springs and good restaurants, a great place to call home during your fishing trip to Ouachita. From Hot Springs, head west three miles on US 270, then travel twelve miles north on Highway 227 to the park.

CONTACTS
Lake Ouachita State Park, www
   .arkansasstateparks.com/lakeouachita
Hugh Albright, guide, 501-767-2171
Mountain Harbor Resort, www
   .mountainharborresort.com

Spring River

- **Location:** North central Arkansas
- **What You Fish For:** Smallmouth bass, walleye, rainbow trout
- **Highlights and Notables:** Like its sister Arkansas rivers, Crooked Creek and Buffalo River, Spring River is a beautiful stream, clear and cold and did I mention beautiful?

I don't know how ineffectual one has to be as a canoe paddler/captain to tip over your canoe in slow-moving water but I guess if there is a place to register, I have to sign in. Lance always warns me that I generally fail as a canoeist and he's right. I'm either top heavy or unbalanced, maybe both. I spill. Spring River is cold, y'all.

There are many reasons why Spring is in this book. The north central Arkansas river is spring-fed by nine million gallons *per hour*. The river is clean and cold. Spring River is accessible, easy to reach, plenty of launch sites. You can imagine how scenic this river must be, flowing through hardwood forests, under bluffs, cascading into waterfalls in places, chopping into chunky rapids in some places, moving along slowly, tranquilly in others.

The fishing? Pretty good. I haven't found many rainbow trout that fight better than Spring River 'bows. They thrash and roll and jump and this feistiness against the placid water is striking, surprising, stirring. The trout hold in the foamy falls, under ledges, and in the long, deep pools. Walleyes are a big deal on Spring River. I know, surprised me too. I've just trout fished on the Spring but I hear that some awfully big walleyes are caught each year, up to 12 or 13 pounds, caught in Spring River Lake. You can also catch smallmouth bass (very, very good fishing for brown bass), largemouth bass, brown, brook and cutthroat trout, muskies (in the deep slow pools), and in fact I've caught one of the longer, prettier brook trout I've ever caught out of a tangled mess of bankside roots on the Spring River.

The Spring River has nearly sixty miles of beautiful canoe fishing but most concentrate on the seventeen miles between Mammoth Spring and Hardy. Both Mammoth Spring and Hardy have digs and eats but I like the vintage 1940s feel of Hardy. It's one cool historic resort town built on the banks of the Spring River. Nearby Cherokee Village is a little too touristy for my blood.

Spring River is ideal for doing that father-son thing, that family thing, that fishing buddies thing, that spouse outdoors thing. If you fly fish, Spring is perfect for both fly fishers and conventional anglers. Lastly, Spring River is good all year long and like I mentioned, has canoeability, at least for those of you who can canoe well. Access is from US 63, which parallels much of the upper Spring River.

White Oak Lakes

- **Location:** Southwestern Arkansas between Hope and Camden
- **What You Fish For:** Largemouth bass, crappie, catfish
- **Highlights and Notables:** A pair of trophy bass lakes that somehow remain relatively unknown

White Oak Lake lies east of Hope but have hope, friends, this is one gem you can put your faith in. They call it White Oak Lake but they're just funnin' because it's two, two, two lakes in one. A dam splits the body of water into two bodies and each has its own nature. So let's call it what they are (is?): White Oak Lakes. The second biggest Arkansas Game and Fish Commission-built lake (lakes?).

Upper White Oak Lake covers 1,032 acres and Lower White Oak Lake covers 1,645 acres. The Upper is known for its shad population, water lilies, and heavy vegetation. Concentrate on the weedbeds. The Lower is being managed as a trophy bass fishery and has a 16- to 21-inch slot limit and creel regs. You'll see anglers fishing in the coves and under and around the docks. In both lakes, you'll find dead timber, floating vegetation, islands, points, cypress trees, riprap, and channels, ideal habitat.

What are they catching? When I tell you, you'll scratch your head wondering why this out-of-the-way set of lakes with a super state park flies under the radar. They're catching lots of Florida-strain bass in a timber-filled lake, bass up to 8 pounds or better. They're catching crappie to 3 pounds and bream over a pound. And if that's not enough, back in 1985, in a week span, two channel catfish weighing over 22 pounds were caught. The lake underwent a fertilization program a while back and it's apparently working.

On the western arm of the Upper White Oak Lake sits award-winning White Oak Lake State Park replete with campsites, marina, boat rentals, hiking trails (ubiquitous in Arkansas state parks). This area is alive with wildlife and you'll have an excellent chance to spot great blue heron, egret, osprey, and green heron. Bald eagles are seen sometimes in the winter. From Prescott, go twenty miles east on Arkansas Highway 24, then turn for the blink of an eye south on Arkansas Highway 299, then go two miles southeast on Arkansas Highway 387 to the park.

White River

- **Location:** Northwestern and north central Arkansas
- **What You Fish For:** Brown and rainbow trout (some cutt, some brook)
- **Highlights and Notables:** The fish are bountiful, the river green and fertile, the banks forested, your chances at a huge trout better than average, and the combination of all of this make this arguably the top trout stream in America.

For as much press as the White River receives—"Number one river in America for trophy trout" proclaims one national outdoors magazine, "World's biggest browns" headlines another—I think this massive fertile fishery gets shortchanged in two respects: 1) few writers give the White its due in terms of beauty; 2) the river is much more productive than you think.

Is this the best trout stream in America? I think so.

The White has it all. World-record size trout; your average size trout is not average at all; an angler can catch great numbers of trout in a day; 150 miles of diverse trout water, stunning mountain scenery, homey riverside villages with cafes, diners, and restaurants with succulent vittles, culture (give up the hillbilly thoughts—the Ozarks have a lot more to offer than you think); great public access; rich food sources for trout that rank with any other trout river; and for as much pressure as the White River gets, it is in no danger of being loved to death. It all adds up, folks.

The White River is a tailwater best known for its large brown trout. The White is subject to high water flows, but is defiant to the heavy angling pressure. This powerful river courses hundreds of miles past dense forests and low-slung mountains. When shrouded by a gentle fog in the early morning, the White River has an otherworldly quality. Great limestone bluffs squeeze against the wide, gentle river. Thickly forested hillsides slope down to the banks.

The only distractions are the numerous trout docks, resorts, and other establishments along the river. Maybe the powerboats cruising up and down the river disturb the aesthetic a bit but you overlook that soon enough. I know what you'll think when you first see the White: sure doesn't look like a trout stream. You've fished with tall snow-capped mountains all too often to get over the stereotype but in case you haven't noticed, more and more of our undisturbed wild waters out west have houses and development on the water's edge. Water's not very clear is it? It clears up, wait a bit. No, the water's not gin-clear like so many Rocky Mountain streams but this one's loaded with trout-growing juice. Get over it. Some folks think bass lakes are beautiful and have learned how to over-look the docks and shoreline development. Show up in the fall when the trees are awash in orange and red and yellow and you'll be a thunderstruck believer in the beauty of this Ozark river.

No doubt that in these waters swim giant browns as big as 50 pounds, the big 5-0. The White is famous for large browns, up to 40 pounds but the staple game fish is the rainbow, stocked by the millions, the fish most likely to be caught. Anglers report catches of cutthroats up to 10 pounds. Brown trout over 15 to 20 pounds are caught many times each year, and the angler who doesn't catch a 2- to 5-pounder needs to stay on the river just a little longer or hire a guide because they're doing something wrong. Rainbows typically run from 9 to 16 inches and we've had days of catching thirty rainbows or more and all were 2 pounds or heavier.

Still, it's the wild trout in here that make headlines and make hearts jump.

Browns run from 10 to 18 inches, and many will be larger than that. A 19-pound rainbow was caught in the cold water of the White River in the 1980s. In addition to the brown and rainbow trout, there are a few cutthroats and brookies stocked in the White. The growth rates are phenomenal for all species because of the amazing fertility of the system. Crustaceans like crayfish, sowbugs, scuds, and minnows (dace, shiners, chubs, and sculpins), and at times in the year, threadfish shad, form the base of the White River trout's diet.

More of this *number one trout river in America* theme: For such a huge system, the pressure doesn't outweigh what it can stand, and with its richness in food sources (in some part due to the makeup of the land with its limestone mountains and lots of annual rainfall, and the filtering/running over the land part brings in minerals that aid the crustaceans and fish), with so much river, so much access, with its central location in America, with being served by bait-and-tackle stores and fly shops and guides and lodges and eateries, with each angler owning a real opportunity to catch a 10-pound trout with a slot-machine's chance at a world-record fish, with year-round angling—now add all that up and there is still one big reason that this is the number one trout river in America: the river fair to fly fishers and conventional anglers alike.

You get around on the White River in johnboats and, more and more, western-style driftboats. When the water's right, you anchor up and fish, you get out and wade the gravel bars. Fly fishers should abandon dry fly fishing and get out the streamers and sowbugs and squirrel nymphs. Conventional anglers should stock the tackle boxes with stickbaits and crankbaits.

The river has been impounded in several spots to form three major reservoirs (Bull Shoals, Table Rock, and Beaver) and a long, narrow lake (Taneycomo). Don't be too surprised to catch smallmouth and largemouth bass, catfish, or sunfish either, as they are plentiful in the river. Below Bull

Shoals there are 100 miles of undammed river. And my little whispering sidenote is the Beaver tailwater. Below Beaver dam, the river is underfished and underrated—most of it public but with few access points. Things are only going to get better, too, with new slot limits in 2006 and other changes, and you watch, this is the emerging section of big trout water.

Ask ten anglers how to get to the White River from Little Rock and you'll get ten different routes. Here's an easy one: From Little Rock, travel west on I-40 to US 65. Travel north on US 65 to Clinton where you will turn northeast on Highway 16. Continue north to Mountain View, then continue on Highway 5 into Mountain Home. The trip should take less than five hours.

CONTACTS

Blue Ribbon Flies and Lodge, Mountain Home, 501-425-0447

Cotter Trout Dock, Cotter, 501-435-6525

Gaston's White River Resort, Lakeview, 501-431-5202

Stetson's on the White, Flippin, 501-453-8066

Sportsman's Resort, Flippin, 800-626-FISH

Duane Hada's The Woodsman, Fort Smith, 501-452-3559

White River School of Fly Fishing, Eureka Springs, 501-253-7850

ILLINOIS

City Fishing

CHICAGO

If you'd have seen the Illinois River a couple of decades ago, you'd have been hesitant to drop a dead body in the polluted water much less think about fishing it. Chicago-area fisheries have really cleaned up their act and the Windy City has some pretty good fishin' holes now.

Lake Michigan is one of the top smallmouth fisheries in the country. If you want to catch a trophy smallmouth, this is one of the top places to start. (Chinook and Coho salmon, steelhead, lake trout, and brown trout are other prey for anglers.) The water clarity is so much better nowadays (thank you, invading zebra mussels) and with riprap shorelines providing ideal bronzeback habitat, the population is flourishing. Diversity Harbor is a popular launch point. Wherever you launch, consider that your background will be the magnificent Chicago skyline, the contrast of fishing water with steel and glass. Amazing scenery.

The Illinois River holds walleyes, saugers, smallmouth as its big three draws, but anglers also drop lines for largemouth bass, crappies, white bass, and panfish. The river is wide and navigable,

fertile instead of contaminated, made more so from sewage effluent that is put into the river. The white bass run in the spring is popular and worthy.

The Kankanee River is an interesting nearby smallmouth fishery south of the city. In places 100 yards wide, this is your traditional medium-sized, shallow, average-gradient, well-oxygenated limestone and slate river. The river and its numerous wild smallmouth bass are less than an hour's drive from Chicago.

Smallies as long as 19 inches are not unusual in this cream soda–colored water. You catch them in and around riffles, runs, flats, pools, holes, slots, gravel bars, deadfalls, islands, vegetation of all types, old dam remains, dams, highway bridges, railroad trestles. Wading is easy but you have to watch out for dropoffs. Access is easy. The Kank is rarely crowded. Canoeable.

The Kank is not just a haven for smallmouth (topwater heaven for bronzebacks as big as 5-pounds, 15.5-ounces, the river record) but also for walleye (14-pound state record), pike (20 pounds), carp (42-pounder), largemouth bass and channel catfish. Walleyes 8 to 10 pounds are not unusual. The river and the road cross each other several times.

Rend Lake

- **Location:** South central Illinois
- **What You Fish For:** Bass, catfish, crappie, you name it
- **Highlights and Notables:** Jack of all trades, master of none. The diversity of this pretty and shallow lake is the reason to visit.

This shallow southern Illinois reservoir is one real good lake. Like Lou Whitaker and Alan Trammell, Rend Lake has no weaknesses, is good at producing all species of fish. Nineteen thousand acres of unrecognized quality lake water, the northern half shallow and timbered, the southern half fuller, more of what you think of as the main lake.

Rend Lake is like the best friend who never reveals your secrets, it's a safe car, a Volvo, the neighborhood diner, the character actor you see in so many good movies but you still don't know his name (Hector Elizondo). No Oscars for Rend Lake. No world fishing records will ever fall here. Everything is pretty good, real good, very good, not great but B+ stuff.

Let's take a rundown of the pretty good fishing at Lake Rend: The crappie fishing is pretty darned good probably the best in the state. The striper fishing is something else, not Texoma, not Ouachita but quality. Hybrid striped bass fishery improving, with numbers down but size of each getting better, better. Largemouth bass fishing, just short of excellent. With a solid population of shad, with cover like riprap and points and laydowns and submerged timber and brush-piles, the bass fishery is healthy. Rend holds few lunkers but the average bass runs 1 to 4 pounds and bass up to 8 pounds are caught each year. White bass and crappie. If you fish for them, they will oblige you. The crappie are slabs of meat, big as t-bones. If there is one superior thing about Rend, one aspect that makes it tops in its field, it's the crappie. The crappie fishery is as good as any in the country. Catfish. You bet. Not record-breaking but close, close.

CONTACTS

Rend Lake Resort, www.rendlakeresort
.com
Rend Lake Sporting Goods, 618-242-2191
Rend Lake State FWA office, 618-279-
3110
Illinois Department of Natural Resources,
Benton, 618-435-8138

KANSAS

City Fishing

KANSAS CITY
Lake Jacomo

Sailboats and windsurfers and pontoon boaters belie just how good the fishing on 970-acre Lake Jacomo can be. I've always thought Kansas City got short-changed by those who didn't know the lay of the land, how pretty this part of the country really is. Located in Fleming Park, Jacomo has boat rentals, boat ramps, dock fishing, a marina, concessions, and gasoline—everything you'd want for a day on the water fishing for catfish, crappie, largemouth bass, carp, walleye, and hybrid bass.

Most community lakes don't have good bass fishing but Jacomo is an exception. If you caught a 5-pounder in Jacomo, I'd be proud of you but not surprised.

Guidebooks and articles about fishing are funny things. They describe the "typical" fishing experience of a fishery. Rivers run hot and cold. Anglers do, too. My brother-in-law and I backpacked about five miles up a river in Colorado one rainy day and were surprised to see a man in his thirties camping beside a fire instead of out fishing in the wet and cold like a trooper. We hailed the camp and took a cup of coffee from him.

We asked about the fishing and he said it was lousy. Worse than lousy.

"It's rained three days straight and I've only caught two fish."

"The weather sucks," we agreed.

He pulled out a book from his tent. It was dog-eared and faded. A copy of a guidebook I wrote—*Flyfishing Southwestern Colorado*. I started to admit that I wrote the thing but held back. I wanted to get upstream and set up camp.

"I should've never come here."

"Rain's supposed to let up by tomorrow," we counseled.

"Won't matter. Ain't no fish in this stream anyhow." He tossed the book in the open tent, the rain soaking the pages. "I'd like to strangle the bastard that wrote that book." I was afraid he recognized me. "Guy said that this river had some of the best unknown fishing in the state. Son of a bitchin' writers."

"I know exactly what you mean. What the hell do they know? Bastards." We three shared a laugh.

We left him and his misery, set up camp a few miles upstream. Then the skies cleared and over the next three days caught more fish on this unknown trout stream than we'd ever caught before. Son of a bitchin' writers, my ass.

I've been there before, of course. On the other side. I've read articles and books about a Shangri-La, where all the fish are big and jump on your hook willingly. Then I go there and get skunked. I have learned not to blame the writer.

It happened the first time I fished the Au Sable. I had read everything I could lay my hands on and with the great Au Sable River, the blue ribbon limestone trophy trout stream, there was a lot to read. I was in college and was on my fish-all-the-American-legendary-waters phase. I was good at catching trout with big attractor flies on western streams, so how hard could the Au Sable be?

Son of a bitchin' writers.

The Muskegon River is an angler's buffet, a variety of fish that will satiate your hunger.

When I was a kid, we used to go to Wyatt's Cafeteria every Sunday after church. You had a Wyatt's in your neck of the woods but it was Piccadilly or Furr's or Morrison's or some other incarnation of the pick-your-food-from-behind-glass-and-have-an-aproned-worker-put-it-on-a-tray kind of buffet/cafeteria restaurant so popular in the '60s and '70s. Most visits, I got what was then called veal cutlet but later revealed to be breaded chicken fried steak. With cream gravy. Mashed potatoes (with cream gravy). Buttered roll. Iced tea. Ice box chocolate cream pie.

Sometimes I'd go for the fried Spam or the heaping plate of spaghetti; sometimes I'd go out on a limb and ask for the Swedish meatballs with noodles.

And if Mamaw was in charge or if Mom wasn't paying close enough attention, I'd add Jell-O, a second meat (usually ground hamburger meat made to look like a steak), a piece of buttered cornbread, and pear halves. And I'd sub in root beer for the iced tea.

Like diners, most of those cafeteria places have gone under, given way to bistros, themed cafés and chain restaurants. I loved being able to choose from all the sights and smells. It's why I still like Chinese buffets, I guess.

A buffet of fish where you can select one or, if your Mother's not looking, fish for as many species as you want.

I have a friend named Bob Stewart and he's from Michigan or maybe it's just his family is from Michigan, I can't remember. He's a fishing buddy so I shouldn't be expected to remember stuff my wife Amy normally remembers for me.

Bob was holding court at a campfire with five or six of us sitting in various states of repose. Tom was strumming guitar and lightly humming. He has a nice voice.

"Grandad belonged to an exclusive fly fishing club up in Michigan, no bait allowed, had to pay good money to join, and

his best friend was also a member. Just so happened that his best friend was the best fly fisher in the club, maybe even in the state of Michigan. Every member knew and admitted it."

A couple of heads perked up at the idea that there was unanimity in a circle of anglers. Michigan outdoorsmen are a tough crowd.

"Granddad and his fishing buddy fly fished the private waters of his club for years, his buddy always catching the most trout and the biggest trout of anyone." Bob seemed more truthful on this tale than his normal meandering fables, so I leaned in and got comfortable.

"Most guys in the club attributed Granddad's best friend's fishing prowess to two facts. One, Granddad's friend was a mighty fine angler with a fly and two, and most importantly, that he was a spiritual man, known for taking a small Bible from his fishing vest pocket while on the river and reading scripture. The men would comment on the power of the Good Book."

Tom had quit strumming at this point and the flames danced and threw weird shadows on our curious faces.

"Granddad's buddy up and died one day and the man's wife gave Granddad all of his tackle including the Bible. To honor his fly fishing buddy, he placed the small Bible in his own vest pocket and pledged to always carry it on the water with him."

Bob began circling the fire and his band of merry anglers as he soothed us with this bedtime camping story.

"One day Granddad wasn't catching many

fish on the private river and decided he'd read a bit and took out the Bible, opened it up, and fell against the bank like he was shot."

I was up on my haunches. I love good fishing stories.

"Granddad was stunned to discover that in the middle of the Bible, somewhere between Nehemiah and St. Matthew, there was a hollowed out square, and in it, dirt and three dried up earthworms."

We laughed nervously not sure if we should believe Bob or not.

"Granddad still carries the Bible in his vest pocket and you know what? All the members of the fly fishing club think of him as the best fly rodder in the bunch, and he always catches the most trout and the biggest trout and they attribute his success to his skills and they say that they see him remembering his best friend from time to time because he is often seen off away from everybody reading from the Good Book."

I wouldn't call it a fascination exactly but I'm a fan of black and white movies, old and new. I like the textures, the subtleties between grays. Amy always shakes her head when someone asks me what my favorite color is and I answer, honestly, gray. Gray is my favorite color, thank you very much Adam Duritz.

When I was a kid, Mom used to tell me to use more colors when I would draw with crayons. My shirts all kind of look the same, the color tones only a sliver of the color wheel, gray-khaki to light slate. My favorite movies include *Young Frankenstein*, *Who's Afraid of Virginia Woolf*, *The Third Man*, *The Man Who Shot Liberty Valance*, *Dead Men Don't Wear Plaid* and so on. And I love *film noir*. Color isn't bad. Too much of it can muck up a perfectly good picture.

In the early morning in the outdoors, before the sun is gold, I like to be at the campfire sipping coffee enjoying the monochromatic panorama.

The movies *Sin City* and *Rumblefish* were filmed in black and white even though they are contemporary movies. What stands out is that in parts of the movie, something, for dramatic purposes, is in color. Whatever it is that's in color is so much more important than if lost in a wash of colors, well, I guess it's kinda like how I see trout in the water when my eyesight is so bad. I like the absence of colors so the things I care about are better defined. When you strip away all the noise, you can see what you're looking for (although Chad Huseman says that my ability to spot trout but not see the bear in front of me is kind of an idiot savant thing).

What brings all this up is that on the second morning I ever fished the Rifle River, a beautiful, underrated trout stream in northern Michigan, I had my own little artsy fartsy black and white movie going. I scratched my face on some dark plant that stood face high as I was walking through the forest (that by day I knew was blazing in yellows and oranges and reds but now was all softly muted) to the river but it was early enough that I could only tell I was bleeding because the blood was dark on my hand. Everything was still a calm mix of grays and silvers.

I hadn't landed a steelhead yet even though I had three on the day before. I caught a couple of brown trout that went 15, 16 inches, and what looked like a sucker. The river had more anglers on it than this medium-sized river deserved (more than I deserved, too, I thought) so I wanted to get on the water early and often to make sure I caught what I came for.

Everything looks different in the gauzy gray of morning and I didn't recognize the hole I was looking for, the one where I had seen that one older gentleman catch several steelies the day before. The water was glassy, moving dark and slowly like the blood I saw on my hand moments earlier. Then I saw the hole. It was beautiful, an elongated circle of water backed up and deep, spilling out over sand and gravel, flowing over a huge downed tree. I had dreamt about it the night before, what denizens this deep dark water must hold.

I walked briskly down the shore so I could set up to fish the pool at first light. The quickness of my pace was warming against the chill of fall. Then I stopped dead in my tracks. The old man moved out of the shadows of the trees where he had been laying in wait, ambling, laying claim to the prize, a gentle nod in my direction, the submissive nod back, his eyes soft and telling, early bird and worms, and the light broke through the tops of the trees and his cap was red and all else was gray and pewter and as I shuffled along the bank to find my own deep dark pool, everything came alive in an explosion of colors, the leaves on the trees, the brightly colored streamer hooked in my rod's hookholder, the crimson blood on my hand, and the river, stained green and reflecting back all those colors of the sky and land back at me.

See what color does for you? Not only does it muck up a perfectly good picture, it takes away the best hole on the river.

Au Sable River

- **Location:** Northeastern Michigan
- **What You Fish For:** Predominantly brown trout, as well as some brook and rainbow trout. These are wild trout.
- **Highlights and Notables:** You might get caught up in the laziness of this shaded fertile river and you might get frustrated at all the trout refusing your flies and lures but if you work hard, you'll catch some of heaviest trout you've ever caught. One of the best trout streams in the United States.

I learned the hard way about the prolific hatches on the nine miles of the Holy Waters. I learned how these fish are smarter than your average bear. How perfect presentation plus long leaders plus thin tippet plus matching the hatch didn't equal success.

I loved the atmosphere of the river, the tree-lined banks and the easy, lazy, twisting flow. I didn't love that I only caught four fish in two days on the river. I spooked fish. I had trout rise to my offerings and turn away. I lost flies on submerged logs and overhanging limbs. I had fish on but lost them. All this "bad luck" was my inattention to detail; I hadn't observed what the writers had written.

The Au Sable is easily the best trout fishery in the Midwest and ranks with most any other river in the country. The Holy Water is one of the most famous and most productive stretches of trout water in the country, but less famous, unnamed stretches can be just as rich and bountiful. But not on that trip.

I didn't watch the hatches closely enough. I wasn't as careful with drag as I should have been in that slow-moving water. I waded too much. I got caught up in the whole Au Sable experience—the low-slung riverboats, bankside fly shops, fabled clubs, famous pools, watching the other boats. I did catch quite a few small brook trout in the upper stretch but the further downstream I went, the darker my experience. The French named this water the "river of sand." Amen.

A few years later, I tried the Au Sable again. I focused more, I matched the hatches more closely, and I paid attention to the lies, the feeding lanes. And I caught a lot of heavy-bodied wild trout, one 19-inch brown with a bottom jaw the size of Dash Riprock.

The Au Sable has over 180 miles of great water for trout and in the lower reaches, steelhead. My advice is to hit the Holy Water for a day but give the rest of the river your attention for as long as you're there.

Don't get all caught up in catching the Michigan caddis hatch, the Hexagenia Limbata explosion. Big browns will indeed jump over rocks and through hoops to get to these huge fluttering insects but there's so many fishers on the water and you may not time it right, so don't worry about it.

Likely looking cover holds trout, and there is likely looking cover everywhere. Feeding lanes are obvious, as are the numerous submerged logs, underwater structure, dropoffs and snags. Trees overhang the cluttered banks. The Au Sable is still complex enough, and the trophy trout wise enough, that hiring a guide your first few times is a good idea. If you want to fish a given hatch, wait around, the hatch will happen soon. The Au Sable is a floating river, floated in the low-slung cedar Au Sable riverboats. The Au Sable is a long, big river with more than enough room and good fishing water for everyone.

CONTACTS
Au Sable Angler, www.ausableangler.com
Fly Factory, www.troutbums.com
Gates Lodge and Fly Shop, www
   .gateslodge.com

Boardman River

- **Location:** Northwestern Michigan
- **What You Fish For:** brook, brown trout
- **Highlights and Notables:** You won't catch many lunkers but you won't forget all the wild trout and the angling history and the challenges and hatches.

I had no idea the brook trout fishing was so good. I spent too much of my time catching brook trout on the North Branch instead of concentrating on the glassy flats of the main stem. But it was so much fun, casting through and under the wild overhanging limbs and heavy bank vegetation to plop down a dry and strip back a wild brook trout. Yeah, I made sure to use an Adams at one point to pay homage to Leonard Halladay who created, then cast, the first Adams on this very stream.

The Boardman is middle-sized, shallow and its brown trout are not typically large. The stories you hear about the big browns are no doubt from those times during the infamous Hexagenia hatch when Moby Dick himself would rise from the depths to thrash around and capture these insects as big as hummingbirds.

The river's trout are picky. With clear water and plenty of mayflies and caddis, they don't really need your offerings. While they rise to properly presented, matching-the-hatch dry flies, I think streamers are an underrated way to entice them. I had one nice brown (14 inches) follow every streamer I stripped in front of him but not take it, not until the sun went behind a cloud.

I did best in the swifter section of the river where the trout, while finicky, were heavier and longer. Problem was that it was in this stretch that I encountered more people on the river, only a few of them fishing, more campgrounds and overall traffic. The river looks like anglers who like to spin fish with lightweight gear would do well. The Boardman flows through heavily wooded beautiful scenery and the upper reaches are a pleasure to fish.

CONTACTS

McCool Outfitters, Traverse City, 231-946-4508

Fuller's North Branch Outing Club, Grayling, 989-348-7951

Hawkins Outfitters, Lake Ann, 231-228-7135

The Troutsman, Traverse City, 231-938-3474

Fox River and the Upper Peninsula

- **Location:** Central Upper Peninsula
- **What You Fish For:** Wild brook trout predominantly but also salmon, steelhead, brown trout, rainbow trout
- **Highlights and Notables:** Big country, endless angling options, historic settings, awesome wild trout streams

You're beautiful, like a May fly.

ERNEST HEMINGWAY

While Nick walked through the little stretch of meadow alongside the stream, trout had jumped high out of water. Now as he looked down the river, the insects must be settling on the surface, for the trout were feeding steadily all down the stream. As far down the long stretch as he could see, the trout were rising, making circles all down the surface of the water, as though it were starting to rain.

Big Two-Hearted River by
ERNEST HEMINGWAY

If you know Hemingway, then you know northern Michigan and the U.P. were recreational stomping grounds for his characters and for him in his youth. He fished Charlevoix and Walloon Lakes. He fished all over North Michigan and that includes the Fox River. Supposedly, the Big Two-Hearted River he wrote about was, in fact, the Fox. Part of what got me started traveling the globe fishing was my quest to follow Hemingway and his characters around the world. Idaho, Michigan, France, Spain, Key West, etc. While I don't share his char-

acters' sense of fatalism, I do share their idea of the man of action.

The Fox River is a fine brook trout stream, the finest in the Upper Peninsula. When the Fox joins its parallel sister, the East Branch of the Fox River, together they form the Manistique River. Both rivers hold great populations of fat, colorful, native brook trout.

The Fox is a cold stream, made more so by cooling shadows from overhanging tree limbs and brush. You see both waders and floaters, fly fishers and spincasters in both

City Fishing

DETROIT
Detroit River, Lake Cadillac, Lake St. Clair, western side of Lake Erie

The Detroit River is connective tissue of the meaty lakes, Erie and St. Clair. Less a river and more a strait, this is a much better fishery than most anyone outside of Detroit knows. In the spring, in April, walleyes from Lake Erie move into the Detroit River to spawn by the millions. And anglers show up by the thousands to jig and hand-line for the walleyes that sometimes reach 10 pounds. The river looks like a bathtub with toy boats at times because it gets so crowded but the fishing is hot and heavy beginning as early as February.

The river (strait) is undammed and

as such, allows salmon and steelhead, muskie and walleye free passage between lakes. And if it lives in the Lake Erie, it lives in the Detroit River. Even though the river is highly developed, anglers can find easy access to fish for bass, muskie, the aforementioned walleye, panfish, and so on, and to make it better, you can fish all year long.

Lake St. Clair is a fantastic fishery for muskie and walleye and pike and is known regionally for plentiful smallmouth and an underrated largemouth population. The smallmouth are good-sized and provide plenty of action. The muskie population here doesn't get enough attention outside the region but it's probably one of the tops in the country. Muskie are everywhere here and they eat everything.

The St. Clair River runs into the lake and keeps things moving, turning over, and is another option, too, as the main stem and its channels hold lots of fish including bass. Lake St. Clair is rightfully thought of as one of the best combination fishing destinations in the Midwest but it gets awfully busy in July when the bronzeback fishing is at its peak and twenty to forty-fish days are not uncommon. I recommend the fall on this huge lake (that is actually one of the largest freshwater deltas in the world; the northeast part of the lake is marshy and full of crazy channels).

Lake St. Clair is twenty-five miles long and twenty-four miles wide, only five or six miles northeast of Detroit (off I-94). I have read that there are over 90 species of fish in Lake St. Clair. An interesting part of the lake is the boundary setup: part American, part Canadian (Ontario), and part Walpole Indian reservation. You can select from bays or flats, islands or channels.

And if that's not enough fishing water for you, in less than an hour you could be on Cadillac, Kensington, Square, Mitchell, Cass, Kent, Sylvan, and Pontiac Lakes, the western basin of Lake Erie, and hundreds more inland lakes.

CONTACTS
Capt. Jim Barta, 313-388-5847, www.truefishing.com
Great Lake Research Station, 810-465-4771

of these rivers. You see brook trout by the dozens, not many but some over a foot long.

Think of fishing the Upper Peninsula of Michigan as a holistic journey. You don't go for any one fishery but to grab a handful of wild trout days on wild trout rivers each time you go. Though not as wild as it used to be what with the inevitability of civilization and tourism creeping in, the U.P. is still a wild and exciting getaway. I heard someone call the U.P. untamed. That's the best word to describe it.

Tourists and visiting anglers tend to stay cemented to the southern area of the Upper Peninsula; the lightly populated interior of the eastern and western U.P. can put an angler on waters that might not have been fished in ages. Even though the angler might find solitude in the forests of white pine of the U.P., notably in the Hiawatha, Ottawa, and Lake Superior National Forests, lodging and groceries can be found in the small towns that dot the peninsula, towns which are usually no more than a half hour away. Many of the rivers and streams will have sea-run brook trout, salmon, steelhead, and other big water fish.

I haven't listed all of the streams and not one lake but if you go, you can do some more research if you've of a mind. These are some of the top and most interesting places to fish streamwise.

Big Two-Hearted River

The brook trout stream made famous by Hemingway, east of the Fox. The West Branch of the Big Two-Hearted River has the best fly fishing water on the river, with easy wading, lots of room to backcast, and plenty of eager brook and rainbow trout to tempt. The river is clear but the color of ginger ale and the fishing pressure is light in the upper reaches.

East Branch of the Tahquamenon

Excellent brook trout river close to Two-Hearted River. This is a blue ribbon stream for twenty of its miles, difficult to reach in many locations. The stream is remote and does not receive much fishing pressure. This is a tough hike. The thick streamside brush and the overall narrowness of the stream make for challenging angling.

Manistique River

Located in the beautiful Seney National Wildlife Refuge. The Manistique is a twisty brook trout stream in the upper (although marginal), a much better salmon (Chinook) and steelhead river lower.

Sturgeon River

Flows south into Lake Michigan, a wide lightly-fished river with better than average fishing for brook and rainbow trout deep in the national forests of the Hiawatha.

Whitefish River

This large river holds a number of fun game fish: brook trout, of course, but also rainbow trout and oddly, splake. Beside that, the Whitefish gets runs of brown and coaster brook trout, steelhead and Chinook salmon. The West Branch is a lot of fun with its intimate water and plunge pools.

Escanaba River

One of the prettier, more dramatic rivers with its fast water and rock croppings and steep cliffs and heavily-forested banks. A larger river that can be floated in the lower stretch. Holds brook and brown trout and it's surprising this great trout fishery and its riffles and runs and pools doesn't get more angling pressure.

Little Garlic River

Talk to anyone about the Little Garlic and they'll tell you, if they're honest, about fishing at the falls for steelhead. If they don't tell you about the falls, they are untrustworthy and probably very good fishermen. Brook trout also reside in the Little Garlic (which is near Marquette).

Carp River

This gem has excellent access and can be found in the Hiawatha National Forest and Lake Superior State Forest lands near the aptly named town of Trout Lake. The Carp has lots of casting room and easy wading, up to forty feet wide, tawny-colored like much of the waters in Michigan. There are big trout including nice-sized browns in parts of the Carp, lurking under overhanging banks and in the mix of roots and fallen trees, and in the deep, dark pools; in other parts, you have to be quick with your flies and lures as the river tumbles down through big rocks, so think pocketwater and fat pools. In its lower reaches, the Carp receives steelhead, king salmon, and Coho salmon (even occasional Pinks).

Chocolay River

Lake Superior tributary, canoeable, with good fishing for brown trout and steelhead. This year-round stream also holds brook trout in its upper stretches and has runs of Chinook and pink salmon.

Black River

Twelve miles of charming but rugged stream, twenty feet wide, difficult to walk to from the road, productive for good-sized brook trout hiding under banks, in eddies, and behind big granite rocks.

Fence River

One of the wilder, more remote brook trout streams but worth the effort for the larger than average brook trout in its stained water. Pack a lunch because this meandering sleeper stream is a long ways off.

Little Carp River

An almost too-accessible trout stream in the Porcupine Mountains State Park. The brook trout are easily caught but you'll see too many others on the river with you. Look on the state park map and find other angling options best not named here and left for you to have fun discovering.

Cook's Run

Hooks up with South Branch Paint River. Mosquitos and no-seeums will getcha but

nice water if you like a challenging clear spring creek and angling for colorful natives.

Firesteel River

Your basic U.P. river with good pools and forests and rainbows and brookies.

Paint River

The South Branch of the Paint River is a top-notch trout winding stream holding wild brook and rainbow trout, ideal for canoeing; the North Branch is a lightly fished brook trout stream, one of the better ones in the U.P.

Ontonagon River

One big diverse river with four branches. Brook, brown, and rainbow trout, good access, boatable, wadeable, rapids, waterfalls, and some of the most superior scenery of any Michigan stream. The river in its lowest stretches also gets runs of steelhead, brown trout, and salmon. Wild for much of its course, the Ontonagon River is one of the must-visits for any visiting angler.

Brule River

Not all of the Brule is top-flight trout water. The most popular and best water (funny how those two things so often go together) is that section below Elvoy Creek at M-73 downstream to M-179. The Brule River acts as the border between Michigan and Wisconsin. If you like catching larger than average brook and brown trout, this might be the river for you.

St. Mary's River

Legendary salmon river. Atlantic salmon. The Rapids. This is one big hard-flowing river and while the Atlantic salmon don't run like they used to the river is so diverse, so profound, so incredible, St. Mary's is one river that rises above the rest. Eighty species of fish live here including steelhead, pinks, Chinooks, brown trout, and so many more.

Laughing Whitefish

You gotta love the name. This spastic river thrashes and jumps and rushes forth to its entrance into Lake Superior. Laughing Whitefish holds steelhead, brook trout, and salmon (pink and Coho).

Isle Royale National Park

For the adventurous angler, a quick trip to Isle Royale National Park in the northwest corner of Lake Superior is in order. The only way to the wilderness island is by boat, ferry (the Barf Barge), or floatplane, and reservations are required. There are no roads on the island, but there are foot trails galore. The streams on the island hold rainbows and brooks, and even though they are not monster-sized, the quality of fishing near-pristine waters more than makes up for it. Streams also hold runs of coaster brook trout and Coho salmon. Off the eastern shore of the Upper Peninsula is Drummond Island, a rocky island wilderness with over 40 inland lakes and three stocked trout streams.

CONTACTS
Isle Royale National Park, 906-482-0984, www.nps.gov/isro

Houghton Ferry, 906-482-0984, www.nps.gov/isro/ranger3.htm
Copper Harbor, 906-289-4437, www.isleroyale.com

A handful of other interesting U.P. waters:
　　Jumbo River
　　Presque Isle River
　　Little Iron River
　　Mirror Lake
　　Lake of the Clouds

CONTACTS
Michigan Chamber of Commerce, www.michamber.com
Rainbow Lodge Motel, Store and Canoe Rentals, 906-658-3357
Mel's Guide Service, 906-293-3760
Uncle Ducky Outfitters, 906-228-5447
Bayshore Bait and Tackle, 906-786-1488
Gander Mountain, 906-226-8300
Fast Water Guide Service, 906-932-4038

Grand River

One of the longest of Michigan's rivers, the Grand offers more than 100 miles of prime smallmouth water. Even the tributaries are worthy, such as the Thornapple. At Eaton Springs, the river changes from a slow stream to a fast, smallmouth style river, the kind with boulders and pockets and pools and riffles. Underfished and plenty of water to feel alone.

Manistee River

- **Location:** Upper western part of the Lower Peninsula
- **What You Fish For:** Salmon, steelhead, brook, and rainbow and brown trout
- **Highlights and Notables:** If you like to catch trout, salmon, and steelhead, look no further. This is your do-everything big river.

Michigan outdoors-folk take their fishing to heart. If you've ever seen photos of anglers lined up shoulder to shoulder fishing for salmon on some big Michigan river, it was probably the Manistee River.

The Big Manistee River lies on the western side of Lower Peninsula, one of Michigan's largest watersheds. The big river flows over fifty miles from its headwaters and on into Manistee Lake and Lake Michigan.

The Manistee ranks in the top handful of salmon fisheries of the state, which by default—given Michigan's bounteous salmonid riches—means this is one of the finest in the country. The Big Manistee lies west of the Au Sable just a few miles, and is better known as a steelhead and salmon fishery but the river produces nice trout, too.

The upper reaches have excellent fishing for wild brook and brown trout, while the lower stretches before the Sharon area have big water and bigger fish, mostly brown and rainbow trout. An eight-mile-long fly fishing–only stretch below Yellowtrees Landing has great angling in its

underwater tangles, undercut banks, and heavy vegetation. The Manistee has one of the best Hex hatches in the country, but in June, the river gets fairly crowded. There is easy access all along the Manistee. Matching the hatch works well on the river, but attractor patterns work between hatches, as do nymphs, wet flies, and streamers.

Wild and hatchery steelhead and salmon are seen in late August, early September coming from Lake Manistee. The Chinooks reach 10 pounds easy, 20 regularly and 30 as a bonus. The Coho are smaller with a lower top-end, and like steelhead, run about 7 to 10 pounds each and arrive a few weeks after the Chinook. As if that's not enough action, and good enough reason for bankside crowds, large brown trout

are present and active during the late summer and fall as well.

The Manistee River is big so the river isn't crowded in all places at all times. Above Tippy Dam, no salmon but plenty of browns, rainbows, and brookies. You'd be surprised how large the trout grow in this underappreciated section.

Little Manistee River

Its neighbor to the north, the Little Manistee River, is loaded with eager rainbows, finicky browns and holdover steelheads left from the spring and fall runs. The river has some excellent fly fishing water with log jams, deep pools, undercut banks, riffles, and glassy runs. Feisty rainbows, some lunkers, take attractors with gusto, but the tricky browns will have to be brought to the net with streamers, terrestrials, nymphs, and crayfish imitations.

CONTACTS
Sean McDonald, Century Circle Guide
    Service, www.centurycircle.com

Muskegon River

- **Location:** Western Michigan
- **What You Fish For:** Brown and rainbow trout, salmon, steelhead
- **Highlights and Notables:** If you are a trophy salmonid hunter, make plans to fish the Muskegon.

Not many rivers offer as much as Muskegon River. The Muskegon is the Wyatt's Cafeteria of Michigan.

The Muskegon River is the redheaded stepsister of the Pere Marquette and Manistee Rivers but it doesn't deserve secondary status. Big and wide, the Muskegon flows into the east side of Lake Michigan. Well known in the upper Midwest for its phenomenal runs of steelhead and salmon, you don't hear much about the Muskegon outside of the region, don't see it in many national outdoor magazines. You should.

Maybe better than its salmon and steelhead are its burgeoning populations of heavy browns and rainbows, these solid fish made so by the prolific hatches of the Muskegon River. The water below Croton Dam (approximately thirty-five miles) is the best trout water on the river's 200-plus miles.

A wide fertile river, 150 to 300 feet across (averaging about 175 to 200, I'd say), a foot to ten feet deep on average, the Muskegon doesn't have classic trout water characteristics. The river is often featureless and glassy for much of its course, ideal water for dry fly fishing. You have to look for edges and seams and foamlines; look for underwater rocks and gravel and weeds for holding trout. That said, in places anglers can fish pools and pockets and riffles and runs and those lies hold trout, steelhead, and salmon.

Fished best by boat, fished best with long light leaders, the two best times to be on the Muskegon are spring and fall, when steelies and salmon are active. Below Croton Dam, you can catch a cafeteria buffet of fishes in addition to trout, spring and summer steelhead, Chinook and Coho salmon, northern pike, crappie, rock bass, largemouth and smallmouth bass, sturgeon, and walleye. The walleye and smallmouth fisheries are two underrated options for Muskegon anglers. And above Croton Dam, where so many anglers *don't* go, you can fish for pike, largemouth and smallmouth bass, walleye, trout, catfish, and panfish.

CONTACTS

Steve Kuieck, Riverquest Charters, Coopersville, 616-837-0440, fishon@ riverquestcharters.com

Department of Natural Resources, Muskegon, 231-788-6798

Newaygo Chamber of Commerce (general tourism-related questions), 231-652-3068

Muskegon County Convention and Visitors Bureau, 231-722-3751, www .muskegon.org

Pere Marquette River

- **Location:** Western Michigan
- **What You Fish For:** Steelhead, salmon, brown and rainbow trout
- **Highlights and Notables:** Pere Marquette holds its own with other salmon and steelhead rivers of the Midwest, but behind that big fish reputation is some amazing angling for trout.

I can solve all your problems fishing the bewitching Pere Marquette. How to find the steelhead and how to entice them? How to locate the big lurking brown trout and what will make them come out and play? Salmon. When, where, how? I can tell you. I can solve your dilemma.

Hire a guide.

If you don't, and you're not a local, you don't stand a chance. The Pere Marquette is full of fish but they are underwater mysteries, dark and murky, green shadows. Since the Pere Marquette has some of the best guides in the world working one of the classic trout-salmon-steelhead rivers in the world, you owe it to yourself to have them float the boat, take you to the best holes, teach you their secrets of this complex river.

Trout fishermen are in the minority on this big and beautiful river with the gentle current. Trophy brown trout hide in deep, dark pools and fast, bankside runs. Heavy rainbows can be caught in the riffles and pools. The Pere Marquette's trout find refuge under foamlines, in the whirlpools, at dropoff ledges. Trout are frequently caught weighing between 2 and 5 pounds, sometimes larger. The three hatches to pay attention to are Tricos, Hexagenia, and Gray Drakes.

The Pere Marquette can be floated, should be floated your first few times, and a guide is a good idea for a first-timer, since the river has tricky currents, lots of cover, and too much water to thrash around this wide and often deep and always deceptive river.

In season, both steelhead and salmon make runs up the river, wild torpedos of strength and beauty. The Chinook salmon enter in late summer, 10 to 20 pounds big with some up to and over 30 pounds. They are masters at leverage and if that doesn't work, the magnificent fish turn to their own brute strength. You may hook up with ten to land one.

The steelhead enter in the autumn, fresh, lithe, angry, and acrobatic, and fishing for them continues through winter and early spring. Being on the Pere Marquette in fall when the hardwood forests buttressed up against the river rage in a palette of blazing oranges, yellows, and reds is something you won't forget. The silver slabs will hit flies, eggs, and other furry facsimiles and when they do, hold on tight because you probably won't land but one of every five or six of these tenacious titans when they run.

It's easy to just stop and watch the grizzled veterans who know what the heck to do to catch the steelhead and salmon. They're not in a pair of $300 waders, and their cigars are cellophane wrapped. They're likely in flannel shirts and gimme caps and they're all about the hunt for the big one.

Pere Marquette is a tributary of Lake Michigan on its eastern shore. In the main river—and I should mention that the upper reaches and feeders have some pretty decent fishing—the river spreads out to anywhere from forty to eighty feet and is shallow, no deeper than your average auto repairman, muddy bottom and all. In many sections, you'll salivate at the classic pool-riffle-run configurations where you know steelhead and resident brown trout reside.

There are famous pools all along the river, productive ones like Grayling Hole, Old Reliable, Bridge Hole, and the Snag Hole. The most popular spot on the river is a top-notch producer, Gleason's Landing and the eight miles below it. Access to the Pere Marquette is fair to good depending on where you want to jump in.

CONTACTS
Matt Suspinski, Gray Drake Lodge &
  Outfitters, www.graydrake.com

Rifle River

- **Location:** Northeast Michigan
- **What You Fish For:** Trout, steelhead, salmon
- **Highlights and Notables:** Popular pretty stream with gorgeous northern Michigan scenery: forests and summer homes and plenty of fish

Rifle River is one fine river. Resident and migratory trout reside in her green tea–colored slow-moving waters as well as the steelhead, salmon, and suckers that make their seasonal runs. The resident trout, brown and brook and rainbow, are not typically of any notable size, but the fish on the move can be. The river is wadeable but more so if you float it and then stop and wade—floating helps you get to the good holes and runs because the Rifle doesn't seem to have as much holding water as most Michigan rivers.

The Rifle also has several troutworthy feeder creeks. One larger one is Houghton Creek, a short, narrow brown trout fishery. The Au Gres River receives a steelhead run in the spring, but its healthy insect population helps keep the trout fishing good all year. Attractors work well on this scenic, easily-waded river, as do streamers and sculpin patterns.

CONTACTS
DNR's Southern Lake Michigan Management Unit, 989-684-9141

Saginaw Bay

- **Location:** Eastern Michigan, western Lake Huron
- **What You Fish For:** Walleye, bass, salmon, and more
- **Highlights and Notables:** You won't locate many fisheries that can produce walleyes like this and also give anglers so many other opportunities at large fish.

Troll deep and often, that's the mantra on this lake, at least for walleyes. Huge, close to urban centers, able to produce walleyes like a factory, Saginaw Bay is a stupendous fishery. Smallmouth bass, Chinook salmon, steelhead, lake trout, perch, and others thrive in big numbers in this immense body of water.

Saginaw Bay lies on the western side of Lake Huron. This is big water, the inner bay and the outer bay and you better be able to move around to find and follow the fish. Numerous rivers empty into the bay. Walleyes are everywhere but act in different ways according to the lay of the land, whether shallow and weedy, rocky and deep, or when they move out of the rivers and back into the bay. This is one of the best walleye fisheries in America.

CONTACTS
Bay Area Chamber of Commerce, 989-893-4567, www.baycityarea.com

Johnse Bushlack of Seagull Outfitters says:

We really do have a gem up there in the Boundary Waters . . . and what's so great is that it is so lightly fished and the adventure is getting there. Campers and canoeists are rewarded for their hard work and effort that they put forth to get to some of these lakes . . . for the true outdoorsman or woman, I think they get more satisfaction in the journey to get to these lakes because it's hard work. You've accomplished something after a week long trip in the wilderness.

Bushlack tells us a common story from the BWCA/Quetico:

Paddlers frequently tell us the same story. They were reeling in a two or three pound smallmouth bass and it was giving them a good fight like they always do, then all of the sudden it started stripping line out like crazy and the fight elevated to a much stronger degree. They continue to fight this fish with new-found energy for a few minutes until they're able to get a look at it alongside the canoe. They finally realize what has happened. The two-pound bass had been attacked by a large northern pike (these pike have been anywhere from 34 to 44 inches . . . 10 to 25 pounds). Some of these paddlers have even landed the pike without having ever hooked it.

When pike see another fish in distress (i.e., hooked smallmouth), they see an opportunity to get a cheap meal. Once they latch on to that bass, they are so intent on consuming that fish that they won't let go until the very last minute. Sometimes they will let go right at the canoe, but much of the time, they lend themselves to be landed by the canoeist without ever having a hook in their mouth. That's a pretty cool thing to see. It's Darwin's theory at its best.

Boundary Waters Canoe Area

- **Location:** Northeastern Minnesota, on the border with Ontario, Canada (Quetico Provincial Park)
- **What You Fish For:** Smallmouth bass, pike, walleye
- **Highlights and Notables:** Few places on earth are as remote. This wilderness is a watery wonderland with lakes and rivers connecting every which way, some of the finest fishing in the Midwest.

Let's get this part out of the way. BWCA. That's how you see it everywhere. **B**oundary **W**aters **C**anoe **A**rea. Sometimes, they add an extra W, don't know Y. Look at a map and with adjoining Quetico Provincial Park, the connected lakes and rivers in this one-million-acre wilderness look like a circuit board.

Heading out for adventure

There is no one fishery that stands out as superior to others in this network. They're all good. Moose Lake, Fall Lake, Basswood Lake, and Kawishiwi River are a handful of the more noted fisheries.

Some hold big pike, some walleye, some smallmouth bass, some chunky bluegill. Some lakes hold one or the other, some all. Roadless. Outboard motors are illegal in the Boundary Waters. This is Canoe Country. Pretend you are a French-Canadian explorer-trapper-voyageur; nothing has changed in this wilderness for two hundred years.

Remoteness. Speaks for itself. One hundred fifty miles along the Minnesota-Ontario border.

Solitude. If you don't want to see another soul, none of the other 200,000 annual visitors, you don't have to, there's that much water (although you are still likely to spot an angler or two on your way from here to there; your best locale for loneliness is on the Canadian side). Fly-in, paddle-out options exist.

Starry skies, unmatched scenery. Lake after lake, some connected by rapids and quasi-rivers, canoe trails to many lakes, others reachable only by portage, the deep, dark pine forests impeding, imposing, tall rock faces staring back at you. The clarity of some of the lakes is breathtaking. Camping with all that water, the trees, the rocks, the huge expanse of black velvet night sky is tantamount to church service.

Shallow water angling. The lakes stay cool so you can fish in water not often over your head. Explosive action everywhere you go.

Options. Pike, walleye, smallmouth bass. Sometimes lake trout, largemouth bass. Imagine your options: BWCA has several thousand lakes and streams, most linked. The possibilities are endless.

The adventure of it all. You should really plan well before you enter the BWCA. You need to stay light, know where you'll be going. Bring enough food and supplies for camping but not so much you're weighted down. Two rods? One for lakers and pike and another for smallies and walleye? The choices and planning are sometimes the sweetest part of the trip and if not, then the reward is when you are in the wilderness and your planning and forethought pay off.

Many anglers/paddlers set up base camps just outside or just inside the wilderness and make day trips, quick forays into the wild. Most use Ely, Grand Marais, or Tofte as launching points but there are over sixty launch points, numerous loop trips, plenty of outfitters and guides and border resorts and lodges. Mosquitos, too, need I say more?

CONTACTS

Moose Bay Co.,
    www.moosebaycompany.com
Boundary Waters Canoe Area Wilderness,
    www.bwcaw.org
Quetico Provincial Park, www
    .ontarioparks.com/quet.html

Pine Point Lodge, Crane Lake, 800-628-
    4446, www.pinepointlodge.com
Seagull Canoe Outfitters and Lakeside
    Cabins, Grand Marais, www
    .seagulloutfitters.com

Driftless Area

- **Location:** Southeast Minnesota/northwest Illinois/northeast Iowa/southwest Wisconsin
- **What You Fish For:** Rainbow, brown and brook trout
- **Highlights and Notables:** A stunning collection of spring creeks and clear cold streams that flow through peaceful farms and under limestone cliffs

The Driftless Area. One of the oddest trout fishing locales on the planet. Look at that list above. These upper Midwest locales can't hold trout and even if they did, how good could the fishing possibly be? If you had no idea that this rather large pocket of land was traversed by fertile limestone spring-fed streams that hold good numbers of sizeable trout and the scenery is punctuated by wooded valleys and caves, gorges and verdant farmland, massive bluffs, valleys, towers and hills and dark rich soil, then you are in for a surprising treat. Read on.

The area's name, Driftless Area, comes from the fact this area has no *drift*. When glaciers descended upon this region thousands of years ago, they did not flatten the earth, no apocalyptic leveling; these slow-moving ice oceans did not leave typical

Kevin Garnett taking a nap. Sometimes they're wider, a KG and a Kevin McHale wide. Their quarry ranges from native brook trout, probably the westernmost native brook trout population, to brown trout (the finest quarry in these parts), and the ubiquitous rainbow. The rivers mostly run through pastureland (and are subject to floods and siltation) but also course through deep canyons they cut over time, past stands of trees, barns, through small towns, under bluffs and limestone outcrops. There are some rivers, like the Root River in southeast Minnesota, that serpentine through thickly forested, well, mountains, I guess, reminding one more of Pennsylvania or West Virginia than anything else. It's a mishmash of pastoral versus wild.

Springs that gush from hidden openings after having been filtered through a maze

glacial deposits, known as drift. Drift-less. The land undulates and is green and the rivers run clear and cold. Like a fish out of water, the Driftless Area's trout streams are gaining recognition, and with good reason—they are getting better and better.

If you look at a map, you are struck by how many streams there are in the Driftless. Coulee Country. Bluff Country. Hills that they call mountains, valleys deep and green and wide. This region, whatever we call it, has more than 500 spring creeks, over 3,000 river miles, over 20,000 square miles big. I don't know of anywhere else in the world that has more spring creeks or more fishable spring creeks in such a concentrated location.

Most streams are about as wide as one

of underground caves and aquifers fill the rivers with clean, cold water. Because of the constant temperatures, temps that are near 60 degrees, most streams are fishable year-round. The area's rivers have been assaulted by both poor farming practices (tree clearing, overgrazing) and nature's wrath (floods, erosion). There is an ongoing awareness, restoration, and rehabilitation of Driftless streams.

Wisconsin and Minnesota streams shut down shop at September's end. Iowa streams have no closed season for fly fishing. Some southeast Minnesota streams open January 1 to catch-and-release, while the regular season opens in April. Most of the streams in Wisconsin open for catch-and-release fly fishing starting in March, and the general opener is in early May.

Whitewater River

A must-fish river with plenty of types of water right in its own system. The Whitewater River looks, in places (the Middle Branch for one), like an English chalkstream with green vegetation of all kinds growing in all directions and trees, leafy, shady, placed elegantly along the riverbank. These lush stretches deserve a riverkeeper.

The main stem, in places, is open, almost channelized, and while you can see the rehab work here and there, the main part of the river does not have as much cover or riparian habitat. The tributaries are richer choices despite the fact that each year, so many anglers catch trout 3 to 5 pounds out of the deeper, less pretty main stem. All three forks converge at Elba and form the main stem.

South Fork of Whitewater gets the most votes for the best part of the system. The two main reasons are that South Fork has 1) all kinds of water, riffle-run-pools and the typical slow mirror-surfaced glides and flats of spring creeks and 2) the remoteness of the valley above Holt Spring. Sure, there are other reasons, like ten miles of fishy water, the exciting mixture of heavy woods and limestone bluffs and overall verdant nature, the wildness of the brown trout—and the list goes on and on.

Middle Fork has also had its share of fixing, from cribs to riprap to manufactured pools. It all helped because despite all the fishing pressure (especially in Whitewater State Park), the beautiful stream still produces. North Fork seems over its siltation problems, and its continued improved fishing bodes well.

Trout Run

Here's a gem, a small one that is one of the sleepers of the system. This feeder to the Middle Fork of the Whitewater is narrow, dense, fertile. Not to be confused with the bigger, better Trout Run of the Root River system.

Beaver Creek

Tributary to the Whitewater, Beaver Creek lies in southeastern Minnesota. Most of the anglers gang up on the water that flows through Beaver Creek Valley State Park, and it is fine water and a pretty park but you'd do better to fish one of the two branches or a different part of the main stem. Not far from Winnebago Creek. Anglers catch some big browns in the main river but also in gin-clear (I'd like to figure out some other way to indicate perfectly clear water other than using gin or vodka) East Branch of Beaver Creek.

Kinnickinnic River

Twenty-two miles of angling for brown trout in amazing numbers, present in numbers higher than any other Wisconsin stream. The Kinni is located near the town of River Falls and flows through a deep gorge. Treat yourself and fish the upper for wild brookies. It's one way to get away from all the Twin Cities' anglers (just an hour away).

Trout Run

Feeder creek to the Middle Fork of the Root River in southeast Minnesota, Trout Run is one of the top two or three fisheries in the Driftless. Thick with brown trout, some 3,500 per mile give or take a fish, Trout Run is one quality fishing experience. Sublime. Absurdly good insect hatches. Deep green pools up against limestone bluffs. Pocket water where browns rise to dries. Good access but you can still find your own water.

Rush River

At the edge of the Driftless, Rush River has a reputation for producing large brown trout, one over 13 pounds. The broad river is beautiful with its clear flats and green, medium-deep pools, the way that the trees come right up to the river and lean over, the playfulness of the choppy riffles, the bluffs that buttress the deeper pools. Not as remote as many other of these Driftless streams as it is close to the Twin Cities, an-

glers can fish from numerous access points in over twenty-three miles of river. Crayfish are part of the diet so tie your flies accordingly.

Kickapoo River

Arguably the top Driftless stream. Located near LaCrosse in southwestern Wisconsin, Kickapoo is the Lazarus of the area's streams, nearly dying a slow, silty death to erosion and floods and pesticides and proposed dams and so on. Cooperative management resurrected the river.

With curves like a woman's hips, this is seductive water, big water with big brown trout. This is one of your best chances to catch and land a trout in the 15- to 20-inch range. Brook trout live in the cold upper reaches and rainbows are mixed in here and there. The West Fork of the Kickapoo has some interesting catch-and-release fishing near Avalanche.

South Branch Root River

This is a famous branch, the one that made *Trout Unlimited's America's 100 Best Trout Streams* a few years back. This branch offers all kinds of water, with excellent access including three productive park stretches. The river runs the gamut from meadows to deep pools to riffles to rapids. One element that has made the South Branch famous is the incredible Trico hatch.

First stocked with brown trout in 1888, this large-for-this-area river holds browns that are about as large as you'll find in the Driftless. The South Branch is navigable by canoe. If you make the trip to this trout mecca, the South Branch of the Root River is a must-do. Preston and Lanesboro are your two top towns to lodge.

North Branch Root River

Feeds the South Branch and is ideal for small-stream lovers. The stream has some nice foamy dips and doodles, pools and runs, and flows through the Forestville State Park.

Winnebago Creek

Perhaps not as productive as many nearby southeastern Minnesota streams, it gets fished less and that's enough for some folks to try it.

Timber Coulee Creek

Vegetation-laden southwestern Wisconsin spring creek in what is known as Coulee Country. Wild trout. Narrow confines. Watercress. Thick wavy carpets of knee-high grasses in the surrounding fields; grasses that overhang the stream. A virtual salad of greens growing from bottom to surface. Clear water that moves fluidly, drippingly like Karo syrup. Brown trout that are challenging, difficult, wary, all the usual adjectives outdoors writers use to describe wild trout in spring creek waters. You won't catch many of them and if you do, you don't often catch the big ones and if you do, you did everything right. The usual things right? Accurate casts, stealth, thin leaders, small flies that match the hatch (the profound and ever-changing hatches), great drifts that master the multiple crosscurrents. Timber Coulee is a recipient of major dollars and hours of restoration and rehabilitation (riprap, banks solidification, that sort of thing).

Supposedly the word *coulee* is the French word for ravine. I guess. I didn't look it up, I'm just trusting Bob from Wisconsin on this one.

Rullands Coulee Creek

Tiny spring creek of about five miles that's a miniature version of its sister streams. Rullands Coulee feeds Timber Coulee south of Portland and with its wild brookies and browns, this underfished jewel gets a big thumbs up.

Spring Coulee Creek

Tributary to Timber Coulee, this pasture-stream has great cover for brown trout and some pretty scenery to boot, really beautiful meadow stretches.

Black Earth Creek

A modern rehabilitation success story, Black Earth Creek was almost destroyed by agricultural needs, then restored by volunteers and hard work to exist today as one of the most productive, beautiful and unique of all spring creeks in America. This limestone spring creek is narrow and offers challenging fishing for anglers hoping to land the 20-inch brown trout trophies swimming in its lush lairs and holding under the overhanging ledges full of foliage.

The flow is usually slow and slower, sometimes tricky, so patience and skilled casting are crucial to landing these finicky trout. Most of the insect hatches produce small mayflies and caddis to imitate, usually sizes 16 to 22.

In Black Earth Creek's middle and

lower sections, the large Hexagenia mayfly comes on the water in June, making for some once-in-a-lifetime fishing for thrashing large browns in a small spring creek.

French Creek

Wild trout stream six and a half miles long with surveys showing that an amazing amount of brown trout per square mile live in lower French Creek. In the upper forks, brook trout thrive. On French Creek, you can only use artificial lures and flies and any brown you catch, you must release. Rainbows (stocked) are also found in French Creek and some of the holdovers grow to fun-to-catch size.

North and South Bear Creeks

North and South Bear Creeks are so close to Waterloo Creek (in Iowa) that Sidd Finch could toss a baseball across a spiny ridge and hit either creek. A trail follows much of North Bear Creek as it moves through pastureland and forests. Both streams hold brown trout, and in their deep pools lie some good-sized browns. Bear Creek is stocked only with brown trout and is located just east of Fayette near Highlandville but you'll want to lodge and dine in Decorah.

Bloody Run

This Iowa stream is wooded, regulated, and nice fly fishing water for brown trout. Artificials only and a 14-inch size restriction.

Coon Creek

Way too many instream improvements for this slow-moving river to feel natural, espe-cially at the park in Coon Valley, but what was once mediocre water became productive water complete with handicapped access. The water above Coon Valley is narrow but not as fished, surprisingly good for brook and brown trout.

Coon Creek becomes Coon Creek below where Spring Coulee Creek marries Timber Coulee Creek. Sort of. Bohemian Valley comes into the mix, too, and on some maps, Coon Creek is known as Bohemian Valley. Confused enough yet? The Bohemian Valley Creek does all the required Driftless requisites: is hard to fish, meanders, runs through meadows, past woods, near dairy farms, holds browns.

Castle Creek

Feeder creek to the Blue River in the southwest corner of Wisconsin, this slow-moving, pasture-creek spates with any rain and is usually an off-color anyway. Castle Creek holds a healthy population of brown trout in its rich limestone waters and big deep pools. Sometimes called Fennimore Creek.

Rupprecht Creek

Also known as Rollingstone Creek, this little gem in southeastern Minnesota is less fished than so many others but with its deep water and meadow sections, it's a great getaway from the bigger popular streams.

Big Green River

Southwest Wisconsin meadow-type creek whose brown trout are as large as those that grow in much larger rivers. The Big Green

River is an undersung producer, full of deep runs and super cover. Word is, streamers in the undercut banks pull out the big boys.

Spring Branch

This Iowa spring creek is subtle, rich, an insect hatch heaven. The stream's habitat has been enhanced through habitat restoration, the trout made larger through special regulations, artificial flies and lures only, and a 14-inch minimum. Spring Branch is a popular place and the trout are even more skittish than those in other streams.

Waterloo Creek

In Minnesota, this small-to-midsized creek is called Bee Creek and then it flows into Iowa and through the hamlet of Dorchester where it is managed as a put-and-take fishery. Lower Waterloo is catch-and-release and artificials only. The browns grow thick and fat in this rich pastureland.

CONTACTS

Minnesota Department of Natural Resources, 651-296-6157, www.dnr.state .mn.us

Wisconsin Department of Natural Resources, 608-267-7498, www.dnr.wi.us

Iowa Department of Natural Resources, 515-281-5918, www.state.ia.us

Melvin Hayner, The Driftless Fly Fishing Company, www.minnesotaflyfishing .com

Bently's Outfitters, Prairie, 952-828-9554

Stewart Fishing Company, Red Wing, 651-267-4133

Bob Mitchell's Fly Shop, Bloomington, www.bobmitchellsflyshop.com

Spring Creek Specialties, Madison, WI, 608-241-4789

Fontana Sports Specialties, Madison, WI, 608-257-5043

The Fly Angler, Minneapolis, www .mnflyangler.com

Silver Trout, Black Earth, WI, 608-767-2413

Gander Mountain, Rochester, www .gandermountain.com

Lunde's Flyfishing Chalet, Mount Horeb, WI, 608-437-5465

Rocking K Fly Shop, Coon Valley, WI, 608-452-3678

Planet Trout Enterprises, Madison, WI, 608-273-9153

Bob Blumreich, guide, www.silverdoctor .net

Lake of the Woods

- **Location:** Northern Minnesota, shares border with Ontario, Canada
- **What You Fish For:** Pike, smallmouth bass, walleye, muskie
- **Highlights and Notables:** Whopper-sized lake that holds whoppers of all species

This massive border lake would be in anybody's top-ten list of fisheries for *each* of these species: smallmouth bass, pike, walleye, and muskies. I don't know many other lakes that can say that.

Lake of the Woods has as many lodges

and camps as fish—or so it seems—but the lake never seems crowded despite the fact the lake is close to Midwestern urban centers and the fishery just keeps on growing plenty of big fish. The lake is shallow, weedy, full of reefs. And humongous. Let me elaborate: 65,000 miles of shoreline, 14,000 islands, 65 miles long, 51 miles wide, 320,000 acres just in Minnesota, 600,000 acres across the border in Canada. Any of that impressive?

Impressive more are the quarry, numbers four. Smallmouth bass are so numerous, you can't help but catch as many as you want to catch. They aren't trophy size but they aren't small, either. The smallmouth fishery excels on the Canadian side of the border as do the muskies. The fish of 10,000 casts responds a lot quicker here. Lake of the Woods's muskies are typically 15 to 25 pounds and bigger since they eat walleyes, which with pike do better on the American side of the lake. Weird, huh?

The pike thrive in the shallows, grow up to four feet long. That's a Mickey Rooney size fish. Walleye are the staple fish of Lake of the Woods. Your average catch will run a few pounds weight and you have an excellent opportunity at walleyes over 7 pounds.

Camp or lodge on the lake (some stay in houseboats) but don't expect luxury lodging. These are rustic cabins and lodges meant for the blue-collar anglers.

CONTACTS

Arnesen's Rocky Point Resort, www
 .arnesens.com

Lake Vermilion

- **Location:** Northeastern Minnesota, close to Boundary Waters
- **What You Fish For:** Muskie, walleye, pike, and more
- **Highlights and Notables:** One of those pretty Minnesota lakes that has blue ribbon fishing for several species

I could make a case that Vermilion belongs in this book because of its outstanding fishing for a) muskie; b) pike; c) crappie; or d) walleye; e) smallmouth bass; and f) panfish, but I'd be lying. The fishing *is* good, sometimes outstanding, but the scenery, with its granite cliffs and giant conifers is heart-stopping year-round. *National Geographic* once listed Lake Vermilion as one of the top ten most scenic lakes in America. The sunsets on Vermilion are legendary.

With 40,000 acres and 365 islands, twenty-eight miles long, on the edge of the Boundary Waters Canoe Area, Vermilion has several outstanding tasteful resorts that cater to both families and fishermen. You hardly notice the marina, the resorts, because the lake is largely undeveloped. All the wildlife you could ever hope to see from deer to loon to moose and more. The area is so pristine, you almost feel as though fur traders are about to come tromping through the woods and offer you some pelts.

City Fishing

MINNEAPOLIS-ST. PAUL
Mississippi River, Lake Minnetonka, Metro Park Lakes

It would be too easy to make a play on words about twins or the Land of 10,000 Lakes so I'm going to pass on those and get right to the point: the fishing diversity in and around Minneapolis– St. Paul will feel like you just doubled your angling pleasure, like you've just fished 20,000 lakes. Ugh. Sorry.

Remember from the movie *Fargo* this exchange between one of the deputies and Marge's husband Norm, the wildlife painter?

Deputy: Hi, Norm. How ya doin', Margie? How's the fricassee?

Marge: Pretty darn good. You want some?

Deputy: Oh, no. I got . . . Hey, Norm. I thought you was goin' ice fishing up at Mille Lacs.

Understated Midwestern. Everybody's always about to go fishin' somewhere. And Mille Lacs is the iconic perch lake, the prototypical Minnesota perch lake that, requisitely, also holds walleye. One hundred thirty-two thousand acres. Come winter, you'll see the ice fishing hut city. And come spring, the walleye angling is topnotch.

In fact, if you head toward Brainerd, home of the Paul Bunyan and the Blue Ox, you'll fish more than Mille Lacs— you can fish the Mississippi River. Smallmouth bass and walleye are the primary catch in this part of the Mississippi River but you can also waste a day reeling in catfish, muskie, and gar. Since the Minnesota mentality leans toward lakes, the Mississippi River doesn't get many angling visitors.

White Bear Lake is a nice muskie lake just a twenty-minute drive from the twins. Lake Minnetonka is an outstanding bass lake and 3- to 5-pound bass are commonplace; muskies are the other target. Other area fisheries include little Lake Harriet (in the smack-dab middle of Minneapolis), Whitefish Chain, Mississippi River, St. Croix River, and many small local lakes offering prime bass fishing.

CONTACTS
Minnesota Department of Natural Resources, St. Paul, 651-297-4919

Minneapolis Park and Recreation Board Headquarters, Minneapolis, 612-230-6400

Thorne Brothers Custom Rod and Tackle, Fridley, 763-572-3782

Red Lake

- **Location:** Northern Minnesota
- **What You Fish For:** Crappie, walleye, and more
- **Highlights and Notables:** While you can fish for pike and perch and other species in Red Lake, crappie and walleye are the two main targets. One of the top ice fishing experiences up north.

Known to the Midwest as one of the best crappie lakes anywhere and the kicker is, anglers fish it only as Midwesterners can—through the ice. They limit out at fifteen per day. You might not know it but Red Lake has had the reputation as one of the finest walleye lakes in these parts. Quite the lake, eh?

And a big lake it is, too, with the Upper Red Lake at 108,000 acres (of which more than half are under the management of the Chippewa Indians, Red Lake Band). Minnesota Natural Resources manages the rest of the lake. The total Red Lake is actually two shallow basins and they hold, in addition to crappie and walleye, northern pike, whitefish, and perch.

The walleye population went bye-bye by the 1990s and a moratorium was enacted. The powers-that-be fixed the lake through intelligent recovery and this past year, limited-harvest walleye fishing was started. When it comes back to full form, Red Lake will have a double whammy to offer anglers.

CONTACTS
Minnesota Department of Natural Resources, 651-296-6157

MISSOURI

My brother Matt is nine years younger, the baby of the family. He wears golf shirts and ironed shorts, keeps his desk neat and clean, his hair is always combed, and even his garage and all his tools are in order. We're nothing alike. He was the right age at the wrong time, being a kid when the video game craze took over, when American kids became inert, so he never really took to fishing. But he could kick my butt at Madden Football or Super Mario or any other video game venture.

I wanted him to go fishing with me; perhaps there was still time to save his soul. He fell for it, agreed wholeheartedly, fishing with big brother. He might tell you, if he were to get space in this book (but he won't) that growing up, I played the big brother role all too well. Airplane sounds and circling spoon full of baby food, head-locks and pillow fights and headstart races and since I was nine years older, he couldn't win.

We fished for a number of days, from Mountain Fork River in Oklahoma to Little Missouri in Arkansas and up to the rivers of southern Missouri, tent camping the entire trip, something he had never done. One night over conversation around a camp-fire, he heard something. Initial suspect, me. *Did you throw a rock? Did you set this up? There's something out there, Mark.* And there was. I shined the flashlight and there were ten to twelve raccoons as big as basset hounds, one of them going thirty or more pounds, and they were creeping closer and closer. Matt had never been camping, never been around wildlife that crept up on you, so this was a real opportunity for a big brother, don't you think? When we shined the light back on them, they had opened the cooler and one of the plastic tubs we had left on the concrete picnic table. He went to bed right after that, ready to get lost in the safety of slumber. We heard drums all night (I had nothing to do with them) and I probably shouldn't have told him that there was a rogue Indian tribe not far from the river.

On one southern Missouri river, we were fishing a section with deep runs and deeper pools. Trout were rising but Matt was a newbie at fly fishing (heck, at fish-ing) so his casts were awful, his fly dragged, his line bunched. He spotted a large brown feeding and asked what he should do to get the fly over him. Matt was wearing the

Red Ball chest waders I had as emergency backups because they seemed more heavy duty than my breathables. They were not felt-soled and in suggesting that in order to catch the big brown trout, in telling him that he should step up on a wide flat sub-merged rock, a rock I knew was covered in slippery green algae-like vegetation, by put-ting him on that flat, greased platform, I was a bad big brother. Matt was the good little brother and listened to me. Never listen to your older brother. After he came up for air, sputtering and coughing, a good twenty feet downriver, he waded out, took off the wad-ers, poured out the water, walked to camp, changed his clothes and was through fishing for the trip. I don't think he's fished since.

Lake of the Ozarks

- **Location:** Western central Missouri
- **What You Fish For:** Bass and crappie
- **Highlights and Notables:** The fishing is a 7 or 8 on a scale of 10 but the scenery is off the charts. Here is one of the great lake fishing trips in the country, super for the family.

One of my guilty pleasures, of which I have many and so do you, is the reality television show *Dog the Bounty Hunter*. Dog's no Aristotle what with his mangled bromides and love of the underdog, and in the back of my head I know I should turn back to the History Channel or Discovery or PBS but there's just something about the Dog. One of my angling guilty pleasures is the Lake of the Ozarks. You can't go to this lovely but developed lake and be serious about angling, not in the same way you can if you go to a trophy bass lake like Dixon or a wilderness backcountry trip to a pike lake. Fishing is one of those things you get around to when you stay on Lake of the Ozarks.

Lake of the Ozarks provides the ultimate family lake experience complete with boats (every kind you can think of), waterskiing and other various water sports, floating lazily near the shore, sunning, hiking, shopping, and lots and lots of bass.

A panoramic view from the theoretical center-of-the-lake produces a view of tall bluffs, rocky points, and lakefront homes everywhere you look, each with green grassy lawns and thick stands of trees and boat docks that range from hideous to that-costs-more-than-my-house. Thousands of docks. But that's a good thing.

Docks mean anglers. Anglers mean brush piles. Brush piles mean cover. Docks provide cover. Bass and crappie need cover. Cool cycle, huh?

The bass don't grow to salivating size, nothing much more than 10 pounds but your average Lake of the Ozarks' largemouth goes 1 to 4 pounds. Plenty of 'em. Fishermen will tell you there are too many spotted bass, those notorious slow-growth bass. So Lake of the Ozarks is your top-of-the-line catch-your-limit lake.

The 59,000-acre lake, an impoundment of the Osage River, is made cool and clean and clear by nearly 1,000 springs. The lake has three distinct sections, the upper, middle, lower sections of the lake as well as three arms: Gravois Arm, Grandglaize Arm, Niangua Arm. Water clarity is typically clear, depths deep especially in the lower lake, but the water gets tinged as you head to the upper parts.

One of the best of its kind, where the lake combines fishing, recreation, second homes, eateries, shopping, marinas, motels, lodges, resorts, condos, cabins, campgrounds, and—a sore spot for lovers of nature—incredibly heavy boat traffic in summer, so much so that some say that because of it, the bass don't get fished for much in the heat. Night fishing during summer, a tactic to avoid the boat wakes and noise of day, is popular. Located 35 miles southwest of Jefferson City, the lake is nearly equidistant between St. Louis and Kansas City.

Besides the largemouth, anglers fish for crappie, white bass, catfish, walleye, and my favorite, hybrid striped bass, one of the meanest, fiercest freshwater fighters. Some anglers fish for paddlefish (134-pounder caught here) but man, are they ugly. The fish, not the anglers. Guilty pleasures. There's just something about Lake of the Ozarks.

CONTACTS

Lake Area Chamber of Commerce, www
   .funlake.com/cvb/chambers
Missouri Department of Conservation,
   Camdenton, 573-346-2210

North Fork of the White River

- **Location:** Southern Missouri
- **What You Fish For:** Rainbow and brown trout
- **Highlights and Notables:** The best trout stream you've never heard of

When you go fish this river, and you should, when you talk about it, don't say the full name. Act the local. It's the North Fork.

The North Fork is the best trout stream in Missouri. The North Fork originates in the Mark Twain National Forest and flows through some of the most spectacular scenery in the Midwest. The twelve miles below where Rainbow and North Fork springs enter is where the best action takes place. It is here at the two springs where the river gets cold and doubles in size that the trout fishing begins.

While more like a western stream than any other Ozark river, the North Fork is a big river and not an easy river to wade. It's easy to fall on these slippery rocks and besides, you'll be dodging canoes more than fishing. So hop in a boat of some sort. You see boats of all kinds. Amy and I saw a nice couple in their 50s tump their canoe in this stretch and we helped them retrieve it off a long gravel run. But floatfishing is the best method to fish this river. But if you don't boat, you can still find plenty of wading access. Just be prepared to slip and fall.

North Fork is a designated trophy trout stream where fishermen can cast flies for wild rainbows and holdover browns that average 12 to 15 inches with some that grow to 10 pounds or more. I had a day where almost every fish I caught above Blair Bridge was 18 inches, a carbon copy. The browns were a harvest yellow and the rainbows wore ruby and emerald like sparkling jewels. I caught all of them on nymphs, on Copper Johns to be exact. Sure, the North Fork has solid hatches and at certain times the trout will take dry flies, but day in, day out, you're gonna do better with nymphs.

While the river has a naturally reproducing population of rainbow trout, browns are stocked. But they don't act like it. They are wary and gain color quickly.

I am not going to recommend you make a trip all the way to southern Missouri just for the North Fork. I'd make it an adjunct trip to Crane Creek and the state parks fisheries, or with the White and Norfork Rivers. Or as an excursion from Branson.

Once you're there, the dense forests, overlooking bluffs, low-slung mountains and solitude will make you glad you came.

Many float the river until they find a likely spot to pull up and wade to fish the riffles and runs. Canoe traffic can become fairly heavy in the summer. The upper section is typical Ozark river, warmer, ideal for smallies. The trout water is thought of as the upper float and the lower float. Both are worthy.

You're not on the tourist path and honestly, most of the folks you meet on the river are locals, so you're dealing with a blue ribbon river that few know about. They're off at the Little Red or White in Arkansas. That leaves you all alone with the big browns and wild rainbows.

Top Waters of Missouri: St. Louis to Branson

- **Location:** Central to southern Missouri
- **What You Fish For:** Trout and bass
- **Highlights and Notables:** What a corridor of fishing, the Ozarks, and angling, scenic lakes, and cascading rivers.

Urban fishing. St. Louis: 2.7 million people in the greater St. Louis area. Lots of business and air traffic goes through here. Branson: 7 million tourists annually. I'm speaking to you eleven million people who might be traveling to St. Looey or Branson and want to spend a part of a day or a full day fishing. My good friend Doc Thompson is from St. Louis but he left there as quickly as he could and has been a fishing guide on the Cimarron River for the last fifteen years. He goes back to the Arch City several times a year because he and his family hold Cardinals season tickets.

Branson is the Live Music Capital of the World, so they say. Beyond the kitschy concerts by has-beens and wannabes, Branson has become a full-fledged tourist destination as well as a corporate retreat. So if you are traveling to or through St. Louis or Branson, you're real close to some quality angling. Don't pass it up because that's just bad karma. Here are the hotspots:

Eleven Point

The Eleven Point is the longest cold water trout fishery in Missouri and when you fish it, especially by boat or canoe, you'll be amazed at how fishy it all looks. The river has a wild trout-managed area for five and a half miles of its run from Greer Spring Branch down to Turner Mill. The other fourteen miles are managed as a put-and-take fishery. You can guess which area has the better fishing.

The trout average 10 to 12 inches but reach 18 to 20 inches and bigger. Wading the Eleven Point is best done by floating a boat and getting out to wade. Fish around structure like submerged logs and don't miss running imitations through the deeper pools. The river is wide in spots (to 150 feet across) and runs through the scenic Mark Twain National Forest.

Crane Creek

Everything I've heard about Crane Creek the last couple of years tells me that the water flow is just plain low. A few years ago, the last time I fished there, the water was fine and the fish were plentiful and big. What I'm hearing is that the water is so low that the trout are congregating in the pools and that their size has diminished.

When the flows are good, there are three miles of excellent spring creek fishing for some large, wild, colorful, unusually feisty rainbows. Residing in spring-fed, mossy Crane Creek is the last pure strain of the McCloud River rainbow trout, brought in many decades ago from California. Thirty minutes southwest of Springfield, Crane Creek is a narrow spring creek with a gravel bottom making for easy wading, and plenty of pools and riffles over a streambed of pebbles and under an umbrella of hardwood trees. All trout caught in the Wire Road Wildlife Area must be done so on artificial lures and flies and must be immediately returned to the water.

So until you know what the flows are like (and anglers were still catching trout even in low flows), I can't recommend a side trip to Crane. If they get some rain and the water levels go up, it's fishing time for these wary wild trout.

Maramec Spring Trout Park and Meramec River

Weird that we have to play this alphabet soup game. The spring in the park has an A but the river has lost the A and replaced it with an E. I think. In the park, Maramec has only one mile of fishing in its spring creek with no flies-only restrictions in scenic environs but it empties into the Meramec giving the river another nine miles of coldwater fishing for trophy browns and rainbows to several pounds. The Meramec here is managed as a trophy trout area and for good reason; there are some big trout swimming here (in the river, out of the park, with an E not an A).

Maramec Spring Trout Park (573-265-7801) is one of four state trout parks in Missouri and lies two hours west of St. Louis. I'd skip the park if it's crowded (and it often is) and fish the river that the spring feeds. From the mouth at the confluence downstream for another seven or so miles has some super water. Tall trees line either side of this forty-five- to ninety-foot wide river so you have shady spots for the trout to hide. The river has lovely runs that are as deep as a tall goat. Dark green pools are your bonanza. Average trout, both rainbow and brown, run 11 to 15 inches but 20-inch trout are here, too. This river holds possibly the best insect hatches of all the trout parks in Missouri.

You enjoy clean cool water because Maramec is the fifth-largest spring in the Show-Me State (the spring dumps over 100 million gallons spring water into Meramec a day). Canoe or wade. Either works.

Both the park and the main stem can be crowded at times especially during weekends, opening day, and holidays but you can still find ideal days and your own water especially in the winter. The park is owned by the James Foundation but the trout fishery is managed by the Missouri Department of Conservation, who stocks 170,000 10- to 14-inch rainbows per year. Maramec Spring is open daily from March 1 through October 31. There are no restrictions to tackle during this season. The winter catch-and-release season is restricted to artificial flies and opens on the second Friday of November through the second Sunday of February on Fridays, Saturdays, and Sundays.

Bennett Springs

One time Amy and I were walking (as it was snowing) from a section of this stream by a deep pool by a bridge that had more anglers and gawkers than we liked. We passed a shallow pool and stopped. In the pool were two spawning trout or at least wannabe spawning trout . . . and a snake. The snake slithered sneakily behind the two lovey-dovey fish but before he could do his snake thing, one of the fish turned on him aggressively and chased him out of the pool. I reckon that was the female, right? We also saw an albino frog swimming across another pool. When we got to this one stretch we like, with divots in the streambed where trout hold, I caught a 17-inch rainbow on a midge pupa. Then the snow really started coming down.

Only two miles of stream flow in Bennett Springs State Park and it's narrow and often crowded. Over the years, some really large trout have been caught here and the reputation is one of a big rainbow trout producer. Still, an obese brown trout that weighed nearly 17 pounds and was over 26 inches long and looked more like a sowbelly largemouth was caught a couple of years ago. Bennett Springs always has trout over 10 pounds living in it and the average

size trout has to be around 2 to 3 pounds. Catching them ain't easy with the clear water and being forced to fish spring-creek tactics.

The water at Bennett Springs is so clear that sight casting to the hundreds of visible fish in an afternoon spoils you. One section of the river has fly fishing–only regulations. Bennett Springs fishes well in the winter, too. Regulations allow winter fishing in these state parks, on Fridays, Saturdays, and Sundays from 8:00AM to 4:00PM from early November to mid-February.

Fishing in the winter means catch-and-release fishing only. The colorful stocked trout hold over and grow to some impressive sizes, and you'll see these lazily putt-putting around in the crystal clear water. Anglers can fish runs, flats and glides, small pools, riffles, and cutbanks. The river has several handicapped ramps on some very nice water. Take a gander at the fish hatchery on Bennett Springs, and check out some of the monsters in the raceways. From Bennett Springs the stream flows into the Niangua River and provides another ten miles of solid water downstream. The Niangua below the confluence is good for a few trout and below for smallmouth.

Roubidoux Creek

For fishermen wanting a chance to catch browns weighing several pounds in a small stream, Roubidoux Creek (about three total miles) fits the bill. The creek is wadeable, has good room for backcasting, and runs through Waynesville, and the water from Roubidoux Spring is clean and cold. The lower 2.2 miles of the creek are managed as a trophy trout area, so anglers are limited to flies and artificial lures, and can keep three trout each over 15 inches. The water goes off-color at times but that's actually a good time to be on the water. Fall and winter are the top times to fish here.

Little Piney Creek

Like most of the trout fisheries in Missouri, it too is short but productive. I don't understand why more anglers don't fish Little Piney Creek. On the negative side, there's not a lot of instream cover and the water is as clear as a glass of Everclear. On the plus side, you get choppy riffles and runs deep enough to turn an aqua-green. You get bigger trout than most folks think (15 inches and up—no lunkers though). Little Piney will never be a trophy trout stream nor even a top-flight quality fishery but it's pretty and holds trout and it's not far from our two metropolises.

Most trout at spring-fed Little Piney will run in the 9- to 12-inch range but you'll catch them on both sides of that. Autumn is a great time to succeed on the Little Piney and less crowded, too. The riparian habitat in some places goes right to the water and can catch your offerings. In other places, trees with exposed roots threaten to plop right down in the water if a good rain comes and washes out the rest of the embankment. Little Piney has some big rocks here and there, gravelly areas, lots of wide flats, overhanging trees and brush, V-shaped channel-runs, a dilapidated fallen bridge, a few bend pools, and skinny overall water. It's fun to fish.

The river has both wild and stocked trout and I'm hearing that there may be improvements on the way to create more wild trout water out of Little Piney. Nearby Capps Creek has two miles of fishing for rainbows and browns near Monett. Capps is a sweet little surprise where the picnickers outnumber anglers (but no need to go out of your way just to get here. If you're south of Springfield, drop in). Walk upstream from the dam and enjoy a couple hours fishing.

Lake Taneycomo

More river-like than lake-like, this impoundment of the White River grows trout in a hurry. Overall, the fishery is perhaps the best opportunity in Missouri for anglers to tie into a big rainbow or brown (Bennett Springs fishing is tough, y'all). Half the fun of fishing here in what is technically a river is just sitting and watching the big bruisers cruising in the clear water.

Lake Taneycomo won't make you think of wild places—the shore is lined with lakehouses (riverhouses?) ranging from those small cabins my Uncle Bob can barely afford to those houses big enough that whoever owns them doesn't worry about how much it cost. I think it's kinda pretty in a development sort of way. Located so close to Branson, you won't be fishing alone.

Big fish, especially the brown trout but you'll catch more rainbows. Folks wade the upper (if the generators are not running) and boat both the upper and lower sections. Bank fishing is good up and down the riverlake.

Table Rock Lake

Table Rock Lake has good fishing for big trout as well, but like the other two lakes, fly fishing isn't good except in the lake's spawning tributaries in the winter. The lake is better known for its bass fishing, which for some time now has enjoyed a national reputation. Located six miles southwest of Branson, it's always crowded. Still, at roughly 47,000 acres and with 800 miles of winding shoreline, you can find your own little haunt. Why so crowded? Thirteen campgrounds around the lake, resorts that number several dozen, marinas galore.

Three big checks on the positive side for Table Rock: 1) it is oh-so-close to Branson; 2) since development has been kept to a minimum, the lake's natural beauty, with its thick forests, meadows, coves, and steep bluffs has been retained; 3) the lake is loaded with largemouth, smallmouth, white, and Kentucky bass. Table Rock doesn't produce trophy bass but makes up for it in the numbers and quality of the bass.

The water is clear and lukewarm—scuba diving is popular in this lake. The lake has tremendous forage fish and submerged timber. That adds up to superior habitat to grow bass. Table Rock has populations of walleye, crappie, and catfish worth setting out for, too.

Big Cedar Lodge

If you like Bass Pro Shops, you'll like Big Cedar Lodge near Branson in Ridgedale. A bit of a mini-outdoor-theme-park feel to it but great for families, ideal as a home base to watch has-been crooners in Branson, go to Bass Pro Shops in Springfield, fish a bit in Missouri and a lot in Arkansas. From golf courses to horseback riding to chuckwagon cookouts to swimming to boating to tennis to the spa (yes, outdoorspeople, a spa). You know, an outdoors theme park. A world-class outdoors theme park resort to be sure and set into the Ozark Mountains with a variety of types of lodging. Not for everyone but will be ideal for others (family, outdoors nuts, folks who like Branson, etc.).

Montauk State Park

Here we have a park at the headwaters of the Current River, one of the finer fishing scenes in Mizzou. In the cooler and colder months, you can find your own water in the park and catch some nice trout. In the summer, in the park, under the trees, people play in the spring. You can't fish with people playing in your water. Leave the park and fish the Current below where the Montauk water enters.

You're gonna love the Current but you're going to need a canoe to love it properly. You can wade but wading takes you precariously through water over your head or through heavy brush.

Browns that range from 12 inches to (get this) 25 inches hold in the Current and you'll be surprised how many caught weigh 3 to 6 pounds. The water most of the year is clear and that makes for difficult fishing. When it's murky, streamers are deadly. Deep runs and deeper pools hold these big browns, including a 13-pounder a few years ago.

The Current flows past limestone bluffs and it was under one of those bluffs that Amy once caught and landed a near-trophy brown and it rolled and took with it the last white Marabou Zonker (which was the only thing working) and neither of us caught anything the rest of the day. Some days, streamers are ineffective and you have to turn to size-18 BWOs and other small mayflies. In its lower reaches, the only access is by canoe and canoes there will be, sometimes in numbers. The river has a variety of regulations and restrictions so check first.

Roaring River

Swift-moving river where in 1966 a UFO was spotted and photographed and made national headlines. Located south of Cassville, the Roaring River runs through a state park but below the park is where all the headline-grabbing big-trout action takes place now.

Taneycomo and Bennett Springs are the top two lunker trout producers and I'd place Roaring River third. With its quicker water, choppier riffles, I like fishing Roaring River more than any other Missouri stream. I haven't caught one of the notorious 7- to 10-pound trout but I have seen them, both in the park and in short deep holes below the park. Unlike some of the other rivers below trout parks, the Roar-

ing River doesn't seem as pressured. Sure, the park's got its share of visitors, some 100,000 a year, but for some reason Roaring River proper seems to only have trout and aliens.

Mill Creek

Spring-fed stream with wild rainbow trout near Rolla. No wider than a prone Mickey Rooney in places and wider than two lying-down Shaqs in others, Mill Creek flows beneath an awning of tall brush and big shady trees. Fun little stream with fun little rainbows. Not much of size.

Blue Springs Creek

Another wild trout stream, even smaller than Mill Creek. Blue Springs Creek is a feeder to Meramec River. The sinuous stream should interest fly fishers (too shallow for conventional tackle), especially those who appreciate dry flies, wild trout, and catch-and-release fishing.

CONTACTS
Missouri Trout Hunter, 573-578-2222
Stream Side Adventures, 913-645-1994
Semper Fly Fishing Adventures, 417-331-1775
Thompson Fishing Guide Service, 417-424-BASS
Missouri Department of Natural Resources, Division of State Parks, Jefferson City, 800-334-6946

Truman Reservoir

- **Location:** West central Missouri
- **What You Fish For:** Largemouth bass, catfish, white bass, crappie
- **Highlights and Notables:** Big under-rated bass lake, ideal for anglers who love to fish to cover

The blue, murky, shallow-water lake with a thousand miles of shoreline, so many coves, creeks, rivers, bays, and hidden cul-de-sacs and so many dead trees and stumps and fallen logs, it's as if the gods played an enormous game of Pick-Up-Stix with the surrounding forests. Aka Truman Lake.

Fifty-five thousand acres of catfishing heaven, an impoundment on the Osage, Pomme de Terre, and Grand Rivers located in the heart of the Show-Me State, less than two hours drive from Kansas City. Truman Lake is known for prime bass fishing and it's not as if the largemouth have nowhere to hide. This propeller-chompin' lake has as much cover as any lake I've ever seen. Fishing for blue, channel, and flathead catfish is always good and makes Truman one of the best catfish lakes in the nation.

So big cats and bass, show me what else? Truman Lake and its silt, its stained water holds white bass, bluegill, shark (just checking to see if you were paying attention), striper, hybrid bass, crappie, and especially catfish and an improving resource, walleye.

NEBRASKA

Lake McConaughy Reservoir

- **Location:** Western Nebraska
- **What You Fish For:** Walleye
- **Highlights and Notables:** This long narrow big lake is one of the best places to catch big walleye in the country.

Lake McConaughy at 35,000 acres is one of the top walleye fisheries in the nation. "Big Mac," as it is known locally, yields great numbers of fat, long walleye, many in the 8-pound or better range. McConaughy holds the Nebraska record with a 16-plus pound walleye. The walleyes here fatten up on alewives. That name always strikes me funny and I picture some stout woman in an apron working in a bar serving bawdy anglers. And walleye. My Mamaw has this one old boy she grew up with who was nicknamed Walleye because, well, he was goggle-eyed. So between alewives and walleyes,

I can't quit giggling and conjuring foolish thoughts. Big Mac also holds large lake-run rainbows and healthy brown trout (and it has been stocked from time to time with kokanee and Coho salmon).

Merritt Reservoir

- **Location:** Northern central Nebraska
- **What You Fish For:** Everything, but your main two are muskie and catfish
- **Highlights and Notables:** One of those local/regional delights, a muskie hotspot, a worthy drive from any Midwestern city or town

If you're not living in the Midwest, this dreamy middle-of-nowhere fishery is out of your range. Denver's about as far away as can be considered. Not many outside of Nebraska have ever heard of Merritt; only a few more have heard about its big sister, Lake McConaughy.

Unless you chase muskellenge, *Esox masquinongy*.

You're not listening to me because you might catch pike, bass, channel catfish, walleye, perch, crappie, white bass but the key other than all this high-level variety is the muskie. The state's top catfishery is Merritt. The deep lake has a cool, eerie setting, the Nebraska sandhills. Winter anglers ice fish. Merritt receives steady inflow from the Snake River and Boardman Creek, so drawdown is not typically a problem. You are not listening. None of this matters.

Muskies. It's all about the muskies.

The most elusive, the most tenacious, the most prehistoric and aggressive and smartest freshwater fish in the world. They eat snakes, ducks, mice, frogs, smallmouth bass (in some places in Canada where smallmouth coexist, anglers are scared out of their wits when they are reeling in a bronzeback and a muskie slashes through the water to steal their catch), and small mammals.

You ever met a muskie hunter? They're out to break records. They almost always have facial hair. They love gimme caps and hooded sweatshirts. They have this weird piercing look in their eyes. Muskie hunters are as much predators as the toothy meanies they chase. Once word gets out about these enormous monsters, muskie aficionados will travel from all parts of the world for the hunt.

A muskie caught at Merritt is the state record—41 pounds, 8 ounces. Since 1992, no fewer than six muskie have been caught (and witnessed) that weighed from 40 to 50 pounds. But only a couple were landed.

Nebraska is not in your normal muskie territory. The population of muskies isn't even all that well known (yet) outside of the Midwest. Merritt Muskies grow big on the healthy population of alewives and since not many catch or land these vicious attackers, they grow to giant sizes.

Sure, sure, others will come to 2,900-acre Merritt Lake for the fantastic catfishing and to take a shot at all the other species, all the while dilly-dallying along the white-fine-sand beaches but beware, there are muskies below the surface, and worse yet, muskie-trophy hunters above.

Located twenty-one miles southwest of Valentine. Nearest highway, Nebraska 97.

CONTACTS
Merritt Reservoir Visitor Center, 402-376-2969

Nebraska Travel and Tourism, 800-228-4307

Merritt Resort, Valentine, 402-376-3437

Merritt Reservoir, Valentine, 402-684-2921

NORTH DAKOTA

Devil's Lake

- **Location:** Northeastern North Dakota
- **What You Fish For:** Walleye and yellow perch
- **Highlights and Notables:** Popular, famous, still productive walleye lake

This is one of those lakes that despite articles and publicity, despite angling pressure, can still produce fifty walleyes in a day for anglers. Lots of 3-pounders and 9-pounders are not uncommon. Pike, bass, and perch round out the menu. At one time, Devil's Lake was a big 45,000-acre lake and then it rained and rained and rained and it became a 150,000-acre lake. This gave the lake new habitat and submerged cover and the fishing just got better and better. Ice fishing for yellow perch is about as good as it gets here on Devil's Lake.

Missouri River

- **Location:** Through Montana, North Dakota, South Dakota
- **What You Fish For:** Walleye and more
- **Highlights and Notables:** Fertile, huge river

Big slow wide water, 700 miles of fishable water. Lakes Sakakawea and Oahe and Sharpe and Francis Case are linked together by this massive mighty river. All are good walleye lakes and below the dams, great fishing. Walleyes are the key and bass are plentiful but incidental. I recommend fishing this historic river if you live anywhere within a day's drive or if you end up near it on a business trip or at Aunt Mamie's house.

OHIO

Lake Erie

- **Location:** Northern Ohio (and also New York, Pennsylvania, and Ontario, Canada)
- **What You Fish For:** Smallmouth bass, walleye, steelhead, perch
- **Highlights and Notables:** You could make a case that Lake Erie is the best place to fish on the planet. It certainly is one of the finest for smallmouth bass.

Lake Erie moves with current like a river, but has the heft and breadth of a lake, the gargantuan qualities of an ocean. I didn't

grow up near oceans or big lakes and it was a shock to my system the first time I laid eyes on Lake Erie. Beautiful? Maybe, in a weird global sort of way. Overwhelming? Understatement. It's easy to hear, like we big river guys tell newbies, break it down into sections, just fish right in front of you and don't try to fish it all at once. Whatever.

The lake has a strong current especially on the eastern side of the lake (the deeper side of the lake). This is probably the best smallmouth lake in the world. Smallmouth like to chase down emerald shiners, then when it warms, they dine on golden shiners then go for crayfish, so plan accordingly. You really have to weight it to get it down in that current.

Twenty-pound limits are common, 5-pound smallies are everywhere, 2-pounders are a nuisance. From the West Basin to the East Basin, it's the best smallmouth fishery on the planet. Zebra mussels invaded in the 1980s but they didn't spell doom and gloom. They are water filters and the clarity is better than ever and so is the fishing. Five pounds for a smallmouth is becoming a common size. That's crazy. Hire a guide your first go-round, learn the techniques and hotspots, and then go out on your own.

I'm not hyping. The smallmouth are some of the heaviest and largest in the world. Three to 6 pounds. Six is a whopper anywhere else and it is here, too, but how about a real chance at a 7-pounder?

How about an 8-pound bronzeback? You can catch them with any kind of tackle including fly gear. You can catch them from kayaks and boats and the shore and wading and piers and float tubes.

The central and eastern basins are the best for bronzebacks (and this includes Ohio, New York, and Pennsylvania). Go for offshore drops and humps in the shallower western basin, the islands and shoals are good; other places, look for the usual smallmouth haunts because Erie has them—dropoffs, rockpiles, rocky points, break walls, piers, etc. When the light is right, in the spring, you can find them in the shallower water, the sandy flats. There's a variety of fishing regs for each state's part of this monstrous lake, so check before you head out.

The carp? Pick a shoreline, any shoreline, any of the endless miles of it. The carp are there in the shallows, up to 25, 30 pounds.

Spring and early summer is perfect time for both pike and muskie. Yellow perch puts food on the table and it's hard not to catch them if you want to—find a large school and work it.

Erie has held its share of IGFA records for various species. Erie is the shallowest of the five Great Lakes. Smallest of the five. Best fishing of the five.

Erie has some of the country's top warmwater fishing and is one of the best smallmouth fisheries in the world. Tributaries flow into the huge lake, rivers where monstrous steelhead and gargantuan Chinook salmon go to pitch woo. What else can you catch?

Largemouth bass in the weeds of the bays. Carp (hey, don't make fun of these guys—they give you another option, you stalk them in the shallows and they grow pretty darned big). Muskie, northern pike, steelhead (wild and stocked); lake trout, but the populations are in flux, not doing so well right now. Because it's so big, near so many populated areas, access points are a dime a dozen (except for New York where most of the shore is privately owned). The average depth is around sixty feet in this rocky lake. Rocks mean walleyes, especially in western Erie but found all over, many in the 6- to 9-pound class. And the rivers that dump into Erie are walleye prime-time fisheries even though the population has declined the last few years.

CONTACTS

Ottawa County Visitors Bureau, www
.lake-erie.com

Bob Troxel, www.lakeeriesmallmouth.com

Jay's Fly Shop, London, Ontario, Canada,
www.jaysflyshop.com

Grindstone Angling, Waterdown, Ontario,
Canada, www.grindstoneangling.com

Angler's Mail, Cleveland, OH, 440-884-
7877

Mad River Outfitters, Columbus, OH,
www.madriveroutfitters.com

Lake Erie Ultimate Angler, Erie, PA, www
.lakeerieultimateangler.com

We'd had days on the Mountain Fork River where we each caught and released enough trout that we lost count and spent a lot of time joking and laughing. This wasn't one of those days.

It was cold and wet and the fishing was dead. We never knew if the rumor was true (but we figured it was) but we heard for years that the Broken Bow woods were one of the top marijuana-growing regions in the country. You'll believe it too if you ever go there and see how thick and expansive these forests are. There could still be moonshine being made in those hills for all I can tell.

Ken Cole decided to stay at the Cold Hole in the drizzling cold rain casting to this one fat, finnicky fish while we fished upstream. He kept putting one hand in his pocket, then the other. When he spoke, his words came out in cartoonish ice fog.

"Y'all go on ahead. I'm gonna catch this pig."

When we came back two hours later, we'd only caught a handful of trout between us, and Ken's bamboo rod was bent over like an old man. He threw us a look that in one frozen communique told us that he had not moved during this entire time and had just now hooked up with the lunker. The fat rainbow jumped out of the water, tailwalking, its emerald and pink sides flashing shades of the rainbow like a prism tossed in the air.

With one shake of its head, the 3-pound rainbow threw the fly and splashed down into the deep blue pool. Ken grinned that impish grin of his.

"He got away." We nodded. "But at least I got him for a minute."

Sometimes, that's all you get on the Mountain Fork. And since you're just glad to be fishing on such a scenic, challenging trout stream only three hours from the Dallas Metroplex, less from Oklahoma City, hooking up and losing a 20-inch trout is a mighty fine feeling.

How good is the river? I know a guy, who knows a guy who caught and released a 27.5-inch brown trout last year. This same guy, who shall remain nameless because he says he will take me to the exact spot this fish was caught, has seen 10-pound browns holding in this river. (Yes, he has shown me photos of these fish.) In case you don't believe the rumors, a trout weighing nearly 10 pounds was caught and certified this past year in Zone Two. They're there and they are getting bigger and more plentiful each season. Guides on the Mountain Fork are seeing 20-inch fish caught every third trip now instead of every three months a few years back.

While most anglers fish Spillway Creek (a diversion of Mountain Fork River that later empties into the main stem, and is excellent in its own right), if you want to go after the big ones, if you want to fish the 100-yard wide stretches of the river, if you want to catch lots of trout, then fish downstream of the state park in sections two and three.

As Ken Cole, of Flies by Night Outfitters, who holds fly fishing classes and personal instruction on this river, shares, "There's twelve-plus miles of fishable water on the Lower Mountain Fork. What was hot yesterday, last week, or during the same weather period last year, can turn into the Dead Sea for no known reason. Just because fish are rising and there are caddis on the water, doesn't mean the rise is to caddis." Cole pauses for emphasis.

"Especially on this river."

Tanks

Bobby Boswell teaches with me at North Heights. He's an Oklahoma boy and if you're from Texas, that says a mouthful right there. Texans have a problem with Oklahomans in that Sooners don't have the inferiority complex that Texans demand from their neighboring states. Bobby's no exception. He's perfectly okay with his Oklahoma-ness, his drawl that, while similar to a Texan accent, is a little more nasal, a bit more rural, his disdain for all things metrosexual, frou-frou. From his gray flattop to his worn jeans, Bobby is elemental, old-school, like those ranchers in their cowboy hats and boots who meet for coffee at the diner near the town square in almost any Oklahoma (or Texas) small town.

Bobby grew up fishing like most boys of the South do: climbing over barbed wire fences and fishing Farmer Bob's tank. If you're not from the South, you might not know what that means. Elsewhere, tanks are ponds.

Fishing tanks/ponds is one of the special treats an angler can enjoy. You have this intimate body of water all to yourself and the odds are, if you've played it correctly, that this murky tank/pond hasn't been fished in years. Maybe you'll land the big bass who eats the bullfrogs and small ducks and perch that live (or lived) here. Somewhere near you, even if you live in the big city, you can find a farmer willing to let you fish his pond. It's worth it. The primer fishing experience for most Americans is worth revisiting.

At a southern tank, you have to be prepared to not fish as much as you do to fish. Fishing tanks/ponds take you back to your boyhood—that's the fun of fishing them. There's likely a shade tree nearby that's calling out your name for a quick nap or for you to see how high you can climb. There are birds to toss rocks at, frogs to catch, ants to avoid. And cottonmouths, aka water moccasins.

Imagine Bobby and his two brothers on an Oklahoma tank, with or without permission, it hardly matters because after all, what rancher/farmer in his right mind cares if you fish his old hog tank anyway? The three boys give up catching perch as soon as the Okie sun turns hot so they swim. And swimming with them is a water moccasin. I've been attacked twice by these watery poisonous serpents and one tried to get in the canoe with me. If he had gotten in, Papaw was all by himself on that one, because I was bailing on him.

Anyway, the three boys *catch* the water moccasin and start playing with him. This snake goes three feet, thick as a baseball bat. They notice a bulge in the hissing snake but it doesn't stop them from swinging the snake like a bolo and eventually, to their surprise, the snake vomited out a thousand baby water moccasins it had been holding inside. These kids were brave but hey, nobody ever said Oklahomans were smart.

Ponds or tanks, Texas or Oklahoma, Maine or Colorado, if you've fished them, you know the secret appeal.

Lake Eufaula

- **Location:** Eastern Oklahoma
- **What You Fish For:** Largemouth and smallmouth bass
- **Highlights and Notables:** Ideal family getaway and an emerging smallmouth bass fishery

East of Henryetta (home of Dallas Cowboy hero Troy Aikman), in east central Oklahoma, this heavily-used 102,000-acre lake on the Canadian River is one of the best crappie lakes in the country. If you don't want to fish for crappie, you might get a hankering to fish for gar.

Eufaula has had fair to middling bass fishing in its shallow, dusky water, a reputation more for largemouth than smallmouth but the bronzeback fishery has surpassed its bigger cousin. Stocked only in the early 1990s, the lake is now producing smallies up to 7 pounds.

Traditionally a family weekend lake, Eufaula is busy. Somehow, any angler you talk to, any family you see (their boat often beached on the sandy shore) is catching fish, has a nice stringer. In the spring, anglers move into the shallows and coves and fish for crappie. Eufaula crappie are slabs-o-meat, fat fish 1 to 3 pounds chunky. While you're jigging in the coves and shallows, the white bass (called sandies here in Baja Texas, too) have moved in to chase shad, schools on schools.

Eufaula has muddy water and it has clear water, like different lakes. The lake does not have much underwater cover, very little vegetation. So catfish and gar obviously do well here, too. In the clear water, the rocky points, the riprap, the smallmouth thrive (as do walleye). Eufaula reminds me of so many Texas impoundments with varied fishing, recreational opportunities, an ideal lake for families to play and fish and swim. Plus, I think the smallmouth fishery is going to bust out this next decade.

CONTACTS
Eufala Cover Marina, www .eufalacovemarina.com
Lake Eufaula State Park, Checotah, 918-689-5311

Mountain Fork River

- **Location:** Southeastern Oklahoma, north of Broken Bow 10 miles. The river is three and a half hours northeast of Dallas, Texas.

- **What You Fish For:** Stocked rainbow and brown trout with limited reproduction

- **Highlights and Notables:** This year-round twelve-mile tailwater is loaded with a diversity of holding water ranging from pools to runs to wide, lake-like flats, a few riffles, pocket water with plenty of underwater cover, and even some undercut banks.

What a bizarre trout stream. Above Broken Bow Lake, it's the standard southern smallmouth fishery, clear cool water and lots of rocks and boulders and bronzebacks the size of small terriers. But in the twelve miles of cold water below the dam, big brown trout and broad-shouldered rainbow trout swim amongst the cypress knees and great slabs of slick black rock.

Browns to 9 pounds have been caught in the middle section of the river. I've seen one over 10 pounds cruising the sloughs near Presbyterian Falls but I'm not telling where until I catch him. The rocks are slippery, the water levels fluctuate due to releases from the lake, and reaching the lower river at Presbyterian Falls can be a driving adventure. But that 10-pound brown is waiting in a slough for one of us. If you catch him first, take a picture and send it to me.

The Mountain Fork River, as incongruous and juxtaposed as it seems for a quality trout stream, flowing less than an hour from the red-siltiness of the Red River border of Texas and Oklahoma, is an angling haven for fly fishing addicts located in the south central United States. The river has for years been a great weekday and weekend, year-round getaway for fly fishers in Oklahoma City, Little Rock, and Dallas who need a trout fix in between longer sojourns to the more famous trout streams of Colorado and New Mexico. But the river is rapidly becoming a destination spot as the quality of its angling continues to improve, as anglers become more aware of this emerging stream, and as more guides and fly shops serve the fishery.

The Kiamichi Range of the Ouachita Mountains provides a pleasant backdrop to fishing in the pools and riffles of this clear, diverse tailwater. In the fall and early winter, the trees and riparian habitat are alive with reds and oranges, and this is when the fishing for rainbow and big brown trout is at its best, but anglers can drop a line for trout in this tailrace all year long. Come spring, the trees burst out in a palette of greens.

The Mountain Fork River will never be a trophy trout factory like the White or Little Red Rivers in Arkansas. But no trout stream in Arkansas will ever have the exciting dry fly fishing that Mountain Fork provides throughout the year, especially in January and February, two of the river's top dry fly months. Both pine and cypress trees line this beautiful tailwater. Fly fishermen will find plenty of hatches but matching the hatch is difficult until you learn the river and its diverse hatches.

CONTACTS
Rob Woodruff Guide Service, 903-967-2665, www.flyfishingfork.com (I think Rob knows more about the Mountain Fork and Lake Fork than anyone in the world)
Orvis Dallas, Dallas, TX, 214-265-1600, www.orvis.com
Blue Drake Outfitters, Dallas, TX, www.bluedrake.com
Ken Cole, Flies by Night Outfitters, 214-969-1030
Bass Pro Shops Outdoor World, Grapevine, TX, 972-274-2018
Three Rivers Fly Shop (across from the entrance of Beaver's Bend State Park), 580-494-6115
Jesse King, guide, 580-241-5644
Beavers Bend Fly Shop, 580-494-6071
River's Edge Fly Shop, Oklahoma City, 405-748-3900
Beavers Bend State Park, 580-494-6538

I bobbed out in the middle of Lake Oahe for hours, trolling a Woolly Bugger behind me. Lake Oahe is big. I was using my flippers and kept thinking that I could make it across this ocean of a lake from the cove where we put in to the cove I could see on the other side. In six hours of float-tubing, fighting the subtle current, I had floated out, circled around, and ended up at the same cove. I reeled in smallmouth bass, trout, and salmon. And in a scary moment, a 25-inch pike that the guide said was way too small to confirm my diagnosis: ferocious.

Bullshit. Dude had teeth like a vampire.

Hugh Gardner and I met legendary angler Tony Dean, enjoyed the Midwestern humor and hospitality, and fished for just about every species over a few days and we each caught some of each. Except Chinook salmon. I kept trying and failing. All around me other anglers had stringers of Chinooks. One time, right after Hugh hooked and released an 8- to 10-pounder, I cast into the pod of Chinook and came back with a 7-pound catfish obviously feeding on the salmon eggs. We went back, ate walleye at the lodge café and Hugh poked fun at me for my lack of Chinook. Oh well, if all you're lacking is some Chinook on any given day, I figure you're ahead of the game.

Black Hills

- **Location:** Western South Dakota
- **What You Fish For:** Brook, brown, and rainbow trout
- **Highlights and Notables:** Under-fished network of clear, cool freestone streams teeming with trout

Where is the perfect place out west where you can fish most all day, keep the kids occupied, and make your spouse happy with all the collaterals?

If you really want to get away from it all, then Spearfish, South Dakota, with its isolated location nestled in a broad valley, with its rich western history, with its proximity to several national parks and monuments and ample outdoor opportunities (including the spectacular Spearfish Canyon), is a great hidden getaway for you and the family. This special hideaway has it all, from fields of colorful wildflowers, precipitous canyons, incredible mountain scenery, and blue ribbon trout streams. You'll feel as though you've been thrust back into the real Wild West, in a town formed by the discovery of gold.

Not many anglers are aware that South Dakota is home to some of the prettiest and best trout fishing east of the Rocky Mountains. Most associate western South Dakota with the colossal visages of U.S. presidents carved into Mount Rushmore.

But most tourists don't know that a few presidents also made this area their fishing mecca. Both Calvin Coolidge and Theodore Roosevelt regularly fished these intimate streams.

The Black Hills are home to over 400 miles of trout streams and fourteen lakes. Sportsmen can cast fly lines in year-round solitude surrounded only by ponderosa pine forests. Brook trout populate the headwaters of the streams, while wild brown trout and stocked rainbow trout inhabit the main stems of the Black Hills waters. The Black Hills are in fact the highest slopes east of the Rockies.

This is a dry-fly fishing haven, one where anglers can catch lots of 10- to 14-inch wild brown trout or search for one of the 25-inch browns lurking in the water's darkness.

This region's streams are similar to those found in the West, but smaller in size and, as a bonus, lightly fished. The trout are also on the lighter and smaller size but the trophy trout hunter can certainly find some attractive prospects.

Would you believe the better-than-average (or luckier-than-usual) fisher occasionally catches brown trout that weigh over 5 pounds from these little rivers? Some of the smaller rivers produce unusually large trout relative to their small stature, owing in part to fertile habitat, few anglers, and great cover like undercut banks and thick watercress. Most streams are smallish but several do have long stretches of twenty-five- to thirty-foot width.

The Black Hills offer scenic mountain fishing in clear streams, deep canyons, and cold lakes. Many anglers comment that many of the narrow, spring creek–like streams remind them of rivers in the East. Some of the better streams you can fish from Spearfish are Rapid, North Rapid, Castle (a slow-moving river below Deerfield Lake), French, Beaver, Redwater, Box Elder, Little Spearfish, Crow, Elk, and Cox Creeks, along with the Cheyenne and Belle Fourche Rivers.

The difficulty in fishing many of the South Dakota small, clear, spring-fed streams is that many are technically challenging. To most anglers, this is intriguing enough to give it a try. Fishing over plentiful but picky trout away from the harangue of crowds is just what many are looking for.

Spearfish Creek

Anglers will want to tackle the pride of the Black Hills, Spearfish Creek—one of the prettiest streams in America. Its upper section runs through a wooded canyon, and in its lower stretches, it flows through calm meadows.

Spearfish Creek has the potential to be a first-class fishery, with good public access except for the lower section, which is largely private. The windy little road through the steep limestone walls of Spearfish Canyon is a beautiful drive.

The stream is gin-clear and loaded with brown, rainbow, and brook trout. It holds one of the finest populations of wild rainbow trout in the Black Hills. The canyon stream has easy road access but despite the fact the road sees its share of traffic, it's not too difficult to find a stretch all to yourself. The river

The river is a playground.

has nice hatches of baetis, midges, and little black stoneflies.

The water varies from wide, long, flat glides to churning, narrow, deep runs, so anglers have to constantly change from dry flies to nymphs to achieve success. Fishing a dropper rig is an efficient method to cover the changing characteristics. On the long flats, you'll need to keep a low profile and be stealthy since these stretches are slow and extremely clear.

CONTACTS
Spearfish Chamber of Commerce, www
  .spearfish.sd.us
Dakota Angler and Outfitter, Rapid City,
  605-341-2450

Custom Caster, Lead, 605-584-2217
Rapid City Scheels, Rapid City, 605-342-
  9033

Rapid Creek
Like the Spearfish, Rapid Creek also has the potential to be a first-class fishery, with good angling for browns (and some rainbows and brookies) in pocket water and nice pools both above and below Lake Pactola. The scenery is first-rate and, except for the steady automobile traffic, proves a wonderful angling destination. With all the cars touring the canyon, you would think this medium-sized stream would be crowded, but there are always long stretches of water to have all to yourself. Rapid Creek is the largest stream in

Pocket water, riffles, a trout angler's delight

the Black Hills, reached from Highway 44 (Rimrock Highway) west out of Rapid City in the central part of the region (although you can fish the creek through town below Canyon Lake). The stream is similar in looks and size to Spearfish, but the reservoir tailrace has created a section of river where larger trout reside.

The upper reaches, above Pactola Reservoir, are scenic but not nearly as productive as the tailrace below the lake. The spectacular valley with its 100-foot granite walls makes it worth a half-day trip.

The drive alone through the canyon is jaw-dropping, so spending a couple of days wading and fishing Rapid Creek is even better. Keep an eye out for wildlife in the canyon ranging from bighorn sheep, deer, beaver, and goats to rattlesnakes.

Anglers can find access at Silver City above the lake. A hiking trail follows the river above and below the lake, allowing easy access. It is on this river where you have the best chance to hook into a 20-inch brown. Wade carefully and watch for finning fish. If you keep your eyes open, you will be sight casting to large trout.

The section below the lake holds plenty of monster browns as well as fat rainbows and even sizable brook trout. Working streamers hard in the big pools is your best method to land the lunkers. Hatches are sporadic and rarely thick, so most of the trout are opportunistic feeders and will rise readily to dry flies.

Because of its proximity to Rapid City, Rapid Creek sees a few more anglers than other Black Hills streams. It is not at all unusual to see businessmen fishing right after work in those stretches nearer town.

Look at a map of the Black Hills region and you will see streams crisscrossing it every which way. The largest feeder stream is Castle Creek above Deerfield Lake, a nice little walk-in stream loaded with brown and brook trout.

Slate Creek is a worthwhile and little known tributary of Castle Creek, difficult to access but holding larger fish in its waters than it should. French Creek, in Custer State Park, surprisingly holds lots of trout in its riffles. Spring Creek is shallow and accessible, and in its clear, low waters reside amazingly big brown and rainbow trout that rank among the most finicky in the Black Hills.

Grace Coolidge Creek is a small, productive stream flowing out of Center Lake in Custer State Park. The creek holds brook and rainbow trout in its small pools.

Many small streams are off the beaten path and require a bit of a hike, but that ensures you'll have them all to yourself. The Black Hills region has so many lightly fished, unspoiled streams that it would be difficult to fish all of them in a decade of summers. And if you ever fish these waters once, you might be tempted to come back each summer to give it a try.

Lakes

The Black Hills have fourteen lakes that hold a mix of rainbows, browns, brookies, cutthroat trout, lake trout, and splake. If you want to tackle other species, you can find largemouth and smallmouth bass, pike, walleyes, crappie, bluegills, panfish, perch, and catfish in other Black Hills lakes. The lakes are floatable with different watercraft including float tubes, but wear Neoprene waders since they are so cold. Spin-casting outfits should be ultralight, no more than 6 feet with 2-pound mono. For trout in the lakes, I recommend a 9-foot for 5- or 6-weight line, but if you pursue pike, walleye, or bass, go with an 8-weight outfit.

The largest lakes are Pactola Reservoir, Deerfield Lake, and Sheridan Lake. Other productive lakes include Canyon Lake, Horsethief Lake, Legion Lake, Center Lake, Bismarck Lake, Sylvan Lake, and Stockade Lake.

Deerfield Lake is a remote year-round lake near Hill City holding rainbows, brookies, and splake, some of which reach 6 to 8 pounds. Most lakes can be floated from a belly boat or other personal watercraft, and some allow boats. Fishing from shore works well, too, on the smaller lakes. The state-record brown (22 pounds, 3 ounces) and lake trout have both been caught in Pactola Reservoir. Other area lakes worth fishing include Sheridan, Iron Creek, Mirror, and Angostura Lakes. Custer State Park has four trout lakes: Stockade, Sylvan, Legion, and Center Lakes. Canyon Lake is located in a city park in Rapid City.

CONTACTS
Spearfish Chamber of Commerce, 605-642-2626
Rapid City Chamber of Commerce, 605-343-1744
Black Hills Badlands and Lakes Association, 605-355-3600

Lake Oahe

- **Location:** Central South Dakota
- **What You Fish For:** Lake trout, rainbow and brown trout, steelhead, salmon, and more
- **Highlights and Notables:** This gargantuan moonscaped lake is overwhelming, from its vastness to its plethora of species to the trophiness of each.

Lake Oahe is a special fishery. It lies below Lake Sakakawea, one of several impoundments of the Missouri River. Oahe is a huge lake with 376,000 acres, 2,250 miles of shoreline, a lake that runs from south central North Dakota south into South Dakota. Anglers fish for lake trout, rainbow and brown trout, and steelhead and salmon in Lake Oahe.

Hugh Gardner and I flew into Pierre in the fall about a lifetime ago and I heard locals call their quaint little town "Peer" instead of the obviously correct two-syllable Texas way of saying it: Pee-Air.

Lake Oahe is humongous. It's as big as some European countries. I don't really know which European countries but I've been in quite a few and I've boated, floated in, and driven around the Oahe, and it's bigger. It's got to be bigger than Monaco.

There are coves and inlets everywhere. Oahe is developing into an angling hotspot. The brown trout are increasing in numbers, and with the profundity of food, they could grow to great sizes but still go largely unnoticed. Anglers are still discovering all the other secrets this large lake holds. We fly

fished and tried some conventional tackle, too. We did pretty good both ways but I think that the fly fishing potential for the lake is limited. The lake is mostly known for its superb walleye fishing. We did pretty good fishing off the riprap at Oahe Dam.

Chinook salmon in the fall? Big rainbow and brown trout in the spring? Come to this massive impoundment of the Missouri and fish one of the most prolific game species fisheries in the nation. The lake, and its hundreds of miles of moonscape shoreline and otherworldly coves, also offers fantastic angling for walleye, catfish, and pike. And now the smallmouth fishery is being touted as being one of the best in the Midwest. Both the tailrace and the sprawling lake are productive. Chinook in the 2- to 10-pound range are caught regularly, especially when they spawn in the shallow coves in the fall. The rainbows in the tailrace grow large on disabled smelt that pass through the dam turbines.

Lake Sharpe

- **Location:** Central South Dakota
- **What You Fish For:** Walleye, smallmouth bass
- **Highlights and Notables:** Combo walleye-smallmouth destination, known for quantity

Located in central South Dakota, Lake Sharpe is one of best walleye lakes in the Great Plains, which means one of the best walleye lakes in the world. Sitting in unremarkable rolling land, this impoundment of the Missouri River fills to 56,000 acres and moves and acts and looks more like a river than a lake. Eighty miles of river-lake between Lake Oahe and Ft. Thompson Reservoirs, where the focus is always on walleye but the up-and-coming fishery is the smallmouth which is relinquishing catches that average 1 to 3 pounds.

I'd treat Sharpe and Oahe as a combo-trip, hitting both humongous, prolific lakes on the same vacation. Sharpe has been producing days of seventy-five walleyes for some happy anglers. (I know, that probably means thirty or forty but Sharpe is good enough to have met those numbers.)

The lake has had good-to-great small-mouth fishing for years but the smalls have been getting bigs lately. Gizzard shad makes for super forage for game fish in Sharpe. Walleye fishing has been slightly up and down the last few years but always in the good-to-great range.

The lake seems get good spawn out of most of its species.

Hire a guide. They know where the walleyes and bronzebacks are on this vast, long lake, how they hold, how they respond to weather and temperature changes, and you don't want to waste time. Besides that, maneuvering the serpentine lake is tricky, dangerous at times, with sandbars and submerged obstacles reaching out and touching newbies. Reach out and hire a knowledgeable local guide, catch tons of smallmouth bass and walleyes, and fish Oahe while you're in the neighborhood.

CONTACTS
Walleye Charters, www .southdakotawalleyecharters.com
Pierre Chamber of Commerce, 800-962-2034
South Dakota Game, Fish and Parks, 605-773-3381

WISCONSIN

I am balding.

I always told Amy that when the pen-insula on the ol' crown became an island, when that narrow strait of wispy brown hairs disappeared and left the one-inch by one-inch patch all lonely, I would be going Bruce Willis on her. No, not dating a woman half my age but shaving it off and keeping it about one-eighth of an inch long.

I did this thing. I looked like a gourd. Bruce

Willis and Michael Jordan have beautiful craniums. I do not. The island is back. Amy jokes that it now looks like the Bikini Atoll.

Sometimes, you think you know what to do, what's best, what things are but you don't know until you see it, do it, experience it. Such as the St. Croix.

I am balding but I like the St. Croix. Makes little sense to me but neither does shaving my head.

City Fishing

MILWAUKEE
Sheboygan River, Milwaukee River, Lake Michigan, Menomonee River, Peshtigo River, Root River

If you asked twenty anglers from around the country to write a top-ten list of the cities with the best angling in and around the city, you'd get the expected answers—Denver, Dallas, Orlando—but I'm willing to bet not a single list would include Milwaukee. And each one of them should. It's just hard to fathom how many angling opportunities exist in and around Milwaukee (including some fine fishing in the local parks).

Milwaukee Harbor produces some surprisingly good catches of brown trout up to 20 pounds and bigger (record is more than 30 pounds).

So many tributaries of Lake Michigan are seasonally the best steelhead rivers in the world, there are too many to list. The Sheboygan, Pigeon, and Milwaukee Rivers are productive, and the Root River would rank in the world's top 1,000 without the urban designation. Heck, the Menomonee is startlingly rich and fertile. And there are many who believe that the once-downtrodden Milwaukee River will one day be a bet-ter steelhead stream than the Root. Strong words but this just goes to show you how loaded the region is with lakes and rivers of note. The springtime brings about a transformation for Lake Michigan tributaries as they become playgrounds for Lake Michigan rainbow trout-steelhead of great size.

Lake Michigan is a large part of Milwaukee's being. The lake is an ocean, the sixth largest lake in the world. Western Lake Michigan is where Milwaukee anglers toil and trouble. There are many many many charter boats in the area that will take you out for any number of hours for any kind of species for any number of people. You can catch fish year-round. The brown trout fishery is top-rate, 1- to 4-pounders common and enough 10- to 20-pounders keep you on edge and coming back for more; small-mouth bass are in great numbers and strong and healthy; Coho salmon, Chinook salmon, steelhead, lake trout (once decimated, now somewhat re-covered), walleye, yellow perch—those are the main targets but you also catch pike, carp, drum, catfish.

Urban Fishing Program
Milwaukee maintains fishing in more than 20 small lakes and lagoons in the

County Parks. Call the Wisconsin DNR Urban Fisheries Hotline at 414-263-8494.

CONTACTS
Smokey's Bait Shop, 262-691-0360

Dick Smith's Bait Shop, Delafield, 262-646-2218

The Fly Fishers, www.theflyfishers .com

Laacke & Joys, 1433 N. Water St., 414-271-7878

Fishin' Hole, 3115 E. Layton Ave., 414-481-6888

Bait Mart/Sportsmen's Den, 414-464-2287

Buttrum's Sporting Goods, www .buttrum.com

Jack's Jigs, 2545 S. Delaware Ave., 414-482-2336

Bois Brule River

- **Location:** Northernmost Wisconsin
- **What You Fish For:** Trout, salmon, steelhead
- **Highlights and Notables:** No weaknesses. The Bois Brule is one solid river, pretty and fruitful.

The spring-fed Bois Brule (Brule River) fishes quiet and placidly in its boggy upper waters and offers pocket water fishing in the whitewater stretches of its lower reaches until it enters Lake Superior, one of the best salmonid rivers in the state. It has nice holding spots for brook, brown, and rainbow trout, in its meandering stretches all the way through its faster gradient where it receives steelhead and salmon. When the browns and rainbows come up from the lake to spawn, it is possible to tie into trout weighing over 10 pounds (heck, the migrating browns average almost 5 pounds).

The river has good hatches of mayfly and caddis. The upper two-thirds of the river can be easily wadefished but for those unfamiliar with the river and its variety of insects, diverse habitat, and multitude of trout lies, I recommend hiring a guide. Much of the Brule is fished by anglers in canoes. Cedar Island is the storied section of the river where several presidents came to fish. Access is tricky so you'll need to check in with local shops or hire a guide.

CONTACTS
Brule River State Forest, 715-372-4866

Brule River Classics, 715-372-8153

Door County
Near Green Bay. Smallmouths the color of Packer green, water as blue as the sky. Loaded with smallmouth structure (think rocky) and loaded with bronzebacks that grow fat, including 6-pounders. For size of fish, Door County rivals the more well-known smallmouth hotspots.

Namekagon River

- **Location:** Northwestern Wisconsin
- **What You Fish For:** Brook, rainbow, and brown trout
- **Highlights and Notables:** A perfect trout stream, ideal for those who like more intimate, wilder environs for brook trout or more challenging angling in bigger water for browns and rainbows

The Namekagon River is a National Wild and Scenic River, rough and tumble water with pools and riffles full of trout, one of the best trout streams in the state. The kicker is that this 100-mile-long river holds some awfully big brown trout. Brook trout are found in the upper river and feeders, hatchery rainbow mixed with the wild browns in the lower river. The "Nam" is heavily wooded with brush hanging over the banks, downed

timber providing perfect hiding holes for big beautifully colored browns.

Most of the Namekagon is easily wadeable but in warm months, you'll share the river with canoeists. Cable and Hayward are nearby towns with lodging and dining plus you can find lodging along the river.

CONTACTS
St. Croix National Scenic Riverway, 715-483-3284
Pastika's Sports, 800-244-2159, www.pastikas.com

St. Croix River

- **Location:** Western Wisconsin and eastern Minnesota
- **What You Fish For:** Smallmouth bass
- **Highlights and Notables:** One of the best twenty-five smallmouth rivers in the country

This river looks innocuous.

This river is one of the top twenty-five smallmouth rivers in the nation.

St. Croix was one of the original eight Wild and Scenic Rivers, so designated because the river was outstanding, remarkable, scenic, recreational, geologic, historic, cultural, and had fish and wildlife. The St. Croix National Scenic Riverway. That's a load of river, huh?

I am told the walleye fishing is solid on the St. Croix. I wouldn't know. I fished Clousers and caught so many smallmouth from my johnboat in two days that this rugged river with all the boat traffic became a secret fave of mine.

John Edstrom, Headwaters Fly Fishing Company, guides on the St. Croix. He tells me this story to illustrate the fun of the St. Croix:

"I was on a float trip with my good friend Tom Andersen. This was a guide's day off so to speak. We were casting surface poppers to bank side lies for smallmouth bass and that day the fishing and the catching were good. We floated up alongside a large sweeper. Tom dropped an excellent cast to the upstream side of the tree when out from the deep comes a 44-inch or larger muskie."

John continues.

"The large predator fish slowly followed the popper and stopped, just short. A three-way staring contest began with the fish staring at the popper, Tom staring at the fish, and John standing on the very gunwale of the boat yelling 'Will one of you do something?!' The stare-down continued until Tom realized that he was dangerously outgunned with his 9-foot #6 rod and smallmouth bass fly. He very calmly pulled the fly away from the fish and we continued our float catching sev-

eral smallmouth bass. At the very end of the float I hooked and boated a beautiful smallmouth bass with a huge tail and big shoulders that was just under 20 inches. Just a typical float on the St. Croix—you never know what is going to happen."

CONTACTS
National Park Service, 715-483-3284
John Edstrom, Headwaters Fly Fishing
   Company, 763-493-5800, www
   .headwatersflyfishing.com

Southwest

COLORADO

Tom Hauge used to be my friend. He is a hippie/geologist. I don't know what happened. He broke up with Penny and I guess that I was too much a part of that newly-censured life. Tom was a neophyte to the sport of fly fishing at that time (he called it sly-fishing and liked the idea of fooling fish). Tom was a quick study, one of those quiet know-it-once-you-see-it/read-it/do-it types. He listened to directions silently, nodding every so often. Tom caught a 4-pound brown out of the Animas, under the Purple Cliffs, in the snow, hard driving white biting snow with a touch of sleet. A muddler, as I remember. Stripped hard through the cobalt water and icy sky that had dropped right on top of the river. I caught two 10-inchers.

Four pounds. Long as a French baguette. Tom's fingers had a million tiny cuts on them from the ice that had built up on the line and guides. I know those slices didn't hurt as much as losing Penny because he went with me to dinner at a Chinese joint on main street Durango and shared some noodles and egg rolls over lies about the size of the fish. I miss ol' Tom. Losing good friends is a weird thing.

■ ■ ■

I once cried while fishing the Arkansas River. It was one of those times when I'd had a lot of crap going on in my life, stuff I'd let get to me, stuff that was my fault, and then a friend had died and there I was, knee-deep in the Arkansas, not catching a damn thing and not caring either, tears running down my face.

I don't remember all the whys and why nots (I could remember if I had a few Scotches but I don't have any Scotch at the house right now and I'd need a drinking buddy to talk to so let's go with the idea that I can't remember) but I do remember that I didn't call home for a couple of days, ate chili cold from a can, slept in the back of the Blazer and ended up catching a lot of fish. I get a funny feeling in my gut every time I go back.

Funny how fishing is escapist, takes your mind off your troubles—so they say and we all know this is usually true. I fish the Arkansas and I get sad each time and it's okay. No escape. Solace, maybe. Espe-

cially this one spot I'll fish with my daughter Sarah one day when she feels like fly fishing again like she did until she gave it up one day out of the blue. It's a comfortable stretch of riffles right under this bluff where I always seem to pick up a couple of decent browns.

A couple of years ago, after a fruitless journey through outlet shops, they tried to sell me supposedly-deep-discounted kitchenware and fashion jeans and Nike tennis shoes, my wife and I stood on the bridge at the outlet mall in Silverthorne overlooking the Blue, the shallow clear Blue and we watched two teenage fly fishers move up several hundred yards and miss three or four

nice trout. When they got to within spitting distance of the bridge, they sight-cast to one whopper who took their offerings thrice but they never hooked up. A few minutes later, a ten-year-old with a spinning rod tossed out a jig of some sort and hooked up with a heavy fish on the other side of the river. I scrambled down and helped him land the trout. Had to weigh at least 4 pounds. I convinced him to let it go.

This is the kind of river I could take my boss to, my principal, Shawn Neeley. He's a big ol' boy, lately taken to riding bikes and swimming and running and participating in mini triathalons, a shock to those of who look at his frame and then back at the tiny bike seat, then back at what used to be a college lineman's body now a principal's body and we wonder how in

the world that bike seat doesn't get lost in darkness. Did I mention how these triathletes think about streamlining when they swim and ride and run? Imagine the guy that plays on *King of Queens* in Speedo biking-shorts. I don't have to imagine, I've accidentally seen him when he runs on the treadmill. I have photos in case my teaching job is ever in jeopardy.

Anyway, Neeley is a good sport and loves to fish and has always chunked bait or flipped jigs. It's fly fishing time and we love rookies. The Blue River below the lake is an ideal transition river to let him catch a few on lures and then teach him how to cast the longrod. Maybe he's tired of spincasting for carp. People do get tired of things, you know? Mr. Neeley, you say the word, and we're on the Blue.

■ ■ ■

The coldest night I ever spent in the out-doors was in a tent with my brother-in-law and most frequent fishing buddy, Kenny Medling. We were fishing the Middle Fork of the Conejos, ten miles back or more and camped out at about 11,500 feet. We caught out on the trail coming back from the river in the evening in the rain, stupidly without our gear, and got soaked. Then it got cold. Deadly cold. Ice and snow. We shivered all night long and never really went to sleep, fearful that this was getting bad. I kinda remember cuddling. Survival mode, okay? When we tried to get out of the tent about four in the morning to make a fire, we had to break the ice sheets covering the tent first—they slammed to the ground, breaking into huge chunks. It was the middle of June.

We broke camp and hiked out five miles at five in the morning. You'd think such a chilling experience would have been the highlight of our trip when we shared the fishing excursion with friends and family back home. Instead we told them about the forty fish we each caught one day and the 4-pound brown Kenny landed in a big unnamed pool. It's that kind of setting, that kind of river.

My fishing buddy McPhail and I love the Conejos, try to fish it as often as we can. Mac thinks we always find signs when we fish, especially when we fish the Conejos. One time, we found a dead rabbit by where we pitched our tent. Sacrificially-dead, mind you. Rabbit's foot and all that. Best sign? We catch a lot of browns here as well as rainbow and cutthroat.

I've been on this river and caught lots of

Colorado

fish. I've been on this river and caught no fish whatsoever. I've fished all the feeder streams of the Conjeos many times yet I hesitate to mention them here because I want them all to myself, they're that good. First Meadow is an easy walk, see the waterfall, fish the slow water, get eaten by mosquitos. No biggie.

Okay, I'll admit. Elk Creek, Second Meadow. To die for. There. You got it. Now you convince someone to hike that freakin' trail with you and see if they're still your friend afterward.

■   ■   ■

I took Kenny and Chase and his friend Cooper to Hermosa one Labor Day weekend. Now Chase is six-foot-five and goes 230, 240 pounds. His foot is in the neighborhood of a size 12 but it seems to grow bigger every few months.

At the car, as Chase struggled to put on his wading boots, Kenny asked his twenty-year-old son "Chase, I know you said your boots still fit but if you want, you can wear mine—they're too big for me anyway and I know Uncle Mark has another larger pair you can try."

If you have been around young men, you know that tone they can adopt, that "you're really not as bright as you think, Dad" tone that they profess with the rolling of their eyes and shrug of their shoulders.

"No, Dad, I'm fine. These boots are okay, all right?"

Chase is a fine young man and we get along great. He is smart and sweet (he'll hate that but it's true) and courteous and any father would be proud to have him as his son but I guess all young men have to battle their fathers, even temporarily or sporadically, like a predisposed genetic code. And lucky for Kenny, even luckier for Chase, is that the young man typically makes good decisions and is more mature than Kenny and me put together at that age.

It's a good hike from the parking lot back into Hermosa. The trail is packed but it's up and down, far from the river then up above the river looking down, then riverside. And you want to walk past those lazy bums who quit hiking the minute they got to a close access. So we walked and walked and walked.

Then we spread out to fish.

Hermosa Creek is drop-dead gorgeous. Pamela Anderson in her prime. The water gurgles and percolates around gray-white rocks, dumps and drops into plunge pools, slashes under cut banks, wiggles and riffles, dances and dips. Dry fly nirvana.

The trout are bigger than they ought to be in a stream this size. None of us caught one 20 inches and I haven't in the last ten years of fishing Hermosa but we all caught several that went 16 to 18 inches and Cooper caught one laying against his rod that by the photo he took on his razor-cell-phone, went awfully close to 19 or 20 inches long. They rise willingly to dry flies, hatch or not. Just get a good presentation, decent drift over new water, and you'll get a strike.

So back to Chase. I find him sitting on a rock, his boots off, his white tootsies shining in the afternoon sun.

"What's up, big guy?" I queried cleverly.

"Check this out." He pointed to the back of his heels. Or what used to be the back of his heels. Each heel had an area the size of two business cards that was bloody and pulpy, big open holes, a flap of dead skin hanging harmlessly.

"Jeez, Chase, what happened?"

"The boots. Too small." He nervously chuckled.

"You're old man is gonna . . ."

"I know, I know."

The looks on Kenny's and Cooper's faces when they saw Chase's heels—priceless. The look on Chase's face when his father was treating the heels and poured antiseptic on the open wounds, priceless. The fat, wild trout that rose freely to western-style attractor dry flies, well, I'd pay good money to do that part again.

"Flaps" says he's ready to come back and fish Hermosa again and he's got new wading boots to wear this time. Funny how smart Dads are sometimes.

I have a blackmail photo of Kenny fishing the South Platte on a 90-degree day in May circa 1996 and he is wearing no shirt. He hates that picture. Heh heh.

Weird how quickly we grow old and you can measure it by trout streams. Kenny's nineteen-year-old son Chase fished the Frying Pan this past spring break and he caught and landed a 19-inch brown trout. On his own. No Dad, no Uncle Mark. On a ski trip. With all of his frat boy buddies skiing their little hearts out on the slopes at Aspen. The young man has great priorities even if he doesn't have wading boots that fit.

So I'm finishing the book. I'm a couple of days away and I'm writing in the loft looking out at a mountain that at one time used to be a ski run. I'm here with my mother and her husband of four months, Don Maroney, a former running back at T.U. (Texas University varsity, 1954–56). It's weird when your Mom changes names, has a different husband, but Amy and I like the guy and Mom likes him and they're like lovebirds all the time and guess what? Don wanted to learn to fly fish. He's got some positives going, I'll say that. We knew this going into the first day of fishing because we'd spent two weeks with Don and Mom in cramped cars traveling the countryside of Spain, Andorra, and France just a month before.

So Don goes all out, reads up on the sport, buys wading boots, dons his vest, we give him a fly box and accessories. Time to go fishing.

I put him out there and we did the beginner lesson thing. He nodded a lot and tried really hard to make his arm and wrist match up with his brain and what all I had told him. Don, bless his heart, tried and tried but it's tough for some, like patting your head while rubbing your stomach. My biggest obstacle in training him enough to match him against those wily trout was my mother who, I found out last year when I taught her to cast, is a natural. Mom couldn't help herself and in between my tips and advice, and sometimes over my tips and advice, provided her new husband with more "don't do thats" and "do thises" than I'm sure he wanted to hear. Don, bless his heart, has the patience of Job. Got to— he married Mom, after all.

After an hour of whipping the water into a froth and believing he was ready, the biggest part of fly fishing, I put Don on a fresh pool and let loose the reins a bit. Darned if he didn't have four or five fish on after ten or twelve casts. Lost every one of them because we hadn't gotten to the setting the hook or playing the fish part yet (although Mom was talking him through it).

After another couple of hours of hitting and missing, Don needed a break. So we busted out the picnic basket, enjoyed Bing cherries/crackers/cheese/pepperoni/grape tomatoes/strawberries and wine under clouding skies. Well, Don didn't drink any wine. He didn't want to drink and wade, I guess.

Don had that look in his eyes. I've seen it before, mostly in men. It's a predator thing. The Hunter.

I figured he was ill-equipped to catch a large trout but might just have enough balance with the training wheels to give it a go by himself, no constant chatter by an instructor. So how was I going to get Mom to leave his side?

Five minutes after he cast after lunch, he was fighting (not really playing, but fighting) his first trout. His rod tip was too low, he backed up about thirty yards of river, but by Jove, at the end of it all, he had a bouncy baby brook trout at least 6 inches long, colorful as the rainbow in the distance. Snap snap, pictures all around and Amy and I left him and Mom to fish by themselves in the wide openness of East Fork.

Endnote: You never know how it's gonna be with a new guy in the family but to give you a clue what a swell egg he is, check this out. The skies opened up from the dark gray bank of clouds and dropped an inordinate amount of rain and sleet and hail in about ten minutes' time. Amy and I backtracked to find Mom and Don and they were soaked, Mom more than he. Don made sure to let us know, as he should (and much to Mom's chagrin) that they had each caught trout, that they had had a splendid day on the water, that he was hooked on the sport, that he still had the fly on the line, and most importantly, that Mom, despite her new felt-soled Simms boots from Duranglers, had slipped and fallen on her tuchis, splash, right in the cold water of East Fork Hermosa Creek. The only thing she hurt was her dignity. Welcome to the family, Don.

Animas River

- **Location:** Southwestern Colorado around Durango
- **What You Fish For:** Rainbow and brown trout
- **Highlights and Notables:** One of the more dramatically scenic rivers in its upper reaches; in its middle stretches a blue ribbon fishery

The Animas after runoff is a beautiful river. The river runs yellow but clear with rocks as big as Quonset huts strewn about the river as if tossed there by giants. The

Except for spring runoff, the Animas is wadeable and productive.

deeper runs and pools are green, the weird amber-green of a Manet painting with the moving water seemingly a collection of dots and small brush strokes that shimmer and change color depending on the light.

Wide but wadeable. I was wading and slipped on a rock by the old Kmart in the early 1990s and did one of those Keystone Kop routines, kinda like Cary Grant in that fishing movie, and then thought I had righted myself on the slippery rock only to take one more step. Heels up, head under water. Cold as hell.

Durango is a cool town. It's one of the few cool Colorado mountain towns that isn't overrun with Californication (yet). It's historical and western and has great atmosphere and attitude. Amy and I used to say that if we ever bought a vacation home, we'd buy one in Durango. Last year we put our money where our mouths are. One of the reasons we did it was because I love the Animas.

A decade ago, the Animas River of southwestern Colorado was thought to be just another sad story, another great river in decline. And it was.

Formerly one of the top brown trout fisheries in the West, the Animas River is now successfully recovering from years of abuse from mining pollution. This wild freestone flows through awe-inspiring southwestern scenery, through wide valleys and steep canyons, past rugged mountains, continuing south from its headwaters on into New Mexico.

There used to be big brown trout pulled from the river, but now 1) the river is heavily stocked with rainbows and 2) there's not a prevailing meat-on-the-table philosophy in this neck of the woods any more. The brown trout fishery is on the rise, and so is the lunker part of this fishery and occasionally browns are caught which are best measured in pounds rather than inches, even in the city limits of Durango. The rainbow trout that live in the Animas are known for their athleticism and heft. In town, through town, under bridges, alongside barber shops and Wal-Mart and sidewalk

For a special fishing excursion, take the train (Durango and Silverton Railway) north out of town toward Silverton. You can prearrange to be let off about five miles above Hermosa to be picked up later in the day, the next, or even several days later. Most anglers and hikers who get off the train hike east from the dropoff point into the Weminuche Wilderness.

cafés, the fishing is productive if not weird. It's just strange fishing under the sentinel of a couple from California drinking Merlot and eating posole. Eat at Serious Texas BBQ. The pulled pork sandwich with raspberry chipotle. And really, the fishin's good in town.

The Animas is a year-round but is best fished early (February, March, and April) prerunoff and postrunoff (July, August, September, and October). In a heavy snowpack year, the Animas can be swollen from April to July, making fishing virtually impossible.

Below Durango, the river flow slows, and it meanders through open meadows, coursing through canyons, through reservation land. Anglers need to have a reservation fishing permit to fish this section. The fishing pressure is diminished but the fishing for big brownies, if you can get flies deep to them or in the undercut banks, can be phenomenal. Don't try to fish it in town during runoff. It's dangerous from the cur-

rent but mostly due to the armadas of blue or yellow or red rafts and kayaks splashing down the frothy river. Fish it the other ten months instead.

CONTACTS
Duranglers, Durango, 970-385-4081
Gardenswartz, Durango, 970-247-2660
Don Oliver, Durango, 970-382-0364

Arkansas River

- **Location:** South central Colorado
- **What You Fish For:** Brown and rainbow trout
- **Highlights and Notables:** Riffle after riffle, pocket water galore under craggy mountains, chock-full of feisty brown trout

From the headwaters of the Arkansas River near Leadville, to the town of Canon City, the Arkansas River provides over 100 miles of quality trout fishing, especially for brown trout, the predominant species in this fast-flowing, classic western stream.

Even though the river looks inviting to wade, fishing from the bank can often be more rewarding. Cast to the pocket water along the banks, and try not to hook the hundreds of rafters drifting by from morning to late afternoon. If you do wade, be careful because many of the areas are treacherous, and water levels can rise quickly, stranding the unaware angler on the wrong side of the river. Wear felt-sole waders for solid footing.

The Collegiate Peaks area is one of the most beautiful stretches of wilderness in the West, with a string of 14,000-foot peaks standing sentinel over clear trout streams, stands of fluttering aspen, dense forests of pine and ponderosa, huge blocks of pink granite, and colorful alpine flower fields. This surrounding scenery is one of the drawing cards to the Arkansas River drainage.

Following the Arkansas River from Salida to Pueblo Reservoir, the river courses through a deep canyon, through the magnificent Royal Gorge. Trout fishermen can fish the Arkansas River all the way to and through Canon City, with public access primarily on the south bank in the city. The spring fishing is legendary, but the river fishes well all summer and then it kicks up a notch come fall. Bring a box of caddis patterns. Or if you are a spincaster, bring Rapalas, Panther Martins, and Rooster Tails. And hold on tight.

The river courses through a deep canyon, the magnificent Royal Gorge. Texas Creek is just upstream from the gorge, and downstream from Stockyard Junction to Texas Creek is some of the best fishing on the whole river. Access is fairly well-marked with signs, and several pullouts are located along the Arkansas. Along the section down from Salida, anglers can fish the many feeder streams and small lakes in the higher elevations in the Sangre de Cristo mountains.

The Arkansas River has good fishing from Buena Vista to Salida, and US 285 runs alongside the stream offering excellent access. Browns Canyon has perhaps the best fishing for lunker browns on the whole river. The best access to this section of the Arkansas can be reached Hecla Junction on Highway 24.

CONTACTS
Royal Gorge Anglers,
    www.royalgorgeanglers.com
ArkAnglers, www.arkanglers.com
Arkansas River Fly Shop, 719-539-4223
Dvorak's Kayak and Rafting Expeditions,
    719-539-6851

Blue River

- **Location:** Central Colorado by Breckenridge and Silverthorne
- **What You Fish For:** Brown and rainbow trout
- **Highlights and Notables:** While the upper reaches are pretty and small and rehabbed, the real destination is the lower tailwater where the lunkers live. For novelty's sake, you can fish for nice trout near the discount mall in Silverthorne.

The Blue River costs me more money to fish than any other in America. It's right by outlet malls and somehow, my wife always goes with me to fish the Blue. It's close to skiing and we love Breckenridge. And Breckenridge has some really cool shopping, too, as well as having a few of our favorite restaurants.

So why the Blue River? Especially since not much of this trout stream provides a wilderness experience unless fishing in plain sight of discount shopping centers and the cars zooming along the interstate is your idea of wild country. But the reason to visit the Blue is the big fish. The Blue has big fish, plain and simple.

Located in central Colorado near the ski town of Breckenridge, this year-round, north-flowing tailwater produces behemoth trout courtesy of its population of mysis shrimp. Midge fishing in winter is popular, if not difficult, just below Dillon Reservoir, but in the fall, they get antsy and romantic and less finicky. The biggest browns are picky eaters and require drag-free drifts. The ten-mile stretch between Dillon and Green Mountain Reservoirs offers plenty of public access and you can fish a small stretch all afternoon and not cover all the trout lies.

The Blue has quietly become one of the most productive year-round streams in the West, with browns and rainbows growing to incredible sizes. Mysis shrimp from the dam is the culinary culprit. You won't be angling by yourself, the wind can kick up at times, and the multiple hatches can be tough to figure out. But did I mention that the fish are really, really big?

The Blue is a Gold Medal stream with nearly forty miles of browns and rainbows that grow to incredible sizes. And the fish are as big if not as plentiful as more fabled western rivers. Below Dillon Reservoir in the lower Blue, 10-pound trout are not an uncommon sight. I've seen bigger ones holding in lies and refusing everything I cast to them. Don't let it be said that Blue

Not for everyone, but you can fish while your significant other shops the mall

browns, rainbows, and even brook trout are easy to fool. They're not.

The Blue looks and acts bigger than it really is. You can see big fish but they're not easy to catch. When the weather gets bad in winter, layer up and hit the stream because that's often the best time to land a whopper. Rainbows average 13 to 17 inches.

The river gets crowded from time to time since it's less than two hours away from Denver. There's plenty of room to spread out and no shortage of trout lies. The water is manageable but in places the rocks on the streambed are slippery and rounded and awkward.

The Blue had a rough stretch not that long ago where a half-decade drought seriously affected the quality of the fishery. Access is good along the river and Division of Wildlife access points are well-marked but from Green Mountain Reservoir to the Colorado, public access is limited. From Dillon to the Colorado confluence, the Blue has special regulations because of its Gold Medal status. Right below the dam, the Blue is designated Wild Trout Water (catch-and-release only).

In the Silverthorne area, the tailwater is as wide as seventy to 100 feet. The river is not deep and the water flows go up and down according to releases. Everything in town is public and most of it further downstream is too. The private land is pretty well marked. All the way down to Green Mountain Reservoir, some eighteen-plus miles, the Blue has great fishing and great holding water including riffles and pools and runs as deep as you are.

Around Breckenridge, the upper Blue

A Texas angler with a sizeable brown trout caught below the dam on the Blue

is freestone, open and artificial and small and kinda weird to fish. The north-flowing river is shallow so it's had a good bit of instream rehabilitation, dams, weirs, reinforced banks and the like. Still, we've caught some nice 15-inchers in deep pools and pocket water. Bubba Gumps in town is a kinda weird but tasty place to catch a lunch, too.

CONTACTS
Blue River Anglers, www.blueriveranglers
.com
Breckenridge Outfitters,
www.breckenridgeoutfitters.com
Jackson Streit's Mountain Angler,
www.mountainangler.com

This Web site lists almost all the shops and guides you'll ever need in Colorado: www.colorado-weekend-getaways.com/ flyshops.html

Cochetopa Creek and Cebolla Creek

Small Idyllic Streams
Typical of Colorado

- **Location:** Southwestern Colorado
- **What You Fish For:** Wild trout
- **Highlights and Notables:** The joys of small stream fishing

Small streams need love, too.

All this talk about big fish and big water, there are those of us who often prefer to bring out our 2- or 3-weight flyrod and cast small flies to small wild fish on small streams. Count me in. If you're not a small stream aficionado then you either haven't tried it or you haven't done it right.

Two of my favorite small streams in the entire world, the Cebolla and Cochetopa. Creeks more than streams. I know what you're thinking—No, I'm not really worried about sending crowds to these two gems because they're both just so darned far from any place and besides, you'll get mesmerized by the bigger water on your way there if you do venture to southern Colorado.

Cochetopa

Cochetopa may not have the biggest fish but with the remote location, the beautiful valley setting, the miles and miles of available river (nearly forty miles of wild trout water) and wild wild trout, you could spend a week fishing it and enjoy every lit-tle foot of it. Size isn't everything and while it's fun to catch the larger ones, it's all about relativity. The size of the fish versus the size of the water. On Cochetopa, you'll be surprised by the size of the browns and rainbows, up to 14 inches (and I've lost one bigger). Most run about 9 or 10 inches but they're solid, healthy wild trout.

Nothing will get in your backcast's way on this meadow stream. Cochetopa Creek sits in a valley with mesas on either side and you can see the rugged mountains in the distance. You're not close to any big city; Gunnison's the closest town and while I love the village, there's not much to it. So you've got Cochetopa to yourself.

Start with being stealthy because as you can see, this creek ain't wide and she ain't deep but she is clear. Tie on a long thin leaders and oops, don't false cast over the creek or they'll run like that every time. You're gonna need accurate casts with that small Elk Hair Caddis I just handed you. Let's work on good presentation, drag-free drifts, and keeping your flyline off the water as much as possible.

See that glide right in front of you? There are two trout feeding, taking something every few seconds. Cast to their left and up above them, then mend, softly. Lift, man, you had one. You have to watch them and your fly at the same time. You'll get the hang of it before long—hey, look at those two deer over there.

Okay, let's work on the cutbanks. Cast as closely to them as you can. You can even land your fly on the bank and let it gently slide off. Oh, you missed another. They flash out pretty quickly from under those banks. If we don't hook one soon, we'll tie a dropper nymph below the fly and we'll get some in the deeper glides and from under the banks, which, by the way, recede back farther than you think. Rule of thumb: Use dry flies all day long and you'll catch lots of trout. Put on a dropper nymph and you'll catch even more trout, your call.

You don't have many features to choose from: glides with undercut banks, pools in the bends, not much of any submerged cover or bankside brush either, just big open grassy valley meadow stream. The hatches are decent, good enough that the trout look up and not so good that they refuse your offerings. I like emergers and wets and streamers fished downstream in quarters and swung under banks if they're off feeding.

Hit the cutbanks during the sunny part of the day; early and late, think middle and seams and shadows. Come mid to late summer with a meadow stream, you're going to think terrestrials and I try grasshoppers like the other optimistic anglers but I always do better with Stimulators and especially black ant patterns.

So if you are a good caster and light on your feet, you will catch more trout than you can shake a 3-weight at and have a joyful time doing it. Cochetopa is an ideal place to teach another angler or wanna-angler, but an even better stream to make yourself a better angler. So it's out of the way, not close to anything except vacationing Texans. You pronounce the creek "coach-a-taupe" (rhymes with rope) and

the fishing is good deep into autumn. The Cochetopa has great access, all three kinds: road access, public access, easy access.

In the upper reaches, brookies and cutthroat thrive but there is more brush and cooler weather and tighter casting. For a diversion, go up one or two of the even smaller feeder creeks and catch twenty fish in two hours. Use 2 to 4 weight although I like to have my 4 to 5 in the car in case it gets windy, which it does from time to time.

Streams like the Cebolla and Cochetopa Creeks can produce trout much bigger than their waters would indicate, with some thick-bodied wild browns lurking beneath undercut banks and streamside alders and willows.

Travel east on US 50 from Gunnison, then south on Highway 114 which parallels the stream and in its midsection, the road and river pass through a tight canyon.

Cebolla Creek

Onions. Wild onions. That's what Cebolla means in Spanish. Like Shrek says, there are layers and layers to peel back with this little gem. Cebolla Creek (pronounced say-vo-ya) is one of the unsung trout streams in the state—small, off-the-beaten path, full of wild trout, one of the best dry fly streams I've ever fished.

Cebolla is a canyon-meadow freestone creek, a high country jewel that has its headwaters at over 11,000 feet (oh, those sweet feeders) and at its lowest stretches flows at 7,000 feet elevation as it flows into Blue Mesa Reservoir. For a stream with

such great roadside access, with such cold winters, being so shallow, the creek's wild brown trout population holds up amazingly well.

These wild trout are fighters, aggressive brown blurs. Uncharacteristically for browns, they attack dry flies with reckless abandon and they do so consistently. Tight casting conditions. Treat the river and the fish with TLC and you'll catch more browns on dries than you've ever done before. The biggest trout I've seen in these small waters went over 20 inches but the longest I've heard caught is 18. No doubt about it, the fish are bigger than you'd expect in this shallow water.

Here's what this little river looks like: Beaver ponds into curvy shallow riffle-ly glides and bend pools and bunch pools then more beaver ponds, beaver-pond plunge pools followed by slow-moving tailraces and braids and island channels and spring-creek-like runs and cutbanks and full-blown riffles then more traditional pools and cliff pools and runs and more cutbanks then deep glides and pocketwaterpocketwater- pocketwater and pools. Sweet.

The creek is no stranger to angling pressure during the summer. Despite the numbers of fishermen, Cebolla stands up well. While the stream is less than fifteen feet wide near the headwaters, it collects numerous feeder creeks along its way north and eventually becomes a fair-sized river.

Some days, early or late and especially when the sky is cloudy or overcast or hazy, the browns take any dry fly and I'm not talking perfectly presented, either. You can fish a long run and if you play your cards right, you might catch five or six out of it. You missed twenty or thirty or forty more in that run, so dense is the trout population in Cebolla. Even when the sun is high and it's hot, you can draw dry fly strikes and always get them on beadheads.

More than most high country small streams, Cebolla enjoys prolific hatches, especially of caddis. The stream holds primarily brown trout with some rainbow and cutthroat trout. There are brook trout in the upper reaches. South from the Cebolla State Wildlife Area, the Cebolla has plenty of pullouts and public access. Plenty of campgrounds in the area, especially near the headwaters.

Primarily a brook trout stream in the upper reaches, anglers enjoy dapping and slashing attractor dry flies on its pocket water and plentiful beaver ponds. You will often have to drop lines over streamside brush or in a steep canyon but this upper section also has some nice open areas from which to cast. There are some sections of private water, but anglers can fish in almost ten miles of public water. Trout in this section of the Cebolla are brookies and browns and they rarely exceed 12 inches.

From Gunnison, travel west on Highway 50 then turn south on Highway 149 toward Lake City. Look for the sign to Powderhorn (Highway 149 east at Gateview on the dirt road) then turn left. Travel south through Powderhorn for about 15 miles to the Cebolla State Wildlife Area.

CONTACTS

High Mountain Drifter, Gunnison, 800-793-4243

Colorado River

- **Location:** North central Colorado
- **What You Fish For:** Rainbow and brown trout
- **Highlights and Notables:** Wild trout on an underfished, scenic mountain river

I have fished the Colorado only twice and I cleaned up both times. The first time, I hit the river in the dead of winter while my wife and two other couples swished down the slopes out at Breckenridge.

The first day that January was cold and overcast and intermittently sleeting. I was properly layered and wore my fingerless wool gloves. Ice formed in my rod-guides and on my line and my hands grew numb. I'm not much of a skier so a bad-weather day on a river is better for me than any deep powder day on a mountain.

None of the twenty-five-plus wild trout, browns and rainbows, I caught that day under gray skies would have measured over 16 inches. None measured under 12, either. When the sleet would let up, the midges came off but more important, the Blue-Winged Olives dramatically hatched, in numbers I'd never seen before.

When I got back to the ski lodge, they weren't back yet, out shopping I figured. I showered under the hottest shower in the world and when I lathered my hair, my hands stung like a million bees. Under the light I could see why. The ice on the line, strip after strip, cast after cast, had made a million tiny cuts on my hands. When they got back, I numbed them again, this time with Jack and Coke.

The next time and last time I visited the Colorado was during late June. I would like to say I was smart and planned my trip around the salmonfly hatch but I didn't. Pure luck.

The salmonflies gathered up in several clouds, like Harry Potter and his Quidditch team huddling up for a pep talk while hovering. The big, clumsy bugs would dip and descend awkwardly, some landing on the river's surface, others missing it by an inch. Others would light briefly on a bush then chug off again, only to fall quickly like a helicopter out of gas.

The day was hot and breezy. I caught more that day than the winter day a few years before. The river was crowded with other boats and all those anglers looked like they were lost in reverie doing the same thing I was doing. The rainbows were the strongest I'd seen save maybe some of the Gunnison River rainbows and they pulled like their lives depended on it.

The Colorado River is a Gold Medal stream which flows through both high plains and rocky canyons. Fishermen first have to get access to this interesting river, since much of it is private, and the reward will be a lot of trout 15 to 20 inches long. The fishing is not particularly challenging any time of year, so I'm told.

I keep thinking about timing a trip to go back but I'm afraid I'll mess it up with perfect planning. Those kind of trips never go as well as the organic, spur-of-the-moment kind. There ought to be a lesson somewhere in there but darned if I can find it.

This Web site lists almost all the shops and guides you'll ever need in Colorado: www.colorado-weekend-getaways.com/flyshops.html

Conejos River

- **Location:** South central Colorado
- **What You Fish For:** Brown, rainbow, cutthroat, brook trout
- **Highlights and Notables:** Rugged, scenic western stream with rich feeder streams

Mac crossing the Conejos isn't quite as dramatic as Washington crossing the Delaware but Mac could outfish him any day.

Named by Spanish explorers, the Conejos River means the river of rabbits. The Conejos offers the fullest fishing experience of all the wild rivers in the Southwest. The feeder streams are big and productive enough that it'd be worthwhile to visit them alone. Most require at least a hike, and you'll need a full-fledged backpacking expedition to get to the best parts of them. But if you want true wilderness angling in pristine forests and wide meadows, hit any one of these tributaries. Some say that if you were ever going to run into a grizzly bear—the last of which was seen in the state of Colorado in 1979 not far from the Conejos drainage—it will be in the backcountry of the Conejos. Wild, wild, wild.

What's it like fishing the Conejos? You find yourself choosing between miles and miles of where to wet a line on this thirty-foot clear stream with little competition from other anglers. You select a fly while abundant insects hatch. Choose from meadows and canyons. Glance up to see the Pinnacles towering overhead. Catch browns and rainbows that are colorful, thick-shouldered and athletic. Fish one awesome pool-run-riffle stretch for two hours and catch or miss ten fish and you can't believe it's been that long when you look at your watch.

While the river fished inconsistently during the 1980s and '90s, historically it was not uncommon to pull brown trout as long as your arm. The river has had instream improvements and better management and is fishing better than it has in two decades. Few rivers in the Southwest this size are as unspoiled. Few are as beautiful.

You have to want to come to the Conejos River. You don't pass through on your way somewhere else. The drainage is far enough from Denver and Albuquerque that you don't get the weekend city anglers. The area has so many things to do, so many fishing and recreation options, it's a great family spot.

In places, the Conejos is big water. Wear waders. Use a five-weight rod. On the other hand, the tributaries and island channels make for fun intimate small water. Bring out the three-weight and wade wet. The river offers beaver ponds, deep pools, overhanging trees, fallen timber, sandbars, gravelbars, cliffs, pinnacles, bends, pools-riffles-runs, undercut banks. Every trout lie you can think of. And the hatches are good but not so prolific that the trout will be picky or refuse your offering. That said, the river does have a phenomenal couple of hatches—the golden stones in late spring, early summer and a steady summer hatch of caddisflies.

So the Conejos is wild and remote. The river is jewel to fish. Its feeder streams are sizeable and numerous. The mountains are covered in pine forests. You have the Pinnacles. Lake Platoro is one of the finer high country lakes you'll ever see. Lots of campgrounds. Always a place to camp.

The Conejos is more crowded than it used to be but that's not saying much compared to other comparable western rivers. The fish are not as big as other name-brand rivers but they're plenty big. Highway 17, west of Antonito, runs beside the river for over thirty-five miles. You turn right (north) onto Forest Road 250 and this road parallels the river for over twenty-five miles.

Fox Creek Fly Shop, 719-376-5881

Cottonwood Meadows Guide Service, 719-
376-5660

Delaney Butte Lakes

- **Location:** Northernmost central Colorado, ten miles west of Walden
- **What You Fish For:** Brown and rainbow trout
- **Highlights and Notables:** If you
  can survive the elements, you might
  just catch the largest trout you've ever
  caught.

You'll catch as many trout on the Delaney
Butte Lakes as if you have "been owed
one." All the times you've been wronged or
suffered come back to you in fish. But you
have to suffer a bit on the lake first as an
initiation.

The weather on these bare-naked lakes
can be intimidating, brutal, and vengeful.
Winds that not only don't stop, they seem
to increase proportionate to the amount
you notice and/or complain. Wind this
high (8,100 feet) means cold this high.
Storms sneak up over the mountain and
drop torrents of rain on your head. Rain
this high means lightning strikes because
with no trees around, you are the tallest
thing around.

Why is it worth all this trouble?

Big brown trout.

Three shallow lakes above 8,100 feet elevation: North Delaney Lake (165 acres),
South Delaney Lake (150 acres), and the
ever-popular East Delaney Lake (65 acres).

Big brown trout. Twenty-five inches
is notable but not enough to mention in
nearby hamlets. Heck, the browns *average*
15 to 21 inches. Rainbow trout grow big
enough to bite off your toe.

North Delaney Lake is a Colorado Gold
Medal Water, recognition for its quality
fishing. The other two are not far behind
in quality either, just slightly smaller fish.
All three lakes are restricted to artificial
flies and lures only and there is a two-fish
limit. On North Delaney Lake, if you catch
a brown trout between 14 and 20 inches,
you must put that fish back in the water
forthwith. No dilly-dallying.

North Lake is the premier lake of the
three and here's how to work your voodoo
that you do: Pitch streamers and scuds until your arm falls off. If there's a hatch, it's
likely damselfly. Any other hatch will just
be torture for you. Keep slugging it out
with subsurface setups. If you are a spinner, spinners and spoons are your ticket to
fame and fortune. Floating the lake is an
ideal way to work the water except that you
better keep an eye out for the unmerciful
bursts of weather. Neat thing is that you
can easily work the shore, even wade a bit.

While North is the tops, East gets second billing and undeservedly South Lake
gets stuck at the bottom with it population
of rainbow and Snake River cutthroat. Use
this to your advantage. The cutts and cuttbows hit often, hit hard, and are surprisingly sized.

City Fishing

DENVER
Cherry Creek Reservoir, Chatfield State Park, South Platte River, Quincy Reservoir, Clear Creek

Few cities of this size offer so many fishing opportunities actually in the city and with any degree of quality. Cherry Creek Reservoir, Chatfield State Park, and close to one hundred other fisheries all rest or flow in the greater Denver area and anglers can catch everything from trout to bass, and yes, of quality. Cherry Creek Reservoir is a pretty lake in southeast greater Denver, loaded with walleyes. It's a solid walleye fishery. At Quincy Reservoir in Aurora, the state-

record tiger-muskie was caught, a 40-pounder at that.

Pull shad-imitating plugs or a worm behind a bottom-walker sinker for eating-size walleyes in Cherry Creek Reservoir, southeast of Denver near the intersection of I-25 and I-225. It's a boater's bite in May as walleyes have pulled off the shorelines into water fifteen feet deep or deeper. Best trolling zones are along the face of the dam, in the old Cherry Creek channel near the intake tower and just out from the west-shore buoys. At sunset, the bluegill and crappie bite picks up. Cast minnows or night crawlers. A $6 State Parks Pass gets you in the gate off South Yosemite Street. Contact: Colorado Division of Wildlife in Denver, 303-291-7227.

Clear Creek
Clear shallow foothills stream just west of Denver that seems to go on and on forever. I first fished Clear Creek when the I-70 rush to ski/fish/relax mad-rush traffic jam got so bad that I pulled off at the Georgetown exit. We stayed at a cute inn, Kip on The Creek and I have no idea if it's still there by that name but we watched the clear stream out of our bedroom window and despite the fact that there was very little cover or structure, decided to give it an afternoon try. We each caught several brook trout, all

on dry flies, with the roar of the interstate behind us.

Several times over the years, I've used the traffic-is-too-heavy excuse to get on Clear Creek. It's shallow with a few pools and loaded with small browns and brookies. Clear Creek begins up near the Loveland Ski Area, flows through Georgetown (where you have always busy Georgetown Lake), Silver Plume, and Idaho Springs then turns and follows Highway 6 through Golden. At Idaho Springs, there are more pools and heavier browns.

We're not talking great trout fishing but the water is clear and cold, the trout are wild and colorful and in stretches, decent-sized, and besides everyone else is in a traffic jam and you're not.

Other hotspots around Denver: Sloan Lake across from Mile High Stadium for catfish and panfish and seasonal trout; Chatfield Reservoir, Chatfield Ponds, Clear Lake. Throughout the city, if there is a pond or a lake or a creek or just about any body of water, the DOW (Division of Wildlife) stocks it (trout, muskie, wipers). And then there's always the fly fisherman's standby, the South Platte River at Waterton and Cheesman Canyons (for more on South Platte, see the entry).

Dolores River

- **Location:** Southwestern Colorado near Dolores and Cortez
- **What You Fish For:** Depends on the water releases—trout, hopefully
- **Highlights and Notables:** A cautionary tale

I really don't like the Dolores. She stood me up in the early '90s after a promising beginning as a fertile tailwater, a drought as it were. She snakes lovingly, frothily in places like a freshwater fishery, but she is fickle and protects her trophies beneath her multicolored waters like Grendel. This is a cautionary tale.

The Dolores River is a recent trout fishery, resulting from the 1986 construction of the McPhee Reservoir. The twelve-mile fishery promised to become a great trout stream, producing large wild trout in a matter of a few years, but a severe drought in 1988 caused the river great harm and killed a large percentage of the trout. Drought throughout another ten years brought more devastation to the Dolores and while things are on the upswing, only time will tell if it will recover to its pre-1988 form, when trout averaged about 14 to 18 inches. That said, it's one helluva fishery again.

This freestone tailwater has cutthroat, rainbow, and brown trout in self-reproducing populations, but is supplemented with fingerling plantings. The high desert countryside is rugged and bleak, resembling nothing like a setting for a trout stream—that's part of the charm. Keep your eyes peeled for wildlife. Deer, turkeys, eagles, even bears. Turkeys scared

the hell outta me one cloudy day, sneaking up on me or me on them.

The river is fishable year-round, but spring runoff makes the river brownish-red and swollen. Upstream sections freeze over in winter, but the feeding lanes on the tailrace close to the dam can be productive. Summertime brings great dry fly fishing, and fall has excellent fishing for large browns. The Dolores is a challenging river with solid hatches and tremendous holding water, but too many anglers make the mistake of not taking the fish seriously. The clear water and educated trout mean that you should use long leaders, be cautious, and match the hatch. Fish the Dolores because it *is* challenging. Fish the Dolores because it runs through wild, desolate high desert country and the angler-to-quality-water ratio is in your favor. The Dolores is one of the more unique trout waters I have fished. And in the winter, you walk in and have the entire river to yourself. Fish the Dolores because she may be a temporary sanctuary, her population of trout annually ravaged by irrigation needs—many would say, "Hey, it's an artificial trout fishery anyway, so get off your high horse." Maybe so.

Durango Area

- **Location:** Southwestern Colorado
- **What You Fish For:** Trout of all kinds, all sizes in rivers and creeks and lakes
- **Highlights and Notables:** The scenery ranges from high desert to alpine, all of it breathtakingly beautiful. The perfect home base for the trout angler, with his or her buddies or with a family.

Durango is one of the coolest mountain towns in North America, located in one of the most scenic valleys in the West. Amy and I always said that if we could have a second home in any mountain town in the west, we'd pick Durango. True to our word, we love Durango so much, we now have a five-bedroom second home in the area.

Durango is an outdoor recreation lover's heaven that harkens back to the West with its cowboy saloons and turn-of-the-century Victorian charm. You are likely to see dreadlocked bohemians playing Frisbee in the park, cowboys riding horses across a field or lean, tanned extreme cyclists pedaling up steep passes. Durango attracts folks of all sorts. Including us, whatever that suggests.

All trout fishers need to know is that Durango is an infectious high-energy town, where high desert meets the mountains, where within a couple of hours drive, anglers can reach some of the top trout waters in the west including the Animas, San Juan, Piedra, Pine, Florida, and Dolores

Rivers, Vallecito and Lemon Reservoirs, and a host of lesser known trout-filled creeks and alpine lakes.

The Piedra River

- **Location:** Southwestern Colorado, in between Durango and Pagosa Springs
- **What You Fish For:** Wild trout
- **Highlights and Notables:** Wild freestone river, unusually athletic wild rainbows and browns

The Piedra River is a canyon river, less than an hour drive east of Durango, with fat browns and foot-long stocked rainbows swimming in its forty miles of pocket water and deep pools, best fishable in late spring and through summer and fall. The Piedra flows through isolated granite box canyons in some of the wildest country in the West.

Think rocks. Lots of big rocks. And rocks mean stoneflies. Lots of stoneflies. The Piedra, which means "rock" in Spanish, muddies quickly, but if you are on it when it is clear, you should expect some of the best stonefly hatches in the state, including some fantastic salmonfly hatches. But the key to success on the Piedra is to fish every likely lie and to make sure to nymph.

I've had days on the Piedra when almost every fish I caught was a heavybodied 14-inch trout—every trout as fat as a rolled-up Sunday *New York Times*. They come up from two or three feet of water in pool after pool. They leap in the air, stare me down, and slam back into the water. I have dreams about those days.

Anglers are likely to see wildlife along the river—bears, elk, deer—but you're not likely to encounter other fishermen along the medium-size stream. The Piedra is in wild country, very little of which is accessible by vehicle, so getting there can be tricky. Anglers should expect to hike a bit to get to the Piedra's deep holes and glassy pockets. The Piedra has two gravel road accesses from both the east and west sides. The east side road runs upstream for twelve miles. Several trails reach the river from the road.

Great place for a multipiece rod since you'll likely be hiking a good bit. Anglers can wade wet with Neoprene socks and felt-soled wading boots. Some anglers pack in lightweight breathable waders but since you scramble on rocks and hike and such, you've got to be careful not to tear them up.

Hermosa Creek

- **Location:** North of Durango
- **What You Fish For:** Wild rainbow, brook, and brown
- **Highlights and Notables:** Hike-in wilderness stream ideal for teaching beginning fly fishers or for vets who want to catch strong wild trout on dry flies in a forested canyon creek

The Spanish named this creek Hermosa, which in English means "beautiful," and it is an apt description. This tributary to the Animas River, located north of Durango, is tailor-made for dry fly enthusiasts. For a smaller-sized fishery, Hermosa has some of the better insect hatches around.

Hermosa Creek is an important feeder creek to the Animas River, running through meadows covered in wildflowers, in a wooded canyon, past thick green forests, its cold transparent waters coursing through true wilderness on its way to meet its larger sister. Hermosa is where the Durango fishing guides get away for a fun day off to pick pocket water for eager brook, brown, and rainbow trout. This is my favorite Durango-area fishery (at least that I'm willing to write about).

East Fork Hermosa Creek

- **Location:** Feeds Hermosa Creek north of Durango, near Durango Mountain Ski Resort
- **What You Fish For:** Small wild trout, cutts, and brooks
- **Highlights and Notables:** Windy meadow stream both easy and challenging, beautiful, and maddening.

Another option for small stream fishing is the East Fork of Hermosa Creek. This is great fly fishing water, packed with small, feisty, colorful brook trout and sometimes Colorado cutthroats. This is also challenging angling, the water nearly invisible, the trout skittish, the casting demanding. Undercut banks and overhanging bankside cover hide these brilliant but diminutive natives. East Fork is a spring creek that snakes slowly across thick grassy meadows and hilly slopes.

I took the following people to East Fork one June day when the stream was full and the fish were hungry:

Amy—my beautiful, smart wife who loves to fish

Mother—my beautiful, smart mother who had just learned how to fly fish

Tammy—my beautiful, smart sister who was just learning to fly fish

Mike—Tammy's ex–college wrestler husband who was also just learning to fly fish

Kyle—Tammy's oldest, my hardcore fishing nephew, talks all the time, age 17

Will—Tammy's middle kid, fishes focused and quietly, age 16

Felipe—Our foreign exchange student Mom and Dad met and brought back from Brazil who came over at age 13 and never left. Mom calls him her "little souvenir." He had never fly fished before.

Martha—Felipe's beautiful, smart Columbian fiancé (now wife) who wanted to learn to fly fish. She caught more fish that day than any of the other beginners.

Quite a crew, huh? The East Fork, at ten or twelve feet wide at its widest, shouldn't be enough river to put this many people on it and still have fun, right? The meadow stream held us all and did so with flying colors. Everybody learned to fish with a fly rod, everybody caught five to ten trout or more, everyone raved about the quality of the scenery and the water and the fish and fly fishing and couldn't wait to buy their own gear, to go fly fishing for trout again. We converted so many in one day. Surely that's worth some extra jewels in my angling crown.

Other stream options in the area include the Pine and Florida Rivers—the upper stretches of each are small, scenic, and public; the lower stretches of each are fertile and productive and require anglers

pay a fee. Wilderness streams are abundant around Durango. Tributaries to the Animas, Piedra, San Juan, and Dolores Rivers are worth your attention. Cascade and Lime Creeks are fun day-trips north of Durango, perfect for those who like dry fly fishing for feisty fish in forested clear streams. The road back into Lime Creek requires a vehicle that's been serviced and has a good spare tire.

Junction and Lightner Creeks

Lightner and Junction Creeks are two small streams within ten minutes of Main Street. Junction Creek is where Mom caught her first trout on a fly, a 13-inch rainbow from the big pool (you'll know the one when you see it).

Lime Creek

Stephen Meyers wrote eloquently about this clear cold brook trout stream, one of the prettiest in the state. I once told McPhail that if he fished hard all day, as good an angler as he is, he'd catch ten or more an hour. We fished only three hours there and he caught over thirty brook trout, two well over 12 inches long. It's a real gem but hard to access with a normal vehicle, back in the boonies.

I taught my nephews Kyle and Will to fly fish on this forgiving creek. The same Kyle and Will who jumped a country mile when two grass snakes crossed their paths on the Cimarron. Kyle wants to be a fishing guide. He already ties flies better than I do.

Will can cast and hit a spot as well as most adults. Kyle knows insects and flies better than many guides. I taught them well. And they caught over ten fish each in less than an hour before the rains hit and we had to take shelter. The water is as clear as cellophane, multicolored cobbled bottom, ideal for beginning anglers.

Cascade Creek

Near Lime, this may be the rockiest stream in the southwest part of the state. Plenty of pocket water and willing trout but hard to wade. North of Durango.

San Juan River

And if those weren't enough options, the world-famous San Juan River lies less than an hour drive south across the border into New Mexico (see entry).

Area Lakes

Like lake fishing? Take a spin on Vallecito Reservoir (2,723 surface acres), a lovely high country reservoir that sits at 7,662 feet (see entry). Vallecito Reservoir has breathtaking scenery, the big lake surrounded by twenty-two miles of forested shoreline and sloping mountains gently falling into the clear, cold water. The lake is used as jumping off spot for hikers, campers, and anglers to get to backcountry of Weminuche Wilderness. While out in the middle of nowhere, there are always folks around. And plenty of cabins, motels, lodges, campgrounds, groceries, gas, and other what-nots. The lake holds some awfully big browns, plenty of stocked catchable rainbows, and self-reproducing pike.

Lemon Reservoir (622 surface acres at 8,145 ft. elevation) has light fishing pressure compared to many other big lakes in southwestern Colorado. It is a pretty lake, surrounded by green forests that are lit with fire and color in the fall. The lake has excellent spring and summer rainbow trout fishing. Two other area reservoirs with top-notch fishing include McPhee and Groundhog Reservoirs, both westerly of Durango. Alpine lakes worthy of your attention in the Durango area include Emerald Lakes, Ruby Lakes, Clear Lake, and Highland Mary Lakes.

CONTACTS
Blue Lake Ranch, 16000 Highway 140, Hesperus, 81326, 970-385-4537, 888-258-3525, BlueLake@frontier.net, www.BlueLakeRanch.com
The Strater Hotel, 699 Main Ave., Durango, 800-247-4431, www.strater.com

Blue Lake Ranch and the Strater Hotel are the two best places to stay in Durango. They both give you the Durango/southwestern Colorado flavor. The Strater Hotel is downtown on Main Street, a Victorian-style hotel with antique furniture, bedside diaries, charming atmosphere. Louis L'Amour used to stay there and write books—it's got that kind of energy.

Blue Lake Ranch is out west of town in the high desert mountains with stunning views of the La Plata mountain range. The ranch has guest rooms in the palatial size house or in casitas, smaller well-appointed comfortable homes with tasteful southwestern décor. Until we got a place out here, we stayed at either Blue Lake or the Strater.

Now we send all our friends there if we run out of room at the house. Both lodgings are always getting written about in magazines as "one of the best" of this or that. We like them as much for their owners and staff as we do their rooms.

Blue Lake Ranch even has a lake on the property with some nice-sized trout that nobody ever fishes for. You should.

Eat lunch at Serious Texas BBQ (their pulled pork sandwiches).

Eat dinner at any of these and you'll be happy: Seasons (where Amy and I spend every anniversary dinner), Red Snapper, Randy's, Kennbec Café in Hesperus. I like Gazpacho's for Mexican food but it's too spicy for some, so try Francisco's.

The Blue Lake Ranch

East Fork of the San Juan River

- **Location:** Southwestern Colorado, north of Pagosa Springs
- **What You Fish For:** Wild rainbow, brown trout
- **Highlights and Notables:** A real secret stream with heavy, active trout in big pools and roily pocket water. And I hear great things now about West Fork, too.

McPhail's gonna be mad I wrote about East Fork. I promised him I wouldn't write about this little masterpiece of nature. I had to. It's one of the gems of the West. I don't want to see you on the water, though. Just enjoy reading about it. Here are some reasons why I had to include it: East Fork is off the beaten path but close to a great home base (Pagosa Springs). East Fork is a medium-sized dry fly water that's hard to get to in spots but if you're not feeling chipper, the road follows the river. You get pocket water with fat fish. Beat that. East Fork holds lots of fish. Beat that. And you get scenery Ansel Adams would love.

McPhail and I were told by the wives (on a nonfishing-take-the-wives-to-Durango-and-be-romantic trip) not to stay and fish all day. We promised.

They knew better.

East Fork water is like one of those shimmery-sequined coats that Liberace wore. Depending on the light, the water is cobalt under gray clouds and then it's linen-gauzy-white in the bright light of noon and then it's peach-puff and salmon against the big rocks and finally, in the evening when the sun drops below the canyon walls, East Fork becomes cadet and tranquil.

One reason I don't feel like I totally betrayed Big Mac is that you won't be able to get to some of the water we fish. You're not that stupid. You won't slide down a four-hundred-foot-high scree 60-degree mountain slope. You won't jump from the big gray boulder the size of a woolly mammoth across the fast deep roily water and hope you land safely on the little gray boulder the size of a Dell computer. You'll stay in the safe spots and catch lots of stocked trout and you'll see two dummies deep in the canyon tandem-fishing each long run that comes out of a perfect pool. We'll be laughing and releasing trout and wishing we had remembered to bring some water and wondering how the hell we're gonna get back out.

We caught maybe ten fish each that September afternoon. We should have caught more. Neither of us was on our game. We were dredging at first, thinking nymphs were the ticket since we saw few risers. We used droppers, hoppers, or Stimmies on top and a small attractor dropper beadhead on bottom. We were fishing to the deepest parts of each big pool, of each cutbank, of each run. We avoided the skinny water, the sides, the eddies, the riffles.

After missing about five fish each, pretty heavy fish that laid in wait in the shallower water and went after our dry flies like my fat Uncle Bob on a chicken-fried steak, we figured things out. We're writers after all, so we're not really all that smart and it took a while to decipher the river in the fall.

At four o'clock, we knew we still had at least an hour of solid hiking just to get to a place in the canyon we could hike up and out. Then we'd have a thirty-minute walk back to the car. Another thirty or forty minutes to break down the rods and drive back to Pagosa Springs. And we were supposed to meet them at four.

But we were catching fish. Twelve to 16 inches. Wild ones. On dries. With perfect lies ahead of us as far as we could see.

So we each lit up a Macanudo and sat on a rock and thought long and hard about our promise. About how this wasn't even supposed to be a fishing trip. At the end of our little smoke session, we realized that we should do the right thing.

We fished all the way up to some distant point until it was six o'clock, hiked out, didn't break down the rods or take off our waders, and drove like a bat out of hell back to the hot springs in Pagosa where the girls had been soaking all day. We were silent on the drive back, each with that little nervous smile we all wore when we were devious teenagers coming home after curfew.

We knew we were in trouble when they didn't give us a smile or flip wave or eye contact when we pulled up in the parking lot two and half hours late. East Fork is worth it, trust me.

CONTACTS
Backcountry Angler, Pagosa Springs, www.backcountryanglers.com
Let It Fly Shop, Pagosa Springs, 970-264-3189
Bow and Arrow, Pagosa Springs, www.skiandbowrack.com
Wolf Creek Anglers, Pagosa and South Fork, www.wolfcreekanglers.com
Capt. Scott Taylor, High Country Fishing Charters, Pagosa Springs, www.highcountrycharters.com

Frying Pan River

- **Location:** Central Colorado near Basalt and Aspen
- **What You Fish For:** Rainbow and brown trout
- **Highlights and Notables:** Fat, trophy-size trout, canyon scenery, blue ribbon fishery, one of the top trout streams in the country

The Frying Pan River at Basalt Colorado, only twenty-five minutes from Aspen, is one of my favorite rivers in the world. The fish are big, the canyon narrow, the river cold. Pound for pound, this fairly small tailwater might be the best trout stream in the country. Some canyons have walls that rise so high and block out so much light that they suffocate. The Frying Pan's red canyon walls have dancing light and colors, texture and depth, warmth and softness. These canyon walls comfort and insulate.

It's cliché to say that fishing this place or that place is therapeutic. The Frying Pan for me has always—here it comes, big cliché finish—has always tempered my nerves, calmed me down, made me feel at peace. The truth is sometimes told in bromides and saws and clichés. Some facts about the Pan:

The big plunge pool beneath Ruedi Dam is known as the Toilet Bowl.

The Toilet Bowl is where the lunkers you've read about live. They grow to gargantuan obesity feeding on mysis shrimp that escape Ruedi Reservoir.

Mysis shrimp is not the only thing the big trout feed on in and close to the Toilet Bowl. Think midges, in all shapes, colors, stages, and sizes.

Year-round fishery. Limestone walls make for a fertile insect hatchery. The Pan has as varied and prolific hatches as any tailwater I've fished. The *average* size trout caught in the Toilet Bowl is 4 pounds. Designated a Gold Medal Water, the Frying Pan flows out of Ruedi Reservoir for fourteen quality miles.

Frying Pan River is known for its football-shaped rainbows, kind of a worn-out description I know, but it is true. The trout caught in the upper two miles of the tailwater, any fish that's over 16, 17 inches, has a belly. They're as big around as they are long (almost). Throughout the other twelve miles of the Pan, the rainbows and browns range from 12 inches to 16 inches but the river holds an amazing amount of 16- to 22-inch trout.

Unless you're glutton for punishment, get in and get out of the Toilet Bowl. This water immediately below the dam is wide and slow, riffley with deep pools, and anglers might be bumped by big brassy fish as well as other anglers (especially in summer). The Pan gets crowded by fishermen anxious to cast into the feeding lanes or even sightcast for the big 'bows. Five-pound trout are as common as dollars in this section so it'll be difficult to leave. Do it anyway.

Spend an hour or two there, maybe an entire morning in the winter when the crowds are sometimes lighter, but move on. The Pan has so many different kinds of habitat, structure, trout lies that you need to fish each section to see what it's like. You can move downstream through the Flats, a shallow section that at first glance appears fishless; next stop, Bend Pool, then Two Rocks, then the Boulder. Sounds fun, right?

Keep downstreaming: Bridge Pool and Baetis Bridge. In this stretch you just fished, you could have found trout around every rock, in the braids, against the islands, in the channels, in the runs, in the pockets, in the riffles, and, of course, in the big pools. The river has changed its personality from slow tailwater to fast freestone, big boulders here and there, holding water everywhere. You will find more cover, islands, and submerged rocks, beautiful red sandstone walls cut by years of erosion by the river, and in late spring and early summer, more stoneflies.

You keep moving downstream and you'll find that you are away from the crowds, the fish seem wilder, the insect hatches heavier and more frequent and diverse, and the canyon walls soothing.

You can fish the Mean Joe Green Pool. You gotta fish a pool named after Mean Joe Green. Thanks, Joe.

The Pan runs cold (often in the 40s), so Neoprene waders used to be the rule but now breathables and layers are the common sight. Nymphing is successful all year round, with dries being most effective from May through September. This is an easy wading river, and it also has two handicapped access points. There are few trout fisheries in the nation of this quality combined with this kind of easy access. For even more solitude (but smaller fish) try fishing the headwaters of the Pan above Ruedi Reservoir. Lodging can be found in nearby Basalt or Aspen, and there are plenty of camping opportunities in the area.

CONTACTS
Frying Pan Anglers, www.fryingpananglers
   .com
Taylor Creek Fly Shop, www.taylorcreek
   .com

This Web site lists almost all the shops and guides you'll ever need in Colorado: www.colorado-weekend-getaways.com/flyshops.html

Gunnison River/Black Canyon

- **Location:** Southwestern Colorado
- **What You Fish For:** Wild brown and rainbow trout
- **Highlights and Notables:** Deep gorge float trip where you angle for humongous wild trout

You will swear you are on another planet, or at least are situated just above the bowels of the earth about to be swallowed up. It's eerie down there. Granite walls rising up from the banks, caressing the tiny sliver of blue sky above. Cold, blue-green-clear big water. The narrow corridor is a whitewater's paradise and as much in the wilderness as any river in the West. The river and the canyon are spectacular. Breathlessly beautiful. The Black Canyon of the Gunnison River.

The river gets write-ups every now and again. The river has gone through some ups and downs the last thirty years (whirling disease in the '90s) but it's up again and I am amazed that this fertile, otherworldly fishery doesn't get any more attention that it does.

Unless you are a strong hiker and don't mind taking risks to get in and out of the Black Canyon—precipitous, switchbacking trails if you can call them that—you are committed to a two- to three-day float trip once you enter the canyon. You won't want to leave.

The Gunnison itself, from the quirky mountain stretches that are clear and bouncy with wild colorful trout darting from pool to run, to the wide flat pocket water, to the deep gorge and below, well, it's a long, productive, diverse fishery, as diverse as any I know of in the Southwest. Gold Medal River. The fish in the deeper waters grow to bragging size, 10 pounds, and with that kind of fishery, wouldn't you think Gunnison would be even more high profile?

The upper twenty miles, that part of the river above the haunted terrain of Blue Mesa Reservoir, is a mixture of public and private land, about half and half, usually well marked. With so many angling options around the upper Gunnison, with as much Gunnison as there is to fish, the fishing pressure is light. Really really good dry fly fishing on the main upper river and on its tributaries.

Below the impoundments, near Montrose, you get the Black Canyon, you get all public land but you can't access the big river very well. Black Canyon National Park. No guides allowed in the park. Bust out the checkbook and hire a guide—don't risk the trails to the river. Too hairy.

The Gunnison River rainbows are among the feistiest, most colorful I've ever caught. They pull like gangbusters and have spirit. But where we used to catch more rainbows than browns, it's about even or close enough and the browns are getting bigger on average. The Black Canyon, except in times of big stone hatches, is not a dry fly river. You nymph with a variety of subsurface offerings including weighted stonefly nymphs, or you crash big streamers.

What are the highlights: Remoteness, solitude, spectacular gorge, abundant wildlife including eagles. The Gunnison is difficult to fish. Nevertheless, these finicky fish have been what has kept fishing pressure low. Catches of brown trout regularly exceed 5 pounds and 25 inches. Fourteen miles of river—takes two to three days.

The Gunnison River is a Gold Medal River with a twist. Access is so limited on this river, at least the Black Canyon section of the Gunnison, that once an angler completes the difficult eight-hour descent into the canyon, the next takeout point is two to three days away as one floats the river. There are other trails to the Gunnison (from Peach Valley Road), but they too are strenuous, too dangerous. Because the river is so tough to reach, it is a highly productive fishery. The Black Canyon of the Gunnison River has more numbers of big trout (16 to 25 inches) than any other waters in the state. Rainbows and browns over 4 or 5 pounds are not uncommon.

Spin fishermen have a lot of success on the Gunnison using spoons, spinners (Mepps, Panther Martins, and Rapalas), and plugs in the deep pools and slow water. Spin fishing is at its best when the water is high and roily. Fly fishermen should carry in heavier lines (5 and 6), and maybe a sinking line of some sort. Hatches of insects are heavy but unpredictable. June has a monster stonefly hatch, and July and August will find caddis and mayfly (bluewing olives) hatches.

Nymph fishing is how the guides who regularly float the river put their clients into big fish. The best way to fish the Gunnison in the Canyon is with a guide, fishing both from the boat and from the shore while your guide prepares lunch or dinner. There are quite a few guide services serving the Gunnison, the nearest in Hotchkiss and Montrose (for a complete listing of guides and shops, check the directory in this chapter).

The river is wide and deep and the rocks are slick, so wear your chest waders and felt soles. If you camp while in the canyon, be aware that water levels fluctuate greatly, so set up camp above high water marks. Watch for both golden and bald eagles, and peregrine falcons. Fishing the Black Canyon is a true wilderness adventure. The Gunnison River from Almont to Austin covers over seventy-five miles of water, but that part of the river not in the canyon pales in comparison. Erosion and other factors have contributed to the demise of a once-fine trout stream.

Lake Fork Gunnison

This feeder river to the Gunnison is one of the undersung rivers in Colorado. The river is medium-sized, runs through a magnificent canyon, magical green pools deep enough to submerge a two-story log cabin. There's big fish in the Lake Fork, browns and rainbows, brooks, and some cutts. Per-

Steamboat Springs Home Base Angling

Steamboat Springs, the town which bills itself as "Ski Town USA," is known for its "champagne snow" which falls in depths of over 325 inches each year, providing some of the finest deep powder snow skiing in North America. But Steamboat Springs has much more to offer than simply incredible downhill skiing.

Steamboat Springs is a small village with roots in the Wild West, surrounded by tall mountains, punctuated by blue rivers coursing through its wide green valleys. Around town, visitors will see authentic cowboys in worn boots and sun-baked Stetsons walking along the weathered storefronts that look right off a studio lot set. At the ski village, they will discover a first-rate ski resort with all the modern amenities. High-speed quad chairs lift skiers to dizzying heights. Steamboat Springs is where the Old West and contemporary mountain living come together.

Known for its excellent snow sports and summer trout angling, this isolated mountain vacation spot, where cowboys still punch dogies and adventure travelers from around the world meet, is a great family getaway all year long. Steamboat Springs was named for the hot springs that make a sound similar to a steam train.

The town has grown considerably in the last couple of decades due largely to the fact that the secret is out of the bag. The Yampa River, as it comes down out of Rabbit Ears Pass into the verdant Pastoral valley, forms a picture-postcard sight, one you will want to return to, year after year.

The area boasts over 500 miles of streams and ninety lakes. The Yampa and Elk Rivers are the centerpieces of trout fishing of the Steamboat Springs area. The Yampa River ranges from tailwater sections to foamy freestone stretches to slow meadow sections. The river holds brown, rainbow, cutthroat, and brook trout as well as whitefish. The improved instream habitat of the Yampa as it flows through Steamboat Springs now houses plenty of trout.

Three lakes not to miss while you're in Steamboat are Steamboat Lake, Pearl Lake, and Stagecoach Lake. The Flat-tops Wilderness (235,000 acres), twenty miles south of Steamboat, offer unlimited angling opportunities on lakes and small streams. Mt. Zirkel Wilderness to the north holds the promise of fishing remote alpine lakes in solitude.

Trappers Lake is one of the most beautiful high country lakes you will ever see. The picture-postcard lake is loaded with brook and cutthroat trout, some of bragging size, too. You can also shuttle-hike from Trappers Lake on the Stillwater and Bear River Trails to Little Trappers Lake, Mosquito Lake, and Stillwater Reservoir past the Chinese Wall escarpment, then atop the Flat Tops plateau for some amazing views (and excellent angling). And just from Trappers Lake as a base (at the parking lot), anglers can hook up with fish on several area lakes and rivers including McGinnis Lake, Skinny Fish Lake, Boulder Lake, Big Fish Lake, Big Fish Creek, Frasier Creek, and the North Fork of the White River.

A short hike on Fish Creek Trail twenty miles east of Steamboat Springs will put you on scenic Fishhook Lake to fish for trout. The hike is only three miles roundtrip. Fish Creek is a fun little stream for dapping for trout and Lake Elmo and Lost Lake are within easy hiking distance.

CONTACTS
Bucking Rainbow Outfitters, 970-879-8747
Buggywhips Fish and Float Service, 970-879-8033
Straightline Sports, 970-879-7568
Steamboat Fishing Company, 970-879-6552
Steamboat Lake Guides and Outfitters, 970-879-6699
Steamboat Springs Sporting Goods, 970-879-7774

sonal best, 22 inches but big as round as peasant loaf of bread. My brothers-in-law have each caught trout in the mid-twenties on the Lake Fork.

The river is a patchwork of clearly-marked public and private land north of Lake City, easily accessible from Highway 149. This is the lower Lake Fork Gunnison. The river flows from the mountains above Lake San Cristobal, wide and clean and cold, the upper Lake Fork, enters the deep, cold lake, exits and runs through the hamlet of Lake City and courses north to enter the Gunnison River system.

Amy's family began coming to Lake City and the Lake Fork Gunnison back in the late 1930s, my family since the 1940s. We keep the tradition up each summer. I haven't missed visiting Lake City for two decades. You'll excuse me if I don't give away all the secrets of this amazingly productive getaway, my favorite haunts. If you see me on the Lake Fork or on Henson Creek, stop and talk and I'll tell you more then.

CONTACTS
High Mountain Outdoors and High Mountain Drifters Guide Service, Gunnison, www.highmtndrifter.com
Dragon Fly Anglers, Crested Butte, www.dragonflyanglers.com
Three Rivers Resort, Almont, www.3riversresort.com
Almont Anglers, Almont, www.almontanglers.com
Dan's Fly Shop, Lake City, www.dansflyshop.com
Sportsman Outdoors and Fly Shop, Lake City, www.lc-sportman.com
Gunnison River Expeditions, Montrose, 970-249-4441
Black Canyon Anglers, Austin, www.gunnisonriverfarms.com

Troutfitter, Crested Butte,
    www.troutfitter.com
Black Canyon National Park, Gunnison,
    www.nps.gov/blca
Gunnison Gorge Recreation Management
    Area, Montrose, www.recreation.gov/
    detail.cfm?ID=(1694)

Horsetooth Reservoir

- **Location:** North central Colorado
- **What You Fish For:** Smallmouth bass, walleyes, perch, rainbow trout, crappie
- **Highlights and Notables:** All about potential. This stark lake may soon be producing big smallies.

Keep an eye on this Lolita, fellow anglers. Horsetooth, with its four separate dams, is located west of Fort Collins in north central Colorado. At only 1,850 acres and often drawn down, the dam was fixed and refilled in 2004. Walleyes and smallmouth are going to flourish now (so the writer predicts) with its new cover and nutrient-rich water. They also put rainbow trout, largemouth, and crappie. If we're talking about Horsetooth in a few years, my bet is that it's because of the brown bass and the yellow pike.

CONTACTS
Lory State Park, 970-493-1623
Horsetooth Reservoir, Loveland, 303-679-
    4570

Rio Grande

- **Location:** Southwestern Colorado
- **What You Fish For:** Rainbow, brown, brook, and some cutthroat trout
- **Highlights and Notables:** The quintessential western trout stream

I believe the mighty Rio Grande flows through the prettiest scenery in Colorado. The water is as clear as air, the air is clean, the mountains majestic, and the trout plentiful. And the river holds some whoppers.

To wit: Picture me on a Rio Grande guided raft trip fishing for big brown trout with guide Chris Gentry and my brother-in-law Kenny. Kenny is squatty and thick and makes Sasquatch look agile. Chris is tall and lanky and moves around with the alternate grace and clumsiness of a Weimaraner puppy.

Ten minutes into the trip, Kenny was casting beautifully from the bow of the boat, his high-dollar, eight-foot rod held high. Chris remarked that it sure seemed that Kenny liked taking risks—he had been tossing big Stimulators right at the shoreline, then letting the fly float dangerously close to overhanging branches. Chris's comment sounded to me like a courtesy warning, but Kenny laughed it off and kept up his wild-man casting.

At first I thought someone had fired off a shot at us. The crack and then pop startled both Chris and me, and we looked up to see Kenny holding a four-foot section of rod. The other four feet were somewhere in the river.

He had snagged a branch, and when he went to pop it off, instead of leaving the fly and a bit of tippet hanging from the tree, his fancy rod broke in two places. Kenny looked like he'd just shot his best bird dog.

We had no extra rods—and I sure wasn't giving him mine—so he duck-taped what was left of his expensive rod, shook his head, and got back to the business of fishing. To our surprise, for the next hour Kenny caught fish after fish, his stiff pole never bending as he played the trout. His casting improved every few feet downriver, and despite the fact it looked like he was trying to chop wood instead of delicately land a size-10 fly, he got fairly good at it. His mending left a bit to be desired, but I did have twice the rod he did.

The clincher was when Kenny hooked up with another fish. Since he had no rod-tip to bend and give a clue how large it was, we only realized its size when we netted it: 20 inches and 2.5 pounds of brown trout. On a four-foot fly rod. With a grin as big as Colorado. Neither of us had ever seen anything like it. That's how good the Rio Grande is—break a rod, catch a big-ass trout, and have a blast.

So you have a freestone stream in wilderness setting with numerous tributaries.

Colorado

This is beautiful and rugged country where the nation's second longest river begins its southward trek, the river swelling with tributary after tributary, surrounded by interconnecting trails and alpine lakes. Deep runs, big pools, riffles, all kinds of water flowing through narrow canyons and broad valleys.

You're in some of the most primeval scenery left in the lower forty-eight. One of the great things about this upper section of the Rio Grande is that despite its remoteness, despite its lack of angling pressure, the river is easily accessed by road and trail.

Roaring Fork

- **Location:** Central Colorado
- **What You Fish For:** Wild rainbow and brown trout
- **Highlights and Notables:** Tumbling, rumbling rowdy freestone river loaded with fat wild trout

I used to think this was one of the most underrated streams in the West. Sure, the tumbly freestone river got the occasional article in this outdoor mag or that one, but this western gem received nowhere the recognition a fishery this good should get. It's that good.

Every time I go to the Roaring Fork, the last decade anyway, it's got more folks in it than I expected and they're all fishin' and slippin' and slidin'. They're catching fish, they're wearing their Orvis and Simms duds, they're slippin' and slidin' on the greased-bowling-ball rocks, and yet there's still plenty of water for me. They're slinging woolly buggers from driftboats but they're so far ahead, I can barely see them and besides, there are a million pockets they just drifted past without hitting so I've pretty much got the river to myself. So it's not underrated, it's just underpublicized. And that's a good thing.

The Roaring Fork meanders down from her headwaters in the 12,000-foot Independence Pass before becoming a rough and tumble freestone river, sixty miles to its confluence with the Colorado River. I've seen Independence Pass with several feet of snow on her in late July. This is some wild country.

Aspen is ritzy. The river begins above Aspen and continues to Basalt.

Basalt is now a rich folks' haven. Maybe not ritzy but you can see the money. It used to be a two-horse town, actually a two–fly shop town, quaint and accessible. Not anymore. This area has changed greatly the last two decades but don't let

For the most part, the Fork is fished best by nymphing, not dry fly fishing. If you are a solid nympher or a big-nymph nympher or better yet a streamer-stripper, you'll have good angling. The Fork is an excellent winter trout fishery, maybe the best in the state. Throughout the summer is when dry fly fishing comes alive with *Pteronarcys californica* hatches (a large stonefly), and abundant mayfly and caddis hatches.

The Roaring Fork is the sister river of the Frying Pan, and like the Pan, is designated a Gold Medal River. Rainbow and brown trout tend to run about 13 to 16 inches but on good days, I don't seem to catch many less than 17 inches. I haven't caught a true 20-inch trout yet but I've had two fishing buddies do so and then relentlessly brag about the rest of the day. They haven't been back with me since. And anglers do catch trout bigger yet, 20 to 24 inches long.

that scare you. The Roaring Fork is worth it. You can still find reasonably-priced lodging. You can skip the gourmet lunches or après-ski martinis. You can brown-bag it. You can always stay in Glenwood Springs or Carbondale (but what would be the fun in that?).

You can fish the Roaring Fork every day of the year. A freestone. 365. Can't touch that. A freestone river, fully fishable every day, loaded with character and big fish. Even though Basalt, where the Frying Pan empties into the Fork, has lost some of its small-town fishing town charm, this is beautiful country with two of the best rivers in the world flowing through these mountains.

CONTACTS

Roaring Fork Anglers, Alpine Angling, Glenwood Springs, www.alpineangling.com

Roaring Fork Outfitters, Glenwood Springs, 970-945-5800

Frying Pan Anglers, Basalt, www.fryingpananglers.com

Taylor Creek, Basalt, www.taylorcreek.com

Oxbow Outfitting, Aspen, 970-925-1505

Pomeroy Sports, Aspen, www.pomeroysports.com

Rocky Mountain National Park

- **Location:** An hour and a half from Denver, north central Colorado
- **What You Fish For:** Greenback cutthroat, brook, brown, and rainbow trout
- **Highlights and Notables:** The spectacular scenery and the native greenback cutts

You don't go to Rocky Mountain National Park to catch big trout. You go for the magnificent scenery. You go for the solitary angling. You go to catch the rare and beautiful emerald jewel, the native trout indigenous to the park, the greenback cutthroat. Amy and I go each year because there's just something about it, even about the towns around it (Estes Park, Grand Lake, Granby) that reaches us.

Rocky Mountain National Park is simply spectacular. The wildflowers in the summer are a palette of colors blanketing meadows and rolling hills. With fog hanging low over Big Thompson River as it flows through the meadows of Moraine Park, where an elk feeds near the banks, the scenes are as though you are on your very own postcard.

But the park can be crowded during the spring and summer, especially since it is only an hour drive from Denver. Rocky Mountain National Park is a family vacation hotspot with nearly three million visitors per year. But there are ways to avoid

the crowds. Most folks stay at the popular access points but with 414 square miles or 265,727 acres, if you get off the beaten path a bit by walking a few minutes, by hiking, by backpacking, or by riding astride a horse, you can get away from all the commotion. The park holds over 150 lakes and hundreds of miles of rivers.

The forty-eight-mile drive from Estes Park through the park to Grand Lake takes over two and a half hours depending on traffic and how long you stop to admire the views. The park has a diversity of terrain, from the junipers and pines of the 7,000-foot lower areas to the firs and spruce of the rivers, to the aspen of the high country, to the alpine tundra of the even higher country, where peaks reach to the skies some 14,000 feet high. This is one of the prettiest places on the continent.

The great scenic road that cuts across the park, Trail Ridge Road, is the main artery through the park but with all the crowds, there are simply not enough roads for all the vehicles. This lack of access is a good thing for exploring anglers. This lack of access makes Rocky Mountain National Park ideal for hikers and backpackers willing to trek off the road to find trout, solitude, and pristine wilderness. Visitors can hike over 350 miles of trails in the park.

As beautiful as the park's waters are, they are not superb trout fisheries in the traditional sense. I think that even with the increase of angling pressure in the park, the fisheries are better than they were a few

years ago. But the growing season is short at this high altitude, only about three months long. This means your average catch in the stream will likely be 8 to 10 inches long and the usual trout caught in a lake will run about 10 to 12 inches.

The reasons to fish Rocky Mountain National Park are the diversity of water ranging from tiny trickling brooks to alpine lakes to quick rushing creeks to foamy canyons to slow-moving meadow streams; to catch and be in awe of the beautiful and rare greenback cutthroat trout; to marvel at the resplendent scenery; to hike and fish the backcountry; to fish without any one else around. And your choices of fisheries in the park seem endless. You can't fish 'em all in a lifetime of summers.

Anglers can catch four species of trout in the park—brook, brown, rainbow, and cutthroat. The Holy Grail of these four trout is the greenback cutthroat trout. Outside of Colorado, this colorful trout, whose range is the farthest east of any native trout, is hardly known.

The greenback is probably the loveliest of all cutthroats. The trout has blood-red gills, big spots, a blushing pink belly, and greenish hues on the side. They sparkle like prisms in the water.

A great thing about Rocky Mountain National Park is that if you want accessible lakes and streams, you can find them right along the road or off an easy trail. If you want solitude, you can hike difficult, rarely-hiked, lonely trails leading to clear lakes and rarely-fished trout hotspots. Trails are

the maelstrom. Leave your nymphs and streamers at home and fish only from your dry fly box. Fish a couple of streams in the morning and hike to a secluded lake to cast to cruising trout in the afternoon.

So where to go? Your main fisheries—and that means those streams and lakes where other fishermen will be—include the Colorado, Big Thompson, Cache la Poudre, Fall and Roaring Rivers, and North St. Vrain Creek.

The better lakes include Chasm Lake, Lake of Glass, Mills Lake, Peacock Pool, Lake Haiyaha, Loch Vale, Sprague Lake, Sky Pond, Lake Estes, Marys Lake, Fern Lake, Upper, Middle, and Lower Hutcheson, Pear, Ouzel, Sandbeach, Fern, Odessa, Spruce, Loomis, Lilly, Lawn, Big Crystal, Lost, and Husted Lakes. These are just some of the inventory of good fishing lakes.

The park has 147 lakes but only forty some-odd lakes hold self-reproducing populations of trout. Cold water temperatures and lack of spawning habitat prevent reproduction in high altitude lakes. Supplemental stocking is done only to restore native species to altered waters.

usually well-marked. If you want to camp "out there," you will need to reserve one of the 250 backcountry camp sites and get a permit. If you don't like hiking, contact a local livery and mount a horse to go exploring the backcountry.

So what can you expect from the fishing opportunities in the park? Anglers will encounter a diversity of water types that run the gamut from winding little brooks with deep undercut banks and long slicks; choppy canyon water chock-full of pocket water and big pools; and the headwaters of major rivers like the Big Thompson where anglers fish in lush valleys under the sentinel of tall, snow-covered, craggy peaks. We're talking majestic views.

It's all about the scenery, the solitude, about sanctuary. If you are a good angler, you might catch twenty fish in an afternoon. You might catch a 10-inch greenback, release it back into the cold clear water, and watch as the green and red colors vibrantly swirl away from you back into

CONTACTS

Estes Park Mountain Shop, Estes Park, 970-586-6548

St. Vrain Angler, Longmont, 303-651-6061

Estes Angler, Estes Park, 970-586-2110

Alkire's Sporting Goods, Greeley, 970-352-9501

Angler's Roost, Fort Collins, 970-377-3785

St. Peter's Fly Shop, Fort Collins, 970-498-8968

Lyons Angler, Lyons, 303-823-5888

San Luis Lake

- **Location:** South central Colorado
- **What You Fish For:** Carp
- **Highlights and Notables:** Fly fishing for carp is one of the hottest things going. Here's a good place to try it.

If you have ever driven through the San Luis Valley, you are struck by the number of potato farms, the hulking mountains of the Sangre de Cristo Range on either side of you, and the small towns surrounded by such amazing overall mountain beauty. You would not, under any circumstances, think that this valley, one of the largest in the world (the locals claim it is but I'm too lazy to verify it and it doesn't seem all that important anyways), would hold a lake known for its carp. You read it right. Carp.

After all, the mighty Rio Grande traverses this big valley, one of the most famous trout rivers in the West. Light out from Alamosa in most any direction and in no time, you'll be fishing to trout. Light out twenty-five miles northeast of Alamosa and you'll hit San Luis Lake, a shallow, sandy lake and it's loaded with carp. Big carp.

Sometimes the lake is murky, sometimes clearish. Rainbow trout has drawn locals to San Luis for years but the carp and its thriving population should be the real draw. The

Sanchez Reservoir, not far from Alamosa, is another southern Colorado lake with good carp fishing.

carp feed in schools, they move in and out of the shallows, they feed where you can see them and sightcast to them.

You may or may not have experienced the thrill of catching and fighting a big ol' carp. A 10-pound carp can whip a 10-pound rainbow trout's ass, no contest. They thrash and roll and pull and even sometimes make awkward jumps. You can catch 5- to 10-pound carp all day on San Luis Lake. If you're so inclined that is.

South Platte River

- **Location:** North central Colorado, an hour and a half from Denver
- **What You Fish For:** Rainbow, brown trout
- **Highlights and Notables:** Up and down scenic fishery that somehow, through it all, remains a popular, viable top-flight trout river

The only thing wrong with the South Platte River is that so many other fly fishers are in on it. This is one fine river, full of big trout. In the winter, the South Platte is less crowded (only an hour and a half from Denver) and if you are inclined to hike, scenic Cheesman Canyon provides excellent angling to trout holding in pocket water and big pools.

The South Platte is in trouble, you'll have heard over and over the last decade, maybe even two, I've lost count. The river has a lot of friends but it sure seems to have its enemies, too.

The South Platte from Deckers and below lies in a wide open park, subject to cold winter winds. Finding your own turf is easier than in Cheesman. Both in the canyon and in the park, the fish are both hefty and discerning.

Beginning anglers will probably not fare as well as seasoned fishermen. The river has tricky currents and clear water, and the trout, while not skittish, rise and refuse patterns with regularity. Any kind of drag, even on nymphs, will put the trout off. Fish small midge larva patterns on long leaders for the best results.

Whether nymphing with golden stonefly dressings in Cheesman or Waterman Canyons, with their steep walls, or casting tiny #24 dry fly trico patterns to cautious lunker rainbows and browns in the gentle tailwater meadows of the Spinney Mountain Ranch section of the Platte, or wading in the shallow, freestone section of Chatfield State Recreation Area, this legendary trout stream is a consistent producer and beautiful to boot.

The famous sections of the river, for instance the Spinney section, require patience and skill to catch these wary, football-shaped trout. Spotting them is usually no problem, since the Platte has a great trout population. These fish are foolhardy, and every day they see expert fishermen from around the world testing them with perfectly-placed mayfly imitations. An interesting side note is that even though these educated trout are wary, they will often feed at an angler's feet, they are so used to wading fishermen. The South Platte gets fished

by a lot of front-range anglers, and at times, the river can be crowded in the more famous sections.

In the Cheesman Canyon section of the South Platte River, the angler will feel as though he is fishing an entirely different river from the meadows of South Park. There are deep holes to explore, the river runs faster, boulders and pockets and nymphs are the order of the day. The hatches aren't very dependable in the Cheesman tailwaters, due largely to the erratic water releases.

CONTACTS
Blue Quill Angler, www.bluequillangler.com

This Web site lists almost all the shops and guides you'll ever need in Colorado: www.colorado-weekend-getaways.com/flyshops.html

Taylor River

- **Location:** Southwestern Colorado
- **What You Fish For:** Rainbow and brown trout
- **Highlights and Notables:** The tiny stretch of river holds some of the biggest fattest trout on the planet, world record sizes.

I'm one of the legion of anglers who have never caught one of the gargantuan trout on the Taylor River tailrace. These fish hardly even look like trout. They are fat,

fat, fat, deep and broad and fat. The Nutty Professor's got nothin' on these whoppers.

Oh, I've hooked two big ones, long and big-headed and with shoulders as wide as Orson Welles, but lost both of them. Each had to be over 15 pounds or bigger. I've caught both a cutt and a rainbow that each went 7 or 8 pounds from this fly-only section, but they are just minnows on the Taylor. I suspect the Taylor has the biggest, fattest trout of any river in the Southwest. And the techniques border on insane.

One fine day, I got tired of casting size 18 patterns and changing flies to size 20 and changing flies to size 22 and going down to 24 mysis shrimp patterns (these tasty morsels make these trout porcine).

I went old-school and tied on a Gray Ghost. I had tired of the size 24-game where, in plain sight, these monstrous trout would feed in a lane, and when my offering came by, perfectly presented I might add, they would nod disdainfully in my direction as though saying "C'mon, fella. Gimme a break." These are easily the most educated, dismissive trout of any I've ever fished and that includes Henry's Fork and Silver Creek and the Test.

We had waded upstream closer to the dam. Beside a boulder the size of a bison, I could see a trout nosing up every so often, feeding. He was bigger than any trout I'd ever knowingly cast to. He looked as big as a king salmon, give or take 10 pounds.

I cast up and over, stripped it across at a 45-degree angle and the nosey trout hit it like a redfish. Freight train. Zipped out line through the run, up a pool, across some riffles, and ducked under a rock overhang. Then the fish stopped and waited for me to reel in my line, walk through the run, wade through the pool and stand quizzically over the overhang pool wondering how to raise this *monster*.

Kenny and David came over to puzzle with me. The fish was on the bottom, resting, waiting me out. I tightened the line, bent the rod over like my grandpa, then let it go slack, hoping to move the trout. Nothing.

The three of us laughed, nervously. Kenny splashed his rod tip in the pool to shake the fish up. Nothing. David waded deeper into but the dropoff was too steep. Another Grendel's underwater cave.

Out of nowhere, there was a pop, the line snapped. Game over.

Don't make a trip to go to the Taylor near Gunnison as your sole destination unless you are a masochist and you don't have much to do. There is precious little public water here but that doesn't stop eager anglers from shouldering up in the six-tenths of a mile of perfect water. The fish, while piggish, are also defiant. The last few state records have come from the Taylor, 23 inches long and 32 inches in girth. Or maybe it was the one that measured 40.25 inches long with a 29-inch girth. I don't know any more. This place is more like a freakshow.

CONTACTS

High Mountain Drifters Guide Service, Gunnison, www.highmtndrifter.com

Dragon Fly Anglers, Crested Butte, www.dragonflyanglers.com

Troutfitter, Crested Butte, www.troutfitter.com

Willowfly Anglers, Almont, 888-761-3474

Trappers Lake

- **Location:** Northwestern Colorado
- **What You Fish For:** Wild cutthroat and brook trout
- **Highlights and Notables:** Remote blue ribbon lake that you fish as much for the heavenly scenery as the colorful cutthroat

Trappers Lake (9,627 feet elevation) is one of the most beautiful high country lakes you will ever see. The picture-postcard lake is loaded with Colorado cutthroat trout, some of bragging size, too. The lake is isolated and loaded with insects so the cutthroats grow bountiful and long.

Glaciers formed this beautiful and heavily-photographed Trappers Lake in the Flattops Primitive Wilderness Area. This 300-acre, 180-foot-deep blue-ribbon fishery does receive relatively heavy fishing pressure but special regulations, including the use of artificial flies and lures only, assist in maintaining the fishery's wild cutthroat trout population, the largest population of native Colorado cutthroat anywhere. The Flattops Wilderness Area has no road access, so reaching the streams and lakes is done only by hiking or by horse.

The average cutt runs about 11 to 15 inches and doesn't vary much out of this range. You occasionally catch one 17 or 18 inches but not much bigger. You know, the fishing is good, the insect hatches varied and prolific, the trout beautiful but if you come here, come here for the scenery. It's that good. I've missed fish more than once because I was just looking around, gazing at the big cliff-block of lava rock standing one thousand feet or more above the lake, imposing its will and sometimes its shadow. Or I was staring at the forests of fir, spruce, and pine reflected in the stillness of the water.

Midges and *callibaetis* are the predominant fish food here. Scuds, mayflies, and caddis are other players in the food chain at Trappers. No motor boats allowed, so you'll have to wade (to get away from the overhanging limbs) or use a boat or personal watercraft (like a bellyboat or pontoon). I like to wade here. There's something stable and satisfying about having my feet on the ground at a mindblowingly gorgeous place like this.

Waders. Make them chest waders. If you are thick-skinned, breathables are fine but the water is pretty chilly. By early June, you can usually be on the lake. Brook trout are pesky and, like always, they'll overpopulate a fishery in no time so you're allowed to keep them.

If families playing in and around the water are bothering you, you can also shuttle-hike from Trappers Lake on the Stillwater and Bear River Trails to Little Trappers Lake, Mosquito Lake, and Stillwater Reservoir past the Chinese Wall escarpment, then atop the Flat Tops plateau for some

amazing views (and excellent angling). And just from Trappers Lake as a base (at the parking lot), anglers can hook up with fish on several area lakes and rivers including McGinnis Lake, Skinny Fish Lake, Boulder Lake, Big Fish Lake, Big Fish Creek, Frasier Creek, and the North Fork of the White River.

CONTACTS
Trappers Lake Lodge, 970-878-3336

Twin Lakes

- **Location:** Central Colorado
- **What You Fish For:** Lake trout
- **Highlights and Notables:** High country setting, big lakes

These pretty glacial lakes, upper and lower, resting below Independence Pass near Leadville, provide some of the best fishing for mackinaw anywhere in the state. And the mountain scenery is stunning, Mt. Elbert looming in the background, Colorado's tallest peak.

Twin Lakes waters are freezing cold. Max depth of sixty to seventy feet, about 1,700 acres large. Rainbow, brook, and lake trout swim in these cold waters, but what you want to concentrate on are the plentiful, hearty lake trout. The mackinaws reach double digits on a regular basis and in the spring, you can catch them in the shallows. If you haven't done that trick, you're missing out.

Twin Lakes is high up and can get cool and even cold on summer days. The night temperatures, if you camp at any of the several campgrounds around the lake, get nippy. There are also plenty of hiking trails nearby and Twin Lakes is near so much in the Arkansas River Valley.

Twin Lakes is located southwest of Leadville and northwest of Buena Vista, along Colorado Highway 82, east of Independence Pass.

CONTACTS
US Forest Service, Leadville, 719-486-0749

Vallecito Reservoir

- **Location:** Southwestern Colorado, north of Bayfield
- **What You Fish For:** Pike
- **Highlights and Notables:** Lovely alpine lake that holds big pike

I have a getaway house ten minutes from Vallecito. We chose the Bayfield area for two reasons: 1) it's a lot cheaper than Durango, eighteen miles to the west, and 2) lakes like Vallecito and Lemon, rivers like Los Pinos, Florida, Piedra, Vallecito, Animas, San Juan, Hermosa, Lime, Cascade, and Junction are all less than an hour's drive away. Vallecito is the closest to my driveway as any of them.

Pinos and Vallecito Creeks are amazingly beautiful clear mountain streams—worth hiking in to to see the wilderness scenery and to catch lots of wild trout—that feed deep Vallecito Reservoir. If you ever fish Vallecito, you'll be hunting pike. Long, mean, toothy pike. In a big ol' alpine lake (7,750-foot elevation) that covers, when full, over 2,700 acres. Others might waste time fishing for stocker-size rainbow trout but there are too many other better trout fisheries in the area than to spend too much time tossing Power-Bait to these guys. Pike, it's all about the pike. And the scenery.

Vaya-see-toe is the common close-to-correct pronunciation but you'll hear everybody butcher it in many other ways. To catch the big pike that others catch, the 4.5-foot-long northerns they catch, fish early in the season and in shallow water with structure. I saw in one of the tackle stores last year, someone had caught a pike that weighed in the neighborhood of 18 pounds. I see them catching pike at the inlet of the Pine River (aka Los Pinos), around the stumps, off a ledge, anywhere the waterwolf can lurk. The lake is good for anglers from shore, although there is plenty of reason to get out in the boat and be mobile.

Okay, I'm lying about the fish other than pike. See this lake is ten minutes from my house. If you read down this far, then you can read between the lines (rainbow and brown and kokanee and smallmouth are to be had and if you do it right, you can catch some mighty big versions of each) and I once saw a dead elk floating at the inlet of the Pine, and ice fishing is popular (and maybe nobody is reading these parentheticals).

NEW MEXICO

I call him Burly. He is, of course, or I wouldn't call him that.

Picture this: snowy wintry New Mexico day and we are five and we are about to descend into a 600-foot-deep canyon. Red River. Three of us are fly fishers. Doc, McPhail, me. One is a recent convert so we won't call him yet a fly fisher. He is Crane. Burly is the only true rookie. We love rookies.

Long hike in. We crowd the narrow trail, thin out then crowd again at switchbacks. Burly, at 6 feet, 2 inches, doesn't cover as much ground as 6-foot-3 Crane. His legs just don't look as long. Maybe Burly's one of those torsos-longer-than-they-should-be kinda guys. Their descent into this increasingly white wonderland/underworld is tentative, like going down the stairs of a friend's dark basement to see if any of the rat traps have a new resident. Plus, it's cold as hell and getting colder.

I've seen the look before—the "we've been walking an hour and we're still not there yet" look. Their furrowed brows, especially Burly's because he is bald so his forehead can really wrinkle up sharpei-good, showed that it wasn't just the distance traveled or the steep incline but a concern for fishing in weather normally reserved for malamutes.

Doc Thompson is my friend, so he says, and he is a fishing guide. Without asking, he gives fly casting lessons to Burly and Crane. McPhail and I fish. Burly and Crane act in-

terested, give a moderately decent showing and they are thrown to the Red.

Burly fishes the confluence. He fishes downstream in the pocket water and has no chance in hell of catching a thing but he looks pretty good doing it. He is wearing heavy Neoprene waders which he later tells us chapped his inner thighs on his too-short legs.

Crane is into it. He has fished Rio Embudo once before and caught a trout. He has his own rod, his own heavy Neoprene waders, the kind with the wading boots sewn in, the kind that give you blisters on your shins and ankles and tops of your feet. He is oblivious to his misery as the snow begins to bother visibility.

McPhail fishes upstream, working around the big gray woolly mammoth–sized rocks. He catches a big one and we rush to look. Twenty inches at least and fat as the cigar that Burly smoked at Simpatico Lake near Bayfield, Colorado, the cigar so big and strong that it brought Burly to his knees after the hike and made him puke his guts out at the recreation center in the Forest Lakes subdivision. Nice-sized rainbow, Mac.

Doc catches an even bigger rainbow, colored so red and dark and green and fervent, the fish looked fake. What Dreams May Come. Twenty-two inches and several pounds fake.

Burly. He's Drew Perkins and he's big and bald and looks slightly Marlboro Man–esque. Burly is from Abilene and it's because of friends like this I win at poker, I have a great life, and I go on fishing trips with newbies. Burly had it tough last year, the last few years actually.

Drew and his beautiful wife Chandra (and that's not a token nod of a compliment either, she's a babe) lost a newborn and then had their second child fight against a rare form of liver disease. Raise hundreds of thousands of dollars or the young man age 3 doesn't survive. Heart-wrenching stuff. Drew and Chandra and Canon are so likeable, so genuine, so pure, the community at large raised the needed amount and many times more than that. Canon is healthy and now has a kid brother Creed and luckily both inherited their mother's looks.

So what we have here is a natural year-round trout fishery worth its weight in trout anywhere in the Southwest. You can fish this gem when the snows are heavy or melting into sludge or when the summer heat hits, you need to visit the maelstrom of blue-green deep canyon waters of the lower Red River. From the rim at 7,000 feet elevation, the trails drop 800 feet into the canyon. At times, you feel like you are in a life-size terrarium, isolated in the red and green and tan and gray colors of the canyon with a narrow strip of blue sky hanging above the narrows at the rim.

Guide Doc Thompson never yells, quiet as the proverbial mouse, but he yelled at McPhail that cold afternoon in February to hurry up with the pics and put the hawg back in the water. Doc's protective of his fishery's fish. Bully for him. Mac was none too pleased, though. The snow started big and wet, didn't even give us time to argue about whether or not it was a good idea to hike out or not. It was coming down like fleece, thick and white, heavy enough to cover my eyeglasses and paint us all alabaster in just minutes.

The hike that was treacherous downhill was even more so up, covered as it was by the snow. We are Amarillo boys and although all of us are in good shape (if I say so myself), this was our first day in altitude so we were sucking air with every labored step. Watching Burly and Crane slug it out in those heavy sloppy waders was secretly funny. The hike out always takes a lot longer than the hike in and a lot longer than you think.

Burly didn't catch a fish, didn't come close. He whipped the water into a froth, caught up in the trees but by the end of it all, he started to get the hang of it. We had converted another angler to our band of brothers and the pain in my lungs felt okay, both when I breathed and when I laughed at the horrahing back-and-forth as we wheezed up the trail.

■ ■ ■

This secluded, green-carpeted paradise is where we like to congregate in the fall, my fishing buddies and me. We set up on Latir Creek and pay the fee, it's easier that way and we're closer to the water that way. Besides, you can catch some beauties out of little Latir.

We set up three or four tents, do the whole guys-out-camping thing. Campfires and drizzle and bears and fish and scrambled eggs and tired old jokes and farts. Ken Cole has all the gear but we subsidize because we have to justify to our wives why we bought it in the first place. It's not very manly to tell them that Ken

has all the stoves, chairs, tables, utensils, and he'll take care of us. Even though he does.

Terry Moore was already dying of cancer that one year when Kenny was driving Terry's red pickup like a maniac, which he is, on those dirt roads. The meadows beside Comanche is where Terry was christened Bearbait, because instead of fishing, he just lay in the field napping and snapping pictures all day. Said he felt "tired." He didn't know then and we didn't know then that his hip was already being eaten by the cancer or else we wouldn't have hoorahed him as much. Probably.

One of our brood was still drinking heavily on those camping trips and none of us knew how bad it was for him. Amazing how people can hide such bearish behaviors and consequences. He since got the drinking under control and in my own selfishness, I've wondered about the next camping trip and how we'll handle campfire time where we usually lace the coffee with something a little extra. I also wonder if Burt Rutherford, who stands 6 feet, 4 inches tall, will still bring his daughters' pup tent that goes about 5-foot-10, or if he minds his feet sticking out so much the cheap bastard will break down and buy a new one.

I wonder how my best friend of thirty years Lance will do this next year at Valle Vidal. He learned to fly fish at Rio Costilla, much to our delight. He was a walking disaster but still managed to catch the largest Rio Grande cutthroat of the entire trip one year, a 17-inch beaut. Lance bought his own gear—he tore up my wading boots

City Fishing

ALBUQUERQUE
Jemez River, Sandia Lakes

Albuquerque is growing like crazy but it's still kept a lot of its original flavor—a mixture of Spanish, Mexican, Indian, cowboy. Central New Mexico is arid, mountainous, hot in the summer, harshly beautiful.

Because it has a major airport and it's either on the way for many to smaller towns with great fishing or a stopover or for business trips, you can find decent to good fishing for an afternoon or for a whole day. Sandia Lakes are three small lakes set in a park along the Rio Grande River and they're stocked with trout, largemouth bass, and catfish. This would be your afternoon off, fishing just to be fishing and enjoying being outside. Shady Lakes are pay-to-fish lakes, the main lakes stocked with bass, bluegill, and catfish. There are also two smaller trout. The lakes are open from April to October. Please call 505-898-2568 for more information. You also have Conservancy Park Lakes. If you need a real trout stream fix, head to the higher country and try the rivers of the Jemez (see entry).

and nicked up my rod—so he seems fairly serious about the sport. He'll have to fix his own bird's nest this go-round. And Harry, that dashing rascal who made his bucks in the petroleum business and for some reason invested part of it in the fly rod business—Harry, he'll bring his latest rods, Hexagraph Fly Rods, and we'll all try them out and love them and then not want to give them back to him (and some times we don't. I fish with "loaners" of his still today and love him and no, Harry, you can't have them back. Squatters rights.).

Valle Vidal. Kenny, Harry, Lee, Jerome, Tom, Garrett, Doc, and the list goes on. I set up these get-togethers and I don't ask just anybody into the Valle Vidal. It's time for Crane and Mac and Burly and Dino and Coach James and maybe even A-Dub.

I don't know about A-Dub. He's never fly fished in his life, he's a tennis player, and he's like that impish nemesis character in Li'l Abner with the cloud over him all the time—Joe Btfsplk—so what am I thinking? We *have* to ask him along. Kicks and grins. A fly fishing newbie.

Rio Chama

- **Location:** Northwestern New Mexico
- **What You Fish For:** Wild brown trout
- **Highlights and Notables:** Underrated wild diverse trout stream

The Chama River is a patchwork of public and private waters. Long stretches are pri-

A section of riffles on the middle Chama

vate. Access is difficult in places, and places of entry aren't always clearly marked. The river is in plain sight coursing right along the highway but you can't get to it without a long drive back around and all around.

The Chama, when accessed, has miles and miles of amazing water, diverse water. The private water, which takes up the largest percentage of the river, helps keep the rest of the river productive, saved from public abuse.

The fish are big. Plentiful.

What hatches. What dry fly fishing. Gorges and meadows. Big pools and riffles. The scenery stupendous. Parts are fishable year-round. Parts are wild fishing at its best.

Wilderness. Parts of the Chama are as wild as any other southwestern river. Tail-

waters. Tailwaters need water. Sometimes they get it. Sometimes they don't.

I've been lost trying to find my way in and out of the river. I've been found, fish after fish, bliss. One hundred miles of beautiful, challenging, enigmatic river.

The Chama River enters New Mexico from Colorado as a small stream, and along its way to several impoundments picks up water from many feeder streams. The upper Chama is a typical western freestone stream flowing through meadows, canyons, beaver ponds, teeming with trout. The middle and lower sections are wider, deeper, with two impoundments releasing water to form productive tailraces.

I like the Chama in the fall. October. Sure, it's the brown trout spawn then, but it's more about the colors and the chill and the solitude. The river is low and clear and the fish skittish after a summer of taunting but if you stay 007, you can catch them fattened up, mad as hell they got caught and you can do so without the madding crowds of summer.

The Chama holds solid hatches of stoneflies, mayflies, and caddisflies. I'd like to tell you these trout are not selective and for the most part, I'd be telling you the truth. If you can cast decently well, if you can move without splashing like a water buffalo, you can catch fish on the Chama. Still, I've had those days on this river where matching the hatch meant zilch and being stealthy meant using Harry Potter's Invisibility Cloak. So go into this knowing that most days these trout are not picky but that on any given day, you might get skunked.

CONTACTS

Outback Angler & Sporting Goods, Chama, 505-756-2300
High Desert Angler, www.highdesertangler .com
Santa Fe Flyfishers, fishing@ santafeflyfishers.com
Ed's Fly Fishing Guide Service, www .edadamsflyfishing.com
Lodge at Chama, www.lodgeatchama.com

Cimarron River

- **Location:** Northeastern New Mexico
- **What You Fish For:** Wild brown and stocked rainbow trout
- **Highlights and Notables:** Awesome dry fly stream set in an intimate canyon setting

I've been fishing the Cimarron going on two decades now. You know, it's funny. I fish all over the country, in the big wild rivers of Montana and Wyoming, in the pristine backcountry of Idaho and Utah, in bigger, better-known waters in New Mexico and Colorado, but there's just something about the Cimarron that keeps drawing me back. It's like a comfortable pair of jeans. Your best girlfriend. A worn leather jacket.

The Cimarron uncannily reproduces the same fishing story time after time, year after year. You stand in the knee-deep water and wonder how in the world you're going to get a cast under the over-hanging brush where two browns are spashily taking zipping caddis off the water. You forget that the road lies fifty yards to your left, forget about city life. Your first cast, a bow and arrow, misses, but the browns keep feeding. Your second is close enough and the strike, the run, the splash, the fat 12-inch brown in your hand. You creep out of the brush to the road and walk twenty yards to the next pool, a deeper, greener pool and you climb down into the cool, clear water and you don't even notice it's midafternoon and you forgot to eat the crackers and jerky in your vest. All is right with the world. Again.

Flowing from Eagle Nest Lake is one of the most underrated wild brown trout fisheries in the West, the Cimarron River. Electroshocking surveys have determined that this tailwater holds over 4,000 catchable-size trout per mile. I doubt that there are many rivers of this small size that attract so many anglers yet still remain so productive.

This narrow river flows through Cimarron Canyon for over twelve miles, winding its way past thick forests and heavy streamside brush. In places, the river fishes like a spring creek. Anglers should plan on bringing extra flies to the Cimarron, because if you aren't losing flies on overhanging brush, submerged logs, or underwater boulders, then you aren't getting to where the fish are hiding. And come spring and high water, the Cimarron is the ideal first stream primer with its abundant stonefly hatches and intimate nature.

There are so many pockets, slicks, riffles, and pools to try, and since the river isn't deep, fish will come from the bottom to take a fly—and they always seem to be looking up. Anglers can catch trout on dry flies in all sorts of weather, from bright sunny days to cold rainy days, thanks to a protective canopy of trees covering most of the water.

The Cimarron isn't wide. It is thirty feet at its widest, wadeable throughout. For its size, the Cimarron produces lots of catchable fish, many running 16 inches or bigger. A 9-pound, 29-inch brown trout was caught in the tailwater a few summers ago. Still, the average-size brown runs about 9 to 13 inches.

traveling the highway in the background. Besides, much of the river isn't as close to the road as it appears.

What sets the Cimarron apart from most southern Rockies fisheries is the abundant insect population. Whether the river is high or low, there always seems to be an ongoing hatch.

CONTACTS

Doc Thompson's High Country Anglers, Cimarron, 505-376-9220, www.flyfishnewmexico.com

Ed Adams, www.edadamsflyfishing.com

Los Rios Anglers, 505-758-2798

Dos Amigos, Eagle Nest 505-377-6226

Los Pinos Fly Shop, Albuquerque, 505-884-7501

High Desert Anglers, Santa Fe, 505-988-7688

Van Beacham's Solitary Angler, Taos, 505-758-5653

What is amazing about the Cimarron is that it continues to hold so many trout, and so many plump, athletic, colorful brown trout, despite the number of anglers. One of the keys for success is getting away from the bridges and other access points. I advise anglers to walk for five minutes away from a crossing, head around the next bend, and fish in relative solitude.

If you take the time to find a pullout without other cars, then walk up or downstream a bit, you can have long stretches of stream all to yourself. The river's rushing and gurgling will drown out the autos

Jemez Area

- **Location:** North central New Mexico
- **What You Fish For:** Rainbow and brown trout
- **Highlights and Notables:** Seven mountain rivers of all shapes and sizes and a productive lake all within an hour's drive of each other

Anyway, I've written several magazine and newspaper articles over the years about the Jemez drainage, and yes, I did lose a fly box near Fenton Lake one trip with McPhail. I love the Jemez area, especially as a winter diversion. Not a single one of the streams would rank in anyone's top five in New

Mexico, but collectively, for the proximity to Albuquerque and Santa Fe, for the diversity of waters all so close, for the wildness still there in the upper reaches, it's a hit, a real winner. So I've written the pieces: about Jemez—here's McPhail's version. *I've caught as many fish there as he has but he thinks he's all that—let's see.*

All it took was one glance at my topography map and my buddy Mark Williams had me convinced. The opportunities for us to net trout might never be more abundant than in the Jemez Volcanic Field in North Central New Mexico.

"Looks like an enormous bear track," I quipped.

Williams nodded. "Where there's bear, there's trout."

Appearing as though some mythical, six-toed grizzly stomped his monstrous paw print into the ground sometime before mankind existed, the Valles Caldera (home to the Jemez Drainage) seemed to remain a bubbling, underground cauldron of volatile gasses and molten magma.

Studying the atlas, I realized this trout-laden caldera spanned a colossal 175 square miles, with seventy-five miles of streams, plus stillwaters. I questioned how much of it Mark and I could fish effectively during our short stint. The task seemed to border on the impossible, even if we had more than the five days our wives had allotted us. But Mark was starved for adventure and bent on fishing all of it, and I was with him. So, brandishing our three-weight weaponry, we dared this bear-paw of a landmass to show us what it had to offer in the way of trout.

Williams and I disagree about a great many things (boxers versus boxer briefs, all-season versus all-terrain, hickory versus mesquite, Aggies versus Fighting Irish), but on the Jemez Drainage we concur. There's nothing in the Southwest quite like it, and certainly nowhere else in New Mexico can we experience such a bounty of fisheries in such close proximity. We've since returned numerous times, and no matter the season, the weather, or time of day, the Valles Caldera always enlightens us with option after option. So when the two of us get that sudden urge to fish for wild trout inside a dormant volcano that geologists say will someday blow its top again, he and I grab our fly fishing accoutrements and head for the Jemez.

A BRIEF HISTORY

Calderas, or collapsed volcanoes, often become world renowned for their romantic scene-scapes and sprawling vistas. Crater Lake, Yellowstone, Santorini—all famous for their extraordinary panoramas. In similar fashion, the Valles Caldera jostles for due recognition among those fabled names.

When the magma chamber beneath the once-towering volcano released its fury, what crust above eventually collapsed, and a hoop of dome-shaped mountains lingered. What remains of this ancient volcanic pile is a stunning ring of eruptive-looking knolls enlaced by tumbling, trout-sustaining creeks. The largest remaining lava dome, Redondo Peak, transcends its siblings at 11,254 feet above sea level—3,000 feet above the caldera floor.

Today, the sacred hoop of mountains diverts runoff and natural springs into an intricate web of angling offshoots, with streams flowing in every direction, some maintaining their integrity year-round. Since the upsurge that sent rock and ash flying as far as the Midwest over a million years ago, the Valles Caldera has slowly eroded into this geologic trout fortress situated in one of the most enchanting areas in New Mexico.

Earliest written accounts of the area come from the Spaniards who arrived in 1541. Here, they encountered the Jemez (pronounced Hay-mess) Nation, a peaceful tribe of Puebloans whose regional numbers may have reached 30,000. Certainly, theses denizens fished for the once-thriving, native Rio Grande Cutthroat (*Onchorhychus clarki virginalis*).

But to the Indians' misfortune, several waves of Spanish expeditions wrought war and disease. The Jemez gave way to revolt and uprising due to forced Christianization and attempts at congregating them into one or two villages by the Spanish. Through tribal unity, the Jemez Nation eventually grew strong enough to cast the Spanish from the area, protecting their hallowed grounds and rivers.

But in the early West, peace was always short lived. In due course, mining, cowboys, and sheepherders found respective claims in the area, leading their thirsty hordes trampling through the rivers. Railways and road building no doubt played pivotal roles in diminishing the numbers of Rio Grande cutthroat as well, forcing sediment and contaminants into the streams, degrading their delicate ecosystem.

In the early 1900s rainbows and browns were introduced into northern New Mexico, also a detriment to the already over-harvested native cutthroat. Until then the Rio Grande species thrived alone in these waterways, but trout fishing for them in the lower Jemez region was likely a tougher prospect than panning for gold. Records indicate that swift floods punctuated by prolonged droughts made the area too erratic to reliably grow crops. It is safe to assume that until instream improvements and reliable fish stocking programs began, the lower Jemez basin suffered as trout habitat.

By now, every stream around the caldera has evolved to support superlative numbers of fish, with the Rio Grande cutthroats showing some signs of a revival in recent years. Each river here is as distinct as the pattern of spots on a trout's skin . . . no two are exactly alike. Inside this confined geographic area, anglers can identify their favorite characteristics in at least one of these Jemez waters—the serenity of float-tubing a glassy trout lake, dapping dry flies in a step-across creek, shooting elegant casts with bushy dry attractors, or nymphing deep pockets and boulder-hopping box canyons. No doubt, the Jemez Drainage has a stretch customized to anyone's discerning taste.

Fenton Lake

Fenton Lake once served as a resting and nesting area for migratory waterfowl and also as a refuge for other wildlife. Since then, Fenton has earned state park status. Fly fishing for cruising browns and stocked rainbows was how Mark and I

#10 parallel to the banks can fool resident browns. Realistic hopper patterns splashed on the edges work, too. Fish early, and again late in the day.

Early September through mid-October is also conducive to big numbers. There will be fewer anglers, and cooler temperatures prevail, spurring easier fishing. Woolly Buggers will still be productive.

Nonmotorized floatation devices are allowed on the water, and the northwest bank was recently fortified in several areas to make fishing easier, safer, and wheelchair accessible. Fenton is the choice for float tubers and kayakers, beginners, kids, and the physically challenged to catch lots of browns and stocked rainbows, with some reaching 18 inches.

Day-use fees of $5.00 per vehicle apply, and overnight camping is $10 per night, with five electrical hookup sites running $14. From Highway 4, turn north on NM 126 at the San Antonio Creek bridge near La Cueva and continue for about ten minutes.

Rio Cebolla

Fishing the Rio Cebolla demands precision, Zorro-like stickwork, and an ideal presentation every cast. We found out the hard way that the difference between expert and idiocy couldn't be more diminished than on the banks of the Cebolla (pronounced se-voya). On numerous occasions (more than I care to admit), this runnel made me feel silly for even attempting to fish it. But with practice and keen instruction from Williams (a skilled fencer back in his col-

rested and nested here after long hours of hike-fishing.

Fed by the Rio Cebolla filtering in from the valley at the northeast, the man-made dam at the southwest end creates a thirty-five-acre brown trout haven. When the Jemez River and supporting cast of creeks muddy up from sudden showers, fishers find sanctuary at Fenton Lake State Park.

By midwinter the lake freezes over, and fishing through holes in the ice helps locals escape the wintertime doldrums. But late spring and the onset of insects are what beckon most fly fishers to visit.

In early May, damselflies are prolific. Fishing olive Damselfly nymphs #6 to lege days), the trout in the meadow downstream reinvigorated my ego.

In arid years, the upper Cebolla above Seven Springs Hatchery is tough fishing and trout are often sparse. Closer to Fenton, the river picks up and trout are plentiful. Only slightly more significant than Peralta Creek, the wild browns (and Rio Grande cutthroats in the headwaters above McKinney Pond) are almost always willing partakers. If your fly is the precise size and drifted flawlessly, five to ten trout an hour are feasible statistics.

Let a Parachute Adams or a Royal Wulff #14 to #20 alight near cuttbanks and spills, letting them glide all the way through the pool. Nearly every inch of bank, riffle, and pool here produce action, especially where we fished farther downstream. This creek entertains curious anglers from Fenton Lake, so make it worth your while by hiking downstream at least ten minutes before indulging.

After a few hours on the Cebolla, Williams and I found ourselves dapping, shooting line and bow and arrow casting like masters, lazerbeaming flies into impossibly tight spaces—between two fallen branches, under overhanging scrub oaks, between tall, opposing stands of prairie grass. Rio Cebolla will force you to be a tactician, and by the time you leave, you will be.

From the north side Fenton Lake, drive up the northwest shore to the dead end near the bathroom. As the road curves right, turn uphill and find the unnumbered parking area. Hop out and cross the gate on foot, following the creek until you feel like turning back to fish upstream.

East Fork of the Jemez

The East Fork of the Jemez is one of those waters that cultivated my partiality for small, intimate streams. For me, catching wild, aloof trout that are holding just a rod-length away is truly special. When that happens, I know I have somehow appeased the trout gods. Mark assured me they would be smiling upon us this day.

For most, the East Fork is the highlight of the Jemez system. Its magnificent entrance is marked by Battleship Rock, an awe-inspiring, hull-like rock formation created by the convergence of San Antonio Creek and East Fork of the Jemez. These tributaries create the Jemez River.

Battleship Rock Trailhead (six miles north of Jemez Springs on Highway 4) begins at the formation's base and sidles along streamside, or close thereabouts. Smaller paths often stick closer to the river as East Fork slithers through the country's most beautiful wilderness.

I found East Fork canyon a magical place. I swore I'd been transported to the northwest, perhaps Oregon or Washington. Fallen obsidian monoliths cluttered the canyon. Wondrous surprises hid behind these slick, black stones. Pool after pool held numerous trout, often teeming side by side. Most of mine taped out at 12 to 14 inches, with a few prowling in the deeps reaching 16 inches. Wild browns were most common, and rainbows are stocked regularly near Battleship Rock.

Plunges yawned at ten to fifteen feet wide. The heads of pools scoured down four to five feet deep, shallowing up at the tail where a fine gravel bottom offered sure footing. Be sure to fish pools thoroughly with a #16 to #18 Pheasant Tail nymph or Beadhead Prince about fourteen inches below a big Doc's Cork or a puffy Stimulator. This will coax those elders out when dry fly action tapers off.

Cunningly approach rock ledges and watch for rises under shelves, or at the sides of pools where vertical rock faces jut up from the stream. Cast into the froth and let them swing down the smooth walls.

September is prime time. Most fly fishers have swapped their rod and reel for remote controls. While football reigns, the East Fork is murmuring her lonely autumn song to few anglers. But you won't be alone. The area is popular with hikers and campers who can unintentionally sully your water. They, too, love sightseeing on East Fork, appreciating the stark contrast of the brilliant foliage against the blacks and grays and greens of the canyon. Be patient and courteous to all nature-goers.

Also fish East Fork from late spring to midsummer. The occasional shower can cause a day or two of chocolaty runoff, which nearly all of the Jemez fisheries experience.

If you hike far enough upstream, you'll fish a fantastic meadow until reaching the boundary of the Baca Ranch, where you should turn back. To fish the Baca Ranch, you must enter and win a beat through their lottery system. (For more information on the Baca Ranch lottery, visit www .vallescaldera.gov.)

As an added bonus, the East Fork also bestows fly anglers the possibility to fish during winter. Supplemental flows from natural springs keep 200 yards of East Fork from freezing. Near the east entrance of the box, tepid pools allow trout to remain active and hungry for beadheads like tiny red Copper Johns or Pheasant Tails. Snowshoes, Neoprene waders and felt bottoms with studs are advisable in winter. And you might think twice about fishing the East Fork without a partner in any season, but especially when ice or snow is present. Felled trees and slippery conditions can make for a treacherous outing whether it's freezing or not. More than once, Williams had to help me up from the deck after I slipped on the rocks.

"I'd hate to leave you lying for the bears to get you," he remarked.

"I have the keys to the truck in my vest. You wouldn't get very far without me."

He agreed and we fished on, heeding caution.

Rio Guadalupe

Rio Cebolla and Rio de las Vacas converge at the abandoned town of Porter, creating Rio Guadalupe. Productive stretches of this river flow below NM 485 in the canyon—a fissure-like crevasse where steep walls, deep pools, and rushing falls make for excellent brown trout fishing. From Highway 4, turn north on NM 485 and park in the turnout before the canyon's entrance.

In the box, rock-hopping was dangerous but thrilling, as the same smooth rocks found at East Fork were present on the Guadalupe. But here, the gushing water was far more intimidating. "Hefty browns nestle down in these parts," according to Albuquerque-based guide Robert Trammel. In order to fool them, anglers should expect awkward body positions, negotiating boulders and navigating rip-roaring pocket water. Weighted nymphs are essential when dry fly action fizzles.

Trammel notes, "Most years, early June produces a giant stonefly (*Pteronarcys*) hatch. Sink dark-colored stonefly nymphs like a #6 Beadhead Stonefly eighteen inches below a fat, well-dressed Stimulator or Sofa Pillow in the pockets and pools. Reliable caddis and mayfly hatches also occur from spring through summer."

NM 485 passes through old railroad tunnels near Guadalupe Falls, then abruptly turns into FR 376. This dirt road parallels the fifteen to thirty foot-wide river for about ten miles. Most summer days, dry fly fishing is great from the falls upstream. Follow FR 376 upstream to find eager browns. Focus on deeper pools, passing on mediocre water. Stimulators, Light Cahills, Pale Morning and Evening Duns, BWOs and caddis patterns in sizes 16 to 20 fool even the wisest trout.

Special Trout Waters regulations apply in the section from Llano Loco Spring upstream to the bridge at Porter, 1.3 miles of fishing. Artificial lures and flies only with single, barbless hooks. Release all trout immediately, with none in possession.

Rio de las Vacas

Following NM 126 past Fenton Lake, Mark and I experienced a growing sense of melancholy as the river slowly abated. After passing Seven Springs Hatchery, we were tempted to turn back half a dozen times. Our fortitude paid off as Rio de las Vacas suddenly appeared. Rejuvenated by the stream's subtle, meadow-winding nature, from the Jeep we spotted trout rising in pools.

Parts of this classic freestone creek reside within the boundaries of private property. Finding the public stretches of this quaint stream is easy and reaps rewards of easily wadable, gradually sloping banks, long, narrow pools and ten- to fifteen-foot-wide riffles that hide wild browns, rainbows, and even Rio Grande cutthroats in the headwaters above the Girl Scout camp.

On the Vacas, the trout can sense your presence. Their lies are unassuming—

behind petite rocks, in the slim shade of trees, beneath menacing aquatic vegetation. Your approach on the Vacas must be low and slow.

May and September are the best months, when extended casts and faultless presentations are essential. Use 7X tippet and size 16 to 20 Hi-Vis Parachute Adams or Comparaduns, or #12 to #14 Doc's Super Caddis. Since aquatic hatches are sparse, have some hopper and terrestrial patterns.

Trammel relayed reports of a possible chemical spill in upper Vacas that may have damaged the ecosystem. Only time will tell. The lower Vacas might still be productive, and can be reached by turning north off of Highway 4 onto NM 485. Proceed through Gilman, following the road that parallels Rio Guadalupe past Porter, where the Vacas (west) and Cebolla (east) converge.

Peralta Creek

Because of its isolation, few fishers visit Peralta Creek. But for the physically fit angler who loves solitude and wily trout, Peralta is bliss. A true step-across rivulet, Peralta varies between one and four feet wide. We drove up FR 280 off Highway 4, fifteen miles west of Los Alamos. There a well-marked, rough gravel road, FR 280 eventually dead-ended after about six miles, testing the two of us with a 4.5-mile lung-buster of a hike to the stream. The payoff for this fantastic voyage, you ask? Lots of brookies and a fine population of one of the purest strains of Rio Grande

cutthroats in the Southwest . . . exactly what Williams and I live for.

Once at creekside, we moved upstream toward the canyon, fishing the frequent pools and cutbanks with a sneaky approach and perfect drifts. Lengthy casts of fifteen feet or more were occasionally possible, but the streamside vegetation became a nuisance, necessitating shorter flicks of line . . . more my style. Once in the canyon, two-foot-deep pools were everywhere, and successful casts were contingent upon our approach and presentation.

Size 16 to 20 Adams, Elk Hair caddis, and Royal Wulffs produce slashing strikes. Although rarely longer than your hand, the blush, vibrant colorations of these trout are intoxicating. Please practice your quickest catch and release technique when you land Rio Grande cutthroats. Don't forget to save some water, a lot of energy, and enough daylight for your strenuous hike out. And it wouldn't hurt to let someone know where you'll be fishing for the day, just in case.

San Antonio Creek

San Antonio Creek embodies the best of both worlds—wide open meadows and deep pocket-water canyons. In spring, the upper San Antonio meadows are the place to be in the afternoons, from 2:00PM on. A green caddis hatch can be matched with olive Elk Hair caddis. Attractors like yellow Humpies also trick trout. Presentation here doesn't seem to be nearly as crucial as with other Jemez waters.

The upper part of the creek above San

Antonio Campground is particularly popular; novice anglers find it easy to cast, and catching numerous stream-bred browns is undemanding. The secret is also out about the canyon water just above Battleship Rock, with a particularly fine stretch gurgling below Dark Canyon Rest Area. Easily reachable by foot, hike from the rest area downstream, then drop in and fish back to your vehicle.

The ubiquitous obsidian boulders coupled by the deep, winedark pools make traversing upstream a chore. Most anglers won't explore too far. Take advantage of others' lack of adventure and trudge on, being especially cautious with footing.

The Dark Canyon pools will take your breath away, but stealth remains imperative. One technique we enjoyed on this stretch was scaling the giant rocks to spot fish before fishing the massive plunges. Remove your polarized lenses to keep from spooking fish with reflections. Peek over the rock ledge down into the pools. When fish appear, it was exhilarating. And once we saw them from this vantage point, trying to remain quiet and calm while climbing down was nearly impossible. Keep your wits about you when you go.

Stimulators, Humpies, and Elk Hair caddis are about all you'll need, other than small versions of Woven Stones, various Copper Johns, and Hare's Ear nymphs to sink behind them. Fish the heads and edges of pools. Making flies appear realistic is the key here, principally during prolific black caddis hatches. A little twitch can make all the difference.

Jemez River

Wintertime streamer and nymph fishing is a favorite season for locals on the namesake of the area, thanks in part to a few low-elevation natural springs. Late April to early May is a fine time for fishers to visit the Jemez as well, as is September through early November.

Much of the river is featureless. Flat, straight water with a few riffles gives novice fly casters the opportunity to present fat dries to stocked rainbows. Use Irresistibles, Parachute Adams, a green or yellow Humpy, and Royal Wulffs in sizes 14 to 18; smaller flies are rarely needed. Instream improvements create slow-moving water above the logs, and deep, foamy spillways below. Dries followed by nymph-droppers, such as Princes and Pheasant Tails, generated more strikes than Roger Clemens. When Mark and I left the Jemez, we were totally satiated.

Because of the geology, moderate water temperatures, and the elevation of the river basin, the Jemez River isn't the prettiest fishery in the area, but worth pulling off Highway 4 near Battleship Rock into one of several turnouts for an attempt at landing some fish.

North Central New Mexico. North of Albuquerque and west of Los Alamos, the Jemez River and the East Fork of the Jemez are accessible from Highway 4. Fenton Lake State Park rests on NM 126, as do fine stretches of Rio de las Vacas. Rio Cebolla parallels FR 376, and fish Rio Guadalupe along NM 485 and FR 376 north of Jemez Pueblo. Peralta Creek is ten miles off Highway 4 down FR 280 at the end of a foot trail.

CONTACTS
Southwest Fly Shop, 505-891-0944, www.southwestflyfishing.com
Robert Trammel, The Reel Life, 505-268-1693
Charlie's Sporting Goods, 505-275-3006
High Desert Angler, www.highdesertangler.com
Los Rios Anglers, www.losrios.com
Vince Homer, 505-771-3132
This is an adapted version of the article that first appeared in *Southwest Fly Fishing*, 2006. Best mag of its kind on the market.

Red River

- **Location:** Northern New Mexico
- **What You Fish For:** Rainbow, brown, and cutthroat/cuttbow trout
- **Highlights and Notables:** Canyon stream, a real southwestern gem, pools and pocket water, resident wild trout, and when they get the urge big trout run up the Red from the Rio Grande

When the world above is a winter wonderland, the canyon is a refuge. And in summer, when the heat is like Hades, the canyon is cool and hidden from the oven above. Descending along developed trails into the basalt-walled canyon is strenuous hiking. The views of the heavily-bouldered, freestone-river are eye-catching. You just know there are some whoppers in those deep stairstep pools.

And there are. The lower Red River is the primary feeder stream to Rio Grande, the main spawning tributary for wild browns, cuttbows, and rainbows of the mighty river. The Red holds its own healthy resident population of colorful wild browns and cuttbows but the prizes are those migrating lunkers, up from the big river to spawn in these spring-fed waters.

The river cut a canyon through the basalt over eons of time with its watery knife slicing ever downward. The clear water churns over boulders, dropping off rocks and plunging into foamy pools. Some of the rocks are as big as kiva ovens. Others are the size of watermelons. And you won't believe the size and depth of some of these pools even though the river isn't all that wide.

Numerous warmwater springs feed the river below the hatchery keeping the water temperatures in the high 40s and low 50s in the fall and winter. In the summer, the canyon water around can reach mid-60s.

These springs increase the volume of the river tremendously, tripling or quadrupling the flow.

The Lower Red River is four miles of some of the wildest water in New Mexico. When you hear the term "lower Red River," this refers to the Red River upstream from the confluence with the Rio Grande to a half-mile below the hatchery. Four miles doesn't sound like a lot of water but you won't cover all this water in a day of hard fishing. These four miles fish like ten or twelve miles, so productive is this fishery. Every pocket holds fish.

The Red River is one of those streams where you can do just fine on your own or you can do a lot better with someone looking over your shoulder, someone reminding you that despite the two fish you just caught in that big pool, you missed two other opportunities to catch even bigger trout. That someone should be a guide.

As Doc Thompson likes to say: It's a whole different world down there. You will lose track of time and where you are. To fish the lower Red River, you really need to want to fish it. This is not a drive-up river. You'll need stamina, want-to. This is for those who need adventure in their fly fishing or vice versa, one of the last of the wild rivers in the Southwest, ideal for a get-away trip when all the tailwaters are full of Neoprene-wading anglers from all parts of the world.

CONTACTS

Doc Thompson's High Country Anglers, Cimarron, 505-376-9220, www.flyfishnewmexico.com

Ed Adams, www.edadamsflyfishing.com

Los Rios Anglers, 505-758-2798

Dos Amigos, Eagle Nest, 505-377-6226

Los Pinos Fly Shop, Albuquerque, 505-884-7501

High Desert Anglers, Santa Fe, 505-988-7688

Van Beacham's Solitary Angler, Taos, 505-758-5653

Rio Costilla

- **Location:** Northeastern New Mexico
- **What You Fish For:** Rio Grande cut-throat
- **Highlights and Notables:** Green-rimmed caldera with a fertile, stunningly beautiful blue stream that holds the rare RG cutt

Anglers looking for incredible panoramic vistas of ancient volcanoes, pristine meadow streams, and wild trout should look no further. While everyone else is standing shoulder to shoulder on the San Juan, Big Hole, or Green Rivers, you could be controlling a couple of miles of this stream, fishing for native Rio Grande cutthroats. And you can even take a leisurely lunch and not feel as though you'll lose your stretch.

Valle Vidal. One of those places that induces good times and memories.

The isolated Rio Costilla runs for miles through a wide valley, curving back and forth through the caldera. The waters are clear and shallow, alternating between long, flat stretches where the cutts hide under deep cut banks, and foamy, deep bend pools where the big trout lie in wait. The roads in are long and rough, preventing most anglers from making the trip. But the Rio Costilla is a special stream that simply cannot take the pounding of other streams—the trout and riparian habitat are too fragile. The river opens in early July to protect the spawning cutthroat and stays open until mid-December.

Trout anglers are always searching for

the ideal trout stream. This perfect river would flow cold and clear, be off the beaten path, and hold populations of big and wild trout. For a topper, wouldn't it be nice if this river ran through a verdant caldera, home to extinct volcanoes? There is such a spot, tucked away in the middle of nowhere where anglers can get away from the madding crowds and fish for rare trout.

Even though Valle Vidal is remote and isolated, a trip to the region is worth the effort. And it does take some doing. That's why it's not overrun with other recreationalists. You have to want to go to the Valle Vidal; it's not something you pass through on the way somewhere else.

The Valle Vidal Unit of the Carson National Forest consists of 100,000 acres between the villages of Cimarron and Costilla. Valle Vidal is a large grassy bowl rimmed by small rolling mountains covered in aspen and fir. Wildlife abounds in the unit, everything from rattlesnakes to elk, bison to bear, deer to the aforementioned wild trout.

Several trout streams run through this caldera but the two blue ribbons you'll want to concentrate on are tiny Comanche Creek and its bigger sister, Rio Costilla. Their confluence, with Comanche Peak standing sentinel over the junction, is the stuff postcards are made of.

Anglers will be rewarded with some of the best angling for wild cutthroats anywhere in the Southwest. New Mexico Game and Fish electroshocking surveys show that over 4,000 trout per mile inhabit

these waters. The fish you're after? The rare Rio Grande cutthroat.

The Rio Grande cutthroat is the prettiest fish you'll ever catch. Their sides are splashed in aqua-green and royal purple. Their gills have been painted with iridescent blood-red slashes. In the water, against the pebbly bottom, they are invisible. In your hand, they are wiggling Monets. In the bigger water, they average about 11 to 15 inches long. In the lesser water, they average 8 to 12 inches long. You will catch Rio Grande cutts, hybrids (rainbows breeding with cutts), and rainbows. Regulations protect the cutthroats and it's a good thing, too. Rio Grande cutthroats inhabit less than 7 percent of their original habitat.

It's a quirky place to fish. The low-slung green mountains that rise gently up from the caldera through which the Rio Costilla runs will remind you of Paradise Valley in Yellowstone National Park. The fishing season doesn't begin until July 1 in order to protect the spawning cutthroats. You'll see thousands of grasshoppers on the banks and in the fields. You might hear anecdotes about longrodders catching fifty cutts on a Dave's Hopper. But the guides will tell you that another quirk of this fine fishery is that in spite of the hot fishing days and plentiful, juicy insects, you might go all day and not catch a fish if you're not in tune with the fishery.

The Rio Costilla usually has good flows from July to September because irrigation needs ensure consistent flows. After September, flows are reduced but so are the number of anglers. Fall can offer some of the best fishing of the year albeit in low water conditions. Comanche Creek is a step-across stream snaking through open fields, a tiny trickle of water that at first looks like it doesn't even hold trout. Bully for you. It does. Let others bypass this gem. That's the beauty of this narrow meandering creek—no one bothers to fish it. The Comanche holds plenty of Rio Grande cutthroats ranging from fit-in-your-palm size to wow-I-had-no-idea-that-size-fish-lurked-in-here size (roughly translated that means the fish range from 6 inches to 14 inches).

Fish Comanche as stealthily as you would if you were stealing your sister's diary while she sleeps or you'll quickly be discovered. One trick is cast from several feet back off the stream, letting your last two or three feet of tippet drop softly on the water but the butt end fall on the grass. Stay low and off the water, look for the deepest holes and the most undercut banks. Oh yeah, if you fish the upstream from where the paralleling road departs, the wind can really kick up.

Shuree Ponds are best fished with nymphs and streamers. The water is clear and the big trout look like cruising submarines. The rainbows and hybrid Rio Grande cutthroat in Shuree Ponds dwarf those you'll have been catching in the river. Some anglers make the trip into Valle Vidal just to go after these behemoths.

CONTACTS

Doc Thompson's High Country Anglers, Cimarron, 505-376-9220, www.flyfishnewmexico.com

Ed Adams, www.edadamsflyfishing.com
Los Rios Anglers, 505-758-2798
Dos Amigos, Eagle Nest, 505-377-6226
Los Pinos Fly Shop, Albuquerque, 505-884-7501
High Desert Anglers, Santa Fe, 505-988-7688
Van Beacham's Solitary Angler, Taos, 505-758-5653

Rio Grande

- **Location:** Northern New Mexico
- **What You Fish For:** Rainbow, brown, and cutthroat trout, pike
- **Highlights and Notables:** Rugged canyon river, mighty and unforgiving. The trout grow strong and sturdy, some topping 10 pounds. The pike eat the strong and sturdy trout and grow bigger than 10 pounds.

On one trip into the Rio Grande in New Mexico, Kenny and I brought along my best friend of thirty years, Lance. We hopped the big rocks along the river, watched a dead cow float in the chocolate milk–colored water and caught several hefty rainbows and browns. Lance got tired because he's not much of a fly fisherman, more because of his frustration level than skill, he won't give it a chance, so he went back to the Troutmobile to take a nap.

We had to keep one nice trout, a 16-inch rainbow because it was bleeding badly, having taken a Woolly Bugger deep. Kenny and

I scrambled out of the canyon, up the big rocks, jumping from one to the other, high enough to notice two folks across the river. They were approaching a natural hot spring, a blonde woman and a balding man.

The man stood and watched as the blonde disrobed. Naked. On the banks of the Rio Grande. In plain view. She saw us and waved in all her nudity. We waved back.

A third person came into view as we sat down on a big rock, stunned. She was a redhead and was as pretty as the naked woman who now sat on the edge of the spring pool. She, too, took off all her clothes. The blonde said something to them and they all three turned our way and they waved to us, across the muddy river, where two miles away in the parking lot Lance was missing out seeing two lovely naked nymphs bathing at a pool, a myth being played out before our eyes and we did the only thing we could do—waved back at them. The river was too roily and dangerous to swim across.

Like Lot and his wife, we walked out of the den of sin, certain that if we looked back, we'd turn into pillars of salt. We looked back. No salt.

We gave the trout to a bohemian couple camping riverside, their German shepherd sniffing the fish and trying to steal it. We woke Lance and told him the tale. He wanted to descend back into the canyon and see for himself but Kenny and I were veterans by now. This was a once-in-a-lifetime scenario and Lance missed his chance. You guys know the old proverb: If you snooze, you lose.

The Rio Grande cuts a mighty path on its seventy-mile southward course from Colorado, through the wide valleys of New Mexico. The Rio Grande is a wide free-stone river with deep pools, wide glides, boulders, big pocket water, and riffles, inaccessible except in a few places due to the 600- to 1,000-foot-deep canyon. Various springs feed the river.

Pike have become the winter draw on the river. Look for deep, slow pools, fish rainbow trout streamers and hold on. Trout lovers can drop a line for big browns and fat rainbows and a decent population of cutthroat trout. Cast around rocks, along current edges, foam eddies, and at the head and tail of pools.

This is big water. In a big canyon. With big fish. Don't take the hike in lightly.

The headwaters of the mighty Rio Grande begin in the San Juan Mountains in southern Colorado. There the river flows past 13,000-foot rugged peaks, through alpine meadows and narrow canyons as it moves south toward New Mexico. Along the way, the land opens up, flattens out, and the river collects water from feeder streams and the Rio Grande grows big and swollen. It's not all that far past Pilar where the trout no longer live and the river makes its turn toward Texas and its long run to the Gulf of Mexico. That said, there is plenty of roadside access and good trout fishing around Pilar.

The Rio Grande has lots of trails over a fifty-mile section. The trails down into the chasm where the river runs are steep, rocky, not for the faint of heart. Running the river in a raft is an adventure but offers anglers float-by looks at some of the finest trout holding water in the West.

Hike into the Rio Grande by 10AM when the sun hits the water. Fish the heavy water, catch a lot of browns and rainbows, begin the arduous hike out by 4PM when the sun creeps away, leaving you in cold shade and with a long hike out.

It's a good idea to bring a daypack with food, water, and a jacket. In case of a bad fall (not to scare you, but this is the wilderness), I bring a first-aid kit. And always fish with a buddy. Better yet, hire a guide and let them show you the ropes of how to locate the 10-pound browns and the 20-pound pike swimming the pools of the Rio Grande.

San Juan River

- **Location:** Northwestern New Mexico
- **What You Fish For:** Rainbow and brown trout
- **Highlights and Notables:** This high-desert tailwater is just amazing. Amazingly consistent, amazingly productive, amazingly fertile. The river grows big fat trout all year long. One of the best trout streams in the world.

Kenny cussed more than I ever heard him cuss that evening I caught the 10-pounder. She was finning near a rock below the Cable Pool in the middle of March with the snow in the air and the water low. Fin out of water. Next to a big male. Size 22 Disco Midge. Cast from her right back passenger side, above her, saw the slight move, the white mouth and it was on. 7X tippet and a big-ass rock. Not a good combo to land a mad 25-inch fish.

Kenny got up on her in a flash, net out. I let her run, put her on the reel, got her head up, reeled her close and then she was out and we did it all over again. This was one big momma. She leaped, tailwalked, and then oohs and ahhhs from some standersby. Great, I had a crowd.

Ten minutes later, she's in the net, Kenny's net, the big trout's body a gallimaufry of greens and purples and a red color so intense, it was as though the trout had been side-swiped with the paintbrush from *What Dreams May Come.* Her tail stuck

out of the net a good ten inches. Several anglers waded out to where we were, snapping a couple of quick trophy pose photos before we released her. She swam off, we shook hands, grinned, waded back to the parking lot in the dying gray evening sky.

Next morning. Parking lot. Putting on our gear. SUVs with Texas plates in most every parking spot when Kenny's sailor-mouthed tirade began. His net was gone. He remembered that he had meant to find a cord to tie it to his vest but had forgotten to do so. When he let go the big 'bow the night before, both the trout and his net floated off to nether places, never to be caught again. What goes around comes around and that day, on the far side of the Texas Hole, in front of seventeen anglers fishing shoulder-to-shoulder on the near side, Kenny caught no fewer than twenty

trout when no one else was catching a thing (and why should you if you have no more gumption than to fish shoulder to shoulder?), caught them on an RS2 emerger variation he tied himself and each fish was a carbon-copy 18-inch fighting beauty.

Colorful high-desert canyon walls line this cold, wide river, one of the premier trout streams in America, a fishing mecca located in the remote northwestern corner of New Mexico near Aztec and Farmington. The tailwater is full of heavy trout and focused anglers. It's a popular winter destination, with an armada of watercraft and decked-out fly fishers fighting over three and a half miles of regulated water.

Not to worry, the river is so profound, so fecund, that all you need is to locate your very own fifty-yard radius and you'll be casting to a day's worth of fish. In your staked-out territory, you can cast to long glides, backwater flats, runs, deep pools, channels, riffles and lots of unremarkable, hard-to-figure water. Don't fret, thar's fish down there. The odds are good you will hook up with an 18-plus-inch trout, maybe longer, but the odds are lesser, even for seasoned vets, that you will land the fish.

The population is predominantly rainbow and brown trout. More rainbows reside in the upper section, more browns in the lower section. Rainbows and cutthroats average 13 to 20 inches with many over 20 inches. Expect to hook-up with several in the 2- to 5-pound range. The brown trout population has increased the last few years, especially in the lower section of the quality waters and below it. The browns get big, too, but aren't as plentiful. Ten-pound browns are caught in the river every now and again. San Juan trout are broad-shouldered and use their strength to take out line and make your reel scream.

Armed with a day's lessons of how to catch the Juan's fabled fish, you can cast away in the Texas Hole with forty other Orvis-clad anglers; cuddle up to fellow fishers at the Cable Pool; or slip and slide on the slippery bottom cursing at how easy it was to drift drag-free midge larvae through riffles and runs when you were with the guide the day before.

The river has seen some drastic environmental challenges the last few years and these won't end soon. Low water flows will likely continue to haunt anglers (and shops and guides) for a number of years to come. But the San Juan is resilient and despite low flows each winter, the insect populations have stayed healthy and so have the trout.

CONTACTS
Abe's Motel and Fly Shop,
 www.sanjuanriver.com
Anasazi Angler, www.sanjuantrout.com
Rizuto's Fly Shop, www.rizutos.net
Soaring Eagle Outfitters,
 www.soaringeaglelodge.net
Rainbow Lodge and Resolution Guide
 Service, www.sanjuanfishing.com
Andy Kim, www.fly-fish.com

The Pecos Wilderness New Mexico

These aren't the tallest mountains or the most rugged peaks or the least trafficked trails but there's something about the Sangre de Cristos in the Pecos Wilderness in northern New Mexico that's hard to put your finger on. If you ever hike in, if you ever drop a fly on the Mora or the other feeder creeks to the Pecos River, if you ever camp a night on the Mora Flats, you'll be hooked. There's magic in them thar hills.

The upper Pecos watershed does provide solitude for anglers although if you hike and fish the Mora Flats, you're bound to run into another angler or a horsepacking group. The mountains run about 13,000 feet and they are towering and magnificent, standing sentinel over this meadow stream. The Mora is cold, clear, and challenging to fish.

The Pecos River headwaters hold buttery browns, colorful cutthroats and cuttbows. Mora Creek is one of the most popular and while not large, isn't a jump-across creek either. Anglers can catch some nice fat browns in Mora Creek. Take one fly box, load it with dry flies and enjoy the fast action in the pools, runs, riffles, and undercut banks. Stick in a handful of beadheads and a couple of Woolly Buggers because you want to make sure that you don't leave any big fish in the deep pools untempted.

Two ways to find the upper Pecos: One is to hike upstream from the Mora Campground, but to reach the uppermost section of the stream, anglers will need to hike or backpack in from the Iron Gate Campground on Trails 249 and 250. Other streams in the upper Pecos to consider for some adventurous angling include Willow, Holy Ghost, Panchuela, and Jacks Creeks.

The season is short in the Pecos high country, June to August. The Pecos Wilderness offers angling in numerous high country lakes and anglers can usually find fish feeding on top. Three of the most popular (read: the easiest to reach) are Stewart and Spirit Lakes and Lake Katherine, all three along the Windsor Trail, six to eight miles from the trailhead. They hold heavy rainbows and cutthroats. Other productive lakes include Johnson, Lost Bear, Enchanted, Truchas, and Pecos Baldy Lakes.

Anglers can access the Pecos Wilderness off of I-25 just east of Santa Fe at the Glorieta exit. Turn north on NM 63 at the town of Pecos and you will drive riverside to Cowles. Remember, though, if you go, you'll feel the enchantment of this place.

What: Backcountry wilderness full of lakes and streams. **Where:** Northern New Mexico. **Gear:** Pack a multipiece light rod.

The Brazos River is where sophisticated, then-fly-shop-owner Manuel Monasterio (he's now a respectable stockbroker in Santa Fe) thought he hooked a nice striper but pulled in a dirty catfish as long as his arm. Where Charles Carter started out on a canoe trip with a so-called friend and they ended up arguing so much that after five miles of down-streaming, he turned the canoe around and paddled back upstream so he could leave his new enemy. Where we turned in a guy who was using a motorized toy boat to fish for stripers (he caught one, a nice one, and you'd think it would have capsized the boat but there he stood, smiling, temporarily, holding up his 10-pounder). Oh yeah, where Oregonian and fly fishing clerk/guide Jerome Butler tipped over into the cold morning water trying to step into his float tube.

■ ■ ■

Lance told us that Michael Chiklis was 27 years old and we laughed. At the time, Chiklis was the star of *The Commish* and he was bald. He didn't have the look of a guy in his late twenties; rather, he looked closer to 40. We were sure Lance was mistaken and I should have known better, for Lance is seldom mistaken.

Michael Chiklis was indeed only 28 at that time but for the entirety of the fishing trip on the Guadalupe, the five of us were merciless in that locker-room way that guys gang up on guys who slip up and show a weakness. Lance took it well but for the last thirteen years, Lance has returned the favor.

The five of us plus the mistake-free Lance were: my brother-in-law David and three of his Exxon coworker buddies. We did the Austin thing, eating Tex-Mex at Chuys with all of its kitschy Elvis stuff, and since we were staying on the river near Gruene, we had to visit the dance hall and the Grist Mill. We were fishing up and down the river, sometimes at Bean's Camp, sometimes at the TU water, sometimes in float tubes and rafts working our way downstream.

We were doing best with caddis emergers when the trout were obviously feeding on emergers. The trout were slashing, their dorsals and backs out of the water and then they were coming completely out of the water. A submerged Elk Hair wasn't working as well as a Goddard with Xink on it. Green caddis pupa and any kind of emerger were

the happening flies. Only one of us caught a trout of any size, a 16-inch rainbow. In most streams where trout are stocked, you can catch the hatchery fish rather easily. Not so in the Guadalupe. This is a technical river for trout.

In places, the water was crazy shallow and the fish were holing up under cutbanks, in V-shaped channels, under ledges and any deeper water they could locate. In those cases, we had to add splitshot and get the flies down on the bottom.

Lance caught one nice 12-inch rainbow by accident, casting to a rising small trout but getting his cast nowhere near, five feet to the right, in a patch of open water in a cluster of cypress knees where the trout exploded out of the water to smash his fly.

At Bean's Camp one morning, we six fished with about fifteen other fly fishers. Almost like opening day on an Alaskan stream or at Bennett Springs in Missouri, we lined up almost shoulder to shoulder facing the shady bank where the trout were feeding. When one would catch a trout, and it wasn't often, heads turned to ask what that angler was using, what he was doing differently. The trout would hit a fly and then it wouldn't work on any of the others—like the Borg, you can hit them once but after that, the collective changes defenses and what you used as a fly (or weapon) will never work again.

When we were floating in rafts, we should have stopped more often to wade fish but the trance of cypress tree-lined banks, limestone bluffs, and multihued clear, cold water kept us joking and talking and sometimes, weirdly, silent, just taking it all in. We did catch a few Guadalupe bass on streamers. Many anglers love to go after striped bass, especially up by the dam.

And oh yeah, each raft tumped over at least once at any of many low-water dams. Be careful on the real roily ones because they're death traps. Ditto when the dam is releasing water over 400 cfs.

Michael Chiklis is now in his forties and the star of my favorite TV cop show, *The Shield*. Lance doesn't even have to say anything to get me on how we made fun of him on the Guadalupe. Best friends for thirty years, fishing buddies to boot, there's an understood silent code of retribution. I don't have to say anything to let him know that I know that I was wrong and he was right because you know what? What goes around comes around and if he were to make too big a deal out of it, he might fall in the stream next time or hook himself with an errant cast and so on. It's the fishing buddy way, after all.

■ ■ ■

My Papaw and Uncle Bob had that sort of patience and would work the brush and stumps and humps and creek channels for largemouth. Papaw favored Carolina-rigged lizards; Uncle Bob liked to work the plastic worms. It's a hoot to see him talking, cigarette hanging out of his mouth, then setting the hook and getting that big Uncle Bob smile that says I'm good, I told you so, and a lot of other uncle-to-nephew things.

When Uncle Bob would get serious about largemouth, he'd get up early (the only time Uncle Bob gets up early) and fish topwater for the big smashing hits. I'll give him his props. Dude can fish.

■ ■ ■

Mark D.

Hopefully, by the time you get this, you'll hit the big time and forget who I am but knowing you, that won't happen. You have a hard time forgetting friends.

I've always had a funny feeling about you. It's almost like we met too late in our lives. It feels like we've been friends since we were little guys.

The time we had together was good and I want to thank you for being my friend. Check on Suzy and the boys for me now and again. Take the boys fishing when

they are older. When they are older, let them drink a beer or two, smoke a cigar, take naps on the bank of the river. Make sure they know how much I enjoyed being outdoors with nothing better to do than fish.

Take care when you hit it big. Don't change. You promised you wouldn't.

Love,
Terry Moore

The truth is this: Anyone who regularly fishes knows fishing shouldn't be about catching fish, and you know that and I know that, but it always becomes just that. When you hear someone say fishing is fun even if one is not catching fish, I can promise you he or she has either had the best catching day of their lives or they're in the middle of being skunked.

I kept looking over my shoulder at Terry wondering how in the blazes he kept hooking up while I flopped fishless cast after cast twenty yards from his offerings. I gritted my teeth and smiled when he'd reel in another thrashing redfish. We slowly waded across the sandy bottoms and through the wide grass flats of Lower Laguna Madre, the boat anchored a hundred yards behind us. For as far as we could see, water and sky and gulls.

While driftfishing from the boat earlier in the morning, I luckily caught and released a nice red and a couple of speckled trout. I had even landed a flounder, which with both its buggy eyes on one side of its pancake-flat body must surely be one of God's practical jokes of nature. Since we had left the boat my luck had run out, and as we waded across the flats, our feet shuffling to spook any and all stingrays, rationalized that I shouldn't be caught up in the numbers game, this wasn't about catching fish.

I had flown down to the Texas coast from Dallas a couple of days earlier, leaving my family and the North Texas metroplex with the ground frozen under a sheet of winter ice. Wading wet in shorts and short sleeves, sweating, breathing in the sweet smell of salt, I felt a tinge of guilt. All too many years, I spend an obscene number of days on the water, most of the trips during the warmer months, most of the time on rivers fishing for trout. I fish all over the world and even in the winter, I fish great spots like the San Juan, the Green and the White Rivers, but most of the time it's cold, snowy, even miserable weather.

Terry and the guide pretended not to notice I had not landed a fish in hours although Terry shot me a disdaining look and knowing grin from time to time, shaking his head as he hooked another. They jeered me when I finally did hook up with a big bull, its pull like that of a freight train, only to lose it after five minutes of tug o' war, the rod's lazy curve flicked straight by the snap of the tippet. Man, did they give me a hard time then.

Somewhere in the afternoon, I got caught up in the rhythm of Terry's casting, his gentle, wet swoosh of the line, the fluorescent orange cutting across the azure skies like a laser beam. As the day faded, the emerald water and the blue sky merged into gray-ness, the horizon and distant ocean becoming one. It's not about catching fish, Terry and I joked later at the bar. After all, he just had the best fishing day of his life and I had been roundly skunked, so somewhere in the middle, like the sky and horizon, we understood why we were qualified to rationalize that awkward but honest credo. He didn't give me a hard time about my piss-poor luck until a few weeks later when he called me on the phone to rub it in.

I thought about that fishless trip the other day when I was stuck behind a pile of papers at my desk. I reached for the phone to call my fishing buddy, Terry, to ask him if he wanted to get out of town this weekend and hit the water. It still hasn't sunk in yet. Terry died at age 32, from cancer, leaving behind a wife and two young boys. I'd gladly trade a lifetime of fishless days with Terry for the best day of fishing every day of the rest of my life. It's not really about the catching . . . it's all about the fishing.

Lake Alan Henry

- **Location:** West Texas, 65 miles southeast of Lubbock
- **What You Fish For:** Largemouth bass
- **Highlights and notables:** Alan Henry is quite likely the best big bass lake in the nation right now.

I'll say this one time and one time only. Lake Alan Henry is the best bass lake in the country that nobody knows about. There. I said it.

There's nothing harsh about this South Plains lake, this lake with the steep shorelines of brush and sandstone rocky ledges that filter the clear water. Here, the anglers and the bass are not coerced into fighting and feuding. They enjoy easy transactions, fish and fisher. The hunt, the struggle, the fish in hand, the release and they both move on to the rest of the day. West Texas friendliness, the spirit of cooperation.

Few know that this lake of nearly 3,000 acres, with its population of Florida-strain largemouths planted a decade ago, has so religiously held up its end of the bargain. The lake produced more 13-pound bass in 2005 than did the most famous bass lake in the world—more than Lake Fork. Surprised?

The Lake Alan Henry record for a largemouth is 14.94 pounds. [Whoops. Since I wrote this two months ago, the lake record has been upped to over 15 pounds.] So many bass run 8 to 12 pounds, it's ridiculous. Those who fish it know that one day soon, the next 18-pound bass will be caught from these amber waters. If Lake Alan Henry were located near Dallas or Atlanta or Los Angeles, you couldn't unload a boat for days. As it is, weekends are crowded in the same way as a Wal-Mart in a Texas small town is crowded (plenty of room for everyone) but lightly pressured during the week. Hell, no one lives out here in West Texas after all and it's a booger of a drive from anywhere to get here.

Make the drive. Fly into Lubbock, home of the Red Raiders, drive an hour

southeast, unload your boat and start fishing. Go deep, go flats, go to bedding bass, go to cover, go to coves, go to humps, fish the flooded timber, mesquite and cedar, the submerged brush. When you have your fill of 5-, 6-, 7-pound bass, the occasional spotted bass, you eat at Holly's or George's or maybe grab a Subway sandwich, you watch whatever's on local television back at the motel and get to sleep early because there's nothing else to do but sleep and eat and fish.

CONTACTS

Lake Alan Henry, www.lakealanhenry.com
Texas Parks & Wildlife, 806-655-4341
Brazos River Authority, Lubbock, 806-762-6411

ALLIGATOR GAR

Growing up in Texas, fishing off docks, from boats in the shallows, I saw more than my share of alligator gar. They are prehistoric. They look like the marriage between a coelacanth and a small alligator. Toothy mouth combined with a long snout. Droopy fins. Scales like medieval iron-mail. Alligator gar are u-u-u-g-g-g-l-l-l-y. They are trash fish. Worse than carp.

We'd see them off the dock, especially at night under the lamp, cruising like an ironsides submersible. I never thought anyone would purposefully fish for these things. They do.

Those who catch them say they are amazing fighters. They thrash and pull like

the dinosaur that they are. Like tarpon, some have the temerity to say.

Those who catch them use bait; they cut up other trash fish like carp or drum or buffalo. The teeth force anglers to use stainless cable leaders and some don't even use bait or lures. They use braided rope that gets caught in the fish's scary teeth.

Those who catch alligator gar claim some of these mutants they land weigh as much as 250 pounds, sometimes more.

Those who catch them talk about sight-fishing. Yeah, like casting to a skyscraper. Fun, fun.

Those who catch alligator gar are mental.

You can pick almost any Texas lake, Sam Rayburn and Livingston stand out, and if you search the shallow grassy slow water areas, you'll come upon alligator gar. You're a fool but have fun because that means you're not in my way of catching large-mouth and sandies.

CONTACTS

Scott Swanson and FishQuest,
    www.FishQuest.com

Lake Athens

- **Location:** East Texas
- **What You Fish For:** Bass
- **Highlights and Notables:** The fishing is good or better, the scenery high on the scale but the Texas Freshwater Fisheries Center is the real reason to visit Lake Athens.

Folks from outside the Lone Star State are always surprised to learn that Texas has 4,960 square miles of inland water, ranking it *numero uno* in the forty-eight contiguous states. Texans like to be first in anything and everything, as you probably know. And if you know a Texan, you probably get annoyed at them being so danged Texan. There are over 6,700 reservoirs in Texas. That's a lot.

Texas has more quality bass lakes than any place else in the world. California and Mexico and Florida might be able to make cases but they wouldn't hold up in a court of piscine law. Lake Athens is not one of Texas's top ten bass lakes but any lake in the top twenty-five in the Lone Star state is still one of the best fisheries anywhere in the world.

Lake Athens is a pretty little wooded lake, 1,800 acres and loaded with 2- to 8-pound largemouth bass. The lake record largemouth weighed 13.81 pounds. Two things that separate Lake Athens from other Texas lakes: 1) great for fly fishing (and popular with fly fishers) and 2) the Texas Freshwater Fisheries Center, which houses a state-of-the-art hatchery. The Visitors Center is a must-see for any angler with its museum (so cool), various aquaria of fish, a catch-and-release pond, educational programs and more. Visitors can see any Texas freshwater fish in its natural habitat. Plus the center has frequent fishing and casting lessons. This is a hoot.

Texas is seriously hot in the summer and it gets mighty hot on Lake Athens. Fishing and ambient temperature. The lake has sub-

City Fishing

AUSTIN
Lake Austin, Town Lake, Lake Travis and Bull Creek

In a recent tournament on Town Lake to catch a record carp, a lucky or very good angler did just that, landing a 43-pound carp. The man won the money for first prize totaling . . . now listen closely . . . $250,000. For a carp. One can also angle for largemouth bass, catfish, and sunfish in Town Lake, right in the heart of Austin. I saw one writer called it "urban backcountry angling," which is true in Austin because it's got to be the most forested big city in the nation.

Bull Creek feeds into Lake Austin. Big deal you say? Bull Creek is one nifty little creek, especially if you just want to catch a few hours of stream-time during downtime. Within minutes of downtown, out west of town, in the rock-strewn hills and the canyons dotted with stands of trees, it's almost wild out there, and through this runs Bull Creek. The clear cool creek cascades over rock ledges and tumbles down waterfalls and flows past limestone cliffs.

East of 360, the creek deepens and you can and should be in a float tube, personal watercraft, canoe, raft, or other floating device. Bull Creek gets deeper and wider and the trees descend right upon the water, making bank fishing difficult. The river has been reborn with lots of clean up, restoration, harmony with nature, that sort of thing—tires and washing machines gone. The creek has good-to-great access with numerous creekside parks along its course providing easy access and a great place to be seen catching fish. You have to compete with bikers, hikers, bathers and floaters, Frisbees, and dogs.

Lake Austin sits on the Colorado River, all 1,800 acres of it. Scenic but developed, the lake holds big bigmouths, some of the largest largemouths in the area, up to and over 10 pounds, cash money. Drop a line also for catfish, bluegill, and redear.

Lake Travis is where Austin money buys second homes on the wooded rocky steep shore. Hilly and woodsy, Lake Travis doesn't produce big fish but you can have a whale of a day fishing for white bass (sandies), Guadalupe bass, largemouth bass that aren't large but are plentiful, and catfish. Watch out for boats and skiers.

merged timber and plenty of aquatic vegetation. Like all Texas lakes, it has riprap near the dam. The shore is green with beds of hydrilla, Eurasian watermilfoil (aka milfoil), and alligator weed. The lake has a full-service marina, double boat ramp and in nearby Athens, a quaint town, you can find good diner-type food and motels. Lake Athens holds lots of tourneys so at times it seems busy.

CONTACTS
Texas Freshwater Fisheries Center, 903-
676-2277

Brazos River

- **Location:** Near Mineral Wells down to just west of Houston
- **What You Fish For:** White bass, stripers, carp, and more
- **Highlights and Notables:** Clear and long, the Brazos is the essential Texas stream, floatable and fishable, loaded with all kinds of game fish.

The Brazos River below Possum Kingdom Lake is a lousy trout fishery. But the stripers and carp in this medium-sized tailwater two hours west of Fort Worth grow big and fight hard. And I have lots of stories from this water, too.

On trout stocking days, anglers line up to pitch salmon eggs and corn at the new inhabitants. When you see these opportunists, head for the dam to cast to the splashes of feeding stripers or walk downstream to fish the slow side channels for carp and striper. Many recreationalists canoe the Brazos, fishing for perch and river bass, especially in the spring and summer. White bluffs overlook this pretty tailrace.

The Brazos is a super winter fishery, the Texas weather rarely turning cold and the river and tailraces providing amazing fishing for white bass, stripers and spotted bass. Just don't count on good trout fishing.

The Brazos gets impounded by Granbury Lake and Lake Whitney and then Waco Lake. Eight hundred miles of river, this Brazos, starting in New Mexico and winding through hot Texas.

The best stretch is probably below Whitney for stripers and black bass as well as smallmouth, spotted, and sand bass but it's also productive between Granbury and Whitney, too, for stripers and smallmouth (the smallie fishery is getting better and better). The Brazos River below PK (you won't hardly hear a Texan call it Possum Kingdom) and Whitney are two of the more scenic areas in Texas with their limestone bluffs and rolling hills and live oak and cedar and clear water. Remember white bass are called sandies or sand bass in Texas.

The Brazos River at Possum Kingdom Lake

During weekdays, few fishers venture onto the clear waters. The weekends and summers are when these waters see visitors, anglers and tubers alike. If the Brazos is a fine winter fishery, things really heat up from spring through summer. You can fish for the 8-inch trout in one of Texas's few trout fisheries; that's your choice. But the stripers will probably get to them first, and it's those big boys I'll be chasing.

Choke Canyon Reservoir

- **Location:** South central Texas
- **What You Fish For:** Largemouth bass
- **Highlights and Notables:** Fertile south Texas big bass lake

It's funny when you hear reports of a lake's early demise, in this case by drought, and you know, sure as shootin' that it's gonna rain again that close to San Antonio and when it does, all new terrain will be flooded and the lake will be a big hit with bassers again. Choke Canyon Reservoir (also Choke Canyon Lake) went through this little scenario the last decade and it's fishing as good as ever now.

Located about an hour's drive south of San Antonio, near the town of Three Rivers, this impoundment of the Frio River has everything the visiting bass angler could want. Launch ramps. Camping facilities. Remoteness. Several species of fish in healthy populations and a lot of baitfish for them to dine on. Brush everywhere, in the shallow flats, on the banks,

Baylor Lake
I think I can, I think I can. The little lake that could. Small municipal lake near Childress somehow produces big fish, lots of 10-plus pounders, even up to 15 pounds. A municipal water supply lake.

in the open fields—you expect to see javelinas charging out of it any second ready to tear your foot off. They're out there, you know. So are alligators. I'm not even funnin' you.

This 26,000-acre lake is best fished in winter and spring but even in the heat of the Texas summer, anglers can catch bass in these clear waters. Maybe you won't beat a world or even state largemouth bass record (lake record is 13-plus pounds) at Choke Canyon but you will have a blast casting to all the submerged structure—timber and brush, diving lures off the points, wiggling crankbaits through the coves. The fishing has been hot and heavy the last few years with lots of bass and lots of big fat bass and you keep hearing every

day about someone landing another 10-pound black bass.

Choke Canyon Lake has so much timber and brush, hydrilla and grassbeds that you better have a trolling motor to get back to where the bass are holding. And with all the shallow water with structure, Choke Canyon is excellent for fly fishers. The lake has dynamite fishing for white bass especially in the Frio below the lake. Blue catfish grow well here and anglers will also find channel and flathead catfish, alligator gar, and crappie.

And I'm not kidding about the alligators. You couldn't get me in a float tube on Choke Canyon Reservoir if I was wearing a suit of conquistador armor.

Pettrigrew Ranch, Texas
Seventy-acre gravel pit, clear as vodka, chock-full of bass. Popular with serious anglers who know how to cast and land bass. Dallas fly anglers love this place. Pettigrew Ranch, Route 1 Chatfield, TX 75105, Home: 903-345-7331

City Fishing

DALLAS
Lake Fork, Ray Roberts, Joe Pool Lake, Trinity River, Lake Lewisville

I lived in Dallas for fifteen years and my family calls Big D home so I can speak with some authority about it and its surroundings. The idea many nonnatives have, the one that Dallas-area anglers all live in Garland and that their bass boats with all the bells and whistles are pulled behind three-quarter-ton pickup trucks and the combination cost of those two items doubles the price of the house (or in another version, the mobile home) is just not totally true. Oh, the idea is true in fact because I've fished with those guys and gals but Dallas has fly fishers and saltwater lovers and those who love crappie and catfish and stripers and bluegills and sand bass and anglers of all ilk.

Is there bass mania in DFW? Go to Bass Pro Shops or Orvis Dallas some day when an angling expert is holding court and you'll see. See if you can be the first to launch from the boat ramps at any area lake in the morning. The Metroplex has so many lakes and rivers and private ponds within an hour or two drive that you could fish a different one each weekend and still need a few more weekends after year's end.

Lake Fork is the nationally reputed bass king and this superior lake is less than two hours drive away (see Lake Fork entry). Benbrook Lake (3,770 acres) is only ten miles southwest of downtown Fort Worth and this small lake isn't bad for largemouth bass, hybrids, sandies, channel and blue catfish, and crappie. Grapevine Lake (7,280 acres) is an underrated largemouth bass lake, managed by the Corps of Engineers, Trophy Club, and the city of Grapevine. The lake is loaded with timber and docks and all kinds of bass housing. The lake sits right next to DFW Airport. Joe Pool Lake (7,470 acres) is a newer lake in the Arlington–Cedar Hill area with the skyline of Dallas looming large in the distance. I haven't found it to be a great largemouth lake even though you hear reports every now and again of some nice days and nice fish. With all the submerged timber, you'd think it would be a good bass lake. I hear enough experts and locals talking about the excellent fishing, and they're also whispering a lot so maybe it will grow into it (or has and nobody's talking loud enough for me to hear). Joe Pool sits in rolling hills and is one of the more scenic lakes in the area.

White Rock Lake (1,100 acres) sits in a fancy schmancy part of Dallas and it looks like anything but a productive lake. With the anorexic north Dallas joggers huffing and puffing around the lake, the huge palaces overlooking the lake, the Lexus and Hummer SUVs buzzing about, you'd be hard-pressed to believe that if you tossed out a lure, you'd have a good chance at catching some decent largemouth bass. My (nameless) buddy fishes White Rock Creek, which it is also known as, and catches some big-ass bass but none of us are certain that it's public so I am not going to say any more about it. Lake Lewisville (29,592 acres) is north of Dallas near Lewisville, one of the numerous suburbs around DFW. It's a recreation lake for the most part and the habitat's not the greatest for largemouths but fishing for catfish, crappie, and sand bass is fair to middlin'. Ray Hubbard (22,700 acres)—I grew up fishing this lake with Papaw and Uncle Bobby but we mostly caught sandies and catfish while we ate Vienna sausages and saltines and drank Cokes. I hear the hybrid and largemouth fishing is pretty good if you know where to go. Actually, his name is Bud and he knows where to go and he fishes humps and points and has caught two bucketmouths over 10 pounds. So it is pretty good. Shhh. I know the crappie and catfish angling is still solid and I'd guess this is one of the better all around lakes in the area.

There are those hearty souls who fish the Trinity River and its feeders. You see there 1977 Chevy pickups and 1975 Country Squire station wagons parked by bridges and overpasses. You're talking mostly catfish and sunfish and carp and the like, even though I have a friend who swears by the sand bass in one local creek. The Elm Fork is a good one if you just have to river fish while in the Metroplex.

Devils River

- **Location:** South Texas
- **What You Fish For:** Smallmouth bass
- **Highlights and Notables:** Primitive setting, the largest bronzebacks in a river you'll find anywhere

I got scared on this river. We were alone, isolated, in the middle of nowhere, hell, in the middle of the desert, in a canyon, in a prehistoric desert canyon, a dark prehistoric desert canyon with dangerous roily water and chutes, in a land with scorpions and rattlesnakes and *chupacabra* and *la lechusa* and *la llorona*. You laugh but you haven't traveled the river of the devil just yet, have you?

Chupacabra isn't real of course. This creature is the goat-sucker, the creature that kills cattle and goats and other livestock by sucking out their blood. Chupacabra has a number of incarnations but the most common sightings say the beast is a cross between a winged-alien and a coyote. This is an urban legend unless you are on the Devils River and your imagination is running wild. Lechusas are witches to be sure and sometimes they are half woman, half bat; other times half woman, half owl. Witches smitches. You laugh but float the Conservancy water toward evening and see if any of the millions of bats in nearby caves don't get the hair on the back of your neck standing as they swoop and flutter like so many bad 1960s horror movies.

La Llorona: witch, siren, harlot, virgin. Another urban legend popular in south Texas and across the border. She is a *bruja*, a mother/wife who in one version of this *leyenda*, after discovering her husband cheating, drowned her own children in a nearby river in a moment of jealous insanity. She steals children's souls and at night, you can hear her cries coming from the river.

The Devils River.

Enter at your own risk.

Why would anyone want to brave one of the wildest rivers of the North American continent? After all, public access is limited. No amenities exist (period). Mean, aggressive landowners post lots of warnings and they mean what they say. Heavy rains create flash floods of a biblical nature. The rocks and limestone will break your boat or your back or your spirit. Your leaders will fray and abrade from the submerged rocks. They are tenacious. This is the descent into hell, the journey to the heart of darkness. Kaiser Soze probably has a house on this river.

First, I'll get this pun out of the way; any article you ever read about this primitive river uses it. Man, these smallmouths are great fighters, they really fight like the devil! Okay, there. So why endure all the Dantean circles?

The smallmouth bass are why you come

here. Devils River bronzebacks are spirited bass. Originally introduced to Lake Amistad, they moved out and into the Devils River where in the cold water and numerous rocky hiding places, they excelled. They grew plentiful and big although they are not typically as deep as other name-brand river smallies. But they are more aggressive, mad at being caught, ornery as the land around them. A 20-inch smallmouth is realistic. A 5-pound smallmouth is realistic. What's probable are lots and lots of 16-inch bass and your biggest a 3-pounder. And if you get lucky, you can catch some tenacious largemouth bass, too.

The waters are clear because the river is spring-fed, because the water that comes into the river flows through limestone. The water has a slight greenish tint but don't think that this bit of color means the water is not clear. The river has pools and runs, both deep and shallow, and periodic rapids. Bass hide in the crevices and under ledges. In low water times, anglers will have to portage canoes over shallow spots. These brown bass will take poppers and other assorted lures and flies but if you fish deep, especially with streamers, you will catch more fish.

When I say Devils River is remote, that's an understatement. Not that long ago, I heard or read somewhere that only about two hundred anglers a year float down the Devils River. I think there are more now but probably no more than, on average, one angler per day annually. Maybe fewer if you factor in those who get taken by chupacabra, lechusa and la llorona while on the river.

CONTACTS

Devils River Outfitters, 830-395-2266

Texas Parks and Wildlife Department, 800-792-1112

The Nature Conservancy, www.nature.org

Falcon Lake

- **Location:** South Texas, border lake with Mexico
- **What You Fish For:** Largemouth bass
- **Highlights and Notables:** Timber-filled lake with Tex-Mex charisma loaded with hawgs

The four best places in the world to catch largemouth bass are California, Florida, Texas, and Mexico. With Falcon Lake, you get two of the four in one fell swoop.

Tell me if you've heard this before. Drought. Lake dries and dries until it is only one-fifth of its original size. Anglers stay away because they can't get their boat into the lake. In the exposed and new shoreline, trees and vegetation grow. Rain, rain, rain. The lake fills back up and it acts like a new lake, a freshly-flooded lake with lots of standing timber and shallow hiding places for juvenile bass. That's the story of Falcon Lake the last decade. Stories of the lake's demise were premature. In fact, the lake still fished well despite shrinking to less than 20,000 acres.

Falcon Lake has all the ingredients for a bass-angler's heavenly destination:

Seventy miles southeast of Laredo, this 78,000-acre lake is warmer in winter than its counterparts to the north.

- Remoteness. This Rio Grande impoundment is a real getaway. You feel like you're going somewhere. The border of Mexico-Texas runs down the middle of the lake.
- Lots of largemouth bass.
- Lots of *big* largemouth bass. Florida-strain, what else?
- Heavy cover, diverse underwater terrain, forage fish, vegetation.

Texans have some great legacies of entitlement. For instance, they believe they have a birthright to owning land and also skiing the mountains in New Mexico and Colorado. Good barbecue and Tex-Mex food. Texans also feel entitled to fishing any of five or ten bass lakes near wherever they live. Heck, depending on where a Texan lives, they might have five to ten world-class lakes within a two hour drive from their house. This means that however good Falcon Lake is, and baby, it's that good, any Texan driving his bass boat from Dallas or Houston or San Antonio is going to have to drive right past other lakes of similar quality. That means fewer fishermen on Falcon Lake. That's better for you, right?

Falcon Lake isn't producing the numbers of 10-pounders of Lake Fork (but 8- to 10-pound largemouths are in Falcon and do get caught) but you will catch an unusual number of 1-, 2-, and 3-pound corpulent bass (more 3-pound bass than you have ever caught) and with all the heavy cover now, you'll need to bring your bigger rod.

The spring and fall bring topwater smashes from the stout bass in the shallows.

The lake has a little bit of everything in terrain, ranging from coves to flats to submerged huisache to deep points. And you can have acres of this fertile, shallow water all to yourself. More importantly, you can get a great selection of cold Mexican beers and hit a taqueria or two in Laredo.

Fayette County Lake

- **Location:** Central Texas, southeast of Austin
- **What You Fish For:** Largemouth bass
- **Highlights and Notables:** The average bass is about 4 or 5 pounds and at Fayette, you can catch lots of them.

There are those who say that this "little engine that could" can only do so much. Fayette County Lake has the highest bass density in Texas and we're not talking small bass either. The average largemouth catch is 3 to 6 pounds. Them's big fish, friends. What the whispers say is that while the lake produces an unbelievable number of prize catchables, they have a top end. These folks believe that Fayette County Lake won't ever be in the running for a state record.

They might be right, who knows?

But let me ask you this—is a lake where you can go fishin' and use just about any strategy and tackle you want, and still catch ten or twenty bass all between 3 and

6 pounds—is that one helluva day of fishin' or not?

Fayette County Lake is small, only 2,400 acres, a warm-water discharge cooling pond power plant lake. This small (but big) lake has all kinds of habitat—humps and bumps, grass, flats, flooded timber and more. Slot limits help keep the average bass 3 to 6 pounds and guides will tell you that the lake has lots of 8-pound bass and some up to 10. The lake record largemouth bass is 12.25 pounds. *I think I can, I think I can, I think I can.* Fayette County Lake is located ten miles east of La Grange off Highway 159.

Lake Fork

- **Location:** East Texas
- **What You Fish For:** Largemouth bass
- **Highlights and Notables:** Most believe this to be the best big bass lake in the world.

Few fisheries could hold up to the worldwide recognition that Lake Fork receives for being the best bass fishing lake on the planet. One study reports that over 365,000 visit the lake each year.

Lake Fork is the best bass fishing place
 in the world. Many think so.
There may be lakes where the bass are
 bigger. But I doubt it.
There may be trophy bass lakes with
 better scenery. I don't think so.

Lake Fork brings it all together. Big bass
 boats. Bigger fish. Possible records.
 Bring your A-game. Your best rod.
 Two tackle boxes. Ten-dollar lures.
Lake Fork is bass fishing heaven. High-
 tech electronics, GPS, beer.

I have not caught a double-digit largemouth on Lake Fork. The biggest, 6.5, maybe 7 pounds. I am not embarrassed. This is a tough lake. When I fish here, I do catch fish but most of them are 5, 6 pounds. I have friends who fish it regularly and they tease me since so many of them have 10-pounders to their name. Bully for them. The 18.18-pound state record is bound to eventually fall and with the fertility and structure, Lake Fork has as good a chance as any other to break it. I hope one of my friends breaks it.

East of Dallas, an hour if you drive fast like so many in Big D, an hour and a half for normal folks, sits Lake Fork, all 27,000 acres of beautiful bass bonanza. The lake hasn't kept up with the various Mexican and Californian lakes that jump up each year with a 19- or 20- or 21-pounder; 18.18 is impressive but where are the sowbellies breaking the two-oh mark?

Lake Fork produces regularly, if not spectacularly, 10-pound bass a commonstance. Sure, the lake hit a lull in the '90s but it was but a nap, everything's good in east Texas again. Submerged timber and heavy vegetation, tire reefs and manmade brush piles, boathouses and docks. The lake has structure, Texas-style. Other ingredients include Florida-strain largemouth, harvest regulations, hydrilla, a friendly Texas Parks and Wildlife.

The lake has held a majority percentage of the Texas top fifty largest bass list. Lake Fork has supplied more than its fair share of the Share-A-Lunker bass. At one time, the lake provided twenty- to forty-fish days, now ten- to twenty-five-fish days. With a guide. Did you know that over 300,000 people fish this lake each year? The best anglers from all over the country, all over the world come to Lake Fork to see if they can break the code. Now that's pressure for a lake this size. Still, the topwater action can be awesome and so can night fishing when the boat noise settles down.

If you've never spent a day in July in east Texas, then you don't know hot. The fishing just isn't as consistent nor as productive during the summer as it is in fall, winter, and especially spring. The lake has cabins, food, boat rentals, and ramps and guides. Canton First Monday has one of the more incredible flea markets you'll ever see (once a month).

You know, one of these days, it might just be me who catches the next state record in Lake Fork, heck, maybe even the world record, not that I care about those things. I'll just hire Rob Woodruff for a day or a week and I'll go trophy hunting. And when I do, I wonder what my fishing buddies are gonna say to me then.

Lake Fork's bass slot limit is 16 to 24 inches. You may keep five bass under 16 inches or you may keep four bass under 16 inches and one bass over 24 inches per day. Please practice "Catch-and-Release" and "Safe Handling" of all bass, and be courteous on the lake. Texas Parks & Wildlife info, call 800-792-1112. Computer generated license, 800-895-4248, Visa and MasterCard only. If you catch a fish weighing 13 pounds or more, call 903-681-0550 to donate it to the Budweiser ShareLunker program.

CONTACTS
Texas Parks and Wildlife, Tyler, 903-593-5077
Greater Quitman Chamber of Commerce, 903-763-4411
Rob Woodruff Guide Service, www.flyfishingfork.com, 903-967-2665 (I think Rob knows more about the Mountain Fork and Lake Fork than anyone in the world)

Gibbons Creek Reservoir

- **Location:** 20 miles east of Bryan in central Texas, Brazos Valley
- **What You Fish For:** Largemouth bass
- **Highlights and Notables:** A productive power plant lake with lots of heavy bass

In all the annual hubbub of early morning debates at coffee shops and tackle shops over which Texas bass lakes are the top ten in Texas, and therefore the world (if you ask any Lone Star angler), some of last year's or last decade's greatest bass lakes get lost in the shuffle. I grew up fishing on power plant lakes and there was always a pattern. The lake would open up and fishermen would fish the hell out of it and in two or three years, the luster was off and they'd be lining up at the boat ramps at the newest lake *du jour*.

Dad didn't fish much but he did like fishing in the winter at power plant lakes, their steam coming off in the gray cold sky. We'd leave early, Dad with his thermos of hot coffee, me with my pillow. Monticello was his fave. He later fished Gibbons Creek with me when I was a young adult and he caught the biggest fish I'd ever seen him catch, a solid 5- or 6-pound largemouth out of a sister trio of submerged trees. He was a Carolina rigged-worm fan. It worked for him one time and he was a guy who stuck with what worked. We didn't talk much during the morning before he caught the solid fish, nor did we talk much when we loaded the boat before lunch. I didn't catch a single fish that day. Dad liked fishing power plant lakes but he didn't like fishing them for long. Dad also liked them because he built power plants and every engineer would rather look at a power plant and cooling pond than forests or lake houses.

Gibbons Creek is small, only 2,500 acres, an impoundment of two small Brazos Valley creeks. Over the years, the lake has produced a number of 10-pound bass. We're not talking clear water here; it's more the color of lukewarm Shiner. Good amount of standing timber. The current lake record is 16.17 pounds. When Dad was bed-bound in his last year, terminal cancer, he and I talked during one rainy afternoon about our trips to Monticello and Fairfield and Gibbons Creek. I never went to Fairfield with him and to Monticello only three times that I remember but I didn't bring any of that up. I pretty much remember every word that quiet old fart said to me on those trips and whatever he wanted to remember on his part was okay with me. Weird thing is he asked if I remembered that big bass I caught on Gibbons Creek. I didn't know what the heck to say so I said nothing. I just nodded. Closed on Wednesdays.

CONTACTS
Texas Municipal Power, Bryan, 409-873-2424
TPWD Fisheries Office, Bryan, 409-822-5067

Hill Country

- **Location:** Central Texas
- **What You Fish For:** Guadalupe bass, spotted bass, carp, stripers, bluegills, smallmouth bass, and much more—even trout
- **Highlights and Notables:** I haven't seen many places or regions in the United States with so many quality angling opportunities—Yellowstone, Driftless, Boundary Waters, the Hill Country. The rolling hills and wildflowers and cool, clear streams defy description and the fishing is underrated, underfished.

Any excuse you can find to go to the Texas Hill Country, well, that's a good excuse.

I lived in Austin and I lived in San Antonio (twice) and I kinda figure I'll live in or near one of those cities again in my life. It's one of those places that when you're a kid, there's an overload of stuff to do, when you're going to college it's the coolest town in America, and when you're old, it's the perfect area in which to retire.

In the late 1960s, we lived in apartments right on the Colorado River in Austin, Texas. Town Lake Apartments or something like that. I took my five-year-old sister Tammy to shore to fish the river and we caught a perch. I went back to the apartment while Tammy kept vigil over the fish and I brought our glass bowl complete with our pet goldfish. The perch and goldfish barely fit together in the glass bowl and Tammy whined for me to let her carry it through the pool area, up the stairs, and back to the apartment.

I knew better. She got giddy and wasn't watching where she was going and she fell and there was glass and blood and screaming and in the end it turned out okay, all she needed was a few stitches but it could have been much worse. We threw the goldfish and the perch back in the river.

Austin is the capital of the Texas music, artists like James McMurtry, Joe King Carrasco and the Crowns, Shawn Colvin, Kelly Willis, Charlie Sexton, Nancy Griffith, and so many more. Willie and the boys made Austin their musical home as have so many other top musicians over the years, including songwriters like Gary P. Nunn and Ray Wylie Hubbard.

The cool hip town has the best bookstores and music stores and coffeehouses and restaurants and cafés and bistros in the Lone Star state as well as some mighty fine Tex-Mex. The town is home to the NCAA football national champion Longhorns but don't hold that against it. If you can stand the heat of summer, Austin ought to be added to your list of must-dos.

The Hill Country is a land of rugged rolling hills, limestone bluffs, clean clear cold streams seemingly everywhere, caves and

springs, cool people and people who want to be cool. Bluebonnets and spring flowers and wildflowers; German and Czech and Mexican populations that settled this area (and that means the Hill Country has great festivals). The Hill Country has the best Tex-Mex food in the state as well as the top barbecue and dance halls and country music and live music. Oktoberfest in New Braunfels is not to be missed. Ice-cold local micro-brewed beer. Mmmm good. Hippie Hollow (ask about this secret and you'll find out the secret). Wadefishing and canoeing and kayaking and float tubing and boating and tubing opportunities (tubing is a specialized activity perfected by college-age kids and generally performed during the summer months on area rivers).

Fredericksburg, Bandera, Boerne, Wimberly, Canyon Lake, Gruene, New Braunfels, Marble Falls, San Marcos, Kerrville, Llano, Salado, Luckenbach, Hondo, and Lampasas are just a few of the neat historic Hill Country towns to visit. In recent years, the Hill Country has become the center of the Texas wine industry.

Guadalupe River

The Guadalupe River is a beautiful limestone river, flowing from Canyon Dam near Gruene (eat at the Grist Mill, dance and drink at Gruene Hall), sparkling clear and cold, offering over ten miles of good trout fishing for those who choose to pay a small fee to gain access. The record for rainbow trout on the Guadalupe is a 8.25-pounder and the brown trout weighed 7.1 pounds.

These are atypical. You will catch mostly rainbow trout and for their length, they will be fat. The trout are getting chubby on caddisflies and crayfish and minnows in this fertile limestone stream.

The ten-mile trout fishery keeps getting better and better, more and more big fish, and it survived the big flood of 1998 and fire ant attacks and increased fishing pressure. Some locals say that there are signs of natural reproduction in this, the southernmost trout stream in America.

The trout section of the Guadalupe (below Canyon Dam) is difficult to access. The state accesses are not very good fishing spots. You can pay a fee at several accesses and they are more hit than miss. You can wade the high-water mark once you are in the river. Beware that when the weather heats up in the spring and all through summer, armadas of drunk college kids and noisy kids will float by and cover the stream and fishing becomes more of a combat sport.

The Guadalupe warms up quickly so about fifteen miles downstream from Canyon Dam, the trout are all gone. In both the upper and lower Guadalupe, anglers can fish for smallmouth bass, Guadalupe bass, largemouth bass, spotted bass, sunfish, catfish, and carp.

Llano River

Amy and I fished with Woody and Beverly Vogt here one spring weekend. One of those Hill Country getaways that spoils Texans. Rich, spicy food, indulgent sweets, a little wine, too much shopping, stay in a quaint bed and breakfast, and the husbands get to fish. Woody and I were disappointed that we missed the white bass run.

But that didn't stop us. We hit the spring-fed limestone stream outside of Mason (I think it was at the James River Crossing) with our fly rods in hand. I was excited to catch Guadalupe bass, a green bass that acts much like a trout and will take dry flies and poppers and will jump and fight much harder than its weight would suggest; and I was excited about catching largemouth bass, some of which get to 5 to 8 pounds in this clear water. Heck, the Llano holds Rio Grande perch, catfish, sunfish, and several other species, so I wasn't too worried.

Amazingly clear water; so clear that a couple of times I couldn't tell exactly where

to step next and nearly tripped. I've heard others say it's so easy to wade because it's clear but I wear bifocals and am about half blind so that's the way it rolls for me. And the Llano has the most undulating, oddly colored (pinkish) river bottom of any river I've seen, granite and limestone. The rock croppings are everywhere. Mesquite and other scrub brush cover the rolling terrain. I think Woody caught two or three bass and we each caught a Rio Grande perch but here was the highlight of our trip (other than that old leather suitcase Amy bought to go with our other four old leather suitcases) was (drum roll, please) . . . carp.

I know, I know. Carp. But they were feeding right across from where we weren't catching fish and the day was growing dark and it was more of a dare. I caught my carp, after fifteen or more casts right in front of the big boy, on a jig-type of fly. When we hooked up, he went into an alligator death roll and then changed over into bulldozer mode and wore me out until I finally landed him and his copper-colored prehistoric self. Seven or 8 pounds. Ugly as hell.

The best way to tackle the Llano is to float it, especially in a kickboat or float tube. The Llano River is one of the wildest, most beautiful rivers in Texas. The forks above Junction are fishable and you'll be angling all by your lonesome. Even on the main stem, you won't see many anglers except maybe in the parks in and around Llano but the fishing is solid there, too. A lot of friends of mine tell me they float the Llano and catch thirty to fifty fish in a hard day's float. Try it and see. Maybe you can catch the white bass run, or land you some feisty bass . . . or maybe even a big ol' carp.

Blanco River

Another classic Hill Country spring-fed limestone stream with the same old boring incredible scenery and ho-hum array of fighting fish. The Blanco River is lined with big green shady trees, runs clear and cool, and has the usual limestone crevices, flats, ledges, pockets, and pools. This river might be the slipperiest river in Texas, the limestone bottom is like walking on greased lizards. The water is as clear as any other Hill Country stream but it does have a light green tea color.

Access is limited on the Blanco so the most efficient way to cover it is to float it. Because of the private land, the Blanco is not as pressured as other Texas Hill Country streams. You may not see another fisherman on your trip. Combine the vistas with

the solitude and the opportunity to catch lots of large smallmouth, large largemouth, and the usual fun diversity of other fish (the Guadalupe bass, hybrids from Guadalupe and smallmouth bass, perch, for starters) and you have a worthy destination.

The Blanco is sometimes a big wide deep river and sometimes the water is barely there. The fishing can be good when it's low. The water is clear and the fish are everywhere and the water is so clear you have to be stealthy and cast to shadows and will regret moving too quickly. When you do hook a smallmouth, it might be one of the big ones, a 20-inch or bigger, a 4-pound, colorful-as-a-small-Texas-town-carnival big one. Here's a secret . . . in the big pools, in the most remote stretches, you might land a largemouth that goes 5 to 8 pounds and fights like Marciano.

Some use rafts, some float tubes, most use canoes. Get ready to swim at some point. The smallmouth bass eat from a buffet of insects, crayfish, and minnows. Even the sunfish get big and beautiful on the Blanco. Every pool, every run, every cutbank seems to hold fish on the Blanco. You'll find out because the water is so clear, you can see them to sightcast to them. If you fly fish, streamers are the only way to go.

Frio River

I think the Frio River is the prettiest river in Texas. Sure, it favors many of the other Hill Country rivers with its limestone bed and limestone bluffs and clear spring-fed water and bald cypress trees and tons of fish, but the Frio has something special.

For one thing, it's cold as ice even in the summer. I bathed/swam in it *sans* clothing one trip, so I can vouch for how cold it is. Its remoteness also makes it special.

As the river moves south from Leakey toward and past Uvalde, the river moves through Garner State Park (eye-candy but crowded) and down into desert-like settings replete with Texans' favorite vegetative pest, mesquite. All alliterations aside, the fishy Frio has large pools with large largemouth. While the Frio is a shallow river, you will find deep pools and runs here and there. Don't miss fishing the heck out of them. You won't miss them because the water is so clear, maybe the purest cleanest water of any stream in Texas, that you will see the fish in them with no problem.

More than most Hill Country rivers, watch out for trespassing. The landowners take their land as seriously as their brethren did in the late nineteenth century. Drive west on US 90 out of San Antonio for about an hour to Sabinal. Turn right on State 127 then go to Concan. Turn right on US 83.

Colorado River and Its Tailraces

Uncle Bobby and I got to Bend State Park on the Colorado River by midmorning. A March morning. What that means to any angling Texan is that the white bass are running. We waded in the green water, he with his ultralight spinning gear and me with my fly rod. He killed me. Uncle Bob may be many things—he is a large boy, a fat man who never grew up. He is a smoker. He laughs at people's misfortunes. He's awfully laid back. But he is one helluva fisher-

man. And a good uncle, too, except for the time he took me waterskiing my first time, me not being a good swimmer then, and after all the instructions on how to get up on two skis (yes, it was that long ago), he forgot the most important direction.

The most important direction, which would have been a good thing to know while I was holding on for dear life after I fell and was being towed under the water in ever-deepening depths, was to *let go of the freakin' rope if you fall*. Thanks, Uncle Bobby.

So he cleaned up with his little flipping technique and array of silver spoons and slabs and roostertails and what not. I caught and released what I thought were a lot of white bass but for every one I caught, Uncle Bob caught two. My only consolation was that Uncle Bob is top-heavy and slipped and for a second or two, he went fully under. Uncle Bobby's so laid back, he didn't sputter and spit, he just wiped his hair from his face and cast back to some overhanging limbs, his wet cigarette still hanging from his lips.

The Colorado River is the major drainage of the Hill Country flowing into Lake Buchanan about an hour north of Austin, then continuing in a lake-tailrace pattern through six impoundments collectively known as the Highland Lakes (Lakes Buchanan, Inks, LBJ, Marble Falls, Travis, and Austin). Each of these lakes is beautiful and has good-to-great fishing. The tailraces of the dams are even better fishing than the lakes (except for Lake Buchanan), holding a variety of fish including white bass, black bass, smallmouth bass, striped bass, catfish, Rio Grande perch, Guadalupe bass, bluegill, and some other species including carp that inhabit the slow water and back eddies below these dams.

In most of these tailraces, anglers can find shallow wading but some places are slippery and felt soles are helpful. Given water releases and the accompanying danger and unknown, it's best to be careful. Some use float tubes or belly boats or kickboats to get into the bigger water. Downstream of Austin, the Colorado grows wider and slower and bigger as it drops out of the Hill Country.

Pedernales River

The small tributary to the Colorado River about an hour west of Austin is a hoot to fish. Pedernales State Park is the centerpiece of this clear limestone stream that begins up near Harper, runs past Fredericksburg and Johnson City and through the park. This is a lesser stream but ideal to spend a few hours on while your wife shops in Fredericksburg, a cool little historic German town with too many antique stores for me to feel safe to take *my* wife Amy to anymore. The area is known for its vineyards, too, if that helps any.

Get away from the splashers and swimmers in Pedernales State Park and hike away and catch largemouth and Guadalupe bass and sunfish and catfish. None of them are of any size but they're plentiful. Oh, occasionally you can catch a largemouth big enough to surprise. Take your lightest fishing outfit, say a 2 to 3 weight fly rod, and you'll have a blast catching sunfish and bass. Other Hill Country fisheries

worth looking into: San Gabriel, Medina, Lampasas Rivers and Choke Canyon and Canyon Lakes.

CONTACTS
Austin Angler, Austin, www.austinangler
   .com
Gruene Outfitters, Gruene, www
   .grueneoutfitters.com
Capt. Scott Graham, www.flyfishingtexas
   .com

Lake Meredith

- **Location:** The panhandle of Texas
- **What You Fish For:** Several species, but the two big draws are carp and smallmouth bass
- **Highlights and Notables:** Carp, carp, carp

Lake Meredith is more than you think it is despite how ugly it looks. Located forty-five minutes north of Amarillo on the Canadian River, even most panhandle natives don't think fondly of this red-cliff bastion with the crazy currents and ruddy water.

Lake Meredith. What is the truth about this stark muddy lake? Sometimes you have to reveal the truth to your own countrymen. Let's get the guest.

You can catch walleye to rival most any other walleye lake. Good odds that most Texans don't know this about this Lone Star lake. Lake Meredith is one of the top smallmouth bass lakes in the state. Catfishing, understandably, given the murky

City Fishing

HOUSTON
Lake Conroe, Texas Coast, Lake Livingston, Galveston

Lake Conroe is worth a fishing trip even if you weren't in Houston for some other reason than fishing. First, it's a beautiful lake, heavily forested, top-quality golfing and resorts, lakeside lodges, numerous campgrounds, nine full-service marinas, jetskis and big boats, an ideal place for a family vacation.

Twenty-one thousand acres and only fifty miles from downtown Houston (but you should know that that doesn't mean just an hour drive, because the I-45 corridor is solid from Conroe to Houston with traffic and strip malls). This impoundment of the West Fork of the San Jacinto is as sexy a bassin' destination spot as so many other Texas hawg lakes but the largemouth fishing has been solid for years here. In the 1990s, every time you looked up someone was hauling in a 13-pounder bass. The hard-hitting hybrid bass is another game fish to tackle on Conroe.

On weekends and holidays, Houston recreationalists come out in droves, zipping their jetskis all around, skiing behind jet boats, cruising in their deck boats, floating in inner tubes and blow-up air mattresses. It's busy and hot and fun but not especially conducive to angling. But on weekdays, when every other Texan is working, you can play hooky and have the lake to yourself.

Fish the brushpiles is all I have to say. Conroe shocks folks every now and again with a run on 10-pound bucket-mouths (usually caught by a dock) and they get big on the excellent forage food base (but cover is lacking and that's why you fish the docks). If you like crappie or big catfish, Conroe has 'em.

Other area lakes include: Lake Houston, where angling for catfish and white bass is adequate to good, black bass only fair; Lake Livingston is a fine, heavily wooded bass lake but it's much better known for the catfishing and huge cats than anything else; Fayette County Lake lies between Houston and Austin (see page 322); Gibbons Creek Reservoir sits near College Station, 2,500 acres, a hydrilla-laden lake where anglers catch much bigger bass than you'd think (it's a sleeper trophy bass lake; see entry). My family lived here for the last two decades—eat at Goode's Barbecue (get the pulled pork).

Jonesing salt anglers can get their fix at nearby Rockport, Port O'Connor, Freeport (and the jetties), and Texas City for flounder, redfish, and trout. East and West Galveston Bays are prime spots for speckled trout, shark, whiting, and more. Matagorda is only a two-hour drive and that area has world-class fishing for reds and specks.

water, is top-notch. And carp, the underrated humpback, the bonefish of freshwater, thrives in Lake Meredith. Sand bass do well, too.

State-record smallmouth bass approaching 8 pounds taken on a Popping Bug. State-record yellow perch weighed in at just over 1 pound. State-record walleye that tipped the scale to almost 15 pounds. World-record largemouth for 6-pound tippet class was taken from Meredith's stilling basin at 14.14 pounds and 26.125 inches in length.

Truth: them's good records, girls and boys.

More truth: The lake is in drought and is down at least thirty feet, maybe more.

So what game fish do most Texans mistakenly think of when they hear Lake Meredith? They think of the 14-pound largemouth bass caught in 2000. Aberration. Illusion.

If you haven't fished for big carp, you're missing out. The thrill is in the hunt, finding and then sight casting in the shallow to fish as big as your Aunt Mary. Compared to other lakes as productive as Meredith,

fishing pressure is nil. If you fish March, you'll catch walleye 4 to 6 pounds up to 8 pounds.

Rattlesnakes live on land around the lake.

Winds kick up in the panhandle of Texas and can be dangerous.

Truth, truth, truth but people see only what they want to see. Let me tell you straight up, and this might hurt, cut to the bone: Lake Meredith, even in drought, even though it's not the most beautiful lake in the world, is one of the top lakes in Texas, one of the better lakes in the four-state region.

So when you make your mind up to fish Lake Meredith, and you should if you like walleyes and smallmouth and carp and catfish in great numbers and in great size,

then you face some truths that you can live with.

There's even a great bed and breakfast on the north shore of the lake (Sanford) called Three Falls Cove. It boasts its own private fishing tank that's filled to the brim with largemouth averaging 4 pounds. Three Falls Cove has recently finished construction on a lavish, five-room lodge with some A+ amenities. There's no place else like it anywhere near the lake, so make your reservations here in advance (www.threefallscove.com, 806-878-2366).

NOODLING IN THE SOUTH

I'll admit it. I've noodled before. I'm not proud of it. But I promise, after the first time, I never noodled again. My noodling days are over.

I had to see what this noodling was all about, this most primitive, elemental form of fishing. And easily the most idiotic, too.

The first time I heard about this *mano a pescado* variation of fishing, it was from my father. Apparently, without the aid of drugs or alcohol, at age 16 or so, he and some of his fellow teenagers got a wild hair and the urge to go to the muddy river and noodle. Dad located a big sunken log and stuck his hand under the log, willingly, mind you, until he located the grotto of a mouth of a huge catfish. The cat clamped down on his forearm and he lifted the whiskery fish out of the water to the applause of his buddies. Dad kept the fish to take home for dinner.

This is low-brow fishing at its best (worst?). When Dad told me about this knucklehead thing he did, for surely that's the word he would have used had I been the one to pull a stunt like that, I did not believe him. This sounded right up there with snipe hunting, Santa Claus, and "this spanking is gonna hurt me as much as it hurts you."

Reach in and grab a demon from the dark depths. Yeah, right.

So I mentioned it to some buddies in Longview, friends who rode motorcycles in the river bottoms and did other crazy extreme things. They knew exactly what I was talking about even if they didn't call it noodling. They didn't really have a name for it. But they decided I needed to try it. Crap.

On the way to the muddy river, they tell me it's all about touch, all about feel. Look in holes in the bank, under big rocks, in and under stumps. Try wiggling your fingers as

bait to make them mad or something like that. They might bite or nip or thrash or worse. You might lose some skin. Gloves? Gloves are for sissies.

As I waded out in the brown-red water, I began to think about what could be in the dark hole in the stump under the murky water? I imagined snapping turtles, snakes, muskrats, beaver, cottonmouth (water moccasin for non-Southerners), alligators, and anything else wet and slimy and alive and mad that I am sticking my hand in their home. I even had thoughts that my hand might get caught in the crevice and I'd either drown (the best option) or get gnawed while underwater. I worried that at best, I might pull out my arm to discover whatever my hand was in had bitten it off.

Big catfish? I once saw a 100-pound catfish in a live well in some bait and tackle shop at Cedar Creek or Tawokani or some Dallas are lake. I was twelve. The fish could have eaten me.

Oh yeah, Mark. Better stay in water that's not over your head or if it's too big, it'll take you under and you won't get up.

The last few years, noodling is everywhere. Apparently, it's a southern thing. There may be some other neighboring states that practice this moronic type of angling but they don't brag about it. I have heard about it happening in every southern state from Kentucky to Texas to Oklahoma to Alabama to Georgia to Missouri to Arkansas to Mississippi. I am not indicting any certain segment. This is not another caricature of the rebel flag–waving gun rack pickup–driving white folks—it's really not. Hey, I went to school with some of those guys and they were not stupid enough to try to catch a 50-pound catfish with their bare hands (not without a weapon of some sort).

There's a book that deals with this weird fishing, *Noodling for Flatheads: Moonshine, Monster Catfish, and Other Southern Comforts*. A movie called *Okie Noodling*. There's a DVD on the market about hot southern chicks pulling up big cats with their hands called—and this is for real—*Girls Gone Grabblin'*. I kid you not.

Grabbling is another name for noodling. So are hogging, graveling, tickling, dogging and stumping. There's a noodling tournament in some small no-name town in Oklahoma. There's even an Okie Noodling Queen.

I normally name my fishing companions but when I called these school buds and talked about this chapter, they told me that they both have families and respectable jobs and always use rods and reels nowadays and could I not use their names. Fair enough.

So there I am, rebuffed at my request for a stick or a reprieve and I'm feeling around the hole at the bottom of the stump with my Chuck Taylors and I'm scared. All that comes to mind are lines from Beowulf when he chases Grendel into her underwater lair. Blame my English major background.

The swirling/ Surf had covered his death, hidden/ Deep in murky darkness his

miserable/ End, as hell opened to receive him.

There was something in the hole and it was alive.

Steams like black clouds, and the groves of trees/ Growing out over their lake are all covered/ With frozen spray, and wind down snakelike/ Roots that reach as far as the water/ And help keep it dark. At night that lake/ Burns like a torch. No one knows its bottom,/ No wisdom reaches such depths.

I need help, guys.

I swam/ In the blackness of night, hunting monsters/ Out of the ocean, and killing them one/ By one; death was my errand and the fate/ They had earned. Now Grendel and I are called/ Together, and I've come.

It was a two-man job pulling out a cat that weighed in the teens. Actually, I kinda gave up when my two buddies took over.

In my research, decades after I had tried my hand (and kept my hand) at the sport, I discovered that noodling can be dangerous. Duh. Not just missing digits dangerous but apparently there are people who do find the cottonmouths and alligators or just plain drown. Besides that, it's not exactly legal in many states and where it is, there are seasons. Seasons!

I don't have a river listed for noodling.

Go south, find a muddy river and a stump, and tackle the devilish fish on your own.

CONTACTS
Catfish Grabblers,
   www.catfishgrabblers.com

Richland-Chambers Reservoir

- **Location:** North central Texas
- **What You Fish For:** Largemouth, hybrid, sand bass, crappie
- **Highlights and Notables:** Locals know this is a killer lake. Now you do, too.

Richland-Chambers is one of the best all-around lakes in Texas which, by default, makes it one of the best lakes in the world. Forty-six thousand acres of hybrid bass, sand bass, and largemouth bass hiding in water to seventy-five-feet deep, hiding around stumps and grass, points and creeks, flats and logs. Fish topwater, fish crankbaits. Richland-Chambers Reservoir has it all.

Tag team two east Texas lakes. Here's the plan: Fly into Dallas. Fish Lake Fork for a day and Richland-Chambers the next day.

Next tip: Follow the birds. If you follow the birds, you'll find the fish (the sandies). Since it's so darned hot during summer midday in North Texas, the sandies tend to be active early and late. Some guides on Richland-Chambers make their living taking out folks just to get their daily limit of sand bass.

I know anglers who fish for largemouth and hybrids all day long, fishing shallow (stumps and humps) early and late, deeper during the day. Many locals love Richland-Chambers for their consistent angling for big blue catfish. A 20-pound blue is fairly common.

Should I mention that there aren't many lakes better for crappie fishing than this one? You'll get on some great beds here and pull in lots of nice crappie for dinner (wonder why we don't say "lots of nice crappies"?).

The largemouth fishing is good, not great, and it takes anglers with patience to get on them. Located on Richland and Chambers creeks, east-southeast of Corsicana on US 287. The lake has changed a lot in the last nineteen years since it opened. You see so many more homes on the lake and if you're not loaded, you won't be able to afford one.

Sabine Lake

- **Location:** On the coast of both Texas and Louisiana
- **What You Fish For:** Redfish, speckled trout
- **Highlights and Notables:** What a crazy fishery, big flat lonely fertile water.

It's purgatorially hot this spring day, sweltering. I'm on Keith Lake, wading, specks tailing. I'm daydreaming back to yesterday, the Badlands, the lonely flat water, the ban-ner day, more specks than I've ever caught in a day. Sightcast to catch them. Shrimp patterns.

Sabine River inlet this morning, where the river runs through it. Two largemouth bass, nothing big but the greener one fought like a banshee, exploded from the flat reflective brackish water like plate-glass breaking. Two speckled trout, one pretty damned long. An angler with a red beard and a gimme cap in a Pathfinder near us caught a bowfin and I was glad I didn't.

I'm hungry, I'm thirsty. I'm tired, I'm sunburned. I'm reminded of my deficiencies as a long-distance fly caster as I miss the pod of feeding trout two feet to the left. I want to blame the wind but there is no wind, where's the wind? Two birds, diving and it's purgatorially hot and sweltering.

Sabine Lake. One of the unique fisheries of America. Eighteen miles southeast of Beaumont on the Texas-Louisiana border. A forty-mile estuary, a primordial stew of nutrients from the Neches and Sabine Rivers, known for its amazing collection of big fish, everything from largemouth bass to striper to bowfin to trophy-sized speckled trout to redfish to a famous flounder fishery (say that three times real fast).

Why such a fertile productive water complex? Take two rivers and bring in their rich fresh water. You have their two inlets. Bayous flow into the bay on its east side. You have lakes interconnecting to the main body. You have two marshes, one is the largest in North America, the other riddled with canals and channels. Introduce a fecund forage base of anchovies, crabs, killfish, shrimp, and juvenile sportfish, throw in good nursery habitat and you have all the ingredients for one incredible fishery.

In the Badlands, you are not alone. The eastern side of Sabine Lake is wild and remote and nicknamed for that desolate wilderness of South Dakota. You are not alone even though you may not see another angler all day as you navigate the flats. You might find company with alligators, share a plot of earth with feral hogs, cruise the backwater with mink and nutria (some Cajuns actually eat these things) and otters and birds, birds, birds. It's on the flats when I wished I cast a fly rod as well as Dave Hayward and Marcos Enriquez, two well-known Texas longrodders and lovers of the salt.

On the northwest side, there is a marsh—the Bessie Heights Marsh complete with canals and bayous. The southwest corner connects Keith Lake, good wading, good access. West side, piers and jetties. There are places in this watery wonderland where an angler can sightcast to tailing trophy trout in no more than half a foot of water. Watch for feeding birds, terns and gulls probably, to find trout and redfish feeding and churning. The flounder mass migration in the summer is a joy if you like fishing for the lively bottom dwellers.

Sabine Lake is nineteen miles long, up to nine miles wide, averages about eight feet deep. The lake record speckled trout is an 11.50-pound 30.5-inch fish.

Sam Rayburn Reservoir

- **Location:** East Texas
- **What You Fish For:** Largemouth bass
- **Highlights and Notables:** One of the most consistent big bass producers in Texas and the nation

I'm forty-six and I can't remember when Sam Rayburn wasn't considered one of the top lakes in the United States. Largemouth Bass Virus affected the lake in the 1990s but Sam Rayburn has emerged as strong as ever.

Located on the Angelina River, this 114,500-acre impoundment in the heart of East Texas has consistent big bass production. The beautiful wooded lake owns or has owned dozens and dozens of record fish. The lake record is a largemouth that weighed nearly 17 pounds.

A big lake, the biggest reservoir located entirely in Texas, Sam Rayburn has over 550 miles of shoreline and is up to eighty-five feet deep with an average depth of around twelve feet. The nutrient-rich lake just looks like a bass lake. Looks fertile. All those lily pads and brush piles and stumps. The lightly-stained water the color of weak green tea. Standing timber means also fallen timber and that means bass haunts. Hydrilla is one great sign and it carpets sec-

tions of the lake like Astroturf. Sam Rayburn has many arms, like the Hydra and creeks and bayous and old channels—so many that in spite of the fact this is one busy lake, only two hours from Houston, visitors from around the country, tournaments galore, you will have no problem at all finding lonely water.

While the trophy bass hunters are mixing and matching structure to lures, you could be chasing after the other healthy populations of fish in the lake. Sam Rayburn is one of the top crappie lakes in Texas. The lake has super fishing for white bass, stripers, and catfish.

Sam Rayburn Reservoir is the quintessential bass lake. I'm going to top it off by telling you what you always hear about quintessential bass lakes: 1) You will catch lots of bass; 2) You will catch bass that average 2 to 4 pounds; 3) You have a real good chance, if there's a chance that you're real good, of catching a trophy bass over 10 pounds.

777 Ranch, Texas
Thirty-two miles west of San Antonio, near Hondo, this fabled hunting/fishing ranch has thirty ponds and lakes, the prize of which are largemouths, up to 14 pounds. www.777ranch.com, 830-426-3476.

Squaw Creek Reservoir

- **Location:** Central Texas
- **What You Fish For:** Largemouth bass
- **Highlights and Notables:** Not many lunkers but plenty of heavy bass. This shallow lake is ideal for fly fishers.

This 3,228-acre impoundment is one of the best fly fishing lakes in Texas, one of the top topwater lakes around. Squaw Creek is a power plant lake (nuclear no less) near Glen Rose and Granbury. The Comanche Peak nuclear power plant lake.

So what are we talking about? Smallmouth bass that reach as big as 3 to 4 pounds and largemouth bass that reach 7 to 8 pounds. Lots of both. These are heavy bass, deep and feisty. Anglers can also catch catfish, sunfish, crappie (is there any freshwater fish that's better eatin' than a mess of crappie?).

Lots of standing timber, a rock and timber shoreline, a ledge dropoff near the banks, Squaw Creek is ideal for topwater nuts. Squaw Creek has clear water for a Texas lake, too. You can imagine that Squaw Creek fishes well in the winter since it is shallow. Squaw Creek is warm since it has discharged hot water going into it. Two places not to miss that most anglers do miss: around the docks and the tailrace below the lake.

This is a good wading lake but nice to float, too. I suggest a 7- to 8-pound weight fly rod or medium-weight spin outfit to go with as tough a leader/monofilament as you can afford. Squaw Creek Park has days and

hours it is open so call Park management 817-573-7053.

Texas Coast

- **Location:** The Texas coast, from Port Mansfield to the Louisiana border
- **What You Fish For:** Redfish and speckled trout and flounder are the three predominant targets but there's much more
- **Highlights and Notables:** Just shy of 400 miles of some of the most productive saltwater on any American coast

Lower Laguna Madre. Port Mansfield is a funky blue-collar town. Not funky in the way that cool college towns like Madison or Austin are funky. Funky like . . . funk. Old,

breezy, laid back, sleepy, fishing . . . village. It differs from Rockport, from Corpus, from Freeport but while Texans can tell the difference between the towns and the water, there's a comforting familiarity up and down the coast.

Speckled trout, redfish, and flounder are the main sporting fish that swim these waters. These waters include everything from big broad flats, rich grassy beds, and narrow channels. Here, in the gut of the Laguna Madre, anglers can sightcast and strip flies to tailing reds while wading the shallow flats north of the East Cut, chunk hardware near deep dropoffs where the fish lay in wait and cast from the front of the boat while looking at the oddly bird-covered Bird Island.

I was drinking Miller Lite that night even though I don't drink Miller Lite but hey, that's what the guys bought and you gotta drink what's on hand. Nighttime and we were watching Phil Shook cast off the dock to visibly feeding specks under the big light. There's not much else to do at night in Port Mansfield.

Phil was catching them every other cast, stripping flies and it was so easy, he and Doug Pike and some other writer/angler type, maybe Joe Doggett, maybe Terry Moore, I don't know because like I said, we were drinking beer, anyway, they each started trying new flies just to see what wouldn't work. I don't think they ever found one that the specks would refuse. By the way, Phil Shook wrote the book on fishing the Texas coast, literally, twice: once *Flyfishing the Texas Coast* from Pruett Press and another time *Flyfisher's Guide to Texas* from Wilderness Adventures Press. Pike and Doggett know more about fishing Texas than just about anybody except maybe Phil.

The Texas coast is one of the top saltwater destinations in the world but it's difficult to call 370 miles of coastline a "destination." The coast is protected by barrier islands, an estuarine system that is complex and loaded with saltwater opportunities. The coast offers every kind of imaginable salt habitat—lagoons, bays, rivermouths, sand and grass flats, shell bars, bayous, lakes, marshes, islands, piers and jetties, creeks, estuaries, oil platforms, and on and on. The choices you are faced with when planning a trip to the coast or when you wake up during a Texas swing are overwhelming. So choose one and fish—Baffin Bay, Port Isabel, Rockport, Port Aransas, Port Mansfield, Matagorda Bay, San Luis Pass, Copano Bay (secret little spot), and so on. They're all great.

Padre Island is the longest barrier island in the world and in turn, this long island creates the estuary environment for redfish and other game fish. The flats. Average depth a little over two feet. *That's* the best place to catch the redfish (red drum). That's the place to sightcast for these big honkin' drums. Heck, Laguna Madre, the shallow body of riverine-like water behind Padre Island is 136 miles long. That's a lot of water to cover in a lifetime.

The redfish. Red drum. *Sciaenops ocellatus.* They're as big as Jethro Bodine and they look about as dumb until you try catching them. When you see the tail, the brass-colored tail with the black circle, your heart races and you know that you will at least boat one or two that are average Texas size—6 pounds. But you also know that you might catch one that lifts you up at Safari Club to new heights.

The Texas coast means these fish: redfish and speckled trout. These two are the big draws but you can also catch flounder,

black drum, ladyfish, sheepshead, grouper, mackerel, bluefish, false albacore, amberjack, croakers, skipjack, sailfish, marlin, kingfish, ling, pompano, bonito, red snapper, warsaw . . .

And tarpon. Sometimes. The tarpon used to promulgate the Texas coast forty years ago and then they left and they're back now, or so it seems. It's an undependable fishery at this point.

Three things drive the Texas fishing machine right now: 1) redfish. Texas is likely the top place on earth to catch lots of redfish and lots of big redfish; 2) flats. Texas has more miles of firm fishable flats than any other state except Florida and those of the Lone Star state are much more easily accessible; and 3) while you are better off with a guide, fishing the Texas coast is an easy do-it-yourself trip.

Shameless plug for my fishing buddy

here: If you want to fish the Texas coast, buy Phil Shook's book. It has it all in there from redfish to specks to offshore. Texas flytiers are some of the most innovative and effective designers in the country. The East Cut Popper, the Matagorda Fighting Blue Crab, and the Laguna Critter. Classic crab and shrimp patterns work well, too.

CONTACTS

Capt. Chuck Naiser, Rockport, 361-729-9314

Capt. Eric Glass, 956-761-2878

Capt. Bill Hagen, 956-792-8482

Capt. Chuck Scates, www.chuckscates.com

Capt. Joe Mendez, www.sightcast1.com

Capt. Scott Graham,
   www.flyfishingtexas.com

This site is a great resource to find fishing guides in the state of Texas including the coast: www.sportsmansresource.com/flocalxtexas.htm#guides

Rio Grande Valley site lists numerous coastal fishing guides: rio-grande-valley.com/portmansfield/businesses/fishinguides.htm

Lake Texoma

- **Location:** North Texas, southern Oklahoma
- **What You Fish For:** Stripers
- **Highlights and Notables:** Arguably the top striper lake in the country

Doug James was a legendary football coach in the panhandle of Texas, one of those tough ol' birds who was no-nonsense, old-school and made men out of boys. James is a colleague of mine, teaches government and economics and other sundry subjects. He is one of those dominant personalities whose strength is belied by the fact he doesn't get animated or loud. A speak-softly-and-carry-a-big-stick-type. His burr cut is now gray where once a beautiful perm sat (I saw a photo from the late 1970s) and I guess if you had to describe his physicality, you'd say burly. He is a man accustomed to control and I've only seen one thing that takes him out of that mode: Lake Texoma.

This is what he has to say about the

great lake but you have to read it with a syrupy-sweet Texas drawl: "I tell ya how good Texoma is—the first time I fished Texoma a number of years ago, Texoma became the last lake I've fished since. I don't fish anywhere else, it's that good."

It's that good, folks. This is the land of big hair, Cadillacs and pickups, barbecue and fishing at Lake Texoma. Lake Texoma is the premier striper destination in the world. You'll hear that mantra and it's true but don't be lulled into thinking that's the only thing to fish for in this humongous lake. Lake Texoma is a big honkin' lake, an impoundment of the Red River nearly 90,000 acres big, up to 100 feet deep on the Texas-Oklahoma border not far from Sherman and Denison and only seventy-five miles north of Dallas.

Here's the most important thing I can

tell you about Lake Texoma. The lake is two-thirds in Oklahoma. Do not, I repeat, do not go fishing anywhere near the imaginary water boundary without having a dual license. They'll catch you. I promise.

So what's so special about Lake Texoma that folks from all around the world go to fish it? The stripers are plentiful and they are big. These striped bass are self-populating, a rarity for this species for an inland freshwater body. Lake Texoma is particularly suited to aid striper spawning. A combination of current and salinity make this an ideal lake for stripers to reproduce.

You need a boat, three rods rigged up for each angler, a dual license, cool beverages, and nerves of steel. One rod needs to be a heavy rod to go down deep. One needs to be a medium-weight to get action for those topwater lures. The other is to be rigged up with something other than what you're casting so you can switch out quickly.

How big do these bad boys get? Feeding on a diet of shad and steroids, Lake Texoma's stripers regularly reach 10 to 25 pounds and big stripers over 30 are not uncommon. Guides say that the average size runs 2 to 4 pounds. They're probably right. I catch very few less than 2 pounds and quite a few bigger than 4 pounds.

Don't even bother bragging to anyone if you catch five or six stripers that go 6 or 8 pounds. I can't tell you how many photos I've seen in local bait shops and grocery stores and gas stations of two grinning anglers showing off a huge cooler full of stripers. It's not hard to catch a bunch of stripers on this lake. And it's not hard to get a 15-pounder on the end of your line, either.

Even in the heat of summer, if you get up early enough, you can find the schooling stripers chasing shad. Best place to look is in the lower reaches of the lake close to the dam. They can be amazingly close to the shore, a frenzy of shad and foamy water. They tend to move up the lake and pick up more stripers along the way until the serious Texas heat shows up.

Doug James starts grinning and talks quickly when I ask him about what it's like when the stripers are schooling. "Oh man, let me tell ya, when you're in the middle of the lake, and there's about fifty, maybe even a hundred boats all circled up and the shad are popping the water because those stripers are after 'em, well, it's exciting, I tell ya." I've been there with Texoma's stripers going top-crazy so I know what he means but it's fun to get him going.

The water's all choppy and you'll be surprised how loud it is, like sticking your head in the washing machine. You can toss out a Pencil Popper or Chug Bug or Zara Spooks, walk a Top Dog and catch the big voracious feeders on topwater or just underneath. Some use live shad. It's not unusual for boats to follow the stripers herding these baitfish uplake for hours and for the school of stripers to number over a thousand. It's a sight to see. When the stripers settle down and go deeper, anglers switch to slabs and spoons and jigs and when they go deeper still, they bring out the downriggers.

Toledo Bend Reservoir

- **Location:** East Texas and a bit of Louisiana
- **What You Fish For:** Largemouth bass
- **Highlights and Notables:** Large fertile legendary bass lake

Toledo Bend is a humongous reservoir that impounds the Sabine River on the Louisiana-Texas border (although most all of the lake is in the Lone Star state). Toledo Bend is spooky. It's big. It holds so many big fish, it's spooky. And big. So many arms and creeks and coves and bays, what with 1,200 miles of shoreline, no angler could cover all this water in a month of summers.

Toledo Bend has been a national largemouth bass destination for years and because of that, many have moved on to the latest big-bass fishery sensation. They're missing out. Toledo Bend has held its own against every newcomer for four decades. Papaw took me there in the early 1970s and one evening that all-too-quickly turned to night, we got lost. I mean big-time grandfather-has-to-stop-and-ask-for-directions-late-at-night lost. But we caught a lot of bass then and I have caught lots of bass in subsequent trips over the years.

What makes this East Texas lake so productive is a combination of just about everything you'd want in a designer bass lake. Submerged timber, rocky coves, dropoffs, points, hydrilla and other aquatic vegetation, water lilies, fed by a major river and also by creeks on both sides, flooded terrestrial vegetation, creek channels, whew. It's tiring listing everything on this monstrous lake. Suffice to say this is fishy water with something for everyone.

These are heavy-bodied Florida-strain bass and not the easiest to catch. Still, when you do, they seem to fall in the thick 4- to 7-pound range. The lower parts of the lake seem clearer than other parts and there are some arms that are just plain muddy at times. Fly fishers seem to favor the southern end of Toledo Bend. The lake has some good striper fishing and is known for its bluegill and redear sunfish, too. One other reason to hit Toledo Bend is that Sam Rayburn Reservoir is just a few miles to the southwest.

CONTACTS

San Augustine Chamber of Commerce, 409-275-3610

Sabine River Authority, Burkville, 409-565-2273

White Bass

- **Location:** In Texas rivers and lakes
- **What You Fish For:** The sand bass (also known as the white bass)
- **Highlights and Notables:** On ultralight tackle, they fight hard and they always make good eatin'.

I grew up calling these fish "sand" bass. In central and south Texas, they're called white bass. White bass are small. I love 'em. You ought to as well.

Some time in the late winter in Texas,

usually in February and throughout April, depending on factors of light, water flow and temperature, these deep-water fish, the *Morone chrysops,* move into the shallows of lakes and make runs up rivers. For the angler, this means catching white bass after white bass with lightweight equipment.

Papaw and Uncle Bob were sand bass aficionados and they took me out on Lake Tawakoni and Cedar Creek Lake from the time I was three. We'd concentrate on points of land that jutted out. We'd look for swooping birds. We'd watch for clusters of boats. Papaw watching all the while drinking his Schlitz and smoking his L & M cigarettes. "Well," he'd drawl, "let's go catch some fish." His one-syllable words extended into two and three syllables like hot taffy dripping in the hot sun.

When we found a school of sandies hitting the surface, chasing baitfish, we'd pull out prestrung rods and toss out surface lures. We'd each catch two, three, four, or five and then the sandies would go a little deeper; we'd switch to our rods that had shallow subsurface lures and catch a few more. Then the school would be gone and we'd see the surface choppy with scared baitfish a few hundred yards away; we'd start the engine, move over and we'd do it all over again.

In the heat of the day, the sand bass go to deeper water, so we'd string up slabs and deepwater lures, bouncing the heavy lures off the bottom until we'd tie into the school. The white bass stage behind dams, up tributaries, in the shallows of lakes. You'll find them in the shallower waters early in the day and in the evenings.

If you catch one weighing 2 to 3 pounds,

you've caught one of the biggest white bass in the fishery. Mostly, they'll run a half-pound to a pound and if you use lightweight tackle, they put up a good fight. I practice catch-and-release fishing 99 percent of the time but I'll admit, a batch of white bass, battered in cornmeal and fried, makes for a tasty Sunday afternoon meal.

The best white bass fishing lies south of DFW and east and north of San Antonio, north and west from Houston, a triangle of sorts between the three big Texas cities. There are many lakes and rivers that have great white bass fishing in Texas but here are a few of my favorites: Lake Buchanan, Lake Travis, Colorado River (especially near Bend), Pedernales River (pronounced perd-a-nall-ays by Texans), Llano River, Richland Chambers, Lake of the Pines, Lake Bob Sandlin, Canyon Lake, San Gabriel River.

West

ARIZONA

I'm skeptical of claims of fifty to 100 fish. I've counted before when I've fished with others and kept silent about my counting and the lot of us were catching lots of fish, from trout to white bass, and almost without fail, their memory was fuzzy and there were not as many in the hand as in the brain. It's awfully easy to include in your count the ones that got away in the same way that a released fish gets bigger every time you tell the story.

Think about fifty fish for one angler in one day. Let's suppose you fish for eight hours, an outdoorsman's work day. That comes out to 6.25 fish in hand per hour. Roughly one fish every ten minutes. For eight hours. A fish in hand, not caught and

Sierra Club–released. One hundred fish in a day means you caught 12.5 fish every hour, or one every five minutes. If you add in the time you took getting set up, wading from place to place, smoke breaks, pee breaks, lunch, you lose an hour or more. So if you caught 100 fish in let's say seven hours, you landed a fish every four minutes. Come on, guys, let's get real. I've caught a lot of fish in a day's time and I've had two-hour stretches where I know I caught thirty fish but for eight hours, the catch rates just don't add up for any but the most amazing places at the exact right time of day and year with the ideal lure, fly, or bait.

Arizona anglers are some of the most organized, knowledgeable, knowledge-sharing

WEST

anglers in the country. Their Web sites are loaded with good stuff. Their forums are friendly and focused. These guys love to fish.

I am convinced that some people are catching upwards of fifty fish in a day. Not on a regular basis. There's still a good amount of benign miscounting going on where they're really catching twenty and thinking forty but I'm a believer in Theodore Roosevelt Lake. The word on the street is that if you want to catch lots of decent-sized bass, Roosevelt is your man. He speaks softly and carries a big Ugly Stik.

The Lakes and Rivers of the White Mountains

- **Location:** All over eastern and north-eastern Arizona
- **What You Fish For:** Rainbow and Apache trout are the two main species but you also catch cutts, browns, and brook trout.
- **Highlights and Notables:** Not many areas in America have so many quality trout lakes this close together.

The White Mountains are both majestic and spiritual. These gentle mountains rise from the desert floors, from searing heat to cooling breezes. Retreating glaciers carved out U-shaped park-like valleys with wide meadows and steep-sided canyons. The forests are thick with Englemann Spruce, white pine, ponderosa pine, aspen, fir, and corkbark. The White Mountains aren't as tall as many ranges, nor as rugged. The tallest mountains barely rise to 11,000 feet.

But this is spectacular alpine scenery with miles of pristine forests, aspens, and wildlife. The land here is rugged, wild, feels like it is unexplored. Herds of elk and wild horses roam freely and if you keep your eyes open, visitors will see turkey, deer, and sometimes, even bear. When you are on a river or a lake in the White Mountains, you are miles from a real city, from a hospital, even from a gas station.

Four rivers (Black, Blue, White, and Little Colorado) have their headwaters on the slopes of an ancient volcano, Mount Baldy (11,403 feet), the second highest peak in Arizona. Mt. Baldy is a sacred place and off limits to all non-Apaches.

But because of the geographic isolation, few anglers (compared to Colorado, for instance) fish these waters. Trails and old forest roads lead deep into the backcountry past high-altitude riparian habitat, through vertical breaks, along singing creeks, through big rock pinnacles. This is remote but intimate country, primitive, a place where an angler can drop a line in a stream where no one else has fished in a year or more, maybe longer. The hues of green and orange of the grassy hillsides and dark forests are cut clean by twisting blue rivers, dotted by turquoise lakes.

Both the state and tribal game and fish departments are stocking the rare Apache trout in the streams, not just in the headwaters. In the right sections of some streams, anglers can catch big fish in relatively small water. And you can catch the bigger fish in lakes. Some lakes and streams are fishable year-round. But there's no Lees Ferry here and most of the fish in the streams are in the 9- to 12-inch range.

You can fish in the spring before other states' trout fishing turns on. The big draw in the early season is the mountain lakes, especially those along the White River system. They hold big fish in spectacular

State Records

Trout, Brook	4 lbs. 15.2 ozs.	Sunrise Lake	10/20/95
Trout, Brown	17 lbs. 0.0 oz.	Last Chance Bay, Lake Powell	5/1/71
Trout, Cutthroat	6 lbs. 5.0 ozs.	Luna Lake	10/1/76
Trout, Native/Apache	5 lbs. 15.5 ozs.	Hurricane Lake	6/10/93
Trout, Rainbow	11 lbs. 1.0 oz.	Nelson Reservoir	4/1/79

mountain settings. The big boys are holding in these stillwaters. Big rainbows, big Apache trout.

The streams and lakes of the White Mountains offer perhaps the best trout fishing area in the state, containing more than 600 miles of fishable streams and over twenty-four major trout lakes. Anglers can fish for rainbows, browns, and in an ever-expanding number of fisheries, the Apache trout. The White Mountain Area is located in the eastern part of the state, and much of the best fishing is on private Indian lands, fishable to the public by daily fees.

The trout waters of Arizona are under-fished, underpublicized, and remote, making them the sleepers of the Southwest. The White River is the crown jewel, especially the North Fork. The river was originally called the Rio Sierra Blanca, which in Spanish means the White Mountain River. Twenty-five miles of the former Rio Sierra Blanca from headwaters of Mt. Baldy to its confluence with East Fork offer prime angling for feisty trout.

Imagine a place where the mountains are green and forested, the weather cool in the summer, and you can choose from thirty quality lakes every morning. Anglers are few and far between. The fish are big and plentiful and include leviathan Apache trout.

The variety and numbers of lakes in the White Mountains is staggering. This area is blessed with so many great trout fishing lakes, it would take several summers for the ambitious angler to effectively fish them all. Most are perfect for a belly boat, personal watercraft, or small boat. The Apache Reservation lakes in the White Mountains of Arizona are but a stone's throw away from one another. Some are little more than quaint, intimate ponds.

Others sprawl across huge, open valleys between verdant, bulging knolls. With each lake possessing its own individual characteristics, adventurous anglers are offered a wonderful variety from which to choose in a relatively small geographic location.

Most locals fish these lakes as though they just graduated from the Kmart "Salmon Egg Baitcasting" course, complete with matching Zebco rod and reel. This means you will encounter families chugging weighted bait as far as they can from the shore on the more popular lakes. Most of these lakes will require that you get out in them—float tube, personal watercraft, small boat. That way you can avoid the bait casters and find the fish.

The variety and numbers of lakes in the White Mountains is staggering. This area is blessed with so many great trout fishing lakes, it would take several summers for the ambitious angler to effectively fish them all. The lakes are stocked with Apache, rainbow, and brook trout. The Apache trout and Apache/Rainbow hybrids often exceed 20 inches.

Black River

- **Location:** Eastern Arizona
- **What You Fish For:** Brown, rainbow Apache trout, smallmouth bass
- **Highlights and Notables:** Wild and remote stream that holds both trout and bass

I once caught so many fish upstream of Burro Creek that I got tired of fishing. I

know that sounds crazy but I set down my rod, took out a sandwich, sat on the bank and enjoyed the wildness and angling success of the Black River.

I went through all my Adams Parachutes (I had three left, size 12, 14, and 16) and when they tore those up, I tied on a tan Elk Hair Caddis. They tore that up. Anything I put on, the trout attacked. The meadows were alive and green. Hoppers flew up from the grass as I walked along. I fished clear, deep beaver ponds. I didn't see another human all day long. And in my opinion, the middle canyon section of the West Fork has better habitat and bigger fish. So imagine the kind of trip you can plan.

This gem of a trout stream forms the border between the San Carlos and White Mountain Apache lands and requires a special daily permit for fishing and camping. Most of the best fishing on the Black River is to be found in the spruce and fir forests in alpine settings in the White Mountains. One of the side benefits for the angler is that the Black River is one of the best smallmouth streams in the state. The trout fishing ain't bad, either.

The Black River runs through some of the harshest, loneliest, and most scenic country in the West. You have a good chance of seeing deer, elk, bear, and even bighorn sheep. In the summer, the two forks, the East and West Forks, are usually low and clear. Apache trout inhabit the upper stretches of the rivers, rainbow and browns the middle sections, brown trout the lower mountain stretches, and a mix of bass and trout the lowest stretches. Mac and I fished the river in a rainstorm and

quit right after a lightning strike hit close enough that the hair on our necks and arms stood up. Talk about idiots. But we were catching fat trout on beadheads. You know what I mean, don't you?

Blue River, White Mountains

- **Location:** Eastern Arizona
- **What You Fish For:** Brown trout, Apache trout
- **Highlights and Notables:** Another wild and remote freestone trout stream you'll fall in love with

One hot summer day on the Blue, a fishing buddy and I had thrown everything we

While the trout do hang in the obvious places, like around the rocks, fish the open slicks, too. Black River

had at the trout and come up empty. We sat on big streamside boulders watching six black cows feeding in the meadow and we began reflecting on what factors conspired against us and we were on number forty-one when we noticed in the distance a dark storm rising up from the afternoon swelter.

The storm was long, flat, rectangular, sitting off the high desert floor like a big black block of coal. Lightning flashed out in long silver lashes. The weird shape, the blackness of the cloud looked surreal. It was an impressive sight. And it was moving toward us with increasing swiftness.

We sat in the truck less than ten minutes

A buttery spotted Apache trout

later, the heavy anvil of the storm dumping rain on us, lightning dancing all around. In epiphany, I looked at my brother-in-law and exclaimed, "Darn. I should've gotten out my camera and got some shots of the storm as it moved toward us."

Kenny thought for a minute and said, "You know, the storm will always be more vivid in here" as he tapped his head with his finger. And he is right. I can still see the powerful weird storm over the Blue River today. This is wild country and you will take some of it with you always.

Technically, most of the Blue River runs through the Blue Range of farthest eastern Arizona but enough of it is in the White Mountains to want to fish it when you visit the great lakes and the North Fork. The Blue River always seems to run shallow when I fish it. The river suffers from many problems including overgrazing and erosion, sediment buildup, and warm temperatures in midsummer, and parts of the upper river can dry up in lean snowpack years. The river hasn't been stocked with

trout the last few years so it's up to the wild trout to reproduce in adequate numbers (and they will, as wild trout always seem to do when returned to a natural cycle on lightly-fished rivers).

The fishing is so spotty in the Blue that without a guide or local advice on current conditions, it's a crapshoot on whether or not you'll have success. Why in the world mention it then? I mention the Blue River because the river has over fifty miles of trout water running through stunning mountain scenery. You won't run into another angler all day. The brown trout are stream-bred. And in places, for instance the upper Blue near the New Mexico border or near the Strayhorse Creek confluence, the fishing can be phenomenal.

The Blue River is best fished in the spring and fall, while the heat of the summer and the low flows can make fishing inconsistent at best. You will mostly catch brown trout but might catch an occasional rainbow trout. And if you walk past the herds of cows and find a beaver pond or a section with deeper water, you have a good shot at getting into some heavy-bodied fish.

The Blue is easily accessible from a crisscrossing of roads from Alpine to Pigeon Creek. The Blue River Road parallels the river for most of its run. With this much access, you'd think the river would be inundated by anglers but it's not. Even with the road beside the river, I always feel like I am secluded, out away from it all.

In this flat clear shallow stretch, McPhail caught and released eight Apache trout feeding on a midday hatch.

North Fork, White River

- **Location:** Eastern-northeastern Arizona
- **What You Fish For:** Apache trout
- **Highlights and Notables:** Classic western freestone stream with added element of indigenous trout, the Apache trout

Two years ago, McPhail and I fished two days on the North Fork of the White River, up and down it, and everywhere we went, we caught Apache trout on dry flies. Rum-colored, spotted Apache trout. Maybe the largest between us was 14 inches. Most were 10 to 12. We rarely saw other anglers and that could be because we hiked in far away or walked the trail away from obvious access points but when we did see others fishing, it was easy to find new water.

In the years I've fished it with Kenny, same story. Lots of Apaches on dries, not many anglers except by campgrounds and accesses. Amazing scenery. A manageable freestone stream with all the different kinds of lies.

The North Fork of the White River is a typical scenic western freestone stream that seems more properly placed in Colorado or Montana. Plenty of pools, followed by riffles, punctuated by undercut banks, fallen logs, small rocks, submerged brush and shallow glides. The water runs clear and cold. Trout tend to hold around any structure, even in the divots in the bottom of the stream or camouflaged next to underwater vegetation. I catch many trout on the North Fork during the heat of the day by fishing to shady spots under overhanging limbs or dapping with nymphs in the deeper pocket water.

The North Fork is where I always catch a lot of Apache trout. The chief appeal of this eastern Arizona trout stream are the trout themselves. In addition to brown trout, you can catch these increasingly rare Apache trout, a lovely native gradually losing its range in Arizona's waters. The North Fork has about twenty-plus miles of public access, clear water punctuated by choppy riffles and shallow pools, flanked by thick stands of evergreen forest. Think dry flies. Think small rods. Bring a camera.

By western standards, the North Fork of the White River is not a big river, somewhere more between a creek and a stream. The fish aren't large by western standards either. In its twenty-five miles of accessible river, anglers will encounter other fishermen and lots of campers.

So why go to the North Fork of the White River?

The fish, the fish. The rainbows are stockers so don't get excited about them. The browns are beautiful and chunky but those aren't the fish you're after. The Apache Trout. Native and rare but now flourishing, found only in Arizona. Buttery silver and a little brassy with dark spots splattered on them as on a paint canvas. A beautiful fish.

Ranging from fifteen to thirty feet wide in its upper reaches where the trout fishing is best, the North Fork flows through evergreen forests of spruce and pine and under the sentinel of 11,000-foot moun-

tains, including the prominent Mt. Baldy. The North Fork's clear water is punctuated by choppy riffles, flat glides, shallow pools and undercut banks. In places, the willows along the bank are thick.

You might catch a 15-incher on this river but the odds are you won't. But what you do catch can almost always be done with dry flies. The dry fly fishing is superb but you'll need fly boxes loaded with both western attractors and match-the-hatch patterns for when the trout are finicky. Hatches include golden stoneflies in spring and early summer, caddis, various mayflies, and baetis throughout the summer.

Because the North Fork sees lots of anglers, mostly in the area near and above the town of Whiteriver, the river is heavily stocked. Don't let this fool you or dissuade

you. The river runs through pristine forests. All you need to do to get to the wilder areas is to hike up or downstream away from the easiest public access, away from where the road crosses the river.

Fishing is mostly put-and-take as it nears Whiteriver whereas wild browns and cutts thrive in the upper reaches. You make the call which direction you head.

Earl Park Lake

Earl Park Lake is where I have seen the largest brook trout south of Maine and Canada. This fish was pushing 23, 24 inches. McPhail caught him. For a minute. We had seen him cruising parallel to the shore, figure-eights, big as a toy submarine, as cocksure as Tony Soprano.

McPhail led him, nice cast, rolled over, laid out, stripped in right past him, big Woolly Bugger, olive. Big white mouth, tug-of-war, the only time I've seen a brook trout dive, dive, dive. They fought for a few minutes, the big fish came to hand and he was one of those fish whose eyes peered at us like he was a dog, and some of you know what I'm talking about, too. Like he knew. Then McPhail held him loosely by the tail, moved him back and forth, and the big brook gently, slowly, confidently swam away and then began his figure-eights again as if nothing had happened. Grendel returning to the lair.

Earl Park Lake is one special lake. This is one of the best fly fishing lakes I've ever fished. Apache, brown, rainbow, and brook trout thrive in this fertile clear broth of a lake. Catch-and-release only.

Fly fishermen love this tree-lined lake.

Smaller Sister: The East Fork of the White River

Smaller than its sister stream, the East Fork of the White River flows clear and cold for over thirty miles, chock-full of brown and Apache trout holding in foamy riffles, pocket water and deep pools. The river width ranges from twelve to thirty feet wide and is loaded with big rocks. Seeing fewer anglers than the North Fork, the East Fork holds some surprisingly large brown trout.

You won't hear many anglers talk about the East Fork. Much of this rocky river is off-limits to the public and the upper stretches run through ground sacred to the tribe and is also used as spawning habitat for apache trout.

This rugged water has stretches of as good pocket water as you'll find in the West for a small stream. Because Route 55 mimics the course of the East Fork for a number of miles, running alongside it, anglers have easy access to the river, sometimes too easy. But most anglers fish within site of their parked vehicle. And with all the holding water, there always seems to be good fishing a quarter-mile from any parking turnout.

Only six miles of the East Fork are public but with so many rocks and boulders, anglers can fish a short stretch for hours, dapping and picking at the pocket water. At times, the East Fork, with its litter of rocks and boulders, is more reminiscent of eastern streams.

The East Fork has some boulders as big as a stagecoach and pocket water galore. Holding in these small pools, under the ledges of overhanging rocks, hiding in deep foamy water are bigger browns than most folks know. Anglers will also catch some stocked rainbows. The Apache trout tend to run 10 to 14 inches.

With all the trees and brush and tall grasses so close to the bank, you'll need to use your array of casts and get out in the water (flip casts, roll casts, steeple casts). Employ stealth, lean on rocks, hide in the shadows, and hit every likely lie. I sometimes catch four or five fish from a twelve-foot radius on this productive little stream. The East Fork is closed above Reservation Route 30. Stay on public accesses and return all Apache trout to the water.

The scenery is spectacular, the large Apache and rainbow trout rise willingly in shallow water to dry flies and the regs say you must release all fish you catch. Why wouldn't they like this lake? Located near Hawley, this forty-seven-acre lake, anglers can fish from the shore but the best method to fish for lunkers is from a float tube or other personal watercraft. Long leaders, great presentations, lead the cruisers.

Earl Park Lake has earned the reputation for being the "pearl" of the Apache Reservation trout lakes. Even throughout prolonged dry spells, Earl Park remains constant because of its depth and its loyal feeder, Trout Creek. Although it is the first Apache Reservation "catch-and-release" lake, the place experiences very little fishing pressure.

The primary reason is that anglers must purchase three pieces of documentation to fish: an Arizona fishing license ($26 for a five-day out-of-state), an Apache Reservation permit ($6 per day), and a Private Water permit for Earl Park Lake ($10 per day). All three are available at the Sunrise General Store on Highway 273 (800-772-7669), but buying all three can mean the difference between steaks for dinner or hot dogs.

Another reason there isn't much pressure is due, in part, to its close neighbor, Hawley Lake. Earl Park visitors must pass by this breath-taking recreation area. Hawley's allure acts like a spider's web, allowing only the most determined and strong-willed fly fishers to escape its grasp and drive the extra few miles to Earl Park. And with no private water permit needed,

many simply settle for Hawley Lake to save a buck.

Perhaps the final reason Earl Park sees few fishers is that it is a catch-and-release, artificial-lure fishery. Lurking beneath the mirror surface of Earl Park Lake, anglers will find four species of trout—browns, rainbows, brookies, and Apache trout, allowing competitive anglers an opportunity to catch a "grand slam," which is common. Trout over 18 inches are frequent, with recent catches that stretched the tape to just over two feet.

Hawley Lake

The trout ended up being no more than 16 inches. Pretty muscular but nothing unusual for a White Mountains lake. Big shoulders, little head. This trout took McPhail for a ride. The Belly-Boat Express. Mac's not a small guy so the fish was strong and while Mac didn't move at a very fast pace in his float tube, he was pulled from one place to another. Impressive.

Hawley Lake is one of the prettiest of the White Mountain lakes. Two hundred fifty to 300 acres depending, this cold clear lake sits at 8,200 feet elevation. Twice, I've had it hail then snow on me while fishing Hawley—in the middle of the day in summer. It always seems cold here. Hawley has some hawgs, rainbow and brown and cutthroat and brook. I've lost a big brook trout while trying to get it into the net. You'll need a daily fishing permit.

A-1 Lake

This high-altitude lake (8,900 feet) on the White Mountain Apache Reservation pro-

vides good fishing for rainbows and brookies in its twenty-four acres with easy roadside access. Located about twenty miles east of Pinetop, this is a good option to cruise in your personal watercraft (rafts, bellyboats, kickboats, canoes). Anglers can fish from the shore and still have easy casting room.

Becker Lake

Irrigation impoundment near Springville, Becker Lake (6,910 feet) is eighty-five acres in the middle of grassy plains two miles northwest of Springerville. I read somewhere once that an outlaw is buried at the bottom of the man-made lake. Becker Lake opens in the spring, closes at the beginning of winter, with the off-time for fishing creating a trophy trout fishery. The lake's not much to look at but a spring helps keep the water clear and the temper-

ature steady, and as a result, the rainbow trout in Becker Lake grow rapidly and to impressive sizes.

Big Lake

Big Lake is a 500-acre lake in the White Mountains, 9,000 feet above sea level. That's a pretty big lake for such a high elevation. Big Lake holds rainbows, cutts, and browns, and is best fished by boat or float tube. The lake experiences windy conditions, so be prepared. Big Lake is an extremely fertile fishery. Dry flies are useful in the shallows and sinktips are handy to get down to the fish when they aren't looking upward. Anglers do hit the lake in great numbers and it is popular for campers and families. Despite the pressure, the lake is one of the best producers in the region. Big Lake has excellent facilities.

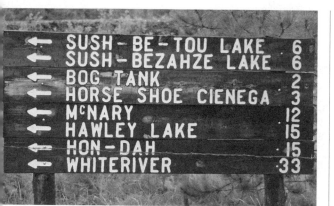

Bunch Reservoir

In recent years, these three Greer Lakes have been on the low side, not a bunch of water. When full, Bunch (8,260 feet) is forty-four acres big. The Greer Lakes are just a couple of miles north of Greer. If you catch trout, you'll catch browns and rainbows but it's been years since I've heard of anything big out of this one.

Christmas Tree Lake

This forty-acre "fly-lure-only" impoundment five miles south of Hawley Lake on Route 26 holds obscenely fat native Apache trout and some brown trout, but has fee fishing per day and a limit of twenty anglers per day (first come, first served). Christmas Tree Lake has good dry fly fishing especially at the inlets of Moon and Sun Creeks. If you want a chance to catch a monster trout, a record trout, Christmas Tree Lake is the stillwater choice for you. Just get up early.

Concho Lake

Located fifteen miles west of St. Johns near Concho, this is a shallow lake (six feet deep) stocked with rainbows; forty-one acres.

Crescent Lake

Crescent Lake (9,040 feet) lies just north of Big Lake, but it doesn't seem to me as prolific as its southern neighbor. With 120 acres, it is shallower, sometimes windy, and holds some big rainbow trout and some of the larger brook trout in the region. Fish the upper end of this pretty lake—rolling green hills, big meadows—with nymphs and wet flies. There is a marina and boat rental available.

Cyclone Lake

Thirty-seven acres; elevation, 8,100 feet. Three-and-a-half miles south of Arizona 260 off Arizona 473 (Hawley Lake Road). This lake is well known among anglers for rainbow, cutthroat, and brown trout. In the past few years, White Mountain Game and Fish has closed Cyclone to the general public but has opened it to private groups and organizations through the Rent-a-Lake program. Ditto Hurricane Lake.

Drift Fence Lake

One of my faves. Few are more scenic and the fly fishing is ideal because it's so shallow (which also means that winter freeze takes the fish and forces annual stocking). Drift Fence (8,900 feet) is fertile and the fish grow quickly. Usually not many lunkers but you can have a great day here catching lots of 1-pounders.

Fool Hollow Lake

Lower elevation-lake (6,260 feet) near Show Low mixes bass and catfish and walleye and sunfish with rainbow trout. One hundred forty acres in Fool Hollow State

Park. Too crowded for my tastes but it has good facilities.

Horseshoe Cienega Lake

Cienega means meadow and this is one of the meadows-turned-lakes. This 120-acre lake (8,100 feet) is popular, one of the most fished of the reservation lakes. Lots of spin and bait anglers. In the summer, the lake becomes weedy but don't let that discourage you—weeds mean a haven for insects especially damselflies, baetis and callibaetis. The state record brown trout of 16 pounds, 7 ounces was caught here. Horseshoe Cienega has some great dry fly fishing at times. The hogs are finicky, a mix of Apache trout, rainbow-Apache hybrids, rainbows, and browns. Sometimes, lure anglers have better luck because they get down deep. Bog Lake is right across the highway from Horseshoe Cienega.

Hulsey Lake

Pretty bumpy road to get back to Hulsey Lake (8,620 feet). This four-acre lake north of Alpine is stocked with rainbow trout. Good spring choice, not much good when it gets hot.

Hurricane Lake

Between Reservation Lake and Drift Fence Lake, Hurricane (9,000 feet) is nineteen acres of kick-ass fishing fun. Fly and lure only for these whoppers. I've seen another guy in a float tube next to mine catch and land an Apache-rainbow hybrid that was somewhere around 26 inches long. When I caught and landed my 17-inch hybrid, he rolled his eyes or so it looked to me. Limited number of anglers per day. Requires a special permit to fish for these Apache and rainbow-Apache hybrids.

Lake Sierra Blanca

Little lake (five acres) that sits at 8,440 feet six miles northwest of Alpine. Shallow lake that runs six feet deep or less and like Drift Fence Lake, winter kills the fish. The stocked rainbow trout grow rapidly with all the insects in this weedy lake and you shouldn't be surprised to catch a 14- to 16-incher. Good for fly fishing.

Lee Valley Reservoir

This picturesque forty-acre lake is restricted to lures and flies, and has a possession limit, so check regulations. Anglers fish here for rainbows and Apache trout, brook trout and for a change of pace, grayling. Lee Valley Lake (9,420 feet) lies at the foot of Mt. Baldy and is one of the most scenic lakes in the state. Lee Valley Lake can be reached along Highway 273.

Luna Lake

One hundred twenty acres; elevation, 7,900 feet. Three miles southeast of Alpine, off US 180. Close proximity to Alpine makes Luna Lake especially popular among both locals and vacationing fishermen. Rainbow, cutthroat, and brook trout fill up the nets here, and although most are just 9 to 12 inches, you'll occasionally see one caught in the mid-teens. Full facilities are available at Luna: campgrounds, picnic tables, restrooms, trailer hook-ups, and boat launch.

Lyman Reservoir

Lyman (6,000 feet) is a big boy, coming in at 1,400 acres. There are no motor restrictions so the lake is recreational and has too many zooming boats and splashy water-skiers on it. Lyman has a hodge-podge of fish, from rainbow trout to channel catfish, crappie, largemouth bass, walleye, and bluegill, to name a few.

Mexican Hay Lake

There's a reason the word "hay" is in the name of this lake. The lake is often so dry it is just a hayfield in a meadow. Even when the snowpack is heavy, the lake is only about ten feet deep. Located about fifteen miles from Springerville on Highway 273, Mexican Hay Lake doesn't hold any trophy trout but plenty of catchable-size rainbows.

Shore fishing is almost impossible for the weeds so you'll need a float tube. I only mention it because when it had water one year, I cleaned up and I can't forget how good that day was.

Nelson Reservoir

This sixty-acre lake gets a lot of bait casters standing on the shore. Nelson Lake (7,410 feet) lies five miles south of Springerville. I've heard about some big fish caught here but the two times I spent a few hours here, all I saw were bland stocker rainbows.

Pacheta Lake

Pacheta Lake (8,200 feet) offers the chance to catch big browns but is some-what tough to reach due to difficult roads, six miles southwest of Reservation Lake.

The lake's remoteness helps keep away all but the serious anglers. Sixty-eight acres and nestled in a dense forest, this is an excellent getaway fly fishing lake with a decent chance at a 20-inch brown (the rainbows and Apache trout aren't typically as big here). Float tubes and canoes make fishing here easier.

Pratt Lake

Here we have a small, hard-to-find natural lake that has lots of fish in the 20-inch class. Pratt is southeast of Springerville in the far eastern section of the state. You notice that I'm not writing much about Pratt (wink wink).

Reservation Lake

This lovely mountain lake (9,000 feet) offers 280 acres of solid fly fishing for brown and brook trout. Fishing is best from a small boat or float tube but there's plenty of shoreline room for casting. As pretty as it is and the fishing as good as it is, it's not very crowded. Dry flies work well in the shallows, especially at dusk.

River Lake

One of the Greer Lakes. Fifty acres and when full, which hasn't been lately, about twenty feet deep. For what it's worth, years ago, we used to catch big stocked rainbows from here but I haven't fished it in years. If the level is up, it's worth a go.

Show Low Lake

One hundred-acre lake in Show Low that is much better for a day outing with the family than for the serious fisher. Show

Low Lake (6,500 feet) holds record-setting walleye along with rainbow trout and catfish. Lots of facilities.

Shush Be Tou (aka Big Bear Lake)

Pretty eighty-acre lake (7,800 feet) east of McNary that is a good spring choice for Apache, rainbow, brown, and brook trout. Companion lake Shush Be Zahze (Little Bear Lake) is next to Big Bear.

Sunrise Lake

This is a big lake for the area, some 900 acres when full. Sunrise Lake is perhaps the crown jewel of White Mountain lakes, complete with high altitude (9,100 feet), big fish and lots of them. Sunrise holds big rainbow trout and the average size runs from 11 to 15 inches. The lake is also stocked with graylings, some of notable size. Even the brook trout can reach 2 pounds here in this fertile lake. Sunrise is located thirty miles east of Pinetop. Since the lake isn't ringed by trees like other lakes, the wind can be a problem at times. One time, McPhail and I were doing pretty well here when the weather changed all of a sudden and it began to rain; then it turned to something in between sleet and hail, some weird cross that Mac dubbed "slail."

Tunnel Lake

Third of the Greer Lakes; forty-four acres. Shallow lake that fattens up fish in a hurry, ideal for fly fishing when the lake is close to full. When healthy, the lake holds some good-sized (but stocked) brown and rainbow trout. Nothing around the shoreline

Little Colorado

Rainbow, brown, native, and brook trout. Good access and trails. Super dry fly fishing. Good early in the season before it gets low. Twenty-plus miles for fishing. Nearest Town: Springerville, for lodging and restaurants.

Permits

You do not need an Arizona fishing license when you fish on tribal lands. You do need a permit. Do not fish without one. Call or contact the White Mountain Apache Tribal Game and Fish 602-338-4385. P.O. Box 220, Whitewater, AZ 85941. An annual adult permit costs $80.00, a summer permit $50.00, a daily permit $5.00. Children ages 10–14 pay $2.50 per day, $25 for the summer, or $35 for the year. Children under 10 fish free but must be with an adult holding a fishing permit. Permits may also be purchased at the Sunrise Sports Center and Salt River Canyon Trading Post. During the summer months, you can secure permits at Reservation Lake, Horseshoe Lake, and Hawley Lake. There are several off season reservation sources in the neighboring town stores.

CONTACTS
Wager's Fly Shop, Cottonwood,
   520-639-2022
Babbitt's, Flagstaff, 520-779-4521
Bob's Fly Fishing, Greer, 602-735-7293
Hon Dah Ski and Outdoor Sport, McNary,
   602-369-7669
Alta Vista Anglers, Phoenix, 602-277-
   3111

to impede your casting and you really don't need a float tube or boat here. Can be windy at times.

Big Bonito

Length: eleven miles. Flows through the Bonito Prairie. Bonito is the Spanish word for pretty. Canyon stream. Brown and rainbow trout. Great pools. Special permits from the White Mountain Apache Tribe required.

Canyon Creek

Length: thirty miles. Artificial lures only in upper stretches. Permits are required for fishing. The creek has been awfully low the last few years but when the water is good, so's the angling.

Cibecue Creek

Length: twenty miles. Entirely on the reservation. Stocked with Apache trout. Some of the biggest browns in the state have been caught here in these pools.

Roosevelt Lake

- **Location:** Less than two hours east of Phoenix
- **What You Fish For:** Largemouth bass
- **Highlights and Notables:** Emerging bass lake close to a major city

One of six Salt River Project lakes, Roosevelt Lake is a popular lake with Phoenix residents since it lies a mere hour-and-a-half drive to the east and has good facilities (campgrounds, restrooms, ramps, etc.). This high-desert man-made reservoir holds 17,000 acres when full and around it has cacti and gnarly hills and rocky granite cliffs. It's a beautiful lake in that harsh way desert lakes are pretty by contrasting features. The Salt River feeds the lake and comprises one main arm, the Tonto Creek the other arm and as such, it can be divided by characteristics into two lakes.

The lake got lower and lower and shrank and shrank in the 1990s due to drought and drawdown. Recently the lake received watery bounty as the skies opened up and raised the water level to bring in nutrients and new cover. That makes for explosive fishing. If Roosevelt could maintain higher water levels—a difficult task given how this lake feeds new subdivisions and is subject

Canyon Creek Anglers, Phoenix,
    602-277-8195
Mountain Outfitters Fly Shop, Pinetop,
    520-367-6200
Pine Top Sporting Goods, Lakeside,
    520-367-5050
Paradise Creek Anglers, Pinetop,
    520-367-6200
Lynx Creek Unlimited, Prescott,
    520-776-7088
Scottsdale Flyfishing Company, Scottsdale
    602-368-9280
4J's Troutfitters, Scottsdale, 602-905-1400
Troutback Flyfishing, Show Low,
    602-532-3474
Arizona Flyfishing, Tempe, 602-730-6808

to desert conditions—it could become a name-brand bass lake. Other than largemouth, the lake holds smallmouth bass (7 pounds is the record), bluegill, channel and flathead catfish, crappie (lots of crappie), and a few more.

CONTACTS
Tonto National Forest Service,
     602-225-5200
Regional AZ Game & Fish, 602-981-9400

Lees Ferry, Colorado River

- **Location:** North central Arizona, close to the Grand Canyon
- **What You Fish For:** Wild rainbow trout
- **Highlights and Notables:** One of America's most prolific trout fisheries in perhaps its most unique settings

Ken Cole always says that you can tell a place is going to be a great fishing location if you tingle when you first lay eyes on the water. The hair on my neck raised like a Rhodesian ridgeback as the jet boat zipped upstream. Ken was right. Great location.

You're bound to feel small standing in a river flowing through an ancient ocean in the desert under prehistoric cliffs that rise a thousand feet into the blue sky. Oh sure, this is an artificial trout fishery created in the early 1960s, forming Lake Powell and this incredible tailrace below it. But there is no other place on earth like it to cast for trout.

The trout that swim this tailwater are

stout and athletic, made so by a rich soup of fish food (scuds, shrimp, and midges). Dry fly fishing is rare on the Colorado (except maybe the largely unknown dry scud hatch, heh heh.) Almost all of the time, perhaps 93.7 percent of the time, fly-anglers will be using nymphs but that's just a guess, a figure I throw out to emphasize how just about nobody fishes dries here. The river is clear and the riverbeds covered in waving green algae. Gravel bars extend out from sloping points.

Anglers will need a boat (a powerboat) to get upriver and most folks hire a guide. You'll need one the first time out. Every time out, as far as I'm concerned. They know the special techniques that work on the Colorado. They know how to change up strategies depending on changing water levels. They know to tell you to quit wading where you should be casting. You'll catch more 12- to 18-inch rainbow trout than your tired arm can handle. And you've always got a chance to hook up with a monster rainbow, one in the 22- to 25-inch range. Landing that monster is another story.

I say all this not because I was stubborn my first two hours on the river and not because I didn't listen to my guide, it's just that it's all so foreign, so river-specific that there's no need for you to waste any of your precious time since I've already wasted mine for you.

Fishing here is weird. Everything is so grand, you feel so small. You're riding in a jetboat, for goodness sakes, and the imposing cliffs keep you in shadows most of the

City Fishing

PHOENIX
Salt River, Lake Pleasant

Dry heat, my fanny. I've cooked food in my oven at 115 degrees and it's not all that humid in my oven. You don't sweat, the locals tell you, talking about the benefit of dry heat. True, you're all dry because you are being baked like a Cornish hen.

The Salt River is the kind of name you'd expect for a river near Phoenix. The fact it has water, cold water in fact, and that this cold clear water runs through a lovely canyon and has catchable trout in it, well, that's a bit surprising don't you think? Saguaro Lake releases cold water to form the Salt River tailrace, a mere forty-five minutes away from downtown Phoenix. Locals sometimes complain the river has too many suckers and that the flows are too low, but the stocked trout are fun to catch, and this is a viable put-and-take fishery, a winter fishing option where you can fish with steep canyon walls rising above you, wildlife all around you, get away from whatever's bugging you in Phoenix and land yourself a few trout. The Salt also has populations of smallmouth and largemouth bass and bluegill. Give the Salt more consistent flows and this could be a productive, interesting tailwater.

Another Phoenix phishing phancy is Lake Pleasant, an excellent winter bassin' spot only thirty miles from downtown. This impoundment of the Agua Fria River is a desert treat, fertile, loaded with 4- to 6-pound largemouths, and noted for its frequency in producing 10-pounders. Some of the new-lake honeymoon has worn off but this is still a fine lake.

day, and this is the gateway to the Grand Canyon so it's just odd to fish most of the time to ankle-deep water for large trout. Colorful mostly-wild rainbow trout that average 13 to 17 inches and weigh between 2 and 4 pounds. Anglers used to occasionally catch browns, cutts, and brookies which were once stocked in the river but I honestly don't know if they still do.

You cast to fish you see. Not much blind casting at all. Even a 17-inch Lees Ferry rainbow can take you into your backing. I just don't know of a trout river this big, this powerful, this good where you can do so much sightfishing. And certainly not all that *and* do so in a locale this primitively beautiful.

I'd love to tell you that the river is still a trophy trout fishery, but with all the changes and water fluctuations and problems who knows from year to year what this river will be. The Colorado has been at the summit, in the valley and has climbed back up again. With the cooperation of many people and agencies, the future is bright.

The fishing can be technical, it can be challenging. Still, I've seen beginners (maybe not true rookies but neophytes nonetheless) catch twenty and miss another twenty in a hard day's work.

Pile casts. Long leaders. Thin tippet. Dead-drifting midge larva or scuds. Indicators (although I still like a dry fly as indicator but when in Rome . . .). Heck, two of the most important and easiest aspects of catching trout here is to be careful wading and to sight cast to one trout without getting all hyped up over the pod of 16-inchers finning in front of you.

I like high-stick nymphing. You can see the trout take the fly and it's like underwater dry fly fishing, with little or no slack in the line. It doesn't work here. You have to dead-drift, up and across, mending all the while, doing everything you can to avoid drag. Sometimes you can cast ten times to a trout and if you don't spook it, if you get in a delicious presentation, you just might hook up. Mend, mend, mend is the mantra.

The Colorado fishes well all year. The mornings in winter are cold and last well into the day. The day in the summer brings the heat early and only splashing cold water on your face can cool you off. The river has some of the best guides you'll ever run into, ethical, courteous, knowledgeable. The digs are typically moderate but clean. Stop by the colorful, wind-carved Vermil-ion Cliffs and sample the area's one-horse, funky flavor.

Access is limited. Little walk-in fishing. Anglers can fish at the boat launch. To go upstream, you'll just have to go by power boat. There is a handicapped access at the Lees Ferry Ramp.

By the way, the hair on the back of my neck still tingles every time I see the Colorado River.

CONTACTS
Cliff Dwellers Lodge, 800-433-2543
Lee's Ferry Lodge, 928-355-2231
Marble Canyon Lodge, 928-355-2225
Each lodge hosts a full-service fly shop.
  Lee's Ferry Anglers, (800) 962-9755
  Ambassador Guide Service,
  800-256-7596
Marble Canyon Fly Shop, 800-726-1789

Oak Creek

- **Location:** North central Arizona
- **What You Fish For:** Rainbow and brown trout
- **Highlights and Notables:** Beautiful canyon stream near Sedona, cool green water under red sandstone

Even though Oak Creek is intimate but somehow big and has some good-sized trout in its pocket water, you'll want to put this one on your list because of the overall local scenery. Oak Creek will immediately go on your list because it's just so darned pretty.

Pink. Orange. Cream. Move into Sedona and everything is red. Everywhere you look. Red. Big cliffs everywhere you look but in the spaces between, you can see forever across the high desert. Austere rugged otherworldly wild country.

Red Rock Country.

And then there's this spectacularly green deep ribbon that runs through it all. Oak Creek.

Oak Creek Canyon is wooded, filled in the summer with the green of oaks and pines. In the fall, reds and oranges that mimic the rocks and cliffs mixed with yellows and green evergreen pines.

In the summer, Sedona is hot, the burn-your-lungs kind of hot. Cool down in the canyon while it's hot up top. And you want to start your fishing above Slide Rock State Park, the lowest end of the really good trout water.

Stealth needed. Big rocks. Long clear placid pools. Trees come up to bank and sometimes hang over and form shade canopy. Felt-soled boots a must. Slippery footing. Lots of scrambling over rocks. The river holds trout in the 9- to 14-inch range with some going 16 to 18 inches. I've seen bigger but Oak Creek is so intimate that it usually takes the perfect cast and perfect presentation to catch the 18- to 20-inch trout in this skinny pocket water and shallow pools.

The water gets low in the summer but I like spring and fall on the river anyway.

It's just too crowded in the summer with swimmers and hikers and car traffic. If you do fish in summer, the weekdays are better than the weekends.

This is one of those places you go on vacation with the wife, the kids. There's plenty to do. Brownie point heaven. Massages at fancy spas. Swimming and shopping. Fabulous restaurants. Hiking, horseback riding, relaxing. There's a fancy elite rich kinda thing going on in Sedona but it's mixed with a new-age ambiance so there's a cool, comfortable balance.

There's something haunting and lonely about the Fall River. I can't quite put my finger on what causes me to feel that way about it.

Noon. High sun. The fishing has slowed. We move slowly across undulating green waving vegetation. Mesmerizing. I am elsewhere, not on the boat, not on Fall River. I am not noticing the pastures we pass, Mt. Lassen looming in the distance, I'm in a trance.

Dad had a seizure in church a couple of months earlier. Two days in the hospital and today, begins to feel all too familiar. The doctors discover cancer in my father's brain, lungs, bones, liver, kidney, and lymph nodes. Stage four cancer. They mention that he has about ten months to live. Best guess. Miracles need not apply.

Dad was not a fishing dad, not the Andy Griffith dad. He has always been the John Wayne dad, the type-A, pioneering, bigger-than-life statue of a man. Fishing wasted valuable work time, church time. As I became more successful as a writer, he was a doting, proud father but since the books and articles were about fly fishing, a sport that he knew nothing about, he was detachedly excited.

I took him on one trout fishing trip, a failed affair on the Bow River in Canada during the worst runoff they'd seen in years. We fished from a boat, with a guide, and he caught nothing during the ten hours we were on the water.

My maternal grandfather, we called him Papaw, died two years before from this same cancerous route, lungs to brain to body. He taught me how to fish for sand bass and catfish in the muddy waters of Cedar Creek Lake. I lost my close friend, Terry Moore, who wrote so eloquently and honestly of his own journey through cancer for the newspaper he worked for. He broke the news about his cancer to me and my brother-in-law Kenny Medling while we all were on a fishing trip in New Mexico. I fished the winding banks of Big Blue Creek in Colorado for years with my father-in-law, Fred Becker, a stalwart giant of a man, who died a few years ago of this same lung and brain cancer. My favorite memories of each of these now dead friends are all tied inexorably to fishing. Fishing and death.

And now that Dad, who is sixty-two years old and dying, deals with this singularly focusing reality, I find myself numb and selfish. I desperately want to be nine years old again and have him come pick me up early from school and have the rods in the back and say, "Son," in his best Duke impression, "we're headin' to Colorado and pardner, we're gonna fish 'til we can't fish anymore." I want one more fishing trip with my father where he and I both hook up with a fat rainbow at the same time and smile at each other with awkward, Cheshire grins.

We had a big disagreement Christmas a year before; the argument was painful, hurtful on both sides. We were both wrong, both big idiots. We both said we were sorry but things haven't been the same since. I know one last fishing trip where we waded in the cool, refreshing waters would heal all wounds. Fishing and death. They are haunting me.

My father was still dying of cancer a year after they said he ought to be dead. That sounds cold but the big lug was beating the odds.

Four close friends and relatives, all of them fishing buddies, died of cancer in the last decade and my thoughts of them, my experiences with them were inexorably tied to fishing. Their deaths made me want to hang up my waders.

So here I was a year later, in the Yucca Point part of Kings River, fishing a pool the size of Aaron Spelling's mansion. I was doing okay, missing more than I should but subconsciously knowing where the trout were, not an easy feat in this stretch of Kings where an angler might fish several hundred yards and not see a trout.

Dad is not and never was an angler. He was all about work and being a dull boy. Recreation was for those who were lopside-headed or lazy or liberals. I reckon I'm all of those from time to time, especially when I was seventeen and living under Dad's roof.

I discovered he had cancer (he had a seizure in church), when the sheriff found me angling for trout on a river in New Mexico. My father nearly died that day. Our dialogue opened up a bit after that, and to my surprise we found ourselves talking more frequently and with no hostility.

Sixteen inches. Wild brown. Long skinny body, narrow head, long jaw. On top. Stimulator. Didn't want the Prince. I moved up.

This last year has been an emotional and cultural renaissance for me in many ways. I like my Dad. And I think he likes me, too.

I asked him to go fly fishing with me umpteen times over the last decade and he always declined. I wanted to show him how much fun fly fishing can be, how beautiful brook trout are, how good I am with a fly rod and at reading water and spotting trout and all those sorts of counterpart elements he wanted to show me when he built birdcages or sheds or apartment buildings or shopping malls. He owned a construction company for twenty years.

A deer in the edge of trees. I sit and watch. A good-sized trout swirls at something fifty feet upstream. I'll get him later.

For two years, a glacial age ago, I worked for him as a project manager, overseeing the turnkey completion of several million dollars worth of jobs, including two grocery stores. I hated it. I didn't feel comfortable reading blueprints. I didn't understand much about the business since I was an English major and I felt intimidated by my father's knowledge and success. I was a fish out of water.

The deer, drinking. The fish, feeding. I didn't even feel good about going out of state, out west, to fish, even if it was to get paid for articles, for research. Leaving him like that. In that bed. In that altered state. Can't get up anymore, still has his dignity.

Dad hates fishing. I know that now. He doesn't want to feel uncomfortable wasting time recreating any more than I wanted to be building strip centers.

He doesn't know how to cast well. He

isn't schooled in the sport. So I was both right and wrong in my persistence in trying to get him back on the river.

I wanted to show off, to bond, to wash away our past. It was a nice gesture but wrong-headed.

The cigar in my shirt pocket might be crushed so I inspect it and it's okay so I smoke it. The deer is gone and so is the big feeding trout.

This last year, Dad and I talked every day on the phone as he deals daily with mortality and pain. We joke about a lot of things.

I tell him that I write about him sometimes in my articles. I ask about the dove cage he is building. I share corny jokes with him (he likes Baptist jokes best of all—it's the deacon in him).

He always asks about my latest book or article, about where I have gone fishing or where I am going, about my school and schooling.

But I know now I don't need to get him back on the water to cleanse anything soiled in our relationship.

We're wading through this father-son thing and he's got his construction and logic and I've got my fishing and writing and things are going to be okay. The big trout is on the end of my line, jumping, diving. In my hand he is not as big as I thought he was, a 12-inch rainbow. It's a long hike back to the car.

I camped my last trip and thought how I would have loved to have taken Dad to this really big green pool up from Yucca Point where I know he would've tied into a big

one and we could have shook hands and nodded at his trophy and talked about it over a roaring campfire.

Barrett Lake

- **Location:** Southern California, close to San Diego
- **What You Fish For:** Largemouth bass
- **Highlights and Notables:** Catch-and-release angling on a quality lake close to a major city

You call Ticketmaster if you want Padres tickets or Chargers tickets or front row seats to the latest retirement concert tour for the Rolling Stones or to fish Barrett Lake. Yep, you read correctly. This lake is so good you have to purchase tickets just to fish it. Not much about this city water storage reservoir for San Diego is normal. Don't bring your own boat to this lake that has only barely been open ten years (1995) because the only boats allowed are the ones you rent.

This catch-and-release only bass lake is different than other quality California bass lakes. If you think California bass, you think Florida, right? In Barrett Lake, the most common catch will be a northern-strain bass, not the faster-growing, bigger Florida strain. Why not? Because the anglers like catching bass and Florida strain, while known for getting much bigger than their cousins, don't take angler lures as often. Oh, artificial lures and flies only.

Barbless. No bait. Release all fish immediately.

Not enough weirdness for you (come on, this is California, after all)? Well, only 100 anglers are allowed on the water per day. Anglers wait at a gate for an escort to the boat dock and office. They must use aluminum rowboats but they do let you bring a small motor up to 25 horsepower or you build your muscles by rowing. The boats come with the price of admission and use 5-horsepower motors. So no jet-skis or skiers or stupid fast boats (not like other California lakes at all, is it?).

Barrett is a treat. At only 811 acres at full pool, you wouldn't think 100 anglers each day would even care about taking the time to call Ticketmaster and travel forty-plus miles east of San Diego and then wait in line. Anglers consistently catch 2-pound largemouth bass. A lot of them. Threadfin shad and bluegill thrive in this clear water and make the bass fat fast. And now Colorado River smallmouth have been introduced and the crappie population has been solid for years. I've seen bullfrogs along the shore, big ones, and they sure don't make the bass skinny.

Barrett Lake has steep shoreline (no development at all) littered with big boulders and shrub brush. Many anglers follow the boiling, roily water from the largemouth chasing shad. At times, the largemouth act like white bass or striper hanging in schools. They like the shade, too. Work the arms and brush and tight banks, the weed-beds and rushes, the rocky structures, the submerged cottonwoods.

Lake Berryessa

- **Location:** Northern California
- **What You Fish For:** Largemouth bass
- **Highlights and Notables:** Catch ten bucketmouths in the morning, drink wine from a vineyard in the afternoon

Like its neighbor, Clear Lake, fishing at Lake Berryessa is a prime northern California experience, a Napa Valley journey. Located about fifty miles south of Clear Lake, this gives you a *Sideways*-like excuse to fish and drink from one end to the other.

Unlike Clear Lake, Berryessa is man-made and the fishing is more about quantity, fewer 10-pound bass. The water is clear in places, tea-colored in others. You'll see waterskiers in the summer but that just gives you a casting target, right?

This highland impoundment holds smallmouth, spotted, and largemouth bass, all in good numbers. What you don't catch in trophies, you'll make up in numbers. Twenty-six miles long and three miles wide, Berryessa is deeper than Clear Lake and while at times Berryessa has super topwater action, trolling deep is a common strategy to lure bass. You might read in the lake records that a 17.5-pound bass was caught here. Don't be fooled, anglers fish for bass in schools and for numbers rather than the catch-the-big-sowbelly game.

The smallmouth fishery is better than many know and the angling's not bad for kokanee or spotted bass (getting better all the time). Rainbow trout, catfish, crappie, silver salmon, and bluegill are other Berryessa residents. East of the Napa Valley, Lake Berryessa offers anglers year-round recreation opportunities.

California Delta

- **Location:** Northern California coast
- **What You Fish For:** Largemouth bass, striped bass
- **Highlights and Notables:** World-class angling for big bass in a quirky labyrinth of salt and freshwater

The elite bassin' holes include Lake Fork, Huites, Castaic, Dixon, El Salto, Alan Henry, and a delta? Yep. The California

Guide Bobby Barrack showing off why the Delta is considered one of the finest bass locations in the world

Delta, as good a bass fishery as any other in the world.

So what and where is this supposed amazing delta? At the mouths of the Sacramento and San Joaquin Rivers, northeast of San Francisco, a plexus of sloughs, canals, channels, cuts, ditches, creeks, and lakes held in check by Sacramento, Benicia, and Stockton, the largest saltwater estuary on the planet.

I can get lost in any city or town on any continent. The concrete and glass of cities are my Kryptonite. I don't get lost in the outdoors, the wild, for some reason. You can take the best navigator in the world and put him or her in the California Delta and if they are without a GPS and a map, they're a goner.

The water is murky and shallow, driven by current and tides, an expanse of vegetation such as hyacinth, tule and hydrilla, 1,600 miles of braided fertility, a complex waterway ideal for growing all things fishy. Largemouth bass and striped bass are at the top of the maze's game fish targets. The largemouth fishery gets better each and every year despite the ongoing overhead safety risk from speeding boats and jetskis (I don't exaggerate much about this, even though I am obviously joking, but these guys are nuts). Anglers have as good a chance at catching a trophy bucketmouth (a 10-pound is a trophy, okay) in the delta as any other bass fishery.

How big do they get in the delta? The biggest ever caught is 18.62 pounds, landed and weighed. Several 15- to 17-pound bass caught. Florida-strain largemouth bass. And there are more 5- to 8-pound largemouths than you can shake a stick at. The average bass goes 2 to 4 pounds. What a great place to catch a big black bass on a surface lure or fly. Experts write and friends tell me that they expect the next world-record bass to come from the delta.

In addition to the largemouth, you get striped bass, sturgeon, king salmon, shad, crappie, and catfish, stripers being the most common catch, often when you are casting for black bass. Stripers are caught all year but are particularly busy in April through June. Hard-core striper addicts think fall and winter are best to track down striped bass in the delta. Twenty pounds is a fairly common delta striper but hold on tight if you're in a float tube or kick boat or canoe because a 40-pound striped bass can motor you along a canal pretty good. Salmon and steelhead pass through the delta on their way up the rivers.

Some anglers fish from the shore, some in float tubes or personal watercraft, some canoes, some boats with motors such as tricked-out bass boats. All of them work for certain kinds of water but all have weaknesses, too. Float tubes are stealthy, easily transportable, maneuverable but the wind blows them around and besides that, a big fast boat or jetski can't see you in a low-profile belly boat right before it runs you over.

So you have to worry about other boaters, but you have other things to think about. The wind. The tides. The current. The fog. Always know where you are. Carry a GPS and a map and a lifejacket. This is serious backcountry. It's "hire-a-guide" time your first go-round.

Trout streams have named pools. California Delta has named areas, Frank's Tract, Little Frank's Tract, Snug Harbor, various marinas, and so on. Not many places on earth have the kind of diversity of game fish like this and in as unique a setting either.

CONTACTS
California Delta Chambers and Visitors Bureau, 209-367-9840, www .californiadelta.org
Bobby Barrack, www.bobbybarrack.com
Randy Pringle, www.100percentbass .com/Guides/Randy%20Pringle/ randys%20home.htm

Lake Casitas

- **Location:** Southern California, near Ventura
- **What You Fish For:** Largemouth bass
- **Highlights and Notables:** In the pantheon of top bass lakes in the world, Lake Casitas was once the king. While not the greatest, it's still great.

Ruth on his way down, DiMaggio on his way up. Jordan out, Shaq in. Nicklaus getting old, enter Tiger Woods. And so it goes. For every superstar who can never be replaced, there is always a great player ready to replace him in the Valhalla of Superiority.

So it goes with "the greatest bass lake on earth" titles. Lake Casitas, while still a major player on the bass-producing tour, is no longer the cleanup hitter, the quarterback, the top scorer on the court/field/arena.

Okay, enough bad sports analogies. At one time, not that long ago, scenic Lake Casitas was the hottest bass lake in the country, popping out hawgs like a Jimmy Dean factory. Only 2,500 surface acres set in high desert mountains, Lake Casitas was the darling of the late 1970s and early 1980s, regularly reporting hundreds of 10-pound largemouth annually. Many thought the world-record bass would come from this clear Southern California body of water since the lake record was caught in 1980, a 21.19-pound bucketmouth just a pound off of the 1932 record of 22 pounds, 4 ounces.

Then, inevitably, old age caught up with this superstar (sorry, I couldn't resist). Angling pressure, catch rates, and size of catch declined, then the drought cycles came and before you know it, Casitas is only producing 10-pound bass a dozen times a month or every two months or some such crazy number. Boo hoo.

Casitas is still an All-Star lake, albeit a designated hitter (too easy, I know), but it can still hit home runs (stop me, I'm out of control). Not many lakes in the West produce as many 10-pound bass as Lake Casitas and there is every reason to believe that with the recent water levels up from rain, with new restrictions and protective limits, and given that trout stockings will continue (feeding time), this lake will continue to rank in the Hall of Fame pantheon (ouch).

CONTACTS

Lake Casitas Marina, 805-649-2233
Marc Mitrany, guide, 800-572-6230

Castaic Lake

- **Location:** Southern California, an hour north of L.A. near Valencia
- **What You Fish For:** Largemouth bass
- **Highlights and Notables:** One of the legendary big-bass lakes of America, still producing

At one time, Castaic Lake produced the second biggest largemouth bass ever caught, 22 pounds and ½ ounce. This southern California bass lake went nuts in the late '80s and early '90s until it shut off for a while when predatory striped bass entered the lake and made it tough on the largemouth bass population. It's back to high form even if it hasn't regained its former glory. The numbers of anglers are legion who have a double-digit bass to their credit from Castaic; and many of the biggest largemouth ever caught in California were caught out of these waters and we're talking bass that weigh more than your average seventh-grade boy can curl with dumbbells.

Located forty miles north of Los Angeles, Castaic is without a doubt in the canon of anybody's list of the best bass lakes in the world. Some say the fertile, year-round aqueduct lake is past its prime as world-record candidate but I'm not as quick to post it over to the great-gone-to-just-good-bass-lake just yet. With rich food sources like crayfish and threadfin shad, with all the deep water and coves and shallow hotspots, and with all the 2- to 10-pound bass still being caught, I'm not ready to mark an X through the name.

The lake is two lakes with the lower lake (Castaic Lagoon) allowing only nonpowered boats and canoeing. Castaic holds largemouth, smallmouth, and striped bass and gets regular stocking of striper food, er, I mean hatchery-raised rainbow trout. The so-called upper lake is for boating, skiing, other fast water boat sports and fishing. Castaic Lake is heavily pressured with both fishermen and recreationalists.

The upper lake is roughly 2,500 surface acres with thirty miles of shoreline. The lower lake is just three miles around and covers about 200 surface acres. Both hold big largemouth. The entire thing they call Castaic Lake does. Let's hope that everybody else keeps writing it off and we'll reap the benefits.

CONTACTS

Troy Folkestad, guide, www
    .folkestadfishingguide.com
J&T Tackle, 805-630-4711

A good source of info is www.castaiclake
.com

Clear Lake

- **Location:** Northern California, close to Berryessa
- **What You Fish For:** Largemouth bass
- **Highlights and Notables:** Napa Valley lake full of large black bass

Clearly, this is a good lake. Let's clear this up, okay? Stupendous bass fishery, is that clear? I am so tired of seeing the intros to Clear Lake always punning the lake's name. It's clear to me that writers need to come up with some other way to introduce this wine-country lake.

The largest natural lake in California sits in Napa Valley, the most naturally romantic largemouth bass setting in America. A couples hotspot, so to speak. So many vineyards, winetasting rooms, cute little towns, shopping, and gourmet meals, how can she mind a little fishing?

Largemouth denizens of beautiful Clear Lake are on average some of the biggest black bass in the country, about 3 to 5 pounds. This relatively shallow lake also holds bass over 10 pounds so it's a super combination, like *pasta con filetto alla crema e funghi* with a local Beaulieu Vineyard Georges de Latour Private Reserve Cabernet Sauvignon (Napa Valley) 1991. Hey, this is California after all, and where else can you mix bass fishin' and taste?

Clear Lake bass can be caught with finesse or by going hard at them; everything seems to work including jumbo minnows. Topwater lures (especially frogs) retrieved

Crowley Lake

- **Location:** South central California
- **What You Fish For:** Lahontan, brown, and rainbow trout (Kamloops, Eagle Lake, and Coleman)
- **Highlights and Notables:** The combination of alpine scenery and top-flight fishing makes Crowley a worthy trip.

The mountains are big and massive and shadowy and granite and the lake is a blue inkblot in the flat valley, two incongruous primitive friends. There is only high desert and sage and snow on big mountains and blue deep water. And a primordial bouillabaisse of Kamloops, Eagle Lake, Coleman, brown, and Lahontan trout. We have an alpine lake, big and bad. And crowded.

Oh, those opening days. This Eastern Sierra stillwater fishery four hours north of Los Angeles has a top-notch rep and still keeps up its end of the bargain. That's why you'll discover anglers by the thousands fishing the lake the first day of the season. There's room for all, fish for everyone. The beautiful scenery is perfect for cameras and float tubes and boats and pontoon boats; conventional and fly anglers alike have success.

Nearly 7,000 acres large and close to 7,000 feet in elevation, Crowley Lake receives an amazing bounty of riches annually, some years getting as many as a brain-jarring half-million trout planted in its waters. Cool thing is the trout are stocked early and late so that thousands

over the weed mats of summer draw blasts of bass. The lake is all about structure, rockpiles, rocky banks, pilings, vegetation, channels, good light to the bottom, residential channels with docks perfect for flippin'.

Just 110 miles north of San Francisco Bay, Clear Lake has 110 miles of shoreline and when at pool holds 44,000 acres. Tag team this lake with Lake Berryessa and the beauty and uniqueness of the Napa Valley.

CONTACTS

Lake County Chamber of Commerce,
    800-525-3743, www.lakecounty.com
Randy Pringle, www.100percentbass
    .com/Guides/Randy%20Pringle/
    randys%20home.htm

upon thousands of trout have a chance to grow all winter before the spring rush hits.

The lake holds big fish, both stocked and wild. Each of the strains of rainbow trout acts differently from the other in terms of location and behavior and spawning and growth so you get a diversity of options throughout the year right there. Owens River and other streams run into the lake and with them come wild trout including a self-sustaining brown trout population. Lastly, Lahontans, which are native to the Eastern Sierra Nevada, have been reintroduced back into the lake.

Most flyrodders find that midges in their nonadult form (pupa, larva) are the most effective method to bring the trout to bear. One clue is the midge hatches so big and dark and in such big clouds that it looks like the air above a tribe of Bigfoot smoking foot-long Cuban cigars.

CONTACTS

Brock's Fly-Fishing Specialists,
    760-872-3581
Kittridge Sports, 760-934-7566
The Trout Fly, 760-934-2517
Tube Tenders of Crowley Lake,
    760-934-6922
Rick's Sport Center, 760-934-3416

This Web site has lots of additional info: www.mammothweb.com

Lake Davis

- **Location:** Northern California
- **What You Fish For:** Trout
- **Highlights and Notables:** Beautiful lake, a cautionary tale

Like so many other Lake Davis aficionados, I was perplexed and pained to hear about the purposeful and controversial poisoning of the lake by the California Department of Fish and Game in 1997 to eradicate the non-native predator, the pike. They were rightfully worried that if pike got downstream, they could decimate the trout and salmon populations. Anything that had fins died. Millions of trout were restocked, tens of thousands of trout over 5 pounds were planted and the plan was to return Lake Davis to a trophy trout fishery.

A couple of years later, after tens of thousands of gallons of poison didn't do the trick, the pike were back in full force. The Bay-Delta watershed's salmon and trout and striped bass and other endangered species were again at serious risk. Seven years later and after limited control efforts (screens on the dam gates, electroshocking, plunking the pike on the head, etc.) and harvesting more than 40,000 or some such large number of pike, the waterwolf was still cruising and looking for fish to bite in half. What to do? There's talk of draining the lake, of using explosives, of repoisoning the lake. Tough to rid these pike.

At one time, Lake Davis (4,000 acres) was a top-flight trout lake full of 1- to

3-pound rainbows and browns with some lunkers swimming away from your lures and flies. The damselfly hatch was the best in the world.

Cautionary tale. Enjoy it while you can. You never know when your favorite fishin' hole will go belly-up even if only for a decade or so. The Sacramento River suffered a major chemical spill in 1991. The Red River in New Mexico was once one of the top brown trout dry fly streams in the West until molybdenum killed most everything downstream of the molybdenum plant. The list goes on and on and on. Lake Davis may soon be back to form, pikeless and ever trout full.

Diamond Valley Lake

- **Location:** Southern California, between San Diego and Los Angeles
- **What You Fish For:** Largemouth bass
- **Highlights and Notables:** Newest bass hotspot

I get the feeling some time that one of the games California anglers play is a lot like finding new music artists. You know the game. You're listening to Saturday morning college radio and a song comes on and you love it, you've got to find out more. First time I heard Rickie Lee Jones. Ani DeFranco. Stanley Jordan. REM. Kelly Willis. Gillian Welch. You get the idea.

So you buy the 8-track or vinyl or cassette or CD or whatever the newest technology is and you listen to it over and over and you love it and that artist is yours, belongs to you, you discovered him or her or it but you make the mistake, a mistake you know better than to make—you tell some of your friends. And before you know it, your friends love her/him/it and you don't mind all that much until all of a sudden that artist, you realize, is no longer yours. There's nothing wrong with your artist—he/she/it still makes great music but it's just time to move on.

Same with hot new California bass lakes. They seem to come one or two a year. Anglers find them and love them and catch lots of big fish and then after a while, they realize the lake's not theirs and they move on to the next lake/music artist.

Meet Diamond Valley Lake. The newest bass crush, a real up-and-comer. You've heard this tune before: new reservoir, awesome growth rates, big bass early in the life of this 4,500-acre lake (opened 2003). Great potential, should produce some big hits, a star in the making, that's what the experts are saying. This lake is different, more structure, deeper, up to 250 feet. Sure, this one flew under the radar for a little bit but this talent had to rise to the top of the charts.

This star is a high-desert reservoir in the Los Angeles metro area and it is loaded with Florida-strain largemouth bass and rainbow trout, a combo that has a history of success.

When everyone gets tired of hearing Diamond Valley Lake sing, go and visit her yourself. The songs will still be good and all the fair-weather fans will be at the next hot bass concert.

CONTACTS
Diamond Valley Marina, 800-590-5253, www.dbmarina.com

Dixon Lake

- **Location:** Southern California near Escondido
- **What You Fish For:** Largemouth bass
- **Highlights and Notables:** In March 2006, a 25-pound hawg was caught. Controversy ensued but this little lake produces huge bass.

Just when I thought we could all get off the Dixon Lake-will-produce-the-next-world-record-largemouth-bass bandwagon, the strangest thing happened. The new world-record largemouth bass was caught in Dixon Lake. Sort of.

Before we go there, let's visit Dixon Lake. Florida-strain bass live in this reservoir near Escondido in southern California in a canyon surrounded by green and brown hills covered in chaparral and oak. The lake makes sure their largemouth bass have plenty to eat including rainbow trout and bluegills and little babay ducklings. Eighty feet deep and in a pretty Southern California setting, Dixon Lake's waters are clear and disturbed only by rental boats with electric motors. At one point, Dixon Lake had produced three of the top fifteen biggest bass ever caught. Dixon has several IGFA line class records. Nice lake, huh?

Dixon Lake covers 72 surface acres.

The most famous and top bass lake in America is probably Lake Fork in Texas and it's considered on the smaller side at 28,000 acres. Dixon certainly looks larger than 72 acres but it still looks and feels like a small lake.

Seventy-two acres? How in the world can Dixon Lake give us so many big bass? And now back to the new world-record bass. In March of 2006, two buddies caught and boated a bass that weighed—hold on to your hats ladies and gents—remember the world record is a bass caught in 1932 in Georgia that weighed 22.25 pounds—an amazing 25.1 pounds!

Twenty-five pounds is one fourth of Salma Hayek: 19.5 pounds bigger than the 72-ounce steak at the Big Texan restaurant in Amarillo that offers you the 4.5-pound steak for free if you eat it all in an hour (you also have to eat all the accoutrements, too). Twenty-five pounds. That's three pounds bigger than the world record that had stood for seventy-plus years. This is bigger than McGwire breaking Maris's single-season home-run record. Maybe bigger.

But it may or may not count. These two buddies didn't weigh it with a certified scale, instead just using a hand-held digital scale. And they released the biggest bass of all time back into the blue waters of Dixon. Controversy ensued after this when all they had to show for the world record was some photographs and a bit of film, hardly what a skeptical fishing community needs to pop corks on the Champagne for the most important fishing record on earth.

You may have seen the photograph. Big guy extending his arm to the camera holding by the lip a fish that looks the size of a Weimaraner. The two anglers are not Johnny-come-latelys because between the two of them, they had already caught many of the top bass ever caught in Lake Dixon.

Plus they had witnesses to this monster bass. And the angler claimed he had caught this same fish before, three years prior, back when it weighed only 21.7 pounds. Did I mention that the plot thickens? There is talk that the fish was foul-hooked, further complicating this potential record. There's even more controversy to this record, and if you want to read the drama that goes with both catching a world-record fish and the ensuing cynicism and rumors, then find an article about the catch—they're everywhere on the Internet.

Bottom line? Dixon Lake produced a bass that weighed well over 20 pounds and probably much more, probably broke the biggest record of them all. The fishing pressure is likely to be crazy for the next year or two until anglers start chasing bass at the next hot lake. So wait a couple of years and then visit little Dixon Lake to try to catch the big bass.

CONTACTS
Lake Dixon, 760-741-4680
Campground Reservations, 760-741-3328

Fall River

- **Location:** Eastern California
- **What You Fish For:** Trout
- **Highlights and Notables:** One of the classic western rivers, a must do for any serious angler

There are those who believe that this spring-fed, crystal-clear river ranks with any other trout stream in the nation. It does. Fall River meanders for seventeen miles past private land on its way to Pit River. The only way to fish for the huge rainbow and brown trout in this flat water is by floating in a boat with an electric motor or by float tubing.

If you stay at one of the many lodges on the river, not a bad idea, they provide access. Guides can get you on and honestly, if you're a first-timer, hire a guide. So, getting on the smooth-surfaced river is the first tough chore, the second is catching these wary leviathans. The water is so clear sometimes you feel like you are floating on clouds. You can see the wild trout, congregating, feeding, ignoring you.

The average size trout caught on the Fall approaches 16 inches. Many reach 10 pounds and 5-pounders are commonplace. Rainbows outnumber and usually outsize the brown trout in the river. In general, the trout are just plain big. Little heads and fat bellies, as big in girth as length it seems sometimes.

Insect hatches on Fall River are some of the most consistent and heaviest of any river in the West and fly fishermen can dry fly fish all season long. Pale Morning Duns begin the season, followed and overlapped by Blue Winged Olives, tricos, caddis, finally culminating in the exciting Hexagenia hatch in the fall. Even during the middle of the day in the heat of summer, hatches occur and trout rise.

Long, delicate leaders are required to even get the cunning trout to take a look at the fly. Nymphing can afford the angler a somewhat heavier leader but be ready to clean the moss off the fly after every cast. Except for the hex hatches, and the occasional green drake, matching the prevailing hatch will require small flies, sizes 18 to 22, and thorax and comparadun patterns are often necessary to fool the fish.

They've seen a lot of flies. The river restricts the angler to artificials only and there are other regs, too. This is one of those rivers where 10 percent of the anglers catch 90 percent of the trout. Those anglers who are both experts and not haunted by waters will be the catchers.

CONTACTS

The Fly Shop, Redding, www.theflyshop
.com

Fish First, Albany, www.fishfirst.com

Vaughn's Sporting Goods, Burney,
530-335-2381

Clearwater Trout, Dunsmuir, 415-381-1173

Dunsmuir Fly Fishing Company, Dunsmuir, 530-235-0705

American Fly Fishing Company,
Sacramento, 800-410-1222

Hot Creek

- **Location:** Eastern central California
- **What You Fish For:** Wild trout
- **Highlights and Notables:** One of the densest trout populations anywhere, a real classic stream

Like a blue slinky wriggling across the lush green valley floor, Hot Creek curves back and forth toward its watery marriage to the Owens River. Snowy mountains surround one level of this vista, high desert and sagebrush a lower level. Funny how much fuss is made over a fishery that has such a short menu, less than six miles, and where most of the best water is fishable but private. Oh, you can fish the two miles of private water on Hot Creek Ranch, but you'll pay. Close to two hundred per night to stay in one of the riverside cabins or over three-hundred-twenty-five smackeroos for a day's guiding.

And on Hot Creek Ranch, you can only fish with barbless dry flies. That's all. No substitutions. No nymphs. No lures. Just dry flies. Been that way for over fifty-six years.

It's worth it, of course, if you can afford it. This section has traditionally held big trout. You get the western spring creek repertoire: tricky crosscurrents, the need for stealth, matching-the-hatch skills and casting accuracy.

Hot Creek is not wide and is not deep (I guess I could say it's narrow and shallow, huh?). The surface is flat and smooth with only a few riffles scattered here and there. Below the ranch and below a public stretch, there are hot springs that give the river its name. Browns and rainbows swim in these clear waters, more browns now than twenty years ago. Hot Creek holds anywhere from 4,000 trout per mile on up which is a down figure compared to surveys from a decade before.

So the negatives? Short stretch to fish. Costs money to fish Hot Creek Ranch. The public section is one of the more heavily fished in the state. By late summer, the weeds make fishing difficult. The wind kicks up at times. Catching fish requires a certain skill level. The river is being threatened by development and drawdown. Hot Creek has big trout but I hesitate to call it a trophy trout stream any longer. Fifteen to 17 inches is a big trout on Hot Creek nowadays. I know from friends that there are bigger fish but the fishery doesn't seem to support as many 20-plus-inch trout as often.

Absolutely beautiful, awe-inspiring scenery. Famous, a classic stream. More trout per mile than most other rivers in the world. Great hatches and lots of invertebrates. Almost every trout you catch is 13 inches or longer and they're plump. Wild trout, by the way. Even though the public stretch sees lots of anglers, you don't need much water to call your own to find fish.

Hot Creek, hot damn. Give it a go.

In the mile-long public stretch, anglers are restricted to a single barbless fly and all fish must be returned to the water.

CONTACTS

Hot Creek Ranch, Mammoth Lakes, www
   .hotcreekranch.com

Rick's Sports Center, 760-934-3416

Eastside Guide Service, 760-934-2517

Kings River

- **Location:** Eastern central California
- **What You Fish For:** Wild brown and rainbow trout
- **Highlights and Notables:** Canyon stream, sequoias rising above it, loaded with dry fly–wanting wild trout

The Kings River is one of the undersung fisheries of America. You probably haven't even heard of it. Over sixty fishable miles of beautiful, trout-rich canyon stream tucked away on the western slope of the Sierra Nevada southeast of Fresno in the middle of California. The granite walls that rise up from the canyon floor reach heights of 5,000 feet into the sky and Kings Canyon is arguably the deepest canyon in America. The sequoia redwoods, their red-orange and green contrasting against the big gray rugged walls, are enormous living things.

Because the geologic wonder tied to great fishing, my geologist/fishing brother-in-law David wants to make Kings Canyon a road trip with me. We will, too, one day soon.

Some say the seventeen miles of the South Fork of Kings River from Boyden Cave upstream to the end of the road past Cedar Grove are the best section of the river system. Possibly. It's certainly beautiful and productive with its incessant pocket water where big gray rocks break through the surface in a snakey line like tops of a prehistoric dinosaur lying down in the river. In places here, it is difficult to wade because of submerged rocks the size of barbecue pits and wheels of cheese and diesel truck tires.

Other sections have more traditional pocket water, riffles, runs, and very very nice pools. Trees come right up to the water. The trout are wild, browns, and rainbows, averaging in South Fork about 9 to 14 inches but more 9 than 14. The water is clear and not particularly fertile and the hatches are fair-to-middlin' which, as any veteran trout angler knows, means that the trout can't afford to be selective. In a deep hole, you will find a 15- to 20-inch trout but they won't be heavy. The browns tend to have long heads, thin bodies. Rainbows tend to be smaller, colorful (but don't be fooled, the rainbows get big, too).

Highway 180 follows the river the entire seventeen miles of this upper stretch so you have easy access—good turnouts—but sometimes the road moves 100–200 feet away and folks are lazy so those are the places to hike into.

Further downstream, where the Middle Fork enters Yucca Point and the flow grows and the river gets bigger, from forty-five to 140 feet wide. Yucca Point is tough to reach and lightly fished (must take a real trail). You will see so much fishable water you won't end up walking as far as you should. The catch is that you should go ahead and fish the fishy water but keep moving until you hit fish, all the way down to Pine Flat. If there are really big fish, they're here in this bigger water. The pools (big big pools) and runs and glides are unusual for a canyon stream (so wide here) and the trout are pickier than they ought to be in this big lovely water.

The tailwater below Pine Flat used to be great water with big fish and a great rep, and then experienced a serious fishkill and subsequent bad conditions. The tailrace seems to be on the road to recovery and I just read where the state is now planting brood fish, big fish. Word of warning, the drive around Pine Flat Reservoir has to wind around the arms of the lake and takes forever.

You simply have to put Kings River on your list of destinations especially if you like hiking (the Copper Creek trail upper

City Fishing

LOS ANGELES
Piru Creek, Piru Lake,
Deep Creek, Castaic Lake,
Inshore/Offshore

L.A. is many things. The people sit in traffic jams, lay on the beaches, write screenplays, wait tables but there aren't many in the City of Angels who fish, not even on weekends. Sure, the piers are chock-full and the bass lakes are busy but the saltwater is a wide open frontier. You have several harbors to choose from: Dana Point, Oxnard, Long Beach, Redondo, King Harbor, Ventura, Marina del Rey, Newport Beach. You might find a sea lion laying in wait and then ambushing the fish you just caught, you get the fish head.

Halibut fishing is prime up and down the southern California coast. Getcha some sardines and start casting. Go for rocky points, reefs, kelp forests.

The white sea bass fishery keeps getting better and better. Bonitos average 4 to 5 pounds and on the right days, you can catch twenty to thirty of them. If you fly fish, you can catch most all of saltwater species and also, you just have to stop in at Bob Marriott's—it's huge and a carnival of longrodding fun. The beach fishing is pretty darned good (one good one is Redondo Beach, near the mouth of Santa Ana River).

Catalina Island waters are underrated but hold so much for the angler—white sea bass as well as mako shark, blue shark, kelp bass, bonito, barracuda, sand bass, mackerel, ladyfish, yellowtail (also perch, croakers, halibut, jack, lizardfish, smelt, opaleye). Catalina has long been known for its big-game angling so the prolific life around the island isn't anything new. It's just most folks don't know about it.

Piru Creek, Lake Piru, Deep Creek—three of the better trout fisheries within an easy three-hour drive from L.A. Piru Creek has been and still is under threat of urban sprawl and only action and vigilance from local associations and state programs has kept Piru from becoming a thing of the past. Piru Creek is a wild trout fishery just one hour from Rodeo Drive. As if . . . You know, if you're on Rodeo Drive and shopping, you have no business trout fishing an hour later.

What else is close by? Kern River, West Fork of the San Gabriel River, each less than an hour theoretically from L.A. Both are blue ribbon–type trout streams.

reaches and the Yucca Point section above Pine Flat for starters); if you like diverse habitat; if you like wild trout; if you like catching lots of wild trout with the prospect of catching big trout; if you like dramatic, unique scenery, accessible angling, underfished blue ribbon quality fishing. Fresno and Visalia and Clovis and Sanger are ideal towns to use as home bases and the area has several campgrounds right on or near the river.

Mammoth Lakes

- **Location:** Eastern central California
- **What You Fish For:** Brook, rainbow, brown, and the rare golden trout
- **Highlights and Notables:** Heavenly alpine scenery, as gorgeous as any mountainous area in the country—super family getaway or backpacking excursion

The scenery definitely outweighs the size of the fish, no doubt about it. The Mammoth Lakes are ideal for the solitary backpacker, fishing buddies doing day trips to lakes from a base camp, family vacations, serious anglers who love high-country adventure.

While the trout are not world record-breakers, you'll be surprised enough (the Alpers trout—stocked whoppers that weigh as much as 10 pounds) that you'll want to keep fishing. The beauty of the Sierra Nevada mountains will make you not want to leave.

Sitting on a blue lake with reflections of the blue sky and clouds and the gray rocky spires and cathedrals of the surrounding mountains, their broken teeth cutting through the blue sky and clouds, a chill in the air, the pure air, several trout circles near the shore . . . does it get better than that? Mammoth Lakes are numerous and offer up brown, brook, rainbow trout (and the elusive rare golden trout). Near Mammoth Lakes, the town (sounds like a movie) sit Lake Mamie, Lake George, Lake Mary (the most consistent), and Twin Lakes, popular, accessible, trouty lakes. And I like the small creeks of the Mammoth Lakes area, fun dancing little things with wild trout ready to pounce on dries, inlets, and outlets as well as the occasional alpine tarn that you're surprised holds fish, small secret gems. Other lakes to explore include: Barrett, Crystal, Horseshoe, McLeod and TJ.

CONTACTS
The Troutfitter, Mammmoth Lakes, www .troutfitter.com

McCloud River

- **Location:** Northern California
- **What You Fish For:** Wild brown and rainbow trout
- **Highlights and Notables:** My favorite river in the Far West, a glorious fishing experience; fishing in a clear canyon river where the most beautiful wild rainbows live

Oregon to the north, Nevada to the east. The McCloud River is stuck up in the northern most part of the great state of California. This is my favorite river in the Far West. I love the wildness of the river, the way I can fish a 100-yard stretch for hours because the McCloud is so rich, so bountiful.

I love the amazing canyon through which the river rushes, most of the time clear as gin, remote and sassy. I love fishing around rocks. McCloud has rocks rocks rocks. I love the sensory explosion—the great woodsy smells and wild terrain and it's so woody and green and lush and tight and wild that you swear every shadow holds a black bear or a mountain lion or Sasquatch.

The McCloud River is a classic freestone stream in its upper reaches, flowing swiftly through meadows, plunging over falls, past boulders. The renowned lower section below McCloud Dam is faster and larger, characterized by cold clear water, prime pocket water, and relatives of the hard-fighting McCloud strain of wild rainbow trout. Hard to believe but you can be on the McCloud and not ever see an angler but the river has so much in the way of trout lies, so much great water, that it can serve anglers and still seem underfished. And there is excellent trail access, too.

Pull on your felt-soled waders. Walk the trail and come to the river. Get in. The shock comes when you feel how impossibly cold the foamy rushing water is, this river fed by springs from volcanic landscapes in northern reaches of the state. Because of the thick forested banks of pine and fir and alder, the sun breaks through the canopy only now and again and you still can't believe that the water is this cold. Pay attention. Your mouth is agape as everywhere you look is a run or pocket water or impossibly deep big wide long pools. And it's all fishy.

You're overwhelmed by it all but start casting. You'll be sightcasting to brightly-colored browns and explosively-colored rainbows that run 9 to 15 inches. If you play it right, you're going to tangle with a trout or two that is best measured in pounds.

These are smart fish most of the time and that challenge is just one more component of why you've found your new favorite canyon stream. The trout are not typically lunkers because McCloud's cold water doesn't equate with fast growth rates. So what you're catching is really big medium-sized fish over and over and over. Some of these athletic fish grow up to 8 pounds. You have a real chance at breaking off a big boy when the browns migrate from Shasta Lake in the fall.

Here's the clincher. The McCloud grows sledgehammers for trout. They hit as hard as any trout in America. And they come from a line of rainbow trout that is as storied as any other in America: the McCloud strain of rainbow trout, known for its beautiful reddish sides and rambunctious nature. The McCloud River rainbow lineage harkens back to 1874 when the eggs from these trout were collected and sent to stock various rivers in the East. Their red-banded sides, often crimson in color, are their dominant trademark.

The McCloud can be fished in any number of ways. The river has significant hatches throughout the year. You've got your usual western hatches of caddis and mayflies. Golden stonefly and salmonfly hatch in late spring with October caddis coming off in autumn.

I have heard locals say that the fish of the McCloud don't like the sun but I haven't found it to be true when I nymph deep enough, even in the sun. I also have had locals tell me that if you fish dries during summer (read: not during the stonefly hatches of spring or the caddis of fall), you will typically catch smaller trout. This turns out to be true for me.

I watched a local twitching his streamer past the boulder over and over and the 5-pound trout kept going after it and re-treating until the old gentleman finally found the right twitch to make him take it. I am guessing 5 pounds because the angler never took the brilliantly-colored brown out of the water, releasing the behemoth gently from his leathery mitts. Big fish.

You are wading and you are stepping over rocks and smaller rocks and gravel and you're scared you're going to fall because it's slippery on the rocks and the fast water that beats against your thighs makes so much noise it sounds like a train. This is the part where the writer includes the caveat that no angler ever follows: "bring a wading stick/staff." Come on. Who wants to tote one of those things around? Chances are that if you get out there a bit, if you have any sense of adventure, you're going to take a fall, a slip, and

get cold and wet. I'm serious about how the smells stick out on the McCloud. It's sensory overload. Enjoy.

CONTACTS

The Fly Shop, Redding, www.theflyshop.com
Fish First, Albany, www.fishfirst.com
Clearwater Trout, Dunsmuir,
   415-381-1173
Dunsmuir Fly Fishing Company,
   Dunsmuir, 530-235-0705

Milton Reservoir

- **Location:** Eastern California, the Sierras
- **What You Fish For:** Brown and rainbow trout
- **Highlights and Notables:** Milton is all about the picture-perfect scenery.

My pick as the poster child for Sierra lakes. There might be prettier lake higher up, farther back but you can reach this one *and* it has great fishing (instead of spotty fishing like so many backcountry lakes). Small Milton Lake, not far from Truckee, is one of the most scenic high country lakes you'll ever see and mightier than its size.

Reflections from the green-forested mountains that come right down to the stillwaters of Milton Lake are photo-orgasmic. Managed as a trophy trout for wild rainbows and wild browns, Milton Lake produces fine fat trout but they are smart and wary. When these smart fine fat wary fish are sipping insects from the surface all at once, it reminds me of another Milton who wrote that "their rising all at once was as the sound of thunder heard remote." (*Paradise Lost,* book II, l. 476)

Don't overlook the feeder creek (Milton Creek) and its wild trout to 10 inches but read (*big*) between (*browns*) the (*enter*) lines (*creek*). The lake has special regs, artificial flies and lures with barbless hooks.

Lake Nacimiento

- **Location:** North of Los Angeles, near San Luis Obispo
- **What You Fish For:** White bass (and to a lesser extent smallmouth and largemouth bass)
- **Highlights and Notables:** White bass fishing is outstanding.

When I was younger, I couldn't help it, I would begin laughing in church. Not every time—I was more respectful than that and besides, Mom and Dad put the fear of God into me. But every so often, if I happened to think of the last time I laughed in church, which I tried hard not to do, I would begin. Didn't take much to trigger this inappropriate behavior.

The laughter would start gutturally, inside and low. Then in bursts, Mother's stern look, then I would lean forward and try to catch Tammy's eye and she would laugh as little sisters should, and the more Mother shooshed me, the louder my hilarity became. The necessity of silence formed a tension for me, instinct fighting convention.

Once, at our church in Lake Jackson, the preacher stopped down Sunday sermon to scold me for my guffawing. The harder I tried to stop, the more bellylaugh I produced until eventually, it became a wheezy diaphragmatic surge. You can imagine how proud my mother was of me that day.

So what's so hilarious about Lake Nacimiento? It's kinda hard to explain so let me set all this up for you.

Lake Nacimiento is not your typical California lake. No world-record largemouth bass, only catchable size here. Not really all that good of a largemouth fishery anyhoo rather a nice winter option. The lake is a solid smallmouth fishery, a pretty lake that lies less than three hours' drive from San Francisco and San Jose. Five thousand-acre Nacimiento has more arms than a busload of Hecatoncheires, canyon walls steep and rocky, pine and oak lining the shore.

White bass. That's the sell for Lake Nacimiento. That's the laughing point. Let's keep going. The white bass are the healthiest population in the lake. Each is a 1- to 3-pound tenacious fighter.

The shad pop is good, too, and the white bass in the spring follow them around and herd them into shallows, into coves. Most of the time, anglers have to find the white bass hanging out in much deeper water than is fun for fishermen (the lake runs from twenty-five to seventy-five feet deep) but when the shad and bass are moving, Geez Louise is it fun.

Lake Nacimiento's holding features run from river pools, runs, flats, rocky points, extensive shoreline (steep and rocky in places, gentler in others), shallow runs clear like a river.

Fifteen casts in a row, I caught a white bass. Fly fishing. A four-weight. In water that ranged from two feet deep to a few inches deep. The water was as clear as a western river so we could see the shad as they frenetically swam for their collective lives, some of them leaping up through the thrashing water and landing on the bank. Insanity churning in a foot of water.

We kept catching white bass, cast after cast, like hitting softballs tossed by third-graders. We kept moving up into coves then back out and following the birds and the foamy maelstrom and we were catching so many, so often, I can't really explain it, but I started laughing. What was church for the white bass was becoming church for me.

I could hardly cast but when I did, lost sheep to the shepherd. What should have been a reverent experience for an angler, catching fifty, sixty, seventy fish in a few hours time, bass on top, became a goofy laughfest, a testament to the sometimes absurdity of fishing. Or maybe of catching.

CONTACTS

Nacimiento Ranger Station, 805-238-2376

Hole in the Wall Fly Shop, Arroyo Grande,
   805-481-0767

Central Coast Fly Fishing, Carmel,
   831-626-6586

Prime Time on the Fly Guide Service,
   Fresno, 408-778-0602

Lake Nacimiento Resort and Marina,
   www.nacimientoresort.com

Owens River

- **Location:** Eastern central California, near Nevada border
- **What You Fish For:** Rainbow and brown trout
- **Highlights and Notables:** Owens is one of the best trout streams, one of the finest spring creeks in the world, large trout and lots of them. Public access is limited.

Here we have one of the classic spring creeks in the world, one of the finest, one of the most beautiful, one whose electroshocking surveys shows that any square mile of the Owens River holds a mind-boggling 10,000 trout. Now for the bad news: not much of this fifty-mile-long blue ribbon fishery is open to the public. Wait, there's still good news: if you don't mind paying and getting reservations in advance, you can still get on the best parts of the Owens.

The Owens takes its sinuous path through this valley after being born in pure springs from way up high. Sounds heavenly. It is.

It's the fault of writers, and here I am guilty, for perpetuating the idea that a place is what it is and is only that thing that it is even if it is more than that. Make sense?

City Fishing

OAKLAND AND SAN FRANCISCO (BAY AREA)
Lake Chabot, San Francisco Bay, Putah Creek

San Francisco Bay is a real fishing destination that just happens to be part of (adjacent to?) one of the coolest, more romantic, scenic, culinary, cultured cities in the world. Nothing against Oakland which shares the Bay. Oakland is a very nice city.

The Bay is known for its world-class striper fishing but anglers can also concentrate on halibut and king salmon (even occasionally a shark). The striped bass are found all over the Bay from the middle of the Bay between the Bay Bridge and the Golden Gate Bridge, to the Berkeley Flats and Treasure Island, to the Oakland Airport to Alameda, the Pumphouse Flats, around islands, around wharf pilings and bridge abut-ments, around rocky points, just off the beaches, in flats and over hard shell mounds, East Bay, South Bay, you name it. The Bay stripers can be fished from the shore or off the piers in many places (ideal for the businessman or -woman who needs an afternoon in the outdoors) but the most efficient way to find the schools is out boating. San Pablo Bay can be good fun for schooling bass in the fall.

Halibut are caught in a lot of the same water as striper, from five or six feet to twenty-five feet deep. Both stripers and halibut follow schools of baitfish and if there are fleeing baitfish, there are diving hungry birds circling overhead.

Putah Creek is always under attack from city creep and other evil things. Flowing from Lake Berryessa to north and east of San Francisco near Davis, an hour or less drive away, Putah Creek is a small to middling tailwater trout stream, a wild brown and wild rainbow

trout stream with some hatchery 'bows stuck in for grins, ideal for nymphing and enjoying the beauty of mountainous northern California. You'll be really surprised with some of these trout when a 5-pounder breaks you off.

Putah fishes well in fall, winter, and spring but is available year-round. Summer sees low flows. The pools ought to be your target—long wide slow lovely pools. Or the long slow flat wide lovely flats that act like pools depending on flow (and that's a real concern on the Putah).

Drinking water reservoir Lake Chabot (300 acres) is an outdoorperson-slash-yuppie's dream with oodles of jogging, biking, and parkland trails in a lovely hilly park. No swimming, no gas-powered motorboats on Chabot. Trout fishing is popular especially in the cooler months. Hard to believe but this little lake has produced a 17-pound largemouth bass. Catfish, crappie, and bluegill round out your catch. Lake Ralphine in Howarth Park (a 152-acre community park located on Summerfield Road in eastern Santa Rosa) holds trout, bluegill, catfish, and

bass. Other area lakes include Lake Vasona, Lake Cunningham, Quarry Lakes, Lake Temescal, Lake Merrit (in downtown Oakland), Lafayette Reservoir, Del Valle Reservoir, Lake Merced, Foster City Lagoon, Lake Borundi, Stevens Creek Reservoir, Lexington Reservoir, Loch Lomond. You get the idea if an angler wants to play hooky one afternoon, it won't be for lack of nearby choices.

Nearby rivers (less than two hours of driving) from SF/OAK include the Russian River, Stanislaus River, Consumes and Mokolumne Rivers, Navarro River. Think steelhead and trout. Beautiful scenery, moderately tough angling because of the rocks and steep sides.

CONTACTS
Lake Chabot Fishing Outfitters, Castro Valley, 510-892-2177
Orvis San Francisco, 415-392-1600
Flyfisher Supply, 415-668-3597
A-1 Fish, 510-832-0731
Capt. Todd Magaline, Blue Runner Sportfishing, www.bluerunnercharters.com

Owens River is a spring creek but only a part of it acts like one, looks like all the pictures you see with the featureless spring creek surface, the wavy vegetation, the patient angler. But you've also got pools and pocket water in its highest reaches, gorges, tailraces below the spring creek part, and more.

We've got some public land in the upper Owens, which runs from its origins at Big Springs down to its entry into Lake Crowley. There is public land, some below Lake Crowley and then in the gorge and again below Pleasant Valley, but the showpiece is the spring creek meadow water of Arcularius Ranch and Alper's Owens River Ranch. The fish outnumber the anglers 10,000 to perhaps ten or twenty. You've got a fighting chance.

That said, let's focus on the water that best represents what this river has to offer: the spring creek water of the upper Owens. Try to remember what you think was the longest leader you've ever tied on. Now mentally add a few feet more because you will need all the fish fooling help you can get. These behemoths know more about fly fishing than you do.

These salmonids will know if you are trying to get by with a pupa pattern instead of a larva. They'll know if your Woolly Bugger is being stripped too fast or without conviction. They'll know if your silhouette seems out of place. Be David Copperfield. Disappear. Stay low and out of sight. Cast accurately and match the hatch and keep your drifts drag-free. Did I mention that the wind can be a real pest at times? Nothing to it. On the upper stretches, artificial flies and lures only, no barbs.

The water below Crowley ends up run-ning through a scenic gorge and access is limited, difficult and as such, not many anglers end up in the gorge. Although roads do parallel parts of the river, this is mostly park-and-walk water, slide-and-scramble water not for the faint of heart. In places, it reminds me of the hike into the Red River in New Mexico. This is for the adventurer, the angler who likes to fish where others fear to tread, cleat, or felt. You might consider putting on your hiking boots and sticking your waders and boots in a backpack with a couple of water bottles and a lunch. You have nineteen miles of solitude in the gorge. You'll find that the trout are still leader shy (but not as much as the upper section) and not quite as big (a whopper will surprise you every so often) but you can catch them on dry flies and these are spirited healthy wild trout.

The Pleasant Valley high-desert tailwater below the lake holds some big fish (known

Fishing private waters

for its large browns) and is a great option during the winter. The Lower Owens takes a tortuous route, curling this way and that, and in its deep bend pools lurk some of the largest fish in the Owens. Many think this is the best water on the entire river. Maybe so. It's all good to me.

CONTACTS

Alpers' Owens River Ranch, 760-648-7334

Trout Fly, 760-934-2517

Trout Fitter, 760-934-2517

Rick's Sports Center, 760-934-3416

Kittredge Sports, 760-934-7566

Wilderness Outfitters, 760-924-7335

Brock's Flyfishing Specialists and Tackle Experts, 760-872-3581

The Matlick House (fly fishing bed and breakfast close to the Owens), 800-898-3133

Sacramento River

- **Location:** Central California
- **What You Fish For:** Rainbow trout
- **Highlights and Notables:** One of the true big-trout rivers in the West A brawling river with large trout that go spastic when caught. An amazing bountiful trophy trout river.

You're bound to see the play on words if you've ever read about this river—THE SAC IS BACK, the headline will proclaim wittily. The Sacramento River is many things. The Sac is big and long and fertile and accessible. The Sac is two rivers, the upper and lower, each with its own set of assets and appeals.

You're bound to feel puppy love when you see the Upper Sac. You remember puppy love, right? Infatuation. You can think of nothing else, hormones raging, all about beauty and immediate gratification. Paroxysms of lust. That's the Upper Sac with its long runs, pocket water, riffles, and deep, glassy pools. Boulders litter the banks and riverbed and the tall forest is right upon you. Deep provocative canyon. Oh man, those big beautiful boulders. The upper Sac is puppy love with all that flashy scenery and heavenly trout lies and trout quick to respond to your gentle touches then all of a sudden, they're gone, burning your line.

The Lower Sac is love, mature. Bold. Big hips. The curvy trout are much more deceptive, cocksure, only willing to play this silly game if you do everything just right. The river is fuller, deeper. Bring candy, work hard, honesty is the best policy but there you are deceptive of course and in the end, perhaps you have seduced a big beautiful lower Sac trout and perhaps you are going home alone. You are willing to put in the time, the study, to wait. If you do hook up, these denizens run and jump and dive and pull and take you for a ride. Love, mature.

The upper Sacramento. Dry fly fishing is great, plain and simple. The trout rise to caddis, mayfly, and stonefly hatches throughout the season. Nymph fishing is productive when hatches are absent. The river's trout respond to man-made flies, flashy lures, and good old bait of any sort.

The Upper Sacramento suffered from a major chemical spill in the early 1990s that wiped out almost all aquatic life for thirty-five to fifty miles of the river. This fishery has returned to its former self.

Over forty miles of this trophy trout stream are easily accessible from I-5, which parallels the river for much of its course. Even with roadside (and railroad track walking) access—not many great rivers have this kind of access—the river rarely seems crowded. My favorite stretches are where the boulders sit in the middle of the river and you have to pick pockets and tightline small pools, work around the rocks.

Stay in Redding, the hub for the trout-spokes of California. Within an hour to two hour's drive, you can fish Pit, McCloud,

Hat, Fall, and upper Sac, to name but a few. The lower Sacramento runs through town. Redding is geared toward the serious angler. The Fly Shop is as good a shop as there is anywhere in the world. They know their own waters and most of the waters around the world. Ask any one of the guides and they'll tell you that the Sac ranks with any other trout river in the world.

The lower Sacramento rightfully gets most of the press. Long a bastion of fishing for everything except trout—such as shad, stripers, salmon, steelhead, sturgeon, you name it—but in the last twenty years, the trout fishery has become the draw, producing good numbers of surprisingly large, hard-fighting rainbows. The lower Sac is big water, the largest waterway in California, considered by many to be one of the

best trout fisheries, one of the top tailwaters in America. The lower Sac, from Sacramento to Red Bluff, has an underrated and underpublicized Chinook salmon run, with kings up to forty and fifty pounds. Sure, the locals know about it and the traffic is heavy at times but it's here in the lower forty-eight and cheap.

The river produces heavy-bodied, muscular rainbows from 14 to 18 inches long, trout that are strong and will, without fail, take your line in a blur and often get into your backing. The football-shaped 'bows as long as 24 to 27 inches are freaks of nature, similar to those caught in the Bow or the Taylor or the Frying Pan.

Riffles are everywhere in this strong river, and nymphing them with caddis larva and pupa is the most popular technique. The water is intimidating at first, so big and wide; some long wide stretches are flat and featureless. At first glance. Take another look. There are quicker currents against slower, a hump of a rock, the edge of a submerged ledge, a slight run over a deeper V, against the bank. Find the riffles, the rapids, it's not tough. And in the spring and summer, you should be in a boat anyway, so cover water, cast, cast, cast.

Too many anglers, most of average pedigree, have fifteen to thirty-five trout days on the lower Sac. The largest I've landed was about 18 inches but I watched jealously as others around me, locals who knew the tricks, caught several bigger than mine. They just lifted their bigger fish for a photo and smiled at me.

CONTACTS
The Fly Shop, Redding, www.theflyshop
.com
Clearwater Trout, Dunsmuir,
415-381-1173
Dunsmuir Fly Fishing Company,
Dunsmuir, 530-235-0705
Ted Fay Fly Shop, Dunsmuir,
530-235-2969

Middle Fork San Joaquin River

- **Location:** Eastern central California
- **What You Fish For:** Wild trout
- **Highlights and Notables:** Awesome scenery, great dayhiking or backpacking fishing trip

I am always on trails, so it seems, trails leading up a river, to the head of these rivers. I like it up there. I like where things begin. I like the hiking as much as I like the fishing. I like to look at the dirt trail as I hike, my combo wading boots-hiking boots damply treading, one foot after the other. I like blank spaces on the map.

It's not as quiet as you think up the river, in the wild. You hear the leaves talking, the birds chattering, the stream becoming a river, and as you sleep in your tent, you hear things that go bump in the night.

You can't be hostile up there. You can't be petty or jealous or nervous.

You are fishing pools, if you struggle through the bramble and over the rock, to

City Fishing

SAN DIEGO

One day in Amarillo this past spring, I noted just how perfect the weather was, 83 degrees and sunny, not too hot to sweat, hot enough to feel right to wear shorts. I thought how great it would be to package this day and repeat it everyday, 365 days a year. And then I remembered it's already been done and it's called San Diego.

San Diego has an unrivaled collection of small-lake, big-bass within an hour's drive. San Vincente, Hodges, Dixon, Miramar, and Barrett Lakes stand out as premier performers. Dixon and Barrett are both covered in this book and with good reason—in Dixon Lake was caught the new unofficial world-record largemouth bass. Other area lakes deserving your attention include El Capitan, Murray, Sutherland, Upper and Lower Otay, Henshaw, Wohlford, Marona, Guajome, Cuyamaca, Jennings, Loveland, Santee, Poway, and Ramona.

If freshwater doesn't float your boat, San Diego is the launching point for fishing expeditions to Baja Mexico for wahoo, dorado, yellowtail, yellowfin tuna, marlin, and other species of game fish. Anglers can also fish from piers and shore in the local harbors Mission Bay, Oceanside, and San Diego Bay. Popular local angling ideas include topwater fishing for barracuda and bonito, bumping for seabass and calico bass, trying to intercept migrating fish like Bluefin, albacore, yellowtail.

One of the more interesting targets is the mako shark, offshore, of course. Makos reach 1,000 pounds but the range of what you will catch runs from 15 to 130 pounds with makos weighing regularly 200 pounds (world fly record is 149 pounds so you might/could break it, right?). You can also fish for thresher and blue sharks in the blue waters off of San Diego.

Fly fishers have made this predatory

creature one of their new favorite quarries for the novelty of it, for the fact they jump and jump fifteen to twenty feet in the air, but more than that, the fact that mako sharks are among the hardest fighting fish you can hook into, some say, pound for pound, the fiercest, strongest. They might run 150 to 200 yards, they might roll, they might spin. They will be gnarly and mean and fearless. And Conway Bowman is the only man on the west coast who knows where they are and how to catch them. He's famous, you see, for this Dr. Doolittle-ness.

If you choose to make the mako take your fly, you'll need a 14-weight flyrod, big flies and big brass ones.

CONTACTS

Conway Bowman, Bowman Bluewater, 619-822-6256, www.bowmanbluewater.com/info.htm

Rich Oldham, Andy Montana's Fly Shop, www.andymontanas.com

trout that may not have been fished to all season.

I like the trails and the upstream, the urge to move upstream, and I like the trout because they are wild and they are often native and they play the game of dry fly and release, flick and flirt. I go there, up there, I don't mind hiking many miles in a day to get to fishing or as I fish, nor do any of my spawning-salmon fishing buddies, I go up there and I never really find anything but I keep going up there anyway.

What I found near the head of the San Joaquin was a golden trout that rivaled any trout I've ever caught. The golden trout was 9 inches tops, as pretty as the one Rio Grande cutthroat that McPhail caught on the Rio de los Pinos (way up the Rio de los Pinos). I think this trout was pure because I think I caught a golden-rainbow hybrid a couple of miles back downstream and this one upstream was cleaner, more copper-colored, more agitated, more brightly colored, the red side-streak redder. He jumped out of the plunge pool to take an Adams Wulff.

The San Joaquin River is prettier than 99 percent of the rest of all Western rivers. The fish aren't big (they're not small either). The Middle Fork is one of the finest midsized Western streams—the adventurous angler can catch wild trout: rainbow, brook, brown, golden, and golden-rainbow hybrid. The trout are neither wary nor leader shy. If you cast, they will come.

West of Mammoth, in the Sierras, the Middle Fork has some roadside access and plenty of trailside access. Cars coming in are restricted to entering the gate to the campgrounds near Devil's Postpile before 7:30AM and after 5:30PM to keep the pressure off of these wild trout. Still, roadside means more put-and-take than wild; roadside means too many anglers for my blood.

Walk. Walk upstream, in fact. You'll be reminded of Yosemite.

You can walk downstream, too, but that doesn't seem as metaphorically pleasing. Below Lower Rainbow Falls, the trail becomes bushwhacking and the fishing is terrific and the way I figure it, this stretch is upstream from the lower stretches, I'm just getting there in descent rather than ascent.

Whether it's the Middle Fork of the San Joaquin or another trout stream, another headwater. Maybe I'll find something up there one day.

Shasta Lake

- **Location:** Northern California
- **What You Fish For:** Trout, salmon, bass
- **Highlights and Notables:** Houseboat Capital of the West, one of the most scenic mountain lakes you'll ever visit

If you travel to Northern California with buddies or with the family, grab a pen, not a pencil, and write down two to three days on Shasta Lake. The beauty of this mountainous region is hard to beat and Shasta will provide you with that beauty plus some solid angling for trout, salmon, and spotted bass. The only way to enjoy the 30,000 surface acres of photogenic Shasta Lake is by houseboat—the lake is often called the "Houseboat Capital of the West."

Shasta Lake has 370 miles of tree-lined shoreline packed with green vegetation—like green felt put down around the lake, like Shrek building the perfect lake on his model railroad set. This year-round fishery has solid angling for rainbow trout (including Kamloops) and brown trout, the average trout going about 1 to 4 pounds. Spotted bass (8.6-pound lake record) are the predominant bass catch at Shasta although the lake also holds largemouth and smallmouth bass.

More than a dozen marinas and thirty or forty resorts ring the lake. Shasta receives lots of people, more houseboats than any Western lake but Powell or Mead perhaps, but the deep cold lake is big enough to get lost in its coves and rivers. Anglers can also catch landlocked king and silver salmon, catfish, sunfish, crappie, and sturgeon. The lake has excellent angling and scenery in its four major tributary arms, McCloud, Pit, Sacramento, and Squaw. Pick this lake if you want a family outing.

Trinity Lake

- **Location:** Northern California
- **What You Fish For:** Smallmouth bass
- **Highlights and Notables:** Alpine scenery and top-shelf smallmouth angling

Not that this is saying much but Trinity Lake is the best smallmouth lake in California. Nah, it's saying a lot because Trinity Lake combines excellent smallmouthing with a scenic alpine setting and lots of water to try.

Trinity Lake, located forty-five miles northwest of Redding, near more popular Shasta and Lewiston Lakes, at the southern tip of the Trinity Alps range, produced the state record for a smallmouth bass that checked in at 9 pounds 1 ounce. Smallmouth average 1 to 2 pounds with 4- to 5-pounders showing up from time to time.

Underrated is the trout fishery, loaded with warm-weather plantings of catchable size rainbows that average 9 to 14 inches. The browns are fewer but larger and it's not uncommon to catch a brownie 18 to 20 inches long. Trinity also has largemouth bass.

The lake is twenty-two miles long, so despite the fact that there are plenty of campsites and amenities, resorts, the cold lake has enough room for everybody. This is partly because the lake is long and narrow so you get spaced out (not that kind of spaced out), partly because the lake covers 17,000 surface acres and has 150 miles shoreline, and partly because you can get lost in the coves. Trinity Lake is a super home base to fish northern California or to take the family. I think it's a fine fishing-buddy lake, too. Work the rocks and the dam and up the arms for smallmouth action. Trinity River feeds the lake and it is a great river in its own right. Additionally, you can hike into the Trinity Alps Wilderness and fish any of fifty lakes in serene backcountry solitude, just you and the creatures of the forest. Did I mention this is Bigfoot Country?

Truckee River

- **Location:** Eastern California, western Nevada
- **What You Fish For:** Trout
- **Highlights and Notables:** Challenging western stream that flows through dramatic mountain scenery

Amy was winning. Not big like my mother does every single time but she was ahead, twenty or thirty bucks. I lost my fifty at the slots and it was time to fish. Amy accused me of willingly losing, giving up quickly so I could slide out of the casino and wade the Truckee. She was dead wrong. I really wanted to win. I chose slots because there was no strategy. The fishing and gambling gods would have to fight for my attention. The fishing gods won.

Flowing from Lake Tahoe is the Truckee River, which traverses through twenty miles of California forests before entering Nevada at Reno, then runs its course to Pyramid Lake. The Truckee River holds rainbows

and browns which on the average grow to 12 inches, but many reach 20 inches and several pounds.

The fishing gods were good to me.

I wanted easy fishing, as little thinking as possible, something rhythmic. So I fished with a black Woolly Bugger. I cast it around the big rocks and the pocket water and swung it into the dropping-off deeper water, where the pastel-blue water turned cobalt. I could see the trout move underwater and follow the streamer, then pounce on it. Between the heavy fish accustomed to the strong currents and the strong currents themselves, it was hell getting in each hefty trout.

I went back that night happy, content in the flashing memories of several fish so fat they seemed ready to split their skin. One rainbow was not even 20 inches but weighed more than any similar trout I had ever caught.

The fishing gods bid me not to gamble that next morning but instead, to fish. So I did. I caught two fish all day. Both 12-inch rainbows. I saw lots of other trout,

lots of big trout. They rose all around me. They rose to my dry flies. They nosed at my nymphs. They swiped at my streamers.

But they ignored my pleas.

And so did the gambling gods. I lost another fifty that night.

I had not been on top of my game and I knew it. Fishing, that is. So I did a better job at matching the hatch. I was more careful on my presentations. I looked for oxygenated bouncy water the trout would retreat to in the midday summer heat. That day was a two-phase day. Yellow sallies and tan caddis. I played the stage game of the two insects and I had a field day. The largest trout I caught was in the neighborhood of 17 to 18 inches and I caught him on sight, swinging a muddler minnow right in front of his nose.

I was on my game, the fishing gods were smiling.

The Truckee is a river with a mission, a river of intentions. It begins high in the mountains and begins its rush to leave California, coursing, flowing until it empties into Pyramid Lake in Nevada. It's a simple river. The Truckee holds an amazing amount of fish, heavy mass. These fish are not easy to catch. Simple.

Downtown Reno has good fishing. Really. Amy caught a 15-inch rainbow not far from the pretty college campus. Electroshock surveys show the river supports over 2,000 fish per acre in town. I read somewhere that the river in other sections holds three to four thousand trout per mile. The better waters of the Truckee are those below the town of Truckee, and they are harder to get to, requiring some walking into the canyon. The results can be rewarding. If you want results on the Truckee, you ought to hire a guide for a couple of days to decipher this gem. Big trout, rainbows and browns, are what draws the adventurous angler to this wild trout water. Many of the trout are in the 2- to 3-pound range, but some 10- to 15-pounders have been caught.

CONTACTS

Mountain Hardware & Sports, Truckee, 530-587-4844

Randy Johnson's Johnson's Tackle and Guide Service, 530-525-6575

Rob Anderson, Reno Fly Shop & Truckee River Outfitters, www.renoflyshop.com

Ralph & Lisa Cutter's California School of Flyfishing, 530-587-7005, www.flyline .com

Frank Pisciotta's Thy Rod & Staff Guide Service, 530-587-7333

Reno Fly Shop, Reno, NV, 702-825-FISH

Truckee River Outfitters, 530-582-0090

Outdoor & Fly Fishing Store, 530-541-8208

Swigard's Hardware, Tahoe City, 530-583-3738

Whiskeytown Reservoir

- **Location:** Northern California
- **What You Fish For:** Kokanee salmon, brook trout
- **Highlights and Notables:** Mecca for kokanee salmon anglers

If you are a sucker for Kokanee, and I don't know why anyone would be, this might be your spot. Kokanee silvers come off each June through September and make all you guys happy. Whiskeytown has some very nice-sized brook trout (stocked) as well as Chinook salmon, crappie, bass (spotted, large, and small), and catfish. Not far from Redding, chunked with underwater islands, prone to windiness.

Happy snagging.

Yosemite National Park

- **Location:** Eastern central California
- **What You Fish For:** Trout
- **Highlights and Notables:** Scintillating scenery, myriad lakes and rivers to fish

I really tire of hearing or reading about how the fishing isn't all that great in Yosemite National Park. You know, it's not anywhere near the level of Yellowstone National Park and it might not be on par even with Smoky or Shenandoah National Parks but Yosemite is as good as or better than Rocky Mountain or Glacier National Parks and has a lot better fishing than what you hear or read. Read this.

Are you telling me that if I gave you fifty-eight fishable streams and 100 fishable lakes and I set these trout fisheries in the most dramatic scenery on earth, that you wouldn't at least take one trip to this place?

I'll include mild weather, 1,000 miles of trails, few other anglers, and wild trout only, trout that will pound dry flies. I am making this fantasy FishWorld a joy to fly fish complete with rough and tumble, cold, clear streams.

Now, there aren't any lunkers and there are very few fish you'd call big. Some lakes have some nice-sized trout (2 to 4 pounds) but for the most part, fish in the park are going to run about 8 to 12 inches. Rainbow, brown, and brook—wild trout only, like I say. Some of the brook trout are pretty nice-sized for these size waters.

Yosemite National Park. Legendary for all its outdoor landmarks—Half Dome, El Capitan, Mirror Lake, Yosemite Falls, Glacier Point, Vernal Falls, Bridalveil Fall, Yosemite Valley. You get waterfalls and giant sequoias and mountains that rise jaggedly to 13,000 feet, verdant meadows everywhere you look.

Most streams are more creek than river, freestone, clear, cold rushing over big

lumpy shelves of gray-black-white granite. You have pools and riffles. You have pocket water around the big rocks and in the canyon sections. You have hiding fish near granite boulders and fallen trees. In the meadows, the streams have traditional lies like undercut banks and long glides and the occasional bend pool.

My favorite is probably Bridalveil Creek. You might know it from the photographs where it falls over Bridalveil Fall into Yosemite Valley and hooks up with the Merced River. I know it from its frothy plunging water that drops over granite into foamy pools, then forms bubbly edges, then moves into kind of a run-pool-thing, then tails out and plunges again and again and again.

The highlight of your Yosemite experience should be fishing Tuolumne Meadows. The grasses are so tall, you can't see the river until you're upon it. This is high country, 8,600 feet elevation.

The Lyell Fork rises near Mt. Lyell, and flows downstream through Lyell Canyon and meets the Dana Fork where their union forms the Tuolumne River. These two forks of the Tuolumne are perhaps the best two streams in the park (although Bridalveil is still my fave). Dana Fork of the Tuolumne River is a joy, eight to fifteen feet wide, shallow, clear, bouncy. Lyell Fork, a feeder to the Tuolumne, is a fun place to spend the day, some nice browns and rainbows. Both rivers have excellent access and aren't heavily fished.

Rainbow trout are native to the park but golden have been previously stocked. There is now no stocking at all in YNP. In Yosemite Creek, you may still be able to catch some trout with golden trout in their heritage although they'll be rainbow-golden mixes. Merced River is the best known river of Yosemite and fishes well in the park. The Merced gets very good outside the park, too. Some other creeks you might ought to take a look at: Fletcher, Eleanor, Rancheria, Ryell, Rafferty, and Ireland Creeks.

The lower the elevation, the better the fishing is a rule of thumb you'll hear, but I've broken that rule several times. That old saw is more correct than not but it shouldn't keep you from exploring the high country. Cathedral Lake is good for small brookies and you have over 100 fishable lakes to choose from, but don't just hike to any ol' lake without first checking to see if it's barren or not. Over half of the park's 268 lakes are barren.

Mountain lions have gotten worse over the years so keep your eyes and ears open. I recommend fishing with a buddy. And in Yosemite National Park, visitors must

always keep an eye out for black bear. They're smart and resourceful and persistent. Make sure to check park fishing regulations.

CONTACTS

Sierra Fly Fisher Tours, Bass Lake,
    559-683-7664
Graham Hubner, Southern Yosemite
    Mountain Guides, 800-231-4575, www
    .symg.com/featured_guides.htm

NEVADA

Papaw and Mr. Cooksey and I had been fishing right off the bridge all night long. I had fallen asleep some time during the middle of dark even though I had promised Papaw back at the house that I was big enough at twelve years old to go out with the big boys and stay up.

Papaw had places on a lake since before I could remember, one a stilt house a half-mile from the water, the other a waterfront custom-built job that came with age and money. When I was twelve, we were in the stilt house with its used furniture and spider webs and Formica kitchen table.

Cookie Cooksey was one of Papaw's best friends and he and Louise were at the stilt house so much when we were there I kinda thought they might be related to me.

Papaw and Cookie had caught a ton of fish all night long. When I had fallen asleep, I hadn't caught a thing. I woke up when Papaw said in his low drawl, "You gittin' up or what?" I popped up embarrassed that he caught me sleeping and that it was dawn. I should have seen it coming but I didn't then. Papaw offered me a Coke and while I was slugging it down, Cookie got excited.

"Hey, Mark, I think you got one."

I reeled in and holy early morning fog, I had a nice fat white bass hooked cleanly in the mouth at the end of my line. Before I could even take it off the hook and put it in the live well, Papaw had the engine started and we were headed back home. At least I caught one. I found out from Papaw years later, when I was in my 30s, that before they woke me, Cookie and he conspired to take a fish they'd already caught, hook it, and give me the satisfaction they knew that little competitive boy needed. I sure miss Papaw.

I saw this played out at Lake Mohave one summer. It didn't work out because the kid was smarter than me. Dad distracted the kid, put the fish on when the kid wasn't looking, had him get excited and reel it in and the kid fizzled the generous gesture by saying loudly, "Dad, this fish is dead. You must've put him on. That sucks." This X-Box generation is way too cynical, don't you think? Had I caught Cookie and Papaw in their trick, I'd have said nothing and been tickled pink they thought enough of me to lie to me to make me feel good.

Crittenden Reservoir

- **Location:** Northern Nevada
- **What You Fish For:** Rainbow trout
- **Highlights and Notables:** Remote high-desert lake, a secret gem full of large trout

If you are a high desert lake nut, then you need to stick this one on the list you keep on the fridge with that chipped Beefeater magnet. Crittenden Reservoir is private and is not very well known but in certain circles and in Nevada. This shallow clear lake is known for trophy rainbow trout, those football-shaped kind you hear about but the kind you never catch yourself.

The lake is an irrigation lake so between heat evaporation and drawdown, the water levels fluctuate; the lake when full is about 250 surface acres. Crittenden grows big trout because of super insect hatches and other fishy foods (caddis, mayflies, midges, dragonflies, damselflies) and because it's not all that deep so sunlight keeps the plants going which keep the insects going which keep the fish fat.

Located near nothing in northern Nevada, bring your belly boat, personal watercraft, or small boat but don't bring any bait. Crittenden restricts anglers to artificial lures and flies only. The lake also holds largemouth bass (a 5-pounder was caught before but most are not impressively sized) and cutthroat (which means you have the inevitable cuttbow hybrids). Focus on the heavy rainbows that go from 12 inches up to mid-20s with some whoppers getting up to 10 pounds large.

For information about regulations and other information, check out www.ndow .org. Remote, there are no towns close, no shops close, and the two best home bases are in Wells or Wendover (I'd take Wendover in a heartbeat). Crittenden Reservoir is located seventeen miles north of Montello off State Highway 233.

East Walker River

- **Location:** Western Nevada and eastern central California
- **What You Fish For:** Brown and rainbow trout
- **Highlights and Notables:** This fertile trout stream runs through high-desert mountains and provides mile after mile of freestone fun fishing.

While essentially a tailwater, the East Walker River doesn't act like one or look like one. Sure, you can use tailwater flies to imitate tailwater insects like midges and scuds, but you can always be successful swinging huge streamers through the undercut banks.

The East Walker comes into Nevada from California, from Bridgeport Reservoir, itself a notable trout fishery. Think hills and sagebrush. Grasses and scrubs cover this rolling basin—brown in fall and winter, green at river's edge in warmer months. The banks are overgrown and wild and the heavy riparian habitat snags flies and gets in your way and forces you into the river. Challenging and fun.

Not many lunkers live in these waters like the old days but you can catch solid 10- to 14-inch trout with a good chance at a heavier, longer trout (4 to 7 pounds). That's really the draw here—catching 15- to 20-inch heavy-bodied browns that live in hard-to-reach quarters in this tight river. That and the fact that it also fishes well in the off-season.

Not a big river, more stream, the Walker runs about twenty-five to forty feet wide. The canyon sections do have some big deep pools but on the whole, the Walker is not all that deep. The tailwater does have plenty of hiding places in both its canyon and meadow stretches. Cutbanks, riffles, runs, flats, and pools. Rocky banks and cluttered tall clumpy streamside brush make it seem isolated and provide solitude despite the fact that highways and roads follow the better portion of the Walker. The river is blessed with a fantastic amount of public access, much of it made so in the last decade.

Rainbows and browns both naturally reproduce here but the river is still supplemented by plantings. The Walker holds twice as many browns as rainbows and the river is known for these chunky browns but don't shortchange the 'bows. They love the riffles and provide super action.

The East Walker has gone through some tough times the last decade, dealing with silt, low snowpack years, lower flows, disruption of forage and spawn, but it's back and it's healthy. The stream sees a lot of anglers in the summer so think about that off-season I mentioned. You'll need a full fly box loaded with everything from size 22 midges to various mayfly, stonefly, and caddis patterns. Gardnerville, Truckeeville, Reno, Tahoe, Bridgeport, and Hawthorne are all good home bases.

CONTACTS

Truckee River Outfitters, 530-582-0900

Angler's Edge, 775-782-4734

East Side Guide Service, 760-924-8177

Reno Fly Shop, 775-825-3474

Tahoe Fly Fishing Outfitters, 530-541-8208

Lake Mead

- **Location:** Southern Nevada
- **What You Fish For:** Striped bass
- **Highlights and Notables:** Exotic, strange, and mysterious striper fishery with more water than you can fish in a lifetime

Let's get a few things out of the way up front. Lake Mead is big (try 150,000 surface acres and 110 miles long) and deep (how does 465 feet deep strike you?) and elaborate (I think several hundred miles of shoreline qualifies). We have here the largest man-made reservoir in the U S of A. Lake Mead lies in two states, Nevada and Arizona and has some electric fishing

for several species. The lake is a short drive from Las Vegas; the lake and the national park it's in see millions of visitors annually. And stripers are the fish target of choice.

Lake Mead is beautiful in that extreme-contrasting-colors-way that high-desert reservoirs are beautiful. Lake Mead has the usual dazzling display of reds, ochres, ambers, grays that stand out against the deep blue water, but the best color is at sunset when everything gets a gauzy pink (the same fuzzy burnt sienna lighting you might expect when the sun goes down on the planet Mars).

With so much water in front of you, around every cove, at the base of every sheer cliff, it's hard to remember, easy to forget that this is desert and that water is so valuable. This huge impoundment is located on the Colorado River roughly thirty miles southeast of Las Vegas, Nevada, in the Lake Mead National Recreation Area. This 1.5 million-acre park is the fifth most visited national park in the country (oh how they love to tout that this park is bigger than Rhode Island; heck, my backyard isn't far off that claim) and you won't be surprised when you see just how many people are on the water, on the beaches, at the marinas, restaurants. You'll see them on sailboats and houseboats and yachts and swimming and waterskiing and picnicking.

Lake Mead is so big you can get away and find your own little parcel of water (is there such a thing as a parcel of water?), so big you can get away and wonder where all the people disappeared to.

Stripers. Not that many big stripers but just a heckuva lot of stripers. Most of the stripers flop around in your boat weighing about 2 to 5 pounds. Fishermen have taken 40-pounders on Lake Mead but I don't want to mislead you—it's doubtful you will. Anglers catch stripers that weigh 10 pounds to make them keep fishing for the 2-pounders. Quantity over quality on Lake Mead but the stunning scenery makes up for it. And you will catch a lot of striped bass and that's a good thing. Other species include largemouth bass, smallmouth bass, rainbow trout, channel catfish, carp, crappie, and bluegill. In the tailrace below the dam live some pretty good-sized rainbow trout.

Anglers follow the striper boils so topwater fishing is very good on Lake Mead. If they're not making the water choppy, you have to go deep to get them.

The carp are big and a nuisance. The tilapia tastes really good on the grill. It's hot hot hot in the summer. The lake has great shoreline access and easy boat access. Marinas are everywhere. Fun everywhere. Lake Mead is a must-do.

CONTACTS
Lake Mead National Recreation Area,
    Boulder City, 702-293-8907

Lake Mohave

- **Location:** Southern Nevada
- **What You Fish For:** Striper and a laundry list of other game fish
- **Highlights and Notables:** Big lake that holds all kinds of fish to drop hooks for

Lake Mohave is probably better in most respects than its bigger more famous sister Lake Mead but somehow it flies under the radar. And you may see this lake spelled Mojave as well. No biggie. Mohave is a largemouth haven (or is it heaven?). You might have heard that Mohave's striped bass fishery is one of the tops in the West and it is but I think its largemouth bass fishery is one of the underrated in the West. Four- to 8-pound largemouth are not uncommon. And if that's not enough, you could go to Lake Mohave and only fish for smallmouth bass and come away whistling Dixie.

Lake Mohave has the typical unique flooded high-desert reservoir terrain loaded with postcard-ready vistas, lonely coves, tan-sand beaches, bulky bluffs, strange rocks of all colors, and that aquamarine water. This narrow-bodied impoundment of the Colorado River covers 181,000 acres and has over 200 miles of shoreline so it's huge. Located in high desert on the border with Nevada and Arizona, Lake Mohave, along with Lake Mead, is part of the Lake Mead National Recreation Area. Like Lake Mead, Mohave is a houseboat lake.

A 63-pound striper, the state record, was caught only a few years ago. That could have been you. If you go and go hard at it, you should catch a few in the 10- to 25-pound range. Forty-pounders are taken several times each year. Could be you.

If it were you and you didn't want to fish for the large plentiful stripers or the large largemouth or the large smallmouth, you could also try your hook at stocked rainbow trout, catfish, tilapia, crappie, bluegill, and red ear sunfish. You could even fish in the tailrace below the dam for big rainbows.

Lake Mohave is an easy drive from Las Vegas, and not far from the south end of the lake is the gaming town in the middle of nowhere, Laughlin. Laughlin is so hot in the summer when the wind blows it's like a convection oven. So get inside quickly to the A/C and cold beverages and let the only thing that's hot be your hand. Three marinas service Lake Mohave: Willow Beach for the north, Cottonwood Cove sorta in the middle, and Katherine Landing in the south part of the lake just above Davis Dam.

CONTACTS
Lake Mohave Resort, 520-754-3245

Lake Havasu
If not for Mead and Mohave, Havasu in both Arizona and California might rank higher for its productive striper fishery.

Pyramid Lake

- **Location:** Western Nevada
- **What You Fish For:** Lahontan cutthroat trout
- **Highlights and Notables:** Remote high-desert lake, one of the last places you can catch the rare, primitive Lahontan cutthroat trout

There is something haunting and lonely about fishing here. Perhaps it's the high-desert setting, treeless, remote and brown. Perhaps it's the ghostly wind that howls across the blue lake so frequently. Maybe it's the dark depths that hold secrets nearly four hundred feet deep. More than likely it's the prehistoric memories that float up from this ancient lake, an Ice Age lake, and the only living remnant is the Lahontan cutthroat trout. Whatever it is, this is a spooky place.

Pyramid Lake is one of two leftover lakes of the once great lake, Lahontan Lake. The cutthroats of the present-day Pyramid are Lahontan but they are only cousins of the giants that used to swim in these waters, a lesser strain of fish. The original race of Lahontan became extinct by World War II. A decade ago, a Lahontan was caught that weighed over 21 pounds. Five pounds is a common cutt now, just off the average (2 to 4 pounds). Great fishing.

Easily, Pyramid Lake is one of the West's best trout fisheries. The combination of history and angling quality make it so. You're going to like how in the cooler months, the Lahontans feed right there in front of you and aren't always hard to catch. That changes in summer when they move around more, move away from you and your casts. But if you persist, you will catch a few and you might catch a big solid colorful trout so you can say you did, you caught one of the rarest trout on earth.

Pyramid Lake is a big lake. The blue-green alkaline lake is twenty-five miles

City Fishing

LAS VEGAS
Colorado River, Lake Mead,
Lake Mohave

Here is where the power comes from. The Colorado River, the seventh longest river in America. Majestic 726-foot high Hoover Dam. This is cactus country, bare and desolate. Lake Mead is 110 miles long with 822 miles of shoreline blessed with red cliff canyons and hide-away basins and coves where striped bass are the main fish to catch, but also crappie, largemouth bass, catfish, bluegills, and carp. Lake Mohave's profile reads about the same. Both these massive impoundments lie a short drive from Las Vegas and if you've lost your shirt and still have some money left to buy a fishing license, there are few better fishing locations. See the full entries for more details.

long, eleven miles wide with over seventy miles of shoreline. Tumbleweeds and sage dot the hillsides. A paved highway runs along its western shore and improved dirt roads run around most of the rest of it. The western shore is busier because it's easier to access. And it's kind of weird the first time you see it. Stepladders.

Yes, stepladders. They are common place. Anglers use stepladders to get more height, to get longer casts. It's de rigueur. You might see twenty stepladders bunched all together, anglers on top of the water like a miracle. I watched this one energetic caster, early 20s, really getting after it one windy day and he got to rocking trying to cast back to the dropoff off the shore, rocking so much that he went over headfirst, into the cold mysterious waters of Pyramid Lake. I was silently laughing. Coulda been me twenty years younger.

The eastern side is more difficult to reach and where you need to be.

The wind. You have to deal with it. A little choppy surface is good, the fish still feed and they can't see you. But at times, the wind is ferocious. Heavy fly rod outfits, 9-foot, 7- or 8-weight rods are necessary. A lot of longrodders make long casts, double haul, muscling sinking lines or shooting heads through the wind.

Anglers will need to purchase an Indian fishing permit. You can find some lodging at the lake as well as camping sites. Pyramid Lake is just a little over thirty miles north of Reno. Sometimes wind kicks up so much you better go back and gamble.

You can look around Pyramid Lake and tell you're out of time, out of place. You can feel the tension between eras. There's a sadness here about what once was, what

will never be again, of time, epoch time, passing and the red watery fish are counterfeit reminders. Take I-80 in Reno/Sparks by way of Route 445. The lake is about forty miles from Reno on Route 445.

CONTACTS
Reno Fly Shop, 775-825-3474
The Gilly Fishing Store, 775-358-6113
Mark, Fore & Strike Sporting Goods,
    775-322-9559

Ruby Lake

- **Location:** Northeastern Nevada
- **What You Fish For:** Bass and trout
- **Highlights and Notables:** One of the best combo (trout/bass) lakes—the West

Strange. Odd. Weird and wonderful.

More marsh than lake, Ruby Lake sits in the Ruby Valley which is less valley and more the basin of a former ancient lake, Franklin Lake, which was a monstrous 300,000 acres and 200 feet deep. Ruby Lake lies on the east side of the rugged Ruby Mountains in the northeastern part of Nevada, fed by 150 springs.

Ruby Lake National Wildlife Refuge. That's where Ruby Marsh sits, twelve feet deep on average. The sagebrush uplands and lush wetlands surrounding the picturesque lake belie the productivity of this stillwater trout fishery. Water is managed to provide the premium nesting and feeding habitat for the migratory waterfowl and water-dependent birds. The great diversity and numbers of birds is fascinating, as anglers can watch many species such as ducks, geese, coots, bald eagles, trumpeter swans, sandhill cranes, and many other birds.

Another weird part. You fish in collection ditches that collect a network of springs. A series of dikes and a collection ditch run along the western side of the lake to help collect the waters. This filtration makes the water in Ruby Lake (and nearby sister Franklin Lake) gin-clear. This collection ditch acts and fishes like a spring creek.

Ruby has brook trout of size and a 12-inch squaretail is fairly common. The lake is known for its tiger trout, a cross between brown trout and brook trout but these are no longer stocked. You'll read that the state record for tiger trout weighed in at 13 pounds 13 ounces and came out of Ruby in 1998 but I hear a 20-pounder was caught a few years before.

Browns and rainbows in the lake grow

big, too, many exceeding 5 pounds. Ruby Lake has also produced a 4-pound brook, a 10-pound rainbow, and a 25-pound brown trout. The trout are stocked so it's the hold-overs that become the lunkers. Largemouth bass also inhabit the lake and they reproduce naturally in the lake but the bass fishery has been in decline for years and management keeps tinkering with it to bring it back to snuff. The biggest reported bass caught weighed in at a hefty 9 pounds.

About half of the lake is limited to dike fishing only. You'll have to keep a low profile and make accurate casts. You'll also be slushing through bullrushes and cattails and muddy bottoms. But fishing the edges of this beautiful lake is the best way to catch trout. Angling pressure is typically light. To be fair, weekends can be somewhat testing, but midweek fishing usually means solitude. Ruby is remote and recent changes have made it less a recreational-boating lake than years before.

The nutrient-laden lake is a rich soup of aquatic foods, giving the trout population plenty to eat. It's hard to go fishless at Ruby Lake. Hatches are sparse so worry about presentation of lures and flies rather than matching the hatch. Ruby Lake can be waded, worked with a float tube, or fished from a small boat.

Fishermen can reach the lake from Elko (65 miles) on 228 to Jiggs, stay south on the gravel road for three miles then take a left over Harrison Pass to Ruby Valley. From there, turn right and a five-mile drive will put you at Ruby Lake. The roads are rough enough as it is, but they get muddy when it rains.

CONTACTS

Clearwater Flyfishing, Inc., Las Vegas
  702-388-1022
Reno Fly Shop, 294 E. Moana #23, Reno,
  NV 89502, 702-827-0600
Nevada Commission of Tourism, Carson
  City, 702-687-4322
Nevada Department of Wildlife, Reno,
  702-688-1500
Humboldt National Forest, 976 Mountain
  City Highway, Elko, 702-738-5171
Ruby Lake National Wildlife Refuge,
  P.O. Box 60-860, Ruby Valley, NV,
  89833, 702-779-2237

Wild Horse Reservoir

- **Location:** North central Nevada, north of Elko
- **What You Fish For:** Brown, cutthroat, rainbow trout, largemouth and smallmouth bass, yellow perch
- **Highlights and Notables:** Remote, high-desert lake full of fat, hard-hitting trout

You ever not wanted to fish? You just had enough of fishing or getting away or escapism or recreation?

Me neither.

I was excited to fish Wild Horse. I hadn't read much about it. It was a gearhead lake, not a fly fishing lake, I was told.

We'd been fishing for over a week, nice long summer trip, a Nevada round-up of sorts and Amy and I had caught a lot of trout. North Fork Humboldt. East Fork

Jarbridge. East Walker. Truckee. Carson. Great time so far. Some of the time, we'd camped. Some of it, as is her deal to go on these fishing trips, we stayed in bed and breakfasts or nicer hotels and did the shopping or touristy thing. We'd enjoyed Elko and its cowboy-*cum*-gambling ambience. And here, in north central Nevada, sixty-some odd miles north of Elko, we are out in the middle of nowhere, out in the middle of the high desert. Rolling brown mountains. Sagebrush. Big blue sky and mountain ranges that cover you like a sheet.

We are struck by how big this lake is. A couple of boats trolling. Might be more in the distance. The west side looks shallower, weedier, fly fishy-er. This is a big lake. Looks bigger than the 2,800 acres the literature says. Bluish-green. Fertile looking. Pastel-green colored hip-high vegetation comes right up to the shore.

I got the feeling and I was right that I was fishing by myself today. I am fishing by myself, kicking my way around in my float tube. It's windy so I'm kind of treading water. Amy is taking pictures, piddling around. I am trolling with a black Woolly Bugger, sinktip. I'm kicking for no more than ten minutes and I catch and land two trout, a cuttbow and a brown. Hard-hitting. Thirteen inches or so each. Girthy.

I'd read that the rainbows could get big in this high-desert irrigation reservoir, feeding on the typical high-desert lake

Nevada Fish Records

Fish	Angler	Weight	Length (inches)	Date	Location
Arctic Grayling	George Delich	15 ozs.	13.75	1978	Desert Creek
Largemouth Bass	Michael R. Geary	12 lbs. 0 ozs.	26	3/8/99	Lake Mead
Smallmouth Bass	Steven Loveridge	6 lbs. 4 ozs.	20.25	5/17/02	South Fork Reservoir
Spotted Bass	Dustin Osborn	4 lbs. 2 ozs.	19.25	8/13/00	Rye Patch Reservoir
Striped Bass	Allan S. Cole	63 lbs. 0 oz.	49	3/15/01	Lake Mohave
White Bass	Greg Ackerman	4 lbs. 0 oz.	19	5/13/84	Lahontan Reservoir
Wiper (Whiterock) Bass	Larry L. Allen	13 lbs. 10 ozs.	28.25	2000	Lahontan Reservoir
Bullhead	Steven K. Bowman	3 lbs. 5 ozs.	16.25	1990	Clover Creek
Carp	Larry L. Frazier	30 lbs. 8 ozs.	36	1976	Lake Mohave
Channel Catfish	Harry Stephens	31 lbs. 1 oz.	40.5	1980	Lahontan Reservoir
White Catfish	Jean Bianchi	16 lbs. 15 ozs.	31.5	1981	Humboldt River
Black Crappie	Henry Herman	3 lbs. 2 ozs.	16.1	1976	Lake Mead
White Crappie	Paul C. Grant	2 lbs. 13 ozs.	16	2000	Weber Reservoir
Sacramento Perch	John Battcher	4 lbs. 9 ozs.	17	1971	Pyramid Lake
Yellow Perch	Warren T. Goodale	1 lb. 8 ozs.	13.3	1987	Dufurrena Ponds
Northern Pike	Kelly H. Malaperdas	27 lbs. 0 oz.	44	1978	Comins Lake
Coho Salmon	Charles W. Caskey	8 lbs. 12 ozs.	30.3	1974	Lake Mead
Coho Salmon	William Musso	8 lbs. 12 ozs.		1974	Lake Mead
Kokanee Salmon	Dick Bournique	4 lbs. 13 ozs.	25.7	1973	Lake Tahoe

Nevada Fish Records (Cont.)

Fish	Angler	Weight	Length (inches)	Date	Location
Bluegill Sunfish	Shane Goodale	2 lbs. 1 oz.	12	1998	Dufurrena Ponds
Green Sunfish	Joe Burgess	1 lb. 6 ozs.	12.5	1992	Tule Springs Lake
Redear Sunfish	Larry Cross	1 lb. 8 ozs.	13	1999	Colorado River
Brook Trout	Richard Baker	5 lbs. 10 ozs.	22.8	1980	Bull Run
Brown Trout	Dennis Mangum	27 lbs. 5 ozs.	33	1984	Cave Lake
Bull Trout	Rex Schelburne	4 lbs. 6 ozs.	22	1985	Jarbridge River
Cutthroat Trout	Ben Barlow	23 lbs. 8 ozs.	38	1977	Pyramid Lake
Golden Trout	Don Capps	15 ozs.	14.5	1969	Hidden Lakes
Hybrid Trout	Lloyd Lowery	24 lbs. 10 ozs.	36	1976	Pyramid Lake
Mackinaw Trout	Robert Aronsen	37 lbs. 6 ozs.	44	1974	Lake Tahoe
Rainbow Trout	Mike Soskin	16 lbs. 4 ozs.	31.5	1971	Lake Mohave
Tiger Trout	Brian Howard	13 lbs. 13 ozs.	28.75	1998	Ruby Lake
Walleye	Billy Foster	15 lbs. 4 ozs.	33	1998	Lahontan Reservoir
Mountain Whitefish	Maurice L. Kiplan	2 lbs. 14 ozs.	16.25	1999	Walker River

These state fish records for Nevada come from the official state agency responsible for tracking records. If you have heard of a new record, please let us know at warden@hotspotsporting.com. If you would like to include Record Fish, Fishing Reports or other content on your Web site, please see Hot Spot WebData.

repertoire. Five to 10 pounds. The big one that hit my Woolly Bugger hit more like a bass than a trout and he bulled down like a hybrid striper. Strong. I read that Wild Horse held largemouth and smallmouth bass along with illegally introduced yellow perch.

It was weird as I floated, this large trout redfishing on me, the waves rolling into me and getting me wet, Amy on the shore taking close-up pictures of something on a bush, boats puttering in the distance, and these brown mountains contrasting with the blue sky, like a preppie boy's oxford shirt against his khakis.

I don't think I have caught a heavier 5-pound rainbow. Amy never heard me hollering at her to take a pic, too windy, too noisy, too distracted. So I cradled the trout in the cold water and watched it swim away.

The next day, Amy said she wanted to fish again, a small river if I could find one. Kingston Creek, here we come.

Wild Horse trout average about 13 to 15 inches and they're round and thick; 20-inch trout, especially rainbows, are not uncommon. Wild Horse is the source of the East Fork of the Owyhee River, which is a spunky brushy stream right below the lake. You can find boat ramps, campgrounds, motel, a lodge on the lake. Some areas of access to the lake run through tribal lands and require a day fee.

CONTACTS
Tanya Wells and Chris Drake, Nevada
  Department of Wildlife, www.ndow.org
Denio Junction, Denio, 775-941-0371
Idaho Angler, Boise, ID, 208-389-9957
Reno Fly Shop, Reno, 775-827-0600
Nevada Division of Wildlife, Elko,
  775-738-5332

UTAH

The Grand Canyon is big and deep and colorful but it's a lot like seeing bison at Yellowstone. The first day there's a lot of "Cool," and "Look at all those buffalo" but by the third day you just want the big cowlike animals to get the heck off the road. Ditto with the hoodoos and multihued rocks of the park. We were on a fishing trip and we hadn't caught nearly as many as we'd have liked.

A coyote walked up to us as we took pictures of the South Rim. He didn't scare us but glanced at us for a photo op then sauntered on into the dense woods. The drive from the park into southern Utah is through one of those dry American deserts you see complete with gila monsters, sidewinders, and two dead gringos without enough sense to cross it. One of the spookiest, loneliest three-hour stretches in the United States especially when foolishly done from midnight to three in the a.m. I never said we were rocket scientists.

Sometimes, when you plan a trip, sitting down with the maps and guidebooks, the excursion takes a life of its own, becomes entirely too unwieldy until you resume control and pare it down to more reasonable expectations. When Chad McPhail and I planned this fishing trip to Arizona, Utah, and Colorado back in the spring, it turned into a monster and we never regained control.

We lost one of the three tubs strapped to the rack of McPhail's Jeep just this side of Albuquerque in the most tremendous wind and rain and dust storm either of us had ever seen—or foolishly driven through. And both of us have lived in Odessa, too, so this was a booger of a storm, the big red wall cloud kind. The tubs had all our food for the trip and some other valuable odds and ends and by the time we wheeled around on I-40, at a convenient exit no more than two or three miles down the road, a truck with bad intentions and a mean-looking trio had loaded our tub and was about to take off with it. While McPhail bravely distracted them, I grabbed the tub and tossed it in the Jeep. Recovery over courage any day.

Our budget was small, allocated to fishing licenses, camping fees, and gasoline. At two dollars and up per gallon, we knew we needed to save our dollars and not fritter them away at convenience stores along the way buying pink things, little pecan pies, and bad truck-stop coffee. (*Funny, Williams. You bought hundreds of those damn pies, leaving me to float most of the gas bill*

home—Love you, too.) Instead, the first two nights, we had to waste a collective hundred and twenty bucks on bad motels, the lightning and rain were so bad.

No gas stations, no nothing. Just nothing. Nothing but eerie unearthly landscapes. Ridges and benches and copper-hued hills. Nothing out there but some Indian roadstands and clusters of mobile homes and nothing else.

McPhail and I were driving through northern Arizona and one of the fiercest stretches of extreme geography in America and doing this incredibly stupid feat in the middle of the night. Chupacabra and other nocturnal supernatural creatures were watching us.

The southwestern region of America is odd. The area's been in drought for over seven years now. They've suffered forest fires. So when we got to the White Mountains of eastern Arizona, we encountered this paradox—voluminous amounts of snow and hail and rain coupled with trickling streams, roads closed to wildfires, pine beetle–destroyed forests, and dried-up lakes. Especially the Mogollon Rim waters were dry as a bone. Fine. Besides that, we were off budget, nearly hit deer on the road (twice), and we forgot to buy a license for Earl Park Lake which meant that when we watched the 5-pound rainbows cruising the edges, we had to only take photos because the office was thirty miles away and also closed for the night. (*Don't make that mistake when you go! The time we spent to get a license the next day and come back was fishing time and you shouldn't waste water time.*) So the eastern Arizona part of the trip was not a thing of beauty. We did catch thirty or forty Apache trout at the East Fork of the Black River, had a hey-day at the North Fork, and caught a few here and there, but most everything else was drier than the preacher's mouth at an outdoor summer revival.

We found this groovy remote creek we won't name (because we want to go back and fish it without you there) and as we hiked down into the canyon, we stepped over a freshly removed bloody deer leg. At the bottom, we found the freshly killed deer. We fished a bit, then, when we heard whatever killed the deer, we left. We may not be rocket scientists but we're not totally stupid.

Let me condense the trip for you:

- I'll tell you this part as delicately as I can: McPhail and I stopped at a rest stop in Glendale, Utah. You might know this one—in the middle of nowhere, clean as a whistle but with extraordinarily short stall doors. McPhail sat in the Jeep while I took some reading time. When the two buses of Korean tourists pulled up and the hordes piled out and raced to the bathrooms, he could only laugh. I could only walk out sheepishly.
- Utah is drier than Arizona and so are its rivers. So are its stores. (Get it?)
- Mammoth Creek is a gem, one of the finest streams we've fished. Go there.
- You can't get good coffee in southern Utah.
- You can't easily get a fishing license in southern Utah.
- Yes, these are two stories you'll have to get out of one of us when you see us on the street.

- The least likely looking angling spot was the best. Scrub brush, high desert, 100-degree heat, two more dead animals, a big snake, and tall grasses. East Fork of the Sevier River. The browns fed all day and we caught them all day, mostly on beadheads but the water was so clear, it was like dry fly fishing underwater. Easily fifty between us.
- Joe's Valley Reservoir, Fish Lake, Panguitch Lake, Fremont, and another twenty fisheries over the next three days. Straight Canyon Creek relinquished to us ten fighting rainbows all over a foot long in just two hours of angling. Utah beat us with the wind and deserts and drought but we got in a few punches of our own.
- And if that's not enough, we fished all the way back through Colorado the last day of driving home. San Miguel, Uncompahgre, Lime Creek, and so on. We accidentally became automobile participants in two Independence Day parades in Ouray and Silverton. We pulled into Amarillo early morning with over fifty fisheries under our belt, 2,755 miles behind us. Nobody said we were rocket scientists, after all.

Flaming Gorge Reservoir

- **Location:** Northeast Utah
- **What You Fish For:** Brown trout, lake trout
- **Highlights and Notables:** This canyon reservoir just keeps getting better with age.

The Gorge no longer produces brown trout or mackinaws that approach world-record size. You know what? Big deal. This famous scenic world-class reservoir in northeast Utah and southwest Wyoming is only getting better, getting better in that same way that Diane Lane and Carla Gugino and Teri Hatcher and Sheryl Crow all did; they got better with age. Flaming Gorge is better than ever.

Flaming Gorge is gorgeous. Even without the trophy-size fish. So you catch a 19-pound laker or an 8-pound rainbow—you're gonna be disappointed? In these unique surroundings?

If you've never been to Flaming Gorge, the scenery alone is worth the visit. The eerie hoodoos, the red sandstone cliffs, the sun's colors on the cliffsides that change like one of those revolving multicolored lights that used to shine on your grandmother's aluminum Christmas tree. At Flaming Gorge, water is a million colors of blue and green, one second the surface is cobalt and shimmering, the next clear as windows.

The fish that brings anglers to the Gorge is the rainbow. Because the lake is fertile and the forage base solid, the rainbow trout are heavy in the belly. When you read most articles about Flaming Gorge's rainbow trout, almost without fail they write that the "rainbow trout are shaped like footballs." Why is the comparison always to footballs? Why not rainbows with bellies like basketballs? Or like wicker baskets shaped like elliptical pumpkins? Like potbellied pigs? A snake that ate several baseballs?

Most trout at the Gorge are fat and average about 12 to 20 inches with your occasional biggie up to 7 or 8 pounds. Anglers are often surprised by how many 18- to 20-inch rainbows they land. The lake's rainbows naturally reproduce but also receive supplemental stockings.

The smallmouth bass are not big but they are plentiful, about 1 to 2 pounds with some smaller. These tough little dudes stay near structure like the rocky shoreline. Kokanee salmon never get me all that excited but FG has plenty—they hold deep, they feed on plankton, and they don't hit flies. Lake trout are big but hard to catch; they hold deep so trolling and downriggers are the weapons of choice. The browns are down—where once lived one of the top brown trout fisheries in America now lives not so many browns. In the shallows, some sightfish for carp. Yep, carp. Bonefish of freshwater.

At 6,100 feet elevation, if you don't wear sunscreen, you're going to burn and burn bad. Wear a hat, lather up. The reservoir (42,000 acres) goes on for ninety miles above the dam and offers over 360 miles of shoreline. The lower third of the Gorge lies in Utah and is the more scenic section, deeper, steeper. The Wyoming section, the upper two thirds, is scenic and then flattens out as you go north and becomes warmer, siltier. Salt Lake City is your fly-in point—three and one half hour drive. Rent a boat, hire a guide, you need to get out and adventure. You will see all kinds of boats and water-skiers and jetskiers and all manners of watersports enthusiasts.

Located in the Flaming Gorge National Recreation Area—okay, darn it, I thought I could get to the end of this without mentioning the Green River, that amazing tailrace that flows below Flaming Gorge (talk about your potbellied pig–shaped trout!)—both the Green River and Flaming Gorge Reservoir are in the National Recreation Area. Lodging is available in both Dutch John and Manila as well as the aforementioned National Recreation Area.

CONTACTS
Flaming Gorge Lodge, 435-889-3773
Flaming Gorge Recreation Services,
   435-885-3191
Old Moe Guide Service, 435-885-3342
Trout Creek Flies, 800-835-4551
Mark Wilson, Red Canyon Lodge, www
   .redcanyonlodge.com

Green River

- **Location:** Northeastern Utah
- **What You Fish For:** Rainbow, brown, cutthroat trout
- **Highlights and Notables:** Arguably, one of the best trout streams—America Splendid canyon scenery, huge trout, and lots of them.

The Green River in northeast Utah is by far the best overall trout fishery in the United States. The river runs through a topographical gallimaufry, wide expanse of arid desert, colorful canyonland, and remote mountain wilderness. The Green River is a green-colored river flowing past red and rust and tan colored canyons, a palette of colors, a year-round fishing wonderland.

Why do I proclaim Green River as the best overall trout fishery? Especially when I say the same about the White River in Arkansas? Hair's difference—Green is the best for fly fishing, White better for *both* spin and fly.

While Utah's overall trout fishery doesn't rank with her Western neighbors, and has fewer miles of trout streams, the state does have the best trout stream this side of Alaska. That being said, anglers who have not had their flylines tightened by thirty big Green River trout residents in an afternoon should know that the river gets crowded.

Because of its international reputation, anglers flock to the tailwater. They float in all kinds of watercraft, fishing for rainbows colored like prisms. They fish for healthy, hefty browns and brookies and cutts. And most of the boat traffic on this amazing river are recreationalists, not anglers. So how does the river manage under such stress?

Unequaled. Fish surveys have found that some sections of the Green River hold nearly 30,000 catchable trout per mile. Let that sink in for a minute. Most sections of the river hold considerably less than that but the overall trout-per-mile survey figures always rank this river as the most productive in the nation. I've read recently that the surveys show only 8,000 or 15,000 or 20,000 per square mile recently (depending on what you read) but what's 10,000 fish one way or another. It's still the largest concentration of sizeable trout I've yet seen. Big fish, lots of them, amazing scenery.

I sat there on a big rock by the launch watching. All these people, these fisher-people. Middle-aged white men with paunches mostly but there was a colorful mixture, a cross-section that surprised me, with parts of the world represented. Five women anglers, too. Bully for them. Now this mix wasn't as universal as a Star Wars bar, but there were folks from all walks of life getting strung up to fish.

Sometimes still today, fly fishing takes a bad rap for being elitist or separatist or something or 'nother. The sport is wide-spread and crosses all lines, races, sexes, ages.

So anyway, I'm sitting there and I'm not really into it, the day, the fishing. None of the people I was watching were laugh-able nor were they Visigoths nor were they mean. Just average nice fisher-people. I had been carrying a cold and it was a cold day and my throat was scratchy and while I can fight through illness and I can fight through most any pain, I was just feeling blah and I couldn't shake that feeling.

We launched and I saw all those trout, so many and the story should say that due to the river's curative powers I forgot all about feeling blah, my throat and stopped up nose, but the truth is, I felt bad all day and got worse by the end of the float. But I caught a 22-inch brown trout that was as beautiful a brown as I have ever caught and that sorta made up for me feeling so crappy.

The Green River is a tailwater fish-ery and this is big water with deep pools, riffles, long runs, current seams, and back eddies enough that a guide is a great idea for the uninitiated fisher. There aren't many accesses, either. The three major access points are at the Dam, Little Hole, and Browns Park. There are some difficult trails leading to the water's edge, and a trail that follows the river downstream on the north bank for most of its fishable course.

Rainbows make up the highest percent-age of the trout population, but you also catch cutthroat, brook, and brown trout as well as cuttbow hybrids. Rainbows tend to be the trout most caught in the upper section, whereas browns and rainbows are about equal in the middle, and browns tend to dominate in the lower section. The holding cover changes for the trout, and to the angler's eye, based on the water levels. In the lower reaches, there is more flat wa-ter, and many boulders to cast to.

All along the river, there are pools deep enough to sink a two-story building, and plenty of others that would cover a care-less wader's head. Some of the more pro-ductive and better known areas of the river include Secret Riffle, Dripping Springs, Little Hole, Two Holes Down, Anticipa-tion Rapids, the Merry Go-Round, Kong's Bed, Diving Board Rapids, Honey Hole, Rock Garden, Dead Man Rapids, and Can of Worms Shoal.

The river is broken into three sections, imaginatively named Sections A, B, and C. Section A is the most popular, the one that has the 8,000 to 30,000 trout per square mile numbers and it goes seven or so miles down to Little Hole. Section B starts there, at Little Hole and eight miles later, Browns Park, end of Section B. Section C begins here, ends seventeen miles later, right at the border of Colorado. This is the sleeper fishery, where the fish are fewer and the big browns eat anything that moves.

The river is as scenic as any trout stream anywhere, as it cuts through a red sandstone–walled canyon, whose walls are dotted with ponderosa pine, pinion pine, juniper, white pine, and cedar. As the sun arcs across the sky during your float trip, you will be entertained by an ever-changing kaleidoscope of colors on the sloped 1,000-foot canyon walls. The water is so clear, your heart will thump as you peer from behind polarized glasses and see a tumbling, turning mass of colors and fins, which upon closer inspection reveals you have sighted a pod of rainbow trout feeding on scuds in the moss.

Wading is done from shore and boat, but extreme caution should be taken because the river can rise quickly and strand an angler. There are dangerous rapids, so if you float yourself, talk with locals and use common sense.

Floating can be done in drift boats, rafts, kickboats, and even float tubes. Utah law requires boaters to wear lifejackets when floating the river. If you plan to float yourself, talk with outfitters and read up on the river, because there are some places, like Red Creek Rapids, where previous knowledge will keep one out of harm's way. Float tubing can be dangerous.

The Green River yields catches diplomatically, without prejudice, without fear of camouflage Neoprene waders or gimme caps or Patagonia fleece or chewing tobacco. The river is often invisible and the trout move around like hovercraft. The days provide beauty and light, many trout or big trout, dry fly or nymph, float or wade. The overwhelming numbers of trout portend well for your success. And why not, the Green River is the best overall trout fishery in America, after all. Except maybe for the White River, okay?

CONTACTS

Denny Breer, Trout Creek Flies & Green River Outfitters, www.fishgreenriver.com

Western River Flyfishers, Salt Lake City, www.wrflyfisher.com

Trout Bum 2, www.troutbum2.com

Flaming Gorge Lodge, Dutch John, www.fglodge.com

Spinner Fall Fly Shop, Salt Lake City, www.spinnerfall.com

Old Moe Guide Service, Park City, 801-649-8092, www.fishwestoutfitters.com

Eagle Outdoor Sports, www.eagle5.com

Green River Drifters, www.greenriverdrifters.com

Green River Outfitters, www.greenriveroutfitters.com

For more information on guide services for the river and for a list of authorized guides, contact the Ashley National Forest, Flaming Gorge Ranger District, P.O. Box 157, Dutch John, UT 84023

Upper Green River

- **Location:** Southwestern Wyoming
- **What You Fish For:** Wild trout
- **Highlights and Notables:** Off the beaten path angling option, underrated trout fishing in big country

I couldn't help but think I was close to where Hugh Gardner had spent time in the rainbow commune in the 1960s. He was writing for *Esquire* then or maybe he was working on his PhD. Or maybe that was when he had gotten caught up in the hippie village thing while researching them for his PhD. Doesn't really matter. Hugh was here.

Southwestern Wyoming is a big place but it feels kinda homey, like you ought to know the farmer-rancher-hippie-trout bum on the 1,000 acres next to you. Diners are greasy and slow and filled with high cholesterol specials. You'll see cowboy hats on guys who know how to rope and ride.

Gardner is an outdoor writer of sorts, a fishing buddy at one time, a character always. He's odd and complex and spread out, just like this corner of the world. While the Flaming Gorge tailwater of the Green gets all the national attention, the upper Green quietly meanders through a mix of public land and private ranches with the public water found only by the Adrian Monks of the world, its trout population growing stronger each year.

Above and below Fontenelle Reservoir, the Green River holds fat rainbow, cut-throat and brown trout. The best way to fish this scenic river is by hiring a guide.

Trout will average 12 to 16 inches but in the lower elevations, you can be surprised by a lunker every now and again. The Green's headwaters begin in the Wind River Mountains to the north and along its southern course to the Flaming Gorge Reservoir, highways run alongside the 100-plus miles. Between the two Green River Lakes and Pinedale, there is much more public land so you can drive and park and fish, rinse, repeat.

Many private ranches are open to courteous inquiries about fishing on their land. Public accesses can be crowded at the height of tourist season but most of the time you'll have entire stretches to yourself. Most folks you'll meet on the river will be locals or townies from another nearby Wyoming village. But you'll need to get on this as of yet undiscovered stretch before everyone else hears about it. Shhhh!

CONTACTS
Denny Breer, Trout Creek Flies & Green
    River Outfitters, www.fishgreenriver.com

Lake Powell

- **Location:** Southern Utah and northern Arizona
- **What You Fish For:** Striped bass, smallmouth bass, largemouth bass
- **Highlights and Notables:** One of the most eye-popping lakes in the world

The first time you lay eyes on Lake Powell, you will stand there and say nothing, mouth agape. Like we did. Guaranteed. Overwhelming. Awesome. Inspiring. Intimidating.

It's as if a John Ford Western turned into color—ochre and blue only—and the monumental cliffs and rock formations were submerged by an apocalyptic flood, only the tallest geologic compositions stand above the watery world.

This high-desert lake is one of the great fishing destinations in the world. Even if it had no fish. Lake Powell (3,700 feet elevation) is the result of the Glen Canyon Dam across the Colorado River over forty years ago, the largest man-made lake in the lower forty-eight.

Cliffs taller than a ten-story building. Sloping rust-colored shorelines, weird striations on rock faces that look like they carry prehistoric messages. And yeah, there are rock-faced human messages, petroglyphs, too.

Nearly 2,000 miles of shoreline; 800 feet deep at its deepest; 185 miles long. There are so many tributary canyons and coves and hideaways you couldn't count them with your fingers and toes and your fishing buddy's fingers and toes and the houseboat operator's fingers and toes and those of the dozen college kids partying on that houseboat just around the cove you're in. Seriously, think about that. Nearly 2,000 miles of shoreline. It's otherworldly. You hear that word a lot when people describe Lake Powell. Otherworldly. And it is.

As far as a fishery goes, some say it's the best bass lake in the West but I think there are better. You're fishing for stripers mostly or else smallmouth and largemouth bass and while there are great numbers here, the sizes don't compare with some other top lakes. But quantity? It ranks right up there with any of them to be sure.

Stripers average about 4 to 6 pounds and if you figure out what you're doing, you have days where you wear your arm out bringing all of them in. The three top draws are black and brown bass and the stripers but anglers can also chase after trout, walleye, crappie, bluegills, catfish, and pike.

Two-pound smallmouths are common. Largemouths aren't trophy class but they are big on average. The lake doesn't have a great population of forage fish but it does have enough shad to keep the fishery in the neighborhood of amazing. Most of the lake is clear but some canyons are gritty and cloudy.

This is brown arid steep extreme country, more desert than anything else. Limited cover and not much vegetation. Shad imitations are the key for stripers (topwater and then deeper), concentrating on fishing the rocky sloping edges. You can also watch for the shad boiling on the surface and then follow the schools. When the stripers are boiling for shad, fly fishing is an ideal method. You can fly fish well here but not many do.

This is a boating lake with lots of boaters and they fish well but you can fish from shore and still have success. Powell does not have many vehicle access points.

Lake Powell is houseboat heaven. If you want, you can find floating parties, college girls with their bikini tops off, and flotillas of houseboats strung together in social commune. Imagine anything you've ever seen float—you'll see it on Lake Powell. Four million visitors come to this red sandstone–walled lake every year. You need to be one of them.

Don't come for a day. Stay a week.

Strawberry Reservoir

- **Location:** Central Utah, 80 miles from Salt Lake City
- **What You Fish For:** Bear Lake cutthroat, rainbow trout, smallmouth bass, kokanee salmon
- **Highlights and Notables:** Popular, productive lake full of fat rainbows and rare Bear Lake cutts

The low-slung pewter hills that ring the lake want to be mountains and change like the seasons. Summer and they are white, the hot light, the white bark and green leaves of aspen and the white hills shimmer emerald like the waves. Autumn and they are gray, the cool sky, and the aspen are gold and they shimmer topaz like the waves and the hills are mountains.

Strawberry Reservoir sits at 7,600 feet elevation and for these parts, is a large lake at 17,000 acres. Popular lake. The Berry. Where middle-aged men sit in inflated rubber tubes and kickboats getting charlie horses from the exertion and the cold water and the wind.

Where anglers catch Bear Lake cutthroat (subspecies), rainbow trout (steril-

ized to prevent crossbreeding), smallmouth bass, and kokanee salmon. Where the Utah state-record cutthroat got hooked and landed. Twenty-seven pounds. Where 10-pound cutthroats are real. Where 17-pound cutthroats are real and alive and swimming in these blue waters.

The rainbow trout are so fat, even the 14-inch rainbow trout, fat from the richness of the waters, that the fat rolls over your hand as you hold them. Kokanee salmon are a big draw here, too. Folks flit around Strawberry Reservoir in pontoon boats, walking and hiking, picnicking, camping, just out enjoying the stark beauty of it all.

Strawberry Reservoir has gone through many changes over the years, from clearing out rough fish with rotenone to degradation from overgrazing the area to seemingly ever-changing regulations. One thing remains: The relatively shallow lake (20 feet deep on average) produces big fish quickly.

They cruise along the shore, fill the channels, hang off the points and around the weedbeds, and then move up into the bays. By late April when the ice breaks up, the float-tubers and kickboats get out in the calf-cramping cold water and fish up by the dam. They might flirt with dry fly patterns that imitate midges and mayflies and caddisflies but that approach is ephemeral, fleeting. Think nymphs and streamers on Strawberry. You want to imitate the scuds and damselflies and sowbugs and nightcrawlers and other creepy crawlers moving in this fertile water. You do see boats, anglers getting whipped

City Fishing

SALT LAKE CITY
Provo and Logan Rivers

Salt Lake is different and let's leave it at that. It's got enough good-enough restaurants, is growing and becoming more a rounded city, and is set in one of the prettiest city locales in America. The Beehive State doesn't have many large rivers but it is long on secluded lakes and fertile streams. The great thing for the angler is that so many fishing holes are located within a few hours' drive from Salt Lake City.

Utah is a harshly beautiful state, with a tremendous diversity of terrain ranging from deserts to mountains. The Wasatch Metro area has a whopping 1.5 million residents. But few major metro areas in America have such proximity to so many quality trout fisheries. Here are two of these top-flight trout getaways.

The Provo River

A year-round tailwater canyon stream that originates in the Uinta Mountains, meanders through the Heber Valley, collects in Jordanelle and Deer Creek Reservoirs, and ends up in Utah Lake. The Provo was once known as the West's premier brown trout river. Then channelization, heavy angling pressure, water diversion, and a handful of other problems sent the river into decline. Since then, regulations and renewed environmental consciousness have led to a comeback of the brown trout population.

Although rare, the biggest browns can even reach 28 to 30 inches. If you look down at the big pools, you can often see big trout in the 22- to 24-inch range holding, feeding. Along the Provo, anglers will find hidden beaver ponds, streamside willows to catch their flies, and thick forests. The Provo River holds wild brown, rainbow, and native cutthroat trout.

The browns average 12 to 16 inches with plenty of trout reaching 20 inches long and like any brown trout water worth its reputation, the Provo holds some lunker brown trout as well, famous for its 5-plus-pound big boys.

The Provo has lots of pocket water, runs, often fast and roily, with riffles, deep pools and long glides, and flatwater. The sections below the impoundments fish small like typical tailraces. The Provo runs past gorgeous mountains, tranquil agricultural fields, and through a stunning canyon, providing over sixty miles of quality fishing. The Provo River is often crowded, or at least it seems that way, and is only an hour south of Salt Lake City. There is plenty of public access. But if you see anglers knee deep in its tricky-to-wade waters, just walk twenty or thirty minutes from the turnout and you'll discover your around by the wind in their drift boats, motorboats, and small rowboats.

Adjunct trip: The Strawberry River is a sweet little stream that flows below lemon-colored cliffs and is a fly fisher's dream to fish. Shallow, rocky, clear and cold, anglers can only use artificial flies and lures. Lots of fun casting to the tight pocket water and around fallen timber.

There are few lakes in the country that combine this kind of quality angling for trout with the unique colorations and spectacular scenery of Strawberry. That's something you take away from any visit here—the colors. From the lemon-cream of the promontory cliffs to the brilliancy of the dogwoods to the saffron cutthroat to the amazing kaleidoscopic sunsets, this fishery is a palette of colors. For campground reservations call the National Recreation Reservation Service toll-free at 877-444-6777. To reserve the group pavilions call MCM at 435-548-2554. For other general user information, call the USFS Heber Ranger District at 435-654-0470 or the USFS Strawberry Visitor Center at 435-548-2321.

Underrated in Utah: Survey of Some of My Favorite Underfished Utah Streams

- **Location:** Southern and central Utah
- **What You Fish For:** Rainbow, brown, cutthroat trout
- **Highlights and Notables:** Utah is underrated as a trout fishing destination. If you like solitude and small stream angling, you need to get to Utah.

Note to reader: The parentheticals are by my fishing buddy and runnin'-around friend Chad McPhail, Amarillo Independent School District's Teacher of the Year, writer and author and overall raconteur. I wasn't gonna let him write any rebuttals but he knows secrets.

Desert Land. (Scarily deserted.) Canyons and hills and dryness. (Just rocks and dust, mostly.) Arid. (Spit and it dries before it splats.) Jaw-dropping scenery. The hoo-doos and spires that John Ford films featured. Not trout country.

Not so fast.

The hinterlands of southern and central Utah, as remote as they are, hold some surprisingly productive streams. Utah is the biggest state in the union, Texas and Alaska included. Seriously. If you added up all the square miles and then tacked on the verti-

cal rock and the holes in the ground and the big blue sky and the lack of people, you'd find you've got the largest state. You can drive and drive and you stay amazed at how much wild country is in one state. It may also be the most rugged, remote and wild of all the states, too.

Now, these trout oases in southern and central Utah are not big streams. Neither are they step-across streams. They are streams that, because of the lay of the land, because of the high desert landforms, because of their remoteness, don't get a look-see by many anglers. (Boulder Mountain alone has nine lives—far too unwieldy to tame into one day, as I found out.) Southern and central Utah trout streams can do that, take on a life of their own, unexpectedly, rewardingly.

Anglers who drive through this remote

country might have stopped for a few minutes roadside at this or that river and caught a couple of trout but most likely drove away thinking this place was drier than the preacher's mouth at an outdoor summer revival.

McPhail and I found this cool remote creek in southern Utah and as we hiked down into the canyon, we stepped over a freshly removed bloody deer leg. (I got hungry all of a sudden.) At the bottom, we found the freshly killed deer. (I got scared all of a sudden.) We fished a bit, then, when we heard whatever killed the deer, we left. We're not rocket scientists but we're not totally stupid, either.

At the next creek, a branch of the Sevier River, we had fish a-jumpin' but we also found a freshly killed calf. We still fished it because 1) the fish were a-jumpin' and 2) each of us was confident the cougar would eat the other of us first. *(Williams had a bum knee, so he was delusional if he thought he could run faster than me that summer.)*

One day, in between rivers, at Piute Reservoir, we saw and photographed the tallest, biggest dust devil we'd ever seen, some two hundred feet tall. (. . . *300.)* As we left the state park, the dust devil bisected our path and attacked the Jeep, rocking it and pelting it with sand and rocks and evil spirits. We had no idea the dust devils packed that much punch. Downstream from the lake, five or so miles, ten minutes later, we left the tailwater because it was more tail than water and on our way out, no lie *(Really, he's not lying!)*, the dust devil crossed our path and pelted us again, broadside.

The spirits protect their fertile waters with ferocity in this part of the Rockies.

Anglers won't need big tackle or chest waders. Wade wet and you'll be happy you did. The summer temperatures regularly hit the mid-90s. Use ultralight rods for these small to medium-sized rivers. Some days, because the streams don't see lots of anglers, you can stick to attractor flies. Other days, because the rivers are often low and clear, you'll need to match the hatch, downsize your flies.

Mammoth Creek

A winding gin-clear high-country stream that has deep green pools, undercut banks, aspen forests, and miles of solitude. The browns are beautifully spotted and heavy in the shoulders. This is a real find though for parts of it, creeping summer home subdivisions appear to threaten the wildness of the stream.

A feeder creek to the Sevier River, Mammoth Creek is located about fifteen miles south of the small town of Panguitch. You'll see plenty of posted water but above and at the hatchery you'll find plenty of public access, and about seven and a half miles upstream from the canal diversion above the hatchery is public until you reach summer home area, though much of the stream is private. In this section, anglers are limited to artificial flies and lures and can only take two trout between 10 and 15 inches. All others must be immediately released.

The river curves back and forth, so working a mile of river on Mammoth can

take hours. Big wide open spaces. Wild brown trout. Rolling green fields and white-trunked aspen forests. The sweet scent of pine trees. The stream flows at almost 8,000 feet elevation.

In the upper reaches, you'll catch some hatchery rainbows and a few wild brookies but the draw on Mammoth is the population of feisty, plump wild browns. They're not typically big, at least in yarn-telling terms. But most are 8 to 12 inches long and fatter than a baguette. Still, I have fished to and have not caught several that approached 2 or 3 pounds.

The hatches are sparser here due to the altitude and a lack of heavy streamside vegetation. This means the fish are less picky and rise easily to well-presented flies. If you use nymphs, the water is clear enough that you can see trout follow your fly. (*I watched two race to mine that were at least four feet under . . . caught 'em both, too.*)

The bottom of the river is sometimes sandy, silty but has enough rocks and boulders that the trout have hiding places. There's no need to wade the river, though you'll need to cross every now and again. A few sections have deep blue foggy pools that tail out into gravel flats. Some of the banks raise up three or four feet over the river but your footfalls and shadows will spook the trout so move with care. I have found smaller Stimulators with a dropper nymph are killer here, imitating both caddis and terrestrials.

Mac kicked my ass this day, catching three to my one. And he caught over twenty so you do the math. (*I'm not good at math, so no thanks. But I'll agree on the 3 to 1 ratio.)*

From Salt Lake, take I-15 south, Highway 148 southeast through Brian Head, Highway 143 east where you pick up the upper reaches of Mammoth Creek.

East Fork Sevier

In between Cedar City and Boulder, in the middle of nowhere, amidst low-slung hills, in the wild high desert as well as dark canyons flows the lonely East Fork of the Sevier River.

This is a true gem of a trout river, lazily meandering under rugged cliffs and flowing through copper hills with bursts of green riparian habitat exploding on its banks. *(Some of it requires either napalm or at the very least a machete to negotiate.)* Loaded with brown trout, I've not fished many streams where the trout cared less about me and more about the prevailing hatch, usually a caddis hatch. *(The trout here literally cared not a wink about how close our approach was. Often they would swim between Williams and me, just look up at us like a puppy and beg for our bugs.)*

The East Fork Sevier doesn't get much fishing pressure. It's too remote. Some might look at it and be displeased that it doesn't fit the mold of your traditional trout stream. The willows and wild roses and other viney, clingy plants and bushes are overgrown. The boulders are big and scattered. In the summer, it gets hot as all git out.

But what a sweet stream.

One day, McPhail and I hit this least likely looking angling spot and he winced suspiciously at the scrub brush, the high desert surroundings, 100-degree heat, two dead animals we passed on the trail to the river, a big snake, and tall grasses. The East Fork of the Sevier River. The browns fed all day and we caught them all day *(I caught that chubby cutthroat too, Williams . . . you always leave that out.)*, mostly on beadheads but the water was so clear, it was like dry fly fishing underwater. Easily fifty between us. He was hooked. He caught more than me, I'll admit it. *(I was on, what can I say?)*

The headwaters begin near Bryce Canyon National Park. Above Tropic Reservoir, the fish are small, typically cutts and brooks. Johns Valley Road parallels this upper section. While scenic enough, head north along SR 22 to Black Canyon. Fur-

ther downstream and north, SR 62 follows the Kingston Canyon section.

The Kingston and Black Canyon sections fish well. In Black Canyon, some of the pools are as big as Roman baths. You have to get down and deep with streamers to have a chance at the whoppers in these pools. They don't catch easily. I have only fly fished this river but the pools call out for spinning lures if you ask me.

Kingston Canyon runs from Otter Creek confluence to near Piute Reservoir.

The Division of Wildlife Resources and Bureau of Land Management post public accesses well along the East Fork. Keep an eye out for private land especially on the Kingston stretch and around Antimony. There is restoration along the river.

I like the calmer water that snakes green and clear before and after the canyons. Small pools dumping into a few runs and lots of riffles. You can see trout holding in almost every conceivable lie. Stay back, work upstream, keep your leaders long and thin, fish above the feeding trout and you'll be rewarded with hookups with beautiful brown and cutthroat trout.

Your average catch on the East Fork? A 10- to 16-inch brown trout. You'll hook some cutthroats, too. I've hooked a 19-inch brown but lost him at the bank. I would say he was 20-inches but I didn't measure him before he jumped off and I've claimed too many 20-inchers that got away over the years. So he was 19 inches. (*It was 20—I saw it.*) There are others that big in the East Fork as well. Trout limit, six. For the section of river from the BLM property boundary (about four miles south of An-

timony) upstream to the confluence with Deer Creek, special regulations include the use of artificial flies and lures only and a limit of two trout.

You reach East Fork from Salt Lake I-15 south to cut over on Highway 70 east to Sevier, then south on Highway 89 or I-15 south then cutoff on Highway 50 then Highway 89 to Sevier. From there, travel south on Highway 89 to Kingston. Turn east to Kingston and you move upstream.

Fremont River

This is a classic freestone stream in central Utah. The upper section has one of the prettiest meadow stretches I've ever seen. The blue river winds back and forth, almost touching itself on the curves like the Ouroboros, the classic symbol of the snake that eats its own tail, an icon symbolizing the eternity of time and the boundaries of the universe. (*I liken it to a Celtic knot.*) It's like you are in your own universe in places on this lovely stream.

You catch rainbow and brown trout on the Fremont River in a patchwork of private and public accesses. And the fishery suffers from whirling disease, though the state has taken proactive measures. Anglers must be careful not to transport fish, and wash their boots and waders well so as not to spread the disease. Still, the Fremont is such a joy to fish that it's worth the effort. (*Not much effort required on this angler's part to exit the Jeep and enter the water.*) In the upper stretches, where the river curves like keyholes, green and clear, it's so scenic, so postcard that you don't care if you catch a fish or not. (*Like seeing a famous*

movie star in Vegas . . . you don't care that you didn't get to talk to them—AT LEAST YOU SAW THEM, BY GOD!) The upper section runs parallel to FR 36.

The river sees its share of anglers and campers and you won't likely find hours of solitude like you will on East Fork Sevier. But the river is fun, noteworthy and classic. One of the top areas for catching browns is the stretch from Mamoit Springs to Mill Meadow Reservoir. Above the reservoir, casting is tight, narrow but worth it for the skilled caster.

Below the reservoir, the river is dewatered for irrigation but picks up again on DWR land at Bicknell Bottoms and due to springs, there is ample water and good habitat for sizeable browns. This section fishes well in the fall when the browns are active. Not all that long ago, this marshy area used to hold big browns, behemoths in the 5-pound range but between flooding and whirling disease, these are far and few between.

As a sidenote, the lower Fremont River that courses through six private miles of the Red River Ranch is special water, albeit costly. The cloudy green waters that run beneath red rock cliffs hold some big fish. When you're through catching big fish for the day, you return to a world-class lodge for great eats and sleep. You would have seen it and the big fish if you watch the Outdoor Channel and *Flyfishing Masters*. Phone: 702-838-6669/Fax: 702-838-6689.

You can reach the Fremont from Salt Lake City on big ol' I-15 to Highway 50 south. Turn Salina, then south on 89, east on SR24. From here you can go east on SR 25 to the headwaters below Johnson Reservoir or continue south along SR 24. You can find campsites along the river or camp at Fish Lake which has campgrounds galore, and then you can fish small creeks and two lakes on your way east to the Fremont.

Cottonwood Creek in Straight Canyon

A surprisingly big and productive canyon stream chock-full of big pools, turning runs and glides and foamy pocket water. This tailwater runs out of Joe's Valley Reservoir.

There are boulders as big as Victorian homes in Straight Canyon. (*Think Graceland!*) The water in a single pool might range from clear to aqua to turquoise to cobalt to black, so deep and varied are they.

The stream holds feisty fish that range from 10 to 15 inches. The largest I've caught has been 18 inches long and surprisingly, I haven't seen many that size in these big waters. I've heard anecdotes that purport there are leviathans in these big pools (*of course*).

The first time I fished this stream, I got

out of the car and looked down fifty feet below, studying the huge pool. Holding and feeding around one big rock were seven big trout, ranging from 13 to 17 inches. I scrambled down the scree and caught three of the seven on beadheads. Would it surprise you that Cottonwood Creek has become one of my favorite medium-sized streams? (*It's in my top three as well!*)

I've had good luck dredging the deep pools with streamers, Woolly Buggers, woolly worms, and Muddler Minnows. (*I like the red Copper John for the same job. Lethal in deep dark water.*) What you'll find though is that contrary to convention when fishing big deep pools, these fish respond well to dry fly patterns. The hatches aren't great on the Straight Canyon section and

the fish suspend not as deep as you think. Running a big dry fly, such as an Elk Hair Caddis or Stimulator or Royal Wulff with a dropper two-feet below it is a surefire strike-getter in these pools, starting at the head and running through to the tail.

The pools are so big, don't give up easily if you're not getting strikes. Work close to the boulders, find the seams, the edges, the different colored water, the microcurrents. Change to a different nymph, add splitshot. Each pool holds fish. I've not fished a big pool yet without catching a 13-inch trout and having several other strikes.

The fishing in Cottonwood Creek outside of Straight Canyon is poor. There isn't much holding water and the water itself is cloudy and white. Stick with the beautiful waters of Straight Canyon, the waters that flow right out of Joe's Valley Reservoir before entering Cottonwood Creek proper (this is where the Straight Canyon water and Cottonwood Creek join). Fish above this for best results. From Orangeville, go west on SR 29 upstream.

You can reach Straight Canyon at Cottonwood Creek from Salt Lake City by traveling south on I-15, go east/south on Highway 6 to Orangeville, then turn back west on SR 29. Joe's Valley Reservoir has ample campgrounds and pretty good fishing.

Panguitch Creek

This is water that ought to be fished more often but because of the popularity and quality of Panguitch Lake, this excellent trout water is often overlooked. Access runs throughout its flow but some accesses are more difficult, more rugged than others.

You get meadow sections and canyon stretches. You get solitude. You get lots of access, some easy, some difficult. The canyon stretches require a steep descent. All the anglers stay on Panguitch Lake, fishing their hearts out while few take the time to explore the rich canyon water of Panguitch Creek. While the lower section of Panguitch Creek holds wild brown trout, the predominant fish throughout is your basic stocked rainbow trout.

The word "Panguitch" is an Indian word that means big fish, but you won't find many in this fun stream. *(Don't look at us . . . they were already gone when we got there!)* The average trout will run 9 to 12 inches. In some of the undercut banks and deep pools, you'll get surprised by bigger fish.

Just up the road from Mammoth Creek, Panguitch Creek flows out of Panguitch Lake, joining Mammoth and Asay Creek to form the main stem of the Sevier River. You fish Panguitch Creek because you are going to fish Panguitch Lake or because you are in the neighborhood fishing Mam-

moth. *(I second that notion.)* I like walking into the roadless canyon section, roughly five miles of lonely water, ideal for the adventurous angler who wants to fish water that doesn't see a dozen fishermen all year.

The stream follows along Highway 143 for several miles below Panguitch Lake, and flows through both private land and portions of the Dixie National Forest. The area along the highway is stocked with hatchery rainbow trout. Further downstream, it leaves the highway and flows through a roadless canyon for about five miles, mostly on National Forest lands. The lower reach supports a population of wild brown trout. *(There's a well-groomed public restroom along this stretch of Highway 143 where Williams got peeked in on by an entire busload of antsy, ready-to-burst Korean tourists. Ask him about it some day.)*

Located about three hours south of Salt Lake City, you can reach Panguitch Creek by taking I-15 south then take 143 east. You're there. You can camp in the high country of 8,250 feet elevation at lovely and fertile Panguitch Lake.

Yellowstone National Park

- **Location:** Northwestern Wyoming and small parts of Idaho and Montana

- **What You Fish For:** Yellowstone cutthroat trout are the key but also rainbow, brown, brook trout, grayling, whitefish

- **Highlights and Notables:** There is no place on earth where so many quality fishing rivers sit in such close proximity. This ought to be on everyone's list of must-visit fishing destinations but if you don't go just to fish, at least drop a line in a river or two during your family sightseeing vacation.

Three million visitors descend upon the park each year and if you fish famous Buffalo Ford on any day after July 15, when the Yellowstone River opens up, you'd think all three million of them are standing right there. On stretches of the famous rivers in the park, the anglers often outnumber the trout.

The rivers that course through the park's boundaries are legendary—the Firehole with its steam rising, the Madison with its choppy riffles, the meandering meadows of the Gallatin, the roaring falls of the Gibbon, the slow-moving crystal waters of Slough Creek, and the powerful waters of the mighty Yellowstone.

Fishing all of Yellowstone National Park's trout waters cannot be done in a week, a year or a lifetime. It's worth a try. What fishermen can do is sample a little bit of each type of water in the park. Whether it is backcountry fishing in solitude or standing in the Yellowstone River at Buffalo Ford with both trout and anglers all around, Yellowstone National Park offers such a variety of water character every angler will be satisfied.

You would think that with over 2.2 million acres and a thousand miles of rivers, there wouldn't be crowded water. But most anglers fish near the access points, the road crossings, the parking lots, the campgrounds, the bridges, where the river parallels the road, and they like to fish the marquee rivers.

What that tells you is that if you get out and walk a bit, you won't see other anglers. Sure, go see the sights, fight the traffic both on the road and on the river, even make certain to fish the legendary waters. But the overlooked quality trout waters are the small to medium-sized streams. To note, a small stream in the park is not always what the average angler thinks of about a small stream. Slough Creek and Soda Butte Creek are both as big as some so-called rivers in Colorado.

Finding the lesser-known and smaller streams makes the YNP experience fuller, more fun. Take a look at a Yellowstone National Park map and you will see all the little blue squigglies. Read any book on the park, and you'll rarely read about the smaller streams (although many streams are ten to twenty feet wide, full of deep pools, tons of fish). Imagine that when you look at that map, all those blue squigglies are potential day trips, half-day excursions, chances to catch twenty or thirty or forty fish in a day.

Imagine that those blue squigglies present a new world, a fishing canvas you have probably never seen before because no one fishes it, you get to choose the hues and brush-strokes, and the masterpiece is yours. You'll find few photos of Duck Creek in the big magazines.

There tend to be surprises along these lesser-known streams, too. I've found a thermal hole along Little Firehole with elk bones in it, have seen an eagle, several moose, bears (black and grizzly), and have come across lot of other surprises. If you don't mind catching twenty-two inches of trout (two 11-inch trout added together), then stuff the day pack, grab the lightweight rod and start hiking.

A few summers ago, my brother-in-law Kenny and I did just that when we took his son Chase and our nephew Bryan on a two-week trip to Yellowstone National Park. The drive from Texas was long, even longer with two fourteen-year-old boys and after twenty hours, we were ready to get there (and to never hear that plinkety-plink music of Nintendo GameBoy ever again).

To be fair, riding in a vehicle with anyone for twenty hours straight is a daunting task, sure to test your mettle. One guy I took on a trip years ago surprisingly pulled out a pistol and shot at an antelope we passed. Another passenger picked his nose for an hour. And another never once offered to pay for gas. So how tough could it be with two teenagers? Besides, anyone who has ever geared up for a road trip to go fishing or hunting knows that the getting there, the anticipation, is almost as fun as the being there.

Kenny and I like to think we are teaching them about the outdoors, passing on a tradition, acting as role models. They like to think that when they are away from Momma for a few days, we are their servants, driving them places, purchasing large quantities of food and acting as their hired hands. (Sort of like how we would have liked our dads to have treated us, no doubt.)

The boys are good anglers, can cast well, and generally catch fish but they grew up feasting on the easy pickin's of stocked rainbows and eager brook trout of southern Colorado rivers. And since Yellowstone is the fly fishing mecca, full of hungry trout and unparalleled scenery, we figured the benefits of the park would outweigh the long drive.

Early July and all the rivers we wanted to fish were still a little high. We had little choice but to put these teenagers on the fickle Firehole or mercurial Madison Rivers or take them hiking into the back-country and onto the smaller streams not affected as much by runoff. They bombed on the big rivers and the finicky fish. So we loaded them up with Pop Tarts and beef jerky and hiked them in the backcountry early one morning.

The sky looked fake. It was a little too sky-blue, the clouds a bit too puffy, kind of like a bad oil painting at a starving artist sidewalk sale. We were watching Bryan cast to four or five cutthroats holding over a sandbar, oblivious to his splashes and shadow.

In the last hour, he caught four cutts from the little meadow creek, each one a wholesome 12 inches long and more colorful than a painter's palette. He hooked up again as we watched, his 4-weight rod bent over like Grandpa's back, the kaleidoscope of a fish twisting and jumping against the fake blue sky.

Chase came over to admire his cousin's catch. The boys reluctantly posed for a picture. The inevitable question "whaddya catch'em on?" and Bryan, with some hesitation, replied "I caught him on a Malcolm X Caddis." We snickered not wanting to show him up. We'd save that for later.

We ate a lazy snack that day on Cascade Creek, the lazy meandering feeder stream to the mighty Yellowstone River. Cascade Creek is typical of the underfished streams of the park. Since all the other bigger rivers in the park were blown out, swollen from melting snow and recent rains or too tough for neophytes, we turned to Plan B and fished the smaller streams of the park and we had one of the best days of angling we ever had. We saw nary a soul on the banks of clear brooks which flow through verdant valleys or race through canyons.

We fished Nez Perce Creek on a sunny day, angled next to backcountry hot springs, walked entirely too close to a grazing bison, hooked and released entirely too many trout. Even if they were only 10 to 14 inches long, no one else we talked to back at camp or at the stores was catching trout on the big rivers. We drove past serious anglers wading the dangerous high waters of the major rivers. We left those swift waters behind for isolation and steady dry fly fishing (and catching) on twisting meadow pools and runs of Obsidian Creek and upper Gibbon River.

We braved rain and wind and mosquitoes to fish for lunkers, and I mean big lunkers, on the marshy twenty-foot-wide, three-foot-deep Duck Creek. Never heard of it? Maybe only Yellowstone River itself holds larger fish of the rivers in the park.

We had great luck tackling the small streams of the park, and despite our best efforts to screw up the fishing trip, Lady Luck was on our side. How about fishing for four hours on Obsidian Creek, where we parked the Suburban on a small turnout, all kinds of cars and RVs passing by, only to come back and find that we had left the tailgate wide open. We saw this error from a quarter-mile away, and since we had thousands of dollars of equipment in the truck, and more importantly all of our food for the two weeks, that was the longest walk we ever made. We were astonished to find everything right where we had left it. And we were able to con the teenagers into thinking it was their fault, too.

So despite the heavy runoff and persistent bad weather, we caught lots of fish. We got to see streams and forests few folks ever see in the park. It was fun to sit back and watch the boys fish, to witness how much better they had become since we had first put a fly rod in their hand.

Small streams are excellent teachers. The pupils catch a lot of trout so their tactics and casts are rewarded. We'd chuckle when Chase would get into his predatory mode. He would zone out, lean forward, and for hours on end, he'd cast and move, his eyes always peeled for rises and subtle movement. Small streams are not as intimidating as the larger rivers.

Yellowstone's big streams are the semester tests. You need to fish them to see where you rank in the class. Challenge the broad-shouldered behemoths of the Yellowstone. Finesse the finicky fish of the Firestone. But don't limit yourself to the big-name rivers or you'll be missing out on the full Yellowstone National Park angling experience.

On our sojourn with the boys, we had difficulty convincing the two teens that they needed to be scared of grizzlies, that bison can outrun them, not to walk too close to the thermal areas, to brush their teeth and so on. Don't you do the same. And when you are in the less-frequented areas where the small streams flow, you have a better chance of encountering wildlife. But at that age, young men have a certain cockiness that defies description or counsel.

We hoped that our explorations of the wilderness that these small streams coursed through showed the boys a genuine affection for the outdoors (even if we ourselves craned our necks silently watching out for their safety at every grizzly sound we heard crackling in the forest) but the boys are now driving cars on the main drags of Texas towns and much more interested in girls and hotrods, so the outdoors is secondary.

I think back to one lunch the four of us shared in the park two years ago. So there we were, the four of us, not on a big stream, but sitting in a meadow by a little stream, a step-across stream with undercut banks and bend pools, snacking on summer sausage and cold water, laughing loud enough that the wolves could hear us.

Earlier in the morning, on our easy hike along the small stream, while we were catching fish after fish, we ended up at a lake. The fishing in the lake was poor for the wind whipped up but we got to see something few people ever see.

A huge bird, like a stealth bomber, appeared out of nowhere and swooped down on the lake. It was an eagle, big enough to carry off one of the boys. Her talons were out, she hit the water, rose quickly and held one of the 14-inch trout we were trying to catch. None of us said a word, just watched, slack-jawed at the rare sight.

We finished our lunch, put the trash in our pack and got back to fishing. The fake sky looked like one of us could reach up and scratch it with a fingernail, and for a moment, as if we were posing for our own postcard, everything in the world seemed just a bit more real by contrast.

BASIC INFO

Fly fishermen should bring two weights of flyline, one for the delicate touch, one for the inevitable windy conditions. Spinning fishermen will do fine with a 7-foot rod and 4- to 6-pound test line. Spinners and jigs will catch cutts all day long, and bubble-fly rigs do well, too. Fly fishers need a full box of flies, since the park has great numbers of insect hatches, including mayfly, caddis, stonefly, as well as grasshoppers. Dry, wet, and nymph fishing will be successful depending on what river you are fishing. You have to be willing to experiment.

Like much of the West, the weather can change for the worse rather quickly in Yellowstone National Park. Always have raingear and an extra jacket handy. Insect repellant is another necessity to ward off mosquitos and horseflies.

Lodging and camping in the park means either reserving a cabin or rooms up to a year in advance, or getting to the campgrounds on a first-come, first-serve basis. There are eleven National Park Service Campgrounds, but in the summer they fill up quickly. If you cannot locate lodging in the park, try West Yellowstone to the west, the Wapiti Valley to the east or to the north, Livingston and Gardiner. There is lodging of any kind and price. Many stay in Jackson to the south.

Visitors can enter the park through five entrances, and driving through Yellowstone National Park will surprise many drivers. Just looking at a map of the park will not fully disclose how long, and often how difficult, it will be to get from point A to point B.

The interior roads are not superhighways, and the cars on the road are more likely to be recreational vehicles than sportscars. Throw in the endless stops by vehicles looking at the amazing numbers of wildlife in the park, interminable road construction, and endless winding, curvy roads, and driving from one side of the park to the other can sometimes take several hours. Plan accordingly before taking off to fish your new favorite river. Make time to look at the sites and wildlife along the way. Better yet, set aside a couple of days to do nothing but sightsee and ogle the landscape. Be ready to spot herds of elk and buffalo, as well as the occasional moose, antelope, trumpet swan, deer, and the grizzly bear.

For the most part, humans have little contact with the park's grizzlies, but prevention is still warranted, especially if hiking in the backcountry. Travel in groups, make lots of noise, and avoid known bear habitat. Visitor centers have useful advice and publications about how to avoid contact with bears. Give the same respect and consideration to the geothermal sites around the park.

Since fish are considered to be an integral part of the total ecosystem, no stocking takes place in the park. Opening and closing fishing dates protect the spawning natural populations of trout. Other restrictive management techniques include excluding the use of bait except on a few streams, placing size and limits of trout on certain streams and lakes, and enforcing catch-and-release fishing on many of the park fisheries.

The innovative fisheries management of Yellowstone National Park in particular, and the region in general, makes it possible for these wild trout to maintain healthy populations. Yellowstone National Park has the greatest concentration of wild native cutthroats in the world. Almost any stream or lake will surprise the fishermen with the colorful, hard-fighting strains of Yellowstone (and some westslope) cutthroat.

For years, it cost nothing to fish in the park, but anglers are now required to secure a Yellowstone National Park license and pay a small fee for a fishing permit. Anglers do not need a state fishing license. Fishing permits are available at all ranger stations, visitor centers, and Yellowstone Park General Stores.

Anglers sixteen years of age and older are required to purchase either a $10 ten-day or $20 season permit. Anglers who are age twelve to fifteen years are required to obtain a non-fee permit. Children eleven years of age or younger may fish without a permit if supervised by an adult.

You should also pick up a map of the park at the visitor center so you can have at hand all the fishable streams, which lakes hold fish and other important tidbits.

As of the summer of 2001, all native sport fish species in Yellowstone National Park became subject to catch-and-release-only fishing rules. The native species affected by this change are the cutthroat trout and its several subspecies, Montana grayling, and mountain whitefish.

The fishing season in the park begins on June 15 and ends October 31 on most waters. Anglers must use lead-free split-shot, jigs, and weights. There is a dizzying array of regulations so pick up park fishing regulations and make certain to look over the numerous restrictions which vary from stream to stream.

The park is divided into four sections by a network of roads called the Loop Roads.

1. **Northwest:** *West Entrance* (West Yellowstone, Montana) ▪ Madison Junction ▪ Norris Junction ▪ Canyon Junction ▪ Tower Junction ▪ Mammoth ▪ *North Entrance* (Gardiner, Montana)
2. **Northeast:** *East Entrance* ▪ Fishing Bridge ▪ Canyon Junction ▪ Tower Junction ▪ Mammoth ▪ *North Entrance* (Gardiner, Montana) ▪ Cody, Wyoming, is one hour east of YNP's East Entrance.

3. **Southeast:** *South Entrance* ▪ West Thumb ▪ Fishing Bridge ▪ *East Entrance* ▪ Jackson, Wyoming, is one hour south of YNP's South Entrance.

4. **Southwest:** *South Entrance* ▪ West Thumb ▪ Canyon Junction ▪ Norris Junction ▪ Madison Junction ▪ *West Entrance* (West Yellowstone, Montana).

General Park Information, 307-344-7381

AmFac In-Park Lodging, 307-344-7311

Advance Campground Reservations, 307-344-7381

Mailing address: National Park Service, Information Office/Chief Ranger's Office, PO Box 168, Yellowstone National Park, WY 82190

Lodging in the Park

Old Faithful Inn, open from early May to mid-October

Old Faithful Lodge Cabins, open from mid-May to mid-September

Old Faithful Snowlodge, open from mid-May to early October and from mid-December to mid-March

Lake Yellowstone Hotel, open from mid-May to the end of September

Lake Lodge Cabins, open from mid-June to mid-September

Grant Village Lodge, open from mid-May to mid-September

Canyon Village Lodge and Cabins, open from early June to the end of August

Roosevelt Lodge Cabins, open from early June to the end of August

Mammoth Hot Springs Hotel and Cabins, open from mid-May to early October and from mid-December to early March

Cities 5 to 10 Miles from the Park

Gardiner, Montana, 406-848-7971

West Yellowstone, Montana, 406-646-7701

Cooke City/Silver Gate, Montana, 406-838-2272

Cities Within a 2-hour Drive of the Park

Cody, Wyoming, 307-587-2297

Dubois, Wyoming, 307-455-2556

East Yellowstone/Wapiti Valley, Wyoming, 307-587-9595

Jackson, Wyoming, 307-733-3316

Big Sky, Montana, 800-943-4111

Billings, Montana, 406-245-4111

Bozeman, Montana, 406-586-5421

Livingston, Montana, 406-222-0850

Red Lodge, Montana, 406-446-1718

Idaho Falls, Idaho, 208-523-1010

Eastern Idaho Visitor Information Center, 800-634-3246

There are so many quality fly shops around Yellowstone National Park, there is not enough room to list all of them. Here are some of the top area fly shops:

Idaho: Henry's Fork Anglers, Inc., Michael Lawson, St. Anthony, 208-558-7525

Wyoming: Bressler Outfitters, Inc., Joe Bressler, Wilson, 307-733-6934 Westbank Anglers, Reynolds Pomeroy, Teton Village, 307-733-6483

Montana: Arrick's Fishing Flies, Arrick Swanson, West Yellowstone, 406-646-7290, Blue Ribbon Flies, Craig Mathews, West Yellowstone, 406-646-9365, Boyne U.S.A., John Kircher, Big

Sky, 406-995-5000, Bud Lilly's Trout Shop, Jim Criner, West Yellowstone, 406-646-7801, Gallatin River Guides, Steve French, Big Sky, 406-995-2290, Greater Yellowstone Flyfishers, Robert & Chad Olsen, Bozeman, 406-586-2489, Jacklin's, Inc., Bob Jacklin, West Yellowstone, 406-646-7336, Madison River Outfitters, Brad Richey, Yellowstone, 406-646-9644, Montana's Master Angler, Tom Travis, Livingston, 406-222-2273, Park's Fly Shop, Richard Parks, Gardiner, 406-848-7314, Yellowstone Angler, George Anderson, South Livingston, 406-222-7130

Bechler River

Beautiful river. Caught one of my biggest YNP non-cutthroat trout in the Bechler. In the southwest region of the park. Takes some considerable hiking (five miles) but can be worth it because it receives very little pressure. The river is deep and clear, with undercut banks, runs, meadow stretches. The river holds fish 10 to 15 inches with some lunkers.

Dries and typical patterns work on this river, but the biggest obstacle would be the mosquitos. They can be terrible. Everything is wet, standing water, marshy boggy areas. Still, the Bechler is hardly-fished and holds some big trout, and could be an option if runoff or rain has got fishermen by the neck in a different part of the park. Wildlife sightings are common on the river and on the trail. Wading requires caution because of the many deep holes. Lots of waterfalls, photo ops.

Cascade Creek

Meadow stream full of cutts in the north central part of the park. Take the Howard Eaton Trail one-half mile west of Canyon Junction. The stream parallels the trail more or less. Cascade Lake lies at the end of the trail about five miles in.

Fan Creek

West side of park, twenty-plus miles north of West Yellowstone. Reach this Gallatin feeder from Fawn Pass Trail onto the Sportsman Lake Trail. Fan Creek is a great place to see moose or bear. Fan Creek is a smallish meadow stream but holds some nice cutts and rainbows with a few solid browns, Fan Creek is a great place to catch pure-strain cutthroat trout. The best fishing is about three miles upstream from the Gallatin in a meadow stretch. Fan Creek Trail parallels the river and the trailhead is located at a pullout off Montana Highway 191. Expect 7- to 12-inch trout but don't be surprised, as I have been, by a 17- or 18-inch cutthroat pounding a hopper or ant pattern. Additional tributaries within the Park are Bacon Rind and Specimen creeks, which meet the Gallatin downstream from the mouth of Fan Creek. Expect small trout, but each stream's meadow stretch holds surprises.

Duck Creek

West side of park, up Highway 191, then east on Duck Creek Road. Wide, shallow stream that winds its way back and forth, slowly, through wide grassy fields. Most anglers bump nymphs up tight to the bank and on bottom to reach the athletic, big rainbows and browns and brook trout. Big wide fields, lazy curves. Duck is either on and the fish are feeding and being catchable or under the cuts and hiding wherein you have to dig them out. One of the prettiest rivers in the park.

Obsidian Creek

At Indian Creek Campground south of Mammoth near the Gardner River. Small brook trout for sure but it's a great place to teach kids how to fish. The river stops and starts in the down-timber forest then smoothes out through the open meadows.

Cougar Creek

On the west side of the park, take Highway 191 north, then east on Cougar Creek Road. Met a mad moose here a few years ago right when I hooked up with a nice brown (probably in the mid-teens). I don't know what was the bigger surprise—seeing the moose up so close all of a sudden or not catching the same little brookie I had caught at every slack bend pool. He crashed through the streamside brush and I ran a 9-flat 100.

Specimen Creek

Feeder stream to the Gallatin River. Take the Specimen Creek Trail from Highway 191 north of West Yellowstone. Fish this more for the thick brush scenery than the big fish. Catch rainbow and cutthroat hybrids in the two rugged forks of the creek.

Nez Perce Creek

Medium-size meadow stream that enters the Firehole River less than six miles south of Madison Junction. Fishing is good for brown trout and the occasional rainbow and brook trout. We've always seen bison in and around the stream. Concentrate on the water above the bridge to Spruce Creek (where you'll find fun fishing for small brookies and a few browns and rainbows). You can park at Fountain Flats Road and fish the four and a half miles upstream or take the Mary Mountain Trail. If you see Mary Lake on the map at the stream's headwaters, don't think of fishing it. It has no fish.

Cache Creek

In the northeast section of the park, on the Northeast Entrance Highway. Take the Lamar River Trail or Cache Creek Trail. Underfished even though its confluence with the Lamar lies near the highway. Anglers can expect to catch rainbow and cutthroat bigger than in many similar-sized streams.

Soda Butte Creek

In the northeast section of the park, this diverse stream parallels the Northeast Entrance Highway. Soda Butte Creek has lots of changing characteristics ranging from a bumpy run in its upper reaches to a wide, meadow stream as it meets up with the Lamar. The rainbows and cutts are above average in size. Awe. That's the word for the scenery.

Pebble Creek

A trib to Soda Butte and there are times when you can't tell which one you are on. A little bit of pressure because of the campground but the scenery is some of the tops and you can still catch lots of fish (not like the old days but still a lot).

Thorofare Creek

Any number of Upper Yellowstone streams like Thorofare Creek are wild and remote and are perfect-sized, loaded with trout fresh from spawning but you cannot fish them not until July 15. The pressure is almost nonexistent because the streams are in the smack-dab middle of bear country.

Upper Gibbon

At Virginia Meadows, at the Norris-Canyon Road river crossing on the downstream side. The brook trout are small but plump. This is a good place to learn how to cast or fly fish.

Others

Glen Creek, Indian Creek, Panther Creek, Blacktail Deer Creek, Hellroaring Creek, Aster Creek, Beaver Creek (near Heart Lake)

Most of the lakes in the park require a hike, and each has its own quality of fishing. A float tube is worthwhile on many of the lakes, if the fisherman doesn't mind hauling it into the backcountry several miles. Yellowstone Lake (88,000 acres) is the world's largest alpine lake, teeming with 15-inch heavy-bodied, buttery-colored native cut-

throat trout, fishable from the bank, from boat, and by wading out from shore. The lake is so deep, that most trout feed close to shore. Spin and fly fishermen alike enjoy success on this productive lake. Boaters beware the daily winds which whip up. This lake is cold, extremely cold, and you don't want to end up in the drink. Shoshone, Lewis, Grebe, Wolf, Cascade, Heart, and Trout Lakes are worthwhile angling destinations, with Wolf and Grebe Lakes offering grayling fishing. Yellowstone Park has a number of more lakes, most which take a hike to reach, so consult guidebooks and topographical maps.

Yellowstone Lake

At 87,450 acres, this is the largest alpine lake in the world. The sea-like lake averages 140 feet deep and at its deepest 320 feet. It's vast, like an ancient sea. Don't think you have to get out to the middle like so many neophytes do—you fish for cutts in close, cutts that are foraging, cruising.

This fishery is amazing, the best cutthroat factory in the world. Some of the monsters I've seen cruising the shallows would make you sweat. In the evenings, dimples from rises look like it's raining. The wind is bad a lot of the time but fish still feed.

Fun time: You can stalk trout.

You'll be surprised by how many are on the lake but not fishing, just taking in the scenery. If you are in a boat, check out the shoreline and the backbays. You can float tube the lake but the wind really makes it tough unless you find a sheltered area.

Shoshone Lake

Shoshone Lake is a big lake for the park, coming in at 8,050 acres, deep, too, with depths of nearly 200 feet. The lake is remote (as in very remote) but is ideal for backpacking, accessible by three trails. You catch brook, cutthroat, and brown trout mostly with lots of lakers, too. I recommend fishing the channel in the fall when they move from Shoshone to Lewis Lake (Lewis Channel). You can fish from shore or from a float tube. Check this out—you can paddle to Shoshone from Lewis Lake. Cool, huh?

Cascade Lake

Anglers can take either of two trails to reach here—two and a half miles each, both pretty flat and easy. You'll be hiking to catch grayling and cutthroats but beware, this lake can get windy. I once saw an osprey take a fish on Cascade; it just swooped down, splash, and talons full of trout. I like the Cascade Creek trail up to its headwaters. Cutts are about 10 to 13 inches but the osprey pulled out one bigger than that. Grayling a bit less in size but iridescent.

Trout Lake

Close to Lamar and Soda Butte, Trout Lake lies in a big meadow. This is a fishery where the cutts and bows get big, 14 to 18 inches and 3 or 4 pounds (and bigger). Like many park lakes, Trout Lakes gets windy at times. Great for float tubes (but you must get a boating permit) and

about as picturesque as it gets with Mt. Hornaday in the background. The trail is less than a mile long but steep and it winds through scenic high country. Go after July 15 because most of the cutts are spawning in the outlet.

Grebe Lake

Mosquitos will eat you up at times at Grebe. Easy to reach Grebe on a three-mile trail. Float tubes are ideal, so just strap it on your back and hike up the easy trail. This is your best shot in the lower forty-eight to catch a grayling in this lake that sits in tall grassy meadows slash marsh. The Grebe is the headwater of the Gibbon River. And it has rainbow trout, too, in case you're interested. Wolf Lake is just another two miles beyond Grebe Lake and this gem holds both rainbow trout and grayling. Grizzly Lake is located in the northeast section, full of brook trout. Grizzly is fun and a good choice for beginners. Joffe Lake, close to Mammoth, is just chock-full of brookies, and is also great for kids and beginners.

Heart Lake

This eight-mile hike takes you about halfway between Yellowstone Lake and South border. You'll have to spend the night because it's not a day trip. It's a real trip into the backcountry but worth it because of the big trout, large cutts, and lake trout. You can even, at times, take lakers on dries. You are in with the bears so be alert and smart. This is really worth the hike.

Lewis Lake

In southern part of the park, Lewis Lake holds brook, brown, cutthroat, and lake trout. One of only two lakes that allow motorized watercraft (Yellowstone is the other). Lewis is one of your better big fish lakes.

McBride Lake

Close to Slough Creek's First Meadow, full of cutthroats. McBride Lake is difficult to reach, with not many anglers because it's an unmarked trail. When you get there, if you get there, it's easy pickin's.

Practicalities

Species: brook, cutthroat, rainbow, some browns, and maybe even a grayling if you're lucky. You might catch a whitefish if you're unlucky.

Gear: Lightweight rod 2- to 4-weight but even a 5-weight would be fine. Leave the 6-weight in the car. Hip waders or just wading boots and Neoprene socks would work well. Fanny pack (first aid, flies, tippet, lunch, water, polarized sunglasses, insect repellant), weather gear for rain and cold. Bring a bear whistle, bear bell, and even bear spray.

Permits, regs: It is a good idea (ought to be a requirement) to read through the fishing regulations of Yellowstone National Park. The streams and lakes are under a dizzying web of varying regulations and restrictions. Some rivers are permanently closed, others have sections permanently closed, while other streams are not fishable until certain dates. Few streams allow keeping cutthroats although brook, brown, and rainbow trout have size and creel limitations. Only four streams in the entire park allow the use of bait. So do yourself and the park a favor, and familiarize yourself with the rules.

Any person twelve years of age or older fishing in the park is required to have a valid Yellowstone National Park fishing permit. The permit must be signed. For anyone sixteen years of age or older, a permit fee is charged (minimal charge of $20.00 for a season, $10 for a week). When supervised by an adult, children eleven years of age or younger may fish without a permit.

The park has four streams that have special regulations for children. At Obsidian, Panther, and Indian Creeks and part of the Gardner River near Norris-Mammoth Crossing, kids eleven and younger may fish with bait.

The general fishing season in Yellowstone National Park is open each day from 5:00AM to 10:00PM, beginning on the Saturday of Memorial Day weekend through and including the first Sunday in November. There are several exceptions to the general opening date so check the regulations (which are almost all tied into cutthroat spawning).

Anglers may not use toxic weights (jigs, lead split shot, softweight ribbon) in the park. Only nontoxic weights may be used.

Reasons for fishing smaller park streams

Gets you in practice for the big streams
See country most don't see

Intimate

Sometimes challenging but often easy pickins'

Perfect for beginners

Perfect for families

Perfect for dry fly purists

Perfect for teaching someone

Perfect for getting away from the crowds

Perfect for fishing to trout that might not have seen an angler all season

Perfect for defeating runoff. They give you a second choice, an adjunct trip to the big river.

Perfect for traveling light (no vest)

Tactics and strategies

The fish aren't all that much smaller and are the same size in some cases. The main stem of the Gibbon River doesn't produce big fish. The feeders to the Firehole have fish that move up during summer when the main river heats up.

And streams like Soda Butte, Cache, Slough, and Duck Creeks hold some big trout.

Hatches are less important but don't totally discount them.

These fish see few anglers and are not as skittish (except when it's shallow and clear, as on Slough Creek).

Don't go a-fishin' up just any creek without knowing if it is fishless, where it goes, without letting someone know where you are—some streams have no fish.

Lots of these small streams come from

or are near lakes, ideal for taking lunch or varying the fishing.

Think dry flies, light leaders, stalking, kneeling, varied casts, staying low, and dapping.

Go with a buddy.

Yellowstone River

This mighty river runs thirty-five miles north to the boundary from Inspiration Point and offers some of the best angling in the park. If you want to hike into the canyon, it is a descent of 1,500 feet, but the payoff is getting to fish for the biggest fish in the park. This area is spectacular, dramatic scenery.

Further downstream around Tower Junction into the Black Canyon of the Yellowstone, the scenery compares favorably to the Grand Canyon section. The descent is less strenuous, and the fish are still big. Can't really wade these parts, rather you have to fish them from the bank. Like the Grand Canyon stretch, anglers will find lots of pocket water and of course, big fish. The hike is around a half-hour to two hours to reach the river. Near Mammoth, the river leaves the canyon and offers easy access.

The Yellowstone River is a big, complex, wild river that often intimidates anglers because of its 150 to 400 foot wide stretches, its greenish-blue deep, swift waters, and the abundance of aquatic food available to the native cutthroat, brown, rainbow, and brook trout inhabiting the depths. From the Yellowstone National Park boundary, the undammed pristine river provides at least 120 miles of high quality trout fishing in some of the most scenic places in the West. This is a difficult river to read, but if fishermen fish the edges, fish around boulders, in the seams, in the back eddies, in the riffles, along different currents, and around structure—in other words, break the big river down into smaller more manageable components—then the Yellowstone can prove to be one of the more rewarding experiences an angler can have.

The Yellowstone is fishable all year long, but the types of fishing depend on the month. The only month usually not fishable is June, at the hefight of spring run-off, and although this is a later runoff for a large trophy trout stream, it means that the river is good when other rivers are suffering from low water and high temperatures. In the early spring, before runoff, large weighted nymphs and stonefly patterns will catch fish. During runoff, the salmonfly hatch occurs, a hatch that is often difficult to follow or find, but for those who do locate this phenomenon, the sight of 5-pound cutthroat slashing the surface in a race with other big trout for the three inch salmonflies will give goosebumps. Bring several versions of salmonfly patterns, in both dry and nymph forms, to best match this exhilarating hatch. Caddis and mayfly hatches come and go through July and August, but the Yellowstone doesn't require matching the hatch, as high-riding attractor flies will do the trick. Wulffs, Humpies, Trudes, Adams, and Goofus all work well. In the later days of summer, grasshopper patterns are effective, and in fact, certain patterns, like a Dave's Hopper, will fool trout all summer.

Do not discount dapping dry flies in the winter, for many anglers fish with the midge hatches of February and March with snow on the banks. Muddler Minnow patterns, both wet and dry, are one of the best all-around flies on the Yellowstone, acting as a surface critter, and imitating the bountiful sculpin underwater. Wet fly patterns worked on the Yellowstone for decades, but the substitute nowadays is to use Woolly Buggers, leeches, and other streamer/nymph patterns. Wet flies can sometimes be a killer in the right hands.

Since the Yellowstone is such a big river, covering as much water as possible will translate to success. Covering a lot of water means that fishermen will have to make hundreds of casts, and that means no 7-foot whippy rods or else someone's arm will fall off. This big-boy river requires big tackle. For dry fly fishing, a 9-foot, 6- or 7-weight rod outfit is best, and for nymphing, a 9½ foot, 9- or 10-weight outfit. Sinking lines or tips help get the flies deep quickly. The bigger tackle also helps fight the furious winds which whip up much of the summer. Spinfishermen need to cast to the stiller waters, otherwise their quick retrieves will not allow the lures to sink deep enough to reach fish. The Thomas Cyclone, Daredevil, and Panther Martins are the anglers' favorites for the Yellowstone.

Because the Yellowstone has walkable, stable banks, and because the trout tend to congregate within casting distance of shore, bank fishing is popular. Because the Yellowstone has walkable, stable banks, and grizzly bears love the Yellowstone River area, you need to do your grizzly-bear-avoidance thing.

The most effective way to cover a lot of the water, and awesome scenery, is by float fishing. There are several put-in points along its course, and I would recommend a guide for your first trip, but the Yellowstone River doesn't require a high-level oarsman, except during runoff and you definitely need a guide if the river's running high.

Hotspots: From the canyon to the lake, the river is often crowded, but when you stand in the middle of the river at Buffalo Ford and big fish nip at your waders searching for food, it is worth fighting the other fishermen. Remember that trout on the Yellowstone River average 17 inches. The river from Tower Junction to Mammoth is primarily stonefly and caddis water. The best part of the river in the park, Buffalo Ford, does not open up until July 15. *Species:* Yellowstone cutthroat, rainbow, whitefish, and some brook trout. *Tackle and techniques:* Respect this river, especially in the canyon sections, because the currents are powerful, the dropoffs and holes, deep.

Flies: Think stoneflies and big attractor patterns. *Regulations:* All tributaries to Yellowstone Lake do not open until July 15 to help protect cutthroat spawning and to prevent human-bear confrontations. Be sure to check regulations for closures. There are several sections on the Yellowstone River which are permanently closed to fishing such as the dangerous LeHardy Rapids section. *Directions:* The Yellowstone bisects the park from south to north and while the road from the lake does parallel the river more or less, much of the river can only be reached by walking/hiking.

The Black Canyon of the Yellowstone River

You'll hear veteran anglers from Montana or Wyoming tell you over a cup of coffee, and with complete sincerity, that they have chased the mighty salmonfly hatch up and down rivers for the last twenty years and never caught it just right.

Oh sure, they've fished over water where the remnant shells of the *Pteronarcys californica* were attached to overhanging alders and the occasional trout ravaged the surface for the big offering.

But the creases in their faces tell you that the stories of tossing Sofa Pillows onto the water indiscriminately and having big trout, lunkers mind you, fight off other lunkers for the right to swallow these two-inch flies, are the stuff dreams are made of.

I have caught the salmonfly dream hatch. I caught the dream when I wasn't chasing it and the dream was big, the dream of a lifetime. Sounds corny, I know. You should've been there.

Yellowstone National Park, 1990. Fourteen days in the park, fishing whatever famous stream struck our fancy. The four of us decided over the campfire that the next day's fancy was the Black Canyon of the Yellowstone, a one- to two-hour hike into some of the wildest terrain in the country, one of the best undiscovered and unknown angling destinations in the world.

David and Kenny, my most frequent fishing buddies (and brothers-in-law), led the way along Hellroaring Creek Trail, slogging down the hill in the drizzle. I hung back with my friend Woody, in his late forties and carrying way too much stuff in his

Descending the trail into the canyon

backpack. The rising sun cut through the clouds and heated up the morning.

Woody is anal. He likes things his way or the highway, that kind of guy. Good guy but demanding. It's why he's successful in business. Dave and Kenny don't take kindly to orders or order. They like freedom and chaos. Woody organized dinner at camp into phases, gave each of us duties, barked out commands, even complained when we didn't cut up the potatoes a certain way. His Suburban was packed to the brim, a smaller version of his house, I guess. His backpack was a smaller version of his Suburban which was a smaller version of his house.

Woody ain't in great shape. A decade later, something we wouldn't know at the time, he would have quadruple bypass (maybe even quintiple) surgery and nearly

die. I still talk to him and he's doing fine today. But at that time, which in this book is *this* time, he was huffing and puffing and at the start of the hike, very alive, burdened as he was with his 75-pound backpack. Descending trail. Easy hiking. Except that Woody was top-heavy and nearly went over a couple of times.

When we reached the river, we were tired and ready to fish. We never even had a chance to shake the willows to see if the salmonflies would sputter out. The clouds of fat insects descended on the river like a settling fog.

The salmonfly is orange and salmon in color, about two inches long, plump as your thumb. These prehistoric-looking creatures are so clumsy and odd-shaped that they look like they were put together with spare insect parts. Their flight is a series of random leaps and jerks, splatting down on the water so hard they often splash.

We tied on big salmonfly patterns, Sofa Pillows, and Stimulators, sizes 2 and 4. The salmonflies had been landing in the middle of the current along the near bank so we spread out and cast our imitations (slung would be more the word) into the run.

Every cast caught a trout. I am not lying. These were cutthroats and big ones at that, averaging 18 to 22 inches with broad shoulders.

Each of us yelped from time to time as a really big one exploded from the depths to chomp off our floating pattern. I hooked and landed one trout that measured 25 inches.

We each lost bigger ones than that.

We fished for several hours and got tired. The current is strong in this big river and it was taking several minutes to land each fish. We ate lunch, debated on whether or not to head on back. Each of us had caught and released forty or more fat trout.

How do you leave a scene like that?

We didn't. Would you believe we each ran out of salmonfly patterns? The trout either tore up everything we had or ripped it off.

Here's the weird part: Woody wanted to leave.

We said no way. We're catching monstrous fish with huge-ass flies on a wilderness river. Shut up already.

Dinner. We've got to get back and start dinner.

Did I mention that Woody wasn't catching as many fish as we were?

Pteronarcys californica, this clumsy chunky orange insect causes havoc on the river.

Woody is a very good fly fisher and has caught lots of big fish but that day was not his day. And he had lost a big trout when Kenny tried to help him net the whopper he was playing (or more correctly, that was playing him). So he was slightly bent out of shape. Red in the face. Fished off by himself for a while. Kenny felt bad about it for days but didn't know what else different he could have done.

As we were casting to still-rising leviathans, Woody started tossing rocks where the fish rose.

Seriously.

Kenny is a high school wrestling coach and Dave is wiry and neither is a stranger to scrapping. It was all I could do to talk them out of making Woody into bear bait. I yelled some things at Woody (to save his life) and we kept fishing, catching but the mood was odd. At least he quit throwing rocks at the fish.

The cutts wouldn't chase a size-12 Orange Stimulator either, much preferring the chunky delicacy to the smaller snack or other fat patterns. So when we ran out of patterns that favored the hummingbird-sized salmonflies, we hiked back out. Ascending trail. Difficult hiking. Woody nearly keeled over backwards a couple of times. Dave and Kenny were way ahead, I stayed back with Woody. I thought the poor guy was gonna die.

He didn't.

In the cold of the night, we sat around the campfire 'til the early hours of the morning, trying to comprehend how we had been so fortunate as to enter this kind of fairy-tale angler's day. Woody went to bed around midnight. We stayed up with strong coffee and cigars until the fire died down and it got cold as hell.

We've each told our various versions of the eight hours on the Yellowstone so many times around other campfires that what really happened that day is fuzzy, sort of like a dream. I know I am not absolutely positive about every single detail any more. I also know that Woody's version is short a few details I am sure about, but his story is just as warm and cozy and dream-like. Just different.

But we all do agree that that day was as real as the heat from the fire, and three of us believe the version I just told you is as accurate as we can recollect. From time to time, we even admit we still dream about that day.

Firehole River

You've seen the pictures. The eerie steam rising from the river. Boiling hot water flowing from a bubbling pot emptying into the winding stream. Buffalo feeding on the banks just over your shoulder. Big fish caught on impossibly small flies. It's all true. The Firehole is otherworldy.

The Firehole is one of those rivers that when you first see it, you lose your breath. For one thing, the smell is a little overwhelming at first. The other thing is that you are now fishing in one of the most scenic unusual spots on the planet Earth.

The Firehole is one of the classic streams, legendary through performance and fishing mythology, made more so by its eerie appearance with its steaming geysers and fumaroles, the sulphur smell, and the river's snakey course.

You fish it and you're so taken with its uniqueness, with its otherworldliness, with worrying you might step through thin crust and burn your leg off, that you don't really care if you catch fish anyway. You're just glad to be there.

A decade ago, Kenny and I are at one of the geysers near the Firehole, taking pics and taking it all in. We are fascinated every time; the park has a hold on us. So there we are and a dude walks up to a steaming geyser pool, looks at his friends, sticks his hand in the pool and his laugh turned to a scream. He went running to the parking lot, his friends running after him, and we could only guess that they were off to a first-aid station. It shouldn't take sticking a body part in a heated pool to figure out they are dangerously hot.

The Firehole has a variety of water types ranging from pocket water, deep banks, and the famous meadow stretches. The water can reach upper 70s, even 80 degrees, making fishing difficult if not impossible by late summer. The Firehole fishes best early and late in the season because of the increased water temperatures. I've seen days in May and June when the hatches were so good, the fish in such a splashy frenzy, that you could stand on the bank and watch no fewer than five to ten fish rising (almost jumping out of the water) at any one second in a twenty-yard stretch. The water was alive with feeding fish (anyone say caddis emergence?).

I like the canyon stretch too because the water seems cooler and there are fewer anglers. Pocket water in the canyon makes it easier to figure out where the trout are in wait. In the meadows, wade carefully and don't forget to cast (carefully and closely) to the banks.

Overall, this is one tough river to fish. At times, the fish are gone, upstream to colder water. When you find the fish, they're usually skeptical, cautious. Rainbows, browns and they are educated. There are no lunkers and the trout average only 9 to 12 inches. If you catch a huge one from the Firehole, you'll be looking at a 3-pounder.

Concentrate on deeper water and near the incoming streams like Iron Springs Creek and the Little Firehole and Nez Perce Creek. You can fish up either of those because when the water gets too hot, the fish move up into these feeders. Fish the banks, the riffles and glides (if deep enough), and enjoy the most scenic river in the park. The fishing pressure is heavy. You always see an angler near a cloud of hot fog coming up from the river, looking like an old Abercrombie and Fitch poster. *Directions*: Anglers have excellent road access since the Grand Loop parallels almost the entire river. Access is great.

Gallatin River

One summer, the two of us split up from Kenny and David leaving them in the meadows the Gallatin while we went to Cougar Creek. Woody and I caught a few smallish cutthroats and brookies in the turning slow waters of Cougar Creek, fought off the charge of a cow moose with yearling, and got eaten alive by mosquitos while Kenny and David enjoyed three hours of closing evening on the Gallatin with the finest hatches and rises they'd ever experienced.

Between them, they claimed they'd caught upwards of fifty to sixty nice-sized trout, 11 to 17 inches long, four species of trout and including whitefish and if that wasn't enough, they'd seen no fewer than five crazy-intense hatches over that same three hours. Should've been here. Fishing action of a lifetime.

Yeah, right.

We got the film developed that next morning and we hated them. All true.

This winding river is just plain fun. Anglers can cover the river easily with a fly rod with no trees on the river to hinder backcasts. Most of the fishing occurs along the highway. The river meanders back and forth and runs about twenty-five to fifty feet wide. This is easy and relaxing fishing, one of the best dry fly rivers in the park. This is a good midday or all-day option.

Not much hiking required except that

which one hikes along the river, and from the road. Fishermen can hike on trails to get to the upper reaches.

Because it's not easy to get to if you're staying in the park, the fishing pressure is light. The Gallatin is thought by most to hold small fish, and while to some degree this is true, there are some nice-sized fish especially in the bend pools and downstream where the river straightens out and gets choppy. In the uppers, the water is easy to read, the trout right where you think they are and if you present your fly well, easy to catch. *Directions:* The only problem is getting there. Anglers must drive to West Park Entrance, out of park, go north on 191 for eleven miles to reenter park, then drive on for another twenty-four miles to reach the Gallatin.

Gardner River

Located in the northwest section of the park, the Gardner is a classic pocket-water stream. The Gardner has an awful lot of fast, broken water with lots of rocks holding trout all around them. The river is on the shallow side, ideal for dry fly fishing.

The lower end of the river has rainbows, browns, and brook trout averaging 9 to 12 inches, and the best stretch is that water just up from the park boundary. There's a trail going into Gardner Canyon and you'll usually have the river to yourself. I have caught one 17-inch rainbow in this section and have seen some similar-sized trout finning. I like to toss dries in the pockets and riffles but I keep an eye out for flat water where I can sightcast to a bigger trout. A dropper rig works well for me on the Gardner.

Usually good in June when it starts to clear, the Gardner is a good way to get away from all the pressure on the bigger-named rivers of the park. High floating flies, like hoppers and Wulffs and large weighted nymphs, are the ticket here. The lower

stretch is accessible by car and trail; the upper section above Osprey Falls by trail only. In the lower section, large stoneflies (dry and nymphs) will bring savage strikes. Cautious angling can make for twenty to thirty fish days in the right conditions.

Gibbon River

The Gibbon is a good first-day river to fish, especially the upper and middle sections, since most anglers need some practice time to get the kinks worked out. The river is medium-sized and easy to wade. Below Gibbon Falls, fishermen can find some secluded pools and runs, and canyon fishing, so they can get used to all the water they'll be fishing over the week.

In the upper reaches, the Gibbon is a beautiful mountain stream, full of eager decent-sized brook trout and the surprisingly easy-to-catch grayling. In Elk Park, anglers might find some large trout in the pools and deep runs. At National Park Meadows (near the junction of the Gibbon and Firehole) there are legendary big trout but spotty areas, areas that are inconsistent. Lots of big fish but tough to catch. Below the falls, big trout will sneak a strike at streamers, but if you catch them they can be hard to land.

Below Gibbon Falls (an eighty-four-foot drop), the river rushes up around the huge rocks, offering the angler plenty of pocket water and nice pools. Below the falls, big trout will sneak a strike at streamers, but if you catch them, they can be hard to land as they like to dive under rocks and dash downstream.

Three of us moved up this part of the river, putting in a mile below the Falls and wading up. The water was strong, the rocks slippery, and despite the fact it was the middle of a bright day, everything was dark in this canyon. We got to one spot where the only way to keep moving upriver was to

straddle a fallen tree that lay across a deep blue pool. Everything else was too deep and powerful to wade. The fallen tree lay close enough to the sheer cliff that once one of us could begin crossing, he could lean forward and use the cliff with his hands to shuffle across.

This is one of those situations we all have in our lives, one of those places we've seen before with the Keystone Cops and on *Amazing Home Videos*. A skinny-ass little dead tree over a big deep deep pool and you have to lean forward, hands against a slick forty-foot cliff. This was no different than the guy knocking out the support on an overhang with a sledgehammer while he himself is stupidly under the overhanging porch; no different than Charlie Brown kicking the field goal with Lucy holding; as predictable as Wile E. Coyote lighting the fuse to an Acme Rocket.

The skinny-ass little dead tree cracked in half as I was halfway across the big deep deep blue cold pool. I went in chest first and the only thing that kept me from losing

both my life and my rod was the fact that the water was so cold and deep and scary that I pitched my rod to Kenny and David and came out of the pool like a wet cat all in the same motion. Wile E. Coyote soaking wet, waders filled and all. I'm surprised Kenny caught my 9-foot Hexagraph rod because he and David were doubled over in laughter.

Karma was alive and well that day. I caught a 2-pound brown on a bucktail streamer, an orange-spotted brown that attacked the fly like a barracuda. Biggest fish of the day. They said they'd take that trade-off any day.

Further downstream, the Gibbon spreads out and deepens, still easy water, with meadow fishing and canyons. There are undercut banks, deep pools, shallow riffles and runs and glassy smooth water, all kinds of productive water.

Section of the park: West. *Species:* Grayling in the uppermost section, brown, rainbow, brook trout. *Hotspots:* In Elk Park, lunkers hide in the pools and deep runs but are near to impossible to catch without a good hatch. At National Park Meadows (near the junction of the Gibbon and Firehole) there are legendary big trout but spotty areas, areas which are inconsistent. Lots of big fish but tough to catch. The upper section is riffle-run, and a few pools, mostly in meadow stretches. *Tackle and techniques:* Wear chest waders if you are getting into the deep water. Neoprene okay but lightweight waders are fine in midsummer. Use light leaders and tippets.

Flies: One of the better dry fly rivers in the park. Need to fish heavy, big nymphs in the deep pools. Small dry flies to match the hatch in the slower sections, big streamers in the heavier water. *Regulations:* Below the falls is fly fishing only. *Directions:* Grand Loop Road runs along most of it.

Hebgen Lake

- **Location:** West of the park, in Montana, along Highway 287
- **What You Fish For:** Rainbow, brown, cutthroat trout
- **Highlights and Notables:** Classic Western lake known for large trout that "gulp" insects

You'd be hard-pressed to find a more complete trout lake. Not too big but big enough. Alpine lake but not so high up that you have only a two-month season. Great scenery with lots of mountains all around. Large trout in at three flavors: how about cutthroat, rainbow, and brown trout. Let's make these fish big and . . . mmm . . . make them willingly sip on dry flies. We'll need great hatches in that case. And good habitat and structure and fertility.

Hebgen Lake, created at your request.

You may know of this lake already. Only ten miles from Yellowstone National Park, Hebgen is the one they call the "Gulper Lake." Some say this is the best dry fly fishing lake in the country. Anglers seem to like catching browns and rainbows from 1 to 5 pounds, cutthroats 1 to 2 pounds, maneuvering the bays in their float tubes.

The mountains come right up to the edge of the lake, ringing the sixteen-mile long lake on the Madison River. You might see an osprey nest in one of the trees like I have many times and you might see an osprey diving for trout, like I have and you might, like I have, be jealous of the size of trout that the osprey is carrying away.

The upper bays and creek mouths are local faves but you'll see anglers on the shore and boats trolling in the middle of the lake. Lots of float-tubing water but it's often windy; you can find sheltered bays and you can also use pontoon boats or other sturdier personal watercrafts or boats.

There are not many, if any, trout lakes in America that have more special and profound hatches than on Hebgen. Chironomid (aka The Midge), Trico, callibaetis but also caddis flies (always flitting around in summer). The chironomid are good-sized early in the season and a good way to imitate them is the Midge Cluster or Griffith's Gnat. The Trico and callibaetis are the insects the trout gulp. You can hear the gulp, sort of an audible sigh, trout comfort food. Visit two or three fly shops in West Yellowstone and ask the local experts what flies they recommend for Hebgen. There are quite a variety of "gulper" patterns and other flies peculiar to the needs of the Hebgen trout.

Hebgen Lake may have great dry fly fishing for a lake, but the angling is still technical and tough. If you dry fly fish, you'll be sightcasting to rising fish. Short of rising trout, you need to work emergers and pupa and streamers and other nymphs.

If you are not a fly fisher, don't give up hope. Many non-fly fishers do well trolling. They do well with rapalas and Panther

Martins and jigs. There are so many trout, so many big trout, that you can always find a way to skin this cat (not Schrodinger's). Either way, you'll find that Hebgen trout don't stay in one place and it's one reason why float tubers don't do as well consistently. You have to follow the fish.

Hebgen Lake has campgrounds but if you don't want to rough it, West Yellowstone is the place to stay, with any and all kind of lodging to meet any budget or desire. Access to Hebgen Lake is excellent. Highway 287 parallels Hebgen Lake for much of its length on the north side, allowing for easy road access. Additionally, several other roads provide access to the south side of the lake, where numerous campgrounds are also found.

Lamar River

Paradise Valley. Few valleys in the world are as scenic as the glacially-formed Lamar. In between forested mountains, meadows carpet the valley as the blue Lamar pulses in lazy curves back and forth on its way to the Yellowstone River. Irregular smooth green-brown hills run beside the river like sleeping gods.

The Lamar River is a mysterious river.

It's not that I have any crazy stories to tell about this freestone stream in the under-touristed northeast part of the park, because I don't. I always have a great time here, a peaceful long day. The Lamar doesn't get ready for fishing until all the others in the park have confessed. The mystery is why more people don't rank the Lamar with all the other fabled Yellowstone rivers. The Lamar is sick. Sick in the way that teenagers say it today (phat is so last decade, Dad), which means kick-ass. The Lamar's trout are heavy-bodied and average about 13 to 15 inches long, which ranks with the other rivers in the park. Most of the cutthroats we catch are 15 inches, the rainbows and cuttbows are about 16 inches, so I don't know why it doesn't get more press (but I'm glad).

The Lamar is mysterious as well because if there's any rain or sleet or hail or drizzle anywhere around, the river muddies up with silt. The river can be flowing clear and then it storms out of sight, up high, and before you know it, the river is running cloudy and the fish have turned off.

So you have meadows. You also have gravel bars and undercut banks and riffles and runs and wildlife. It's rare that I fish the Lamar and don't see elk or bison and a couple of times, heartbeat heartbeat, I've seen a grizzly lumbering along the treeline in the distance. And you have solitude especially compared to the other high-traffic park waters.

You can wade and you'll want to wade because it's such a wadeable river but you shouldn't wade the Lamar. The fish are spooky and they're in skinny water and there's not many deep holes for them to hide—they are holding against the banks and in the pocket water, around boulders and not as much in the riffles like you've been taught in Reading Water 101.

Watch your shadows, your footfalls and you'll be surprised—you don't think that with a western freestone rowdy shallow river like this you'd need to use long leaders and be so stealthy but you do if you want to max your chances. You have to watch for fish. Pay attention ahead of where you are walking (or crawling). Get your flies to the deep runs against the banks. You can also sightcast more than you think—watch another twenty to thirty yards ahead than you think. When you see a deep run, work it—it will hold several fish and the biggest in that stretch. Ditto for pools.

It's a better nymph river than you'd believe. Tie on dry flies with droppers, bounce nymphs off the bottom, work terrestrials close the grassy banks (grasshoppers and crickets especially). Sure, there are periods of time, days when dries work well, but consistently, you'll do better with nymphs. The salmonfly hatch in July can be great dry fly fishing but that goes without saying, right?

This is an enigmatic river, subject to runoff and rain, at times easy to fish, other times frustratingly impossible. Still, it is an underfished, often great trout fishery and (hint, hint) one of the best fisheries in the West come autumn.

Madison River

David rested on his elbow on the banks of the Madison like a shah watching his harem dance. He has that way about him. Woody Vogt was in the middle of the Madison casting from riffle to riffle. Kenny was downstream wading up, his goofy grin showing under the brim of his straw cowboy hat. I had the camera in hand, waiting. We were waiting for something to happen on the Madison. Something always seems to happen on this fabled river.

The first place a buffalo charged me was along the Madison in the park. Bluff charge, they call it. Scared the hell outta

me. I was sightcasting to feeding 10-inchers in the placid waters of the meadows when the one prone dusty buffalo I had been earlier taking pictures of decided that he'd had enough of me usurping his paradise.

Early July in the '90s, we saw eight to ten bison swim across the Madison and later I wondered if they stepped on any fish. Three years later, I saw a cow and calf swim across the Madison. I know it shouldn't seem like a big deal to watch buffalo swim but tell me honestly, have you ever seen it in person?

One time a father and young son were fishing in the park, close to where we were fishing and it was obvious they were newbies so we went over and helped. The father knew nothing about fly fishing and was relieved, glad for the help. His thirteen-year-old was decked out in discount gear but was lacking the right flies and didn't know how to cast.

For the next couple of hours, we gave him the abbreviated version of how to fly fish—we coached him, instructed him, taught him to tie a couple of knots and Kenny helped him bring in his first trout, a magnificent 8-inch rainbow so we all whooped it up and the kid had a smile as big as Texas. Then we found an extra fly box, donated ten or so flies each to make thirty and the kid was on his way. The father shook our hands entirely too eagerly, thankful thankful thankful. Something always happens on the Madison.

Here is maybe the most famous river in the West. In the park, the river has two distinct personalities. In the upper half, the river is characterized by weedy channels, pocket water, deep water, flats, gravel bars, downed trees, thick weed beds, big boulders, ledge banks, and more weed beds. The surface is often glassy, indecipherable.

In the lower half, the Madison runs out of the park and the river is wide and fast, a current of quick riffles but still chock-full of weeds and structure (fallen logs, big rocks, not many pools).

Created by the confluence of the Gibbon and Firehole Rivers, the Madison flows for another 140 miles where it ends in namesake after it joins the Gallatin and Jefferson to form the Missouri River.

For trout cover, the Madison outside the park has pocket water, riffles, eddies, undercut banks, boulders, underwater structure, side channels, braids, beaver ponds, and more. Not many deep pools. Typically, the river has movement, and is rarely slow, meaning that these fish have lots of well-oxygenated water and resulting energy. Don't be surprised when these trout take enough line off the reel to go into the backing, and cause your palms to sweat. The river flows through a wide valley coming out of the park, through ranchlands, and through a canyon, all the while with mountain ranges rising up on either side.

Out of the park, the Madison trout isn't always turned off by awkward presentations, and in fact, might investigate the fly for several passes before either sucking it down or being spooked. The water moves along at such a quick clip that they can't afford to be too picky or the food they see will pass them by. Short, upstream casts are all an angler needs for technique, since a long cast will inevitably cross a multitude of cross currents, and the fly will be dragged and swung and will be little more than an ornament on the end of the line.

If you are floating the river, you'll probably be casting to the bankside runs, landing flies on the edges of the current, dropping flies near the few, big instream boulders. Beginning fishers can do well on the river, tossing big attractor dry flies onto riffles, and reasonably expecting to land several 12- to 14-inch trout during the day, but to catch the bigger trout, well-seasoned fishermen match the hatches with the smaller flies, fish with nymphs, emergers, and wet flies, or try innovative patterns.

The big river supports an amazing number of trout, and an even more amazing number of trout fishermen. Madison is famous but its fish aren't necessarily big by Western standards—10 to 13 inches on average with a big one coming in at 17 to 18 inches. The river's 12-inch rainbows are fat and deep. Madison River saw whirling disease affect its population fifteen years ago but has recovered nicely.

The Madison River has a variety of characteristics and water types, insect hatches, and moods. One could fish any mile section of the river for a year and still not know it fully. The river's trout are plentiful and often finicky, sometimes requiring match-the-hatch angling from an increasingly sophisticated fishing crowd. But part of the charm of the river is that in some areas, attractor patterns work better than close imitations. Fat trout respond eagerly to salmonfly patterns as big as pillows when the famous stonefly hatch is on. Beetles, ants, and hoppers thrown against the banks in the meadow sections are deadlier than any other. Large streamers stripped in during fall's spawning run yields trophy brown trout.

So the river is many things for many people. If you want it to be gulper stream, head to the Hebgen area. If you want to toss salmonfly patterns to bigger trout, then get to the river at the end of June and while away the hours chasing the durned hatch. I like fishing in the park not far from where the Gibbon and Firehole join to form the Madison. The scenery is overwhelming, the water flat and challenging and the trout demand your best game. *Directions:* Main park road follows the river for twelve of its fourteen miles in the park.

Slough Creek

The park ranger we met at First Meadow on Slough Creek wore his shorts (a little too short) and his short-sleeved shirt (cuffed) like he designed the uniform. Comfortable in his skin. He knew everything about anything to do with the park. He knew where this bear roamed and that section of river held this kind of trout and just about anything else we asked. But our most important question was:

"WHAT CAN WE DO TO GET THESE STUPID HORSEFLIES FROM BITING US AND RIPPING OUR SKIN OFF?!!"

The park ranger was one of those sneaky confident quiet types. He asked if we had bothered to put on any insect repellant and the four of us nodded because as we talked to him the horseflies were biting us and ripping our skin off. He had nary a one land

on him. We had welts on our necks and arms and hands and even on our scalps.

"Boys, what you just put on then was insect *attractant*." Sucker smiled a big toothy grin, turned, and walked off.

This is how bad it was: the big cutts that cruise the clear but tea-tinged pools were rising to our Elk Hair Caddis patterns, fighting well and being healthily released but the horseflies were biting us and ripping our skin off so after thirty minutes of catching huge cutts—and I'm talking 16 to 20 inches, fat as my Uncle Bob—we quit fishing and walked back to the car. Next day, we didn't slather on insect repellant, hiked back into First Meadow and the horseflies didn't bite. Neither did the cruising cutts we disappointedly cast to over and over. Guess you can't have everything.

Slough Creek is arguably the most scenic river in the park. Rugged snow-peaked mountains in the background, green meadowed banks and cold, clear water. Yellowstone cutthroats are known for their penchant for dry flies but to catch them on dries in Slough Creek, you must be stealthy. The water is incredibly clear, and anglers can spot the trout and cast to them in deep glides and pools. Problem is, the trout can see you and your line too. If the sun is shining it is hard to get them to bite, even though they will rise if you stay out of sight and provide a good presentation.

The First Meadow has lots of fish, anglers have lots of success, especially on dries, but the fish tend to be smaller than in the Second Meadow, the further hike. Still, the trout in this section tend to be close to 14 inches long.

The Lower Meadows section is heavily fished but there are still large lunker cutthroats in this section. Lots of riffles. They are wary but landable. The water is incredibly clear, and anglers can spot the trout and cast to them. If the sun is shining it is hard to get them to bite, even though they will rise unless the dry fly is in some shadows.

The Second Meadows has the biggest fish but fewer of them and harder to land. The cutts are known for their penchant for dry flies. The Absaroka-Beartooth Mountains in the background are postcard-perfect.

You're going to have to hike to get to either. The lower meadow sees a lot of traffic so go on up. The First Meadow requires a forty-five-minute strenuous hike. Don't hike from the campground but start from the trailhead one-quarter mile before the CG. The Second Meadow requires a three- to four-hour hike. Start your hike on the north side of the entrance road to avoid steep trail. There is no road access. Third Meadow is eight miles and best as an overnight trip.

I've found over the years these things about Slough Creek: 1) First Meadow trout taunt you with their visibility and size but since they see so many more anglers than do Second Meadow trout, they are *muy dificil*; 2) Stay low. Lower than that, even. Hide when you can. Just because Slough Creek trout don't run for cover when they see you lulls anglers into thinking that they can stand on the bank and sightcast and still catch fish. Don't let them see you. I sometimes lie down to fish a particularly good pool; 3) Because the water is so ridiculously clear, you can watch them take your fly. It's easy to react based on the supposed take but you'll find yourself a tad slow or a tad fast if you're not careful. Timing is everything; 4) Longer, thinner leaders; 5) Don't spray on insect repellant. Offer it to your buddies.

Section of the park: Northeast. *Hotspots:* Good fishing from underrated Lower Meadows to the smaller, more difficult Second Meadow. The Lower Meadows section is heavily fished but there are still large lunker cutthroats in this section. Lots of riffles. *Species:* Cutthroat (and some rainbows and cuttbows). *Tackle and techniques:* No need to wade in the Upper Meadows. You can fish the Lower Meadows in hip or chest waders. Neoprene waders might be too hot. Hiking boots are really all you will need since this is meadow fishing.

If you want to catch these cutts, you've got to go small (6X tippet and small flies) and during the summer months, usually match the hatch. Meadow fishing, undercut banks, runs and riffles and glassy pools. Keep your shadow off the river for these are finicky fish. *Flies:* The hatches can be prolific. *Regulations:* Fly fishing only. Catch-and-release only. *Directions:* Start hike at trailhead halfway twixt the highway and campground, then follow Slough Creek Wagon Trail. There is good fishing below the campground, too. Breathtaking scenery.

Northwest

IDAHO

From the drift boat I see the moose, chocolate in the greenness of the banks, sanctuary, my fly dragging, and the guide telling me but I am lost, lost and fuzzy, lost and thinking of *Saving Private Ryan* and music and the funeral, and I see the snow on the mountains, but I am hot, the peaks so high and steep and Sisyphus must live there, and the guide, the irascible guide, a doorstep darkener, choleric commander, yelling, yelling over Edith Piaf who is singing in my head, *tu es partout*, the sparrow, the amazing blue blue blue of the moving water but how can it be clear and still have color I think, the boat as confessional, I should be bitter Dad died but I am not, guide at his pulpit, rowing, the bank a blur, divining, and then I cast, I guess because I don't

remember casting and under the tree and in the shadows and the big fly hit and the big fish hit and it was all tumble and jostle and splash and then water dark and deep, glassy beads on the slick back, hang in the air, suspended.

For over twelve years, I let my barber in Dallas, Lee, cut what little hair I had left. His prices increased even as the amount of hair he cuts decreased. He and I have gone on two trout fishing trips together, both about ten years ago, and I don't have the guts to go with him again.

Lee's not very good at cutting hair nor is he much of an angler, but he talks a good game and makes things fun. My friend Chuck and I took him angling with us on an early summer fishing trip. We never did it again.

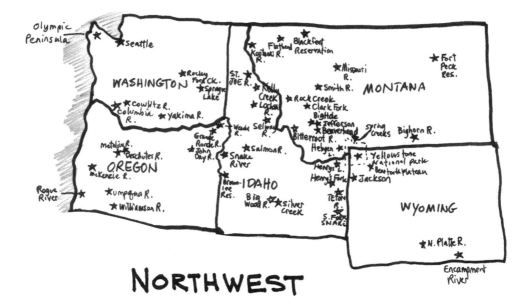

NORTHWEST

Chuck and I had timed the trip to hit the golden stones coming off out West. Golden stoneflies are one of the underrated hatches, a generic name given to several similar stoneflies.

The name applies to those stones that are yellowish in color and hatch after the salmonflies appear. They often hatch when the water is muddy from run-off but if you fish the clear water on the edges, you can have a field day. And the golden stones are dependable from year to year.

For some dumb reason, we let Lee drive his big four-wheel-drive SUV instead of me driving my own fishing SUV, the Troutmobile. Since I know where I'm going (and when), I like to drive my own truck on our trout fishing jaunts.

As Lee drove through the wide flats, Chuck and I lulled off into daydreams before we heard the two gunshots.

Lee held a pistol in his hand, the gun stuck out the passenger-side window, right across where I was seated. Lee laughed as he pulled back the pistol, holstered it, and slid it back under his seat. The antelope herd he fired at ("just in their general direction," as he put it) scattered frantically.

Chuck and I should have done the same but we were locked in.

Chuck hid the pistol in his duffel packed in the back of the truck. We fished for three days and one day, Lee the Barber developed an obsession for finding Love Lake. When we pulled up to the lake, he jumped out, pulled off his wedding ring, a real nice gold diamond ring, showed it to us as we clambered out of the truck, then ceremoniously kissed it and tossed it high into the air. With a plop, the thousand-dollar ring dropped into the cold alpine lake. I debated whether or not to dive in after it.

On our last night, we tried to go over a steep mountain pass but it was closed down because an eighteen-wheeler had gone off the side and rescue units were at the scene. We went into a small hamlet and ate some overcooked steaks and rubbery baked potatoes, then drove back to where the sheriff had blocked off the road. Second in line.

We waited for four hours, told stories of high school glory, catnapped, and finally the sheriff pulled up the sawhorses. Just as we were pulling out, a sports car came out of nowhere and tried to enter the lane in front of us.

This ticked old Lee off in the worst way. In a blur, Lee pulled out a sawed-off shotgun (which we didn't know he had) from under his seat and was trying to get the window down so he could stick the gun out at the guy driving the sports car.

The sheriff was off to the side and never saw a thing, but the driver did see the gun and stopped dead in his tracks. Lee put the gun away and Chuck looked back at me with an implied facial expression that we'd never go a-angling with this wild man ever again.

And like I said, we haven't. But he still cut my hair until I moved to Amarillo. I was afraid not to let him. I'm a little apprehensive about finding a barber here on the Golden Spread. And I'm definitely not taking him fishing with me.

Big Wood River

- **Location:** Southern central Idaho
- **What You Fish For:** Rainbow and brown trout
- **Highlights and Notables:** One of Idaho's best freestone medium-sized trout streams with excellent access from the highway, close to major ski areas

To the south of the White Clouds Lakes Area, is the Big Wood River, a popular but productive freestone stream near Ketchum. Cottonwoods on banks. Rocky and steep up top, gradient becomes slower. Thick streamside brush. Islands and side channels with loose banks, steep banks, brush right up to the banks.

Big Wood River has decent fishing pressure but it is spread out so you don't often feel rushed. The river has both stocked and wild browns, rainbows, and some brook trout too. This is a wading river with a short window for floating. Lots of ski-and-fish combo types end up on the river.

Magic Reservoir sends up migrating browns fall and rainbows spring. Big Wood ain't tough fishing most of the time—an uncomplicated angling friend, fishable most of the year (April and May are runoff). Downed cottonwoods provide super trout cover, hint hint.

I do kneel or hide down behind brush but mostly I just make longer casts and so did Doc when he fished here but then again, Doc kneels anywhere he fishes. Doc is an overkneeler.

Everything adds up—cool stark scenery, cool flowing water, lots of hatches, lots of fish, consistent angling, good growth rates, uncrowded, lots of fish per mile, excellent access. The river is good for newbies but has enough action to remain interesting for vets.

Adams Parachute is the top fly. I have never streamer fished here but they ought to work. Typical rainbow, the hold in faster water. Good presentation or even mediocre works much of the time but they'll throw you a curve every now and then. The river is more difficult and stronger to cross than you think especially with the cobbled rocks rolling around.

Even though Highway 75 borders the river, much of the access is private, but permission is often granted. Around Bellevue, on Highway 75, one can find fairly easy entry. Once you get into the river, it is easy going since the Big Wood is a wadeable river. The Big Wood has good fishing year round, including some excellent winter fishing for mostly wild rainbows (generally considered to be descendants of the redbanded trout), some brown and brook trout. The average size fish in the Big Wood approaches 13 inches, but anglers catch many from 16 to 20 inches and anglers report lunkers in the mid-20 inch range. Part of the Big Wood is subject to catch-and-release and barbless hook restrictions, so check the most recent regulations. The creeks entering the Big Wood are a good way to get away from the crowds and still catch a lot of trout.

Many anglers try the "Canyon" below Magic Reservoir, but the fish are wary and difficult to catch. Magic Reservoir is a fishery for the seasoned veteran to consider. The brown and rainbow trout grow big and finicky. There are hatches of Green Drake and Golden Stoneflies, and grasshoppers in the grassland sections. The nearest community is the Sun Valley area, a major tourist area with a number of fly shops, outfitters, and lodging.

CONTACTS
Lost Rivers Outfitters, Ketchum, 208-726-1706
Sun Valley Outfitters, Sun Valley, 208-622-3400
Silver Creek Outfitters, Ketchum, 208-726-5282

Brownlee Reservoir

- **Location:** Western central Idaho, eastern Oregon
- **What You Fish For:** Smallmouth, crappie, catfish
- **Highlights and Notables:** The diversity and continued quality of Brownlee angling make this impoundment a worthy listing.

It's easy to write off famous people, famous athletes—people, places, or things that are on top. We love rooting for the underdog.

Brownlee Reservoir, a huge warmwater impoundment in the Snake River Canyon has been on top, been considered the best fishery in the West for several species, holding many state records. The lake separates Idaho and Oregon and is one of the most heavily fished in the region, has water level fluctuations, and has lost some of it luster from the 1990s. Brownlee Reservoir is the largest of three Hells Canyon lakes on the Snake, some 15,000 acres, long (fifty-seven miles) and narrow.

Known for quality fishing for crappie, catfish, and especially smallmouth bass, Brownlee Reservoir just keeps rolling along. The lake is down, *they* say. The fish aren't as big, not as plentiful, *they* say. *They're wrong.* The catch rates and average size of smallmouth is still as good as any other lake in the western United States. The steep rocky shorelines of the lake are still ideal smallie habitat.

Yeah, we're talking about an established fishery so the luster has worn off for writers and anglers but Brownlee still has potential, has not tapped it out. The lake still produces incredible numbers of quality bronzebacks.

The perch fishing is top-flight, crappie A-plus, catfishing for flatheads and channel cats superior. The fishing for the rest of the species is average at best—largemouth bass, bluegills, blue catfish, sturgeon, red-eared sunfish, pumpkinseed, rainbow trout (mostly a winter fishery), brown trout, and walleye.

If anglers have a fishing license in either state, they can use the facilities of either state to put in or take out boats, but they cannot fish from the shore, dock, or a docked boat in the state which they do not hold a license.

CONTACTS

Brownlee Reservoir Charters, www .brownleereservoirfishing.com

Henry's Fork of the Snake River

- **Location:** Eastern Idaho
- **What You Fish For:** Rainbow and brown trout
- **Highlights and Notables:** Henry's Fork of the Snake River is generally considered to be the best dry fly fishing stream in America, maybe the universe.

Henry's Fork took a beating in the late 1980s and 1990s as it suffered from a variety of ailments. The river has been up against other threats over the last twenty years, with friends of the river turning back proposed hydroelectric plants, creating buffer zones between the river and over-grazing cattle, and fighting to gain better release patterns from the reservoir so that the Fork doesn't go high and dry in the winter. Henry's Fork is regaining some of the stability and prolific insect hatches that made it a world-class fishery. The last few years have seen more juvenile trout, better hatches, and less sedimentation of the river.

Henry's Fork is a complex river, one which makes the fisherman work hard for his catch. You have a better than fifty-fifty chance of the river kicking your ass on any given day. I mean skunked. Zero. Don't laugh, it could happen to you, too. Yeah, it's

happened to me. I think I'm batting about .300 and since this isn't baseball, the river is winning.

Because the Henry's Fork is so legendary, so complicated, so diverse, so rich with insects, so profound in its fishery, so Western, so beautiful and aesthetically pleasing it has become, with the Madison River, the icon of Western streams and undoubtedly, with Silver Creek, the epitome of the challenging fishing river.

There are typically an amazing number of hatches which occur on the stream (even though the last couple of years have seen a decline overall in hatches), and to complicate matters, a multitude of them might be hatching at any one time. That's the great thing about the Fork, for almost any time of day, there's usually a hatch to fish. The trout grow big, up to 10 pounds and bigger. The average size trout you are likely to land approaches 15 inches. Twenty-inch trout

are a dime a dozen, it's just darned hard to catch them. The Fork's trout are primarily rainbow, with a smattering of brown trout, although in the lower river, the brown trout population is bigger. Brook trout are found in the upper river.

The river fishes like two different rivers: the first is the Box Canyon in the upper flow, from Island Park Reservoir downstream to Last Chance, where anglers face heavy currents, big rocks, and slick wading; and the second about four miles from Last Chance to the Railroad Ranch area, a five-mile stretch in Harriman State Park, where the river fishes like a meadow stream. At one time this was probably the most fertile and productive section of trout water in the world. The river has excellent fishing in other stretches of 120 miles, but this two-part section is by far the best.

Henry's Fork supports mayfly, caddis fly, and stonefly hatches of the first degree. Many pedigreed fishermen have come to the Fork and have been humbled by the diversity of the hatches, the delicacy in matching them, and by the frustration of trying to get the rising trout to take their delicately-matched fly. Brown drake hatches, you might do well and if you do, don't put on your stoic face. Dance. Flail your arms. You've bested the best. The Fork isn't an easy river to fish. Drag-free floats are difficult to attain in the tricky currents. Landing a Henry's Fork trout is a task in itself, for they are strong and aggressive.

In early June, the salmonfly hatch starts in the Box Canyon, and by using big, weighted stoneflies, the angler has a chance of landing some of the monsters that lurk in here. You nymph in the Box. You use streamers or big ugly nymphs. Look up and around. This is one beautiful canyon. You can float this section, or do like most, and fish from shore and wade a bit. Good access throughout.

The Railroad Ranch is a gentle, meadow stream that barely moves, wide and wadeable, tricky invisible surface currents. This section is loaded with big rainbow trout usually rising to anything but your imitation. You can sightcast if your heart can stand it. Tie on the longest leader you can stand and then add two feet of tippet. Find your lowest riding flies. The best time is during a hatch when the trout are rising. Don't get carried away. Find a fish and stick with him. Good luck, you're gonna need it.

The hatches they rise to include Green Drake, Blue Winged Olive, Black Quill, Pale Morning Dun, Grasshoppers, Caddis fly, just to name a few. The trick is to figure out which of these they are keying on, and during what stage. These are selective trout, but if you tie on the right fly, make a perfect cast, have no drag despite the thousands of tiny currents, hold your tongue right, then the rewards can provide a lifetime memory. Anglers can float or wade this section. Parts of the river are catch-and-release after a certain time of year, so check the regulations. Most fishermen practice catch-and-release fishing as a matter of course. And as you release, you're ecstatic. You fooled one. High fives all around.

Despite recent troubles with Island Park Dam water releases, Henry's Fork of the Snake River is a special river. The river will provide you with the best day of frustration you've ever experienced.

CONTACTS
Mike Lawson's Henry's Fork Anglers, www.henrysforkanglers.com

TroutHunter, www.trouthunt.com

Last Chance and Island Park, 208-558-7755, www.islandparkchamber.org

Idaho Travel Council, Boise, 800-VISIT-ID, www.visitid.org

Staley Springs Resort, www.staleysprings.com

Island Park Chamber of Commerce (for lodging options near the Box Canyon and Harriman State Park), 208-558-7755

Henry's Lake

- **Location:** Eastern Idaho
- **What You Fish For:** Brook trout is the main target but you also catch rainbow, cutthroat, and cuttbows.
- **Highlights and Notables:** Some of the largest brook trout in the West, but heck, almost any trout you catch in Henry's Lake is large. Don't miss this one.

If, for some reason, someone in authority, perhaps supernatural, perhaps with Fish and Game, came to me and said "Mark, you have to fish only one trout lake the rest of your life. We need your decision right now," I would think for about thirty seconds (because there are some very good trout lakes) and then I would reply "Not fair," and they would counter with "Time's almost up and if we don't get an answer, you'll have to watch reality television the rest of your life."

"Henry's Lake, sir," I'd quickly say.

Henry's Lake (2,500 acres) is a shallow lake in eastern Idaho, known as Hank's Pond, and is one of the best trout lakes in the West. Headwaters for Henry's Fork of the Snake River, the lake is famous but for the one million fish in its waters and their amazing sizes, you'd think it would be even more of a destination.

Bank angling won't net much and shore angling is limited to boot, so the best way to cover the lake is by boating or floating. Bring your belly boat, kickboat, pontoon, aluminum skiff, or other one-man showboat and get to kicking and paddling.

The lake has big fish, holding cutthroat, cutthroat-rainbow hybrids, and brook trout of prodigious size. Brook trout in Henry's Lake often weigh over 2 pounds, sometimes weighing as much as 5 pounds (even bigger but let's keep this real, okay?). This is one of the best places in the West to land a trophy squaretail. The hybrids have been known to reach 8 to 12 pounds.

If you fish hard for a couple of days, here is what you can expect: Wind in the afternoons. Weeds on your flies. At least one trout close to 5 pounds. Nymphs and streamers work consistently better than dries. Sinking and sinktip lines get to the fish better than pinching weights. At 6,500 feet elevation, the weather can change quickly and you'll be caught without your fleece or jacket at least once. Frustration and relief that the lake closes at 9:00PM each night.

You'll bump into other anglers because the lake is only twenty minutes from the west entrance to Yellowstone National Park and as such, is crowded.

Your scuds and Krystal Buggers work better than most anything else. The season on the lake is from mid-May to October 31 but sneak away to Henry's Lake at the first suspicion of autumn's dense colorful approach if you can. You have the lake to yourself and the fish are actively feeding and you can hear their slurps and sips and the brook trout are moving toward the streams to spawn.

Kelly Creek

- **Location:** Northern Idaho
- **What You Fish For:** Westslope cutthroats
- **Highlights and Notables:** Wild remote freestone stream with wild cutthroats of size and abundance

Kelly Creek is where my 12-year-old nephew Chase wanted to establish his independence. He wanted to fish by himself. No adults (read: his Dad and Uncle Mark) telling him what to do—"Watch your backcast, you almost hooked that bush" and "Try a little closer to the rock" and "tie your shoelaces" and so on. Dad and Uncle stuff, you know.

Kelly Creek is in wild wild country. We warned him of all too real critters and other dangers. We tried to counter his continuing demand to fish alone. "You don't know how to even tie on a fly, do you?"

He begged. Kenny shrugged and smiled. We let him.

He did okay for a bit, hooking but not landing two pretty nice cutthroat in a nice long pool. He looked back several times to see if we were keeping herd over him but we were sufficiently hidden and he didn't catch sight of us. He was sufficiently spooked.

Chase got hung up. On a limb. Brown, three feet long. He picked up the limb he hooked and dropped it like a hot potato. Shrieked, too.

The kid practically jumped out of his waders. The limb was a dead deer leg, just feet from the rest of the carcass. He fished with us the rest of the trip.

Kelly Creek is possibly the best creek in America. This wild freestone stream runs through some of the most spectacular backcountry in the world. The combination of several factors makes me say this:

First factor: westslope cutthroats averaging 15 inches that jump and turn and slash and thrive in great numbers.

Second factor: Kelly Creek is both challenging and easy fishing. It switches on you in a heartbeat and keeps you on your toes.

Third factor: solitude—the river will be yours.

Wide enough to be called a river in many states, Kelly Creek is one of those special fisheries I did not want to put in the book but knew that if excluded, I knew I'd be called on the mat for keeping secret one of the best rivers anywhere. Luckily, the stream is in the middle of nowhere, has no towns within forty miles of it, so I'm still likely to be able to fish this gem with few if any anglers around.

The westslope cutthroat isn't as colorful as other cutts but honestly, a cutt is a cutt is a cutt. There's just something magical about natives and even more so, cutthroat. Most of Kelly Creek's fish are 9- to 14-inch but they do have lots of trout 16 to 20 inches and they live in the hard to reach spots, the deeper pools, the deeper seams, underneath that overhanging branch next to the boulder where you have a one-in-a-million casting chance and you might catch a 17-incher but the 22-incher laughs in your face.

Kelly Creek has incredible trout homes. Turn pools and quick runs, rocks and logs, gravel bars and boulders, long narrow pools chuted by huge rocks. The stream has long flats that aren't quite riffles and not yet runs. And the sexy pocket water, man oh man. The water is clear but has a green tinge, like diluted Gatorade.

What makes the stream a challenge at times are the strong currents and the tricky crosscurrents. The trout will rise willingly to big fluffy western attractors at times but then turn off and get picky, taking only lesser-dressed imitations that match the prevailing hatch. They'll turn off to drag and sloppy presentations at times after pretty much slashing at any decent offering.

The creek has nice hatches but not prolific. That's a good thing because they don't have the right to turn down too many things that look like food. Kelly Creek has the usual western hatches—stoneflies, caddis, and mayflies. Kelly Creek is a secluded and scenic catch-and-release fishery, limited to single barbless hooks with artificial lures or flies only. That regulation right there makes the fishery healthy. A destination in its own right, I suggest making a week trip to fish the Kelly, Clearwater, Lochsa, and Selway. If you hike long enough, hike up Cayuse Creek, feeder to the Kelly.

Chase is now twenty, a handsome young man with a good head on his shoulders even though he attends the University of Texas (we tried to make him an Aggie), wants to be a film director and is a good egg (even though we don't let him know that). We took him back to Kelly Creek recently. He stands 6-foot-5 and weighs 225 and the young man isn't scared of anything, least of all a detached deer leg. On the way to the river, he took some ribbing from us about deer legs and he chuckled, that coming-of-age chuckle that conveys humility, suggests he thinks he could take us but still manages to forecast his future actions as a father and uncle when he deals with rites of passage for his son or nephews. I like that Kelly Creek's waters are a liquid legacy for our family.

Chase fished for a while by himself, caught quite a few fish (he showed us with his digital camera) and never looked over his shoulder once. (Yeah, we peeked.) He ended up fishing with Kenny and me most of the time, catching some nice trout, helping us land ours, and genuinely seemed enjoy our company. He's growing up nicely and he didn't even want to fish by himself anymore. There's just something about sharing solitude if you know what I mean.

Lochsa River

- **Location:** Northern Idaho
- **What You Fish For:** Cutthroat trout
- **Highlights and Notables:** Beautiful wilderness river full of big cutts

In the language of the Nez Perce, the Native Americans indigenous to this land, the word Lochsa means "rough water." Amen.

I was a traitor to Kenny on this river. He and I were fishing, the trout were rising to caddis and the day was sunny. We leap-frogged pools, staying within sight (and bragging vision rights) and I was about to walk wide around his pool when I noticed him fiddling with his leg.

As I approached, I saw two remarkable things: 1) Kenny's leg was impaled on a sharp branch of a fallen log and 2) a fat trout was rising at the tail of the most beautiful pool I'd ever seen. Normally, my fishing buddy instincts would take over and I would have helped him remove his leg from his entrapment. It was an ugly bloody wound, weird looking. It looked like Kenny had super-glued a four inch sharp stick to the front of his calf muscle.

He had stepped over the log and half-fell, caught himself, and realized he wasn't going anywhere. The long skinny sharp branch went through clean as an arrow.

Here's where I departed from my normal help-Kenny-once-again nature. I don't know why I bailed but this is what happened:

1. I said something warm and fuzzy, like "Ouch, man, I bet that smarts" or "I feel your pain." That led him to believe I was sympathetic and might actually help him.
2. Without him noticing, I cast to the middle of the dark pool, drifted in the rising trout's lane and then caught the 19-inch cutthroat, got its head up, brought it in, netted and held it up for him to see as he broke the stick off from the log and stood there looking helpless with a small tree protruding from the front of his leg.
3. I said nothing when he asked me, "Did you just fish my pool?"
4. I just hung my head.

It was the wrong thing to do, taking a man's pool, catching his big trout. There are plenty of pools up and down the river. I didn't need to steal his. I should have been performing emergency surgery on his calf muscle. But damn, that fish was fat.

He yanked the stick out and bled like a stuck pig. I leapt two pools ahead of him for the rest of the day and both of us caught a lot of cutthroats. Fine ones. Great colors. They ranged from 12 to 16 inches.

They held in deep runs. Dark pools. Pocket water. In the riffles. These beautiful cutts were everywhere and we caught lots. But none were as long or heavy-bodied or soulful as the stolen-pool trout. Kenny still whines about the stolen trout to this day. And he has two nice scars to prove it happened, to throw it in my face. I don't even say a word, just let him babble. I still got the fish after all. Rough water.

The reason you don't see the Lochsa on everyone's list of top trout rivers in America is because this diamond is so far away from anything and everything. If the vodka-clear Lochsa wasn't so far from Texas, I'd fish it a lot. Not much has changed about this river since Lewis and Clark floated it in 1805. The highway that runs along the river wasn't there of course but it is named the Lewis and Clark Highway. And given how easy it is to access the Lochsa, the fishing pressure is low. Nearby Kelly Creek doesn't get much fishing pressure and I'm of the opinion that the Lochsa gets even less.

Westslope cutthroats and rainbows of good size populate the river. Chinook salmon and steelheads move into the river when it's their season. Come spring, the great rapids and drops and fast water means that whitewater enthusiasts show up and clog up the river.

The Lochsa is a sanctuary, one of the greatest unknown fishing getaways in America. You're as likely to see MT or WA plates as those from ID. If you see TX, find me and fish with me. We can leapfrog pools.

Middle Fork, Salmon River

- **Location:** Central Idaho
- **What You Fish For:** Cutthroat trout
- **Highlights and Notables:** One of the top two or three most beautiful float trips in America and one of the best cutthroat streams

I packed three knee braces, the heavy one I use when I have tweaked the knee because I wasn't wearing any support, the midweight which I wear in anticipation of a hard day's wading and the lightweight that I like to wear when the knee ought to get tired. All three stayed packed for six days, five nights. I caught hundreds of trout and the knee never once hurt. The healing waters. The righteous waters.

Art is all about context. Is the beauty around me on the Middle Fork *art* or the *context*?

Clearwater River

Primarily a steelhead fishery in each of its four reaches and at times, a fantastic fishery. When the steelies are off, fishing can be good for rainbow and cutthroat trout. The trout don't grow to gargantuan proportions because the granite formations the river runs through don't give much mineral nourishment to the food chain. The Clearwater's steelhead are typically reared in hatcheries but are still strong fighters.

This isn't Pynchon or Joyce, this is simplified, elemental, primitive, primeval. The ultimate wilderness float fishing trip, the granddaddy of them all. This is the poster child for those frontier getaways you read about, the six-day trips where you are so isolated, in such reverie that you forget all about who will win *American Idol*. You don't consider the office because you have no chance at talking on a phone. The Middle Fork is where you really do decompress and think about the simpler things in life.

So bountiful, so beautiful, so unique, so wild it makes you wonder why you ever go fishing anywhere else. You have to suppress the urge to catch a dozen fish while they make shore dinner and set up camp because after a while on the Middle Fork, what's another dozen fish on top the hun-dred or two hundred you have already caught on the trip?

I cannot describe how pristinely clear the water is—super super invisible water but with a heavenly-aqua aura about it. As you drift, in a raft or driftboat, you see them in the water, suspended as if in blue clouds, the wild westslope cutthroats and wild rainbows, foot-long prisms, active finny changing slabs of colors. Leaping hearts, breath shortened, pools of swirling trout holding in a pod like salmon.

The Middle Fork of the Salmon River has the best dry fly fishing anywhere. I can say this without worry of competition. You can be an absolute beginner and catch more fish than you've ever dreamed of. The riffles and eddies are guaranteed to provide lightning-quick strikes. The trout take anything and everything, just plop a big western fly in front of them and voilà! Twenty-five to 100 fish in a day, no lie (but don't count, this is a fun river). Now there are no trophy trout, just wild and pure and 8 to 18 inches long (a rare 20-inch cutt). Twelve to 15 inches are the norm.

Screaming fly reels murmur scratchily from the pull and run of an 18-inch west-slope cutthroat, not a hatchery fish but a strong-bodied, strong-willed survivor. You catch these natives in chutes and over gravel bars, around boulders, and in the slow water in front of the little parks where a deer might be watching you. You catch them only with barbless artificials and you release them the second you catch them (okay, get a quick snapshot then release). But wait, there's more: rapids and riffles and gin-clear pools and riffles that sparkle like a floating bed of diamonds—green water but clear—rock bottom and eddies guaranteed to get a strike or twelve.

The Middle Fork is one of the top ten whitewater trips in the country. True wilderness, a steady 3,000 foot gradient drop, 100-plus miles of northerly-flowing river you can get to by plane or trail (a tiny bit of this river you can make by gravel road). Total lack of access. The trails are bad-ass. Fly in to mountain air strips if you have the co-jones. This is the Frank Church River of No Return Wilderness and the river starts high with thick stands of aspen and Douglas fir and lodgepole pine then runs through scattered rock outcroppings, bare brown dirt, ponderosa pine randomly strewn on the mountainside, then chugs through canyon

and vertical walls and sagebrush. You will probably see deer and elk and bear and cougar and bighorn sheep and coyote and otter on your journey.

Do not float it yourself, the river will kick your fanny. These are sobering rapids, narrow chutes. You can get on the river by permit only and you're not going to get one anyway. Do you really want to waste perfectly good fishing time worrying about death and destruction in the labyrinth of boulders and rocks and narrow places in the canyon that threaten to smash you between rock walls?

Not only is the Middle Fork one of the top wilderness trips, one of the best float-fishing excursions, the best dry fly fishing rivers, one of the finest waters for catching a hundred trout or starting a neophyte, this is also the pinnacle of the shore camping experiences.

Consider this: After a shore-cooked camp breakfast (food always tastes better in the wild), you load into the boat about 9:00 or 9:30 and you fish and catch fish until midday. Stop. Fish while the outfitters prepare lunch. Fish again and fish on. Then you make camp about 5:00 or 5:30 and you shore fish or wade fish or hike or sit in a hot spring or just chill and they set up tents and cook dinner for you and not just any dinner but grilled salmon and roasted corn salsa or Dutch oven pizza or some other open-fire gourmet-style delectable dinner. With excellent wine. And dessert. Your most toughest choice will be whether or not to sleep comfortably in your tent or dream under the stars.

Al and Jeana Bukowsky of Solitude

River Trips have been guiding on the Middle Fork since 1972. This is a team that has guided the Orvis Perkins trio, worked with Hollywood celebrities like John Wayne, Susan Sarandon and Tim Robbins, and a couple of guys named Jimmy Carter and George Bush.

How's the fishing compare now to then, Al?

"There's no comparison. Back then, you could keep ten and today, it's all catch-and-release. There are more fish and more bigger fish today than way back then."

How big, Al?

"We catch more 18- to 20-inch cutthroat now and there was a 23½-inch cutt last summer, bigger than any fish we had in the good old days."

Any advice, Al?

"Don't count fish."

Any rules of the river, Al?

"I always say we either have a good day or a great day, that's how good the Middle Fork of the Salmon is."

Thanks, Al.

I have never once used a nymph on the Middle Fork. Had I, I am positive that on a good day, one hundred trout would have been just a number I passed by midafternoon (but who's counting?). Most trips are five- or six-day trips and they provide anything you'll need (including showers and toilets of a sort). You can fish with an Elk Hair Hopper or Stimulator or Royal Wulff all day long and catch all the fish you care to catch. The only thing stopping you will be the dazzling scenery and your desire to get in touch with the depths of your soul.

CONTACTS

Al and Jeana Bukowsky, Solitude River Trips, www.rivertrips.com

Salmon River

- **Location:** Central Idaho
- **What You Fish For:** Steelhead, trout, etc.
- **Highlights and Notables:** Huge evocative rambling river, as dramatic as you'll find in North America

The trout fishing is marginal at best. The scenery is superlative at worst, otherworldly at best. The canyon is one of the largest in the world, tree-lined with sandy beaches, clear warm water, abandoned gold mines, ghost towns, history along its shores. Fish the Salmon because this is one of the premier floatfishing trips in the world; adjunct to this trip are the steelhead, good-not-great but quality enough when combined with the rest, must-do.

The Salmon River has its headwaters in the Sawtooth Mountains where it flows for nearly 200 miles north to North Fork. Highway 75 follows the river and gives anglers good access in the upper reaches. Trout fishing isn't terrible in this stretch, worth a day's angling, underrated but not blue ribbon.

From North Fork to the river's main tributary, the Middle Fork of the Salmon, the Salmon runs through a narrow canyon. A road parallels the river for most of this stretch but access varies. From this area downstream for the next few hundred miles, the river is fished by boat, usually jet boats. This river which holds most anglers' attention for the steelhead runs it holds, average size 5 to 10 pounds, fall and spring.

The lower Salmon River, the longest undammed river in the lower forty-eight, is still accessed mostly by boat, but there are some roads which lead to the canyon, a breathtakingly enormous canyon, replete with natural amphitheaters, eerie hoodoos, cathedrals. The river is big and dangerous in the main stem, but because of its relative sterility, does not support the same numbers of trout as the upper section. The steelhead runs are up and down, up in recent years. If this is your first time to fish the Salmon River, I suggest contacting a guide or outfitter to get the most out of this unique wilderness experience.

Anglers would do well to look at the many tributaries of the Salmon River along its course for even more trout fishing. In the lakes basins, there are hundreds of al-

pine lakes dotting the map, offering fishing under the jagged peaks for golden, brook and rainbow trout, such as Crater, Ship Island, Skyhigh, Glacier, and Gooseneck Lakes.

Selway River

- **Location:** North central Idaho, south of Lochsa River
- **What You Fish For:** Westslope cutthroat
- **Highlights and Notables:** Primitive river, thick forests, wild fishing experience for wild cutts

Think prehistoric. Primeval. Before time. The Un-Civilization. Raw. Fierce. Untamed.

The Selway River is all these things. This clear rushing river is untouched.

Cradled by the Selway-Bitterroot Wilderness and the Frank Church River of No Return Wilderness, two of the most pristine wildernesses in North America, the Selway runs through dense forests of pine, fir, and cedar, through a rugged canyon, past craggy granite summits on its rendezvous the Lochsa and from this mating comes the Middle Fork of the Clearwater.

The Selway River is difficult to access. Only two roads reach the wild river, Selway Falls Road and Magruder Corridor Road. You might see a few anglers at these access points but not many and you can get away

from them just by walking a bit. The way to get back to the really wild sections is by way of hiring a bush plane to drop into one of the backcountry airstrips of the Selway Bitteroot Wilderness. Many meet up with guides and backcountry camps (fishing, elk, backpacking).

Those who come to fish expect to catch the pure natives, the westslope cutthroats. They expect to catch a lot of them. They expect these natives to slash at any offering, these beautiful fish with their sides of copper or goldenrod or brass depending, as colorful as the Basque flag with their brilliant red slashes and green backs. These natives average 10 to 15 inches but not many of them grow bigger than this in the cold fast Selway waters.

This river is tough to wade. The Selway is invisibly clear but has these big, irregular rocks everywhere; some are boulders, spaced so they are ankle-traps, and negotiating these can be tricky and dangerous. You might want to walk the banks (and there are trails on both sides) but the banks are overgrown and pose casting problems. So you're going to have to wade.

You'll want to concentrate on the big deep holes and you'll do well in them but don't overlook the riffles and runs and pocket water and deep flats. Trout hold everywhere and hit everything. The Selway is an ideal finish to a Grand Slam of the Lochsa, Kelly Creek, and the Clearwater.

Silver Creek

- **Location:** South central Idaho, near Sun Valley
- **What You Fish For:** Brown and rainbow trout
- **Highlights and Notables:** You could argue that this lovely spring creek, with its intricate cross-currents and challenging angling, is one of the best fishing holes in the world.

So this guy is fishing Silver Creek and he doesn't stand a chance in hell of catching a fish. I tell you this not to make fun of the guy, although I'm certainly not above that, but to show you that if you read about Silver Creek and you go there ill-equipped in strategy, technique, preparation, and the willingness to fail, you don't want to be a happy *pescador*.

This guy is fishing, using an alibi of a fly rod, one of those 1970s mass-market specials, fiberglass thick as a Polish sausage, probably a 7- or 8-weight. His flyline slapped the mirrored surface like athletes with wet towels in a locker room. His rod tip never bent so he cast with his entire arm moving the rod back and then furiously pushing his arm forward. Trout were rising upstream and downstream but in his thirty-foot arc, made frothy by his slap-casts, nothing moved. I felt sorry for the guy and was considering talking to him and seeing if he'd be amenable to some basic advice (like anything I was going to tell him would alter the fact that casting that broomstick could put his fly in position to catch a Silver Creek trout).

Just as I had enough of the poor guy flailing about and was ready to get up from my sitting position, he tossed the rod down and started cussing, ranting, and raving, stomping around. Man, I've been there. Get some lessons and start off fishing a smaller creek, dude.

Silver Creek flows along slowly, like melted pewter. She is a high desert, meadowy spring creek, rich as Croesus. The fishery holds primarily rainbow trout, a good brown trout population and a few brook trout. These fish are small-headed, big shouldered, heavy-bodied trout. Wild trout. And the wild trout grow big and smart and mean on Silver Creek, and there are trout over 20 inches and up to 28 inches in here. The average-size fish caught will run between 13 and 18 inches. A 20-inch trout is not uncommon, but catching one is.

There are not enough superlatives to describe how eerily beautiful or fertile this clear, cold spring creek truly is. The river snakes through open fields with lush green streamside vegetation. The river meanders slowly, so slowly at times the river seems to be motionless. At other times, it shimmers like a mirror. But this illusion will be shattered when the hopeful angler casts a small dry fly onto the glassy silver surface, when the confounding cross-currents will be evident.

The slow flows will trick you, like a magician. You think you see it but it's in the other hand. You believe you have the hang of it and then poof! Gone. The spring creek

has muck for a bottom in most places, and the water depth near the banks can be unusually deep, deep enough to surprise the unwary wader, like magic. The Magus. Conchis. Just as cruel.

When I am fishing Silver Creek and no one is around, there is an inevitable music I hear in my head. The tricky currents are moving across the surface like so many instruments, part of a symphony but many playing the same note. I hear Phillip Glass's *The Photographer*—it's not traditional and it's not easy but it has its rhythm and repetition like a mantra ah ah ah ah ah.

Anglers have so many stop-starts, it's not a beautiful fishing experience. I mean, it ought to be but you get moss on your fly over half the time, your fly drags eleven of twelve times, you finally get a strike and you miss. Even when you figure it out, you aren't really sure if you were allowed to catch some fish to set you up for next time or what.

Not all fishing stories end the way you want them to and not all fishing stories even have an ending. Some just go on for years. Sometimes you know the answer before you have a fishing story, like a *Columbo* show—but you still enjoy the ride. What's cool about Silver Creek is that you know how it's going to end. You're not going to catch any fish. If you do, you beat the odds. If you land a big one, get a picture. You'll need one to prove it to your friends.

So you go to Silver Creek. You are one heckuva fly fisher, even your buddies say so. You bring your best fishing buddy. Now close your eyes and let's daydream:

The morning is wet and cold and the Polarfleece you got wet when you slipped and fell and later hung over the back of the chair to dry didn't. You said last night the two of you would eat a quick breakfast, a Pop Tart maybe, but this morning, with the clouds low and the air damp, the two of you decide to stop at the diner for something hot.

When you make the river, you wished you'd gone for the cold quick meal because, as you stand and watch, the trout are rising in the green water, sipping, everywhere you look and you can hear the subtle slurps and the water falling off the trout's backs.

You two fish all day, moving up the river, stopping and casting to rising fish. Your casts are things of beauty but doggone it, the millions of currents singing their song are sure messing up your tune. Two times a trout moved to your fly but stopped short. You talk to several anglers along your upstream hike and they're not having much better luck. One older gentleman in his seventies is fishing with his son, in his fifties. The son lowers his head when he confesses his old man has caught five fish, he none. All on wet flies. Old-school.

You and your friend work the banks, work the channels between islands, cast over and over to any feeding lanes and the current edges. You've seen some of the famous spots along the creek over the three days so far, Kilpatrick Bridge, the S-Turns, confluences with Grove and Loving Creeks, Purdy Ranch Pond, the Old Larkin Ranch. You've seen trout as big as you've ever seen on a river before. Some of the lunkers were cruising in the wide flat water that's more lake than river. Over three days, each of you has caught and landed two trout, each about 15 inches. All rainbows. But not a trout at all today. And daylight is dimming.

You turn and ask your buddy, why do you think the big brown, the 17-inch one, why did it take the downwing when mayflies were all over the water? He harrumphs knowing it's a stupid question and that it'd be more efficient to figure out where we're going to eat for dinner tonight.

This is the part where you sigh and sit on a log and light a cigar and reflect but you don't do that. You're okay with all of this. You earned it and you can walk away from it since it's a part of you, it's a part of Silver Creek and you can go back to the motel and sleep well tonight.

Located in south-central Idaho, Silver Creek is close to Ketchum, Sun Valley, and Hailey, off Highway 75. The best public access to the spring creek is through the Conservancy property. All a fisherman needs to do is sign in at the Preserve headquarters. The private water of Purdy Ranch holds big trout and must be floatfished by belly boat, but the public may not trespass the high water mark. Other access is at the Highway 20 crossing, the Point of Rocks, Priest Rapids. Fishable all year-round, but the best fishing is usually from June to October.

If you are a seasoned veteran and haven't fished Silver Creek, you owe yourself a day of near-misses, squishy wading, sunburn, and watching large trout refuse your best casts. It's like facing a Nolan Ryan fastball. You probably won't hit it but 1) what if you do and 2) this is one of the Hall of Fame

South Fork, Boise River

Solid winter trout fishery, so close to Boise (just an hour) and other towns, that most people don't give the river the credit it deserves. This wild rainbow trout fishery has parts which provide only marginal fishing, but the twelve-mile section below Anderson Ranch Reservoir and the thirty-mile section below Danskin Bridge are some of the more exciting and picturesque trout waters in Idaho. The section below the dam receives heavy pressure because a road follows it closely, but the second section can be accessed only by boat. The South Fork of the Boise isn't a large river by Western standards, but the enticement of catching large wild rainbows in riffles, runs, and pocket water make the South Fork a nice day-out from Boise.

trout streams in the world. If you're scared, go to church.

Once you get to the creek, there are few places to grab a bite or rest your weary bones. Lodging, restaurants, and groceries are plentiful to the north in Sun Valley and Ketchum, and twenty miles to the south in Wood River Valley. There are campgrounds near Silver Creek at the Sportsman's Access near Picabo. Access to Silver Creek is best found at the Silver Creek Preserve. There are other access points along the river as well. Float tubes are a great way to approach and fish this creek. Highways 20, 93, and other side roads make access possible.

CONTACTS

Conservancy Visitor's Center, 208-788-2203

The Nature Conservancy, Sun Valley, 208-726-3007

Ultimate Angler, Sun Valley, 208-483-2722

Ultimate Angler, Boise, 208-389-9957

Silver Creek Outfitters, Ketchum, 208-726-5282

Lost River Outfitters, Ketchum, 208-726-1706

Bill Mason Outfitters, Sun Valley, 208-622-9305

Sun Valley Outfitters, Sun Valley, 208-622-3400

Silver Creek Outfitters, Ketchum, 208-622-3400

St. Joe River

- **Location:** Northern Idaho
- **What You Fish For:** Cutthroat and smallmouth bass
- **Highlights and Notables:** Lovely river loaded with catchable cutts

Idahoans rave about the St. Joe. Half of it has great trout fishing, the other half great bass fishing. I've fished it twice. I am not an Idahoan but I have to admit, the trout part is wholly correct.

Besides, the St. Joe River empties into

Lake Coeur d'Alene after flowing from the Bitteroot Range on the Montana-Idaho border for 140 miles and you'd be hard-pressed to find a more spectacular landscape for a Western river to run through. Neat fact: St. Joe is the highest navigable river in the world at 2,200 feet. The river is one of America's Wild and Scenic Rivers and why not.

The best stretch for fly fishing is from Avery upstream where the river is much smaller and has clear water, riffle-run-pool configurations, and is secluded. I didn't see a soul (or at least a fly fishing soul because there were quite a few kayakers) for two days as I stayed in pretty much a half-mile stretch and caught westslope cutthroat and stocked rainbow on fluffy western patterns in pools, riffles, and especially in the runs and pocket water. I didn't catch one cutt over 14 inches, I don't believe, either trip but I had a blast.

The water below Avery is big enough to float and fish but next time I go back, I'd like to backpack into the upper reaches. St. Joe is easy to get to since SR 50 runs right beside it. Catch-and-release regs apply to the upper fifty miles of the river (from Prospector Creek up). St. Maries and Avery have minimal supplies but you can camp on the river or make the drive from Coeur d'Alene, which is one of the most beautiful villages you'll ever see.

CONTACTS

Idaho Department of Fish and Game, Lewiston, 208-799-5010

Blue Goose Sporting Goods, St. Maries, 208-245-4015

St. Joe Outfitters & Guides, St. Maries, www.stjoeoutfitters.com

Teton River

- **Location:** Southeastern Idaho
- **What You Fish For:** Cutthroat trout
- **Highlights and Notables:** The Teton is one of the most spectacular rivers that Nature has to offer. Lots of cutthroats for dry fly fishers, too.

The Teton is seductive. She has you at hello.

If the Yellowstone is just too crowded for your taste, drive west to the Teton River near Driggs, Idaho, not far away at all. If you don't take the time to drive west to the Teton River near Driggs, Idaho, you are missing out on what has to rank as the most beautiful river in the world. I don't know if it is or not, but it has to be considered in the running, it's *that* stunningly overwhelming. The Grand Teton Mountain Range is craggy, skyward, pointy, angular, snow-covered, dramatic, shadowy.

The seductive Teton is located in eastern Idaho and is canyon stream at times, meadow stream at times. The spring-fed river's manna is the cutthroat trout. Eager to please, colorful as a painter's palette, the cutthroat is the ultimate symbol for the wildness of the Rocky Mountains. These natives rise willingly to dry flies. Teton also holds rainbows, hybrid cuttbows, brook trout, and whitefish.

Official List of Idaho Record Fish

People who fish Brownlee Reservoir and nearby waters know this is a good area to fish if you want to have a chance at breaking a state record. Below are the Idaho state records for fish as of June 2004, according to Idaho Dept. of Fish & Wildlife. The following information was obtained from the Idaho Fish and Game Web site.

Trout Family

Species	Weight	Length	Girth	Location	Angler	Address	Lure	Test	Date
Atlantic Salmon	13 lbs. 6 ozs.	29.75"	17.75"	Deadwood Reservoir	Garrett Buffington	Emmett	Jensen Krocodile	6#	10/15/95
Brook	7 lbs. 1 oz.	23.5"	15.5"	Henry's Lake	DeVere Stratton	Idaho Falls	Worm	6#	8/16/78
Brown	26 lbs. 6 ozs.	36.5"	24.75"	South Fork Snake River	Farrell Oswald	Idaho Falls	Sculpin	6#	4/16/81
Bull (Dolly Varden)	32 lbs.	—	—	Pend Orielle Lake	Nelson Higgins	—	—	—	1949
Chinook (fresh water)	42 lbs.	41.25"	29.75"	Coeur d'Alene Lake	Jane Clifford	Coeur d'Alene	Hootchie	30#	9/13/87
Chinook (ocean run)	54 lbs.	—	—	Salmon River	Merrold Gold	—	—	—	1956
Coho	6 lbs.	23.5"	—	Cascade Reservoir	Ted Bowers	Horseshoe Bend	Z-ray Green	12#	9/19/92
Cutthroat	18 lbs. 15 ozs.	—	—	Bear Lake	Roger Grunig	Montpelier	—	—	4/30/70

Species	Weight	Length	Girth	Water	Angler	Location	Bait	Line	Date
Golden	5 lbs. 2 ozs.	—	—	White Sands Lake	George Wolverton	—	—	—	1958
Grayling	2 lbs. 7 ozs.	18.125"	—	Nez Perce Lake	Velma Mahaffey	Lemhi	Horse Fly	4#	6/21/92
Kamloops	37 lbs.	—	—	Pend Oreille Lake	Wes Hamlet	—	—	—	1947
Kokanee	6 lbs. 9.5 ozs.	24.5"	14.5"	Priest Lake	Jerry Verge	Spokane, WA	—	—	6/9/75
Lake (Mackinaw)	57 lbs. 8 ozs.	49"	32.5"	Priest Lake	Lyle McClure	Spokane, WA	—	—	11/14/71
Lake Whitefish	3 lbs. 5 ozs.	22.125"	11.25"	Pend Oreille Lake	David Fowler	Coeur d'Alene	Treble Hook	4#	5/3/98
Mountain Whitefish	5 lbs. 14.4 ozs.	22.5"	14"	Island Park Reservoir	Robert Hall	Glenns Ferry	Caddis Fly	8#	1997
Rainbow	19 lbs.	—	—	Hayden Lake	R.M. Williams	—	—	—	11/47
Rainbow/Cutthroat Hybrid	24 lbs.	35.5"	24.5"	Pend Oreille Lake	Irwin H. Donart	Nampa	Bucktail Fly	12#	11/21/91
Sockeye	5 lbs.	24"	—	Redfish Lake	June McCray	Boise	—	—	8/8/70
Splake	10 lbs. 3 ozs.	28"	16.5"	Ririe Reservoir	R. Lee Davison	Rigby	White Rooster Tail	8#	5/31/04
Steelhead	30 lbs. 2 ozs.	44"	—	Clearwater River	Keith Powell	Lewiston	—	—	11/23/73

Official List of Idaho Record Fish (Cont.)

Other Species

Species	Weight	Length	Girth	Location	Angler	Address	Lure	Test	Date
Black Crappie	3 lbs. 8.96 ozs.	17.5"	15"	Brownlee Reservoir	Jason Monson	Middleton	—	—	6/8/03
Bluegill	3 lbs. 8 ozs.	—	—	C.J. Strike Reservoir	Darrell Grim	Nampa	—	—	1966
Bluegill/ Pumpkinseed Hybrid	1 lb. .03 oz.	9.875"	10.25"	Star Lane Pond	Kevin Graveline	Eagle	1/16 oz. jig	4#	5/8/01
Bullhead Catfish	3 lbs. 14 ozs.	20.5"	11.875"	Brownlee Reservoir	James Winter	Gooding	Dead Minnow	10#	5/25/86
Channel Catfish	31 lbs. .05 oz.	38"	23.5"	Mann Lake	Kenny Decker	Kooskia	Nightcrawler	30#	8/25/01
Flathead Catfish	58 lbs. 8 ozs.	48"	31"	Brownlee Reservoir	J. Newberry/ K. McCormick	Star	Snell Hooks	20#	8/23/94
Green Sunfish	5 ozs.	7.375"	6"	Hauser Lake	Tom Fulton	Post Falls	Rubber Worm	12#	5/26/94
Largemouth Bass	10 lbs. 15 ozs.	—	—	Anderson Lake	Mrs. M.W. Taylor	—	—	—	—
Ling (Burbot)	14 lbs.	—	—	Kootenai River	P.A. Dayton	—	—	—	1954
Northern Pike	38 lbs. 9 ozs.	49"	23.75"	Coeur d'Alene Lake	Dennis W. Hicks	Post Falls	Spoon	10#	4/11/92
Northern Pike	38 lbs. 9 ozs.	49.75"	23"	Hayden Lake	Walter Estes	Spirit Lake	Smelt	80#	3/19/02
Pumpkinseed	14 ozs.	9.75"	10"	Chase Lake	Bob Russell	Coeur d'Alene	Wedding Ring	8#	1977

Species	Weight	Length	Girth	Location	Angler	City	Bait	Line	Date
Smallmouth Bass	8 lbs. 5 ozs.	22"	19.25"	Dworshak Reservoir	Dan Steigers	Juliaetta	Power Grub	6#	10/14/95
Sturgeon (Rod & Reel)	394 lbs.	—	—	Snake River	Glenn Howard	—	—	—	1956
Sturgeon (Set Line)	675 lbs.	—	—	Snake River	Unknown	—	—	—	1908
Tiger Muskie	38 lbs. 7 ozs.	48.25"	22.5"	Hauser Lake	Douglas Butts	Eureka, MT	Mepps Bucktail Yellow	30#	6/16/01
Walleye	16 lbs. 2 ozs.	32.5"	19.5"	Salmon Falls Creek Reservoir	Bill Sorensen	Kuna	Mr. Twister	8#	6/7/96
Warmouth	9.6 ozs.	8.75"	8.5"	Snake River	Marvin Stevens	Twin Falls	Slip Bobber/Worm	—	6/23/88
White Crappie	3 lbs. 1 oz.	17"	14.5"	Crane Creek Reservoir	Leslie Greenwood	Council	Worm	10#	5/27/01
Yellow Perch	2 lbs. 9.6 ozs.	15.5"	—	Wilson Lake	Jerry Hamblin	Burley	—	—	1/3/76
Nongame Species									
Carp	37 lbs. 8 ozs.	44"	25.5"	Brownlee Reservoir	Jere Bower	Boise	Shad Rap	12#	6/13/88
Chiselmouth	1.16 lbs.	14.25"	8.375"	Salmon River	Justin Powell	Nampa	Worm	10#	4/15/03
Largescale Sucker	8 lbs. 2.56 ozs.	29.25"	17.75"	Cascade Lake	Terry Sunderland	Boise	Worm	12#	4/2000
Peamouth	1.06 lbs.	14.75"	7.75"	Clearwater River	Robert Riek	Peck	Worm	6#	5/4/04
Pikeminnow	7 lbs. 14.24 ozs.	25.25"	16"	Snake River	Emil Nowoj	Asotin, Wa.	Jig	8#	5/7/04
Tench	4 lbs. 14 ozs.	21"	—	Spokane River	Scotty Brueher	—	—	—	2000
Tilapia	1 lb. 10 ozs.	13.5"	11.5"	Snake River	Stephen Gobel	Twin Falls	Worm	6#	2/10/01
Utah Sucker	7 lbs. 11 ozs.	25.5"	—	Portneuf River	Craig Curtiss	—	—	—	1999

The trout can reach prodigious sizes, even the native cutts. I mean really big. Some grow well into the mid-20-inch range. Most of the trout you land will be 12 to 16 inches but many hit that 16- to 19-inch slot. Large wild trout on dry flies in a world-class setting. The guides will warn you that these trout can be challenging and they're right but comparatively, not that tough, and most of the time, catching trout goes as smoothly as the glassy surface you are floating. The upper Teton is, after all, what many once called the best dry fly river in the West.

This blue ribbon fishery went through tough times (degradation, silting, a big flood) but it's coming back and coming back strong.

I'm not sure that most anglers know this is a spring-fed, spring creek–like river and instead most have in their mind the choppy fast-moving water, an angler at the bow casting. Teton River has that but much of the river (the Upper Teton) slow-moving and fertile, loaded with insects and sipping trout.

The Narrows. Enter at your own risk. Below the slow spring creek comes the drop, the boulders, the rapids, the canyon. To reach the roily river in one section, guides lower catarafts to the water from 1,000 feet above. Make sure you read that correctly. If that's not Butch and Sundance enough for you, some of the rapids are such killers that you may be asked to get out while your guide maneuvers the treacherous section. To top it off, this crazy Narrows part of the Teton may fish better than any other part—the catch rates are great and the trout are huge.

Soft and easy. Rough and hard. The Teton, femme fatale.

CONTACTS

Reel Women, Victor, www.reelwomen.com

Teton Valley Lodge, Driggs, www .tetonvalleylodge.com

Henry's Fork Anglers, Island Park, www .henrysforkanglers.com

Coy's Wilderness Fishing Trips, Jackson Hole, WY, 307-733-6726

Hyde Outfitters, Island Park, 800-428-8338

MONTANA

I was in the Corps of Cadets at Texas A & M University my freshman year. I bounced out that year with a sparkling 1.0 GPA. One tradition, one of thousands in College Station, a remnant of the "good old days" is called quadding. This is a practice that I can't imagine is still in practice in Aggieland but I don't know for sure.

Here's how quadding works (worked):

1. A junior (serge-butt) or senior (zip) would tell us freshmen (fish) to go grab

an individual. The serge-butt or zip had his reasons for picking this unfortunate fellow and it usually involved some sort of public slight.

2. They'd give us a name, a dorm, and a time.

3. The twelve of us would ambush the unsuspecting fellow and carry him back kicking and screaming to our dorm, having changed him into swim trunks or shorts.

4. Two fish would have filled a fifty-five gallon trash can to the brim with water. They stationed said trash can on the second floor near the window at the stairwell.

5. The ten remaining fish force this struggling corps member to his back, his legs open toward the open window above. The two stairwell fish, on the command of said serge-butt or zip, begin pouring the water in a solid stream toward the prone prisoner's privates where it would hit him with such breathtaking force that his screams would shut down immediately. The heavy stream of water would continue to punish the violator until the water ran out, at which point the fish would relinquish their hold and run away.

Weird tradition, this Corps of Cadets payback, huh? A long way to get to my point, too. The Big Hole takes your breath away, hard, like that heavy rush of water from the second floor window, but there won't be a gaggle of freshmen holding you down. If you're an angler, you're not going to know what to say as you catch big fish af-

ter big fish. If you fish the Big Hole during the salmonfly hatch, not even the quadding metaphor works. Takes your breath away.

When Kenny wasn't looking, I purloined a Kenny's Special Adams Parachute, one of his own inventions. He'd been catching more than I had on the Kenny's Special, and he hadn't offered me the fly yet. I'd been fishing to match the yellow stones I saw in the air but that the trout weren't taking.

We'd both gotten over our going-to-a-new-place anxiety first thing that morning when ten minutes after we launched and strung up and tied on, he landed a 15-inch brown. He had caught at least five more than I had at that point and I needed to do something or I'd hear about it all day long. To some, stealing another angler's fly deserves flogging. With fishing buddies, it's no big deal. And I started catching fish on Kenny's Special Adams Parachute, one nice brown about 18 inches, long body, big head.

■ ■ ■

Think someone you know doesn't fart? Cuss? Well, next fishing trip with a new try-them-on-for-size fishing buddy, do this: ride in a car for eight hours eating nothing but Paydays and drinking Big Red sodas, wade across a dangerous river holding hands with this possible-partner-to-be, eat at a greasy spoon or out of the same can of chili over a campfire, laugh at their stupid jokes, help them remove a hook from their thumb, catch them letting out a silent-but-deadly without them having the common courtesy to open the tent flap or roll down the window—you figure out quickly if this is someone you want beside you in a deep run.

If you want a concentrated version of the regular fishing trip to test out a potential angling mate, go on a weekend backpack fishing hike. Nothing like blisters and bears and tasteless freeze-dried foods to show off the dark side of a person.

After a fishing trip, you both know if you're ever going to do it again. It's a given, one way or another. Kenny and I have been on so many fishing trips together that we finish each other's sentences. In fact, we more often just kinda intuit what the other guy is thinking and wanting to say, somehow we just know and we don't have to do much more than grunt or nod.

Example: White Mountains, Arizona. I came with new camping gear (we share most all that kind of stuff—you bring the deep fry and I'll get the propane), and Kenny was fighting a headache and it was dark before we ever set up camp and Kenny was grunting, head down, eating while I was eating from the cookware and I complained that my chili tasted funny. I also whined that he had taken more than me.

"Idiot," he stopped eating and drawled. "Did you remember to take the plastic wrapping out of your new little pan?"

I hadn't. Cellophane does not a good meal make.

Each of us has his roles in the partnership. I'm the Wal-Mark of the duo. I bring most everything either of us would ever need and when he needs it, I have it. He

fights bears. When Terry Moore joined us as a fishing buddy, the only other member we've unofficially allowed (other than our brother-in-law David), we immediately charged him with camp cooking, bringing the liquor and being bear-bait. The nickname stuck by the way. Bear bait.

After a few years, Kenny's corny jokes are kinda funny but I don't dare let him know that. Kenny has removed hooks from my body including the one he yanked out of the back of my head—the fly imbedded in the thin skin a few inches back from my big ears on the right side—and I have tended to his wounds. He always gets cuts or scratches or impales himself on some part of nature. A blind trust develops in a good fishing buddy setup, a locker room mentality of what's said there on the trip, stays on the trip.

No whining (except if it's life-threatening or we're missing out on catching fish).

No lying. Be honest.

So we've been through thick and thin—he's thick and I'm thin. I think back to being stranded on that Western lake with little hope of getting out but swimming or climbing the sheer cliff. We swam.

I remember Kenny doing the River-Runs-Through-It for me a few years back on South Clear Creek in Colorado when a particularly large brown (22-inches on that small stream is more than particularly large, I guess) took me downstream on my three-weight and easily dashed through two deep pools.

Kenny was neck-deep (he doesn't have a neck, but you get the picture) with his net in his chubby hands held high above his massive cranium. He never went under but he would have, he's that kind of fishing buddy. He landed the monster and went back to fishing and neither of us said much about how wet he was or how stupid that was.

We fish until dark on most any river we visit. We make camp in the dark, in the rain. We clamor in the woods picking up what we hope is campfire wood. We get up early, fish hard, wade through deep water, jump from big rock to smaller rock, hike up steep scree slopes, all stupid stuff for men with families.

I heated water in the popup while Kenny was casting to early rising trout on the San Juan one February, snow falling. I washed my hair outside and had two pots of water, one hot, one cold. Kenny came back amazed to see me washing my hair—I had hair then—in the cold morning air. I told him it wasn't that bad, I heated water and if he wanted, lean over and I'll pour it on your head while you lather that mane of yours. He fell for it. I poured the entire pan of cold water on his big noggin.

You have to use your noggin to catch trout on the Bighorn. I recommend hiring a guide for a day or two to decipher where they are holding, what techniques and flies are happening and hot. The fishing can be easy but most times, the trout are selective and the fishing is challenging.

For three days, Kenny and I caught fish, the largest a 22-inch rainbow so fat he looked like he was ready to burst. It was July and it was hot, hotter than anyone would expect in Montana. We were both tanned with a hint of red in our cheeks.

Kenny freckles, I tan more. Wide-brimmed hats would have kept our ears from frying in the baking sun. We had a blast. We caught a lot of fish, few under 14 inches, most around 16, 17. We were working for our trout, moving around, then setting up shop, switching out flies to match hatches, cross-talking about this and that. We don't "advise" each other because each of us thinks he is the better angler. We just share information.

Our meals were unmemorable, the lodging Kenny's pop-up camper. We both agree it was one of our best fishing trips.

■　■　■

We left the Bighorn and had two other rivers to hit on our way back to Texas. We ate Pop Tarts, beef jerky, drank Coca-Colas, had a huge Frito pie at a roadside stand somewhere in northern Colorado and sang aloud to Willie Nelson all the way home. I looked over one time at Kenny's big head and remembered a line Randy Denham had said about him— "Hey Kenny, the Egyptians called and they want their Sphinx back." Kenny at one point let the boat get away and had to slosh like a madman to retrieve it. Neither of us said a word. We didn't have to. He knew he was an idiot.

So why do I keep going on these suicide trips with this man? After all, whenever I go fishing with him, adventures (or should I say, misadventures) happen.

I occasionally feel sorry for the guy. I remember when Kenny bought an expensive new reel, jumped from the bank to a big rock in the middle of a river, fell and damaged the reel. Moments later, he hooked up with a heavy fish, half of his reel fell off into the water, and he retrieved the line hand over hand thinking that at the end of the retrieval he'd find the other half. All he came up with was the end of his line. You know what they say about fishing—a hook at one end and a fool at the other.

The Bighorn can sometimes skunk you, make you feel the fool. But most times, if you work hard, pay attention, you can have the proverbial field day. Over beers one night, Kenny and I rambled on about past fish and future fishing destinations, wives and past girlfriends, hopes and dreams, and jobs and money and right after the last beer, we kinda figured out the meaning of life. By morning, we forgot what it was or I'd share it with you.

Kenny the erstwhile philosopher was present and guilty at the Crystal Lake Debacle, the Alpine Loop Bicycle Marathon, the Shortcut Hike that Became the Longcut, and the Battle with the Bear at Wounded Knee Creek.

I've hiked hundreds of miles with this guy; waded through thousands of gallons of water; rafted (foolishly) dozens of rivers with him; fished over a hundred streams and a handful of lakes with this teacher-coach-outdoor writer; and I've avoided bears and moose when he went out of his way to find them. We have slept in the rain, woke up to the snow, cast in the lightning, woke up to a herd of bugling autumn elk outside our tent, broken down in the summer in 100-plus degree heat, traded and loaned fishing gear, tried out and purchased rods and reels, eaten fresh grilled brook trout and also many cans of chili and ravioli and tasteless freeze-dried meals.

He's my fishing buddy and good ones are difficult to come by, even if he's goofy and risky. You know, he catches fish and he fights bears and I'll go fishing with him anywhere, anytime.

Beaverhead River

- **Location:** Southwestern Montana
- **What You Fish For:** Brown and rainbow trout
- **Highlights and Notables:** Classic Western stream with trophy trout but beware, despite the fact you've heard this river's name mentioned with the other classics, this one is more challenging than you'd think. The payoff is there if you work it right.

The Beaverhead. Conjures images of the west. Big brown trout. Twenty-inch trout. A classic Western stream. Fertile. Fifty-miles long. Tailwater. All true.

I should warn you that the Beaverhead is not the trout mecca where you pull up, get out, and start catching fish. The Beaverhead is incredibly challenging. Selective browns. Tiny flies. Lots of streamside habitat to steal your flies. Narrow in places. And with its trophy trout reputation, the Beaverhead can get awfully crowded. All true, too.

The Beaverhead is best known for its smooth-surfaced upper reaches where anglers float in low-slung boats in the fast, tricky current short casting to 3-pound trout lying in wait under a tangled web of willows and cottonwood overhanging the undercut banks. Anglers will lose many flies and leaders to the brushy banks, but to catch Beaverhead browns, one must be aggressive and toss flies and lures into the thick trout habitat.

I have always floated the Beaverhead. The river is tough to wade, impossible to wade unless the flows are low. There are deep pools, limited access from the shore. I like floating the Beaverhead. The Beaverhead doesn't have the scenic mountain ranges reflecting on the water surface but it has sagebrush and low hills, narrow canyon and flat valleys. I like that. Sure, the highway is in plain sight at times and there are obstacles to deal with, but I think it's a fun float. You have to cast well to get up under the overhanging brush and limbs. You have to watch out for weeds. The river turns and tosses and makes it difficult to anticipate what's next. Fun float. Anglers will want a guide because the river is tough to read, the currents difficult and sometimes dangerous to navigate, and various stretches of the river hold more trout than others.

These guides will tell you that the back eddies of the big pools hold some large browns. They have me cast to this backwater and I see rising trout and for some reason it's not where I do well. Others do.

I do better at guerilla fishing. I'm decent at getting casts under the limbs and around the fallen logs. I do well in the tight spots. I also lose a helluva lot of flies. Beaverhead hatches include caddis, PMDs, BWOS, stoneflies (goldens and yellows),

and craneflies. I lose imitative flies to each one of these insects.

The Beaverhead is not for beginners. Trying to entice these wily 15- to 20-inch brown and rainbow trout requires all of an angler's skills. You'll want to tie on as strong a tippet as will fit through your little flies and also not break as soon as you hook up with a lunker as you're sailing down the river in a strong current.

The upper sixteen miles has the best fishing of the river. You'll fish with streamers and nymphs unless you see hatches and even then, the trout are sophisticated enough to taunt and tease. Then again, I've seen the Beaverhead in full hatch mode with trout biting any fly I threw out there. Rare but it happens.

Work the banks, work foam lines, work any edges, the backwater (yeah, right) and good luck. The Beaverhead will likely kick your butt. That's the fun of it. Butte and Bozeman are the closest plane flights in to fish the Beaverhead. You'll probably make Dillon your home base.

Big Hole River

- **Location:** Southwestern Montana, southwest of Butte

- **What You Fish For:** Rainbow, brook, brown, cutthroat, grayling

- **Highlights and Notables:** There are those who believe the Big Hole is the best trout river in the world. Might be. The trout are boastful yet magnanimous. The river holds titans that will stare you down as you net them and put fear in your heart as they swim slowly, confidently away.

The Big Hole is a 150-mile long tributary to the Jefferson River. Plain and simple, this is one of the best trout rivers in the United States. I think that this is one of the most awesome rivers to behold, too. You'll be awestruck. Dumbstruck. Struck by lightning. From the towering mountains in the upper section to the river-cleft canyon to the sweeping green valley, the Big Hole has as beautiful and as diverse a landscape as any river in Montana.

In the upper section, my favorite section, the prettiest scenery of the river, the brook trout are bigger than most anybody knows or talks about. Fifteen-inch brook trout on a Royal Trude, hookjaw and all. This upper water holds brook trout and rainbows and cutthroats and some browns and most especially grayling, the last meaningful river-residing population of grayling in the lower forty-eight. So make the upper Big Hole part of your trip because of 1) the

beauty; 2) the ease of catching fish; and 3) grayling.

With the Beaverhead, the Big Hole merges and forms Jefferson River. Before it gets to that marriage, the river changes characters more than a New York street corner. Flats, runs, riffles, canyons, meadows, big valleys and big mountains, and wide open spaces. In the lowest stretch, the must-float-this-big-puppy stretch, the river braids and undercuts banks and this is where the biggest browns and rainbows lurk.

The Big Hole River is famous for its salmonfly hatch which begins in early June and lasts into early July but the staple diet for trout is caddis, whose clouds sometimes darken the skies.

So let's review (and add some new things) why you should make the Big Hole a top-five fishing trip on the list you've been making as you read this book:

Super insect hatches especially salmonfly and caddis. Lots of trout, small and medium and large. Six species of game fish: brown, rainbow, brook, cutthroat, grayling, and mountain whitefish. Don't roll your eyes, give whitefish a chance. Great tributaries for adjunct trips. The River Wisdom. Big Hole River used to be called the River Wisdom. Wise up and come here and fish. Holes are valleys in nineteenth century frontiersmen lingo.

The river is thought of in three sections: upper section from Jackson to where the Wise River comes in; middle from Wise to Glen; and lower section from Glen to confluence with Beaverhead at Twin Bridges.

Good access in most parts, not as good for wading in spots, better in others. Float trip best. Fishing the Big Hole can be crowded until the salmonfly hatch is over (it's that good).

CONTACTS
Complete Fly Fishers, 406-832-3175
Bugs & Bullets, 406-782-6251
Fran Johnson's Sports Shop, 406-782-3322
Montana Fly Company, 406-835-2621
Sunrise Fly Shop, 406-835-3474
Great Divide Outfitters, 406-267-3346
Frontier Anglers, 406-683-5276
Uncle Bob's Fishing Supplies, 406-683-5565
Montana Troutfitters, 406-587-4707
The Bozeman Angler, 406-587-9111

Bighorn River

- **Location:** South central Montana near the Wyoming border
- **What You Fish For:** Brown and rainbow trout
- **Highlights and Notables:** This is real easy. A simple river. Big-ass trout.

The Bighorn is no-frills, big Western river fishing at its finest. The Bighorn is a fishing buddy river. The best way to get to know someone is to go on a three-day fishing trip with them. A week's better but if you don't like them, you risk jail-time for what you might do. Three's plenty.

Most anglers *sans* fishing buddies don't properly acknowledge that a significant portion of any fishing trip, of any worthwhile fishing trip, necessarily involves adversity. Sometimes pain. Danger. Stealth.

Adversity breeds honesty.

Maybe it reveals it, instead. Regardless, if you take a face-first header into a cold pool because of slippery rocks, you should right yourself and laugh with your fishing buddy and suck it up and see if you have anything at the end of your line. On any fishing trip to a canyon stream, one of us is bound to say "go ahead and jump—you can make it." If we don't, well, like I said, adversity breeds honesty.

The Bighorn is considered by many to be one of the top two or three trout fisheries in the nation. This belief prevails despite that the Bighorn River takes a constant pounding year-round from the numbers of fly fishermen who flock to the tailwater as a result of the glowing reports in articles and books and television fishing shows.

Great hatches. Fishable year-round. Consistent fishing. Rainbows and browns that average 16 inches. One of the best places in the USA to catch a trophy trout. Outstanding dry fly fishing.

Plains rivers are not always beautiful but the Bighorn is an exception. This tailwater is clear and cold, pursuing its course through wide open spaces, flanked by rolling hills and isolation in the upper river, then the Bighorn and Pryor Mountains rise from the flat land. Few trees save cottonwoods drink from the river. With the blue hue of the Bighorn, the mixtures of greens and browns on the landscape, and the rainbow of colors of the trout, the experience is colorful.

The Bighorn tailwaters below Yellowtail Dam might be the best chance for a fisherman to land heavy-bodied 3- to 4-pound browns and rainbows on a regular basis. Heck, the average trout caught on the river is over 16 inches. Landing trout over 20 inches is not unusual. There are fewer days where an angler catches twenty to forty trout in a day but the size of the trout remains deep and wide and long. Some blame drought, some blame other things and all this could change by next year. But the river will still produce big trout one way or another.

The most popular stretch is the thirteen-mile section below Yellowtail Dam. It gets crowded, folks. Combat fishing.

The Bighorn acts much like a spring creek in places, with a weedy bed and big fish that feed on scuds, sowbugs, aquatic worms, chironimids, caddis flies, and may-

flies. Anglers come to this cold fishery in hopes of landing the purported trophy trout with every cast, and even though the Bighorn supports an amazing amount of trout biomass, the predominate brown trout and hatchery rainbow trout (several generations removed since they no longer stock the Bighorn) are under greater and greater stress from overfishing, high water levels, large trout mortality, and other factors. Special regulations have been introduced to counteract some of these problems, and more may be forthcoming.

This is a boating river but not necessarily how you're thinking. With limited public access, the only way to cover water is to be in a watercraft. The Bighorn moves slowly, ponderingly, so you'll see kayaks and canoes and float tubes and pontoons in addition to the drift boats. You put in with a boat, find a good spot to park it, then get out and wade fish (although in high water, you better be watchful where you step).

The lodging and dining options in the towns along the Bighorn are spartan, utilitarian. Nightlife is nonexistent. I recommend one of the many lodges on the river because if you're going to be thinking only of fishing on a trip, and on the Bighorn you should be thinking of little else, you might as well be on the river. And the meals are better, too.

CONTACTS

Bighorn Angler, www.bighornangler.com

Big Horn Fly and Tackle Shop, www
   .bighornfly.com

Bighorn Trout Shop, www
   .bighorntroutshop.com

Ellyn Nadeau, Michael Mastrangelo, Fort Smith Fly Shop and Cabins, www .flyfishingthebighorn.com

Bitterroot River

- **Location:** Southwestern Montana
- **What You Fish For:** Rainbow, brown, brook, cutthroat trout
- **Highlights and Notables:** Great hatches, diversity of ideal lies, big trout

The Bitterroot is a perfect example of the ideal Western stream. Loaded with riffles and runs, pools and glides and structure, structure everywhere. And the river has great hatches, too, especially the strange-

sounding "Skwala" hatch. This is a special enough hatch that it's worth devoting some time to in this book, a hatch integral to catching Bitterroot trout during certain times of the year. What's a Skwala? Chuck Stranahan's Flies and Guides fly shop owner and guide Chuck Stranahan talks.

"It happened again last week," Stranahan shares. "A well-meaning angler came into the shop and asked for a Skwala emerger. This would be a knowledgeable request during a mayfly emergence."

"Skwalas are stoneflies," Stranahan told him. The angler understood. His expression changed a couple of times. Then they kidded a little about how the trout would don their little trout equivalents of scuba gear to go slithering up into the streamside rocks to take the emerging stoneflies.

The Skwala hatch is misunderstood, no doubt. You hear some talk about how you can toss out any big attractor and the trout will rise from the depths to splashily attack the fly. Many don't know what the heck a Skwala is but they know they want to be on the river when the Skwala is hatching. Stranahan knows that the *skwala parallela* is a golden stonefly–sized bug that hatches in many west-slope rivers during the pre-runoff period, but provides fishable numbers of bugs in only a few. Of them, the Bitterroot River in Western Montana sees this bug as an annual "super hatch."

More olive stonefly than anything else, they can range in color from greenish-gray to fatigue green. They are often confused with similar (but different) stoneflies. Know this, though—they are angler-friendly if you play your cards right.

Start with nymphs. "Any #8 dark stone-fly nymph will do for the nymph, which can be especially productive before the trout key on the adults," says Stranahan. "Several local variations of standard salmonfly nymphs, scaled down, and featuring a peacock herl body, are deadly when the water temps hover around 47 or 48 degrees."

What about dries? Stranahan informs that "on the Bitterroot, good fishing occurs between spurts of nasty weather. The water temperatures gradually warm up to hatch-producing levels from the departure of winter until full-blown runoff, usually from mid-March until early or mid-May. There are multitudes of hatches; many of them can be profuse. It is not uncommon to be searching the surface with a dry #8 Olive Stone tied to 3X tippet, and find a bunch of big trout working hard on #16 Blue-winged Olive mayflies."

Stranahan knows that one of the big mistakes anglers make is to get in a hurry. He knows that "the temptation is to cast right into them. Sometimes it works. But very often the angler who is equipped with the big stones and nothing else will wish he packed his baetis emergers and 6X as well."

I agree with Stranahan when he says that "the Bitterroot offers the best prerun-off dry fly fishing I've experienced in any non-tailwater river in the West." It's top flight. And while the Skwala gets most of the attention, it isn't the only show in town. "But it's the one that gets the trout—and the anglers—going. They lie in wait, in the slow nondescript edges where the current washes the nymphs close to shore, and scarf down. Tread lightly, and carefully

drift a big bug. This is not dredging." And if you do it right, you'll have 20-inchers busting the surface instead of an 11-incher.

"At this time of year," Stranahan offers, "when the big Olive Stones are on the water, trout that would ordinarily sulk on the bottom come to the top. They aggressively crowd the juveniles off the feed lanes, and they feed aggressively. Places where a 12-incher would be welcome during midsummer will now produce fish that run 14 inches and above. Smaller fish scurry for cover, and are uncommon. Healthy trout to 14 to 18 inches are the norm, and fish over 20 inches on the dry fly are more numerous now than throughout the rest of the year."

These active big fish produce a frenzy among anglers that Stranahan cleverly calls "a local form of March madness" when they get behind the fly-tying vise. "Adrenaline and enthusiasm are the precursors to fly design. Some of the results have foam egg sacs that could be used to clean whitewall tires. There are gaudy combinations of parachutes and rubber legs and bright foam and dull dubbing and elk hair and synthetic wings that cause me to wonder just how much stuff can you load on a hook."

While the Bitterroot trout may take some of the crazy imitations early on, they wise up and anglers will have to more closely imitate an egg-laying olive female Olive Stone with peacock herl egg sac and golden olive abdomen tied to lay flat in the water and a sparse, fluttering wing on top.

Unlike the methods most use for stonefly fishing, anglers can't get away with splashy casts and short leaders. Stranahan warns "the water is usually clear and cold, as the stream meanders slowly at winter low levels in its bed. Stalking, a stealthy approach, and headhunting are usually the order of the day."

Another Montana river with a famous name, but the Bitterroot doesn't receive the intense fishing pressure of other Montana trout streams. The Bitterroot provides over seventy-five miles of scenic fishing sheltered for most of its run by the steep, rugged Bitterroot Mountains to the west, and to the east, by the forested Sapphire Mountains.

Anglers can easily float or wade the Root, and finding where the rainbow, brown, cutthroat, and brook are hiding is no problem whatsoever since the riparian makeup of the river is a smorgasbord of logjams, deep pools, riffles and runs, and undercut banks. Target where your fly can get lost and you'll find the trout.

CONTACTS

Chuck Stranahan, RiverBend Flyfishing, Hamilton, www.chuck-stranahan.com

Anglers Roost, www.anglersroost-montana.com

Blackbird's Fly Shop and Lodge, Victor, 406-642-6375

Blackfeet Reservation Lakes

- **Location:** Northwestern Montana
- **What You Fish For:** Trout
- **Highlights and Notables:** Harsh climate and harsher scenery keep away the riff-raff. Only serious anglers make the long journey to catch the goliath trout of the Blackfeet Reservation's numerous lakes.

Star Trek. You've watched the original and you've watched TNG (The New Generation). I like them both but some folks choose up sides with a passion. Doesn't matter.

Remember any of a hundred planets where the Enterprise landed or beamed. Like when Captain Kirk and Dr. McCoy were trying to escape from a forced-labor camp on the planet Rura Penthe in the movie *Star Trek VI: The Undiscovered Country.* They had to trek through bitter cold and gale-force winds with that traitorous shapeshifter who was really Iman, David Bowie's wife.

Or the time in *Star Trek II: The Wrath of Khan* when Commander Chekov beams down to a wasteland of a planet supposedly devoid of all life for Project Genesis only to find that Khan (not Chaka) has survived, with revenge on his mind, since Captain Kirk marooned him fifteen years earlier.

Inhospitable. Barren. Wasteland. Elements beyond man's control. Some of the biggest trout on the planet. Destination: Blackfeet Reservation in the remotest part of Montana.

Did I mention that the Blackfeet Reservation is stark, vast, hard? I should also mention that the lakes are blue and fertile and contrast greatly to the harshness. And their denizens are as enormous as any found in more famous trout fisheries anywhere in the world.

So many lakes and so many big fish and Blackfeet's waters are still so unknown. You can read that the Blackfeet Reservation usually has about fifteen to twenty available lakes depending on water and viability that range from one acre to 2,000 acres. You can hear that these lakes and ponds and reservoirs are so loaded with scuds and freshwater shrimp and leeches that trout on average weigh more than your typical poodle, somewhere around 5 pounds and that anglers report that they often catch twenty-five to fifty trout a day. These are heavy, deep, broad-shouldered trout. Many locals who fish these lakes often believe that a 5-pounder is about as good a catch as a minnow, that anything under 10 pounds isn't worth the effort. Anglers also report that they catch trout as long as 30 inches. So what's holding you back?

For one, it's not an easy destination to reach; 1.5 million acres east of Glacier National Park on the border of Canada. For another, this prairie is windy. Not windy like Chicago or Amarillo but constant, violent windy like the planet where Khan was marooned. This is rough country where the lakes have no natural reproduction and have to be stocked frequently. The streams haven't been developed yet as fisheries. Anglers don't have many lodging choices very close.

The mountains are in the background as you stand or float any of fifteen lakes, all within forty miles of each other, so while the immediate scenery is spare, the vistas are stunning. The streams are not developed but there are good reports about Cutbank and Two Medicine Creeks; besides which, almost nobody fishes them. The spring-fed lakes are fishable by March and April after ice-out and despite the bone-numbing cold and the boisterous winds, anglers have a field day with hungry big trout.

Giant rainbows make your heart stop when you seem them motoring in the shallows. When you hook one, they fight like the one night Buster Douglas was a tiger in Japan. These big, ferocious trout are the payoff for fighting the elements.

Duck Lake is probably the best known of the reservation lakes. Others you'll want to fish include Mission Lake, Hidden Lake, Goose Lake, Kipp Lake, Lower St. Mary Lake, Four Horns Lake, and Cooper Lake. Mitten Lake is a tough lake to get to but has a rep for long, hefty, feisty rainbows. Callibaetis is a major hatch on most of the lakes but freshwater shrimp is the number one fish-fattener. Scuds and leeches are also major players in the trout diet. The lakes have hatches of caddis in May, damselflies starting in June (which the fish dearly love), Pale Morning Duns by late June, and various terrestrials by August. You can find midges, too. The wind blows year round.

By October, the lion comes to town with winter ferocity and ends fishing.

If you fly fish, you should bring the works—sinking lines, sinktips, intermediate lines and floating lines and I know most bring a 5- or 6-weight but I think a 7-weight isn't too much when the wind is up, maybe even an 8-weight. Campgrounds on the reservation or in Browning at a motel or Babb or Cutbank or you can even stay in Glacier National Park.

In order to fish the Blackfeet Indian Reservation, an angler must buy a tribal license but won't have to possess a state fishing license. Cost to nonmembers of the tribe is $60 per year, and includes a boat authorization sticker and float-tube authorization sticker. A one-day license costs $25. A float-tube sticker is an additional $20, and a boat sticker an additional $20.

CONTACTS

Blackfeet Nation, Browning, www
   .blackfeetnation.com

Blackfoot River

- **Location:** Southwest Montana
- **What You Fish For:** Brown trout
- **Highlights and Notables:** A water-cooler river, the stuff of legends

The Blackfoot River is an iconic trout river, epitome of Western streams in many ways. *Warning: this next sentence is a writer's opening, the hook that you have seen in various guises any time you have read about the Blackfoot since 1992.*

Here we go: Made famous by Norman Maclean's novella and Robert Redford's movie, *A River Runs Through It,* the Blackfoot River has enjoyed a resurgence of popularity which had waned as did the river's quality of angling. Sorry. It had to be done.

The Blackfoot River has suffered from environmental woes over the last few decades, including sedimentation from logging and mining, overharvesting, and a string of low water flows. Concerned citizens, environmental groups, and companies have joined forces to pour money and means into preserving and restoring quality to this scenic river. The Blackfoot is back.

The trout are not as big as they were in Norman Maclean's day and they probably never will be. But the Blackfoot River is in the best shape it's been in for quite a while and no one who fishes it will walk, drive, float, hike, or fly away disappointed. Except for the river not holding the lunkers like it used to, a visit to the Blackfoot is so pristine, so wild, so powerful, it will be reminiscent of the way things used to be, mindful of how things should be.

The worst part of the Blackfoot River for anglers is all the use it gets for things other than fishing. Rafts and kayaks and all forms boat/craft. Float-tubing families and teens. Watersplashers. Picnickers. Most of them play in the Clearwater Crossing to Johnsrud Park section so you have dozens and dozens of miles from which to not see any obstacles except logjams. The Blackfoot receives a lot less fishing pressure than rivers of similar high quality.

The trout of the Blackfoot is now the brown trout. About the only time you'll catch rainbows is in the lowest stretches. For large browns bring your streamers, or hit a big seasonal hatch like the salmonfly or golden stonefly. Blackfoot browns can be selective but at times, the smaller ones, the 10- to 14-inchers, rise willingly to dry flies.

The 'Foot has a variety of different types of trout water, and any means of catching trout will work, from spincasting to baittossing to fly fishing, depending on regulations, of course. The river runs through dense pine forests, a colorful canyon, dumps into pools the size of city blocks and as deep as skyscrapers. The unspoiled habitat of the Blackfoot and the quality of the fishing and the immensity of this wide river combine to provide one of the finest Western river experiences.

CONTACTS

Kingfisher, Missoula, www
   .kingfisherflyshop.com
Missoulian Angler, Missoula, www
   .missoulianangler.com
Grizzly Hackle, Missoula, www
   .grizzlyhackle.com

Clark Fork River

- **Location:** Western Montana
- **What You Fish For:** Rainbow, cutthroat, and cuttbows trout
- **Highlights and Notables:** Catch this productive river on its way up.

Sleeper stream alert.

In the last twenty years, the Clark Fork has struggled to reach more than just a marginal trout stream. It has been trying to recover from years of massive mining pollution that wiped out trout and virtually all other aquatic life. Sewage from nearby towns comes into the river causing a chemical overload, oxygen saturation, and heavy algae growth. Doesn't sound like your kind of river?

Well, don't judge too quickly, because this immense river has recovered and is once again a quality fishery. The fishing public still thinks of the Clark Fork in the old light and that means fishing pressure is some of the lightest in the state proportionate for a river that fishes this well. Clark Fork is one of the top rivers in the state and therefore the West and few know about it.

The Clark Fork is 285 miles long. Over that course you can imagine how diverse the terrain is—arid plains, narrow valley, past dense ponderosa pine forests, stretches where the trees stand right on the river's edge, mountain ranges looming in the distance, mountains so close they appear to drink from the river. The catch includes rainbows, cutthroats, cuttbows, and

A hefty rainbow, typical for the Clark Fork

the accidental bull trout. Rainbow trout average about 12 to 15 inches with some real heavy long fish caught and landed. Twenty-inch rainbows are showing up at the end of angler's lines more and more. The cutthroat and cuttbows are chunky, average about 12 to 14 inches and like the rainbows, some big ones are being brought to net and hand. Let the bull trout be.

Floating the river is the best way to get to the productive stretches, especially when the salmonfly hatch occurs in early June. Access is excellent along most of the river since I-90 follows the river for its fishable course. Guide and former host of ESPN's *Trout Unlimited* television show where he fished around the country, Tim Linehan knows the Clark Fork well and thinks that the river reminds him a lot of the Kootenai. The biggest difference is that the Clark Fork offers "more consistent early season action (March, April, early-May) due to a fairly prolific skwala stonefly hatch." Ah, the Skwala (see the Bitterroot entry).

CONTACTS

Clark Fork Trout & Tackle, www .clarkforktrout.com

The Grizzly Hackle & Trout River Coffee Company, www.grizzlyhackle.com

The Kingfisher Flyshop, www .kingfisherflyshop.com

Tim Linehan, Linehan Outfitting Company, www.fishmontana.com

Flathead River

- **Location:** Northern Montana
- **What You Fish For:** Westslope cutthroat
- **Highlights and Notables:** Primitive setting, native cutthroats

The river doesn't fish as well as it did in the good ol' days. You can still catch your share of cutts, maybe five to ten in an hour, which, I know, is super, but believe it or not, the river used to be even better than that.

The marriage of the Middle and North Forks of the Flathead River comprise the main stem, now that the South Fork River lost much of its lower course to the Hungry Horse Reservoir. The Flathead River has some of the clearest, prettiest-looking trout water and habitat you'll ever see, but this is nutrient-poor water, and yet, the river still holds a good population of cutthroat trout (now catch-and-release only and that's helped a lot). They're not big, they're not small—10 to 16 inches with some a bit bigger.

The migrations of bull trout and cutthroats that take place each spring as thousands of spawning fish leave Flathead Lake for gravel beds and smaller streams is another quality aspect of this wild river. Fishing the South Fork in the primitive Bob Marshall Wilderness is exquisite backcountry fun, especially because of all the sections or branches, this one has the most fish per mile. The Middle Fork has decent fishing for cutts and bull trout (but sees too many floaters), but the North is very sporadic in its quality.

The Bob Marshall Wilderness with native cutthroats is a touchstone to the past. The Bob might just be the wildest area in the lower forty-eight. You have an entirely too good a chance of seeing a grizzly bear. And you will catch lots of cutts.

CONTACTS
Glacier Anglers, West Glacier, www.glacierraftco.com

Fort Peck Reservoir

- **Location:** Eastern Montana
- **What You Fish For:** Everything from sauger to walleye to bass
- **Highlights and Notables:** Not all good things come in pretty packages.

This eastern Montana fishery is the anti-Orvis lake. Off-color and silty, this humongous prairie reservoir isn't catalog-cover pretty nor are the over fifty species of fish that swim its fertile soupy waters. No breathable waders, no superfine fly rods, no Range Rovers. This is a blue-collar lake made for hard-core anglers and world-record fish.

Fort Peck Reservoir is 250,000 acres huge, the largest body of water in Montana but when you're on it, it just seems to go on forever and in every direction, upstream, over there, up this arm, down that one, through the odd and fascinating Missouri Breaks for a hundred miles, with 1,500 miles of shoreline. It is monstrous. It is fed by the monstrous Missouri River. Monstrous both.

So are the fish. Lots of state records. Known for outstanding walleye fishing, that's just touching the muddy surface of Fort Peck. Let's list: Sauger (and of course saug-eye, a walleye-sauger hybrid). Smallmouth bass (underrated). Lake trout, white crappie, black crappie, paddlefish (40 to 80 pounds), yellow perch (fried, preferably), burbot, lake trout (5 to 10 pounds and up), rainbow trout, catfish, carp, Chinook salmon, coho salmon, pike (up to 25 pounds).

If you are after big fish and possible state records or lots of fish and variety of fish on the end of your line, Fort Peck should be your pick. Tim the Tool Man Taylor would have made the journey to fish here. He'd have had a big fast boat and four tackle boxes full of lures and other assorted fishing fanatic tools, gee-gaws and necessities.

In case you're not impressed yet, anglers have caught 16-pound walleye, 31-pound Chinook, 5-pound coho, 15-pound saug-eye, 20-pound drum, 8-pound sauger, and a 26-pound channel cat.

Missouri River

Twenty-five hundred miles long. Part of this historic river has been designated a National Wild and Scenic River. The Missouri River itself is a major fishery but it acts like several different rivers since its long course is affected by impoundments, changes in topography, and the influx of so many different kinds of feeder streams. The Missouri River is a big, wide river, and it has over 150 miles of trout fishing, but the river has had problems with depleted trout populations the last few years, and drought has been a bane for the Missouri the last half-decade.

Jefferson River

- **Location:** Southwestern Montana
- **What You Fish For:** Brown and rainbow trout
- **Highlights and Notables:** Not as famous as its sister rivers, the Madison and Gallatin, the fishing is often as good or better.

When the Jefferson is not low, when the river is right, the river is powerful, driving images into your brain like a hammer. A slow big hammer driving stakes into the ground.

The Jefferson moves like molasses through grassy valley and arid brown country, past canyon and lowland, determined to avoid its marriage with the Madison and Gallatin, avoiding the union that makes the Missouri. The Jeff is one of the three rivers forming the Missouri and it differs from its sister rivers in that it lumbers along for over seventy-five miles.

The river is formed by the confluence of the Big Hole and Beaverhead Rivers. The brown trout that predominate the Jefferson have had to face tremendous low-water stress since the drought of 1988, and 2005 was terrible and there is not much immediate hope now. There is an ever-increasing demand for irrigation purposes.

Feeder streams load sediment into the Jeff, causing turbidity at times, and making the river murky. The Jefferson doesn't see as many anglers as do other nearby rivers, and even though the Jeff is a sleeping giant, its recent low-water times have downgraded its overall quality.

When water levels are high, fishing in the upper reaches can make for some nice trophy trout hunting. The river is fished best by floating, but wading the river in spots is easy. The river does have undercut banks and deep bends, making wading a wet proposition and therefore unlikely. Like most southwestern Montana rivers, 12- to 15-inch trout make up most of the catches but most of what you catch are browns (and brown trout from 3 to 10 pounds are not unusual). What is unusual is that insect hatches are sporadic on the Jefferson, due largely to the fluctuating water levels.

So if the Jefferson suffers so much, why is it in this book? On the positive side, the Jefferson River has darned good fishing for brown trout with very little angling pressure, especially the upper section between Cardwell and Twin Bridges. Fall fishing for moving browns is excellent. On the negative side, if the river were better managed, it would be as good as its sister rivers. Who

knows. In a few years, with the right people involved, it could happen.

CONTACTS
Complete Fly Fishers, 406-832-3175
Bugs & Bullets, 406-782-6251
Fran Johnson's Sports Shop, 406-782-3322
Montana Fly Company, 406-835-2621
Sunrise Fly Shop, 406-835-3474
Great Divide Outfitters, 406-267-3346
Frontier Anglers, 406-683-5276
Uncle Bob's Fishing Supplies, 406-683-5565
Montana Troutfitters, 406-587-4707
The Bozeman Angler, 406-587-9111

Kootenai River

- **Location:** Northwestern Montana
- **What You Fish For:** Rainbow trout
- **Highlights and Notables:** As good as this Western tailwater is, you'd think it would bank more print. Kootenai is one of the best in the West.

First things first: The Kootenai River is pronounced "Koo-ten-nee." This big river flows in the extreme northwest corner of the state, bold and wide. Many anglers have never even heard of the Kootenai and its huge rainbows (try a 33-pounder in 1997). The Kootenai is not known for its prolific or complex hatches, but that doesn't mean you can disregard the hatches and just toss out big attractor dry flies (like they did on the Kootenai in the old days).

Tim Linehan was for years the host of the *Trout Unlimited* television show and is one of two full-time guides on the Kootenai. Linehan's television show took him all over America and he knows trout and he knows hatches and trout. He's a fly fishing star.

The Kootenai begins in Kootenay National Park in British Columbia, Canada, flows for hundreds of miles into the northwest corner of Montana, through Idaho for a bit, then crosses Canada again, through Kootenay Lake and into the mighty Columbia River. The Kootenai is a big, bad river.

Flow problems of the past are history. The flows that ten years ago plagued the river are more consistent now (due to local TU chapters, guides, and many others). From more consistent flows came more consistent hatches. "Hatches there are now thousand times more consistent," Linehan stresses. "The population of trout is now as good, as healthy as ever."

Here's my take: the Kootenai is as good as any tailwater in the West. This remote river gets shortchanged. I figure those who leave it off their lists, out of their books, haven't fished this gem. More for me.

The Kootenai has good hatches of caddis, blue-winged olive, Pale Morning Duns, Green Drake, salmonfly, and midge. This is a tailwater that doesn't often act like a tailwater. You don't have to use size-22 larva flies or imitate mysis shrimp. The hatches can be very good on the Kootenai, and big 'bows rise to caddis and mayfly hatches and imitations. The dry fly fishing can be as good as anywhere in the state at times.

Linehan shares some insights that work for Kootenai hatches (and are universal enough to use on other rivers, especially big ones). "The first and most common mistake anglers make on the Kootenai is that they are intimidated by big water." And make no mistake about it, when you first see the Kootenai, it's big and seemingly featureless.

"I see anglers casting way too far. There's no need to cast ninety-five feet to the middle." Like most big water, you have to break it down into smaller sections. Linehan points out that when he guides from a boat, "we cast from about forty-five feet out toward the shoreline. The fish are holding in lies near the shore. Yet I see anglers on the shore casting out as far as they can, farther than the boat and they're not putting their flies where the fish are."

Mistake #2: "Anglers spend too much time fishing in marginal water," Linehan continues. "Instead, they should concentrate on where the fish are, on places where the fish feed. Don't waste time floating a big dry in a six-foot-deep run if there's not a hatch and no fish rising. Find seams, think edges, go to the five-acre riffles."

Mistake #3: "Keep your casts manageable and short," Linehan cautions. "This helps your presentation which makes your patterns look more attractive to the fish." This was one of my mistakes (Tim tells me this years after my first time to fish the Kootenai, of course). The best way to fish this endangered fishery is by floating it and casting in and around the big rocks, to the riffles and backwater pools, and to obvious hatches.

Since there's not much to worry about with lots of different hatches going on at one time on the Kootenai, concentrate on each hatch more closely. "If PMDs are coming off, and fish are rising, PMDs is what they are eating," Linehan shares. "Nothing complicated there. What makes it more complicated is that the fish are

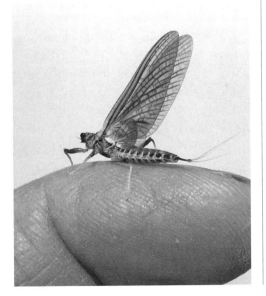

more selective about the stage presentation of the patterns. The fish get on the emerger stage and don't want an adult pattern."

How best to imitate the emerger hatch? While Linehan ties his own emerger patterns and they have local and national recognition, he says that what works well, one of his favorite patterns, is a Matthew's Sparkle Dun with trailing shuck. "Sure, CDC Cripples are great and useful and I tie one that has lots of success, but a good old Sparkle Dun is time-tested and ideal."

So don't make any of the three mistakes, locate the stage of the hatch, and you'll have it covered, right? Not so quick.

"Silhouette is the most important thing on the Kootenai," Linehan provides. "Size is important but if you have an upwing pattern close in size, say an Adams and it's a PMD hatch, they'll take it. If it's a downwing and there's a caddis hatch, they'll take it. You get the idea." His typical pattern for Green Drakes on the Kootenai is not a typical Green Drake pattern at all—try a big ol' attractor, a size 10 Royal Wulff.

Kootenai rainbows fatten up on the dead kokanee salmon spit out of the generating turbines, and they reach weights which have recently reset the state record of 21 pounds. Recent catches weighed 26 and 29 pounds. Wow. If you plan to float the Kootenai, for the most part it is safe and easy. There are some tricky spots and some out-and-out dangerous spots like Kootenai Falls and China Rapids. Check with fly shops and outfitters before rafting the river.

Good presentation, good drift, and match the stage (and silhouette) and you're on.

By the way, Kootenai is served by only two full-time guiding outfitters, Tim Linehan and Dave Blackburn. That only two guides fill the needs of such a big and great fishery tells you how underfished it is. These are both great outfitters befitting the quality of the river.

CONTACTS

Linehan Outfitting Co., Troy, www .fishmontana.com

Dave Blackburn's Kootenai Angler, Libby, www.montana-flyfishing.com

OTHER MONTANA WATERS TO TRY

Montana is probably the best trout fishing state in the nation (including Alaska because you can't hardly dry fly fish in Alaska). The state has the big names, a roll call of great trout rivers—Madison, Yellowstone, Firehole, Big Hole, Bighorn, Jefferson, Bitterroot, Kootenai, Beaverhead, Blackfoot, and the list goes on.

What you don't need to miss out on is the wildness, the intimacy of the wildness in Montana. Make a point to get off the main rivers and fish some of the top small creeks of the state. Because so many fishers from around the world come to fish the big-name big rivers, the smaller ones get overlooked. You don't even have to be a small-stream enthusiast to enjoy the intimacy, the pristine scenery, the isolation. Heck, you can often catch fish that rival the bigger river's average trout in size. And catching/landing a 15-inch trout in a small stream is equivalent in fun and difficulty

as it is to catch/land a 20-incher in a large river.

Blacktail Deer Creek

Set in a big bowl-type valley. Sage. Rolling grassland. Weird low-slung white hills straight out of a sci-fi movie. Blacktail Deer Creek looks too small to have driven all this distance for but you're gonna have to trust me on this one. It's plain and simple. Here, on this manageable stream, with nothing to catch a backcast, you can bring a newbie and they will be able to catch brookies and cutthroats until they "get it." And you can catch fish 'til the cows come home, too.

Crow Creek

"Skinny water" you'll think when you first lay eyes on this bouncy mountain stream. Try it. It's out of the way, loaded with trout, and you won't see another angler. No, there's not many fish of size but this is one of those you fish so you get the beauty and dry fly fishing and the numbers of fish and the wildlife and . . . you know the drill. Pack a lunch, bring your camera and binocs, take one fly box only, make your choice a lightweight rod, wet wade, whistle while you walk, and on and on.

Rock Creek (Not *That* One)

This Rock Creek is in southern Montana near Red Lodge and is not as good as the other Rock Creek. Anglers do have nearly sixty miles of darned good trout river to angle in, a creek with all kinds of diversity in landscape and loaded with cutts, brookies in the upper section, browns and rainbows in the flatter wider section. The water is clear, the dry fly fishing fun.

Boulder River

Fifty miles of Blue Ribbon water and it lies in the spectacular Absaroka-Beartooth Wilderness, is a medium-sized freestone river, known as much for its slippery wading on thousands of slick rocks as for its excellent nymphing for rainbow, cutthroat, brook, and brown trout. Bring your camera to record the rock formations, the green forests, and the incredible number of rocks in this clear river. The fishing is perhaps as good as it gets in Montana.

Stillwater River

Any time you can fish with the Absaroka-Beartooth Mountains in the background, it's a great day of fishing. Stillwater is a bouncy, rumbling stream, so don't be fooled by the joke of a name placed on it. Fishermen will often catch as many whitefish as rainbows and browns and cutthroats, but the river is loaded with trout. The Stillwater is in the pristine Beartooth Range, but still gets a bit cloudy from irrigation deposits. Wading is better than floating this quick stream. The river doesn't hold any lunkers because there are few deep pools, but trout to 16 inches lurk about.

Shields River

Poor access since most of the river is in private hands. Still, you can access the Shields at bridge crossings and there are quite a few bridge crossings. The river draws down in summer from irrigation, has thick riparian habitat, and is narrow, but it's a productive river and has less fishing pressure than most nearby rivers. It can't hold a candle to most other fisheries, but it does provide the angler a less-fished river. It receives migrating spawners up from the Yellowstone in the spring and fall.

Clarks Fork of the Yellowstone River

Turbid where it enters the great river, and most of its quality fishing is in northern Wyoming, but from the border in the south central part of the state for several miles to Belfry, Montana, trout can be caught. The Clarks Fork doesn't hold many lunkers but the desert and mountain valley settings and abundance of small to medium-size trout which are easily fooled by wets and nymphs makes it a worthwhile option.

Others
  Flathead Lake
  Flathead River
  South Fork Boulder
  Big Sheep Creek
  Upper Smith River/Belt Creek
  Little Prickly Pear Creek

Rock Creek

- **Location:** Western Montana
- **What You Fish For:** Brown, rainbow, cutthroat trout
- **Highlights and Notables:** A creek not a stream, this is classic water with nice-size wild trout.

There was a time not that long ago when few folks outside of Montana knew about Rock Creek. This scenic, fifty-mile long, classic mountain stream was a guarded secret, the river where guides went fishing on their day off.

I wish I owned Rock Creek. I also wish that it had less road access and that it wasn't as close to Missoula. *C'est la vie.*

Rock Creek is not the biggest or baddest of the Montana streams but off the record, guides and locals will tell you this is probably the best fishing Montana destination west of the Continental Divide despite what you'll hear about the fishing pressure nowadays. This medium-sized stream has small stream character with a healthy population of wild trout (rainbow, cutthroat, brown), a rich diversity of insect hatches, different types of nat-

ural habitat, and excellent roadside access. The fishing is steady throughout the year, the hatches consistent. Rock Creek is ideal if you have a newbie who wants to learn (and catch fish) and not have to lie about his or her catches, or if you're a long-timer who wants lots of lies and big challenges for big fish.

Before the first time I fished the Rock, I had talked to a few guides and a local and got four different stories on the best way to coax up the big browns and rainbows, the smartest move to land a bunch of cutthroats. Upstream, I heard, were the smaller trout, 8 to 12 inches, mostly cutts and rainbows. Middle, variable sizes, lots of opportunities. Lower river, big browns.

I ended up trying everything I could

and all my techniques worked. I swung big streamers under cutbanks; dropped a sink-tip through the deep deep pools; bounced small dries on top of riffles; and tied on size-6 stonefly adults.

I caught fish with everything I threw out there. I love Rock Creek.

You'll see other anglers on Rock Creek but there are floating restrictions that keep the heavy water traffic out of your way during the summer. You can drive up or down, hike up or down, and find your own long stretch of cold clear fertile water. About the cold water: Rock Creek is one of the coldest rivers in Montana, and also one of the slipperiest.

The stream holds big, wary browns in its most concealed lies, while the abundant rainbows frequent the riffles and runs, but you'll discover that the trout on Rock Creek intelligently use any and all lies, from submerged logs, big rocks, channels, foamy pocket water, choppy riffles, deadfall, canyon walls, deep deep pools, mats of vegetation, and just about any other trout lie, habitat, or characteristic you can think of. They're sneaky and the Rock has a little of everything. Summer is great on the Rock but autumn is best. The colors, the solitude, the beauty. Unbeatable.

Smith River

- **Location:** West central Montana
- **What You Fish For:** Brown trout
- **Highlights and Notables:** One of the top float trips in the West

The Smith River is limestone walls, trout, and not much else. Here, around a shore campfire, with a tad bit of bourbon in my cup, I once solved all the problems of the world on a five-day float on this moody wilderness river but I forgot the solution by the time I made it back to Great Falls. Easy come, easy go.

If you consider yourself an angler; if you are looking for that special trip that evokes reverential murmurs as you fish its waters; if you get high on wild country and big trout, then save up for what many say is the best float trip in America. Lewis and Clark floated the Smith and not much has changed since then. True, you'll see more floaters than they did and more than you'd like to see, more houses on the river but not enough to make you forgot how beautiful or primeval a land you're fishing through.

Just do the float trip. Don't one-day this river. Save up and buy a three- to five-day float. Feel the rhythm, the pace. There's too little shoreline fishing on the Smith to make it worthwhile. If you went all the way to south-central Montana and just fished the Smith from the banks, it'd be like landing a ticket to the World Series but spending all your time at the concession stand. If you must wade, the best place is at the Smith River Access site.

The gray-white limestone cliffs rise up from the twisting emerald-colored river like primitive skyscrapers. They envelope you for most of the sixty-mile float and when they break for short periods, grassy meadows lay down in front of you like blankets. This is the ultimate Western float trip. Campfires on gravelly shores. Dutch ovens. Hot coffee. Shooting the bull with your buddies. Landing whopper wild trout. Light bouncing off the cliffs in a frenzy of changing hues. The feeling you've traveled back in time.

Smith River has tricky currents so if you're a beginning level boater, I'd float somewhere else and hire a guide for the Smith. Besides, the state regulates who gets on and who doesn't and limits the number of floats per year. The Smith is doable if you have a Montana buddy who has a boat and knows what he's doing and you promise to be his camp-wife.

Browns are consistently big. They vary in color. Some have more white background and dark spots, some more yellow with brownish spots. They grow large in this limestone river, partly from food, partly because they don't have hordes of anglers yanking their jaws. Smith River browns hit dry flies like a ton of bricks and they're not slashing at little tailwater size flies. They're gashing at size 6 Stimulators and Madame-Xs and Woolly Buggers with frantic rubber legs and nice-sized caddis, patterns they can sink their teeth into, patterns you can see. Expect to catch browns in the 12- to 15-inch range and bigger; rainbows 10 to 14 inches and bigger. Don't expect lunkers. Expect lots of violent strikes by 1- to 3-pound wild trout. You'll miss more than you catch your first day until you get that rhythm.

The float season is short and difficult to predict. Top months are May, June, and sometimes July and then again in the fall (sometimes). It all depends on flow.

One night as the sun bounced off the walls as Helios ended his race across the sky, I mentioned to a float buddy that the Smith always strikes me as eerie. In the growing shadows, he nodded. When you do the Smith, you'll know what I mean. I've done the Smith four times and each time I find comforting things I remember from before and still make new discoveries and still find it with more questions than answers. I've got plans for this next May because I've got this friend who needs to get away from it all and he's never been fly fishing and if I'm gonna hook him, it needs to be with the biggest baddest float trip in the West.

CONTACTS
Glacier Guides, www.glacierguides.com

Sun River

- **Location:** Central Montana, near Great Falls
- **What You Fish For:** Brook, cutthroat, rainbow trout
- **Highlights and Notables:** A beautiful river with a lot of potential

What could be.

The Sun River has no business, in its present state, of being listed as one of the best 1,001 places on earth to wet a line. Sun River is used to irrigate, has many dams, and gets low way too often during the summer. The fish aren't big.

She begins in the mountains on the

eastern side of the Bob Marshall Wilderness for five miles and then her two forks (North and South Forks) meet up with Gibson Dam and in a bit, Sun River Dam. Along the way, as the river leaves the mountains and flows through canyon and plains, water is diverted for irrigation, nullifying good flows that would encourage natural trout reproduction.

What could be. Sun River is so unknown outside of its area, is so remote and wild, that if the flows could ever be improved, you'd see consistent spawning below the dams and you'd see more trout and you'd see bigger trout. The scenery ranges from spectacular hulking snow-covered mountains to wide rocky arid dusty flatlands, beautiful in its own harsh manner.

As it is now, if you do fish the Sun, fish the upper Sun River, that part above Highway 287 and even more so, above Gibson Reservoir. The Sun River Canyon is wild and woolly, floatable, fishable, and isolated. The two forks both lie in the Bob Marshall Wilderness and to reach them, you must hike. Fishing the Bob is one of the more isolated fishing experiences in the lower forty-eight, and in these forks, you can catch fifty trout and up even if you suck as an angler—brook, cutthroat, rainbow, none of any size but all wild and lovely. As the two forks merge and reach Gibson Reservoir, access isn't as easy but the trout are plentiful, a tad larger, and rise to dries. The water to Willow Creek Reservoir is pretty much unfishable but in the canyon below the water is trout-y and the fish large. Humongous emerald pools with a hint of cobalt and finning fish that are best caught under the water with nymphs and streamers.

What could be with a little help. Nature has done its job setting up a premier trout stream but man is taking away the life source.

Quick story about the Sun in the Bob: My brother-in-law David (big brother to my wife Amy) convinced my other brother-in-law Kenny (married to Amy's sister Betsy) to spend a few weeks in the Bob Marshall Wilderness with him, helping him collect rock samples for his graduate studies in geology. This is long before I was in the family, mind you.

David enticed Kenny with promises of steak and cold beer and other foodstuffs all to be purchased with stipend or grant money. Kenny fell for it hook, line, and sinker even though he was torn between leaving his six-month-old son and his wife Betsy for so long.

Kenny ate Doritos and Fig Newtons and cold canned corn and little else. He slept in ant beds in a sleeping bag with no tent and freezing cold nights. He carried a knapsack that David kept filling with rock samples so it got heavier and heavier, even for my thick-shouldered, bison-headed, pea-brained, no-neck brother-in-law.

David and Kenny detoured from the trail to a big ledge overlooking a whopper of a pool, swirling and green. They spotted ten, twelve, fifteen trout, all big enough to see clearly from ninety-five feet above. I love to hear David and Kenny tell this story because they get to laughing and because they both agree on every part of the story.

Kenny lost his footing on the slanted ledge, shale; yeah, slanted enough that once he got started sliding, and even though he laid down immediately, he kept on sliding toward the edge. David was sitting on the slanted ledge looking down ninety-five feet above the huge pool and turned and saw his pack-mule of a brother-in-law with a rock-filled knapsack, sliding out of control, heading for a freefall . . . *and did nothing.* They both agree on this point.

"I wanted to see if Kenny would sink or swim," Dave chuckles.

"I reached out to Dave and he just grinned and nodded at me," Kenny confides.

Did he stop in time?

Yep, only when he, like the movies, pulled out his rock hammer and jabbed its flat end into a crack. Kenny's feet hung over the ledge. Cliffhanger the Sequel. Kenny shares this secret too:

"I had two weird thoughts as I was sliding toward the edge, toward the fall into the pool. First, I was thinking about my son Chase and wife Betsy and how much I missed them, and two, I was wondering if I would land on any of the trout."

They made it out of the Bob, the near-fall a near-memory, fishing that pool the next day fresh in their minds (they caught all they could) and happened upon a mirage of a café called Betty Hegland's where they ate their first good meal in a month, the best burger, they contend, they have ever eaten in their lives.

They both crack up telling all about the Bob and the ledge and what could've been. That's the Sun River. What could be.

Montana Spring Creeks

- **Location:** All over the state but the most famous are in Livingston Valley in the southwestern part of Montana
- **What You Fish For:** Rainbow and brown trout
- **Highlights and Notables:** The mecca of trout spring creeks

As few as 500, as many as 900 spring creeks flow through Montana. That's mind boggling. These spring creeks are likely the finest spring creeks in the world, and certainly the most famous.

So much prestige is heaped on just a few miles of fishing water, but boy howdy, this is some kind of fishing, not for the impatient, faint of heart, or beginning angler. Casting tiny flies in glassy, clear, still water to huge, discerning rainbow and brown trout can be a humbling experience even for long-time fly fishermen.

Nelson's, DePuy's (pronounced "Duh-Pews"), Armstrong, Big Spring Creeks are the most attractive spring creeks in the state, fee required for the first three and reservations are needed up to a year in advance, but don't let this scare you off. The fee has been below a Benjamin for a day's fishing for some time, and you can sometimes get worked in on shorter notice. Lesser fees are charged in the off-season, too. The selective trout never have an off-season. Paradise Valley. The spring-creek enthusiast's mecca.

Livingston is your home base. Cool town. The residents are better anglers than you are, just admit it up front. They are probably better educated and since they decided to leave the rat race and can fish Montana any time they want, they are happier than you.

DePuy's and Armstrong are different parts of the same creek, but the upper stretches of the creek are perhaps a little easier to land trout. All of the spring creeks maintain a consistent flow and water temperature through snow, rain, or wind. The insects, mostly midges and mayflies, hatch all year long. Tackle for the spring creeks should be light because delicate, short casts are necessary. Three- to 5-weight lines are typical, and 7X leaders are sometimes too heavy.

If that weren't challenging enough, the predominant rainbows, which range from 14 inches to several pounds, turn their respective noses at any cast with drag. They will sip on any of multiple ongoing hatches, not always the biggest or thickest, either. The trout will feed on various stages of an insect's life cycle, so the fully prepared angler will have several fly boxes filled with mayfly and midge patterns, size 16 to 24, in all stages. Crippled and thorax patterns have shown to work well recently. Scuds, sowbugs, and small nymphs like Brassies are crucial to catching fish at times. Some fishermen wade, but stalking and crawling is probably less spooky for the big trout, and certainly less threatening to their redds and spawning habitat.

In Armstrong, DePuy's and Nelson Spring Creeks, rainbows are the main attraction, but browns and cutts do inhabit the waters to a lesser amount. Three of these creeks lie just south of Livingston on private ranchland, and Big Spring Creek (also known as Big Creek and Cold Spring Creek) is a tributary to the Missouri River near Lewistown.

Nowhere else can you get so much for a hundred spot. The scenery, the quality of the fishery, the legacy. Killer.

I have fished the Big Three in summer and in fall. I haven't figured out yet what I'm doing right when I do it right, nor wrong when I am doing it wrong. I take notes on every water I fish but it seems like I have less time to take notes on the Big Three because I am trying so hard to catch fish or figure out how I just caught that fish.

You better not just be a good caster, you need to be an accurate caster and a good judge of where to accurately cast, and a quick mender and a constant mender. It helps if you are a professional entomologist. Pack our fly box with CDC midge emergers, midges, BWOs, and every spring creek fly pattern you can remember. Find the feeding lane, time their rises, put it in their mouth and make it taste like the real thing. I recommend hiring a guide your first time—Yellowstone Angler, Al Gadoury's Outfitters, James Marc, the list goes on.

Notes I've scribbled before, during, and after days on Armstrong, Nelson, DePuy:
Armstrong only twenty-five to thirty
feet wide but seems wider when
you're in it. Right there is the Yellowstone, right there and it flooded
a few years back, 1996. O'Hair's

one and a half miles at the top and DePuy's three miles below open to public with rod fee.

Watch your step. O'Hair's section is riffles and runs. DePuy's has pools big fat pools.

Warm weather, I told myself to think PMD, think stages—and I thought too much and I was dead in the water, I was just practicing my casting and watching caddis and sulphurs.

Armstrong's is wider than I thought—you get in and it's deeper and wider and there's just so much water because you can see fish and you see them all over the place and you know that it's all good, trout lies everywhere, every nook and cranny. Eight miles south of Livingston—the creeks are close but it seems to take fifteen minutes to get to them (only one creek four to five miles total) but it is Big Spring at the top part but somehow called different than Armstrong, O'Hair's—then lower is DePuy's on west side of Yellowstone (Nelson's is on east side)—all these names and so little water.

Moss on the flies—every other cast—it's killing me. I found fish in shallow water as well as cuts and pools and riffles. O'Hair's is faster than the other sections. Size 18 Royal Wulff, baby! Changeup. Seventeen-inch brown, fat, yellow. I knew a Royal Wulff wouldn't work but there was that brown feeding and nudging my other offerings and darn it, it just had to work and it did.

In the middle of a big hatch, adults all over, duns on the water but not hardly any was taking—and still they are feeding—they might not even be keying on that insect especially my imitation. Thank god for the Copper John.

Betty's Riffle, the fisherman's hut, Call of the Wild Ranch-house?—southern mansion style home—out of place. Nelson's—East side—Not many riffles—A big pool—lots of fish feeding in the shallow flat that is big and wide—damn this is clear clear water. This is tougher than the other side but similar in some ways to DePuy's. Brown 16 inches long, skinny with big head, huge spots on a PMD—yes!

THREE OTHER SPRING CREEKS STAND OUT: MCCOY, MILESNICK, AND POINDEXTER

McCoy (near Dillon)

Not all that long ago, there were two spring creeks in a state of disrepair, few trout called these creeks home. New owner, and the new owner fixed them up. Added boulders and narrowed the creeks and re-structured them and made them fertile. Then the owner opened them up to anglers like you and me for a total of three miles of creek and ten ponds, too.

The two creeks hold brown, rainbow, and brook trout. The hatches are Montana good and the trout not yet as selective as trout from Paradise Valley trout. You still have to wade carefully, cast well, but they're easier, no doubt about it. And the creeks hold some really big big browns. Twenty-five- to 30-inch browns are not all that unusual.

Rent a guesthouse or just fish at the reasonable amount of 100 bucks per rod per day. Two beats, 2 to 3 rods per beat per day. Closed October 1 to March 31 for spawning protection. McCoy policy is that you hire either a half-day or full-day professional guide your first time out.

Milesnick

Locals have known about this Gallatin Valley gem for a good while, they just kept their mouths shut. Owner renovated and rehabbed and reshaped, now has deeper places and cutbanks (sound familiar?). Thompson Creek and Benhart Creek curve back and forth and empty into East Gallatin.

We're talking spoooooooky fish, browns and rainbows 15 to 20 inches and mean when hooked. This working ranch (the MZ Ranch) also provides access to five miles of private water on the East Gallatin. Located only ten minutes from Bozeman airport. These things change but as of this writing the rates went seventy-five bucks per rod from June through August and fifty bucks May and September through November. Not open year round. Reservations book early, so get in while you can. Six anglers allowed per day, first come, first served on the water—no beats.

Poindexter Slough

This is one of the few public spring creeks in Dillon worth its weight in brown trout. The creek is off the Beaverhead River at river mile 53. Open year-round, day-use only. Poindexter Slough fishes well with nymphs all year but what differentiates it from other spring creeks in the state is that dry fly fishing is first-rate because the river enjoys prolific hatches of all types all year long. Now, you need to tie on small flies and you need some technical skill, but your medium-level fly fisher can do quite well here.

You'd think that with the river being public, it'd get more pressure than the pay-creeks of Paradise Valley. Not true. Poindexter is underfished.

CONTACTS
Armstrong Spring Creek, O'Hair Ranch, Livingston, 406-222-2979
DePuy Spring Creek, www .depuyspringcreek.com
McCoy Cattle Company and Spring Creeks, Dillon, www .mccoycattlecompany.com
Milesnick Recreation Company, Belgrade, www.milesnickrecreation.com
Nelson's Spring Creek Ranch, Livingston, 406-222-2159
Yellowstone Angler, Livingston, 406-222-7130

OREGON

Deschutes River

- **Location:** North central Oregon
- **What You Fish For:** The red-banded rainbow trout (aka redsides trout)
- **Highlights and Notables:** One of the best trout and steelhead streams in the West

I have a June 1938 *National Sportsman* magazine I bought off eBay. On the cover is a painting of a young angler in a red shirt on the close bank netting a fish. If you get a chance to find this mag, do so if you want to see what an Oregon stream looks like. I don't know if this young man is fishing an Oregon stream or not but it sure looks like your typical Northwest stream. Green deep foamy pool, brush and trees and vegetation right up on the banks and big boulders lining the banks.

This cover looks nothing like Oregon's best trout river, one of the West's top five trout streams, the Deschutes. Nope, this rapid river busts through a stark high desert landscape, rushing over mauve and taupe beds of basalt, through steep tall canyons of drama, a green choppy liquid incubator in the midst of harshness. This brawling snake looks nothing like a trout river, a steelhead haven. Where are the pools, the verdant meadows? Where is the green nurturing aquatic vegetation, the life-green of plants and shrubs and trees?

In midsummer the fish are deep, the sun beating down hot, hot, dancing off the tanned landscape shimmering out-of-focus dust devils. The Deschutes hold "kiss-my-ass" wild trout, braying at the thought of any mortal angler both fooling them *and* landing them in the same cast and retrieve. The redsides, a strain of rainbow trout that wear their anti-authority like tattoos, red claiming-colors. *Oncorhynchus mykiss irideus.*

In June, when the salmonfly hatch descends on the river like locusts, clumsy clouds, Portland (only two hours away) shuts down all businesses for three weeks so that every single resident can have a shot at the river. Not really, but it often

feels that crowded. Then the golden stones come and you lose some of the angling mob and by midsummer, the great dry fly fishing is over and you have to nymph and you have the river more or less to yourself.

The Deschutes is one of those special rivers that has the variety of water types, thick insect hatches, and a healthy population of trout all set in a beautiful part of the world, and destined to become set firmly in the minds of destination anglers across the country. The Deschutes is one of the best trout streams in the nation. The river is equally known, maybe even better known, for its steelhead fishing.

Set in central and north-central Oregon, the accessible Deschutes River flows north after beginning its trek from Little Lava Lake in the High Cascades. The headwaters of the river belie the great size of the river below it, and there is quiet, shallow water for angling for rainbow and brown trout with pine forests thick, enclosing.

I have a bad habit of trying to get to know someone by exploring where they came from. Q & A time. I like to visit their heritage, their hometown, their parents, and I'm sure it comes off as pop psyche but it's not. I like headwaters, beginnings, where things begin. I almost always find time to fish the upper reaches of any river I visit. The fish may be smaller but I usually find wilder scenery, fewer anglers, eager trout. From Little Lava Lake to Crane Prairie to Wickiup to Billy Chinook, the upper Deschutes. I get answers this way and I am happy. The upper Deschutes is pretty and the fish willing and I like it. After Wickiup, the Deschutes is a teenager. After it leaves Billy Chinook, where it is made bold by the Metolius and Crooked Rivers, the Deschutes is an adult.

This is a long complex river, northerly flowing, a river of many moods, many personalities, impounded several times, popular with anglers and recreationalists (like those pesky whitewater enthusiasts). It flows over waterfalls and through pine forest, meadow, desert, and canyon. The upper reaches are nothing like the middle, the seventy-mile stretch known for its trout fishing. In its lower twenty-five miles before the Deschutes slams into the Columbia, well, that's steelhead water. Steelheading heats up in summer when an assortment of wild and hatchery steelies ranging from 4 to 20 pounds.

The most celebrated trout water on the river is that section from below Pelton Dam fifty miles to Sherars Falls, a powerful, cascading stretch of water holding excellent if unpredictable hatches of caddis flies, mayflies, stoneflies, and midges.

The trout of this river have to fight the constant power of the river and are strong fighters. Known to any angler who has ever tied into a Deschutes trout is the redside trout, a native fish with extra oomph when on the end of a line. The trout grow to impressive sizes with the average brown trout running about 15 inches, the average native rainbow about 16 inches or thereabouts. Brown trout are caught weighing over 10 pounds although you don't catch many browns. I think that at times the fascination with the redsides (count me in) overshadows just how good this river is for lunker brown trout.

Redsides top 20 inches every so often but you'll think you have caught one of these from the way they'll run into your backing only to surprisingly find it's just a 15-inch purplish redside in your net. Sometimes you can't believe the fish on your hook isn't a steelhead, these redsides fight so tenaciously. If and when you do catch a 20- to 24-inch redside rainbow, and they're there, well, you probably won't, so don't think about it.

Because the river is rough and the fish are smart, it is a good idea to hire a fishing guide if you are not familiar with the Deschutes. Many stretches of the river can be floated, and in fact, the river suffers in summer from the activity of numerous rafters. Regs say: single barbless hooks. Catch-and-release only. No bait, artificials only.

Places to stay? Cool mountain towns like Bend, Sisters, Salem, but the river towns of Maupin and Madras are closer and are common choices for home base. All have great choices for eats and digs.

A classic. You know it when you see it. The Deschutes deserves to be ranked with Leort, Fall, Hat, Madison, Firehole, Batten Kill, and all the other classic trout rivers of America, so unique, so fertile, so perfect, this tumultuous river of so many colors. And with the added value of having a steelhead fishery (where these migratory rainbows will take flies at or near the surface), the Deschutes has few peers.

CONTACTS
Damien Nurre, Fly & Field Outfitters, www.flyandfield.com
Deschutes Angler Fly Shop, 877-395-0995, www.deschutesangler.com
River Bend Guide Service, 541-553-1051
Deschutes Canyon Fly Shop, 541-395-2565, www.flyfishingdeschutes.com
Oasis Resort and Guide Service, 541-395-2611, www.deschutes-riveroasis.com
Western Fishing Adventures, 503-250-0558
Fly Fishing Shop, 503-622-4607, www.flyfishusa.com

Grande Ronde River

- **Location:** Northeastern Oregon, south-eastern Washington
- **What You Fish For:** Steelhead, small-mouth bass
- **Highlights and Notables:** Combo steelhead/smallmouth bass river that flies under the radar except with locals. Set your GPS and find it.

Reason to fish here: Excellent trout fishing above LaGrande; steelhead on skated flies wherever you find steelhead; king-sized smallmouth angling in the warmer downstream stretches; manageable river, beautiful stretches and great-looking runs of steelhead-type water on end. *Best place to stretch out for the night:* Boggan's Oasis, with its five rooms and hot tub, is at 509-256-3372. *Best home base:* Troy where the Wenaha meets the Grande Ronde. *Best place to fill your stomach:* Shilo Inn Café (lodge, RV, park, gas). *Best place to meet up with way too many anglers:* Confluence with Snake River.

Best place to have the river to yourself: In the rimrock canyon. *Best place to catch a lot or a large steelhead:* At any number of named holes. Hatchery Hole, Troy Bridge Hole (under the span bridge), State Line Hole. *Boat or wade?:* Yes. Even better, boat and wade. Driftboats cover so much more water and you can then get out and wade-fish. *What Grande Ronde means in French:* Big beautiful circle. *Best time to be on the river:* October. *Access:* Easy except in the canyon. Roads intersect and parallel at different points. To reach Troy (and man, is it tiny) from northeast Oregon, you take SR 3 which for a while is paved, and then becomes gravel, and then one lane, and then drops down precariously and gets even narrower. You'll think Troy residents don't want you to come to their town. If you need to reach Troy from Washington, come in on SR 129. *Average size of your basic Grande Ronde steelhead:* 4 or 5 pounds. *Equipment:* Midweight spincasting gear and 6- or 7-weight fly rod. Spinners and streamers. Wading cleats. Floating lines, sinktip lines, sinking lines.

CONTACTS

Dennis Dickson, Dickson Flyfishing Steelhead Guides, www.flyfishsteelhead.com

Oregon Department of Fish and Wildlife, Wallowa District Office, 541-426-3279

Mac Huff, Eagle Cap Fishing Guides, Joseph, www.eaglecapfishing.com

The Shilo Inn Café and RV Park-Gas, 541-828-7741

Tim Johnson, of FishHawk Guides, www.fishhawkguides.com

High Desert Lakes

Sampling of some of the better lakes, Oregon (Bend area and high desert)

- **Location:** All over Oregon, especially central and eastern part of the state
- **What You Fish For:** Trout and bass
- **Highlights and Notables:** Oregon's inventory of lakes is amazing. For the stillwater angler, there are few other regions on earth that contain so many blue ribbon trout lakes as in the Northwest.

Oregon has some of the finest lake fishing for trout in the nation. These lakes of central and eastern Oregon are typically rich in trout food, rich with fat trout. The so-called high-desert lakes are usually windy and remote. Sagebrush rules these rolling hills and where there are no hills rolling, there is vast empty landscape where the wind rushes across the open area like the Huns across the Steppes. Not all lakes are set in such harsh, extreme conditions. Many more are located high in the mountains and surrounded by dense green forests that come right up to the shoreline.

Three of these lakes in Oregon are arguably the three best trout lakes in the America but you probably have never heard of them before. Their foods include snails, leeches, shrimp, scuds, dragonflies, mayflies, caddis flies, midges, and chironomids. Some lakes are so fertile that the trout grow as much as 8 inches or more per year. Anglers regularly catch trout weighing 2 to 5 pounds. A 10- to 15-pounder barely causes a stir and you have an opportunity to catch yet another state record trout over 20 pounds. This is a catch-all section for these lakes, too numerous to mention all here, for some are called Cascade Lakes, some high-desert, but all great and remote and of high quality and all can use Bend (or Sisters) as a home base. I recommend a week-long getaway to try to fish as many of these jewels as possible.

Crane Prairie Reservoir

- **Location:** Central Oregon
- **What You Fish For:** Rainbow trout
- **Highlights and Notables:** The centerpiece of the great lakes around Bend

Crane Prairie Reservoir (4,444 feet elevation) is the centerpiece of the so-called High Desert Lakes. Crane Prairie is one heckuva trout lake, producing large rainbows in excess of 10 pounds and brook trout that weigh as much as a small canned ham from its unusually shallow waters, old river channels, and submerged timber. The lake has oodles of great trout habitat and a rich soup of insects and other trout food which feed these large cruisers. The lake has become a pretty fair bass lake but overall, the sizes of the fish are down a bit.

Arms like tentacles, Crane Prairie Reservoir spreads out over five panoramic square miles, an hour or so southwest of Bend. Bend is close to nowhere but somehow close to all the best fishing holes in the northwest.

Anglers can fish from the banks on Crane, but wading is next to impossible with the yucky-mucky bottom. Boating is the only way to get to all the holding spots, but drive slowly because the lake is full of underwater obstacles like logs, weedbeds, and other snags. Belly boats and other personal watercrafts are ideal for Crane Prairie but remember that the wind isn't an "if," but a "when."

When you look up from Crane Prairie to see Mt. Bachelor looming in the background, you see the standing dead timber all around, you hear the buzzing insect life in the air and on the water, you know you've made a great choice for a day of fishing. You have a realistic chance at a 22- to 24-inch fish but the average for rainbow trout runs about 12 to 17 inches, with a 2- to 5-pounder pretty common. You get the feeling that some real leviathans live in this rich stew, fish much bigger than 24 inches. Big fish and I'm not just giving you the guidebook line; these are really really big fish especially the large rainbows.

One last word about Crane Prairie Reservoir—I've had days where I caught five or ten fish and days where I didn't catch anything. The lake is tough and yields its rewards unwillingly. Beginners will have a rough go with all the things that go bump in the night. They will get snagged and hung up and frustrated. Keep that in mind.

Mann Lake

Mann Lake is crazy remote. This lake (4,150 feet elevation) in the sage flats is out in the middle of nowhere. So there I am floating in this high desert lake, a bit of July wind moving me around as I troll with a black Woolly Bugger for Lahontan cutthroats and I'm daydreaming.

Here's what I was thinking about: My waders have a small leak, right leg, cold water, not that bad really and my mind jumps to a practical joke I pulled on a friend a decade ago.

It was spring but still cold and Chad McPhail asked me to fish a remote western New Mexico high desert lake, Ramah Lake. I couldn't go. He asked if he could borrow some Neoprene waders and flippers. Women won't get this, what I did next but most guys will.

I loaned my good buddy a pair of Neoprenes that had a couple of tiny leaks in both legs. I'd been meaning to patch them up for years but in the meantime had found reasons to buy newer waders and not patch the old. He'd get cold but nothing to worry about and we'd all have big laughs when he got back.

Apparently, the pinholes had gotten bigger over time but not enough to notice until he got into his float tube and into the middle of the windy lake. McPhail reported later, a goofy grin on his face, revenge in his heart, that his legs got chilly and then numb as he tried to quickly paddle back to shore and that task was made next to impossible because one of his flippers came off.

He made it back to shore and went through a series of duck taping the waders, duck taping the fins to his boots and the waders kept leaking and the flippers kept flipping off and his legs were blue and all the while the wind blew him around and he finally gave up. When he got back to town, he told his story to all of us and yeah, we had a big laugh.

The cold water in my waders and the way the wind was blowing me around Mann Lake kept me chuckling at the prank in that daydream-way that makes any movie scene or memory in your head seem to be happening in real time. Sometimes, time gets all jumbled up and you go Billy Pilgrim when you're fishing and daydreaming at the same time.

I hooked a nice one, put him on the reel, landed, and slipped him back into the water. A Lahontan cutthroat, 16 inches long and thick, colorful. Back to reality.

Mann Lake has crazy winds and abrupt weather changes. The lake is fishable from March into November. You're an hour or two from the nearest lodging or services. Kick the tires, fill up the tank and load up the cooler. Hatchery-raised Lahontans are typically 13 to 15 inches but cutts 17 to 22 inches long are common.

East Lake and Paulina Lake

These two sister lakes sit in a caldera, the Newberry Crater, and at this elevation, 6,300 feet, you'd never guess that one lucky angler once caught a 28-pound trout and that anglers regularly catch trout weighing 10 to 12 pounds. Probably never guess that one could catch Atlantic salmon either, huh?

These two gems are a half-hour drive southeast of Bend (there's Bend again). The prime sibling is Paulina Lake, a deep, cold lake with big brown trout. The sexy little sister is East Lake. They're big and beautiful and deep, both ringed by green forests and volcanic rock, each with a resort, each providing fascinating views.

Let's start with East Lake. Record trout is a brown at 22 pounds and some ounces. Landlocked Atlantic salmon that sometimes take dries and grow to 20 inches. Kokanee salmon that average about 16 inches.

East Lake is deep, up to 160 feet, and when full covers 1,030 acres. Cliffs drop into the blue deep holding water but what makes East Lake fun is that there are still shallow edges and dropoff ledges. Submerged hot springs bring trout to its warm releases.

Paulina Lake had a record trout at 27 pounds, 12 ounces and then not long ago, produced a brown that weighed 28 pounds, 5 ounces. Hard to imagine, right? This is a boating lake, and boaters tend to run lures deep, trolling plugs as they putter around the depths of Paulina. Can you say 250 feet deep?

Anglers fish mostly for kokanee salmon (landlocked sockeye) that run 13 to 19 inches and from 1 to 4 pounds. Trolling deep with cowbells is the method of choice for kokanee on Paulina.

Fish are found in the middle channel, around boat docks, hanging off ledges, cruising skinny water. Anglers employ all kinds of methods to catch fish in both lakes, from fly fishing in the shallows to trolling lures deep to bouncing jigs to hooking them on a nightcrawler. Most everything works in these productive lakes.

CONTACTS
Paulina Lake Resort, 541-536-2240

Hosmer Lake

Hosmer Lake is a beautiful, shallow natural lake in central Oregon, complete with green islands, in full view of Mt. Bachelor, a magic place where anglers can only fly fish with barbless flies in its rich, clear waters. At 160 acres, Hosmer looks more like two lakes joined by a narrow channel, like old-timey barbells. The fish are lunkers here but the lake holds some of the bigger brook trout you'll find out West. Hosmer also holds Atlantic salmon. Hosmer has the reputation of being a challenging lake and if you've ever fished for Atlantic salmon, you know why. The water is as clear as the Oregon air so you can see big fish swimming around.

If you catch one of the Atlantic salmon, you must release it immediately—but if you catch one, your jaw will drop at how athletic these guys are, acrobatic jumpers. Hosmer is only ten feet deep at its deepest, making fishing for the big landlocked salmon and brookies a sight-casting delight. Brook trout average about 12 to 15 inches, but reach weights to 5 to 6 pounds. The landlocked salmon average about 14 to 16 inches, with many surpassing 20 inches. Fish underwater with nymphs and streamers to entice both of these selective salmonids, but the brookies will rise to the numerous lake hatches. All Atlantic salmon must be released immediately.

This is a good lake to putt around in a float tube or canoe since gas-powered engines are not allowed and you can only use an electric motor to get from one point to another (no usage when fishing). Thirty-five miles southwest of Bend, Hosmer doesn't have any services to speak of (other than campgrounds) so take care of business beforehand.

Davis Lake

A shallow mountain lake with abundant trout food (insects, leeches, and dragonflies), Davis Lake (3,000 acres) is on the rise. The insect population is so bountiful, the fish are growing so fast, that Davis Lake is now one of the more productive lakes in the state. Rainbows average 2 to 4 pounds and rumor has it there are some 10-pounders swimming about. Fly fishing only.

Wickiup Reservoir

Wickiup Reservoir (10,000 acres) is the largest of the Cascade Lakes, known for its brown trout trophies. While large browns are commonly caught in the 5-pound range, the lake doesn't yield as many double-digit browns as it did two decades ago. Anglers now set their sights on kokanee salmon that run about 12 to 15 inches on average. You might even catch a brook or rainbow trout.

Chickahominy Lake

Chickahominy Lake offers great bank fishing because of its meandering layout; the lake has arms galore. Anglers should concentrate on the drowned streambeds, those channels on the bottom because the trout stay in these channels when they're not cruising the shallows. The fish are small-headed, big shouldered, fat as my Uncle Bob. The lake is surrounded by sage-covered brown hills and lies east of Bend about 100 miles.

Lake Billy Chinook

Kokanee is the main target. Billy Chinook is scenic with its cool-looking cliffs, basalt rimrock, a real lovely lake; 4,000 acres and 400 feet deep. The lake has three arms that are canyons (Deschutes, Metolius, Crooked Rivers). Lake Billy Chinook holds bull trout, big and plentiful rainbow and brown, of which the fishing is underrated. The smallmouth fishing is not all that good. Lots of boat traffic. Other nearby lakes include Little Cultus, Crescent, Sparks, North and South Twin Lakes.

Lava Lake

This high Cascade lake is also known as Big Lava Lake. This spring-fed lake is one-half-square mile big and thirty-feet deep. Lava Lake is fertile, with excellent angling the brook and rainbow that are stocked an-

nually, a real fast growth-rate. We're talking really big brookies, to 19 inches and averaging 10 to 13 inches (the rainbows vary from little to big). Trees shoot up from everywhere and looming mountains provide an ideal backdrop.

Little Lava Lake

Fed by springs under the lake, Little Lava Lake is the headwater of the Deschutes River, 130 acres of brook- and rainbow-catchin' water, Mt. Bachelor's jarring profile in the background. At 20 feet deep, not as good of fishing as big sister lake, Little Lava is heavily forested and not quite as developed.

Cultus Lake

Blue, blue, blue and deep deep deep, up to 180 or more feet deep and that means good lake trout habitat. The lake trout fishery is good all right, mackinaws ranging from 2 to 20 pounds. In 775 acres, Cultus also holds stocked rainbow trout and self-populating brook trout. For top results on this heavily forested lake, employ downriggers for mackinaws, troll deep water.

CONTACTS
The Fly Fisher's Place, Sisters, 541-549-3474
The Riffle Fly Shop, Bend, www .theriffleflyshop.com
Fly and Field, www.flyandfield.com
Sun River Fly Shop, www.sunriverflyshop .com
Patient Angler Fly Shop, www.patientangler .com

John Day River

- **Location:** Northeastern Oregon
- **What You Fish For:** Smallmouth bass
- **Highlights and Notables:** If you like mind-boggling scenery and catching dozens of fat bronzebacks a day, well, this might be the river for you.

There's not a lot I can say about John Day River in northeast Oregon. With the Umpqua River, Oregon has two rivers in the top ten best smallmouth rivers in the world year after year. A John Day float trip is one of those seminal fishing experiences, one of the unique angling journeys, a must-do for any fisherman worth his or her salt. Some think the Umpqua's smallies are bigger and some say John Day has more smallmouth but chocolate or vanilla, potato or potahto, Chevy or Ford, Ginger or Mary Ann. They're both great.

John Day River runs through what looks like a desert. In the summer, it sure feels like a desert. To either side of the river, you'll see a geologic formation that looks like that Wyoming Devils Tower, the one of which Richard Dreyfuss makes a mashed potato (potahto) statue. Canyons carved out of lava by thousands of years of non-stop river. You get the feeling of eons, time, prehistory when you float the John Day.

You camp out under the skies with more stars than Cannes, eat mouthwatering meals and feel the camaraderie that can only be felt camping on a wild and scenic river.

You also get the feeling that you could catch two hundred bass in a long day's work. You can catch fifty. Seventy-five. Even one hundred. Whatever your skill level, you will catch smallies and you will catch enough that you think you caught a lot. The Department of Fish and Game estimates that there are 4,000 smallmouth bass per mile.

You're on your own on this float, usually a three- or five-day float trip. You won't see anybody else but if you do, it will be fleeting, like a mirage.

CONTACTS

Steve and Linda Fleming's Mah-Hah Outfitters, Fossil, www.johndayriverfishing.com

Arrowhead River Adventures, Eagle Point, www.arrowheadadventures.com

McKenzie River

- **Location:** Western central Oregon
- **What You Fish For:** Rainbow trout, steelhead, Chinook salmon
- **Highlights and Notables:** A combo trout/steelhead river of the first degree

I wade fearlessly in the McKenzie despite the deep pools and slippery rocks and big rocks. I have fallen twice this morning, once taking a dunking up to my shoulders in a pool where, to any observer, I looked like I was trying to sit on a big exercise ball on a slick linoleum floor. The boat, the only way to fish long parts of this river, the boat, what I rode in for two days prior, I didn't want to pay for another day. Live and learn.

The sun rising over the trees toward its noon appointment overhead warms me. I pass up easy pickings, the eager smaller brook trout, the colorful-but-not-so-finicky cutthroat to go after the more finicky, bigger rainbow trout.

I am working a big pool, to a large brook trout, at least 16, maybe 17 inches long, about as big a squaretail as I've seen in this river, one of the bigger I've seen in a river out west. Most are palm-sized to ruler-sized. Twice I have fooled this fish with these fur-and-feather imitations only to lose it both times on the hookup—first with a House and Lot, an ugly fury of black thread and white calf tail. The second time, the big fish took then quickly shook off a Bloody Butcher, a gray and red fly meant to swim just beneath the surface. This time,

after sitting and waiting and breathing and smoking a cigar, I have tied on a Humpy.

I false cast a couple of times, my cream-colored line whizzing through the air like a laser light. I have a tricky placement to get to the big trout because I need to set the fly to the far side of the chute coming into the pool and that means the drag will pull the fly within a second. No room for error.

The fly lands perfectly, the broad-backed trout opens its mouth and engulfs the fly. I lift my rod tip and the rod bends, charging the electric tug on the end of my line, that fuzzy pit feeling, the reason I love to fly fish. The trout zips back and forth in the pool but this time I keep the line taut, my eagerness under control and I play the fish to evaluation, stripping the fish in to my hand. I goof up and get the line wrapped around the leather strap in the back and while I try to pull it off, the trout lies on its side, gasping for air, looking like it is trying to say something to me. An explosion of color. Orange fins tipped in white, its back mottled green and brown and gray, ruby spots painted on the trout's side, its belly a buttery hue.

In the western half of Oregon flows one of the most productive trout streams in the West; certainly one of the best combination trout/steelhead streams. The McKenzie River gives its name to the famous drift boat, and float fishing is a great way (the best way) to fish the rough and tumble river. Wading on much of this powerful river can be dangerous, so be cautious.

This is a gorgeous river, flowing through a canyon, past thick forests, big boulders scattered on the shores, in the water, cold and swift and full of fat native rainbow, cut-throat, and brook trout, as well as lots of stocked rainbow and brook trout. Maybe there are the native redsides but they are diluted, distant relatives to their progenitors.

Steelhead and Chinook salmon (a spring run) also inhabit the river and while the trout nor the salmon nor the steelhead get big (this is not a trophy river), they get big enough and offer fishermen quality options. Rainbows run on average about 9 to 12 inches but you'll catch quite a few in the 14 to 16 range, fewer 16 to 18, and a 20-inch trout is kinda rare. These are colorful trout and you'd swear that if the rainbow you are releasing is not a redside, with its side emblazoned crimson, it ought to be. Dry fly anglers beware that the McKenzie is addicting.

The McKenzie River has a freeway, Highway 126, that runs beside it for most of its way, so access is not a problem, but even with the auto traffic and proximity to Eugene, the river's atmosphere maintains a secluded feel. Summer steelhead runs are increasing and provide an additional game fish for the angler. If you go in summer, you'll find the cutthroat eager participants in this fishing game; you'll experience multiple hatches; you will enjoy Eugene's college-town/yuppie feel with its hip restaurants and coffeehouses and bookstores and art galleries.

CONTACTS

Caddis Fly Angling Shop, www
   .thecaddisfly.com
Gorman Fly Fishing, www
   .mckenzieriverflyfishing.com

Creekside Fly Fishing, www
   .creeksideflyfishing.com

This site lists most of the other shops and guides: www.mckenzieguides.com/mgamckenzieriverguides1.htm

Metolius River

- **Location:** North central Oregon
- **What You Fish For:** Rainbow trout predominantly but also brown and brook trout, kokanee salmon
- **Highlights and Notables:** Best spring creek in the Northwest

Even if the Metolius were not the best spring creek in the Northwest, I'd advise you to visit just to stay in Sisters and have an amazing selection and amount of salmonid waters to choose from each day. This is beautiful country. Spellbinding snow-covered mountains, dense green forests of cedar, pine, and fir where Bigfoot lives, rushing clear streams, and high-altitude lakes comprise this area.

The Metolius is a challenging, stunningly scenic spring creek pregnant with insects, profound with trout, fishable all year long. She begins at Black Butte and flows northward for nearly twenty miles then heads east and moves slowly toward Lake Billy Chinook. Nearly forty miles of quality angling of which eleven miles are fly fishing only regulated.

This clear, cold spring-fed creek holds wild trout or at least stream-bred trout because the state quit stocking the river ten years ago. Most of the trout are rainbow trout but the population also contains bull trout, brown, brook trout, whitefish, and kokanee salmon. These wild rainbow trout average 12 to 16 inches with the big boys found in the deeper holes measuring over 20 inches and weighing over 5 pounds. Rumor has it some anglers see trout pushing 30 inches.

Bull trout are protected by regulations. You might catch one by casting into heavy downed timber and deep pools and might land one up to 15 pounds. Please release them carefully and immediately.

The Metolius has to be one of the purest rivers in the country, given its volcanic origins and how many spring-fed tributaries enter this beautiful stream. The river also gets plenty of snow and rain from altitude and summer thunderstorms so the water levels rarely get low. The clear water and big fish mean that you better be on top of your game to catch and land any. Think long thin leaders, matching the hatch, drag-free drifts, more nymphs than dries—you know the drill. Toss into that primer list that you need to not only match the hatch but *match the correct stage of the hatch.* Since the Metolius doesn't have lots of overhead shelter, the sun and clear water make it easy for the trout to see you and be wary. One way to beat that combo is to find any surface riffling or deep green pools. I got lucky one day *not* using the prescribed slack casts but by keeping my line and leader short and under control and hitting likely lies over and over.

The Metolius is tricky as are most spring creeks. Microcurrents work against you, the sameness of the surface with few riffles means you have to watch for rising fish, look for underwater hiding places, work the banks, hits all the seams, fish the pools.

The water temperatures are steady all year and the river runs cold and extremely clear. Anglers' hearts will skip a beat as they spot lunker trout holding in lies. The Metolius River is best fished from the lush banks and by wading, although wading in the canyon section can be tricky. There isn't a lot of submerged cover for the trout in the river, so they hug the undercut banks and bankside structure. Access is excellent to this incredibly rich spring-fed stream, one of the best in the West. Hear this: The tributaries are well worth exploring, too (hint, hint).

CONTACTS
Camp Sherman Store, www
    .campshermanstore.com
The Fly Fisher's Place, www
    .flyfishersplace.com
Sisters Oregon Guide Service, www
    .sistersoregonguide.com/recreation-fly-
    fish.htm

Rogue River

- **Location:** Southwestern Oregon
- **What You Fish For:** Chinook and coho salmon, steelhead
- **Highlights and Notables:** Steelheaders know this is one of the must-do rivers, classic pools, ragingly dramatic scenery.

This was one of those weeks when I sucked as a fisherman. I couldn't get a steelhead to hit my offerings, the Chinook weren't running yet (as if I needed another excuse), I was cold and wet, I was not casting well and my knee was acting up. And then, I broke my 7-weight rod

A 71.5 pound Chinook salmon.

No, I didn't catch it, but one lucky angler did just weeks after I visited the Rogue. And I broke my rod tip walking the river, caught in under a rock and it snapped like a twig, just like my spirits. I caught two steelhead when it was all said and done but it was on a borrowed rod and I'm not sure those fish technically counted for me.

The Rogue River in southern Oregon is famous for its great salmon (Chinook and coho) and steelhead fishing, classic for its scenery, and classic for its perfect pools and runs, mostly wild supplemented with hatchery stock. Early summer begins the world-class steelhead and salmon runs. I recommend floating the trip, drift boat–style, hooking up with a guide because of the wildness of the Rogue and the temperamental nature of the fish. The action continues all summer into fall, and by Christmas the winter steelhead are moving—but some kind of salmonid is living and running in the Rogue all year long.

The upper forks have beauty and trout fishing, as does the Holy Water below Lost Creek Dam and above the hatchery. That section is fly fishing only, barbless, catch-and-release, and some real hogs grow here as well as natives cutts and bows. There are two hundred miles of Rogue but there are also spots that are congested with either boats or shore anglers or both. Medford is one cool town. I-5 runs along side the Rogue. Grants Pass has guides and amenities and most all of the towns along the Rogue tend toward anglers.

CONTACTS
Rogue Fly Shop, www.rogueflyshop.com
Michael Gorman, www.gormanflyfishing
.com
Roe Outfitters, www.roeoutfitters.com

Umpqua River

- **Location:** Southwestern Oregon
- **What You Fish For:** Trout, steelhead, and smallmouth bass
- **Highlights and Notables:** Legendary steelhead fishery now surpassed by its exceptional angling for bronzebacks. One of the more diverse and productive rivers in America.

Off the top of my head, I don't think there is another North American river that would rank in the top ten for both smallmouth bass and steelhead fishing. That's like Cindy Crawford being a supermodel *and* being a valedictorian. For the younger crowd, I guess I should use Shakira and her noted genius level for a strange combination to rival the Umpqua River.

The smallmouth bass fishery was born illegally, introduced by some yo-yo a couple of decades ago. Luckily, the smallies don't seem to have visibly upset the applecart and since the population is healthy and numerous, we can all revel in the fact that these nonnatives are doing well.

The steelhead fishery of this southwestern Oregon river is legendary, the North Umpqua Fork steelhead, these steelhead mighty and muscular, dignified but wild, ornery and difficult, chronicled by Zane Grey and other masochistic sportsmen. The North Fork of the Umpqua River is a challenging stream, thirty-five miles of it, flies only, perhaps the most storied of all American steelhead rivers.

It's funny, because Umpqua steelies are not among the largest of summer steelhead, 6 to 12 pounds, but their fame exceeds their size. Perhaps because of the setting. The North Fork is a deep blue or a light green depending on the light and on your vantage point, but either way, clear, invisible to the bottom, basalt bedrock. Cascades, runs, pools, pocket water, tailouts, ledges, chutes, eddies, glides—if you can think of it, the North Fork has it. And if you wade it, you will fall. Cleats, baby, cleats.

Another reason the North Fork Umpqua is so revered by steelheaders is that you just don't catch many of these silver cruisers. Like fatalistic Atlantic salmon anglers or those hard-core fishermen who chase muskies, the harder the prey, the better the day. These sea-run rainbows are finicky, and when caught, furious. You don't have enough line or enough backing on your whirring reel. So much patience for such a tiny amount of adrenaline. Hell, just getting to the river in one piece is a struggle, what with nasty thick forestation

and blackberries and then the steep slopes and then riprap and then you realize, if you haven't fallen or aren't putting on a band-aid, you have just maneuvered yourself into somewhere that has no casting room and little future.

The North Fork Umpqua just has that look. The river and its surroundings just looks like a classic, like a steelhead stream. *That*, that run right there, that's where a steelhead holds. You know it when you see it but it's hard to put into words. A certain *je ne sais quoi*.

Named pools always reflect the angling community's belief that a fishery is genuine, classic. The North Fork qualifies: Sweetheart Pool. Kitchen Hole. Glory Hole. Hayden's Run, the Camp Water. When a river is really good, writers insert the word "fabled" in front of the word pools. Fabled is just another word for "nothing on the end of your line."

Named flies also reflect the confidence that a river is good enough to beat you, named flies designed for a specific water, specific fish. North Fork: the Skunk, the Black Gordon.

I have heard a million times from anglers that the Umpqua River, especially the North Fork, is the most scenic river in the West. And something you won't hear is that the winter steelhead run is relatively uncelebrated and has gotten better in recent years. The fish are larger, the weather wicked, ideal for those who love adversity.

And if this great fishery isn't enough, the North Umpqua also has coho salmon and spring Chinook salmon. There are those anglers who come from far and wide to fish the Umpqua just for the Chinook runs, runs beginning in later March and going through early July, these salmon able to weigh as much as 40 pounds, an impossible challenge to land in this rough water, like Gilbert Gottfried trying to knock out Chuck Liddell.

On to the mainstem and the South Fork, the warmer water, the smallmouth water. The Umpqua is awesome for your bronzeback jones. Light tackle or fly fishing is the ticket. You can drift a boat or raft but the ideal method in this languid clear warm river is to slip into a belly boat and sneak up on the bass. Wading's out because the water is too clear, the smallmouth too skittish, your sloshing too clumsy.

In the deep clear pools where you can witness the school or pod or conference of 2- to 4-pound smallmouth bass, the brushy banks, the gentle pace of the river, there is usually a lunker. You have to cast and you have to do this with limitations, presentation, drift, observation. Just do it. If you do, then you discover why the Umpqua is considered one of the greatest smallmouth rivers in the country.

Steelhead, world class. Chinook salmon, top notch. Smallmouth, national rep. But wait, there's more.

American shad. May and June, these hard-fighting bullets, these poor man's tarpons, provide excellent action, underrated fishing. Striped bass in the lowest reaches of the Umpqua ambush the smolts of salmon and steelies on their way upstream. Green and white sturgeon in the lower river. Trout. I forgot to mention that the upper river has really good trout fishing and spectacular scenery.

You find the North Umpqua near Roseburg in southern Oregon. You find Highway 138 paralleling the river for more than sixty miles out of Roseburg. Whether you fish for smallmouth and catch in one day more than you can count on your fingers and toes and your fishing buddy's fingers and toes, or whether you cast to steelhead and never catch a one, you take away something special from the Umpqua.

CONTACTS
Roe Outfitters, www.roeoutfitters.com
The Joseph Fly Shoppe, www
   .josephflyshoppe.com

Wenaha River

- **Location:** Northeastern Oregon
- **What You Fish For:** Wild redband rainbow, bull trout
- **Highlights and Notables:** 2,000 feet down, basalt ridges and canyons, sheer, steep, deep. Timber-r-r-r-r. Heavily forested canyon bottom and sides. The Blue Mountains. You won't see a soul but you might find yours.

I doubt you've heard of the Wenaha River. The freestone river doesn't make many headlines, doesn't get many articles written about it. Even if it did get the press, not many people would or could fish it because in Wenaha run about a foot long and are brilliantly colored. You can find them in the stream's riffles, pools, pocket water runs, behind rocks, in front of rocks, they don't seem to care, they hit anywhere, anything and everything.

Wenaha River for twenty-plus miles, a Wild and Scenic River. Flows right through the Wenaha-Tucannon Wilderness, 177,465 acres. You can't ride a bike or go into this wild river on anything motorized. You must hike if you don't float.

CONTACTS

Umatilla National Forest, Pendleton, 503-278-3716

of the long descent into the canyon and besides it's so out of the way, in the middle of nowhere. This river runs through real-life wilderness. That's the river's biggest appeal.

The wild redbands alone ought to be unique quarry enough that you shouldn't feel obliged to fish for bull trout. You can, you know—fish for bull trout. Wenaha anglers are allowed to fish for bull trout and release them immediately. Given the declining numbers of bull trout throughout the West, I'd hope you fish more for redband than bull.

The Wenaha dumps into Grande Ronde. Access to the river is only by trail, and you can find several trailheads, including one at Troy, the nearest town. You can camp along the river but beware rattlesnakes that want to share your sleeping bag. Redband

Williamson River

- **Location:** South central Oregon
- **What You Fish For:** Rainbow trout
- **Highlights and Notables:** One of Oregon's many fine trout streams

In south central Oregon, the Williamson River offers fine trout fishing in slow-moving spring-fed waters. Anglers can find big, big trout, many over 20 inches, more than you think reach weights up to 10 pounds. The rainbow trout (landlocked steelhead) swim the fertile waters of Klamath Lake, but leave for the cooler, moving water of the river in late summer and also move out during spawning.

The Williamson's upper river provides meadow fishing for small brook and rainbow trout. Below the marsh, which colors the water at times, the river is best float-fished. Public access is a problem on both the upper and lower Williamson River, and in some places, the only way to access it is by floating. Boat put-ins are a scarce commodity as well. Parts of the upper and lower river flow through the Winema National Forest, but access from there to other places requires a boat.

WASHINGTON

Columbia River

- **Location:** Borders between Oregon and Washington (and flows through Canada too)
- **What You Fish For:** Walleye, sturgeon, smallmouth bass, rainbow trout, shad, salmon
- **Highlights and Notables:** Remarkable river, grand and powerful and gorgeous

The Columbia is kind of like Brian "Fish" Dolive back at LHS where I graduated. He was tall and handsome, dated the prettiest, nicest gal in school, made straight A's, excelled at sports, had no enemies, was president of every club or organization, was nice to geeks and dopers and kickers and all cliques alike. He was big and beautiful and all things to all people. He even seemed like he was happy.

Brian Dolive had as many friends as the Columbia has tributaries, which is a lot. The Columbia River is all things to all people as well, big and beautiful, the second largest river system in the nation. All at once, the Columbia is one of the best walleye, smallmouth, rainbow trout, white sturgeon, shad fisheries in the country. At one time, the Columbia might have been the top salmon river in the world. You almost always see the adjective "mighty" in front of Columbia and why not, this powerful river is the fourth largest river by volume in North America behind the Mississippi, the St. Lawrence, and the Mackenzie Rivers. The Columbia has ten major tributaries: the Kootenay, Okanagan, Wenatchee, Spokane, Yakima, Snake, Deschutes, Willamette, Cowlitz, and Lewis rivers.

Given how good the fishing is on the Columbia for all these species (and I didn't even mention the Chinook and coho salmon or the steelhead or kokanee salmon fishing that while diminished because of hydroelectric dams and bad farming practices and other sundry things, is still productive) it's a wonder that the river doesn't see even more anglers than it does (which is a lot but this is one big mean system, after all).

You've probably seen the white sturgeon being fished for on television programs because it's so rare and so ugly and prehistoric. The regs are strict but you can still fish for them and have decent expectations of a white 8 to 10 feet. The spring and summer Chinook runs are huge targets, busy times on the river but exceptionally worth it.

I think the most underrated fishery in the river is the rainbow trout—they are typically big and fat, up to 10 or 12 pounds and average 12 to 20 inches, round and broad with small heads and deep red sides. The best place to catch rainbows is in British Columbia near Trail.

Cowlitz River

- **Location:** Southwestern Washington
- **What You Fish For:** Sea-run cutthroat trout, salmon, steelhead
- **Highlights and notables:** One of the best aspects of this big river, other than the fact it's Washington's best steelhead stream, is that it lies equidistant between Seattle (2.5 hours south of the city) and Portland (2 hours north of the city, just south of Mt. Ranier N.P.).

The Cowlitz River is wide and mean, loaded with big salmonids that can break you off and make your heart race every month of the year. Fifty or sixty miles you can call

your own as long as you don't want to call the few hundred yards below Blue Creek Hatchery and at the Barrier Dam—that part belongs to all the throngs. The rest of the river is yours.

Born on Mt. Ranier, ending its course 100 miles later when it meets the Columbia River, the Cowlitz River is a nursery for wild and hatchery fish, holding runs of winter and summer steelhead, resident rainbow trout, chum, coho, (silver) and Chinook (king) salmon, sea-run cutthroat. Something's biting all year long. And some of them are big, 10, 15 pounds or more.

The river has all the requisite haunts big fish need and anglers desire—long gravel bars, side channels are as big as some rivers, pools, back-eddies, entering creeks. Much of the river is private, so you'll be floating it. Located right off I-5, the Cowlitz is worth a multiday visit just about any time of year or as a day trip out of Seattle or Portland.

Olympic Peninsula

- **Location:** Western Washington
- **What You Fish For:** Steelhead, salmon, trout
- **Highlights and Notables:** This assortment of coastal rivers is one of the best areas in the world to catch steelhead.

Hi, my name is Mark and I am a coffee addict.

Every morning, I drink coffee. No exceptions. And I like good coffee. This doesn't mean I run to Starbucks, because I don't. Paying four bucks for a cup of coffee isn't my cup of tea. I like to make my own cuppa joe.

I'm not a big fan of the 8- or 10- or 12-cup coffeemaker (but I am a big fan of Joltin' Joe). The coffee seems bland and lifeless. I'll drink a bad cup of coffee (worst ever was a truckstop in western New Mexico in 1986) because bad coffee is better than no coffee, after all. I've tried coffee presses, percolators, plungers, jugs, espresso machines, boiling coffee at the campfire, four-dollar cups of coffee, and they all meet with my approval, more or less, but the best way, my favorite way, is to use a cone filter in a plastic single cone filter holder and pour hot water over the freshly-ground grounds (water first speeds up the release of caffeol) and voilà! Great cup of java.

I'm no barista and I don't play one on TV but I do know what coffee I like (French roast with a shot of espresso) and know that without it in the morning, I get headaches and I'm grouchy and I'm dumber than usual. And on the Olympic Peninsula in western Washington, I was dumber than usual and I couldn't get my coffee, so go figure.

So I'm on the Hoh (sounds terrible when I write it that way), sitting on this big-ass log but was really a recently-downed tree the diameter of my Uncle Bob. I am listening to the river rush by me, and I'm thinking about the coffee I had in Seattle for lunch and again for dinner and again for breakfast. These cups of coffee were the best cups of coffee I'd ever had, made by angels no doubt. Strong but not bitter, pungent, heavy-bodied without being thick, aromatic, almost like a good wine. If you drink good coffee, you know what I mean. If you drink coffee from McDonald's and you like it, well, we're on different pages. But I missed my coffee this morning, my fault I guess, but I figured I'd have a chance to stop in town but we didn't stop and now I have a headache and I'm not having a good day.

Anyway, I had missed three steelhead, caught nothing all day much to the chagrin of my guide who is getting out the bag lunches and who must think I am more rookie than veteran, and I'm taking a break and I'm lost in thought because the Hoh is that color of Fresca, that color that glacial silt does to a river, a frosty blue-green with tinges of salt and gray. The trees and the jungle (for this is more jungle than forest with all the mosses and odd green misshapen plants and canopy of trees) and the moistness of the ground and the moistness of the air all wrapped around me like a wet blanket. Tree trunks are suffocated by green moss and then green Jurassic-looking fern-y plants growing out of the moss on the tree. The forest smells of musk and spruce and something sweet I can't quite place. If there is a Bigfoot, he lives here. I know the otters do.

I had missed the three steelies and it was my fault. I just wasn't on my game. I resolved, as I sat there listening to the water in its arrhythmic wash, changing on me like Fiona Apple, thinking that the rest of the day would be better. This is one of the most beautiful places I've ever sat in my life.

Olympic Peninsula is one of the best winter steelhead fisheries in the lower forty-eight, home to some of the largest wild winter-run steelheads on the planet. Coho and Chinook begin their runs in these rivers about the same time. These coastal rivers that slice through the western slope of the Olympic Mountains, the Hoh, Sol Duc, Queets, Quinault, Bogachiel. All remote but accessible. The winter steelhead run begins in November and lasts into April.

The guide tells me that on the Hoh, steelhead enter the river all year long, that I should have no trouble finding more, which means that he'll put me on them and I, by God, better do a better job at catching them next time.

Bogachiel and Quillayute Rivers are consistent steelhead streams and some think that the Quillayute system is the finest wild steelhead stream anywhere. Shhh. Sol Doc is north of Bogey, winds and turns, deep pools, tough wading, big boulders. Bogachiel, with its big bars and lengthy runs, hooks up with Sol Doc and forms Quillayute River. Queets River lies between Quinault and Hoh, has great runs, real wild, is less crowded than most, so far away. Quinault to the south of the Hoh December through March is fruitful, maybe the best of all O.P. rivers to catch a big steelhead, but must be fished with a local guide since it runs primarily through Quinault Indian Reservation.

When I caught him from behind the boulder in the slack, I knew he wasn't getting off like the other three. He leapt out of the water after slashing at the flashy big fly the guide had tied on and splashed down furiously and the rod bent and I knew it, I knew what to do and I played him for ten minutes and it seemed like forever with his runs and my shoulders slumped into two charley horses and then the wild steelhead with its burnt red-hued side and sparkling silvery body. Nine pounds. I need some coffee in a bad way, even bad coffee at this point and the guide appears to be smiling and the mist is becoming rain.

The Elwah River, on the Olympic Peninsula, is another good-sized steelhead river that supports rainbow trout, and also has runs of sea-run cutthroat, coho, and Chinook salmon. The quality steelhead fishing of the peninsula is hard to match for sheer numbers of blue-ribbon streams in one area, like the aforementioned as well as the Skokomish, Duckabush, Dosewallips,

Salmon, and Calawah Rivers. Some of the better streams with rainbow and cutthroat populations include Skokomish, Dosewallips, Gray Wolf, and Elwah Rivers, Tshletshy, Cameron, Godkin, and Grand Creeks. These are the larger rivers but there are many more smaller streams worthy of exploring. Be sure to check with park and forest officials to familiarize yourself with the dazzling array of regulations governing the area.

The rivers are a breeze to reach from Seattle, Tacoma, and Olympia. Three-hour drive from Seattle. In the northwest corner of the peninsula, Forks is where the fishing headquarters are located, a small village with enough blue-collar to middle-class lodging and eateries that you'll be happy.

CONTACTS
Wild Steelhead Coalition, Kirkland, www.wildsteelhead.coalition.com
Washington Department of Fish and Wildlife, wdfw.wa.gov
Lake Quinault Lodge, 800-562-6672
Quinault River Inn, 800-410-2237

Rocky Ford Creek

- **Location:** East central Washington
- **What You Fish For:** Rainbow trout
- **Highlights and Notables:** You'll see as many Idaho plates here as you do those from Washington. Funky, challenging spring creek with lunker rainbow trout who will drive you nuts ignoring your offerings.

Rocky Ford Creek is arguably the finest spring creek in Washington. She is a slow-moving, (too) popular, shallow, weedy spring creek in sagebrush country where reeds line the banks, the alkaline flats beyond the reeds, horizontal until basalt cliffs in the distance. Rainbow trout grow to titanic sizes here and in this shallow water, appear as large as the Titanic. I know they stock brood fish and I've heard they've stocked triploids (like steers—no reproduction, so they fatten up). Rainbows over 20 inches are regularly sighted but rarely caught. (Derisively, I have heard some say these are tame fish.) If you do catch rainbows on Rocky Ford, it will be because you followed all the rules (fly fishing only, catch-and-release only, no wading at all, barbless hooks only) and obeyed spring creek tactics 101 (presentation, small flies, long leaders, stealth, no drag).

There are less than three public miles on Rocky Ford, with private property well marked. Located in eastern Washington above the town of Ephrata, fishing is open year-round. There is also public access to the lower mile and a half plus parking off of Highway 17. Public access begins below the upper hatchery. To get to Rocky Ford Creek from northern Idaho, travel west on I-90 to Moses Lake. At Moses Lake take Highway 17 north until you reach Trout Lodge Road.

City Fishing

SEATTLE

Lake Washington,
Puget Sound,
Snoqualmie River,
Lake Sammamish,
Cedar River

Renton is a Seattle outskirts town, south of Lake Washington. The Cedar River runs through it, this northwestern-style-yuppie link of riverfront parks, the river moves easy and effluent past bicyclists and joggers and picnicking families, under bridges and concrete ramparts. The river is open again after years of being closed much to the delight of Boeing workers. Rainbow trout and sockeye salmon are the big catches (and there are some big big rainbows, too) but you'll hear of other things being caught as well including the last three steelhead left in the river. Steelhead are occasionally caught but they're rare.

Seattle is more than great bookstores and coffee haunts and high-tech companies and rainy days. The Emerald City is arguably the prettiest city in America, what with the backdrop of the jagged Cascades and the blue waters dotted with islands that is Puget Sound. The city is also properly situated to be near

many rives and lakes that hold trout, salmon, and steelhead. Puget Sound itself is quite the fishery as are the rivers that run into it: cod, flounder, halibut, and the famous salmon fishing. From the beach, you can angle for salmon, steelhead, and sea-run cutts in its calm and protected waters. You can hire boats and guides to get you into the Sound and find fish, too (although things get awfully busy come salmon season). Seattle has numerous lakes and parks where one can angle for all kinds of fish.

The Yakima and the Snoqualmie Rivers are the two most prominent rivers near Seattle (see the Yakima entry for more on this fine trout stream). The Snoqualmie is green, lush, and mountainous, while the Yakima is sagebrush and arid. Snoqualmie offers year-round trout fishing as well as seasonal salmon fishing (the king fishing can produce some whoppers), steelhead, and sea-run cutthroat. Think pink. Bright pink flies. The Snoqualmie has fun feeder creeks too, lush forests, big boulders, clear cold water.

CONTACTS
Emerald Water Anglers, 206-545-2197, 206-601-0132, www. emeraldwateranglers.com

Sprague Lake

- **Location:** Eastern Washington
- **What You Fish For:** Trout, bass, crappie, walleye
- **Highlights and Notables:** An up-and-down lake that, when on, makes memories

Year-round lake (1,840 acres) that is a blast to fish for rainbow trout, smallmouth and largemouth bass, crappie, catfish, and even walleye. I have caught 20-inch rainbows in Sprague.

The lake is inconsistent and at times, you can't catch a thing (even when they are jumping out of the water all around you) and other times, you catch everything, every species of fish that swims in its cool waters. If you can't fish Sprague, or don't like the summer mosquitos, then investigate further into Washington lakes. The high country lakes are a different experience—Washington has so many where the size of the trout and beauty of the mountains will overwhelm you. Start with Snow Lake for amazing scenery. Western Washington has about 1,600 high lakes (2,500 feet elevation or higher) and east of the Cascades, 900-plus lakes are 3,500 feet or higher. That's a good start.

Yakima River

- **Location:** South central Washington
- **What You Fish For:** Rainbow, brown, cutthroat trout
- **Highlights and Notables:** Solid consistent year-round trout performer, worthy of a visit

The most underrated (whatever that term really means) trout fishery in the Northwest is, hands down, the Yakima River. Anglers in Washington state are so tuned into great salmon fishing locations that they usually bypass/overlook/forget about the Yakima. Just two hours from Seattle, you can be on the river in a plane ride and a fast car trip.

When my daughter Sarah lived in Spokane and we'd go to visit her, the Yakima was always the tail-end adjunct sidetrip back home on my way to Dallas.

The Yakima River has everything you'd want out of a big western trout stream: seventy-miles of water of all sorts, wild rainbows as the predominant species along with browns, cutthroats, and some brookies, crazy-beautiful scenery complete with forests and mountains, canyon section (requisite for the ideal trout stream, right?), and the list goes on and on. The Yakima is a tailwater that doesn't always act like a tailwater.

Out-of-staters will read "trout stream in Washington" and they will think rain. Fair enough. But east of the Cascades, rain is sometimes a distant memory. Don't let the thought of cloudy wet days keep you away from the best trout stream in the state. The Cascades form a serious buffer to the rainy

weather of the western half of Washington. (I hear the word "buffer" and I can't help but think of the scene in the *Godfather II* where mobster Willie Cicci tells the congressional panel "Buffer? Yeah, the family had a lot of buffers.")

The Yakima has solid hatches but they'll fool you if you don't pay attention (sounds like my wife talking to me now). When water is released in midsummer and on into the fall (in order to irrigate the apple groves), the river gets up in a hurry and this increase affects the hatches. You can wade in three seasons but boating is your best bet for consistent angling.

Like so many traditional western streams, the Yakima is split into thirds—upper, middle, lower. They're all good. The scenic Yakima flows east from the Cascades

in the central portion of the state, providing angling opportunities for wild trout to 5 pounds and it does so twisting and turning more than Chubby Checker. The best sections include the river between Yakima and Cle Elum, especially the canyon section near Cle Elum and from Keechelus to Roza Dam. You won't catch many 20-inch trout on the Yakima but you'll have a field day dry fly fishing for 11- to 16-inch wild rainbows.

Many float the river, dropping big stonefly nymphs in its full waters. The river has an amazing diversity of insect hatches, ranging from several types of stoneflies, including the big salmonfly *Pteronarcys californica,* the Skwala, caddis flies, and some mayflies. The Yakima mayflies hatch early and they include green drakes, blue-winged olives, and pale morning duns. Attractor patterns make for best dry fly fishing in the state from July to early October.

Fall fishing sees thick clouds of caddis flies, and combined with the brilliant colors of the tree-lined banks, this is the best time to fish the Yakima. Fishing is excellent all through winter and into March when the golden stoneflies begin hatching. In addition to the less-crowded water in the winter, the Yakima's flows are low enough that wading can be managed. Anglers are restricted to artificials and single barbless hook and a long stretch is managed for catch-and-release only.

CONTACTS
The Evening Hatch, 509-962-5959
The Worley Bugger, 509-962-2033
Chuck Cooper, 509-962-5259
Bob Aid, 425-643-2246

WYOMING

Kenny and I had done our Yellowstone fishing trip we love to do every year or two. *Let's take a few days on the Beartooth,* we both agreed. We needed it. This backcountry setting was one of my first long backpacking trips. I learned many things during various trips to Beartooth, most every time with my fishing bud and bro-in-law Kenny. Here is a quick rundown of what I (we) learned:

Poop rolls downhill. Take a tent—don't sleep outside. Value of a bear bag and rope and distance. The jinx kicks in. It's not about the fishing.

POOP ROLLS DOWNHILL

Look, there are actually books about this subject, how to take care of business in the woods. It's an easy thing, a natural thing but it can sure expose your weaknesses. I was a young man so that's my excuse. I'd had a wonderful day of fishing and Nature called and I found a good hill with a bit of cover, hid, pointed my toes downhill and got to work. The title of this paragraph explains the rest of the story.

TAKE A TENT—DON'T SLEEP OUTSIDE

Kenny thought he'd save weight by leaving the tent behind. We usually share a two-man tent and if he left it behind, that meant I would be outside, too, so I found my weight-loss in other ways. I carried my one-man tent, not quite a bivy, not quite a tent. Kenny jinxed himself and I loved it.

"What if it rains?" I asked the bison-headed fishing buddy of mine.

"Ain't gonna rain," Kenny retorted.

"It could snow."

"It's not going to snow."

"It might." I knew that repetition often tricked him.

"If it snows, I'll just snuggle deeper in my sleeping bag."

"You ought to at least take a tarp to have a lean-to," I suggested. "And the mosquitos will tear you up."

"I'll be fine, just shut up."

So I shut up fully confident that the fishing gods had been listening.

Even in early July, snows hit the Beartooth Plateau, and those who are sleeping near lakes, with more regularity than someone who didn't bring proper shelter would like to believe.

Kenny caught a lot of brookies in this one no-name lake, we each ate a mediocre freeze-dried dinner (this was back before they turned tasty), and as we settled in to sleep, under a clear starry sky, I joked with Kenny about how he might want to bed down under a tree in case it rained during the night. He chuckled at my complete ignorance and said no, he thought he'd sleep under these twinkling stars and enjoy the clean cold air. No less than six inches of snow fell on us after the skies opened up and pelted us with rain and hail first.

VALUE OF A BEAR BAG, ROPE, AND DISTANCE

I *always* keep my food separate from my camp, cook hundreds of yards away from my bed, tie up my goodies in a tree in a bear bag. But I only do this because I didn't always do this. Food gone, torn up backpack, ripped tent, bear tracks everywhere. Live and learn.

THE JINX KICKS IN

I mention this in other chapters, this thing I do where I like to get Kenny riled up. I predict how many fish I'm going to catch that day. I tell him that he is not going to catch a single fish. I tell him I'm gonna land the big one. And so on. Superstitions be damned.

This jinx I like to play with at the start of fishing trips had its genesis at a lake near Louis Lake, the name of which shall never be spoken by me again. Kenny caught several grayling while I took photos. Then he caught brook trout and rainbow trout and cutthroat trout and one of the cutts was pretty good size. He suggested I get in on the action. In the Beartooth, you can usually catch a fish on every cast so I deferred, took more pics, then when I was good and ready, strung up and cast.

And cast and cast and cast. Fishing in the Beartooth is easy, fellow anglers. There's no way you can't catch fish unless you're fishing a lake that has no fish.

Kenny had one of those days where someone you know really does catch 100 fish. I got started late and with Kenny on one side of the lake, me on the other, us circling in a weird boxing match, the fish rose on his side and retreated from mine. The fishing gods laughed like thunder that day and I caught two small brook trout only at the end of the day when the lake boiled from all the rises. I'm sure Kenny slept like a baby that night. He paid for it years later with the no-tent decision. The fishing gods are incredible, aren't they?

Beartooth Plateau

- **Location:** Northwestern Wyoming
- **What You Fish For:** Trout of all species, grayling
- **Highlights and Notables:** One of those perfect getaways for fishing buddies, inspiring scenery, clean air, lots of trout

You don't go fishing in lakes that sit at 10,000 feet to catch trophy trout. You don't go fishing way back there, way up there to get away from it all, either, that's a cop-out, the easy answer. No, you go fishing in lakes that sit at 10,000 feet to find things. For me, I find resignation, submission to something bigger than me. Beartooth Plateau will convince you of many things, and if you are looking, you'll find it there.

If you like an exhausting drive to the middle of nowhere, a long tiring hike up and down trails, possible altitude sickness, the only amenities the ones you stuffed in your backpack, and fish that aren't really all that big and alternately hard to catch or jumping on your hook (all depending on the time of day), then Beartooth Plateau is the place for you.

The Beartooth Plateau Lakes can be found in northwestern Wyoming and southern Montana near Yellowstone National Park. Hundreds of lakes to choose from. Dozens of small streams. Not all bodies of water in the Beartooth hold fish but most do and most are teeming with trout and/or grayling, and some are stocked with Snake River and Yellowstone cutthroat, brown trout, golden trout, lake trout, splake, and mountain whitefish.

We drove in, past the top of the world, nodded indifferently at the waterfalls you see on the way, cared nothing about the steep dropoffs from the road and we somnambulistically fished roadside lakes—US 212—for a bit at first for small brook trout, our minds not in full wilderness mode, and we hardly noticed the other folks, families and kids fishing these same roadside lakes with us.

We found the trail and hiked and hiked and kept on hiking, walking right past perfectly good remote lakes. Wildflowers covered meadows and with heads down to the trail, we walked and walked.

We sat above the blue bowl of a lake for an hour looking down on it, not talking. Some signal shared—we descended, tied on flies, fished, shoulder to shoulder. The sun a golden sphere slamming slowly into the granite peaks while we set up camp.

Over the campfire, Kenny spoke first, sotto voce.

"You believe that people in heaven know what's going on down here? That they can see us?"

"Fred, right?"

"Yeah, Fred."

It was a quiet, lonely two days. We spent a lot of the time away from each other, much of it not fishing. Signal shared again—we just kind of knew it was time to go and we packed up camp at the same time, silently, the only sounds the slick shuffle of the sleeping bag shoved into the compression sack, the hissing of the fire when the water hit it, our feet knocking little rocks and pebbles.

I don't know if I believe in heaven or that people in heaven can know what goes on down on earth. I'm a Baptist turned Episcopal so I'm pretty messed up when I wrestle with the angels. I do know this. Fred passed away not all that long before our trip—not long before we buried our father-in-law, not long before the man who was surrogate father to both of us reentered the earth, this angel who played advisor to the two men (related, friends) who grew up with stepdads—and we were sure looking for him out there somewhere in the Beartooth.

By the way, Beartooth Lake is a great lake and I lied about not being able to have a chance at big trout or even trophy trout in the Beartooth Lakes. Here is the *one* place you can do just that. Okay, maybe you can find a lake here and there that hold some cutthroats that are big, but really, other than Beartooth and these handful of secret lakes, the fish are on the small side.

CONTACTS

Beartooth Plateau Outfitters, Inc., Cooke City, MT, www.beartoothoutfitters.com

Clark's Fork Ranger District, Cody, 307-527-6921

Wyoming Game and Fish Department, Cody, 307-527-7125

Encampment River

- **Location:** Southern Wyoming, northern Colorado
- **What You Fish For:** Brook, cutthroat, and brown trout
- **Highlights and Notables:** Pocket water and pools in a lovely canyon

I'm not going to sit here (at my computer) and tell you that the Encampment River ranks right up there in trout density or has trophy trout and therefore is one of the top trout streams in the world. Three species of trout (brook, cutthroat, and brown), solitude, wild scenery, productive feeder streams, and a beautiful hike—those things make Encampment special enough to include.

The Encampment begins in Colorado, flows north into Wyoming. Your target areas are the alpine valley under the Continental Divide where the Encampment begins and the canyon that the clear cold river rushes through before becoming an ordinary river that passes through farm and ranchland. Think Routt National Forest in Colorado and Medicine Bow National Forest in Wyoming.

You have to hike into the canyon and brothers and sisters, it's worth the effort. The canyon doesn't get much angling pressure, the browns are thick-bodied and rise to dry flies, the river is shallow for the most part, about thirty feet wide and the trout lies include pocket water around the big boulders, wide glides, riffles, pools, and oh-so-beautiful green runs. This is attractor dry fly heaven. And when you catch a cut-

The trout in the North Platte get about as fat as any trout in any river in America. They grow as big as any trout in America. I think, and I'm not really going out on a limb here, that the North Platte is as good as the San Juan and the Green for the consistency of catching large trout. It's only short the scenery.

The scenery's not bad—I like high desert—but I'd be lying if I said it was equal to the dramatic landscapes of any number of other blue-ribbon trout streams. You come to fish the North Platte's Miracle Mile and Gray Reef for the behemoth trout. These trout are the proverbial footballs you always read about, see in the photos in the fly fishing magazines, like those in the Frying Pan, obesely big in the middle, round in girth like Falstaff.

You have over 150 miles of river to fish on the North Platte. The upper reaches in Colorado are wilder, rougher, tougher, less visited (meadows, canyon, boulders, heavy rapids) and it flows through the wild Medicine Bow National Forest and out through a glacial valley. The river is variously impounded and the tailwater trophy trout teasers are the Miracle Mile and Gray Reef, short fertile tailraces that flow through flat lands for ranching, replete with cottonwoods and cows and lots of wind.

How a river this productive can be so relatively unknown is mind-boggling. This is one of the top float-fish trips in the nation, with its year-round angling and the opportunity to land numbers of 15- to 22-inch trout with a solid chance at a linebreaker. How often is it that we find a trout fishery that has improved significantly, con-

throat, they have a fluorescent cut on their gillplate that is so bright and 1980s pink, it's unnatural. Fifteen miles of wilderness fishing. And the West Fork is just pure backcountry pleasure.

North Platte River

- **Location:** Central and southern Wyoming
- **What You Fish For:** Rainbow and brown trout (some Snake River cutts)
- **Highlights and Notables:** Miracle Mile and Gray Reef, two of the best trophy trout-catching stretches of river anywhere in the world

sistently over the last two decades? Since the slot limits initiated in 1982, the number of catchable trout per mile has doubled and the quality of fishing has appreciably increased.

This is one productive river, providing excellent nymph fishing, decent dry fly fishing, and spin fishing. The river has several personalities, in part shaped by the varied topography through which it flows. The Platte runs through a gorgeous, forested canyon in the Medicine Bow National Forest, through the Saratoga Valley, through wide expanses of ranchland and through high desert plains.

The North Platte is fishable year-round. In the winter, the two tailwaters have their best fishing but the weather can be dreadful. In the early spring when runoff is high, the tailwaters have a steady flow, unaffected by the swollen waters. After the river has lowered and cleared, the seventy-five-mile section around Saratoga has excellent angling. The fall spawning run of the brown trout is crowded but top-notch fishing. The

river is so large and diverse, that whatever time of year chosen, the North Platte can respond in kind.

The Miracle Mile is an eight-mile section of tailwater between Seminoe and Pathfinder Reservoirs and this is generally considered to be the richest stretch of the North Platte. This area has plenty of pools, runs, riffles, and deep channels but finding feeding fish that will bite is challenging. The variety of aquatic food for the trout makes choosing a fly a daunting task. The Miracle Mile has great insect hatches especially in summer but the crowds hatch too.

There are an immense number of trout in the river. Some studies suggest the river supports over 4,500 catchable trout per mile. Most range between 12 and 16 inches. The odds of landing a trout 16 to 22 inches are good on the Platte and trophy trout over 5 pounds are common. Catching a trout that weighs between 15 and 20 pounds is a reasonable quest. Anglers will catch mostly rainbows and brown trout but from time to time, they'll land a beautiful copper-colored Snake River cutthroat. The browns are wild and most of the rainbows are wild, too, but the river does receive regular stockings. The trout are thick in the Mile and sightcasting to feeding trout is a common technique. Ditto for the Gray Reef tailrace, a thirty-mile blue-ribbon stretch below Gray Reef Dam.

Gray Reef is similar to the Miracle Mile but has most constant flows and seems like better dry fly fishing. This is floating water, drift boat or kick boat, for there's not much public access or wading water.

Good roadside access in the Miracle

Mile but floating it covers so much more water. Some of the best wading is in the Miracle Mile and you do see a lot of walk-and-waders. Good roadside access and parking lots along the river. And about the scenery, it's pretty in its own harsh way what with low hills in places and they have some juniper and pines growing here and there on them.

The river is a bug factory and most of its bugs, like the omnipresent scuds, are found near the riverbed. So are the trout. Running large stonefly nymphs through a run in the spring or generic mayfly and caddis nymphal forms through a pool in the summer can result in some explosive action. Fish the pocket water, around the boulders in the channels and seams. Use weighted nymphs or sink-tip lines. The riffles of the Platte are full of trout when the hatches are right. The banks hold trout when the sun is full, and a well-placed fly to the bank under the cover of willows usually draws a strike.

Also remember that in Wyoming, landowners own the streambed, so don't get out of your boat and wadefish unless you have permission from the owner. Many floatfishermen choose to float then put up and wade nice-looking spots. After runoff wading is easy below Saratoga thanks to a firm gravel bottom. Chest waders are best until the fall when the river is low enough to wade with hip waders.

CONTACTS

Great Rocky Mountain Outfitters, Inc., Saratoga, 307-326-8750

Riverside Tackle, Riverside, 307-327-5751

Platte Valley Anglers, Saratoga, 307-326-5750

South Side Tackle, Cheyenne, 307-635-4348

Lou's Sport Shop, Laramie, 307-745-8484

Platte River Fly Shop, Casper, www.wyomingflyfishing.com

Grey Reef Outfitters, 307-232-9128

South Fork Snake River and the Jackson Hole Area

- **Location:** Western Wyoming, southeastern Idaho
- **What You Fish For:** Cutthroat and rainbow trout
- **Highlights and Notables:** One of the top four or five float trips in America. Mind-numbing mountain scenery and eager wild beautiful cutthroat trout. The Jackson Hole area is one of the most popular (and rightfully so) angling destinations in the West.

And now, introducing the Snake River (aka the South Fork of the Snake River).

The South Fork Snake River may be the best river in America to take a friend, a son or daughter, a wife, your fishing buddy, or a perfect stranger to catch a wild cutthroat trout. You have proximity to Jackson Hole. You have a plethora of guides. You have dozens and dozens of miles of perfect trout water. And all this set in the most beautiful mountain scenes on the planet. The majesty of the Tetons, the wide valley, the

wildlife, it all adds up to a spectacular fishing experience.

The South Fork is born in Wyoming and rushes to Palisades Reservoir and then it escapes for sixty-six miles until it merges. The Henry's Fork and the South Fork of the Snake meet up and form the Snake River. Even though the Henry's Fork of the Snake gets the lion's share of the press, the South Fork of the Snake River and its fertile waters produce trout every bit the equal of the sister river.

South Fork cutthroat grow fat and deep-bodied and the brown trout grow just plain big. The state record was caught in these turbulent freestone waters, a huge brown that weighed over 26 pounds. The area below the Palisades Reservoir begins the quality water of this fishery. Over its course, the big water of the South Fork of the Snake River runs fast and wide, acting nothing

like a tailwater and while most parts can be waded, the only way to do the South Fork correctly is by boat. Most anglers float the river (and you should too) and since it is a popular river, be prepared to share the water, especially when the salmonfly hatch is on in mid-July.

I am one of the few who hasn't fallen in love with Jackson Hole. I can see the beauty of the western town in the big valley (the hole). I can also see the chain stores. I don't like boutiques. I always feel like an outsider. This despite my recognition that Jackson is one of the ideal home bases anywhere from which to fish Western rivers and lakes. Props. Maybe I'm just being a hater because I don't have millions of dollars.

That said, my biases aside, Jackson Hole *is* the perfect Western fishing home base. From the diversity of fishing choices to the overwhelming number of choices—from the hip coolness and western chic of the town of Jackson Hole to its array of lodging options to the succulent gourmet food or earthy grains or meaty buffalo burgers of the local restaurants—this is a great place to call temporary home. There is enough of the Old West left to feel like you're in the Old West. Jackson Hole is the crown jewel of the West, the mountain village to which you'd bring a foreigner to get a better feel of what America is all about. (Yeah, yeah, hard-core mountaineers are sneering now but isn't America all about that weird dichotomy of commerce and nostalgia?)

Millions of visitors come to this area every year, romping in the great outdoors of some of the most picturesque countryside

in the world. The Jackson Hole and Yellowstone areas are trout-rich, and when one includes the quality streams and lakes of eastern Idaho and southern Montana into the mix, this region is probably the best trout-fishing locale anywhere on earth. Quite simply, there is water, water, everywhere. The vistas anglers will see while fishing the coldwater fisheries are so awesome the distraction will often cause them to miss strikes.

The Teton Range towers over the huge, enclosed basin called Jackson Hole, its snow-capped craggy peaks magnificently rising over the green, rushing waters of the Snake River and its many tributaries. This is truly postcard scenery. You've seen this pose by Nature on any number of postcards, greeting cards, and calendars.

Northwest Wyoming has an amazing diversity of world-class trout streams, but even more amazing are their topographical settings. Anglers will fish rivers running through wide, open valleys, near bubbling hot fountains and spewing geysers, coursing through dense forests, cascading over fifty-foot falls, meandering lazily across thermal basin meadows, and tumbling through deep chasms and canyons. The kicker is that the fish are mostly wild, typically larger than average, and prolific in numbers. The chances of catching heavy-bodied trout are great, and to catch wild trout in wild surroundings is a thrill every fisherman should experience.

The Bridger-Teton and Shoshone National Forests (a combined 4 million acres) and parts of the Targhee National Forest and the Grand Teton National Park (1.7 million acres) surround Yellowstone National Park. They provide superb fishing opportunities.

Float fishing the Snake River is one of the great rides in the world—bobbing in a raft in the wide, swift, green waters past breathtaking canyon walls, through inaccessible rugged terrain, tossing heavy nymphs and streamers in its deep runs and deeper pools.

The South Fork Snake River Yellowstone cutthroat. A large one, say 18 inches, will have teeth you can see. This trout will be fat, its bronze sides making fat-rolls over your hand as you gently hold it, two or three hundred tiny black spots all over its sides. Its gills will be yellow and pink with a hint of red in one spot. The trademark jaw will have a fluorescent red-orange slash. The fins are translucent tissue-paper orange. This might be the prettiest fish in the world.

Did you happen to notice the state record for Idaho brown trout? Caught right in the South Fork's rich waters, a monster weighing 26 pounds and 6 ounces. For the most part, the browns and cutts (and sadly, now rainbows) average about 14 to 18 inches. This isn't hyperbole when I say that if you drift fish a solid day in the summer or fall, you have an excellent chance at catching fifteen to thirty fish (more if you're a good flyfisher) and a handful or more will be between 16 and 24 inches. When you go back to the office, you won't have to lie about catching 100 trout over a three-day trip.

The cutthroat trout are not all that finicky. Yeah, they have their moments of selectivity but they tend to be opportunistic feeders, relying on their beauty to get by in life more than their brains.

South Fork Snake River is a big river with all the requisite perfect-mountain-river trout lies. Wide dancing riffles where you can see rainbow trout noses poking out taking caddis. Deep green runs where you can spot the shadow of a huge brown. In the tails of pools, in water too shallow to hold trout stick the dorsals of ten, twelve cutthroat. The South Fork is sometimes angler sensory overload, so much so, you don't even look up from casting to the banks to notice the canyon walls or the trees or that deer drinking. And you are catching fish (because you can't not catch trout on the South Fork) and you are catching fish typically with large splashy dry flies like Madame's X or Turck's Tarantula or a big Stimulator. Dry flies all day long.

Beginning anglers, line up now. I know of several veteran fishermen who don't find the South Fork challenging enough for them. The fish are too easy. They're missing the point. I wondered if some of them were a little threatened by the river because when you're on it, you realize that this is big water, a tad intimidating at first. And South Fork is so clear, that you can't drift two feet without seeing trout—like a glassbottom boat ride.

Make sure to fish the twenty-plus miles of the Canyon including the twelve-mile roadless area. There are few stretches in America as wild and scenic and perfect as this. I suggest a camping trip there. Make it the full Western experience.

The South Fork has ample access, crystalline water, native cutthroat, hatches of

Fishing Flat Creek, Hoback, and Gros Ventre Rivers, three tributaries to the Snake, give the angler a chance to try some different approaches to some characteristically different streams. Flat Creek (and one can take this name literally) is a strange creature, a small, flat, meandering stream with little cover for the cutthroats it holds and even less riparian habitat along its undercut banks. This means that the fisherman is exposed, so stalking feeding trout is the best method to fish this interesting creek. The starkness of the land also means that the wind has no obstructions and can and will whip furiously across the meadows. The fun of Flat Creek is that its trout are a wary bunch, ready to light for cover if bumbling anglers stumble along the cushiony banks, and just as ready to feed on the steady diet of insect hatches on the river.

Hoback River is a swift feeder stream, underfished due to its tendency to grow muddy after rains. It runs through canyon and meadows and holds a decent population of cutthroats. Gros Ventre River receives less fishing pressure than the Snake River, and is too narrow to float, so anglers can find some isolated stretches. Like the Snake and Hoback, the Gros Ventre has a fine salmonfly hatch in the middle of July. Also, like the other two, attractor patterns entice strikes in the absence of hatches. Near Lower Slide Lake, a good trout fishing lake in its own right, the Gros Ventre has productive pocket water.

caddis, mayfly, and especially stonefly, and is but an hour's drive from Jackson (half-hour from Idaho Falls). South Fork Snake River is a classic fishing hole, one of the best of its kind in the world.

There are numerous private sections, lodges, ranches on and just off the Snake you might consider. Lodge at Palisades Creek, Crescent H Ranch, Spotted Horse Ranch, Snake River Sporting Club (the model for private luxury high-toned riverside home-ownership in Paradise, er, Jackson), Flat Creek Guest Ranch, and the list goes on. This area has whatever level of luxury or budget you desire.

I don't mean to downplay the Snake River in Idaho at all. In this book, I cover Henry's Fork, the South Fork, and several tributaries. The Lower Snake River runs fast and deep in Hell's Canyon, North America's deepest and most dramatic gorge. Most anglers rarely consider fishing the Snake in the Canyon for anything but sturgeon and steelhead (e.g., at the confluence of Grande Ronde for steelies). A mix of huge numbers of wild and hatchery steelhead make their way to Clearwater, Salmon, and other feeder streams. Because of the attention on other fish, rainbows can be taken with little angler competition.

The best way to reach it is by boat in this big, running water. The Snake in the canyon is one hecukva fine smallmouth fishery, too, 1- to 4-pounders living right amongst the steelhead and 5- to 10-foot long sturgeon (sure there's bigger, but these are the average size). Don't overlook fishing the many tributaries of the Snake where the rainbows and steelhead run upstream.

CONTACTS
Snake River Angler, Moose, www
    .snakeriverangler.com

High Country Flies, www.highcountryflies
    .com
Jack Dennis Sports, www.jackdennis.com
Three Rivers Ranch, 208-652-3750
Drifters, Inc., 208-483-2722
Lodge at Palisades, 208-483-2222
Heise Expeditions, 208-538-7312
South Fork Outfitters, 877-347-4735
Teton Valley Lodge, 800-455-1182
Hyde Outfitters, 800-444-4933
Snake River Sporting Club, Jackson, www
    .snrsc.com

ALASKA

It's not as though I (or any other writer) can tell you much new about Alaskan waters. You know there are huge fish "up there." You know fishing Alaska has been on your dream list for some time now. You know that this is the world's last great wilderness, that every stream and lake and bay are thick with sporting fish. You see a monthly article in every outdoors and fishing magazine on the rack and on Sundays in the newspaper. Alaska has that much to offer.

If you fished every summer day and every fall day for the rest of your life, you'd still never come close to covering all the water in this big state.

Next summer, I am visiting my friend Lee Leschper, fellow Aggie and outdoor writer who lives just outside of Anchorage and taunts me constantly, incessantly by sending me e-mails describing the photos he attaches which inevitably show him and his big moustache holding yet another salmon or trout as big as my nephew Bill. I'm going to visit him in his home in Anchorage and he's going to show me his home waters. No lodge, no real guide, just two guys out in the bush hoping to catch big fish and not get eaten by bears.

Alaska has been the trout fisherman's dreamscape for decades. Because there is so much wilderness, so many rivers and lakes (3,000 rivers and 3 million lakes), man's gluttony has not yet been able to spoil the tens of thousands of miles of pristine trout and salmon streams, places where anglers can fish for twenty-four hours a day during the summer, if they desire. Much of Alaska is still uncharted, many of the streams and lakes accessible only by boat or plane or horseback. The waters of the

ALASKA

BERING SEA

NORTON SOUND

Fairbanks
•Mt. McKinley

YUKON TERRITORY

Anchorage

BRISTOL BAY

Iliamna L.

Alagnak R.

ALASKA PENINSULA

KODIAK ISLAND

KENAI PENINSULA

Sitka

Ketchikan

BRITISH COLUMBIA

GULF OF ALASKA

Aleutian Islands

Hard to draw islands

last great wilderness (okay, Russia, too) are home to the largest bear population in the world, and as such, great caution is needed when fishing for the lunker rainbow and cutthroat trout, some lake and brook trout, Dolly Varden, grayling, char, and five species of Pacific salmon (silver, king, red, chum, and pink).

This is a land with no forgiveness, and the waters are best fished with the services and wisdom of a guide. Learning the seasons of the spawning runs, the techniques needed to land the different kinds of fish, how to reach these great untamed rivers is all too much for the beginning Alaskan angler. In recent years, lodges and guides have realized the need to protect rainbow

trout, and more and more they are encouraging catch-and-release fishing, or at the least, respecting the fish enough by keeping only what the angler can eat.

To the first-time visitor, choosing how and where and when to fish the Land of the Midnight Sun is a daunting task. The potential angler must select which month to fish from the many productive ones available. Do I fish for the silver salmon (coho) migrating in the fall, or the steelhead run in October, or try for trophy grayling in May? It's like being the proverbial kid in a candy store figuring out which month to visit Alaska, but once that chore is done, the fisherman must then pick from exquisite, first-class lodges, fixed camps, tent

set-ups, guided boat services, fly-in planes and helicopters, and wilderness resorts. Seven-day stays are customary, but more and more lodges and guides are offering shorter day packages, 3- and 4-day stays. Lodges are available with limited services so as to keep the prices down, as well. And if that's not enough choices, you might be one of those do-it-yourselfers looking to hire a bush plane for day trips or for good angling near Anchorage.

The weather can be (will be) ornery, so paying upwards of $5,000 for a one-week package can cause headaches if the fly-out plane is grounded. July and August are the most reliable weather months. Typical costs for a one-week stay run from $1,500 to $5,000 (and even more, depending) and these lodgings and airfare don't go down in price, only up.

Most of the lodges and guides are respectable, even outstanding, overwhelmingly so, 98 percent or so but the sheer numbers of these available in Alaska mean that a few bad apples are inevitable. Be sure when perusing the avalanche of brochures and catalogs and online touts likely to come your way once you've requested just one, that the lodges and guides provide referrals. Make a list of your interests, set your budget limitations, then call and talk to the owners. If you don't call and you end up with a lemon of a trip, you have only yourself to blame.

- Do they have local fishing if the weather grounds the plane?
- How many daily hours will guides be available?
- What's a typical day like at your resort/lodge/camp?

▪ What is the ratio of guides and staff to guests? How many other guests might I be sharing the lodge or camp or boat with? What kind of boats are these? How much running time each day?

▪ What kind of equipment do I need? What if mine breaks? Do you have repairs or extra gear? What brand of equipment do you use? Do you charge for flies and do I need to bring my own?

▪ Are meals included? (You might be surprised but go ahead and doublecheck.) You say all-inclusive? What all does this include? Does it include licenses, tag fees, and other services?

▪ What types and how many of each can I reasonably expect to catch? Don't give me the numbers for the best day ever. What's realistic? (Let them know that you are a realist and you don't mind paying for the chance to catch fish but that you want to have some lowdown before plunking down big bucks.)

▪ What if I want to ship some of my fish (salmon) home? How much does it cost?

In some of the more remote camps, it might behoove the inquisitive angler to ask if there are running water, toilets, and hot showers.

There are a number of books, articles, brochures, and services, as well as travel agencies, that can supplement your investigation. Just chatting with the guides, pilots, and lodge owners can tell you if their personality meshes with yours, so take the time to check it all out before spending a king's ransom.

Alaska does have a great many rivers and lakes that can be approached by the casual and car-bound fisherman, but the truly great fishing experience is in the backcountry, by way of bush plane, helicopter, horse, or boat. Alaska's highway fisheries receive a lot of angling pressure, but the willingness to hike a few miles can steer you away from the crowds.

Consider fishing from sunset until sunrise (even though the sun never sets in the long days of summer). The roads are nothing to brag about, but they are not the gravel pits some make them out to be. Still, many of the areas are not connected by roads, like the Far North, the southeast, and southwest regions of the state.

Fishing Alaska on a budget is becoming more and more popular, but somewhat limiting. A number of excellent fisheries exist within easy driving distance of Anchorage. If you do decide to fish on your own, consider driving along the Alaska Highway where you can pick and choose your spots

to fish, to catch a bush plane, to spend the night.

The northern fishing areas are unreachable except by bush pilots but in the southern region of the Great Land, finding quality fishing for trout and salmon requires a little bit of research, and some gumption to get there. A number of reference guides are in print and are tailored to the fishing-on-a-dime crowd. Fishing along the highway might not provide the same quality of fishing or wilderness experience as getting away to the more remote sections of Alaska, but great angling is all a matter of relativity. Average fishing in the Last Frontier beats most anything else in the continental United States.

The kind of sportfish you chase will determine the kind of tackle you'll need. The typical fly fishing setup effective for the mainland, for instance an 8½-foot, 4- or 5-weight, will suffice when fishing the backcountry, and the smaller rivers and lakes, but a 9-foot, 7- or 8-weight will be

necessary to land trophy trout, and many of the salmon species. The 9-foot, 7-weight is a good all-around outfit, but many anglers prefer a longer rod, or a heavier line.

Larger salmon like the king, require a 9- or 10-weight line since the fish grow big and they are often caught in swift currents. If you've got room in your bags, and you probably won't, slip in a lightweight pack rod to take advantage of some backcountry fishing or angling for grayling. Make sure your reel is able to hold a lot of line, up to 225 feet, as well as a fair amount of backing. Leaders should be kept strong, no less than 4-pound for the smaller streams, as much as 12 pounds (or more) when fishing the larger fisheries.

The Alaskan fisherman, to be properly prepared, should not only bring fly rods peculiar to certain fishing conditions, but also various fly lines. A basic floating line is essential, and either a sinktip line or a sinking line you can turn to on a separate reel can mean the difference between getting deep enough to land twenty fish, or going over their head and being fishless. Many anglers prefer two or more weights of sinking lines, as well as floating lines with sinktips.

To catch many of the coldwater species in Alaska, you have got to go underwater with your offerings, and at different depths. Alaska is not dry fly heaven. This is why many of the more successful fishermen are the ones who cast salmon eggs or colorful lures with spinning gear into fast runs. Except when fishing for king salmon, the best all-around spinning rod is a medium action rod loaded with 12- to 15-pound test. Some of the best lures for Alaska are effective for more than one species of fish, and they come in the usual assorted colors and sizes; many of the most popular lures are local ones.

The best advice is to check with your guide, lodge owner, fly shop, and the guy you know who went to Alaska last year and found a can't-miss lure. Some of the more popular lures include: daredevil, glo-bugs or salmon eggs (spin-n-glo), pixie, tee spoon, mepps spinners, rooster tail, spoons, spinners. Bright colors seem to work well in low-light conditions.

Fly patterns for Alaska can be a tricky subject. Some anglers prefer to be prepared for any aquatic feeding habit of their prey and load up their vests with every color and pattern stuffed in fly boxes until the bulging pockets on their vest threaten to tear open. Others select a few basic patterns and learn

to work these well. Dry flies will not be as important in fly boxes as in other states.

The insect hatches are not often prolific on the state's cold, pure waters, meaning that dry fly fishing can be spotty. Attractor dry fly patterns are regular producers for trout and grayling, classics like the Royal Wulff, Elk Hair Caddis, Griffith's Gnat, Humpy, Adams, Irresistible. Matching the hatch can sometimes occur but not often so just bring some basic dun and caddis patterns for topwater action. In late summer in certain areas, beetle, grasshopper, and black ant patterns draw trout to the surface. Black gnat and mosquito dressings also work well at times.

The fun fly—the mouse. A large mouse pattern cast along the banks can result in splashy takes from lurking rainbows. There is nothing like tying on a fly that has heft,

Alaska

one that feels like you're tying on a chocolate chip cookie or a furry key chain. So heavy, you'll not adjust for it with your first cast and you'll nearly hook your ear, or your guide's ear. When it lands on the water, the mouse pattern makes a watery thud, and when you start stripping in, your heart races. Two casts, five, ten and then you see the dorsal fin and hear the *Jaws* music as the rainbow trout that must go 32 inches long is chasing that big deerhair mouse pattern. Fish on.

Wet flies like streamers can be come-to-the-rescue flies when all else fails. For salmon, large streamers are a given, but they also work on big rainbow trout. Zonkers, Muddler Minnows, sculpins, leeches, and Woolly Buggers are the best of the lot. Nymphs work in more rivers in more conditions than any other fly offering,

the best being Bitch Creek, Hare's ear, Zug bug, glo-bug, Prince nymph, and Woolly Worms. Walk into a fly shop and you'll find the usual smorgasbord of brightly-colored, innovative flies, all purported to be great fish catchers, so this list can certainly be supplemented. Salmon flies have the same kind of variety, but the basics that work over and over across the state include flash flies, smolt, and fry dressings, Everglows, Krystal bullets, polar shrimp, Babine special, Iliamna Pinkies.

The weather is fickle in Alaska, and even though the snowy temperament of the great state is exaggerated, with daily temperatures in the summers generally mild and in the high 60s, extreme weather can strike immediately, and anglers need to be prepared. Dressing in layers of warm clothing is the only way to protect from overheating on those rare 80-degree days, and to be able to shed clothing as the weather warms. Layering also allows the recreationalist to add layers of clothing and warmth when (and I mean when) the day turns cold and rainy. And windy. I mean windy, too, because the winds kick up often during the summer. And wet. Rain is a commonplace occurrence, heck, an every-day occurrence in many parts of the state.

There are high quality technologically-advanced clothes available from all the fly shops and outfitter shops, useful but expensive items like Polarfleece pullovers and pants. Wool shirts and pants will also suffice to keep out the cold. Rain gear is a must, because parts of Alaska receive heavy rain during the year.

Other distractions in this vast frontier include: The largest and fiercest mosquitos anywhere in the world, so bring industrial-strength insect repellant. Devil's club, a tall, wicked thorny plant which when brushed up against, will cause welts, so wear long sleeves when walking through the countryside. Glacial silt that muddies up perfectly clear water. Alaska Time Zone, one hour later than Pacific Standard Time. And lastly, bears, bears, bears. Alaska has lots of 'em, and if you fish enough of the right waters, you are bound to cross their path. This is their land, so respect them and their terrain. Attacks on people are rare, happening usually when humans are doing things they shouldn't be doing, like walking along streamsides in thick brush, coming too close to a sow and her cubs, having food near camp, and straying too close to a carcass. There are some excellent publications

put out by the state and federal governments instructing outdoor enthusiasts how to behave to avoid contact with bears.

Alaska has two national forests, the two largest in the United States, the 17 million acres of the Tongass National Forest, and the 6 million acres of the Chugach National Forest. For the most part, fishing on national lands in Alaska is not as productive as elsewhere in the state. This is one huge state, nearly 600,000 square miles big, roughly one-fifth the size of the lower forty-eight states.

Alaska is like a land before time, almost prehistoric in its wildness and unspoiled lands. The topographical diversity is amazing, ranging from coastal rainforests, volcanic uplands, glacial fjords, tundra meadows, wide stream valleys carved by glaciers, dense forests and tall snow-capped mountain ranges, some of the highest in the world. Seventeen of the twenty highest peaks in the United States are in Alaska. Wildlife watching will subtract from fishing time as

anglers encounter moose, bear, caribou, and bald eagles, to name only a few. To cover all of this and the thousands of miles of fishable streams, and millions of lakes in one chapter is impossible. There are scads of books on Alaska fishing which willingly suggest that the only way to properly research Alaska is by fishing it. Trying to fish any one region fully would take a lifetime, this land is so vast.

There are some well known trout rivers like the Situk, Copper, and Tikchik Rivers, but these celebrated waters are three of several thousand. The Ilimniak Lake is famous, but celebrity doesn't always guarantee good fishing. Salmon runs are better in some years than others, better in some rivers than others. Alaska is a land of change, and the most effective way to catch your

share of fish is by combining timing, luck, and skill.

To wet your whistle, here are some highlights.

Bristol Bay Area

Possibly the most popular angling destination, Bristol Bay has it all, the salmon smorgasbord. All five species. And grayling. And rainbow trout. And pike. And Arctic char. One of the reasons to book your trip at a Bristol Bay area lodge or camp is that you have so many choices each day of type of fishing, species to fish for—you can make a seven-day stay seem like seven different trips.

So many of the best Alaskan rivers run through the Bristol Bay area, the Copper, Talarik, Nushagak, Agulawok, American, and Brooks, and they hold the quintessential, poster-child of Alaska, those big thousand-spotted colorful leopard rainbows you see on fishing calendars. You've no doubt, if you've ever read an outdoors mag, seen a review or an article or an ad for Bristol Bay Lodge. You've no doubt seen photos of bears crossing the river in the background with an angler hooked up with a typical aggressive Bristol Bay area rainbow trout. Bears bears bears.

Alagnak River

This southwestern Alaska river that dumps into Bristol Bay is best known for its coho salmon but it's just about as good producing large rainbow trout. But if you like silvers, this might be the best river to go about finding them—and with all the lodges, camps, and outfitters on the river, you won't have any problem finding a place to hang your hat. Note: Coho are underrated and provide feistiness and will match your willpower.

Don't underestimate them just because they don't reach king salmon sizes.

Nushagak River is another Bristol Bay relation and this brawling river is famous for having the largest king salmon run in all of Alaska, plenty of 20-pounders. If you desire great numbers of hookups with kings, this is your river. You have many choices of lodges and camps on the river.

Sitka

Located in the southeastern part of the state, on Baranof Island, one of the numerous islands of this part of the state, this port town has awesome overall angling (king, coho, halibut, lingcod) with a healthy selection of lodges and charters to choose from including Talon Lodge, Dove Island Lodge, and Kain's Fishing Adventures. What's great about Sitka is that it's big enough that real live commercial airlines fly into it (from Seattle, for

instance). Fish for halibut and salmon in the same day. By the way, lingcod are one of the ugliest fish anywhere. They hit hard and pull like a diesel truck, a fight sort of like a huge redfish (but uglier).

Kenai River/Kenai Peninsula

The Kenai River has seen its share of anglers over the years, and like the old gray mare, just ain't what she used to be, but this beefy river can still hold its own with most any rivers in the world you can name especially if you're naming king salmon rivers. Because the Kenai is just a short drive from Anchorage (three hours if you're not in bad weather), the bait fishermen come out in droves, boats like fleets, and they drop hooks for the 50-pound kings that still run the river. This is one popular, productive river.

Ketchikan

This southeastern Alaska town is a great home base to fish for Chinook and sockeye salmon, halibut, lingcod, rockfish, and steelhead, but the king is the king salmon. You fish in big open water for big broad-shouldered salmon. From Ketchikan, you can also find numerous quality lodges, and Prince of Wales Island is within striking distance. Prince of Wales has plenty of rivers to choose from and they hold steelhead, sea-run cutts, salmon, and Dolly Varden.

CONTACTS
FishQuest, www.fishquest.com

HAWAII

Uncle Stan and Aunt Di have had a second home (or maybe it's a third home) in Hawaii for about twenty-five years. I never knew what a lanai was until I went out on their balcony in Honolulu. They have had several places there over the years, condos and homes, one of which was right next to Jim Nabors. Gollleee.

I have a confession. I have been to Hawaii on more than one occasion and I have never been to Pearl Harbor. Terrible, I know, but the most opportune time, my first time, I was eighteen and my Dallas Cowboys were playing the Los Angeles Rams in the NFC Championship game and it was being televised at nine in the morning and Mom threw a fit because I simply refused to go with the family to Pearl Harbor but my staying there helped bring them enough mojo that they beat the Rams 28-0 and went to the Super Bowl. One day, I will go to Pearl Harbor.

Dad wasn't happy with me that day or the next night at a fancy restaurant in Honolulu when I ordered steak and lobster. I had never eaten lobster and I had always seen guys in movies ordering steak and lobster but little did I know that it was the most expensive thing on the menu and it was Dad's night to buy dinner for our family and the other two families with us. I've seen deposed third world dictators who were in better moods than Dad was the next few days. He said nothing when I ordered my first six-dollar hamburger (six bucks for a burger?!) but since it was only one-tenth the price of the steak and lobster, I guess I did okay.

- **Location:** Central Pacific Ocean
- **What You Fish For:** Billfish, giant trevally, tuna, snapper, wahoo, and mahi-mahi
- **Highlights and Notables:** The waters off Kona provide anglers with some of the finest marlin waters in the world, especially for big blue marlin of trophy size.

The fishing in Hawaii is awesome and so is the scenery and before we ever get to the smallmouth bass, largemouth bass, peacock bass, trout fishing, or the inshore fishing of Hawaii, we have to talk about how Hawaii is the greatest giant blue marlin fishery in the entire world. In a word: Kona.

The perfect marlin waters off Kona Coast of the big island of Hawaii are leeward, calm; the steep dropoff zone for the marlin's magical cruising zone is a seashell's throw from shore; the food sources plentiful, everything has come together to make this the fertile stomping grounds for blue marlin. These are giant Giant Blue Marlin, THE place to try for a grander.

Granders are caught in all seasons but the best time to be on a boat luring a 400- to 1,000-pound Giant Blue to your lure or fly or bait is in July and August (May through October is great, July and August superlative). Check this out: In these very waters, several marlin up to and exceeding 1,600 to 1,800 pounds have been caught and landed. Hawaii (more typically Kona) has dominated the line-class records for blue marlin the last thirty years.

Anglers in the know think that if there is a one-ton blue marlin to be caught in the world, it will happen here in Hawaiian waters. Outfitters from Hawaii, especially Kona, are innovators for many of today's techniques and lures and tricks to catch marlin. Moving from a kill fishery to a tag fishery bodes well for the future.

Black and striped marlin are not quite an afterthought, but with all the eyes on the prize that is the Giant Blue Marlin, you can fish for these and many other offshore species (bigeye tuna, yellowfin tuna of size, albacore, shortbill spearfish, skipjack, wahoo, and the ever-present, always-fun, delectable mahi-mahi) and have the time of your life.

With their volcanic construction and steep dropoffs, all the Hawaiian Islands have excellent angling for billfish but it's like comparing a good Dominican maduro to a true Havana cigar. If you want the best, fish Kona. Otherwise, you can still catch 500- to 600-pound blue marlin and all the other assorted offshore quarry (all year long), then go back to the mainland of your island and do the Hawaiian tourist thing. Don't discount bottom or inshore

Captured and released

fishing, either. Maui and Kauai hold giant trevally, tuna, snapper, wahoo, and mahi-mahi in their waters.

Trout in Hawaii? Peacock bass, too?

- **Location:** Kokee State Park, Waimea Canyon, west side of the island of Kauai for trout; all over the islands for bass
- **What You Fish For:** Rainbow trout, peacock bass
- **Highlights and Notables:** The scenery supercedes the fishing to be sure, but the scenery of Hawaii beats the heck out of most any fishing.

I am totally serious when I commit the Hawaiian Islands to the global spectrum of interesting freshwater fishing locales.

Interesting, not always great, just so I'm clear. Fishing in freshwater in Hawaii is a neat thing to do.

So let's start with the Kokee Public Fishing Area. For two months each year, in August and September, rainbow trout are traditionally stocked in the Kokee Public Fishing Area on the island of Kauai, the state's northernmost island, ten miles north of the town of Kekaha.

The scenery is unlike any other trout fishing locale in the world, set in the mountains amidst lush tropical rain forests. The Waimea Canyon is sometimes referred to as the "Grand Canyon of the Pacific." There are thirteen miles of fishable streams, a fifteen-acre pond, and two stocked ditches. Some of the streams include the Kauaikinana, Mohihi, and Koaie Rivers. These small streams are tributaries to the Waimea River. The interesting thing is that these rainbows are naturally-reproducing. In Kokee's fifteen-acre pond, called Lake Puulua, and in two miles of man-made canals, the trout are planted year round.

In the Wamiea Canyon, you have such a limited time to angle for these stream-bred rainbow trout that you have to time it just right. It rains everyday in what some say is the wettest place on earth. My favorite is the Koaie River where you have to traverse one tough-as-nails five-hour hike on a narrow brambly trail that's barely even there, rats, pigs, slippery slopes and the desire to stay in this lovely mountain setting (complete with waterfalls) for another week or three. Why?

Nobody else fishes in these big long root beer–colored pools where the resident rainbows live, 'bows from 13 to 18 inches, two or three per pool. They get fat on Hawaiian insects and other aquatic what-nots but if you are stealthy, they sure will eat dry flies of a western nature and beadheads of a generic nature. The rain is so frequent and the forest so green and jungley and you so out there in the heart of darkness that with me wearing my camera around my neck, I almost had a Dennis Hopper moment. I also caught a trout that was the size of a baked ham and was easily 20 inches long, not that that matters. (On the private side of trout, on the big island at Kuhua Ranch, the Flyfishing Hawaii club stocks Kamloops rainbow trout in a small lake.)

There are numerous other public fresh-water fishing opportunities in Hawaii. Wahiawa Public Fishing Area on Oahu has Lake Wilson, a 300-acre reservoir that holds bass, bluegill, channel catfish, tilapia. The Nuuanu Freshwater Fish Refuge has a lake stocked with catfish and tilapia. Both are open year round. The Waiakea Public Fishing Area on Hawaii Island has a twenty-five-acre spring-fed pool that holds mullet, trevally, and threadfin. On Kauai alone there are over 150 reservoirs (ponds and lakes) and nine rivers that have been stocked with largemouth and/or peacock bass including Waita Lake (400 acres). Most all are private so you'll have to go through a club or a guide.

You might think the largemouth bass would grow big in this year-round environment but they top out at a couple of pounds (some up to 7, 8, even 9 pounds but those are rare). The peacock in Hawaii can get as big as 6 to 8 pounds but more normally weigh 2 to 4 pounds.

If you decide to fish for trout or bass in Hawaiian waters, you shouldn't go in

with lofty expectations. Think instead of enjoying the beauty of the mountains and canyons, the jungle atmosphere and the puzzled looks on the faces of those you tell stateside that you just returned from freshwater fishing in Hawaii.

CONTACTS

Kauai Freshwater Aquatics, 808-245-7358

Hawaii Division of Aquatic Resources, 808-274-3344

Sportfish Hawaii, Kauai, www .sportfishhawaii.com

Kathy House, Sport Fish Hawaii/Hawaii Fishing Adventures and Charters, www .sportfishhawaii.com

Tom Christy, Cast and Catch Freshwater Bass Guides, Koloa, 808-332-9707

Charleys Fishing Supply, Honolulu, 808-528-7474

Kuhua Ranch Flyfishing Hawaii, Kamuela, 808-885-5941

Kokee State Park, Lihue, 808-274-3444

Bass On Kauai, Hanalei, Kauai, 808-826-2566

Lodge at Kokee, Waimea, 808-335-6061

Canada

CANADA

The Bow River. When I called the guide to set up the trip, I told him two things: 1) Dad's never fly fished before; and 2) Dad's a type-A personality so we needed to catch some fish. It was one of those things where neither of us, Dad or me, wanted for this to really come off; we enjoyed the game of me trying to get him to go and him saying "maybe one day." We weren't especially close and neither of us really wanted to spend twenty-four hours a day together for three or four days.

Mom made both of us say yes. It was Mom's idea. She came up with the idea for a family vacation up north, put together

the trip, and, most important, paid for the trip. Fishing, rafting, horseback riding. In the wilds of Canada. Not exactly Dad's cup of tea. Dad didn't care for fishing (he'd given it up years before), feared rafting, and detested riding horses. Sounds like a lot of fun.

Dad had every right to dislike Canada after the one and only trip he spent visiting our friendly neighbor to the north.

Our Bow River guide took fifteen minutes to instruct Dad on the finer points of fly casting before we slid the drift boat into the cold May waters of this famous trout river. I could see the question mark forming over Dad's gray pate but he played along, nodding as though he understood the difference between loading the rod and stripping line. Clueless but game-faced.

The Bow River is a slow-moving big western river that traverses some of the biggest, wildest countryside you'll ever see. The fish are big and plentiful and, when hooked, put up a fierce fight. Since the river was swollen with spring runoff, we fished with heavy nymphs cast to the rocks and cutbanks. It was hard work for an experienced longrodder like me but it was torture for a neophyte like my father. His ungainly attempts hooked the guide twice, me once, and with the heavy stonefly pattern, he also knocked off his own cap. He smiled and laughed through his own attacks upon us three anglers.

His shoulder and arm wore out after a couple of fishless hours. I caught quite a few and one nice one around 19 or 20 inches long, but then again, my casts were hitting where I aimed. His were shotgun-style and almost as dangerous.

Ten hours later, Dad was exhausted and without a single catch. He twice had fish on but the advice he had received hours earlier on the riverbanks was long forgotten. The guide and I did everything we could but we were fighting heavy brown runoff and a lousy caster.

Dad wasn't upset, had a good time, thanked me and the guide for a great day, but I never coaxed him out on the stream again, despite my repeated efforts. He'd been trout fishing, he'd caught nothing and there was no need to do it again, he had tried this sport of fly fishing for the last time.

Strike one.

Dad told Mom that under no circumstances would he be getting astride a horse this trip. He had had several bad run-ins with horses over the years and at his age, he had seen all the close equine encounters he needed.

Mom won, of course.

Dad rode in the middle on a horse the guide told him was the gentlest of the group. And he was, too. Problem was, my wife Amy's horse was ornery as a hermit and she followed behind my father as we slugged it out in the pouring cold spring rain on a trail that circled the turquoise-colored postcard of a lake, Lake Louise.

I first noticed Dad's horse galloping while we were clip-clopping when I heard his horse whinny. Amy's horse bit Dad's horse. Drew blood. And there Dad went on the narrow, steep trail, holding on for dear life, no doubt thinking about his proclamation he wouldn't mount one of these beasts and Mom's reassurances that this ride would be different.

Dad's horse beat us back to the stables by a good ten minutes.

Strike two.

The Kananaskis River is one of the roily whitecapped rivers you marvel at for its power and beauty but know in your heart you'd never want to raft down its rapids even though you might brag as such. The rapids and whirlpools are heart-stopping. Great thing is, right by the rafting put-in, it's a fairly tranquil-looking river so Dad gave in to Mom's request to spend a couple of hours slowly rafting down a lazy river. Mom is so fun sometimes.

The Kananaskis River is so cold, you must wear Neoprene body suits. And so dangerous, you must top your noggin with a safety helmet. These precautions should have been enough to scare Dad off but he was distracted by his recent equus event.

We hit the Class III rapids as we rounded the first bend. The guide was still lecturing us on how dangerous this river was and how we should not, under any circumstances, leave the boat or drop our oar. And don't fall in because you'll get hurt or die. Dad's eyes popped open at that point. And then we saw the maelstrom ahead.

Everyone in the boat begged the guide to turn back, let us out, stuff like that but before he could respond, we were upon the rocks and the heavy water. We dipped and we flew and we hit boulders the size of Donald Trump's ego. The cold water was shocking but not nearly so much as the fear we all felt inside.

The eddy-slash-whirlpool caught us and wouldn't let go. Dad's end of the boat went under and so did Dad and we swirled around in this death trap while the guide barked instructions nervously and warned us that if we didn't keep paddling, we were doomed.

Dad was under the water all the way and the raft was tilted on its side so that my wife Amy's paddle was out of the water and available for any submerged rafter to grab hold of—so Dad did.

My daughter Sarah, then twelve, fell out of the raft but Dad grabbed her with his free hand. Family in one paw, Amy's paddle in the other. Submerged in cold swirling water, death's door at the bottom of this icy river. Not happy with Canada at all.

Strike three.

The sucking whirlpool relinquished its hold on our watercraft and we bounced and thrashed down the wicked river until we were exhausted from the nervous energy—some call it fear. We made it to safety and Dad informed the family not to ask him to encounter any other fears. Years later, he fondly recounted his day fly fishing the Bow, his mad ride along Lake Louise, and his dunking on the Kananaskis. Funny how time heals all wounds.

I asked Dad to go fly fishing with me umpteen times over the last decade of his life and he always declined. I wanted to show him how much fun fly fishing can be, how beautiful brook trout are, how good I am with a fly rod and at reading water and spotting trout and all those sorts of counterpart elements he wanted to show me when he built birdcages or sheds or apartment buildings or shopping malls. He owned a construction company for twenty years.

I don't cry easily but I had to look away one afternoon when Dad was down in bed with his terminal lung and brain cancer (where he lasted two years longer than they gave him, the strong old fart) and he had been telling me how he wished he had been a better father (he was a great father) and how he wished he'd have done this for me and that with me and he said "I wish I'd have let you take me fly fishing one more time and I could have caught something." I told him he was a great father (and he was) and that he did more for me and with me than any son had a right to expect and then I kissed him on the cheek and went to the bathroom and cried like a baby.

I cast a stimulator behind the big rock on the far side. It was one of those tricky casts across a river, across multiple currents into a swirling backeddy that if I had analyzed before I cast, I would have messed up completely. The wind was up and there was no way in Alberta I had a chance to reach that rising fish on the other side of the river by the big rock and I knew it and the one angler I saw on the entire river, the fifty-year-old gentleman who seemed to be following me upriver, on the other side, the one who had come to an impasse and wouldn't be able to scramble over *these* rocks, well, he knew it, too. I saw it in his eyes. Nobody in their right mind would even try a stupid cast like that. But instinctively, and that's not always a good thing with me, I saw a fish rise, I lifted and cast to it and I caught the damn thing. Seventeen inches of ruby red rainbow.

I am not a great caster. I'd say a 6 or 7 on a scale of 10 with a 6-weight or less. But on that windy day for thirty feet, for one cast, I was one bad dude.

ALBERTA

Bow River Drainage

- **Location:** Western Canada, southern Alberta Province
- **What You Fish For:** Rainbow, cutthroat, brown trout, grayling
- **Highlights and Notables:** A classic western-style river, big, floatable jaw-dropping scenery, and huge trout

You'll feel like you've gone back in time if you trek to the Bow River, one of the legendary rivers of North America. This is big, dramatic ancient country. A land etched by time, mountains shorn by glaciers.

Alberta where the Bow River runs is a land of retreating glaciers, icefields as big as some states, hoodoos carved by erosion, jagged sharp mountains whose summits look like knives carved from flint, canyons with so many colorful wildflowers like nature's spilled paintbucket, waterfalls and rivers, alpine lakes and ridges of rock debris, marshy floodplains and open prairie, heavy forests of pine and fir and spruce.

Don't go just to fish the Bow and Crowsnest. This is a two-week tour.

Alberta is loaded with memorable images, a notable geographical and cultural mix. Cowboys, sunny weather, oil and gas, cattle, railroads, wheat farms, home to Winter Olympics—Calgary is a modern town like Fort Worth, maybe even Dallas. Alberta is a mix of European and Indian cultures. So naturally, my family all thought it seemed a lot like Texas, especially West Texas, until we got further north into the mountains and then we thought it looked an awful lot like southwestern Colorado (which until then, we had collectively thought was the prettiest part of North America).

Banff is one of the ultimate mountain towns in the world. The Post Hotel in Banff National Park is a world-class hotel with its red tin roof, known for its European luxury in the midst of forested mountains on the Bow River. The Fairmount Banff Springs Hotel has few others in any mountain setting in the world to compare with this stately hotel.

Lake Louise and Lake Louise Village are breathtaking locations to visit. The Fairmount Chateau Lake Louise is that huge white castle-like hotel with the blue roof that favors a French noble's palace with its stunning location on the edge of the turquoise lake—the lake sits in a bowl with the mountains sloping steeply into the bowl of blue water. Jasper is north, wilder, more remote. Elk feed and walk around this ski resort town.

The Bow River courses through three geographic zones and runs past all of the above scenery. Big mountains, foothills, and prairie. The river is a weird blue, glacial silt, and fertile, and holds big rainbow and brown trout. The upper Bow River, the

For Dad, the best part of his Bow River float was lunch.

headwaters down to Calgary, is the most beautiful but least productive section of this fabled river. In its upper reaches, the water is fast and clean and nutrient-free and holds small trout. Below Banff, the browns grow big but they are not as bountiful as the stretch from Calgary downstream 100 miles. Still, if you enjoy the most scintillating scenery in the Western Hemisphere and don't mind working a little bit for lunker brown trout and small brook trout, the upper Bow might be for you. I like it a lot and have found the river to have good enough caddis and mayfly hatches that the fish love them but the hatches aren't so solid that the fish are picky. So when the hatches are on, dry fly fishing is excellent. And the sizes of these trout are a pleasant surprise.

If you fish in the park, you need a park fishing license. (I know, because I was taking pics of my mother fishing in the park or rather pretending to fish because up until

Post Hotel on the Bow River

2005 she'd never fly fished and the park rangers came down to see what was going on.) The Bow's feeder streams are not heavily fished but they are not blue-ribbon either. Ghost River and the Kananaskis look good but aren't and that's too bad because the Kananaskis is one of the most beautiful, inviting, trouty-looking streams you'll ever see. The Elbow River, Jumping Pound Creek, and Highwood River are worth fishing and are worth investigating. Maligne and Sparrow Lakes near Jasper have excellent and scenic fishing. Lake Minnewanka in Banff National Park offers fishing for large lake trout. There are various lakes in each park, both easy to reach and requiring a long hike, that hold trout, too.

The long stretch below Calgary, the trip I took Dad on for ten hours, is the famous Bow River, the slow winding prairie river known for trout you write home about. Postcard-sized trout. Consistently insanely big trout. Maybe not White River Arkansas size trout but persistently producing 18- and 20- and 22-inch trout. Browns and rainbow.

Now I say consistent and persistent only if you figure out how to fish the lower Bow River. You have to play by the rules. I recommend hiring a guide for a day or two to get to know the changing conditions. Get ready to nymph with beadheads and San Juan worms and mayfly nymphs. Be ready to employ streamers in high water, deep pools, cutbanks. Dry flies are not imitating large insects very often (the exception is the golden stonefly); instead you'll be sightcasting tiny Tricos and smaller mayflies to rising trout. I use my typical dry fly on top, nymph on the bottom dropper rig. You can wade or float the river but below Calgary, most only wade while on a float trip.

Throughout the course of the Bow, in Calgary, in Banff, in Lake Louise, in Jasper, you will see lots of tourists and buses and young hiker-bohemian types and mountain climbers and floaters and canoeists and kayakers, but this is such big country, you won't notice them for long. You will also see elk walk calmly through Banff; in the wild see grizzly, moose, bighorn sheep, deer, and antelope and if you're unlucky, rattlesnakes.

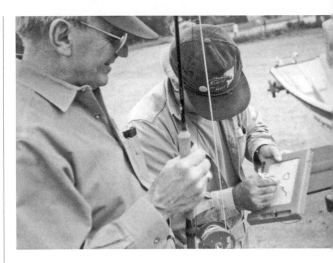

CONTACTS

Upper Bow Fly Fishing Company, www.upperbowflyfishing.com

The Crowsnest Angler Fly Shop & Guide Service, www.crowsnestangler.com

McLennan Flyfishing, www .mclennanflyfishing.com

Alpine Anglers, www.alpineanglers.com

Banff Fishing Unlimited, www .banff-fishing.com

Fish Tales Fly Shop, www.fishtales-flyshop .com

Green Drake Fly Shop and Mountain Fly Fishers, Canmore, 403-678-9522

Monod Sports Ltd, Banff, 403-762-4571

Roberts Fly Shop & Fishing Co., Cochrane, 403-932-5855

This site lists many of the guides and shops that service the Bow River: www.lfghp.com/alberta.html

Crowsnest River

- **Location:** Western Canada, southwestern Alberta province
- **What You Fish For:** Wild rainbow trout
- **Highlights and Notables:** Stunningly beautiful classic western trout river with excellent access

Sometimes, you feel like you know someone the minute you see them or meet them. You can't explain it, can't put your finger on it, it's on the tip of your tongue but unspeakable. You just know it.

The Crowsnest was my friend from the second I laid eyes on it. The river and its mountains and the long, wide runs that riffle on top looked like some place I had fished before or maybe some place I had always wanted to fish or maybe even some stretch of river in one of my dreams. Yeah, I dream about fishing.

The Crowsnest isn't famous worldwide

nor is it a complete secret. For its productivity, the Crowsnest is among the more underrated trout rivers in the world.

Consider this: dry fly fishing for wild rainbows 14 to 17 inches long in a Rocky Mountain–postcard environment with much less fishing pressure than similar quality trout streams. Located in southwest Alberta, a two-hour drive southwest from Calgary, the Crowsnest River just looks fishy. If you are a trout fisher, if you have been on a few rivers in your time, you'll get the Crowsnest right off the bat. There's nothing mysterious going on. The trout hide in the right places; the river has classic water, easy-to-read lies.

The Crowsnest does that character change thing so many of the western rivers do—the river begins at the headwaters with mountains close and wild moving downstream through a wide meandering valley where the mountains have retreated to mere spectators. Then the mountains slide forward close to the river making the river tighter, faster, through a narrow chute less than 100 yards wide at Turtle Mountain; then the river widens again to become lake-like (and this is where most anglers begin to take the river seriously probably because the trout get serious). Trout to 5, 6, 7 pounds but that's more the exception than the rule; still, the trout are bigger here than upstream. Then the river flows out of the mountains and the land is farming land, ranch land, rolling instead of steep, and there are falls and the trout are larger still and finally the river comes to rest in Oldman Reservoir. Whew.

Fat, muscled rockets, wild and colorful, these rainbow trout of the Crowsnest. The river is surprisingly fertile in its lower stretches where the growth rates are rapid. Outstanding insect hatches contribute to this growth, quality diverse hatches of mayfly, stonefly, caddis. The *Pteronarcys californica* and golden stones are two pulpy hatches to try to hit. The water flows are stable on this, one of the most beautiful trout rivers you'll ever see.

The upper Crowsnest is an average fishery compared to the lower but for my money, with its great scenery, solitude, and plentiful trout willing to smash dry flies, I'll always make sure I spend some time there. Sure, the trout are smaller but they're not minnows. Ten to 14 inches with the occasional 16-inch trout. That's still a lot of fun for a day's work in my book (and this is my book). In the upper, you catch cutthroat, brook, rainbow, and even lake trout that move up from Crowsnest Lake. The brook trout from time to time can get long and fat, more colorful than Dennis Rodman.

The lower Crowsnest, for quite a number of miles, is where you find the lunker action. Trout to 20 inches, and this isn't brochure fodder either. You won't hardly catch a rainbow under 14 inches long. This river isn't going to grow a 20-pounder, or should I say 20-pounders, but the average to above-average trout are solid, fat and healthy. Ideal wading water—fifty feet wide—but wear felt-soled waders because the rocks are slippery.

Accessibility is just one more additional positive factor for the river that is just over the Montana border. Anglers can access the river at more than a dozen bridges.

Royal Canadian Pacific Fishing Excursion

Here's a unique trip that combines train travel, the majestic scenery of the Canadian Rockies, and a sample of blue ribbon trout fishing opportunities in southwestern Canada. The tour puts you in luxury 1920s- and 1930s-vintage cars. You eat fancy food, look out the windows at gorgeous landscapes, talk fishing with the other fishing nuts, and when you stop at your next destination, the fly fishing guides pick you up and take you to the Oldman river, the lower Bow River, a variety of rivers in the Crowsnest area, and the Elk River.

You eat gourmet meals, three squares a day, both on and off the train. The cars travel aboard business cars built by Canadian Pacific Railway for use by corporate executives, royalty, and dignitaries. Some of the previous notable guests on these cars include Sir Winston Churchill and Lady Churchill, the royal family (King George VI, Queen Elizabeth, Princess Elizabeth—prior to her coronation). Not bad company. You begin and end in Calgary, four nights on the train. The trip per person costs about $6,600 per person and that's ballpark.

CONTACTS

Royal Canadian Pacific, 133 9th Avenue SW. Calgary, AB, T2P 2M3, Canada, 877-665-3044, 403-508-1407, info@cprtours.com, www.cprtours.com

Nancy Mozayani and Royal Canadian Pacific, www.royalcanadianpacific .com

---

Highway 3 parallels the river for miles. A bike-walk trail traverses the banks in several places. Even though you'll find some private water, there are enough bridges and other public areas that provide plenty of easy access and you can wade in the high water mark.

The Crowsnest River is more popular now than a decade ago—partly due to the tough times the Bow went through, to exposure, word gets out from anglers and writers alike. But compared to big-name, big-fish American trout rivers, the pressure will seem like nothing. There is a winter fishery on the Crowsnest, too, because Chinook winds make it warm in winter and fishable on the lower fifteen miles. (Did I mention that since Crowsnest Pass funnels wind through it, the summer can see awfully windy days at times?)

Crowsnest is remote but not too remote—you still have lodging and amenities you won't have in a true wilderness setting. This is wilderness, don't get me wrong, but there are enough humans in the area to provide comfort. I found comfort. I caught twenty to forty fish a day in the upper rivers; fifteen to twenty-five a day in the lower. Wild trout. With times where I'd go hours without seeing another soul.

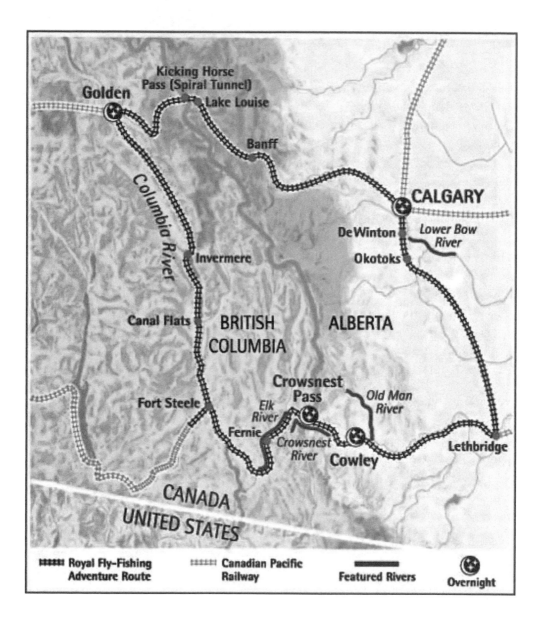

The Crowsnest Angler Fly Shop & Guide
   Service, www.crowsnestangler.com
McLennan Flyfishing, www
   .mclennanflyfishing.com

Oldman River

The Oldman is a must-fish on your trip to the Crowsnest or the Bow River (which it feeds). One of the more scenic rivers in its upper reaches, the upper Oldman is one of those special scenic clear, rocky, dry fly cutthroat streams similar to what America had fifty years ago in the West. The river has a deserved reputation for big rainbow as well and in the lower stretches, both rainbow and cutthroat reach 14 to 18 inches and bigger. Below the Oldman Dam, where Crowsnest lost valuable river miles, the Oldman becomes a productive tailwater.

Castle River

A tributary to the Oldman River, the Castle River is a steady stream of cutthroat and rainbow. This wild stream and its branches, West and South, are most noteworthy, clear and cold and with isolated stretches, both creeks full of eager cutt. In fact, West Castle River has produced an Alberta record for heaviest cutthroat, a whopper that weighed in at over 9 pounds.

You can float and should float the lower Castle because of the sizeable numbers of rainbow and cutthroat and because of the sizeable rainbow and cutthroat. If I told you that some 28- to 30-inch trout had been caught here, I bet you might think about it. The upper Castle is beautiful, floatable, loaded with cutt in the 11- to 16-inch class.

North Raven River (Also Called Stauffer Creek)

North Raven River is one of the finest spring creeks in Canada, fifteen miles of blissful hell, the resident brown trout fat and fine, and they have no intention whatsoever of accepting your fur and feather sacrificial offering. The slow fertile river feeds the Red Deer River in southern Alberta.

The North Raven has all the typical plusses and minuses of a quality spring creek trout fishery. On the plus side, the river is mineral-rich with calcium which in turn nourishes the cycle of plant-insect-fish. The fish are of size, enough to make your brow bead with sweat when you see them ignoring you in the heavy stream vegetation. The North Raven fishes well during runoff when no other rivers do. But as with most spring creeks, the negatives, while fewer, weigh more. The trout are so selective, so finicky, so alert and aware and educated and spoiled, that to catch one, the stars must be aligned. Also in or around the Raven system is South Raven River, a bucolic trout stream; Prairie Creek, a popular meadow brown trout fishery.

Red Deer

Think big browns, long dark-spotted, long-jawed brown trout on a tailwater (much less). The Red Deer is aqua-blue, rocky-shored, wide, shallow, tree-lined. Big river, big fish. Brown trout average 17 to 22 inches. Seriously.

The brown trout are not "everywhere." There's no "you shoulda been there yesterday." You have to work to find them, work to catch them, work to land them. But they're not leader shy. They're not wader shy. They're gorgers, feeders, real trough-eaters. They're huge. But there's not as many of these large predators as you find, let's say, with your normal rainbow-brown mix in your normal Western river, neither is it as sparse as New Zealand. They are spread out, findable by their feeding rings.

North of Calgary, fishable in the winter, closed from part of March into May, these browns love hatches, love dry flies. From the early season Skwala hatches that bring about long dashes by huge brown trout to the naturals and sizeable stonefly imitations, to Golden Stones to Pale Morning Duns to caddis to Blue-Winged Olives to Tricos to Brown Drake to hoppers. You can imagine what the surface is like during *Hexagenia* hatch in July. And Red Deer has heavy hatches of each to go with its heavy browns. Most drift-boat this river (the best way to cover the water, reach more fish, except in low-water years this isn't always easy or possible), some wade (tough in places) but all catch browns that on average are bigger than your average brown. *On dry flies.*

Ram River

Think of this premier wilderness river in terms of North Ram and South Ram. Think of this as the premier cutthroat stream in all of western Canada. Think of this edgy pristine fishery as a place where an angler can catch more trout than George Burns had birthdays. Think of this as one of the truly stunningly beautiful mountain rivers you'll ever see.

From the Ram River's headwaters to the falls below the confluence of the North Ram, anglers will find and catch only one trout species: westslope cutthroat trout. The Ram, north and south, holds a grade-A pure strain of westslope cutthroat. No hybrids. Thirteen to 17 inches on average, which is just about the perfect average size. Dave Jensen guides on the Ram (and obviously cares deeply about this special fishery) and explains, "The lower reaches of the watershed hold high populations of trout while upper reaches produce a few, exceptionally large cutthroat trout due to the low availability of wintering habitat." The westslopes aren't native to the Ram but they are to Alberta's other mountain rivers and specifically the North Saskatchewan drainage into which the Ram empties—the impassable waterfalls and chutes of the Ram made it impossible for the cutthroat to move upstream.

South Ram is rugged and you have to be dogged to want to fish it, heck, even reach it. Backpacking off of Highway 732 is the way to reach the South Ram—but wait, bulletin, this just in: helicopters will pick you and set you down in pristine wilderness. The 1,400-foot-deep canyon through which the South Ram flows is as inaccessible and wild as any country you're bound to ever fish in. And eerily landscaped to boot.

With its quick descent, the South Ram dumps into perfect plunge pools, dances through riffles, meanders through congregations of boulders, surges through runs. How big, the cutthroat that inhabit these ideal trout lies? Jensen confides, "While only a few fish in excess of 22 inches are seen each year, westslope cutthroat trout up to exactly 26 inches have been caught on the South Ram River." Jensen suggests, "Perhaps the finest attribute the South Ram River has is its reputation as the purest remaining population of westslope cutthroat trout in Alberta." South Ram is at once big and powerful but fragile and intimate.

Access to the South Ram River is sixty-four kilometers south of Nordegg on the Forestry Trunk Road (Highway 732). The entire river lies in the Rocky Mountains Forest Reserve.

North Ram is easier to access but no less productive. Shallower, better for dry fly fishing, you'll find more familiar surroundings in this valley-wide. Meadow sections with undercut banks. Runs dumping into pools. Riffles bouncing out of turns. Easy to wade, easy to spot where the trout ought to be, and when the water is lower, easy to spot the big cutthroat trout. Sightfishing for big cutts in wild country. Does it get any better than that?

Access to the North Ram River is from

the Forestry Trunk Road (Highway 732) twenty-seven kilometers south of Nordegg. The entire river lies in the Rocky Mountains Forest Reserve.

Dave Jensen of Ram River Alberta Fly fishing books flights directly with the helicopter company on a bulk rate, meaning that anglers can fly with them, raft the river to the best pools, and have a fly fishing guide and lunch provided for less than you can fly in on your own booking directly.

Jensen also has a remote fly-in retreat location (complete with cabins) on Fortress Lake, a lake in Hamber Provincial Park, immediately adjacent to Jasper National Park. Fortress Lake, dominated by towering peaks, is considered by many to be one of the top three brook trout lakes anywhere. Jensen has exclusive rights to the lease for the entire provincial park and the lake averages 3- to 5-pound brookies, with the lake record at 12. It too is a heli fly-in location, twenty-six kilometers from the nearest road.

CONTACTS

Dave Jensen, Ram River Alberta Flyfishing, www.reddeerriver.com, www.flyfishalberta.com, www.fortresslake.com (did you ever see a guide with this many web links?)

Kootenay Fly Shop & Guiding Co., Fernie, BC, www.kootenayflyshop.ca

Alberta Bow River "Must Be Nice" Drift Co., Calgary, 403-271-9108

Country Pleasures Bow River Orvis Shop, Calgary, www.countrypleasures.com

Crowsnest Angler, Bellevue, www.crowsnestangler.com

Dave Brown Outfitters (formerly Elk River Angler), Fernie, BC, www.davebrownoutfitters.com

Fish Tales Fly Shop, Calgary, 403-640-1273

Stream Weaver Flies, Red Deer, 403-343-8699

BRITISH COLUMBIA

Dean River

- **Location:** Southwest British Columbia
- **What You Fish For:** Steelhead and salmon
- **Highlights and Notables:** The dean of steelhead rivers, this wide brawny river's steelhead are considered to be among the strongest fighters in the world.

Think summer steelhead runs. Southwest British Columbia. One of the most scenic rivers in Canada with the jagged tall peaks of the hulking Coast Mountains overlooking the wide blue river, the Dean leaves Nimpo Lake and rushes to the Dean Channel by Bella Coola. (Aside: Nimpo and Anahim Lakes are superb trout fishing locales.)

The lower Dean gets most of the attention for its strain of summer steelhead, sometimes considered to be the strongest strain anywhere. Acrobatic fighters that run from a couple of pounds to 20 pounds with quite a few over the magic 20-pound mark. Average size about 10 pounds.

In June, the river receives runs of Chinook salmon (as big as 50 but more likely 15 to 20 for you and me), and in August, coho salmon (up to 15 to 20 pounds). Good access for waders, but most boat and there's a lot of fly-in action. The lower few miles of the Dean see plenty of anglers so if you want more by-yourself fishing, time to go upstream. And as if for kicks, Dean River steelhead have a penchant for surface and near-surface lures and flies. Stellar fishing lasts from June into October. Lots of regs so make it easy and hire a guide; stay at a lodge.

CONTACTS

Dean River Lodge, www.mooselakelodge.com/deanriver.html

Moose Lake Lodge, Anahim Lake, 250-742-3535

Lower Dean River Lodge, Bella Coola, www.lowerdean.com

Elk River

- **Location:** Southeastern British Columbia, real close to the border with Alberta
- **What You Fish For:** Westslope cutthroat
- **Highlights and Notables:** Unbelievably beautiful mountain scenery, a river that is probably the finest cutthroat river in North America

At the risk of starting controversy similar to what happened when *Fly Fisherman* magazine published an article on the Elk River, I'm including North America's top westslope cutthroat river. In 1997, one of the writers of the Elk River article complained that the article he himself contributed to had led to the demise of Elk River in many facets including catch rates, sizes, pressure, and so on. This writer suggested that Americans coming over the border to fish Canadian waters might have to suffer some accessibility limitations in the future. Proprietary dude, isn't he?

Another writer/angler who contributed to the Elk River article responded by agreeing that the cutthroat were indeed more wary and that pressure had increased, but he pointed out that the cutthroat population was in better shape than before the article, catch sizes were up, pressure had increased but only minimally, the cutthroat were better protected and thriving under stricter regulations, and that the Elk River "explosion" had in fact helped the local fishing economy, especially in Fernie. And now, new angler fees have been added to every day's fishing, some twenty-one bucks a day, give or take a nickel.

This is in addition to the regular fishing license. The fees are to be used to make the Elk a better river (although it sure smacks of a way to keep foreigners out, doesn't it?).

All this fuss over a little ol' wilderness cutthroat river? Yeah, because Elk River in British Columbia is really that good. To be fair and not send droves (hordes?) to the river and mess it up for everyone, especially the locals, I will keep the Elk River section to a minimum.

A four-hour drive southwest from Calgary or a two-hour drive north of Whitefish, Montana, will put you in Fernie and into lodging and dining and on the river.

The Elk River's westslope cutthroats run 12 to 17 inches with trout on either side of these numbers. I'm not going to say there's a great chance to catch a 20-inch native but . . . you can figure it out on your own. Beautiful fish with their tiny black dots spread across their golden bodies like stars across the sky. But in negative.

The Elk River is beautiful and wild and offers miles and miles of fishing and deserves whatever protection we need to give her to protect and preserve and enhance the river and her fish.

CONTACTS
Crowsnest Angler, Bellevue, AB,
   www.crowsnestangler.com
Dave Brown Outfitters (formerly Elk
   River Angler) Fernie,
   www.davebrownoutfitters.com
Fly Fishing Canadian Services,
   www.flyfish-canada.com
Kootenay Fly Shop & Guiding Co.,
   www.kootenayflyshop.ca

Trusty Creek Trout and Trail,
   www.telusplanet.net/public/k-kwiebe/
   trusty1.html
Elk River Guiding Company, 877-423-
   7239, www.elkriver.ca

Iskut Chain Lakes

- **Location:** Western British Columbia
- **What You Fish For:** Wild rainbow trout
- **Highlights and Notables:** Isolation, stark beauty, and big, wild rainbow trout

Only knuckleheads need apply. Why else would someone fly into Vancouver and drive 400 miles toward the great unknown up north, over a highway that is as much a highway as Tara Reid is an actress, to fish for trout you know won't be over 2 or 3 pounds in a land where there are 1) absolutely no amenities; 2) no people; and 3) a good chance that if you screw up, you die or become horribly disfigured?

The land is breathtaking, weather-worn mountains wearing snow caps, rivers stained copper from the peat bogs, black and brown bear outnumbering the residents, jagged rugged mountains and boreal highland, the Tahltan people, the Athabascan Nation, as old as the land and as tough as the bears. You just think you've been in some wild country before.

To the point. Spatsizi Plateau Wilderness Park and the Mount Edziza Provincial Park press against these lakes, this chain of lakes, the waterway of the Iskut River joining the lakes like a blue diamond necklace fifty-five miles long.

The main lakes of interest are Natadesleen, Kinaskan, Tatogga, Ealue, Eddontenajon, and Kluachon Lakes. Wild rainbow trout. You will feel guilty catching so many 14- to 18-inch trout. They will impale themselves on just about anything you toss, throw, cast, skate, or strip. The highway runs beside all the lakes.

Isolation. Absolutely, positively, guaranteed you will be the only person or persons on these lakes. No one else from Canada wants to fish them, not with all the other "better" choices so much closer, with so many more big fish. This is the Far North, after all.

Difficulty. The Stewart-Cassiar Highway (aka Highway 37, aka the Death March) has more pocks and holes and gravel than a 1940s movie heavy's face.

Prehistory. The land is relatively unchanged since the Tahltan Indians first moved into this area to hunt for moose, caribou, and deer thousands of years ago. You can feel the gentle pressure of wind and fire and rain upon this land.

No trophies. The winters are harsh and long, the summers short, and the food supply limited. But there are thousands and thousands of trout with your name on them.

There is a good chance you will see one or more of these animals while driving the "highway": moose, wolf, goat, beaver, fox, eagles, bear, Stone's sheep, grouse. Also, the people of the Far North are proud of their edible mushrooms (I don't do 'shrooms).

If you want to be out in the sticks, in the middle of it all, stay at Tatogga Lake Resort (Wilderness Oasis). Iskut is the town to visit with Tahltan natives, huge by Far North standards—post office, grocery store, gas station.

The sky seems bluer, the spruce forests greener, the air cleaner, colder, so clean it will take your breath away until you get your bearings.

CONTACTS
Northern BC Tourism Association, Prince George, 250-561-0432

Prince Rupert

- **Location:** Western British Columbia on the coast
- **What You Fish For:** Salmon (five species), halibut
- **Highlights and Notables:** Great base location to enjoy Canada, catch salmon, especially the huge kings. Halibut capital of the world.

Grab your atlas and look up Canada. I want you to find Vancouver. Excellent. Now move your finger up the coast. There, up, up, keep going, there, on the mainland from the big island, stop. You've found Prince Rupert.

Chatham Sound. Dixon Entrance. Migrating through are some of the largest Chinook salmon in the world. Come June and July, anglers get in drift boats and jet boats and boats of all kinds, even tugboats,

or they wade, all in hopes of landing one of the giant kings destined for the Nass or Skeena River systems. Eighty-pound kings, thank you very much.

That's it. Nothing fancy. Trophy salmon from April to August, burly sea-beasts that typically come to the net weighing 20 to 40 pounds. The 80-pound kings are not the norm but 50- to 60-pounders are there, in numbers, waiting for you.

Prince Rupert is one of the coolest, best, nicest cities in the world. Small but big, beautiful but fits into the land. Fjords, islands, mountains. Museums, natives, wilderness, grizzly bears, ecotourism, Tsim-

shian peoples who have lived here on the coast for 10,000 years, houses on stilts, humpback whales, and so much more. Less than 20,000 people, located at the mouth of the mighty Skeena, blessed with fine dining, accommodations from budget to luxurious, this is an outpost in the Pacific Northwest wilderness and yet it remains wild itself.

Prince Rupert is a jumping-off point for other fishing trips but is one of the top salmon home bases in the world. It calls itself the "Halibut Capital of the World" and the "City of Rainbows." Salmon as big as they come, this side of Alaska, in an unusual friendly community you won't forget.

CONTACTS

King Pacific Lodge, 888-592-5464

Fred Hutchings, Triple T Charters, www
.tripletcharters.com

Queen Charlotte Islands

- **Location:** Western Canada, west of Prince Rupert
- **What You Fish For:** Five species of salmon
- **Highlights and Notables:** One of the last frontiers for salmon, a real out-there place

One of the last frontiers for salmon, "discovered" in the 1980s, this is still "out-there" water, not quite like bush plane-water or fishing in Mongolia, but close. Of the 150 islands in this archipelago (don't you just love to say that word), the main focus for fishermen concentrates their attention on four islands: Hippa, Graham, Moresby, and Langara.

Not even truly discovered as a viable sports fishery until the 1980s, this locale picks up salmon near maturity on their way to move up the rivers of western Canada and America. You want me to tell you about a watery expanse where anglers are pioneers and catch 40-pound salmon eager to fatten up and eat just about anything, right? Did I mention you drop hooks for five different salmon species? Oh yeah, baby.

Queen Charlotte Islands lie on the northern tip of British Columbia, Chinook salmon heaven, a summer fishery. Screaming reels. Jumping kings, fresh and strong and motivated to be somewhere else. Fifty-, 60-, 78-pound Chinooks (called *tyee* here) are catchable and have been caught more frequently than you can believe. The average Chinook runs about 25 pounds, hard fighters. Catches? Kings, of course, but also coho (5 to 14 pounds), with lesser action for pink, sockeye, and chum. Catch halibut from the Chicken Yards (nothing big like Alaskan waters, 30 to 150 pounds) and also yelloweye, cabezon, lingcod, black and blue rockfish.

The Continental Shelf makes its presence known here, stirring up vital nutrients. The day is made up of you, the big water, the seals and whales and sea lions, few other anglers and salmon, your thoughts or the vacancy of thoughts. You mooch, you drift, you troll, you drool.

CONTACTS

Queen Charlotte Adventures, 800-784-1718

Skeena River System

- **Location:** Southwestern British Columbia, from Prince Rupert inland
- **What You Fish For:** Salmon, steelhead
- **Highlights and Notables:** The best steelhead river in the world, the best river system for steelies in the world

SCOUTING REPORT

1. The greatest steelhead river in the world, hell, the greatest steelhead river system in the world begins west of the Spatizi Plateau, moving southerly, fertile mother, receptive to her daughters. The average Skeena steelhead weighs 10 pounds—the strongest, largest strain in the world. Another allure: Skeena River steelhead go after skated flies, even walking flies, so anglers can use floating lines. Before reaching the Pacific Ocean at Prince Rupert, this collection of feeder streams (over thirty streams have steelhead runs) and main stem comprises a steelhead fishery that has no peers.

2. South, south, south. Through valleys carved by glaciers, mountains topped with snow, deep green primeval forests of spruce, pine, and aspen. You are out there, here.

3. Enter the Sustut. Here, the most remote of the Skeena steelhead tributaries. Wilderness. Access tricky, difficult. Two lodges in the lower Sustut, Suskeena Lodge and Steelhead Valhalla Lodge, reachable by plane. Ten-pound steelhead in pristine setting. Not as many big steelhead as its sister rivers, but 15- to 25-pound ironheads not unusual. Best times, late August into October, right when the weather gets mean and nasty.

4. Enter the Babine. Probably the most famous steelhead river in the world. Fly-in only; no roads lead to Nirvana. Three lodges on the Babine: Silver Hilton Lodge, Babine Steelhead Lodge, Babine Norlakes Lodge. Every week, several 20-pound steelheads are boated (and released). Jet-boated, the way to get up the river. The Babine is the trophy steelhead river where each season, fish over 30 pounds are caught. Rainbow trout, too—May, June, July—Rainbow Alley—rainbows 2 to 8 pounds by the dozens. Come August's end, the steelhead. You might hear that the Kispiox has the largest steelhead in the world (on average) and I'm going to write that very thing in a moment but because the Babine has such great returns, the river has *more* big sea-runs than any other Skeena river. And sockeye salmon. And grizzly bear. Wilderness, tough access, likely the wildest of all Skeena rivers.

5. If you hold a 10-pound steelhead in your two hands, you get the idea how big a 10-pound steelhead really is—this silver monster is as big around as your thigh.

6. South runs the Skeena, bigger now with its drinking of the feeders.

7. Enter the Kispiox. Have you ever heard that the Kispiox has the largest steelhead in the world? Yep, true. You can tell where they hold. You can wade. Boat but do not fish from the boat. The forest primeval comes right up the bank and makes you have to get out a bit to cast. Can you steeple-cast fifty feet? Twenty- to 25-pound steelhead a reality. Fifteen-pound *average* steel-

head. The Kispiox steelhead, for various reasons (I just don't know), gains weight quicker and is bigger around than any other steelhead. This just might be the best steelhead river in the world even though the Kispiox is the smallest of the Skeena streams. Nowhere else do you have a better chance at catching a 30-pound steelhead. Logging roads parallel the fishery above the Indian village of Kispiox. The river is clear September to November and this is the greatest time in the world to fish the greatest steelhead fishery in the world (possibly, right?).

8. South and enter the Bulkley River along the Yellowknife Highway, under the watchful eye of the Bulkley Mountains. Has picked up Morice River. The Bulkley-Morice is the easiest Skeena trib for the nonguided (self-guided) angler. Easy access from Highway 16/Yellowknife Highway, which parallels the river a lot of the way (and access from logging roads as well). Like to catch 20-pound steelhead on a fly? This popular river near Smithers is one of the top fly fishing steelhead rivers anywhere. Cleated waders and a staff. September and October are the finest months to be on the river. Lots and lots and lots of fish, not as big on average as the other steelhead in Skeena sister rivers. You can still catch a trophy but the draw here is the frisky one- and two-year-old salts that go after flies on or just under the surface and they do this in broad smooth pools. That's a hoot.

9. The Lower Skeena, big and powerful, smooth and wide, on broad shoulders flowing southwesterly. Chinook and coho salmon runs.

10. Enter the Copper (Zymoetz), the Kalum (Kitsumkalum), and the Kitimat Rivers. Three sisters. Terrace is your home base. The Copper, glacial-tinged water, pools shaped by gods. Early season fish move in from the tidal waters, aggressive, they hit surface flies. The steelhead are not as large but plenty big enough, 8 to 15 pounds and up. Copper, access good. Kalum, not as good (but fishes well in winter).

11. The Skeena in all its might moves through Prince Rupert.

12. From Prince Rupert into the ocean and there are Queen Charlotte Islands, Haida Gwaii.

13. Northern British Columbia. Railways, grizzlies, whitewater rafting, horseback riding, snowskiing and snowboarding, backcountry adventures, the finest steelhead rivers in the world.

CONTACTS
Sustut
Steelhead Valhalla Lodge, 250-847-9351
Suskeena Lodge, 250-847-9233

Babine
Babine Steelhead Lodge,
    www.fishbabine.com
Babine Norlakes Lodge, 250-847-6160
Silver Hilton Lodge, 415-897-4997,
    www.silverhilton.com

Kispiox

Bear Claw Lodge, 250-842-6287

Terrace Northcoast Anglers, 250-635-6496

Sportsman's Kispiox Lodge, 250-842-6455

Kispiox Steelhead Camp, 250-842-5435

Kispiox River Resort & Campground, 250-842-6182

Wilfred Lee, 250-842-6350

Gordon Wadley, 250-847-5933

BC Fisheries Office, Skeena Region, 250-847-7260

Bulkley and Morice

Driftwood Lodge, 250-847-5016

Frontier Farwest Fishing Lodge, 250-846-9153

Bulkley River Lodge, 250-287-3256

Denise Maxwell, 604-552-2181

Robert Hull, 250-847-1847

Ray Makwiechuk, 250-845-2982

Copper (Zymoetz), the Kalum (Kitsumkalum), and the Kitimat Rivers

Northwest Fishing Guides, 604-635-5295

The River's Edge Lodge, 250-635-2540

Spey Lodge, 250-635-1514

Vancouver Island

- **Location:** Southwestern Canada, British Columbia
- **What You Fish For:** Salmon, steelhead, sea-run cutthroat
- **Highlights and Notables:** Self-proclaimed "Salmon Capital of the World." The ambience of this special island combined with the stellar salmon fishing makes this a must-do.

They call this the "Salmon Capital of the World." This is where Roderick Haig-Brown wrote about his home river, the Campbell. Famous landmarks and icons like the Tyee Club, Island Pool, the Hump, Lighthouse Pool, and Seymour Narrows. This is where millions of salmon run every year; where your fall runs of sea-run cutthroat and steelhead last through winter; where large Chinook and coho and pink and sockeye run through Discovery Passage and up through Campbell River and the Gold, the Cowichan, the Marble, the Stamp. Salmon come from all over to run up the rivers of this Pacific Northwest island of Vancouver.

Fishing Vancouver Island is not always your middle-of-pristine-forest salmon fishing experience—you'll see thousands of anglers, hundreds of boats in Discovery Passage when the salmon are running. But you do have deep green forests, dark canyons, stunning rugged mountains, ocean and bay and big brawling rivers where most of the time you can get away from it all. On the island, in the bay, up the river you could find yourself on a water-taxi, floatplane, car, 17-foot Boston Whaler, helicopter, afoot. You have numerous choices in lodges and guides and towns. You can hire guides or do it yourself (after a day on the water with a guide). You can wake up, eat breakfast, and be on a river in fifteen minutes. You have interesting historic towns, fishing towns (Victoria, Campbell River, Courtenay), pleasant, accommodating people, whale-watching, bear-watching, glaciers, totem poles—and the overall Pacific Northwest ambience is tough to beat.

And so is the salmon fishing.

July brings Chinook and sockeye and they can last into September. After the Chinook comes the pink, which can also last until September. After the pink run (and take just about any pink fly or lure), the coho and they just keep on running until Christmas. Chum are in season all year long (and don't discount the chum like so many do—in the fall, chum put up a good fight, leap and splash, and weigh 10 to 20 pounds or more).

Heck, if you time it right, in the spring, you just have to find time to go a-fishin' for the sea-run cutthroat, what with these big honkers all up in even the smallest of streams. How about heli-fishing into wild coastal streams for wild sea-run cutthroat that weigh several pounds? Summer steelhead on the western edges of Vancouver Island heat up in the cool streams in May, steam things up through July before they peter out. Brown and rainbow trout and even Dolly Varden reside in V.I.'s rivers as well. Discovery Passage has year-round salmon fishing. So you can fish fresh or salt, take your pick from five species of salmon, or angle for trout. There are just too many angling options.

Chinook salmon that weigh 20 to 50 pounds, sometimes bigger, run through Discovery Passage and into the rivers. The coho tease you at 4 or 5 pounds and then rip off line as a 25-pounder. You can go where the fishing is the hottest, saltwater or freshwater.

The legendary Campbell River is a must-fish. While no longer the premier steelhead river it once was, the salmon and trout more than make up for it. Better trout fishing than you know but the steelhead fishing pales in comparison to what it used to be, and it used to be among the best, the stuff of legends.

This river is timeless. Like all great rivers. They are parts of the past, the present, and the future. They are stories and fish and rocks and water, always water.

Campbell River

Roderick Haig-Brown wrote in *A River Never Sleeps*, "I still don't know why I fish or why other men fish, except we like it and it makes us think and feel."

When you lay eyes on the Campbell, you will think and you will feel and you will know why it is you fish. The wet fluid legacy wraps around the hand you've dipped into the water; you hear the murmurs, millions of bits attach and millions more trickle away and flow over the rocks and past the banks where the salmon swim upstream. This, my friends, is why we fish.

Large Chinook and coho or the pink and chum salmon bend your rod, you shift in the boat, thuds of your feet, broke off again, hooked again, the kype, the hump, the landscape blurring in your periphery, the smell of clean salt, of your guide's cigar, of coming rain and this is why we fish.

Gold River

The Gold River is an angry beautiful stream, difficult to float on your own because of its rumbling water bursting through canyons and narrow passages.

So hire a guide. The Gold is fun to wade, clear cobble-bottomed flats and big green pools, and offers year-round fishing for steelhead for its two annuals runs, catch-and-release only. This short stream moves quickly, powerfully, known especially for its winter run, excellent access, and winter popularity.

Cowichan River

Say the secret word, win a hundred dollars. "Trout." Brown trout to be exact. Large brown trout to be even more exact. The browns are big but difficult to catch. The large brown trout are mixed in with cutthroat and rainbow trout (some pretty nice ones from the lake) in this wooded river, a river with some awesome stretches of riffles and pocket water, rocks on the riverbottom the size of picnic baskets. The steelhead fishing is solid, winter and spring, and salmon run up as well. You can wade the Cowichan but it's powerful and you better stay alert. Most drift the river anyway because access is limited. Cowichan Lake is worth your time, hint hint.

Other Important Streams

The other main Vancouver Island rivers to consider include Stamp (rich but too crowded for my blood), Ash, San Juan (near Victoria), Salmon (winter steelhead-ing), White, Marble, Nitinat (near Victoria, Mahatta, Nimpkish, and the Quinsam), a smaller, more intimate river that feeds the Campbell where maybe you too can see a bear cross the river and catch salmon all day long.

CONTACTS
Campbell River Tourism,
   www.campbellrivertourism.com
Directory of lodgings,
   www.campbellrivertourism.com.
Silver King Lodge, Campbell River, 250-286-0142

MANITOBA

Nueltin Lake

- **Location:** Straddles the Northwest Territories and Manitoba provinces, east of Kasba Lake
- **What You Fish For:** Pike and lake trout
- **Highlights and Notables:** Remote world-class lake with world-record-size pike and lake trout

World-class fly-in lake/resort time.

Nueltin Lake is near the top of the list for remote fly-in lakes. Why? Let's take a look at what you expect out of a remote fly-in lake:

CHECKLIST

Expensive. You wouldn't expect a world-class fly-in resort vacation not to cost you some Benjamins, now would you? How could you brag to your buddies with a straight face? If it were cheap, everybody would go.

Remote and beautiful. More virgin islands and bays than you care to count. Wildlife like moose and caribou and wolves and bears. What's remote fishing without the chance of some big animal crossing your path?

A chance at a world-record fish. In this case, lake trout (56-pound is the lake laker record; plenty of lakers 12 to 25 pounds and many 25 to 40) and pike (50 inches and over; lots of pike 12 to 20 pounds). Even if you don't catch a world-record, you have a fighting chance at catching the largest mack or pike you've yet caught. You will come home with photos of you and big fish. Extraordinary angling *in the shallows.*

A near-guarantee that you'll catch a lot of fish, usually big fish (in this case lake trout and pike). You will come home with photos of you and lots of fish.

Some species of game fish that everybody overlooks that are well worth fishing for but that you, like everyone else, can overlook as well. In this case, grayling, 2 to 4 pounds.

You don't have to do diddly-squat. They spoil you rotten. You don't want to go home and wouldn't except that, like I said, it's expensive and if you stay the summer, you'll be broke.

Few anglers fish these waters. There are places on this lake that are so far from anything, few if any anglers fish that area in a season.

Food to remember at the lodge. Succulent fresh shore lunches.

A lounging area with drinks, a place to play poker and repair lures and tie flies and share tall tales about the day's fishing.

Built-in regret. You won't want to go home. You won't want to fish your normal waters. This was too good.

Guides who are professional but friendly, who know how to find fish and are committed to the health of the fishery and to deciphering how to give to you the type of experience you need and don't even know you need.

The fishing at Nueltin Lake is completely catch-and-release, to only use barbless single hook lures and flies. Nueltin empties northerly with a good current throughout into Sealhole Lake, a little-fished lake (where no-telling-what lives in there) but not before passing river inlets and bays and the Narrows where the lake narrows (imagine that). Two thirds of the lake is in the Northwest Territories, one third in Manitoba, 125 miles long, up to thirty miles wide. Short season opens in June and ends when it gets too cold. Anglers fly into Winnipeg and then catch a plane to the private Treeline Lodge airstrip. You get around the big lake via boats, float planes, and sheer determination.

God's River

Brook trout and pike are the two major draws for anglers. God's River and God's Lake are two outstanding fisheries. Fly-in locale with roductive rapids. Some of the brookies reach Labrador sizes and the average goes about 3–4 pounds.

Kasmere Lake lies at the south end (but west) of Nueltin Lake, a good half-hour float plane trip away, and has its own luxury ten-person lodge. Kasmere Lake is worthy of angling attention in its own right, twenty miles long and loaded with pike in weedy shallows, lakers that will take topwater lures, and more grayling than you can shake a graphite stick at. There are other accommodations (what they call minilodges) at the Narrows, at Windy River, and at Shannon Lake at the far south end.

CONTACTS
Nueltin Fly-In Lodges, www.nueltin.com

Silsby Lake

- **Location:** 450 miles north of Winnipeg
- **What You Fish For:** Northern pike, walleye
- **Highlights and Notables:** Camp-record pike weighed in at nearly 54 inches. That good enough for ya?

Silsby is one of Canada's finest trophy pike fisheries, with pike caught regularly that measure 40 to 50 inches or more. But wait, there's more. Anglers not only catch scary humongous pike, they catch lots of scary humongous pike.

You fly in to Silsby Lake and from the air, you can see the structure and habitat and shallow bays that make it such a great pike lake. The best time to visit is from May to September but if you can, hit it right after ice-out.

CONTACTS
Fishquest, www.fishquest.com

NEW BRUNSWICK

Look, I know New Brunswick has a lot more to offer than just landlocked salmon (like trout) but these four lakes are worth mentioning: Utopia Lake, Chamcook Lake, Digdeguash Lake, and Magaguadavic Lake. All of these are great for landlocked salmon in the 1- to 4-pound range.

New Brunswick also has some underrated angling for bronzebacks. Digdeguash and Utopia Lakes aren't good just for Atlantic salmon but also for a healthy population of smallmouth. Ditto Oromocto, Palfrey, Skiff, Spednik (a rising smallie hotspot), Harvey, East Grand Lakes. Not many 6-pounders but plenty of 1- to 4-pound smallmouth bass. The best thing is—fishing pressure for smallmouth is almost nonexistent.

Miramichi River

- **Location:** Eastern Canada, on the mainland coast, west of Prince Edward Island
- **What You Fish For:** Atlantic salmon
- **Highlights and Notables:** This famous river is not what she used to be, nor is she deceased. Still a worthy destination, one of the prettiest rivers you'll ever fish.

At one time, the Miramichi was considered the world's best river for Atlantic salmon. This is a beautiful, big, rich river, one that over the years has about as many angler days as any other North American Atlantic salmon river.

You wade out in the riffles, position for the big pool, hope, pray, wait. The fall version of the Miramichi is the most gorgeous river in eastern Canada. While the salmon are not as frequent as they used to be, the number of big salmon seems to be holding its own or even increasing. There are also runs of shad in the spring, anadromous brook trout in early summer.

NEWFOUNDLAND AND LABRADOR

- **Location:** Eastern Canada
- **What You Fish For:** Brook trout
- **Highlights and Notables:** The largest brook trout in the world, remote wild mecca for adventurous serious anglers

So much of the landscape will remind you of Alaska, it's eerie. Rugged, rock-strewn, thick forests, wetness everywhere, wild land that seemingly goes on forever.

The brook trout are so big, it's scary.

The hatches, the Hex, the Green Drake, the Brown Drake, can be so thick, it's hairy.

Ted Williams, Lee Wulff, Joe Brooks—all kinds of angling legends loved Labrador.

The weather. It rained on my four of five days one time. You just never know.

Labrador.

One of the must-visit trout fishing locales in the universe. The typical brook trout goes about 4 to 5 pounds, 20 to 22 inches long. Petch's Pond, Little Hairy, The Nursery, Johnny's Lake, and so many other fishing hotspots, icons. The locals also call the eastern brook trout the speckled trout. And squaretail.

I had this one squaretail on the English River that taunted the dickens out of me. He or she, I couldn't tell, was holding in a pool behind a rock, water clear as day. Feeding on something on the surface but I saw no hatches. I tried an Adams. A stimulator. A Royal Wulff. Then I went streamer on the big speck. Then deerhair mouse. Surely I could move the green-mottleback with a deerhair mouse. All the other fish I'd cast to that morning had attacked my flies voraciously like Iron Mike on an ear. The fish looked up at the huge fuzzy fly and then back at me with one of those you-gotta-be-kidding-me looks. Had that brook trout taken any of my offerings—and there was no indication that was ever a possibility—it would have easily been the biggest brook trout of the trip. Instead, I had to settle for a brook trout just under 6 pounds, a dark trout with the yellowest spots I've ever seen. That's how good Labrador is.

Crooks Lake Lodge

Here's the pitch:

While there are locales that provide bigger average size (such as the Minipi giants averaging 5½ #, up to 10 #), or destinations that boast fantastic numbers of smaller (mostly 1–2 #) brookies, Crooks Lake offers consistent, high quality fishing for wild brook trout of a very impressive average size.

Here's the reality:
True.
True, Crooks Lake may not produce the 6- to 10-pound brook trout that other lakes and streams of Labrador do, but the

lake and nearby Eagle River hold speckled trout that rival any fishery for average size (about 4.5 pounds) and consistency. Ten to twenty 4- or 5-pound brook trout in a day is not unusual.

Cooper Camps

Talk about tradition. Cooper's Minipi Camps. Three camps: Ann Marie, Minonipi Lodge, and Minipi Lodge, the newest and most modern. You fly into Goose Bay Labrador through Montreal, Toronto, or Halifax, and catch a float plane to the Minipi headwaters. If you're not with Cooper's, you ain't fishing these waters (the Minipi River, the two lakes, and feeders).

There may not be a better place in Labrador (and therefore on the planet) to catch a 5-pound brook trout on a dry fly. And in Minipi watershed, the drakes are big and heavy, and so are the rises.

Brook trout as large as 10 pounds. Lots of IGFA tippet-class records for fly rods. Lakes are shallow for the most part (and that means manageable). Hatches are world class. They've been catching and releasing for decades. Five- to 7-pound brookies are not uncommon. You need a 6-weight rod for brookies, even a 7—a brookie! You use big humpys and big lemming and big mouse and big stimulator patterns. The *Hexagenia* hatch is great; the northern lights are cool.

Part of this system are Anne Marie, Petch's Pond, The Nursery, Johnny Lake, Minonipi, and Little Hairy. The Minipi River system in particular regularly coughs up squaretails between 3 and 8 pounds (remember, we're talking about *brook trout*), and record-setting monsters pushing 10 pounds have been hooked in these waters. What are you waiting for?

Anne Marie Lake

Like Lovers Lane or Lovers Lookout or Lovers Point, we all had a makeup spot in our hometown and so does this fertile lake, with its own spawning amorous formation, Loverboy Rock (aka Loverboy Run). This tree-lined, dark green, lily-padded lake is known for its prolific mayfly hatches especially the Brown Drake in midsummer and the Green Drake in August. Caddis show up throughout the warm months. A stimulator gets hits all summer long. Hard to get skunked at Anne Marie. One of the Minipi Camps.

Awesome Lake

The name fits. Awesome Lake and its main feeder, the English River, are the showpieces for Labrador and its world-renowned brook trout fishing. Fed by streams and brooks, not loaded with big hatches, the water clear as Evian. Fly fishing only. Barbless hooks only. Catch-and-release on all trout 3 pounds up.

Even with the clear water, even though you can easily spot the big brook trout and they in turn can spot you, they aren't spooky. Only wary. You'll hear how anglers tempt these squaretails with mouse and lemming patterns but you'll consistently draw strikes with streamers. It's not unusual for big brook trout to take smaller brook trout and in this clear water, you can see it all happen before you. Outdoor writer Len Rich used to own the lodge and sold it but his words in his articles and e-mails suggest just how much he loved it.

These brook trout are fighters and you'll enjoy lots of hookups so get your game face on. Fish the inlets and outlets. Three- to 4-pound brook trout are common. You want 5 to 6 pounds? You can do it if you're good enough. Seven- or 8-pounders? Sure, but give up the dream, you're probably not that good.

English River

This feeds Awesome Lake, medium-sized, good trout fishery, then leaves Awesome, and goes into Hamilton Inlet and Lake Melville, and then below the outlet, even better fishing. Dark gray rocks with orange lichen stick up out of the water like humps of time and brook trout lurk around them. The pocket water was designed by trout gods. The size of the brook trout will astound you as well as how they bend your 7-weight.

Big River

The best way to fish Big River is Big River Camps, a northern Labrador fishing operation near the North Sea on a bend in the tannic-colored river. Short season of a month and a half for Atlantic salmon, char, and brook trout; you can fish right out the front door of the main lodge or hit other stretches and other waters in Inuit-style canoes.

Goose River

Nearby, the Goose River has one of the largest remaining runs of bright Atlantic salmon that keeps happy anglers coming back year after year. The allure of wild Atlantic salmon up to 15 pounds can do that to you.

Osprey Lake

Sixty-three miles in Labrador doesn't measure the same as sixty-three miles on I-25 north out of Colorado Springs. You can't travel sixty-three miles in any direction by road. These are air miles. Osprey Lake is sixty-three air miles from Goose Bay, southeast.

If you like isolation, 6-pound square-tails, big flat water, and a chance at a 10-pounder, Osprey Lake may be for you. Fly fishing only. Catch-and-release fishing only. The lake has held several line class records for brookies.

Crooks Lake

Five miles long fed by rivers and streams, holding speckled trout from a pound to 6 pounds. Pike to 20 pounds help keep the population in check. Sixty miles southeast of Goose Bay on the upper Eagle River system.

Eagle River

Southwest of Goose Bay, you fly into the headwaters for the Eagle River. Brook trout average about 3 to 4 pounds and you'll go after them in flat, slow-moving lakes such as Crooks, Parks, and No Name. Bucktails work well traditionally in the Eagle, especially in between hatches.

Park Lake

Here are the headwaters of the Eagle River. Back to snuff after a few changes in ownership, accessible only by air, this remote island-dotted lake holds the typical outrageously sized brook trout as well as northern pike. In late August, Atlantic salmon come back to Park Lake to spawn. Fly fishing only. Barbless hooks only. Catch-and-release standard. You fly into Goose Bay and from there you will fly by float plane to your destination.

CONTACTS

Awesome Lake Lodge, 877-677-3363, www.awesomelake.com

Awesome Lake Fishing Lodge, Happy Valley-Goose Bay, www.fishinglabrador .com

Newfoundland and Labrador Department of Tourism, St. John's, www.gov .nf.ca/tourism

Len Rich, Mick Emmens, Awesome Lake Lodge, www.labradoranglingadventures .com

Newfoundland Department of Tourism, Culture and Recreation, 709-729-5604

Osprey Lake Lodge, www.ospreylakelodge .com

Cooper's Minipi Camps, Happy Valley-Goose Bay, www.minipicamps.com/ home.htm

Hanover Fly Fishers (an international guide service), Richmond, VA, 804-537-5036

Park Lake Lodge, Goose Bay, www.parklakelodge.com/contact .html

NORTHWEST TERRITORIES

Great Bear Lake

- **Location:** On the Arctic Circle
- **What You Fish For:** Lake trout and grayling
- **Highlights and Notables:** Hands down, the best combo lake in the world for lake trout and grayling

This is one of those fishing trips of a lifetime. World-record possibilities on your lure or fly every cast while around you, nothingness, the top of the world.

This is one of those trips you save up for, the trip that has the requisite exotic peoples, remote location, fly-in airstrips, lodges you share with anglers from around the world, shore lunches, the works.

Northwest of Great Slave Lake on the Arctic Circle sits Great Bear Lake, a virtual ocean of a lake, the best fishery in the world for lake trout and grayling, no contest. Whatever words the English language has for "big" are inadequate. Leviathan, behemoth, titan, giant, monster, gargantuan, huge, large, substantial, Herculean, great, whopper—nope, none of those effectively describe how "big" these fish are here. In fact, none of the English words I know for "big" describe how large Great Bear Lake looks or feels or fishes.

The lake is nearly 200 miles long. That's twenty miles longer than the three-hour drive from Houston to San Antonio. Great Bear Lake is the fourth largest lake in North America (only Huron, Superior, and Michigan are bigger). Great Bear Lake is the eighth largest lake in all the world, 12,000 square miles large (big? humongous? titanic?).

So what's the fuss all about? Great Bear Lake is where you go to catch the biggest lake trout in the world. Sixty-pound lake trout were caught several times each season for the last few seasons. Lake trout of 65 and 66 pounds have been caught since 1995. In 1995, the lake produced a 72-pound mack. In 2001, an angler landed a 74-pound laker. The year before, unofficially, in 2001, an angler caught a 78-pound laker. Fifty-pound lake trout are caught numerous times a season. Is there an 80-pound laker out there? No doubt about it.

Great Bear Lake is likely the finest grayling fishery in the world as well. Either in the lake or in the numerous tributaries, the grayling population is bountiful and beautiful and the biggest on earth. The heaviest grayling of all time came from these waters, 5 pounds and 15 ounces. The rivers that flow into the lake are loaded with grayling and at times, glorious times, you can catch them with dry flies. You can catch grayling with anything anytime all the time. Eighteen- to 21-inch grayling are fairly common. That's uncommon anywhere else, guys and gals. And too many people report catching 50, 100, even 150 grayling in a day—no lie.

The lake owns so many line records for its fish that I'm not sure if the records outnumber the annual total of anglers each year. There are so few anglers each year it's silly. Maybe 500 or 1,000 tops on a lake that is 200 miles long. Some water obviously never gets fished in a year. The lake holds more fish than the population of New York City but only sees the number of anglers of Groesbeck, Texas (salute).

Formed by glaciers, Great Bear Lake is located on the Arctic Circle so you can't forget that in the summer, the sun never goes down. Light leaks from the distant horizon 24/7. The lake is iced over from November to July, so the fishing season is short. Some say that since there is no development and the lake was never commercially fished, it's the most pristine big lake in the world or maybe it's the biggest pristine lake in the world, I don't know. The Taiga Plain surrounds Great Bear Lake, which means that when you are there, you believe the earth is flat. Whatever green you see is shrubbery (thank you, Monty Python) and a few trees.

Two other fish to think about while you're at Great Bear: northern pike and Arctic char. The pike are plentiful if not big. The Arctic char fishery is one of the tops on earth and the highlighted rivers include Tree and Coppermine, and the char get as big as 15 or more pounds.

Other things to think about: Bring warm clothes, several changes so you can layer. Those early morning boat rides are freezing and you never know when a quick storm will pop up while you're on the water. You stay in one of five lodges on the lake. They are comfortable and friendly and they take care of all your needs. First-class operation. Great shore lunches. The guides enforce catch-and-release fishing and use barbless hooks to protect this amazing fishery. Fly-outs available. Did I mention that there are no roads for hundreds of miles, that wolves are often seen around the lake, that you can also meet up with muskox, moose, grizzly bear, and caribou?

You have a fantastic chance of boating a 20-pound lake trout and a 30- to 50-pound laker is not out of the question. If you don't fly fish, you'll be trolling with plugs and spoons to catch them and you will. Early-season anglers love to entice lakers in the shallows to rise to surface lures and flies. You might catch the next world-record grayling. You will have the best fishing of your life.

CONTACTS

Plummer's Arctic Lodges, www
.plummerslodges.com

Tree River

- **Location:** Top of the world, the Arctic Circle
- **What You Fish For:** Arctic char
- **Highlights and Notables:** This is the river you come to so you can catch the world-record Arctic char.

The largest Arctic char ever caught and landed came out of the Tree River, a 32-pound monster. The only way to fish here is to be a guest at the Plummer's Lodge, 230 miles away, and you come for the night, stay, in rustic riverside tents, and baby, you are in the middle of nowhere, no cliché, no exaggeration. The Tree River runs fast and blue-green, cascading past hills on its way to the Arctic Ocean.

Each year, several anglers catch char 20 pounds and up, but the rapids make landing one of these beauties difficult. The Arctic char is one of the most colorful, beautiful fish in the world. The Nunavut Territory is where the Tree River empties, a land of another time, of muskox and caribou and bears, and especially of the native people of the Nunavut, the Inuit. And the Tree River is likely the best place in the world to angle for an Arctic char that you could call trophy size or world-record size.

CONTACTS

Plummer's Arctic Fishing Lodges
    (the only outfitter on the river),
    www.plummerslodges.com

Kasba Lake

In the "Land of the Midnight Sun" is a mini-Great Bear, specializing in huge lake trout and grayling. Blessed with hundreds of islands and reefs and thousands of miles of shoreline, it's an angling paradise. The lakers aren't world class but they range from 15 to 25 pounds and up to 40. Grayling grow big, to 3 and 4 pounds, and in great quantity, and live in the lake and in the many feeder rivers. You catch a lot of fish (including pike) and while you probably won't break a world record, you'll probably bust wide open your own records.

Mosquito and Dubawnt Lakes

You fly in to fish in the Barren Lands of the Northwest Territories, in the middle of pristine wilderness, in the middle of the tundra, in the middle of hundreds of clear unspoiled lakes and streams, some of which have never been fished before. You fish both lakes for humongous lake trout (numerous 40-pound lakers each year) and grayling. The two home base camps are Mosquito Lake Camp and Dubawnt Lake Camp.

Coppermine River

The Inuit word for this river means "place of rapids." *Kugluktuk.* What an amazing river. Rapids and falls. Water that is a weird color, milkily blue and yet cobalt blue. Bloody Falls. Arctic char. The Arctic char in Cop-permine don't get as big as those in Tree but they're plenty big enough. Seeing the Inuit village of Kugluktuk is worth the trip itself.

Great Slave Lake

- **Location:** Southern Northwest Territories
- **What You Fish For:** Pike, grayling, lake trout
- **Highlights and Notables:** Mecca for pike anglers

Few places on earth are as remote and wild as Great Slave Lake. This is a powerful land with a powerful pull, the result of the tension between starkness and beauty, the vastness and primitiveness. This is the Land of the Midnight Sun. Northwest Territories. One of the last true wild places on earth. Think caribou, muskoxen, Northern Lights, native Indian tribes, tundra—and also think big fish.

Pike, pike, pike. That's your mantra. This huge lake, the fifth largest in North America, may be the mecca for big pike hunters.

Don't overlook the grayling or the lake trout. Grayling average over 2 pounds and 4-pounder is not uncommon. Lake trout? Big. You fish long enough, you'll have caught twenty, thirty lake trout in the 10- to 20-pound range and you'll have a good chance at a whopper over 30 pounds. The rivers emptying into Great Slave Lake hold great numbers of grayling. Big grayling, as big as you'll find on the planet.

Think creek mouths. Grayling feed there and pike feed on grayling. Easy.

Great Slave Lake is massive, Canada's second largest lake, fifth largest in North America, stretching across 280 miles. This baby's deep, too (1,970 feet), one of the deepest lakes in the world (did I mention one of the biggest, too?). You'll probably stay in Yellowknife, a bigger town than you think but small enough that you don't lose that "I can't believe I'm really at the end of the world" feeling. And the people are some of the friendliest on earth.

I know grayling aren't big but I wouldn't bring a 3- or 4-weight unless I also brought a 5- or 6-weight. And for lakers and pike, fly rod outfits in the 8- to 10-weight class are ideal; heavy-action spinning rods with 15- to 20-pound test line. The weather can get crazy in a heartbeat, boat rides can take a lot longer than you think, so bring layers of weatherproof clothes.

CONTACTS
Bluefish Services, 867-873-4818
Barbara Ann Charters, www.fishingcharter
    .com/greatslavelake
Frontier Fishing Lodge, www
    .frontierfishing.com
NWT Arctic Tourism, 800-661-0788

ONTARIO

Lake Scugog

- **Location:** Southern Ontario
- **What You Fish For:** Muskie, walleye
- **Highlights and Notables:** One hour from Toronto, Scugog is a solid choice, a great day on the lake.

While Scugog is one helluva fishery, it's in the book mostly because it's just an hour drive from Toronto. Sure, the relatively shallow lake is good, sometimes great, for muskie and walleye but the combination of good-great and proximity to a major urban center is the kicker.

The lake is shallow, and it is surprising how many walleye are cruising the shallows, schooling and feeding in the flats, hanging off a hump (but it's not a deep hump). You ought to hire a guide and let them find these walleye and muskie for you; that way you can concentrate on—picture this now—reeling in a good-sized walleye and out of nowhere you see a green shadow and a swirl and slash and your walleye is cut in half. Muskie, big as a wolf. Average size 36 to 44 inches.

Scugog has such good forage, such good habitat and structure, so many walleye, it's no wonder the muskie population is amazing. Dark murky water, trees all around the lake, walleye everywhere but not big, perfect eating size. You look for the rippled surface of skittish baitfish and you have your walleye school. Spinnerbait, let it fall and bam, hookup.

Perch, pickerel, and largemouth bass complete this fishery. The bass do well in the weedy water and they average a couple of pounds—a big Scugog bass is 5 pounds. Perch are the winter prey, finning under the ice and shanty town.

Algonquin Provincial Park

Brook trout by the dozens, not Labrador size but you do see trophies 4 to 6 pounds caught in this labyrinth of lakes and rivers not far from either Detroit or Buffalo. Super place to spend time in a canoe, paddling around and catching squaretails.

Lake Simcoe

Clear water, rocky shores, shoals and reefs, and a great diet make this one of the top trophy smallmouth lakes in North America. Lots of 4- to 6-pound whoppers but you have to be cautious and slick to fool 'em in this clear of water.

Grand River

If you like tailwaters full of fat brown trout that feast on prolific hatches, this southern Ontario stream just might be your kind of river. The river wasn't always this fertile (maybe fertile in another way, since it got more than its fair share of human runoff, if you know what I mean). Today, it's probably the top brown trout tailwater river in eastern Canada.

QUEBEC

Gaspé Peninsula

- **Location:** Eastern Canada, between Ontario and Newfoundland (especially the Gaspé region)
- **What You Fish For:** Atlantic salmon
- **Highlights and Notables:** The combination of Quebec charm and ambiance with the top-quality angling for Atlantic salmon makes this one of the great fishing destinations in the world.

No place else, nowhere, has so many rivers with so many Atlantic salmon. This is truly the Atlantic salmon capital of the world. This part of Canada is a long way from anywhere (where isn't, in Canada?) and the Gaspé region, the finest of the salmon areas of Canada, is beautiful to boot, with its aqua-green clear rivers and rocky coasts and bucolic seaside villages. The food is rich, exquisite, inexpensive (remember, Quebec thinks it's still attached to France so the food is delicious).

Leaping robust salmon? *Oui.*

Thirty-pound salmon? *Oui.*

Forty-pound salmon? *Oui, oui.*

Fifty-pound salmon? Once in a lifetime.

I've never really liked or appreciated canoes. I fall out. I nearly make others fall out. They sit so low I feel like I'm underwater. Canoes are the transport of choice for many of the guides in Gaspé. Oh well.

The lodges and guides of the Gaspé Peninsula are all about the clients. They have this thing down. From the comfortable lodgings to the great food to their knowledge of the fish and rivers to their insistence on doing whatever it takes to make you happy— they want to make you happy with salmon although this water is perfectly good trout water. If you live in the Northeast, you can reach Gaspé Peninsula in several hours by car. If you live in the Northeast, you might fish these rivers enough that you don't feel you need a guide. If you are visiting, hire a guide; there is no other way to do it.

The Atlantic salmon. Gaspé Peninsula. Dry fly fishing. From wherever you are, you can have five to ten world-class rivers an hour's drive away.

The Atlantic salmon spawn and then return to the ocean, unlike their Pacific brethren. With these leapers, you need patience, lots of patience, sometimes a season's worth. And more patience. Sometimes, you find a pool, salmon splashing like little kids all around you and nothing you toss brings one to hand. And then you have one of those days—you wish you didn't—when you get spoiled and half your casts end up with a hookup. If you really want to be an Atlantic salmon purist, you shun those happy pools, those memorable days because you know that the way of the salmon angler is one of penance and self-mortification and denial.

So you cast and cast and cast and cast. You dead drift; twitch retrieve; hit the salmon on the nose. Nothing. You strip some more and he follows. Nothing.

Reposition, downstream, quarter swing, hit but patience, wait, wait, and then lift. Nothing. Some days, you raise them, you hook up, they leap and you lose them. Other days, you hook up and they race from your pool to another and it's over just like that. And even other days, you'll swear there is not a salmon in the pool. You are wrong, of course, but it hurts so good.

Labatt's Blue, one of the strangest-looking flies ever tied. When it works, it's the most beautiful ever tied. Atlantic salmon anglers don't go into a day expecting much. Fulfilled expectations. So much sight fishing, so few rewards. That's the beauty of the futility of this sport, this species. Bow to her majesty.

The Petite Cascapedia River is perhaps the signature river of the region. On the south coast of the Gaspé Peninsula, Petite Cascapedia is the big time Atlantic salmon river. What green water, like liquid emeralds! What icy cold water! What big Atlantic salmon! Pebbled bottom. Gravel bars. Deep pools. Mountains in the short background. Underrated for sea-run brook trout. Four fishing zones.

Some of the rivers (like the York) are a funky Kool-Aid electric blue color but still clear—almost New Zealand color and clarity.

Grande Cascapedia. You ought to see the size of the nets the guides use on this river. It's like being on safari to capture a gorilla and then seeing a cage large enough to hold King Kong. Frightening. More frightening is that they net salmon whose tail sticks out of these honkin' huge nets.

Great, they fish from canoes here. You switch out fishing and share a rod. Saves money. I like wading. And you can.

Grande Cascapedia is the salmon river for big salmon. It has good access, good numbers, and each year a handful of 50-pounders are caught. Boated or brought-to-hand 30- to 40-pounders are probably more numerous here than any other Gaspé Peninsula river.

The following Gaspé Peninsula rivers are standouts, outstandingly beautiful, profound salmon fisheries, a laundry list of heartaches and beautiful pools. Each has its own history, own personality, own challenges:

York River (spooky big salmon, unusually colored water, canoe heaven)
Dartmouth River (the falls are worth fishing here even if you catch something)
Forillon River
Grande River (if you read articles and books, you've read about this classic stream)
Malbaie River
Pabos River
Cap-Chat River (getting hung up salmon fishing is odd, but the banks are full of trees . . .)
Matapedia River (imagine pools that hold 100 to 200 salmon, some of them topping 40 pounds)
Nouvelle River (a river in restoration and coming along nicely)
Madeleine River (a real coastal river, unbelievable scenery)
Sainte-Anne River (the mountains descend upon this green dry fly river)
Bonaventure River (nearly 100 pools to fish in this heavily forested river)

By late July or August, the rivers are low and the fish are spooky. If you plan on using your two-handed spey rod on these small- to medium-sized rivers, you'd better do it in June when the water is high.

Gaspé rivers are divvied up into sectors or zones. Some sectors have limited rod access and some have unlimited rod access. This is all divined by a lottery whereby anglers apply for the sacred permits. Applicants must now be present to win, no more flooding the lottery by the outfitters. If you win (yippee), you can have two rods for two or more days—a rod for you and a rod for a buddy. The ZEC is the river management authority that runs this show. But the outfitters still get rods on the water—they have ten guaranteed daily rods for various rivers. There's more to this shell game but if you want to fish, hire a guide and he or she will get on the river somewhere.

CONTACTS

Malbaie River Outfitters, 603-472-4043 (Oct. to May), 418-645-3965 (June to Sept.) www.malbaieriveroutfitters.com
Camp Bonaventure Sporting Lodge, 418-534-3678, www.campbonaventure.com

Gaspé Salmon Destinations, 418-534-3678, www.gaspesalmon.com

Ann Smith, Quebec Sporting, 866-747-5511, www.quebecsporting.com

Gaspé Salmon Destinations, 418-392-4575, www.gaspesalmon.com

Gouin Reservoir

- **Location:** South central Quebec
- **What You Fish For:** Walleye
- **Highlights and Notables:** Whopper of a walleye lake

I didn't grow up fishing for walleye (Texas doesn't have many walleye haunts) and even though I've jigged next to rocky shores for them and cast crankbaits and spoons and spinners to them, I'm positive that I'll never catch walleye fever like those who grew up fishing for and eating walleye.

On the shield lakes located in south central Quebec, Gouin Reservoir will satiate any walleyed wonders' thirstiest imagination. This lake is enormous and made more so by the navigational nightmares of hundreds of islands, peninsulas, bays, and fingers; 3,000 miles of shoreline. Sixty by forty miles big. Sizeable walleye, 1 to 6 pounds, you'll catch by the dozens. Ten-pound walleye have been caught in this "gi-normous" lake. Where there's walleye, there's usually pike and Gouin is no exception. Not trophies but 10- to 20-pounders. You can fly in by float plane or haul your boat over questionable roads. Eat some walleye for me.

Gaspé isn't the only region in Quebec where one can angle for salmon. Other quality rivers include: St. Jean North Shore, Escoumins, Moisie, Aux Roches, Godbout, Trinite, Kedgwick, Sainte-Marguerite.

The St. Lawrence, big and bold, is a worthy fishery if you like big fish, big shipping boats, and hefty rivers. How hefty? Try an average width of two miles and max depth of more than 200 feet deep. The river begins at the northeastern end of Lake Ontario and then flows 700 miles to the Atlantic Ocean. St. Lawrence River drains over 30,000 square miles of the Great Lakes Basin.

This border river between the United States and Canada has a great variety of game fish—muskie and smallmouth and walleye are top dawgs but you can also catch pike, perch, bullhead, largemouth bass, and all sorts of panfish.

SASKATCHEWAN

Lake Athabasca

- **Location:** Northwest Saskatchewan bleeding into Alberta
- **What You Fish For:** Lake trout, walleye, grayling, pike
- **Highlights and Notables:** One of the best all-around lakes in the world, in the top five for four species

The vast lake has been among the most productive, best all-around lakes in the world for years and years and it's just now getting its due. Lake Athabasca is so big, it acts more like a sea than a lake. Athabasca is the ninth largest lake in North America, the fourth largest in Canada (entirely in the country's borders), the nineteenth biggest lake in the world. The massive lake covers 3,064 square miles. Never heard of it, have you?

A 102-pound lake trout. Can you even imagine a laker that big? This lake has produced one (albeit a commercially caught one). The lake record for a lake trout on rod and reel is still a whopping 58 pounds. Locals will tell you that several 50-pound lake trout are caught every year (and Athabasca's lakers are beautifully colored—where most lake trout are color-free, these are mustard and coppery). Lakers that weigh 20 to 30 pounds are common and this isn't hype. In the shallows. For rizzle.

All-around lake, remember? Great walleye fishing, tremendous grayling population, and the lake probably holds world-record-size grayling if anyone really went after them instead of going after lakers, walleye, and pike. Pike. In the bays, in the shallows, ahhh the pike.

Trophy size pike. Pike 15 to 30 pounds with 40-pounders spotted swimming the shallows like subs. Fifty-inch pike and longer. Twenty-pound pike are caught with amazing regularity. These pike have strong backs with mottled big backs and orangey fins. Guides will put you on these leviathans with orange Mepps with a soft plastic trailer using a stop-and-go retrieve, making long casts in the shallows.

Around this Saskatchewan lake (two thirds in here, one third in Alberta), in the middle of the summer, everything is green. In the next outer ring lie the rolling lowlands, the baby hills. This is wilderness, nonpolluted land, a complex ecology. In Athabasca, all fish grow quickly with so much to eat, so many places to take cover, the abundance of structure. Still, the water quality is the key. Fertile. Double hookups are common, I mean really common, especially for the green-gold walleye.

Rocky treeline shores, reefs and islands, water clear but tinged brown-green. Good weeds and inflowing streams. Sandy beaches and sand dunes. Sand dunes? Yep. This is unique wild scenic country where your fishing guides, usually Indian guides, make memorable shore lunches, fried walleye and fried potatoes and corn. Mmm good.

So what keeps anglers from flocking to Athabasca? Hard to say but these factors certainly play a part. The lake has commercial fishing for walleye so that taints the perception of wildness. In fact, that the walleye fishing is still so good for the sportsman is a tribute to how profound the walleye population actually is.

Weather and wind can whip havoc on Athabasca in the same way it does on one of the Great Lakes. Not that many lodges and outfitters and guides, given the lake's productivity. The sand dunes are the largest active sand dunes in Canada and lie on the southern end (they are one reason the southern end is shallow and not as fishy.) The lake's regs include catch-and-release only (except for shore lunches) and barbless hooks. You need titanium leaders for pike.

Lake Athabasca is undersung and underpriced. Be among those who see this lake for what it is before everybody else does.

CONTACTS

Lakers Unlimited, www.lakersunlimited
.com

Tourism Saskatchewan, www.sasktourism
.com

Milton Lake

- **Location:** Milton Lake Lodge is situated on the north shore of the lake, 40 miles south of the Northwest Territories border, in far northeastern Saskatchewan
- **What You Fish For:** Lake trout, Arctic grayling, northern pike
- **Highlights and Notables:** Each of the species is first-class quality, living in virgin waters that see low fishing pressure.

Milton Lake is just another remote world-class pike-laker-grayling Canadian lake, the kind that you save and plan for and then find yourself going back to, over and over. One cool thing about Milton is that you can catch all these species within minutes of the lodge. You don't have to take long boat rides just to get to the good spots. You can cast out from the rocky shore in front of the lodge and catch trophy fish.

Another bonus is that the Porcupine River and East Porcupine River are close to the lodge, and both are excellent choices to break away for a day of fly fishing for grayling. Milton enjoys sheltered bays and islands, ideal hiding spots for pike. The lake trout spawn fishing in mid-September is as good lake fishing as you can find anywhere. Huge lakers on the move, in the shallows, sightfishing. Your nerves will be rocked.

CONTACTS

Scott Swanson and FishQuest (Silsby Lake, Manitoba—Milton Lake, Saskatchewan), www.FishQuest.com

Selwyn Lake

- **Location:** Northern Saskatchewan
- **What You Fish For:** Lake trout, pike
- **Highlights and Notables:** Consistent catches of big mack and heart-stopping casting to shallow-drafting northern pike make Selwyn Lake a real angler's delight.

Shallow water trophy pike. Accessible only by float plane. Seldom fished. The best shore lunches in Canada. One of the finest catch-and-release fisheries in the world.

Stalking 20-pound pike in clear shallow water is anticipatory, heart-racing, thrilling. You, on the 18-foot Lund boat, cast nervously to lead the skulking predator. Canadian bonefishing.

Pike are only the secondary target for visiting anglers in these remote waters. Lake trout are the true quarry, the fish that put and keep Selwyn Lake on the map ('cause it's so far north, it's almost off the map). Lake trout record for Selwyn, a robust 56 pounds. Each year, 40-pound mack are caught. A 20-pound laker is a more realistic goal and that's a horse.

The common report for Selwyn anglers is that they caught about fifteen to thirty-five fish a day. They caught and released at least one fish 15 to 20 pounds. They had a blast catching 3- to 4-pound grayling while a delicious shore lunch was being prepared. And they've already booked for next year.

Selwyn Lake is forty-five miles long, eighteen miles wide, with 135,000 acres to boat and fish. The lake is shallow (hence the pike) and it is deep (up to 300 feet deep, so lakers have their habitat covered) and has multiple tributaries (the living quarters for the 3- to 4-pound grayling that most anglers overlook). Islands by the dozens are scattered around the big lake. Dangerous reefs lurk under the blue rippling surface. The lake is ringed by thick forest.

Anglers who haven't caught huge pike in shallow water before are in for a life-changing experience. The anxiety of first spotting the hulking cruiser, then making a worthy cast in front of the bruiser, then the moment right before the take when the white of the mouth is the only color you see, then it no longer matters because it's a blur of color and action and splashing water and survival. The lake produces lots of 41-inch-long pike and they're caught with spoons, spinners, poppers, and streamers. Pike 10 to 25 pounds are common everyday occurrences.

The lake is open from June through September. Bring warm clothes and mosquito repellant because you're gonna need 'em. Arrive from Saskatoon via Stony Rapids to Selwyn Lake Lodge, the only full-scale operation on the lake.

CONTACTS

Selwyn Lake Lodge, www.selwynlakelodge .com

Wollaston Lake

- **Location:** Northeastern Saskatchewan
- **What You Fish For:** Northern pike
- **Highlights and Notables:** Giant northern pike that can eat you

Lost on Wollaston Lake is coming to a theatre near you. In the leading role, husky, heavy Northern Pike paces this action-packed movie with his daring moves and physical presence. This water-wolf plays a master assassin, an ambusher lying in wait to viciously attack any intruders. Supporting roles in this underwater adventure drew some of the finest names in show biz. Costars in this thriller include Wall Eye, Mack N. Awe, and Gray Ling.

Wollaston is the third largest lake in Canada, a star in its own right, famous for the giant northern pike that swim in its bays and skinny backwater. Locals like

to fish for these jackfish right after ice-out when they move into the shallows. Many consider Wollaston to be one of the top northern pike lakes anywhere and with good reason—each year, fishermen catch over a thousand pike that measure three and a half feet or longer. Ten-pound pike, commonplace.

Big lake, big fish. Over 2,700 miles of shoreline, nearly 400 islands. Remote as any lake but accessible by way of a long, lonely road hours from anywhere. Only a handful of lodges operate on the lake. Fly-in, fly-out trips available.

You'll catch pike even if you are an incompetent nincompoop, and if you fish for walleye, you'll catch walleye hand over fist. They are not typically large but they are numerous, thriving in these cold, clear blue waters. Lake trout are plentiful, too, large but not trophy-sized. As an afterthought, 2- to 4-pound grayling are in inlet rivers but more so in nearby rivers by way of fly-out trips. One thing about Wollaston that brings anglers from far and wide is that they always get nonstop action for four quality game fish. Oh, that and the 40-inch and bigger northern pike. Drive from Regina on a long, lonely road, gravel Highway 905. Fly from Saskatoon to the lodges by charter plane. There are two lodges on the lake, Wollaston Lake Lodge and Minor Bay Lodge.

Mexico

There is something haunting and mystical about these Mexican backcountry lakes.

Kenny and I finished up a three-day trip on the Cimarron in northern New Mexico. Wet, tired, satisfied with catching 11-inch browns on dry flies from morning 'til dusk, we grabbed a bite at the Creamee, the usual big greasy burger and a shake. We sat at a booth, red vinyl with tears and stains. This was the day we had met up with the crazy angler and his dog from hell. We gassed the Troutmobile as the sun set.

We drove out of town. I don't believe in ghosts and I need to make that perfectly clear. As we drove out this New Mexican

dusty mountain town, something caught our attention on the south side of the highway. Something jade. Lighted.

Floating.

We drove past it, jerked our heads to look at each other and each of us had dropped open our mouth, our eyes wide open like a Munch painting, like Wile E. Coyote in midair before he plummets to the ground. I braked, stopped the car, slowly reversed until we were in front of an abandoned gas station. Dirty white adobe filling station. Pumps removed. A beautiful Mexican teenager in a diaphanous white prom dress floating in the doorway, surrounded by a green fuzzy light.

Did I mention that I don't believe in ghosts?

Neither of us spoke a word. I could hear heavy breathing and I wasn't sure if it were mine or Kenny's.

Kenny and I slightly alter our story every time we tell about our encounter after this point. But we do agree on all the facts up to when we got out of the truck. Through oral tradition, mostly around campfires with a captive audience, we have come to name this dark-skinned beauty with the emerald aura, Our Lady Guadalupe of the Gas Pump.

Kenny opened his door first and rushed toward the mystery. You would expect this from this thick-maned high school teacher. He has no fear. He did this once when a 500-pound black bear crossed the road high along Henson Creek in southwestern Colorado. He chased the bear. He ain't smart.

I followed (and I mean followed). I have fears. I don't chase bears. Or ethereal beings floating in doorways of abandoned gas stations. *Fantasmas.*

She was beautiful. Seventeen, maybe. Kenny said it looked to him like she was wearing a prom dress. I always say that to me, it looked more like a wedding dress, more angel than demon. She wore no veil. The young lade wore no smile. Her big black eyes were sad. *Triste.*

Kenny says that we walked right up to the doorway and she disappeared. The big lug might really believe that, too, but that's not what we did. We inched toward the Lady Guadalupe, our feet shuffling in the red dirt, like a bad Scooby-Doo cartoon, me peeking out around his big shoulders. I kept my eyes from catching her distant stare, not believing that she was even real but not wanting to take any chances either. I've read about Medusa and other evil spirit women who can control men with their eyes. Dated one once, too.

As we neared, the Lady shifted, turned toward us. Kenny swears he never noticed but he has tunnel vision. My heart jumped. Then she vanished.

My high school students are incredulous that despite seeing this hovering haunt, I have not come around to believing in human spirits caught in the nexus. They point out that since Kenny and I surveilled the building inside and out, looked for a projector in the fields around the gas station (thinking we might be punked) and came up empty, there is no other explanation than to believe it was a ghost. Not all is what it seems, I tell them. The world was flat once, remember?

The students conjecture that the Lady Guadalupe of the Gas Pump was killed horrifically by a jaded lover or struck down by a passing car or some-such type of un-doing. I can compartmentalize with the best of them, so my wife and family tell me. I can forget ugly things I said, danger-ous things I tried, unfriendly people I met, my first marriage, entire college semesters. I don't try to rationalize these events. In-stead, I just forget them. It's a gift.

I can also lock away in some closet in my brain the image of a seventeen-year-old girl floating on air. *Verde*. Out of sight, out of mind.

This is the foundation for my constant sightings of witchy women. They manifest around the world, not at every fishing stop but enough that they keep me on my toes. I find I do look for them but even when I don't, they find me.

Most every society has such dramatic creatures in their folklore, the Lilith myth. These women are seductresses, often winged, taunting, destructive. It's an out-dated primitive legend to be sure, this idea of a succubus. More peculiar to Mexican folklore is that of the haunting mother.

La Llorona is one of those haunted mothers, a woman who, in her grief over be-ing jilted by her husband, killed her children and herself, all drowned in the river. My class googled La Llorona one slow afternoon and the second site we pulled up stopped me in my tracks. The kids say I turned white (I'm normally olive). On the screen was a picture of the Cimarron River and La Lloro-na's story. Here's the site so you can see for yourself: www.legendsofamerica.com/HC-WeepingWoman1.html.

I am not a folklorist or anthropologist or any other kind of person who studies peoples or cultures or civilizations. I have a passing interest in this stuff and have al-ways regarded malevolent spirits as ways to control the kids or ignorant populations, as in "Don't do this or the boogeyman will get you." La Llorona didn't seem far off from the Lady with the Serpent, a goddess from Mexican mythology who speaks with snakes and has twin sons who fight a lot.

■ ■ ■

Kenny and I have never lied to each other about how many fish we catch or how long or big or tiny the fish were. Some of this honesty is that we so often fish together and have for closing in on twenty years now, some of it is that we know the other angler so well, his skills and weaknesses, and also because catching a small fish or falling in the water or breaking a rod is funny and real.

This particular myth came from a trip out of Amarillo zigzagging to northern New Mexico and later southern Colorado by way of Clayton, New Mexico. After fishing at the Dry Cimarron in the morning, the Cimarron in the afternoon, we camped for one night at Clayton Lake, not far from the preserved dinosaur footprints the lake is famous for.

On these five-to-ten outings, we might bathe once or twice but we do brush our teeth twice a day and we sometimes remember to splash water on our faces. We drove to the public restrooms that next morning needing to brush teeth and splash water, still in need of coffee and breakfast.

She wore a pink bra and Daisy Dukes, the faded jeans kind that Pamela Anderson made famous when she was still just a Labatt's girl. She was twenty, tops, with long tanned legs, a flat stomach and wild, blonde hair, the kind you'd find on a hard rock band groupie. She was bent over drying her hair with a towel, and even bent over, her stomach was flatter than West Texas. When we pulled up, she unceremoniously lifted up, stopped drying, flashed a big white smile at us, the kind girls who've had a few beers at a dancehall do when they want you to ask them to dance. Neither of us said anything but I know I put on my best "I've still got it" face. I didn't know if I still had it, but I was quite sure she did.

Kenny and I married sisters, Betsy and Amy, two beautiful German-American girls from Amarillo, Texas. They are pretty and funny and we lugs couldn't have done any better, trust me. We married up. We've never strayed and never would. They've been married over twenty-five years, we've been married seventeen. So there, that's out of the way.

But this pink bra–wearing tanned goddess was ten feet in front of us, we two thirty-somethings, flashing her smile, among other things. Medusa all over again.

Embarrassed, perhaps at the forcefulness of her stare or the fact we stared instead of turning our heads, we puffed out our chests and got out of the Troutmobile. We both muffled our greetings, the words coming out a dead language cross between "hiya doin" and "good morning" so we ducked our heads and walked quickly toward the men's room.

"Hey right back at ya." We stopped in our tracks. We did not look at Circe, frozen by her song. "You boys fishin' or what?"

We still get goofy little smiles when we talk about this story, especially when we get to this part. We always spin this yarn in the car after disposing of the requisite two hours of river talk or around the campfire with fishing buddies. But never in front of the wives. We didn't do anything wrong but our smiles would say what we were thinking at the time (and now, come to think of it).

We didn't reply to the witchy woman. She wasn't wearing a shirt, she was tanned and flawless, she was young, and she was actually talking directly to us. We just nodded, tucked our chins and went into the bathroom, breathless. We giggled like schoolboys disbelieving that on a grubby, grimy fishing trip we should run across a babe in the woods. We splashed water on our faces, more to take the shock off than to get clean, tugged down our caps and conspiratorially, we exited excitedly to go back to the car and perhaps, this time, respond.

She was gone, of course.

This is the kind of story you tell your fishing buddies. They get to advise how they would have handled it, play killjoys by telling us we're so ugly she was just being nice, kid us about how silly we acted and so on. It's great campfire fodder. But we know that they are vicariously there with us. Their goofy smiles give them away.

She became known as Coyote Girl.

Baja California

- **Location:** Western Mexico, peninsula on the Gulf of California
- **What You Fish For:** Black, blue, and striped marlin, sailfish, roosterfish, wahoo, mahi-mahi, and yellowfin tuna
- **Highlights and Notables:** Easy to reach from North America, lots of flights, inexpensive, beautiful, diverse species

Occasionally, I'll admit, I like the lodge or resort scene. Everything in the room is expensive and fits in some sort of classy theme and the sheets are Egyptian with lots of thread count. The lodge has a gourmet chef who whips up delicious five-course meals. And the bar is fancy and shiny with no barflies or shady ladies or salty old fishing bums.

But I'm a spartan angler. I like a clean comfortable room I didn't have to pay much for, in fact, I like it where I can feel like I got a bargain. If I can share it with a fishing buddy (and split the cost) and have him keep his crap on his side of the room and not snore too loudly and not complain when I keep my flashlight on to read at night, then so much the better. I just want to be near the water and fish all day. I don't really ever take advantage of the lodge or resort—I don't read in the sitting room (or sit in the reading room); I don't lounge by the pool, I don't really stop to admire the fishing antiques or cherry-wood furniture.

Baja California is a fishing hole, a big fishing hole, where you can easily find a bar complete with barflies and shady ladies and salty old fishing bums. Sometimes, you need that to feel like you're on a fishing adventure. You need to drink a cold beer instead of sipping a single-malt Scotch. You need a cheap cigar instead of a Cuban. You need a hard day of fishing where you're plain worn out but not ready to quit talking about it. You sometimes want a relaxed, naughtier, edgier pace, not that artificial kind you sometimes get at a secluded lodge where you are spoiled but that kind you get when you wonder if you might get in a fight at the bar (and you're glad you have big fishing buddies like Kenny and Mac). Baja can give this fishing spirit to you and then some. Sure, you can find your rich-boy lodges on Baja and they're great and all, but—well, either you know what I mean or you don't.

On the cape of Baja California, you get the Sea of Cortez and the Pacific Coast. On either side, you can find some of the best fishing in the world. Depending on where you are, you can strain your back reeling in black, blue, and striped marlin, sailfish, the strangely combed roosterfish, wahoo, mahi-mahi, and yellowfin tuna. And that's just the tip of the cape for what all you can catch.

The beach fishing is infinitely more interesting than offshore; you have so many choices and you can run up and down the beach to different habitat, different species.

Marinas open up, charter boats emerge overnight, every sleepy little fishing village eventually becomes a new home base on Baja. Southern Baja (Loreto, Cabo San Lucas) has been written about for years and deservedly so. The end of Baja has unusual access to both sides. But northern Baja has better than respectable fishing. Ensenada, La Salina, San Felipe are excellent bases for this part of Baja so you can fish from the rocky shores for rockfish, barracuda, and bonito, or go into the blue and catch tuna, marlin, mahi-mahi and yellowfin tuna.

Still, southern Baja is where most of the action takes place. The East Cape is the crown jewel. Anglers love southern Baja largely because there is year-round fishing with several species always "hot." Comparatively inexpensive, close, easy, plenty of cold cerveza, this is angler's paradise. Not heavily developed with resorts (although the high-rise hotels, condos, and tourist traps of Cabo and La Paz are disconcerting and annoying—even Loreto is growing, you can tell) but the fishing infrastructure is well established. I know I'm not a Cabo San Lucas fan (for all the wrong reasons) but it's a world-class. Ditto Loreto. Magdalena, Las Arenas, and La Paz are three more hot headquarters but you can also fish out of San Juan de la Costa, Punta Chivato, Bahia Concepcion, Bahia San Nicolas, Bahia Agua, and others. You can select between luxury lodges and beach camps and everything in between. You can even drink the water. It's safe.

Pez vela = sailfish
Dorado = dolphin
Pez gallo = roosterfish

Those are a few of my fun fish. Sails are fun but it does get a little boring at times especially if you're bringing up quite a few or if the mahi are too plentiful or if you aren't raising any sails at all. Dorado (mahi, dolphin) are fun but they get pesky after awhile unless you aren't catching many but the ones you catch are 30 pounds and up. Roosterfish, well, they don't bore anybody one little bit. In some places on Baja, you can cast for roosterfish from the shore and while wading.

Baja's beaches are the big sell. They give you variety of fish but you are also challenged. You work for your catches. Light tackle anglers have found these beaches and inshore options, and they are starting to outnumber those who troll offshore for bigger prey. They even scoot up and down beaches, all of which are public in Mexico, on ATVs nowadays, able to keep a low profile, able to find cruising roosters and dancing jacks, able to move from place to place without wearing themselves out in the hot sand. Some paddle kayaks, some hire guides and fish from pangas. It's all good.

What else can you catch on the beach other than 50-pound roosterfish? Pargo are an underrated game fish—if you ever hook one you'll know it because they shoot off and break off on the rocks. If you lose one, must've been a pargo. Or it could actually be a Sierra mackerel whose teeth cut you off before it can even get to the rocks. Heck, you've got ladyfish, cabrilla, skipjack, pompano, triggerfish, corvina, and so many more aquarium fish, you'll have a ball wondering "what the heck is that?"

Magdalena Bay

Mag Bay is pretty special. One hundred or more miles along the Pacific Coast of Baja where you fish for snook snook snook from pangas in the estuary coves all around the bay (because mangrove trees cover the shoreline). The bay itself is covered in mangrove trees. Corvina and leopard grouper jump out at your Clousers in the little hidden *esteros* as well. Pompano, too.

Where the Pacific kisses the bay, you can also fish for barracuda, amberjack, pargo, yellowtail, cabrilla, and more—you never know what's at the end of your line. Further out in the blue, you can take tuna, marlin, wahoo, and mahi. Sometimes you get big pounding surf but Mag Bay is so fertile and productive, it's worth the few days you have to sit in the bar with some buddies and shady ladies.

CONTACTS

Baja on the Fly, www.bajaonthefly.com, www.bajafly.com

Fishing International, www.fishinginternational.com

Fishabout, 408-356-5899, www.fishabout.com

Ricardo's Fleet, 011 52 613 135 0025

Jose Torres Fishing Charters, www.fishloreto.com

Loreto Bait Cooperative, www.bajabait.com

La Paz Sportfishing, lapazsportfishing.com/index.html

Baja Big Fish Company, www.bajabigfish.com

Baja Anglers, www.baja-angelrs.com/Fishing/index.html

Cortez Yacht Charters, 619-469-4255, www.cortezcharters.com

Minerva's Baja Tackle, www.minervas.com 011 52 624 143 1282

Bass Lakes of Mexico

La Llorona. La Lechusa. La Bruja.

The first time I heard about fishing for bass in Mexico was sometime in the late 1970s when Papaw and his friends loaded up a trailer with fishing gear and drove eight or ten hours from Dallas and got stopped at the border, turned away. I don't remember what it was that forced their quick return to Dallas, their failure to reach Lake Guerrero, then the hot lake, but Papaw never really came clean about it.

That made me want more than anything in the world to go fish bass lakes in Mexico.

A few things to remember when you visit Mexico on a fishing trip:

> The folks speak Spanish. Most of these lakes are in remote areas where very few speak English, not even that many of the fishing guides speak more than a few phrases of English. That said, they do speak fishing but it wouldn't hurt if you'd take the time to bone up on your high school Spanish you have since forgotten. Remember to pack a fleece or sweater and rain gear. In the mountains,

it's cold, wet, and hot, sometimes all in the same day. The lodges at the bass lakes offer packages of all kinds, especially in conjunction with bird hunting. The lodges range from simple fishing huts to luxury lodges. Not all lodging has air conditioning, though that seems to be changing more and more.

The meals are typically good to great, service that used to be spotty has gotten better to serve the American sensibility. More and more, the state and local concerns have realized the value of what the bass fishery does for their economy. Changes in behavior, regulations, and attitudes toward this resource continue to make the bass fishing better now and better for the future.

You are in the middle of nowhere so bring what you need. There are no 7-11s out there. And you won't find much else at these lodges for recreation but fishing and hunting.

You need proof of citizenship, a valid passport or birth certificate, and valid photo identification.

Most of the bass lakes are best fished September to May more or less.

Lake Huites

High in the Sierra Madre Range (in the Sierra Madre Occidentals, which means western), this is Mexico's most scenic lake, just down the road from the incredible Copper Canyon. The blue lake is nestled green-brown spasmodic mountains,

hewn rough as my Granddaddy Williams's gnarled brown welder hands. When the water levels are up, which in recent times has not been the case, Huites is as good a bass lake as El Salto or any other.

Lake Huites is a mountain bass lake that at one time, not that long ago, was considered the best in the world. You say the name with a near-silent puff of breath on the first syllable: Wee-tayz.

The lake saw the typical Mexican lake cycle. Nothing here in the middle of nowhere at first but a lake, fast-growing fish, and some adventurous anglers. Then come the lodges, resorts, camps, stores, shops, and guides servicing the lake (although I want to emphasize that there are some enterprising, caring guides and lodge owners who have been there at some of these lakes from the start and care greatly about their fishery). The locals find that they have a bounteous treasure in their own Sierra Madres and they net the fish, and wouldn't you? Then come the 100-fish days, the record-breaking bass rumors and legends, and most of it is true. Then you have degradation in some form or another; in this case, water drawdown and gill nets. The powers-that-be are working to fix both problems.

Huites has amazing structure, great fertility, stupendous growth rates, 10-pounders on topwater lures. Anglers have a chance at a world-record bass and fifty-fish day. The average bass is 2 to 3 pounds. The bass fatten up on shad and tilapia.

You fatten up your soul catching black bass of size that in the soft gray mountain mornings explode from around submerged trees to thrash at your poppers, buzzbaits, and other surface lures. During the infernal heat of the day, you fish hard and you fish deep to humps and coves and brushpiles, to schools of big bass and you catch big bass until your arm tires out, or siesta, whichever comes first.

The lake record is 15 pounds and 11 ounces as of this writing and every day, lots of 6- to 12-pounders are caught and released. The best thing about Lake Huites bass is that whether you fish topwater or love crankbaits or spinnerbaits or even worm fishing, you can catch more bass than you dreamed.

Located on Mexico's West Coast, outside the city of Los Mochis, in the state of Sinaloa in northwestern Mexico sits Lake Huites. She is 600 feet deep, 30,000 acres when at full pool. Twenty-one miles long and on the mountain sides, boulders as big as Mayan temples sit and watch you fish. The river that Huites impounded is the Fuerte which in Spanish means strong or strength.

Aesthetics and wildness and silence and solitude. Those are the virtues of Lake Huites. That and the big bass, of course. The local villages are dusty and worn, teeming with folks who live in a different century. The trees and brush and mountains and the submerged buildings of flooded towns are monuments to a different time. You might see cows on the banks, donkeys on the road, eagles in the air.

At Guerrero, where I finally got to visit after Papaw didn't, after his tantalizing secret about why he and the guys never made it to this then–bass fishing heaven, Kenny and I caught a few small bass and went back home. The lake at that time was in its throes of disintegration, years before things started to turn around.

We sat in the heat on a boat not catching fish and we were miserable. In the air flew a bird the size of a small child, an eagle, and it circled effortlessly high above us. We looked at each other and back up to the eagle and again, a transfigured spirit above us, taunting us, no fish, no fish, no fish, the wind whispered.

■ ■ ■

A fishing trip legend among my friends is Coyote Girl. She does exist. She was not a ghost. Not at first anyway. We created her. Myth-makers that we are.

On long fishing trips, as we sit in the car eating up the last of the Tom's Pecan Pies, we run out of things to talk about. We would have already dissected the river we're heading to, the hatches, the possibilities of big fish, of wild trout, of changing jobs.

Later, around the campfire, we'll go much deeper, sometimes with the influence of a beer or two, and talk about our best ex-girlfriends, our best near-death-while-driving story and so on. But in the tenth hour of a fishing trip in an SUV filled with smelly fishing gear, having listened to five repeats of the one cassette tape left in the player (we forgot to bring our cassette holders with our Willie Nelson so it's usually Phil Collins, or Seals and Croft, or Dan Fogelberg, and one can only listen to "In the Air Tonight," "Summer Breeze," or "Wisteria" so many times), it's time to invent.

Myth-making.

This is a common practice among anglers. The fish that got away. A magic lure or fly. The 100-fish day. A 20-pound fish on 2-pound leader. That sort of thing. Coyote Girl was the eagle at Huites or maybe the doe-eyed vixen in the dusty village. It's gotten difficult to tell anymore.

Lake Guerrero

Growing up *bebe*.

In the 1970s, Lake Guerrero became the world-rumored best bass lake on earth. You never really knew anybody who went down there and had 100-bass days and several 10-pounders. You never really knew anybody who did these incredible things but your father's friend knew somebody or you read about it in a magazine. Catching 100 big bass a day was all true but we didn't have Internet and online postings and online photos and not as many people traveled out of the country just to fish, so it sure sounded like a dreamy otherworld, that if true wasn't some place I'd ever go and if I did, all the fish would be caught and I'd have none left for me.

Turns out, I was kinda right. Commercial angling and poor harvest practices and poaching and degradation of the water and so on and so on added up to more than the lake could take to maintain its world-class status. Located in northern Mexico, in the state of Tamaulipas, northeast of Ciudad Victoria, Lake Guerrero has come back to life. Guerrero will probably never be back as the *It* girl but it is back to being a good

bass lake, one of the better 100 in the world, a mature, user-friendly lake.

You still have majestic scenery. Better regulations and enforcement (bag limits) are in place now. Catch-and-release is a more typical practice now. Heck, from McAllen, Harlingen, and Brownsville, we're talking just 150 to 200 miles, and it's still worth that kind of drive. You still have what made it a top-five lake—submerged timber, rocky points, clear water, islands, thick vegetation on the banks, great topwater action in spring and fall, year-round fishing, lodging ranging from utilitarian to deluxe including one lodge especially for fly fishers, Hacienda Las Palmas.

You can still bump the stumps for ornery largemouth bass. The lodges are still making ice-cold Margaritas and serving hand-cramping cold *cervezas*. In recent years, catches of 13- to 16-pound largemouth have been reported. The lake's water level is up twenty feet or more. Your average bass will go about 1 to 4 pounds but anglers report many days with thirty, forty, and fifty in a day and after all, you'll be catching them in another world, *los pescados grandes*.

Baccarac Reservoir

The likelihood is that Baccarac has jumped the shark. This is one of the older Mexico bass lakes, famous in its day but now tired. One year, the veterans mumble, they caught 200 8-pound bass. It's tough getting old.

In 1994, the lake produced two 19-pounders, surprising because even then the lake was in decline. I fished a few years after those two were caught and I could have done better on Greenbelt Lake in the Panhandle (that's not a compliment). The lake holds the Mexican record with a bass that came in at 19 pounds, 2 ounces. Murky reports claim bass weighing 24 pounds were once caught at Baccarac.

Baccarac is a beautiful lake, dotted with hundreds of islands, cradled in forested mountains, twenty-five miles long and five miles wide. It is cool on the terrace over coffee, cooler on the boat ride in the morning but hot as hell during the day.

The lake is not dead by any means. Nor has it miraculously reemerged as some of the guides on the lake would have you believe. I figure somewhere in between is the truth. An 18-pound bass was caught in 2005 so there is life in this aging star yet. From time to time, anglers catch hawgs but they don't catch 100 a day any more. And as good as Baccarac once was, as loaded with habitat as it still is, you just get the feeling that maybe, somehow, some way, the lake might cycle its way back to being worth a fishing trip. Wishful thinking maybe. But the big bass being caught every now and again give us hope.

Lake El Salto

Unbreakable. The land looks unbreakable. Tough wooded mountains, craggy peaks in the distance, undulating green bumpy hills that look like rock-creatures taking a nap. Sinewy trees cover mountains, trees that look like tall mesquite and giant huisache. The land looks built to last.

Tops of trees stick out like watery monster fingers. Floating grass mats look like tiny green islands. In the early morning when all is pewter, the water reflects the day to come like a magic mirror. The day bodes well.

Lake El Salto is easily the best bass lake in Mexico and ranks right up there with any other bass lake in the world. Let's look at why El Salto is held in such high regard.

Prime habitat. Submerged timber and brush, lots of points and ledges and edges, bumps and humps, plenty of wide flats, coves, steep bluffs, fertile water—a little bit of everything. This is the lake you'd draw up on the blueprints of your perfect bass lake. El Salto is loaded with forage fish for bass food. So we have a habitat-plus-forage base and let's toss in Florida-strain largemouth.

The bass. They are numerous. They are huge. They are numerously huge, if that makes sense. The El Salto bassin' fool can honestly expect to have the best bass-fishing day of his or her life. No hype. The average bass is 4 pounds. Let that sink in. Four pounds of silver-green meanness every time you reel in a fish to your net.

The reported growth rate is 2 pounds per year. Let that, too, sink in.

The last five years, El Salto Lake anglers reported catches of fifty to 200 bass a day. You never know about these figures (I normally don't trust these kinds of numbers but I heard about days like this from an awful lot of people I trust), but if you just halved these incredible numbers, you'd have an amazing first five-year run.

El Salto relinquishes 4- to 8-pound bass regularly. Some anglers have caught five or six or more 10-pound bucketmouths in a day. That's a trophy bass six times. Ten-pound bass are more common in El Salto Lake than any other bass lake I know. There are 6- to 15-pounders left and right and middle. Twelve-pound bass, says one reputable guide/operator, are caught by more than one third of his clients. I am sick that I have spent time on all the other big-name Mexico lakes but haven't gotten on El Salto and have to rely on others, but I do know this much: A 5- or 6-pounder is a cinch, slamdunk, a certainty for anyone with a rod.

Fourteen pounds is the lake record by the way. All these 5- and 6- and 7-pounders will take you under cover and break you off, by the way.

The last ingredient you need on any great bass lake is a conscience. The people involved with the water, from the natives to the government to the guides to the anglers themselves, they all must care enough about the resource to take care of its future. El Salto Lake has a conscience.

El Salto Lake is 24,000 acres when full, half of that after irrigation use by end of summer. You come to El Salto by way of Mazatlan, the nearest city of size. So you fly into Mazatlan, the Billfishing Capital of the World (as if you didn't know that), then you fish the Pacific for sailfish, roosterfish, tuna, and other fighting fish of the sea, then you get your fanny the ninety miles up to El Salto Lake.

Located in northwest Mexico, not far from the coast, in the state of Sinaloa, in the coastal foothills of the Sierra Madre, northeast of Mazatlan lies this irrigation impoundment of the Elota River. You fish from dawn to dusk with the guides of El Salto, stopping for lunch and Margaritas for 2 to 3 hours of break and/or siesta (take the siesta if you never have—a real treat. You do it when you lay on the couch on Sunday afternoons anyway).

The fish here are very aggressive and will bite any kind of bait, but topwaters and crankbaits are the most popular. They take it all—on top or down deep, all kinds of lures and techniques and tactics, and the water is murky clear and they aren't as shy as many Florida-strain bass. These bass hide, dive for cover, play obstacle course so your mono-leader needs to be strong. Prepare to lose lures and flies. You need a good drag, quality equipment.

Don't get too excited if you see gill nets—they're for tilapia, stocked by the government (as a commercial enterprise) to assuage the folks who were displaced when they were moved from their homes and their land flooded in the impoundment. I don't know if many or any anglers try this other bass fishery but reports are that Rio Elota holds bass, too, stocked before the impoundment.

An interesting aside—one must-shoot photo-op on the lake is the cemetery that was flooded to fill the lake, complete with tall gravestones rising eerily out of the water. If, when I go, I see a woman or eagle or snake by the watery graves, I am turning that boat around and going back for Margaritas.

For the time being and the foreseeable future, El Salto Lake wears the crown, *el rey de Mexico.* Unbreakable.

CONTACTS
Hook Sportfishing Charters, 800-583-8133
Angler's Inn, Mazatlán, Sinaloa www.AnglersInn.com

Lake Agua Milpa

Three hours from Puerto Vallarta, Lake Agua Milpa is an accessible scenic bass lake of 70,000 acres, and it is on its way up the legend status bar. You really can catch thirty, forty, even seventy-five bass a day. The largemouth bass are growing, ranging from 2 to 10 pounds big and your average catch will run about 2 to 3 pounds. Rumor has it, some 15-pound bass have been caught.

Agua Milpa impounded the large river, Rio Sanbago, in 1997. The water is not just clear, it's cobalt blue, the surroundings lush tropical plants and trees layering the mountains. The spawning bass are protected from March to May by no-fishing regulations. The best times to come to Agua Milpa are September through June.

This lake sits in—imagine this—the rugged Sierra Madres Mountains in the coastal state of Nayarit. You can fly into Puerto Vallarta or Guadalajara or Tepic (only forty-five minutes from Agua Milpa).

CONTACTS
Bob Mauldin, B&B Mexico Bass Fishing, www.wheretofish.com

Lake El Cuchillo

One of the newer not-yet-known-but-soon-will-be-lakes, El Cuchillo is being managed with great gusto to be the next trophy bass hotspot. As proof of this direction, the lake restricts commercial fishing, meaning there will be no nets and no nets means the bass fishery has a chance to flourish. Another bit of proof, the ten-year-old lake is a state park, a first, to be used only for recreation.

Located an hour drive south of McAllen, Preso Cuchillo impoundment in the state of Nuevo Leon is already producing bass weighing 8 to 10 pounds. With this kind of attention to management, Cuchillo may turn out to be the next hot lake in Mexico.

Lake Comedero

We're talking huge for Mexico lakes, nearly twice the size of El Salto and running neck and neck with El Salto in numbers of big bass caught. Comedero suffered from low levels for a long time but the rains have raised levels and raised quality of fishing again.

Nearly four hours (a little over a 100 miles if that tells you about the drive) from Mazatlan, Comedero is more distant from the big coastal city than El Salto so it doesn't receive as much pressure. The record hawg at this remote mountain lake with the muscular mountains all around is over 18 pounds and the requisite yarns exist about fish caught many times heavier than that. The truth we know is that 10-pound trophies abound in clear-watered Comedero.

Comedero is one of the oldest bass fishing Lakes in Mexico and has gone through some of the ups and downs that Mexican lakes go through. The 100-fish days only occur every now and again—the lake is more about producing lots of big black bass now.

■　■　■

We were camped on the Middle Fork of the Conejos River in remote southern Colorado. We had a tough hike in, loaded down with forty-pound backpacks, still snow on the ground in spots, muddy and wet in other spots. We didn't see another soul in the ten miles we backpacked, only elk and deer. This is wilderness angling, our favorite kind of fishing trip—the promise of wild trout, the possibility of some lunkers, no other anglers, and days that run into other days so we won't be exactly sure how long we've been in the backcountry.

We only stopped to set up camp because the skies darkened and then opened up, first with heavy rain, then with messy sleet and finally with big white snowflakes that floated down as lazily and erratically as the G.I. Joe on a parachute I used to drop from the roof of my house when I was nine. We were soaked and tired, our hoods tight over our heads, as we set up the tent while snow piled up on our shoulders and heads so that we looked like puffy white ghosts.

We ate soggy bagels and went to sleep. The howls of the coyotes were as close to us as we'd ever been to coyotes. Live ones, anyway. They sounded close enough to be in camp. We both woke with a start, then settled back in our sleeping bags. Kenny's line began the myth, "Well, I guess she followed us. Coyote Girl wants us."

Ever since then, Coyote Girl has taken on a Mexican-goddess type of dimension, a devil woman of beauty and deceit, who lives in the mountains, who bewitches outdoorsmen. Our fishing buddies see her on their trips, too. Sometimes she howls at night, other times she appears at convenience stores, general stores, and taco wagons.

McPhail and I ran into her twice in Arizona and Utah, once on a backcountry trail along a small stream where she, as a thirty-year-old woman with short hair, bounced along the trail holding hands with her girlfriend; and a week later at a coffeehouse in St. George.

We see Coyote Girl in her different incarnations and disguises wherever we travel in the mountains now. She is sometimes blonde and tanned, sometimes old and worn, she was a barfly at a dive in Chama, New Mexico (you could tell she had once been a high school beauty but the ravages of liquor, cigarettes, and time had done the ol' girl in). The last two times we saw her, she was young and flirty in a bodega selling cigarettes in Mazatlan and a few days later, she was a mother of three, standing in a doorway wearing a faded print dress, sweeping the floor of her whitewashed house.

Like I said, I don't believe in ghosts. But I do know that I have to wipe this goofy smile off my face when my wife comes in my study while I am reliving one of my fishing trips.

CONTACTS
Where to Fish.com, www.wheretofish .com/mexico.htm
Bass Fishing Mexico, www .bassfishingmexico.com

Cabo San Lucas

- **Location:** Western Mexico, southern tip of Baja California
- **What You Fish For:** Billfish, mahi-mahi, roosterfish, jack crevalle, and much more
- **Highlights and Notables:** Easy to reach from the United States, a trendy, consistent angling hotspot.

I don't want to shortchange Cabo San Lucas. This has been a popular angling locale for a long long time. I have friends (especially Bob Brown) who go back year after year. They love the billfish (black, blue, striped marlin, and swordfish). They love the plummeting offshore canyons. They love the marlin tourneys. They love the rugged big scenery. It's an area steeped in fishing, geared toward sportfishing.

I can't explain it but the one time I fished it, Cabo just didn't do it for me. The chase for striped marlin, the area's claim to fame, was exciting. It might have been the boat, the attitudes, the lousy place I stayed. I wasn't feeling all that good. Like I say, I don't want to shortchange Cabo. This is one of the feeding lanes from the conjunction of currents from the Sea of Cortez and the Pacific Ocean.

Cabo San Lucas has some beautiful mahi-mahi (I did catch quite a few and was pleased), ample populations of jack crevalle, amberjack, ladyfish dorado (on a popper, and that was a blast), roosterfish (missed out, which is nuts because not many places have more but my guide/captain didn't want to listen to me and we trolled too much but wah wah, I know), wahoo, and tuna. The pangas are fun, these sixteen-foot skiffs where each one looks as though its seen better days. Huge craggy stone monoliths rise from the ocean, like the famous arches at Land's End. It's a pretty pretty place so I can't knock that aspect (although it has grown a lot from its sleepy little Mexican fishing village days).

And another thing. I ended up on a boat one day, through odd circumstances, with someone whose initial odor portended tempestuous seas. He had a bulbous nose and from his filthy Neiman Marcus–level clothes and the smell of body odor mixed with bourbon, he was a walking movie caricature of a drunk rich white guy. He played his part well, bellowing, swaying, burping, annoying, interrupting, and dominating. He didn't catch a fish all day. You know, half the fun of these trips is meeting new folks, making new friends and fishing buddies, sharing the fishing experience. I'd love, as a Texan to tell you this rich old drunk fart was from Jersey or New York but he was from Dallas, Texas, my hometown. Fella, if you read this, you know who you are. Thanks for all the good times that day.

When I go back, and I will go back, this time I'm going after roosterfish like every other fishing nut who goes to Cabo. Maybe I'll be the drunk loud Texan this time.

Give Cabo a go if you are into marlin and big boats. Just avoid all drunk Texans and crotchety captains.

CONTACTS

Baja Anglers Fly Shop, 888-588-3446 (I want to emphasize that this was not the outfitter with the crusty old guide.)

This site has a solid list of guides and charters: www.bajaquest.com/bajasports/charters.htm

Cozumel

- **Location:** Eastern Mexico, east of the Yucatán, south and east of Cancun
- **What You Fish For:** Billfish, bonefish
- **Highlights and Notables:** If you've never caught a sailfish, you're chances are greater than most here in Cozumel's waters. Plus you can party and lay in the sun to celebrate your first.

Early reports from the damage Hurricane Katrina did to the Cozumel fishery, inshore and offshore, are encouraging. Years ago, Cozumel was a jewel-shaped island that played second-fiddle to Cancun since pretty much all you could do there was scuba dive, tan, and drink. Cozumel has grown up some since then and there's a lot more you can do and it's still jewel-shaped, Marquis-cut in fact. The fishing game has improved, too, with catch-and-release the unwritten law for billfish.

The billfish fishery has been around for a while, firmly established, with guides who speak English (kinda) and know all the different methods to catch these acrobatic beasts. Large numbers of sailfish let the currents take them past Cozumel in April, May, and June. The average sailfish off Cozumel averages about 30 to 50 pounds, ideal for fly fishing and light-tackle gear. White marlin run 50 to 70 pounds on average while blue marlin are found in the deeper water and some go up to 200 pounds. Deep-sea fishing has been around for a while and anglers have their best shot at a billfish from February to June, especially for the tailwalking sailfish.

Years ago, when I used to go there with either my wife Amy or a couple of buddies, we'd swim and tan and drink. We also waded the flats hoping to find the bonefish we'd heard the locals talk about but nobody fished for (no guides for flats then). We did. The bonefish are not big but they are plentiful. There are several guides for flat fishing on the island now but I've yet to fish with one. I did try to hire a flats guide but they were all full up at both Thanksgiving and Christmas last year so I fished on my own, sorta. Hired a local nonguide who knew the waters and had a boat. We did pretty good, thank you.

We also waded on the north end, a little less than hip deep, we fished two lagoons of three over the six-day stay. We caught quite a few smallish bones, almost all on Crazy Charlies and we tied into several schools each day. You can't get far in these big lagoons and we'd have done better by boat. The wind whipped up the water and at times, it was blind casting but for the most part, these are amazingly clear water. If I didn't have good buddies with good eyesight, I wouldn't have seen as many bones as I did.

The bones averaged about 2, maybe 3 pounds. The largest we caught went about 5. Even smaller bones take line and zip like caged furies. I caught one smallish 'cuda, surprised a little how hard he hit and that he was there in the first place. I've also heard that the clear lagoons out at Isla de la Pasión hold nice schools of bonefish in the 2- to 5-pound class.

There are also *palometa* (permit) to 20-plus pounds and *sabalo* (tarpon) 15 to 30 pounds that frequent these three lagoons and other shallow Cozumel waters as well (of which there aren't all that many shallows/flats). I have yet to tie into either one. I've heard about snook, too (5 to 15 pounds), and they live in the mangroves in the lagoons. I love these new things coming to light, discoveries. I might as well start planning a return fishing trip, er, I mean romantic husband-wife getaway.

Cozumel is an inexpensive tropical get-away with enough to do if you want but plenty of nothing to do if you don't. Cozumel is not nearly as developed as Cancun nor is it as good a fishery. It's pretty. I like the white sandy beaches and the clear blue-green water. Plenty of flights into the island. Your wife will have plenty to do while you fish. Go eat at La Choza for casual and Pepe's for a step up and try any of many taquería/loncherías for a cheap great lunch. But I like fishing Cozumel mostly for the following reasons:

1. It's cheap and easy to reach.
2. There's a good chance of catching a lot of bonefish in one day.
3. Few others go to here to fish.
4. Drinks are cheap, Cuban cigars are cheap, and the restaurants are excellent if you like fresh seafood and authentic coastal-style Mexican food, and if you avoid the cruise ship area, nothing much is crowded.
5. There's a laid-back 1950s vibe going on even though there are more families at the all-inclusive hotels dotting the island.
6. If you absolutely, positively have to catch a sailfish, this is one of the the best places in the Western Hemisphere to do that. Sailfish on light tackle. Anglers can also fish for kingfish, blue and white marlin, swordfish, mackerel, bonito, jacks, mahi-mahi, dorado (consistent numbers, big fish), snapper, barracuda, and wahoo, and my brothers-in-law report that groupers big enough to eat small children lie just off the reef.

7. Did I mention anything about the sun and drinks and sandy beaches?

All that said, I haven't been here often when rain didn't get me. It's often muggy. You can tell when the cruise ships unload because the population pretty much doubles (but stay out of the tourist trap stores and the bars like Carlos 'n Charlies and you'll be okay). You'll also be on Cozumel time, which means that things move slowly and if it doesn't get done today, it might get done tomorrow or at worst, later in the week. There's a sense of disarray and not just in the guided fishing community.

Check this out: Mom is scared to death of birds. We piled seven people in a Jeep to take a tour around the island, see the rain forest and the ruins. Dad got out of a ticket with the local po-po with a smooth breeze bribe. Mom had to sit in my lap in the back of the Jeep and as we passed under the canopy of trees, a dead bird fell into my mother's lap as though ordained by the prankster gods. She tried to jump out of the moving vehicle with me holding on not knowing she was fending off a dead bird. Between the screaming and shrieking and near-leaping, Dad stopped the Jeep without Mom taking a header on the road. Fun stuff. And the dead bird had beautiful feathers.

Cozumel is thirty-three miles long, nine miles wide. Sailfish swim offshore in great numbers. You can catch sailfish and you can do it easily and you can do it on light tackle or fly rod. Trolling is the popular way to hook into a sailfish and this takes place mostly in the twelve miles of deep water between the island and the mainland. Plug casting to teased billfish is becoming an accepted method, too. Your hotel can hook you up with charter boats and guides.

They tried to get me to learn how to scuba dive. They knew I had no interest in breathing underwater, unnatural and so stupidly and obviously dangerous as it is. This is Amy's family, especially David and Kenny. Luckily for me, on the morning of scuba training in the pool at the Cozumeleno, the instructor found out about my chronic asthma (cough cough) and told me I would not be allowed to submerge myself to the mercy of barracuda and *tiburón*. Things underwater can eat you, you know.

Puerto Vallarta

- **Location:** Western coastal Mexico
- **What You Fish For:** Giant marlin and tuna, sailfish, amberjack, roosterfish, dorado, bonito, wahoo, pargo (Pacific dog snapper), sierra, and cubera snapper
- **Highlights and Notables:** Stunning scenery, trophy fishing for giant marlin

I was thirty minutes late to my first wedding. That's a bad omen, I guess. My cousin Jay and my best man Lance pulled a fast one and got me in the car, drove out of town about twenty minutes all the while hoorahing me and joking about how I was making a mistake and we were pointed to-

Puerto Vallarta

ward Vegas so just give the word. Just guys having fun. Then we all realized it was already 3:15 and the wedding began fifteen minutes ago. And we were fifteen miles from the church. The wedding was called off by the time we got there and it was some real smooth-talking by my buddies (that can't be good can it? Manipulating a man of the cloth?) and the wedding went on as planned. For better or worse.

I got married the second time and it took. Eighteen years now and going strong. Amy and I took our honeymoon to Puerto Vallarta. She had no idea they had such good fishing or that part of my scheme was fishing and she was naturally insistent that I concentrate on making the new bride happy and fishing some other time. I didn't fish Puerto Vallarta on that trip. Amy loves to fish and she went back with me and we did it right. Fishing, that is. And we did the honeymoon right, too.

I speak Spanish. I'm fluent but I'm not really good at conjugation. I speak hillbilly Spanish. I understand it well and I make Spanish-speakers understand me although I've been told my Spanish hasn't gotten much better than when I spoke it with my friends in Puerto Rico in the early '70s. Beats ol' nothing.

But I get cocky in a Spanish-speaking country. Amy and I were sunning on the beach in Puerto Vallarta and Amy decided she wanted one of the panchos a man was hawking. Let me handle it. I'll get him to come down. The seller and I dickered for a while and I won. He was asking 25 bucks and I got him to come down to 15. Great deal. We got sunburned and walked back to the hotel through town and Amy tapped my shoulder and pointed to a poncho blanket just like ours in a store window. Five bucks, two for nine.

Both times we've gone to Puerto Vallarta together, we bought into one of those package deals where you get seven nights lodging at a moderately nice hotel and all the crappy food you want to eat. Daiquiri Dick's fruity drinks and appetizers became a big player for us each time after a few days of hotel buffet food. Puerto Vallarta is absolutely stunning but like so many Mexican resort towns, you can have luxurious white sandy beaches and deluxe hotels only to find a few hundred yards away ramshackle *barrios* and seedy folks. You get a lot of Old Mexico with touristy Mexico but also a fair dose of poor Mexico.

For the most part, the colonial resort of Puerto Vallarta on the western Mexico coast is a joy to visit, this the backdrop for the great movie *Night of the Iguana*, the story of a defrocked Episcopal clergyman (Richard Burton) who has to deal with the obvious shortcomings of his own life while acting the shepherd/babysitter to a gaggle of gray-haired Baptist women. This movie and the behind-the-scene tabloid shenanigans between Burton and Liz Taylor while in the coastal fishing village (not yet resort) put Puerto Vallarta on the proverbial map. Black and white movie but Puerto Vallarta and its surrounding lush green tropical jungles never looked more starkly beautiful.

So other than the beauty and Old World charm and amazing sunsets and sunny days and white beaches and reasonable cost and ease of access from the United States, why consider PV for a fishing trip?

Big game fish. Trophy game fish. Giant marlin and tuna. Astonishingly fertile waters for marlin and tuna. And sailfish, too. Heart-stopping action.

Sure, you can catch amberjack, roosterfish, dorado, bonito, wahoo, pargo (Pacific dog snapper), sierra, and cubera snapper and they'd all be worthy quarry any other day but in the convergent waters of Banderas and El Banco Bays, with all of the necessary food sources to entice these monsters of the deep, with the ideal currents, the proper underwater layout, why even think about anything but buckling up and hooking into one of these pewter Poseidons.

The jazz that goes down when you see the lurking shadow, the underwater beast stalking your sacrificial offering is undeniable and exhilarating. Your heart beats like a drum. The smash and crash and tumult that follows happens all at once and also in slow motion. The rest is dissonant fatigue, the threshold of a marathoner. You don't give up, you can't give up. If you surrender, they defrock you and you're stuck in purgatory taking little old ladies on tours for eternity.

I shouldn't make light of the inshore opportunities or the diversity of your angling options or the possibility of landing some big fish on light tackle. A 200- to 300-pound yellowfin tuna on the end of your rod is one of the unique must-do angling experiences, and Puerto Vallarta offers with some of the finest inshore-offshore angling in the Pacific, and you get to enjoy haggling with beach vendors to get the best price on a poncho to boot. Or save time and money and buy the twofer in town.

Ixtapa-Zihuatanejo
May be the top roosterfish fishery in Mexico. Located on Mexico's Pacific mainland coast. Overlooked fishery where you can catch sails and dolphins, but it's all about the large roosters.

CONTACTS

Vilma's Yacht Services, www .vilmasyachtagency.com

Paradise Village Marina, www .paradisevillage.com/marina.htm

Margarita's Restaurant and Bar, Punta de Mita, 011 044 322 779 6279

Capt. Danny Gomez, Dhamar Sportfishing, www.dhamarsportfishing.com

Capt. Danny Osuna, Marla II Sportfishing, 01 152 329 295 5073

Capt. Tony Ocaranza, Yolaray Sportfishing, 01 152 322 292 1317

Yucatán Peninsula

- **Location:** Eastern Mexico
- **What You Fish For:** Bonefish, snook, tarpon, permit
- **Highlights and Notables:** Besides the beautiful beaches, green jungles, ancient history, and colorful umbrella drinks, here lies one of the great bonefishing spots on earth.

You have to make time to visit Mayan ruins. I'm serious. Don't visit the Yucatán and just fish. You'll be missing out on the history, the ambience, the essence of this part of the country.

So let's discuss why the Yucatán Peninsula is so interesting as a world-class fishing destination.

1. The cost is reasonable. Cheap, you might say. Not that you can't find expensive luxury lodging because you can.
2. Mexico is a lot of fun. The food, the music, the people, the lay of the land, the Cuban cigars, tequila, the aforementioned archaeological aspect, and so much more. And by the way, the food isn't your Tex-Mex chili con carne variety either but a tasty mixture of fresh seafood, lobster ceviche, black beans and mole, plantains, and other succulents.
3. Inshore and offshore fishing are to die for. Tarpon, bonefish, and permit, the trifecta of the Caribbean, and it's not unusual to catch all three in one day.
4. Flights from most anywhere to Mexico are easy and cheap.
5. The variety of fish, the combination of offshore and inshore fishing, the quality of both, the relatively inexpensive costs, the ease of travel, the beauty and culture, experienced guides, excellent lodges, established fishing infrastructure, a light-tackle paradise but the area is so vast, it's lightly fished, and well, do you need any other reasons to visit?

Sometimes, under the spell of the white sandy beaches, aqua-blue flats, and too many cold cervezas, I get this crazy idea I'd like to live here. I know Amy would never go for an authentic Mayan-style house, one of those thatched-roof jobs. I could live in one of those blue clapboard, shingle-roof houses near the beach, Parrothead-style but again, Amy probably wouldn't see the value in this simplified lifestyle. I'd love a luxury thatch-roof bungalow like those at Boca Paila but that's out of my price range. So given her needs (and she is quite practical and easy-going) all I need is a two-room condo, preferably with an ocean view. Nothing fancy, just clean. A terrace where we can catch a breeze and have a drink or two.

Since I don't want to have to run this harebrained idea past Amy anyhow, I'll table it for now. Heck, it's inexpensive enough and close enough that I can catch a flight down there on a whim so forget I ever mentioned it. But don't think you won't think the same thing once you visit.

To give you an idea of what awaits you:

You have many choices all along the peninsula, Quintana Roo, Ascension Bay, Boca Paila, Punta Allen, Cancun, Cozumel, Espiritu Santo Bay, Chetumal Bay, and more, all the way south to the Belizean border. They run the gamut from fishing-is-the-only-thing-to-do in Punta Allen to Cozumel and Cancun's busy (too-busy?) tourism. The Yucatán is ideal for either getting away with the wife (and/or family) for a combo trip or a fishing buddies' road trip with lots of cerveza, not putting on sunblock and getting stupidly sunburned and fishing to your forty-year-old heart's content. Each fishing stop along the Yucatán has its own offerings, its own flavor, but there's something familiar about each.

You have expanses of flats, limestone and sand, hard and flat, easy to wade and rich and loaded with fish. These bonefish are not as big as Venezuela or Christmas Island or the Bahamas or South Florida but these are easier to catch. And while the bonefish may not rank among the world's largest, they certainly place among the most abundant. If you want to take a rookie, this is your spot. Want to catch ten or twenty bones in a day, think Yucatán. Most Yucatán bones run about 1 to 2 pounds but 4- to 7-pounders are commonplace. The bigger bones, the ones that reach 10 pounds, are here, too, but they are not easy to catch.

You have mangrovey lagoons (by the hundreds) where tarpon tear off line and break you off before you can sweat. In these same lagoons and bays, permit lurk. Barracuda cruise. Snook sun. You fish.

Coconut palms sway over white sandy beaches. Coastal mountain jungles breathe thick and green. Channels connect and interconnect and weave and bob and they hook up with lakes and mangroves and islands. Reefs provide shelter for myriad fish. You expect Jimmy Buffet to jump out from behind the bar any moment.

Snook + mangroves = fun. Tarpon run 15 to 65 pounds. Petty crime is alive and well in the populated areas. Renting a car can be more expensive than you first considered. Essentials include a camera and polarized glasses. Bring and wear sunblock if you are smart. Gulf of Mexico to your north, Caribbean Sea to your east. One of the world's largest barrier reefs protects the inland waters from the fullest force of the sea. Right in your backyard jungle is a 1.6 million-acre preserve, Sian Ka'an Biosphere Preserve. Mayan ruins are everywhere. You can be fishing on the flats, look up at a cliff and see the unmistakable gray block pyramid shape. Three hours from Cancun, you can go see the Chichen Itza ruins. A treat is to visit a local grocery store or fruit stand. It's fun to shop and fun to have new fruits and candies to munch on back at the lodge or out on the water.

Permit and the underrated sportfish barracuda that give your rod some bend, if, that is, you can ever get them to take. If you tire of casting into schools of bonefish and catching only 2- to 3-pounders, hardly an afflicted day, the permit of the Yucatán are as numerous and as large as in any other fishing locale you'll visit. In the warm months, permit are plentiful—hanging out waiting to be ambushed in the deeper flats just off the shoals. Seeing them and then perfectly casting to them and then somehow holding on long enough to bring them in, well, that's another story entirely.

The water of the Yucatán Peninsula includes all the blues and greens of the color spectrum but in the flats, the water is clear and blue like swimming pool water. The water so clear, in fact, that with my bad eyesight (good for trout, bad for bones and permit), with my natural clumsiness (I splash when I wade, I can't help it), I do much better on bones out of a flats-boat than I do in the water. I look for nervous water and often I see things that aren't there. When the school or the singled-up bone is close enough, they're too close for me to cast without spooking them. I need eye surgery or a stronger glasses prescription or as the dangling Chads say, a seeing-eye dog. So I get help, I'm not too proud to admit it. And this note: If you are a competent angler, you may catch so many bones the first few days that you eschew them the rest of the trip to catch larger prey. Ain't that a lovely dilemma?

More about water—do you drink the tapwater or risk Montezuema's Revenge? I've gotten the runs once in Mexico after drinking from the tap but it wasn't the first nor was it the last time, but if you want to avoid any chance of it, you can find bottled water at the lodges, the hotels, most restaurants, and most stores.

Something else, girls. If you're not an avid angler, then listen up. When your husband/boyfriend/boy-toy asks you along on these fishing trips (especially the warm-weather exotic types), I am sure his intent is in part honestly wanting you along, another part wanting an excuse to go fishing. Maybe he's honest about this, maybe not. He wants to see you shopping as well (within reason of course), wants to see you on the beach sunning and enjoying an umbrella drink. But unless you are Cathy Beck and can rival your husband's fishing skills, 1) don't fish with him 100 percent of the time and 2) if you do, do *not* under any circumstance make a big deal if you catch the bigger fish. Leave him some dignity. Thanks, Ames, for leaving me mine (and she's an avid angler, to boot).

I guess to be fair, I should reverse that above paragraph in case there are women who fish and have husbands/boyfriends/boy-toys who don't. Reverse it.

I failed to mention, and should, that the offshore fishing, this bluewater treat that so often gets rightfully overlooked by those of us who love flats fishing, offers some of the finest sailfish angling in the world. Isla Mujere and Cancun and Cozumel are the three top sailfish and marlin hotspots. (Plus you can find dorado, bonito, and other fish offshore.)

Bottom line: If you fish and you haven't yet fished somewhere on the Yucatán Peninsula, book the trip now. I feel somewhat like a drug dealer knowing full well that once you taste the beaches, the water, the food, the exotic *sopa de lima* that is this region of Mexico, you'll be back, you'll jones for it, you'll develop this weird "I don't want to leave" creepy feeling. Like I have.

CONTACTS

Lodges like Boca Paila, Casa Blanca, and Playa Blanca are served by numerous U.S. sporting-travel agents, such as Frontiers (800-245-1950; www .frontierstravel.com) and Angler Adventures (800-628-1447) and just about any reputable sport-travel agent. See list below—all first-rate outfits.

Boca Paila Lodge, www.bocapaila.com

Pesca Maya Lodge, www.pescamaya.com

Casa Blanca Lodge, www.casablancafishing .com

Ascension Bay Bonefish Club, www .ascencionbay.com

Cuzan Guest House, www.flyfishmx.com

Playa Blanca Lodge, 800-771-2202

Paradise Lodge, www.tarponparadise.com

SeaClusion Villa, www.seaclusionmexico .com

Alpine Angling & Adventure Travel, www
.RFAnglers.com

Angler Adventures, www.angleradventures
.com

Angling Destinations, www
.anglingdestinations.com

Blue Drake Outfitters, www.bluedrake
.com

Cabela's, www.cabelas.com

Frontiers Travel, www.frontierstrvl.com

John Eustice & Associates, www
.johneustice.com

Kaufmann's Streamborn, Inc., www
.kman.com

Leisure Time Travel, www.leisuretimetravel
.com

Leland Fly Fishing Outfitters, www
.flyfishingoutfitters.com

Rod & Reel Adventures, www
.rodreeladventures.com

The Fly Shop, www.theflyshop.com

The Orvis Company, www.orvis.com

Travel Adventures, www.travela.com

Westbank Anglers, www.westbank.com

Caribbean

CARIBBEAN

BAHAMAS

- **Location:** East of the tip of Florida, north of Cuba
- **What You Fish For:** Bonefish is the reason for the season.
- **Highlights and Notables:** Vacation plus superior bonefishing equals one of the world's top fishing destinations.

I want you to buy someone else's book about the Bahamas. The Vletases book. Here's why: So I'm getting a great tan, fishing for the second day in a row with not a single bonefish to my name. My guide is pissing me off because apparently, I've pissed him

off. I'm supposed to be a pretty good angler, hotshot writer, and all that and all I can do is screw up. I can hear it in his voice.

I am not casting worth a durn. I've got a new rod and new reel and new line and that shouldn't be an excuse but it is anyway and I'm mad and embarrassed that I am performing so poorly and then he's in my ear, all the time, *cast at 2 o'clock, no, see them? See them? Can't you see them? Try over there, 10 o'clock, fifty feet, lead them about ten feet, cast, cast, you spooked them, they're gone*—and so on. I sure wouldn't have wanted to put up with me. He'd put me on so many bonefish and I had messed up even the easiest casts and approaches.

I guess it's hard to guide for any length of time in the Bahamas, no matter how much sunscreen you lather on, without eventually looking weather-beaten—maybe they look that way because they have to instruct guys like me and you every day on where to cast, where to cast again, where to cast even better, where we'll go next after spooking that school. My guide was twenty-five going on ninety based on his wrinkled tan skin. He was really nice when he wasn't irritated at me.

I thought to myself about the anglers I've talked to who said they got bored catching so many bonefish. I can't remember who they were or I would hate them at this point.

I try several tricks as the blue water and the hot yellow sun are enveloping me, suffocating me. I clear my head. I think of pretty places but none are more beautiful than the aqua flats through which we are floating. I come up with a silent mantra but I forget it by the third cast: *I hate this sport.*

We have waded, we have poled. We have switched from my rod to his rod. Back to my rod. I'm holding my tongue to the other side. I tossed the cigar. I have told myself ten times, "It's time to get down to business, quit thinking so much, it's like your golf swing, when you analyze, you paralyze, maybe I'll try obeah."

And then, it happened.

A school of small bones. Instructions. Cast. Hookup. Run, reel, run, bone to hand. Two pounds. I am okay again. And so is my guide. I can't wait to drink a cold Kalik at the lodge. I might even try a conch fritter. *I love this sport.*

The Bahamas are one of the premier fisheries in the world, especially for bonefish. This is the Commonwealth of the Bahamas, and they speak English, are self-governing, laid back, controlling more than 700 islands and cays (keys, small islands) of the Atlantic Ocean, an archipelago bordering the Caribbean (but you'd be hard-pressed to tell where one begins and the other ends). North of Cuba, east of Florida, this is where Chris Columbus first made American landfall. Baja Mar. Shallow sea. Bahamas.

The big island of the Bahamas is Andros Island. Nassau, a beautiful tourist trap, and the largest city, sits on New Providence. Grand Bahama owns the second biggest city (Freeport). Hurricanes clobber some part of the Bahamas every summer or so it seems.

The Bahamas is ideal for American anglers for several reasons other than the fact that this is bonefish heaven. It's a quick getaway, close, with direct flights from most major American cities. The Bahamas is not always expensive (it can be if you want luxury).

So many islands, so little time. The fishing in Bahamian waters is good year-round, great most of the time, so when the snow is piling up in your town, it's warm and the fish are biting in the Bahamas.

Where to go in the Bahamas? So many islands have developed ideal fishing and tourist infrastructure, it's a tough choice out every time. Each of the islands has differing offerings, personalities, and lodgings. There are just so many great resorts and lodges and guides.

Clear water, white sands, hard flats, and bonefish, Deep Water Cay

Andros, Bimini (for deep-sea fishing), and Grand Bahama are probably the most legendary fishing hotspots; even with the influx of new resorts and angling pressure, they've held their own and maybe even gotten better. Let's face it, with 700 islands, you have to choose from the most extensive bonefish flats in all the world. There are still unexplored fishing waters in the Bahamas, islands that don't see many anglers all year long.

The Bahamian bonefish is known for being large and being finicky. Ask me about the choosy aspect. The average size might be the largest average size bone in the world, 5 to 7 pounds. The waters hold many 10-pounders but also many that challenge the world record. Bahamian bonefish, when hooked, are reel-screamers, tearing off line and putting you into your backing quicker than you can say Bimini. You don't only catch bonefish in the Bahamas; other hot species include barracuda, sharks, tarpon, permit, grouper, and snapper, and more reef species than you can shake a Sage rod at. Offshore yields gigantic blue and white marlin, giant tuna, amberjack, and other bluewater species.

Acklins Island

Remote fishing location. Endless flats for bonefish (creeks too), deeper channels for tarpon and permit. For the serious angler.

CONTACTS
Acklins Island Lodge, 800-593-7977,
    www.acklinsislandlodge.com,
    info@acklinsislandlodge.com

Abacos

The Marls. These mangrove islands stretch on into infinity. There may be no other place in the Bahamas that has more bonefish per square foot of clear beautiful water. Cherokee Sound has easy wading flats. Easy access by plane. If you are a hardcore fisher and want to access the central and southern marls, you stay at and go through Nettie's Different of Abaco, the Great Abaco Fishing Club. If you have family or like a little more pampering, you don't. Hers is one of the best fishing experiences in the Bahamas, maybe anywhere.

CONTACTS
Nettie Symonette, Nettie's Different of
    Abaco, 877-505-1850, www
    .differentofabaco.com
Pete and Gay's Guesthouse, 242-366-4119
Rickmon Bonefish Lodge, 242-366-4477,
    www.rickmonbonefishlodge.com
Treasure Cay Hotel Resort and Marina,
    www.treasurecay.com

Andros

The pinnacle of bonefishing, many say. Bonefishing capital of the world. You just might catch (or at least see) the largest bonefish you've ever caught (or have seen). If the 6- to 15-pound type of bonefish is in your plans, plan on Andros.

The bigger bonefish hang out in or near the deep water and the local guides know right where to take you if you are huntin' for trophies. They also know where to take you if you are a starter-kit and want to learn how to catch 1- to 5-pound bonefish. There aren't many other places in the world with this kind of bonefish habitat ranging from the obvious flats to creeks to mangroves. The Big Yard. I don't want to discount the offshore angling for dolphin, sailfish, tuna, and wahoo, nor the other flats swimmers like permit, tarpon, and barracuda, but really, it's about the bonefish on Andros. Check out Joulters Cays on the less-fished north side.

All the lodges but Flaming Cay are on the east side.

CONTACTS
Andros Island Bonefish Club, www
    .androsbonefishing.com
Tranquility Hill Fishing Lodge, www
    .tranquilityhill.com
Nottages Cottages, www
    .bigcharlieandros.com/index.html
    (one of the best Bahamian fishing
    guides, Big Charlie Neymour)
Bair's Lodge, www.bairslodge.com
Bonefish Bay Club of South Andros, www
    .bonefishbayclub.com
Mangrove Cay Club, www
    .mangrovecayclub.com
Tiamo Resorts, www.tiamoresorts.com
Flamingo Cay, www.flamingocay.com
Kamalame Cay, www.kamalame.com
Stafford Creek Lodge, www
    .staffordcreeklodge.com

Berry Islands

Known more for its offshore fishing and deep dropoff water, the Berries do have miles and miles and miles of flats. Chub Cay is known as the "Billfish Capital of the Bahamas." Chub Cay Wall, Eel Garden, the Canyons, all popular bluewater locales. Berries are known for all the millionaires that live there.

CONTACTS
Tropical Diversions Resort, www
    .tropicaldiversions.com
Chub Cay Club and Marina, www
    .chubcay.com

Bimini

Only fifty miles from Miami, Bimini doesn't have the extensive flats of many other Bahamas islands. Bimini has enormous fish. From the large bonefish and permit to the wahoo, tuna, and sailfish, Bimini is Bahamas-Big-Fish-Central.

One of the drawing cards of big fish is the cero mackerel, world-class size. Bimini has set several records for these and dozens for other species. And then, of course, the offshore whoppers and the tournaments that always seem to be going on in Bimini.

CONTACTS
Bimini Big Game Fishing Club and Marina, www.biminibiggame.com
Bimini Sands Resort & Marina, www
    .biminisands.com

Cat Island

Pink sand, remote locale, untamed island has the usual awesome Bahamian bonefish flats and creeks but the sleeper fishery here is the wahoo. They grow 'em big at Cat Island—does 100 pounds sound big enough for you? The offshore fishing is solid, too, especially for marlin and tuna.

CONTACTS
Hawk's Nest Resort and Marina, www
    .hawks-nest.com
Pigeon Cay Beach Club, www
    .pigeoncay-bahamas.com

Crooked Island

The beautiful wadeable shallow waters of Acklin's Bight is the piscatorial highlight of Crooked Island. This is a wide expanse of flats between Acklin and Crooked Islands. Cliffs, reefs, abundant bird life, bonefishing, inshore and offshore angling that rival anything in the Bahamas.

CONTACTS
Pittstown Point Landing, www
    .pittstownpointlandings.com

Eleuthera-Harbour Island

Eleuthera means "freedom" in Greek. A popular spot for do-it-yourself fishing for bonefish and other fish. That's got to be a bad thing. Hire a guide. Eleuthera has plenty of rocky spots, dropoffs, creeks (especially around North Eleuthera), bays, and of course flats. Amy's dream hotel is here, on Harbour Island, the Pink Sands Hotel, a real luxury hotel complete with pink sandy beaches, and apparently, she tells me, I'm taking her there this year. Fine with me. The bonefishing's great there.

CONTACTS

Pink Sands Hotel, www.islandoutpost.com
Rainbow Inn, www.rainbowinn.com
Duck Inn, www.theduckinn.com

Exuma

Known as much for being a leading yachting anchorage as it is for flats and reef fishing. Two islands make up Exuma, Great and Little Exuma. Miles and miles of white sand beaches mean awesome wade fishing for bonefish.

CONTACTS

Peace and Plenty Bonefish Lodge, www
    .ppbonefishlodge.net
Barraterre Bonefish Lodge, www
    .barraterrebonefishlodge.com

Grand Bahama Island

One of the more developed islands of the Bahamas, Grand Bahama, the amazing flats have remained productive and reports still show the bonefish are heavy, on average about 5 pounds. If you want a family vacation with all the big resort activity and to fish while you're on that vacation, don't select Nassau. Choose Grand Bahama. That is, if you really want to have a world-class fishery (inshore and offshore) plus all the Bahamas tourist activities. If you don't want a family vacation but want world-class fishing plus a variety of excellent restaurants and shopping, then Grand Bahama is the place to go. Double digit bonefish. It has it all.

Deep Water Cay Club is a famous fishing lodge with white sandy beaches on a remote cay that both offers fishing packages to the public and equity membership in the club. The place is first-rate and so is the water, some of the best flats in the world. We're talking average bones in the 5 to 6 range with numerous 7- to 10-pounders you'll see. Record for the lodge is 13.5 pounds. There aren't many saltwater establishments that rival this one.

CONTACTS

Deep Water Cay Club, www
    .deepwatercay.com
Pelican Bay Bonefish Club, www
    .pelicanbaybonefishing.com
North Riding Point, www
    .northridingpointclub.com

Great Inagua

If you rearrange the word *inagua* you get *iguana* and that's how they named Great and Little Inagua. Anagram. Common to these shores. The Inaguas are at the southernmost of the Bahamas and Great Inagua is the third-largest island. Morton Salt produces millions of pounds of salt in the Salinas here. World's largest colonies of flamingos live in the Inaguas. Everlasting flats and ragged shorelines, even an inland lake (Lake Windsor) with tarpon, the Inaguas are remote and special for anglers, something different, the most consistent tarpon fishery.

CONTACTS
Morton Main House, 242-339-1267
Ezzard Cartwright, guide, 242-339-1362

Long Island

Seventy-six miles of the prettiest unspoiled tranquility you've ever seen. Long Island is both serenity (white beaches of fine sand, rolling hills, peaceful bays) and power (rocky crashing beaches, caves, and bluffs). However beautiful other Bahama islands are, this one takes it to a new level with breathtakingly gorgeous beaches. And the flats fishing is superb, but tides decide if you wade or skiff. Stella Maris is an ideal hideaway with stunning architecture and amazing history (Columbus made port here).

CONTACTS
Stella Maris Resort Club, www
    .stellamarisresort.com
The Triple Seas Bonefish Lodge, 242-357-
    1067 (cell), 242-337-0443 (home)
Samuel Knowles Bonefishing, 242-337-
    1056
Chez Pierre, www.chezpierrebahamas.com

Mayaguana

Here's your Bahamian wilderness. Your virgin getaway. Where you can find water that never sees anglers. At least not anglers as capable and good-looking as you. Mayaguana is at the easternmost of the Bahamas, as remote as it gets. Curtis Creek, Blackwood Point, and Abrahams Bay are the three flats that are the most productive at this point, but who knows what you and your guide will discover in these relatively new fishing grounds? Come to think of it, a wild place like this might be ideal for the do-it-yourselfer.

CONTACTS
Baycaneer Hotel, www.baycanerbeach
    .com
Frontiers Travel, www.frontierstravel.com
Angling Destinations, www
    .anglingdestinations.com
The Fly Shop, www.theflyshop.com
Angler Adventures, www.angleradventures
    .com
InterAngler, www.interangler.com
Waders On, www.waderson.com
FishQuest, www.fishquest.com
So many guides and outfitters and
    lodges and resorts and booking
    agents, I couldn't possibly list them
    all here.
Kim and Stephen Vletas penned the end-
    all, definitive book for fishing the Baha-
    mas. If you fish the Bahamas, you must
    own and read their book, *The Bahamas
    Fly Fishing Guide* published by Lyons
    Press.

BERMUDA

- **Location:** Western Atlantic Ocean, a good ways east of the Carolinas
- **What You Fish For:** Bonefish, barracuda, etc.
- **Highlights and Notables:** Easy to get to, vacation spot, ideal as an adjunct trip to a holiday or business trip

Growing up, I always thought that Bermuda was a place, not a bunch of places. Bermuda is a chain of islands, some 138 of them. You won't find it listed in a book of Caribbean Islands (again, like I once thought) because it's not. It's northerly, in the western Atlantic Ocean, humid in the summer, cool to cold in the winter.

The fishing spots of the Bermuda Islands are both twenty-five miles southwest, Argus Banks and Challenger Banks. At Argus, the water depth falls from twenty-five to 710 fathoms faster than you can say "Bermuda Triangle." The fishing is iffy, dependent, sometimes good, you can do good but you could do better and it's for yellowfin tuna, wahoo, blackfin tuna, Almaco jack (great on a fly rod), bonito, rainbow runners, and maybe, probably, possibly not but maybe, a blue or white marlin.

If you're in Bermuda on business or pleasure, you should try fishing for bones and 'cuda in the deeper-than-most flats on the northern shore, around Somerset, Whale Bay, Bare Butt Bay (no, I did not stutter-type) on your own, or hire a charter to try a day of offshore angling. Bermuda is hardly the place to which you'd want to plan a first-class fishing excursion.

CAYMAN ISLANDS

- **Location:** South of Miami 500 miles
- **What You Fish For:** Bonefish, tarpon
- **Highlights and Notables:** The fishing is superb but this is superb fishing in jaw-dropping scenery.

The bonefishing is pretty good but the fact that this pretty-good bonefishing is located in the Cayman Islands, the Caribbean's most beautiful waters, makes the bonefishing even better. Sun, lounge, eat, drink, dive, and fish. The perfect laid-back (albeit expensive) vacation.

There's tarpon, too.

Triumvirate: Grand Cayman, Cayman Brac, and Little Cayman.

Location: Less than 500 miles south of

Miami, Florida, and a couple of hundred miles west of Jamaica.

Species: Bonefish, tarpon, yellowfin tuna, blackfin tuna, blue marlin, dolphin, wahoo.

Little Cayman: Best bonefishing of the three.

Cayman Brac: Bonefish average about 1 to 5 pounds.

Grand Cayman: More about the big game here. Plenty of charter boats for hire. They'll take you out past the reeds to the Wall where the depths go from shallow to Jules Verne in a heartbeat; or the Cayman Banks west of the island. The blue marlin are neither abundant nor huge, averaging less than 200 pounds. Small bones in a few flats with Head of Barkers flats a first option for doing it yourself. Tarpon are caught in all kinds of water including mangroves, as well as ditches and canals not far from Georgetown. Most are juveniles.

Flights: One hour flight from Miami. Several major airlines fly into Grand Cayman. You take Cayman Airways to the lesser two.

CONTACTS

Cayman Islands Department of Tourism, 420 Lexington Avenue, Suite 2733, New York, NY 10170, 212-682-5582, 708-678-6446, Fax 212-986-5123

DRY TORTUGAS

- **Location:** West of the Key West, Florida
- **What You Fish For:** Bonefish, tarpon
- **Highlights and Notables:** An American national park (surprised?). Solitude in waters every bit as productive as the more crowded waters of the Keys.

Casting a crappy 80-feet in what is not quite a double haul (more a 1¾ haul) versus some really sharp 40-foot casts. That's my dilemma. I cast a fly rod okay-to-good in fresh, less-than-okay-to-okay in salt. On the flats of Dry Tortugas, which means the "Not-Wet Turtle," I can get by—and so can you—with not being the best caster in the world (or even on that particular flats stretch you are fishing).

What the heck and where the heck is (are?) Dry Tortugas?

To begin, the tiny smattering of low-slung islands known as the Dry Tortugas is a national park (betcha didn't know that) that lies as the crow flies seventy-five miles west of Key West, Florida. Uninhabitable. Reefs and shoals and flats as far as the eye can see. Sunken wrecks. A year-round fishery for more game fish than you can count on your tanned fingers and toes only one and a half to two hours by boat from Key West.

The reef you see is the last undamaged coral reef in America. As a national park, no commercial fishing takes place. Dry Tortugas is one of the last great fishing frontiers.

You can charter a boat, take your own boat (full up with supplies and radio and other essentials because there is *no way* to gas up or get *any* food or water or anything but sand, salt, and fish), or fly in on a seaplane. No accommodations except what you came in on. Fort Jefferson, the only building on all of these islands, a former fort and prison, is the centerpiece of this national park (on Garden Key Island). I have heard that one or some of the guides can get you in the fort for a night and in the a/c. I don't know for sure about this. I'm a camper myself. And no mosquitos.

You can camp on the beach or grass if you want. If you don't know the trip, I recommend hiring a two-day charter that will navigate your way to the Tortugas where you can camp at Garden Key or provide a mothership with a comfortable boat to sleep on.

Since there are no resorts or condos or huts or population at all, you can deduce correctly that the fishing pressure is light. Speaking of light, this is a light tackle enthusiast's dream. The water is green melon and Prussian blue but clear, so clear you can see to the bottom, you can witness schools of fish swimming about. You won't likely see any other boats or people moving about. That's what's so great. You own this joint. So what can you catch? Man, the list is endless, the action nonstop and furious.

And by the way, the IGFA record book is lousy with record fish from these waters all the way to Key West. Pretty amazing most folks have never heard of Dry Tortugas. The list of opportunities is amazing: wahoo, tarpon, permit, barracuda, sailfish, king mackerel, yellowtail snapper, grouper of all kinds, amberjack (50 to 60 pounds and up), cobia, blackfin tuna, mutton snapper, jack crevalle, African pompano, horse-eyed jack, dolphin, and more.

Jumping tarpon, wearing out your body on amberjack, cranking in king mackerel, hanging on for dear life with wahoo, sight-fishing to permit—you can do this and more all on light tackle, no bigger than 20-pound tackle. Wet your whistle at the Dry Tortugas.

PUERTO RICO

- **Location:** East of Dominican Republic, west of the Virgin Islands
- **What You Fish For:** Marlin, sailfish, bonefish, peacock bass, largemouth bass
- **Highlights and Notables:** Easy to find flights from America, a quick plane ride and once you're there, you'll fall in love with the beaches, mountains, food, and people. And the fishing.

Water. Always about water or the need for water.

I lived for three years in Ponce, Puerto Rico, on the south side of the island. Dad was project manager for H. B. Zachry at the power plant. For a ten-year-old boy who spent three years on this rich adventure-laden island, Puerto Rico was heaven.

I loved Tio Tom's barbecue (pig, spit-roasted) but the drive on the way through the mountains to San Juan to visit El Morro on serpentine two-lane roads (no guardrails) with Sea-Land 18-wheelers honking as they rounded corners on their way from San Juan, loaded enough that they often swayed from side to side, scared the hell out of me each time and always ended with me throwing up on the side of the road. Mom would have a glass of water for me ready for the upchuck.

I loved empanadas, a fried meat pie that we called *impapadillas,* purchased from food kiosks that seemed to be everywhere. The best ones had cheese and pep-

pers in them and cold water was the only way to take the delectable sting out of your mouth. Mom would give us a couple of dollars when the fruit-and-vegetable-cart man would come down the street to buy fresh avocadoes and two dollars when the shaved-ice-cart man would rattle down our *calle.* (Dad, who spoke no Spanish, once said to me that he didn't know who or what *Calle* was but the Puerto Ricans sure were proud of it because it was on almost every sign in the commonwealth. *Calle* means street.)

More than once, in Ponce, in our little concrete block house in Quintas de Monserrate, I stole drinks of Don Q Rum from my father's liquor cabinet (and threw up more than once). Chuck Osucha and

Right out your hotel window on the beaches of San Juan, you can see where you can go catch tarpon and other game fish.

Charles Glantzberg and Tom Butz and I used to take our BB guns and fishing poles and hike into the mountains behind our house and shoot lizards and fearfully try to catch iguanas and we would catch colorful little fish from the creek with bacon, and we'd find a shady tree and eat pomegranates and kumquat-type fruits we'd pick from wild trees in the rain forest jungle.

Yeah, Mom and Dad would force the family to go to El Yunque rain forest or take a boat trip at night in Phosphorescent Bay where you could see any living thing glowing blue in the inky-dark water.

Snorkeling off the white sandy beaches at Mayaguez, I needed my good friend, a virtual man-child, Clay Hanks, to hold my hand through the clear water because I had not yet learned how to swim at age eleven. Thanks, Clay.

My brother, then four, fell into the hot coals where the men were slow-roasting an entire pig and he cried so loudly no sound came out and the men's faces had horrified expressions as they saw the three glowing embers embedded in his shins. When Matt did finally emit a sound, it curdled the blood and reached your soul. The water they tossed on his leg made steam rise and the poor little kid just screamed and screamed.

I often sailed with one of my friends in their catamaran, with other teen boys and girls, to Coffin Island and we anchored off shore, swam to the rough sandy beaches and climbed to the top of the peak; all the while, I kept my eye on the bikinis the teen girls wore.

I learned how to swim more or less (my sister Tammy says "less" is more like it) at the ritzy Intercontinental Hotel pool in downtown Ponce. My instructor grew impatient with my fear, and in front of my mother—and much to her dismay—tossed me in the deep water and pushed me back everytime I dog paddled to the safety of the lipped edge. My mother was further embarrassed because I kept hollering out to the instructor, in between taking in great gulps of chlorine-laced pool water "I hate you blub blub blub" and "I can't swim, he's killing me, Mom, blub blub blub" and "I wish you were blub blub blub dead."

Beisbol was king in Puerto Rico and I remember Dad with tears in his eyes twice in Puerto Rico, both times when someone meaningful died—once when we found out native Roberto Clemente had perished in a plane crash and the other when Dad's father, Grandaddy Williams, lost his life in a pickup truck crash.

Dad took me twice to the American Airlines Celebrity Pro-Am golf tourney and it was there I got autographs from Willie Mays and Joe DiMaggio and Joe Namath. My hero Johnny Bench told me to shut up, can't you see he's trying to hit, when I asked for his autograph and Del Unser was in the middle of a backswing.

Puerto Rico. I thought I was done with the crowded beautiful schizophrenic little nation that's not quite a country or a state. Growing up, I watched the political rallies that would go mobile, on the narrow roads, that would go four or five cars abreast, their white flags with logos representing their political affiliation hanging from their antennas. Water shortages from strikes.

Speaking of water shortages, Dad should have killed me but he stood up for me. Age thirteen, I went to shower before we were going as a family (ugh) to see *The Ten Commandments*. No water, the shortage hit again. We got home four or five or ten hours later, it seemed like an eternity but not as long as the fear felt in my chest when we rounded the corner to our concrete block house and saw water running from under the front door and filling the street with a minor river. The water had come back on while we were at the movie, that interminable movie that even had an intermission, and I had forgotten, in my teenage absentmindedness, to turn the faucet back to off. I wished Moses was standing beside me to make the waters part.

Dad opened the front door and like a really bad movie, water rushed out. All the rattan furniture in our house was floating. I wanted to die and Mom was quite willing to help me achieve it. Dad told her to leave me alone and he got to work and we all got to work, moving furniture to the front yard, squeegeeing out the house. I never loved that old man more than that quiet few hours.

Across the street from our mostly white, foreigner, new-house neighborhood flowed a river. And on that river lived two families. In shanty huts. They drank from and bathed and washed their clothes in the river.

Years later, I am back in Puerto Rico. Several times. I am working on articles about Juan Gonzalez and Pudge Rodriguez, about Latin American baseball in general, on a book about Juan Gonzalez, with Juan touring the barrio where he grew up, and for *SPORT* magazine covering a celebrity All-Star softball game. I am running around interviewing Ruben Sierra, Tony Perez, Dona Clemente (Roberto's wife) and Roberto Jr., the Governor, Magic Johnson, and other Puerto Rican dignitaries (*leyendes de beisbol*), getting interviewed on the radio and hoping my Spanish was up to par, eating Cuban food with Luis Mayoral, and watching athletes at the disco cheating on their wives with hoochie mamas.

And fishing.

The first marlin I ever caught, not all that far from where I used to play golf at the Cerromar, El Conquistador, and Dorado Beach (and shoot over 100), and where I first met Chi Chi Rodriguez. Less than two miles offshore, depths drop to 1,000 feet. The blue marlin are leapers, huge and powerful and menacing and beautiful. Summer is the time to be on offshore here but the rest of the months are good for everything else.

You can catch mahi-mahi, dolphin fish, wahoo, kingfish, bonito, barracuda (Dad never told me there were barracuda in these waters while I was twelve and snorkeling and being a scared bad swimmer), and various pelagic species including sometimes white marlin. The big blue marlin is the key. The northern shores of Puerto Rico are so good for blues that they christened themselves the "Blue Marlin Capital of the World." The island of Culebra (means "snake") is a new hotspot to fish flats for bonefish and permit. Culebra is quiet and nontouristy. The flats of Luquillo are popular for barracuda. Heck, in the lagoons right near the airport, I've hooked five or six 10- to 20-pound tarpon in an afternoon. The guides are good (for the most part) and can put you on fish (albeit on the smaller side).

Bass fishing was pretty popular on the island as I remember and the Puerto Rican largemouth bass (*lobina*), with its year-round eating season, can grow an inch a month. Nowadays, tarpon (*sabalo*) fishing is the hot action while peacock bass (*tucanare*) and tilapia fishing are sizzling. Vieques is another island off the Puerto Rican coast where more and more fishing friends are finding solitude and good fishing. Bonefishing in the flats and tarpon in the lagoon mouths.

First, remember that P. R. is a notch above a third-world country. And you're on Puerto Rican time, which is much slower and more relaxed than even Margaritaville time. Regulations and maintenance and vigilance are not staples of Puerto Rican commonwealth government so you will run into lots of variables, some good, some not so good.

Puerto Rico has about twenty-five lakes stocked with bass, catfish, and a few (seven at last count) with peacock bass and tilapia. Peacock bass lakes: Carraizo, Guajataca, La Plata, Cidra, Dos Bocas, Patillas, and Carite. Quality? The average Puerto Rican peacock bass weighs about 1 to 2 pounds, a 6-pound a huge catch. Compare this to the commonwealth record bucketmouth which is 14 pounds. Your best bet to find the best inland fishing is to contact one of the many fishing clubs on the island.

Hire a guide to take you into the lagoons and mangroves and mouths of rivers to chase tarpon so you can bow to the silver king and snook, too. Sabalo run up to 150 pounds in these shallows, ideal for heart attacks and fly fishing.

San Juan will be your best place to lodge. This colonial city has history galore, so leave time to visit the fortress El Morro, walk through the narrow cobbled streets, play at the casinos, snorkel in the clear blue water, eat at a fancy restaurant, eat an empanada from a local vendor. Some of the hotels are world-class but San Juan has lodging for all budgets.

CONTACTS

Fishermen of Rivers and Lakes, P.O. Box 2161, Hato Rey, Puerto Rico 00919
Federación of Lake Fishermen, P.O. Box 3813, Hato Rey, Puerto Rico, 00919
Caribbean Fly Fishing Company, 787-450-3744; www.viequesflyfishing.com

TURKS AND CAICOS

- **Location:** A logical extension of the Bahamas but not the Bahamas—southeast of the Bahamas, north of Dominican Republic
- **What You Fish For:** Bonefish, barracuda
- **Highlights and Notables:** Scintillatingly beautiful beaches and water, the fishing for bones good enough to pull you away from drinks on the sandy shore

This is one of the better bonefishing locations in the Caribbean. I would easily recommend the trip but I don't want to compare it to crème de la crème like the Bahamas or Los Roques. Neither is this a trip where you fish while you are on vacation. This is a real-life fishing destination where you can vacation (the islands are typical Caribbean take-your-breath-away scenery) or you can *just* fish. Turks and Caicos is easy and quick to reach from any eastern city. Traveling anglers always need another sandy beach on their horizon so here it is.

The guides sure feel like the bonefishing is extraordinaire, with some charging nearly $800 a day to take you to the flats

Turks and Caicos

to fish for the bones. The bonefishing is pretty good here, folks, but not that good. Of course, you can find reputable and affordable outfitters in Caicos.

There are thirty islands in this Bahamas chain that is not part of the Bahamas (British West Indies) and is not very well known. Provo (Providenciales) is the main tourist island hangout, built up way too much, with lots of guesthouses and resorts and high-rise hotels and shopping. Provo's flats fishing is nice for 4- to 6-pound bones with the occasional double digit fish or close enough to it. Provo is also ideal for snorkelers and skin divers (is that what they are still called?). Barracuda hang out in the flats, too, but you're more or less on your own finding them.

Turks and Caicos lies north of Haiti and southeast of the Bahamas and overall, from food to drinks to lodging (excluding silly guide rates) is one of the least expensive Caribbean fishing vacations you can do, but I have talked with folks who did things up right and spent way too much money on the main island. You don't have to if you don't want to. North Caicos is especially inexpensive, laid back and do-it-yourselfish. South Caicos has fewer folks, bigger and more numerous flats, and with the right guide, you'll be on more bones more often. With a guide, you can realistically expect to catch ten to twenty a day with the odd day less or more. Some have complained about the limited number of qualified guides in the islands and others complain about—now get this—how the bonefish are not easily spooked enough. Too easy in other words. Jeez.

The Turks and Caicos offshore ops include blue marlin but even though the islands are on the migration route, the blue marlin are just not all that big. So you have hard sandy bottoms (that sounds funny to me) for bonefish and barracuda. If you could find a kayak on the island, I think you could get around nicely on the flats of Provo and have a nice shot at finding the bones. You can get flights direct to Provo, and Sky King is a short fifteen-minute flight to South Caicos.

CONTACTS
Ocean Bay Hotel Condominium,
   Whitby Beach, North Caicos,
   649-946-7113
Catch The Wave Charters, Providenciales,
   649-941-3047
Barr Gardiner, Providenciales, www.provo
   .net/bonefish
Bibo Jayne, Beyond the Blue, Melbourne
   Beach, FL, www.beyondtheblue.com
Marta Morton, Harbour Club Villas &
   Marinas, www.harbourclubvillas.com

British Virgin Islands

- **Location:** Caribbean, east of Puerto Rico, north of the U.S. Virgin Islands
- **What You Fish For:** Bonefish, marlin, permit, tarpon, and others
- **Highlights and Notables:** Underrated, known more for its sailing ops than anything else. The British Virgin Islands are as good a deal, for the combination of price and quality of bonefishing, as you will find in the Caribbean.

Wish you were here.

You should have been here yesterday.

Nature's Little Secrets, the British Virgin Islands.

Forever began in the BVI.

I don't want to go home.

The British Virgin Islands fly under the tourist and angling radar, a secret collection of verdant specks, some fifty or sixty-odd idyllic green islands rising up through the aqua-blue Caribbean shallow waters east of Puerto Rico replete with coral atolls, reefs, and islets, where no building is taller than the tallest palm tree. Most tourists pass on visiting BVI and focus on the touristy, expensive, cruise-ship laden ports of the U.S. Virgin Islands. Let them. You want bonefish? You want marlin? Fly into San Juan, catch a jump plane over to Tortola (Turtle

Dove) and get busy doing nothing. Funky. Laid back. Low key. As beautiful as any islands anywhere in the world. Friendly folks and low crime. No high-rise hotels, no casinos, no crowds. Where Robert Louis Stevenson found his inspiration for *Treasure*

British Virgin Islands

Island. And the best word to describe these emerald jewels—mystical.

Island time. You hear about it for other islands, where time slows down, people are late but don't worry about it. Island time was obviously invented in the British Virgin Islands. And you won't mind one bit.

Catch the ferry from Road Town to Anegada. Hire the only fishing guides on the island, the only coral island in this bevy of beautiful volcanic isles. Garfield and Kevin Faulkner. Brothers in arms. Legacy to the founding fathers of the is-

land. Funny and handsome and knowledgeable and competitive. The island is less than thirty feet high at its highest point, a thick-jungled retreat of only 250 or less full-time inhabitants.

The white sandy beaches and clear green and blue waters and miles and miles of flats. These expansive flats are what make this a bonefishing heaven and an altogether different fishing experience than fishing the sister islands of the U.S. Virgin Islands. These big wide flats run about one to two feet deep and through them roam schools of bonefish, sometimes 100 in number, and these silver streaks average 4 to 6 pounds. And it's great fishing, good weather, all year long.

You haven't heard about the bonefishing in Anegada have you? Have you heard that they catch 10- to 12-pounders, too? To give

The rain tickles at first, feels good against the sun behind us. Then the waves precede the fiercer winds and I think Kevin is a smart man and we need to get to shore pronto. Noelle hooks into a bonefish, and good, the teal flats spitting up sprinkles of waterdrops from the running fish.

The bone runs, Noelle tries to lift the tip of the rod but this fish is game, a runner, girthy and powerful. Kevin's firm voice tells her to keep that tip up or else and she does for a while but I have to put a finger in the middle to help, a spotter for a lifter, just enough help to let it still be all her own.

Run and pull, reel and lift. Fifteen minutes before the bonefish comes to hand. Kevin hands the fish carefully to Noelle, Amy and Christi and me with cameras at the ready, click click and the 6-pounder says

you an idea of how productive this fishery is, here's a microcosm:

The sky bellows gray clouds that blow out like smoke from a giant and the wall of dark force fills the horizon behind us. We are fishing near Conch Island, a man-made reef of used conch shells. The stillness belies the impending power.

Noelle Casagrande fishes from the bow, an experienced angler on shore, not from a boat. The flats are murky and high from the surge, the winds of the morning. As the winds increase, the boat rocks, Noelle's footing becomes more and more unsure. She is casting a Gotcha, letting it sink, retrieving and letting sink, retrieving and letting sink, blind casting. You can't see an inch under the water and Kevin is about ready to pack it in.

It's a real storm headed our way.

enough and it is enough and the fish powers its way out of her hands and into the pitted water and the rain comes down and we are wet and happy and tired and ready to go back to eat shrimp and drink Bushwackers and watch the world pass us by.

Here's the reason to make BVI the season: You can catch bonefish 'til your arm drops off, quality bones the equal of most any Caribbean destination, and because the costs are lower all around, you can stay a day or two or three longer fishing, napping, eating, and enjoying the other aspects of Island Time. Jost Van Dyke, Beef Island, Marina Cay also have reputations for excellent bonefishing.

The lodging options range from quaint quiet inexpensive beachside villas to affordable midrange hotels to braggin'-rights for humongous villas with panoramic views. I recommend doing things the local way, get to know the islands from the people who live there—stay at the Jewels of the BVI, a charming collection of intimate inns of all types nestled in her green mountainous bosoms and on her sandy shores.

If you go, you must enjoy a rum drink at Pusser's (probably a Painkiller) on Tortola, visit the Baths on Virgin Gorda, see the wreck of the Rhone, drink with the British Royal Navy like we did all day on the beach at Myetts (hey Daisy!), and make sure to listen to fungi, eat lobster at the Rock Café and drink more rum. BTW, when you order a *Carib* beer, it's Care-Rib with no Spanishy flair. Everyone swears by the conch fritters but they're not my cup of tea.

You can fish for everything from wahoo to yellowfin to mahi-mahi to tarpon to tuna to kingfish and even permit but as an adjunct fishing trip, I suggest going fishing for 900-pound marlin (and other billfish) in both the North Drop (just thirty minutes off the north coast of Virgin Gorda) and the South Drop, providing probably the largest regular marlin fishing in the Atlantic. The tarpon fishery is unknown, sounds great and I intend to go back and find out the old fashioned way.

CONTACTS

Garfields Guides, Garfield and Kevin
    Faulkner, home: 284-495-9569, cell:
    284-496-9699

British Virgin Islands Tourist Board, 284-
    494-3134, 800-835-8530
Some of my favorite inns and villas:
Mongoose Apartments
Fischer Cove Beach Hotel
Villa Majesty
Turtle Dove Cottages
Guavaberry Spring Bay
Seven Jewels Manor
Marta Morton, Harbour Club Villas and
    Marins, www.bonefishing.tc, www
    .harbourclubvillas.com
Paola Calabria Dean, Silver Deep, www
    .silverdeep.com

Central America

BELIZE

- **Location:** Central America, right up against Mexico and Guatemala, Caribbean side
- **What You Fish For:** Permit, sailfish, and bonefish
- **Highlights and Notables:** Permit and bonefish mecca. Turneffe Flats is one of the richest bone hotspots anywhere.

My friends Aaron (A-Dub) and Dez Witt did the Peace Corps thing for a couple of years in Belize and got to know the country much more intimately than those of us who visit for a few days and stay in comfortable lodges and fish all day. They rave about how friendly the people are, how comfortable they are in their own skin, how you have to get on Belizean time instead of thinking like a fast-paced American.

The Witts are travelers and athletic (how did Aaron land such a hot wife)? so they'd get out each weekend and visit Mayan ruins, climb mountains, raft rivers (Aaron tells a great story about rafting through a dark cave followed by a rapid descent—something akin to a waterfall in the making). They visited nature preserves and tell great stories about howler monkeys and jaguars and the like.

Aaron was born twenty years too late. He's a beatnik, an anachronism. He looks like Shaggy from *Scooby-Doo* but he's smart as a whip. Laid back, little goatee, dry quick wit (not witt), helluva tennis player, but definitely not an outdoorsman or sportsman.

Aaron didn't even want to go fishing. Like I say, he is not a fisherman. Aaron's Dad visited, wanted to do some fishing, hired a boat to take him offshore and he made Aaron go with him. Reluctantly.

Aaron caught a marlin big enough to make anyone proud and also a sailfish.

Belize.

It rolls off the tongue, easily, like water lapping sand.

Belize.

Stress-free. Laid back. Rich culture. No standing army. Cockroaches as big as birds.

On the east coast of Central America, tucked between Mexico and Guatemala, Belize is the only English-speaking country in Central America (reason: former British colony) and was known as British Honduras until 1973. Guatemala has always considered Belize as its own and still makes tenuous claims of ownership today. Only a quarter of a million people live in this tiny country.

Belize is the best place on earth to fish for the elusive permit. Belize has the second longest barrier reef in the world, behind only the Great Barrier Reef. Behind this reef are islets and islands by the hundreds. It's hot and muggy; from May to November is the rainy season. One of the best

Proud angler Aaron Witt with his first billfish

things about Belize is that it's just a two-hour flight from Houston or Miami. Belize has all the requisite Caribbean game fish/eyepopping habitat—flats, cays, channels, mangroves, and river mouths.

It's about the permit in Belize, that elusive predator. Belize is the best place in the world either to catch your first permit or to catch your largest. The permit are typically 10 to 15 pounds but you have legit shots at permit upwards of 35 pounds.

It's also about the bonefish on Turneffe Flats (and other places, of course, but this is the top spot). And it's about wade fishing in Belize since the flats are firm (coral in southern Belize) and the fish are in the flats or on the edges. You won't fish from boats (shallow water skiffs) very often here save for the softer flats, and if you are permit fishing, sometimes. Fly fishing is popular but light spinning tackle is fun here, too.

The tarpon are the smaller side but you can sure catch them. Catch tarpon, bonefish, and permit all in one day and you have the Caribbean Grand Slam. To me, a Grand Slam needs four elements or the metaphor doesn't work. And I could also care less about artificial awards or designations—I don't care about being forty versus being thirty-nine and one day from being forty. I don't care much about a trout being 19 inches or 20 inches, it's still a nice fish. But I do care about being handed the huge check for the Publisher's Clearinghouse Sweepstakes, and I care about jumping tarpon. Belize tarpon fishing is exciting and you can jump several a day with a good guide. These tarpon don't reach the magic 200-pound mark but they're big enough for you and me. These run 50 to 100 pounds with some in the 130 range.

The bonefish are not trophy size either and since Belize doesn't have vast flats like its northern neighbor Mexico and its Yucatán wadeable flats, bonefishing ranks third in Belizean targets. That said, anglers do catch and release 107-pound bones so it's not as though they're minnows. Your average Belizean bone goes about 1 to 5 pounds. Good spot for beginners since if you put in a full day fishing, you see a hundred bonefish, mostly in schools but some larger singles. You might see 100 bonefish in a single school, that's how prolific the fishery is in Belize.

Other flats fish besides bonefish, permit, and tarpon include grouper, barracuda, and snapper. The reef fishing is excellent for large wahoo, barracuda, grouper, and king mackerel (trolling, usually). The offshore fishing, while not world class, is underrated—not fully developed, the marlin and sails not as plentiful; the fishery could be good, could be marginal, could be amazing—it's still being understood. Best served by motherships because of the great distances from Belize City.

The two best fishing lodges are a study in contrast:

Blue Horizon Lodge is a comfortable lodge but nothing fancy. This is a lodge for serious anglers who care little about paying for all the amenities. Blue Horizon is an angling retreat—meat and potatoes—you're not paying for any extras. The food

> In the rivermouths, you can catch snook, baby tarpon, jacks, and grouper.

is simple and comforting. Lincoln Westby and his guides are the tops in Belize.

Turneffe Flats Lodge lies thirty miles off the coast and is known for being located on one of the most famous flats sections in the world. You're on foot much of the time on the shallow, easily waded flats. The lodge is modern, recently remodeled, fine food, more along the lines of what saltwater anglers have become accustomed over the years. Beachfront cabins for sixteen.

A few other worthwhile lodges aren't total fishing-crazy lodges so if you want a more balanced trip, consider these: El Pescador Ambergis (family-oriented), Turneffe Island Lodge, El Pescador Punta Gorda (eco-friendly).

The tarpon season runs from mid-April to November, peaking in June to September. Outstanding scuba, snorkeling, swimming, and Mayan ruins add to the Belizean appeal. Ideal for a partner/spouse/friend who doesn't fish. Belize has outstanding diving, snorkeling, sightseeing, etc. Moonlight fishing for tarpon is efficient and popular. English is the official language in Belize, although Creole is commonly spoken. Valid passport required. Use 8- to 10-weight rods for permit, 7 to 8 for bones, 11 to 12 for tarpon.

CONTACTS

Don Muelrath, Fly Fishing Adventures, www.flyfishbelize.com, www.flyfishingadventures.org

El Pescador, Ambergris Caye, www.elpescador.com

The Inn at Robert's Grove, Placencia, www.robertsgrove.com

Chaa Creek Lodge, San Ignacio, www.chaacreek.com

Journey's End Resort, www.journeysendresort.com

Turneffe Flats, www.turneffeflats.com

Turneffe Island Lodge, www.turneffelodge.com

Action Belize, www.actionbelize.com

Belize Outdoor Expeditions, www.outdoorbelize.com

Belize River Lodge, www.belizeriverlodge.com

Blue Horizon Lodge, www.worldangler.com/blue.htm

Belize Fishing Adventures, www.flyfishbelize.com

InterAngler, Santa Fe, NM, www.interangler.com

FishQuest, www.fishquest.com

COSTA RICA

- **Location:** Central American country lodged between Panama to its south and Nicaragua to its north

- **What You Fish For:** Sailfish as well as snook, tarpon, billfish

- **Highlights and Notables:** The sailfish fishing compares favorably with other world-class locales but don't underestimate the angling for tarpon. Fishing for tarpon on the Rio Colorado is one of the weirdest, richest river experiences to be found.

Can you even imagine a place on earth where you might average fifteen to twenty or more sailfish bites per day on your trip? Okay, Guatemala, but other than Guatemala. Me neither. Costa Rica is one of the top billfish locations going, a new "Billfish Capital of the World."

But that's not all Costa Rica has up its jungle. How about flats-type fishing for roosterfish and snook? Or river fishing for tarpon? All world-class I might add. Warm friendly people. Billfishing par excellence on Pacific side. Snook and tarpon on the Caribbean. Blues, blacks, stripes, *but think sailfish*.

FRESHWATER AND CLOSE IN

It's a little intimidating sometimes, fishing a famous place, a place where the quality of fishing matches its rep. Not overwhelmingly so, just a knot in the stomach a bit.

The Rio Colorado experience, for instance. Silver kings in a big river. A big brown powerful river. You lose a rod while casting. More knots in your stomach.

Hundred-pound tarpon are a common occurrence at the mouth of this river and out in the Caribbean near the Rio Colorado. They move by the hundreds, sometimes the thousands. Some of the baddies reach 200 pounds. You see them chasing baitfish, then you blind-cast heavy weighted flies into the brown foamy frenzy and hold on. Aha. Now that's a tarpon. I can tell by the way he broke me off in seconds flat. Again. A jumper. Gone in sixty seconds.

Costa Rican tarpon are found in these stained ocean-meeting rivers. They are the Colorado, Parismina, and Tortugero. Some run up all the way into Lake Nicaragua. The freshwater tarpon angling has been distressed and diminished by many factors but there are few places that compare.

The snook (*calba*) factory runs hot and heavy in September and October but like tarpon, you can take them all year long. You can always catch native fish like *guapote, machaca,* and *mojara*. This Caribbean side is the low jungle, with rivers emptying murky brown water. Not much sightfishing on this side—blind casting to tarpon. You can also find inshore schools of dorado, schools of bonito, and when the bonito are popping the surface and you cast in a popper and clean up.

SALTWATER

Drake Bay is between Golfito to the south and to the north, Quepos. Remote and wild with beautiful scenery (sandy white beaches, rocky shores), real sailfish country. The snook world record from these waters.

Near Isla de Cano. Marlin, too—lots and lots. Yellowfin tuna, anyone? You reach the resort by floatplane or boat so you are by yourself. Like Pez Vela, you might catch a roosterfish that sets records. Drake Bay has great fishing lodges and clean, comfortable accommodations.

Quepos is another one of the sailfish capitals of the world. You'll see iguanas and monkeys and toucans and lush jungle. Set on the side of a mountain with some upscale lodging if you want it. Here you catch three species of marlin, wahoo, dorado, big eye tuna, and yellowfin tuna. And don't let the howler monkeys at daybreak wake you up.

In southern Costa Rica, on the famed Osa Peninsula, anglers can select from three super lodges: Roy's Zancudo Lodge, Golfito Sailfish Rancho, and Crocodile Bay Lodge. Golfo Dulce—The Sweet Gulf. North of the Panama border. This is one big-ass gulf.

Unbelievable lineup of fish: Marlin—black, blue, striped. Sailfish—ten to fifteen raised sails a day not uncommon, 100 pounds on average. Wahoo, dorad, yellowfin tuna. These are your top choices but you can also lay into grouper, cubera, snook (three species), some of the largest roosterfish in the world, bluefin trevally, tripletail, bonito, amberjack, bonefish, snapper (no fewer than five species), pomapano, crevalle jack.

The reef fishing has baitfish and that means lots of sportfish. The river mouths are always good (especially—or unfortunately, as the case may be—dorado, some real whoppers). Rocky spots, covers, shore and beaches, flats, humps, sandbars all fertile spots.

Outfits 20-pound, 50-pound, four teasers, two from bridge, two from cockpit, bait and switch. The pumping, the pressure, the tired arms, the charley horses, the back strain, the sunburn, the blisters. I must have seen Crocodile Bay Lodge on television fifteen times and now, here I am. A sailfish to the boat, it all happens so quickly and the circle hook—easy release and it's gone. Passport required and visa not required.

CONTACTS

Crocodile Bay Lodge, www.crocodilebay
.com

Roy's Zancudo Lodge, Playa Zancudo,
www.royszancudolodge.com

Trout in Costa Rican mountains? Yep. Americans stationed in Panama found a way to stock some of the high mountain streams of Costa Rica for their own angling pleasure. The government has continued stocking trout over the years and small trout thrive in the cool, clear waters today. The Rio Savegre is the most popular trout stream but you can also find them in the Rio Chirripo, Rio Copey, and Rio Toro.

Golfito Sailfish Rancho, www
.golfitosailfish.com
Rancho Pacifico, www.ranchopacifico
.com
Aguila de Osa Inn, www.aguiladeosa.com
Silver King Lodge, silverkinglodge.net
Casa Mar Lodge, www.casamarlodge.com

Rio Parismina Lodge, www.riop.com
Rio Colorado Lodge, www
.riocoloradolodge.com
On the Fly, www.nowfishing.com
InterAngler, www.interangler.com
Waders On, www.waderson.com
FishQuest, www.fishquest.com

GUATEMALA

- **Location:** Central America
- **What You Fish For:** Sailfish are the big draw.
- **Highlights and Notables:** This is arguably the best place in the world to raise sails.

It's a small world.

So I'm eating at Randy's, the best Amarillo restaurant, and it's not even located in Amarillo. Randy's is in Wildorado, a good twenty minutes west of Amarillo on I-40. Not many good eating joints in Amarillo. Now, if you want a burger or pizza or mediocre steak, you can get those in spades. In Amarillo, you can also find on every street corner a used car lot, a church, and a dollar store.

Out to eat with three couples: Dino (my honey-colored Eritrean friend) and his wife Cindy; Chad (the Crane) Huseman and his wife Terri; Drew (Burly) Perkins and his wife Chandra. And my wife Amy, of course.

We four couples were enjoying Randy's of Wildorado. Dark, stately, great prices on some dishes, you don't care about the prices on others because Randy's is just so darned good. Great wine selection. Super bar.

We're visiting with each other, drinking (red table wine, a shiraz I think), eating appetizers (artichoke dip, onion straws) waiting on our meals (they're fast for a gourmet-style restaurant) when I noticed a guy at the bar was chuckling at some of our lame jokes and playful banter.

The meals came (Parmesan-crusted chicken for me) and as we talked to the man at the bar, we found out he was Randy himself, owner of the establishment as well as full-time farmer. Only in the Panhandle.

Randy Allred, restaurateur/farmer was the ninth wheel and he and we were enjoying getting to know each other. Turns out, Randy has a son, Doug Cavin, and Doug owns a fishing travel company. He also sells seeds. Like I said, only in the Panhandle.

Randy calls Doug up, it's late and we've all been drinking and we're working on the brandy and getting ready for the check at this point, and Doug drives to his father's restaurant and he and I start talking fishing. Especially Doug's passion, fishing Guatemala.

I go home and Google Doug and find out the dude has all kinds of fishing records, line class records, fishes all over the world, too. Instant friendship.

So I ended up finding another fishing buddy and since I've fished Guatemala only once, and Doug has fished it a lot and frequently and recently, I thought I'd let him have his say on the fishing. Unlike many in the biz when they write about their locale *especial,* Doug isn't big on hyperbole, just the facts. A real Panhandle country boy.

Doug Cavin has this to say about Guatemala:

Guatemala represents one of the greatest sport fishing opportunities available today. Most people's idea of billfishing includes riding around in a boat all day and maybe seeing a fish or two along the way. This is not the case with Guatemala. An average day of fishing off the Pacific coast of Guatemala produces double digit shots at a billfish each day.

March of 2006 was a record setting month for Guatemala with both the conventional and fly fishing world records for catches in a day being shattered. The old conventional record of eighty sailfish being caught and released in one day (also in Guatemala) was shattered by the new record of 124 sailfish caught and released in one day by one boat. The old fly fishing record was also shattered in March. The old record of twenty-seven sailfish caught and released in one day (also in Guatemala) fell to the new record of fifty-seven.

Both of these records are still unofficial but it still goes to show the potential of this tremendous fishery. Pacific sailfish are the main attraction in Guatemala, but other species are a possibility. Blue marlin, dorado, yellowfin tuna, and wahoo are the most common other offshore species with roosterfish, cero mackerel, cubera snappers, and a tremendous population of hungry jack crevalle round out the inshore opportunities.

Fishing for sailfish should be the main objective of anyone that travels to Guatemala, but plan a day of inshore fishing to sample all the area has to offer. Most of the captains who fish the area are ready for any of the other offshore species if they appear while fishing for sailfish. The seas in Guatemala range from one to four feet on average, and the fishing grounds are close compared to some other destinations—average runs are four to forty miles depending on where the blue water and bait are each day.

There are a lot of misconceptions out there about the safety of Guatemala. I have traveled there and never felt uneasy about any aspect of the trip. I did a lot of research before my first trip and I couldn't find anything negative from anyone who had gone on a fishing trip in Guatemala. Now, could you get in trouble if you tried?

Yes. If I ask that question about your home town, what would the answer be? Any time you travel abroad you should exercise caution and stay in the areas that are recommended. The travel to Guatemala is easy and quick. The trip to the Pacific coast from Guatemala City is approximately a one and one half hour trip.

There are several different options for lodging and fishing in Guatemala. I represent The Great Sailfishing Company, which is one of the newer operations. They have two different lodging options. First are the private villas. These villas are very nice and have all the amenities of home with a chef, waiters, and cleaning crew for each villa. Option two is the Villas del Pacifico Resort, which is an all-inclusive resort. I would put it in the same class as the three- to four-star resorts of the Yucatán in Mexico. Most of the fishing is done out of thirty- to forty-foot sport fishing boats. These boats are nice and very maneuverable when backing down on a hot sailfish or marlin.

Guatemala is one of the finest fishing destinations available today. It is not only for the experienced angler, but a great place too for anyone to catch their first billfish. On an average day you can expect a minimum of ten opportunities at a sailfish. Guatemala is also a great place to target sailfish on a fly due to the number of opportunities per day. Other species are available offshore, but they should be considered a bonus if you happen across one. The inshore fishing, on the other hand, is worth a day of your trip. Roosterfish are *the primary target, but the cero mackerel and jack crevalle are plentiful and can add a lot of excitement to your day.*

Travel to Guatemala is easy, very safe, and moderately priced. The lodging and boats in Guatemala are first-class. Several different lodging and fishing packages are available.

Thanks Doug. I look forward to going to Guatemala with you some day and hooking up with some big ones.

I have found that Guatemala lives up to the hype but that they have a bit of an inferiority complex, numbers-oriented, still determined to prove that they and not X, Y, or Z are the true billfish capital of the world. Hey, it's the hot new billfishery. Iztapa, Antigua. Pacific sailfish in big numbers November through May. The seas are calm—there you are trolling with rigged ballyhoo, the bait and switch, satisfied in knowing that you raise more sails than you can imagine because the Guatemalan waters are rich in bait due to swirling currents or is it water temp or maybe the shape of the sea floor or that billfish are all catch-and-release nowadays? Happy because they have the greatest day-catch rates in the world.

You'll lose more sails than you bring in but how about ten to fifteen sails hooked in five or six hours? What gear? Twelve- or 14-weight fly rods, 300 yards backing, 500 grain shooting head, 60-pound bite tippet streamer tandem hooked need a great reel with excellent drag. Bring your passport. Enjoy.

CONTACTS

Doug Cavin, Doug's Fishing Adventures, Wildorado, TX, 806-426-7454, www .dougsfishingadventures.com/
Randy's of Wildorado, TX, www .randysofwildorado.com/home.htm
Baja On the Fly, bajafly@bajafly.com
Sailfish Bay Lodge, 513-984-8611, 800-638-7405
Guatemala Lodge, www.sailfishbay.com
The Great Sailfishing Company, www .greatsailfishing.com/en/indexeng .html
Pez Aguazul Pro Sportfishing, www .guatemalaflyfishing.com
Sailfish Guatemala, www .sailfish-guatemala.com
South Fishing, Inc., www .captainhookguatemala.com
InterAngler, www.interangler.com
Waders On, www.waderson.com
FishQuest, www.fishquest.com

HONDURAS

- **Location:** Central American country bordered by El Salvador, Guatemala, and Nicaragua
- **What You Fish For:** Inshore for bonefish, snook, tarpon, jacks, triggerfish; offshore tuna, sailfish, marlin, wahoo, dolphin, snapper
- **Highlights and Notables:** Remote, developing fishery, awesome potential, a labyrinth of lagoons and rivers, ideal for snook and tarpon and native game fish

My friends rave about *Boston Legal*. *Grey's Anatomy*. *Survivor*. *The Amazing Race*. *The Office*. Over the years, they've tried to get me to watch *E.R.*, *Everybody Loves Raymond*, *Coach*, and a slew of others that for various reasons, I just couldn't commit to. I finally fell for *West Wing* and I was disappointed in myself because 1) I had to watch the previous two years' episodes to get the backstory; 2) if you get into a show, you have to commit weekly time to it, and not just that half-hour or hour but time worrying about not going to dinner until it's over or finding a blank tape to videotape it for later and there goes another one to two weekly hours of my life; 3) there's a certain emotional energy that goes into a relationship with a TV show and I already had *Ab Fab* and *Twin Peaks* and *Northern*

Honduras

Exposure and *The Shield* and *The Sopranos* (along with my Mavs, Cowboys, Rangers, and Aggies) that I was married to and I am married, too, so I sure didn't need other distractions. And then *West Wing* ended, just like that.

I've been avoiding Honduras for years now.

I don't have a reason of epic logic. I just didn't have enough time or enough interest. I might have been tainted by early reports—negative—about the quality of guides and the usual new fishery problems and distractions. I know that, for the most part, the Honduras fishery has matured, has fewer problems. To fish the lagoons and flats of Honduras might still be an adventure fishing trip but hearing newer reports, the place has worked most of the really bad bugs out.

I am aware that Honduras is exotic in that way that Central American countries often are—the lodges provide all the comforts of home contrasted by surroundings that are simpler, reflective of unchanging culture. Natives handline fish, pick bananas; your rod and reel cost more than several of these families make in a year or two years. The food is of the water, the jungle, the mountains. Jaguar still kill cattle. I am aware that you can catch cubera as big as 56 pounds or 78 pounds or who knows how much bigger? I am aware that in Honduras the wahoo grow to weigh as much as Eva Longoria. I am aware that the fishin's for grouper, tuna, barracuda, jacks, mackerel, triggerfish, and more. Why I haven't visited yet, I just don't know.

I know there's great fishing. I know I love tropical getaways. I know I'll get to Honduras one day and if I decide I ever want to watch *E.R.* or *Boston Legal,* heck, there's always reruns.

I was visiting with Jason Balogh the other day. Jason guides on the Snake and in Honduras, a real fishing bum, can't get enough angling. "I was thinking that the best thing about fishing the flats of Honduras," Jason told me, "is the opportunity to stalk permit on foot. There aren't too many places in the world where you can do that." Jason is right, you know. Jason did his best to turn me around, to come to Honduras, to try this show. So I'm working on a plan to get there next year. Here's part of his pitch:

Mango Creek Lodge

On the eastern side of Roatan Island, the quieter and less populated side of the island, which pirates and buccaneers once called home port, sits Mango Creek Lodge. The lodge was originally built as a luxury retreat and then four over-water cabanas were built and it became a fishing lodge. All of the buildings are built out of local hardwoods, mostly mahogany, by local craftsmen. It sits on twenty-two acres of coastal jungle at the mouth of a freshwater creek, Mango Creek.

The lodge owners, Patrice Heller and Terry Kyle, actually patrolled the flats on the eastern side of the island to keep the locals from netting all of the fish off the flat. They in turn gave these same locals money-making opportunities, such as bringing loads of sand for a beach, so they could support their families.

The fishing is very good and getting better. More fish show on the flats each year, thanks to no more netting. Most of the fishing is fly fishing for bonefish, permit, tarpon, snook, jacks, and triggerfish. There are some trolling opportunities for tuna, wahoo, and dorado outside the reef as well. All of the guides are knowledgeable locals who are capable fly fishermen. These guys love to fish and will fish you sun up to sundown if you'd like.

The flats are shallow marl flats behind the reef. The fishing is mostly wade fishing. There are about a dozen flats they fish. A few of the flats are large, but most are smaller in size. In my opinion, these flats could not hold up to extensive bait/spin fishing. The reefs around the island are in great shape.

The lodge runs day trips to the nearby island of Guanaja. These are weather permitting because of an hour and a half boat ride across open water. The flats around the southern side of Guanaja have great fish populations because the locals on this island realized the value of not netting many years ago. The bonefish numbers are astounding. There are also good numbers of permit, triggerfish, and jacks on these flats as well. In the channels and cuts of the main island swim tarpon and snook.

You won't get to Mango Creek by car or bus because there are no roads to it. You come by boat from Oakridge. Isolation, baby. The reef system, besides the stunning diving and snorkeling opportunities, holds a great number of fish.

Brus Lagoon

Another Honduras hotspot is the Brus Lagoon. Brus Lagoon is not the Blue Lagoon after rains. Chocolate Lagoon is more like it. Cannon Island is a resort on Brus Lagoon, an ideal location to base your operations to try to catch tarpon in the 200-pound range (maybe above it). Some competent anglers jump as many as five tarpon in a day.

We're talking part of the Miskito Coast tucked away in a remote part. You don't reach it easily by land with all the hillsides covered in jungle. This is the largest tract of virgin tropical rainforest in North America. You fly in. Five rivers empty into this lagoon, but there are smaller lagoons, too.

The Miskito Indians still live here, primitively, subsistence living, in rough houses. Living with them are iguanas and jaguars and macaws and banana trees. The land is hilly and green dotted with thatched huts, the water with dugout canoes. Vegetation is like an arboretum gone wild. Cannon Island is nine miles long, two miles wide. Pirates played here. Cannon Island has two remnant cannons from the British or pirates or someone with cannonballs.

Lost River has tarpon and snook in it, in water the color of my faded tan guide-weight shirt, the other one Amy always wants me to throw away. You look for man-groves in this slow-moving river. In addi-tion to tarpon and snook, you might land *mojarra,* a panfish type of fish, and *guapote,* similar to bass, and the *machaca* which looks like a prehistoric shad. The Patuca River is a few miles away and has tarpon all up in it, and so does Rio Tilasunta.

Warunta Lagoon

Near the northern border of Nicaragua, on the Miskito Coast of Honduras, is Wa-runta Lagoon, part of an expansive lagoon system, river system. Snook, snook, snook. Warunta Lagoon, where jaguars take live-stock from the indigenous Indian and howler monkeys roar in jungle treetops.

We're talking remote as in very remote. The lodge is built over water in the Laguna de Caratasca region. Most of the fishing is done in freshwater lagoons and rivers. These shallow lagoons hold both snook and tarpon as do shorelines and deeper holes and, of course, the numerous riv-ers. You fish sunup to sundown. Honduran snook average less than 10 pounds. Hon-duran tarpon average less than 50 pounds. Caratasca Lagoon in southeastern Hondu-ras is another burgeoning adventure-laden fishery.

CONTACTS
Jason Balogh, Honduras on the Fly, www .hondurasonthefly.com
Trek International Safaris, www.treksafaris .com
Warunta Lagoon Lodge, www .waruntalagoon.com
Mango Creek Lodge, www .mangocreeklodge.com, www .hondurasonthefly.com
Cannon Island Fishing Club, Brus Lagoon, 503-643-9224
Pan Angling, www.panangling.com
InterAngler, www.interangler.com
Waders On, www.waderson.com
FishQuest, www.fishquest.com

NICARAGUA

- **Location:** Bordered to the north by Honduras, to the south by Costa Rica
- **What You Fish For:** Tarpon, snook, and more
- **Highlights and Notables:** Remote, primitive country and fishery where you can angle for some of the largest tarpon in the world

Nicaraguan tarpon are bigger than Larry Holmes after he retired.

The behemoth tarpon are the big punch, what draws your attention to this burgeoning fishery that was off-limits because of war. But don't think that tarpon is the only game in the jungle on the east coast of Nicaragua.

Rio Indio Lodge is the classiest, safest way to go, a first-rate luxury angling lodge on the Miskito coast (the same coast that extends from Costa Rica). Sure, you go ocean for tarpon but you go river and bay for snook and guapote and mojara and rainbow bass and grouper, to name a few. Tarpon to 250 pounds have been caught so you can either target them and feel the power or you can not target them, catch feisty 10-pound snook, gigantic grouper,

and tiger guapote (a mean-as-hell toothy perch), and be happy but still be thinking about what could have been.

Despite the fact you can stay in world-class digs with fancy new boats and fancy new tackle and eat well and sleep well, you are still in a country whose infrastructure hasn't returned to prewar days when it was then only iffy at best. This is one of those fishing adventures. And FYI—the San Juan River and other Nicaraguan rivers and mouths were once well known for their tarpon fishing. Then came the Civil War in 1976.

You can stay in more moderate accommodations with San Carlos Sport Fishing and guide Philippe Tisseaux who has a modest lodge where the San Juan River meets up with Lake Nicaragua. His guide company claims to average nine tarpon hits a day. That's good, guys.

CONTACTS

Rio Indio Lodge, www.rioindiolodge.com

San Carlos Sport Fishing, www
.nicaraguafishing.com

InterAngler, www.interangler.com

Waders On, www.waderson.com

FishQuest, www.fishquest.com

PANAMA

- **Location:** Connected to South America by way of Colombia, bordered to the north by Costa Rica
- **What You Fish For:** On one side, you fish for tarpon and snook; the other side, marlin and sailfish and much much more.
- **Highlights and Notables:** Fertile waters, bigger fish on average than other places, everything from roosterfish to sailfish

One thing about fishing saltwater I don't like. My feet.

You have to deal with feet when you play in the sand and salt. On charter boats, I don't like the idea of walking around barefoot. Never did it growing up, not gonna start now, not on a boat, only maybe on the beach. But what shoes to wear? My legs then get tanned and my ankles get tanned and my feet stay white. I don't have nice-looking feet to begin with. They look like God gave me slabs of pork meat and then meat-cleavered Fred Flintstone–like slices to make toes. I'm a slender dude but I have chubby feet, short plump toes. That's not a good look.

I don't like flats booties because no one makes them where they fit right and not chafe and give any arch support. They might, I guess, but I haven't found 'em yet. And like I say, I hate the above-ankle tan I get. Deck shoes are passé. I kinda like those slip-on Keds but they don't dry

quickly. I'm always on the lookout for the right shoes to wear on boats and to wear on flats. No luck yet.

Panama doesn't do flats, not very well anyway, not enough of them. Panama doesn't do sightfishing. Panama does shorelines and reefs and deep blue water. Panama does world-class fishing. Panama does it for me and will for you too. Panama is one of the world's greatest fishing destinations.

Panama is an intercontinental isthmus, linking Central America to South America. An isthmus, famous for its forty-eight-mile canal with its locks and malaria (then, not now) and famous for wide-brimmed hats that took the name. An isthmus with the Caribbean Sea wetting its north shores, the Pacific Ocean dampening the south shores, and both seas connected by that famous canal. So what does Panama offer? Abundant fish. The fish are bigger than your average fish whatever species you're thinking about. The water is typically calm (I have been known to get seasick from time to time). Reasonable prices if you desire but you can pay a lot for some of the lodges and feel like you got your money's worth.

Options galore. Great food. Fresh, tasty grub. Diversity of fish. Record-setting fish. Or is it fish-setting records? IGFA pages love Panama. You're close to the fishing grounds. Panama is wild country. *There's Toucan Sam sitting on that branch over there.* Since it's wild, even though the fishing infrastructure is sound, you can occasionally get a spotty trip (or a fishing adventure, as we like to say). Spring is sailfish time. The people are friendly, the outfitters knowledgeable, enthusiastic, and they take care of you.

Panama might not be the place to take a saltwater newbie. The casting can be long and arduous at times, some outfitters want to troll too much, the atmosphere is one of veteran anglers, real hardcore, not much sightfishing, let's-fish-10-to-12-hours-a-day types. Dawn to dusk Fish, eat, sleep, fish.

Without the expanses of Bahamian-style flats, how does Panama do it? Shallow to deep habitat. Dropoffs. Underwater mountain ranges and amazingly big humps, seamounts hundreds of feet high. Bays soupy with fish. Islands above and below sea level with record-setting surrounding waters. Reefs fertile with the ocean food chain. The Pacific side is better than the Caribbean but don't discount the north side because in its rivers run tarpon and snook.

The snapper are unquestionably, doggedly big, the yellowfin tuna as huge as Roy Campanella, some as unwieldy as Nate Newton. Tuna taken on top, if you please, world-record class. If you tire of these gargantuans, tackle something bigger, like blue marlin or black marlin or striped marlin or sailfish. The marlin are caught more frequently and in larger size than just about anywhere else you can go. Sailfish are year round and it's not unusual to raise ten or more sails a day, multiple hookups included.

If you are tired of something that big, try roosterfish, big 'uns. Wahoo in the 20- to 40-pound range. Try for a record cubera snapper because they are here, just off the reefs, take them on poppers. On these reefs, milkfish too.

If you need a jones for the catch-a lot-of-fish part of your brain, run out from the reef a bit and catch more dorado than you ever dreamed of, nuisance fish some say but then some think sailfish a nuisance when they're chasing blues. You might catch a record dorado, too, by the way, since these dolphin run 15 to 40 pounds with 50s noted.

What else is on the docket? How about snook, blue trevally, pompano, rainbow runner, grouper, jack, mackerel? The list of suspects goes on. On any given day, you can catch multiple species, the largest of a kind you've ever caught, more of one species (wahoo, roosterfish, tuna, marlin, dorado for starters) than you've ever caught in a day or a trip, or you can catch a world record.

The hotspots include Ladrones Islands, Montuosa Island (where an underwater volcano sits), the Deep Drop, Coiba Island, Pinas Bay, Isla Boca Brava, Hannibal Bank (but outfitters will tell you there are many better places, even as good as this underwater hump is), and Pedasi.

Coiba Island

Coiba Island is a large island off the Peninsula de Azuero with many smaller islands nearby, structure everywhere, fishes all around the structure. Your predominant catches will be yellowfin tuna, cubera snapper, roosterfish, black marlin.

Pesca Panama is an outfitter to look up if Coiba hits your fancy. Part of an archipelago of Montuosa, Jicron, Jicarita, and many other smaller islands that all surround the Hannibal Bank, Coiba Island enjoys little fishing pressure, endless other tiny islands and underwater structure and an unspoiled bounty of nature and fish. You fish to schools of yellowfin tuna, wahoo, dorado, cuberas, amberjack, and roosterfish. Anglers report catches of up to forty yellowfin in a day. The roosterfish slash and attack topwater plugs. You can do the sailfish thing, the marlin thing—but the yellowfin tuna angling is so good, that's what you'll want to do mostly.

Pinas Bay

Pinas Bay is on the Pacific side, east. Here is Tropic Star Lodge, one of the finest in Central America and it sits in the middle of the Darien Jungle, 150 miles from Panama City, 100 miles from any road. Brothers and sisters, you are truly in the middle of nowhere and what a fine place to be. The Darien Jungle is impenetrable across the eastern part of the country all the way to Colombia (a country to which Panama used to belong). You get blue marlin and sailfish and inshore fishing. You get rocky shorelines for trolling and casting.

Tropic Star Lodge, nestled in a cove with its beautiful beach, is one of the fabled bluewater lodges. One hundred twenty or more world records have been set in Pinas Bay (mostly billfish)—now light tackle is the hot thing.

You might fish off Zane Grey Reef (yes, named after the famous writer who loved fishing this area). You might meet up with marlin that thrash their heads back and forth when hooked under charcoal-lined clouds on the horizon, gray rain almost slate, the silver topped ocean, all dark blues and grays and slates and everything jumbled up in the madness of the marlin. And then, just what you don't want, the big marlin dips and dives and then sounds. The fight won't be a quick one now.

Or you might see waves, choppy white tiny waves coming right at the boat, a stampede of bonito just offshore. You might catch a 50-pound snapper or an amber over 40 or a rooster nearly 60. But you'll catch something and many things and big things and plenty of them and you'll eat well and it'll be such a jumbled juxtaposed journey because you're in the Darien Jungle, after all.

Gatun Lake

Lake Gatun is notorious for peacock bass (pavon) by the numbers, not by size; 2- to 3-pound peacock bass (of the butterfly variety) are the norm, a 5- to 6-pounder a bragger, 7 to 9 pounds a trophy. The lake is a refuge lake from the construction days of the Panama Canal, 160 square miles of islands and stumps. Think light tackle, especially think fly fishing. Streamers work best, dropped near cover, rapid retrieve, aggressive strikes, headshaking takes, frenzied dives.

You can imagine how much fun it is to catch twenty-five or fifty of these finny nuclear missiles. They fight as hard as your tackle will let them so go light, use shock tippets, strip quickly, and enjoy the battles. You get to see the Canal, fish in the jungle, see local wildlife like caiman, iguanas, monkeys, and parrots, and catch peacock bass. It's inexpensive, close to the city and fun as all get out.

Isla Boca Brava

Panama Big Game Sportfishing Club rests here. All you ever hear anybody talk about is the delectable food they prepare and how great it is. Then they get around to talking about the fishing. The owners are in the restaurant biz, and it's obvious from the time your fingers start snapping up the hors d'oeuvres at the bar until the last course at dinner. The chatter about food is not a reflection of the quality of the fishing rather a testament to what kind of grub they serve up. Sails, snapper, tuna, dorado, the savage *pez gallo* (roosterfish), and the vicious cubera— you can catch it all from this camp and its shallow green water or deeper blue water.

Panama Big Game Sportfishing Club is the third full-time saltwater fishing operation in Panama, this one right there by the legendary Hannibal Bank. The combination of gourmet-level food and world-class angling make this a must-stop for any serious bluewater angler.

Pedasi

No billfishing here. No high-powered energy, no expensive lodges, no pressure. Remote and *tranquilo*. Order of the day is light tackle fishing for Sierra mackerel and blue trevally and roosterfish and many other species.

CONTACTS
Capt. Lee Allen Campbell, Panama
    Big Game, www
    .panamabiggamefishingclub.com
Capt. Julian Jay Gustin, Pesca Panama,
    www.pescapanama.com
Tropic Star Lodge www.tropicstar.com
InterAngler, www.interangler.com
Waders On, www.waderson.com
FishQuest, www.fishquest.com

South America

ARGENTINA

- **Location:** Southern South America, bordered by Chile to the west
- **What You Fish For:** Dorado, trout
- **Highlights and Notables:** It doesn't get any better than Argentina. The top lodges, the top lodge food, the top lodge wines, the top trout fishing, the top dorado fishing. One of the last frontiers for big-game trout

Dorado

Dorado just might be the maddest fish in the world when caught. They tug and pull and thrash and bull and jump and manhandle and threaten. Their sharp teeth cut line, destroy baitfish, lures, and flies. They put all their power into the initial fight. They impose their will. If you can keep them on after the primary burst, you'll find a golden treasure at the end of your line.

One of the leading experts on the golden dorado is my friend Garrett Veneklasen, international angler, explorer, writer, author, one of the first to explore much of the angling potential in both Central and South America.

This is what Garrett has to say about the fish he knows so much about:

Freshwater dorado (Salminus maxillosus *and* S. hilarii) *are a distinct migratory game fish not to be confused with the saltwater dolphin fish (which is also called* el

dorado *in many Spanish-speaking countries). Physically, the freshwater dorado is best described as a prehistoric golden trout or salmon with the jaws of a pit bull terrier.*

Ichthyologists have appropriately given the southern species of dorado the Latin name Salminus maxillosus. *Salminus, meaning trout-like, and maxillosus referring to the fish's immensely-powerful jaws. Dorado are hard-hitting, incredibly strong, acrobatic fighters that attain weights in excess of 30 pounds. They are,*

in short, South America's hyped-up version of a "tropical trout."

Dorado are commonly found throughout a massive watershed between southern Brazil/Bolivia and Northern Argentina. Incredibly, freshwater dorado remain a relatively little-known game fish in the United States.

The two top places to catch freshwater dorado are in Argentina—the established fishery of the Ibera Marsh and the newest, La Zona.

La Zona (Uruguay River)

Argentina's Entre Rios Province. I don't hunt anymore (long story) but you can cast and blast here, like many other Argentinian trips. In this case, for dorado and doves, pigeons in the same day. The accommodations, luxurious, no other word for them. Food and Argentinian wine? If you've done the Argentinian sporting trip thing, you know this is probably the best grub and wine in the world.

You take a river, let's say the Uruguay, you dam it (let's say the El Salto Grande) create a tailwater (start calling it La Zona) and you know what? You have a fishery where the dorado grow as big as they can grow. Don Causey, owner and publisher of *The Angling Report* calls La Zona "Fishing's Jurassic Park . . . the fish are so huge and numerous, like something out of prehistory."

La Zona opened (reopened) and immediately became one of the latest "you can't believe this new fishery" fisheries. Each time out, anglers were unofficially besting the line-class records for dorado. And these fishermen were catching big dorado by the dozens, golden dorado up to 50 pounds. There's even a report of a dorado from La Zona that topped 60 pounds.

This is Argentina so the scenery on La Zona must be beautiful, right? Not exactly. The dam is big and concrete and looming. The water is the color of caramel. The boats are comfortable and a little out of place. From the boat, you go up to the dam, float downstream while casting big flies with 300-grain sinking lines with a heavyweight fly rod, then run back up to the dam, over and over. This is not for everyone.

You go to La Zona because you want to catch the largest dorado you've ever caught. Or you go because you like exotic fishing, or trophy hunting, or cast-and-blast, or fighting big freshwater fish. Or because you like to fish the latest international hotspot. You fish La Zona because of the surface frenzies of the dorado, striper-style bait chasing. You do the Ibera Marsh or Patagonia, Argentina, for scenery and clear water.

J. W. Smith of Rod and Gun Resources first clued me in to the amazing goings-on at La Zona. He told me that since La Zona opened April 2006, literally scores of fish exceeding the largest fly-caught IGFA record have been caught, including one that weighed more than 50 pounds. "That is nearly triple the previous record! On top of that, at least one fish has been caught on bait casting tackle that exceeded the previous world record by nearly 10 pounds," Smith told me in almost a reverent whisper.

Fierce, toothy predator brought to hand, ready to be released

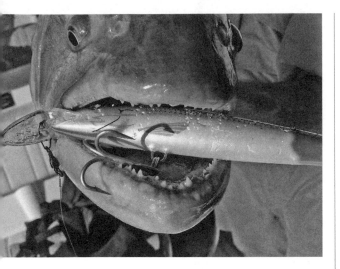

The guides are quite experienced and the fishing is done from new, spacious twenty-two-foot center console boats—all first class. Fly fishermen, spincasters, and bait casters can all expect to hook/jump anywhere from ten to thirty dorados each day. These aggressive fish are a real handful once hooked—guests have experienced dorados fighting over lures, had them run completely under the boat leaping eight feet in the air on the other side, and have even seen a hooked fish leap high out of the water and a second, competing fish leap in the air, crash into the hooked fish and knock the lure out.

In order to keep the fishing quality at this amazing level, only four boats (two Argentine and two Uruguayan) are allowed in La Zona per day and fishing is allowed only Monday to Thursday. Larger groups can divide their time between the fishing and the excellent bird hunting.

Less than ten minutes away from the river is Los Tres Sietes, the lodging for this trip. Dorado fishing, pigeon, and optional perdiz (partridge) hunting guests are accommodated in an elegantly converted polo pony facility and grounds. The food is delicious and stylishly presented by owner and chef, Julieta Gaviña, who was trained at the elite Maussi Sebes culinary academy in Buenos Aires.

J. W. Smith on rodgunresources.com says, "South American golden dorado are magnificent iridescent golden fish that strike viciously, leap maniacally, burn off line, and destroy tackle and lures. Most dorado run from 5 to 10 pounds, sometimes as large as 20 pounds. In the fabled, highly-restricted La Zona on the Uruguay River, the dorado routinely go 30 to 40 pounds with world-record setters exceeding 50, even 60 pounds." Seasons run best from September through April.

The Ibera Marsh

The dorado here are nowhere near as large as those dinosaurs at La Zona but the experience is entirely different. Wild, lonely landscape, wide glassy flats, a labyrinth of lagoons, grassy marshes, the low horizon, the amazing sunsets. The water clear, clean.

The Ibera Marsh Wildlife Refuge. Nearly three times as vast as the Florida Everglades. Some say it's the largest body of freshwater in the world. That's hard to wrap your brain around isn't it? Ibera isn't swampy. There is current, and the water is cool to the touch. Like a slow wide spring creek.

The dorado of Ibera don't reach La Zona

size but they live in more natural surroundings, they live in clear water. When you cast your large saltwater Deceiver and the dorado attacks it, often, like a massive gold rainbow trout, they jump in the air and try to shake loose the hook. Fury in midair.

If you don't cast well or strip well or play the fish well, all you catch is the 7- to 10-pound hard-fighting dorado. Boo hoo. The largest fish caught in the marsh was 30 or so pounds. If you're on your game, you have a chance to bust that record up.

TACKLE

Conventional gear that you feel won't leave you with half a rod. A wire leader is essential. Seven-inch jerk baits, Rattle Trap–type lures, spoons and jigs are most productive. Eight to 10-weight fly rod and either a 200-grain, 24-foot sink tip line or a full floating line depending upon water conditions. A heavy steel leader is a must, as these fish will chew through 100-pound line like it is sewing thread.

Dorado take a variety of streamers, sliders and even Atlantic salmon—style Bombers during ideal conditions (all on 3/0 heavy long shank hooks). Northern Argentina, Paraguay, and Bolivia have the strongest populations of dorado. Passport required.

CONTACTS

Rod & Gun Resources, Kerrville, TX,
    http://www.rodgunresources.com/index
    .shtm
InterAngler LLC, www.interangler.com
Waders On, www.waderson.com
FishQuest, www.fishquest.com

ARGENTINA TROUT FISHING

Argentina trout fishing is expensive and far far away. The country is lightly populated in the areas you'll want to fish and the accommodations luxurious, accommodating, and, well, not cheap. The scenery runs the gamut from beautiful to stunning to stark.

Much of the scenery will look vaguely familiar—high desert, semiarid, rugged peaked mountains, scrub brush, sometimes it favors eastern Oregon, eastern Washington, parts of Montana and Wyoming and California—but somehow, you can't quite put your finger on it, it's different, unique. So few buildings, so few people, so little traffic, the cattle and sheep outnumber

Dorado, Bolivian-style

It is not unusual in clear Bolivian rivers where the dorado live for an angler to get ten to fifteen hookups in a day. Bolivian dorado run from 5 to 25 pounds. There are also game fish you'll want to pursue including pacu that get up to 30 pounds, yatoranas, muturos, and surubi (giant catfish). Rod & Gun and Interangler are just two of many fine agencies that set up trips to Bolivia for dorado.

An emerging country for exotic fishing. No place else in the world has fisheries where you can catch more peacock bass than Bolivia. They are not as big as Brazil's or Venezuela's but you catch more of them and with less angling pressure.

people. In some places, say around the Rio Grande, the lay of the land is one of Alaskan-style expanse, fairly flat, little vegetation, everything brown or pale green, rolling wide-open land. If you can save the money and you are one of those anglers who wants to trade money for memories, you need to start an Argentina piggy bank.

The Andes. Gauchos and ranches (known as *estancias*). The southern sky. Volcanoes. Cliffs and bluffs and the Pampas and so much more, this Argentina. Big trout, so many big rivers you can't believe it, sort of like Alaska. You are at the end of the world, bottom of the earth, fishing Tierra del Fuego, angling in Patagonia.

The browns get all the press but you can also catch whopper brook trout (like in Lago Espejo) and rainbow trout. You can fish desert spring creeks in the middle of nowhere, wide thin rocky streams, rivers that plunge angrily through canyons, deep brawling unwadeable rivers—Argentina has every kind of river and stream you can think of, and all of them are dreamy.

The two regions you'll want to concentrate on, the places to fish are Patagonia and Tierra del Fuego, the Land of Fire. Some of the finest rivers include Rio Malleo, Rio Caleufu, Rio Limay, Rio Traful, Lago Espejo, Rio Chimehuin, Rio Collon, the Rio Carrileufu with its landlocked salmon, a spring creek like Arroyo Pescado and two of the best brown trout rivers in the world, the Rio Gallegos, and of course, the heavy hitter, the Rio Grande.

The Rio Grande is simply one of the best trout rivers in the world. Born in the Andes of Chile, crashes down the mountains and onto the foothills, slowing down on the grasslands. Giant brown trout. Think of *huge* brown trout, no, think bigger than that—yeah, 15 pounds, 20 pounds, even 30 pounds. And one estimated to weight close to 40 pounds was caught in recent years.

The brutish browns begin life in these mountains, in these feeder streams, and then in this big river move out to the Atlantic and back again each November. A 5-pounder is like a 12-incher elsewhere. The average brown is about over 8 pounds, closer to 10—larger than just about any other place on the planet—you'll be surprised by how many catches will run close to or over 15 pounds.

Dry flies? Excellent choice. You will try surface lures and they will work enough times that you'll use them more than you should and when they smash your fly, you'll jump like you do when you come upon a covey of quail. Open the streamer box, too, and wait for the freight train.

The air that surrounds the Rio Grande is the cleanest-smelling air you'll ever breathe. The water cold, cold and clear, clear. The wind is constant but overrated. Don't make the impossibly long cast; keep 'em short and tight and you'll do fine. The key is maintaining line control. The river swings slowly back and forth, easy to wade, easy to fish, pool after pool after pool. You fish in beats on this private river, ensuring that the trout aren't overfished. Catch-and-release practiced, strictly enforced. Each cast, your heart will pound because you know you may catch the largest brown trout you've ever caught, maybe the largest *ever* caught. That's the thrill of this harsh, unforgiving river.

The rivers in Tierra del Fuego are nutrition-poor, including the Rio Grande, and perhaps that's why these fish hit flies so aggressively. They're hungry and opportunistic. Some of the top Rio Grande lodges include Estancia Maria Behety Lodge, La Villa de Maria Behety, Estancia Despedida Lodge. A real wilderness experience is the Lago Fagnano and Rio Azapardo, in the farthest southern part of Tierra del Fuego. While you can catch the big sea-run browns, thick resident rainbows, you can also catch brook trout that reach sizes of 7 or 8 pounds.

The Rio Gallegos lies just north of Tierra del Fuego (it's an island, did you know that?), and has superb angling for sea-run brown trout. The Gallegos is challenging because the river is clear and fine and shallow, not fast-running or having deep pools like the Rio Grande. Think technical. Think strategy. The average size brown is just slightly smaller than those of the Rio Grande, if you consider a 7-pounder small in any way, shape, or form. The top end sea-run is not much over 20 pounds but you'll catch more browns in the Gallegos or so it seems. You can also catch steelhead. An adjunct trip is a feeder stream to the Gallegos, the Rio Penitente, known for its dry fly fishing for huge brown trout in shallow water.

The ranch-slash-lodge of Estancia Arroyo Verde sits on the Rio Traful, one of the best rivers in Patagonia. The mighty Andes rise in the background, broad plains and valley beneath, gin-clear Rio Traful flowing through the expansive postcard-like land. Your targets are heavy browns and rainbows and landlocked salmon. You won't fish in a river with a more magnificent setting. Other world-class fishing lodges on the Gallegos are the Estancia Carlota and Estancia Guer Aike.

So consider seriously a trip of a lifetime to the land of gauchos and dogs and cattle and sheep and volcanoes and beautiful profound rivers. This is not a cheap trip, you'll encounter a language barrier but the lodges are the best in the world and so is the food and the wine and so are the rivers so forget that the length of the air trip is long 5,000-plus miles from Washington and New York. Hook up with a booking agent and find out more about this wild frontier. Don't overlook some of the lakes in Argentina, prolific fisheries like Lago Cinco, Lago Tres, and Lago Cholila. Almost all of the booking agents have trips to Argentina so check with them for more info.

CONTACTS
J. W. Smith, www.rodgunresources.com
The Fly Shop, www.theflyshop.com

BRAZIL

- **Location:** Eastern South America, big and beautiful
- **What You Fish For:** Peacock bass, payara, cuiu-cuiu and other bizarre, exotic, native fish
- **Highlights and Notables:** Perhaps the Granddaddy of all big fishing trips. Exotic locales straight out of a movie with huge rivers and rain forest and animals and natives. And oh yeah, exotic huge mean fish like the peacock bass, perhaps the finest freshwater game fish on earth

Where do you begin and end when you discuss fishing Brazil? You could start with floods and high water of the last year and how it disrupted fishing. But that's temporary. You could talk about the famous peacock bass that thrive in the Amazon's waters and smash your topwater flies and

Your comfy streamside lodging

lures with a tenacity unlike any other freshwater fish. That's what everyone wants to hear about. You might want to hear stories about how a jaguar cornered a woman in a tent or how a giant snake wrapped around a camp mate in the river and several anglers had to rush to save him or how a piranha caught hours before still bit down and severed the tip of a guide's finger. Thanks, Garrett.

But you're like everyone else and you're preoccupied with the peacock bass that you might not notice when the articles start describing the flora and fauna and animals and birds. Or the thousands of miles of unexplored (virgin) rivers. Or the native fish like the ferocious payara, and unusual unique local fish like the matrinchã and juatarana and arawana and traira and cuiu-cuiu and more. Whatever vision of fishing Brazil sticks in your mind, you know that it's one of those top five destinations on earth.

You better also notice some of the flaws that make this an adventure fishing trip. Water. Lots of it. Brown water. Blue water. Black water. White water. Water in the Amazon. In case you've had your head in the sand, the Amazon is the biggest wilderness on earth (save maybe the icy environs of Antarctica), the world's largest rain forest, and this dense flora-fauna-packed jungle is crazy wild. You'll need to plan according to the wet season and the dry season. You'll need shots. You'll need to be conscious that things go wrong when you go south so you

Writer Larry Larsen with one of the larger peacocks you'll see. The size of the lure is about as long as from fingertip to elbow.

These fish just look mean and nasty, like they're members of Hell's Anglers. They have a palette of colors and the big spots. They have teeth only a dentist could love.

Whether you fish with a fly or a lure or bait, this is the fish that sits at the top of your wish list. You can catch them with conventional tackle or flygear and they'll smash whatever lure or fly you toss their way. Amazonian anger in full raging display. Skill at garnering a predatory attack is not a requisite. You can be a neophyte or a crappy angler and still get them to slash and smash. Landing the beasts is another element all together.

Still, getting them hooked takes some understanding. It's easy to strike too quickly, think they've gone for it hook, line, and sinker when in fact, all they have done is attempt to stun your offering. Sometimes, many times, you can cast again, vary your retrieve, alter your drop-in point just a bit and you can entice another strike. Then you must employ patience and *not* set the hook right away. Wait, wait, now. Hard set. Once on, they try everything from jumping to headshaking to diving for cover to eliminate the fool at the other end. You might reel in to find your lure's hooks straightened out, the lure demolished, the lure vanished. You might have hooked a peacock bass and been able to get it close to the boat to land it only to discover your bass still has plenty of energy and poof! Bye bye.

Despite how difficult it is to land a peacock bass, most first-rate outfitters take you to rarely fished waters, to bass that have rarely if ever seen a lure or fly, and you

need to choose a reputable booking agent-outfitter.

If you are a booking agent worth your salt, you have connections to some kind of boss peacock bass trip to the Amazon. You might be in a group, probably will be with a group and you need to ask your outfitter how many will be in your group and what that means to you. How many guides per client? How much fishing time per day versus travel time to get to your spot? The less travel time, the more times your lure can be in the water and have more chances to have the treble hooks straightened out.

So let's talk peacock bass fishing. This is the end-all, the Shangri-La, the Mecca, top dog of fishing for this most aggressive colorful predator. You've seen the pics.

will come away, if you are any kind of angler at all, with five or ten or more catches a day, many more misses than that. It's not unusual to catch twenty to thirty peacock bass each day, from 3- to 6-pound "butterflies" to the 12- to 25-pound "barred" or "pacu" super-lunkers. Anglers always have an opportunity to catch a real monster.

Peacock bass are cichlids. We call them peacock bass in the same way we call a sunfish—a sunfish, or a perch—a perch. Kind of a catchall reference. There are two types of peacock bass species in Brazil—the tucunare (the big pacus that average 5 to 7 pounds and reach those monster sizes, some 20-plus pounds) and the butterfly tucunare (the most common and the smallest of the three recognized species of peacock bass).

In northeastern Brazil, the Xingu River, a whirling tumult of agitated water, a den of multiple species of Amazonian frenzy, predator central. You might catch five or ten or a dozen species in a single day. You can catch peacock bass, hard fighters although they don't reach prodigious sizes like in other Amazon rivers. You can catch these pacu, the hard-fighting payara, and also cuiu-cuiu (an armored catfish), bicuda, traira, jacunda, matrinchã, tiger surubim (aka cachara) and

black piranha to name a few. The prime time to go is August through March.

Depending on your location in Brazil, you can coax to your lure or fly the pacu, pirapitinga, jacunda, apapa, tambaqui, pirarucu, bicuda, picua, piranha, aruana, pescada, and many more. The Amazon is huge and the rivers are many and the outfitters and lodges are ever-increasing. The Amazon and Orinoco and Paraguay and São Francisco River basins are the top destinations.

The Rio Negro and the Xingu River are the two best, Rio Negro for peacock bass, Xingu for multispecies. These are the crème de la crème but a fishing trip in Brazil can be many things. You might stay in a lodge and go out by boat each morning. You might stay in a shallow-draft floating barge or a mobile cabin and where you go, you fish. Lagoons and untouched rivers and structure and schools of peacock bass—the guides are good and while there are always horror stories of bad trips, if you stick with a reputable agent and outfitter, your problems should be minimized.

CONTACTS
Rod & Gun Resources, www
.rodgunresources.com
Fishquest, www.fishquest.com

CHILE

- **Location:** Western South America, long and narrow
- **What You Fish For:** Trout, salmon (including coho and Chinook)
- **Highlights and Notables:** Chile doesn't get the same kind of press as Alaska or neighboring Argentina but the quality of the fishing and lodging stands up to both.

At the bottom of the world are bold broad-shouldered mountains that look like they support the weight of the entire earth, Atlas revisited. Kurt Vonnegut once had one of his characters say about a neighboring South American country, it must be nice to live in a country so long and narrow. Chile is that, long and narrow, 2,600 miles long, 111 miles on average, narrow. Few folks live in Chile, a wild mountainous coastal country, mild climate, the elegant city of Santiago, the graceful, sky-reaching, snow-blanketed Andes Mountains.

Chile is not a do-it-yourselfer. You will fish on private ranches, private waters, exclusive with very little angling pressure, dramatic scenery, and huge resident and sea-run trout. For the quality of scenery, the size and abundance of trout, the established infrastructure of lodges and guides and ease of transport, there may not be another fishery in the world that sees less fishing pressure. The nation's southernmost thousand miles is the best Chilean trout

locale, browns and rainbows, sea-run and resident, lakes and rivers. You combine big fish with amazing and unique scenery and that's why you travel to Chile (because—and this is an important because—even though we're talking trout that average 1 to 4 pounds with numerous trout running 5 to 10 pounds or better, you do have weather and finicky fish and plain tough fishing and that means that often in Chile, you're not going to rack up big numbers as you try for big fish).

What regions, what rivers should you consider? River of Swans, Fundo el Salto, Estancia Rio Cisnes, Rio Baker, Rio Simpson, Rio Cisnes, Rio Nirehuao (so many resident browns, you won't believe it), Futaleufu River, Rio Grande, the Chilean Fjords, El Saltamontes (grass-hopper), Posada del los Farios (Spanish for brown trout), Dragonfly Lodge, Patagonian Chile, Tierra del Fuego, the Lake District (Puerto Montt/Puerto Varas, a ninety-minute jet flight south of Santiago) and the Coyhaique region (accessed via Balmaceda airport, a three-hour jet flight south of Santiago). A litany of some of the finest fishing waters and lodges in any hemisphere. You can even stay on a luxury yacht to fish the fjords, a floating mobile lodge.

The scenery ranges from the high-range flatland to deep chasms to dramatic mountains similar to the Rockies to wide valleys to sparse lowlands to snow-capped volcanoes. Their hot season, in the Southern Hemisphere, is the Northern Hemisphere's cold season. Even with all this going for it, you won't find an overwhelming number of lodges and camps to choose from. Chile, in many ways, for all its tradition and deserved reputation for quality fishing and lodging and food and wine, is still a fishing wilderness.

The brown and rainbow trout (and some brookies) are not native to Chile but they thrive. These trout live in the short, western-flowing rivers and they get fat and happy. In the southern coastal rivers of Chile, anglers can also fish for salmon and steelhead; one of the best is the Rio Puelo. Many of the rivers are wide, some deep and unwadeable, some shallow and wadeable. You may not have a huge choice of freshwater fish but you do have diversity in trout waters. Some rivers green with their banks choked with temperate rain forest will remind you of those in misty Oregon and Washington, others make you think of the muscular streams with lean mountains of Montana and Wyoming, others look like moonscape, unlike anywhere else you've fished. Some rivers need a 7-weight rod to fight the sea-run trout and salmon. Some spring-fed lakes and intimate wild rivers need but a 4-weight. Some rivers are known for huge browns but you'll catch few of them. Others are known for being top-notch dry fly streams or hit-or-miss on the spawn run or for producing big numbers of big browns, and you even have a few spring creeks. You get it all in Chile.

Going in, know that you will be a guest and recipient of some of the best lodges and food and wine anywhere in the world. Besides the huge trout and spectacular scenery and uncrowded waters and a sense of Lewis and Clark, it's why you spend all that money to fly to Chile for a week. Oh yeah, you get to enjoy never-ending wind, too.

Each of the lodges has access to many many rivers and lakes, numerous miles of water. Each generally expects you for a week-long vacation but most will accommodate you for however short or long you need to stay. You can visit more than one lodge on your journey to sample different waters and terrain and many anglers even include an adjunct trip across the border to fish Argentina. Each is set up to please and they will, too—with gourmet meals and amazing wine and a variety of packages and diversity of fishing options. Peak season is January to March, but fishing can be superb from mid-November to mid-April.

CONTACTS
The Fly Shop, www.TheFlyShop.com
Estancia de los Rios, www.fly-fish-chile
   .com/Estancia/estancia.html
Dragonfly Lodge, www.thedragonflylodge
   .com
Río Azules (the 50-plus foot-long Hatteras
   yacht, Río Azul), www.fly-fish-chile
   .com/fjords/fjords.html
Patagonia Baker Lodge, www.pbl.cl/
   esidebar.htm
John Eustice, Cinco Rios Lodge, www
   .johneustice.com/chile/cinco_rios/
   cinco_rios.html
El Saltamontes Lodge, Coyhaique,
   011-56-67-232779

El Patagon, www.southernchilexp.com/
  CHILE Hotel_and_Lodging/
  EL_PATAGON_LODGE/el_patagon
  _lodge.html
Cameron Lodge, www.anglingclassics
  .co.uk/Argentina%20Sea%20Trout.html

La Posada del los Farios, www.flyfishing
  travel.com/chile/laposada.html
Rio Futaleufu Lodge, www.exchile.com/
  flyfishing.html
Estancia de Los Rios, Puerto Varas,
  Fax 011-65-233-585

SURINAME

- **Location:** Northeastern South America, on the coast, sandwiched between French Guiana and Guyana
- **What You Fish For:** Weird-looking fish you've never heard of including the wolf fish, surubi, and animar
- **Highlights and Notables:** If you want to catch fish nobody's ever heard of before, fish that will draw oohs and ahs when you show off photos, Suriname is your new best friend.

The wolf fish. A scary prehistoric looking fish out of your dreams, sharp teeth and powerful jaws capable of amputating your finger, your hand . . . or worse.

Humongous catfish including the redtail and the surubi.

The *Animar*, a fierce fish with big teeth, big jaws, scaly like a carp, a jungle river fish that thrashes and rolls when caught. Startling with its bowfin tail, greenish silver color, the orange-red tail, specks all over the green body, a dogfish look to it.

Tucanare, as the locals call the peacock bass.

Black piranha and the pacu, cousins to piranha.

Trapun, anyumara and kubi.

Without a map, I betcha don't know what continent Suriname is a part of. Say your choice out loud. Answer: South America. Suriname, the smallest country in South America, sits between French Guiana and Guyana and is one of the least traveled countries in the Western Hemi-

sphere. The country is an amalgam of international cultures and languages, eleven spoken, and guess what? Spanish is not one of them. Hindi and Dutch are. The Dutch heritage is strong but you'll see such a variety of ethnicities and religions your head will spin, Brazilian to Javanese to Maroons, Hindu to Jewish to Muslim. You will come away with one inevitable impression of Suriname's population: friendly.

Most of the population (half million or so) lives in cities on the coast, most in the capitol city of Paramaribo. Not densely populated at all, mostly made up of tropical rain forest. The Suriname tropical rain forest is virgin. Through this tropical rain forest run myriad serpentine unexplored rivers where only natives live in obscurity. Ecotourism is a thriving business.

Suriname is one of the fishing frontiers. From this statement, you should expect a fishing adventure. Developing nation, undeveloped fishing. Not many guides to choose from and that means "adventure." Wink wink. If you don't know what I mean by that, Suriname fishing is not for you.

The best time to visit Suriname is in one of the two dry seasons, February through late April and again from August to early December. The climate? Hot and humid.

In the midwest region of Suriname, in the middle of the pristine and uninhabited Amazon rain forest, you will find Suriname's latest, most exclusive lodge Kabalebo Nature Resort, accessible only by air. Kabalebo Resort is one of the more developed lodges in Suriname, trustworthy, knowledgeable. Kabalebo offers two lodges and

Uraima Falls, Venezuela

a bush camp. The main lodge is a seventy-minute flight from Paramaribo.

The lodge has ten twin-bedded rooms with air-conditioning or without and most importantly, a private bathroom with hot and cold running water. The resort offers an all-inclusive local meal plan as well as a bar (second most important). The second lodge is built on a rapid on a river, two and a half hours from the main lodge, holds up to ten folks, ideal for anglers. The bush camp is just that—you sleep in tents or hammocks and you bathe in the river, the same river where you catch piranha.

Saramacca River and Lake Brokopondo (tucunare) are two other fishing destinations. For the huge sportfish, you'll need 80- to 130-pound monofilament—no stretch.

Swamp fishing is a wild card. The locals know the swamps and the fish and you won't so it sounds like an ideal adventure. Visa and passports are required. In the heartland of the country is the rugged beauty of the Central Suriname Nature Reserve, one of the largest in the world. While you can find most anything you need in the capital city, you won't find much elsewhere, so come prepared. You're on your own for the most part, on an adventure, traveling in a country where the Amazon is as wild as it gets. I'd go the resort route first and explore on your own at a later date.

CONTACTS
Kabalebo Resort,
www.natureresortkabalebo.com

VENEZUELA

- **Location:** Northern South America, bordered by Guyana to the east, Brazil to the south, Colombia to the west
- **What You Fish For:** Peacock bass, payara and other exotic freshwater species, bonefish, billfish
- **Highlights and Notables:** Las Roques should be on any saltwater angler's must-visit list, a genuine classic spot for bonefish. The fishing for peacock bass runs a tad behind that of Brazil but is still blue-ribbon quality.

Los Roques

Controversy abounds. Are guides really crossing illegally into national park waters? Yeah, it sure looks like it. Not all guides,

but there did seem to be a concerted effort to skirt the rules. What about Venezuela's new government and their anti-American stance? Does this posture cause anglers any risk? Not yet. Probably not in the future, either. Not personal safety, anyway. You could find yourself without a plane to get there if things escalate between the countries and Venezuela blocks flights to and from the United States. But this is all conjecture at this point.

Now that those two things are out of the way, let's talk fishing. The bonefishing is hot, has been for years. Venezuela is beautiful, laid back, and has world-class fishing. It deserves a place on your dream list.

When you talk to someone who does Las Roques, you can tell it's a sickness. They have fallen in love and can't get enough. They don't want the exotics like Christmas Island or Seychelles. Key West and the Bahamas are too domestic. They want their Las Roques. Dave Rittenberry owns Riverfield's in Amarillo, the preeminent sporting goods store, fly shop, hunting center. He's smitten with Las Roques. What gives?

Las Roques is eighty-some-odd miles off the coast of Venezuela, Gran Roque the kingpin of the islands and yet they have no automobiles and only one town, El Gran Roque. The flats are easy to wade, the water ridiculously clear and heavenly-colored, the season long and consistent (ten months). The bonefish are as big and plentiful as the other bone-

La Guaira Bank

Come spring, billfish to this fabled bank. You want to catch your first billfish or catch fifteen to thirty in a day? La Guiara Bank is one of the best anywhere for blue marlin and white marlin and especially sailfish.

The payara have these teeth that look straight out of a monster movie, two bottom teeth that are obviously too long, too big for the fish's mouth (which is chock-full of other big choppers). Vampires would be jealous, these two teeth are so fierce and long and sharp. The saber-tooth tiger would be green with envy.

Payara look prehistoric. They have the pent-up fury of eons, for they will shatter rods, snap lines, straighten hooks, take you into your backing, bite lures in half, and break your heart. They live in the Amazon's rivers, fast water preferred (although they do live in lakes such as Guri Lake) and when they hit a lure, they devastate it, slam it. When hooked, they leap acrobatically, twisting in midair like a tarpon. One of the top trips to find your destiny with a menacing payara is to Uraima Falls on the Paragua River, a scenic set of falls unlike any other in the world, a river that currently holds the IGFA's all-tackle record for payara, 39 pounds. My friend Scott Swanson of Fishquest puts together an amazing trip to Uraima Falls Lodge to fish for the payara and another local jungle denizen, the aymara. The season runs from December to May.

CONTACTS

FishQuest, www.fishquest.com

Pez Raton Lodge, www.pezraton.com

Posada Mediterraneo, www
.posadamediterraneo.com/en/index
.html

Macanao Lodge, www.macanaolodge
.com/english.htm

Frontiers International, www.frontierstrvl.com

Eduardo Pantoja, Chapi Sportfishing,
www.chapisportfishing.com

The Fly Shop, www.TheFlyShop.com

Angler Adventures, www
.angleradventures.com

Urban Angler Ltd., www.urbanangler.com

fishing paradises. The accommodations run the gamut but they are established and reliable. The guides are some of the best in the world. It must be the charming laid-back Venezuelan vibe that causes this addiction. It's only eighty miles from Venezuela but it's light years away from the political demonstrations of recent times.

Over 300 islands and cays in the archipelago provide endless fishing habitat. Boats run you to your spot and drop you off and then another boat picks you up so there's no backtracking. Cool. You get your large bones singled up or lesser bones schooled up. Las Roques has barracuda in the flats, small tarpon, permit, snapper. But the bonefish average 4 to 5 pounds and you might land a 10-pounder so why bother with anything else?

Europe

ANDORRA

- **Location:** In the Pyrenees, scrunched between Spain and France
- **What You Fish For:** Brown and rainbow trout
- **Highlights and Notables:** Crowded in the main village-city of Andorra la Vellà, you'll fish all by yourself in the remote high country lakes and alpine streams of the pristine Pyrenees Mountains.

Andorra is a country, tiny and high. Not many outside of Europe have ever heard of it. Tourists come and go but you'll want to stay to play in her trout streams and high country lakes in the Pyrenees Mountains between Spain and France.

On some maps, Andorra looks more like a region than a country. At only 180 square miles and with a population of only 65,000, Andorra doesn't get much attention. What mostly happens in this mountainous country's borders is tourism and shopping, tax-free shopping (cigarettes, wine, electronics, almost anything you can think of but you do have limitations on what you can bring out—Douanes [Customs] will definitely check you when you least expect it). Several ski resorts. And fishing.

Andorra hasn't been ravaged by shopping centers and McDonald's and advertising signs though the country is in a serious growth spurt, enjoys twelve million visitors (though they mostly come for skiing and shopping), and even though they are working to expand their highway system, they do have traffic jams. Driving during the day in Andorra la Vella, the

Europe

ICELAND
LAPLAND
SWEDEN
NORWAY
FINLAND
EST.
LAT.
LITHUANIA
RUSSIA
SCOTLAND
NORTH SEA
DEN MARK
BALTIC SEA
IRELAND
WALES
ENGLAND
NETHER-LANDS
BELGIUM
GERMANY
POLAND
BELARUS
UKRAINE
NORMANDY
PARIS
CZECH REPUBLIC
SLOVAKIA
FRANCE
SWITZ.
AUSTRIA
HUNGARY
SLOVENIA
ROMANIA
PYRENEES
ITALY
CORSICA
ANDORRA
BARCELONA
SARDINIA
HERZE.
SERBIA
ADRIATIC SEA
MAC
BULGARIA
BLACK SEA
GA.
PORTUGAL
SPAIN
MADRID
ALBANIA
MAC
GREECE
TURKEY
LISBON
MEDITERRANEAN SEA
SICILY
CROATIA
SLOVENIA
CRETE
CYPRUS

main town, is not for the faint of heart nor the reading-signs-in-Catalonian-quickly-as-they-whiz-by-challenged.

The mountains are clean and primitive, the only signs of humans are the huts you see from time to time (twenty-six huts). The meadows are full of flowers and horses and cows; the mountains with clear streams and blue lakes. The likelihood is that you will fish any of sixty lakes without having anyone else fishing the same one you're on. Most of the lakes are at least an hour's hike away from a road.

No airport, no train goes into Andorra. A three-hour drive from Barcelona. This iso-lation is key to the uniqueness of the country, of the fishery. Most inhabitants speak Catalonian but also Spanish, French, and English. It's truly an international place.

We had an adventure getting to Le Hospitalet, the closest train depot, right across the border in France. Buses run there during the week but on Sunday evening, it's a crapshoot. We rolled and lost so we spent 80 euros to hire Mahlki, a Moroccan-born Andorran taxi-cab driver–tour guide to drive us out of the chaos in Andorra la Vella and to the isolated little French depot town.

If I were you and you end up wanting to fish Andorra, maybe as an adjunct on a trip

The streams are quick, small, rocky, and clear. You'll sometimes see a local fishing with the long rod native to these parts, small hooks baited with tiny worms or parts of worms. If you fly fish, smaller attractor flies do great on these high altitude streams but have as backup some lighter-dressed flies, too. Some of the streams to consider include Valira del Nord, Madriu, Valira d'Orient, Riu de la Coma, Ransol, and Rialb and Incles. Lakes you don't want to miss include Montmalus, Estany de la Nou, Engolasters, Cabana Sorda, Juclar, Illa, Pessons, and Tristania. Many of these lakes have suitcase-sized rocks ringing them that abrade your line, and trees and shrubs that reach out and grab your backcast. The lakes are spectacularly clear and cold.

Most of these fisheries are about half-hour to a couple of hours normal hiking from the road; a few, like Lake Engolasters, are right on the road.

The weather is warm but changing. Storms can crop up in a hurry and the evenings and nights are cold. Since you can't get to Andorra by train or airplane, rent a car and drive there from your home base or take a bus and rent a Jeep in Andorra. In the high clear sunny blue mountain sky, sitting beside a lake eating a picnic of cheese and sausage and wine is about as good as it gets. Foie gras, fresh bread, cherry tomatoes, fresh apricots, a wheel of local cheese and olives, too, if you're so inclined, would make it even better. A local red table wine finishes things off nicely.

through southern France or northern Spain or Barcelona, I'd certainly visit Andorra la Vella, maybe even stay in town if you like shopping and good eating (the country is known for its 250 quality eateries) but after that newness wears off, and it has for us, I'd stay in Ordino or one of the other smaller towns and get to the fishing quicker and easier. Heck, the best way is to camp at one of the lakes or rivers.

You fish Andorra because it is one of the last pristine, high-country fisheries left in Europe. All public, all available, all have fish, all are clean and pure. The scenery is alpine and breathtaking. No big trout, not really. On average about 9 or 10 inches long. A whopper goes about 14 to 15 inches.

AUSTRIA

- **Location:** Central Europe, bordered by many countries including Germany and Italy
- **What You Fish For:** Trout, grayling
- **Highlights and Notables:** One of the most beautiful countries in the world, I recommend fishing Austria as you tour the snow-topped mountains and charming villages, catching lovely trout and prism-like grayling.

If you live in Europe, I could see Austria being a fishing destination. If not, I would

Poster promoting Austrian fishing

recommend fishing as an adjunct to a trip to this beautiful country.

The Alps. The Austrian Alps. Few mountain ranges rival this range for beauty. The Austrian Alps cover the southern and western half of Austria. Austria isn't always on the American vacation radar but it should be. The architecture, music, history, food, and shopping make it worth a two-week visit. Brush up on your German, that's the national language. Austro-Hungarian Empire, the Hapsburgs, Freud, Mozart, and Brahms.

Mountainous Austria has an unfair amount of tumbling crystal-clear freestone streams, the most famous of which is the Traun River. The Traun's heydays are in the past although it's still a beautiful and moderately productive river.

The trout and grayling don't grow to prodigious sizes, a 2-pound rainbow or brown is good-sized for Austrian waters but they are abundant and beautiful and they live in some of the most gorgeous mountain scenery in the world. These same mountains make for some of the top snow skiing anywhere and that's what most folks think of when they think of outdoor sports in Austria. The same spectacular scenery you saw in the movies like *Heidi* and *The Sound of Music*, you'll see just about anywhere you travel in Austria.

Some of the top waters include the Torrener Ache, Mur (near Torrener Ache),

Lammer, Krimmler Ache, Gebestroiter, Moser, Grosse Drau, and Villgraten.

One great thing—close to most any river you fish, you have picture-postcard towns nearby with a range of accommodations. You need two permits for most any river or lake, a private permit and a state license. Many of the hotels have access to water but you have to stay with them to get on it—which, I might add, I don't mind one little bit. Since there are no public waters in Austria, you gotta pay somebody.

Most Austrians don't fish so most anglers you meet on the rivers and lakes are from out of the country. When Austrians do fish, they tend to chase carp and pike. And the coarse fishing is supposed to be pretty darned great, too, but you don't go all the way to Austria to fish for coarse fish.

Most rivers are accessible by road, but that also means you find other anglers. Get away from them after you try for the bigger trout and walk upstream into alpine reaches and enjoy the scenery. Mid-July to September provides the best fishing. Most rivers have fly-only regulations for trout, grayling, and char.

One of the most notable hotels that offers trout waters is the charming Braurup Inn in the mountain town of Mittersill. The inn offers over 135 kilometers of fishing (catch-and-release only) including the River Salzach (great rainbow, brown trout). Plus they have access to lakes, know Austrian fishing, and they even have a fully-stocked fly shop to boot.

Here is the Austrian tourism board fishing pitch:

Proud angler with an Austrian rainbow. Note the snow.

No fewer than thirty fine hotels in incredibly beautiful regions throughout Austria are waiting to cater and care for holiday guests. Whether you love the rugged mountains and wild streams of Vorarlberg, Tyrol, and Salzburg, or the lakes, picturesque rivers, and gentle hills of Carinthia, Styria, and Upper Austria, "Fishing in Austria" has something to offer everyone. Anglers seeking all types of fish—from pike to minnows—will enjoy themselves just as much as will fly fishermen casting their nymphs, while allrounders can always find mixed fishing waters to suit them.

Competent Care and Advice
Hoteliers are always happy to answer any important questions you may have, such as where to get the necessary fishing permit, where it's possible to refrigerate the fish you catch, or what to watch out for when fish-

ing in a particular lake or river. If you'd like to learn to fly fish, you can have a personal, experienced fishing instructor to help you get a lot of fun and pleasure out of the sport, right from the start. The right bait is easily available through the hotel.

Alternatives and Culinary Delights

But fishing isn't the only attractive activity. Austria's magnificent natural surroundings have many other sporting opportunities to offer visitors, ranging from swimming to rambling or cycling. Golfers and tennis players will certainly be able to find a hotel to cater to their interests, where they can bask in a sense of well-being while enjoying their favorite sport. Last but not least, the many traditional Austrian culinary specialities are an essential ingredient in enjoying a well-rounded holiday. And, in many a hotel, the chef will prepare and serve up the pike-perch or trout which you caught just a few hours ago.

What could be more pleasant than fly fishing for trout in crystal clear water, surrounded by breathtaking Alpine scenery? Or peacefully sitting by an emerald lake, waiting for a prize wells or pike, and then landing one with a flick of your rod?—

"Fishing in Austria," Austria Tourism's, holiday specialist, offers you relaxation and adventure rolled into one. So just what does "Fishing in Austria" have to offer the holidaymaker?

You'll find all our details, secret tips & the latest news on our homepage. Would you like to order your own catalogue, or to receive more information? Then simply contact "Fishing in Austria."

CONTACTS

Austria Tourism, www.fischwasser.com, Hauptstraße 203, A-9210 Pörtschach, 0043-(0)4272/3620-30, Fax: 0043-(0)4272/3620-90, hermann.striednig @strafinger.at

Hotel Braurup, Mittersill, 0043/6562/6216

Fishing associations own or control much of the fishing waters of Austria. The two main associations are: the Austrian Fishing Association (ÖFG) and the Association of Austrian Workers' Fishing Clubs (VÖAFV).

Österreichische Fischereigesellschaft, Elisabethstrasse 22, 1010 Wien 1 (Austria) Verband der Österreichischen Arbeiter-Fischerei-Vereine, Lenaugasse, 14, A-1080 Wien (Austria), Telephone: 0222 403 21 76 403 97 54

CORSICA

- **Location:** Island off the coasts of France and Italy in the Mediterranean Sea; north of Sardinia
- **What You Fish For:** Trout
- **Highlights and Notables:** This is novelty fishing, catching fish in a stunningly beautiful place where you wouldn't normally think trout would live. Trout in the streams of Corsica? That's surprising. Exactly.

Honestly, everything I know about fishing for trout in Corsica is second- and third-hand knowledge. I didn't even know Corsica had worthwhile inland fishing until the other day. We're on this journey of fishing this Mediterranean island together. For me, Corsica and its high mountain trout streams are on my summer destination list for next year. I like adventures, I like hiking, I like the idea that not many fish these rivers in the mountains and it could be hit or miss. Hit or miss is okay with me.

I love the Basque, the Catalans, the Andorrans, and I am guessing that the Corse, who wish feverishly for their independence from France, will be the same feisty independent unique highland people.

So I turn to David Lynch, not the moviemaker as far as I know, but of www.bluedome.co.uk/corsica/index.html. He knows the difficulty in obtaining info about Corsica fly fishing. And he's been there, done that.

Dave has this to say about the Corsican wild brown trout fishing:

My knowledge was a little limited and I could only recall that Napoleon Bonaparte was a son of Corsica and the GR20, one of the world's toughest mountain walks, ran across the Corsican peaks. I also knew that Corsica had some great rivers.

The information from the Internet started to give a picture of a beautiful island with a culture that encompassed colonial France and patriotic Corse to create a unique breed of people. The desire for independence from France is still much in the thoughts of the Corsican people and the central region where we stayed was a very Corsican place to visit. Graffiti calling for independence from France adorned many walls.

Our destination was Corte, the capital of old Corsica, and our hotel was in one of the most spectacular locations in Europe. Home for the week was to be Le Refuge Hotel in the Gorges de la Restonica. The hotel is perched between the narrow road and the raging Torrente Restonica, which pushes several thousand gallons a minute down the granite bed of the gorge. Great food is the order of the day at Le Refuge and we could see the pounds pile on after the first meal.

Sometimes it is only when sipping a glass at home do you get a true picture of what was good, bad, and indifferent about your fishing exploits. I am still going over the Corsica experience and probably will do so for years to come or until I can get back there and apply the lessons learnt on this trip.

The Rivers

Corsica has the cleanest rivers in Europe. There is hardly any industrial activity on the island and the levels of recorded pollution are tiny. The rivers are stocked by a group of twenty or so local fishing organisations in association with the local department for the environment. From information gleaned across the various fishing Web sites it claims that the survival rate for trout stocks is the best in Europe and from what we eventually saw I can believe it.

Arriving at a new destination with a complete absence of local knowledge can be challenging. Even finding the fishing shop in Corte took three days.

We saw lots of dry riverbeds even in May before the summer heat kicks in. Spate rivers make up the majority of river forms and they tend to be highly seasonal. The waters tumbling down the Restonica could be seen to be falling through the week we were there in spite of late snow on the peaks. Sadly there are no fish in the Restonica; it would have been wonderful if there had been any.

No fish—no problem. I checked my list of possible venues and found that there were three rivers that were noted on the French Web sites—The Tavignano was first up and it was not too far from Corte. The roads on the island all follow riverbeds so doing a visual inspection is quite easy. The Tavignano is a gem of a river with several Genoese arched bridges still in use as the road follows the river from Corte to the coast at Aleria.

We travelled the whole length of the river and spotted a couple of likely places to wet a line later in the day. Lunch was from a boulangerie in Ghisonaccia on the busy N198, which runs along the eastern coastline.

Back to the river: I had spotted a track off the main road just a mile or so from the Pont Genois bridge. It led from the main road along to an ancient stone cottage behind which was a sandy beach and a lovely stretch of river fed from a tumbling riffle of clear water. The river had excavated a deep pool which then ran over a bed of granite cobbles and away to the sea. Fantastic!

My partner laid out the sunbathing gear and settled to watch my efforts. A quiet walk along the eighty yards or so of easy bank fishing gave me some concerns. Once again there was no visual sighting of any fish. The river was in great condition and crystal clear until it fell away into the depths of the main pool.

The only thing to be seen were a few tiny pin fry hiding behind the boulders in the shallows and a few pond skaters. Everything was here, clear, pollution-free water, ample insect life along the wooded banks, no obvious predators, no one fishing apart from myself, yet no fish.

I put my travel rod together and selected a small, black dry to try and mimic the local flies that could be seen here and there in the margins of the river. My first few nervous casts were clumsy but I have done worse and still caught fish. The result was nil. Over the next ninety minutes I went through my full repertoire of emergers, dries, nymphs and lures to no effect. The river seemed to be empty. I could not see anything apart from water.

It had been stated on one of the Web sites about outdoor activities on Corsica that although the rivers were in great condition there was a huge amount of illegal poaching. We can't back this up but this was not the first "blank" to arouse some suspicions about where the fish had gone. In spite of a poor start we had received a taste of what Corsica could offer and the next destinations promised something better.

The Gravona and Prunelli Rivers and Lac de Tolla

Another day and another journey across the island toward Ajaccio and three potential opportunities to try the fishing. The drive from Corte south-westwards takes you through some of the most spectacular mountain scenery that Corsica has to offer. The N193 is the main highway and is best described as a modest UK A road. The route, however, is unlike any in Britain. The villages along the road are "old style" Corse and cling to steep, wooded mountainsides as the route snakes toward the highpoint at Vizzavona. The village is famous as a stopping off point for the GR20, Europe's toughest high-mountain walking route. A station for the narrow-gauge railway also serves the walkers at Vizzavona and the surrounding forest offers home to eagles, wild boar, and countless streams and brooks.

From Vizzavona the road tracks down toward the Gravona Valley and the coast. Most of the steep spate rivers flowing into the Gravona were very low and pointed toward the coming summer heat. The main river itself still held a good flow of water and we began to stop at suitable points to look at the clear water as it fell to the sea.

At one point I was able to walk as stealthily as I could for about half a mile along the river. Passing by some good pools and shallow riffles as well as past huge granite boulders in midstream.

Not a single fish to be seen anywhere.

I returned to the car in a state of serious disappointment. It seemed inconceivable that such a beautiful river could be so devoid of fish. Yet we had looked with care at four different sections and seen nothing. I was all for giving up and returning to Vizzavona to do some walking and cover some of the other aspects of our visit. My partner would hear none of it and insisted we continue and drive up the N196 then onto the D3 and up the Prunelli valley to Lac de Tolla.

Lac de Tolla

Off we go as the afternoon heat starts to climb. Another visit to a small boulangerie in Bastelicaccia for refreshments and we are away.

The Prunelli River cannot be seen for most of the drive but what you do see is another lush valley full of vines and fruit trees. We keep driving but no lake appears. The villages are ticked off as we climb higher toward the mountains and it dawns that Tolla is going to be a dull, empty alpine lake. How wrong can you be? Lac de Tolla lies below the village of the same name and is ringed by pines and farmland in spite of sitting at close to 800 meters above sea level. The water is blue and the Lac is formed by a huge dam placed to provide drinking water and power to the west of Corsica.

We sat on the balcony of the only bar in town and examined our choices. The drive back was about three hours and we had arranged to meet some friends for dinner. It was red hot and the fishing was likely to be as bad as the rivers. Take some pictures and then turn for Corte seemed to be the best bet. As we got ready to go a car arrives and two smiling Corsican fishermen got out. A decent pike in lovely condition was brought from the boot (trunk) of the car and ourselves, the barman and a few others gathered to congratulate the fishers' skill. This is big news in a place as small as Tolla!

It was discovered that the specimen was a mere "tiddler" and the Tolla pike were known to grow to huge sizes. The barman explains the size of the resident fish with his arms outstretched in classic "fisherman's tales"-style, also the "truite" were magnificent specimens and would break my rod.

That statement made up my mind, Liz would stay and read her book and I would just manage to get about ninety minutes of fishing. After the lack of fish in the rivers I did not really expect to see a thing apart from water. Mistake. I stood close to edge of the water at a small bay. A watersport centre was starting to prepare canoes and kayaks for the coming season. In the margins I could see several deep-bodied brown trout cruising in the deep, weed-free water.

My hands shook with anticipation as I put the rod together, reel, leader, and lastly a fly. A buzzer seemed like a sensible place to start. The water was slightly green but it was alive and deep. Fish at last.

As I looked for a suitable spot to start my campaign, a little black dog joined me. He seemed to grasp what I was about and would not go away. As I got ready for my first cast he was watching where the line went and had seen all this before. He examined my technique without comment but got slightly agitated with every new cast, settling down as the line was retrieved. It was good to have a companion to help me along.

After a dozen casts, the line tightened and a minor fight ensued which brought me a tiny brownie that although heavily outgunned still fought to break my rod. The dog went berserk and barked like mad until I had the fish in the net. I should have taken a picture, as this was my first brown trout and my first fish on Corsica. I had aspirations of the bigger specimens that still cruised past every ten minutes or so. The little brownie was carefully returned to fight another day. And that was it, not a sniff of anything else. I tried the buzzer variations and then started to go through the "menu," changing positions and tactics every twenty minutes or so, my small, black companion always alongside. I could still see the fish cruising along in a lazy Mediterranean-style and as my agreed return time drew closer, a few rises could be seen but no more interest in my offerings.

As I tackled down, the fishing dog realised that the day's entertainment was over and scooted away up a path toward the village. I trekked back and told my tale before throwing all the gear in the boot and starting the return journey.

Lac de Tolla held much promise and a visit of only a couple of hours is not enough to even scratch the surface. The lake is wide, long, and deep and is holding some fine fish. This is where a return trip to Corsica started to be planned!

Casting a Nymph in the Last Chance Saloon

Our last day on Corsica started with a shopping session in Corte and coffee in one of the little bars. I bought a handsome, Corsican-made pocketknife as a souvenir. The plan for the day was to drive to Ponte Leccia and take the N193

east toward Bastia and a day at the seaside. The roads were very quiet, a bit like Sunday in the UK. The first port of call along the N193 was to be Ponte Nuovo. This was the place where the last stand by Corsican patriots took place against the French. The Corsicans were routed and many were killed, as the cause for Corsican independence was lost. The old bridge was later damaged during a bombing raid in World War II but it is still a place of great importance to native Corsicans. I pulled the car into the wide lay-by (pullout) just over the new road bridge and looked down into the waters of the Golo River. I looked right down into the deep left channel to see three trout keeping position in the steady flow of the river. The fishing gear had gone into the car as something of an afterthought. I had not expected to fish on Corsica again but this was what I had brought the kit here for, brown trout swimming in a clear river just waiting for me to present the right fly.

There lies another tale. In the run up to the trip I had built up a small selection of wet flies, nymphs, and bugs to make my fishing a complete success. Sadly that particular box of flies was still sitting on a corner of my desk while what I had in my vest pocket was my all-purpose UK Stillwater fly collection. I cannot blame my lack of success on this one fact but it was one of those stupid mistakes that will always be remembered with deep anguish—stupid sod that I am.

Liz agreed to me having a casting session if we could find a place to fish. Otherwise we would continue to the west and enjoy a day at the beach. I would find a place to fish this river if I had to dynamite a path myself. I did not need to worry; someone had already done that for me.

About three kilometres away from Ponte Nouvo the new road winds its way along the gorge; just before the road starts to climb is a small mustard-colored hotel and a hundred metres further is the remains of a small access road that was constructed to aid the new road building. We parked here and the pathway led to a flat section of riverbank about 300 metres long. This section of bank had been supported with huge lumps of rock to stop the river undercutting the new road.

The water was clear and flowed steadily into the curve of the bank. Liz and I watched a dozen fish of all sizes rise to take at the surface and just below it, too. In the deeper water the huge natural boulders in the riverbed gave shelter to larger fish that were taking passing food items in an unhurried, confident way.

Game on! An hour was my allowance, so I carefully put my thoughts to the problem of getting my first brown trout from a river. Floating line, floating braided leader, nine feet of fluorcarbon and my best guess at what these fish would find interesting. My error with the fly boxes left me with very little choice. I had a couple of wets and the best one to me, not that I eat them myself, was a gold beaded nymph. My only thought being that it was a big one.

I carefully and quietly scrambled down the rocks to one that gave me a flat platform about three feet above the river.

Steady, get some line out. Remember the lessons and let's fish.

My first cast went right across the flow of the river, good cast but too far. The fly sparkled in the water and I tried to judge the depth. The water is so clear that it could be three feet or thirty!

I started to reduce the amount of line and then stopped for a while to study the river and the fish. A large brownie had taken station at the shoulder of a huge, submerged boulder. An even larger head kept appearing from the furthest side of the boulder and I decided to try for one of them. The line went out a couple of times before I realised that I should reduce the leader. In it came again and I took off three feet and replaced the gold beaded what-not.

This time the line went out perfectly. The current brought it in line with the far shoulder of the rock and I watched as both fish sighted the bright sparkle of the fly coming toward them.

The smaller fish was higher in the water and came forward to the fly. The larger fish showed more of himself and then turned away never to be seen again. The smaller of the two fishes took his chance and turned to the fly and then quickly turned away to take station again in the current.

That was the end of the fishing. Time had almost run out and in spite of changing the fly a couple of times there was no interest from the fish.

Wrong menu, spooked fish, or whatever, it was time to pack up and consider a return match in the spring of 2006, late April seemed about right.

We drove to the beach, a tiny place called Aghione, which we found by accident down a sidetrack. A small beach café served a great meal and we looked out across a bay that was several miles wide with only thirty other people for company. Elba was visible in the veil of the heat mist and I wondered if Napoleon could have seen his home from his exile there.

Conclusions

Firstly let me say that I am going back to try the fishing again! Corsica is a different destination than expected. The roads are quieter than we thought they would be and the mountains and rivers are without reservation—stunning. Food and accommodation are good everywhere and there is a huge range of options for both. Local knowledge proved to be a major problem when it came to finding anywhere to fish

and when we finally found the Corte fishing shop the owner and his pals did not want to offer any useful information.

A visitors' fishing ticket is available but we could not find out where one could be purchased so we fished anyway.

Our visits to the various rivers did not exhaust the islands potential by any stretch of the imagination. There are dozens of other rivers that could produce some great fishing. The coastline is also another area that is largely uninhabited and undeveloped. You could spend months exploring Corsica and still not see everything.

CONTACTS

Corsican Places, www.corsica.co.uk/ default.aspx is a great company to deal with and very much a Corsica specialist.

Thanks to Dave at www.bluedome.co.uk/ corsica/index.html.

CROATIA

- **Location:** South-central Europe, bordered by Italy, Slovenia, Hungary, and more
- **What You Fish For:** Trout and grayling
- **Highlights and Notables:** Your money goes farther here than in other European countries and the scenery and fishing are as good or better. The history is so rich, you'll be surprised.

Wild trout and grayling in a country you probably know nothing about. Formerly a part of Yugoslavia, Croatia obtained its independence recently, in 1991. Why go to Croatia to fish when you've never heard of it, you don't read articles about the fishing, and the country is new and just getting on its feet?

Croatia is a beautiful mountainous country with productive clear cold streams. And the streams are not crowded (yet).

Part of Rome, the Holy Roman Empire, a kingdom of its own, in cahoots with Hungary, part of the Ottoman Empire, part of the Hapsburg Empire, member of a triad confederacy, unionized with Serbia, part of Yugoslavia, under Russian control, in the middle of the Serb-Croat conflict of the 1990s.

Croatia is situated between central, southern, and eastern Europe. Shaped like a crescent, the country has lots of neighbors: Slovenia, Bosnia, Herzegovina, Hungary, Serbia, Italy, and Montenegro.

Croatia has a crossroads location connecting the Balkans to central Europe. The infrastructure of the country has struggled to meet the demands of unemployment and bureaucracy in a post-Communist economy and then, as the country's economy grew, had growing pains.

The country has beautiful diverse terrain, ranging from its rocky shores on the Adriatic to forested mountains to lowland plains and rolling hills. Its villages are red-roofed, packed together.

The fishing? Surprisingly healthy con-

Croatia has the Adriatic Sea on its western border and this colorful sea has prime fishing for shark, bluefin tuna, swordfish, amberjack, and dolphin.

sidering the country suffered through so much military conflict and governmental oppression. The rivers and lakes are some of the least polluted in Europe. The streams are conducive to fly fishing. Spring-fed Kupa River is one of the top streams for grayling and brown trout, green and cobbled, and while it's not always wild (it flows past villages but in parts, it's wild), the fishing is excellent. The Danubian salmon still swims in some of these rivers as well. Kupica River and Curak Creek (a canyon stream) are tributaries of the Kupa and they too have superb angling for browns and grayling and have a more wilderness feel. The Gacka and Cetina Rivers are two more top trout streams.

ENGLAND

- **Location:** Western Europe, off the coast of France and Belgium
- **What You Fish For:** Trout
- **Highlights and Notables:** Storied rivers, birthplace of fly fishing, English charm

Rightly or wrongly, this exchange is treated as fact: As the story goes, Lady Nancy Astor, the first woman to ever serve in the British House of Commons once chided Winston Churchill "Winston, if you were my husband, I'd poison your tea." He responded "Nancy, if I were your husband, I'd drink it."

Now how can you not fall in love with a country that produces men like that?

England is intimidating to me. I've been an Anglophile since I was a kid, read everything I could get my hands on about English history and culture, studied maps, literature. I love London but it overwhelms me. I can't really explain it.

When I read WWI or WWII histories, I pay unusual attention to the British perspective. I know I shouldn't but I secretly admire the British Empire and how worldly they were, how they effectively imposed their culture on so many different cultures. And they taught these countries how to speak the native language of England, which, if you are American and have ever visited England, you know is not English, it is not the same language the rest of us speak.

The rivers of England intimidate even more. The lakes confuse me. I have cut my fly fishing teeth on Western streams. Big bushy flies. Fast rocky rivers. High country streams. Sure, I've fished numerous spring creeks in America and other locales but English chalkstreams are different enough that I'm flummoxed and wherever I've fished them, I've come away with few landed fish, and a healthy respect for those who fish them regularly. The rivers are cultivated, manicured, babied—the English rivers have riverkeepers, for goodness sakes. You can't wade in many of them. I'm American. I need to wade, I need to nearly drown. I don't wear tweed or Barbour or driving caps. Fishing English demands patience and refinement and alterations. One thing I found when fishing Europe is that, in typical American bravado, I could catch fish in their rivers as well as they could. Nope. Wrong. Can't do it. That's why these guys from England and France and Czech Republic and Poland and Portugal win these world fly fishing championships. They are damned fine fly anglers. If you think that on our home waters we'd whoop 'em, well, you'd be wrong. They go to American waters and they kick our butts there, too.

Honestly, I want to tell you that England is one of the top fisheries in the world for trout or salmon or something but I can't consider the private lakes enough pull to pay all that money to fly across the pond. Most of the places you fish are for stocked trout. That doesn't turn me off, not a deal breaker, but for destinations I have to pay well for, it's not a turn on either. The Test and Itchen are icons, comparable to any other trout streams in the world but they are hard to access, difficult to fish, not ideal for many anglers.

Fly fishing was born here and if you fly fish, that ought to be reason enough to fish England. Do a "Fishing England" trip one of three ways: Go with your best fly fishing buddy, one who can understand the history behind the rivers and sport, the long complex history of England, and who is a pretty fair angler. He or she cannot mind getting skunked. He or she needs to appreciate the poetry, the art, whatever tired cliché you want to use for that time period when you feel connected or changed or humbled.

Or: You go on vacation to England, stay a few days in London, tour the Lake District, take the car for a spin on the wrong side of the road to visit some castles and along the way, you integrate a day here and a day there angling.

Or: Do England budget-style and map out streams and lakes, stay in budget lodg-ing, enjoy fishing across the countryside, alternating chalkstreams, and freestoners.

But this is a dreambook. Fish the Test and Itchen, maybe the Frome, Lambourn, Avon, Kennet, and Blagdon Reservoir. And remember these things:

There's a price to pay to fish in England. It's not a cheap sport. From licenses to ghillies (guides) to lodging, it's costly.

Chalkstreams cost money to fish but there are some bargains if you look away from the Test and Itchen.

Spring is the finest time to fish in England but summer and fall are excellent if the weather and water cooperate and you make good choices. Flies are bigger than you think (oh sure, you need your smaller ones especially for chalkstreams, like CDCs but you'll be surprised). Insect hatches, like the mayfly, are bigger than you'd expect.

You usually fish beats. Most beats have fishing huts to cool your heels.

While many rivers are well-groomed, that doesn't mean there aren't sections that are wild and have thistles. On chalkstreams, you fish upstream and you fish only with dry flies. You usually do not wade.

River Test

Such greenery and Englishness, it's as though it runs through the land of hobbits. The Shire (Hampshire) lies just under eighty miles southwest of London. The River Test should be fished even if you suck as an angler, even if you don't catch a single fish after a hard day's fishing on the river. And that's overrated. You can catch trout and grayling on the Test. You need a good guide, some decent hatches, and to play by their rules and you can have a field day.

The upper Test starts near the town of Ashe, in the Hampshire, and just gets bigger with feeders (imagine that) and goes on some thirty-nine miles long. Spring-fed, laden with rich green cultured riparian habitat only the wet English countryside could produce, diverted and rerouted over centuries along its route, the Test has excellent hatches and is, for lack of a better term, very English. Everything you hoped for when before you got on the stream. The upper holds many wild brown trout but not many of significant size—that's the middle section (the one where the most exclusive fishing club in the world, the Houghton Club with its twenty-plus members, has its private waters). You begin to pick up more stocked trout in the middle section.

The Test gets lots of pressure from anglers all over the world who want to test their skills, walk through its garden-like banks, become one with the touchstone, and fish where the sport began. While the majority of the fish might be stocked, they do run 1 to 5 pounds stocked and that's not all bad. All the other stuff makes up for that aspect.

CONTACTS
Orvis, Stockbridge, 011-44-1264-810-017
Roxton Sporting Limited, www.roxtons.com
Bob Bailey, 011-44-1488-658905
Alex Walker, 011-44-1985-212325
Nick Hart, www.hartflyfishing.demon
  .co.uk
John Horsey, www.johnhorsey.co.uk
Famous Fishing, www.famousfishing
  .co.uk

FRANCE

First and foremost, the angling in France is mostly about trout and salmon but the days of Gaul being a world-class salmonid fishery are long gone. Today, you're more likely to find French anglers tackling carp. That said, the fishing experience for those who dap and cast in France is world-class because of the ambience, the food, the culture, the history, and—surprisingly to many who don't know France—the people, the lovely French people.

Angling is tradition in France, each region proud of its rivers and lakes, its own techniques and equipment. Perhaps only in a few places in England can you find the same streamside elegance as on a French river. I happen to like the chalkstreams of

Normandy and swift clear cold rivers of the Pyrenees the most, but I could have easily included fishing in the Jura, the rivers that feed the Rhine, the Rhone, the Loire, the Seine. At one time, the Atlantic salmon fishing in French rivers was as good as it got but over time, the populations have dwindled.

Vallée de Campan

- **Location:** Southwestern France, near south of Tarbes, north of Bielsa, right on the border with Spain
- **What You Fish For:** Brown trout
- **Highlights and Notables:** A beautiful small-to-medium freestone river ideal for dry fly fishing, beginners, and enjoying a day in the Pyrenees Mountains

We met up with our guide Mariano Cruz in the Vallée de Campan in southern France and immediately hit it off with him. He was exactly what we needed for our first foray into the French high country. Spanish-born but having lived his life in this valley in France, and having watched enough American television, his three languages allowed him to converse with us and anyone else we met.

He spoke Spanish (with an Andalusian accent which was fun for me, because I have a Tex-Mex Spanish accent when I speak Spanish). We communicated easily but he always made a point to help Amy understand what we were saying. He is witty, too. And he spoke enough English to bridge the gap. We spent 'til late evening with him fishing the Adour, the Adour-Payolle, and a secret perfect stream

I am not allowed to name or he gets to kill me. The rivers were knee-deep, cobble-bottomed, clearing from runoff, and cold. We could see trout holding but they were picky and the casts needed to be precise.

The hatches were sparse that day although Mariano told us that the mayfly and caddis hatch throughout the warm months. We caught many browns, nothing of great size, on mostly generic nymphs on droppers below dry flies but we were amazed at the incredible scenery, reminiscent of many spots we fish in the American West. We decided that it was in fact more beautiful because it is in Europe (this is where we fell in love with countryside Europe by the way). The browns were thick as thieves, the water cold and a bit off-color from early June runoff, and we had had only breakfast and were as hungry as all git out.

Mariano took us to a bar/café at the top of the mountain (so it seemed) for a very Pyrennees-style lunch of cured canard (duck) breast, cured ham, olives, and ternera and frites (rare veal steak and French fries). From our covered table, we watched two different herds of sheep and one herd of cattle feeding within twenty yards of us. The owner was French Basque and did not speak Spanish so each time he brought us another plate of food, the best I could do was murmur lowly something I hoped sounded like "merci." Spanish and French cooks do not cook the meat, huh? Simply let each side hit the fire, then turn it over? Despite the pool of *sangre,* the meat was delicious and we savored the lunch and the fishing.

At one point on the river, I was standing next to Mariano watching him cast skillfully

to tiny pockets. He caught and released a fat little brown trout and as we stood chatting about the fish, he greased up his fly with some floatant he had in a film canister. I reached in with my finger and swiped some, smelling it because it had a bit of a funky odor, then dabbed it on my fly and my tippet. With a smile, Mariano asked me how much my floatant cost me, how many bottles of floatant I bought each year.

Knowing where he was going with this, I beat him to the punch and asked if he made his own floatant. Indeed he did. When the farmers milk the cows, a residue is left, a milky cream, which when put in a film canister, looks just like what I had dipped my finger into. I nodded at him, realizing that he was not funning with me. I dipped my finger in the river and wiped it on my shirt. Mariano said he is friends with all the farmers in the valley and they save the residue for him. He said he spends nothing a year on his

floatant while I must spend nearly fifteen or twenty bucks a year.

Mariano was the perfect fishing and travel guide, helping us understand some of the cultural differences. When we asked him over lunch what kind of fast food he ate, he thought for a minute and told us how he selects a cow for slaughter each quarter year from a local farmer. He chooses a cow he has watched and knows, and this way (as Mariano taps his head), "I know what kind of cow I will be eating. Only grass." He broke down the cuts of meat, telling us that "in France, we eat all the cow, even the brain, the tongue, and the nose. I have the snout salt-cured, sliced very thin and I keep it in the refrigerator." Amy and I looked at each other with wide eyes. "That," he paused for dramatic effect and popped in an olive, "is my fast food."

Gave d'Oloron, Gave de Pau, Gave d'Aspe

As we drove back through France the next day, the pilgrims walking the road were thick, so our driving slowed, the *niebla* (fog) settling down over the mountains like a blanket. Even French drivers were using caution!

I saw the Gave d'Oloron after two days of heavy rain and my heart sank. It was high on its banks, swollen, and I knew that overnight, its tributaries would keep feeding water from on high. So I figured then I wouldn't get to fish it.

Jean-Michel Boyer was to meet us at three. We ate lunch at a local bar and found out some subtleties of the French language. Amy thought she ordered a salad with fruit but instead it was a salad with

fruit of the sea. The beautiful salad arrived complete with octopus legs draped all over the lettuce, and in it were other lovely creatures of the sea. Surprise.

We still had few francs in our pocket and the banks were closed but we found one little bank that opened from 2:15 to 4:30 and changed money there. In the countryside, there are few banks, and where there are banks, the hours are short. Change your money at a bank in a big city or at the airport or before you fly over.

We met the young Frenchman and luckily, even though he spoke little English, he did speak pretty good Spanish. He agreed the Gave d'Oloron would be tough fishing (nymphs only and dangerous wading) so we decided to visit the Gave d'Aspe and Gave d'Ossau. Jean-Michel was a super guide,

driving us around for hours, stopping for us to fish and take pictures, winding around those high country roads, talking about the fishing on the Gave de Pau and Gave d'Oloron and techniques and so on, showing us the rare Egyptian vultures, telling us about the nearly extinct Pyrennean bears. We visited even some very small streams at the top of the mountains (including the exquisite little stream, the Gave de Lourdios) where the scenery was nothing short of dramatic, heavenly.

The Gave d'Aspe was amazing looking but the only way we could fish it was dunking nymphs with lots of split. Two rainbows, 12 inches each, wild as the hairs in my ears. Rocky, quicky, clear, and fishable from the bank or wadeable when you have normal flows.

We loved Biarritz where we stayed the day and night before Paris. I love Gateaux Basque now. The fromage quiche is exquisite. We love the food overall. I loved driving fast but in control. I loved the scenery and the history and the people and the fishing. I've been back to fish the Gave d'Oloron and the Gave de Pau since that day, and did poorly at the first, well at the second. We're planning to go back again next summer.

Risle River

The Anclou reach of the Risle (pronounced reel), one of the storied rivers of France, and there I am sitting on a stool, ten feet from the glassy surface, drinking local red wine, munching on leg of lamb that just came off of Nick Toldi's little grill. Neither Amy nor I had ever eaten lamb of any sort so this was a stretch for two Texans.

Delicious. Touch of herbs, pepper, juicy. I spread boar's pâté on the bread.

The occasional brown trout rose in the river right at the bank's edge and it was torture to sit and eat instead of stringing up the rod. Such is the order of the day on a French chalkstream. Leisurely take your dinner and wine and dessert and coffee until the late hatch brings up the fish.

More protocol. Don't wade. Bank fish, only cast to rising trout.

And we ate more of the smoky sausage, then bacon as thick as a steak, grilled, covered in herbes de Provence, then came the rain, then the coffee and chocolate éclairs and then the cigars and Calvados and then rolled in the fog, white puffy fog that crept across the fields like a division of ghosts.

And Nick talked about former famous anglers who fished these waters, Charles Ritz and Frank Sawyer, Skues, and others.

I see some fat browns, big noses in the feeding ring-rises, and I have takes, subtle ones, nudges to my lightly-dressed flies but catch nothing. The glare on the water was merciless and then there was dusk. At eleven in the night, still twilight, Nick catches a 12-inch brown. One trout to hand, a memorable fishing experience.

You can't visit Normandy without a day or two on the Risle, the queen of the region's "fly-only" chalkstreams. And you can't visit Normandy without visiting the D-Day villages and beaches where the solemnity and importance will impact you as greatly as it did me.

The Andelle

We met up with Nick and a client of his, Kenichiro Eitaka, a Japanese businessman who lives in Paris. We met at the Andelle River in Normandy. Ken has a big smile, is easy to like, is absolutely eaten up with fly fishing.

The Andelle River lies just an hour drive from Paris, a half-hour more if you're driving instead of Nick or some other native Frenchman. The trout are not of great size. The river is not wide nor is it deep.

Then why fish the Andelle?

For starters, the angling history of the stream. How about an eighteenth-century castle on the river's banks? A 1,000-year-old abbey, complete with legends and

ghosts, sitting on the banks of the Andelle. Famous past anglers of the Andelle include G.E.M. Skues, Frank Sawyer, Louis Bouglé, Georges Hardy, Dwight D. Eisenhower, Frank Hemingway, Winston Churchill, and Odette Pol-Roger (of champagne fame).

The streamside meal. Nick opens the back of his SUV and he rustles around in his wooden boxes. He pulls out a table, sets up chairs, covers the table with a checkered tablecloth. We tear off chunks from the fresh baguette, crisp on the outside, warm and soft on the inside. We pop cherry tomatos in our mouth, from the vine, sweet as sugar. We eat slices of cheese from the Alps. We spread whipped goat cheese with herbs on our bread, nibble on thin-sliced sausage, sop our bread in Nick's piperade, a thick, spicy, tasty tomato and pepper sauce.

At one point, when the soft goat's cheese spread is almost all gone, Ken talks about how he hates to eat anything from sheep or goats and Nick informs him he has just eaten a passelfull of it and Ken covers his eyes, then his mouth, and says "Oh, no," and we think he must be allergic or something but it turns

from the rising brown trout tell us it's time to fish. The difficulty in catching these trout demands your best effort but when you are in the zone, as Nick and I were when we started at the bridge by the castle, the Andelle is friendly. We caught browns in long wide glides that had no discernible currents or visible underwater lies. Only the ring-rises and splashes gave their location away. We also caught fish tight against the bank, in between the tangled roots of trees, in the few riffles, and many in the short runs.

The Andelle is famous and typical chalk-stream of Normandy, a tributary to the river Seine. Private beat, fly fishing only, catch-and-release only, barbless hooks only. No streamers allowed. Nymphs tolerated but in the Normandy tradition on chalk-

out he just really thinks goats and sheep are dirty and doesn't like to eat anything to do with either. But he lived through it.

Conversation. We talk with Ken and Nick, each of us sharing fishing stories. Nick's story is from a wayward angling trip to Sweden. Ken's story takes us to the delicate rivers of Hokkaido. Mine is a goofy tale of Mark screwing up on a Western river yet again. We marvel at Ken's custom bamboo rod, a real work of art. Ken gifts me with an expensive pin of a mayfly for my vest. The air becomes cool and gray.

The wine. Two bottles of white wine, local. That fuzzy feeling, warm all over. You can't go wrong drinking French wine in France, especially with a Frenchman selecting what you drink.

The coffee. Strong and hot and too tasty to expect such an after-dinner treat while sitting on the banks of a river.

The Calvados. The drink of the Normans, an apple brandy that warms your mouth, your throat, your stomach.

The gentle circles on the smooth surface

streams, dry fly preferred and to rising fish only. The season runs from mid-March to early October. Additional "category one" trout and grayling rivers close to Paris include the Iton and the Rouloir.

CONTACTS

Nick Toldi, Gourmetfly, www.gourmetfly .com

Arkadi de Rakoff, Risle River, Normandy, www.clubfishfrance.com

HUNGARY

- **Location:** Eastern Europe
- **What You Fish For:** Trout, grayling, pike, carp
- **Highlights and Notables:** Dental work and fishing. Seriously.

I have fished Hungary before and while I enjoyed Hungary, and enjoyed the fishing, at no time did I think it was one of the best 1,001 places I'd ever fished. I love the history and atmosphere and people but the fishing is average to pretty good. The Danube and Tisza Rivers are popular fishing spots for Hungarians and Europeans but compared to other rivers in Europe, they come in second. That said, if you were going to be in Hungary anyway, say, for dental work, you would do well to recover over a couple of weeks and fish each day to aid your recovery.

Weird I know but this is real and legit. Dental work and fishing. So you get your fangs fixed and fish for fish. How can you beat that combo?

I am told that dental treatment in Hungary is up to 60 percent cheaper than in the United States. Flying to a foreign country for tooth-fixing is apparently more common than we think, the name given for it, dental tourism. Yikes.

The pitch is that you save lots of money on the million-dollar smile (bridges and crowns and veneers) by traveling to the Hungarian resort town of Mosnmagyarovar, receiving dental treatment, and, during recovery, enjoy the spa, day trips to Bratislava in Slovakia, to Budapest, Vienna, the Hungarian baroque towns of Sopron and Gyoer, to the 1,000-year-old monastery of Panonhalma, enjoy a dinner or wine tasting in a twelveth-century castle, play golf, ride a bike through the meadows and forests alongside the Moson Danube, an arm of the Danube or, of course, fish. Part of the sell is that the dental work is so cheap that the savings cover the cost of your fishing trip and then some. This company/dentist supplies everything from a rental car to fishing licenses to accomodations.

Mosnmagyarovar lies less than an hour's

drive southeast of Vienna and sits on the Moson Danube arm of the Danube. The area is heavily forested, lush land with numerous streams and lakes including three large productive lakes, Lake Balaton, Lake Tisza, and Lake Velencei.

Posh Journeys sets up the dental-angling adventure and puts you in touch with experts who arrange for the licenses as well as for a local guide. Fish species include trout, grayling, several species of carp, pike, and several other species of fish native to these waters. I am told that soon they will also offer dental tourism-fishing trips in the Czech Republic as well.

I haven't done this trip. Not that I don't need some dental work. I checked into the quality of the dental tours and everything I found said we're talking quality medical services. Heck, if you have to have some expensive dental work and you like to fish, well, why not turn that pain into angling fun?

CONTACTS

Helga van Horn, Posh Journeys, 775-852-5105, poshjourneys.com

Florian Scheuer, www.dental-offer.com, fscheuer@dental-offer.com

Tim Baldwin, (sets up trips in the Czech Republic), www.praguetoursuk.com

ICELAND

- **Location:** Western Europe, an island in the northern Atlantic
- **What You Fish For:** Atlantic salmon
- **Highlights and Notables:** If there is a mecca for Atlantic salmon today, this is it, this otherworldly looking island of a hundred salmon rivers.

Iceland as a fishing destination is not for every angler. Despite the fact that this volcanic island has (some say had) some of the best Atlantic salmon runs in the world, 100 rivers to choose from. Despite the fact that Iceland's streams are the least polluted of any in the world. Despite the fact that Iceland's rivers have (some say had) some

of the finest brown trout and arctic char fishing in the world. Despite the fact that in the Land of Fire and Ice, you can cast a lure or fly pretty much all day and night long—Iceland is also the Land of the Midnight Sun and in summer, the sun never seems to set.

Fishing Iceland is on the expensive end of the cost spectrum. The weather is capricious—cold and windy despite the fact Iceland has a moderate climate. Many (some say most) of Iceland's rivers are not public, the fishing rights owned by those other than me and you. Because Iceland's fishing is/was so great, the angling pressure now exceeds the available fisheries.

Iceland is easily the most expensive

country to travel in all of Europe. The sales tax is high, duties are high, rental cars are high, food can cost you an arm and a leg if you let it. Rod fees are expensive (because they are so limited). If you fish for salmon, everything escalates in price. If you fish for browns, for instance at fish farms that have streams with brown trout and no salmon, you can cut your costs significantly.

To me, you go fishing in Iceland for two reasons: 1) you are a seasoned angler with dough who enjoys a challenge and needs another notch on his or her belt or 2) you want to angle a bit while you are touring one of the most beautiful pristine countries on earth.

The Atlantic salmon are there and in better numbers and healthier than most any other country but the numbers are down and it was never like Atlantic salmon played the numbers game anyhow. You hear anglers say that on average the salmon don't rank size-wise with those of Gaspé and other areas. You have to catch the salmon first—you have as good a chance of warming up with the Red Sox before a game and their letting you take grounders at third, and grabbing a hotshot down the line and firing a strike to the first baseman. It could happen.

Fishing an Iceland river, with its greenery on volcanic rock, is like fishing on another planet. And Atlantic salmon, like all fish native to Iceland, have taken on mystical qualities, mythological proportions; not unusual for a country whose livelihoods are so tied to fish and fishing, for a country that has fish as such a part of its diet.

Iceland is breathtakingly, stunningly drop-dead gorgeous. Rivers flow across green fields and craggy volcanic rock, geothermal activity bubbles, waterfalls tumble, snow-capped hills they call mountains rise to the clouds. Clean to a fault, the islanders have disease-free fish, pollution-free rivers and lakes, an ecologically minded population (heck, much of Iceland is heated by geothermal means). The population also enjoys hot springs and pubcrawls. There's something hobbit-like, Shire-like, heck, Middle Earth–like about Iceland.

The brown-trout showpiece of this fantastic island is the Laxa I Husavik with its postcard rapids. The Laxa has a thirty-kilometer stretch for fly fishing only. The river is wide, full of islands, and flows out of Lake Myrvatn. The most productive months are June, July, and August, but early fall is underrated. Streamers are the ticket on the Laxa. Arctic char in Lake as well. Another world-class brown trout fishery is the Laxa Myvatnssveit.

The other namebrand Atlantic salmon rivers are the Laxa I Adaldal, the Grimsa, the Nordura, Hitara, Hofsa, Midfjardara, and the Ranga. The Laxa I Adaldal is known for its 30-pound salmon but there aren't many of them caught each year. The pools are named and have as much character and personality as any angler fishing them. The pools have a mysterious power to unhook your salmon or send all the salmon to another pool.

A little controversy—catch-and-release practice is just now taking hold in Iceland—getting better all the time but there are those who do kill and keep the salmon. This is a personal choice for all and while I myself catch and release, I understand consumptive behavior and don't automatically mark it as negative. Some of the most conservative, ecofriendly people I know eat a fish now and again.

All imported fishing equipment must be decontaminated upon entry and it's not cheap. They don't want any contamination of their fish or rivers or basically anything.

CONTACTS
Angling Club LAX-A, Reykjavik, 011-354-557-6100, arnibald@ismennt.is

IRELAND

- **Location:** Western Europe, island west of England
- **What You Fish For:** Atlantic salmon, trout, coarse fish
- **Highlights and Notables:** Guinness. Castles. Old bridges. Green fields, green hills. Pubs. Fresh air. Friendly faces, friendlier people. Great whiskey. Writers and poets. Wild fish

Funny how so many folks I meet nowadays claim to be part Irish. Wasn't such a happy connection 100 years ago in America. The generic bit is "Yeah, I'm Scotch-Irish" kind of covering both Ireland and Scotland. Oh, by the way, I'm part Scotch-Irish, too.

The Atlantic salmon fishing just isn't what it used to be, not in Ireland. The trout fishing and coarse fishing are as good as ever. I'd still recommend trying a day or two or three on a salmon river because of the history and the aura—sort of like playing a round of golf at St. Andrews.

There are hundreds of choices of where to fish Ireland. Almost every stream holds trout or salmon or sea trout or some sort of game fish. You can fish hundreds of loughs. That's lakes to you and me. You can fish tumbling mountain streams, rumbling salmon rivers, flat lowland streams or meanderingly slow limestone streams. You can fish for pike as long as your leg, or brown trout as long as the pike (that is, as long as your leg), or Atlantic salmon that if you could just catch it would be as long as the trout that is as long as the pike that is as long as your leg. Landlocked salmon also live in these lakes but they rarely get as long as your leg. Most of the Irish water is owned or controlled by associations or clubs or lodges; some is open to the public and a very little bit is so private you have to be a lord or wealthy or something like that to fish it.

You might want to go ahead and invest in a two-handed or Spey rod or a long one-handed rod. That's what the local experts use so much of the time and you don't want to get caught up in a game of fly rod–envy, after all. And they use a three-fly setup, too,

wet flies. Buy the best raingear you can afford (Gore-Tex is best but so gauche and American—maybe try Barbour) because it rains or sprinkles or drizzles more than most tropical rainforests. And in summer, you can fish until well after supper since it stays light until after when Jay Leno normally comes on.

If you get to the point of planning a trip to fish in Ireland, you must buy Peter O'Reilly's definitive guide *Trout and Salmon Rivers of Ireland: An Angler's Guide* (Stackpole Books.)

Peter O'Reilly is my segue into Delphi Lodge. This writer/angler has put on fishing programs at the lodge and he knows his stuff. One of the showpieces of Irish fishing is the celebrated Delphi Lodge, a country house from the 1830s, set in a breathtaking valley in the wilderness of Connemara. This lodge is an ideal example of how genteel yet wild, bold, and beautiful fishing Ireland can be.

The lodge has twelve bedrooms all with private bathrooms. Many of the rooms enjoy lake views. Green mountains all around. The house is picture-postcard perfect for what you'd expect an Irish fishing lodge to be. Charming, elegant, informal—all kinds of paradoxes—not unusual for anything Irish, right? Their food is exquisite and just plain tasty. The wine list varied and deep. If you are ornery and don't like to be around friendly people, they have five cottages to choose from.

The Delphi Lodge offers incredible fishing on several lakes and a dazzlingly productive river that you'll want to package up and take home with you. The river has over twenty pools, hardly ever goes spate, feeds the lakes, is emerald green (as it should be). Delphi is secluded, unspoiled, wet, wild. The major Delphi lakes are Doolough and Finlough. The lodge sits on and overlooks Finlough, a dainty little lake, deceptively productive. Doolough is massive by comparison, deep, and awe-inspiring. Two other lakes include Glencullin and Tawnyard Loughs. The season is long at Delphi, February 1 to September 30.

The main technique at Delphi (and still many parts of Ireland) is fishing the wet fly. Most fishing on the river is with single flies. In early spring, tube flies and waddingtons (from 1 to 3 inches long) are often used, though some people use single or double-hooked flies from size 4 up to size 8. For the heavier flies in the early part of the sea-

Dolough at dawn

son, consider using a double-handed rod of up to 14 feet in length, although many anglers only use 9- to 11-foot single-handed rods, suitable for an 8-weight line. Floating, intermediate, and sink-tip lines are all used with success on the river.

On the lakes, only single-handed rods are used, ideally 10 to 11½ feet in length and suitable for ⅞-weight lines. A second or third dropper fly is usually added to the cast. Single-hooked flies are the norm, from size 6 up to size 12 or even smaller during the summer. Bring all your fly boxes because, as they say "while there are plenty of local favorite patterns for sale at Delphi, we have no monopoly of wisdom on the highly subjective issue of fly selection."

Waders are not needed because wading in the river is not permitted. There is a great team of experienced ghillies (guides) at Delphi. These are mandatory on Doolough, optional on Finlough, and unnecessary on the river. The river, being quite small, has very obvious pools and a most useful Delphi fishing guidebook is available that explains each of the pools. Fishing on the lakes is almost entirely from boats, with drift-fishing the principal technique. Lifejackets must be worn (by law).

All salmon killed must be gill-tagged with tags that are provided when you purchase your State license and logbook. State salmon licences and tags are available at Delphi. Logbooks must be completed and returned to the local fishing authority. Hatchery-origin salmon, which are recognizable by their clipped adipose fin, must be killed for research purposes and may be taken home or eaten by the captor. A smoking facility is sometimes available locally, depending on the length of your stay. Wild salmon, however, must be released alive, unless it is your very first salmon of the season. All sea trout must also be released alive.

Catching salmon is the idea behind salmon fishing, but it is not the end-all. You are fishing, deciphering, gathering intel, changing strategies, altering techniques, studying the water, the hatches, the fishes' movement. A 10-pound salmon, not rare, is still a big deal, a notable event. You spend a week at Delphi and you will have a fighting chance at going home bragging about the salmon you caught—different from some salmon locales where you go home bragging about the salmon you almost caught.

Most fishing guests stay for a week, from Saturday to Saturday, and all-inclusive packages are the norm. Shorter stays are sometimes possible, though priority is always given to those who stay for the week. Day permits without accommodation are rarely available and may only be booked a maximum of forty-eight hours in advance.

Priority for fishing tickets is given to those staying at Delphi (fishing-only day tickets are only released at very short notice). Fishing at Delphi costs €75 per day in February, August, and September. €100 per day in March, April, and May and €125 per day in June and July. Guides cost €80 per day (normally shared by 2 rods). Unless otherwise indicated, the beats ro-tate on a half-daily basis between the River, Finlough, and Doolough. If the lodge does not let the full weekly packages, they may split these in half. If you are interested in a half week, contact them—they are awfully friendly folks. The lodge always keeps a spare boat on Doolough which may be booked at half price.

Boyne River

In the Irish Midlands flows the Boyne, one of the top wild brown trout streams on the Emerald Isle. The Boyne is an excellent dry fly stream but challenging because it's a chalkstream, English style. Easy to reach, easy to wade, fertile beyond belief, big wild brown trout.

Like English and French chalkstreams, the best fishing takes place either during a hatch or in the evening; any other time, angling is tough. The fishing is controlled privately by angling associations. It also enjoys the reputation as one of Ireland's finest salmon and sea-run trout fisheries.

Boyne flows through countryside with horses and cattle herds, past historic sites, archaeological sites, prehistoric Newgrange pyramids, early abbeys, and medieval castles. Wild browns average over a pound and 2-pounders are common; 3 to 5 pounds are not uncommon.

This is a wide, deep river in lower stretches and there are some big ol' trout there. Avoid the deep flats. Wets work well. Top hatches include caddis and BWO (prolific) and mayflies including a mayfly that favors our Green Drake, midges and black gnats. Local dry fly patterns include Grey Duster, Klinkhammer, black Gnat, Grey Flag, Spent Gnat, and wets that include Wickham's Fancy, Black Pennell, Mallard, and Claret. The River Boyne also has a run of Atlantic salmon and sea trout. The best fishing for these is during the summer months July, August, and September.

Suir River

In southeast Ireland flow the Suir, through typical Irish countryside, the green green countryside. This limestone river is fertile and famous and one of the best in the country. Super insect life. The Suir is the second longest river in Ireland and flows southeast from Devils Bit Mountain for over 100 miles.

The Suir is a large river with big pools and slicks and firm gravelly bottom (easy wading), forty to sixty-five feet wide at source and 150 to 200 feet wide toward the mouth. The Suir is noted for its dry fly fishing and (like the Boyne) often likened to English chalkstreams and other spring creeks. Excellent hatches all season—spring sees small mayflies and midges and some caddis; summer sees BWO, spur-wings, caddis; fall sees midges and dropper rigs.

The River Tar is a major tributary to the Suir, a classic chalkstream with slicks and riffles. The Tar holds abundant trout, one of the densest populations per mile in Ireland, but few grow large.

The Nire River is another productive tributary to the Suir, a spate river, clear as my Mom's iced tea (clear with a hint of peat bog). The Nire is a quick rocky river with deep short runs and fun pools. Stoneflies, mayflies, caddis, and in late April and May, the Nire has a wild hatch of Hawthorn flies (a black terrestrial). This fast river actually holds some nice-sized fish, a whopper per pool, some over 20 inches and the browns are beautifully colored.

OVERALL

The season runs from beginning of March until end of September, a seven-month season. Lots of rain even in summer. Water is high in spring (fish with nymphs except dries in hotter parts of the day and in the summer). Fall is low water and even tougher. Recent years didn't see lots of rain.

Hatches: caddis, mayflies (March Browns, BWO, Spurwings which are like PMDs), midges, stoneflies and also Hawthorn flies, Heather Flies, Black gnats, Reed smuts (blackflies). You must have these five flies: Klinkhammer Special, Elk Hair Caddis, Comparaduns, Beadhead pheasant tails and CDC Emergers.

Equipment 9-foot, 5-weight with floating line for bigger rivers. Three- or 4-weight works fine on the smaller rivers. 5X to 8X tippet and longer leaders than U.S. streams (9 to 15 feet). Bring and wear chest waders even if you're on a stream where you cannot wade—you won't get as wet or cold that way. Waders need felt soles.

You can dry fly fish but it's still kind of a new way of thinking in Ireland. Midges come out at dusk. Fish until an hour before midnight.

Access to Irish rivers is easy. All are privately owned (individuals, fisheries associations, fishing clubs) but while you don't need a state license for trout, you do need one for salmon. You'll also need a permit or license from your lodge or guide or tackle shop or even from the local pub. More and more, catch-and-release fishing is the common practice.

OTHER WORTHY WATERS TO CONSIDER INCLUDE

Blackwater River, with its stained tannic water and where it runs right by a castle. Both salmon and trout swim in the Blackwater; the Lough Corrib, one of Europe's best salmon and own trout fisheries. You can stay in a 700-year-old castle that has a panoramic vista across Lough Corrib. Drop-dead gorgeous. The Lake is open to the public and ghillies

(local fishing guides) can be booked at the Porter or Activities Desk. Ghillies can accommodate up to three fishermen in one boat and are available for half- or full-day's charter; Lough Carra, Lough Ennell, Lough Conn, and Lough Currane. That's just a starter kit.

CONTACTS
Delphi Lodge, Galway, www.delphi-salmon
  .com
David Byrne, Boyne River, dbyrne
  @flyfishingireland.net
Deel & Boyne Angling Association,
  (Europe) 00-353-44-74595, (U.S.A.)
  011-353-44-74595
Longwood Anglers Association, (Europe)
  00-353-46-9546119, (U.S.A.) 011-353-
  46-9546119

LAPLAND (FINLAND, SWEDEN)

- **Location:** Northern Europe
- **What You Fish For:** Trout, salmon, grayling
- **Highlights and Notables:** Fish with Santa and his reindeer. Fish Europe's last wilderness, Samiland.

Lapland isn't a destination trip for every angler. If you live within a plane ride of only a few hours, a summer mountain fishing trip is ideal. The Laplanders love ice fishing so if that's your bag, a winter trip might be in

order. Fishing Lapland should probably be an adjunct to a tour of Lapland, Finland, Sweden. A family vacation.

Lapland is a place of mind as much as it is a geographic place. The northernmost provinces in Norway, Sweden, and Finland carry the name Lapland but the real Lapland is where its people live or range. Laplanders once ranged far and wide across Europe and into Russia. Traditionally, these were the Sami people. Reindeer and wolf and bear and colorful clothing and Arctic Circle and all that. The western portion of Lapland holds fjords, deep valleys, glaciers, and mountains. Farther east, the terrain drops into a low plateau, replete with marshes and lakes. The extreme eastern section—tundra. The climate is subarctic. Vegetation is sparse. So are people. There aren't many places in Europe less populated.

While many Lapland rivers and lakes are easy to access by road or a short walk, many more require lengthy trips, long hikes, longer boat rides, real effort.

Grayling, trout, char, and salmon. Brown trout grow large. Pike fishing is popular in the lakes. And I'm not about to travel all the way to Lapland to fish for perch but by God, they love perch fishing and from the pictures they showed me, they catch huge perch so if perch is your thing, by all means, Lapland may be your heaven.

Some of the rivers are so deep you swear you'll never find fish. Some of the rivers are so torrentially choppy you swear the fish will never see your lure or fly. The areas you fish are so remote and wild you hope nothing happens to your guide or you know this is one of your last days. The water that comes from glacial melt so green, you swear nothing could live in it. I wish I had learned better from that guy in Poland who tried to teach me the Czech method of nymphing. You need those kinds of mad skills on Lapland rivers.

Laplanders love to fish. They love to talk and to eat. They are annoyingly friendly and chipper. The Northern Lights. The days are long in summer, twenty-four hours a day for fifty days straight, light still early in the morning, so what better way to spend time with new friends?

Mosquitos can be awful, trust me.

West Lapland holds the wild Kapsajoki, Tornio-Muoniojoki (salmon) and Miekojärvi-Raanujärvi-Vietojärvi, great angling options, adequate accommodations. East Lapland has Kemijärvi Lake known for its large pike. Rivers worth fishing include Nuorttijoki and Kairijoki, the Luosto ponds, and the large man-made lakes, Lokka and Porttipahta. In Northern Lapland you can catch fish in the Juutua area, at gigantic Lake Inari (and nearby small lakes for arctic char and whitefish, grayling, etc.) and in legendary Teno River (border river between Finland and Norway) where you angle for salmon, grayling, and trout. The River Juutua in Inari village is famous for fly fishing as well.

Greger Jonsson of Lapland Fishing recommends Lake Avaträsk, situated just ten

kilometers from Dorotea. This lake will make both old and new pike competitors happy. The fact that it is quite shallow and has a number of small islands is a guarantee for rich fish production. Locals love the lake for its big pike and perch.

Jonsson also likes to take clients to the River Långseleån, a small and easy river for fly fishing, about fifty kilometers from Dorotea. The river is dominated by grayling (90 percent) and a small stock of brown trout (10 percent).

I am not totally convinced but I'm closing in to a point where I believe that Lapland is one of the top destinations for grayling trophy hunters. Grayling can be found from the forest region to the mountains. The Superpuppan is the most commonly used dry fly for grayling. The water is so pure and clean and there are *so* many rivers and lakes that go largely unfished, and the grayling caught are typically 2 to 4 pounds, there must be some 5-plus-pounders in these waters. If you go grayling, you might want to go to Lapland.

Big grayling can be found in many rivers and lakes in Swedish Lapland. A growing fashion is to fly fish for grayling in lakes, by the use of float tubes. A couple of top grayling waters include Kultsjön and Ammarnäs. But you can also find good places for grayling in Gafsele and Rännudden—in fact, Rännudden is only ten minutes away from the rivers where the World Fly Fishing Championship was held in 2001. Rännudden is also host for the Lapland World Cup Fishing 2002.

The most famous rivers for salmon and seatrout in the county Västerbotten are the Byske älv, Lögde älv, Rickleå, and with the mighty mountain river Vindelälven as an up-and-comer. In fact, driving a car by the coast in the county of Västerbotten, you will pass a river with salmon and seatrout every thirty kilometers.

Jonsson informs me that in forest rivers like the Byskeälven, the fishing for seatrout starts in the second half of May. The peak season for salmon is normally June, but July and August are also good months. The fishing for seatrout is allowed in most rivers from mid-May to mid-September. During the period May to June 18 all salmon caught must be released.

The most commonly used rod for seatrout and salmon is a two-handed fly fishing rod, 11 to 13 feet, but many locals also use one-hand rods. The Byske river can be quite rocky so a wading stick is necessary if you are not used to wild rivers. Commonly used flies are Thunder & Lightning and GP Special. In the beginning of the season a sink tip/sinking line can be a good choice due to spring floods, and in the late season a floating line will do fine. Spin fishermen are recommended to use Rapalas and spoons like the Tasmanian devil.

I don't know many digs but I can recommend the Tenon Eräkievari on the River Teno (perhaps the best salmon river in Europe) on the border of Finland and Norway. This riverside lodge offers comfortable lodging with full or half board. At the Eräkievari, there are two rooms for four persons and seven rooms for three persons available. You get showers and toilets, always a plus in remote areas. How about a sauna and a fireplace after a hard day's fishing for perch or trout? They have a restaurant as well.

CONTACTS
Magic Lapland, Patrick, www.magiclapland.se, magiclapland@telia.com
Heikki Nikula, Hotel Inarin Kultahovi, www.hotelkultahovi.fi
Tenojoki Erakievari Lodge, www.personal.inet.fi/luonto/tenokievari
Greger Jonsson, Lapland Fishing, www.laplandfishing.com

Anne Harju, Inari Event Lapland & Inari Info, inari.event@saariselka.fi, www.saariselka.fi/inarievent

Other recommended Lapland recreation sites worth visiting: www.inarilapland.org, www.poronpurijat.com, www.tenonerakievari.com, www.arctictravelinfo.info, www.saariselka.fi/lakeandsnow, www.ivaloadventures.fi, www.nellim.fi, www.kaamasenkievari.fi, www.nuorgaminlomakeskus.fi

NORWAY

- **Location:** Northern Europe, bordered to the east by Sweden
- **What You Fish For:** Trout, grayling, salmon
- **Highlights and Notables:** The scenery is overwhelming, powerfully dramatic, the rivers dauntingly wide and strong, the fishing a shell of what it once was but good enough because you get with this fishing the scenery and the big rivers.

My friend Jorgen has the greatest beard since Paul Prudhomme. Red in its splendor, full in its coverage, velvety not bristly, symmetrical, covering what looks like a babyface. Juxtaposition. Some beards look as though they've been cultivated or as if the act of growing it were a struggle. Not Jorgen's. It's so natural, it looks like he must have been born with it. *Infante con barba rosa.* Barbarosa.

He came to fly fishing late. He does everything tardy. Norwegian blood runs through his veins and how could he not have that Nordic lineage with a name like Jorgen Wouters. Pronounce it correctly and it sounds something like this: Yore-gin Vow-tours. Hard G. The Norwegian Night-crawler.

Jorgen was my editor when I was the so-called expert angler at Gorp.com. Gorp was one of the biggest, if not the biggest, outdoor adventure Web sites going in the mid- to late-90s. Out of New York. The Texas hick and the NY sophisticate. Jorgen is one helluva writer and if he weren't so lazy, he'd pen that next Great American novel I know he has it in him.

Jorgen is not the first Norwegian friend I've had. Tom Erik Bockman-Pedersen was my friend-bandmate-classmate-neighbor in Puerto Rico. We wrote songs and copyrighted them and performed in our band (The Incredibles) for the neighborhood (Quintas de Monserrate) at fifty cents a head. The Pedersons were a logical, even-mannered family. Tom Erik's mother was the cleanest woman I ever saw in my life. The house was immaculate. She cleaned and washed her driveway everyday.

Norway is one of Jorgen's favorite places to fish. He loves to go back to the old country and speak his native Norwegian and fish his home waters. He loves to show off how good he has become at fly fishing when he only picked up a rod in the last decade. He fishes with his father and speaks fondly of it. What a sentimental softie.

Jorgen's choice for the top Norwegian river?

After all, Norway is famous for its brown trout and Atlantic salmon. Big rivers, rivers that will drown a man. Big flies for big fish. This is Viking fishing. So what river does my Scandavian Scavenger love? Not the fabled Laerdal. Stjordal, Vosso, Tana, Orkla, or the Gaula? The Aa? The Namsen?

Nope, he loves the legendary Alta.

My friend Jorgen gets caught up in journalism and forgets what I told you—he can write. This is what Jorgen has to say about his favorite Norwegian river:

Norway

Nineteenth-century English aristocrats once piloted their yachts across the North Sea to fish for salmon in Norway. The lakselordane (salmon lords) were the first outsiders to discover what the natives have known for centuries: Monster salmon swim in Norway's bountiful rivers.

Overfishing, pollution, and loss of spawning grounds have decimated many Atlantic salmon fisheries. But Norway remains an incredible exception to the rule, especially in the north. For far above the Arctic Circle flows the mighty Alta, arguably the finest Atlantic salmon river on the planet. Alta salmon average more than 25 pounds, and whoppers topping 50 pounds are regularly taken.

Besides the matchless fishing, Norway boasts some of the most eye-popping scenery on earth—scenery directly responsible for the superb fishing. Glaciers high atop mountains feed bottle-green rivers that roar down narrow valleys before pouring into fjords. Violent forces of unimaginable power shaped Norway's rugged beauty, as if Thor himself blasted the landscape into being with his thunderous hammer. It's a trip you'll never forget, but don't spend too much time taking in the breathtaking scenery or a Viking-size salmon may rip the rod right out of your hands.

That's my friend, the Vaunted Viking.

At one time, Norway's brawling rivers produced the largest Atlantic salmon in the world. This is no longer true. Numbers and sizes are both down significantly. The world's Atlantic salmon fishery is down by 60 percent or more and while various countries and commissions try their best to solve this problem, the fishing is not all that good right now. Check back in a few years. If you go, lower your expectations for salmon, fish the Alta or one of the other legendary salmon rivers, check with local fly shops and tackle stores about the best brown trout or Arctic char fishing. If you like fishing for cod, halibut, torsk, ling, coalfish, haddock, pollack, and redfish, then you might consider northern Norway's other options, including saltwater. This is still a great country to play outdoors in. Enjoy.

PORTUGAL (INCLUDING THE AZORES AND MADEIRA ISLANDS)

- **Location:** Western Europe, west of bordering Spain
- **What You Fish For:** Inshore you fish for trout and coarse fish, offshore in the Azores and Madeiras, you fish for blue marlin.
- **Highlights and Notables:** Underrated fishery, country. Beautiful scenery with a vast impressive history and friendly people

You ever know someone a really long time but they are so guarded, or maybe not guarded but they just don't reveal much or they don't care about revealing much about themselves and as such, you know them but don't know much about them? This small western European country is humble, nonplussed, satisfied. Portugal is unassuming but with its history and culture, food and wine, beaches and low cost, scenery and architecture, the temperate climate and the laid-back people, you should plan to fish here just for the excuse to visit Portugal.

The rivers hold trout and salmon, barbel and *achiga* (bass), carp and catfish, perch and shad, but Portugal doesn't advertise it, few natives talk about it, few guides work the waters, and the fishing infrastructure so common to civilized countries with good fishing holes is almost nonexistent. The rivers of Portugal are tailor-made for fly fishers but good luck finding a fly fishing guide.

Dear anglers, you're pretty much on your own fishing inland Portugal. No, the best-known, properly served fishing while in Portugal is in the sea, inshore, offshore, the Madeira Islands, the Azores. So first, the salt.

This stately coastal country enjoys 630 miles of ocean shoreline but its claim to fishing fame is its deep sea fishing. The continental shelf descends precariously about sixty miles off the Portugal coast, diving to over 3,000 fathoms. The shelf acts as a table where the small fish hang out and get eaten by the big fish. Here are your target fish: mackerel, sea bass, bluefish, mako shark, salmon bass, albacore, amberjack, bonito, dolphin-fish, skipjack tuna, spearfish, wahoo, and the big boys like marlin (white and blue), bigeye tuna (150 pounds common), bluefin (800 to 1,200 pounds), swordfish.

The marlin fishery received lots of attention over the years for its humongous blue marlin that tipped the scales at 700-plus pounds but the fishery has seen its ups and downs. Still, the green-blue waters of the Azores and Madeiras of Portugal are one of the best places to catch large Atlantic blue marlin, possibly the greatest sportfish that ever lived, and there are many reputable charters and guides available. They'll take you in the Azores to Nazare, Peniche, Sines, Sesimbra, Eagres, Tavira, Lagos, and Faro. The best time for marlin is May

through October. An underrated fishery in Portuguese waters is the wahoo, a real fighter that's best fished for in the fall.

The Madeiras lie off the coast of Portugal to the southwest, an archipelago that only in the last twenty years developed their offshore sportfishing industry. You've probably tasted Madeira's wine at some point. You will want to drink it in a toast if you hook and land one of the blue marlin monsters that swim only ten miles from their coast, some topping out at 1,200 pounds. Funchal is the keystone home base for fishing in the Madeiras.

The Azores are farther away from Portugal, volcanic islands in the North Atlantic and like the Madeiras, the islands drop off steeply and deeply just off shore. An inter-

esting aside: The Azores, in their volcanic uprisings, have lakes and rivers with *trout*. Yeah, you read that correctly. I haven't fished for trout in the Azores yet but it's quirky and random enough that I will next time I'm there. Most are on San Miguel and Flores.

Lagoa de Fogo (the Lake of Fire—come on now, don't you want to be around the water cooler talking about your trout travails at the Lake of Fire?) and Lake of Lomba are two lakes stocked with trout. Rivers include Bispos, Faial da Terra, Salga, Coelhas, Machado, Carneiros, Ribeira Grande, Alegria, Tambores, Pulgar, and Ribeira da Praia, and on the island of Flores, trout are in these streams Ferreiro, Grande, Silva, Moinho, and Fazenda.

And then I hear, last minute, that Madeira has or had a trout hatchery and their lakes and rivers also hold trout, that some of the rivers hold some big browns that are never fished for. I'm getting online in a few minutes to make plans for next year.

You might not catch anything of size and they'll be hatchery trout but you have to figure you will be the only person in the Azores fishing for trout. And you'll be fishing in volcanoes. And you'll be on some of the most beautiful, charming islands in the world.

Back to Portugal. You'll see locals fishing from the Portuguese beaches, in the surf, for mullet, eel, bream, shad, bass, sole, mullet, and mackerel.

Now back to the inland fishing in Portugal. Sea-run brown trout, Atlantic salmon, brown trout—and they live in some of the most beautiful rivers in Europe. The Portuguese love to fish, you see them on the river's edge. The rivers run clear and cold, down mountains, through valleys, and canyons. The insects feed the trout. Fly fishers find that the trout and the depleted salmon stocks willingly take flies, the trout to dries and both take subsurface flies with reckless abandon. If you nymph like the Czechs and Poles, you will catch more trout than you can count in Portuguese. But overall, the trout fishery isn't kept up, poaching is a problem, and the stocks not maintained.

The trout fishing season runs from the first day of March to the last day of August.

The Alge River in northern Portugal is one of the best trout streams. The Serra da Estrela is known to have some productive streams and lakes like Lagoa Comprida. This is a journey, trout fishing in Portugal, Prosek-style. Find a villager, a bartender, a travel agent, a friend of a friend, and piece it together, until, lo and behold, you have found a pool with trout. The Mondego, one of the larger trout streams, the Minho, the Limia, the Alva (a slow tailwater)—the list goes on. I have fished one Portugal stream for trout (the Alge) and had spotty results. Finding out much more is a crapshoot.

If you fish for trout in Portugal, the trip will be a self-serviced one, you doing most all the research. Don't go plan a big trout fishing trip to Portugal. Fish for trout in Portugal as an adjunct to visiting this storied, interesting country.

Like any European country, licensing is intricate and serendipitous. Start at the local municipality for the river you plan to fish. Even when you have a license, you need to make yourself aware of seasons, restrictions, etc.

Other rivers that hold trout or supposedly hold trout or used to hold trout include: Ocreza River, Ponsul River, Nisa River, Sor River, Seda River, Alcacovas River, Xarrama River, Campilhas River. To note: Most all Portuguese rivers have barbel, and many hold carp and black bass.

CONTACTS
Sun Fly Fishing, Coimbra, www .sunflyfishing.cjb.net
Nuno Breda, www.portugalfishingadventure .com, www.portugalfishingadventure .com/NunoBredaE.htm

SLOVENIA

- **Location:** South central Europe, bordering Italy, Croatia, Hungary, Austria, and the Adriatic
- **What You Fish For:** Trout and grayling
- **Highlights and Notables:** Under the radar, Slovenia ought to be put at the top of your list if you like trout fishing, mountains, history, beauty, and something entirely different.

You would think that a country with such beauty and so many mountains and so many crystalline trout streams would be more in the angling consciousness than it is. Funny how a little border conflict some call war can throw a country's reputation off. If only a little while. It's long gone now.

Slovenia is the real gem of angling travel for me. In case you can't tell from other entries, I love trout and I love mountains. To discover a country with so many quality

waters, with wild trout (the fabled marble trout), with such friendly people, enchanting villages and a storied past and interesting architecture, well, it is in my top ten finds. It was there, others knew about it, but I didn't.

Did you know that Slovenia—is a republic? is half the size of Switzerland? has the Alps in its country?

Did you know that Slovenia—has everything from mountains, lakes, waterfalls, forests, caves, hills, plains, rivers, and the sea? has a population of two million people? has tourism of over two million a year? is also known for its great wines and delicious traditional food?

Did you know that Slovenia—is modern enough with a solid enough infrastructure that Slovenia is connected with the rest of the world by a modern highway network, railway system, international airports, and ports? That said, there aren't so many roads that tourists are zipping all over the countryside accessing the rivers you and I are on.

Did you know that Slovenia—is in the center of Europe and borders Italy? Croatia? Hungary? Austria? the Adriatic Sea? got its independence from Yugoslavia in 1991? has grayling? has the indigenous trout to the Adriatic river system, the marble trout?

Did you know all that? Me neither, and I like to read up on all this stuff. Slovenia slipped under the radar while I was paying attention to the Serbs and Croats. I remembered once I saw it that the Soca was the famous Soca of the former Yugoslavia (and the Slovenia region of the former Yugoslavia).

Slovenia is a pleasant mix of Adriatic and Germanic. Maybe a touch of Swiss

I believe and you will believe, is the most beautiful river in all of Europe. Marble trout (*Salmo trutta marmoratus*) are native to the Soca, this subspecies of the brown trout, this Adriatic native, this trout that is unusual looking with its ivory marbling and mottling over brownish green trout skin. The tributaries are just as productive or better (Lepenja and Tolminka), quick small streams excellent choices for midday angling and dry fly fishing. The waters are so clear, you need your felt-soled ballet shoes to sneak up on them. Fish in the 10- to 16-inch range

or Italian Alpine. Mediterranean meets High Country. It's got its own thing going, like Croatia on steroids. If you have ever thought of fishing Austria (a little costly) or Germany (tough to access rivers) or Switzerland (it's the Swiss), put Slovenia in front of them on your list. The country has personality, a diversity of waters, an abundance of waters, the weirdest colored rivers I've ever seen this side of New Zealand, and more trout than you can believe. Sunning on the Adriatic and fishing in the afternoon should be enough to convince your significant other. To cinch the deal, Slovenia has trophy trout, 10-pounders. The overall fishing is superb, ranks with any other European country, and many American states, and countries around the world. No, it's not New Zealand or Argentina or Alaska. But it beats a number of the other noted ones.

Slovenia fishing is provocative.

The Soca River is the most prominent river name that comes up in Slovenia fish-talk. The river, the Slovenians believe, and

Lithuania

An underrated trout underfished little country in eastern Europe. Walked over through history, most recently before its independence from Russia, it's time for this trout fishing secret to bust out the next few years. Wild brown trout, wild grayling. How do 700-plus rivers and 3,000 lakes strike you for potential?

One of the first fishing stops need to be Dzukija National Park, in the southeastern corner of Lithuania, thick with forests and cold, pure, clear streams. The two largest rivers of the Dzukija are the Nemunas and Merkys Rivers. The Varena, Ula, Neris, and Zeimena are other productive park streams. You don't always have roads or even trails beside these two substantial rivers so this is a real fishing adventure.

were plentiful and silvery. In deep pools, you can spot trout that easily weighed 8, 9, 10 pounds or more, sometimes just showing a glimpse of a tailfin. Twenty-inch trout, for those who care, are in Slovenian rivers with about as much frequency as any other fishery you can think of.

The rivers worth fishing are too numerous to name and I plan to go back and fish them all—Sava Bohinjka, Idrijca, Krka (a chalkstream), Unec (a southern, slow moving river), Unica (known for grayling and browns), Radovna—they all look good, reports are good. Brown trout, rainbow trout, and grayling (and I hear char) live in these aqua-blue mountain streams. And the Slovenians already believe in river and fishery management and catch-and-release and barbless hooks. Hooray.

You can get by with hip waders, wade wet if you can stand cold water like I can (and to keep down my travel gear weight). Breathable waders would be the best way to go, just roll them down, easy to pack. Bring plenty of dries and nymphs but be ready to pay for some of the innovative and numerous Slovene patterns.

CONTACTS

If you want the best Web site about Slovenia, check out my main man, Luka Hojnik, and his site www.flyfish-slovenia .com

SPAIN

- **Location:** Western Europe, between Portugal to the west, France to the east
- **What You Fish For:** Trout, catfish, barbel
- **Highlights and Notables:** What history. What ambience. What scenery and food and language and culture. And the fishing is good to great.

And when he struck his first cod, and felt the fish take the hook, a kind of big slow smile went over his features, and he said, "Gentlemen, this is solid comfort."
STEPHEN VINCENT BENET (1932)

Rio Ebro

- **Location:** Eastern Spain
- **What You Fish For:** Wels catfish, black bass, carp, largemouth bass, zander, pike
- **Highlights and Notables:** Trophy catfish and carp

Not only is the Rio Ebro one of the best catfish rivers in Europe, it's arguably one of the best in the world. I have even heard some Europeans say this river is the best fishing spot in Europe, no matter what spe-

The Rio Ebro is a large river and moves across eastern Spain, southeasterly over five-hundred miles, through mountains and valleys and *embalsas* (impounded lakes) before emptying into the Mediterranean Sea. Anglers have unlimited choices of digs and eats along the course of the river.

CONTACTS
WadersOn, www.waderson.com
Fishquest, www.fishquest.com

Pyrenees Mountains

High in the Pyrenees Mountain range of northern and eastern Spain are trout fishing streams and lakes where you can fish all by yourself; streams flowing under the gaze of fairy-tale castles that stand sentry over you like the Roman armies that used to inhabit this ancient land. These are among the wildest, most scenic trout streams in Europe, flowing under the sentry of the imposing peaks of the Pyrenees, set amongst the first race to populate Europe, the hospitable but mysterious Basques or the fiercely independent but oh-so-friendly Catalonians in a mountainous land so medieval, sheep-herding is still a viable and common way to make a living.

cies. The targets are the trophy cats as big as 300 pounds as well as the trophy carp that reach sizes of 15 to 30 pounds. Most anglers think of trout or barbel when they think of fishing in Spain, and most every region in Spain has quality trout rivers and lakes. But don't overlook these whopper Wels catfish.

Historical villages, olive farms, spectacular scenery. And to think that the Wels catfish, these legendary beasts, were not a part of the Rio Ebro systems until the mid-1970s. While you do have a chance at a 200-pounder, going after a world-class catfish ought to be secondary to your pursuit of the largest cat you've ever caught. These are true monsters, drippingly fat, coming to both bait and lures.

Unlike most other areas of Europe, fly fishing for trout in this isolated pocket of Old World Europe doesn't cost an arm and a leg. Much of the best water is public, and the stretches that are not can be fished for a small fee. Licenses to fish public water are inexpensive (although confusing).

Fishing the Pyrenees is less about the size of the fish or the deciphering the prevailing hatch and more about the substance of fly fishing in a land that hasn't changed since knights rode about on horseback. To be sure, anglers will find the freestone streams full of chunky browns, some fairly sizeable. I found a small river in the eastern Pyrenees with rainbow trout (stocked) whose average size rivals any similarly-sized American stream. And the scenery across the Pyrenees is as magnificent as any in Western Europe. But you fish here for the ambience and history and culture and food.

Digs are cheap despite the high quality of lodging and the incredible regional cuisine these hotels serve (often as part of the price of the hotel). Most nice hotels

run from $30 to $70 a night double occupancy, so dinner for two is often worth what you're paying for the room alone. The Pyrenees are only an hour-and-a-half flight from Paris or Madrid, so any angler on a trip with the wife or family, or on business, would find getting to these ancient mountains extremely do-able.

Don't think you can look at the map and see sixty miles from one town to the next and believe you can get there in an hour. You can't. There are no straight roads in the Pyrenees. You never know when you're going to run into 100 sheep crossing the road. And when you factor in your lazy lunch at a sidewalk café, a two-hour four-course meal, you won't have time but to fish one river a day anyhow.

On a two-week visit, you can fish in ten different streams, stay in six villages, meet locals almost none of whom will speak English, eat incredible food, fish where Ernest Hemingway and his characters caught trout, and drive as crazily as the Europeans (if you don't, they'll run you over).

This is the land of which Hemingway wrote in his classics *The Sun Also Rises* and *Death in the Afternoon,* the land where both Papa and his characters drank hearty red wine, ran with the bulls in Pamplona, watched bullfights in Roman arenas, and caught brown trout in the unspoiled Irati River. The fishing and the ambience have changed little since.

Guide and friend Nick Toldi of www .Gourmetfly.com explains that fifty years after Hemingway fished in these waters "not many things have changed here, at least for the setting. The very small villages are incredibly well kept and preserved. The mountains are wild and beautiful, like the wonderful beech forests of Ibañeta and Monte Iraty." Toldi reminds me that the river is spelled Irati, and the mountain, Iraty.

How good is the fishing in northern Spain along the Pyrenees? Toldi shares that the quality of the waters is so good that in June 2003, "this network of rivers and a high lake was used for the Fly Fishing World Cup. If one finds the results of the competition he can try to measure his own performances to those of the different teams that were competing. In any case, the traveling sportsman will find very pleasant remote nature to spend excellent outdoors moments."

My wife and I have fished these Spanish Pyrenees for years now and have found adventure and wilderness at every turn. When I first spoke with Toldi on the phone years ago, he sold me on the trip when he told me "there is an outstanding harmony between the landscapes and the unique local architecture. This area is the most primitive place in western Europe today." Toldi was dead on.

Now to the fun part: I mistakenly put gas into our diesel van—hey, give me a break, they label diesel "gazole"—and my wife and I had some nervous moments.

We left France, knowing that I had goofed up, only to get stranded on a lonely mountain top five kilometers from the Tunnel of Bielsa, that goes into Spain. For two hours in this remote location, cars passed us without stopping and the only company we had was some bleating sheep and mooing cows.

I eventually started the car and we limped into Bielsa through this interminable tunnel and called Budget to come trade cars with us. The car quit running because in France, they like to fake out Americans by not labeling any of the petro pumps with the words "diesel." Our car was a diesel. I had five choices at the pump and made these assumptions:

1) the pump labeled "gazole" was gasoline
2) like America, the diesel nozzle is a different size than the gas nozzle and as such, won't fit in both
3) since most cars in Europe are diesel, I assumed that four of five possible choices would be diesel

I was wrong on all counts. I filled the diesel tank with a healthy half tank of gasoline. The next two days were rather interesting. Ever try to cram diesel into a full tank of gas?

We limped across the border, and stayed in the Hotel Bielsa that next night (nicer than most American hotels and it has a great view over the river and cost a ridiculously low amount of only $30 for the night). We took off the next morning, apprehensive about traveling with a troubled car through wild country. We also met some new owners of a tapas bar, a couple who had moved from crowded Madrid, and made quick friends with them.

We nervously stopped for a couple of

hours at an eleventh-century fairy-tale fortress standing guard on the promontory village overlooking the junction of the Rio Cinca and Rio Ara (where we left the car running, taking no chances. We also stopped at every station to put in more diesel). This is a must-stop side trip to get the real feel of Old World Europe.

The car, full of a nice combination of diesel and gasoline, clumsily sputtered into Boltana to get our licenses for Aragon and Spain as well as to secure a permit to fish private club water. The drive along the Rio Ara is as scenic as any we have in the United States. High mountains, frontier ghost-towns, thousand-year-old churches. The river was high and blue, too high from recent rains and runoff to fish comfortably. We stopped a couple of times to take pic-

tures but left the car running (not taking any chances).

Rios Ara and Cinca

We made Sarvise by early afternoon, enough time to get settled in and take the rods to the river. We walked and fished toward the quaint village of Broto but the river was so high and the sky so blue and the day so hot, the trout were uncooperative. We caught two small trout the entire day.

We stayed at the charming and folksy Hotel Casa Frauca, a magnificent building with an interesting history (rebuilt from photos after it was destroyed by the government in the Spanish Civil War). Like most of the hotels in northern Spain, you eat at their restaurant for two reasons. First, there are few if any other choices in towns so small the sheep outnumber the residents. Two, the food is as good as anything you'll get in bigger European cities. A double room cost us 6,500 pesetas per night or around $35 American. A fishing license for Rio Ara was 1,287 pesetas each (less than ten bucks). That's my kind of budget.

Visitors will find the fish thick and feisty. Toldi advises that the lower Rio Ara "boasts an excellent reputation and runs free of any dam or any other kind of regulation of its course."

I had difficulty fishing the Ara in late June because it ran so high. Toldi agrees, saying that for the same reason "I have never been able to fish the Ara under Broto because it often runs high and responds quickly to rain. I have just been able to admire the majesty of its course reaching sometimes a width of eighty to one hundred meters. I have been luckier with upper reaches of the Ara around Torla. These are narrower rivers flowing in a more frankly high mountain surrounding. There you are under the notch of Roland on the slopes of the Vignemale peak and at the entrance of the national park of Ordesa and Monte Perdido. These names are magnets to the visitors of Aragon."

There are so many waters in northern Spain, the Rio Ara is just one of the fine ones. Toldi recommends the rivers near Jaca, but also suggests the Cinca heading to the parador hotel of Bielsa. There are excellent rivers above the town of Jaca, heading to Navarra. I found that just about every road crosses a river and I saw only one other angler the entire trip.

There are *cotos,* private club water but open to the public only on certain days with certain restrictions. There is also plenty of public water. You must buy your permits from places that don't advertise. You must buy a license from a different entity. That's why I suggest hiring www.gourmetfly.com to take care of all this and reserving your lodging for a modest fee before you ever cross the pond. There's no other agent who knows fishing Europe like Nick.

This is generally a region of difficult fishing. Due to the clarity of the water, trout are quite spooky. As for your physical shape, no long mountain treck is required but the river is often found under quite steep meadows. Wet wading on the rocky soil is more comfortable with felt soles but going down the slope with often slippery wet grass is tricky with the same felt soles. So far, no one has found a real satisfactory solution. The highest streams are best fished with a rather short rod, because you will often be wet wading under a tunnel of trees.

All towns of Navarra have a nice historical center even if very small. Towns like Ainsa, Jaca, or Pamplona are all worth a few steps and a drink at one of the old tavernas. "What strikes everybody" Toldi reflects, "is the beauty of the landscapes seen from the main roads, the feeling of being in a remote preserved region, as when you get to a village, there is no industrial area or shopping centers or ugly modern suburbs, you are most often just directly bumping into nice villages. Then there are other highlights like monasteries, scenic canyons, or breathtaking views."

Rio Irati and Rio Urrobi

We drove through Jaca in the northern Spanish frontier the next morning, through all kinds of different-looking countryside and enjoyed the often-desolate vistas. We stopped in the tiny Basque village of Garralda. Along the way, we began to see pelegrinos (pilgrims), sometimes walking three abreast in the road. Bicyclists, sometimes very old men, were also performing the Catholic pilgrimage of Santiago de Compostela. Scallop shells on backpacks, shells on leather necklaces, shells atop walking sticks. The scallop shell is the symbol for Saint James (Santo Iago). An amazing sight to see so many dedicated worshippers. We zipped right past them, in and out of them zooming like a good European—I was beginning to drive and think European at this point.

We had eaten food on this trip that we thought we would never eat—we ate duck breast, we ate goat cheese and cheesecake made from goat cheese, we tasted foie gras, we ate boar, venison, ternera so rare it mooed. But we loved it all. We fished the upper Rio Irati where Hemingway and his characters fished the first evening after a lunch of tapas (the specialty of this house was chorizo sandwiches and frites). We caught many plump 6- to 10-inch brown trout, and one heavy trout probably 13 or so inches took my fly but broke off in the submerged limbs.

We took the traditional late Spanish dinner and I enjoyed more ternera (bloody steak) but especially enjoyed the verdura soup (a thick vegetable soup) and roasted red peppers appetizer. A double room cost us 8,500 pesetas per night, around $45 per night with tax. Our bill for two nights of sleep, two breakfast, and two full dinners added up to around $180 American. How can you beat that? (Note that it's all Euros nowadays.)

By midmorning, after eating breakfast in a *panaderia* (Spanish for bakery) in Auritz, we fished the tiny meadow stream, Rio Urrobi. The trout were small but as we fished up to the ivy-covered ancient bridge from the thirteenth century, the water got deeper and the fish got bigger. Gray duns and Red Quills were hatching everywhere and the water was spotted with rises.

After a lunch in Roncesvalle, at a castle-like building not far from where the great warrior Roland fell, we hit the middle sections of the Rio Irati. We drove past the cottage where Ernest Hemingway used to stay when he fished the river. We found two different ways to the river near two small Basque towns, complete with white square houses and colorfully painted shutters with Basque names over the doors.

The river has a tea-colored tint to it but was so very clear, with such long, still pools, that the fish were awfully skittish and it took patience and long leaders and skillful wading to even draw a rise. Around four or five, the clouds moved in, the insects started hatching (an amazing variety of stoneflies, mayflies, and even some caddis), and we started landing more and more trout. These were nice-sized, heavy-bodied fish, stuffed from eating insects, especially the 1½-inch long golden stoneflies that were landing erratically everywhere. And the idea that I was fishing where Jake Barnes had fished and napped was pretty cool, too, I'll admit.

A long dinner of *trucha y jamon* (trout and ham), a great bottle of Navarran wine, some brandy, and the strongest coffee in the world, and the great day was complete.

Toldi is high on the Rio Irati as well. "Truly, it is one of the most beautifully kept regions of Northern Spain and the surrounding deserves the Hemingway (and Gourmetfly.com) endorsement. Like most European waters, the Irati is difficult to fish when no surface activity is visible and becomes quite easy to understand with a good hatch and fish rises to observe."

Want to know the difference between American anglers and European ones? He casually confides, "With long 8X tippets and #16 or #18 CDC dries most anglers should have fun." 8X tippets and fun in the same sentence? Most Americans have never fished with a 7X tippet (which is nearly invisible, I might add, so an 8X is ridiculous to recommend, but Nick is correct so you ought to listen). I will return to these waters next summer packed with 8X (if I can find a spool, that is) and armed with more patience. Buena suerte, amigos.

Access to public water in Europe is tricky to us Americans but not at all to Europeans. Finding parking on the narrow roads is difficult enough. But if land is not marked with some sort of warning, you can respectfully cross it to get to public water.

The choices, even for a small section of the northern Pyrenees, are overwhelming, so much so, we have several times hired the services of www.gourmetfly.com to help us set up our trip. Each go-round we begin by e-mailing the proprietor/fly fishing guide/travel guru named Nick and describing our basic travel desires. We write Nick that we want to fish small and big and everything in between. We want to see the countryside, stay in clean hotels. Amy wanted to make sure all of our rooms had a private bathroom and toilet. I just wanted to be close to the rivers.

Nick is always honest with us about some of our plans. He will tell us "this drive is too long from that town to fish those two rivers in a day. No, you don't want to take the train from Paris. You won't have time to drive into Pamplona." That sort of thing.

Nick and www.gourmetfly.com provide info about which roads to take, where to turn, how to find the hotel, the best restaurants in the town. He secures rooms at these hotels without you needing to put down a deposit. Nick secures fishing licenses which are waiting for you at your hotel. He provides a detailed itinerary with directions and instructions on the rivers you will fish, tells you about local and regional history in the area, suggests techniques and fly patterns and equipment—he even provides adjunct trips in case the weather is bad or the water is high. One trip, we paid a little over 300 bucks American to get a two-week itinerary, secure hotel rooms, twenty-plus pages of detailed fishing information, history, and culture. He even sets up our itinerary with plenty of alternate plans, hoping to fish as many as ten rivers, but with runoff and season rains, knowing that we might only fish four or five. One of our trips had us circling from Biarritz to Pau to Ainsa to Sarvise to Garralda to Navarrenx and back to Biarritz. We could not have done the trip without his preparation.

The food is different. If you are squeamish or finicky or stuck on fast food, get over it. The meat choices are about the same at all the eateries: lamb, salmon, steak, fish (hake and trout the most common), and duck. Appetizers run the gamut from foie gras (enlarged goose liver) to olives. Breakfasts are light, usually a croissant or bread or pastry with coffee and fresh-squeezed orange juice. Lunches are also often light. But dinners are a different story. In Spain, the restaurants we ate at usually didn't begin serving until 8PM, sometimes later. The meals consisted of several courses and almost always included desserts. These dinners often last two hours or more. Know that the coffee is not like American-style coffee and is strong. Because there are no fast-food joints, we kept groceries with us in the car.

Do you need Band-aids or shampoo or cough syrup or batteries? Get 'em in Paris or bring 'em from home. There are few stores that carry those types of things. You buy meat at the meat market, bread at the bakery, cheese from the market.

These small hotels in the smaller towns are large old homes, sometimes several hundred years old, converted to hotels. The rooms are often oddly-shaped and have a strange assortment of period furniture. The rooms were always clean, even the one in Navarrenx we didn't care for (the halls and hall walls and lobby were drab and worn-looking). The bathrooms in all of these hotels are very small (as are the Europeans of this region we met). If you like hotels with personality, rooms with character, then you will love staying in these hotels, looking out shuttered windows, flinging them open each morning to see a fog-covered field with a shepherd tending sheep, the mountains all around you. If you like Paris or New York–style quality, this may not be your bag.

They don't drive on the wrong side of the road. That's Great Britain. But they do drive fast and pass a lot and have no fear. We rented a compact car that was upgraded to a van, an Opal SUV contraption, which was half van and half sports car. It cost us about $300 unlimited for two weeks and got great gas mileage. I mean diesel mile-

age. Traffic signage is usually clear but you have to pay attention to the arrows.

In these Pyrenees, don't expect the same services you receive in the United States. You won't get lunch. You won't get flies supplied. You also don't pay as much, with most charging about 150 American dollars for one or two persons. Half-day rates are usually available. We found our guides to be knowledgeable, courteous, friendly, eager to please, and excellent anglers, useful almost as much as tour guides as fishing guides.

Aiguablava, Costa Brava

I'm not sure there is a prettier place in Europe. Aiguablava is on the Mediterranean, the east coast of Spain, just south of the border with France. Catalonia.

You might know the Costa Brava (the Brave Coast), the crowded beaches of Lloret de Mar and Tossa de Mar, the Roman ruins of Empuriabrava, the history and architecture of Girona, the majesty of the mountain setting of Montserrat monastery that purportedly holds the Holy Grail. But the isolation and undeveloped beauty of Fornells, Begur, and Aiguablava in the northern Costa Brava is where I go. Close to France. No crowds. Breathtaking beauty—rocky cliffs, emerald water, mountains sloping into calm *bahias*.

Amy and I stay at the Hotel Aiguablava. The whitewashed hotel sits on a rugged cliff, juts out into the blue-green cove, and the mountains sneak right up on the hotel. The grounds are green and flowerful and peaceful. I write with my laptop on a breakfast bistro-style cast-iron table, the rising smoke of both my espresso and cigar in front of me, and I sit on the patio that overlooks the gardens and the blue-green cove and the bobbing boats of all colors and sizes and the sea breeze washes over me and I never want to go home.

I write about the fishing in eastern Spain. The odds-and-ends fish you catch in the shady rocky coves. The trout that fill the clear mountain streams. I write with the buttery garlic breath of Fornells crayfish I had for lunch. Sure, I had sweet juicy fresh cherry tomatoes and fresh bread I dipped in olive oil and cheese that tasted smoky and creamy we bought in a wheel from a local vendor in town. Amy is in the room getting ready; we're going to the beach this afternoon. Pals. White sand and crashing azure waves and yeah, topless sunbathers. Not Amy, no way.

On the beach, we'll see folks of all shapes and sizes, bathing suits of all cuts and types (yes, including the Speedo bikini for men, a big player on Spanish beaches). After we're burnt to a crisp, we'll take tapas at this bar on the beach, in the shade, with the breeze, the bar with the *pa amb oli* (bread with olive oil and tomatoes) and spicy chorizo sausage and the plate of assorted olives I like so much. And that's kinda what fishing vacations are like in Spain—a series of sun and meals and drinks, a variety of meals and drinks, broken up by a few hours angling and then back to meals and drink.

I fished one day with Bruno Goulesque, after the daily Hotel Aiguablava breakfast we won't miss, the Aiguablava breakfast in the windowed dining room that looks out over the Mediterranean. I drink three cups of coffee, thick black strong coffee. One cup is straight, café solo. The next is coffee and espresso mix and the third is usually just espresso. Some days, I have hot chocolate, Spanish-style, thick and sweet, instead of the third cup of joe. We vary our choices from the three tables of goodies. One day I mix and match a chocolate croissant, an *embutido* (a platter of mixed meats, sausages), two slices of fresh pineapple, goat cheese, and grapes. And oh yeah, a glass of fresh-squeezed orange juice because Spain has the best tasting o.j. in the world.

Bruno stands about 5-foot-something and I want to be nice here so I say "something." Let's just say it's more than five and less than seven. He is short and muscular, forty-something going on eighteen, a childlike wide-eyed view of the world, a bundle of raging electrons, never still. Impish smile. A fishing guide in warm months, a ski instructor in the cold months. We were

to fish in the Segre River drainage in eastern Spain.

Heavy rain had put the main stem in spate form so we drove up the mountains, through the mountains, through a toll road, and came to a tiny village where a feeder river flowed right through the heart of town. The water was too narrow, too skinny to hold any fish worth all this trouble.

I was wrong. In a big way.

The Llobregeta River. Town of Llobregeta. This feeder to the famous Segre River flowed weakly and green through town, a good fifteen feet below the street and sidewalk. Amy and Mom and Don and I peered over the edge and looked down and I lost my breath. We saw trout everywhere. Everywhere.

Five across the river holding in water so shallow, two dorsals break the surface. At least four of them are in the high teens, one might be over 20 and I'm being conservative. There were dark silhouettes by the chute of water falling into the big pool where four more trout outlines finned.

Bruno and I entered below town and throughout the day and into the evening, stopping for a leisurely lunch of tapas at the only bar open in town that day, we each caught fifteen or more fish. We took turns at first, I missed more than he; we each made long casts to rising trout, sightfishing in six to twelve inches of water, long flats. The takes were explosive in the shallow water and the thick trout kicked out the fly easily in this thin water.

The longest trout I caught was in the high teens but weighed more than your usual rainbow. Girthy mean trout, rainbows and browns, all caught on dry flies. Bruno lost one trout we saw hanging in a two-foot wide run that was scary big, several pounds. He lost it when the brute shook his head and broke him off like he was a Catalonian downing a plate of paella. Next time, Bruno wants to take us to a hidden set of lakes in these eastern Pyrenees, an hour walk in, fish bigger than those we caught that lovely day on the Llobregeta. And he knows this little bar with some of the best local wine in the region. But after the long day trip, we hustle back to Hotel Aiguablava to enjoy the promontory sea breeze on the terrace, evening drinks before dinner, and later, maybe a romantic walk on the beach by the pulsing waves.

CONTACTS

Nick Toldi, Gourmetfly.com, 33-6-83-25-
8409, www.gourmetfly.com, nick
@gourmetfly.com

Hotel Aiguablava, www.aiguablava.com

Costa Brava Tourism, Girona, www
.costabrava.org

Canary Islands, Spain

- **Location:** Off the northwestern coast of Africa
- **What You Fish For:** Marlin
- **Highlights and Notables:** Undeveloped sporting fishery where you could catch a world-record marlin

You don't think of the Canaries and fishing in the same thought. You think of skimpy bathing suits, men in Speedos who shouldn't be, partying all night long and water sports. The archipelago and its clear and deep waters could have great fishing. It's untapped, unexplored, in its infancy. No one knows for sure.

Blue marlin and tuna (bigeye, bluefin at 1,000 pounds, and yellowfin) have been caught that either set or challenge world records. Ditto swordfish, bonito, wahoo, and albacore.

Thousand-pound marlin are in the books, 1,600 and up are anecdotal from commercial fishermen. How big do they grow in these Canarian waters? Find out for yourself.

Asia

HONG KONG

- **Location:** Southeastern China
- **What You Fish For:** Barramundi, grouper, wahoo, tuna, sailfish, and more
- **Highlights and Notables:** Adjunct trip to Hong Kong, not a true destination spot. Business and pleasure in one of the world's busiest port cities

I know you don't associate fishing opportunities with China's Special Administrative Region, Hong Kong, but you'd be surprised how consistent the action can be. Hong Kong isn't an angler destination but if you're in the city for business or pleasure and need to fish, you will find ample angling. The South China Sea, twenty to fifty miles out from one of the world's busiest, most populated cities, holds bluefin and yellowfin tuna, dorado, wahoo, sailfish. You can try to local sportfish, the Japanese seabass and the seerfish. The estuaries and rivers and even Hong Kong Harbor provide quality fishing. Inshore quarry includes barramundi and grouper.

Popular harbors include the harbors of Kowloon, Tsim Sha Tsui, Kwun Tong, and Hong Kong Island.

The local reservoirs have decent to good freshwater angling ops including lakes that hold snakehead, largemouth bass, tilapia, goldfish, and carp. You'll need a special license for freshwater fishing (available from the Water Supplies Department of the Government of the Hong Kong Special Administrative Region, www.wsd .gov.hk). Open season for fishing in Hong Kong's reservoirs runs from September 1 to March 31.

CONTACTS

Po Kee Fishing Tackle Co Ltd, Hong Kong, 852-25441035, www.pokeetackle.com

INDIA

The Mahseer of India

- **Location:** Southern Asia, Pakistan to the west, Nepal to the east

- **What You Fish For:** Mahseer

- **Highlights and Notables:** The mahseer is a majestic fish, exotic and stately and large and Himalayan. If you are a trophy hunter or a world-traveler, the mahseer should be chiseled onto your tablet of must-dos.

The mahseer. Looks to me like a huge carp. A giant mutant minnow. Scales as big as pancakes. Your tackle isn't good enough, heavy enough for the electricity that occurs when the monster takes your offering and shatters your world as it rushes powerfully up or down the torrential Himalayan river in which you are angling. You just thought you had a chance to bring one to bear.

When it comes to mahseer, Misty Dhillon is *da man*. I know of no other guide/outfitter who is so closely tied to one sportfish, who knows so much about a sportfish and its history as does Misty. I am confident that few people have even heard of the mahseer, even most sportsmen. The combination of exotic locale, huge size of the fish, the powerful nature of the fish and the history behind it is an enticing proposition for any angler.

So let Misty and his graceful words introduce these watery beasts to you:

If you are interested in fishing for the mahseer of India, need any kind of information on the mahseer fishery, if you're planning a trip to fish for this mighty creature, you need to call Misty.

CONTACTS
Misty Dhillon, guide, and Mickey Sidhu,
  The Himalayan Outback, www
  .himalayanoutback.com

The great Indian subcontinent is enclosed in the north—stretching to the northeast by the grand Himalayas and in the south delimited by the Indian Ocean. It's been home to various civilizations in the past 10,000 years, the foundation place of Hinduism and Buddhism. A land of colossal history where one is overwhelmed with culture, places, shrines, forts, languages, crowded markets, and lively cities.

In the midst of the vast subcontinent, which has such diverse landscape, and in the many rivers which drain the nation, swims a classic game fish, still unheard of, by a lot us, the Mighty Mahseer of India.

Undeniably, the mahseer is one of the fiercest fighting freshwater game fish that exists. Pound for pound it has unparalleled strength and endurance. They do have a transitory likeness to the carp and the barbel of the English waters, but as they say, the similarity soon ends in the turbid waters of the Himalayan foothills.

Often weighed against the lordly salmon for their sporting competency, the mahseer have overjoyed generations of anglers and time after time lived up to being called the "Mighty Mahseer." The legacy of this absorbing sport was brought into the country by the English during their reign in India and was passed on over the years to the Indians.

The eighteenth century brought about a few accounts on the mahseer by some expatriot anglers who were captivated by the excellence of sport the mahseer had to offer. Over the decades the word of its sporting abilities spread. The mahseer of the south, which grew larger than their northern cousins were obviously given awareness, and any avid angler who traveled to this part of the world would try his hand at the mahseer of the South.

The early nineteenth century saw a number of records being broken and the word on the mahseer's mightiness had spread far and wide. A number of anglers acquainted with the southern waters of the Kabbini and the Cauvery made the most of the so-called golden era of mahseer fishing. The Van Ingens, famous Dutch taxidermists from Mysore, established many records, as they were perhaps the most frequent anglers on those waters. In 1922 the Van Ingens were guides to possibly the most eminent team of anglers ever seen on the Cauvery, one including the Prince of Wales (later Edward VIII).

The Kabbini and the Cauvery were soon known for their heritage of monstrous fish lurking in their turbid flow. J. Detwet Van Ingen still holds the record of the largest rod-caught Mahseer of a 120 pounds caught on the 22-3-1946 [that's 3-22-1946 for us American chaps—MDW].

After India achieved its independence, the angling scene suffered a setback, as the population shot up and India was soon one of the most populous nations of the world. Pressures on all resources were high and the new government did not have an understanding for the sport; besides, the government then had other priorities. The years 1947 to 1978 could be said to be the neglect period of angling in the subcontinent.

The transworld fishing expeditions brought about the much-needed breakthrough in terms of the initial conservation efforts for the mahseer of the Cauvery in the '80s. It was the reintroduction of these forgotten monsters to the angling world. Robert Howitt, one of the team members, soon convinced the government to protect a stretch of the river Cauvery by announcing a complete ban on killing the mahseer.

This ban led to the quick revival of fish populations of the Cauvery, which were previously suffering the effects of uncontrolled poaching in the region. The years ahead saw prestigious events like the Mahseer Maharaja World Cup at the Cauvery and the consistent enforcement of controlled angling with minimal impact to the habitat of the fish. Over the year, efforts are following up the example of the Cauvery and the results are showing.

"There he stood the Mahseer off the Poonch beside whom the Tarpon is a Herring and he who catches him can say he is a fisherman."
—RUDYARD KIPLING

The Himalayas are indeed the perfect setting to take a mahseer, and if one is keen on the spinning or the fly, this is the place. Needless to say, there are few freshwater fish in comparison to its sporting aptitude and which inhabit such torrential waters.

Prior notes on fishing for the mahseer in the north mention the capture of some giants, too. A. St. J. Macdonald's book, *Circumventing the Mahseer*, mentions fish over 55 pounds caught by him and others including a 75-pound fish in the early nineteenth century (though he goes on to say that there would be few anglers in the north who could count the 50-plus-pound fish they've caught in their life on more than five fingers).

A 50-pound fish in the north is considered a trophy. These mahseer are taken best on a lure or a fly, something not true of the southern giants. The southern giants are taken on a local form of millet flower (ragi), this paste is hardened and dressed on a 6/0 hook before it's hauled into the current.

A lot of the former accounts on the mahseer of India have focused mainly on the mahseer of the north, the Himalayan mahseer, due to the enormity of area they are to be found—their distribution, the multiplicity in techniques they could be taken on and as they were to be found in all the rivers in the north and in the river which drained the rain forest of the east.

India has quite diversity of these fish, spread throughout the subcontinent, to be found in all rivers, though perhaps the commonest of them all are the Himalayan mahseer. This fish occurs all throughout the north, northeastern, and even parts of central India. The Himalayan mahseer are one of the two most popular game fishes of India, the other ones are their larger more elusive cousins of the south called the humpbacked mahseer. The fish are to be found in the Coleroon river system of southern India, primarily the rivers Cauvery and the Kabbini. These fish are given superior status due to the size they attain. Above and beyond these two common types of mahseer there are six to eight types of acknowledged species of Mahseer, which are said to have comparable sporting features.

The mahseer inhabits the torrential rivers and perennial rivulets of sub-mountainous terrain. In the course of the Himalayas, they could be found up to an altitude of 2,500 feet above sea level. The following rivers are considered to be the strong holds of the Himalayan mahseer: the Ganges and its tributaries, the eastern and western Ramganga, the Maha Kali and its tributaries, the Kosi, the Beas and its tributaries, the Sutlej and its tributaries, the Bhramaputra and its tributaries, Ravi and its tributaries, Yammuna and its tributaries, and the Indus, which flows into Pakistan. Due to the diversity of regions they are to be found in and the assortment of techniques they can be had on, fishing for them makes a particularly interesting pursuit.

The Himalayan mahseer grow to enormous proportions and prior accounts pertain to them exceeding lengths of 7 feet. Nowadays that would be a rare occurrence, though 50-pound fish is considered monstrous.

Mahseer have a prismatic range of shades on their large scales. In addition to their beautiful exterior, they have a firm appearance, too. For the ones of us who have experienced their first rush, for those of us who recognize what the mahseer feels like at the end of the line, we know that perhaps the most significant sporting feature of the fish and the most intense adrenalin charge is felt when a fish takes the bait and begins the rush. It's more sudden than you expect it to be, very impetuous, rash, impulsive, reckless. Sometimes it can be terrifying since the bait is taken very rapidly.

In the north of India, the best time to undertake the large snow-fed rivers is from February through the middle of May, as they are most liable to be clear and the water at a reasonably low level. By mid-April the river begin to rise progressively and the real snowmelt comes in by the end of May. This timing slightly alters from year to year as and when the summer approaches.

All chief river systems have a particular window period they produce the best fish in. Another good time to fish these snow-fed rivers is post-monsoon, from the middle of September through the middle of November. Confluences predominantly during this time produce fine results, principally when the rivers are changing color and just about begin to maintain their usual color subsequent to the monsoons.

Most fishing in the north is preferably done in the region of confluences, due to the kind of results they have produced over the years and for obvious reasons, mostly post-monsoon when the receding river gives the fish an indication to move down. The fish, after laying their eggs, are exhausted and hungry and start their journey down to the lower reaches of the river. This is considered to be one of the best times to be fishing in most waters of north India. Predominantly, spinning is the most killing way to fish. As a generalization it would be right to say that the best months to be fishing in the north would be March and October.

The enormity of the Himalayan mahseer's territory leaves even currently some rivers and their confluences untouched by anglers. With that said, deep pools, which are in abundance, too make great spots for the fishing both on spinning and on baits. What usually makes it harder though is the flow, which the mahseer for understandable reasons uses utterly to its benefit. The flow of some of these rapids one fishes in is so intense that one can hardly hear anything.

The mahseer of various regions of the country over time have adapted themselves to lakes as well. A fine example of this could be seen in the natural lakes of Kumaon, this region lies in the north Indian state of Uttaranchal, over the years it has adapted itself to the many man-made reservoirs in various parts of the country, too.

By and large mahseer fishing is compared to fishing for the salmon, for the similarity in methods more so in fishing for the northern mahseer than for the southern fish. The kind of tackle used for spinning or fly fishing for that matter would generally be used for catching large salmon. Truly the appeal of mahseer fishing in the north is on either taking the mahseer on the big river on spinning or the smaller clearer streams on the fly.

The mahseer prefer taking in clear water, in fact the clearer the better. The rougher the better, too, he'd rather take in turbulent water. Thunder or rain may or may not hold back his unpredictable craving. Feeding habits? It is a remarkably omnivorous fish. The mahseer is noted to be a discontinuous feeder. Green filamentous algae and other water plants taken in with intent or while seizing aquatic insects on them, figs, other things thrown by humans, other insects, fish, etc. have been recorded from the stomach of mahseer.

JAPAN

- **Location:** Eastern Asia, east of Russia, China, and Korea
- **What You Fish For:** The rare yamame and amago trout
- **Highlights and Notables:** Serene alpine streams, small and dainty like the rare wild trout you fish for, the Amago and the yamame trout

Imagine a Japanese painting come to life. A mountain stream, gurgling and surging, foamy swells that break against big gray boulders. A big azure sky broken by tufts of white clouds. Beautiful green-blue pools, waterfalls that drop fifteen to twenty feet, then spread out slowly into wide clear beautiful green-blue pools. Cherry blossoms hanging on trees, puffs of pink petals. And the trout swimming in the beautiful green-blue pools, the yamame.

The yamame mimics the cherry blossoms on the trees with the parr markings on its side, the cherry blossoms that fall

lightly on the water's surface. The yamame is striped light mauve, dotted with black spots on its back each painted carefully, peach-colored fins. The yamame is a living breathing swimming painting. The cherry salmon.

The yamame is not a trout at all, but a landlocked Pacific salmon found in only Japan, Russia, Korea, and Taiwan. The fish looks much like and feeds much like a brook trout; and like the brook trout, doesn't grow very large. Five to 8 inches is the norm and a 10-inch yamame is the largest in the beautiful green-blue pool.

I won't pretend here to be Benhke or Prosek but as I understand it, the amago is another name for this species, a similar but slightly different fish. Yamame has black spots while amago has black and red spots. Both spawn September to November. The amago has a slightly more southerly living ability. Amago—*Oncorhynchus masou rhodurus.* Yamame—*Oncorhynchus masou formosanus.* There is supposedly a sea-run yamame that reaches 2 to 5 pounds. Yamame live in headwaters, rushing mountain streams, and they live with other trout (stocked rainbow and others). They are easy to catch on both dries and wets but you must be stealthy and use long leaders.

You probably wouldn't plan out a trip all away across the planet just to chase these colorful beauties through the mountains of Hokkaido or Honshu. My friend Kenichiro Eitaka has fished these streams for yamame for years and he is reverent in his words about the fish, the mountains, the streams. Kenichiro knows that just to catch a 7-inch yamame, he needs to be conscious of all the factors. Kenichiro isn't unusual for Japanese anglers, either—he ties flies flawlessly, knows his hatches, stays as technical in technique and equipment as he can (whether he needs to or not). And he smiles a lot because he truly enjoys the sport.

It's all about the uniqueness of the fish because the size isn't enough to warrant excitement. If you're in Japan on business or pleasure (funny how those two things don't always mean the same thing) you might as well go ahead and fish for yamame and see how beautiful Japan is beyond the Tokyo city limits.

MONGOLIA

- **Location:** Central Asia, as big as Alaska, bordered by Russia to the north, China to the south
- **What You Fish For:** Taimen, lenok, grayling
- **Highlights and Notables:** One of the world's best adventure fishing trips, a real wilderness, cultural-shock type of trip for the world's biggest salmonid, the rare taimen

The taimen.

Looks like a tri-cross between a salmon, brown trout, and bull trout.

The taimen is the largest salmonid in the world, up to and over 50 inches long, weighed in tens of pounds—the average Mongolian taimen runs about 10 pounds and 30-some odd inches long. The taimen is found only in Mongolia as well as a few (increasingly rare) remote places in Russia and China. The largest on record is—get ready for this—a taimen that weighed 231 pounds, taken in 1943.

They eat mice. Ducks. Lemmings. Prairie dogs. Rodents. Small children. You sight fish for these river wolves with big hairy flies that look like floating beards. You fish for one of the world's greatest game fish, one of its rarest game fish. And you do so in a land before time.

Mongolia is one of the most unique of all fishing destinations. Not only is your prey unusual and rare and mighty, but the land around you, the jagged mountains, the expansive forests, the nomadic people, the rolling steppes, rugged canyons, pastures and meadows that go on for as far as the eye can see, even the Gobi Desert. What a secretive country, so isolated, so remote, so unique, so magical. This is as odd, as unfamiliar a fishing trip as you can take. Culture shock awaits you. You'll sleep in a ger (yurt), those circular moveable nomadic Mongol dwellings. A true adventure—the landscape, the people, the culture, the food, the fish. The big blue sky and the pure air and the green grasslands enrapture you, cleanse you.

Where not overfished, these Mongolian rivers abound with taimen, grayling, and lenok, a trout-like native fish. Don't go all the way to Mongolia and get so hung up on taimen that you don't put away the 9-weight rod and bring out the 5-weight to catch lenok (a part of the salmon family that looks like a trout but has a downturned sucker-like mouth) and grayling. These rivers vary in size and construction but many have easy wading with a rocky or gravel bed, lots of interesting structure, long deep runs, and big wide pools. That said, some of the rivers are wide and deep and unwadeable. That's much of the fun of this fishing trip—the variety of the land. Sometimes you'll get the notion that this is wide-open Wyoming or Montana but you know better; there's just something that smells different, feels different. You get around by all-terrain vehicles, rafting, or even by horseback. You get there by way of an MI8 Russian helicopter, an adventure in itself. Along the way, you might spot a Mongolian wolf running along a ridge or crossing the river.

What's so great about the taimen? Savage surface attacks. Even on dry flies. And you don't have to be delicate in your presentations. The taimen aren't scared of your splashy strikes and, in fact, like them better. Pop your poppers, slap your mouse patterns, splash your bass bugs, wiggle your Verminator. Violence is part of the adrenalin rush. The attack is visual, heart stopping, otherworldly. When they run, they sometimes leap and to see a fish that big, that muscular propel itself high out of the water, body writhing, it's breathtaking.

Why else fish for taimen? They have strength and pulling power beyond their size. How about the rarity of this dignified creature? You'll hear anecdotal stories from perfectly believable guides who swear they've been reeling in 20-pound taimen only to have 100-pound taimen attack the hooked fish and take sizeable chunks of it. Taimen live a long time, sometimes twenty-five or thirty years or more so they have the population density and growth rates are always low, the species always easily threatened.

Bring both a big rod and medium rod—the big rod for taimen and the medium for lenok and grayling. You can do well with either conventional tackle or fly fishing outfits. Some anglers use a spey rod for these river wolves. Most all outfitters now practice catch-and-release fishing and most make you use barbless hooks. Bully for them. A few of the top rivers include the Uur, Urgol, Eg, Delger, Bator, and Chuulut Rivers.

Don't expect to catch a lot of taimen on your trip. You may go a day without one. This is akin to fishing for steelhead or Atlantic salmon—it's more about the arduous journey than anything else. Still, you can have those days, those special frameable days, when you do catch more than one taimen, perhaps a bevy of taimen, a lifetime of memories.

Passport is required. The guides will speak English but you won't hear but a smattering from anyone else you meet. The weather ranges from blistering hot to freezing cold and everything in between. Best times to go are from June to September but midsummer can see high water.

CONTACTS

Fishquest, www.fishquest.com
Fish Mongolia, www.fishmongolia.com
Interangler, www.interangler.com
Sweetwater Travel, www.sweetwatertravel .com
Orvis, www.orvis.com
Frontiers Travel, www.frontierstrvl.com

RUSSIA

- **Location:** Northern Asia, west to east, a monstrous and diverse landscape

- **What You Fish For:** Brown and rainbow trout, Arctic char, Atlantic salmon, other species of Pacific salmon

- **Highlights and Notables:** Frontier. The only comparable place is Alaska, and in many ways, Russia is Alaska decades ago, not fully developed, wilderness and adventure, both good and bad. One of the great fishing trips in the world

Remember George Carlin on Rowan and Martin's *Laugh-In*? Carlin's skits were hit or miss, the Hippy Dippy weatherman—hit. The Indian Sergeant, miss. In another skit, Carlin played a sportscaster who would read the scores from his shuffle of papers: "And tonight's scores were 2–1, 8–4, 3–2, 12–5, 4–3, 5–1 and 10–0." You never could match the scores with the teams.

Without a guide or camp, you will have no earthly idea where to go, what to do, how to act.

Even with a guide or camp or outfitter, anything you can think of that can go wrong, has a better than even chance of going wrong. And then there's the things that there is no way you could possibly imagine because you're not Russian, can go wrong. That famous Russian fatalism, perhaps even nihilism, seems prophetic. And too bad, because there is still so much of Russia that is just aching to be explored, new angling opportunities.

If you want to understand what can go wrong with deciding to plan a fishing trip to Russia—and this is the tip of the iceberg, believe me—look no further than what happened in the spring of 2006, a transportation mess of Russian proportions, a real screwed-up situation. The airline service that flies between Russia and Anchorage went bankrupt, leaving hundreds of anglers who had plans to fish Kamchatka stranded, without a way to get there short of the slow boat to China.

Everything you take for granted, don't, even with the first-class camps. Communications, awkward at best, nonexistent at worst. Comfort on helicopters or planes, not gonna happen. But the camps have come so far from what it used to be—in the beginning days, in the early '90s when Russia opened up after the fall of Communism, the wilderness was being explored and that meant snafus. Plenty. In the genesis, you might end up with a guide meeting you at the rendezvous, and you might not. That's why you should only go through a respectable, established booking agent and camp. Do your homework. Things are

so much better but you still need to be prepared. This ain't Montana or Colorado or even Alaska. You are dealing with the Russians and their government and their distance from each other.

I am not going to generalize but sometimes the Russians you meet are friendly but they are survivors. They are often warm but also vodka-hot; eager but downtrodden. They've been crapped on all their lives and there still exists a sense of doom, reasonable distrust of all things politic and a healthy dose of fatalism. Now I'm talking about some of the people you meet along the way, not necessarily those who work your camps. They're making money and making friends and hell, they fish for a living so they are happy and they are in the throes of westernism. Bully for them. You have to ask yourself before you plan and plunk down bucks—is the fishing in Russia even as good as the fishing in Alaska? Comparable, not better. Similar, a little different and that's because of the culture and a few different fish (like the cherry salmon and the white-spotted char).

The food has gotten better in the camps but along the way, you might have to eat Russian food which is plain and simple and, well, you don't see Russian restaurants cropping up all over the place, do you? The weather, don't forget the unpredictable weather.

But a fishing trip to Russia is one of the ultimate water-cooler bragging trips and you want to take it. So we're going to discuss the two areas best supported by infrastructure, such as it is in Russia. Two of

the more developed, maturing as it were, fishing spots.

Kola Peninsula

The Arctic Circle. Tundra. Heavy forest and endless views. Endless day (or is it endless nights because the days don't end?). That's how far north you'll be. Bring layers of clothes because one day it can be cold, gray, and rainy, the next you'll be fishing in shirtsleeves.

The Kola Peninsula is known for Atlantic salmon. Is this the best Atlantic salmon fishery in the world? The rivers of Kola Pen-

insula may not get salmon as big as some other fisheries, say the Gaspé, but they are big enough and wild enough and abundant enough, and in a wild enough place, that you'd be hard-pressed to say no.

The Kola Peninsula is desolate even for Russia, bare but not barren. Atlantic salmon is the king here and the Ponoi wears the crown. Kola has a hundred rivers but none are more productive, that we know of, than Ponoi. The largest river on Kola, it runs dark, tannin, the color of Coca-Cola. That means limited visibility.

So far north and remote are you that you will see the Sami, Laplanders, who live on the river. These natives are the only folks you will see. The Ponoi has lots of tributaries of all sizes so it just gets bigger and bigger. The black river does not have many pools or runs or rapids for long stretches which are kind of a requisite for Atlantic salmon anglers. You just cast and reel in. Ten salmon in a day is not unusual at all for the Ponoi. For the rest of the world of Atlantic salmon fishing, yes, unusual. You catch and release salmon which tells you that they are serious about their fishery. The runs seem to be only getting better. Not many caught that are 30 pounds but those behemoths are there.

You use floating lines to catch big Atlantic salmon.

You can skate dry flies for salmon that are aggressive, that haven't seen many flies or lines or boats.

The fishing season is long and consistent.

The River Varzina is the queen of the brown trout fishery and that's saying a lot because there's a lot of quality competition. Varzina is an amazing vessel for these big-backed fish, loaded with big browns 20 inches long, more in the high twenties than you'll see just about anywhere else in the world. These brown trout live in a big river so they are strong fighters, even the 16-inchers. Did I mention that weekly, anglers catch browns that push or top 30 inches? There are five types of brown—no, not big, bigger, biggest, even bigger, and holy crap— just five different subspecies or variations. The river also holds pink salmon and Arctic char.

There are ninety rivers on the peninsula and two dozen sporting camps (with solid reps). Military helicopters are the way you get to and fro. Varzina and Ponoi are the big names, but you also have quality rivers like Penka, Drosdovka, Zili, Umba, Varzuga, Kitsa, Pana, Kharlovka, and Sidorovka. Varzina River Lodge is one of the top out-fitters. You'll fish below tundra lakes that have huge gray protruding rocks. In the rivers below them are the heavy rivers with trout and salmon. Some rivers are 600-plus feet across. By the way, the mosquitos can be oh-so-bad.

Kamchatka Peninsula

I know the fishing biz has gotten better but there was a time when Kamchatka was like a *I Love Lucy* episode and you were just waiting for what was going to go wrong. And it would. (Don't get me wrong, Kola had its problems, too, including legal battles for fishing rights.)

It's too bad that occasionally, even after things have been cleaned up, hardships and slipups still occur in Kamchatka. The steelhead and rainbow fishing is as good as the best in Alaska. That's what you'll have to decide about going to Russia—the fishing in Alaska is as good as Kamchatka and it doesn't have nearly as many goofups and weird things. This is an adventure fishing trip and you should expect some adventure along the way.

Kamchatka. It has that exotic adventurous ring to it, doesn't it? Huge rainbows. Colorful char and abundant salmon. In a frontier roadless setting on eastern Russia, untouched until fifteen years ago, a stone's throw from the Aleutian Islands. That should tell you something.

Ring of Fire.

That means Kamchatka is volcanic. The wild place has geysers, hot springs, volcanoes, calderas, thermal activity. You can witness Earth's hot steam rising. Things could explode any day now. So could the fishing while you're there and that's why you go on a fishing adventure like this.

Resident rainbows that rival Alaskan rainbow in size and appearance. Sea-run rainbows that bear resemblance to steelhead—they are more vibrant, colorful, wilder than the residents. They are stronger and have an urgency to their life. Skated mouse patterns draw heart-stopping strikes.

Brown bears scare the crap out of you. They won't hurt you, probably. But every sound in the brush, every splash will get your breathy attention.

You also get cherry salmon in some streams (not the Zhupanova River though) as well as sea-run taimen—in Zhupanova you do get Pacific salmon and grayling and the weird East Siberian white spotted char (zundzha). You get from one place to another in Russian military helicopters. Cedar Lodge is one of the top outfitters on Kamchatka. The Ozernaya River is one of the up-and-comers for trophy rainbows; many are saying in whispers that this just might be the next great Russian rainbow river.

CONTACTS

Mark Firth, Roxton, Bailey, Robinson, Ltd., Hungerford, United Kingdom, www.rbrworldwide.com

Frontiers International, www.frontierstrvl .com

Gordin Sim, The Kharlovka Company, www.kharlovka.com

Varzina River Company, www.varzina.fi

Arni Balduresson, Club Laxa-a, www .looptackle.se

Kent Lindval, Fishing North, www .fishingnorth.com/english.htm

Wild Salmon River Expeditions, 425-742-1938

The Fly Shop, www.TheFlyShop.com

The Best of Kamchatka, 877-707-0880

Flywater Travel, www.flywatertravel.com

Kamchatka Travel Waters, www .kamchatkawaters.com

Blue Drake, 866-350-4665, www .bluedrake.com

John Eustice, www.johneustice .com

SOUTH KOREA

- **Location:** Eastern Asia, peninsula east of China
- **What You Fish For:** Trout
- **Highlights and Notables:** I can barely recommend fishing for trout in South Korea as a stand-alone trip, rather a tie-in to an Asian vacation or visit for those wandering souls who like to venture out in the unknown.

It's funny writing a guidebook. Friends and acquaintances and perfect strangers find out about it and they ask if I've heard about this honeyhole or that one. South Korea was never in my purview until it was too late. The most I knew about the country was from watching *M*A*S*H* and reading about the war. Trout and largemouth bass fishing in South Korea?

Apparently so.

I doubt the fishing is world class or even all that good so it's the novelty of it that makes me include it in the book. The Gangwon Province is a mountainous region with clear cold streams running down from the peaks and they hold trout planted in the 1960s. This region has most of the trout streams but a couple are located in the southern part of the country in the Jiri Mountain Range.

I have read, too, about catching several local river fish in addition to rainbow trout—the mandarin, a scary-looking elongated fish that looks like a pike in fatigue camouflage; a brook perch that looks like a warped smallmouth bass; the lenok, also called the Manchurian trout; and masou trout, the cherry trout, a native trout that I'm sure Prosek and Behnke know all about, a trout supposedly among the most beautiful in the world. I even hear there may be taimen in some South Korean rivers.

So I don't know much about the fishing in South Korea. There are no inland fishing guides in the country. The only guided trip I can locate is through the fishing travel agency www.waderson.com which has put together daily guide trips out of local cities.

CONTACTS
Waders On, www.waderson.com

SRI LANKA

- **Location:** Southern Asia, island off the southern tip of India
- **What You Fish For:** Inland you fish for trout but the lowland, inshore, and offshore fishing have real potential.
- **Highlights and Notables:** Fly fishing for trout in the mountains and valleys of Sri Lanka is a risky, high-reward real angler adventure.

High in the mountain streams of this Indian Ocean island, live trout. These rivers flow rocky and lush and the trout are colorful but not typically big. Nuwara Eliya is the best town to make your home base from which to set out and fish the cool jungle rivers or grassland streams. You can find plenty of comfortable enough accommodations including bungalows for rent near rivers.

Most of Sri Lanka's trout fishing is restricted to fly fishing only. Dry flies aren't the rage since adult insects landing on the water don't comprise much of the Sri Lanka trout's diet. Browns and rainbows, stocked many years ago by those trout-loving Brits are the trout of the island. They average about 9 to 14 inches (but heavy) in the rivers of Nuwara Eliya but you will hear reports of 20-plus-inch fish caught. Some of the top streams include Nuwara Eliya, Ambawela, Bulu Ella, Portswood Dam, Agra Oya and Gorge Valley Rivers, and the top Sri Lankan stream, Horton Plains. Trout fishing is now controlled by the Nuwara Eliya District Fishing Club. You get your licenses from the Honorary Secretary, Nuwara Eliya District Fishing Club, Court Lodge Estate, Kandapola.

Native fish you can angle for in the lowland jungle rivers include the mahseer (that huge native carpish fighter) and a freshwater shark called the walaya. The inshore and offshore fishing in and around Sri Lanka (I keep wanting to write Ceylon, its former name) provide some pretty hot fishing but not world class—tuna (yellowfin, bluefin), dolphin, marlin, and other billfish as well as trevally, wahoo, bonito, cobia, grouper, mackerel, barracuda, giant perch, and others.

Caveat: Monsoon season runs twice. Heavy rains unlike what we see in America. And the guiding/outfitting infrastructure is in its infancy.

THAILAND

- **Location:** Southern Asia, bordered by Myanmar (aka Burma), Laos, and Cambodia
- **What You Fish For:** Mekong giant catfish, Siamese giant carp, and other native fish and introduced Amazon species
- **Highlights and Notables:** A connecting adventure to a Thailand trip. Between the interesting culture, architecture, and food, and the friendly people and the curious game fish, it's a worthy destination.

My father, Gary Don Williams, served in Thailand during the Vietnam War, 1963–1965, Army Corps of Engineers. Much of the time, he spent living in thatched huts, no air-conditioning. He built bridges and blew up bridges. He got to use that fresh civil engineering degree from Texas A&M University (whoop) right out of school, building things. Learning demolition was just a little bonus.

Dad didn't talk much about Thailand or the war. He'd go in ten year spurts where nothing, then one day, he'd get out his uniform or his slides and talk about the experience. Dad didn't talk all that much, especially to me, so I listened, relished, nodded. He told me how great the people of Thailand are, how beautiful the country is, how much history you saw everywhere, how happy folks were who had next to nothing. Dad said that their reputation for hospitality was deserved. Dad loved Thai food but then again, he'd eat most anything. He described humidity that was beyond belief and how they'd have to use mosquito nets to avoid weird-looking bugs as big as poodles. They played a lot of poker and smoked a lot of Lucky Strikes.

His favorite story was how some higher up brass had a room with no view, just thick jungle, so he ordered Dad to knock down a few trees so he could see out. Dad said he and a buddy laid more plastic explosives in that forest than you can imagine. They were out to clear the land, blow up every tree in the marked off area just to please the brass. The blast was surprisingly potent, a monstrous boom. Dad said it was like the explosion in *Butch Cassidy and the Sundance Kid* when they blew up the Pinkerton safe *and* the money inside the safe and the railcar. Every tree was gone even those out of the marked area, just disappeared. Guy had a great view.

You can imagine a son would ask this— *Dad, did you ever shoot or kill anybody?*

I shot my pistol a couple of times when we heard gunfire from the jungle but it was so dark I know I didn't hit anything. And we shot at beer cans sometimes. I was pretty good.

Dad said he and some of the guys would occasionally fish in the river and catch what looked like a mutated catfish. Dad said Thailand, despite the war, was one of the most peaceful serene places he'd ever visited.

Thailand is a country rich in history and culture. Also fishing. We have another fishing adventure. Siamese giant carp, Mekong giant catfish, and the giant snakehead, a fish that looks like it swam in ancient oceans eons ago.

Bung Sam Lan Lake sits in Bangkok and is the most famous and best fishing lake in all of Thailand. This freshwater lake that used to be a swamp is well known for its Mekong giant catfish and Siamese giant carp, which are rarely found anywhere else in the world. Bung Sam Lan is stocked with Mekong catfish that become monsters, weighing anywhere from 15 to 200 pounds. These cats are as strong as Russian weightlifters or those guys built like blocks of stone you see on late-night ESPN2 who pull 18-wheelers with a cable in their teeth. Bung Sam Lan also holds

striped catfish, giant Siamese carp, and several other introduced Amazon species. Catching Mekong catfish is a slam dunk.

So you fish in the city and then it's time to head out to the jungle. There's this jungle reservoir that holds giant snakehead. The giant snakehead is a freaky fish. Long and cylindrical and made for ambushes, the giant snakehead teeth are sharper and more vicious than Mike Tyson. They are weirdly mottled in mostly black but with amoebas of fluorescent green and pink. Big black evil eyes.

Giant snakehead don't just take your lure or your fly. They smash it. They attack it with demonstrative topwater strikes. I am mean, I am king of this lake.

Avid angler Scott Swanson, Managing Director of Fishquest (the booking agent who puts together this trip) says this about the giant snakefish and the lake: "The Khao Laem Reservoir is near the Burmese border and it's there, in a huge valley covered by a tropical forest, where this fifty-mile-long artificial lake was created by damming part of the valley where three rivers meet.

"In this lake," Swanson informs us, "there are a thousand coves and channels, creating perfect habitat for hundreds of different species, one of which is the snakehead. This region is totally wild and there are few tourists, hotels, or lodges, only local small fishing villages. Arriving there in the early afternoon, we'll settle into a typical teakwood floating house. Then we'll head out on the lake to spend the rest of the afternoon topwater fishing.

"Fishing boats here are powered by Yamaha engines. The boatmen-guides are all snakehead experts. The giant snakehead runs about 8 to 35 pounds and is a unique and amazing predator. There is no fish to be compared except maybe peacock bass. Giant snakehead can grow to nearly 3 feet long, and are extremely tough and hardy predators. It is considered to be one of the best fighting freshwater fish." You can also catch striped and cobra snakeheads, as well as jungle perch and striped catfish (10 to 35 pounds), giant Siamese carp (40 to 220 pounds), and other Thai species.

They also do couples tours where you fish and see the best of Thailand and

Malaysia. The Thailand trip takes place March to July for snakeheads, year-round for others. Beautiful scenery, delicious authentic Asian food. Dad would have loved this trip.

The typical package includes airport assistance and transfers, internal transportation within the country, four nights hotel in Bangkok, meals, guided tours in Bangkok, six full days guided fishing, assistance of an English-speaking fishing tour leader, private comfortable Thai-style hut or floating house, fishing license, baits and rigs for catfish, ice, mineral water, coffee and tea, fruits of the season.

CONTACTS
FishQuest, www.fishquest.com

Africa

BOM BOM ISLAND

- **Location:** Western Africa
- **What You Fish For:** Blue marlin, sailfish as the main draws
- **Highlights and Notables:** Emerging fishery but still primitive, subject to adventures you hadn't counted on, so come prepared.

Good Good. That's what Bom Bom means in Portuguese. Bom Bom Island, part of the Guinea Islands off the Coast of Gabon is part of Principe Island and Principe Island is a part of the Democratic Republic of São Tomé and Principe, Gulf of Guinea, West Africa.

The fishing for blue marlin and sailfish is good good. Granders have been caught by locals and as many as seven world records have been set in the waters off Bom Bom. Anglers also catch barracuda, kingfish, snapper, wahoo, and bonito.

You fish Bom Bom, you stay at the Bom Bom Island Resort, a comfortable lodge with all the amenities that overlooks a beautiful bay on the north coast of Principe. The crews are competent and know how to bring the sails and marlin to you. Passport and visa required, yellow fever inoculation required, malaria precautions recommended, travel insurance a must.

CONTACTS
Bom Bom Resort, 239 251114 / 251141,
  www.bom-bom.com/PAGES/index.html

EGYPT

Lake Nasser

- **Location:** Southern Egypt, along the Nile River
- **What You Fish For:** Nile perch
- **Highlights and Notables:** If you're a safari-style angler who needs notches on the belt, this is for you.

Does that get your attention? Hey, this trip isn't for most anglers. Egypt isn't on very many fishing lists but the opportunity to catch 200-pound freshwater fish fits a special few.

Lake Nasser is set in a desert. Lake Nasser is a harshly beautiful, otherworldly lake, with spectacular rock croppings and clean clear water and sand-colored bare islands. The lake is vast, expansive, mysterious, incongruous with the heat and sparseness of the surroundings.

Lake Nasser is an impoundment of the Nile River (did you remember from middle school geography that the Nile flows south to north?), the world's largest man-made lake. This desert canyon reservoir provides electricity for all of Egypt. This is wilderness, an amazing place to visit for the scenery alone. Giant Nile perch is just the added attraction. The largest man-made lake with the largest freshwater game fish. Fitting.

Only adventurous souls need apply. This is safari. Okay, you're in a mothership and then a boat and it's safari without the lions and elephants but safari nonetheless. The safari unit is made of two or three fishing boats, supported by a mothership that acts as a mobile camp and rest area. You occasionally see Bedouin tribesmen watering their herds at the water's edge.

The locals know how to catch Nile perch and tigerfish and tilapia and vundu catfish. These guides almost always speak pretty good English. They'll release the Nile perch which is a good indication of the quality of your guides and the fishery. The top seasons are November to January, April to July. As you can imagine, since it's a desert, it's hot. No humidity but the sun beats on you like a big brother.

Nile perch are more closely related to barramundi and snook than the perch you and I grew up catching. Two hundred pounds is big, world-record level but amazingly, there are anecdotal reports of Nile perch caught by locals that weighed in excess of 400 pounds.

Here's the kicker: while most of the time you troll for them, you can (with a spotter) catch them from the shore, sometimes in water no deeper than a basketball goal is high. Slam dunk. Hook one and you'll feel like you took one on the chops from a professional mixed martial arts competitor. Tim Sylvia-size. Red-eyed lasers. Lots of lure repairs. At Lake Nasser, you will run into schools of Nile perch and will cast to individuals and you have an excellent chance of catching one in the 50- to 90-pound range before your week safari is up. A 200-pounder is well within the range

Nile Perch World Records

IGFA (International Game Fishing Association) ratified world records that have been broken on African Angler safaris.

All tackle world-record 230 pounds on 20-pound line class

World-record 213 pounds on 30-pound line class

World-record 210 pounds on 50-pound line class

African Angler Top Twenty

1. 20lbs	Bill Toth	USA	230lbs	IGFA
2. 30lbs	Adrian Brayshaw	England	213lbs	IGFA
3. 25lbs	Franz Retzinger	Germany	211lbs	
4. 50lbs	Darren Lord	England	210lbs	IGFA
5. 30lbs	Peter Bond	England	205lbs	
6. 50lbs	Darren Lord	England	202lbs	
7. 50lbs	Wilma McDermid	Scotland	200lbs	
8. 20lbs	Larry Dhalberg	USA	200lbs	
9. 25lbs	Dietmar Rittscher	Germany	200lbs	
10. 30lbs	Robert Fry	England	200lbs	
11. 30lbs	Colin Campbell	England	195lbs	
12. 40lbs	Olivier Portrat	Germany	192lbs	
13. 30lbs	Paul Burnside	England	190lbs	
14. 30lbs	Rory Collins	England	190lbs	
15. 30lbs	Roger Durham	England	186lbs	
16. 50lbs	Tim Baily	England	186lbs	

Marked IGFA on chart—These are the three largest freshwater fish ever caught on rod and line that have been ratified by the IGFA (International Game Fishing Association) as world records. The 230-pound fish is the existing all-tackle world-record Nile perch and the 213-pound and 210-pound Nile perch are preceding all-tackle world records.

The largest reliably recorded Nile perch from Lake Nasser weighed 392 pounds. The largest Nile perch caught on an African Angler safari was 6 feet 2 inches long and had a girth of 4 feet 11 inches. Gerald Eastmure, a 78-year-old tea planter from India, landed this huge perch. The available scales measured up to 220 pounds which was not enough; this perch has been estimated to weigh 275 pounds plus.

of possibility. Nonstop action for perch and any of a number of Nasser species including the recent record for Lake Nasser vundu catfish: 78 pounds of ugly meanness. Thirty-two species of fish, as well as Nile River crocodiles, are found in the lake. The top lures are Rapala Super Shad Raps, Mag Raps in big sizes. Passport and visa are required.

CONTACTS

World Sport Fishing, Ltd., www
.worldsportfishing.com
The African Angler Pty Ltd., Aswan Egypt,
www.african-angler.co.uk

ETHIOPIA

- **Location:** Eastern Africa
- **What You Fish For:** Nile perch, catfish, tigerfish, and over 200 indigenous species
- **Highlights and Notables:** Fishing in a rich diverse land with guaranteed *Wow* factor and no other anglers

"He who digs too deep for a fish, may come out with a serpent."

ETHIOPIAN PROVERB

Dino Ferraresi is the color of honey. He is Eritrean and Italian, descended from dukes, born in a sliver of primeval land on the East African Horn on the brink of falling into the Red Sea by the push of the neighboring countries of Ethiopia and Djibouti and Sudan. In these lands, one can feel that this is the birth mother of all lands, the lifeblood of humanity, a land lost in time. The Cradle of Man, they call it. This is a big diverse breathtaking land that produced my honey-colored regal friend Dino Ferraresi.

This is a smart man, blessed with the slow wisdom bestowed from a land so oblivious to time's march, or rather—maybe—so in tune with its ponderous surge. Dino is from this most ancient of all lands but gifted with the swift tongue necessary for moving around western countries and not seeming like he hails from a third-world nation. Dino lived for years in Addis Ababa, the capital of Ethiopia. Eritreans and Ethiopians are from the same stock. He teaches math to American high school kids. That proves he has patience, too. Ethiopia is nothing if not a patient land.

So, honey-colored Dino was seventeen and growing up in Eritrea and in the midst of a rite of passage. His father and three friends took this son on a guys-only fishing trip (which I imagine makes my forays at age sixteen with my grandfather, father, and uncle to such mundane places as Lake Tawokoni and Cedar Creek Lake seem like peanuts. We never had a man-eating lion to worry about.).

To the Rift Valley, old as the gods, maker of men, hider of sacraments. They fish Lake Metahara, catch lots of tilapia. They stay the night on top of the gorge, the primeval Awash River hundreds of feet below them, spasmodically rushing through the chasm, they on top eating, elbows on tables, screened in on the sides and top, eating fish in native sauces and chile is the dominant flavor. Dino in his rite of passage with the men and the rich food and bugs are everywhere, noisily attacking the screens, repelled, and this band of angler-adventurers sleep in travel trailers, fenced-in travel trailers and they think it luxurious.

On what passes for a road, they drive back home. Sandro has a full stomach and he is driving, dusty, hot, driving, wishing for a cup of rich Asmaran espresso, thoughts elsewhere and sees a peasant farmer ahead, far ahead but closer, closer, the peasant farmer turns to cross, forcing Sandro to slow down. Peasant relinquishes,

turns back to wait, Sandro speeds up, the peasant changes his mind again, reverses to cross and in the convoluted world of straw huts and metal, cars and primitive earth, the two meet in a violent clash of culture, the chaos of broken bone, blood, and sinew and there is the peasant on red dusty road, tossed like a rag doll by the car, by Sandro and his three friends and the new man-boy Dino whose rite of passage reached the depths of the Awash Gorge.

The peasant lay on the red dusty road and his legs were mangled, bloody, his feet split open cleanly, like machete on pomegranate. The peasant is wearing sandals made from rubber tires, the symbolic sandals of the Eritrean fighters in their cause against ruling Ethiopia; some call the sandals *shida*, some *barabossas*.

His feet and legs are irreparable and Sandro drives for help and the police come by and the situation is grave so they commandeer a passing bus. The men load the peasant on the bus, Dino holding the legs and feet, the feet split, cleaved open to the bone from impact. The men ride with the peasant to the hospital and take the long drive home.

The peasant farmer with the split feet and mangled legs. Amputations, both, they discover. The next day, they discover, the peasant farmer with no legs, dies. Fishing as a rite of passage. Haunting. I've said it elsewhere in the book, water haunts us as no other element does. Water is the giver, the taker. It washes, cleanses, drowns.

Fishing? In Ethiopia? Sounds like swimming in the Sahara. Suntanning at the South Pole.

Ethiopia is a vast land of grasslands, canyons, mountains, rushing streams and great rifts. It is a land of the rock-hewn churches of Lalibela, the Sanctuary of the Ark at Axum, the castles of Gondar, the Coptic Church. Think colors. Ethiopia loves its colors.

Ethiopia is a cornucopia of fascinating and diverse landscapes and tribes of historic people. Ethiopia at one time was called the Island of Christianity. Ethiopia has mountain ranges, big burly rivers. You don't see that in the commercials asking you to send money to starving kids, do you?

As I am writing this, I come across an AP report of a pride of lions that killed and ate twenty villagers and wounded ten others over a week's time. This takes place less than three hours from Dino's home town near Addis Ababa. As you might tell, fishing Africa in Ethiopia is not the cultured estate fly fishing of the western Cape.

Lake Tana in Ethiopia is the largest lake in the country and is the source for the Blue Nile River. The river leaves the lake and soon you have the Blue Nile Falls, and then the river flows southward, then west and into Khartoum where it meets the White Nile that forms the main stem, the Nile; from there, the Mediterranean.

Lake Tana holds secrets from the ages, big blue water with eerie trees shooting out harshly from the slick surface. Lake Tana also holds tilapia, catfish, Nile perch. The catfish are endemic to Tana, to Africa, and they grow humongous. The Nile perch may not be of the size of Lake Nasser but they are as big as grown men. If you go to fish Lake Tana, you are on your own. You will probably not see another angler. The locals don't fish, at least not sportfish. You will likely see hippos, crocodiles, pink flamingos, and any number of wild African animals that will raise the hair on your neck.

You might think about combining a sightseeing trip with a day or afternoon of angling. Lake Tana is located on the north central plateau of Amhara. The lake is the center for fishing, farming, and transportation but for you and me, the lake is the home of thirty-seven islands. These islands are the isolated, watery backbones to Egyptian Christianity, dry land for numerous Ethiopian Orthodox Church monasteries, some dating back to the thirteenth century. Most of these are not open to women.

Trout fish in the Bale Mountains between Adaba and Goba. I know it sounds crazy but in Africa's largest Afro-Alpine massif complete with juniper forests and stands of giant heather and high grassland, you can catch trout. Nine rivers have been stocked with brown and rainbow trout including the Web River near Dinsho. The rivers are diverse and range from waterfalls to narrow clear streams to deep pools. The Ministry of Agriculture purports to have all kinds of info but darned if I've been able to find out much. You do have to gain permits from Department of Agriculture offices in Goba, Adaba, or Dinsho.

Some of the booking agencies that have these Lake Tana, Axum, Gondar, Lalibella trips will know how to put you in touch with some locals (I hesitate to call them guides) who know how to catch the huge catfish and giant Nile perch.

Other Ethiopian lakes that hold the giant Nile perch and big cats and tigerfish and over 200 species and are underfished include Awasa Lake (around eighty miles from Addis Ababa; several nice-to-luxury hotels on the lake shore), Abaya and Chamo Lakes (in the Rift Valley, mountains and savannahs, forests and herds of hartebeest, zebra, and gazelle; tigerfish, giant Nile perch, barbel catfish, and tilapia); Lake Langano, Lake Abyata, Zuquala Lake and Zway Lake.

Ethiopia is a land of extremes and diversity and agelessness. The people are stalwart and tribal and earthly. The water is the source of the Blue Nile and in those waters are primitive African fish. There is not any infrastructure for fishing the blue lakes or rivers. Adventure in a land from before.

GABON

- **Location:** Western Africa
- **What You Fish For:** Tarpon, African cubera snapper, giant African threadfin, Guinean barracuda, and jacks
- **Highlights and Notables:** Behemoth tarpon, some of the world's largest, swim in these wild waters

With the crazy pounding, foaming, pounding, turbid, powerful rolling pounding Gabon surf comes the beast. This isn't clear water, no, not perfectly blue clear flats, but big waves and murky water, in from the whales, toward the gorillas, toward the west coast of Africa. In comes the world's largest tarpon, the King Kong of the silver kings. When you think of a big tarpon, what's the size that runs through your noggin? Two hundred pounds right? That's a whopper, a monster, a gargantuan fish.

Three hundred pounds.

You read it correctly. In these waters just off the coast of Iguela, Gabon on the western coast of Africa are behemoth silver poons, as large as the ocean produces. Gabon is a wealthy country by African standards, not all that scary politically, with petroleum and tourism and investments. Like Guinea-Bissau, the African west coast is the new world-record tarpon frontier.

Big fish on big flies from the beach or boat. The sheltered Iguela Lagoon is your base, your stewpot. Besides huge Atlantic tarpon, you catch huge African cubera snapper, giant African threadfin, Guinean barracuda, and potential world-record jacks. You're at the northern gateway to Loango National Park and you need to stay at Loango Lodge.

In the tannin-colored surf, the ferocious surf, you are turned back from entering the wide open ocean and going after the tarpon so you move to the river mouths and fish for cubera. The cuberas are beasts, real whackers, bullies, bruisers. They are brown to copper-colored with sharp teeth and silver vertical stripes. Fifteen to 30 pounds all day long, every one a struggle and on those rare days, you might land and release an 80-pounder. The giant threadfin looks kinda like a permit caricature, not a threadfin—all these feelers, four on each side—big tarpon tail, feisty fighters; the threadfin is long and mean, a cross between a catfish and a carp, yellow as saffron.

You overcome the heat and humidity of jungle, you marvel at the elephants and hippos, birds of all colors and shapes. September to April season, with peak November to February. Gabon is bordered by Equatorial Guinea and Cameroon and Congo. The language is French and some local dialects, but at the lodge, they speak French and English and Dutch and German and Afrikaans. Gabon is a stable country but fishing is in its infancy so bring anything you think you will need; bring a spare everything. Valid yellow fever inoculation is mandatory—you need a certificate. Malaria area, so prophylaxis recommended. I recommend bringing your own first aid kit. This is still a frontier, after all.

CONTACTS
World Angler, www.worldangler.com
Sportfish Africa, www.sportfishafrica.com

GUINEA-BISSAU

Bijagos Archipelago

- **Location:** West Africa, coastal country tucked between Senegal and Guinea (pronounced gin-ee biz-soo)
- **What You Fish For:** Tarpon
- **Highlights and Notables:** Emerging fishery, still developing, a real frontier fishery, ideal for the angler who wants to catch a world-record fish, in this case, giant tarpon perhaps over 300 pounds

The largest tarpon in the world. Plain and simple. Sure, it's fun to go to the Everglades and catch a 60-pound silver king on a 7-weight in shallow water, but that's peanuts compared to these whoppers. Sure it's fun to fish Boca Grande and land a 100-pound tarpon on heavy tackle but you could catch the biggest tarpon ever caught, here, in these waters.

The largest tarpon in the world.

You probably won't catch one of these 200-pound sea monsters. If you do, you'll have to invest many many hours. This trip to Guinea-Bissau is for the angler who loves the exotic, loves to be on the edge of the fishing frontier, doesn't mind snafus or challenges.

Guinea-Bissau is a tiny country on the western coast of Africa sandwiched between Guinea and Senegal. A safe and stable African country (although you know how that goes). You fish in the Bijagos Archipelago, thirty miles offshore, in and around the eighty islands (thirty main islands), the largest archipelago in African waters.

Here's the list of fish you can catch and this is only what I know (there are others): the giant tarpon, jack crevalle, leerfish, amberjack, barracuda, cubera, ladyfish, Spanish mackerel, needlefish, drum, sharks of many kinds including tiger sharks that reach sizes of over 800 pounds, pompano, cobia, bonefish, permit, Sengalese jack, corvina, African sierra, and more. Whew.

But it's really about the giant tarpon, 250 pounds and bigger. Anecdotal reports of natives catching tarpon over 300 pounds. On a fly? Doubtful. No sightfishing for these beasts. Sounds like a challenge, huh?

You realize you are an anachronism in these remote islands of Guinea-Bissau. The natives are simple and poor and farmers and fishers and friendly and use fishing canoes carved from a single tree. You are titillated and afraid at the same time, giddy that there are still places on earth that have their innocence, that are primitive, that while poor by some standards, are rich by others; afraid that these kinds of places are but fleeting and in another decade or two or three, will somehow be tainted and lost forever.

There may be other operations booking this trip (I know that GP Chasse & Peche books the M'îles Vagues de découvertes camp and I hear good things about this simple camp on the island of Kere; and the Acaja Club and the Tubaron Club, both on the island of Rubane, get good marks, too) but the one I feel most comfortable sharing is the one that www.worldsportfishing .com books, the one that puts you either on the African Queen (seven-day packages and yes, there are eco-type things to do as well as snorkel) or in one of two camps replete with thatched bungalows, baths, and showers.

The African Queen has seventeen cabins, a classic 1950s motor yacht, beautifully built from hardwood and steel, the ideal combination of style and comfort. All the cabins are air-conditioned; she has a majestic state room and dining room with a classic '50s bar area. She tows nine fishing boats along with her and carries satellite telephone and fax and all the latest navigation and safety features, and just for extra reassurance she is powered by twin diesel engines. The cruise begins every Friday from October to June, and after the two hours' crossing to the Bijagos you will be cruising in calm clear seas protected by the islands at all times.

You fish mostly from boats but there is wadefishing, beachfishing, lagoons and mangroves and channels and river-mouths to plink around in as well. And you certainly don't want to miss fishing the dropoffs either. Like many infant fisheries, trolling to make sure you get on fish is a common technique. If you don't want to troll, just let your guides know.

The beach fishing brings big strikes from

jack crevalle but there are no true flats (six to twelve feet deep hardly qualifies). Anglers use all kinds of methods including trolling, dead-bait, live-bait, spin (both heavy and light), and fly fishing. One of the allures of Guinea-Bissau is the diversity of habitat and the variety of fish.

The fishing season is from October to May because the rainy season runs from June into September. Don't come all the way here and use equipment that's not first-rate. Buy a top-notch saltwater reel with at least 200 yards of backing. For tarpon, buy the best reel and rod and put even more backing. If you are tarpon-targeting, you need medium to heavy gear, a 12- to 15-weight fly rod, stiff action spinning rods. For the other fish, if you choose to fly fish, a 9, 10, or 11 works just fine. Sinking line and floating lines, saltwater type to cover your needs. Six hundred grain sinking would be ideal for tarpon. Saltwater spinning reels need at least 300 yards of 20- to 30-pound braid. The best flies and lures include Poppers, Deceivers, Clouser Minnows, Half and halfs, big flies for tarpon (2/0 to 5/0 to 10/0), something in a mullet or shad.

You'll need a valid passport and a yellow fever certificate to enter Guinea-Bissau. Get vaccinated and while you're there, you might as well update your vaccinations for malaria, typhoid, hepatitis, and meningococcal. You'll not need credit cards so change your currency into Euros (and expect your change to come back in CFA francs).

CONTACTS
World Sportfishing, Ltd., www
   .worldsportfishing.com
GP Chasse & Peche, Paris, France, www
   .gpvoyages.com

KENYA

- **Location:** Eastern Africa, bordered by Ethiopia, Somalia, Tanzania, Uganda, and Sudan
- **What You Fish For:** Trout in the mountains; marlin and sailfish

- **Highlights and Notables:** Some of the greatest scenery on earth on one of the wildest places on earth. The inshore/offshore fishing infrastructure is still developing, full of potential.

Wild and sporadic, vastly underfished, parts unexplored, the offshore waters are kind of hit or miss but when they hit, they hit with vengeance, shocking the fishing world. Huge blue marlin, granders. Pacific sailfish numbers to die for. Striped marlin. Black marlin. How about a black marlin that would have been a record breaker? It's been sighted. Three hundred miles of coastline, year-round fishing. Only those sportfishers in the know end up off the Kenyan coast. Even the inshore fishing for wahoo and tuna and dolphin is good around the creeks.

You can also fish for trout in Kenya. There is no established guide infrastructure but high mountain streams do carry trout put there by, you guessed it, the Brits. The Aberdares near Mount Kenya and Lake Rutundu are the best known locations for trout in Kenya.

SEYCHELLES

- **Location:** Off the coast of eastern Africa, east of Tanzania
- **What You Fish For:** Bonefish, milkfish
- **Highlights and Notables:** One of the newest discoveries, a bonefish carnivale. North Indian Ocean islands now one of the finest fishing destinations on the planet

Now this is exotic. The Seychelles.

They are a group of islands, 150 of them—the main ones for fishing purposes, the islands of Alphonse and St. François. Physically notable is the big dropoff not all that far out from the flats where the world plunges to 3,000 feet deep. In addition to St. François, you can fish also at Assumption Atoll and Aldabra Atoll and at remote Cosmoledo.

Seychelles lie in the north central Indian Ocean, off the African coast. Tanzania to its west, India to the northeast, Madagascar to the south. Halfway around the world and near nothing at all. Dwight Yoakum would say Seychelles is 1,000 miles from nowhere. One of the world's (latest) fishing hotspots, a top ten destination. It's difficult to believe that it wasn't until the mid- to late-1990s that Seychelles even made it on the international scene.

On Seychelles, you walk a lot—the beaches, the flats. A lot of wading, some skiff. Islets and islands and spits of land and sand. St. François is the best overall place to call home but the new frontier of Cosmoledo has such incredible fishing that it's hard not to want to venture to this fishing wilderness.

We're talking really really big bonefish—if you fish bonefish, this place needs to be on your list. The bonefishing is as good as anywhere else on the planet, big numbers, large fish. The bones are big and frequent and don't scatter as much as the Keys bones. You get the size of bonefish from the Bahamas and Florida and you see numbers associated with Yucatán and Christmas Island. Bonefish schools come boom boom and then gone and you go find more or you wait and then boom boom. Boom, even I did well with bonefish. And then there's the milkfish.

What's a milkfish?

The milkfish looks like a mutated minnow with an eye as big as Marty Feldman's eye. Milkfish or *pati pati* (legitimately, they are *Chanos chanos*) are found in Indian waters and even as far east as California. Milkfish farming is common in southeast Asia. These aren't farm fish, they fight like the dickens. They have a tail like a fork, a big mouth with lips like Jennifer Lopez's in *Monster-in-Law* after the vengeful peanut-induced allergic reaction–gravy by Jane Fonda. Milkfish are a relatively new pursuit for anglers, especially fly anglers. I missed the rage but I'll be back, I will return.

Milkfish, when hooked, produce high leaps, furious runs, and powerful charges. They eat algae—so how to get them to take a fly? An algae fly, that's how. I'm serious. Milkfish take forever to reel in, and pound for pound, they put up as tough a fight as anyone—stories of broken rods to prove it.

The giant trevally are some of the biggest in the world. They hang out in canals and off reefs. The alpha dog predator. They straighten out hooks. They cut you off on coral and I'm talking 40- and 60-pound tippet so you need stout as you can find. Gangs of GTs weighing 15 to 50 pounds. Hell, bluefins will do damage, too.

Warning. These are for professionals only. Do not try this at home. This is dangerous and should not be tried by those with heart conditions.

What else?

Shallow water—pompano, sharks, rays, Green jobfish, snappers, wrasse, and tropical trigger fish like yellow margin and giant margin that looks like some animated under-the-sea movie, huge noggin, huger nose, brilliant electric iridescent colors only a movie could have in yellows, greens, blues, and oranges. Bluewater species include wahoo, barracuda, billfish, and tuna.

Equatorial caveats: Sun and hydration. Stay shaded and drink water. Fishing from the boat ends at 4PM—no one wants to get caught outside the lagoon at dark—kinda spooked me a little. I was stuffed from dinner and the eight beers from the night before. My head hurt and the sunshine hurt and the reflection from the sunshine on the mirrored flats hurt.

Seychellois people are of African, Asian, and European descent. No visa necessary, just passport. I love this part: no shots needed (I hate shots). A real baby.

Palm-thatched huts—comfortable Pacific chalets in that Brando-Tahiti way. A young fishery (oh, the fish have been there but the anglers have not). Sparkling flats of green water—like Sprite and lime. Good place to learn to fish or fly fish for bonefish. Mostly hard bottom knee-deep sand flats. Air Seychelles from several big cities but you'll log a lot of air hours. Seven- to 9-weight rods for bones, 10- to 12-weight for trevally and milks.

St. François Lagoon, not far from Alphonse Island, is where the bonefishing is mind-numbingly good on its hard flats. We're talking huge bonefish where the average runs 5 to 8 pounds and you have legit sightings of 15-plus pounds. You will see few other anglers wading the shallows. Fishing for the GTs and barracuda is hot at St. François as well and both species are huge, world-class.

Cosmoledo is an atoll with no one there. Deserted. Wild. Eerie. One of the international angling scene's newest darlings. Remote, and bonefish in the double digit range. You've heard it before. Sometimes, it's a viable fishery, sometimes it's not, sometimes it's hype. Cosmoledo is for real and will be for a long long time.

Everything is bigger on Cosmoledo. The bonefish keep to themselves and aren't as early-angler stupid as many new fisheries.

The giant trevally are the real steal, the real deal. A world-record swims in the flats or in the deeper water off the flats of Cosmoledo. Even the milkfish seem larger here than anywhere else in Seychelles.

Another option to the lodges and resorts are the live-aboard luxury yacht charters. One such outfit is FlyCastaway. They visit Cosmoledo. I haven't done a Seychelles mothership so I talked to Gerhard Laubscher of FlyCastaway to find out more about what a trip like this entails. Here's what Laubscher says:

A visit to the Shangri-la begins with a two-hour charter flight from Mahé to Assumption, Cosmoledo's closest island with an operational airstrip. As Cosmoledo is an eight-hour sail from Assumption, we will travel at night so as not

to waste the precious light hours. The rest of the day is spent settling into your cabin, getting your rods ready for battle and even having a few casts at bonefish tailing on the white sands common to this atoll.

Our accommodation for the next seven days will be on the 110-foot Grand Bank schooner Mieke. She is equipped with all the luxuries needed to explore the most remote atolls of the world in comfort. Originally built in 1997 for commercial fishing, the Mieke was revamped in 2004 to become a unique and luxury live-aboard vessel. She boasts six double/twin en suite cabins, an air-conditioned lounge/dining room as well as a spacious aft deck for dinning. Additionally, she is fully kitted for scuba diving and has three outboard tender boats, which makes accessing the flats quick and easy. At any given time there will be at least two FlyCastaway guides with years of guiding experience in the Seychelles onboard to make sure that you get the catch of a lifetime.

A fiery sunrise mirrored by the glassy water leaving the southern entrance of the lagoon welcomes us to Cosmoledo. If seen at high tide, the lack of flats might make you think you were in the wrong place, but as the tide drops at a rate of knots you realize how much water you have to cover. This southern entrance sometimes referred to as a roaring river, makes you quickly realize

how large the tidal shifts are. The charts show a two and a half meter shift, but the experience would make you think that the shift is in the three to four meter range.

The Seychelles sand is unlike most other venues in the world. It's white and hard, making wading easy. This relieves you from the encumbrance of being in a boat, thus allowing you to do your own thing. Having a guide to help you with fly selection, tackle and point you in the right direction on different tides, is handy and maximizes your fishing time, but once this is all done catching a fish after doing everything yourself is gratifying and easily done.

CONTACTS

Gerhard Laubscher, FlyCastaway, www .flycastaway.com

Angling Destinations, www .anglingdestinations.com

Charles Norman, Fish Africa Safaris, www .sportfishafrica.co.za

Alphonse Island Resort, www .alphonseislandresort.com

Waders On, www.waderson.com

FishQuest, www.fishquest.com

Frontiers Travel, www.frontierstrvl.com

John Eustice & Associates, www .johneustice.com

The Fly Shop, www.theflyshop.com

The Orvis Company, www.orvis.com

Westbank Anglers, www.westbank.com

Tigerfish

- **Location:** Zimbabwe, Zaire, Congo, Ethiopia, Gambia and other African nations
- **What You Fish For:** Tigerfish
- **Highlights and Notables:** The tigerfish is the ultimate freshwater prey for adventurous anglers. You fish in exotic primeval locales for an exotic primeval predatory game fish.

The first time you see the tigerfish, you'll swear it's a mutant striped bass with alien choppers. This is presuming, of course, you do everything correctly to entice and land the creature. The tigerfish is built for eating other fish, and often attacks fish as big as they are. The powerful tail, the strong shoulders, the demonic, black fierce eyes, and especially the eight piranha-sharp teeth on the top jaw and bottom jaw, interlocking, sharp and mean, teeth that protrude like the toothy nerd you knew in middle school. The better to eat you with, my dear. And now that nerd is all grown up and can whip your ass.

The tigerfish may well be the most aggressive, difficult-to-land of all freshwater fish in the world. If you hook it, and that's not a cinch because the mouth is so darned tough, the teeth can sever the hookup immediately. If you hook, hold on tight, for the next few seconds are an explosion of fury and leaps and dives and splashing warm brown water. *I don't know where to grab hold of this fish and I'm not sure if I want to.*

They are hazy shimmering yellow, black striped, orange-tinged fins, overall, a wavy mirage of a predator. They hit angrily, a ton of bricks, like a Butkus-forearm shiver, vengeance in their soul. The word "tenacious" does not do justice to the wickedness and power in their savagery. The tigerfish attacks your flashy lure or fly with disdain, with a stick-your-hand-in-the-water-and-see-what-happens attitude. The tigerfish you'll catch will run about 2 to 5 pounds, a few in the 5 to 10 pound range, and a twelver is a large one. Twenty pounds begins challenging the world-record tackle records although tigerfish have been caught by various means weighing anywhere from 30 to 97 pounds. They fight initially like fish many times that size. There exists also a giant or goliath tigerfish that swims in few places nowadays, the Congo for one, with this supersized version weighing as much as 100 pounds. *Did the guide just say 32 teeth?*

There are few places in the world you can catch tigerfish, none of them developed in any meaningful way. Predominantly in West

African rivers, and a few lakes, all the way to Kenyan waters. You should be a seasoned outdoorsperson or an adventure-loving soul, willing to travel into the wildest lands on earth, willing to tolerate heat and surprises and vaccination shots and dangerous animals like the hippo (yes, the hippo, the large gray animal that can capsize a boat). Do you like the thought of seeing leopards? Cape buffalo? Elephants, lions, warthogs, impala, bushbuck, baboons, kudu, zebras, and hyenas? The idea that life is fragile and temporary sticks in your mind like humidity. Calls of lions and safari, after all. The short happy life of Francis Macomber.

The Zambezi and Chobe Rivers are two other of the best tigerfish rivers. Lake Kariba, in a natural preserve teeming with wildlife (rhinos, hippos, crocodiles, etc.), is the top lake for tigerfish although most fish its water primarily for the huge vundu catfish (and they catch them with homemade soap for bait). Mountainous and dotted with islands, Kariba has over fifty species of fish worth catching including pike, kapenta, nkupe, chessa, and more.

The camps that offer fishing for tigerfish are few; reputable and safe and knowledgeable, even fewer. The ones I am most familiar with and will vouch for are Chiawa Camp Lodge (on the lower Zambezi River), Chobe Rapids Lodge, Okavango Delta Lodge, Cindy Garrison's Safari Anglers (I haven't found out if they still offer this trip or not), Zambelozi Island, and Tiger Camp. The Chiawa Camp on the Zambezi River in western Zambia, the fourth largest African river—Chiawa Lodge in Zambezi National Park—one of the top safari camps in Africa. So says Condé Nast, so it has to be true, right?

And now for something completely different: Fishquest puts you onto the rare, hard-to-catch goliath tigerfish, the larger cousin, the one that reaches over 100 pounds. The one that has thirty-two razors for teeth. The one that smashes your fly and absolves it of all sins then takes 200 yards of line while it rockets through the water, leaping in the air every so often, posterizing you. You find yourself in the Congo, fishing for a lurking monster that can bite your lure in half.

Giant tigerfish are hard to catch. If you do, when you do, it's the fight of your life. Imagine catching a 123-pound goliath tigerfish in the African Congo, a country until recently had too much civil unrest and other dangerous nonsense going on to even consider a trip there; 123 pounds is the camp record for Tigerfish Camp. This trip is not for everyone. You need to be able to endure delays and weather and all that goes with a safari-type trip. Your reward is Africa. Your reward is the goliath tigerfish of the Congo and while you probably won't catch one of the 100-pounders, you have a real chance at a 30- or 40-pounder and that's enough satisfaction in itself. A valid passport, visa, and evidence of yellow fever vaccination are required for entry. The official language is French.

Seychelles

headed catfish is another typical exotic quarry.)

Heavy gear is the way to go with no less than 20-pound test, wire leaders to boot and you better sharpen your hooks to ensure more hookups. The cost isn't all that much, in the neighborhood of $400 to $600 per person per day. Most of the camps are first-rate, safari-style and they cater to most every whim. If you've gone safari before, you'll want to include tigerfish in your exotic travels; if you have not done Africa before, this would be a great starter. Either way, the experience of returning to the heart of darkness is undeniably emotionally awesome.

There are other outfitters that can serve you well, too, but do your research before you dole out the bucks. There are many angling travel services that can hook you up with tigerfishing and these camps. (Vundu catfish, a prehistoric-looking armor-

CONTACTS

Grant Cumings, Chiawa Camp (Lower Zambezi National Park), www.chiawa.com

FishQuest, www.fishquest.com

South Pacific

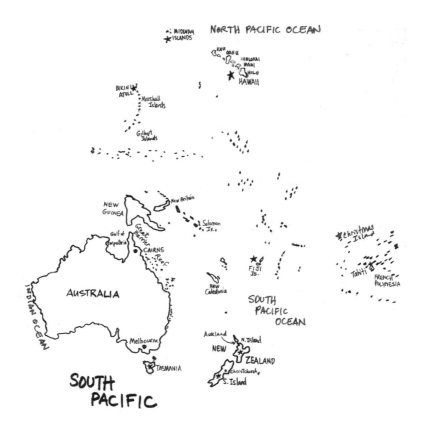

AUSTRALIA

Cairns

- **Location:** Northeastern Australia, Queensland
- **What You Fish For:** Black marlin and other billfish
- **Highlights and Notables:** Granders are not uncommon in these waters and many think a 2,000-pounder will one day be caught here.

Even if you don't catch a grander here, you'll have your memory imprinted with the vastness and beauty of the Great Barrier Reef. One thousand three hundred miles of ever-growing coral beauty and shockingly crystal-clear water. That's what Cairns is famous for—the biggest black marlin in the world and the Great Barrier Reef. You can catch shark at Cairns as well as you can anywhere else in the world and ditto barramundi and over 1,000 other species, but the black marlin is the Rosetta Stone that speaks all languages; the black marlin the demiurge that creates an angler. You are Santiago to the black marlin leaping at the end of your line.

Black marlin, 1,000 pounds. That's the goal.

Cairns supplies. Supplies granders. Supplies world-class records. Supplies 1,300-pound marlin. Supplies dreams.

Cairns is on the northeastern tip of Australia, a port town, the center of the fishing universe in the South Pacific but this is just a jumping-off point. You may have to travel great distances to find your prey. Cape Bowling Green and Lizard Head are two other jump-off points for Great Barrier Reef fishing.

Other Australia Fishing Ideas

Go ahead. Do your best "put another shrimp on the bah-bee" impression. Think of didgeridoos and boomerangs and Aborigines and pints and khaki shorts. Do that and put it behind you. Australia is indeed that and much much more. There are few places on earth where you can find the combinations of beautiful scenery and diversity of angling (both on- and offshore).

Lizard Island
Like Cairns, and not all that far from Cairns, Lizard Island has a big reputation for world record–size black marlin. A reputation as one of the top spots to catch

a grander. Numerous line-class world records caught here. Hope that the elusive (mythological?) two-grander will one day be caught from Lizard's Great Barrier Reef area waters. If you really want to make some hay, let everyone else fish for black marlin and you catch all the other fish of size and note swimming around the reef.

Great Barrier Reef
The main targets around the reef are mahi-mahi, yellowfin tuna, giant trevally, but that's just the tip of the iceberg. You've got over 1,000 miles of reef to fish, off the east coast of Queensland, and you're gonna be amazed at the colors and shapes and sizes of these exotic other fish you catch.

Barramundi
Head for the Northern Territory. Yeah, the dangerous crocodile-infested Crocodile Dundee country. Head for the mangroves in the estuaries and rivers and lagoons and hold on tight. These relatives of perch have that aboriginal/prehistoric look to them and they fight like they don't want to be caught. These predators get as big as 50-plus pounds (don't hold your breath). And don't feed the crocs. These saltwater versions are the kind you see on the Discovery Channel eating anything that moves.

BIKINI ATOLL

- **Location:** In the middle of the Pacific Ocean, northeast of New Guinea, southwest of Hawaii
- **What You Fish For:** Giant trevally, bonefish, and so many more
- **Highlights and Notables:** History and beauty, fishing for numerous species in the middle of nowhere

Marshall Islands, Micronesia

I still haven't figured out my salt attire. In the heat, the all-day sun, the reflective blue water, the chafing and blistering, you have to be smart. Your clothing needs to be functional but still express something about how you feel about yourself as an angler. I have ruled out the Jimmy Buffett floral print shirt with too-short white shorts and slip-on plastic sandals. The deck shoes with tucked-in Polo shirt and pressed shorts is not my style, either. I am considering the lightweight zip-off supplex pants and bug-free pastel-colored Orvis/Simms-style guide shirt with the closed-toe Keen-style sandals everybody is wearing nowadays but you know, while I enjoy fishing the flats and tolerate the rocking-and-rolling of the offshore, I'm just not good enough to pull off that sophisticated look yet. So I'll stick with the wrinkled frayed cotton shorts to my knees, my Keds sneakers that at one time were white, and the generic worn faded fishing shirts I got from Bass Pro Shops or Academy or some place like that. I don't have the perfect salt fishing hat or cap yet.

To a writer, the history and the very name of this emerging inshore-offshore fishery makes it too easy but too difficult to resist making a play on words. Bikini Atoll. A-Bomb and the two-piece swimsuit. A goldmine that long since played out. Now fool's gold. I intend to resist mining.

As a fishery, this remote chain of islands—and remote doesn't even begin to describe how far away from anything this is, but anyway—as a fishery these reefs and flats and dropoffs to the bottom of the earth won't likely produce any world records (well, maybe for trevally), but your trip will be more journey, a week-long confrontation with things darkly past and things blue and future—precariously balanced, ominous and awesome—an experience unlike any other saltwater destination in the world. And you catch lots and lots of fish you know, and lots and lots of fish that look like they are from another planet or even better, unique and different from our own.

The most haunting reminder of how close we came to the destruction of it all, the irony of blowing up a paradise, is the Bravo Hole. Quick history lesson for those of you who are too young to know or who slept through World History class or who have conveniently socked away this necessary memory.

Bikini Atoll is where we practiced blowing up the world.

This tiny atoll consisting of twenty-six islands surrounding a huge lagoon, in the middle of nowhere in Micronesia, these daughters of the Marshall Islands were used by the United States to test nuclear bombs from 1946 to 1958, some twenty or more tests, even after the successful detonations in Japan to end World War II. The largest nuclear test was the Castle Bravo detonation of 1954, an accident of stupendous, horrendous proportions that vaporized three islands and spread fallout across the Marshall Islands, devastating parts of the remaining native population. It remains the largest nuclear weapon ever detonated by America.

The hundreds of thousands killed by the Hiroshima and Nagasaki atomic bombs and the resultant carnage and lingering physical and psychological effects were not enough proof that these bombs were powerful enough or wreaked enough havoc. With the Cold War and improving technology and military momentum, we had to build bigger and better atomic weapons. Because you never know if they're really gonna work or not, we had to watch them explode, just in case.

The other piece of history involving the Bikini Atoll? A bathing suit designer the same year capitalized on the fame of the islands and their setting as a test site and named his two-piece bathing suit after it. Luckily, both the islands and the bikini are in good shape today.

The Bravo Hole is two miles wide in diameter and nearly two-hundred feet deep.

Fish you know: bonefish, snapper, grouper, bluefin trevally, yellow-spot trevally, black marlin, blue marlin, skipjack, barracuda, mahi-mahi (kawa-kawa), giant trevally (GTs that will spool you or break you), wahoo (40 pounds and up).

Fish you don't know: longnose emperor, swallowtail dart, dogtooth tuna, rainbow runners, green jobfish (king snapper), queenfish, milkfish, more reef fish and bottom fish than you can shake a rod at and most are a combination of colors and body parts the likes of which you've never even imagined.

Fish you don't want to know: gray reef shark.

If you were wearing any, the scenery would knock your socks off. You can't help but notice the untouched reefs, the miles and miles of coral reef, unending reef. When you see the reefs, the lagoon, the white sand, your mind will be fried thinking that anybody could think of using this spot for annihilation.

You'll fish walking along the white sandy beaches, over hard flats, in patch reefs, in a skiff, in a dive boat, deep-water trolling or stripping in Crazy Charlies, with light tackle using swimming-action lures or jigging over submerged shipwrecks, you name it, it all works. You can even send lures to the bottom of the nuclear test craters in the lagoon. Outside of the outer reef, the ocean plunges to the darkest inkiest water, plunging to depths where large scary sea creatures live.

If you haven't caught a mahi-mahi before, this green-yellow-blue dolphin fish, you are missing out—a 10-pounder will make your arms tired as you try to bring him or her in, in between jumps and leaps. The colors of the water around Bikini Atoll are the most varied and awe-inspiring of any you'll ever see. From Rogue River pool-green to Florida Keys-at-sunset blue to cerulean to indigo—the vibrant sunglow and teal colors of a mahi-mahi don't even do the colors of this water justice.

Once-a-week flight in and out. You're there for a while, so kick back. Easy to reach. Los Angeles to Hawaii to Majuro in the Marshalls then another two hour flight to Bikini. You might have to stay a day or two in Majuro waiting for a flight though.

The coral will break you off and so will the sharks. Yes, sharks. They congregate and wait. They will take your fish from you on the hook. They will take your lure and put up a fight. You might be wondering if being here is safe. Yes. You can swim, snorkel, fish, eat fish, even live here and the radiation won't get you anymore. You stay in either lodge or guest cabins on the waterfront on the lagoon side. Yes, they have air-conditioning. Sit on the deck when you're not fishing and chill. Enjoy the tranquility. There's nothing else to do anyway.

The variety of fish you'll catch is unmatched, the reef fishing some of the finest in the world, the remoteness of this (one of the least visited locales on earth) place all comprise one of the truly unique fishing experiences. Here is the last new frontier, a new world rising from the one we destroyed. The Bikini Atoll is a living breathing solemn testament, as much a memorial as Sadako's Thousand Paper Cranes.

CONTACTS
Kaufmann's Streamborn, Inc., www
    .kman.com
Robert Reimers Enterprises,
    692-625-3250
Pacific Unique Travel, 692-625-3409
Majuro Charter Boat Association,
    692-625-FISH
Marshall Islands Visitors Authority,
    692-625-3352

CHRISTMAS ISLAND

- **Location:** Island in the Indian Ocean, northwest of Australia, south of Java
- **What You Fish For:** Bonefish, trevally (several types), milkfish, and much more
- **Highlights and Notables:** World-record fish, amazingly beautiful water, remoteness, and a fishing infrastructure all add up to one of the best fishing spots on the planet.

I get nervous when I see bonefish. Actually, I don't usually see them because of the glare and their camouflage and because I'm about half blind. I can hear my trout-fishing buddies now hollering in the background about how I can always "see" trout holding in rivers but hey, my superpowers are limited, okay?

Then I have to make a good cast but it's like stepping in the batter's box for your first at-bat or teeing off in front of a group when you're playing through—you hit it good and all is right with the world. You get over it quickly and whether you blew the cast or nailed it, the jitters are gone and you can get on to the business of fishing.

Fishing Christmas Island (three paragraphs and no holiday references yet, pretty good, don't you think?) is the ultimate salt-water destination trip. Getting there takes a long time, the water's beautiful, the place has history galore, you catch big fish of each species, the island is geared to anglers.

Disorientation. Hard to tell where you

are—you can't tell by jungles or trees or buildings—it's a labyrinth of islands and flats and channels and beaches and more flats and blue water everywhere. One thousand three hundred miles from Hawaii. A monochromatic blue scale of deep blue high sky, white clouds, indigo horizon sky and the light puffy tissue blue water all horizontal, hard to get your bearings. Christmas Island is not all jungley and lush and green. Just kinda flat and lonely; you're definitely there for the fishing. Perfect weather year-round. Good fishing year-round. No hurricanes, no cold fronts, not much rain, no typhoons or cyclones.

Christmas Island on a map looks like a monster, another victim of bomb testing—its tail off to the right, mouth open right to left, the lagoon mouth, ready with teeth of Paris and London, Cook Island its first meal. Christmas Island belongs to the nation of Kiribati (keera-bass). Thirty-three islands make up this country. Great hard-bottomed flats with fine white sand.

Something to think about: the sun will burn off your skin if you don't wear sunblock. Ladies and gentlemen, you are right at the equator and closest to the sun. The water is so aqua, it sometimes doesn't look real—like an overpolarized photo to bring out the greenish blue like someone played too much with Photoshop. And nowadays, English-speaking guides and good boats, not always the case in the past here. The guides are knowledgeable and bossy (in a good way, they want you to catch fish and they see bones you'd never spot) and friendly. The lodges or resorts are not luxury-level digs and the chow won't be gourmet like so many other tropical dining experiences. You're here to fish so get your game face on. The lodging's clean and comfortable and the food is comforting and pretty good. And you're here for a week since that's when the plane from Hawaii comes in to drop off the next bunch of hard-core anglers.

You wade fish most of the time. You might get there by vehicle, you might get there by skiff but you'll be wading to catch your fish. Paris Flats is the big name, the big producing flats, reachable only by skiff.

Christmas Island waters hold bonefish like crazy. Schools and schools. Big 'uns and small 'uns. One- to 3-pound bones and bigger but the larger bones swim in the deeper water; the edges will produce the 6- to 10-pounders. A chance at a world-record bonefish exists any time you cast. One complaint early on in the bonefish fishery's emergence was that the bonefish were not selective. Too easy to catch. That has changed over the years but Christmas Island is still a great choice for a beginning bonefisher. You'll catch your fair share.

A giant trevally (GT) eats bonefish, for goodness' sake, that's how bad these babies are, they run in gangs after all and Christmas Island has lots and lots of GTs, 20- to 30-pounders and much much bigger and by big GTs, I mean large GTs,

too, world-record size. A GT in person is much more menacing than in pictures. To catch a GT is a feat because you have to cast on the spur of the moment, you have to be fishing for the GT and ignore bonefish, and you have to put the fly or lure right in front of them (and this is with the Christmas Island wind, too). And if you hook them, they attack savagely then they shoot to the coral and break you off. Blue trevally and barracuda patrol these waters as well.

The milkfish hold in the lagoon. Milkfish look sort of like bonefish but with an eye ten times too big for their body.

Bluefin, golden, and dusky are the other trevally in the Christmas Island waters. While the giants can reach one hundred pounds, a big bluefin trevally is fifteen, twenty pounds. You probably won't catch any goldens and the duskies don't get big enough to mess with.

You need your passport and visa. Everyone accepts U.S. dollars but Australian dollars are the local currency. You need 60-pound wire or bite tippet for the GTs. And you'll want 7-, 8-, or 9-weight fly rod for bones and a 10-, 11-, or 12-weight for trevally. Conventional gear should be midweight for bones, heavy for trevally. Make sure you have plenty of backing (200 yards). The guides have all kinds of localized fly patterns including a Christmas Island Special and variations of Clousers and Crazy Charlies. Bring what you think works and then use theirs.

FIJI

- **Location:** East of Australia, north of New Zealand, west of the Samoas
- **What You Fish For:** Trevally, barracuda, tuna, etc.
- **Highlights and Notables:** The fishing is a seven, the scenery a ten.

There are 330 islands in this isolated archipelago in the big blue expanse of the South Pacific; 206 of the islands are considered uninhabitable. Fiji is close to nowhere but Tranquility. Once known as the "Cannibal Islands," now Fiji is a wonderful mix of old and new, as multicultural as any country with Europeans, Chinese, Micronesians, East Indians, Fijians, Polynesians, and many others in this mélange of identities. Fiji is expensive to reach by air but cost-effective once you get there. And uncrowded.

If you see the heaven-blue clear water of these islands you will acknowledge that it is the most beautiful water you have ever seen in your life. The beaches are white sugar, the volcanic mountains greens of all hues, the climate the stuff of Pacific gods and goddesses.

Fiji is close to nowhere, I think I mentioned. Double digits in a plane to reach Nadi. From London, including stopovers and connections, twenty-seven hours. You better bring your spouse or significant other to round out this trip and justify coming all the way to Polynesia to fish. The Fiji Islands lie between North America and Australia, 3,000 miles southwest of Hawaii

and 1,800 miles northeast of Sydney. Fiji shares a time zone with New Zealand as well as their perverse friendliness.

Fiji is undeveloped in so many ways and the one you want to know about is the fishery. They're working on the infrastructure, to be sure. What can you catch in Fiji? Giant trevally is one of the top quarries, so too barracuda (at this writing, Fiji holds the world record).

In the deeper water, the channels, all around the barrier reefs, your chase includes bluefin and school travelly, yellowfin tuna, skipjack, *walu* (Spanish mackerel, 50 to 100 pounds), marlin (400 to 800 pounds), dolphin fish, red snapper, coral trout, cod, bonito, mahi-mahi, and various other pelagics. I have read or heard that a near-200-pound sailfish was once caught in these waters. If all you've done is eat mahi-mahi and have never caught mahi-mahi, they fight like the dickens and are as beautiful as brook trout.

From skiffs in the bays, up the rivers, you'll pursue jack crevalle, tuna, barracuda, walu, mangrove jack, rainbow runners (colorful fish that resemble their cousins, the kingfish), and especially wahoo. You may not catch world records or record numbers but you will catch lots of fish in Fiji. There are several fishing charters in Fiji and several of the lodges can hook you up.

The bays, reefs (good thing, because Fiji is loaded with reefs), and rivers are the top areas for fishing in Fiji. You fish here for two reasons: 1) you want to fish somewhere

where no other angler fishes or 2) you are on vacation in Fiji and want something to do other than lounge around on alabaster beaches, snorkel in emerald lagoons, eat fresh fruit in your grass hut, or snooze by the pool.

You need a valid passport to enter but you won't need a visa. The currency is the Fiji dollar, which is about two to one to the U.S. dollar in value. Banking hours are Monday

MV Wai Tadra Rates—Pacific Harbour	VAT Inc.
Full day big game fishing	FJ$1725
½ day reef fishing	FJ$910
Island snorkel trips	FJ$840
Surf Frigates	FJ$920

Note: *Fishing charter rates are for the boat for up to eight anglers and include fishing gear and tackle. Lunch, snacks, and beverages available at your request on all trips. Rates are subject to change.*

Fish Kadavu—MV Wai Tadra from FJ$700 Per Person Per Day!

Includes
- full day fishing
- all gear and tackle
- accommodation
- breakfast and dinner at resort
- lunch, snacks, and beverages on board

This rate is based on 4 anglers for minimum of 4 days. We will happily arrange international flights, mainland accommodation, domestic and island transfers on your say so all you have to do is tell us when you want to get in on the action and for how long.

to Thursday 9:30–3:00, Friday 9:30–4:00. Tipping is not customary but do it anyway.

CONTACTS
Xtasea Charters, www.xtaseacharters.com
Jim Siers, Anglers Paradise fishing Lodge at Vatia Point, Tavua, www.fijifishing.com
I don't normally include rates because of several reasons—especially that they are out of date by the time the book is published—but I thought it would be useful to help you figure out if this is a trip in your budget. For example, 900 Fiji dollars equals about 514 American dollars (as of midsummer 2006).

CONTACTS
Angler's Paradise, www.fijifishing.com

One novel way to fish Fiji is to live on a boat for a day, three days, a week. This option is perfect for those who like to set their own agenda, like to take in the full experience by snorkeling, relaxing, chilling. With over 300 islands to choose from, the potential for live-aboard expeditions, day trips, and cruising is unlimited. This, coupled with the unique configuration of Wai Tadra, an amazing boat (a forty-foot fly-bridge cruiser designed for offshore boating) makes Xtasea Charters your first call to hire a live-aboard boat in and around Fiji.

Featured in *Blue Water* magazine (raved about actually), the Wai Tadra makes you feel as though you are rich. And that's while you are sunning or catching fish or cruising in style to the next island. Rebecca Dickinson of Xtasea Charters sells you with this little teaser:

Destination Kadavu; a rugged, remote and breathtakingly beautiful place that oozes with aquatic adventure and charm. Located just 60 nautical miles south of Fiji's main island Viti Levu, Kadavu is noted for its awesome dive sites and more recently its virgin fishing grounds privy only to a select number of charter vessel operators. With raging currents, canyons, drop-offs, and seamounts galore it doesn't take an avid fisherman to tell you that the chances of hooking up to a host of gnarly fish is high. Well I'm not an avid fisherman and I can tell you that a whole lot of fish were hooked and subsequently weighed. Five brand-spanking-new Fiji records! What more can I say? The editor (of Blue Water) got his story, the anglers got their records, and Fiji fishing received another rave review.

MIDWAY ISLAND

- **Location:** Midway between Asia and America, smack dab in the middle of the Pacific Ocean
- **What You Fish For:** Giant trevally, yellowtail, jacks, wahoo, sailfish, sharks, etc.
- **Highlights and Notables:** One of the top spots anywhere to catch world-record giant trevally. Midway is historic, haunting, beautiful.

While Midway Island is the historic site of the famous World War II battle, this isolated blip on the Pacific radar, over 1,200 miles north by west of Hawaii, has gotten quite the reputation for offshore fishing for marlin and tuna and wahoo. Inshore quarry is excellent for Giant Trevally (I don't know if both words are capitalized or just one or neither but I like the look of anything "giant" to be in big letters.) And the GIANT Trevally are taking away all the publicity from the marlin now what with line-class world records being broken in their turquoise waters.

Even flyfishers do well for the GIANT Trevally with poppers and streamers but you better make sure you have a stiff round butt (both kinds) to handle these GIANT Trevally that run 65 to 130 pounds large and have the propulsive explosion of a torpedo. Additional quarry include yellowtail, thick-lipped trevally, rainbow runner, amberjack (they'll wear your arm out after jumping on your poppers), wahoo, sailfish, kawakawa, queenfish, snapper, and lots and lots of sharks.

You can catch some mighty fish from shore but you'll do better hiring a guide for most of your days. Not many choices but most are good, reputable, and know these waters. Accommodations are modest but clean, all you'll need. You have your choice of restaurants as long as it's the main cafeteria where everybody eats.

Flights are once a week from Hawaii, so this is a commitment. You'll be fishing six solid days but the other visitors will likely be from other pursuits—birders, journalists, amateur war historians, divers, ecologists, shutterbugs, and Joe Tourist. Bring a camera and leave yourself time to observe nature in its Galapagos-style best—the monk seals, the Laysan albatross, the numerous birds of all sizes, shapes, and colors, turtles, sharks, and all this managed as a National Wildlife Refuge. The sunsets are otherworldly and why not, you're in another world.

CONTACTS

Sportfish Hawaii, 877-388-1376

U.S. Fish and Wildlife Service, 808-599-3914

NEW ZEALAND

- **Location:** Bottom of the world, southeast of Australia, you have a North Island and a South Island
- **What You Fish For:** Brown trout predominantly but also rainbow trout
- **Highlights and Notables:** The granddaddy of all fishing trips

This is it. The one. This is the A-list angling destination. The trip of all trips. And why not? Fishing New Zealand is a once-in-a-lifetime adventure. The cost and the distance are so daunting, the idea of doing this twice is unreasonable.

Fishing New Zealand is not a numbers game. The resident trout are probably the biggest you can consistently get to take a fly; in many Kiwi streams, the trout average 7, 8, even 9 pounds. You just won't see or catch many 12- or 15-inch trout. The population densities are low in the rivers so the fish tend to grow larger.

Everything is different in New Zealand. One of the more unique spots on planet Earth. Winter is summer, summer is winter and everything seems backward and like you've gone down the rabbit hole. The river waters are ethereal, like blue sky upside down, liquid azure air. It's hard to explain the texture of the water of these rivers. The colors are straight out of a Crayola box, a Technicolor dream.

You watched the *Lord of the Rings* movie trilogy and noticed the dramatic otherworldly landscapes that range from snow-topped jagged mountain peaks to glaciers to wide lush valleys to fields of gray-hued rock to huge ferns next to stands of fir or jungle-line rivers and wondered it those were special effects. They weren't. That's the magical terrain of New Zealand. That's where Peter Jackson filmed. So unique, such a combination of features, it looks prehistoric. Hey, New Zealand has volcanoes, after all, some active.

New Zealand is a game of sight casting. You don't have to be the perfect caster able to leap buildings in a single bound while casting eighty feet on an arrow. But you should be a competent caster, able to make decent casts and decent drifts more times than not. You can't be a complete beginner and have any hope of going out to fish for the skittish browns and expect to have a field day. And you don't float often, hardly ever. You take helicopters to reach remote stretches of river.

The guides dress like hoboes with their pulled-up socks over their lon thermal underwear, khaki shorts over the leotards, a bandana round the neck, a funky hat on top of it all. The Americans are the ones outfitted as if straight from a fly fishing catalog, breathable waders, colorful guide-weight shirts, new hats. Just wade wet, it's not that cold. When in Rome. . . .

This is not dry fly heaven since you mostly nymph fish and streamer fish but you do also fish with dries—the hatches are underrated (sometimes a great caddis

hatch). The Holy Grail is the brown trout. Big-jawed, big-boned, big around. The browns aren't typically colorful but they are long-jawed, deep, thick as canned hams. The rainbows are so colorful, you'll wonder what pale imitiation it is you've been catching back in the States.

You and your guide—oh, those sweethearts who work so hard on these rivers for you—you and your guide creep up to a crater of a blue-green pool. If you kick a rock, throw a shadow, the two trout that inhabit the big green pool are gone, not to resurface until the morrow. This is a land of outdoorsmen skills. Be prepared to kneel and cast. Be ready to crawl like a centipede.

You'll find that your guide will be high on rocks, rocks as big as bungalows, pointing to feeding trout, advising you where and how to cast, drift, lift. Some of your casts will be longer than you are comfortable with, the drifts will sometimes be un-doable. But you will cast and drift and mend better than you ever have in your life. You must. These guides are the hardestworking guides in show business.

So clear is the water, it's akin to bonefishing, stalking cautious predators in clear water. While the fish you see in the deep pools are sometimes only shadows, sometimes you can see every spot, every fin, sometimes you can even count the number of teeth in the big mouth. If you come to a pool, a riffle, a run that hasn't been fished in a few days, maybe even weeks or more, you have a great chance to catch the whoppers that inhabit the lie if you can only cast and drift well. If the lie has seen anglers recently, that day or the day before, you likely won't catch these trout. Your chances at the fish diminish greatly with each unsuccessful cast. Get it right the first go-round. Get 'er done.

Helifishing is popular, common Down Under. Helicopters can get you into the backcountry quickly, easily, so you can discover unfished water and large trout.

New Zealand is a difficult place to fish on your own unless you have a Kiwi friend who knows the lay of the land. And while the lodges make the trip, the friendly people of New Zealand make the lodges. This isn't guidebook hype—New Zealanders are friendly beyond belief.

So much of your trip is based on the lodges, you need to match your choices with your desires and skills. With each lodge, you get a different type of river, a different type of fishing. Spring creek. Huge lake. Fast water. Backcountry river. How you select your lodge determines your happiness. And these lodges rank with those in Argentina, Alaska, Montana-Wyoming-Colorado-Idaho, Chile as the finest in the world. Everything from intimate bed and breakfasts to luxury lodges and everything in between.

North Island

The focus for trout fishing on the North Island takes place around these areas: Lake Taupo, Tongario River, Rotorua, Cape Egmont, and the Wellington region. Slightly warmer than its southerly cousin, wet wading is the rule.

Three of the top lodges on the North Island include Tongariro Lodge, Poronui Lodge, Rotorua Lodge. The Rotorua Fishing District that includes Rotorua, Waikaremoana, and Gisborne fisheries is perhaps the best freshwater fishing area in New Zealand. The average weight for this expansive region is nearly 5 pounds. The centerpiece of the Rotorua region is Lake Rotorua, a picturesque lake on the shallow side, loaded with catchable wild trout. Some days on the lake find anglers catching fifteen to twenty or more of these fighters.

Ruakituri River in the Rotorua region holds the largest river resident rainbow trout in New Zealand, one of the signature rivers of the country. The river flows into Lake Aniwhenua, an impoundment that fished great its first few years for trophy trout.

The rainbow trout in the Ruakituri River are legendary for their strength and attitude, the feistiest trout in all of New Zealand. Some of the boulders on this heavy-watered river are so gigantic, they are almost like landforms themselves, small mountains. The river character ranges from cascading rapids to slow, cavernous pools and everything in between. Heavy leaders are requisite and even then, you're likely to be broken off by the heavy trout and choppy water. Five pounds is about average for the Ruakituri River trout and trout over 10 pounds don't even cause a stir.

The Horomanga River is another world-class river and it flows into the Ruakituri River. The Horomanga is one of the main spawning streams of the lake and while not a big river, during spawn it holds numerous and large trout. The Whirinaki River begins smallish and intimate then matures through a gorge and scenic blue pools until it flows slow and determined through huge wide pools and across flat farmlands. The rainbow and brown trout aren't as large as in the Ruakituri or Horomanga (about 3 pounds on average), but the scenery is as good as it gets in New Zealand.

Other North Island hotspots include the Makuri (classic NZ stream), Mohaka River (big fish in little water), the Mangatainoka (dry fly heaven), the Manawatu (dense populations of brown trout), Hamurana Springs, Ngongotaha, Waiowhiro, and Utahina Streams, and the Ohau Channel, all entering Lake Rotorua. There are also several worthy lakes on the North Island: Okataina, Tarawera, Rotoiti, Rotoma, Rerewhakaaitu, Tuai, and Kaitawa.

The overall best lake in New Zealand is also its largest, Lake Taupo. Taupo sits in the center of the North Island, well developed, ideal as a home base for fishing and tourism. So many fertile rivers empty into Taupo that it enjoys the bounty, a town on the lake proclaims itself the "Trout Capital of the World." The rainbow trout in Taupo are steelhead-like in appearance, movement, and fighting ability.

Near Turango, the Tongariro River enters Lake Taupo. Tongariro River is thought by many to be the finest of the feeder streams to Taupo, with its named pools, huge trout, and figures like Zane Grey enmeshed in the river's history. You fish from pool to pool to pool, big swirling emerald-green bowls. In addition to Tongariro, you can choose from a plethora of other top-notch rivers: the Waitotaka, Waimarino, Hatepe, Waitahanui, Waikato, Waihaha, Waihora, Whanganui, Kuratau, and Whareroa Rivers. The Waimarino River is perhaps the best of these—you have to hike a lot and that keeps away fishing pressure; the browns average 4 or 5 pounds; and being a river on the smaller side, the dry fly fishing is superb, rises coming even from deep pools and deep runs.

South Island

Not quite as warm, not a twin of the North Island at all, the South Island will remind you of Oregon, Washington, Vancouver with its glaciers and tall mountains and green lush rainforests. Fjords deep and dramatic. Lakes formed by glaciers. Rivers less fertile than those on the North Island. Cooler than the North Island—hey, you've got the Southern Alps, after all. And you fish for sea-run, lake-run, and resident trout and even salmon (quinnat). The prey at the top of the angler's list is the sea-run brown. You walk a lot to traverse the rivers of the South Island and the sizes of the trout are less than those on North Island. The remote backcountry is prettier, if that is possible and that makes up for some of that smaller size.

The northwest corner of the South Island is the Nelson region, mountainous terrain that creates a mild climate, but you also get touristy things like great beaches, wineries, breweries, artists' communities, and national parks. The scenery is indescribably beautiful.

Some of the top lodges include Rotoroa Lake Lodge, Mateuka Lodge, Grasmere Lodge, Owen River Lodge. The Owen River is one of the most famous of the South Island trout streams and rightfully so. The pools are some of the clearest you'll ever see (even though it can cloud up from time to time), what looks like a foot deep might be take-a-dunking deep—this on what you'd have to consider a small stream, delicate and intimate and that's probably why the pressure has deteriorated the river's rep. You still hear about 10-pounders being caught (sighted is probably more the truth) on the Owen but on the whole, I'm understanding the river is no longer as good as it once was—even so, the average size trout runs from a couple of pounds to 6 pounds and that's a nice fish in my book. Stylish Owen River Lodge is a good place to call home to fish the Owen and other area rivers and lakes of the Nelson Lakes District.

Lake Rotoroa Lodge is one of the top lodges in New Zealand, a real luxury getaway with folks who really know the area, really know angling. Located less than five hours northwest of the pastoral town of Christchurch, at the edge of the Nelson Lakes National Park, known as much for its cuisine, wine, and hospitality as the world-class fishing. Imagine having forty pristine rivers within the purview of the lodge, some by hiking, some by vehicle, some by helicopter. Elegance and efficiency. Lake Rotoroa is known for the large brown trout (rainbow trout live in Rotoroa, too, but are the lesser target). The lake isn't bothered by lots of boats or water skiers. Peaceful, prolific, picture-perfect.

Other blue ribbon fisheries of the South Island include the Mataura River (an underrated world-class brown trout fishery), the rocky Hope River, and the Waiau River in Southland with its variety of water and killer fishing for rainbow and brown trout and, to top it off, the river offers a chance at Atlantic salmon that average nearly 3 pounds. Other waters worth visiting are the Mararoa, Aparima, Oreti, Makarewa, Clutha (New Zealand's largest river, full of sea-run browns), Taieri, Catlins, Waikouaiti, Waipori, and Shag Rivers.

The Waitaki and Hakataramea Rivers are two excellent rivers for rainbow and brown trout, each averaging over 3 pounds. The Rakaia River and Waiau River are your best choices for quinnat salmon but don't overlook the sea-run browns that hit 3 and 4 pounds regularly. The Ashburton, Hinds, and Rangitata Rivers are three other local first-class rivers. The Southern Lakes District has an amazing variety of trout waters including the Riwaka, Takaka, Cobb, Wangapeka, Buller (I've heard some negative things recently about the Buller), Travers, Gowan, D'Urville, Sabine, Owen, Mangles, and Maruia Rivers, as well as Lakes Rotoiti and Wakatipu. The Wairau (Marlborough), Gowan (Nelson Lakes), and Montueka (Nelson Lakes) Rivers are sleeping giants, magnificent rivers with brown trout up to 7 pounds, wild rainbows that pull like trains.

English is the official language of New Zealand although Maori is also recognized as an official language. The local currency is NZ dollars and cents. The exchange rates vary according to international monetary conditions. New Zealand's population is about three and a half million.

Air New Zealand offers daily flights both nonstop and direct, stopping in Hawaii, Tahiti, Cook Islands, and Fiji. It's a good idea, if you have the time, to lay over for several days rest on your return trip. Many booking agents handle trips to New Zealand. I have yet to find one who knows more about New Zealand and how to match your needs to your pocketbook and to your dreams like Mike McClelland of Best of New Zealand Fly Fishing.

CONTACTS
Best of New Zealand Fly Fishing, www .bestofnzflyfishing.com

This Web site lists all kinds of fishing resources: www.nzsouth.co.nz

PAPUA NEW GUINEA

- **Location:** South Pacific, just north of Australia
- **What You Fish For:** New Guinea black bass, barramundi, saratoga
- **Highlights and Notables:** The New Guinea black bass is explosive and caught nowhere else on earth.

New Guinea black bass. This is one ferocious water monster. They live in shadowy rivers, the jungle so close, leaves brush your arm as you float by in the brackish water, the air is heavy and hot and sticky. New Guinea black bass attack with a fury, with an anger that is matched by their physical bullying nature. They don't want you to catch them or land them and you probably won't.

The New Guinea black bass has that snide derision of Jack Torrance from *The*

downed trees—they are structure oriented. The bass reach about 50 pounds but a 25-pounder will straighten out hooks, break rods, make unstoppable runs and make for cover and then break you off and break your heart and sometimes, break your spirit.

You can also fish for barramundi and saratoga. The barramundi are worthy game fish in their own right, ambush predators that also like structure. A 20-pounder will give you all you can handle. They attack flies and lures with a vengeance. Saratoga are natives and hang out in similar places to the barramundi. They are colorful and powerful adversaries.

The parts of New Guinea you'll be fishing are primitive. Fishing adventure-level primitive.

CONTACTS
FishQuest, www.fishquest.com

Shining, the pent-up explosiveness of Travis Bickle in *Taxi Driver* and the reckless devil-may-care flippance of Harry Lime in *The Third Man.* Most of these bass have never seen a lure or a fly. They fight like Anna Nicole Simpson hanging on to her tenuous fortune. They are found only here, in New Guinea, nowhere else on earth. They are relatives of the Lutjanid family, related to cubera snapper, mangrove jack, red emperor, and if you know them, you know what fighters they all are.

Fishing for these voracious fish is good year-round. You cast to structure, to

> The Aussies stocked trout in the high country in the 1960s and '70s. The streams are typical high country tumbling streams as they rush down the 11,000 and 12,000 foot peaks. As the rivers flatten out, they widen and form big pools and you need bigger equipment for the heavier trout. Tribes still live in these nether regions and your safety should be a concern. Fishing adventure!

TAHITI, FRENCH POLYNESIA

- **Location:** South Pacific, east of Australia
- **What You Fish For:** Bonefish, marlin, trevally, etc.
- **Highlights and Notables:** Tahiti is one of the top vacation destinations for good reason—the beaches and water and climate and lodgings and atmosphere are perfect. The fishing is pretty good, not great, so I'd recommend fishing Tahiti while you're on vacation, not as a destination per se.

Explorers like Captain Cook and Zane Grey (yes, that Zane Grey) and Marlon Brando (yes, that Marlon Brando) discovered Tahiti. Cook found it for the "civilized" world, Grey for the sportfishing world, Brando simply gave to the world a Tahiti that showcased his own unique flair and isolation as well as the islands' bohemian native romantic side. Because of that exposure he will always be linked to these islands.

Tahiti is part of French Polynesia and there are several archipelagos in the Tahiti system. French is the common language but most speak Tahitian, and English still works. You would get no argument from anyone who has ever been to Tahiti that there is no more beautiful spot on the planet. Now for the good and the bad.

The good is that Tahiti is one of the prime offshore fishing hotspots in the Pacific. Off of Tahiti (reef fishing here is good) and Moorea, anglers for years have been stalking and chumming and rod-bending for huge marlin to match the one Zane Grey caught—a blue that went well over 1,000 pounds. In today's typical Tahiti waters, marlin is usually in the 300- to 700-pound class. Tahiti's nearby open seas also hold bonito and yellowfin tuna. Inshore fishing can be dynamite for giant trevally, blue-finned trevally, striped trevally, and most especially bonefish. Many anglers who have fished the flats of Tahiti and surrounding islands report that they have caught and lost bonefish that would break the world record.

Now for the bad. The marlin fishing is spotty, sometimes hot, sometimes not. Capricious. The bonefishing, when it's good, it's naughty—10- to 13-pound bonefish naughty. When it's bad, there are no bonefish whatsoever. Tahiti, especially in its outer fishing frontier atolls like Tetiaroa and Tuomotos, has some of the largest bonefish on earth. These monsters are silver-i-er and sheen-i-er than any bonefish you'll ever see. Tahiti's other world-class fishing is for trevally and they're hit or miss, too. What gives in Paradise?

The fishing infrastructure (guides and lodges) has been as spotty as the inshore fishing but improving—sorta—still emerging as a structured fishery. The lodges and outfitters are still learning to be guides and lodges. For years now, *The Angling Report* (hello, Don) and *Wild on the Fly* magazine have been reporting various troubles clients have had with missing guides, missing boats, airports closed, government interference, *no* fish. Like a really bad Don Knotts movie. Then you'll hear just the opposite about this bipolar fishery with claims that anglers are catching more bonefish and the biggest bonefish than anyone has ever heard about. Such is the stuff of dreams (and nightmares).

The fishing gods play tricks and the locals swear that a combination of factors has this fishery in a state of flux. They'll tell you how the *El Niño* current brought in warm water and flushed out the game fish, and that all is right with the fishing right now. They'll tell you how the outfitters were new to it all, that the travel agents jumped the gun and made too many early or top-heavy promises. Put this all in the blender, drink a cold Margarita, and call your nearest travel agent and see what's up right this second.

Tetiaroa looks like a giant amoeba from the air, a misshapen blue-green sea creature. Azure lagoons dotted with coral, white sand beaches, sunken volcanic cones, thick palm forests, mosquitos the size of small bonefish, humidity and uncomfortable heat and the biggest bonefish in the world. Tetiaroa is the private atoll owned by Brando and now his family—the Tuamotos archipelago and Anaa are two other angling options that have had hit-or-miss results.

My guess is that they eventually get all of this figured out, the fishery in the remote island flats will turn out to be great with bouts of good and that we can all get along. As it stands now, it's a crapshoot.

CONTACTS
Tahiti Fly Fish, www.tahiti-fly-fishing-cruises.com
Planet Fly Fishing, www.planetflyfishing.com

TASMANIA

- **Location:** Island off the southeast coast of Australia
- **What You Fish For:** Trout
- **Highlights and Notables:** What a collection of lakes. Trout stillwater heaven

I hate sleep. I fight it. I am nocturnal. I stay up until 1 or 2 or 3 in the morning every night and then get up at six-thirty in the

a.m. and teach. When I was a wee tot, Mom would put me to bed and darken the room only to find me a couple of hours later under the covers with a flashlight, reading a book.

I feel like I'm missing out on something if I sleep. I have things to do, things to watch, things to listen to, things to write.

But one cool thing about sleep is when I sleep in a car or on a train or on a plane and

I wake up and I'm somewhere else. I love being somewhere else almost as much as I hate sleeping. I don't do sleeping pills (they never make me sleep; just the opposite). I can't sleep on a plane when I know it's daylight outside (the window-shutters-down trick doesn't work on me). I can look at my watch and I know what time it is and what I would normally be doing. But somehow, on the plane, this trip, I slept. When you go to Tasmania, if you live anywhere else but the southern hemisphere, you've got a long long flight. Sweet dreams.

You won't sleep much in the southernmost state of Australia. There's too much to see and do. Tasmania may be more famous for its devil and tiger but the fishing ranks right up there with them. I just want to say, to let you know in case you didn't that Tasmanian devils are for real and so was the Tasmanian tiger. I say was because the last thylacine died in the Hobart Zoo in 1936.

Tasmania is a mountainous island right across Bass Strait, 150 miles from Melbourne. Good amount of rain, moderate climate, lots of lakes and rivers, most of which hold trout. We're talking about an island that is mostly rural, where the water and air are still pure, that has thousands of lakes, disease-free wild trout.

While Tasmania has trout fishing in many places including both high country and lowland rivers, the best spot is the Central Highland Lake region, the highlight the stillwater angling in lakes. Large cruising trout in weedy shallows. Lightly-fished lakes, guys. Three thousand lakes, even high-country wilderness lakes, beautiful wild snow-melt tarns that test your patience and your mad skills.

The trout in these lakes grow big, marbled brown trout (and some 'bows) but the real fun for angling explorers is that fishing for Taz trout includes lots of stalking and sightcasting on the lakes. You wade a lot but you can find some boat fishing as well.

What's fun for the stillwater angler is the sight fishing for tailing trout, just like fishing for reds in the marsh, bones on the flats. Look for foamy scum lines, edges, structure, wind lanes, weeds, dropoffs. Then you search for nervous water or a tail and you've got your feeding trout. They call it "polaroiding," because to see these feeding trout, you'll need a good pair of polarized glasses. Perhaps nowhere in the world is this sight fishing for tailing trout on lakes more developed than in Tasmania. Catching them in this motionless water, these freshwater flats is another story.

What do they eat? Mayflies, midges, scuds, and caddis, and some local jobbers like (eucalyptus) gum beetles and mudeyes (dragonflies) and lake-living stoneflies. And tadpoles, snails, and little puppy tails.

The best lodge in Tasmania, one of the best Down Under (and some compare it favorably to any other in the world) is London Lakes Lodge. Intimate, private, exotic, the Lodge entertains anglers from all over the world. The lodge is known as much for its hospitality, food, and wines as it is for being the best Tasmanian base for fishing. Your days and nights are full of all kinds of things—the food, the wine, the fishing—but also seeing wildlife on the property (5,000 acres), everything from wombat to platypus to wallaby to quolls and even Tasmanian devils.

London Lakes Lodge has its very own notable trout ponds and a fifteen-kilometer meadow stream between Lake Big Jim and Lake Samuel but if you tire of their waters—a difficult task—you're minutes away from many other dignified waters. The standard approach is to catch big trout on dry flies. A seasoned, fully-accredited London Lakes guide must accompany all fishing on lodge lakes.

Night fishing is popular and useful to get big browns. Ideally, during the day, you want cloud cover, polarized glasses that work, and patience. There is plenty of accessible water from boat and car but there are lonely backcountry places too.

Tasmanians drive on the wrong side of the road (so says this American), so be alert and mindful (you'll end up messing up a time or two, I just know it). Their summer is our winter, and vice-versa. The brown trout season runs from August to April. The rainbow trout season runs from October to May. There are also several trout waters open all year round. The top fishing is from October to March. Trout fishing is closed from June 1 to July 31 in order to allow the fish time to spawn. Leave the felt-soled waders at home. They carry disease and you won't need the nonslip aspect anyway since you'll be wading in lakes. A good trick when polaroiding is to wade slowly. Slower than that. We move too fast, those of who are used to fishing faster waters and easier lakes. No disease in Taz—clean and disinfect beforehand or use their flies and boots and lines. A license is required to fish all Tasmanian inland waters.

Little Pine Lagoon, Lake Sorrell, Great Lake, Arthurs Lake

Unless you are a top fly fisher, this might not be a destination you'd travel around the world to fish unless you have seven to ten days or more to spend on the island or in combination with a trip to Australia or New Zealand. The fishing, while productive and interesting, requires casting skill, sighting ability and patience, three things not always associated with beginners. That said, at places like London Lakes Lodge, the guides and outfitters go out of their way to assist and teach newbies. That said, if you like challenging trout fishing, stillwater angling, there are few spots on earth that offer this kind of experience.

Other productive waters include rivers east of the lakes, uplands, North and South Esk and their feeders, Meander, St. Patricks, Liffey, St. Pauls, Macguire, Elizabeth, Break O'Day, Bumbry's Creek a tailwater, Leven River near Gunns Plains in north central Taz.

Arthur's Lake

This 16,000-acre man-made lake is one of the most popular lakes in Tasmania. Arthur's produces quality fishing from September to April. The trout are wild browns ranging from 1 to 5 pounds but a 6-pound brown is not uncommon. Big brown dry flies work well here. A couple of locals told me the lake doesn't fish nearly as well as it used to. Ten browns in hand ranging from

1 to 6 pounds on big brown dry flies gave me a different impression but they'd know, right? I did hear from a couple of other locals that the lake is still one of the top producers in the Highlands.

Weeds, floating wood, brush, flotsam and jetsam, you can just tell it's fertile; thick stands of dead trees yet the water so clear. Most fish it with boats. I saw some of the largest duns I've ever seen. I never saw beetles but quite a few anglers I talked to were using them successfully. I never have used many beetle patterns and didn't have any stocked so I didn't.

Great Lake

Deep and clear, Great Lake is a vast inland sea on the northern rim of the Great Western Tiers in the Central Highlands of Tasmania. The lake holds an excellent population of wild brown and rainbow trout. The polaroiding (don't you just love that term?) is great along the shore but you won't have any problem spotting the fish where they ought to be (froth lines, rocky points, the flats, slicks).

This is the largest lake in the Central Highlands and it is still underfished. Because it's big and the wind can kick up, smaller boats need to keep an eye on the weather. Great Lake's trout season is different from other waters as it is only prohibited to fish on the lake between June and July. The season opens the nearest weekend to August 1 and closes on the last weekend nearest March 31. Fly fishing only. Locals tell me bad weather brings out the best hatches and the best fishing.

Penstock Lagoon

On the Central Plateau, this shallow productive lake has the obligatory weed beds and finicky fine fish. Both browns and rainbows thrive here in this fly fishing–only regulated forest-ringed, rocky lake. You will not catch as many on Penstock as other lakes but when you do, they are larger than most and fight you like Tasmanian devils.

Little Pine Lagoon

The hatches on this small Central Plateau lake are so thick and varied and persistent, it reminded me of the Delaware River's own prolific hatches. Like Penstock, the fish are smart and wary but Little Pine is loaded with tailing wild brown trout. Hair-rising-on-the-back-of-your-neck, stomach-in-knots kind of wild brown trout. Get in position, take your time and be good on your first cast. I hear October and November are the best months but December brought to hand a nice 5-pounder (the only fish of the day for me). Fly fishing only, easy to wade, typical weedbeds and marshy areas. Not far from Great Lake.

Nineteen Lagoons

The "western lakes" are a remote network of lagoons, connected by what pass for streams or creeks and all this watery system surrounds Lake Augusta. You reach the Nineteen Lagoons area from the Lake Highway at the Liaweenee Canal. Some of the more notable lagoons include Double Lagoon, Howes Bay Lagoon, Lake Augusta,

CONTACTS

Gayle and Michael Hawker, Tasmania Reservations, 800-830-8999

London Lakes Fly Fishing Lodge, 011-61-002-891159

Ken and Marea Orr, Bradys Lake, Tarraleah, 011-61-02-891191

Compleat Angler/Mayfly Travel, Melbourne, Australia, 011-61-3-6211247, 203-655-9400

Michael McClelland, Best of New Zealand Fly Fishing, www.bestofnzflyfishing.com

Frontiers International, www.frontierstrvl.com

Tasmania Trout and Fly Fishing, www.fishingtasmania.com/welcome.htm

London Lakes Lodge, www.londonlakes.com.au

A good site for information: www.discovertasmania.com/home/index.cfm

Carters Lakes, Rocky Lagoon, Lake Ada, and Lake Botsford. You can reach some by car, some by foot. The lakes are similar in that they are each shallow and weedy and clear, but each has its own personality and idiosyncracies. You're in the middle of nowhere and you're up high so the weather can turn bitterly cold in a flash.

Lake Burbury, Bronte Lagoon, Lagoon of Islands are three other options you should look into.

Acknowledgments

I owe a lot to my agent David Smith and to my editor Matthew Benjamin at HarperCollins who saw the need and fun of a book like this.

I also want to thank the following: Nick Toldi of Gourmetfly, Greger Jonsson of www.laplandfishing.com, Patrick of www.magiclapland.se, magiclapland@telia.com, Anne Harju of www.saariselka.fi/inarievent, Heikki Nikula of the Hotel Inarin Kultahovi, Tenojoki Erakievari Lodge, www.personal.inet.fi/luonto/tenokievari, John Garger, Ripp Media, Kathy House, Sport Fish Hawaii/Hawaii Fishing Adventures and Charters, www.sportfishhawaii.com, Bert Deener, Capt. Kelly Windes, Sunrise Charters, www.destin-charter-fishing.com/html/important_info.htm (Destin, FL), Bobby Barrack, www.bobbybarrack.com (CA Delta), Tanya Wells and Chris Drake, Nevada Dept. of Wildlife, www.ndow.org, Dennis Dickson, Dickson Flyfishing Steelhead Guides, www.flyfishsteelhead.com (Grand Ronde, WA), Steve Kuieck, River Quest Charters (Muskegon/St. Mary's River, MI), Steve and Linda Fleming, Mah-Hah Outfitters, www.johndayriverfishing.com (Fossil, OR), Pinepoint Lodge, www.pinepointlodge.com (Crane Lake, MN), John Edstrom, Headwaters Flyfishing Company, www.headwatersflyfishing.com (St. Croix, WI), Terry Cook, Harrison Convention and Visitors Bureau, www.HarrisonArkansas.org, Capt. Joe Greco, Justy-Joe Sport Fishing Charters, www.newyorkfishing.com (Lake Champlain and George), Dave Shindler, Jst Fishin' Guide Service, www.JSTFISHIN.com (Manchester, PA), Sam Williams, Hawks Fishing Guide Service, www.fishingworld.com/iGuide/AL/Eufaula/HawksFishingGuide/ (Lake Eufaula, AL), Billy Darby, Billy Darby's Fishing Guide Service, www.dixiebass.com/billydarby (Lake Eufaula, AL), Blaine Mengel, The Backwoods Angler, www.backwoodsangler.com (Allentown, PA), Randy Pringle, www.100percentbass.com/Guides/Randy%20Pringle/randys%20home.htm (CA Delta and Northern CA Lakes), Marta Morton, Harbour Club Villas and Marinas, www.bonefishing.tc and www.harbourclubvillas

.com (Turks and Caicos), Damien Nurre, Fly & Field Outfitters, www.flyandfield.com (Bend, Oregon), Paola Calabria Dean, Silver Deep, www.silverdeep.com (Turks and Caicos), Rebecca Dickinson, Xtasea Charters, www.xtaseacharters.com (Fiji Islands), Capt. Mike Locklear, www.homossafishing.com (Ft. Lauderdale, FL), Randy Jones, www.yankeeangler.com (Salmon River, NY and Cape Cod, MA), Jim Siers, Anglers Paradise fishing Lodge at Vatia Point, Tavua, www.fijifishing.com (Fiji), Misty Dhillon & Mickey Sidhu, The Himalayan Outback, www.himalayanoutback.com (New Delhi, India), Brian Shumaker, Susquehanna River Guides, www.susqriverguides.com (New Cumberland, PA), Mark Wilson, Red Canyon Lodge, www.redcanyonlodge.com (Flaming Gorge, Utah National Recreation Area), Capt. W. Brice Contessa, Contessa Flyfishing, www.contessaflyfishing.com (Martha's Vineyard, MA), Reese Stecher, Beach Bum Fishing, www.beachbumfishing.com (Outer Banks, NC), Nuno Breda, www.portugalfishingadventure.com and www.portugalfishingadventure.com/NunoBredaE.htm, Sean McDonald, Century Circle Guide Service, www.centurycircle.com (Baldwin, MI), Matt Supinski, Gray Drake Lodge & Outfitters, www.graydrake.com (Newaygo, MI), Rob Anderson, Reno Fly Shop & Truckee River Outfitters, www.reonflyshop.com (Reno, NV and Truckee, CA), Capt. Frank Campbell, Niagara Region Charter Service, www.niagaracharter.com (Niagara Falls, NY), Bill Hilts, Jr. www.outdoorsniagara.com/bill_hilts_outdoors_weekly, Len Rich, Mick Emmens, Awesome Lake Lodge, www.labradoranglingadventures.com (Labrador, Canada), Fred Hutchings, Triple T Charters, www.tripletcharters.com (Prince Rupert, BC, Canada), Harold McMillan, Richard Procoppio, Housatonic River Outfitters, www.dryflies.com (Cornwall Bridge, CT), Gail Arterburn and Millard Reed, an avid fisherman, Denny Breer, Trout Creek Flies & Green River Outfitters, www.fishgreenriver.com (Dutch John, UT), Capt. Jay Gustin, Pesca Panama, www.pescapanama.com (Hannibal Bank/Coiba Island, Panama) (Glendale, AZ), Johnse Bushlack, Seagull Outfitters, www.seagulloutfitters.com (BWCA and Quetico, Grand Marais, MN), Peter Mantle, Delphi Lodge, www.delphi-salmon.com (Leenane Co. Galway, Ireland), Capt. Todd Magaline, Blue Runner Sportfishing, www.bluerunnercharters.com (San Francisco, CA), Bob Troxel, Bob Troxel's Guide Service, Lake Erie Fishing Charters, www.lakeeriesmallmouth.com (Athens, OH), Graham Hubner, Southern Yosemite Mountain Guide, www.symg.com/featured_guides.htm, Rich Oldham, Andy Montana's Fly Shop, www.andymontanas.com (San Diego Bay, Coronado, CA), Rogelio Velasco, Pesca Maya, www.pescamaya.com (Ascension, Mexico), Ellyn Nadeau, Michael Mastrangelo, Fort Smith Fly Shop and Cabins, www.flyfishingthebighorn.com (Bighorn R, MT), Bob Mauldin, B&B Mexico Bass Fishing, www.wheretofish.com (Lake Agua Milpa, Mexico), Luka Hojnik, editor, www.flyfish-slovenia.com, Jason Balogh, Honduras on the Fly, www.hondurasonthefly.com, Capt. Lee Allen Campbell, Panama Big Game, www.panamabiggamefishing.com, Chuck Stranahan of RiverBend Flyfishing, www.chuck-stranahan.com (Bitterroot, MT), Don Muelrath, Fly Fishing Adventures, www.flyfishbelize.com and www.flyfishingadventures.org, Dan Black, Brigadoon Lodge, www.BrigadoonLodgecom (Soque River, GA), Grant Cumings, Chiawa Camp, www.chiawa.com (Lower Zambezi National Park, Lusaka, Africa), Gerhard Laubscher, FlyCastaway, www.flycastaway.com (Africa & Indian Ocean Islands), Nancy Mozayani and Royal Canadian Pacific, www.royalcanadianpacific.com, Patricia Postma, www.natureresortkabalebo.com (Suriname), Jeff Sayre, www.flyfishingthefineyard .com (Martha's Vineyard, MA), Al and Jeana Bukowsky and Solitude River Trips, www .rivertrips.com (Middle Fork of the Salmon, ID), David Lynch (Corsica), Arkadi de Rakoff of www.clubfrance.com (Risle River, Normandy, France), Melvin Hayner, The Driftless Fly Fishing Company, www.minnesotaflyfishing.com (Driftless Area, MN), Herman Striednig, Fischwasser Osterreich, J.W. Smith, Rod & Gun Resources, www.rodgunresources.com, Larry Larsen by way of J.W. Rod & Gun, Little St. Simons Lodge, www.littlestsimonsisland.com (Georgia), Capt. Julian Jay Gustin, Pesca Panama, www.pescapanama.com, Richard Sheard of www.worldsportfishing.com, Curtis Bailey, Kenichiro Eitaka, Joey Hall, Harry Briscoe, John Openshaw of www.waderson.com, Tammy Williams Walker, Mike Walker, Kay Kay Brock, Kyle Brock, Will Brock, Martha and Felipe Nogueida, Drew Perkins, Ken Cole of Flies by Night, Matt Williams, Seth Williams, Doug James, Bobby Boswell, Ed Burge, Shawn Neeley, Mark Leach, Craig Kautsch, Larry Metzger, Dave Rittenberry of Riverfields, Tony and Kay Tarasewicz of the Sportsman Lake City, Colorado, Jerome Butler, Megan Medling, Larry Kingrey of Royal Gorge Anglers, www .royalgorgeanglers.com (Colorado, Arkansas River), Pete and Evelyn Spann, Bobby Spann, Mike Spann, Bob Brown, Jim McKee, Larry Hodge, Texas Parks and Wildlife, www.tpwd .state.tx.us, Jorgen Wouters, Richie Santiago, Aaron and Dez Witt, Tracy Asbury, Outdoor Adventures, www.wvoutdooradventures.com, David Becker, Ben Becker (Norway), Jane Becker, Cindy and Dino Ferraresi, Chad and Shell-Dawg McPhail, Lee Raymond, Don Muelrath, John Garger of Ripp Media, Kit Menis of DPS Sporting Club Development Company, Terry Cook of Arkansas Visitors Bureau, Perry Cooper (Honduras on the Fly), Ken Medling, Chad Huseman, Doc Thompson, Chase Medling, Sarah Williams, Gwen and Don Maroney, the guys at Girls Gone Grabblin', Doug Cavin, Rod Barker of the Strater Hotel, Tom Hawthorne, Larry Kennedy, Manuel Monasterio, Garrett Veneklasen, Marcos Enriquez, Don Causey, Gerald McDaniel, Keith and Kendra Brown, Lee Leschper, Jeff and Cyndie Schmitt, Rob Woodruff, Phil Shook, Ed Adams, Woody Vogt, Vince Homer, Jim Miller of F2K Guide Service, Ralph Cutter, Taylor Creek Fly Shop, Lance Barnette, Shirley and David Alford of Blue Lake Ranch, Tim Linehan, Scott Swanson of Fishquest, Helga Van Horn and Florian Scheuer of Posh Journeys, Brett Pauly of ESPNoutdoors.com, Manuel Martinez of Hotel Aiguablava, John Shewey, Luis Mayoral, Noelle Casagrande and Sabrina Mary Beth Bozek of British Virgin Islands, Don Oliver, Jamie Tedesco of Taos Inn (the Historic Taos Inn), Mike McClelland of Best of New Zealand Flyfishing, Burt Carey, Bud Zehmer, Mike Jones, Steve Probasco, Mark McDonald, Dave Jensen of Alberta Flyfishing. If I forgot anybody who contributed to this book in any way, I'm sorry and I owe you lunch.

Credits

Maps and photos © Mark D. Williams except where otherwise credited.

Photos on pages 199, 205, 232, 253, 255, 256, 264, 268, 269, 272, 665, 666, 667, 734, 736, 767 courtesy of Amy LB Williams; Photos on pages 6, 7 courtesy Richard Procoppio & Housatonic River Outfitters; Photos on pages 13, 34 courtesy of Randy Jones; Photo on page 16 courtesy of Capt. W. Brice Contessa of Contessa Flyfishing; Photos on pages 24, 35 courtesy of Jorgen Wouters; Photos on pages 26, 33 courtesy of Bill Hilts Jr.; Photo on page 28 courtesy of the Backwoods Angler & Blaine Mengel; Photo on page 42 courtesy of Dave Shindler of Jst Fishin' Guide Service; Photo on page 43 courtesy of Brian Shumaker of Susquehanna River Guides; Photos on pages 44, 48, 121, 129, 149 courtesy of Gerald McDaniel; Photos on pages 46, 47 courtesy of Woody Vogt; Photos on pages 50, 53 courtesy of Nicholas Ponzios; Photo on page 57 courtesy of Sam Williams of Hawks Fishing Guide Service;

Photos on page 65 courtesy of Kelly Windes of Sunrise Charters; Photos on pages 78, 83, 85 courtesy of Richie Santiago; Photo on page 79 courtesy of Bert Deener; Photo on page 87 courtesy of The Lodge at Little St. Simons; Photo on page 88 courtesy of Patrick Sayle; Photo on page 91 courtesy of Brigadoon Lodge; Photo on page 114 courtesy of Swain County Chamber of Commerce; Photo on page 121 courtesy of Reese Stecher of Beach Bum Fishing; Photos on pages 138, 141, 148 courtesy of Tracy Asbury of Outdoor Adventures; Photos on page 155 courtesy of Harrison Convention & Visitors Bureau; Photos on pages 157, 402, 567 courtesy of Tammy Williams Walker; Photo on page 181 courtesy of Sean McDonald of Century Circle Guide Service; Photos on pages 182, 183 courtesy of Steve Kujeck of River Quest Charters; Photo on page 184 courtesy of Matt Supinsk & Gray Lodge & Outfitters; Photo on page 188 courtesy of Seagull Outfitters; Photo on page 190 courtesy of Melvin Hayner of The Driftless Fly Fishing Company; Photo on page

212 courtesy of Bob Troxel's Guide Service; Photos on pages 221, 222 courtesy of Spearfish Chamber of Commerce; Photo on page 229 courtesy of John Edstrom of Headwaters Fly Fishing Company; Photo on page 249 courtesy of Kyle Brock; Photos on pages 307, 333 courtesy of Chad McPhail; Photo on page 308 courtesy of Texas Parks and Wildlife and Larry Hodge; Photo on page 311 courtesy of Lee Raymond; Photos on pages 313, 589, 601, 602, 617, 696, 706, 707, 708, 709, 782, 783, 786, 793, 812, 814, 815, 834 courtesy of Scott Swanson & FishQuest; Photos on pages 334, 335 courtesy of Girls Gone Grabbling; Photo on page 343 courtesy of Jane Becker; Photo on page 344 courtesy of Doug James; Photo on page 374 courtesy of Bobby Barrack; Photo on page 378 courtesy of Randy Pringe; Photo on page 392 courtesy of Capt. Todd Magaline of Blue Runner Sportfishing; Photo on page 394 courtesy of Millard Reed; Photo on page 398 courtesy of Rich Oldham of Andy Montana's Fly Shop; Photos on pages 404, 405 courtesy of Southern Yosemite Mountain Guide, Graham Hubner; Photo on page 412 courtesy of Rob Anderson & Reno Fly Shop; Photo on page 414 courtesy of Chris Drake & Nevada Department of Wildlife; Photo on page 477 courtesy of Al & Jeana Bukowsky of Solitude River Trips; Photos on pages 498, 499 courtesy of Ellyn Nadeau, Michael Mastrangelo, and Fort Smith Fly Shop and Cabins; Photo on page 500 courtesy of Chuck Stranahan; Photos on pages 506, 510, 511 courtesy of Tim Linehan & Linehan Outfitting Company; Photos on pages 522, 523 courtesy of Fly & Field Outfitters, head guide Damien Nurre; Photo on page 525 courtesy of Dennis Dickson Flyfishing Steelhead Guides; Photo on page 531 courtesy of Steve & Linda Fleming of Mah-Hah Outfitters; Photo on page 540 courtesy of David Becker; Photo on page 554 courtesy of Kyle Brock; Photo on

page 555 courtesy of DPS Sporting Club Development Company; Photos on pages 560, 561, 562, 563 courtesy of Joey Hall; Photo on page 564 courtesy of Scott Smith & FishQuest; Photo on page 565 courtesy of Lee Leshper; Photo on page 566 courtesy of Ken Sheffield; Photo on page 570 courtesy of Capt. Chuck Haupert of Catchem Sportfishing; Photo on page 571 courtesy of Kathy House and Capt. Tom Christy of Sport Fish Hawaii/Hawaii Fishing Adventures & Charters; Photos on pages 573, 583, 584 courtesy of Royal Canadian Pacific; Photos on pages 587, 598 courtesy of Dave & Amelia Jenson of Fly Fish Alberta; Photo on page 592 courtesy of Fred Hutchings of Triple T Charters; Photo on page 603 courtesy of Labrador Angling Adventures; Photo on page 622 courtesy of Rogelio Velasco & Pesca Maya; Photo on page 633 courtesy of B&B Mexico Bass Fishing; Photos on pages 647, 651 courtesy of Fuzzy Davis; Photo on page 663 courtesy of Marta Morton of Harbour Club Villas & Marina; Photo on page 672 courtesy of Aaron Witt; Photo on page 673 courtesy of Fly Fishing Adventures; Photos on pages 669, 678 courtesy of Doug Cavin of Doug's Fishing Adventures; Photo on page 681 courtesy of Honduras on the Fly; Photo on page 682 courtesy of Perry Cooper; Photo on page 687 courtesy of Pesca Panama; Photos on pages 695, 700 courtesy of J. W. Smith of Rod and Gun Resources; Photos on pages 691, 701 courtesy of Larry Larsen; Photo on page 705 courtesy of Kabalebo Nature Resort; Photo on page 716 courtesy of Austrian Tourism; Photo on page 717 courtesy of Herman Strieding; Photo on page 719 courtesy of David Lynch; Photos on pages 731, 735 courtesy of Arkadi de Rakoff of CLUBFISHFRANCE; Photos on pages 741, 742 courtesy of Delphi Lodge; Photo on page 746 courtesy of Heikki Nikaula & Hotel Inarin Kultahovi; Photo on pages 749 courtesy of Jourgen Wouters; Photos on pages 752, 753 courtesy of guide Nuno Breda; Photo on page 766 courtesy of Luka Hojnik; Photos on pages 755, 756 courtesy of Hotel Aiguablava; Photo on page 775 courtesy of Misty Dhillon & Michey Sidhu of The Himalayan Outback; Photo on page 780 courtesy of Kenichiro Eitaka; Photo on page 792 courtesy of Gary D. Williams; Photos on pages 297, 806 courtesy of Richard Sheard & World Sport Fishing; Photo on page 795 courtesy of Dino Ferraresi; Photo on page 810 courtesy of Gerhard Laubscher & FlyCastaway; Photo on page 813 courtesy of Grant Cumings of Chiawa Camp; Photos on pages 825, 826 courtesy of www.davidgranvillephotography.com and XtaseaCharters; Photo on page 829 courtesy of Mike McClelland, Best of New Zealand Fly Fishing.

Index

A-1 Lake, Ariz., 359

Abacos, Bahamas, 652

Abrams Creek, N.C., 117

Acklins Island, Bahamas, 651

Adirondack Park, N.Y., 24

Adriatic Sea, 726

Aiguablava, Costa Brava, Spain, 766–69

Alabama, 54–61

Alagnak River, Alaska, 567

Alaska, 558–68

Alberta, 578–88

Albuquerque, N.Mex., 282

Algonquin Provincial Park, Ontario, 611

Allegheny River, Pa., 40

alligator gar, 311–12

Amelia Island Plantation, Fla., 64

Andelle River, France, 735–37

Andorra, 713–15

Andros, Bahamas, 652

Androscoggin River, N.H., 18–19

Animas River, Colo., 236–38

Ann Marie Lake, Labrador, 604

Argentina, 693–99

    tackle to use in, 697

    trout fishing in, 697–99

Arizona, 347–69

    fishing records of, 349

    lakes and rivers of White Mountains in, 348–65

    permits in, 364–65

Arkansas, 152–66

Arkansas River, Colo., 238–39

Armstrong Spring Creek, Mont., 518–20

Arthurs Lake, Tasmania, 838–40

Atlanta, Ga., 80–81

Au Sable River, Mich., 173–74

Ausable River, West Branch, N.Y., 22–23

Austin, Tex., 313

Australia, 817–19

Austria, 716–18

Awesome Lake, Labrador, 604–5

Azores Island, 751–54

Baccarac Reservoir, Mexico, 630–31

Badin, N.C., 113

Bahamas, 649–55

Baja California, Mexico, 625–27

Bale Mountains, 802

Baltimore, Md., 106

Barkley Lake, Ky., 98–99

Barkley Lake, Tenn., 130

Barramundi, Australia, 819
Barren River Lake, Ky., 94–95
Barrett Lake, Calif., 372–73
Batten Kill River, Vt., 48–49
Baylor Lake, Tex., 316
Beartooth Plateau, Wyo., 549–50
Beaver Creek, Minn., 191–92
Beaverhead River, Mont., 494–95
Beaverkill River, N.Y., 23–26
Bechler River, Yellowstone National Park, 444
Becker Lake, Ariz., 359
Belize, 671–74
Bennett Springs, Mo., 204–5
Bermuda, 656
Berry Islands, Bahamas, 653
Bienville Plantation Lakes, Fla., 63–64
Bieri Lakes, Tex., 332
Big Bear Lake (Shush Be Tou), Ariz., 363
Big Bonito, Ariz., 364
Big Cedar Lodge, Mo., 207
Big Creek, N.C., 120
Big Fishing Creek, Pa., 40–41
Big Green River, Minn., 194–95
Big Gunpowder Falls River, Md., 104–5, 106
Big Hole River, Mont., 496–97
Bighorn River, Mont., 497–500
Big Lake, Ariz., 359–60
Big River, Labrador, 605
Big Two-Hearted River, Mich., 178
Big Wood River, Idaho, 467–68
Bikini Atoll, 819–22
Biloxi, Miss., 109
Bimini, Bahamas, 653
Birmingham, Ala., 56
Biscayne Bay, Fla., 72
Bitterroot River, Mont., 500–502
Black Canyon, Colo., 261–66
Black Canyon of the Yellowstone River,
    Yellowstone National Park, 451–54
Black Earth Creek, Minn., 193–94
Blackfeet Reservation Lakes, Mont., 502–4
Blackfoot River, Mont., 504–5
Black Hills, S.Dak., 219–23
  lakes of, 223
Black Lake, N.Y., 25–26

Black River, Ariz., 351–52
Black River, Mich., 179
Blacktail Deer Creek, Mont., 512
Blanco River, Tex., 328
Bloody Run, Minn., 194
Blue Lake Ranch, Colo., 257
Blue River, Colo., 239–41
Blue River, White Mountains, Ariz., 353–55
Blue Springs Creek, Mo., 208
Boardman River, Mich., 174–75
Boca Grande Pass, Fla., 64–65
Bois Brule River, Wis., 227
Boise River, Idaho, South Fork, 484
Bolivia, 697
Bom Bom Island, 797
Boston, Mass., 12
Boston Harbor, Mass., 12
Boulder River, Mont., 513
Boundary Waters Canoe Area, Minn., 187–89
Bow River Drainage, Alberta, 578–81
Boyne River, Ireland, 743–44
Branson, Mo., 202–8
Brazil, 700–702
Brazos River, Tex., 314–15
Bristol Bay Area, Alaska, 566–67
British Columbia, 588–99
    Vancouver Island, 596–99
British Virgin Islands, 665–68
Brownlee Reservoir, Idaho, 468–69
Brule River, Mich., 179
Brus Lagoon, Honduras, 683–84
Buffalo River, Ark., 154–55
Bull Creek, Tex., 313
Bunches Creek, N.C., 118
Bunch Reservoir, Ariz., 360

Cabo San Lucas, Mexico, 635–36
Cache Creek, Yellowstone National Park, 445
Cairns, Australia, 817–18
Calcasieu Lake, La., 100
California, 370–405
California Delta, 374–75
Campbell River, British Columbia, 597
Canary Islands, Spain, 769
Canyon Creek, Ariz., 364

Cape Cod, Mass., 13–14
Cape Cod Bay, Mass., 13–14
Carp River, Mich., 178–79
Cascade Creek, Colo., 256–58
Cascade Creek, Yellowstone National Park, 444
Cascade Lake, Yellowstone National Park, 447
Castaic Lake, Calif., 376–77, 386
Castle Creek, Minn., 194
Castle River, Alberta, 585
Cataloochee Creek, N.C., 118
Catawba River, N.C., 113
Cat Island, Bahamas, 653
Catskill Park, N.Y., 25
Cave Run Lake, Ky., 95
Cayman Islands, 656–57
Cayuga Lake, N.Y., 26
Cazumel, Mexico, 636–39
Cebolla Creek, Colo., 242–45
Cedar Creek Lake, Ky., 95–96
Cedar River, Wash., 544
Cedar Run, Pa., 39
Chandeleur Islands, La., 101
Chaquamegon Bay, Wis., 228
Charlotte, N.C., 113
Charlotte Harbor, Fla., 64–65, 69
Chatfield State Park, Colo., 249–50
Chattahoochee River, Ga., 80–81
Chattooga River, N.C., 112–13
Cheat River, W.Va., 148–49
Cherry Creek Reservoir, Colo., 249–50
Chesapeake Bay, Md., 106
Chicago, Ill., 167–68
   area waters close to, 168
Chickahominy Lake, Oreg., 530
Chile, 703–5
Chippewa Flowage, Wis., 228
Chocolay River, Mich., 179
Choke Canyon Reservoir, Tex., 315–16
Christmas Island, 822–24
Christmas Tree Lake, Ariz., 360
Cibecue Creek, Ariz., 364
Cimarron River, N.Mex., 284–86
   private water on, 286
Clark Fork River, Mont., 505–7
Clarks Fork of the Yellowstone River, 513

Clear Creek, Colo., 249–50
Clear Lake, Calif., 377–78
Clinch River, Tenn., 127–28
Cochetopa Creek, Colo., 242–45
Coiba Island, Panama, 688
Colorado, 230–79
   area lakes in, 256
   Durango Area in, 251–58
   Gunnison River/Black Canyon, 261–66
Colorado River, 245–46, 329–30, 411
   Lees Ferry, 366–68
   tailraces of, 329–30
Columbia River, Wash., 539–40
Conasauga River, Ga., 86
Concho Lake, Ariz., 360
Conejos River, Colo., 246–48
Connecticut, 3–7
Connecticut River, N.H., 19–20
Cook's Run, Mich., 179
Coon Creek, Minn., 194
Cooper Camps, Labrador, 604
Coosa River, Ala., 56
Coppermine River, Northwest Territories, 609
Corsica, 719–25
Cosby Creek, N.C., 118–19
Costa Brava, Spain, 766–69
Costa Rica, 675–77
Cottonwood Creek, Utah, 434–35
Cougar Creek, Yellowstone National Park, 445
Cowichan River, British Columbia, 598
Cowlitz River, Wash., 540–41
Cranberry River, W.Va., 150
Crane Creek, Mo., 203
Crane Prairie Reservoir, Oreg., 526–30
Crescent Lake, Ariz., 360
Crittenden Reservoir, Nev., 406–7
Croatia, 725–26
Crooked Creek, Ark., 156
Crooked Island, Bahamas, 653
Crooked Lake, Fla., 73–76
Crooks Lake, Labrador, 605
Crooks Lake Lodge, Labrador, 603–4
Croton Waters, N.Y., 30
Crow Creek, Mont., 512
Crowley Lake, Calif., 378–79

Crowsnest River, Alberta, 581–85
Cultus Lake, Oreg., 530
Cumberland River, Ky., 97
Cyclone Lake, Ariz., 360

Dale Hollow Lake, Ky., 97–98
Dale Hollow Lake, Tenn., 130
Dallas, Tex., 317–18
Davidson River, N.C., 113–14
Davis Lake, Oreg., 529
Dean River, British Columbia, 588–89
Deep Creek, Calif., 386
Deep Creek, N.C., 118
Deerfield River, Mass., 14–15
Delaney Butte Lakes, Colo., 248
Delaware River, N.Y., 27–28
Denver, Colo., 249–50
DePuy's Spring Creek, Mont., 518–20
Deschutes River, Oreg., 522–24
Destin Village, Fla., 65–66
Detroit, Mich., 176–77
Detroit River, Mich., 176
Devil's Lake, N.Dak., 211
Devils River, Tex., 318–20
Diamond Valley Lake, Calif., 380
Dicks Creek, Ga., 83
Disney World, 74–75
Dixon Lake, Calif., 381–82
Dolores River, Colo., 250–51
Door County, Wis., 227
Dorado, Argentina, 693–94
Drift Fence Lake, Ariz., 360–61
Driftless Area, Minn., 189–95
Dry Run Creek, Ark., 156–57
Dry Tortugas, 657–58
Dubawnt Lake, Northwest Territories, 609
Duck Creek, Yellowstone National
    Park, 444–45
Duck River, Tenn., 128–29
Dukes Creek, Ga., 83–85
Durango Area, Colo., 251–58

Eagle River, Labrador, 605
Earl Park Lake, Ariz., 356–58
East Branch of the Tahquamenon, Mich., 178

East Fork Hermosa Creek, Colo., 253–55
East Fork of the Jemez, N.Mex., 291–93
East Fork of the San Juan River, Colo., 258–59
East Fork of the White River, Ariz., 357
East Fork Sevier, Utah, 432–33
East Lake, Oreg., 528–29
East Walker River, Nev., 407–8
Egypt, 798–800
    Nile perch world records in, 799
Eleuthera-Harbour Island, Bahamas, 653–54
Eleven Point, Mo., 203
Elk River, British Columbia, 589–90
Elk River, W.Va., 150
Encampment River, Wyo., 550–51
England, 727–29
English River, Labrador, 605
Escanaba River, Mich., 178
Ethiopia, 801–3
Everglades, Fla., 66–67
Exuma, Bahamas, 654

Falcon Lake, Tex., 320–21
Falling Spring Branch, Pa., 39
Fall River, Calif., 382–83
Fan Creek, Yellowstone National Park, 444
Farmington River, Conn., 5
Fayette County Lake, Tex., 321–22
Fence River, Mich., 179
Fenton Lake, N.Mex., 289–90
Fiji, 824–27
Finger Lakes, N.Y., 26
Finland, 745–48
Firehole River, Yellowstone
    National Park, 454–55
Firesteel River, Mich., 179
Fish Camp Prong, N.C., 118
Fishing Creek, N.C., 113
Fishing Creek, Pa., 39–40
Flaming Gorge Reservoir, Utah, 419–21
Flat Creek, Wyo., 557
Flathead River, Mont., 507
Florida, 62–77
Florida Keys, 68–71
Fontana Lake, N.C., 114–15
Fool Hollow Lake, Ariz., 361

Forney Creek, N.C., 119–20
Fort Peck Reservoir, Mont., 507–8
Fox River, Mich., 175–77
France, 729–37
Fremont River, Utah, 433–34
French Broad River, N.C., 115–16
French Creek, Minn., 194
French Polynesia, 835–36
Frio River, Tex., 328–29
Frying Pan River, Colo., 259–61

Gabon, 803–4
Gallatin River, Yellowstone National
    Park, 455–56
Galveston, Tex., 331
Gardner River, Yellowstone
    National Park, 456–57
Gaspé Peninsula, 611–14
Gatun Lake, Panama, 688–89
Gave d'Aspe, France, 732–34
Gave de Pau, France, 732–34
Gave d'Oloron, France, 732–34
Georgia, 77–93
    north trout waters of, 79–86
Gibbon River, Yellowstone National Park, 457–59
Gibbons Creek Reservoir, Tex., 323–24
Glass Lake, Tex., 325
Gold River, British Columbia, 597–98
Goose River, Labrador, 605
Gouin Reservoir, Quebec, 614
Grand Bahama Island, Bahamas, 654
Grande Ronde River, Oreg., 525–26
Grand Isle, La., 101
Grand River, Mich., 180
Grand River, Ontario, 611
Great Barrier Reef, Australia, 819
Great Bear Lake, Northwest Territories, 606–8
Great Inagua, Bahamas, 654–55
Great Lake, Tasmania, 838–40
Great Slave Lake, Northwest Territories, 609–10
Great Smoky Mountains National Park,
    N.C., 116–20
Grebe Lake, Yellowstone National Park, 447
Green River, Utah, 421–23
    Upper, 424

Greers Ferry Lake, Ark., 157–58
Gros Ventre River, Wyo., 557
Guadalupe River, Tex., 326–27
Guatemala, 677–80
Guinea-Bissau, 804–6
Gulfport, Miss., 109
Gunnison River, Colo., 261–66

Hawaii, 568–72
Hawley Lake, Ariz., 358–59
Hazel Creek, N.C., 117
Heart Lake, Yellowstone National Park, 447
Hebgen Lake, Yellowstone National Park, 459–64
Henry's Fork of the Snake River, Idaho, 469–71
Henry's Lake, Idaho, 472
Hermosa Creek, Colo., 253
    East Fork, 253–55
High Desert Lakes, Oreg., 526
High Rock, N.C., 113
Hill Country, Tex., 324–30
Himalayas, 777–79
Hiwassee River, Tenn., 129–30
Hoback River, Wyo., 557
Holston River, South Fork, Tenn., 130–31
Homosassa River, Fla., 67–68
Honduras, 681–84
Hong Kong, 773–74
Horseshoe Cienega Lake, Ariz., 361
Horsetooth Reservoir, Colo., 267
Hosmer Lake, Oreg., 529
Hot Creek, Calif., 383–84
Housatonic River, Conn., 5–7
Houston, Tex., 331
Hulsey Lake, Ariz., 361
Hungary, 737–38
Hurricane Lake, Ariz., 361

Ibera Marsh, Argentina, 696–97
Iceland, 738–40
Idaho, 465–90
    fishing records in, 486–89
Illinois, 167–69
India, 775–79
    mahseer of, 775–77
Indian Camp Creek, N.C., 118

Indian River, Fla., 69
Indian River Lagoon, Fla., 68
Ireland, 740–45
Iskut Chain Lakes, British Columbia, 590–91
Isla Boca Brava, Panama, 689
Isle Royale National Park, Mich., 180
Ixtapa-Zihuatanejo, Mexico, 641

Jacks Creek, Ga., 82
Jackson Hole, Wyo., 553–58
Jacksonville, Fla., 69
James River, Va., 140–41, 143, 146
Japan, 780–81
Jefferson River, Mont., 508–9
Jemez Area, N.Mex., 287–96
   brief history in, 288–89
Jemez River, N.Mex., 282, 295–96
   East Fork of, 291–93
Joe Pool Lake, Tex., 317–18
John Day River, Oreg., 531
Junction Creek, Colo., 255

Kamchatka Peninsula, Russia, 787–88
Kansas, 169
Kansas City, Kans., 169
Kasba Lake, Northwest Territories, 609
Kelly Creek, Idaho, 473–75
Kenai River/Kenai Peninsula, Alaska, 568
Kennebec River, Maine, 8–9
Kentucky, 93–99
Kentucky Lake, Ky., 98–99
Kentucky Lake, Tenn., 130
Kenya, 806–7
Ketchikan, Alaska, 568
Kickapoo River, Minn., 192
Kings River, Calif., 384–87
Kinnickinnic River, Minn., 192
Kissimmee Chain of Lakes, Fla., 74–75
Kola Peninsula, Russia, 786–87
Kootenai River, Mont., 509–12

Labrador, 602–6
La Guaira Bank, Venezuela, 709
Lake Agua Milpa, Mexico, 633

Lake Alan Henry, Tex., 309–11
Lake Arlington, Tex., 317–18
Lake Athabasca, Saskatchewan, 615–16
Lake Athens, Tex., 312–14
Lake Austin, Tex., 313
Lake Berryessa, Calif., 373–74
Lake Billy Chinook, Oreg., 530
Lake Cadillac, Mich., 176
Lake Calderwood, Tenn., 133
Lake Casitas, Calif., 375–76
Lake Chabot, Calif., 392–93
Lake Champlain, Vt., 49–51
Lake Comedero, Mexico, 634–35
Lake Conroe, Tex., 331
Lake Dannelly, Ala., 56–57
Lake Davis, Calif., 379–80
Lake El Cuchillo, Mexico, 633–34
Lake El Salto, Mexico, 631–33
Lake Erie, 176–77, 212–13
Lake Eufaula, Ala., 57–58
Lake Eufaula, Okla., 216
Lake Fork, Tex., 317, 322–23
Lake Fork Gunnison, Colo., 263–66
Lake George, N.Y., 27
Lake Guerrero, Mexico, 630
Lake Guntersville, Ala., 56, 58–59
Lake Havasu, Nev., 410
Lake Hickory, N.C., 113
Lake Huites, Mexico, 628–30
Lake Jacomo, Kans., 169
Lake James, N.C., 113
Lake Lewisville, Tex., 317–18
Lake Livingston, Tex., 331
Lake McConaughy Reservoir, Nebr., 209–10
Lake Mead, Nev., 408–9, 411
Lake Meredith, Tex., 330–32
Lake Michigan, Wis., 226–27
Lake Minnetonka, Minn., 197
Lake Mohave, Nev., 409–10, 411
Lake Murray, S.C., 124–25
Lake Nacimiento, Calif., 391
Lake Nasser, Egypt, 798–800
Lake Norman, N.C., 113
Lake Oahe, S.Dak., 224

Lake of the Ozarks, Mo., 200–201
Lake of the Woods, Minn., 195–96
Lake Okeechobee, Fla., 71–73
Lake Pleasant, Ariz., 367
Lake Ponchartrain, La., 102
Lake Powell, Utah, 424–26
Lake St. Clair, Mich., 176–77
Lake Sammamish, Wash., 544
Lake Scugog, Ontario, 610–11
Lake Seminole, Ga., 89
Lake Sharpe, S.Dak., 224–25
Lake Sidney Lanier, Ga., 80–81
Lake Sierra Blanca, Ariz., 361
Lake Simcoe, Ontario, 611
Lakes of Danbury, Tex., 319
Lake Sorrell, Tasmania, 838–40
Lake Taneycomo, Mo., 206–7
Lake Tarpon, Fla., 71
Lake Texoma, Tex., 342–44
Lake Tom Bailey, Miss., 108
Lake Travis, Tex., 313
Lake Vermilion, Minn., 196
Lake Washington, Wash., 544
Lake Winnipesaukee, N.H., 20–21
Lake Wylie, N.C., 113
Lamar River, Yellowstone National Park, 460–61
Lapland, 745–48
Las Vegas, Nev., 411
Laughing Whitefish, Mich., 180
Lava Lake, Oreg., 530
La Zona, Argentina, 695–96
Lees Ferry, Colorado River, Ariz., 366–68
Lee Valley Reservoir, Ariz., 361
Letort Spring Run, Pa., 36–37
Lewis Lake, Yellowstone National Park, 448
Lightner Creek, Colo., 255
Lime Creek, Colo., 255–56
Lithuania, 756
Little Carp River, Mich., 179
Little Colorado, Ariz., 364
Little Garlic River, Mich., 178
Little Juniata, Pa., 37
Little Lava Lake, Oreg., 530
Little Manistee River, Mich., 182–83

Little Pigeon River, N.C.:
    Middle Prong of, 119
    West Prong of, 119
Little Pine Lagoon, Tasmania, 838–40
Little Piney Creek, Mo., 206
Little Red River, Ark., 158–60
Little River, N.C., 117–18
Lizard Island, Australia, 818–19
Llano River, Tex., 327–28
Lochsa River, Idaho, 475–76
Logan River, Utah, 427–28
Long Island, Bahamas, 655
Lookout Shoals, N.C., 113
Los Angeles, Calif., 386
Los Roques, Venezuela, 708–10
Louisiana, 99–103
Lower Niagra River, N.Y., 32–33
Luna Lake, Ariz., 361–62
Lyman Reservoir, Ariz., 362

McBride Lake, Yellowstone National Park, 448
McCloud River, Calif., 387–89
McCoy spring creek, Mont., 520–21
McKenzie River, Oreg., 532–33
Madeira Island, 751–54
Madison River, Yellowstone
    National Park, 461–63
Magdalena Bay, Mexico, 627
mahseer, 775–77
Maine, 8–11
Mammoth Creek, Utah, 430–32
Mammoth Lakes, Calif., 387
Mango Creek Lodge, Honduras, 682–83
Manistee River, Mich., 181–83
Manistique River, Mich., 178
Manitoba, 599–601
Mann Lake, Oreg., 527–28
Maramec Spring Trout Park, Mo., 204
Marshall Islands, Micronesia, 819–22
Martha's Vineyard, Mass., 15–16
Maryland, 103–8
Massachusetts, 11–18
Mayaguana, Bahamas, 655
Menomonee River, Wis., 226–27

Meramec River, Mo., 204

Merritt Reservoir, Nebr., 210–11

Metolius River, Oreg., 533–34

Metro Park Lakes, Minn., 197

Mexican Hay Lake, Ariz., 362

Mexico, 621–45

  Baja California, 625–27

  bass lakes of, 627–30

Miami, Fla., 72

Michigan, 170–86

  Upper Peninsula of, 175–80

Micronesia, 819–22

Middle Fork, Salmon River, Idaho, 476–79

Middle Fork San Joaquin River, Calif., 397–400

Middle Prong Little River, N.C., 117–18

Middle Prong of the Little Pigeon
    River, N.C., 119

Midway Island, 827–28

Milesnick spring creek, Mont., 521

Mill Creek, Mo., 208

Millers Ferry, Ala., 56–57

Milton Lake, Saskatchewan, 616

Milton Reservoir, Calif., 389–90

Milwaukee, Wis., 226–27

Milwaukee River, Wis., 226–27

Minneapolis, Minn., 197

Minnesota, 187–98

  Driftless Area in, 189–95

Miramichi River, New Brunswick, 601–2

Mississippi, 108–9

Mississippi River, Minn., 197

Missouri, 198–209

  top waters from St. Louis to Branson, 202–9

Missouri River, 211, 508

Mongolia, 782–84

Monongahela River, Pa., 40

Montana, 490–521

  smaller creeks and rivers in, 512–14

  spring creeks of, 518–21

Montauk Point, N.Y., 32

Montauk State Park, Mo., 207–8

Monticello, N.C., 113

Mosquito Lake, Northwest Territories, 609

Mossy Creek, Va., 141–42

Mountain Fork River, Okla., 217–18

Muskegon River, Mich., 183–84

Myrtle Grove, La., 102

Namekagon River, Wis., 228

Nantahala River, N.C., 120–21

Nantucket Island, Mass., 13–14

Nantucket Sound, Mass., 13–14

Nashville, Tenn., 130

Nebraska, 209–11

Nelson Reservoir, Ariz., 362–63

Nelson Spring Creek, Mont., 518–20

Nevada, 405–17

  fishing records in, 415–16

New Brunswick, 601–2

New Foundland, 602–6

New Hampshire, 18–21

New Mexico, 279–305

  Jemez Area in, 287–96

New Orleans, La., 102

Newport, R.I., 45

New River, W.Va., 151

New York, 21–35

New York, N.Y., 29–31

New Zealand, 828–33

  North Island, 830–31

  South Island, 831–33

Nez Perce Creek, Yellowstone National Park, 445

Niagra River, Lower, N.Y., 32–33

Nicaragua, 685

Nile perch world records, 799

Nineteen Lagoons, Tasmania, 840

Noland Creek, N.C., 119

Nolichucky River, Tenn., 131

noodling, 333–36

Noontootla Creek, Ga., 85

Norfork River, Ark., 160–61

North Bear Creek, Minn., 194

North Branch of Potomac River, 105, 149–50

North Branch Root River, Minn., 193

North Carolina, 110–24

North Dakota, 211

North Fork, White River, Ariz., 355–56

North Fork of the White River, Mo., 201–2

North Island, New Zealand, 830–31

North Platte River, Wyo., 551–53

North Raven River, Alberta, 585
Northwest Territories, 606–10
Norway, 748–50
Nueltin Lake, Manitoba, 599–600

Oak Creek, Ariz., 368–69
Oakland, Calif., 392–93
Obsidian Creek, Yellowstone National Park, 445
Ohio, 212–13
Ohio River, Pa., 40
Oklahoma, 214–18
 tanks in, 215–16
Oldman River, Alberta, 585
Olympic Peninsula, Wash., 541–43
O'Neill Forebay, Calif., 394
Ontario, 610–11
Ontonagon River, Mich., 179
Orange Lake, Fla., 73–76
Oregon, 522–39
 Crane Prairie Reservoir, 526–30
Orlando, Fla., 74
Osprey Lake, Labrador, 605
Ouachita Lake, Ark., 161–62
Outer Banks, N.C., 122–24
Owens River, Calif., 391–95

Pacheta Lake, Ariz., 363
Paint River, Mich., 179
Panama, 686–89
Panguitch Creek, Utah, 435–36
Papua New Guinea, 833–35
Paradise Public Fishing Area, Ga., 90
Park Lake, Labrador, 605–6
Paulina Lake, Oreg., 528–29
Pebble Creek, Yellowstone National Park, 446
Pecos Wilderness, N.Mex., 305
Pedasi, Panama, 689
Pedernales River, Tex., 330
Penns Creek, Pa., 38
Pennsylvania, 35–45
 trout streams, 37–41
Penobscot River, West Branch of, Maine, 10–11
Penstock Lagoon, Tasmania, 839
Pepacton Reservoir, N.Y., 30
Peralta Creek, N.Mex., 294

Percy Priest Reservoir, Tenn., 130
Pere Marquette River, Mich., 184–85
Peshtigo River, Wis., 226–27
Pettigrew Ranch, Tex., 316
Philadelphia, Pa., 38
Phoenix, Ariz., 367
Pickwick Lake, Ala., 59
Piedra River, Colo., 252–53
Pinas Bay, Panama, 688
Pine Island Coast, Fla., 76
Piru Creek, Calif., 386
Piru Lake, Calif., 386
Pittsburgh, Pa., 40
Poindexter Slough, Mont., 521
Porters Creek, N.C., 119
Portugal, 751–54
Potomac River, 146
 North Branch of, 105, 149–50
 South Branch of, 149
Powder River, Oreg., 538
Pratt Lake, Ariz., 363
Prince Rupert, British Columbia, 591–93
Provo River, Utah, 427–28
Puerto Rico, 659–62
Puerto Vallarta, Mexico, 639–41
Puget Sound, Wash., 544
Purtis Creek State Park, Tex., 319
Putah Creek, Calif., 392–93
Pyramid Lake, Nev., 410–12
Pyrenees Mountains, Spain, 758–61

Quabbin Reservoir, Mass., 17
Quaboag River, Mass., 16
Quebec, 611–14
Queen Charlotte Islands, British Columbia, 593
Quincy Reservoir, Colo., 249–50

Ram River, Alberta, 586–88
Ramsey Prong, N.C., 119
Rapid Creek, S.Dak., 221–23
Rapid River, Maine, 9
Rappahannock River, Va., 142–43, 146
Raven Fork, N.C., 118
Ray Roberts, Tex., 317–18
Raystown Lake, Pa., 41

Red Deer, Alberta, 586
Red Lake, Minn., 198
Red River, N.Mex., 296–97
Reelfoot Lake, Tenn., 131–32
Rend Lake, Ill., 168–69
Reservation Lake, Ariz., 363
Rhode Island, 44–45
Richland-Chambers Reservoir, Tex., 336
Richmond, Va., 143
Rifle River, Mich., 186
Rio Ara, Spain, 761–63
Rio Cebolla, Colo., 290–91
Rio Chama, N.Mex., 282–84
Rio Cinca, Spain, 761–63
Rio Costilla, N.Mex., 297–300
Rio de las Vacas, N.Mex., 293–94
Rio Ebro, Spain, 757–58
Rio Grande, 266–68, 300–2
Rio Guadalupe, N.Mex., 293
Rio Irati, Spain, 763–66
Rio Urrobi, Spain, 763–66
Risle River, France, 734–35
River Lake, Ariz., 363
River Test, England, 728–29
River Wye, Wales, 728
Roaring Fork, Colo., 268–69
Roaring River, Mo., 208
Rock Creek, Mont., 514–15
Rock Creek, Mont. (small one), 512–13
Rocky Ford Creek, Wash., 543
Rocky Mountain National Park, Colo., 270–72
Rodman Reservoir, Fla., 76–77
Rogue River, Oreg., 534–35
Roosevelt Lake, Ariz., 365–66
Root River, Minn.:
    North Branch of, 193
    South Branch of, 192–93
Root River, Wis., 226–27
Roubidoux Creek, Mo., 206
Royal Canadian Pacific Fishing Excursion, 583
Ruby Lake, Nev., 412–13
Rullands Coulee Creek, Minn., 193
Rupprecht Creek, Minn., 194
Rush River, Minn., 192
Russia, 784–88

Sabine Lake, Tex., 336–38
Sacramento River, Calif., 395–97
Saginaw Bay, Mich., 186
St. Croix River, Wis., 228–29
St. Joe River, Idaho, 484–85
St. Johns River, Fla., 69, 74–75
St. Louis, Mo., 202–8
St. Mary's River, Mich., 180
St. Paul, Minn., 197
St. Simons Island, Ga., 87–89
Salmon River, Idaho, 479–80
    Middle Fork, 476–79
Salmon River, N.Y., 33–34
Salt Lake City, Utah, 427–28
Salt River, Ariz., 367
Sam Rayburn Reservoir, Tex., 338
San Antonio Creek, N.Mex., 294–95
Sanchez Reservoir, Colo., 273
Sandia Lakes, N.Mex., 282
San Diego, Calif., 398–99
San Francisco, Calif., 392–93
San Francisco Bay, Calif., 392–93
San Joaquin River, Calif., Middle Fork, 397–400
San Juan River, 258, 302–4
    East Fork of, 258–59
San Luis Lake, Colo., 273
San Luis Reservoir, Calif., 394
Santee Cooper, S.C., 125–26
Saskatchewan, 615–18
Savage River, Md., 107–8
Savannah, Ga., 90–91
Schuylkill River, Pa., 38
Seattle, Wash., 544
Sebago Lake, Maine, 9–10
Selway River, Idaho, 480–81
Selwyn Lake, Saskatchewan, 617–18
Seneca Creek, W.Va., 148
777 Ranch, Tex., 338
Sevier River, Utah, East Fork of, 432–33
Seychelles, 808–11
Sharon Harris, N.C., 113
Shasta Lake, Calif., 400
Sheboygan River, Wis., 226–27
Shenandoah National Park, Va., 144–45
Shenandoah River, Va., 146

Shields River, Mont., 513

Shoshone Lake, Yellowstone National Park, 447

Show Low Lake, Ariz., 363

Shush Be Tou (aka Big Bear Lake), Ariz., 363

Silsby Lake, Manitoba, 600–601

Silver Creek, Idaho, 481–84

Sitka, Alaska, 567–68

Skeena River System, British Columbia, 593–96

Slate Run, Pa., 39

Slough Creek, Yellowstone National Park, 463–64

Slovenia, 754–57

Smith Lake, Ala., 56, 60

Smith River, Mont., 515–16

Snake River, Idaho, Henry's Fork of, 469–71

Snake River, Wyo., South Fork, 553–58

Snoqualmie River, Wash., 544

Soda Butte Creek, Yellowstone
    National Park, 445

Soque River, Ga., 80–81, 91–93

South Bear Creek, Minn., 194

South Branch of Potomac River, 149

South Branch Root River, Minn., 192–93

South Carolina, 124–26

South Dakota, 219–25
    Black Hills, 219–23

South Fork, Boise River, Idaho, 484

South Fork Snake River, Wyo., 553–58

South Island, New Zealand, 831–33

South Korea, 789

South Platte River, Colo., 249–50, 273–75

South Toe River, N.C., 124

Spain, 757–69

Spearfish Creek, S.Dak., 220–21

Specimen Creek, Yellowstone National Park, 445

Sprague Lake, Wash., 545

Spring Branch, Minn., 195

Spring Coulee Creek, Minn., 193

Spring Creek, Pa., 41

Spring River, Ark., 162–63

Squaw Creek Reservoir, Tex., 339

Sri Lanka, 790

Stauffer Creek, Alberta, 585

Steamboat Springs, Colo., 264–65

Stillwater River, Mont., 513

Straight Canyon, Utah, 434–35

Strater Hotel, Colo., 257

Strawberry Reservoir, Utah, 426–28

Sturgeon River, Mich., 178

Suir River, Ireland, 744

Sunrise Lake, Ariz., 363

Sun River, Mont., 516–18

Suriname, 705–7

Susquehanna River, Pa., 41–43, 146

Sweden, 745–48

Table Rock Lake, Mo., 207

Tahiti, French Polynesia, 835–36

Tahquamenon, Mich., East Branch of, 178

Tallapoosa River, Ala., 60–61

tanks, 215–16

Tasmania, 837–40

Taylor River, Colo., 275–76

Tellico River, Tenn., 132–33

Tennessee, 126–37
    fishing records of, 134–37

Teton River, Idaho, 485–90

Texas, 306–46
    alligator gar in, 311–12
    Coast of, 331, 339–42
    Hill Country, 324–30

Thailand, 791–93

Thorofare Creek, Yellowstone National Park,
    446

tigerfish, 811–14

Timber Coulee Creek, Minn., 193

Toccoa River, Ga., 81–82

Toledo Bend Reservoir, Tex., 345–46

Trappers Lake, Colo., 276–77

Tree River, Northwest Territories, 608

Trinity Lake, Calif., 401

Trinity River, Tex., 317–18

Trout Lake, Yellowstone National Park, 447

Trout River, Fla., 69

Trout Run, Minn., 191

Trout Run, Minn. (Root River), 192

Truckee River, Calif., 401–3

Truman Reservoir, Mo., 209

Tunnel Lake, Ariz., 364

Turks and Caicos, 663–65

Twin Lakes, Colo., 277–78

Umpqua River, Oreg., 535–37
Upper Gibbon, Yellowstone National Park, 446
Upper Green River, Utah, 424
Upper Peninsula, Mich., 175–80
Uruguay River, Argentina, 695–96
Utah, 417–36
  survey of underfished streams in, 428–36

Vallecito Reservoir, Colo., 278–79
Vallée de Campan, France, 730–32
Vancouver Island, British Columbia, 596–99
Venezuela, 708–10
Venice, La., 101–3
Vermont, 45–53
Virginia, 137–47
Voyageurs National Park, Minn., 190

Wales, 728
Walker Camp Prong, N.C., 119
Ware River, Mass., 16
Warunta Lagoon, Honduras, 684
Washington, 539–47
Washington, D.C., 146
Watauga River, N.C., 122
Wateree, N.C., 113
Waterloo Creek, Minn., 195
Waters Creek, Ga., 82
Wenaha River, Oreg., 537–38
West Branch Ausable River, N.Y., 22–23
West Branch of the Penobscot
  River, Maine, 10–11
Westfield River, Mass., 17–18
West Prong of the Little Pigeon River, N.C., 119
West Virginia, 148–51
  top fishing hotspots in, 148–51
Wheeler Lake, Ala., 56, 61
Whiskeytown Reservoir, Calif., 403
White Bass, Tex., 345–46
Whitefish River, Mich., 178
White Mountains, Lakes and Rivers of, 348–65

White Oak Lakes, Ark., 163–64
White River, Ariz.:
  East Fork of, 357
  North Fork, 355–56
White River, Ark., 164–66
White River, Mo., North Fork of, 201–2
White River, Vt., 51–52
Whitetop Laurel Creek, Va., 145–47
Whitewater River, Minn., 191
Wickiup Reservoir, Oreg., 529–30
Wild Horse Reservoir, Nev., 413–17
Williamson River, Oreg., 538–39
Williams River, W.Va., 151
Willowemoc River, N.Y., 34–35
Wilson Lake, Ala., 56
Winnebago Creek, Minn., 193
Winooski River, Vt., 52–53
Wisconsin, 225–29
Wollaston Lake, Saskatchewan, 618
Wood River, R.I., 44–45
Wyoming, 547–58

Yadkin River, N.C., 113
Yakima River, Wash., 545–47
Yellow Breeches Creek, Pa., 37–38
Yellowstone Lake, Yellowstone National
  Park, 446
Yellowstone National Park, 437–64
  basic info on, 441–44
  Hebgen Lake, 459–64
  practicalities for, 448
  reasons for fishing smaller streams in,
    448–49
  tactics and strategies for, 449
Yellowstone River, 449–54
  Black Canyon of, 451–54
  Clarks Fork of, 513
Yosemite National Park, Calif., 403–5
Youghiogheny River, Pa., 43–44
Yucatán Peninsula, Mexico, 641–45